March 7–11, 2018
Tokyo, Japan

Association for
Computing Machinery

Advancing Computing as a Science & Profession

IUI 2018

Proceedings of the 23rd International Conference on
Intelligent User Interfaces

Sponsored by:

ACM SIGAI and ACM SIGCHI

Supported by:

Adobe, DAYPLA, LIFULL, Yahoo! Japan, and Rakuten

Association for
Computing Machinery

Advancing Computing as a Science & Profession

The Association for Computing Machinery
2 Penn Plaza, Suite 701
New York, New York 10121-0701

ISBN: 978-1-4503-4945-1 (Digital)

ISBN: 978-1-4503-5876-7 (Print)

Additional copies may be ordered prepaid from:

ACM Order Department
PO Box 30777
New York, NY 10087-0777, USA

Phone: 1-800-342-6626 (USA and Canada)
+1-212-626-0500 (Global)
Fax: +1-212-944-1318
E-mail: acmhelp@acm.org
Hours of Operation: 8:30 am – 4:30 pm ET

IUI 2018 Chairs' Welcome

It is our great pleasure to welcome you to the 2018 ACM International Conference on Intelligent User Interfaces (IUI 2018), held in Tokyo from 7-March to 11-March!

It is the twenty-third IUI conference, continuing its tradition of being the main international forum for reporting outstanding research at the intersection of Human Computer Interaction (HCI) and Artificial Intelligence (AI). The work that appears at IUI bridges these two fields and delves also into related fields, such as psychology, cognitive science, computer graphics, the arts, and others. Members of the IUI community are interested in improving the symbiosis between humans and computers, and in making systems adapt to humans rather than the other way around.

The program of IUI 2018 reflects the growth of the Intelligent User Interfaces research community. The calls for contributions attracted 299 submissions from all over the world (a record number for the IUI conference series), 127 submissions of posters and demos, and 22 submissions to the student consortium. The conference committee accepted 68 papers (43 long papers and 25 short papers), covering a diverse range of topics, as reflected in the conference session titles. The conference program will also include 35 posters, 30 demos, and 11 student consortium papers. Building on the tradition of collaboration of IUI with ACM TiiS journal, 4 papers that were published by the journal in 2017 will be presented at the conference and selected papers presented at the conference will be invited to submit extended versions to the journal. In addition, IUI 2018 will feature 7 workshops on topics related to Intelligent User Interfaces.

One of the main attractions of the conference is the 3 keynote talks. James A. Landay from Stanford University will open the conference with a keynote talk entitled "From On Body to Out of Body User Experience." Following this, Masataka Goto from the National Institute of Advanced Industrial Science and Technology (AIST) will present his talk "Intelligent Music Interfaces." Finally, Jennifer Golbeck from the University of Maryland will present her talk "Surveillance or Support: When Personalization Turns Creepy." IUI 2018 will also feature the second edition of the Impact Award, celebrating an impactful paper presented at one of the past editions of IUI.

A novelty of IUI 2018 will be its co-location with IPSJ Interaction 2018, the leading domestic HCI conference in Japan. The two conferences will be held in the Hitostubashi Hall and will be scheduled back-to-back, allowing the participants of one conference to also take part in the other. The two conferences will have a shared day that will feature the keynote talk of James A. Landay and a shared interactive poster/demo session. This co-location of the conferences will expose IUI to the local research community and hopefully attract new participants. We thank the IPSJ (Information Processing Society in Japan), and especially the five special-interest groups that organize IPSJ Interaction: IPSJ SIG-HCI, SIG-GN, SIG-UBI, SIG-EC and SIG-DCC. Without their immense help, this co-location would not have been possible.

IUI 2018 has been a product of a vibrant and supportive community, and a cohort of amazing organizers, who have generously volunteered much of their own time. Their names can be found in the following pages. All the members of the organizing committee have done a stellar job of coordinating the many parts that go into putting together a great conference. We extend our deepest gratitude to the 43 Senior Program Committee members for coordinating the papers review process, as well as the 107 members of the long/short papers' Program Committee and the 90 members of the Posters/Demos Program Committee for providing high quality reviews. The local organizers have worked particularly hard and a special big thank you goes to all the other members of the organizing committee. THANK YOU all!

Most importantly, we thank the authors of all the contributions — technical program, posters/demos, student consortium, and workshops — for providing the content of IUI 2018. The process was competitive and selective, and allowed us to develop the excellent program that is the heart of the conference.

Last but not least, we gratefully thank the traditional sponsors of IUI — ACM SIGCHI and ACM SIGAI — and our corporate supporters: Adobe (Silver supporter), DAYPLA (Silver supporter), LIFULL (Silver supporter), Yahoo! Japan (Bronze supporter), and Rakuten (Bronze supporter). Their generous funding helped immensely.

We hope you find the program of IUI 2018 interesting and thought-provoking. We also hope the conference provides you with a valuable opportunity to share ideas with other researchers and practitioners from around the world, leading to further advancements in the exciting research field of Intelligent User Interfaces.

Shlomo Berkovsky, Yoshinori Hijikata, and Jun Rekimoto
IUI 2018 General Chairs

Margaret Burnett, Mark Billinghurst, and Aaron Quigley
IUI 2018 Program Committee Chairs

Table of Contents

Session 2A: Evaluation of IUIs

Session Chair: Simone Stumpf *(University of London, UK)*

Session 2B: Modeling and Predicting User Behavior

Session Chair: Jeff Nichols *(Google, USA)*

Session 3A: XAI: Explainable IUIs

Session Chair: Vera Liao *(IBM Research, USA)*

Session 4B: Persuasive and Assistive IUIs

Session Chair: Brian Lim *(National Univeristy of Singapore)*

Session 5A: IUIs for Wearable, Mobile and Ubiquitous Computing

Session Chair: Kai Kunze *(Keio University, Japan)*

Session 5B: Intelligent Visualization and Smart Environments

Session Chair: Giulio Jacucci *(Helsinki Institute for Information Technology HIIT, Finland)*

Session 6A: IUIs for Complex Tasks

Session Chair: Alison Smith *(University of Maryland, USA)*

Session 6B: Social Media and Recommenders

Session Chair: Takayuki Itoh *(Ochanomizu University, Japan)*

Doctoral Consortium

Session Chair: Jason Orlosky & Naomi Yamashita
(Osaka University, Japan & NTT Communication Science Laboratories, Japan)

IUI 2018 Organizing Committee

General Chairs:	Shlomo Berkovsky (CSIRO, Australia) Yoshinori Hijikata (Kwansei Gakuin University, Japan) Jun Rekimoto (University of Tokyo, Japan)
Program Chairs:	Margaret Burnett (Oregon State University, USA) Mark Billinghurst (University of South Australia, Australia) Aaron Quigley (University of St Andrews, UK)
Workshops/Tutorials Chairs:	Takanori Komatsu (Meiji University, Japan) Alan Said (University of Skövde, Sweden)
Posters/Demos Chairs:	Li Chen (Hong Kong Baptist University, Hong Kong) Masahiro Hamasaki (AIST, Japan) Masataka Imura (Kwansei Gakuin University, Japan)
Student Consortium Chairs:	Jason Orlosky (Osaka University, Japan) Naomi Yamashita (NTT Communication Science Laboratories, Japan)
Local Arrangements Chairs:	Kiyoshi Kiyokawa (NAIST, Japan) Satoshi Nakamura (Meiji University, Japan)
Sponsorship Chairs:	Casey Dugan (IBM Research, USA) Tobias Grosse-Puppendahl (Porsche, Germany) Makoto Okamoto (Academic Resource Guide, Japan)
Treasurers:	Shinsuke Nakajima (Kyoto Sangyo University, Japan) John O'Donovan (University of California, Santa Barbara, USA) Kenta Oku (Ryukoku University, Japan)
Registration Chair:	Daisuke Kitayama (Kogakuin University, Japan)
Proceedings Chairs:	Matt Dennis (University of Portsmouth, UK) Ben Steichen (California State Polytechnic University, USA) Takehiro Yamamoto (Kyoto University, Japan)
Publicity Chairs:	Yuichi Itoh (Osaka University, Japan) Christoph Trattner (MODUL University, Austria) Yong Zheng (Illinois Institute of Technology, USA)
Student Volunteer Chair:	Takayuki Itoh (Ochanomizu University, Japan)
Webmasters:	Yuichi Itoh (Osaka University, Japan) Tomu Tominaga (Osaka University, Japan)

Senior Program Committee:

Elisabeth Andrè (Augsburg University, Germany)
Joshi Anirudha (IIT Bombay, India)
Lora Aroyo (VU University Amsterdam, Netherlands)
Peter Brusilovsky (University of Pittsburgh, USA)
Andrea Bunt (University of Manitoba, Canada)
Marc Cavazza (University of Kent, UK)
Cristina Conati (University of British Columbia, Canada)
Anind Dey (Carnegie Mellon University, USA)
Jill Freyne (CSIRO, Australia)
Cristina Gena (Universita' di Torino, Italy)
Ido Guy (Yahoo Labs, Israel)
Tracy Hammond (Texas A&M University, USA)
Eelco Herder (Radboud University Nijmegen, Netherlands)
Masahiko Inami (University of Tokyo, Japan)
Giulio Jacucci (Univeristy of Helsinki, Finland)
Anthony Jameson (DFKI, Germany)
Joaquim Jorge (Universidade de Lisboa, Portugal)
Per-Ola Kristensson (University of Cambridge, UK)
Antonio Krueger (DFKI, Germany)
Tsvi Kuflik (The University of Haifa, Israel)
Elisabeth Lex (Graz University of Technology, Austria)
Henry Lieberman (Massachusetts Institute of Technology, USA)
Brian Lim (National University, Singapore)
Hamasaki Masahiro (AIST, Japan)
Wendy E. Mackay (INRIA, France)
Luana Micallef (Helsinki Institute for Information Technology, Finland)
Jeffrey Nichols (Google, USA)
Petteri Nurmi (Helsinki Institute for Information Technology, Finland)
John O'Donovan (University of California, Santa Barbara, USA)
Nuria Oliver (Vodafone/Data-Pop Alliance, Spain)
Cecile Paris (CSIRO, Australia)
Fabio Paterno (CNR-ISTI, Italy)
Daisuke Sakamoto (Hokkaido University, Japan)
Barry Smyth (University College Dublin, Ireland)
Simone Stumpf (City University London, UK)
Maki Sugimoto (Keio University, Japan)
Itoh Takayuki (Ochanomizu University, Japan)
Nava Tintarev (TU Delft, Amsterdam, Netherlands)
Feng Tian (Chinese Academy of Sciences, China)
Ilaria Torre (University of Genoa, Italy)
Matthew Turk (University of California, Santa Barbara, USA)
Jean Vanderdonckt (Université Catholique de Louvain, Belgium)
Nakano Yukiko (Seikei University, Japan)

Long/Short Papers Program Committee:

Aonghus, Lawlor (University College Dublin, Ireland)
Ardissono, Liliana (University of Torino, Italy)
Ardito, Carmelo (University of Bari Aldo Moro, Italy)
Avrahami, Daniel (FXPAL, USA)
Berthouze, Nadia (University College London, UK)
Bird, Jon (City, University of London, UK)
Bogina, Veronika (Haifa University, Israel)
Borgo, Rita (King's College London, UK)
Butz, Andreas (LMU, Germany)
Campos, José (University of Minho, Portugal)
Carrascal, Juan Pablo (Microsoft, USA)
Cena, Federica (University of Torino, Italy)
Ceolin, Davide (Centrum Wiskunde en Informatica, Netherlands)
Champin, Pierr-Antoine (University of Lyon, France)
Chen, Li (Hong Kong Baptist University, Hong Kong)
Chollet, Mathieu (USC ICT, USA)
Čopič Pucihar, Klen (University of Primorska, Slovenia)
Dalvi, Girish (Indian Institute of Technology Bombay, India)
Daly, Elizabeth (IBM Research, Ireland)
De Carolis, Bernardina (University of Bari, Italy)
DeLine, Robert (Microsoft Research, USA)
Dibie, Ogheneovo (Electronic Arts, USA)
Dmello, Sidney (University of Colorado, Boulder, USA)
Dumas, Bruno (University of Namur, Belgium)
Ferrario, Maria Angela (Lancaster University, UK)
Flores-Saviaga, Claudia (West Virginia University, USA)
Funakoshi, Kotaro (Kyoto University, Japan)
Garijo, Daniel (Information Sciences Institute USC, USA)
Garzotto, Franca (Politecnico di Milano, Italy)
Genaro Motti, Vivian (George Mason University, USA)
Ghosh, Sanjay (Samsung R&D Institute, India)
Guerra, Julio (Universidad Austral de Chile, Chile)
Hayashi, Yuki (Osaka Prefecture University, Japan)
Holz, Christian (Microsoft Research, USA)
Hoque, Enamul (Stanford University, USA)
Hsiao, Sharon (I-Han) (Arizona State University, USA)
Huang, Liang (Oregon State University, USA)
Itoh, Masahiko (The University of Tokyo / NICT, Japan)
Jahanian, Ali (MIT, USA)
Kang,Byungkyu (Jay) (Nokia, USA)
Kato, Jun (AIST, Japan)
Katrin, Plaumann (Ulm University, Germany)
Kleanthous, Styliani (University of Cyprus, Cyprus)
Kljun, Matjaž (University of Primorska, Slovenia)
Komatani, Kazunori (Osaka University, Japan)
Koolen, Marijn (Royal Academy for Arts and Sciences, Netherlands)

Long/Short Papers Program Committee (continued):

Koyama, Yuki (AIST, Japan)
Kunze, Kai (Keio University, Japan)
Lanir, Joel (University of Haifa, Israel)
LaViola, Joseph (UCF, USA)
Lee, Doris Jung-Lin (University of Illinois, Urbana-Champaign, USA)
Li, Fuxin (Oregon State University, USA)
Liao, Q. Vera (IBM Research, USA)
Lisowska Masson, Agnes (University of Fribourg, Switzerland)
Lombardi, Ilaria (University of Torino, Italy)
Ludwig, Bernd (University Regensburg, Germany)
Lumsden, Jo (Aston University, UK)
Mac Namee, Brian (University College Dublin, Ireland)
Macbeth, Jamie (Fairfield University, USA)
Malizia, Alessio (Brunel University London, UK)
Manca, Marco (ISTI-CNR Pisa, Italy)
Marivate, Vukosi (Rutgers University, USA)
Mauro, Noemi (University of Turin, Italy)
Mirri, Silvia (University of Bologna, Italy)
Misu, Teruhisa (Honda Research Institute, USA)
Mohan, Shiwali (PARC, USA)
Mokatren, Moayad (University of Haifa & DFKI, Israel & Germany)
Mokryn, Osnat (University of Haifa, Israel)
Nakano, Mikio (Honda Research Institute, Japan)
Nakano, Tomoyasu (AIST, Japan)
Ngai, Grace (Hong Kong Polytechnic University, Hong Kong)
Okada, Shogo (AIST, Japan)
Orlosky, Jason (Osaka University, Japan)
Pau, Giovanni (Kore University of Enna, Italy)
Pielot, Martin (Telefonica Research, Spain)
Prasov, Zahar (The Charles Stark Draper Laboratory, USA)
Ramos, Gonzalo (Microsoft, USA)
Rapp, Amon (University of Torino, Italy)
Rau, Martina (University of Wisconsin - Madison, USA)
Rohs, Michael (University of Hannover, Germany)
Said, Alan (University of Skövde, Sweden)
Santoro, Carmen (CNR-ISTI, Italy)
Santos, Olga (aDeNu Research Group, UNED, Spain)
Sarcar, Sayan (Kochi University of Technology, Japan)
Sari, Eunice (UX Indonesia, Indonesia)
Sarkar, Advait (Microsoft Research Cambridge, UK)
Savage, Saiph (West Virginia University & UNAM, USA & Mexico)
Sayago, Sergio (University of Barcelona, Spain)
Schiavo, Gianluca (Schiavo, FBK - Fondazione Bruno Kessler, Italy)
Schöning, Johannes (University of Bremen, Germany)
Sheidin, Julia (University of Haifa, Israel)
Smith, Alison (Decisive Analytics & University of Maryland, USA)

Long/Short Papers Program Committee (continued):

Sorathia, Keyur (Indian Institute of Technology Guwahati, India)
Spano, Lucio Davide (Spano, University of Cagliari, Italy)
Steichen, Ben (Santa Clara University, USA)
Taylor, Alex (Microsoft Research, UK)
Vatavu, Radu-Daniel (University of Suceava, Romania)
Verbert, Katrien (KU Leuven, Belgium)
Vernero, Fabiana (University of Torino, Italy)
Votis, Konstantinos (Information Technologies Institute, Greece)
Wander, Jeremiah (Microsoft, USA)
Wecker, Alan (University of Haifa & University of Trento, Israel & Italy)
Xiao, Robert (Carnegie Mellon University, USA)
Xu, Anbang (IBM Research, USA)
Yang, Jie (Delft University of Technology, Netherlands)
Yu, Kun (CSIRO, Australia)
Zheng, Yong (Illinois Institute of Technology, USA)

Posters/Demos Program Committee:

Altmeyer, Maximilian (DFKI, Germany)
Ardissono, Liliana (University of Torino, Italy)
Blat, Josep (University Pompeu Fabra, Spain)
Boratto, Ludovico (EURECAT, Spain)
Butz, Andreas (LMU, Germany)
Callaway, Charles (Fondazione Bruno Kessler, Italy)
Cena, Federica (University of Torino, Italy)
De Carolis, Bernardina (University of Bari, Italy)
Demmans Epp, Carrie (University of Alberta, Canada)
Dittmar, Christian (Friedrich-Alexander-University, Germany)
Dumas, Bruno (University of Namur, Belgium)
Durand, Guillaume (National Research Council of Canada, Canada)
Fan, Xiangmin (Chinese Academy of Sciences, China)
Ferwerda, Bruce (Jönköping University, Sweden)
Fonseca, Manuel J. (University of Lisbon, Portugal)
Fujinaga, Ichiro (McGill University, Canada)
Furukawa, Masahiro (Osaka University, Japan)
Gasparetti, Fabio (Roma Tre University, Italy)
Gatti, Lorenzo (FBK-irst, Italy)
Gena, Cristina (University of Torino, Italy)
Genaro Motti, Vivian (George Mason University, USA)
Germanakos, Panagiotis (University of Cyprus, Cyprus)
Gouyon, Fabien (Pandora, USA)
Guchev, Vladimir (University of Torino, Italy)
Hamasaki, Masahiro (AIST, Japan)
Hashida, Mitsuyo (Soai University, Japan)
Herbig, Nico (DFKI, Germany)
Hirai, Shigeyuki (Kyoto Sangyo University, Japan)
Imura, Masataka (Osaka University, Japan)

Posters/Demos Program Committee (continued):

Ionescu, Bogdan (University Politehnica of Bucharest, Romania)
Itoh, Yuichi (Osaka University, Japan)
Jung, Hyunggu (University of Washington, USA)
Karatzoglou, Alexandros (Telefonica Research, Spain)
Kazuya, Murao (Ritsumeikan University, Japan)
Kleanthous, Styliani (University of Cyprus, Cyprus)
Kljun, Matjaž (University of Primorska, Slovenia)
Knees, Peter (TU Wien, Austria)
Kohlsdorf, Daniel (Georgia Institute of Technology, USA)
Kono, Yasuyuki (Kwansei Gakuin University, Japan)
Kosmalla, Felix (DFKI, Germany)
Kuflik, Tsvi (University of Haifa, Israel)
Kuramoto, Itaru (Osaka University, Japan)
Lanir, Joel (University of Haifa, Israel)
Loizou, Styliani Kleanthous (University of Cyprus, Cyprus)
Ludwig, Bernd (University Regensburg, Germany)
Mac Namee, Brian (University College Dublin, Ireland)
Manca, Marco (Manca, Italy)
Marolt, Matija (University of Ljubljana, Slovenia)
Marques, Diogo (University of Lisbon, Portugal)
Matsumura, Kohei (Ristumeikan University, Japan)
Minakuchi, Mitsuru (Kyoto Sangyo University, Japan)
Mitake, Hironori (Tokyo Institute of Technology, Japan)
Munekata, Nagisa (Hokkaido University, Japan)
Nakano, Mikio (Honda Research Institute, Japan)
Narducci, Fedelucio (University of Bari Aldo Moro, Italy)
Okada, Shogo (AIST, Japan)
Orlosky, Jason (Osaka University, Japan)
Parra, Denis (Pontificia Universidad Catolica de Chile, Chile)
Pereira, Lucas (University of Madeira, Portugal)
Pham, Phuong (University of Pittsburgh, USA)
Polignano, Marco (University of Bari, Italy)
Rapp, Amon (University of Torino, Italy)
Rauber, Andreas (TU Wien, Austria)
Sakaguchi, Saki (Kansai University, Japan)
Sakata, Nobuchika (Nara Institute of Science and Technology, Japan)
Santoro, Carmen (Santoro, Italy)
Schiavo, Gianluca (FBK - Fondazione Bruno Kessler, Italy)
Sezgin, T. Metin (Koc University, Turkey)
Spano, Lucio Davide (University of Cagliari, Italy)
Stober, Sebastian (Potsdam, Germany)
Su, Xiaojun (Chinese Academy of Sciences, China)
Sugiura, Yuta (Keio University, Japan)
Taele, Paul (Texas A&M University, USA)
Takashima, Kazuki (Tohoku University, Japan)

Posters/Demos Program Committee (continued):	Terada, Tsutomu (Kobe University, Japan) Tomeo, Paolo (University of Bari, Italy) Uranishi, Yuki (Osaka University, Japan) Vaish, Rajan (Stanford University, USA) Votis, Konstantinos (Information Technologies Institute, Greece) Wang, Yi (University of California, USA) Wauck, Helen (University of Illinois at Urbana-Champaign, USA) Wu, Wen (Hong Kong Baptist University, Hong Kong) Xiao, Xiang (University of Pittsburgh, USA) Xiao, Ziang (University of Illinois Urbana-Champaign, USA) Yamamoto, Goshiro (Kyoto University Hospital, Japan) Yang, Yi-Hsuan (Academia Sinica, Taiwan) Yu, Kun (CSIRO, Australia) Zhang, Amy (Massachusetts Institute of Technology, USA) Zheng, Yong (Illinois Institute of Technology, Chicago, USA) Zhou, Sharon (Stanford University, USA)

IUI 2018 Sponsors and Supporters

Sponsors:

Supporters:

From on Body to Out of Body User Experience

James A. Landay
Computer Science Department
Stanford University
Stanford, CA
landay@stanford.edu

ABSTRACT
Today's most common user interfaces represent an incremental change from the GUI popularized by the Apple Macintosh in 1984. Over the last 30 years the dominant hardware has changed drastically while the user interface has barely moved: from one hand on a mouse to two fingers on a panel of glass. I will illustrate how we are building on-body interfaces of the future that further engage our bodies by using muscle sensing for input and vibrotactile output, offering discrete and natural interaction on the go. I will also show how other interfaces we are designing take an even more radical approach, moving the interface off the human body altogether and onto drones that project into the space around them. Finally, I will introduce a new project where we envision buildings as hybrid physical-digital spaces that both sense and actuate to improve human wellbeing.

Author Keywords
Behavior Change; Ambient Display; Muscle Sensing; Vibrotactile Feedback; Human-Drone Interaction; Smart Buildings

BIOGRAPHY
James Landay is a Professor of Computer Science and the Anand Rajaraman and Venky Harinarayan Professor in the School of Engineering at Stanford University. He specializes in human-computer interaction. He is the founder and co-director of the World Lab, a joint research and educational effort with Tsinghua University in Beijing. Previously, Landay was a Professor of Information Science at Cornell Tech in New York City, a Professor of Computer Science & Engineering at the University of Washington, and a Professor in EECS at UC Berkeley. From 2003 through 2006 he was the Laboratory Director of Intel Labs Seattle, a university affiliated research lab that explored the new usage models, applications, and technology for ubiquitous computing. He was also the chief scientist and co-founder of NetRaker, which was acquired by KeyNote Systems in 2004. Landay received his BS in EECS from UC Berkeley in 1990, and MS and PhD in Computer Science from Carnegie Mellon University in 1993 and 1996, respectively. He is a member of the ACM SIGCHI Academy and he is an ACM Fellow.

IUI 2018, March 7–11, 2018, Tokyo, Japan.
ACM ISBN 978-1-4503-4945-1/18/03.
DOI: https://doi.org/10.1145/3172944.3176183

REFERENCES
1. Jessica R. Cauchard, Jane L. E, Kevin Y. Zhai, and James A. Landay. 2015. Drone & me: an exploration into natural human-drone interaction. In *Proceedings of the 2015 ACM International Joint Conference on Pervasive and Ubiquitous Computing* (UbiComp '15). ACM, New York, NY, USA, 361-365. DOI: https://doi.org/10.1145/2750858.2805823
2. Jessica R. Cauchard, Janette L. Cheng, Thomas Pietrzak, and James A. Landay. 2016. ActiVibe: Design and Evaluation of Vibrations for Progress Monitoring. In *Proceedings of the 2016 CHI Conference on Human Factors in Computing Systems* (CHI '16). ACM, New York, NY, USA, 3261-3271. DOI: https://doi.org/10.1145/2858036.2858046
3. Sunny Consolvo, David W. McDonald, Tammy Toscos, Mike Y. Chen, Jon Froehlich, Beverly Harrison, Predrag Klasnja, Anthony LaMarca, Louis LeGrand, Ryan Libby, Ian Smith, and James A. Landay. 2008. Activity sensing in the wild: a field trial of ubifit garden. In *Proceedings of the SIGCHI Conference on Human Factors in Computing Systems* (CHI '08). ACM, New York, NY, USA, 1797-1806. DOI: https://doi.org/10.1145/1357054.1357335

4. Jon Froehlich, Tawanna Dillahunt, Predrag Klasnja, Jennifer Mankoff, Sunny Consolvo, Beverly Harrison, and James A. Landay. 2009. UbiGreen: investigating a mobile tool for tracking and supporting green transportation habits. In *Proceedings of the SIGCHI Conference on Human Factors in Computing Systems* (CHI '09). ACM, New York, NY, USA, 1043-1052. DOI: https://doi.org/10.1145/1518701.1518861

5. T. Scott Saponas, Desney S. Tan, Dan Morris, Ravin Balakrishnan, Jim Turner, and James A. Landay. 2009. Enabling always-available input with muscle-computer interfaces. In *Proceedings of the 22nd annual ACM symposium on User interface software and technology* (UIST '09). ACM, New York, NY, USA, 167-176. DOI: https://doi.org/10.1145/1622176.1622208

Intelligent Music Interfaces

Masataka Goto
National Institute of Advanced Industrial Science and Technology (AIST), Japan
m.goto@aist.go.jp

ABSTRACT

Automatic music-understanding technologies (automatic analysis of music signals) make possible the creation of intelligent music interfaces that enrich music experiences and open up new ways of listening to music. In the past, it was common to listen to music in a somewhat passive manner; in the future, people will be able to enjoy music in a more active manner by using music technologies. Listening to music through active interactions is called *"active music listening."*

In this keynote speech I first introduce active music listening interfaces [1] demonstrating how end users can benefit from music-understanding technologies based on signal processing and/or machine learning. Music-understanding technologies can automatically estimate *music scene descriptions* [2] in musical audio signals: descriptions such as melody and bass lines, beat structure (beat and bar), and music structure (chorus section). By using the estimated music structure, for example, the active music listening interface *"SmartMusicKIOSK"* [3] enables people to access their favorite part of a song directly (skipping other parts) while viewing a visual representation of the song's structure. Other interfaces enable people to also customize (personalize) music by changing the volume or timbre of instrument sounds in existing music recordings and to browse a large music collection to encounter interesting musical pieces or artists.

I then introduce our recent challenge of deploying such research-level music interfaces as web services open to the public. For example, a web service for active music listening, *"Songle"* (http://songle.jp) [4], has analyzed more than 1,100,000 songs on the web and augments people's understanding of music by visualizing music scene descriptions estimated automatically. Since the current accuracy of automatic music understanding is less than that of human music understanding, Songle features a crowdsourcing interface that enables users to collectively correct analysis errors. Songle is used to provide a web-based multimedia development framework, *"Songle Widget"* (http://widget.songle.jp) [5], that enables music-synchronized control of computer-graphics animation and robots. It makes it easy to develop web-based applications with rigid music synchronization by leveraging music-understanding technologies. Furthermore, by using web-mining and music-understanding technologies, a web service for large-scale music browsing, *"Songrium"* (http://songrium.jp) [6], provides various bird's-eye views on more than 780,000 music video clips on video-sharing services.

In the future, further advances in music-understanding technologies and music interfaces based on them will make interaction between people and music even more active and enriching.

Author Keywords

Music interface; music understanding; music analysis; active music listening; web service; music information research

BIOGRAPHY

Masataka Goto received the Doctor of Engineering degree from Waseda University in 1998. He is currently a Prime Senior Researcher at the National Institute of Advanced Industrial Science and Technology (AIST). In 1992 he was one of the first to start working on automatic music understanding and has since been at the forefront of research in music technologies and music interfaces based on those technologies. Over the past 25 years he has published more than 250 papers in refereed journals and international conferences and has received 46 awards, including several best paper awards, best presentation awards, the Tenth Japan Academy Medal, and the Tenth JSPS PRIZE.

IUI 2018, March 7–11, 2018, Tokyo, Japan.
ACM ISBN 978-1-4503-4945-1/18/03.
DOI: https://doi.org/10.1145/3172944.3176184

He has served as a committee member of over 110 scientific societies and conferences, including the General Chair of the 10th and 15th International Society for Music Information Retrieval Conferences (ISMIR 2009 and 2014). As the Research Director he began a 5-year research project (OngaCREST Project) [7] in 2011 and follow-on 5-year research project (OngaACCEL Project) in 2016, both of which have focused on music technologies and been funded by the Japan Science and Technology Agency (CREST/ACCEL, JST).

https://staff.aist.go.jp/m.goto/

ACKNOWLEDGMENTS

I thank (in alphabetical order) Hiromasa Fujihara, Satoru Fukayama, Masahiro Hamasaki, Takahiro Inoue, Keisuke Ishida, Yuta Kawasaki, Matthias Mauch, Tomoyasu Nakano, Kosetsu Tsukuda, and Kazuyoshi Yoshii, who have been working with me to build music interfaces and web services. This work was supported in part by JST ACCEL Grant Number JPMJAC1602, Japan.

REFERENCES

1. Masataka Goto: Active Music Listening Interfaces Based on Signal Processing, Proceedings of the 2007 IEEE International Conference on Acoustics, Speech, and Signal Processing (IEEE ICASSP 2007), pp.IV-1441-1444, April 2007.
2. Masataka Goto: A Real-time Music-scene-description System: Predominant-F0 Estimation for Detecting Melody and Bass Lines in Real-world Audio Signals, Speech Communication (ISCA Journal), Vol.43, No.4, pp.311-329, September 2004.
3. Masataka Goto: A Chorus-Section Detection Method for Musical Audio Signals and Its Application to a Music Listening Station, IEEE Transactions on Audio, Speech, and Language Processing, Vol.14, No.5, pp.1783-1794, September 2006.
4. Masataka Goto, Kazuyoshi Yoshii, Hiromasa Fujihara, Matthias Mauch, and Tomoyasu Nakano: Songle: A Web Service for Active Music Listening Improved by User Contributions, Proceedings of the 12th International Society for Music Information Retrieval Conference (ISMIR 2011), pp.311-316, October 2011.
5. Masataka Goto, Kazuyoshi Yoshii, and Tomoyasu Nakano: Songle Widget: Making Animation and Physical Devices Synchronized with Music Videos on the Web, Proceedings of the IEEE International Symposium on Multimedia (IEEE ISM 2015), pp.85-88, December 2015.
6. Masahiro Hamasaki, Masataka Goto, and Tomoyasu Nakano: Songrium: A Music Browsing Assistance Service with Interactive Visualization and Exploration of a Web of Music, Proceedings of the 23rd International World Wide Web Conference (WWW 2014), pp.523-528, April 2014.
7. Masataka Goto: Frontiers of Music Information Research Based on Signal Processing, Proceedings of the 12th IEEE International Conference on Signal Processing (IEEE ICSP 2014), pp.7-14, October 2014.

Surveillance or Support: When Personalization Turns Creepy

Jennifer Golbeck
University of Maryland
College Park, MD 20742 USA
jgolbeck@umd.edu

ABSTRACT
Personalization, recommendations, and user modeling can be powerful tools to improve people's experiences with technology and to help them find information. However, we also know that people underestimate how much of their personal information is used by our technology and they generally do not understand how much algorithms can discover about them.

Both privacy and ethical technology have issues of consent at their heart. While many personalization systems assume most users would consent to the way they employ personal data, research shows this is not necessarily the case. This talk will look at how to consider issues of privacy and consent when users cannot explicitly state their preferences, The Creepy Factor, and how to balance users' concerns with the benefits personalized technology can offer.

Author Keywords
personalization; privacy; recommender systems; user preference

BIOGRAPHY
Jennifer Golbeck is Director of the Social Intelligence Lab and an Associate Professor in the College of Information Studies at the University of Maryland, College Park where she is director of the Social Intelligence Lab.

Her research focuses on analyzing and computing with social media, focused on predicting user attributes, and using the results to design and build systems that improve the way people interact with information online. She also studies malicious behavior online, including bot detection, online harassment, and fake news.

She received an AB in Economics and an SB and SM in Computer Science at the University of Chicago, and a Ph.D. in Computer Science from the University of Maryland, College Park.

IUI 2018, March 7–11, 2018, Tokyo, Japan.
ACM ISBN 978-1-4503-4945-1/18/03.
DOI: https://doi.org/10.1145/3172944.3176185

FocusMusicRecommender: A System for Recommending Music to Listen to While Working

Hiromu Yakura
University of Tsukuba
Tsukuba, Japan
hiromu@coins.tsukuba.ac.jp

Tomoyasu Nakano **Masataka Goto**
National Institute of Advanced Industrial Science and Technology (AIST), Tsukuba, Japan
{t.nakano, m.goto}@aist.go.jp

ABSTRACT

This paper proposes *FocusMusicRecommender*, an automated system recommending background music to listen to while working. Recommendation systems matching user preferences have been widely researched even though research has shown that music that listeners strongly like is not suitable background music because it interferes with their concentration. FocusMusicRecommender plays songs that users may "neither like nor dislike" instead of "like very much." It is designed to by default summarize a song automatically so that users can give "like very much" feedback by pressing a "keep listening" button or "dislike very much" feedback by pressing a "skip" button. It uses this feedback, along with users' concentration levels estimated from their behavior history, to distinguish between the preference levels "like" and "like very much." It then estimates the preference levels of unplayed songs and selects the most suitable song by considering the user's current concentration level. The effectiveness of the proposed feedback method and suitability of the recommendation results were verified experimentally and in user studies. Furthermore, it is confirmed that the proposed method can estimate the user's concentration level more accurately than the previous methods.

CCS Concepts

•Human-centered computing → HCI design and evaluation methods; •Applied computing → Sound and music computing;

Author Keywords

Music recommendation; concentration level estimation; background music.

INTRODUCTION

Many people listen to music while working. In the survey of 189 students by Lonsdale et al. [21], 75.7% of the participants confirmed that they listen to music when working or studying, and most of them reported that they listened because it helped them concentrate. The efficacy of music as a study

IUI'18, March 07–11, 2018, Tokyo, Japan

ISBN 978-1-4503-4945-1/18/03...$15.00

DOI: https://doi.org/10.1145/3172944.3172981

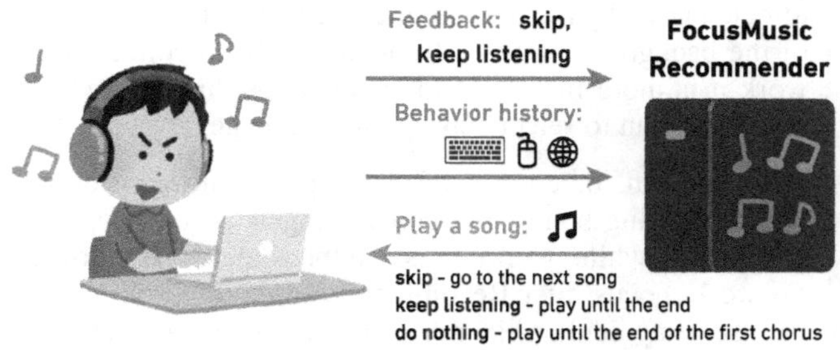

Figure 1. Usage of FocusMusicRecommender. It selects songs automatically according to the user's feedback and behavior history and plays in an abridged manner.

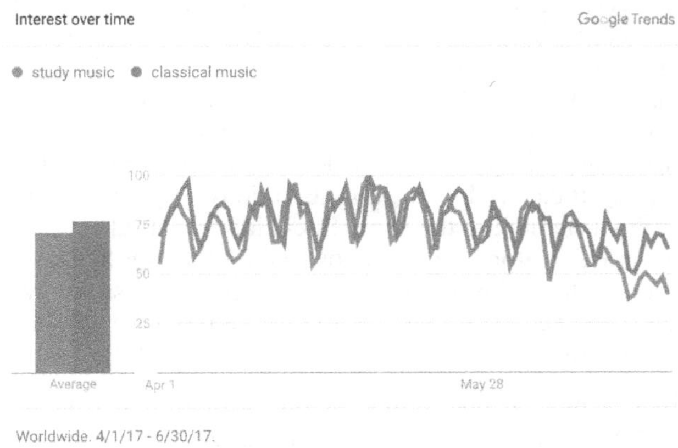

Figure 2. Comparison of the interest of the terms "study music" and "classical music" in YouTube[3]. The search interest of "study music" is as high as that of "classical music," and they drop on weekends.

aid is also suggested by Figure 2 taken from Google Trends[1], which presents the popularity of search queries in YouTube[2]. It shows that the term "study music" is used as frequently as "classical music" which is often used in psychological studies to measure the effect of background music [25, 12, 27, 15]. We therefore propose *FocusMusicRecommender*, a system recommending background music suitable for listening to while working and thereby improve the efficiency and the quality of one's work.

The conventional systems for recommending a song that the user would like the most [28] are unsuitable because a song

[1] https://trends.google.com/

[2] https://www.youtube.com/

[3] This result can be inferred from https://g.co/trends/4Zhu7.

strongly preferred by the user may interfere with the user's concentration. This is supported by a survey by Huang et al. [15] on the relation between concentration level while listening to songs and the preference level for the songs rated using a five-point Likert scale of "like very much," "like," "neither like nor dislike," "dislike," and "dislike very much." They concluded that the concentration level of people listening to songs they liked or disliked very much was much worse than it was in a silent environment whereas that of people listening to songs they liked, neither liked nor disliked, or disliked was not significantly different from what it was in a silent environment. They also concluded that the concentration level was affected more by the user's preference level than by the genre of the background music. In other words, to concentrate on work it is more important to avoid songs that arouse strong emotions than to select appropriate music genres.

The user can, of course, take this point into consideration when selecting songs, but considering how much one likes each song while working is troublesome. As shown in Figure 1, FocusMusicRecommender therefore selects songs the user may neither like nor dislike automatically according to the user's working behavior (mouse operation, etc.) and the user's listening feedback elicited by the songs (skipping, etc.) and plays them continuously.

FocusMusicRecommender also plays songs in an abridged manner by using chorus section information. The song ends after the first chorus section. This was inspired by the fact that many video clips posted on video-sharing services concatenate chorus sections of multiple songs for the purpose of listening while working[4]. It lets a user encounter unknown music efficiently by listening to various songs and does this without burdening the user. In detail, we introduce a "keep listening" button to make it possible for the user to give feedback such as "I want to listen more because it is my favorite song" as well as a "skip" button for giving feedback such as "I want to skip this song because I dislike it" [24].

Furthermore, FocusMusicRecommender estimates the user's concentration level and takes it into account for recommendation. Based on the hypothesis that feedback given when concentrating reflects the preference level for songs better than does feedback given when not concentrating, the system combines the estimated concentration level with the feedback to determine the preference level precisely. In addition, when there are multiple songs judged suitable to be recommended, the system selects one by adjusting the selection criterion according to the concentration level.

RELATED WORK

In this section we describe related research on music recommendation for specific situations, music recommendation based on limited feedback, and estimation of concentration level during working with a computer keyboard and mouse. The situation of working with a keyboard and mouse is not limited to desktop computers and laptops and may be similar to that of working with a tablet or the like, so hereinafter these kinds of devices are collectively referred to as personal computers.

Music Recommendation for Specific Situations

Many methods of music recommendation for specific situations have been proposed [23, 22, 18, 1]. For example, PAPA proposed by Oliver et al. [23] uses the user's heart rate as feedback in order to assist physical exercise. The system plays faster songs (more beats per minute) when the heart rate is low and plays slower songs when the heart rate is high. InCarMusic proposed by Baltrunas et al. [1] is targeted to support driving of a car and changes the selection priority of music genres according to whether the user is traveling an ordinary road or an expressway, whether the user is sleepy or alert, and so on.

Although music recommendation systems using recent machine learning algorithms have been proposed [19, 32], none of them recommend background music suitable for listening to while working because they don't prioritize songs that the user neither likes nor dislikes. That is one of the reasons why Demetriou et al. [8] recommended that the music information retrieval community develop recommendation systems optimizing the user's level of cognitive engagement rather than to meeting the user's preference.

Music Recommendation on Limited Feedback

To design a music recommendation system to be used while working, suppressing the burden of giving feedback is important. For example, Pampalk et al. [24] proposed a method that recommends music on extremely limited feedback from users. It uses as feedback only the skip operation that the user either performed or did not perform while a song was playing: songs that were not skipped are regarded as liked and songs that were skipped are regarded as disliked.

1. For each candidate song, let s_s be the musical similarity to the nearest song skipped and let s_a be the similarity to the nearest song that was not skipped.
2. If there are candidate songs that satisfy $s_a > s_s$, play the one with the largest s_a.
3. Otherwise, play the song with the largest $\frac{s_a}{s_s}$.

This method uses only the two preference levels determined according to whether or not the user skips a song – i.e., "dislike very much" or "not dislike very much" – and thus cannot give priority to songs that are neither liked nor disliked when recommending music to listen to while working.

Concentration Level Estimation

Since FocusMusicRecommender recommends in accordance with the user's concentration level, it should estimate the concentration level automatically. Estimating "concentration" or "interruptibility" level during work on a personal computer has been investigated in several studies [30, 9, 35, 29]. For example, Fogarty et al. [9] used not only the numbers of keyboard and mouse operations but also the door-opening count

[4]Searching "*Sagyouyou BGM* (in Japanese)," which means background music to be listened to while working, in YouTube gives clips that have titles like "*Chorus medley* (in Japanese)" and concatenate summarized version of multiple songs.

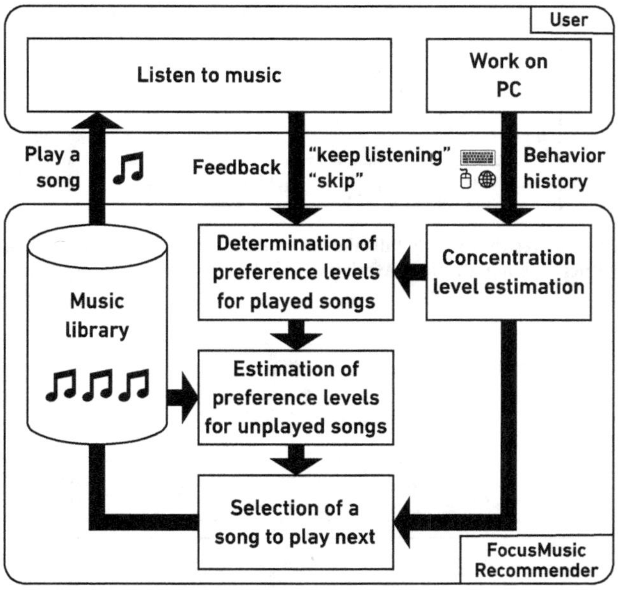

Figure 3. Overview of FocusMusicRecommender. It determines the user's preference levels for songs and selects the song played next according to the user's feedback and behavior history.

detected by a magnetic sensor. Züger et al. [35] used a biometric sensor to measure the user's electroencephalogram, skin potential, and heart rate. Tanaka et al. [29] proposed a method combining the numbers of keyboard and mouse operations and the number of switchings of active applications.

Using physical sensors or biosensors for music recommendation, however, is considered unrealistic in terms of costs and the psychological barriers of users. The method proposed by Tanaka et al. [29] uses features that can be collected without using external sensors, but it uses the number of specific operations in a fixed length of time and therefore cannot be applied during music playback where the length of time is variable because a song may be skipped after only a few seconds.

FOCUSMUSICRECOMMENDER

In this section we describe the overview of FocusMusicRecommender (Figure 3) and describe the methods that determine the user's preference level for played songs and select the songs to be played next.

Overview

FocusMusicRecommender is a system that helps users concentrate by listening to music when working on a personal computer. Although a user could use an automatic playback function in order to avoid the trouble of bothering to select songs during work, random playback or the conventional recommendation method plays songs the user may like very much, which interferes with the user's concentration. The proposed system therefore automatically selects songs the user neither likes nor dislikes and summarizes them by successively playing each from its beginning to the end of the first chorus section.

Many methods of music summarization using chorus section information have been proposed [20, 5, 7]. Along with the user-generated summarized clips described in Section *"Introduction"*, the acceptance of such automated summarization function in music players is supported by the fact that similar functions are implemented in the Walkman portable music player[5] and the continuous playback function[6] of the music browsing assistance service Songrium [13], and therefore it is considered to be effective. Furthermore, the function enables the system to introduce a "keep listening" button, which is necessary to avoid playing songs the user may like very much. Without the function, the system would need to require the user to explicitly input the preference level song by song, which would distract the user from his/her work.

The system therefore determines the preference level according to both user feedback such as "keep listening" or "skip" and the concentration level estimated from the user's behavior history on the personal computer. Furthermore, to choose the most suitable of multiple candidate songs it adjusts the selection criterion according to the estimated concentration level.

Determination of User's Preference Level for Played Songs

In this section we describe in detail a method for determining a user's preference level for played songs. As shown in Figure 4, we first introduce a "keep listening" button to determine the three levels "like very much," "neither like nor dislike," and "dislike very much" and then extend the determination to five levels by using the user's concentration level.

User Feedback from a "keep listening" Button

Getting user feedback from a "keep listening" button extends the method of Pampalk et al. [24], described in Section *"Music Recommendation on Limited Feedback"*, and enables the system to eliminate not only songs the user dislikes very much but also songs the user likes very much. While songs are being summarized the system determines their preference levels according to the following user feedback.

- **Do nothing**
  It plays the song until the end of the first chorus section and judges that the user neither likes nor dislikes the song. Each song is played back at least 30 seconds because it is difficult for the user to decide right after the playback starts whether to skip a song or keep listening to it.

- **Press "skip" button**
  It judges that the user dislikes the song very much, and it plays the next song immediately.

- **Press "keep listening" button**
  It judges that the user likes the song very much, and it plays it until the end.

[5] ZAPPIN Playback: https://docs.sony.com/release/NWZW273S_W274S_guide_EN.pdf
[6] Songrium Smart Player: http://smart.songrium.jp/

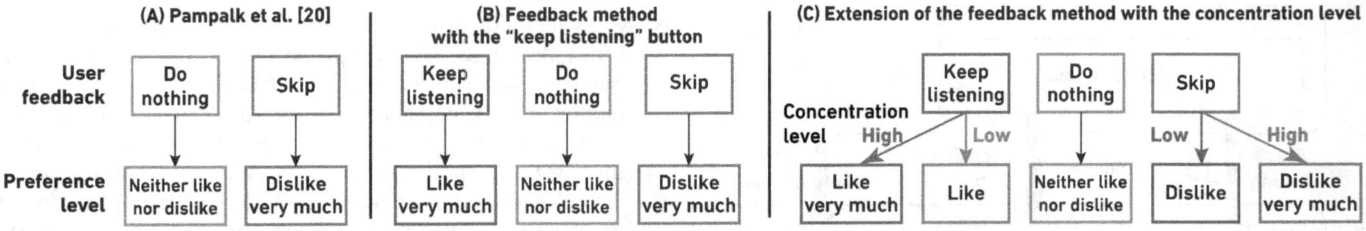

Figure 4. Relations between user feedback and preference levels. (A) From the "skip" feedback, only "dislike very much" or not can be obtained. (B) Adding "keep listening" feedback makes three preference levels, including "neither like nor dislike," available. (C) Five levels, including "like" and "dislike," can be obtained by combining the concentration level.

Table 1. Preference level can be obtained on a five-point scale by combining user feedback and concentration level as indicated in this table and shown in Figure 4(C).

Concentration	User Feedback		
	Keep listening	Do nothing	Skip
High	Like very much	Neither like nor dislike	Dislike very much
Low	Like	Neither like nor dislike	Dislike

Refine Preference Level Using Estimated Concentration Level
After obtaining the preference in "like very much," "neither like nor dislike," and "dislike very much" levels by the method described in Section *"User Feedback from a "keep listening" Button"*, the system determines it in five levels including "like" and "dislike" by using the user's concentration level and the following hypothesis.

> **Hypothesis** User feedback obtained under a high level of concentration expresses the preference level better than feedback obtained under a low level of concentration.

The system determines the preference level by combining the user feedback and the concentration level as summarized in Table 1.

The reason we extend the feedback by using the concentration level is that discriminating liked songs from liked very much songs is more suitable for the problem situation. In detail, according to [15], misclassifying liked songs as neither liked nor disliked may not affect the concentration of the user as much as not discriminating between songs that are liked and songs that are liked very much would. We therefore enable the system to deal with such prioritization by combining the five-level preference with hierarchical classification algorithms [17] as shown in Figure 5. This helps the system to reduce the possibility of misclassifying songs the user likes or dislikes very much as songs the user neither likes nor dislikes, which would interfere with the user's concentration.

Song Selection Method Corresponds to Concentration Level

The system estimates the preference levels of songs that have not been played yet relative to those of previously played songs and plays songs the user may neither like nor dislike. If

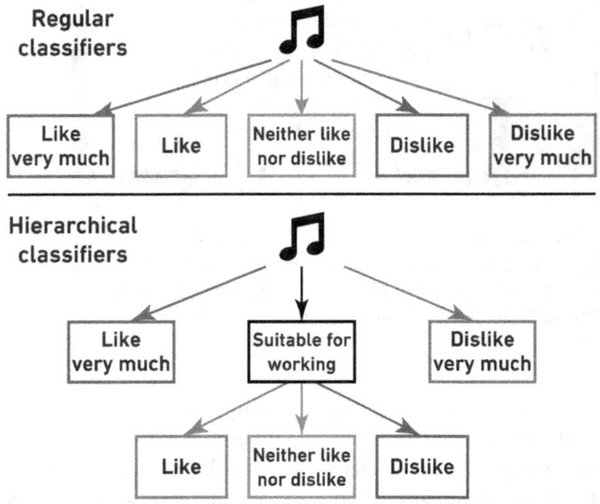

Figure 5. Difference between regular classifiers and hierarchical classifiers in FocusMusicRecommender. The extension of the feedback to five levels enables the hierarchical classifier to treat liked songs, neither liked nor disliked songs, and disliked songs as belonging to a subgroup of songs suitable to be listened to while working.

there are two or more songs estimated to be neither liked nor disliked, the system needs to choose one of them.

For the purpose of enhancing the user's concentration, it adjusts the selection criterion according to the current level of concentration. When the concentration level is high, priority is given to music similar to the song that was played immediately before in order to avoid sudden changes that might distract the user. On the other hand, when it is low, priority is adjusted to play a variety of songs in order to give the user a chance to change his/her mood. These priority adjustments are based on the results of a survey by Wells [34]: 73.3% of the 225 participants agreed that music is useful for changing their mood and that the genres of music that they listen to for changing their mood are very diverse.

IMPLEMENTATION

As shown in Figure 6, FocusMusicRecommender consists of four modules: playback, behavior history collection, concentration level estimation, and music selection. In this section we describe the implementation of each module.

Playback

The playback module plays the selected song in cooperation with the other three modules by using Songle Widget [11], which is an open framework for providing an embeddable

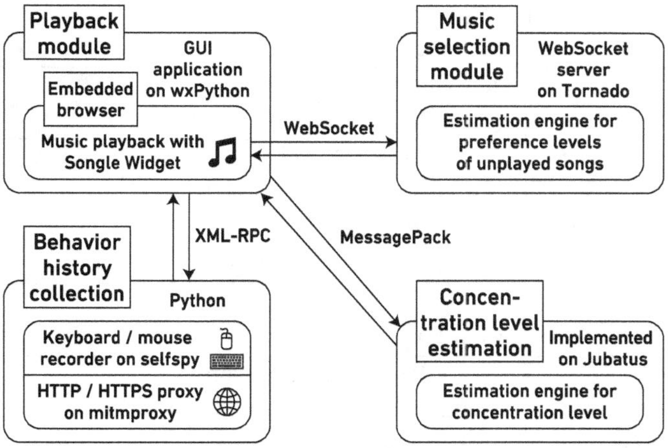

Figure 6. Structure of FocusMusicRecommender. The playback module handles the interface, and the other three modules operate in the background.

music player. Songle Widget makes playback easy by using chorus section information that is estimated automatically and can be corrected manually on Songle [10].

Behavior History Collection

The behavior history collection module records three types of action logs: keyboard input, mouse input, and Web communication (Table 2). The reason we record Web communication, which is not used in existing related methods [30, 9, 35, 29], is that it reflects the work content, such as whether the user is performing a web search or using a social networking service.

Concentration Level Estimation

The concentration level estimation module uses the online learning algorithm AROW [6] with the n-gram of the hash value of the behavior history. This method not only solves the problem described in Section *"Concentration Level Estimation"* but also can use more information such as application name and host name, than would be available if only the number of operations were used. For example, Google and Facebook accesses have different meanings in this method because they produce different hash values, while the counting method treats Google and Facebook accesses equally. This method was inspired by malware detection methods that use n-grams of the hash values of the system call for learning [26, 2].

There are several reasons we use AROW for the concentration level estimation [6]:

- It is suitable when collecting a large amount of labeled data is difficult because it uses passive-aggressive update algorithm and therefore converges faster than other algorithms.
- It is suitable when the feature space is sparse because it uses a confidence-weighted algorithm to take into account the frequency of features.
- It is suitable when the labeled data may contain noise such as the subjective deviance of the concentration level because it uses a mistake bound that doesn't assume separability.

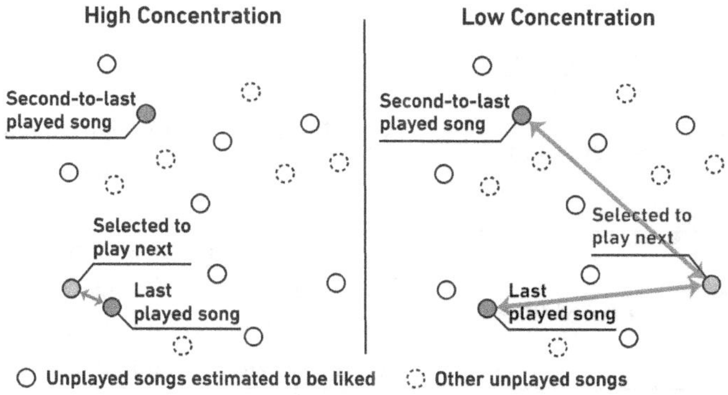

Figure 7. Overview of the song selection method. When the concentration level is high, the song most similar to the last played song is selected. When it is low, the song most dissimilar to the two previous songs is selected.

Music Selection

As mentioned in Section *"Song Selection Method Corresponds to Concentration Level"*, the music selection module estimates the preference levels for unplayed songs relative to those for played songs. This module uses HierCost [4] based on user's preference-level information obtained by the method described in Section *"Determination of User's Preference Level for Played Songs"*. The reasons for using HierCost are that it is one of the hierarchical classification algorithms that can be used for educational and research purpose and also that it is designed to deal with unbalanced data. Even though the number played songs is limited, HierCost's ability to deal with unbalanced data reduces the chance of playing songs that interfere with a user's concentration because they are songs the user likes or dislikes very much but were misclassified as songs the user neither likes nor dislikes.

When selecting the song to be played next, the system changes the criterion in accordance with the concentration level estimated as described in Section *"Song Selection Method Corresponds to Concentration Level"*. Although several recommendation methods [3, 16] consider songs recently played, our proposed method also considers both the estimated preference levels and the current concentration level as follows (Figure 7):

1. To start making a listening history, select the first and second songs randomly.
2. Estimate the preference levels of unplayed songs and list as candidates all songs labeled as "neither like nor dislike." If there are none, select candidates in the order of songs labeled as "like," "dislike," "like very much," and "dislike very much," according to the effect on the concentration level described in [15].
3. Select the third (next) songs from the candidates based on the musical similarity like [24] as follows.
   (a) When the user's concentration level is high, in order to avoid sudden changes that might distract the user, select the song that is the most similar to the last played song (the song with the maximum similarity to the song played immediately before).

Table 2. List of user behaviors collected by FocusMusicRecommender.

Types of Behavior	Collected Information	Examples
Keyboard input	"key [Target application name] [Key]" (Modifier keys are put together in a single event.)	"key Google Chrome a" (Press "a" in Google Chrome)
		"key Microsoft Excel <[Ctrl: v]>" (Press "Ctrl+v" in Microsoft Excel)
Mouse input	"mouse [Target application name] [Event number]" (Event numbers 1 ∼ 7 respectively represent left, middle, and right button clicks and up, down, left, and right scrolling.)	"mouse Firefox 1" (Click a left button in Firefox)
		"mouse Skype 4" (Scroll up in Skype)
Web communication (HTTP/HTTPS)	"web [Request method] [Hostname]" (Only GET and POST requests are collected.)	"web GET www.google.com" (Send a GET request to www.google.com)
		"web POST www.facebook.com" (Send a POST request to www.facebook.com)

(b) When the user's concentration level is low, in order to give the user a chance to change his/her mood [34], select the song that is the least similar to both the last played song and the second-to-last played song (a song with the minimum sum of similarities to the two songs played immediately before). This selection is based on the two previous songs. Otherwise, the problem that songs in two genres are selected alternately would occur, reducing the diversity of the songs played.

4. Go back to 2.

EVALUATION

We first evaluated the accuracy of the concentration level estimation and validity of the preference level determination experimentally and then conducted user studies. In this section we describe detailed procedures and their results.

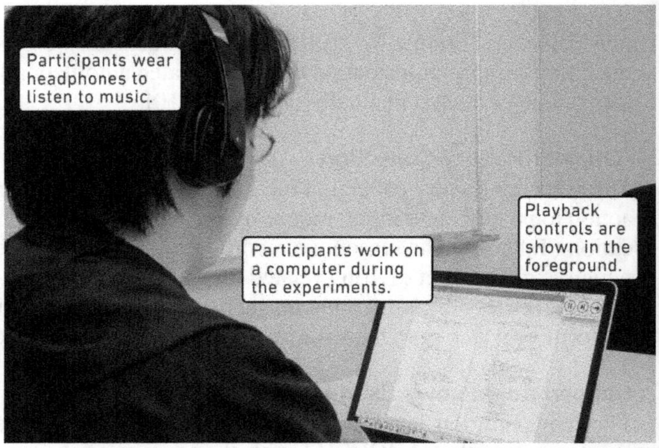

Figure 8. Example of experimental setup. Participants listened to music using earphones or headphones while working on a personal computer in a quiet room.

Data

We used top 50 most frequently played songs with the tag "VOCALOID," which are songs created using a popular singing synthesis software, in the popular Japanese video-sharing service *NicoNico Douga* (`http://nicovideo.jp/`). Our experiments used VOCALOID songs because accurate user-corrected chorus sections for all 50 songs are available via Songle Widget. Furthermore, those songs tend to cover diverse genres[7] because they are created in a user-generated content community [14, 13]. In fact, 15 different tags indicating the genres are used for the songs such as "*VOCAROCK* (tags used for rock music)," "*Vocaloid Japanese-style music*," and "*Mikuno-Pop* (tags used for electro-pop music)."

The similarity between songs was estimated based on three-dimensional musical feature vector calculated in Songrium [13]. First, MARSYAS [31] was used to obtain a 35-dimensional feature vector for more than 98,000 VOCALOID songs. The vector consists of the mean and variance of average values of mel-frequency cepstral coefficients calculated across the entire song (26 dimensions), the mean and variance of local spectral features (centroid, rolloff, flux, and zero-crossings) across the entire song (8 dimensions), and the tempo in the chorus section (1 dimension). Then the first through the third principal components were retained by applying principal component analysis (PCA) to the feature vector for dimensionality reduction.

[7] As of Oct 1, 2017, 141 tags indicating the user-defined music genre of VOCALOID songs are listed in "*NicoNico Pedia*," a Wiki system for topics related to *NicoNico Douga* (`http://dic.nicovideo.jp/id/252926` in Japanese).

Experiments

To confirm the effectiveness of the proposed methods, we conducted two experiments using data obtained from users. The first evaluated the concentration level estimation described in Section *"Implementation"* and the second evaluated the preference level determination described in Section *"Determination of User's Preference Level for Played Songs"*.

Collection of User Data for Evaluation

These experiments involved eight voluntary participants (male students 17 to 24 years old) who were in the habit of

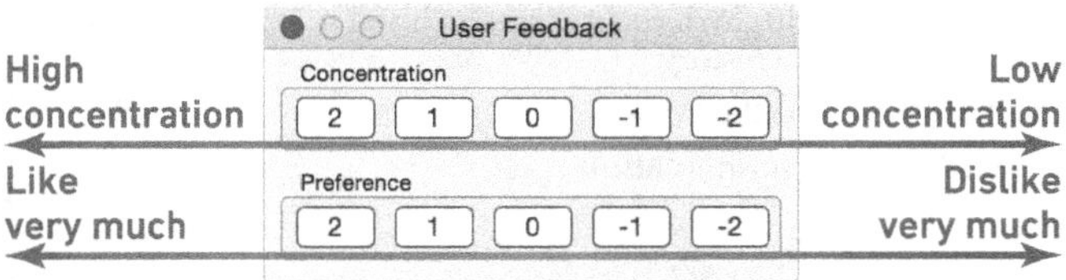

Figure 9. Dialog box used for entering the concentration level and preference level as validation data. The system asks users to enter these data each time a song is played.

Table 3. Confusion matrix of concentration level estimation (five-class).

Estimated Label	User-entered Label 2	1	0	−1	−2
2 (High)	28	18	18	9	5
1	14	39	12	11	9
0	11	10	22	12	12
−1	5	11	15	30	28
−2 (Low)	5	12	11	22	31
Total	63	90	78	84	85

listening to music while working on a personal computer. In a quiet room they listened to all 50 target songs in random order using headphones while being presented with "keep listening" and "skip" buttons. During the experiments, four participants wrote new documents by using word processing applications and the other four worked on programming on a personal computer (Figure 8). Their behavior histories were collected automatically, and they were informed beforehand that the history data is saved in the form of irreversible hashes so that they can work as they usually do.

Their concentration levels and preference levels were also obtained using a dialog box (Figure 9) presented each time a song was played. The method of obtaining validation data by dialog box was used in previous studies of concentration level estimation [9, 29], and as in those studies we used five-point scales ranging from "like very much" to "dislike very much" for preference level and from "high concentration" to "low concentration" for concentration level.

Accuracy of Concentration Level Estimation

Verifying by five-fold cross-validation the correspondence of the estimated concentration level and the validation data that the participants entered, we found that the accuracy was 37.5% in five-class estimation and 70.5% in two-class estimation. Table 3 and Table 4 present the respective confusion matrices.

Although the accuracy of the two-class estimation was lower than that of the method using the physical sensor (76.9%) [9]

Table 4. Confusion matrix of concentration level estimation (two-class).

Estimated Label	User-entered Label High (2, 1)	Low (0 $\sim$ −2)
High concentration	99	64
Low concentration	54	183
Total	153	247

and that of the method using the biometric sensor (78.6%) [35], it was higher than that of the method using features that can be collected without external sensors (58.4%) [29]. Therefore the effectiveness of the proposed method for estimating the concentration level was confirmed.

We compared the accuracy of the concentration levels estimated from behavior history with and without consideration of Web communication history. The result is shown in Table 5, and it indicates that the Web communication history improves the accuracy of the estimated concentration levels.

In calculating the above accuracies of the previous methods [9, 29] and the proposed method, we converted the multiclass estimation results into the two-class estimation results by following the procedure of Züger et al. [35]: a concentration level labeled "neither high nor low" (= 0) is categorized as "low."

Validity of Preference Level Determination

First we evaluated the validity of the "keep listening" feedback describe in Section *"User Feedback from a "keep listening" Button"* by checking whether the preference level of songs the participants wanted to keep listening to was high and that of songs they wanted to skip was low. The result is shown in Table 6, and Pearson's correlation coefficient between the preference level the participants entered and the user feedback is 0.55 ($p < 0.01$). Note that p-value here indicates the probability that the data would have arisen if there is no correlation.

Then we evaluated whether the determination method that combines the concentration level estimation with the "keep listening" feedback appropriately reflects the user's preference level. The result is shown in Table 7, and Pearson's correlation coefficient between the preference level determined by the proposed method and the one that the participants entered is 0.67 ($p < 0.01$). Therefore the hypothesis mentioned in Section *"Refine Preference Level Using Estimated Concentration Level"* was supported and the appropriateness of the proposed determination method shown in Table 1 was confirmed.

Moreover, in Table 7, we can find quite a few "like" and "dislike" songs in the "do nothing" row. It suggests that users at the high concentration level don't pay attention to songs that they neither "like very much" nor "dislike very much" as shown in Figure 4(C). In other words, it confirms that songs disliked, liked, or neither liked nor disliked don't interfere with users' concentration as stated in [15].

User Study

In the user study, the eight participants in the experiments described in Section *"Collection of User Data for Evaluation"* used FocusMusicRecommender and the comparison implementations described below.

Skipping Behavior (SB)

We implemented as a baseline for comparison a system based on the conventional method proposed by [24] that uses the skip operation as feedback. Instead of avoiding songs similar to songs the user skipped, the system

Table 5. Comparison of the accuracy of the concentration levels estimated with and without using Web communication history. The accuracy obtained using Web communication history was higher than that obtained not using Web communication history.

	Without Web Communication (only mouse and keyboard)	With Web Communication
5-class	32.4%	37.5%
2-class	61.9%	70.5%

Table 6. Correspondence between the user-entered preference level and the "keep listening" and "skip" feedback ($r = 0.55, p < 0.01$).

User Feedback	Preference Level: Like very much (2)	Like, Neither like nor dislike, Dislike ($1 \sim -1$)	Dislike very much (-2)	Total
Keep listening	43	64	2	109
Do nothing	13	179	6	198
Skip	1	52	40	93
Total	57	295	48	400

Table 7. Correspondence between the user-entered preference level and the combination of the estimated concentration level and the user feedback ($r = 0.67, p < 0.01$).

User Feedback (Concentration Level)	Preference Level: Like 2	1	0	−1	Dislike −2	Total
Keep listening (High concentration)	22	8	3	2	0	35
Keep listening (Low concentration)	21	33	12	6	2	74
Do nothing	13	45	107	27	6	198
Skip (Low concentration)	1	5	3	35	19	63
Skip (High concentration)	0	2	1	6	21	30
Total	57	93	126	76	48	400

plays songs that are dissimilar to songs for which the user pressed either a "skip" or "keep listening" button. In other words, we extended the binary feedback of [24] shown in Figure 4(A) to the three levels shown in Figure 4(B) in order to avoid songs the user may like or dislike very much.

FocusMusicRecommender Not Considering Concentration Level (FMR-1)

We implemented an alternative version of FocusMusicRecommender that doesn't take the user's concentration level into account. The system estimates the preference level of unplayed songs in the three levels using the feedback shown in Figure 4(B), and thus, the estimation process is excepted to perform like regular classifiers that don't use the hierarchical information. Then instead of changing the selection criterion as described in Section *"Music Selection"*, the system selects the song to be played next randomly from unplayed songs estimated to be neither liked nor disliked.

Table 8. Distribution of the preference levels and the number of operations for the songs played by SB, FMR-1, and FMR-2. The proposed method plays fewer songs that the participants like very much or dislike very much and would decrease the concentration level.

	Preference Level: Like 2	1	0	−1	Dislike −2	Participants pressed "skip" or "keep listening"
SB	43	62	79	38	18	102
FMR-1	30	45	111	34	20	91
FMR-2	22	48	121	38	11	70

FocusMusicRecommender with Concentration Level (FMR-2)

We of course also implemented the proposed version of FocusMusicRecommender. The system uses the five-level preference based on the estimated concentration level shown in Figure 4(C). The system also changes the criterion for selecting songs to be played next in accordance with the concentration level as described in Section *"Music Selection"*.

The participants used each implementation until 30 of the 50 songs had been played under the same condition of work contents and environments, and they commented on the ease of use and their impressions of the songs played. The data collection described in Section *"Collection of User Data for Evaluation"* was carried out at least one month before the user study in order to avoid anomalous results due to short-term preference changes caused by repeated listening.

Result

Table 8 shows the distribution of the preference level the participants entered beforehand in Section *"Collection of User Data for Evaluation"* and the number of operations the participants performed for songs played by SB, FMR-1, and FMR-2. In contrast to the distribution of the population shown in the bottom row of Table 7, the hypergeometric p-value of avoiding "like very much" or "dislike very much" songs in SB, FMR-1, and FMR-2 is 0.1×10^{-1}, 2.4×10^{-7}, and 1.6×10^{-13}, respectively. The results demonstrate that FMR-

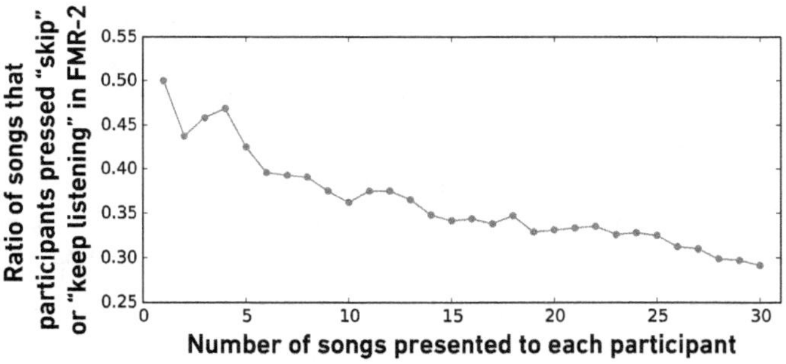

Figure 10. Transition of the ratio of songs that participants pressed the "skip" or "keep listening" button while listening to the recommendation results of FMR-2.

2, which implements the proposed method, played fewer songs that would decrease the concentration level than SB and FMR-1 did and thus is suitable for use during work. This is supported by the fact that FMR-2 caused fewer interruptions due to pressing the "skip" or "keep listening" button than SB and FMR-1 did.

The difference between the results of SB and FMR-1 is due to FMR-1 deciding what song to play by using a learning algorithm to estimate the preference levels of unplayed songs and SB basing the decision on the neighbors of each song. The difference between FMR-1 and FMR-2 is due to the precise determination of the preference level as described in Section *"Refine Preference Level Using Estimated Concentration Level"*. It enables FMR-2 not only to estimate the preference levels of unplayed songs precisely but also to prioritize the levels in accordance with the effect on the concentration level by combining with the hierarchical classification algorithm. In fact, as shown in Table 8, FMR-2 played fewer "like very much" and "dislike very much" songs than FMR-1 even though it played more "like" and "dislike" songs, resulting in fewer interruptions.

In addition, it is suggested the proposed method is resistant to the *cold-start* (*new-user*) problem [33], which is that recommendation systems cannot handle new users. Figure 10 shows that the ratio of the numbers of songs for which participants pressed the "skip" or "keep listening" button dropped as the number of played songs increased and stabilized after about ten songs. This is because HierCost, the classification algorithm used in FMR-2, bases its calculation of misclassification cost on both the hierarchical information and the population of labeled data in order to deal with unbalanced data.

User Comments

The participants commented positively about the songs automatically played by the proposed system, saying things like "I think they were good for concentrating," "they were good choices," "they were moderately suitable for working," "I was able to work comfortably while listening," "although they matched my preference, they never got in the way of working," "I was bothered neither by music nor by my surroundings," "I paid less attention to music than usual," and "I think they became more suitable for working as I made use of the system." Regarding the "keep listening" feedback, comments such as "I didn't feel it burdened me," "I didn't particularly mind it," and "I didn't feel uncomfortable" were obtained. The participants also commented positively about the "automatic summarization" function, saying things like "this function is convenient because I can listen to many songs without being bored."

One participant mentioned that using the "keep listening" button seemed to interrupt work more than using the "skip" button did. It is presumed that this is attributable to the fact that a "skip" button is widely used by many music players and a "keep listening" button is not. The participant also said that "using a 'keep listening' button is much easier than using a precise scale and entering a preference level for each song," and therefore the efficiency of the feedback method is confirmed. Moreover, because an increase in the number of played songs leads to an improvement in the accuracy of estimating the preference level of unplayed songs, the more the user uses the proposed system, the less often it would recommend songs that are not suitable for listening while working. As shown in Figure 10, if the user continued to use it, we would expect the number of button operations to decrease, resulting in fewer interruptions.

CONCLUSION AND FUTURE WORK

We have described FocusMusicRecommender, a music recommender system designed to improve users' concentration while working on personal computers. With a focus on background music for enhancing concentration, we designed the system to give priority to songs that a user may neither like nor dislike rather than like very much. The system's design is also consistent with the fact that the effects on a user's concentration level of liked, neither liked nor disliked, and disliked songs are not significantly different, while songs the user liked very much interfere with his/her concentration.

We introduced a feedback method that obtains the three levels of preference "like very much," "neither like nor dislike," and "dislike very much" while suppressing the burden on the user by implementing a "keep listening" button in addition to a "skip" button. Furthermore, we enabled the preference level to be acquired more precisely by determining the degree of "like" or "dislike" according to the user's automatically estimated concentration level. Hypothesizing that feedback given when concentrating reflects the preference level for songs better than does feedback given when not concentrating, we proposed a method for estimating the preference levels of unplayed songs and selecting the most suitable song by taking into account the relationship between the concentration level and the preference levels. The results of evaluation experiments supported our hypothesis and showed that the proposed system has high recommendation performance and is suitable for use during work.

We also proposed a method for estimating the concentration level from the user's behavior history collected without using physical sensors and confirmed it can estimate the user's concentration level more accurately than the previous methods used in experiments like those described in Section *"Concentration Level Estimation"*. This method can be applied not only for music recommendation but also for avoiding unwanted interruptions while working like the conventional methods.

Future Work

For future work, we would like to expand the experiments with alternative approaches along with increasing the number of the participants and the songs. For example, we are considering a different music selection method that takes into account novelty and diversity of the recommended songs because they are sometimes considered in the quality assessment of recommendation systems. Moreover, since the proposed system plays songs in an abridged manner, we would like to use other musical feature extraction methods that take into consideration the structure and variation in the song.

Furthermore, we would like to explore the new interactions due to using the estimated concentration level. For example, FocusMusicRecommender can prompt the user to take a break when the estimated concentration level stays low. Since it is possible to play songs the user may like very much, as the conventional recommendation systems do, by changing the priority of recommendation described in Section *"Music Selection"*, the system can help the user change the his/her mood seamlessly when he/she accepts the recommendation of taking a break. In addition, whether the user did or did not accept the recommendation is the information that can be used as labeled data for the estimation. In other words, since the system uses an online learning algorithm to estimate the concentration level, it is expected to be personalized and made more accurate by collecting such data.

ACKNOWLEDGMENTS

This work was supported in part by JST ACCEL Grant Number JPMJAC1602, Japan.

REFERENCES

1. Linas Baltrunas, Marius Kaminskas, Bernd Ludwig, Omar Moling, Francesco Ricci, Aykan Aydin, Karl-Heinz Lüke, and Roland Schwaiger. 2011. InCarMusic: Context-Aware Music Recommendations in a Car. In *Proceedings of the 12th International Conference on E-Commerce and Web Technologies*. 89–100.
2. Davide Canali, Andrea Lanzi, Davide Balzarotti, Christopher Kruegel, Mihai Christodorescu, and Engin Kirda. 2012. A quantitative study of accuracy in system call-based malware detection. In *Proceedings of the 21st International Symposium on Software Testing and Analysis*. 122–132.
3. João Paulo V. Cardoso, Luciana Fujii Pontello, Pedro H. F. Holanda, Bruno Guilherme, Olga Goussevskaia, and Ana Paula Couto da Silva. 2016. Mixtape: Direction-Based Navigation in Large Media Collections. In *Proceedings of the 17th International Society for Music Information Retrieval Conference*. 454–460.
4. Anveshi Charuvaka and Huzefa Rangwala. 2015. HierCost: Improving Large Scale Hierarchical Classification with Cost Sensitive Learning. In *Proceedings of the 2015 European Conference on Machine Learning and Principles and Practice of Knowledge Discovery in Databases*. 675–690.
5. Matthew L. Cooper and Jonathan Foote. 2002. Automatic Music Summarization via Similarity Analysis. In *Proceedings of the 3rd International Society for Music Information Retrieval Conference*. 81–85.
6. Koby Crammer, Alex Kulesza, and Mark Dredze. 2013. Adaptive regularization of weight vectors. *Machine Learning* 91, 2 (2013), 155–187.
7. Roger B. Dannenberg and Masataka Goto. 2008. *Music Structure Analysis from Acoustic Signals*. Springer New York, New York, NY, 305–331.
8. Andrew Demetriou, Martha Larson, and Cynthia C. S. Liem. 2016. Go with the Flow: When Listeners Use Music as Technology. In *Proceedings of the 17th International Society for Music Information Retrieval Conference*. 292–298.
9. James Fogarty, Scott E. Hudson, Christopher G. Atkeson, Daniel Avrahami, Jodi Forlizzi, Sara B. Kiesler, Johnny C. Lee, and Jie Yang. 2005. Predicting human interruptibility with sensors. *ACM Transations on Computer-Human Interaction* 12, 1 (2005), 119–146.
10. Masataka Goto, Kazuyoshi Yoshii, Hiromasa Fujihara, Matthias Mauch, and Tomoyasu Nakano. 2011. Songle: A Web Service for Active Music Listening Improved by User Contributions. In *Proceedings of the 12th International Society for Music Information Retrieval Conference*. 311–316.
11. Masataka Goto, Kazuyoshi Yoshii, and Tomoyasu Nakano. 2015. Songle Widget: Making Animation and Physical Devices Synchronized with Music Videos on the Web. In *Proceedings of the 2015 IEEE International Symposium on Multimedia*. 85–88.
12. Susan Hallam, John Price, and Georgia Katsarou. 2002. The Effects of Background Music on Primary School Pupils' Task Performance. *Educational Studies* 28, 2 (2002), 111–122.
13. Masahiro Hamasaki and Masataka Goto. 2013. Songrium: a music browsing assistance service based on visualization of massive open collaboration within music content creation community. In *Proceedings of the 9th International Symposium on Open Collaboration*. 4:1–4:10.
14. Masahiro Hamasaki, Hideaki Takeda, and Takuichi Nishimura. 2008. Network analysis of massively collaborative creation of multimedia contents: case study of hatsune miku videos on nico nico douga. In *Proceeding of the 1st International Conference on Designing Interactive User Experiences for TV and Video*. 165–168.
15. Rong Hwa Huanga and Yi Nuo Shih. 2011. Effects of background music on concentration of workers. *Work* 38, 4 (2011), 383–387.

16. Shobu Ikeda, Kenta Oku, and Kyoji Kawagoe. 2016. Music Playlist Recommendation Using Acoustic-Feature Transitions. In *Proceedings of the 9th International C* Conference on Computer Science & Software Engineering*. 115–118.

17. Carlos Nascimento Silla Jr. and Alex Alves Freitas. 2011. A survey of hierarchical classification across different application domains. *Data Mining and Knowledge Discovery* 22, 1-2 (2011), 31–72.

18. Hao Liu, Jun Hu, and Matthias Rauterberg. 2010b. iHeartrate: a heart rate controlled in-flight music recommendation system. In *Proceedings of the 7th International Conference on Methods and Techniques in Behavioral Research*. 26:1–26:4.

19. Ning-Han Liu, Shu-Ju Hsieh, and Cheng-Fa Tsai. 2010a. An intelligent music playlist generator based on the time parameter with artificial neural networks. *Expert Systems with Applications* 37, 4 (2010), 2815–2825.

20. Beth Logan and Stephen M. Chu. 2000. Music summarization using key phrases. In *Proceedings of the 2000 IEEE International Conference on Acoustics, Speech, and Signal Processing*. 749–752.

21. Adam J. Lonsdale and Adrian C. North. 2011. Why do we listen to music? A uses and gratifications analysis. *British Journal of Psychology* 102, 1 (2011), 108–134.

22. Nuria Oliver and Fernando Flores-Mangas. 2006. MPTrain: a mobile, music and physiology-based personal trainer. In *Proceedings of the 8th Conference on Human-Computer Interaction with Mobile Devices and Services*. 21–28.

23. Nuria Oliver and Lucas Kreger-Stickles. 2006. PAPA: Physiology and Purpose-Aware Automatic Playlist Generation. In *Proceedings of the 7th International Society for Music Information Retrieval*. 250–253.

24. Elias Pampalk, Tim Pohle, and Gerhard Widmer. 2005. Dynamic Playlist Generation Based on Skipping Behavior. In *Proceedings of the 6th International Society for Music Information Retrieval*. 634–637.

25. Frances H Rauscher, Gordon L Shaw, and Catherine N Ky. 1993. Music and spatial task performance. *Nature* 365, 6447 (1993), 611–611.

26. Konrad Rieck, Philipp Trinius, Carsten Willems, and Thorsten Holz. 2011. Automatic analysis of malware behavior using machine learning. *Journal of Computer Security* 19, 4 (2011), 639–668.

27. E. Glenn Schellenberg, Takayuki Nakata, Patrick G. Hunter, and Sachiko Tamoto. 2007. Exposure to music and cognitive performance: tests of children and adults. *Psychology of Music* 35, 1 (2007), 5–19.

28. Yading Song, Simon Dixon, and Marcus Pearce. 2012. A Survey of Music Recommendation Systems and Future Perspectives. In *Proceedings of the 9th International Symposium on Computer Music Modeling and Retrieval*. 395–410.

29. Takahiro Tanaka and Kinya Fujita. 2011. Study of user interruptibility estimation based on focused application switching. In *Proceedings of the 2011 ACM Conference on Computer Supported Cooperative Work*. 721–724.

30. Yoshisuke Tateyama, Yoshio Matsumoto, and Satoshi Kagami. 2004. Concentration detection by eye movements: towards supporting a human. In *Proceedings of the 2004 IEEE International Conference on Systems, Man & Cybernetics*. 1544–1548.

31. George Tzanetakis and Perry Cook. 2000. MARSYAS: a framework for audio analysis. *Organised Sound* 4 (12 2000), 169–175. Issue 03.

32. Aäron van den Oord, Sander Dieleman, and Benjamin Schrauwen. 2013. Deep content-based music recommendation. In *Proceedings of the 27th Annual Conference on Neural Information Processing Systems*. 2643–2651.

33. Xinxi Wang, David S. Rosenblum, and Ye Wang. 2012. Context-aware mobile music recommendation for daily activities. In *Proceedings of the 20th ACM Multimedia Conference*. 99–108.

34. Alan Wells. 1990. Popular Music: Emotional Use and Management. *The Journal of Popular Culture* 24, 1 (1990), 105–117.

35. Manuela Züger and Thomas Fritz. 2015. Interruptibility of Software Developers and its Prediction Using Psycho-Physiological Sensors. In *Proceedings of the 33rd Annual ACM Conference on Human Factors in Computing Systems*. 2981–2990.

Ensemble Recommendations via Thompson Sampling: an Experimental Study within e-Commerce

Björn Brodén
Apptus Technologies
Lund, Sweden
bjorn.broden@apptus.com

Mikael Hammar
Apptus Technologies
Lund, Sweden
mikael.hammar@apptus.com

Bengt J. Nilsson
Malmö University
Malmö, Sweden
bengt.nilsson.TS@mau.se

Dimitris Paraschakis
Malmö University
Malmö, Sweden
dimitris.paraschakis@mau.se

ABSTRACT

This work presents an extension of Thompson Sampling bandit policy for orchestrating the collection of base recommendation algorithms for e-commerce. We focus on the problem of item-to-item recommendations, for which multiple behavioral and attribute-based predictors are provided to an ensemble learner. We show how to adapt Thompson Sampling to realistic situations when neither action availability nor reward stationarity is guaranteed. Furthermore, we investigate the effects of priming the sampler with pre-set parameters of reward probability distributions by utilizing the product catalog and/or event history, when such information is available. We report our experimental results based on the analysis of three real-world e-commerce datasets.

CCS Concepts

•**Information systems** → **Electronic commerce; Recommender systems;** *Collaborative filtering;* Information retrieval query processing; •**Computing methodologies** → **Sequential decision making; Learning from implicit feedback;** *Ensemble methods;*

Author Keywords

E-commerce Recommender Systems; Streaming Recommendations; Bandit Ensembles; Session-based Recommendations, Thompson Sampling, Reinforcement Learning

INTRODUCTION

Dynamically responding to user queries with top-N item ranking is a very common problem on the web, which pertains to search, advertising, and recommendations. A specific use case of interest is generating *item-to-item* (i2i) recommendations for every visited product page with the aim to maximize product sales. Such *non-personalized* recommendations are useful when user profiles are limited or non-existent. This is very typical of online shopping sessions, where most visitors are unidentified [44, 47], yet keen to see meaningful recommendations already on their first page visit (e.g. on a landing page). Such dynamic environments with streaming event data and severe cold-start make conventional recommender systems impractical and call for *reinforcement learning* approaches, whose exploration-exploitation paradigm appears very appropriate [32].

Item rankings can be generated by various predictors that utilize item consumption patterns and/or content features. Learning which predictor (or a combination thereof) is optimal in a given context in an online manner naturally translates to a *multi-arm bandit* (MAB) problem. In its classical formulation, a policy sequentially chooses from a finite set of actions with stationary (but unknown) reward distributions in attempt to maximize the total reward (or equivalently, to minimize the total regret w.r.t the oracle policy). This problem has been extensively studied in the literature, especially since the seminal paper by Lai & Robbins [29]. They introduced upper confidence bound (UCB) policies attaining a logarithmic regret. Another popular but fundamentally different low-regret policy is Thompson Sampling [22]. Being Bayesian in spirit, it is better suited for modeling complex online problems [16], which is why we adopt this method to build our recommender system. Since most work on multi-arm bandits has been theoretical in nature [41], their implementation in real-world scenarios such as content recommendations is still elusive [1]. This is because many of the assumptions made by traditional MAB are violated in practical applications. In particular, we envision the following challenges of implementing bandit recommendations in e-commerce:

Non-stationary rewards. Since behavioral signals in the data evolve with time, predictors of this type are characterized by non-stationarities in their reward sequences. Algorithms that deal with this issue include *switching* and *restless* bandits [10, 15, 36].

Multiple plays. The "top-N ranking" problem dictates that multiple actions need to be taken in each round to ensure that all available item slots are filled. Problems of this type are addressed with *ranked* [28, 39, 42] *cascading* [27, 33] and *multiple-play* bandits [16, 34, 45].

IUI 2018, March 7–11, 2018, Tokyo, Japan.
Copyright © 2018 ACM ISBN 978-1-4503-4945-1/18/03 ...$15.00.
http://dx.doi.org/10.1145/3172944.3172967

Variable availability of actions. In the real world, not all actions are available at each time instance. For example, this may happen when predictors find no correlations between items, or when items themselves are not accessible (e.g. out of stock). Bandit policies capable to accommodate such situations are known as *sleeping* bandits [21, 24, 40].

In this paper we propose a streaming (sequential) recommender system [17], which adapts existing MAB policies to the aforementioned scenarios. Motivated by the fact that many industrial recommenders tend to favor simple algorithmic approaches (e.g. best-seller lists) [38], our solution is essentially an ensemble learning scheme that uses Thompson Sampling to orchestrate the collection of elementary recommendation components. This allows content-based and behavioral signals in the data to effectively complement each other in response to user queries. The proposed model offers a number of advantages to a prospective vendor:

- It allows to easily plug-in/out recommendation components of any type, without making changes to the main algorithm;
- Modeling components as arms helps to overcome the scalability limitation of the more common "items-as-arms" representation;
- Handling context can be shifted to the level of components, hence eliminating the need for contextual MAB policies;
- Elementary recommendation components are easily interpretable and hence allow for more transparent user interfaces that improve user's trust in the system.

The paper is organized as follows. The next section gives an overview of related variants of MAB policies, along with related studies on MAB-based recommender systems. Section *Approach* introduces our approach and details the proposed ensemble algorithm in pseudo-code. In Section *Experiments* we describe our experiments and present their results. We summarize and conclude our findings in Section *Conclusions*.

RELATED WORK

The non-stationarity of arm rewards has been approached from different angles. In the presence of domain knowledge, the shape of the reward distribution may be known a priori. Bouneffouf and Féraud [8] show how to take advantage of this knowledge in UCB1 to tackle non-stationarity in music or interface recommendations. In many cases (including ours), the functional form of non-stationarity is not known. Therefore, automatic detection of abrupt or drifting changes in reward sequences has been proposed in several extensions to UCB [19, 15] and Thompson Sampling [36, 10] policies. These two types of behaviors (i.e. abrupt and drifting) correspond, respectively, to *switching* [15, 36] and *restless* [10] bandits. Garivier *et al.* [15] also show that any policy with a logarithmic regret for the stationary case is bound to $T/log(T)$ regret in the presence of reward irregularities, where T is the time horizon. In fact, the notion of *dynamic regret* has been introduced for drifting reward functions, which is measured w.r.t. a benchmark policy taking the best action for each round in isolation [40].

The multiple arm selection (top-*N*) problem appears to be highly relevant for recommender systems. The most straightforward solution, known as *ranked bandits*, assigns a separate bandit to each slot in the ranking [42, 39]. Lacerda [28] presents an interesting use case for ranked bandits that optimizes multi-objective ranking in recommender systems. More recently, *cascading bandits* have been proposed as a variant of a ranked bandit for modeling position bias in click data [27], and have been evaluated on movie recommendations [33]. Ranked bandits have been criticized for the underutilization of the available feedback, since it cannot be shared between individual bandits [34]. A better approach in this respect is the so-called *multiple-play* bandit, which can fully observe all incoming rewards. It is this approach we adopt in our work. A multiple-play bandit algorithm called $EXP3.M$, originally proposed in [45], has been assessed against two ranked bandit algorithms on movie and joke recommendations, demonstrating that $EXP3.M$ indeed converges faster than the two ranked algorithms [34]. Likewise, Gopalan *et al.* [16] apply Thompson Sampling for the problem of top-*N* arms selection and report a significant reduction in running time as compared to a decoupled bandit policy. They conclude that being Bayesian is advantageous for addressing complex bandit problems, and thus motivate our choice of policy.

Our problem setting, which resembles many other practical situations, assumes that certain actions may be unavailable at times. This has implications on the definition of regret, which is traditionally measured w.r.t. the best action in hindsight and is no longer applicable [24]. The idea then is to choose the best action among currently available actions ordered by their expected reward. Problem settings that exhibit such behavior have been coined *sleeping bandits* and studied in various contexts. For example, Kanade *et al.* [21] present a no-regret sleeping bandit algorithm for adversarial rewards, whereas Kleinberg *et al.* [24] analyze the regret for both adversarial and stochastic cases. A contextual sleeping bandit with stochastic rewards is presented in [40], wherein the author reproduces the result of [24] using contextual zooming.

Bandit algorithms are becoming one of the most promising approaches in the area of recommender systems [32]. Due to their exploratory nature, they are especially effective in attacking the cold-start problem (e.g. [35, 13, 11]). Referring to the e-commerce domain, Bernardi *et al.* [7] characterize this problem as the *continuous* cold-start, meaning that users and items remain "cold" for an extensive period of time. Moreover, existing users have the tendency to "cool down". This observation motivates the use of non-personalized i2i recommendations that we present in this work. We model bandit arms as predictors, which allows us to devise an ensemble method to tackle cold-start. This distinguishes our approach from others mentioned (e.g. [30, 46, 48, 28]), wherein arms represent single items. Whereas an item-as-arm model may be reasonable for few arms (as in [23, 30, 31, 37]), the magnitude of real-world data would likely lead to scalability issues [25].

Recent years have seen successful implementations of Thompson Sampling for recommendations of news articles [12, 43], movies [48], music [18], documents [9], learning courses [37], search queries [20], and dating partners [2]. Convincing attempts [23, 48] have been made to couple Thompson sampling with popular matrix factorization techniques. Closest in spirit to our work is the paper by Tang *et al.* [43], who present an ensemble meta-bandit recommender system. Similar to our approach, they use a hyper-bandit ruled by non-contextual Thompson Sampling to adaptively explore/exploit base contextual bandits that select items to recommend. The same basic idea of using a bandit algorithm for *prediction model selection* in recommender systems has been conveyed by Felício *et al.* [13]. They experiment with UCB1 and ε-greedy policies with arms modeled as clusters of users induced by matrix factorization. Our work differs mainly in how we model arms and attribute rewards. Contrary to some of the aforementioned recommenders that maximize the click-through rate (CTR) (e.g. [43, 12, 30, 34, 28, 1]), we are interested in optimizing the number of sold units. In our experience, this e-commerce objective does not benefit from items that merely attract clicks, and therefore requires a different attribution model. We outline our approach in the next section.

APPROACH

Problem Setting

Following the reinforcement learning paradigm, we consider a typical e-commerce scenario as an interplay between:

- *E-commerce environment* comprised of a product catalog $I = \{i_1, \ldots, i_{|I|}\}$ and (possibly overlapping) user sessions, $S = (s_1, \ldots, s_{|S|})$, each defined as $s = (q_{t_x}, \ldots, q_{t_y}, P_{\tau_s})$, where query $q_t \in I$ represents a product page visit at time t, and $P_{\tau_s} \subseteq I$ is the final purchase order at time τ designating the end of the session (typically, $|P_{\tau_s}| \ll |I|$).
- *Recommendation agent* implemented as a multi-arm bandit with a set of actions $\mathcal{A} = \{a_1, \ldots, a_{|\mathcal{A}|}\}$ and a sequence of states $\Sigma = (\sigma_1, \ldots, \sigma_{|\Sigma|})$. Each action represents a base recommendation function that maps a given query to some subset of the product catalog, i.e., if Q is the set of all queries, then $a : Q \to \mathcal{P}(I \setminus Q)$, where $\mathcal{P}(\cdot)$ is the powerset function.

We will only consider queries and purchases belonging to the same session and will, for ease of notation, omit session indices.

For each query q_t with an associated N-sized recommendation list L_t, the agent takes at most N available actions $A_t = (a_1, \ldots, a_{|A_t|})$, s.t. $|A_t| \leq N$ and $a_i \in \mathcal{A}$, according to some bandit policy π so that the precision at time t: $prec@N(L_t) = |L_t \cap P_\tau|/N$ is maximized. An action can appear more than once in A_t and the recommender does not have access to P_τ at time t, since $t < \tau$.

Each *display* of an action's recommendation in L_t results in a binary *reward* $r \in \{0, 1\}$ after observing a purchase order at time τ. We refer to each successful recommendation (i.e. the recommended item is eventually bought) corresponding to $r = 1$ as a *hit*. The reward of an action that fails to generate a hit is zero ($r = 0$).

In case the same successful recommendation is given by different actions within a session, we face the problem of *attribution*, i.e. deciding which action should get credit for the sale [5]. We follow the *equal* multi-touch attribution strategy, according to which each action that generates a hit is equally rewarded. Alternative strategies include first-touch attribution, last-touch attribution, and fractional attribution (see [5] for details). Since we have no means of establishing which of the displayed recommendations are actually noticed by the user, we consider equal attribution to be the safest choice.

For each action $a \in \mathcal{A}$, we maintain a tuple of running rewards r_a and displays n_a, which represents the agent's current state of knowledge: $\sigma_j = (r_a, n_a)_{a \in \mathcal{A}}$. The agent moves to an updated state σ_{j+1} after attributing rewards at time τ. Figure 1 exemplifies the described mechanism.

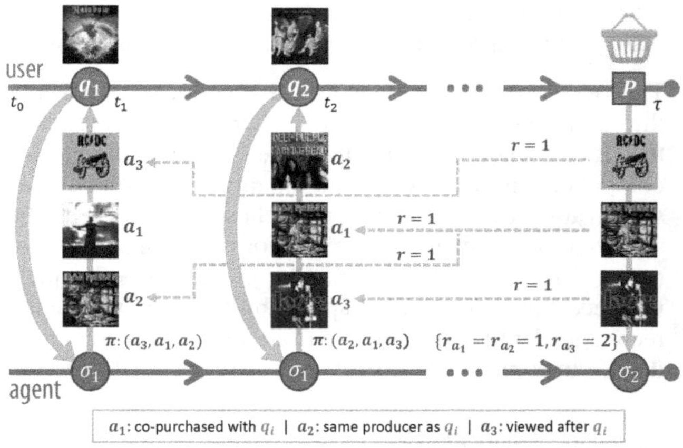

Figure 1. *i2i* session-based recommendations with explainable actions

The ultimate goal of the agent is to maximize the cumulative reward: $r_T = \sum_{t \leq T} r_t$, where r_t is the sum of rewards obtained at time t.

Base Recommenders

As stated earlier, action set $\mathcal{A}$ is an ensemble of base recommendation functions or "components".[1] These are simple contextual predictors, whose output is determined by the input query. Each component defines a graph $G_a((V,E),W)$, where V is a set of vertices representing items, E is a set of edges representing between-item associations (induced by a), and W is a set of edge weights measuring the strength of these associations.

We distinguish between two types of components:

1. **Attribute-based** components connect items via their content features (i.e. metadata). We use elementary components, each representing a particular attribute of the product catalog. Edges of this type are undirected. For example, $N_{G_{color}}(v)$ retrieves the neighborhood of item v containing all items of the same color(s) as v. Optionally, edge weights can be used to measure the number of attribute values that are matched.
2. **Behavioral** components connect items via events (e.g. clicks, purchases, etc.). The edge's weight in this case captures the frequency of event observations, i.e. the strength of the association. The edges can be directed, indicating that the event connecting two items is only meaningful in

[1]The terms 'actions', 'components', 'predictors', and 'recommendation functions' have the same meaning and are used interchangeably

one direction. For example, we use the following four types of behavioral components:

- ***click-click*** *(cc)*: the directed edge $(v, v') \in E[N_{G_{cc}}(v)]$ signifies that the click on item v is followed by the click on item v'.
- ***session-click*** *(sc)*: the edge $\{v, v'\} \in E[N_{G_{sc}}(v)]$ signifies that items v and v' are both clicked within the same session.
- ***purchase-purchase*** *(pp)*: the directed edge $(v, v') \in E[N_{G_{pp}}(v)]$ signifies that the purchase of item v is followed by the purchase of item v'.
- ***customer-purchase*** *(cp)*: the edge $\{v, v'\} \in E[N_{G_{cp}}(v)]$ signifies that items v and v' are both purchased by the same customer (not necessarily in the same session).

The two types of components correspond, respectively, to the terms *content-based* and *collaborative* filtering used in the recommender systems literature. A vendor can engineer components in many ways, for example by introducing personalization (as in 'customer-purchase'), campaigns, best-seller/special offer lists, or more complex feature combinations. Our choice of very granular predictors is dictated by the need for cross-domain applicability, since we want the recommender to operate well on various types of e-commerce data from complete cold-start.

Dynamic Partitioning

It is apparent that bandit arms constructed in this manner are prone to non-stationary behavior, since the size of the neighborhood $N_{G_a}(v)$ may differ significantly from query to query. The problem is particularly profound in behavioral components, as new edges are constantly added to the graph and the weights of existing edges are constantly updated from new observations. This may lead to situations when top-performing predictors (in the long run) get under-explored by the bandit algorithm because of their poor performance at an early stage.

A simple solution to this problem is to dynamically partition a component a (i.e. its output) into several disjoint parts or "sub-components" based on the estimated precision of each candidate item contained in the query response $N_{G_a}(q)$. In other words, we cluster the response with the aim to obtain sub-components each having a distinct but homogeneous precision. Let A_a denote a *partition* of component a: $A_a = \mathcal{P}(a), s.t. \bigcap_{a' \in A_a} = \varnothing, \bigcup_{a' \in A_a} = a, \forall a \in \mathcal{A}$. We can now expand the original action set to the set of sub-actions: $\mathcal{A} = \bigcup_a A_a$, where each sub-action $a' \in A_a$ has a (relatively) fixed reward distribution.

To achieve this, we can use various proxies for precision depending on the type of component. For example, attribute-based components can be partitioned based on the *inverse document frequency* (IDF)[2], as shown in Algorithm 1. The intuition behind it is that the more frequent the target attribute value is in other items, the more difficult it is to make the right recommendation. For behavioral components, we can directly use edge weights $w_a(v, v')$ corresponding to event observations as a proxy for precision. The obtained estimates are then thresholded to obtain the partition of the component's output. Because the event graphs are constantly evolving, partitioning is done dynamically upon each query response, and hence new (more precise) sub-components may emerge with time.

[2]Term frequency (TF) is omitted from calculations as the number of occurrences of an attribute value in the same item is rarely greater than 1

Algorithm 1 IDF-based partitioning

Input: q: query, a: attribute, I: item catalog, K: #subsets in partition
Output: A_a: partition of candidate itemset $V(N_{G_a}(q))$

$a'_1 \leftarrow \varnothing, a'_2 \leftarrow \varnothing, \ldots, a'_K \leftarrow \varnothing$ ▷ empty sub-components
$A_a \leftarrow (a'_1, a'_2, \ldots, a'_K)$
$idf_1 \leftarrow 0, idf_2 \leftarrow 0, \ldots, idf_{|I|} \leftarrow 0$
for all $v \in$ attribute_values(a, q) **do** ▷ for all values of a in q
    $C \leftarrow V(N_{G_{a:v}}(q))$ ▷ candidate itemset induced by value v
    $idf \leftarrow \log(|I|/(|C|+1))$ ▷ inverse document frequency
    for all $i \in C$ **do** ▷ for each item in candidate itemset
        $idf_i \leftarrow idf_i + idf$
for all $i \in V(N_{G_a}(q))$ **do**
    $k \leftarrow$ select_index(i, idf_i) ▷ based on pre-set *idf* thresholds
    $a'_k \leftarrow a'_k \cup \{i\}$
    return A_a

Ensemble Learning Agent

Preliminaries

Our agent extends beyond the classical multi-arm bandit, since it needs to solve the top-N selection problem with varied action availability. The availability of action a for filling the i-th position in the top-N list L_t is subject to the following conditions:

1. $N_{G_a}(q_t) \neq \varnothing$, i.e. the response is non-empty
2. $N_{G_a}(q_t) \setminus L_t[1, \ldots, i-1] \neq \varnothing$, i.e. the response contains at least one item distinct from those already recommended.

Based on the above conditions and the policy π, the agent plays the best among currently available actions. This corresponds to picking one item from the action's sub-graph. The procedure is repeated for each position in L_t. The ensemble learner is therefore characterized as a *sleeping* bandit with *multiple plays*. Both recommendation steps (i.e. choosing an action and choosing an item) can be taken in either deterministic or probabilistic manner.

Because of the partitioning method presented earlier, we can apply any standard stochastic policy to our bandit ensemble framework, henceforth referred to as BEER (Bandit Ensemble for E-commerce Recommendations), where action rewards are assumed to be drawn i.i.d. from some fixed probability distributions. This also means that the selected action can now pick a *random* item from its sub-graph, which helps to diversify recommendations without loss in precision.

A well-studied family of *deterministic* MAB policies is based on the principle of *optimism in the face of uncertainty*. These policies select an action with the highest index corresponding to the *upper confidence bound* (UCB) for the action's expected reward, plus some padding function (e.g. [29, 15, 30]). They capture the intuition that the high bound is either due to the action being under-explored, or well-rewarded in expectation. Other policies balance between exploration and exploitation *probabilistically*. For example, the ε-*greedy* policy chooses a random action with probability ε and the empirically optimal action with probability $1-\varepsilon$, whereas *randomized probability matching* chooses an action in proportion to its probability of being optimal. The latter approach is known as Thompson Sampling and has shown promising results in many practical applications, including top-N action selection [16]. We now give an overview of this policy and then explain how to adapt it for the needs of our ensemble learning bandit (Algorithm 2).

Thompson Sampling

Probability matching is a Bayesian heuristic, which models reward distribution using a parametric likelihood function $P(r|a,\theta)$, where $\theta = (\theta_1, \ldots, \theta_{|\mathcal{A}|})$ is some unknown parameter vector. Our reward system implies a Bernoulli bandit, where parameters θ represents the probabilities of obtaining a binary reward. Given agent state σ at the current step t' and some prior distribution over θ, the posterior distribution is obtained using Bayes' rule: $P(\theta|\sigma) = \frac{P(\sigma|\theta)P(\theta)}{P(\sigma)} \propto \prod_{t=1}^{t'} P(r_t|a \in A_t, \theta)P(\theta)$. We then take an optimal action according to the probability matching principle: $a^* = \arg\max_a \int \mathbb{1}\left[\mathbb{E}(r|a,\theta) = \max_{a'} \mathbb{E}(r|a',\theta)\right] P(\theta|\sigma)d\theta$. Instead of computing the integral, Thompson Sampling draws random samples independently for each action a from the respective posterior $P(\theta_a|\sigma)$ and chooses the action a^* with the largest θ_a. The prior is typically Beta-distributed, since it is conjugate to the Bernoulli distribution: $P(\theta_a) \sim \text{Beta}(\alpha,\beta)$, where $\alpha = \alpha_0 + r_a$ can represent the number of "successes", and $\beta = \beta_0 + n_a - r_a$ can represent the number of "failures".

The randomized nature of Thompson Sampling implies continuous exploration in situations when deterministic UCB policies get stuck in the same action over the extended period of time. This makes Thompson Sampling more robust in various practical scenarios, namely:

- *Delayed feedback.* Because of random sampling, the exploration phase does not suffer from the lack of regular posterior updates.
- *Adding new actions.* One can simply set the new action's prior to the default $Beta(1,1)$ and let the ensemble algorithm continue its exploration naturally. In UCB, the exploration would be substituted by exploitation of the new action until its confidence bound becomes comparable to the bounds of other actions.
- *Non-stationary actions.* When a previously well-performing action starts failing, Thompson Sampling goes to the exploration phase faster than UCB.

All the above scenarios are handled seamlessly without any algorithm parameterization, which is another advantage of Thompson Sampling. However, the existence of the Beta parameters allows to re-shape the reward distributions beforehand, as we discuss next.

Sampler Priming

The parameters $\alpha > 0$ and $\beta > 0$ control the shape of Beta distribution with mean $\mu = \frac{\alpha}{\alpha+\beta}$ and variance $\sigma^2 = \frac{\alpha\beta}{(\alpha+\beta+1)(\alpha+\beta)^2}$. The prior parameters α_0 and β_0 allow us to prime the sampler with some initial frequencies of successes and failures. At time t_0, $\alpha = \alpha_0$ and $\beta = \beta_0$. The de facto choice $\alpha_0 = \beta_0 = 1$ corresponds to the uniform distribution (i.e. uninformative prior). We consider two practical situations when more informative prior parameters can be specified:

1. Recorded event data is available beforehand. This can happen when the recommender system is deployed on a pre-existing e-commerce site. In this case, parameters α and β can be learned directly by running Thompson Sampling through the recorded data.
2. No recorded event data is available. This is the case of newly launched e-commerce sites, where only the product catalog is known. In this scenario, a vendor might attempt to prime attribute-based components based on the statistical properties of the product catalog.

In cases when the direct estimation of α and β does not seem feasible (as in case 2), we might still make assumptions about the means of prior distributions based on some domain knowledge (e.g. product catalog). We can then reason about the variance through the following formula:

$$\sigma^2 \stackrel{\text{def}}{=} \frac{\mu(1-\mu)}{\nu}, \tag{1}$$

where $\nu > 1$ is a parameter expressing our uncertainty about the estimated mean. This parameter is defined as $\nu \stackrel{\text{def}}{=} \alpha + \beta + 1$. Choosing high values of ν (i.e. high certainty) results in more peaky curves, whereas lower values lead to flatter distributions. Knowing the estimates of μ and σ^2 allows us to compute α and β as follows:

$$\alpha = -\frac{\mu(\sigma^2+\mu^2-\mu)}{\sigma^2} \qquad \beta = \frac{(\mu-1)(\sigma^2+\mu^2-\mu)}{\sigma^2} \tag{2}$$

We provide further details about the estimation of μ and σ^2 for case 2 in Section *Experiment 4*.

Algorithm

Our bandit ensemble algorithm based on Thompson Sampling ("BEER[TS]") is summarized in the pseudo-code below.

Algorithm 2 BEER[TS]

```
Input: α_0^(a), β_0^(a): prior parameters ∀a ∈ A        ▷ default: α_0 = β_0 = 1
Output: top-N recommendations L_t, where t is current time step
for all t do
    for i = 1,...,N do
        for all a ∈ A do
            C_a ← V(N_{G_a}(q)) \ L_t[1,...,i−1]        ▷ a's answer to q
            if C_a = ∅ then
                continue                               ▷ do not take "sleeping" actions
            A_a ← partition(C_a)                       ▷ into disjoint subsets
            for all a' ∈ A_a do
                Select index k(a')                     ▷ sub-action to sample from
                θ_a' ~ Beta(α_0^(a) + r_k(a'), β_0^(a) + n_k(a') − r_k(a'))
        a* ← argmax_a' θ_a'
        L_t[i] ← pick_item(C_a*)
        Observe reward r ∈ {0,1} for L_t[i]            ▷ delayed until time τ
        r_k(a*) ← r_k(a*) + r                          ▷ update action rewards
        n_k(a*) ← n_k(a*) + 1                          ▷ update action displays
    Output L_t                                         ▷ output recommendations at time t
```

We note that it is easy to substitute TS with other MAB policies within the BEER framework. The experimental evaluation of different policies is given in Section *Experiment 3*.

One step of Thompson Sampler takes constant time, and the time complexity increases linearly in the number of sub-components involved in the learner.

EXPERIMENTS

Datasets and Evaluation Metrics

We conduct our experiments using two proprietary e-commerce datasets [3] from the *books* and *fashion* domains, and one public dataset [4] [6] with *cross-domain* merchandise. From these datasets, we select 500,000 events of timestamped session data for our experiments. We only consider sessions that culminate in a purchase order. The summary of the datasets is given in Table 1.

Table 1. Dataset summary

Dataset	**Books**	**Fashion**	**Yoochoose**
# Products	91433	19731	52739
# Purchases	134850	50096	101763
# Attributes	45	51	2
# Sessions	58465	21411	55600
Mean session length	8.6 events	22.37 events	9.25 events

In all our experiments, top-N recommendations are evaluated at $N = 5$. The accuracy of such recommendations is traditionally measured in terms of precision and recall. Precision shows how accurate the recommender system is in relation to the number of displays within a session, whereas recall evaluates its accuracy with respect to the number of purchases in a session. Let h_s and h'_s denote, respectively, the number of total and distinct hits in session s. The above metrics can be defined as follows:

$$precision = \frac{\sum_s h_s}{\sum_s n_s} \qquad recall = \frac{\sum_s h'_s}{\sum_s |P_{\tau_s}|} \tag{3}$$

where n_s is the number of displays in session s, and P_{τ_s} is the set of purchased items in session s.

In addition, we report the Normalized Discounted Cumulative Gain (NDCG), which is sensitive to the position at which a hit occurs. For a set of queries Q, NDCG at rank N is computed as follows:

$$NDCG = \frac{1}{|Q|} \sum_{q=1}^{|Q|} \frac{DCG_q}{IDCG_q}$$

where

$$DCG_q = \sum_{i=1}^{N} \frac{r_i}{\log_2(i+1)}, \quad IDCG_q = \sum_{i=1}^{\min(|P|,N)} \frac{1}{\log_2(i+1)} \tag{4}$$

All our experiments report the averages over 10 runs of the simulation.

[3]Provided by Apptus Technologies: **http://www.apptus.com**

[4]Provided by Yoochoose: **http://2015.recsyschallenge.com**

Experiment 1: Standard vs. Modified TS

In our first experiment, we compare the modified Thompson Sampling policy adapted for non-stationary and "sleeping" actions (i.e. Algorithm 2) to the standard Thompson Sampling algorithm. The comparison table is given below.

Table 2. Standard vs. modified Thompson Sampling

Agent	Recall	Precision	NDCG
		Books	
TS (SB+DP)	**0.0581** ↑83.3%	**0.0210** ↑94.4%	**0.0716** ↑94.6%
TS (SB)	0.0562 ↑77.3%	0.0202 ↑87.0%	0.0660 ↑79.3%
TS	0.0317	0.0108	0.0368
		Fashion	
TS (SB+DP)	0.1734 ↑21.3%	**0.0152** ↑13.4%	**0.0483** ↑19.9%
TS (SB)	**0.1760** ↑23.2%	0.0142 ↑6.0%	0.0427 ↑6.0%
TS	0.1429	0.0134	0.0403
		Yoochoose	
TS (SB+DP)	0.2973 ↑10.5%	**0.0419** ↑10.8%	**0.1391** ↑21.4%
TS (SB)	**0.2984** ↑10.9%	0.0409 ↑8.2%	0.1273 ↑11.1%
TS	0.2690	0.0378	0.1146

SB = Sleeping Bandit, DP = Dynamic Partitioning

Table 2 reveals that accounting for "sleeping" actions in Thompson Sampling is a necessary measure for our application, since it improves the accuracy on all three metrics and all datasets. The magnitude of the accuracy gain in each dataset is inversely proportional to the query response rate of each component of the ensemble. If frequently chosen components cannot answer many queries, the "sleeping" mode becomes more important. This claim is supported by our next experiment, where we report the query response rates for the datasets.

It can be seen that component partitioning is able to further boost the accuracy on all datasets in terms of precision and NDCG ranking. In the Books dataset, it also improves recall. In the other two datasets, we observe the typical precision-recall trade-off, with recall suffering small losses yet remaining within comparable value ranges. This can be explained by the fact that sub-components have limited catalog coverage (as compared to an unpartitioned component), and hence can miss some items in P_τ. However, they increase the likelihood of a relevant item being purchased by improving its exposure (precision) and ranking (NDCG) in recommendation lists. We also note that in this experiment we applied the same thresholds for component partitioning in all datasets, and hence it would be reasonable to expect higher scores with dataset-specific thresholding strategies. We leave this analysis for the future. In Table 2, TS (SB+DP) is equivalent to BEER[TS] from Algorithm 2.

Experiment 2: BEER[TS] vs. Baselines

We now compare our ensemble recommendation algorithm against two stand-alone recommenders, namely *best sellers* (BS) and *those-who-bought-also-bought* (TWBAB). Both predictors are based on item (co-)purchases, which is clearly the strongest behavioral signal in a non-personalized context. This makes these predictors highly competitive as baselines for our experiment. We evaluate two variants of BEER[TS] - *with* and *without* the aforementioned baselines as components of the ensemble. In this comparison, it is also worth looking at the coverage of queries by the recommenders. Table 3 summarizes the results of the experiment.

Table 3. Ensemble recommender vs. stand-alone baselines

Agent	Recall	Precision	NDCG	query coverage
		Books		
BEER[TS] incl. baselines	**0.0589**	0.0213	**0.0719**	**1.0**
BEER[TS] excl. baselines	0.0551	0.0275	0.0655	0.7185
TWBAB	0.0324	**0.0365**	0.0366	0.4164
Best sellers	0.0105	0.0085	0.0292	**1.0**
		Fashion		
BEER[TS] incl. baselines	**0.1750**	**0.0155**	**0.0504**	**1.0**
BEER[TS] excl. baselines	0.1704	0.0149	0.0474	0.9825
TWBAB	0.1185	0.0136	0.0277	0.7792
Best sellers	0.0490	0.0119	0.0374	**1.0**
		Yoochoose		
BEER[TS] incl. baselines	**0.2985**	0.0424	**0.1424**	**1.0**
BEER[TS] excl. baselines	0.2953	0.0470	0.1376	0.8999
TWBAB	0.2311	**0.0519**	0.1063	0.7286
Best sellers	0.1211	0.0234	0.0687	**1.0**

TWBAB = those-who-bought-also-bought

Regardless of whether the two baselines are part of the ensemble or not, BEER[TS] vastly outperforms the stand-alone baselines in terms of recall and NDCG. It is also clear from Table 3 that TWBAB tends to be the most *precise* recommender (for Books and Yoochoose). However, this predictor has rather poor query coverage, which is especially evident in the Books dataset, with only 41.64% query response rate. The query coverage of BEER[TS] without baselines is also lower than in other datasets, which is why the Books dataset benefits more from the "sleeping" bandit configuration in the previous experiment (Table 2).

The *best sellers* baseline, on the other hand, is capable of answering every query (past the very first session), since its recommendations are not query-specific. Therefore, the inclusion of this baseline makes it a good fallback method for the ensemble learner. With the addition of TWBAB, the learner can benefit from TWBAB's high precision in cases when it gives an answer. Indeed, we observe that the inclusion of the two baselines to BEER[TS] results in better recommendation accuracy with an excellent query coverage.

Experiment 3: MAB Policies within BEER

As noted earlier, it is easy to substitute Thompson Sampling with other MAB policies within the BEER framework. In this experiment, we run several instances of our ensemble learner powered by various MAB policies. Apart from TS, we consider four variants of UCB algorithms, namely UCB1 [4], UCB-Tuned [4], UCB-Bayes [22], and KL-UCB [14], as well as the pre-tuned ε-greedy and MOSS [3] policies. The resulting scores for different policies are summarized in Table 4.

We observe that Thompson Sampling maintains its top rank for all metrics in all three datasets. In line with the findings of Gopalan *et al.* [16], we conclude that Thompson Sampling is the most effective bandit policy when it comes to solving complex practical online tasks, such as e-commerce recommendations. The strength of Bayesian policies is also evident from the fact that UCB-Bayes is the second best performer.

Table 4. Ensemble learner with different MAB policies

Agent	Recall	Precision	NDCG
	Books		
BEER[TS]	**0.0589**	**0.0213**	**0.0719**
BEER[UCB-Bayes]	0.0578	0.0210	0.0709
BEER[UCB-Tuned]	0.0568	0.0206	0.0694
BEER[MOSS]	0.0567	0.0205	0.0694
BEER[UCB1]	0.0526	0.0188	0.0642
BEER[KL-UCB]	0.0500	0.0195	0.0657
BEER[ε-greedy]	0.0024	0.0117	0.0382
	Fashion		
BEER[TS]	**0.1750**	**0.0155**	**0.0504**
BEER[UCB-Bayes]	0.1701	0.0147	0.0480
BEER[ε-greedy]	0.1697	0.0151	0.0489
BEER[MOSS]	0.1656	0.0141	0.0463
BEER[KL-UCB]	0.1630	0.0149	0.0485
BEER[UCB-Tuned]	0.1602	0.0133	0.0437
BEER[UCB1]	0.1426	0.0114	0.0377
	Yoochoose		
BEER[TS]	**0.2984**	**0.0424**	**0.1424**
BEER[UCB-Bayes]	0.2976	0.0422	0.1414
BEER[UCB-Tuned]	0.2975	0.0421	0.1412
BEER[MOSS]	0.2971	0.0422	0.1413
BEER[UCB1]	0.2955	0.0415	0.1394
BEER[KL-UCB]	0.1794	0.0287	0.0950
BEER[ε-greedy]	0.1211	0.0234	0.0755

Experiment 4: Priming the Sampler

Having established the best policy for orchestrating the ensemble components, we experiment with priming the Thompson Sampler with side information in attempt to give it an additional accuracy boost. As outlined in Section *Sampler Priming*, this information may come from two sources: a) pre-existing user sessions; and b) the product catalog.

Priming with Pre-Recorded Event Data

The deployment of the recommender system on an existing website with some history of past user sessions makes it possible to prime the sampler in two ways. First, the behavioral components can be warm-started with initial item associations from past events. This allows the sampler to take advantage of high-precision behavioral components from the very start. Second, after running the sampler through historical data we obtain the initial posterior distributions for each component, which allows us to assign informative priors to the Thompson Sampler. We evaluate both scenarios by running BEER[TS] through pre-recorded 100K events preceding our test data for each dataset. In Table 5 we evaluate the effect of pre-training behavioral components and priming the component's Beta distributions separately.

It becomes clear that pre-training behavioral components has a noticeable effect on the accuracy of recommendations (even when the pre-recorded dataset is 5 times smaller than the test set). However, the effect of priming the Beta parameters is less evident. This especially holds for datasets with few components, such as Yoochoose.

Catalog-Based Priming

A more challenging priming scenario is when the only available side information is the product catalog. Even though priming behavioral components in this situation is not feasible, we may still make informed guesses about the predictive ability of attribute-based components. One way of reasoning

Table 5. Priming the sampler with pre-recorded event data

Agent	Recall	Precision	NDCG
	Books		
BEER[TS]: pre-trained+primed	0.0632 ↑7.3%	**0.0231** ↑8.5%	**0.0828** ↑15.2%
BEER[TS]: pre-trained	**0.0633** ↑7.5%	0.0230 ↑8.0%	0.0822 ↑14.3%
BEER[TS]: cold-start	0.0589	0.0213	0.0719
	Fashion		
BEER[TS]: pre-trained+primed	**0.1805** ↑3.2%	**0.0159** ↑2.6%	**0.0517** ↑2.8%
BEER[TS]: pre-trained	0.1792 ↑2.5%	0.0157 ↑1.3%	0.0511 ↑1.6%
BEER[TS]: cold-start	0.1749	0.0155	0.0503
	Yoochoose		
BEER[TS]: pre-trained+primed	**0.3115** ↑4.5%	**0.0434** ↑3.1%	0.1464 ↑3.2%
BEER[TS]: pre-trained	0.3096 ↑3.9%	**0.0434** ↑3.1%	**0.1466** ↑3.4%
BEER[TS]: cold-start	0.2980	0.0421	0.1418

about their means is to make them inversely proportional to the average query response size. In other words, assuming that each query response from action a contains one relevant item, the mean μ_a is equal to the probability of that item appearing in the top-1 result. We can express it as follows:

$$\mu_a = \frac{1}{|V(G_a)|} \sum_{q \in V(G_a)} \frac{1}{|N_{G_a}(q)|} \tag{5}$$

where $V(G_a)$ is a set of vertices (items) connected via attribute a, and $N_{G_a}(q)$ is a neighborhood of query item q containing items with same value of attribute a.

The calculation of the variance is done via Equation (1), where we need to set the uncertainty parameter ν according to our confidence in the estimation of μ_a. We envisage several possibilities:

1. Uniform ν. For the standard Thompson Sampling with priors $\alpha = 1, \beta = 1$, we have: $\nu = \alpha + \beta + 1 = 3$. This corresponds to the default variance of $1/12$.
2. Component-specific ν depending on the component's query coverage. For example, $\nu_a = \sqrt{|V(G_a)|} + 1$. Intuitively, the more items (i.e. queries) have contributed to estimating the means, the more reliable that estimate is. Plugging this ν_a to Equation (1) will result in variances reflecting our degree of uncertainty in the primed means.

Another factor worth considering is posterior scaling. In classical Thompson Sampling, all actions start off with uniform priors with $\mu = 0.5$. In most recommendation scenarios, however, it is reasonable to assume that the true Beta means will be much closer to 0. This can be seen in Table 3, where the precision of the best stand-alone predictor (TWBAB) is at best 0.0519. Therefore, we may aid convergence by setting the initial means to lower values, such as 0.05. In case the distributions are not uniform but primed, we can scale the primed means to the interval [0,0.05].

We now evaluate the catalog-based priming of attribute-based components based on Equation (5) and the two aforementioned variance estimation strategies. Behavioral components cannot be primed in this case and hence maintain their uniform distributions, but are scaled as explained above. This time we exclude the Yoochoose dataset from the analysis, since it only has 2 attribute-based components. The results for the two other proprietary datasets (having 45 and 51 attribute-based components) are presented in Table 6.

Table 6. Catalog-based priming

Agent	Recall	Precision	NDCG
	Books		
BEER[TS]: catalog-primed, $\nu_a = \sqrt{|V(G_a)|}+1$	**0.0592**	**0.0214**	**0.0721**
BEER[TS]: catalog-primed, $\nu_a = 3$	0.0587	0.0213	0.0718
BEER[TS]: cold-start	0.0587	0.0212	0.0716
	Fashion		
BEER[TS]: catalog-primed, $\nu_a = \sqrt{|V(G_a)|}+1$	**0.1761**	0.0156	0.0506
BEER[TS]: catalog-primed, $\nu_a = 3$	0.1752	**0.0157**	**0.0508**
BEER[TS]: cold-start	0.1750	0.0155	0.0503

Our results indicate that priming the sampler in the absence of any historical event data is indeed feasible, but the additional accuracy gain obtained in our experiments is negligible (below 1%). While other approaches for the estimation of primed means might yield slightly better results, we conclude that adjusting prior parameters is not crucial for the convergence of Thompson Sampling, as the algorithm learns very fast anyway. However, what helps to warm-start the algorithm, as is shown in Table 5, is pre-training behavioral components using past event data.

CONCLUSIONS

Contribution Summary

E-commerce is one of the most important and challenging application domains of recommender systems, where recommendations must be adaptively computed for each new product page visit. Such an interactive user interface makes it easier for a user of an e-commerce service to find the product(s) of interest as s/he explores the product catalog.

In this paper, we have proposed an item-to-item ensemble recommendation algorithm with Thompson Sampling at its core. This algorithm was designed with a commercial application in focus, making it simple for a potential vendor to introduce recommendation functionalities to new or existing e-commerce platforms. The recommendation components of the ensemble can be constructed automatically from the existing item attributes or user-item interaction types (collaborative signals). At the same time, the system allows vendors to effortlessly integrate handcrafted components into the ensemble, which are immediately picked up and explored by the Thompson Sampler. Such a component-based architecture is scalable, since the number of bandit arms does not depend on the number of items. Furthermore, it allows system developers to deliver *semantically transparent user interfaces* [26], where each recommendation is accompanied with a clear explanation of its source (e.g. behavioral or attribute-based, see Figure 1). An integral part of our recommendation bandit is its adaptation to realistic situations with "sleeping" actions and non-stationary reward sequences.

In a series of experiments on real e-commerce session data, we show that the above adaptations are crucial for the algorithm's operation (with accuracy gains ranging from 83% to 94% for the Books dataset). We further evaluate the strength of the ensemble approach, achieving far superior results in comparison to strong stand-alone baseline recommenders, namely *best-sellers* and *those-who-bought-also-bought*. As we have observed, adding these baselines to the ensemble does not only improve its accuracy, but also attains 100% query coverage. Our comparative study convinces us that Thompson Sampling is empirically the best MAB policy for the BEER framework. We further show that Thompson Sampling handles cold-start gracefully out-of-the-box, as it does not seem to benefit much from Beta parameter priming. This property together with TS's robustness to observation delays makes it a very attractive method for attacking the recommendation problem using reinforcement learning.

Future Work

The proposed ensemble algorithm is as good as the components that it is comprised of. It is therefore worth exploring better strategies for constructing base predictors for the ensemble. When it comes to behavioral signals, we expect that the provision of personalized components based on existing collaborative filtering techniques would be advantageous for the ensemble, provided that user profile data is available. This way we can take advantage of both short-term and long-term user preferences when computing recommendations. With regard to attribute-based components, the next research direction is to develop methods for the automatic composition of high-precision attribute combinations as potential components of the ensemble. In addition, it is worth considering components built from item descriptions and/or images. Finally, it would be interesting to follow the recent success of deep reinforcement learning in playing video games in attempt to adapt it for the sequential recommendation problem in e-commerce.

REFERENCES

1. Deepak Agarwal, Bee-Chung Chen, Pradheep Elango, and Raghu Ramakrishnan. 2013. Content Recommendation on Web Portals. *Commun. ACM* 56, 6 (June 2013), 92–101.
2. Eric Andrews. 2015. *Recommender Systems for Online Dating*. Master's thesis. University of Helsinki.
3. Jean-Yves Audibert and Sébastien Bubeck. 2010. Regret Bounds and Minimax Policies Under Partial Monitoring. *J. Mach. Learn. Res.* 11 (Dec. 2010), 2785–2836.
4. Peter Auer, Nicolò Cesa-Bianchi, and Paul Fischer. 2002. Finite-time Analysis of the Multiarmed Bandit Problem. *Mach. Learn.* 47, 2-3 (May 2002), 235–256.
5. Viktor A. Barger and Lauren Labrecque. 2013. An Integrated Marketing Communications Perspective on Social Media Metrics. *International Journal of Integrated Marketing Communications* (May 2013), 31.
6. David Ben-Shimon, Alexander Tsikinovsky, Michael Friedmann, Bracha Shapira, Lior Rokach, and Johannes Hoerle. 2015. RecSys Challenge 2015 and the YOOCHOOSE Dataset. In *Proceedings of the 9th ACM Conference on Recommender Systems (RecSys '15)*. ACM, 357–358.
7. Lucas Bernardi, Jaap Kamps, Julia Kiseleva, and Melanie J. I. Müller. 2015. The Continuous Cold Start Problem in e-Commerce Recommender Systems. *CoRR* abs/1508.01177 (June 2015).
8. Djallel Bouneffouf and Raphael Féraud. 2016. Multi-armed Bandit Problem with Known Trend. *Neurocomput.* 205, C (Sept. 2016), 16–21.
9. Djallel Bouneffouf, Romain Laroche, Tanguy Urvoy, Raphael Feraud, and Robin Allesiardo. 2014. Contextual Bandit for Active Learning: Active Thompson Sampling. In *Neural Information Processing: 21st International Conference, ICONIP 2014, Kuching, Malaysia, November 3-6, 2014. Proceedings, Part I*, Chu Kiong Loo, Keem Siah Yap, Kok Wai Wong, Andrew Teoh, and Kaizhu Huang (Eds.). Springer International Publishing, 405–412.
10. Giuseppe Burtini, Jason Loeppky, and Ramon Lawrence. 2015. Improving Online Marketing Experiments with Drifting Multi-armed Bandits. In *Proceedings of the 17th International Conference on Enterprise Information Systems - Volume 1 (ICEIS 2015)*. SCITEPRESS - Science and Technology Publications, Lda, 630–636.
11. Stéphane Caron and Smriti Bhagat. 2013. Mixing Bandits: A Recipe for Improved Cold-start Recommendations in a Social Network. In *Proceedings of the 7th Workshop on Social Network Mining and Analysis (SNAKDD '13)*. ACM, Article 11, 9 pages.
12. Olivier Chapelle and Lihong Li. 2011. An Empirical Evaluation of Thompson Sampling. In *Advances in Neural Information Processing Systems 24*, J. Shawe-Taylor, R. S. Zemel, P. L. Bartlett, F. Pereira, and K. Q. Weinberger (Eds.). Curran Associates, Inc., 2249–2257.
13. Crícia Z. Felício, Klérisson V.R. Paixão, Celia A.Z. Barcelos, and Philippe Preux. 2017. A Multi-Armed Bandit Model Selection for Cold-Start User Recommendation. In *Proceedings of the 25th Conference on User Modeling, Adaptation and Personalization (UMAP '17)*. ACM, 32–40.
14. Aurélien Garivier and Olivier Cappé. 2011. The KL-UCB Algorithm for Bounded Stochastic Bandits and Beyond. In *The 24th Annual Conference on Learning Theory*. 359–376.
15. Aurélien Garivier and Eric Moulines. 2011. On Upper-confidence Bound Policies for Switching Bandit Problems. In *Proceedings of the 22Nd International Conference on Algorithmic Learning Theory (ALT'11)*. Springer-Verlag, 174–188.
16. Aditya Gopalan, Shie Mannor, and Yishay Mansour. 2014. Thompson Sampling for Complex Online Problems. In *Proceedings of the 31st International Conference on International Conference on Machine Learning - Volume 32 (ICML'14)*. JMLR.org, I–100–I–108.
17. Frédéric Guillou. 2016. *On recommendation systems in a sequential context*. Ph.D. Dissertation. Université Charles de Gaulle - Lille III.

18. Negar Hariri, Bamshad Mobasher, and Robin Burke. 2015. Adapting to User Preference Changes in Interactive Recommendation. In *Proceedings of the 24th International Conference on Artificial Intelligence (IJCAI'15)*. AAAI Press, 4268–4274.

19. Cédric Hartland, Sylvain Gelly, Nicolas Baskiotis, Olivier Teytaud, and Michéle Sebag. 2006. Multi-Armed Bandit, Dynamic Environments and Meta-Bandits. In *Online Trading of Exploration and Exploitation, NIPS 2006 Workshop*.

20. Chu-Cheng Hsieh, James Neufeld, Tracy King, and Junghoo Cho. 2015. Efficient Approximate Thompson Sampling for Search Query Recommendation. In *Proceedings of the 30th Annual ACM Symposium on Applied Computing (SAC '15)*. ACM, 740–746.

21. Varun Kanade, Brendan Mcmahan, and Bryan Brent. 2009. Sleeping Experts and Bandits with Stochastic Action Availability and Adversarial Rewards. In *In Proceedings of the Twelfth International Conference on Artificial Intelligence and Statistics, number 5*. 272–279.

22. Emilie Kaufmann, Nathaniel Korda, and Rémi Munos. 2012. Thompson Sampling: An Asymptotically Optimal Finite-time Analysis. In *Proceedings of the 23rd International Conference on Algorithmic Learning Theory (ALT'12)*. Springer-Verlag, 199–213.

23. Jaya Kawale, Hung H Bui, Branislav Kveton, Long Tran-Thanh, and Sanjay Chawla. 2015. Efficient Thompson Sampling for Online ï£ijMatrix Factorization Recommendation. In *Advances in Neural Information Processing Systems 28*. Curran Associates, Inc., 1297–1305.

24. Robert Kleinberg, Alexandru Niculescu-Mizil, and Yogeshwer Sharma. 2010. Regret Bounds for Sleeping Experts and Bandits. *Mach. Learn.* 80, 2-3 (Sept. 2010), 245–272.

25. Tomáš Kocák, Michal Valko, Rémi Munos, and Shipra Agrawal. 2014. Spectral Thompson Sampling. In *Proceedings of the Twenty-Eighth AAAI Conference on Artificial Intelligence (AAAI'14)*. AAAI Press, 1911–1917.

26. Andrea E. Kohlhase and Michael Kohlhase. 2009. Semantic Transparency in User Assistance Systems. In *Proceedings of the 27th ACM International Conference on Design of Communication (SIGDOC '09)*. ACM, 89–96.

27. Branislav Kveton, Csaba Szepesvári, Zheng Wen, and Azin Ashkan. 2015. Cascading Bandits: Learning to Rank in the Cascade Model. In *Proceedings of the 32Nd International Conference on International Conference on Machine Learning - Volume 37 (ICML'15)*. JMLR.org, 767–776.

28. Anisio Lacerda. 2017. Multi-Objective Ranked Bandits for Recommender Systems. *Neurocomput.* 246, C (July 2017), 12–24.

29. T.L Lai and Herbert Robbins. 1985. Asymptotically Efficient Adaptive Allocation Rules. *Adv. Appl. Math.* 6, 1 (March 1985), 4–22.

30. Lihong Li, Wei Chu, John Langford, and Robert E. Schapire. 2010. A Contextual-bandit Approach to Personalized News Article Recommendation. In *Proceedings of the 19th International Conference on World Wide Web (WWW '10)*. ACM, 661–670.

31. Lihong Li, Wei Chu, John Langford, and Xuanhui Wang. 2011. Unbiased Offline Evaluation of Contextual-bandit-based News Article Recommendation Algorithms. In *Proceedings of the Fourth ACM International Conference on Web Search and Data Mining (WSDM '11)*. ACM, 297–306.

32. Shuai Li, Alexandros Karatzoglou, and Claudio Gentile. 2016a. Collaborative Filtering Bandits. In *Proceedings of the 39th International ACM SIGIR Conference on Research and Development in Information Retrieval (SIGIR '16)*. ACM, 539–548.

33. Shuai Li, Baoxiang Wang, Shengyu Zhang, and Wei Chen. 2016b. Contextual Combinatorial Cascading Bandits. In *Proceedings of the 33rd International Conference on International Conference on Machine Learning - Volume 48 (ICML'16)*. JMLR.org, 1245–1253.

34. Jonathan Louëdec, Max Chevalier, Josiane Mothe, Aurélien Garivier, and Sébastien Gerchinovitz. 2015. A Multiple-Play Bandit Algorithm Applied to Recommender Systems. In *Proceedings of the Twenty-Eighth International Florida Artificial Intelligence Research Society Conference, FLAIRS*. 67–72.

35. Jérémie Mary, Romaric Gaudel, and Philippe Preux. 2014. Bandits Warm-up Cold Recommender Systems. *CoRR* abs/1407.2806 (June 2014).

36. Joseph Mellor and Jonathan Shapiro. 2013. Thompson Sampling in Switching Environments with Bayesian Online Change Point Detection. In *Proceedings of the Sixteenth International Conference on Artificial Intelligence and Statistics*. 442–450.

37. Minh-Quan Nguyen. 2014. *Multi-armed Bandit Problem and Its Applications in Intelligent Tutoring Systems*. Master's thesis. ÃL'cole Polytechnique.

38. Dimitris Paraschakis, Bengt J. Nilsson, and John Holländer. 2015. Comparative Evaluation of Top-N Recommenders in e-Commerce: An Industrial Perspective. In *14th International Conference on Machine Learning and Applications (ICMLA)*. IEEE, 1024 – 1031.

39. Filip Radlinski, Robert Kleinberg, and Thorsten Joachims. 2008. Learning Diverse Rankings with Multi-armed Bandits. In *Proceedings of the 25th International Conference on Machine Learning (ICML '08)*. ACM, 784–791.

40. Aleksandrs Slivkins. 2014. Contextual Bandits with Similarity Information. *J. Mach. Learn. Res.* 15, 1 (Jan. 2014), 2533–2568.

41. Aleksandrs Slivkins, Filip Radlinski, and Sreenivas Gollapudi. 2013. Ranked Bandits in Metric Spaces: Learning Diverse Rankings over Large Document Collections. *J. Mach. Learn. Res.* 14, 1 (Feb. 2013), 399–436.

42. Matthew Streeter and Daniel Golovin. 2008. An Online Algorithm for Maximizing Submodular Functions. In *Proceedings of the 21st International Conference on Neural Information Processing Systems (NIPS'08)*. Curran Associates Inc., 1577–1584.

43. Liang Tang, Yexi Jiang, Lei Li, and Tao Li. 2014. Ensemble Contextual Bandits for Personalized Recommendation. In *Proceedings of the 8th ACM Conference on Recommender Systems (RecSys '14)*. ACM, 73–80.

44. Bartlomiej Twardowski. 2016. Modelling Contextual Information in Session-Aware Recommender Systems with Neural Networks. In *Proceedings of the 10th ACM Conference on Recommender Systems (RecSys '16)*. ACM, 273–276.

45. Taishi Uchiya, Atsuyoshi Nakamura, and Mineichi Kudo. 2010. Algorithms for Adversarial Bandit Problems with Multiple Plays. In *Proceedings of the 21st International Conference on Algorithmic Learning Theory (ALT'10)*. Springer-Verlag, 375–389.

46. Xinxi Wang, Yi Wang, David Hsu, and Ye Wang. 2014. Exploration in Interactive Personalized Music Recommendation: A Reinforcement Learning Approach. *ACM Trans. Multimedia Comput. Commun. Appl.* 11, 1 (2014), 7:1–7:22.

47. Chen Wu, Ming Yan, and Luo Si. 2017. Session-aware Information Embedding for E-commerce Product Recommendation. *CoRR* abs/1707.05955 (2017).

48. Xiaoxue Zhao, Weinan Zhang, and Jun Wang. 2013. Interactive collaborative filtering. In *Proceedings of the 22nd ACM international conference on Conference on Information and Knowledge Management (CIKM '13)*. ACM, 1411–1420.

Discovering Surprising Documents with Context-Aware Word Representations

Michał Dereziński* University of California Santa Cruz, CA mderezin@soe.ucsc.edu

Khashayar Rohanimanesh eBay Research Labs San Jose, CA khash@cs.umass.edu

Aamer Hydrie eBay Research Labs San Jose, CA ahydrie@gmail.com

ABSTRACT
User experiences can be made more engaging by incorporating surprise. For example, online shoppers may like to view unique products. In this paper we propose an approach for detecting surprising documents, such as product titles. As the concept of surprise is subjective, there is currently no principled method for measuring the surprisingness score of a document. We present such a method; an unsupervised approach for automatically discovering surprising documents in an unlabeled corpus. Our approach is based on a probabilistic model of surprise, and a construction of effective distributional word embeddings, which can be adapted to the semantic context in which the word appears. As the performance of our model does not degrade with the length of the document, it is particularly well suited for very short documents (even a single sentence). We evaluate our model both in supervised *and* unsupervised settings, demonstrating its state-of-the-art performance on two real-world data sets: a collection of e-commerce products from eBay, and a corpus of NSF proposals. These experiments show that our surprisingness score exhibits high correlation with human annotated labels.

Author Keywords
product discovery; text surprisingness; information theory; recommender systems; topic modeling

INTRODUCTION
With the rapid growth of e-commerce, new products are increasingly introduced into the marketplace on a daily basis. A larger subset of these products consists of our daily needs or off-the-shelf products (Figure 1), while a much smaller subset can be attributed as *unique*, *creative*, *serendipitous*, or *surprising* (Figure 2). The latter class of products often provokes an emotive response in users and gives them a more engaging experience. Automatic discovery of this type of products is an important problem in e-commerce for creating an engaging experience for the users and encouraging them to return to the site. One approach to solving this task is through analyzing textual information that is associated with each product (e.g. title, description). Such a task can be framed as follows: given a large corpus (where each element describes one product), detect documents that are deemed surprising. This problem presents several challenges. First, the notion of surprise is not well understood and very subjective, two users may disagree about whether a product is surprising. Second, textual information is fairly limited in this domain. Many products may only be described by their title (typically 10 to 12 words), so the corpus may contain very short documents, making most text processing techniques ineffective. However, we believe that even from product titles alone it is possible to automatically detect items that appear unique and surprising to a sufficiently large population of users.

Figure 1. Examples of off-the-shelf eBay products. Note that in every case, the word co-occurrences in the titles match our expectation.

(a) Black Qi Standard Wireless Charging Case For iPhone 5 5G

(b) Bluetooth Wireless Speaker Mini Portable For iPhone

Figure 2. Examples of surprising eBay products. The highlighted keywords are not expected to co-occur in the context of the product.

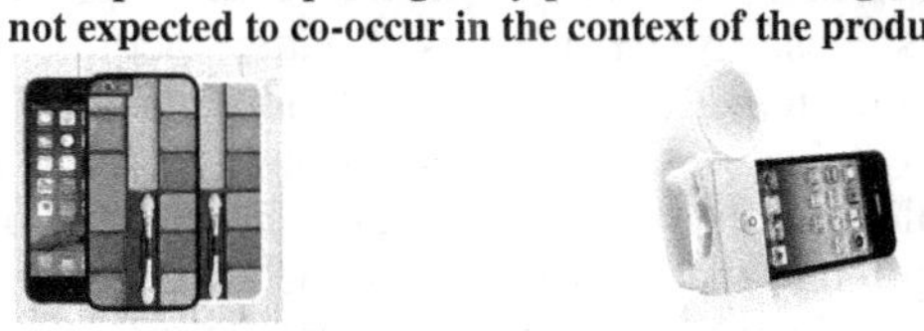

(a) Eyeshadow Palettes for iPhone 6 case

(b) White Silicone Horn Stand Speaker for Apple iPhone 4/ 4S

In this paper we present a probabilistic approach for discovering surprising documents. Unlike existing approaches, this method is shown to be effective even for very short text snippets. We hypothesize that many text forms that could be deemed surprising often express considerable variety in terms of the text describing them. As an example, in Figure 2(a), in the context of iPhone cases, one would not expect to observe topics that relate to makeup. Based on this hypothesis we introduce a probabilistic model for measuring topic diversity based on *Jensen-Shannon Divergence* and show how it correlates with text surprisingness. To make our measure effective for short documents, we construct distributional word representations, which can adapt to the semantic context of the document. We present results evaluating the performance of

*The author was supported by NSF grant IIS-1619271.

IUI 2018, March 7–11, 2018, Tokyo, Japan.
Copyright © 2018 ACM ISBN 978-1-4503-4945-1/18/03 ...$15.00.
http://dx.doi.org/10.1145/3172944.3173011

our surprisingness metric in two different real world domains: (1) identifying unique eBay products based on the surprisingness of their titles; (2) identifying the most cross-disciplinary National Science Foundation Scholarship proposal abstracts (introduced in [1]). Moreover, we compare our model for constructing context-aware distributional representations to other standard text-embedding techniques, including recursive auto-encoders [17].

RELATED WORK

There has been considerable research on the topic of discovering unique, interesting or surprising documents. Researchers have studied different dimensions of this problem in terms of *humor identification* [12, 4, 10], *text aesthetics* [15, 16, 7], and *document diversity* [1, 8]. [12] studies a computational approach for humor recognition by utilizing a set of humor-specific stylistic features such as alliteration, antonymy, and adult slangs. Some of these features, e.g., antonymy, in a limited way capture some sort of text diversity as we do not normally expect antonyms co-occurring in standard text. [4] proposes a semi-supervised approach for identifying sarcastic sentences in Twitter and Amazon. Their approach consists of two stages; a semi supervised pattern acquisition is used for identifying sarcastic patterns, and a classifier uses such patterns as features in a classification task. Such word-level stand-alone interestingness features are related to the word-saliency factor that is discussed in the next sections. [7] studies automatic prediction of text interestingness by utilizing a broader set of features such as word length, repetitions, polarity, part-of-speech, semantic distances, and somewhat simple treatment of topic generality and diversity.

Measuring topic diversity for text has been previously studied by [1] which is the most relevant work to our approach. [1] uses Rao's diversity [13] for measuring document diversity based on a topic model learned over a corpus of documents. As shown in Section "Experiments", we found that this method did not work well for the eBay product dataset. We believe that the primary reason for this is that the amount of useful textual data for each product is often too small to be treated as a document. As made clear in the remainder of this paper, our measure differs from this metric from an information theoretic perspective, allowing it to perform well in this setting. Throughout our experiments, we use the approach of [1] as one of our baselines.

QUANTIFYING SURPRISE IN TEXT

The term "surprise" is not well defined and may vary depending on the domain. However, one concrete and general definition is offered through the probabilistic measure of "entropy" [14]. In the context of a text document, we can think of entropy as measuring the diversity of the topics/ideas which are being conveyed in the text. If we encounter two topics which are not expected to co-occur together, this surprises readers. Our goal is to define a quantifiable metric of entropic surprise in the text domain, which will perform well in practical tasks. Here, this problem is formulated as an unsupervised one, i.e. we expect our model to discover surprising documents in the absence of labeled training data or any user-specific information. We are given a large and representative corpus of documents from the considered domain, but no human-curated surprisingness labels are provided. We also require that the trained model be capable of efficiently scoring new documents as they come in, without the need to retrain on the entire corpus.

As our primary domain of interest is e-commerce, the documents we encounter are very short (e.g. product titles on eBay), often just 10 to 12 words. This makes standard bag-of-words models ineffective, because we cannot retrieve accurate word-frequency information for a single document. To address this problem, we can construct distributional word representations, which capture semantic information by embedding words into a multi-dimensional space of probability vectors.

Distributional Word Representations

As a starting point to obtaining distributional word representations, we run *Latent Dirichlet Allocation* (LDA) [2] to build a topic model from a corpus of documents. We use the set of topics as the contexts. In this case, each word is mapped to a probability distribution over the topics discovered by LDA. We will use T to denote the set of learned topics. As a result of this procedure, each word occurence in the corpus is tagged with one of the topics $t \in T$. From this model we obtain the word-topic-count matrix $\mathbf{X} \in \mathbb{R}^{|V|\times|T|}$ where entry x_{ij} is the number of assignments of topic t_j to word w_i from the vocabulary V. By normalizing the rows of matrix $\mathbf{X}$ we obtain a set of distributional representations, where the i-th row of the matrix gives a topic distribution for the word w_i.

Capturing topic correlations. When building a topic distribution model based on the word-to-topic co-occurrence matrix, the relationship among topics (i.e, topic correlation) may be lost. For example, a product description that is related to two topics such as *Computers* and *Software* should be deemed less surprising then if those two topics were *Computers* and *Clothes*, so our model has to be able to make such a distinction. To address this problem, we define a topic similarity matrix $\mathbf{S} \in \mathbb{R}^{|T|\times|T|}$ where the element $s_{i,j}$ gives the similarity/correlation between topic t_i and topic t_j (e.g. the similarity would be high between *Computers* and *Software*, but low for *Computers* and *Clothes*). Using $\mathbf{S}$ we transform the word-topic-count matrix $\mathbf{X}$, obtaining $\widehat{\mathbf{X}} = \mathbf{X}\,\mathbf{S}^\top$, which effectively diffuses the topic distributions to ones where for every topic assignment, all similar topics are also well represented. To construct the topic similarity matrix for the LDA model, we use the document-topic-count matrix $\mathbf{Y} \in \mathbb{R}^{|C|\times|T|}$ (where C is the set of documents), which is returned by LDA alongside $\mathbf{X}$. This matrix, for each document, has a row vector describing the total number of assignments of each topic. To estimate the similarity of topics t_i and t_j, we compute the cosine similarity between their corresponding columns in $\mathbf{Y}$. Denoting $\mathbf{y}_i$ and $\mathbf{y}_j$ as those column vectors, their cosine similarity is

$$s_{i,j} = \frac{\langle \mathbf{y}_i, \mathbf{y}_j \rangle}{\|\mathbf{y}_i\|_2 \|\mathbf{y}_j\|_2},$$

where $\langle\cdot,\cdot\rangle$ represents a dot product between two vectors and $\|\cdot\|_2$ is the ℓ_2-norm of a vector.

Let $\widehat{\mathbf{x}}_w$ denote the row of matrix $\widehat{\mathbf{X}}$ corresponding to the word w. Applying *Laplace smoothing* to $\widehat{\mathbf{x}}_w$, we define the static representation of w:

$$P_w = \frac{\alpha P_0 + \widehat{\mathbf{x}}_w}{\alpha + \|\widehat{\mathbf{x}}_w\|_1}, \quad (1)$$

where $\|\cdot\|_1$ is the ℓ_1-norm of a vector, while α is the parameter that specifies the strength of the smoothing prior distribution P_0. We obtain a prior topic distribution P_0 by summing up matrix $\widehat{\mathbf{X}}$ along its columns and then normalizing.

Probabilistic Model of Surprise

For the remainder of this section, we assume that a topic distributional model for the words in the vocabulary has been learned. More specifically, we are given a distributional representation over a vocabulary V and topic set T, with P_w giving a topic distribution corresponding to the word w. We will measure surprise for a text snippet $W = (w_1, ..., w_k)$ by analyzing its distributional representation $\mathcal{P}_W = (P_{w_1}, ..., P_{w_k})$. To estimate the surprise induced by $\mathcal{P}_W$, we use a measure of divergence between probability distributions, discussed in [6], which is a variant of Jensen-Shannon Divergence.

DEFINITION 1. *Let $\mathcal{P}_W = (P_{w_1}, ..., P_{w_k})$ be a sequence of distributions (for example, topic distributions for the words in a document). Moreover, assume $\{d_{w_i}\}$ is a set of importance weights assigned to $\{P_{w_i}\}$, such that $\sum_{i=1}^k d_{w_i} = 1$.* ***Jensen-Shannon Divergence*** *of the mixture $\Sigma d_{w_i} P_{w_i}$ is defined as*

$$D_{\mathrm{JS}}(\Sigma d_{w_i} P_{w_i}) = \sum_{i=1}^{k} d_{w_i} D_{\mathrm{KL}}(P_{w_i} \| M),$$

where $M = \sum_{i=1}^k d_{w_i} P_{w_i}$ is the mixture distribution.

Here, D_{KL} corresponds to Kullback-Leibler Divergence (see [3]). As a shorthand, we will also write $D_{\mathrm{JS}}(M)$, when it is clear that M represents a mixture of distributions. It can be shown that Jensen-Shannon Divergence is a direct generalization of Shannon entropy.

Note, that to compute D_{JS} we need not only the distributional representations, but also a set of weights assigned to each of them. Intuitively, the weight d_{w_i} should describe the saliency of word w_i, i.e., how important it is in describing the content of the text (e.g. stop words should get a low weight). We want to quantify the information gain coming from each appearance of the word w_i. This can be described by the KL-divergence between the distributional representation of w_i and the prior topic distribution P_0.

DEFINITION 2. *We define the* ***importance*** *of a word representation P_{w_i} with respect to the prior distribution P_0 as*

$$D_{w_i} = D_{\mathrm{KL}}(P_{w_i} \| P_0).$$

For any text W we define its *static mixture representation* as $M_W = \Sigma d_{w_i} P_{w_i}$, where $d_{w_i} = D_{w_i} / (\sum_{j=1}^k D_{w_j})$.

CONTEXT-AWARE WORD REPRESENTATIONS

Let $W = (w_1, ..., w_k)$ represent a text snippet that we want to analyze. The word w_i has a specific meaning inside of W, that can be significantly different than its meaning out of context. For example, the word *mouse* can be associated with the topic of computers as well as the topic of animals, which are clearly very different. However, in a given context, usually there will be no confusion as to which topic is most relevant. We propose to define a new context-aware distributional representation of w_i that takes this into account (as opposed to the static representation P_{w_i} we have so far). We will represent the context information using the static mixture distribution $M_{W_{-i}}$ (see Definition 2), where W_{-i} is the text W with word w_i excluded. If a topic t has high weight in both distributions P_{w_i} and $M_{W_{-i}}$, then it is relevant to w_i in this context. More generally, if distributions $M_{W_{-i}}$ and P_{w_i} have significant overlap, then those shared topics are likely to explain the text well, and the remaining topics in P_{w_i} should effectively be ignored. If the overlap is minimal, then this indicates unexpected (surprising) content. To model this intuition, we define the following context-aware representation of a word w_i in text W:

DEFINITION 3. *Let w_i be a word in text W, and let P_0 be the prior topic distribution. Then the context-aware distributional representation of w_i in W is defined as*

$$\widehat{P}_{w_i}(t; W) \propto \left(\frac{M_{W_{-i}}(t)}{P_0(t)} + \beta \right) P_{w_i}(t).$$

This can be intuitively understood as follows: we can think of $\frac{M_{W_{-i}}(t)}{P_0(t)}$ as a weight that further reshapes $P_{w_i}(t)$ to take into account the context. The key operation here is the element-wise multiplication $M_{W_{-i}}(t) \cdot P_{w_i}(t)$, which essentially captures the overlapping topics. The prior P_0 is there to adjust for the overall popularity of each topic - if context distribution were equal to the prior, we would expect it to have no effect in this transformation, as is the case here. Note that we apply additional Laplace smoothing with parameter β to account for the case where the word and the context have minimal topic overlap, which is very important because that is what generates surprise. If this occurs, the transformation effectively reverts to the static representation.

Finally, we can define our surprise score by combining the context-aware word representations into a mixture using weights d_{w_i} (see Definition 2):

DEFINITION 4. *We define the* ***text surprisingness*** *of W w.r.t. corpus C to be $D_{\mathrm{JS}}(\widehat{M}_W)$, where $\widehat{M}_W = \Sigma d_{w_i} \widehat{P}_{w_i}(\cdot\,; W)$ is the* ***context-aware mixture representation*** *of W.*

Note that our method can efficiently compute the surprisingness score for a new document without the need of retraining on the entire corpus, making it particularly suitable for many web applications.

EXPERIMENTS

To evaluate the proposed method, we used two datasets:

Interesting iPhone cases. Motivated by the important task of generating user engagement on an e-commerce website like eBay, we collected a number of interesting (positive) and uninteresting (negative) iPhone case product titles as follows. For generating positive examples, we used the data hosted by Pinterest. For generating the uninteresting iPhone case dataset (negative examples), we hired workers from *AMT* to label a collection of nearly 20,000 iPhone cases on *eBay*. We

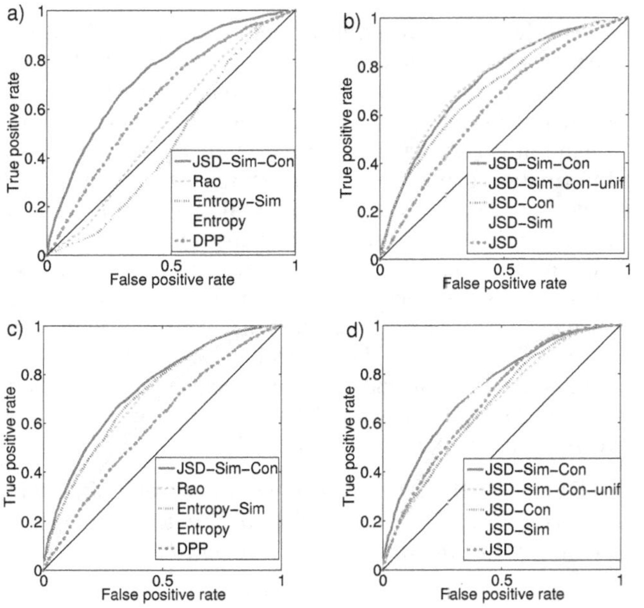

Figure 3. ROC curves presenting the results of experiments on the eBay dataset (a,b) and NSF proposal dataset (c,d). The comparison plots (a,c) show the results for our approach (JSD-Sim-Con) against other methods, while the plots (b,d) show different variations of our approach ("Sim" means applying topic similarity matrix S, "Con" means using context-aware word representations, rather than static ones, "unif" means uniform importance weights, instead of d_w).

then pulled our final dataset from the annotated by selecting only those instances where the annotators all labeled it as uninteresting. The final dataset consists of 2179 positive and 9770 negative instances for a total of $11,949$ instances. For each instance, the product title of the corresponding *eBay* listing was used as the input. In this case we are dealing with very short text snippets, usually 10 to 12 words each. To train a topic model, we used a larger, more broader set of about 2 million product titles, grouped based on *eBay* categorical information into about $8,000$ documents of approximately 200 titles each. We used the Mallet LDA implementation (see [11]) to learn a topic model with 400 topics.

Cross-disciplinary NSF abstracts. For the second dataset we used a set of 61,902 National Science Foundation Scholarship proposal abstracts (see [1] for more details) to evaluate how our diversity measure compares to other methods on larger pieces of text. We used this set for training a topic model, however to get labeled data, we had to generate artificial examples, by randomly mixing pairs of abstracts that we could expect to be either similar (not surprising) or very different (surprising), based on the available meta-data, and labeling them accordingly. We generated 5,000 of those examples with positive and negative labels evenly represented. For this experiment, we trained a separate topic model with 300 topics based on the original NSF abstracts.

Unsupervised Setting

We evaluated our text surprisingness model in an unsupervised learning task on both datasets. The model was implemented as described in the previous sections (labeled by *JSD-Sim-Con* in the plots). We compare out method against other known document diversity metrics: LDA topic entropy, LDA topic entropy using topic similarity (labeled by *Entropy-Sim*), *Rao diversity* (see [1] for details) and a metric based on determinantal point processes (DPP) [9], which measures the spread of word representations in a document as vectors in a Euclidean space.

As seen in Figures 3 (a) and (c), our approach outperforms the baselines, with an AUC around 0.73. Moreover, for the *eBay* dataset the other measures give very poor results. This can be explained as follows: since the text snippets are short, LDA may yield a poor topic inference for such short text and as a result all measures using topic inference directly on the test data would perform poorly. Our technique allows training LDA on a separate dataset, so it is not affected by text length. Interestingly, LDA topic entropy performs much better on the NSF dataset when applied to distributions transformed using topic similarity information, showing the efficacy of this technique. This is further confirmed in Figures 3 (b) and (d), which show gains obtained by separately applying topic similarity and context-awareness techniques to the word representations, as well as using non-uniform importance weights d_w from Definition 2.

Table 1. Classification results for the eBay dataset.

	Precision	Recall	Accuracy
JSD	**0.71** ± 0.01	0.60 ± 0.02	**0.883** ± 0.004
RAE	0.68 ± 0.01	**0.67** ± 0.03	0.881 ± 0.002
LSI	0.68 ± 0.01	0.63 ± 0.02	0.878 ± 0.003

Supervised Setting

In the second set of results, we used the unnormalized vector of mixture topic distribution (described in Definition 2) computed over *eBay* product titles in a supervised classification setting. Table 1 shows the performance of the SVM classifier using our proposed mixture topic distribution as features and compares it to two different baselines, namely, SVM using *Latent Semantic Indexing (LSI)* features (by forming a document-term matrix and performing SVD, see [5]), and a deep learning approach using the *recursive auto-encoders (RAE)* framework described in [17]. These results are averaged over five different cross-validation splits using 0.6 for training and 0.4 for testing. Our proposed approach shows marginally higher accuracy compared to the baselines, but it also achieves a significantly higher precision, which is especially important, given that the goal of this task is discovering interesting products for recommendation.

CONCLUSIONS

In this paper we propose a novel approach for discovering surprising documents, and show that it can be an effective way of discovering interesting products for recommendation. At the heart of this approach lies a model for constructing context-aware distributional word representations. Using this framework, we show that Jensen-Shannon Divergence can be a useful measure of text surprisingness. We provide experimental results in two different real world domains, for which this method outperforms the previously known metrics.

REFERENCES

1. Kevin Bache, David Newman, and Padhraic Smyth. 2013. Text-based Measures of Document Diversity. In *Proceedings of the 19th ACM SIGKDD International Conference on Knowledge Discovery and Data Mining (KDD '13)*. ACM, New York, NY, USA, 23–31.
2. David M. Blei, Andrew Y. Ng, and Michael I. Jordan. 2003. Latent Dirichlet Allocation. *J. Mach. Learn. Res.* 3 (March 2003), 993–1022. `http://dl.acm.org/citation.cfm?id=944919.944937`
3. Thomas M. Cover and Joy A. Thomas. 2006. *Elements of Information Theory (Wiley Series in Telecommunications and Signal Processing)*. Wiley-Interscience.
4. Dmitry Davidov, Oren Tsur, and Ari Rappoport. 2010. Semi-supervised Recognition of Sarcastic Sentences in Twitter and Amazon. In *Proceedings of the Fourteenth Conference on Computational Natural Language Learning (CoNLL '10)*. Association for Computational Linguistics, Stroudsburg, PA, USA, 107–116. `http://dl.acm.org/citation.cfm?id=1870568.1870582`
5. Scott Deerwester, Susan T. Dumais, George W. Furnas, Thomas K. Landaue, and Richard Harshman. 1990. Indexing by latent semantic analysis. *Journal of the American Society for Information Science* 41, 6 (1990), 391–407.
6. B. Fuglede and F. Topsoe. 2004. Jensen-Shannon divergence and Hilbert space embedding. In *IEEE International Symposium on Information Theory*. 31–31.
7. Debasis Ganguly, Johannes Leveling, and Gareth Jones. 2014. Automatic Prediction of Aesthetics and Interestingness of Text Passages. In *Proceedings of COLING 2014, the 25th International Conference on Computational Linguistics: Technical Papers*. Dublin City University and Association for Computational Linguistics, Dublin, Ireland, 905–916. `http://www.aclweb.org/anthology/C14-1086`
8. Jennifer Gillenwater, Alex Kulesza, and Ben Taskar. 2012. Discovering Diverse and Salient Threads in Document Collections. In *Proceedings of the 2012 Joint Conference on Empirical Methods in Natural Language Processing and Computational Natural Language Learning (EMNLP-CoNLL '12)*. Association for Computational Linguistics, Stroudsburg, PA, USA, 710–720. `http://dl.acm.org/citation.cfm?id=2390948.2391026`
9. Alex Kulesza and Ben Taskar. 2012. *Determinantal Point Processes for Machine Learning*. Now Publishers Inc., Hanover, MA, USA. `http://dl.acm.org/citation.cfm?id=2481023`
10. Igor Labutov and Hod Lipson. 2012. Humor as Circuits in Semantic Networks. In *Proceedings of the 50th Annual Meeting of the Association for Computational Linguistics (Volume 2: Short Papers)*. Association for Computational Linguistics, Jeju Island, Korea, 150–155. `http://www.aclweb.org/anthology/P12-2030`
11. Andrew Kachites McCallum. 2002. MALLET: A Machine Learning for Language Toolkit. (2002). http://mallet.cs.umass.edu.
12. Rada Mihalcea and Carlo Strapparava. 2005. Making Computers Laugh: Investigations in Automatic Humor Recognition. In *Proceedings of the Conference on Human Language Technology and Empirical Methods in Natural Language Processing (HLT '05)*. Association for Computational Linguistics, Stroudsburg, PA, USA, 531–538.
13. C. Rao. 1982. Diversity and dissimilarity coefficients: a unified approach. In *Theoretical Population Biology*, Vol. 21(1). 24–43.
14. Carlo Ricotta and Laszlo Szeidl. 2006. Towards a unifying approach to diversity measures: bridging the gap between the Shannon entropy and Rao's quadratic index. *Theoretical population biology* 70, 3 (November 2006), 237–243.
15. Jürgen Schmidhuber. 2010. Formal Theory of Creativity, Fun, and Intrinsic Motivation (1990-2010). *IEEE T. Autonomous Mental Development* 2, 3 (2010), 230–247.
16. Ekaterina Shutova and Lin Sun. 2013. Unsupervised Metaphor Identification Using Hierarchical Graph Factorization Clustering *(Proceedings of the 2013 Conference of the North American Chapter of the Association for Computational Linguistics: Human Language Technologies)*. Association for Computational Linguistics, 978–988. `http://aclweb.org/anthology/N13-1118`
17. Richard Socher, Jeffrey Pennington, Eric H. Huang, Andrew Y. Ng, and Christopher D. Manning. 2011. Semi-supervised Recursive Autoencoders for Predicting Sentiment Distributions. In *Proceedings of the Conference on Empirical Methods in Natural Language Processing (EMNLP '11)*. Association for Computational Linguistics, Stroudsburg, PA, USA, 151–161. `http://dl.acm.org/citation.cfm?id=2145432.2145450`

FontMatcher: Font Image Paring for Harmonious Digital Graphic Design

Saemi Choi
University of Tokyo, Japan
merrycsm@hal.t.u-tokyo.ac.jp

Kiyoharu Aizawa
University of Tokyo, Japan
aizawa@hal.t.u-tokyo.ac.jp

Nicu Sebe
University of Trento, Italy
sebe@disi.unitn.it

ABSTRACT
One of the important aspects in graphic design is choosing the font of the caption that matches aesthetically the associated image. To obtain a good match, users would exhaustively examine a long font list requiring them a substantial effort. This paper presents FontMatcher, which supports users to design digital graphic works harmoniously pairing fonts with an image. The system provides three features, *recommendation, explaination* and *feedback*. If a warm feeling image is given as input, the system *recommends* warm feeling fonts, and then *explains* what is the distinguishing features of the recommendation, e.g. a cursive shape. Users can also provide *feedback* to find fonts which correspond to their intention. Our evaluation results show that the recommended fonts scored better than selected fonts by novices and provides competing results with the ones chosen by experienced graphic designers. The system also provides explanations that help increasing the reliability of the recommended results.

Author Keywords
Graphic design; matching fonts with images; font search

INTRODUCTION
In digital graphic design projects, designers use various elements such as background images and typography elements. Unity in design makes these elements come together as a whole in order to communicate a particular message. In other words, to create effective graphic works, users should consider impressions that each element conveys and should make all the elements match well with each other. Figure 1 shows an example of matching two fonts that give different impressions with an image. The image may convey soft and delicate feelings from the presence of flowers and soft color tones, and the font on the left matches better this feeling as it has a light weight that appears to be carefully written. However, finding a best matching font to a given image is a difficult task. One solution would be to perform an exhaustive font search through a list of fonts that may match well the given image. This is a time-consuming and laborious process for novice users as well as professional designers. According to [13], providing too many choices will not only stress the users but will also decrease their satisfaction and enthusiasm in performing the font selection. Addressing this issue, this paper presents a font search system which leads to an efficient and satisfactory decision-making for the font selection.

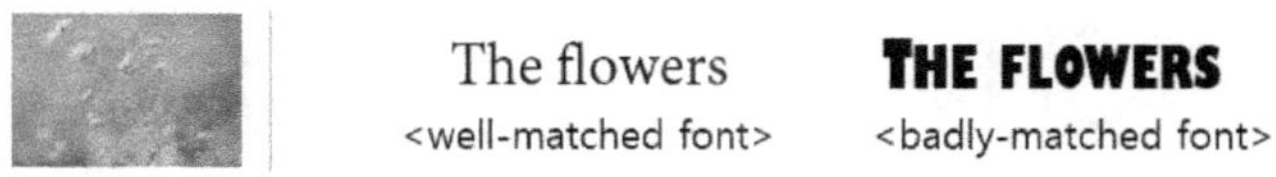

Figure 1. The flower image with soft color tones conveys soft and delicate feelings. We can say that the thin serif font on the left matches well the image as it gives more similar feelings than the thick and angular font on the right.

There are various approaches for searching fonts. Font sharing web sites enable users to browse fonts by categories such as serif and script, and properties (e.g. thickness of letters) [1, 2]. A recent visual font recognition study enabled the identification of fonts from real-world text images such as signboard [14]. These systems are only useful if a user has a clear preference for the fonts to be searched. In [9], the authors proposed a tool that uses machine learning to learn the visual similarity of fonts and allows their visualization in a two-dimensional latent space. The authors of [12] proposed an interface for exploring fonts using binary attributes such as "dramatic" or "not dramatic." Although both studies proposed an interface for exploring large font datasets without a clear preference, their interface still requires a high aesthetic intuition of the user. In this paper, we propose an alternative approach that enables users to explore fonts that match in an harmonious way the feelings the image conveys.

We highlight our key contributions as follows. Firstly, we model font-impression relationship on a two-dimensional semantic space and built a font recommendation system to save users from the effort to explore large font datasets. If a *warm and soft* feeling image was given as an input, the system recommends *warm and soft* feeling fonts. Secondly, our system provides an explanation to support the recommendations made. It has been shown in [8] that providing a recommendation that lacks an explanation, brings about users' lower satisfaction in the recommended results. Explanations why the system recommended the items give the users the feedback that their requests were understood by the system. The explanation our system gives describes what is the important feature of recommended fonts, e.g., *the cursive shape is the distinguishing feature of the recommended font.* Finally, users can also provide

IUI'18, March 7–11, 2018, Tokyo, Japan

ISBN 978-1-4503-4945-1/18/03...15.00
DOI: https://doi.org/10.1145/3172944.3173001

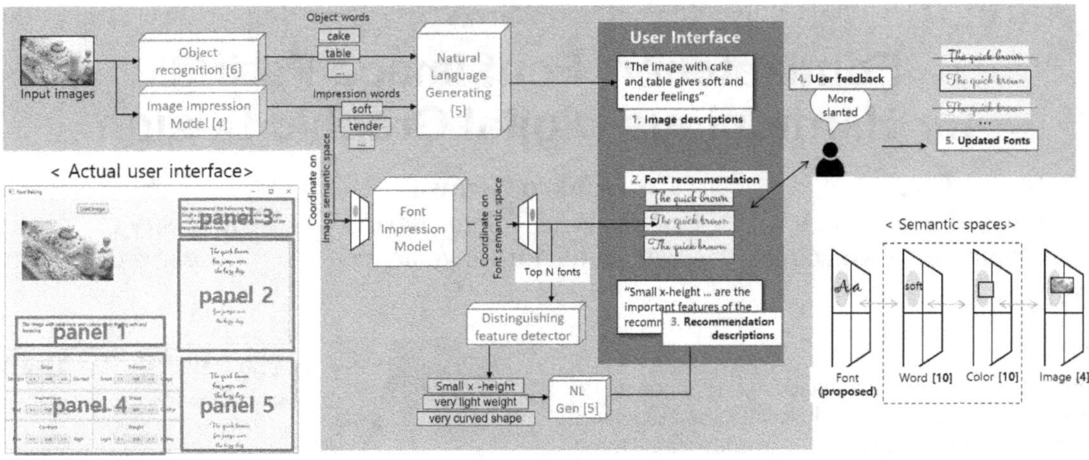

Figure 2. Overview of the system flow. If a user inputs an image, a image description is generated by object recognition [6], impression analysis [4] and natural language generating models [5] in panel 1. Then our proposed font impression model recommends fonts which have similar feelings to the given image (panel 2). Based on the recommendation, the system generates a description for supporting the recommendation (panel 3). Users can give feedback by controlling font features such as *slanted* (panel 4), and the results are updated in panel 5.

their feedback by controlling the typography attributes e.g., *more slanted.* The goal of our work is not only to recommend the best matching fonts but also to make users feel satisfied with the search by increasing the design-domain knowledge via an explainable recommendation system.

OVERVIEW

Figure 2 outlines the features of FontMatcher and the actual user interface. If a user inputs an image, a content analysis tool [6] identifies objects in the image (e.g., cake and table) and an impression model [4] analyzes the feelings the image conveys (e.g., soft and tender). Then, a natural language generating engine [5] outputs a sentence describing the image in panel 1, e.g., *The image with cake and table gives soft and tender feelings.*

The image impression model [4] outputs a coordinate in the semantic space of the input image. Because our font impression model analyzes fonts in the same semantic space, coordinate values are used for calculating semantic distances between the image and each font in the semantic space. Then the system ranks fonts in ascending order by their distance and displays the result in panel 2. At the same time, the system extracts distinguishing features of top-ranked fonts and generates a description in panel 3, e.g., *Small x-height, very light weight and very cursive shape are distinguishing features of the recommended fonts.*

Users can give feedback in panel 4 by controlling six font appearance features, i.e., slope, x-height, alignment, shape, weight contrast and weight. For example, if a user wants to find more slanted fonts than the current recommendation, he/she can select the *more slanted* button in panel 4 and the results are updated in panel 5.

METHODOLOGIES

In this section, we describe our modeling method for mapping fonts on a two-dimensional semantic space, and then introduce two interface features, i.e., how we generate the explanation for supporting the recommendation and how the system processes the user feedback.

Font Impression Mapping

Mapping Space

Kobayashi developed a semantic space consisting of warm-cool and hard-soft axes [10]. He presented two semantic spaces, word and color. On each space, 180 impression words or 1,170 color combinations were located respectively. The bottom right of Figure 2 shows four semantic spaces: font, word, color and image. According to Kobayashi, different objects located in a certain position in different spaces have a similar feeling. He mentioned that not only color, but other objects such as clothes and house designs can be mapped in the semantic space as well. We, thereby, utilize a model which maps natural photographs on the image semantic space [4], and furthermore, we built a model for font mapping on the semantic space to correlate images with fonts.

Font dataset

O'Donovan et al. provided a 200 fonts dataset and 37 attribute scores for each font [12]. We dropped three fonts which have inadequate shapes (e.g. too wide to display in a limited space). We then select a subset out of the provided 37 attributes for model construction. We removed 7 typography limited attributes (e.g. capital, display, italic, etc.) and 18 attributes which were not defined on the semantic space (e.g. angular, attention grabbing, and so on). Consequently, we used 197 fonts with 12 attribute scores in our mapping process.

Mapping method

To map fonts with 12-dimensional attribute scores into a two-dimensional semantic space, we adopt a dimensional reduction method. There are many dimensional reduction methods such as principal component analysis (PCA) and multidimensional scaling (MDS). However, the reduced axes by these methods are not explainable. We, therefore, applied factor analysis that explains the extracted factor with related variables for the modeling process.

The factor analysis of the 12 attributes yielded three factors which explain 85.19% of the variance. Table 1 shows the factor analysis results with varimax rotation. We can find that the first factor comprised of five attributes describes *coolness.* The

Attribute	Factor 1 (coolness)	Factor 2 (warmness)	Factor 3 (strong-soft)	α
formal	**0.892**	-0.015	-0.029	
gentle	**0.803**	0.339	0.354	
calm	**0.762**	-0.032	0.579	.896
fresh	**0.744**	0.449	-0.145	
sharp	**0.719**	0.21	0.327	
friendly	0.599	**0.654**	0.185	
charming	0.091	**0.948**	0.069	.929
happy	0.032	**0.919**	0.065	
graceful	0.334	**0.86**	0.004	
delicate	0.116	0.57	**0.733**	
soft	0.442	0.106	**0.845**	.885
strong	0.031	0.082	**-0.971**	
			KMO measure of sampling adequacy : 0.880	
			Bartlett test p-value < .000	

Table 1. Factor analysis result. The column α shows Cronbach's alpha.

second factor comprised of four attributes describes *warmness*. Three attributes yield the third factor, and we labeled this as *strong to soft*. We used the coefficient matrix obtained from the factor analysis to calculate the 197×3 factor score vector F ($F = X \times B$, where X is the 197×12 attribute score matrix and B is the 12×3 factor score coefficient matrix). According to the semantic space, we can say the third factor F_3 describes the hard-soft axis well. We normalized the 197×1 column vector F_3, and regarded an element of the vector as a font's coordinate value on the hard-soft axis. In the case of warm-cool axis, we observed two factors (F_1 and F_2) explain the axis (coolness and warmness). We therefore performed a linear combination of the first (F_1) and second (F_2) factor score vectors. By doing that, we can represent the two factors in a single axis Y (warm-cool axis). We formulate the linear combination as: $Y(\alpha) = \alpha F_1 - (1-\alpha)F_2$. Then we estimated the optimal α as follows.

$$\alpha = \underset{\alpha}{\operatorname{argmax}} \sum_{i=1}^{5} \frac{w^i_{cool} corr(Y(\alpha), F^i_{cool})}{5} + \sum_{j=1}^{4} \frac{w^j_{warm} corr(Y(\alpha), F^j_{warm})}{4}$$

The first term in the right side indicates the sum of correlation between $Y(\alpha)$ and five attributes' factor scores F_{cool} which describe *coolness*. The second term is for the four attributes' factor scores F_{warm} which describe *warmness*. Here, w^i_{cool} (or w^j_{warm}) is the weight of the attribute i (or j). Each weight value is the value on the warm-cool axis provided by the word semantic space [10]. As a result, we were able to get coordinate values of 197 fonts on the warm-cool axis estimated by the linear combination of the first and second factor scores. Figure 3 shows the result of mapping 197 fonts to the semantic space and some example fonts. For example, if a user inputs an image, the image impression model outputs a coordinate value on the semantic space. Based on the value, the system calculates the distance from the image to each font. Then the system ranks fonts in ascending order by the distance and displays the result.

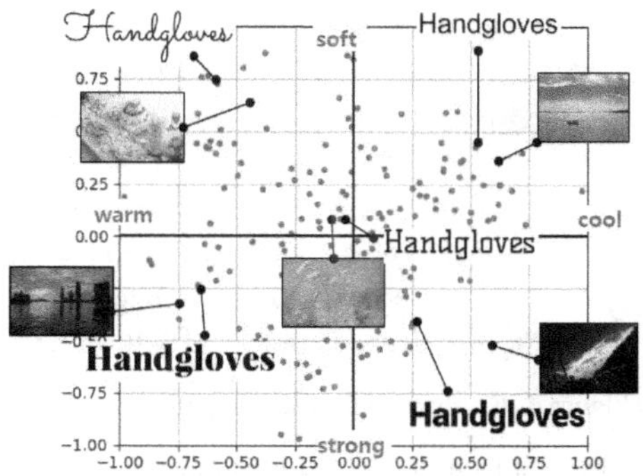

Figure 3. The font mapping results on the semantic space. One blue dot indicates one font. The five images were plotted in the semantic space by the image impression model. The phrase "Handgloves" is a filler text to demonstrate the shape of fonts.

Font Description Generating

Font description comprises of combination of the **font feature word** and *the degree of the feature word*, e.g., *very heavy* **weight**. We defined six font features which are picked up from [7], i.e., *slope, x-height, alignment, shape, weight contrast and weight*. We also defined five stages of degree for each feature. For example, *weight* has five stages of the degree words, i.e., *very heavy, heavy, normal, light* and *very light*.

For recommended top N fonts, we extracted six font features and computed each histogram. The same process was conducted for whole font dataset (197 fonts). After that, we measured the distribution difference between the top N fonts histogram and the 197 fonts histogram by using the KL divergence [11]. Because it returns how much the distribution of the recommended fonts is different from the whole font dataset, we regarded the feature which has the largest difference as a distinguishing feature. Here we adopt three features which returned the highest estimated differences for generating descriptions. Referring to the mean feature value of the top N fonts, we assigned *the degree of the feature* word for the font feature. For example, if the mean weight value of top N fonts is 0.9 (five steps of the degree in 0.2 intervals between 0 to 1), we assign the degree word *very heavy*. We then generated a description which is a combination of the font feature words and the degree of each feature word (e.g., *Small x-height, very cursive shape, and very light weight are the distinguishing features of the recommended fonts*.

Attribute Filtering

For the given recommended fonts, users can give relative feedback such as "*heavier* weight than the recommended one." If a user gives feedback *more* than the current weight score, the system calculates the mean of the weight value of the top N fonts as the current feature score, and then filters out the fonts which do not satisfy the constraint from the ranked font list.

EVALUATION

To evaluate how well the system recommends fonts, we conducted a user study. Four different user groups chose the font that matches in an harmonious way the feelings a given image conveys, then designers examined and scored the image-font

Figure 4. Example of font-image pairing task results

pair. In addition to that, the effect of accompanying explanations was also evaluated.

Effectiveness of the System

Task and participant

Figure 3 shows five different images we used for the user study. Participants were requested to choose best three fonts which harmoniously match a given image. We formed four user groups, designers, novices, random and system and each group conducted five font-pairing tasks. We recruited three designers and three novice users, so 45 font-image pairs were generated per group (3 participants $\times$ 3 fonts $\times$ 5 tasks). For the random group, instead of involving the human intervention, we randomly chose three fonts per each task arriving at 45 pairs. Image-font pairs of the system group are the result of three top-ranked fonts. In total, we obtained 150 font-image pairs for the test. Figure 4 shows font-image pair examples of four different group to the given image (see Appendix for more examples).

Results

Six designers who did not participate in the font-image pair generating task rated the collected font-image pairs, which add up to 838 ratings. Each font-image pair was questioned on a ten-point Likert scale ranging from unacceptable (1) to outstanding (10). Table 2 shows the mean and standard deviation of the ratings across all pairs by each group. We can see that font-image pairs designed by professional designers received the highest score. Next came System, Novice, and Random, respectively. We found that although the system recommendation results were not as good as the designer's font-pairing results, the system made better suggestions than both the novice user and random groups.

Effect of Explanation on User Reliability

Task and participants

We organized three user groups via Yahoo crowd-sourcing service to investigate the effect of the explanation on users' reliability of the recommended results. We provided image-font pairs only for the first group (default), image-font pairs with image description for the second group (image description), and image-font pairs with both image description and font description (image & font description). We used the five sets of three image-font pairs provided by our system in the font-pairing task. Workers rated two questions using a five-point Likert scale, (1) how reliable and (2) how satisfying the image-font pair is. Each worker rated five image-font pairs, and 100 workers were allocated per group, so we finally collected 1,500 assessments.

	Ours	Designer	Novice	Random
Mean	4.95	5.06	4.82	4.19
(SD)	(1.98)	(1.93)	(2.10)	(1.89)

Table 2. Mean and standard deviation of the ratings across all pairs. One-way ANOVA revealed the mean differences are significant ($F(3,146)=6.91$, $p<.001$).

Analysis and results

We analyzed the assessments in terms of user reliability of the recommended fonts. According to [3], satisfying results positively affect user reliability. Because different workers participated to the three different groups, user reliability was biased depending on the individual's satisfaction. To avoid this bias effect, we defined a relative reliability which measures how the reliability of the recommendation results changed in accordance with the satisfaction of the given results. We labeled 1 (or -1) when a worker's reliability score is higher (or lower) than his/her satisfaction score, or 0 when there was no change. The mean and standard deviation of the average relative reliability scores for the default, image description and image & font description groups were -0.11(.48), -0.07(.50) and -0.026(.52) respectively (the higher the better). A one-way ANOVA revealed the existence of a significant effect of the descriptions on the relative reliability ($F(2,1497) = 3.53$, $p=.03$). We can see that the image & font description group rated the highest relative reliability. Next came image description and default. This result indicates that the image description and font description which supports the recommendations brought about a higher reliability of the image-font pairs.

User Comments for the Interface

We invited more novice users and collected their comments. A few examples are listed here: *"The recommended fonts are the exactly same to what I was trying to find" "The image description was helpful. When exploring the font list, I was able to compare the description with fonts. It made font-search easy." "I got to know what font features like 'contrast' means through the system,"* and *"This allowed me to think about how to reflect my preference in feedback."* However, some problem was pointed out. *"I can check and compare a variety of fonts at once with regular font list, but this system gave the impression that the number of fonts is pretty limited." "Some of the recommended fonts did not match the description."*

CONCLUSION

In this paper, we presented a font recommendation system for harmonious digital graphic design. We built a model for font mapping on a two-dimensional semantic space. Combining the font mapping model and the existing image impression model, the system ranked fonts by a semantic difference between the input image and fonts in the semantic space. The system also generated explanation to support the recommendation by a statistical method. From the user study, we found that the proposed system made a better suggestion than novice users. Furthermore, the accompanying explanations brought about high reliability on the recommendation. From these results, we believe that the system can be a good starting point for searching fonts in designing graphic works.

ACKNOWLEDGEMENT

This work was partially supported by Erasmus Mundus TEAM for Information and Communication Technologies and KAKENHI under grant number 17K19963.

REFERENCES

1. Dafont.com. `http://www.dafont.com/`.
2. Adobe. Typekit. `https://typekit.com/fonts`.
3. Berkovsky, S., Taib, R., and Conway, D. How to recommend?: User trust factors in movie recommender systems. In *Proceedings of the 22nd International Conference on Intelligent User Interfaces*, ACM (2017), 287–300.
4. Choi, S., Yamasaki, T., and Aizawa, K. An interactive system based on yes-no questions for affective image retrieval. In *Proceedings of the 1st International Workshop on Affect & Sentiment in Multimedia*, ACM (2015), 45–50.
5. Gatt, A., and Reiter, E. Simplenlg: A realisation engine for practical applications. In *Proceedings of the 12th European Workshop on Natural Language Generation*, Association for Computational Linguistics (2009), 90–93.
6. Google. Google cloud vision api. `https://vision.googleapis.com`.
7. Henderson, P. W., Giese, J. L., and Cote, J. A. Impression management using typeface design. *Journal of marketing 68*, 4 (2004), 60–72.
8. Herlocker, J. L., Konstan, J. A., and Riedl, J. Explaining collaborative filtering recommendations. In *Proceedings of the 2000 ACM conference on Computer supported cooperative work*, ACM (2000), 241–250.
9. IDEO. Font map. `http://fontmap.ideo.com/`.
10. Kobayashi, S. The aim and method of the color image scale. *Color research & application 6*, 2 (1981), 93–107.
11. Kullback, S., and Leibler, R. A. On information and sufficiency. *The annals of mathematical statistics 22*, 1 (1951), 79–86.
12. O'Donovan, P., Lībeks, J., Agarwala, A., and Hertzmann, A. Exploratory font selection using crowdsourced attributes. *ACM Transactions on Graphics (TOG) 33*, 4 (2014), 92.
13. Schwartz, B. The paradox of choice, 2004.
14. Wang, Z., Yang, J., Jin, H., Shechtman, E., Agarwala, A., Brandt, J., and Huang, T. S. Deepfont: Identify your font from an image. In *Proceedings of the 23rd ACM international conference on Multimedia*, ACM (2015), 451–459.

APPENDIX: FONT-IMAGE PAIR EXAMPLES

<Task image>

Ours	Designer
Handgloves	Handgloves
Handgloves	Handgloves
Handgloves	Handgloves
Novice	**Random**
Handgloves	Handgloves
Handgloves	Handgloves
Handgloves	Handgloves

<Task image>

Ours	Designer
Handgloves	Handgloves
HANDGLOVES	Handgloves
Handgloves	Handgloves
Novice	**Random**
Handgloves	Handgloves
Handgloves	Handgloves
Handgloves	HANDGLOVES

<Task image>

Ours	Designer
Handgloves	Handgloves
Handgloves	Handgloves
Handgloves	HANDGLOVES
Novice	**Random**
Handgloves	Handgloves
Handgloves	Handgloves
Handgloves	Handgloves

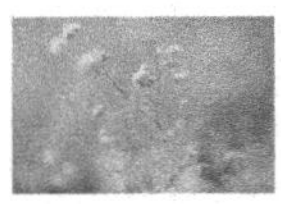

<Task image>

Ours	Designer
Handgloves	Handgloves
Handgloves	Handgloves
Handgloves	Handgloves
Novice	**Random**
Handgloves	Handgloves
Handgloves	Handgloves
Handgloves	Handgloves

AlterEgo: A Personalized Wearable Silent Speech Interface

Arnav Kapur
MIT Media Lab
Cambridge, USA
arnavk@media.mit.edu

Shreyas Kapur
MIT Media Lab
Cambridge, USA
shreyask@mit.edu

Pattie Maes
MIT Media Lab
Cambridge, USA
pattie@media.mit.edu

Figure 1. Alterego seeks to make computing a natural extension of the user's own cognition by enabling a *silent*, *discreet* and *seamless* conversation with machines and people, in likeness to the user talking to her own self.

ABSTRACT
We present a wearable interface that allows a user to silently converse with a computing device without any voice or any discernible movements - thereby enabling the user to communicate with devices, AI assistants, applications or other people in a silent, concealed and seamless manner. A user's intention to speak and internal speech is characterized by neuromuscular signals in internal speech articulators that are captured by the AlterEgo system to reconstruct this speech. We use this to facilitate a natural language user interface, where users can silently communicate in natural language and receive aural output (e.g - bone conduction headphones), thereby enabling a discreet, bi-directional interface with a computing device, and providing a seamless form of intelligence augmentation. The paper describes the architecture, design, implementation and operation of the entire system. We demonstrate robustness of the system through user studies and report 92% median word accuracy levels.

Author Keywords
Silent Speech Interface; Intelligence Augmentation; Peripheral Nerve Interface; Human-Machine Symbiosis

IUI'18, March 7–11, 2018, Tokyo, Japan

ACM ISBN 978-1-4503-4945-1/18/03$15.00
https://doi.org/10.1145/3172944.3172977

INTRODUCTION
The vision of closely coupling humans and machines has been advanced and re-imagined in successive iterations. Input devices have come a long way since punchcards and present day input modalities have enabled computing devices to become an intrinsic parts of our lives. Keyboards (or typewriter style input devices) replaced punch cards to facilitate text input on early computers. The modern age of mobile and ubiquitous computing ushered in the widespread adoption of voice inputs for communication and search applications.

Natural user interfaces (NUI) including gesture-based inputs, touch and voice have been touted as natural extensions of the human persona [5,13,21–23,27]. Despite significant advances made, machines, input modalities and interactivity still exist as *external* artifacts to the human user, in an obstacle to fully realize symbiosis of humans and machines.

We present AlterEgo a wearable silent speech interface that allows a user to provide arbitrary text input to a computing device or other people using natural language, without discernible muscle movements and without any voice. This allows the user to communicate to their computing devices in natural language without any observable action at all and without explicitly saying anything.

In summary, this paper makes three primary contributions:

1. We introduce a novel wearable architecture for a bi-directional silent speech device.

2. We outline the neuromuscular input needed for detecting silent speech.

3. We demonstrate the feasibility of such silent speech recognition based on neural information, and demonstrate the utility of the device as a personal computing platform and interface.

AlterEgo, allows people to privately and seamlessly communicate with their personal computing devices, services and other people, such that users leverage the power of computing in their daily lives, as a natural adjunct to their own cognitive abilities, without "replacing" or "obstructing" these abilities.

BACKGROUND AND RELATED WORK

Voice Interfaces

Conversational interfaces currently exist in multiple forms. The recent advances in speech recognition methods have enabled users to have interaction with a computing device in natural language [1,12]. This has facilitated the advent of ubiquitous natural voice interfaces, currently deployed in mobile computational devices as virtual assistants (e.g- Siri [28], Alexa [29], Cortana [30] etc.). These interfaces have also been embedded in other devices such as smart-wearables, dedicated hardware speakers (e.g - Google Home [31], Amazon Echo[32]), and social robots. Another broad category under voice interfaces are modern telecommunications devices for person-person communication (e.g - smartphones, Skype etc). Although, all the aforementioned platforms offer robust voice based interaction, they share common limitations. There are fundamental impediments to current speech interfaces that limit the possibility of their adoption as a primary human-machine interface. We list a few here amongst others:

Privacy of conversation: Speech is broadcasted to the environment by the user when communicating via these interfaces and therefore user privacy is not maintained (e.g - a phone call with another person; communicating with Siri etc.).

Eavesdropping: Voice interfaces are always listening in on conversations, when not desired, only to be visibly activated later on by a specific trigger-word (e.g - 'Ok Google' activates Google Assistant but the application is on nevertheless).

Impersonal devices: These devices are not personal devices and any other user can intentionally or unintentionally send valid voice inputs to these devices.

Attention requiring: Current voice interaction devices have low usability as a device, a user cannot use a speech interface hands free on-the-go, which is the case oftentimes with immobile dedicated speech devices (e.g - Amazon Echo). Moreover, user proximity to the device is required for optimal speech recognition (telecommunications devices).

Silent Speech Interfaces

There have been several previous attempts at achieving silent speech communication. These systems can be categorized under two primary approaches: invasive and non-invasive systems.

Invasive Systems

Brumberg et al. 2010 [6] used direct brain implants in the speech motor cortex to achieve silent speech recognition, demonstrating reasonable accuracies on limited vocabulary datasets. There have been explorations surrounding measurement of movement of internal speech articulators by placing sensors inside these articulators. Hueber et al. 2008 [17] used sensors placed on the tongue to measure tongue movements. Hofe et al. 2013 [16] and Fagan et al. 2008 [9] used permanent magnet (PMA) sensors to capture movement of specific points on muscles used in speech articulation. The approach requires permanent fixing of magnetic beads invasively which does not scale well in a real-world setting. Florescu et al. 2010 [10] propose characterization of the vocal tract using ultrasound to achieve silent speech. The system only achieves good results when combined with a video camera looking directly at the user's mouth. The invasiveness and obtrusiveness or the immobility of the apparatus impedes the scalability of these solutions in real-world settings, beyond clinical scenarios.

Non-Invasive Systems

There have been multiple approaches proposed to detect and recognize silent speech in a non-invasive manner. Porbadnik et al. 2009 [24] used EEG sensors for silent speech recognition, but suffered from low signal-to-noise ratio to robustly detect speech formation and thereby encountered poor performance. Wand et al. 2016 [26] used deep learning on video without acoustic vocalization but requires externally placed cameras to decode language from movement of the lips. Hirahara et al. [15] use Non-Audible Murmur microphone to digitally transform signals. There have been instances of decoding speech from facial muscles movements using surface electromyography.

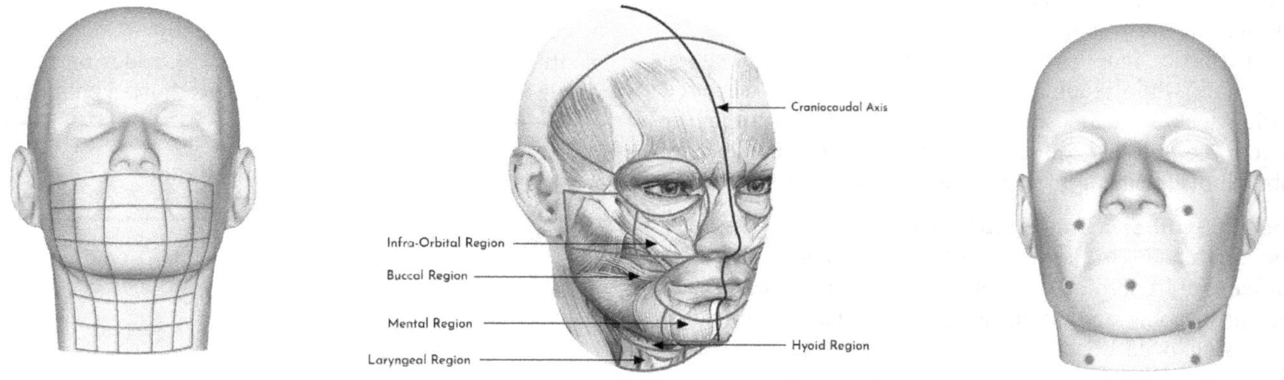

Figure 2. Selection of the final electrode target areas (right) through feature selection on muscular areas of interest (left, center).

Wand and Schultz 2011[25] have demonstrated surface EMG silent speech using a phoneme based acoustic model, but the user has to explicitly mouth the words and have to use pronounced facial movements. Jorgensen et al.[18] use surface EMG to detect subvocal words with accuracy fluctuating down to 33% with the system also unable to recognize alveolar consonants with high accuracy, which is a significant obstruction to actual usage as a speech interface.

ALTEREGO

AlterEgo is a wearable silent speech interface that enables a discreet, seamless and bi-directional communication with a computing device in natural language without discernible movements or voice input (Figure 3-4).

We distinguish our system based on the following points:

1. The first difference is the non-invasiveness of the approach described herein. The system captures neuromuscular signals from the surface of the user's skin via a wearable mask.

2. The existing non-invasive real-time methods with robust accuracies require the user to explicitly mouth their speech with pronounced, apparent facial movements. The key difference between our system and existing approaches is that our system performs robustly even when the user does not open their mouth, make any sound and without the need for any deliberate and coded muscle articulation that is often used when using surface EMG to detect silent speech. The modality of natural language communication without any discernible movement is key, since it allows for a seamless and discreet interface.

3. On a standard digit recognition test, our system achieves a median accuracy of 92%, outperforming conventional methods mentioned above amongst others. Moreover, this is despite the AlterEgo system not requiring any facial muscle movement as opposed to conventional methods that require the user to lip sync the words in a pronounced fashion.

4. This leads to the fourth key point, which is the portability of the wearable device. The proposed device is an ambulatory wearable system which a user just needs to wear for it to function and the device connects wirelessly over Bluetooth to any external computing device.

5. Unlike proposed traditional brain computer interfaces (BCI), such as head based EEG/fMRI/DOT/fNIRS, the platform does not have access to private information or thoughts and the input, in this case, is voluntary on the user's part. The proposed platform is robust on extended vocabulary sizes than traditional BCI since we propose a peripheral nerve interface by taking measurements from the facial and neck area, which allows for silent speech signals to be distilled without being accompanied by electrical noise from the frontal lobe of the cerebral cortex.

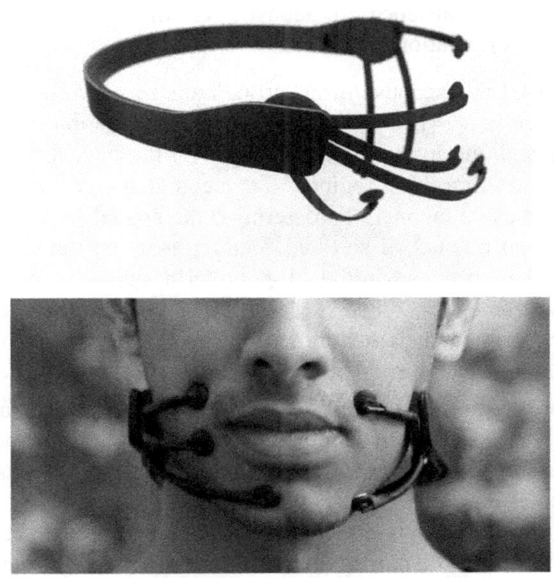

Figure 3. Rendering of the AlterEgo wearable (Top). Front view of the user wearing the device (Bottom).

INDISCERNIBLE SILENT SPEECH RECOGNITION

Internal vocalization, in this text is described as the characteristic inner voice in humans that is usually noticeable while reading and can be voluntarily triggered while speaking to oneself [4], excluding deliberate lip or discernible muscle movement. This is characterized by subtle movements of internal speech articulators.

Speech Synthesis and Electrophysiology

The production of acoustic speech involves a series of intricate and coordinated events and is considered one of the most complex motor actions humans perform. An expression once conceived in the brain, is encoded as a linguistic instance mediated by areas in the brain, namely the Broca's area, and subsequently the supplementary motor area to map into muscular movements for vocal articulation. This cortical control for voluntary articulation is enabled through the ventral sensorimotor cortex which controls the activation and activation rate of a motor unit, via projections from the corticobulbar tract to the face, laryngeal cavity, pharynx and the oral cavity. A motor neuron receives nerve impulses from anterior horn cells in the spinal cord which are propagated to neuromuscular junctions, where a single neuron innervates multiple muscle fibers.

The propagation of a nerve impulse through a neuromuscular junction causes the neurotransmitter acetylcholine to be released into the synapse. Acetylcholine binds with nicotinic receptors leading to ion channels releasing sodium cations in the muscle fiber, triggering an action potential propagation in the muscle fiber. This ionic movement, caused by muscle fiber resistance, generates time-varying potential difference patterns that occur in the facial and neck muscles while intending to speak, leading to a corresponding myoelectric signature that is detected by the system described in this paper, from the surface of the skin in the absence of acoustic vocalization and facial muscle articulation for speech.

Amongst the various muscle articulators involved in speech production [14], we focused our investigation on the laryngeal and hyoid regions along with the buccal, mental, oral and infraorbital regions to detect signal signatures in a non-invasive manner. To determine the spatial locations of detection points, we selected 7 target areas on the skin for detection, from an initial 30-point grid spatially covering the aforementioned select regions. The selection was done on experimental data recorded on which we expand on in following sections. We ranked potential target locations according to the χ^2 filter-based feature ranking, evaluating how signals sourced from each target were able to better differentiate between word labels in our dataset. Symmetrical equivalents of target locations across the craniocaudal axis were ignored in order to avoid feature repetition. In the current iteration of the device, the signals are sourced as 7 channels from the following areas - the laryngeal region, hyoid region, levator anguli oris, orbicularis oris, platysma, anterior belly of the digastric, mentum. The finer positions of the electrodes on the skin, within the selected regions, were then adjusted empirically.

Ranking	Region
1	Mental
2	Inner laryngeal
3	Outer laryngeal
4	Hyoid
5	Inner infra-orbital
6	Outer infra-orbital
7	Buccal

Table 1. Top muscle regions ranked according to the χ^2 filter ranking against a binary-labelled dataset, evaluated in the pilot user study.

Signal Capture, Processing and Hardware

Signals are captured using electrodes from the above-mentioned target areas. In two versions of the device, the device houses either TPE plastic, gold plated silver electrodes (1.45 mm diameter conductive area), in combination with Ten20 (polyoxyethylene (20) cetyl ether) conductive paste (Weaver and Company) for reduced contact impedance, or passive dry Ag/AgCl electrodes (4 mm diameter conductive area). Although both electrode forms can be integrated into the system, the former offer superior data quality. Therefore, we report experiments, data collection and results based on the former in this manuscript, as a controlled variable. A reference electrode is placed either on the wrist or the earlobe. We use bias based signal cancellation for canceling ~60 Hz line interferences and to achieve higher signal-to-noise (SNR) ratio. The signals are sampled at 250 Hz and differentially amplified at 24× gain (Texas Instruments, OpenBCI).

We integrated an opto-isolated external trigger, acting as a final channel stream with high voltage pulses marking starting and ending events of a silent phrase. Subsequently, the signal streams are wirelessly sent to an external computing device for further processing. The signals go through multiple preprocessing stages. The signals are fourth order IIR butterworth filtered (1.3 Hz to 50 Hz). The high pass filter is used in order to prevent signal aliasing artifacts. The low pass filter is applied to avoid movement artifacts in the signal. A notch filter is applied at 60 Hz to nullify line interference in hardware. The notch filter is applied, despite the butterworth filter, because of the gentle roll-off attenuation of the latter.

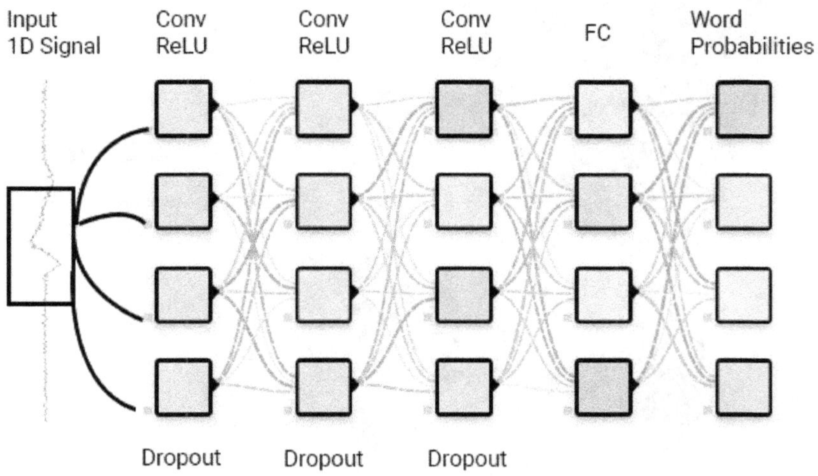

Figure 4. Architecture of the AlterEgo silent speech recognition model.

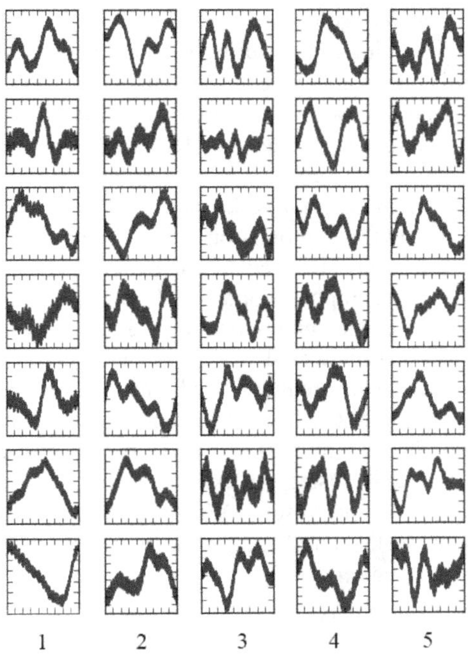

Figure 5. Output of activation maximization on the classes *1-5*, to visualize input signals that maximize the corresponding output activations.

We separate the signal streams into components through Independent Component Analysis (ICA) to further remove movement artifacts. The signals are digitally rectified, normalized to a range of 0 to 1 and concatenated as integer streams. The streams are sent to a mobile computational device through Bluetooth LE, which subsequently sends the data to the server hosting the recognition model to classify silent words. This protocol is in consideration of data transfer speed requirements and power requirements for the system to potentially scale as a wearable device.

Data Collection and Corpus

We created a data corpus comprising datasets of varied vocabulary sizes. Data was collected during two main phases. First, we conducted a pilot study with 3 participants (1 female, average age of 29.33 years) to investigate feasibility of signal detection and to determine electrode positioning. The preliminary dataset recorded with the participants was binary, with the world labels being *yes* and *no*. The vocabulary set was gradually augmented to accommodate more words - for instance, the phonetically dissimilar words *reply*, *call*, *you* and *later* formed another dataset. In sum, the data collected during the study has ~5 hours of internally vocalized text.

In the second phase, we set out to create a data corpus to be used to train a classifier (same 3 participants). The corpus has ~31 hours of silently spoken text recorded in different sessions to be able to regularize the recognition model for session independence. The corpus comprises of multiple datasets (Table 2). In one category, the word labels are numerical digits (0-9) along with fundamental mathematical operations (*times*, *divide*, *add*, *subtract* and *percent*) to facilitate externalizing arithmetic computations through the interface. We expand on other dataset categories in later sections. We use the external trigger signal to slice the data into word instances. In each recording session, signals were recorded for randomly chosen words from a specific vocabulary set. This data is used to train the recognition model for various applications, on which we expand on in following sections.

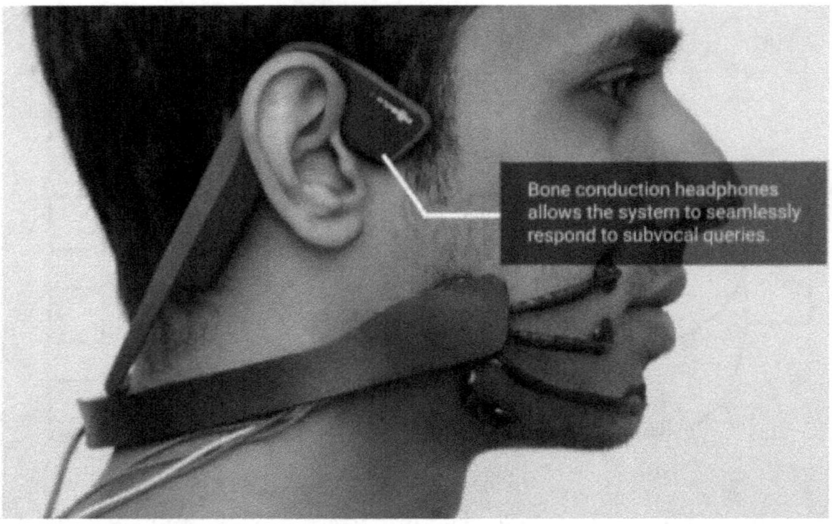

Figure 6. Bone conduction aural output of the AlterEgo system, making it a closed-loop input-output platform.

Silent Speech Recognition Model

The signal undergoes a representation transformation before being input to the recognition model. We use a running window average to identify and omit single spikes (> 30 μVabove baseline) in the stream, with amplitudes greater than average values for nearest 4 points before and after. We use mel-frequency cepstral coefficient based representations to closely characterize the envelopes of human speech. The signal stream is framed into 0.025s windows, with a 0.01s step between successive windows, followed by a periodogram estimate computation of the power spectrum for each frame. We apply a Discrete Cosine Transform (DCT) to the log of the mel filterbank applied to the power spectra. This allows for us to effectively learn directly from the processed signal without needing to hand-pick any features. This feature representation is passed through a 1-dimensional convolutional neural network to classify into word labels with the architecture described as follows. The hidden layer convolves 400 filters of kernel size 3 with stride 1 with the processed input and is then passed through a rectifier nonlinearity. This is subsequently followed by a max pooling layer.

This unit is repeated twice before globally max pooling over its input. This is followed by a fully connected layer of dimension 200 passed through a rectifier nonlinearity which is followed by another fully connected layer with a sigmoid activation. The network was optimized using a first order gradient descent and parameters were updated using Adam [19] during training. The network was regularized using a 50% dropout in each hidden layer to enable the network to generalize better on unseen data. The error during training was evaluated using a cross entropy loss. The neural network was trained on a single NVIDIA GeForce Titan X GPU. We use this network architecture to classify multiple categories of vocabulary datasets.

AURAL OUTPUT

Silent speech recognition of the AlterEgo system attempts to open up a unique opportunity to enable personalized bi-directional human-machine interfacing in a concealed and seamless manner, where the element of interaction is in natural language. This potentially facilitates a complementary synergy between human users and machines, where certain tasks could be outsourced to a computer while the computation still seeming as "intrinsic" to the human user. After an internally vocalized phrase is recognized, the computer contextually processes the phrase according to the relevant application the user accesses (e.g - An *IoT* application would assign the internally vocalized digit *3* to device number 3 whereas the *Mathematics* application would consider the same input as the actual number 3). The output, thus computed by the application, is then converted using Text-to-Speech and aurally transmitted to the user. We use bone conduction headphones as the aural output, so as to not impede the user's sense of hearing.

WEARABLE FORM DESIGN

There are a number of design aspects that were considered with the intention of making the wearable system robust, and usable in a routine setting. Firstly, it is imperative for the electrodes to not shift position so as to maintain signal consistency. Secondly, it is desirable for the electrodes to maintain position on the target areas between multiple sessions of the user wearing and not wearing the device. Thirdly, while the electrodes must not move to stray forces, it is desirable for the positions to be adjusted to the positions of different users via one device that could be worn by multiple users. To that end, the form factor of the device is designed as a wearable that is worn around the back of the head, with extensions landing on the face to record signals from the afore-stated target areas (Figure 4). The band is 3D printed using photopolymer resin with a brass rod supporting it structurally, so as to maximize skin-electrode friction and minimize relative movement. The extensions are brass supports that provide rigidity to support electrodes while also being amenable to deliberate adjustment. Furthermore, the extensions are designed to attach to the frame in a modular manner such that specific extensions and electrodes could be pulled out for further experimentation.

APPLICATIONS

The AlterEgo system attempts to facilitate personal, discreet and seamless human-machine communication. In this section, we briefly present initial application explorations with the AlterEgo interface and demonstrate its utility as a personal cognition augmentation platform.

The current prototype implements modular neural networks in a hierarchical manner to accommodate for simultaneous accessibility to applications. The applications are initiated by internally vocalizing corresponding trigger words, for instance the word *IoT* for initiating wireless device control using the interface. At present, the vocabulary sets are modeled as *n*-gram sequences, where the recognition of a specific word assigns a probability distribution to subsequent vocabulary sets (Table 2).

The probability p_i can be assigned to a vocabulary set v_i based on previous recognition occurrences x_1 to x_{n-1} as $P(v_i|x_{n-1}...x_1) = p_i$. In the current setup, the probability $p_i = 1$ is assigned to vocabulary sets meant for specific applications, in a Markovian dependency arrangement, where each set is detected by a convolutional neural network. This hierarchy reduces the number of word possibilities to be detected within an application, thereby increasing the robustness of the current system.

The applications of AlterEgo can be classified under three broad categories:

Closed-loop interface

This scenario describes silent speech interface with a computing device where specific computer applications respond to internally vocalized queries through aural feedback, thereby enabling a closed-loop, silent and seamless conversation with a computing device. A few example implementations are described in this section.

The AlterEgo system allows the user to externalize any arithmetic expression to a computing device, through internally vocalizing the arithmetic expression and the computer subsequently relaying the computed value through aural feedback. For instance, the user could subvocalize the expression *2581 times 698 divide 2 add 13*, and the application would output the answer *900782* to the user, through bone conduction headphones. The device can be currently used to issue reminders and schedule tasks at specific times, which is aurally output to the user at corresponding times, thereby providing a form of memory augmentation to the user. The device also enables the user to access time using the interface, by silently communicating *world clock* and the name of a city, within a trained vocabulary set (Table 2).

Through such an interface, we explore if artificial intelligence (AI) could be democratized, and could instead act as an adjunct to human cognition in a personalized manner. As a demonstration of this, we implemented human-AI collaborative chess and Go through bi-directional silent speech, where the user would silently convey the game state and the AI would compute and then aurally output the next move to be played.

Open-loop interface

The interface could be used purely as an input modality to control devices and to avail services.

An example application is an IoT controller that enables the user to control home appliances and devices (switch on/off home lighting, television control, HVAC systems etc.) through internal speech, without any observable action. The interface can be personally trained to recognize phrases meant to access specific services. As an example, the internally vocalized phrase *Uber to home* could be used to book transport from the user's current destination using the interface. The interface could also be used as a silent input to Virtual Reality/Augmented Reality applications.

Human-human interface

The device also augments how people share and converse. In a meeting, the device could be used as a back-channel to silently communicate with another person. In the current instantiation of the device, the user can internally communicate 5 common conversational phrases to another person through the interface (Table 2). This could be naturally expanded with further user training.

We have created an environment for the device where applications could be developed catered to specific tasks. The environment asks the user to silently communicate the keywords of interest which is used for training for the application. In addition, the system potentially allows for peripheral devices to be directly interfaced with the system. For instance, lapel cameras and smart-glasses could directly communicate with the device and provide contextual information to and from the device.

EXPERIMENTAL EVALUATION

We sought to evaluate the word accuracy (WAcc) of the silent speech recognition model across multiple users, which formed our core experiment for the multi-user study. To evaluate the robustness of the platform, we recruited 10 participants (6 female) between 19 and 31 years old (μ = 23.6 years) to participate in experiments. None of the participants had any prior experience with the system evaluated in the study. We use the arithmetic computation application as our basis for accuracy evaluation.

Application Initializer	Vocabulary Set	
Arithmetic	0-9, multiply, add, subtract, divide, percent	
IoT	light on, light off, fan on, fan off	0-9
World Clock	Amsterdam, Beijing, Boston, Delhi, London, New York City, Johannesburg , Toronto	
Calendar	previous, next	
Chess	a-h, K, Q, R, N, 1-8	
Reply	0-9, finish	hello how are you, call you later, what's up, yes, no

Table 2. Hierarchical organization of the vocabulary sets.

Figure 7. Examples of some applications or use cases: 1. Calculating totals during shopping (mathematics) 2. Controlling IoT devices 3. Controlling media 4. Temporal augmentation e.g. setting calendar meetings, current time, etc. 5. Responding to phone calls (Receive/reject)

The experiment was conducted in two phases.

First, we collected user silent speech data and evaluated word accuracy on a train test split. Second, we assessed the recognition latency of the interface by testing live inputs on the model, trained using the previous step.

In order to help the users understand silent speech, we showed the user a piece of text and asked the user to read it like (s)he silently read online articles, i.e. read to oneself and not out loud. For each participant, we showed them a total of 750 digits, randomly sequenced on a computer screen, and instructed the users to 'read the number to themselves, without producing a sound and moving their lips'. The digits were randomly chosen from a total of 10 digits (0 to 9), such that each digit exactly appeared 75 times. The data was recorded for each user with the trigger voltages marking word-label alignments.

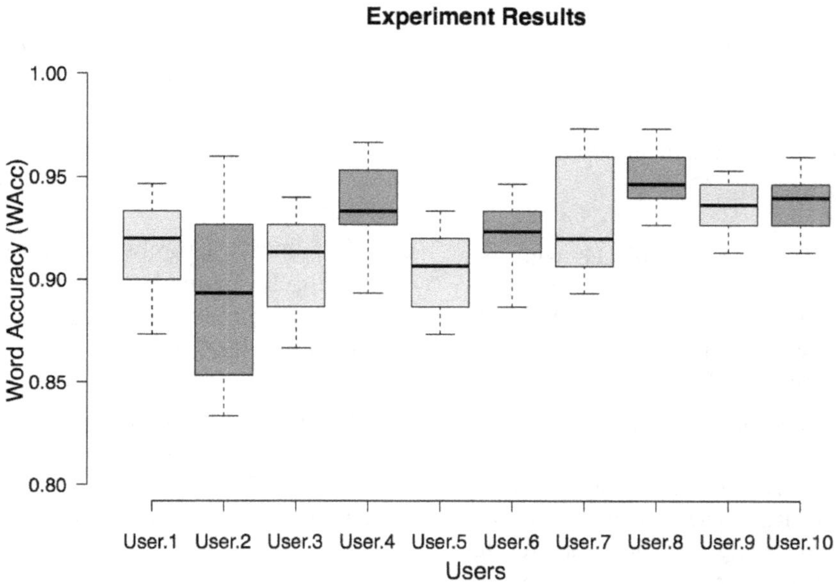

Figure 8. Word accuracy (WAcc) of the silent speech recognition model evaluated on 10 users, using 10 training testing splits of the arithmetic computation dataset. The edges of boxes represent 1st and 3rd quartile respectively, and the whiskers extend to 100% coverage.

Quantitative results

The user data was split according to an 80/20 random split for training and testing for each user. The word accuracies for each user were recorded for 10 runs of training and testing. Figure 8 shows the word accuracies for each user and each run. The average accuracy over all runs for all the users is 92.01%. We conducted live testing for each user to observe the latency of the system for real-time predictions. The latency refers to the computational latency of the silent speech speech system as measured from the end of an utterance until the corresponding transcription is produced. The average latency for the 10 users was 0.427 seconds (3sf).

DISCUSSION

The results from our preliminary experiments show that the accuracy of our silent speech system is at par with the reported word accuracies of state-of-the-art speech recognition systems, in terms of being robust enough to be deployed as voice interfaces, albeit on smaller vocabulary sets. The promising results from the current interface show that AlterEgo could be a step forward in the direction of human-machine symbiosis. We plan to conduct further experiments to test the system for an augmented vocabulary dataset in real-world ambulatory settings.

The concept of human-machine symbiosis has been suggested by several, such as Engelbart [7,8], Licklider [20] and Ashby [2,3] to propose the combination of human and machine intelligence as a goal to be pursued and as an effective computational strategy as opposed to either human or machine intelligence acting independently. Recently, there have been several advances in the area of AI/machine intelligence, prompting anxiety with respect to consequences for human labor and societies [11]. The current viewpoint commonly places machine and human intelligence at odds. Through the AlterEgo device, we seek to move in the step to couple human and machine intelligence in a complimentary symbiosis. As smart machines work in close unison with humans, through such platforms, we anticipate the progress in machine intelligence research to complement intelligence augmentation (IA) efforts, which would lead to an eventual convergence - to augment humans in wide variety of everyday tasks, ranging from computations to creativity to leisure.

FUTURE WORK

There remain many avenues for future work. In particular, we identify the following key future tasks for our silent speech device:

1. *Collect more data to develop a more generalized multi-user silent speech recognition model:* We aim to develop a generalized multi-user system that is user-independent, but can also be tuned and personalized for each user when they start using the device.

2. *Extend the system to include a broader vocabulary of words:* In the current instantiation, we implemented accessibility to multiple vocabulary sets simultaneously, albeit on limited data. Our experimental evaluation was based on an arithmetic computation application. We plan to augment our recognition models to accommodate for a

larger dataset, and plan to follow this with thorough multi-user longitudinal accuracy tests of our system.

3. *Test the system in real-world ambulatory settings:* Our existing study was conducted in a stationary setup. In the future, we would like to conduct longitudinal usability tests in daily scenarios.

CONCLUSION

Silent speech entails that the user communicates with the device by internally talking to oneself instead of actual speech articulation. We akin this to reading something to oneself without moving one's lips, producing an audible sound and without any discernable action.

Silent speech interfaces allow the user to communicate with computers, applications and people as seamlessly as they do through speech interfaces (telecommunications devices, speech based smart assistants, social robots etc.), but without the overhead of saying things out loud. As a result, silent speech interfaces are more private and personal for each user, and do not conflict with the existing verbal communication channels between people. We envision that the usage of our device will interweave human and machine intelligence to enable a more natural human-machine symbiosis that extends and augments human intelligence and capability in everyday lives.

ACKNOWLEDGEMENTS

The authors would like to thank Neo Mohsenvand, Mina Khan, Ashris Choudhury, Jason Robinson for their valuable inputs and feedback on the manuscript.

REFERENCES

1. Dario Amodei, Rishita Anubhai, Eric Battenberg, Carl Case, Jared Casper, Bryan Catanzaro, Jingdong Chen, Mike Chrzanowski, Adam Coates, Greg Diamos, Erich Elsen, Jesse Engel, Linxi Fan, Christopher Fougner, Tony Han, Awni Hannun, Billy Jun, Patrick LeGresley, Libby Lin, Sharan Narang, Andrew Ng, Sherjil Ozair, Ryan Prenger, Jonathan Raiman, Sanjeev Satheesh, David Seetapun, Shubho Sengupta, Yi Wang, Zhiqian Wang, Chong Wang, Bo Xiao, Dani Yogatama, Jun Zhan, and Zhenyao Zhu. 2015. Deep Speech 2: End-to-End Speech Recognition in English and Mandarin. *arXiv [cs.CL]*. Retrieved from http://arxiv.org/abs/1512.02595
2. W. Ross Ashby. 1956. Design for an intelligence-amplifier. *Automata studies* 400: 215–233.
3. W. Ross Ashby. 1957. An introduction to cybernetics. Retrieved from http://dspace.utalca.cl/handle/1950/6344
4. Alan Baddeley, Marge Eldridge, and Vivien Lewis. 1981. The role of subvocalisation in reading. *The Quarterly Journal of Experimental Psychology Section A* 33, 4: 439–454.
5. Richard A. Bolt. 1980. &Ldquo;Put-that-there&Rdquo;: Voice and Gesture at the Graphics Interface. *SIGGRAPH Comput. Graph.* 14, 3: 262–270.
6. Jonathan S. Brumberg, Alfonso Nieto-Castanon, Philip R. Kennedy, and Frank H. Guenther. 2010. Brain-Computer Interfaces for Speech Communication. *Speech communication* 52, 4: 367–379.
7. Douglas C. Engelbart. 2001. Augmenting human intellect: a conceptual framework (1962). *PACKER, Randall and JORDAN, Ken. Multimedia. From Wagner to Virtual Reality. New York: WW Norton & Company*: 64–90.
8. Douglas C. Engelbart and William K. English. 1968. A Research Center for Augmenting Human Intellect. In *Proceedings of the December 9-11, 1968, Fall Joint Computer Conference, Part I* (AFIPS '68 (Fall, part I)), 395–410.
9. M. J. Fagan, S. R. Ell, J. M. Gilbert, E. Sarrazin, and P. M. Chapman. 2008. Development of a (silent) speech recognition system for patients following laryngectomy. *Medical engineering & physics* 30, 4: 419–425.
10. Victoria M. Florescu, Lise Crevier-Buchman, Bruce Denby, Thomas Hueber, Antonia Colazo-Simon, Claire Pillot-Loiseau, Pierre Roussel, Cédric Gendrot, and Sophie Quattrocchi. 2010. Silent vs vocalized articulation for a portable ultrasound-based silent speech interface. In *Eleventh Annual Conference of the International Speech Communication Association*. Retrieved from http://www.gipsa-lab.inpg.fr/~thomas.hueber/mes_documents/florescu_etal_interspeech_2010.PDF
11. Carl Benedikt Frey and Michael A. Osborne. 2017. The future of employment: How susceptible are jobs to computerisation? *Technological forecasting and social change* 114, Supplement C: 254–280.
12. A. Graves, A. r. Mohamed, and G. Hinton. 2013. Speech recognition with deep recurrent neural networks. In *2013 IEEE International Conference on Acoustics, Speech and Signal Processing*, 6645–6649.
13. Jefferson Y. Han. 2005. Low-cost Multi-touch Sensing Through Frustrated Total Internal Reflection. In *Proceedings of the 18th Annual ACM Symposium on User Interface Software and*

Technology (UIST '05), 115–118.
14. William J. Hardcastle. 1976. *Physiology of speech production: an introduction for speech scientists*. Academic Press.
15. Tatsuya Hirahara, Makoto Otani, Shota Shimizu, Tomoki Toda, Keigo Nakamura, Yoshitaka Nakajima, and Kiyohiro Shikano. 2010. Silent-speech enhancement using body-conducted vocal-tract resonance signals. *Speech communication* 52, 4: 301–313.
16. Robin Hofe, Stephen R. Ell, Michael J. Fagan, James M. Gilbert, Phil D. Green, Roger K. Moore, and Sergey I. Rybchenko. 2013. Small-vocabulary speech recognition using a silent speech interface based on magnetic sensing. *Speech communication* 55, 1: 22–32.
17. Thomas Hueber, Gérard Chollet, Bruce Denby, and Maureen Stone. 2008. Acquisition of ultrasound, video and acoustic speech data for a silent-speech interface application. *Proc. of ISSP*: 365–369.
18. Jorgensen, C., & Binsted, K. (2005, January). Web browser control using EMG based sub vocal speech recognition. In *System Sciences, 2005. HICSS'05. Proceedings of the 38th Annual Hawaii International Conference on* (pp. 294c-294c). IEEE.
19. Diederik P. Kingma and Jimmy Ba. 2014. Adam: A Method for Stochastic Optimization. *arXiv [cs.LG]*. Retrieved from http://arxiv.org/abs/1412.6980
20. J. C. R. Licklider. 1960. Man-Computer Symbiosis. *IRE Transactions on Human Factors in Electronics* HFE-1, 1: 4–11.
21. S. Mitra and T. Acharya. 2007. Gesture Recognition: A Survey. *IEEE transactions on systems, man and cybernetics. Part C, Applications and reviews: a publication of the IEEE Systems, Man, and Cybernetics Society* 37, 3: 311–324.
22. A. Nijholt, D. Tan, G. Pfurtscheller, C. Brunner, J. d. R. Millán, B. Allison, B. Graimann, F. Popescu, B. Blankertz, and K. R. Müller. 2008. Brain-Computer Interfacing for Intelligent Systems. *IEEE intelligent systems* 23, 3: 72–79.
23. Sharon Oviatt, Phil Cohen, Lizhong Wu, Lisbeth Duncan, Bernhard Suhm, Josh Bers, Thomas Holzman, Terry Winograd, James Landay, Jim Larson, and David Ferro. 2000. Designing the User Interface for Multimodal Speech and Pen-Based Gesture Applications: State-of-the-Art Systems and Future Research Directions. *Human–Computer Interaction* 15, 4: 263–322.
24. Anne Porbadnigk, Marek Wester, Jan-P Calliess, and Tanja Schultz. 2009. EEG-BASED SPEECH RECOGNITION Impact of Temporal Effects.
25. Michael Wand and Tanja Schultz. 2011. Session-independent EMG-based Speech Recognition. In *Biosignals*, 295–300.
26. M. Wand, J. Koutník, and J. Schmidhuber. 2016. Lipreading with long short-term memory. In *2016 IEEE International Conference on Acoustics, Speech and Signal Processing (ICASSP)*, 6115–6119.
27. Nicole Yankelovich, Gina-Anne Levow, and Matt Marx. 1995. Designing SpeechActs: Issues in Speech User Interfaces. In *Proceedings of the SIGCHI Conference on Human Factors in Computing Systems* (CHI '95), 369–376.
28. iOS - Siri. *Apple*. Retrieved October 9, 2017 from https://www.apple.com/ios/siri/
29. Alexa. Retrieved from https://developer.amazon.com/alexa
30. Cortana | Your Intelligent Virtual & Personal Assistant | Microsoft. Retrieved October 9, 2017 from https://www.microsoft.com/en-us/windows/cortana
31. Google Home. *Google Store*. Retrieved October 9, 2017 from https://store.google.com/us/product/google_home?hl=en-US
32. Echo. Retrieved from https://www.amazon.com/Amazon-Echo-And-Alexa-Devices/b?ie=UTF8&node=9818047011

Aging and Engaging: A Social Conversational Skills Training Program for Older Adults

Mohammad Rafayet Ali[1], Kimberly Van Orden[2], Kimberly Parkhurst[3]
[1]Computer Science, University of Rochester
[2]University of Rochester School of Medicine
Rochester, United States.
[3]University of Utah.
Salt Lake City, United States.

Shuyang Liu[4], Viet-Duy Nguyen[5], Paul Duberstein[6], M. Ehsan Hoque[7]
[4, 5, 7]Computer Science, University of Rochester.
[6]University of Rochester School of Medicine.
Rochester, United States.

ABSTRACT

We developed "Aging and Engaging," a web-based intelligent interface, to improve communication skills among older adults. The interface allows users to practice conversations with a virtual assistant and receive feedback on eye contact, speaking volume, smiling, and valence of speech content. Feedback is generated automatically by analyzing the temporal properties of the conversation using the hidden Markov model. The interface was designed with the assistance of an expert advisory panel that works with geriatric patients, as well as a focus group of 12 older adults. To evaluate its effectiveness, we conducted a study with 25 older adults, each of whom participated in four conversations. Participants' response times to questions, as well as the amount of positive feedback, increased gradually through these interactions, as assessed by human judges. Participants found the feedback useful, easy to interpret, and fairly accurate, and expressed their interest in using the system at home. We plan to enroll subjects with difficulties in social communication; have them use the system over time at home in a randomized, controlled study; and measure any changes in their behavior.

Author Keywords
Aging, virtual agent, social skills.

INTRODUCTION

Ed is 72 years old and lives alone. Recently, he began case management with his local aging services provider at the request of his primary care physician, given Ed's reports of social isolation and loneliness. The case manager visited Ed's home and immediately noticed that Ed rarely smiled and had a flat expression on his face. Ed reported that he had a few acquaintances, but no close friends. The case manager encouraged Ed to visit his local senior center. The manager was delighted to learn that Ed went to the center for lunch one day. However, Ed did not have a positive experience. He felt left out even among the group of older adults. He reported feeling uncomfortable about asking to join a card game. Instead, Ed sat by himself. One gentleman invited him to sit at his table at lunch, but Ed found he had little to say. After eating, the gentleman moved on to a different group. Ed didn't understand why he didn't seem to fit in, but the case manager noted to herself that Ed demonstrated difficulties with conversational skills. Specifically, Ed often failed to make eye contact with her, spoke in a monotone, and said little. When he did speak, he was dour and gloomy. If Ed interacted this way at the senior center, it would explain why he had trouble fitting in. The case manager correctly identified Ed's problem, but how could she help someone who was reluctant to talk to even a counselor?

IUI'18, March 7–11, 2018, Tokyo, Japan

ACM ISBN 978-1-4503-4945-1/18/03…$15.00
https://doi.org/10.1145/3172944.3172958

Figure 1. Aging and Engaging virtual conversation

People around the world are living longer—a phenomenon termed "population aging." According to U.S. Census Bureau projections, the worldwide population of older adults (those who are 65 years old or older) is projected to reach 1.5 billion by 2050. It is, therefore, a high priority to promote healthy (or "successful") aging. This is achievable. Later life is not typically a time of isolation and despair: despite losses in function, cognitive capacity, and social network size, rates of depression decline in later life [1]. Research indicates that some (but not all) negative emotions are experienced less

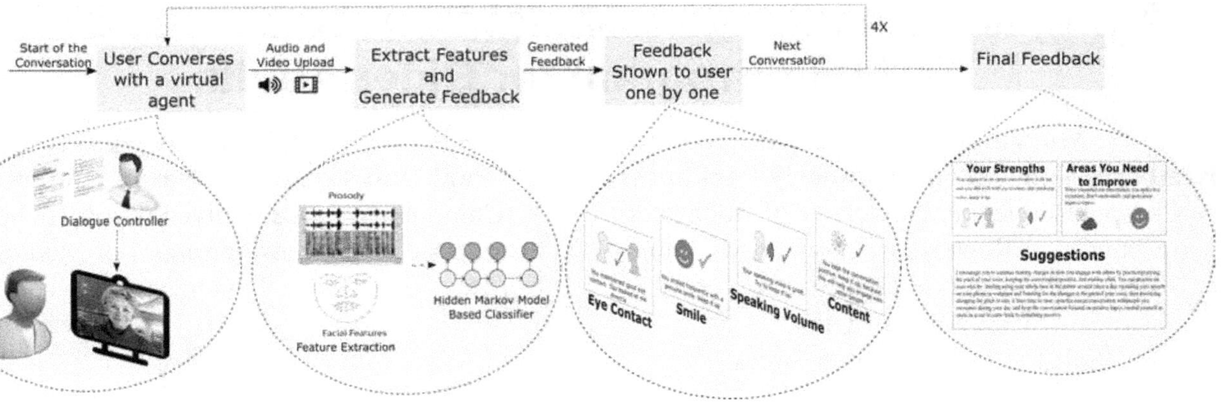

Figure 2. The overall system. Users initiate a conversation, which is driven by a dialogue controller. Conversation audio and video are processed in the server and feedback are generated. Users receive the feedback one by one and move to the next conversation phase. After four rounds of conversation, users receive final feedback summarizing the previous

often (e.g., anger) and that the ability to manage and change one's emotions (i.e., emotion regulation) often improves with age, in part due to increased motivation to experience positive emotions and accumulated life experiences that allow older adults to make effective choices regarding situations to approach or avoid [51]. Research from lifespan developmental theorists [2] has described the best approach to healthy aging as involving an increased focus on the most meaningful aspects of life—typically relationships—rather than a focus on losses or death. Some older adults, however, struggle with the transitions of later life and do become isolated and depressed [3]. A large body of literature has demonstrated that ineffective nonverbal communication impairs the ability to form and maintain positive, supportive relationships [6,7,8,9,10]. Up to 20 percent of community-dwelling older adults demonstrate difficulties with nonverbal communication [11], and yet effective intervention strategies are unavailable to them.

Some computer-based communication skills training programs exist [20,21,28,36,50]. These programs are difficult for older adults like Ed to use, for several reasons. They rely on a capacity for divided attention [36], which declines with normal cognitive aging. They require significant comfort and some experience with technology, which many older adults lack (though research has shown that they do well with technology when given appropriate instruction), and they do not accommodate for age-related sensory changes. In this paper, we propose a conversational skills training system geared toward older adults called "Aging and Engaging." In its initial application, it is designed for older adults who visit senior centers. Not all older adults who visit senior centers are able to have positive and meaningful social interactions, precisely because they lack the conversational skills to do so. Our interface allows them to converse with a virtual assistant and receive feedback on three nonverbal behaviors—eye contact, smiling, speaking volume—and one verbal: valence of speech content. We chose these four behaviors because they are empirically linked to poor social functioning [8,17]. Other communication behaviors, like gesturing, can be affected by physical impairments due to chronic disease. We divide each conversation into four phases, allowing users to receive and reflect on feedback often. In each phase, users interact with the assistant (see Figure 1) for about four minutes. During the conversation, our system captures audio and video and uploads both to our server in real time for immediate analysis. From the uploaded video and audio files, the facial and prosodic features, including smile intensity, volume, and eye gaze direction are extracted. A hidden Markov model–based classifier then classifies the patterns of nonverbal features into two categories: positive and negative. After each conversation phase, our system gives the feedback based on the classified temporal patterns.

Our system performs automated speech recognition, which we later use to perform a sentiment analysis (ratio of positive to negative words, for instance). After each phase, the transcript is uploaded to the server, where our system looks for negative and positive words in the transcript from a pre-populated list. The list of words was generated with direct input from two clinical psychologists who provide regular therapy to elderly patients. Our system gives overall positive or negative feedback depending on the prediction and on the three nonverbal and one verbal cue, after each phase. The four types of feedback come one after another with both text and voice options to improve accessibility. After the end of the conversation, our system generates a summary of all the feedback provided during each phase, identifying users' strong areas, as well as weaknesses. The feedback also includes suggestions for improvement. We employed a dialogue controller using a Wizard-of-Oz technique, which uses an online interface to select dialogues from predefined topics. Figure 2 shows the key components of our system. We aim to develop a system that engages users in conversation, puts at ease, and offers useful feedback that is interpretable.

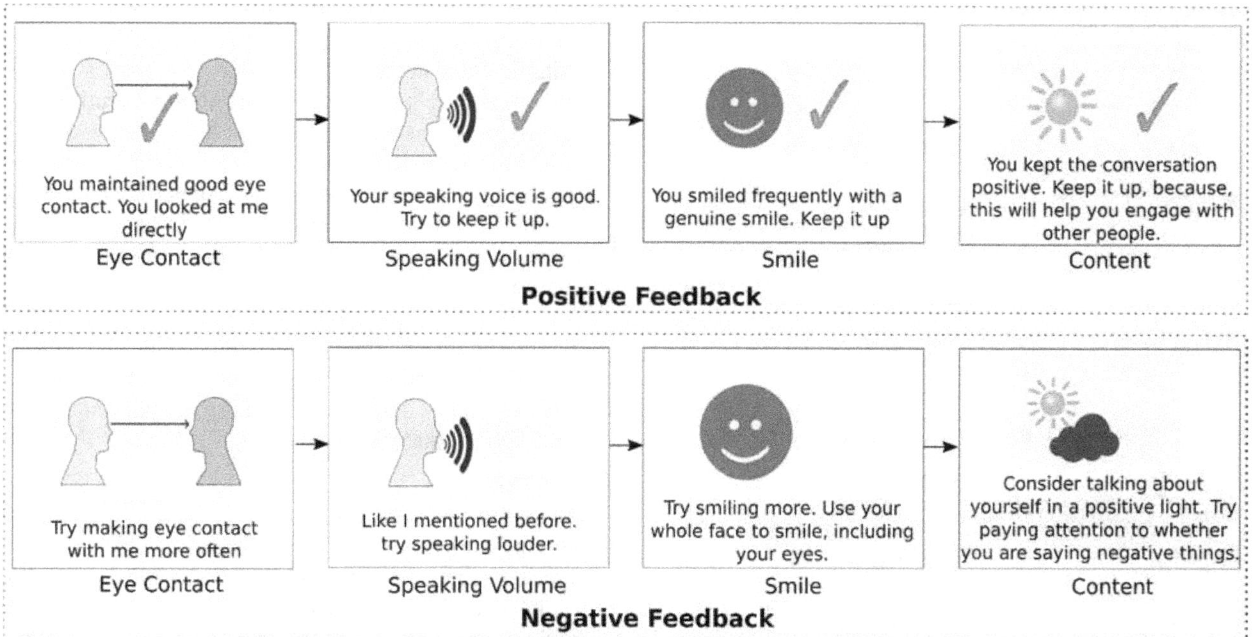

Figure 3. An example of feedback interface for each conversation phase. Users can receive either positive or negative feedback for each of the four conversational skills cues. For example, a user can receive positive feedback on eye contact and speaking volume, and negative feedback on smiling and content.

Our interdisciplinary team developed a semi-automated interface with the input of an expert advisory panel of professionals working with geriatric patients (geriatricians, neuropsychologists, gerontologists) and a focus group of 12 older adults. Our focus group helped in designing the interface and feedback, as well as selecting dialogue topics of the conversations. We conducted a study with 25 participants, each of whom is 60 years old or older. We collected the videos of their conversations with the virtual agent. Later, two raters watched the videos independently and determined whether the system should have provided positive or negative feedback. (Inter-reliability was 0.73.) Our system showed an accuracy of 72 percent, on average, considering the human-provided annotations as a ground truth. The post-study interviews show that our participants found this program useful, easy to interpret, and easy to use. (Further details are provided in the "Qualitative Analysis" section.) They also found, however, that the system's feedback was sometimes inaccurate. Unsurprisingly, participants felt the conversation was not as natural as a face-to-face interaction with another human. According to human evaluations, our participants gradually received less negative feedback as they continued the session ($p < 0.05$) and increased their speaking time (Δmean = 15.79 sec, ΔSD = 4.43, $p < 0.05$). Using the video data and annotations collected, we intend to deploy a fully automated program for use at home in the near future.

RELATED WORK

Prior technologies focused on providing more opportunities for social interactions among older adults. Beacker et al. [18] designed a social media platform, InTouch, to help older adults share photos, text, audio, and video messages within their network. Garattini et al. [19] developed a system, the Building Bridges Device, to create social networks. This device contains a touchscreen computer and a phone cradle that allows users to chat, make phone calls, and broadcast or send asynchronous messages. Their study of 19 older adults over a 10-week span showed no significant decline in usage when paired with face-to-face meetings. That is, when the technology is paired with face-to-face interactions, the attrition rate does not change.

Numerous studies used virtual agents to provide companionship to older adults. The main goal of these projects was to explore different ways of reducing social isolation. This differs from our work, as we focus on improving social skills. Vardoulakis et al. [20], for example, designed a virtual agent companion. They used a Wizard-of-Oz technique to collect data from older adults who were socially isolated. Participants' self-reported ratings showed that they were willing to use the device again. Ring et al. [21] developed a computer program with a virtual assistant that exhibits synchronous non-verbal behavior using the Behavior Expression Animation Toolkit (BEAT) [22]. Their program has two modes: passive and proactive. In proactive mode, the program can initiate a conversation after observing the user with motion sensors. In passive mode, users had to initiate the conversation by themselves. In a one-week study with 14 older adults, the proactive group reported a significantly greater decrease in loneliness than the passive group. Bickmore et al. [23] developed a virtual lab for conducting studies with human and virtual agents. They used it as an exercise coach for older adults. Participants who used

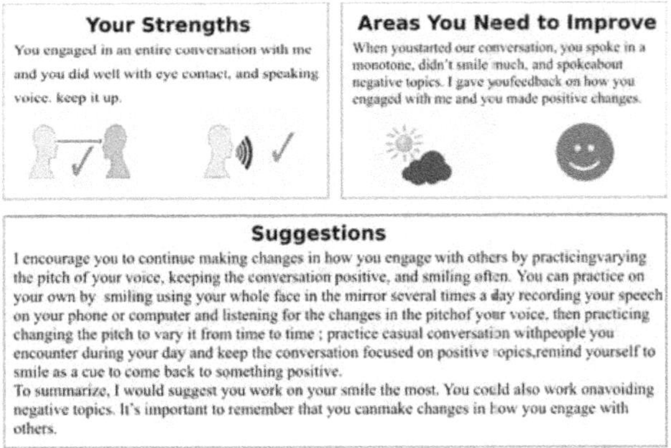

Figure 4. Final feedback interface

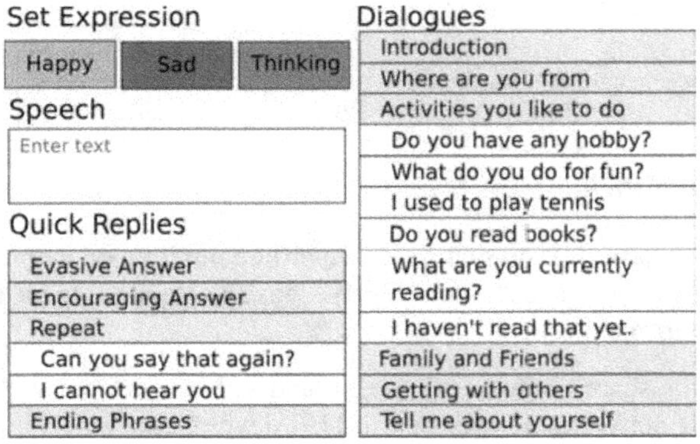

Figure 5: The dialogue controller's interface

the system exercised significantly more. Previous efforts with younger adults focused on giving real-time and *ex-post facto* feedback on nonverbal behavior. These efforts have not been replicated for older adults. Some of the previous studies focus on minimizing the distraction caused by real-time feedback [24,25,26]. (Older adults perform worse when their attention is divided [27].) In the past, *ex-post facto* summary feedback has been effective. In My Automated Conversation coacH (MACH) [28], a virtual agent asks a series of interview questions, providing neutral acknowledgments by mirroring smiles and head nods and then following up with detailed feedback on the user's performance. This project demonstrated the viability of using virtual agents and *ex-post facto* feedback in the context of a job interview. ROC Speak [29] is a semi-automated public speaking practice tool that uses crowdsourced and automated nonverbal behavior analysis. It, too, employed *ex-post facto* feedback, which enabled users to reflect on their mistakes and practice again.

We focus on conversational skills training to help older adults improve social communication. This is significantly different than previous studies [18,19], which focused on developing social networks and reducing social isolation by providing a virtual agent companion. Our system is a coach, not a companion. In the past, the social skills training tools have demonstrated the effectiveness of the automated computer-based social skills training. However, these tools do not focus on the older adults who have particular needs. For example, using MACH [28], the participants, who were college students showed significant improvement on job interviews. Aging and Engaging is inspired by the concept of using a virtual agent and adapted to help improve social skills among older adults. The interface does not feature any graph or numbers, instead, it uses pictures and text to speech technique to deliver the feedback. Unlike past interfaces [24,26,36,50] which aimed to change behaviors among young adults, our interface does not feature any real-time feedback. Our work draws on previous systems that aimed to change nonverbal behaviors [28] but is innovative in that it was designed to meet the unique needs of older adults. Older adults who differ from younger adults with respect to sensory and cognitive processing, including vision and hearing loss [30], as well as declines in working memory and difficulties with divided attention [27].

SYSTEM

In designing a system for older adults, we encountered several challenges. First, we needed to design an interface that is simple and requires minimal training to use. Second, we needed to generate feedback on the nonverbal behaviors of the users. Third, our system needed to give feedback that is generalizable and easy to understand. To understand these problems better, we consulted with a focus group of 12 older adults, each of whom volunteers as companions for isolated peers. They have valuable experience with older adults who are at an elevated risk of having nonverbal behavioral difficulties. We described our concept and showed them a low-fidelity prototype. The focus group offered thoughtful advice on the virtual assistant's appearance, feedback, and dialogue topics. In summary, the focus group made the following suggestions: the avatar should look like an older adult; the feedback needs to be less distracting (i.e., avoid real-time feedback and have feedback appear in sequence, not all at once); avoid too much negative feedback, as it might disengage users; and reinforce positives and demonstrate understanding. We then consulted with the expert advisory panel. This panel consists of a geriatrician, a geriatric neuropsychologist, and a gerontologist with expertise in interventions. The advisory panel made the following suggestions: include short assessment points throughout the intervention in which the virtual assistant can give participants feedback directly—as opposed to real-time feedback, delivered through text and images—and also foster transitions; and the avatar's face should be highly contrasted against the background so that even visually-impaired participants will have no difficulty seeing it. We tried to incorporate all suggestions. We divided the conversation into four phases to reduce cognitive load on users. Our system gives feedback after each phase. Given that increasing difficulty with divided attention is common with cognitive aging [27], many older adults may find it difficult to focus on a conversation and feedback simultaneously [24,33,26]. This may be especially true of older adults with social functioning impairments, like those for whom our program is designed [31]. Additionally, feedback across four stages allows users to adjust their behavior in successive conversations. Afterward, our system summarizes the feedback and provides recommendations for future practice as well as areas to emphasize later (e.g., "vary pitch while explaining something").

Interface Design

Our interface features an older woman from SitePal [32] (Figure 1). We choose this virtual assistant after consulting with our focus group. Also, using the virtual agents for social skills training has been shown to be successful in different contexts and user groups [28,36,50]. During the conversation with the virtual assistant, our system uploads the recorded audio and video to a server for processing. After the conversation, our system uploads the transcript of the conversation to the server to generate feedback. The system automatically takes users to the feedback page. We chose four different dimensions of conversational skills to give feedback: eye contact, volume, smile, and speech content. The attendant behaviors (smiling, volume modulation, making eye contact, etc.) have been shown to foster communication [16,34,35]. A future version of our system may include other verbal and nonverbal cues. The feedback was given using pictures, text, and voice. Figure 3 shows our feedback interface. The top row shows an example of positive feedback; the bottom row, negative feedback. The feedback interface contains a picture and some text. Some studies used pictures to give feedback effectively [36]. We added text feedback because feedback offered through multiple channels is more likely to be effective than that offered through only one channel. We selected this approach in response to the expert panel and the focus group. For each skill dimension, our system offers positive and negative feedback. If the user makes eye contact with the avatar, for example, they receive positive feedback on eye contact. Each instance of positive feedback is accompanied by an animated green checkmark and a "ding" sound. The feedback text is read aloud to the user using a text-to-speech engine. To avoid repetition, the negative feedback text changes across each conversation. For example, if a user does not smile at all during the first conversation, the system will say, "You didn't smile at all. Try smiling more, including with your eyes." If the user does not improve in the second conversation, the system will say, "Like I mentioned before, try smiling more." To show engagement, we programmed our virtual assistant to nod its head periodically (every five seconds).

After every phase of the conversation, our system offers final, integrated feedback. This final feedback summarizes the feedback the user received after each phase. Figure 4 shows the final feedback interface. The final feedback shows, at most, two dimensions in which the user received negative feedback. We decided to show only two cases, as too much negative feedback can lead users to disengage. The system suggests ways for users to improve. For example, if the user receives negative feedback on speech content, our system will say: "Practice casual conversation with people you encounter during your day, and keep the conversation focused on positive topics."

Dialogue and Feedback Generation

Automated understanding of language and responding remains an active area of exploration. In this exploratory study, we decided to go with a Wizard-of-Oz technique to manage the dialogues. A research assistant worked as a dialogue controller. The dialogue controller uses an online interface shown in Figure 5. To avoid delay due to typing, we decided to generate dialogues on predefined topics and list the sentences in the dialogue controller's interface. On the right side of the interface (see Figure 5), we listed all dialogue options and grouped them by topic. After discussing with the focus group, we selected five topics: where the user is from, the activities the user likes to do, family and friends, getting together with others, and the user him or herself. In our study, the first topic (an introduction) was mandatory for all participants, after which we allowed participants to choose any three among the five topics for the remaining three phases. This is how we ensured that each of the participants completed four phases of conversation. The focus group helped us generate the prompts and replies for each topic. On the left side of the controller's interface (see Figure 5), there are buttons for controlling the assistant's nonverbal behavior, including selected dialogue topics, a few quick replies, and freeform text input.

The system records both audio and video of the conversation using the computer's microphone and webcam then sends the stream to our server in real time. On the server, the facial and prosodic features are extracted from the audio and video files using Praat [37] and SHORE [38]. Our features include smile intensity, pitch, volume, frequencies of the first three formants (F1, F2, F3), and pixel differences between consecutive frames. We used a face tracker from Visage technologies [39] to extract gaze direction in real time. To generate feedback, we used a hidden Markov model–based technique. In the past, hidden Markov model was used to model human behaviors and actions [55,56]. The training data was collected from a speed-dating study [36]. The data includes 506 minutes of video from 47 male college students having a conversation with a virtual assistant. The videos contain only the male students' faces. A trained set of research assistants from psychology with experience in social skills training watched the videos to mark those moments where they felt a subject needed to adjust their nonverbal behavior. Specifically, the research assistants looked for appropriate eye contact, volume, and smile. We extracted the features from the training videos and trained three hidden Markov models using the Baum-Welch algorithm [54] for the three nonverbal cues. To predict the feedback (positive or negative), we used the forward-backward algorithm and the features we extracted from participants' videos. Given a sequence of observation, the forward-backward algorithm calculates the posterior probability of a hidden Markov model [58]. To give feedback on content, our clinical psychologists collected some keywords, which we considered negative words in the context of our study (e.g. "died," "lonely"). We consider it as a negative conversation if the ratio of negative words and total words is greater than a predefined threshold empirically chosen after testing it on our research assistants. An example of false positive feedback would be, participant kept the conversation positive but the system gave a negative feedback on the content. A limitation of this approach is that it is unable to detect when a negative word is used in a positive way, and vice-versa. Adding this feature remains part of our future exploration.

STUDY

To assess the acceptability of the interface to its intended audience, we conducted a study with 25 participants who are each 65 years old or older. The average age of the participants was 68.5. Of those 25, six were single, eight were divorced, one was widowed, and ten lived with their spouses. Participants were recruited from a hospital-based geriatric mental health clinic (n=5) (where difficulties with nonverbal behaviors are common) as well as through print advertisements (n=20). All participants were native English speakers. Our participants varied on self-perceived social skills, as we believed more diverse feedback would be most useful at this stage. However, the majority of our participants (67%) were below the 50th percentile on a population-normed measure of social skills (PROMIS Self-Efficacy to Manage Social Interactions). The study took place in a private room in the medical center. Participants first consented to the study with a trained assessor. We emphasized that participation would have no impact on services received from the Medical Center if any, and our research staff had no connection with the clinic. After the consent process, we explained how the interface works. Participants then interacted with our interface by pressing the start button in our interface. During the interaction, participants went through four conversation phases. After each phase, the system redirected participants to a feedback page. After four rounds of conversation and feedback, the participant received the final feedback (Figure 4), which summarized the feedback previously given and suggested areas for improvement. Our research staff did not intervene beyond helping participants open the interface in the web browser. After the interaction, we asked participants a series of questions about the interface, their experience, their demographics, self-perceived social skills (PROMIS) [52,53] any depression or anxiety [44], their social connectedness [45], and their use of computers or other electronics. The study served to collect data since there is no dataset available from any previous studies that target the desired behaviors in older adults. We did not conduct this study as a system intervention. We plan to conduct such an intervention study in the future to evaluate the effectiveness of the system.

Survey Results

We showed the participants four statements and asked them to rate each between one and five, where one indicates strong agreement and five indicates strong disagreement. The statements and their average ratings are shown in Table 1. On average, participants self-reported the interface as easy to use, with a value of 1.96 (SD=1.02). Our intuitive design choices, with minimal button-pressing and voice-assisted feedback, might have made our interface easy to use. Participants also disagreed with the statement about the system taking too long to use, rating it a 4.04 (SD=0.97). We wanted to know more about the opinions of the participants who agreed with the statement, "I feel disconnected from other people" (n=12). Table 1 shows no significant difference in ratings of the interface between participants who felt disconnected and those who did not. There was also no difference in the ratings provided by those who felt like outsiders at social events (n=12) and those who felt lonely (n=20). The participants were further divided based on a self-reported measure of perceived social skills (in Table 2). We did not find any significant difference in the ratings between the two groups. These results are important because they show the interface is acceptable to people who have (or are at risk for) difficulties with social communication [46].

In our study, 19 participants possessed a home computer or a laptop—we called them the "computer user group"—and six participants had no access to computers—the "computer non-user group." These two groups' ratings are also shown in Table 1. The computer non-user group thought the program was easier to use than the computer user group. This may be because the computer user group had higher expectations in terms of feedback speed and system responsiveness. The computer non-user group tended toward not wanting to use the program in their home. But these differences are not statistically significant. The lack of difference between computer users and computer non-users is important because it shows that our system is acceptable to even those who have limited experience with technology. We also looked at the average ratings of the statements after grouping participants based on the presence (or absence) of clinically-significant depression, anxiety, and social isolation, as these are characteristics that often coexist with communication difficulties in later life. Table 2 shows the average ratings. In it, the "yes" column contains the ratings of those who reported elevated levels of depression, anxiety, or social isolation using population-based norms. In these three categories, we did not find any significant differences in ratings between the groups, which, while inconclusive given our sample size, nonetheless suggests that those who feel isolated, depressed, or anxious are not less likely to find the program acceptable. This is important, as those who report these characteristics are most likely to have deficits that could improve the program.

To see how the system performed in terms of feedback accuracy, we compared the system-generated feedback against that of human judges. Two trained research assistants watched each of the interactions individually and decided whether to offer positive or negative feedback. We calculated the accuracy of our system by comparing against these determinations as ground truths. Table 3 shows the average accuracy of the system when compared against the decisions of the two human judges. The inter-rater reliability (Cohen's Kappa) of the two human judges for each feedback dimension is also shown in Table 3. We found that our system-generated feedback accorded most with human judges on eye contact. Some of our participants were not sure where to look to receive positive feedback. Others sat facing the light, which reflected on their eyeglasses, making it difficult to accurately determine eye gaze direction. Some dialogue topics became negative even when participants tried to keep them positive. Our system only looked at the ratio of positive words to negative words, not more complex syntactic structures. There were instances in which participants described a positive phenomenon with negative words and thus received negative feedback on their speech content.

Feature Analysis

We looked at how participants were performing in each phase of their conversation. We took the percentage of participants who received positive feedback according to our human annotators (see Figure. 6a). We saw a statistically significant difference between the first phase of conversation and the last (fourth) phase of conversation ($p<0.05$) on a smile, volume, and content. This suggests that participants were able to reflect on the feedback and change those behaviors more likely to elicit positive feedback. Among the four dimensions, the percentage of participants receiving positive feedback on eye contact changed the least (Δ = 0.31%), whereas smile changed the most (Δ = 83.15%).

We also looked at the average speaking time of the participants during each phase of the conversation (Figure. 6b). Participants' response times increased in subsequent conversations. Average response time for each question during the first conversation was 24 seconds (SD=4.5), whereas the average response time for the final conversation was 40 seconds (SD=4.9) ($p <0.05$). This suggests that, as the conversation progressed, the participants become more comfortable with the interface and revealed more information about themselves.

We further analyzed the affective features of the participants. We extracted the facial action units (AU) [47] features from the participants' videos using OpenFace [48] software. Each of the AU is expressed in two forms, a strength value ("_r") and binary presence ("_c"). Figure 6c shows the difference between the features of the first and last conversation phase where the difference was significant after adjusting for the number of features ($p<0.05$). We observed that the AU01 (inner brow raise) which is associated with a surprised facial expression [49], had an increase in both average and variance in the last conversation phase. In our context, this change may indicate that the participants were becoming more animated as the interaction progressed. AU04 (brow lower), the variance of AU09 (nose wrinkler), and variance of AU15 (lip corner depressor) also decreased in the last interaction. AU04, AU09, and AU15 are associated with the expressions of anger, disgust, and sadness respectively [49]. This might indicate that as the conversation went the participants became more comfortable.

Post Study Interviews

In order get additional feedback to help us improve our system, we included a qualitative interview with our participants (this interview was added midway into data collection, thus we only have feedback from n=15 subjects). We took a phenomenology approach to designing the interview guide, which was developed by one of our study investigators. Feedback was obtained from an additional researcher and the interview guide was edited accordingly. The interview guide included questions focused on participants' experience during the time they engaged with the program and suggestions for improving the program.

Statements	Avg. Rating					
	AVG (n=25)	Disconnected (n=12)	Outsider (n=12)	Lonely (n=20)	Computer User(n=19)	Computer Non-User(n=6)
1. The program was easy to use.	1.96	1.83	2.08	1.78	2.08	1.69
2. Using the program was frustrating.	3.68	3.67	3.83	3.94	3.69	3.67
3. The program took too long to use.	4.04	4.00	4.25	3.89	4.14	3.91
4. I would likely use the program if I could access it from home on a computer.	2.68	2.75	2.58	2.72	2.57	3.33

Table 1: Average ratings from participants in different groups based on interpersonal needs. (1 = strongly agree, 5=strongly disagree)

Statements	Avg. Rating							
	Depression		Anxiety		Social isolation		Social Skills	
	Y(n=1)	No	Y(n=3)	No	Y(n=2)	No	Good(n=6)	Poor
1. The program was easy to use.	1.00	2.00	1.67	2.00	2.00	1.95	1.78	2.11
2. Using the program was frustrating.	4.00	4.00	4.33	3.76	3.50	3.77	3.89	3.44
3. The program took too long to use.	4.00	4.04	3.67	4.09	4.50	4.00	4.22	3.68
4. I would likely use the program if I could access it from home on a computer.	3.00	2.70	3.60	2.81	3.00	2.68	2.67	2.44

Table 2: Average ratings from participants in different groups based on their diagnosis (1=strongly agree, 5=strongly disagree

	Accuracy (%)	True Positive Rate (%)	False Positive Rate (%)	Cohen's *kappa*
Eye Contact	79.60	76.06	3.50	0.84
Volume	72.00	58.50	14.25	0.79
Smile	66.00	60.25	15.35	0.62
Content	68.80	67.91	17.36	0.67

Table 3: Accuracy of feedback compared to human judges

Interviews were audio-recorded with participants' permission and transcribed. We then conducted thematic analysis using principles of grounded theory (including the constant comparative method) to analyze the data [57]. Coding was done by one investigator and then reviewed by another investigator (we used open coding) [57]. Discrepancies between the two raters did not arise as the themes were relatively straightforward and unambiguous. We added user codes with the quotations.

Accuracy of the feedback

All participants commented on their perceptions of the accuracy of the feedback, as they reflected on their performance and suggested areas for improvement. Many participants perceived that the feedback was accurate (n=5).

"Every single thing she said I should try to be better at was absolutely correct." (Subject 2, 69 y/o female, 45th percentile on social skills).

Insight into their behaviors and its relation to feedback accuracy was also raised by several participants (n=3).

"I'm pretty much aware of all those things I don't do well. I don't smile a lot, I don't vary the pitch of my voice. I have a very soft voice." (Subject 14, 74 y/o female, 39th percentile for social skills).

However, an equal number of participants thought the feedback was inaccurate (n=5). This may be the case because the training data was collected from college students, rather than older adults. A key objective of the current study was to obtain data from older participants to better train the system for our subsequent efficacy study. One way in which our older participants differed from many of the younger participants was that most wore eyeglasses, which made it difficult for the program to recognize eye gaze direction. Further, some of the participants were not sure where to look (at the webcam or into the virtual assistant's eyes) in order to get positive eye contact feedback. At first, this frustrated them, but eventually, they understood and looked at the assistant's eye to get a positive feedback. As another said,

"I was frustrated by inaccurate feedback, but once it seemed to be in sync, it was fine."(Subject 11, 70 y/o female, 18th percentile on social skills).

Comfort with the interface

Most participants (n=10) spoke about their level of comfort with the interface given that it was a novel experience for all of them. Some spoke about how they initially felt uncomfortable engaging with the program, but that this improved over the course of the session.

"I got more comfortable as I went on because I wasn't sure how it was going to work at first." (Subject 2, 69 y/o female, 45th percentile on social skills). Another said, "'I think the more it went on, the more comfortable you get with it." (Subject 7, 69 y/o male, 55th percentile on social skills) Many participants also spoke about ways in which the program was easy or difficult to use (n=8). We carefully designed our system using the feedback from our focus group. We had several key design concerns, which included participants' ability to read the feedback, navigate through the interface, and hear properly. We minimized button pressing to make the program more intuitive. Said another:

"The program is easy to use; I didn't need training like I do with other new programs." (Subject 11, 70 y/o female, 18th percentile on social skills).

Useful program for engaging

We asked our participants about how useful they thought the system was. Most participants thought the program could help improve conversational skills (n=12). Our interface allows these people to practice and possibly improve conversational skills without feeling judged by a human. Said one of our participants:

"I know that I could probably improve by practicing. I've never had the opportunity to practice with something like this, which would be an impersonal coach. I started to think of her as a coach who wouldn't react—like a psychiatrist, just listening and letting the person do all the talking." (Subject 14, 74 y/o female, 39th percentile for social skills).

Our participants also said the program could be a great teaching tool. Said another,

"I think it's a great teaching tool. The program is already helpful; it just needs tweaking." (Subject 3, 67 y/o female, 32nd percentile on social skills).

Our participants also viewed this program as a tool that can be helpful to those who are shy and withdrawn, learning the skills needed to connect and communicate with others. This program might also be helpful for those who find it difficult to start a conversation.

"This would be good for people who have issues—who are so withdrawn that they can't communicate. This would help them break out of their shell, and give them instructions on how to move forward." (Subject 8, 65 y/o female, 70th percentile on social skills).

Content of the discussion

We carefully chose dialogue topics after discussing with our focus group. Several participants (n=5) commented on the content of the dialogue.

"I would've done all five conversation topics- they were great. There was nothing intrusive, it was very basic."

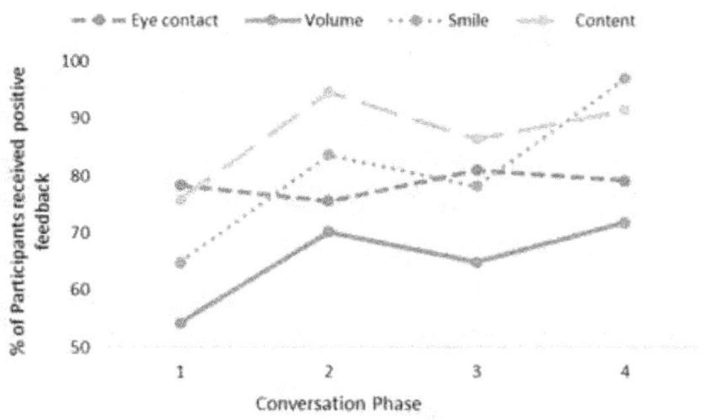

(a)

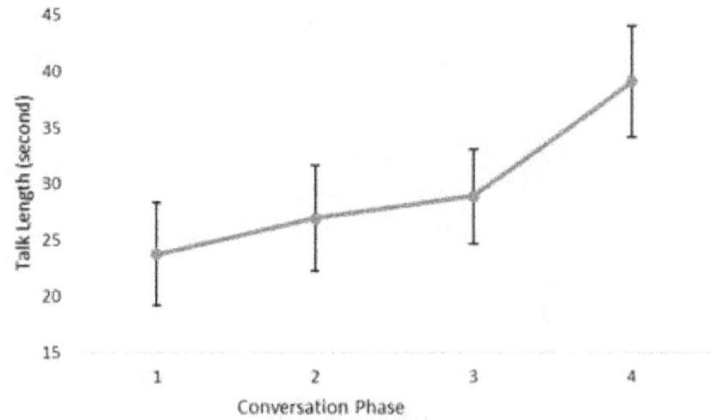

(b)

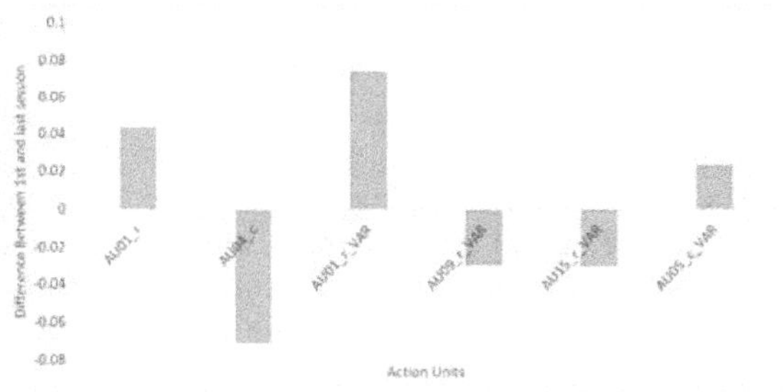

(c)

Figure 6. (a) The trend line of the percentage of participants annotated as positive feedback recipients after each conversation. (b) The average length of the participants' speeches for each of the small conversation. (c) Changes in the average action unit values.

(Subject 18, 62 y/o female, 25th percentile on social skills).

During the conversations, the virtual assistant asked some questions relevant to their selected dialogue topics. Our participants found that the questions the virtual assistant asked were common, natural, and comprehensive.

"I thought the questions were so realistic. Those are the questions I grill people on all the time when I meet them. It was very natural." (Subject 8, 65 y/o female, 70th percentile on social skills)

Some of the participants felt that the conversation was one sided, as the virtual assistant was not able to respond to all the questions the participant asked.

"I gave answers but I didn't feel like I had the chance to ask her questions. It felt strange... The conversation is too one-sided." (Subject 2, 69 y/o female, 45th percentile on social skills)

Suggestions to improve the interface

Two participants addressed the fact that the conversations had no time limit, allowing participants to speak as long as they wanted. It was not clear to the participants how long the conversations would continue. One participant suggested using a timeline.

"A timeline would be helpful—knowing how long each section is going to be, and how far along you are in the program." (Subject 5, 83 y/o male, 61st percentile on social skills).

Another participant brought up the issue of sensory impairment in later life.

"At first I had a hard time hearing, but after she started talking, you kind of get what was going on. It could be part of the hearing problems I have, but once I got into it, I could understand her voice. As it went on it got better." (Subject 7, 69 y/o male, 55th percentile on social skills)

To further improve our program, we plan to consult with the geriatrician on our advisory board for features we could add to better accommodate age-related hearing and vision loss.

DISCUSSION AND FUTURE WORK

Even though the agreement between the feedback generated by our algorithm and two labelers was fairly high, there is room for improvement. The feedback module was trained with videos of college students who are younger than our target population and have different facial, prosodic and behavioral characteristics. We used a hidden Markov model to better understand temporal patterns to generate feedback. In future, we will continue to improve our proposed machine learning model to generate more accurate feedback. Our exploration will include other non-temporal models (i.e., support vector machine) and neural network based classifiers (i.e., recurrent neural network). In this exploratory study, we collected 25 videos of interaction with older adults. We will improve our feedback module by using this new set of videos. Formulating feedback by counting positive and negative words has many limitations. Future work will involve more semantic analysis, using techniques from natural language processing.

The effectiveness of the system (i.e., improving social skills) was not assessed through the preliminary study. The objective of the study was to assess the acceptability of the system in older adults. This type of intervention is acceptable to younger adults. There are no evidence-based reasons to predict that older adults would react differently than younger adults to the prospect of using the program. Some of the end users take part in the design of the system. Some of the older adults we included did have difficulties with social skills. We also included those without these difficulties because we believe a wider range of feedback is helpful. In future, we will recruit participants with social skills deficits.

The study was a one-time visit by the participants. Thus, it was not necessary to remember the information from the previous sessions, and there was none. However, the system remembers the feedback it gave to the participant in subsequent conversations (in the same day) and synthesizes them to produce a final feedback. In future, we will enable the system to remember the past conversation by augmenting the login capability.

Participants appreciated the dialogue we chose. The interactions, however, were one-sided, as the virtual assistant was not able to answer all the questions posed by our participants because we generated a limited number of responses. The transcripts collected from this study will allow us to generate more responses for the assistant. To automate the dialogue controller, we will build a topic-based dialogue module. The automated dialogue module can have conversations on particular topics and the responses will be chosen by pattern-matching. Spontaneous back-channeling was not implemented in our current prototype. In the future, we will incorporate features, such as sharing a smile or nodding appropriately, which can lead to a more natural interaction. This remains an open research problem for us and the virtual assistant community.

Our aim is to build an interface that will become a part of the users' lives. With the initial exploratory study and findings, our next step is to deploy a fully automated system online. We used the Wizard-of-Oz technique as our first step to build the automated dialogue system. This study gave us the valuable data necessary for an automated dialogue manager. It will allow us to run a longitudinal study allowing participants to use our system from home. It is important to investigate how the participants are able to utilize their practice with our interface to improve or maintain their relationships and maintain better health and quality of life. We will have older adults who demonstrate difficulties with social communication (as measured by low levels of social functioning and impairments on standardized ratings of communication behaviors) engage with the program several times and assess their communication behaviors at baseline, at the end of the two weeks of practice, and three months later. Doing so will allow us to measure learning and change over time, as well as maintenance of gains after finishing their sessions. Our study presented here is a necessary first step to this future study.

Further, later life brings with it numerous potentially stressful social encounters, including discussions about end-of-life care, for example. Even older adults with strong conversation skills will likely to have some difficulties with these conversations. Thus, a future direction with our system is to adapt it for assisting all older adults with challenging social situations common in later life, including end-of-life planning, discussions with physicians, discussions with adult children about giving up driving and moving to retirement communities.

CONCLUSION

Our semi-automated interface was designed to benefit older adults who have difficulties with communication skills, including those who are homebound, while avoiding social stigma and minimizing burdens associated with in-person interventions. Since our target users are different than those studied using previous social skills training tools, we spoke with the advisory panel and the focus group in order to make the design choices. Our exploratory study, with 25 participants, revealed key challenges while also underscoring the acceptability and feasibility of the system. Our participants shared their experiences using the interface and, overall, found it useful, intuitive, and fairly accurate. This indicates that such technology might be accepted by many older adults, including those who could stand to benefit the most. Our analysis of the response time and the human annotations revealed that participants gradually spoke with the assistant longer and received less negative feedback as the interaction progressed. The exploratory study provided important insights that we will use in building the next version of this program.

Improving interpersonal skills is a personal experience and should happen with the presence of other humans. Thus, our program is not designed to replace human interaction and companionship. Rather, the program is a tool to be used to improve communication skills in a safe, non-judgmental environment; these skills can then be practiced with other people. Having difficulties with conversation skills can make social interactions stressful, which exacerbates cognitive changes associated with aging that could impede learning new behaviors; using our program allows older adults to practice new skills in a less stressful environment before attempting to use new behaviors with people in their lives. Further, later life imposes a unique challenge for individuals who are homebound and unable to take advantage of help by commuting to a clinic, thus indicating an important role for a web-based automated program. Our program may help these individuals improve their skills, thereby maximizing the time they have with people in their lives and promoting useful and less stressful conversations with spouses and family members. We believe computation has an important role to play by providing fully automated, repeatable, standardized, and non-judgmental "conversational coaching" to individuals who may need it.

ACKNOWLEDGEMENT

The work was partially supported by NSF EAGER grant IIS-1543758 and by a University Research Award from the University of Rochester (Van Orden, PI).

REFERENCES

1. S. T. Charles, "Strength and vulnerability integration: A model of emotional well-being across adulthood." Psychol. Bull., vol. 136, no. 6, pp. 1068–1091, 2010.
2. S. T. Charles and L. L. Carstensen, "Social and emotional aging." Annu. Rev. Psychol., vol. 61, pp. 383–409, 2010.

3. K. A. Van Orden, A. A. O'Riley, A. Simning, C. Podgorski, T. M. Richardson, and Y. Conwell, "Passive suicide ideation: An indicator of risk among older adults seeking aging services?," Gerontologist, vol. 55, no. 6, pp. 972–980, 2015.
4. J. Holt-Lunstad, T. B. Smith, M. Baker, T. Harris, and D. Stephenson, "Loneliness and Social Isolation as Risk Factors for Mortality: A Meta-Analytic Review," Perspect. Psychol. Sci., vol. 10, no. 2, pp. 227–237, 2015.
5. A. E. Schneider, N. Ralph, C. Olson, A.-M. Flatley, and L. Thorpe, "Predictors of Senior Center Use among Older Adults in New York City Public Housing," J. URBAN Heal. NEW YORK Acad. Med., vol. 91, no. 6, pp. 1033–1047, 2014.
6. R. Schwartz and M. D. Pell, "When emotion and expression diverge: The social costs of Parkinson's disease," J. Clin. Exp. Neuropsychol., vol. 3395, no. August, pp. 1–20, 2016.
7. C. F. Keating, "The developmental arc of nonverbal communication: Capacity and consequence for human social bonds.," in APA handbook of nonverbal communication., 2016, pp. 103–138.
8. M. A. Struchen, M. R. Pappadis, A. M. Sander, C. S. Burrows, and K. A. Myszka, "Examining the contribution of social communication abilities and affective/behavioral functioning to social integration outcomes for adults with traumatic brain injury," J. Head Trauma Rehabil., vol. 26, no. 1, pp. 30–42, 2011.
9. J. K. Burgoon, laura K. Guerrero, and V. Manusov, "Nonverbal signals," in Handbook of Interpersonal Communication (4th ed.), 2012, pp. 239–280.
10. J. K. Burgoon and A. E. Bacue, "Nonverbal communication skills.," in Handbook of Communication and Social Interaction Skills, 2003, pp. 179–219.
11. H. M. Geurts, M. Stek, and H. Comijs, "Autism characteristics in older adults with depressive disorders," Am. J. Geriatr. Psychiatry, vol. 24, no. 2, pp. 161–169, 2016.
12. A. S. Young, R. Klap, C. D. Sherbourne, and K. B. Wells, "The quality of care for depressive and anxiety disorders in the United States," Arch Gen Psychiatry, vol. 58, no. 1, pp. 55–61, 2001.
13. M. Heerink, B. Kröse, V. Evers, and B. Wielinga, "Assessing acceptance of assistive social agent technology by older adults: The almere model," Int. J. Soc. Robot., vol. 2, no. 4, pp. 361–375, 2010.
14. K. Laguna and R. L. Babcock, "Computer anxiety in young and older adults: Implications for human-computer interactions in older populations," Comput. Human Behav., vol. 13, no. 3, pp. 317–326, 1997.
15. T. L. Mitzner, J. B. Boron, C. B. Fausset, A. E. Adams, N. Charness, S. J. Czaja, K. Dijkstra, A. D. Fisk, W. A. Rogers, and J. Sharit, "Older adults talk technology: Technology usage and attitudes," Comput. Human Behav., vol. 26, no. 6, pp. 1710–1721, 2010.
16. C. R. Bowie, W. W. Leung, A. Reichenberg, M. M. McClure, T. L. Patterson, R. K. Heaton, and P. D. Harvey, "Predicting Schizophrenia Patients' Real-World Behavior with Specific Neuropsychological and Functional Capacity Measures," Biol. Psychiatry, vol. 63, no. 5, pp. 505–511, 2008.
17. M. Youngren and P. M. Lewinsohn, "The functional relation between depression and problematic interpersonal behavior.," J. Abnorm. Psychol., vol. 89, no. 3, pp. 333–341, 1980.
18. R. Beacker, K. Sellen, S. Crosskey, V. Boscart, and B. Barbosa Neves, "Technology to reduce social isolation and loneliness," Proc. 16th Int. ACM SIGACCESS Conf. Comput. Access. - ASSETS '14, no. November 2015, pp. 27–34, 2014.
19. C. Garattini, J. Wherton, and D. Prendergast, "Linking the lonely: An exploration of a communication technology designed to support social interaction among older adults," Univers. Access Inf. Soc., vol. 11, no. 2, pp. 211–222, 2012.
20. L. P. Vardoulakis, L. Ring, B. Barry, C. L. Sidner, and T. Bickmore, "Designing relational agents as long term social companions for older adults," Lect. Notes Comput. Sci. (including Subser. Lect. Notes Artif. Intell. Lect. Notes Bioinformatics), vol. 7502 LNAI, pp. 289–302, 2012.
21. L. Ring, B. Barry, K. Totzke, and T. Bickmore, "Addressing loneliness and isolation in older adults: Proactive affective agents provide better support," Proc. - 2013 Hum. Assoc. Conf. Affect. Comput. Intell. Interact. ACII 2013, pp. 61–66, 2013.
22. J. Cassell, H. H. Vilhjálmsson, and T. Bickmore, "BEAT: the Behavior Expression Animation Toolkit," Life-Like Characters, vol. 137, no. August, pp. 163–185, 2004.
23. T. Bickmore and D. Schulman, "A virtual laboratory for studying long-term relationships between humans and virtual agents," ... Conf. Auton. Agents ..., pp. 297–304, 2009.
24. O. Kulyk, J. Wang, and J. Terken, "Real-time feedback on nonverbal behaviour to enhance social dynamics in small group meetings," in Lecture Notes in Computer Science, 2006, vol. 3869 LNCS, pp. 150–161.
25. T. Kim, A. Chang, L. Holland, and A. S. Pentland, "Meeting mediator: enhancing group collaborationusing sociometric feedback," in Proceedings of the 2008 ACM conference on Computer supported cooperative work, 2008, pp. 457–466.
26. M. I. Tanveer, E. Lin, and M. E. Hoque, "Rhema : A Real-Time In-Situ Intelligent Interface to Help People with Public Speaking," in IUI 2015, pp. 286–295.
27. S. Getzmann, E. J. Golob, and E. Wascher, "Focused and divided attention in a simulated cocktail-party situation: ERP evidence from younger and older adults," Neurobiol. Aging, vol. 41, pp. 138–149, 2016.
28. M. (Ehsan) Hoque, M. Courgeon, J.-C. Martin, B. Mutlu, and R. W. Picard, "Mach: My automated

conversation coach," Proc. 2013 ACM Int. Jt. Conf. Pervasive ubiquitous Comput. - UbiComp '13, p. 697, 2013.
29. M. Fung, Y. Jin, R. Zhao, and M. E. Hoque, "ROC Speak: Semi-Automated Personalized Feedback on Nonverbal Behavior from Recorded Videos," Proc. 17th Int. Conf. Ubiquitous Comput., 2015.
30. C. Correia, K. J. Lopez, K. E. Wroblewski, M. H. Scheetz, D. W. Kern, R. C. Chen, L. P. Schumm, W. Dale, M. K. McClintock, and J. M. Pinto, "Global sensory impairment in older adults in the United States," J. Am. Geriatr. Soc., vol. 64, no. 2, pp. 306–313, 2016.
31. J. T. Cacioppo and L. C. Hawkley, "Perceived social isolation and cognition," Trends Cogn. Sci., vol. 13, no. 10, pp. 447–454, 2009.
32. "Site Pal." [Online]. Available: www.sitepal.com.
33. G. Leshed, D. Perez, J. T. Hancock, D. Cosley, J. Birnholtz, S. Lee, P. L. McLeod, and G. Gay, "Visualizing real-time language-based feedback on teamwork behavior in computer-mediated groups," Proc. 27th Int. Conf. Hum. factors Comput. Syst. CHI 09, p. 537, 2009.
34. J. L. Hames, C. R. Hagan, and T. E. Joiner, "Interpersonal processes in depression.," Annu. Rev. Clin. Psychol., vol. 9, pp. 355–77, 2013.
35. C. Segrin, "Social skills deficits associated with depression," Clin. Psychol. Rev., vol. 20, no. 3, pp. 379–403, 2000.
36. M. Ali, D. Crasta, L. Jin, A. Baretto, J. Pachter, R. Rogge, and M. (Ehsan) Hoque, "LISSA- Live Interactive Social Skill Assistance," in Affective Computing and Intelligent Interaction (ACII), 2015 International Conference on, 2015, pp. 173–179.
37. P. Boersma and D. Weenink, "Praat: doing phonetics by computer." .
38. "SHORETM - Object and Face Recognition." [Online]. Available: http://www.iis.fraunhofer.de/en/ff/bsy/tech/bildanalyse/shore-gesichtsdetektion.html.
39. "Visage Technologies face tracking and analysis." [Online]. Available: http://visagetechnologies.com/.
40. An assessment of Interpersonal Competence, "Conversational Skills Rating Scale," 2007.
41. E. J. Finkel, P. W. Eastwick, and J. Matthews, "Speed-dating as an invaluable tool for studying romantic attraction: A methodological primer," Pers. Relatsh., vol. 14, no. 1, pp. 149–166, 2007.
42. D. Wendler, Improve your social skills. 2014.
43. "5 Body Language Tricks To Make Anyone Instantly Like You - Personality Development & English Lessons." .
44. W. T. Riley, P. Pilkonis, and D. Cella, "Application of the National Institutes of Health Patient-reported Outcome Measurement Information System (PROMIS) to mental health research," J. Ment. Health Policy Econ., vol. 14, no. 4, pp. 201–208, 2011.
45. K. A. Van Orden, K. C. Cukrowicz, T. K. Witte, and T. E. Joiner, "Thwarted belongingness and perceived burdensomeness: construct validity and psychometric properties of the Interpersonal Needs Questionnaire.," Psychol. Assess., vol. 24, no. 1, pp. 197–215, 2012.
46. A. Struchen, N. Clark, M. Sander, R. Mills, G. Evans, and D. Kurtz, "Relation of executive functioning and social communication measures to functional outcomes following traumatic brain injury.," NeuroRehabilitation, vol. 23, no. 2, p. 185, 2008.
47. P. Ekman and W. V Friesen, Facial Action Coding System: A Technique for the Measurement of Facial Movement. 1978.
48. T. Baltruˇ and P. Robinson, "OpenFace:an open source facial behavior analysis toolkit."
49. S. Du, Y. Tao, and A. M. Martinez, "Compound facial expressions of emotion," Proc. Natl. Acad. Sci., 2014.
50. Anderson, Keith, Elisabeth André, Tobias Baur, Sara Bernardini, Mathieu Chollet, Evi Chryssafidou, Ionut Damian et al. "The TARDIS framework: intelligent virtual agents for social coaching in job interviews." In Advances in computer entertainment, pp. 476-491. Springer, 2013.
51. Isaacowitz, D. M., Livingstone, K. M., & Castro, V. L. (2017). Aging and emotions: experience, regulation, and perception. Current opinion in psychology, 17, 79-83.
52. Hahn, E. A., et al. (2010). "Measuring social health in the patient-reported outcomes measurement information system (PROMIS): item bank development and testing." Qual Life Res 19(7): 1035-1044.
53. Gruber-Baldini, A. L., et al. (2017). "Validation of the PROMIS measures of self-efficacy for managing chronic conditions." Qual Life Res 26(7): 1915-1924.
54. L. E. Baum and G. R. Sell, "Growth functions for transformations on manifolds," Pac. /. Math., vol. 27, no. 2, pp. 211- 227, 1968. L. E. Baum, T. Petrie, G. Soules, and N. Weiss, "A maximization technique occurring in the statistical analysis of probabilistic functions of Markov chains," Ann. Math. Stat., vol. 41, no. 1, pp. 164-171, 1970.
55. J. Yamato, J. Ohya, K. Ishii, "Recognizing human action in time-sequential images using hidden markov model." In Computer Vision and Pattern Recognition, 1992. Proceedings CVPR'92. (pp. 379-385). IEEE.
56. Chung, P. C., & Liu, C. D. (2008). "A daily behavior enabled hidden Markov model for human behavior understanding. Pattern Recognition", 41(5), 1572-1580.
57. J. Corbin, A. Strauss, Grounded theory research: Procedures, canons and evaluative criteria. Zeitschrift für Soziologie 1990, 19(6), 418-427.
58. L. R. Rabiner, "A tutorial on hidden Markov models and selected applications in speech recognition". Proceedings of the IEEE 1989, 77(2), 257-286.

Supporting Spatial Skill Learning with Gesture-Based Embodied Design

Po-Tsung Chiu, Helen Wauck, Ziang Xiao, Yuqi Yao, Wai-Tat Fu
University of Illinois at Urbana-Champaign
Urbana, IL, USA
{ptchiu2, wauck2, zxiao5, yuqiyao2, wfu}@illinois.edu

ABSTRACT
Prior research has shown that spatial abilities are crucial for STEM achievement and attainment. The connection between the digital and physical worlds provided by embodied interaction has been shown to enhance performance and engagement in educational contexts. Spatial reasoning is a domain that lends itself naturally to embodied, physical interaction; however, there is little understanding of how embodied interaction could be incorporated into educational technology designed to train spatial reasoning skills. We propose several guidelines for gestural interaction design in spatial reasoning education games based on an empirical study with students at a local afterschool program using a custom-built computer game for training spatial skills. We present a series of gesture sets derived from an iterative design approach that are easy for children to acquire, show sufficient congruency to specific spatial operations, and enable robust recognition from the system. We also compared children's behaviors when playing the game with our gestural interface and a traditional mouse-based interface and found that children take more time but fewer steps to complete game levels when using gestures.

Author Keywords
Embodied Learning; Embodied Cognition; Gestural Interaction; Spatial Reasoning; STEM Education; Design Guidelines.

INTRODUCTION
There has been a rising recognition that training one's spatial reasoning skills at an early age is a key to success in STEM disciplines [16]. They are believed to be malleable and can be transferred to different tasks with spatially enriched education [15]. Embodied learning, on the other hand, has become a popular topic as researchers believe that it could enhance the effectiveness and engagement of learning [10] by leveraging the embodied nature of human cognition to help enact abstract knowledge and concepts through body activity. Together, [5] presented evidence showing that the relationship between body, action, and space help shape our spatial cognition and identified the elements of interaction in embodied systems that engage spatial cognition. This opens up the opportunity to investigate widely adopted embodiment techniques for spatial ability training in educational interventions.

We explored this direction in the present work by incorporating human gestures with Leap Motion sensors[1] into a video game designed specifically for training children's spatial reasoning skills. We used Leap Motion sensors since they are portable, affordable, and accurate on small-scale movements. The video game was a construction game where players build items by attaching the virtual constituent parts together, tapping into several categories of spatial skills like *mental rotation* [12]. On top of that, we followed the theoretical principle of gestural congruency [14] to map the gesture control scheme for manipulating virtual objects to humans' cognitive framework underlying these manipulations in the real world. We included a user study where nineteen participants were recruited from an afterschool program in the Midwestern US to try out our construction game with both gesture and mouse control schemes, during which we refined the gesture control scheme iteratively from feedback and observations in gameplay.

When designing gesture-based interfaces, it is important to distinguish between whether gestures are used as controllers, by which interface objects are manipulated, and whether gestures can help students learn. This distinction is important because as controllers, gestures are likely not as good as other input devices, such as the mouse, since current gesture sensing technologies cannot provide the level of precision of control as these traditional devices. Our goal is to understand how gestures can help students learn spatial skills, assuming that sensorimotor experiences during the learning process can provide a strong foundation for spatial skills as they are integrated into the cognitive operations of spatial reasoning, providing a stronger perceptual-motor grounding of these operations [2].

Our evaluation is therefore more focused on the extent to which we find evidence that the gesture-based interfaces encourage learning, and how they help engage students during the game. Our in-game behavior data suggested that gestures may encourage more deliberation when performing spatial

IUI'18, March 7–11, 2018, Tokyo, Japan

DOI: https://doi.org/10.1145/3172944.3172994

[1] Leap Motion, Inc. 2017 https://www.leapmotion.com

Game Feature	*Spatial Operation*
Object Alignment	Spatial Visualization
Object Rotation	Physical Rotation, Mental Rotation
Location Matching	2D to 3D Projection, Shape Matching

Table 1. The mapping of construction game features designed and specific spatial operations.

operations, since participants performed fewer rotations when using gestures while completing a similar number of part attachment tasks. The post-game survey results also suggest that gestures were as engaging as mouse control, which aligns with the notion that physical engagement in embodied interaction can have conceptual development benefits in education [10].

RELATED WORK

Researchers have previously applied embodied interaction to systems in the educational context based on the theory of grounded cognition and attempted to enhance the effectiveness of learning conceptual knowledge. Embodied interaction powered with diverse technologies including interfaces designed for gestural input involves more of our senses than traditional interfaces like mouse and keyboard [14]. Lindgren and Moshell used MR (mixed reality) to experiment with adopting body-based metaphors into the process of learning conceptual domain knowledge, where the body movements of students were represented by the behavior of virtual asteroid in a planetary astronomy simulation [11]. They found that students created more dynamic mental models to understand the core concept of the content and proposed that MR could physically engage their learning of a domain. Zhang et al. investigated the effect of five interaction modalities, including gesture interaction, on solving spatio-visual problems, and suggested that physical expressions would affect the quality of the solutions to such problems [19]. Also, [4] incorporated a virtual reality headset and tangible interface in a spatial puzzle-solving game to study perspective taking ability, a subskill of spatial cognition. To further untangle the relationship between embodiment and learning, a hierarchical design framework for embodied learning games was proposed in [13]. However, to the best of our knowledge, no one has yet studied how different factors in gesture design could tap into the cognitive operations for spatial reasoning skills.

CONSTRUCTION GAME

The goal of our construction game focused on understanding players' spatial skills with manipulating virtual objects, in particular their abilities of *mental rotation* and *projection*. The primary game mechanic was to build a set of target objects starting with one "base" part and attaching additional parts one by one. We derived our game mechanics from a prior work of Wauck et al. [17] to shape the relations between different game features and specific spatial operations as summarized in Table 1. For example, determining a part's correct attachment location mapped to *2D-to-3D projection* and *shape matching*, while determining its correct orientation mapped to *physical* and *mental rotation*.

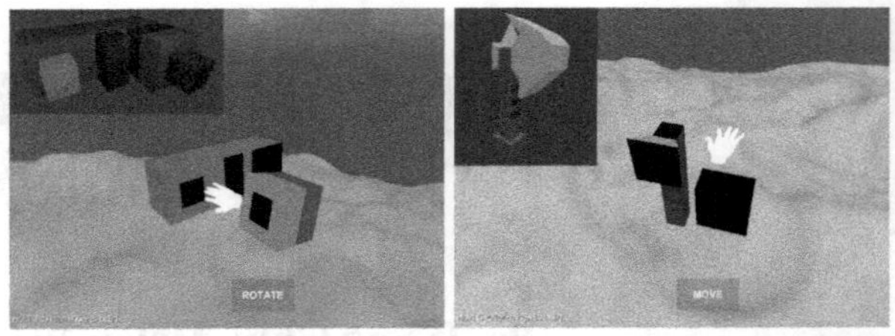

Figure 1. Left: *Easy* level. Right: *Sledgehammer* level. The 2D images on the upper left corners show what the 3D objects would look like when all parts are attached correctly. Rotate and Move modes indicate the spatial operation the player can perform at the moment.

To complete each level, players needed to attach all parts at correct locations and with correct orientations. However, they would not need to decide which part to control, as the parts would appear in a predefined order. The game's interface, as shown in Figure 1, displayed a 2D picture of the complete target object in the upper left corner to guide the player's construction. We designed 4 game levels, each with slightly different training focuses:

- The *Tutorial* level (3 parts) contained basic part shapes, all of the same color, focusing players' attention on distinguishing different shapes to keep things simple. It served as a tutorial level for learning about the game's control.
- The *Easy* level (4 parts) used only cuboids and cubes for part shapes, but varied their colors, forcing players to pay attention to the picture of the completed target object in the upper left corner of the screen when building.
- The *Rocket Boots* level (6 parts) used more complex shapes. The player needed to observe the 2D picture carefully to build the object, as some parts looked like they could be attached at multiple positions on the base part.
- The *Sledgehammer* level (11 parts) was also considerably more challenging than the *Tutorial* and *Easy* levels. All parts except one had the same color. Some parts had similar shapes, as some were occluded by other parts in the 2D picture. To complete this level, players would need to notice subtle details and reason carefully about how the 3D parts matched the picture.

GESTURE DESIGN

Our gesture design focused on two specific operations – *Movement* and *Rotation* – for moving and rotating parts in the game. Initially, we investigated the example in [18] prototyped with swipe gestures of Leap Motion API for the *Rotation* gesture. However, a crucial pitfall of this example we found was the difficulty in distinguishing between the actual swipe gesture and the following movement of the hand returning back to its initial position. This natural inclination to return the hand to its initial position confused the gesture recognition system and caused unintended rotations in game to the frustration of players. Also, the gesture used in the prototype discretized the rotation process, where players would swipe in either of the 6 directions (left/right, up/down, or forward/backward) to rotate the subject in 90 degree increments in the direction of the swipe. This mitigated the fact that rotation in the real world is continuous and the ability to control with continuous visual flow could benefit spatial learning [8]. We present three versions of our gesture control design, V1, V2, and V3, in the following paragraphs. The first three versions were tested with 2 participants each, and we iterated the development of the new version based on feedback received from the post-game survey and from observation during gameplay.

Version 1

The major difference between this version and the aforementioned prototype was *Rotation*. We addressed the two drawbacks of the prototype by changing the scheme based on the following idea. Using hands to build things in the real world, such as a LEGO set, we can manipulate the pieces freely and rotate them in any direction. We redesigned *Rotation* to support such freedom by binding player's hand angle to that of the piece being manipulated. Both *Movement* and *Rotation* would be activated as the player formed a closed fist, and deactivated when the hand opened near a piece in the game. A piece would return to one of the 6 possible orientations parallel to the x, y, and z axes when not rotating. This embodied the player's hand more holistically as the virtual object, in contrast with swiping gestures in the previous prototype.

Version 2

During the gameplay session of V1, the participants had a lot of trouble getting Leap Motion to accurately distinguish between moving, rotation, and releasing from rotation or movement. Particularly frustrating for players were situations in which they had the part rotated properly, but then as they tried to move the part to the correct position, the game detected a rotation operation rather than movement, and as a result, the part became incorrectly rotated. This led us to split moving and rotation into two modes (Figure 1) for the player to switch between by hitting the space key. Both *Movement* and *Rotation* were the same as in V1, but our goal was that the player would be able to perform both operations with confidence.

Version 3

While V2 avoided the confusion encountered between moving and rotation, Leap Motion could not track the hand's orientation in a robust way. We attributed this problem to the hurdle for Leap Motion's depth camera to distinguish different orientations of a closed fist. Hence, rather than turning to other gesture sensing devices, we used a different hand position in V3, namely the opposite hand posture – palm flat and open – to enable moving and rotation. The movement of the open palm would map to the position of the piece in control when in moving mode. When the player tilted their hand in one direction (x, y, or z) as shown in Figure 2, the object would begin rotating in that direction until the player's hand closed back into a fist.

Guidelines

While embodied activities have the potential to enhance learning, we believe that they need to be designed adaptively to fit with the conceptual knowledge we expect the participant to learn. Drawing upon our experience in the user study, we propose the following design guidelines for gestural control

Figure 2. Final *Rotation* gestures. Left to right: *Rotation x, y, and z*.

in spatial skill training games for children: (a) using separate modes for different spatial operations, (b) maintaining gestural congruency to spatial concepts, and (c) using static hand posture for each spatial operation.

First, defining a clear picture of the correspondence between game modes and the spatial operations in Table 1 could help players concentrate on reasoning about one operation at a time, which could reduce cognitive load and frustration. Second, making sure that the gesture performed is congruent to a spatial concept aids the construction of that particular concept and strengthens the action-concept link [10] that can improve learning. We formulated the third guideline based on observations of how the children performed gestures during the study. By using a fixed, static hand posture for each spatial operation, players can focus more on the mapping between large, simple hand movements and the virtual objects being manipulated, while also reducing system errors with camera-based gesture recognition systems like Leap Motion and enabling a consistent (or at least less frustrating) user experience. These guidelines can be used by game designers to develop more effective adaptive gesture sets for spatial games, and by educators seeking to engage participants in higher-order thought processes to acquire new knowledge.

METHOD

The goals of our study were to understand how the gestures designed help and engage children to reason and learn in spatial tasks. We also compared the players' in-game behavior between 1) different versions of the gesture design, 2) the gestural interface and the mouse-based interface. We conducted the study at an afterschool program center and recruited 19 participants through the program director to participate in a 50-minute study session. Their ages ranged from 8 to 12 (median=10, mean=9.84) with 8 of them being female.

Procedure

The participants spent 20 minutes playing each version of the game (gesture versus mouse control) – 40 minutes in total. After playing, they filled out a post-game survey that asked them to indicate their age and gender and rate how easy, fun, frustrating, and tiring they thought each version of the game was and why. We counterbalanced the gameplay order of the gesture and mouse-controlled version. For each control scheme, participants played the *Tutorial* level followed by the *Easy* level, and then were assigned to play one of the more challenging levels: *Rocket Boots* or *Sledgehammer*. If the participant was assigned to play the *Rocket Boots* level for the first control scheme they tried, then they were assigned to play the *Sledgehammer* level for the second control scheme, and vice versa. We playtested gesture versions V1 through

V3 with 2 participants each in the first three sessions and all participants after played with V3, the final version.

In-Game Behavior Metrics

Our primary measures of interest were *completion time*, *number of rotations*, and *number of wrong attachments* in each level since they were related to the difficulty of the tasks and player impulsiveness. We also looked at some other metrics from the data collected, such as the *number of rotations per successful attachment* (the number of rotations divided by number of successful attachment attempts) and the *average time spent between each rotation* (the time taken to finish divided by number of rotations). These two metrics gave us a sense of how children reason when trying to determine the correct spatial relations of the parts, or the case where they perform the rotation operations directly and without bothering to mentally visualize the rotation first.

RESULTS

There were 15 participants that played at least 2 levels with both the mouse-based and gestural V3 interfaces. The other 4 quit before the end of the study due to frustration or because their parents picked them up early from the afterschool program. In addition, we excluded the behavior data from the *Tutorial* level of the game as we provided verbal assistance to the children as they learned how to play the game and demonstrated different gestures for them in this level.

In-Game Behavior Analysis

First, we analyzed differences in behavior between the gesture and mouse control. We found a significant difference in the number of rotations per successful attachment under a repeated measures t-test; players needed fewer rotations to correctly align parts when playing with gestures than when playing with mouse control ($t(27.821) = 2.560$, $p = .016$). Therefore, participants may be performing more redundant rotations with the mouse interface, suggesting that they are using the epistemic mode of immediate "doing" rather than mediated "thinking" [1] when tackling the task. This difference is also consistent with the results that while the number of successful attachments were fairly close for both interfaces in the *Easy* level (mouse-based: mean=4.00, gesture: mean=3.67) and *Rocket Boots* level (mouse-based: mean=5.11, gesture: mean=5.33), participants performed more rotations with the mouse-based interface in the *Easy* level (1.63 times more) and the *Rocket Boots* level (1.77 times more). Interestingly, the only participant who completed the *Sledgehammer* level with gesture controls used only 22 rotations, far fewer than the number of rotations used by those who completed the level using the mouse-based controls (mean=113.2, max=187, min=53). One possible explanation for these findings is that the mouse-based and gestural interfaces may guide the participants to play the game in different ways. Borrowing the analogy from Kahneman's theory of effortless intuition and deliberate reasoning [9], the mouse-based interface could be promoting finding a rapid and heuristic path to the solution, while the gestural interface may be slower yet more accurate and encourage deliberation. It is important to note that the latter over time can become more effortless and rapid [6,7]. In addition, we found that participants performed less rotations along the y axis when using the gestural interface across all game levels, possibly due to the ergonomic limitations of the required open hand posture.

Next, we compared behavior across different versions of the gesture control scheme. Of the four participants using gestural interface V1 or V2, only one completed the *Easy* level, and none of them completed the more challenging *Rocket Boots* or *Sledgehammer* level. The participants using V3 performed better; 50% completed the *Easy* level, and 30% completed the more challenging levels. Also, the number of rotations per successful attachment for V3 (mean=4.91) was less than with the first two versions (mean=9.50). This indicated that V3 facilitated better performance and was easier for the participant to learn to use.

SURVEY

Not surprisingly, most participants reported that the mouse control was easier to use, less frustrating ("*Something didn't work [using gesture]*"), and less tiring ("*Need to move hands a lot [using gestures]*" or "*Arms wouldn't get tired [using the mouse]*"). But when asked how fun they thought using the gestural interface was, participants responded with statements like "*You have lots of fun and more experiments*", "*You get to learn and have fun doing it*", or simply "*Liked to move my hand*", "*My hand is in the game*", etc., showing participants' engagement with the game and using gestures. In addition, some participants (n=4) reported that the gestural interface was either easier to use or more preferable to play with, particularly V3. Even though the participants' familiarity with mouse control may give them an advantage in performance or learnability with our mouse control scheme, the additional learnability difficulties introduced by our gesture control scheme could potentially enhance recall and transfer during the learning process, based on the theory of desirable difficulties [3].

CONCLUSION

In this study, we discussed the design process of our gesture-based spatial learning game, as well as results that supported the notion that gestures can help students learn spatial skills. Although the evaluation involved a limited number of students, the results were in general supportive of the notion that the current design approach is useful for generating embodied games for training spatial skills for children. We expect that a large scale user study with more participants and run for a longer period of time will provide more insights into the details of how these gesture sets can be designed to enhance learning.

ACKNOWLEDGMENTS

This work was partially funded by the Strategic Instructional Innovations Program (SIIP) at College of Engineering of the University of Illinois at Urbana-Champaign and by the NSF grants SES-1419297 and IIS-1441563. We thank Yuan Yao for ideation, and all staff at the Urbana Neighborhood Connections Center for their help with the user study.

REFERENCES

1. Dor Abrahamson and Robb Lindgren. 2014. *The Cambridge handbook of the learning sciences* (2nd ed.). Cambridge University Press, Cambridge, UK, Chapter Embodiment and embodied design.
2. Lawrence W. Barsalou. 2010. Grounded Cognition: Past, Present, and Future. *Topics in Cognitive Science* 2, 4 (2010), 716–724.
3. E. L. Bjork and R. A. Bjork. 2011. *Psychology and the real world: Essays illustrating fundamental contributions to society*. Worth Publishers, New York, NY, USA, Chapter Making things hard on yourself, but in a good way: Creating desirable difficulties to enhance learning, 56–64.
4. Jack Shen-Kuen Chang. 2017. The Design and Evaluation of Embodied Interfaces for Supporting Spatial Ability. In *Proceedings of the Eleventh International Conference on Tangible, Embedded, and Embodied Interaction (TEI '17)*. ACM, New York, NY, USA, 681–684. DOI: http://dx.doi.org/10.1145/3024969.3025033
5. P. G. Clifton, J. S.-K. Chang, G. Yeboah, A. Doucette, S. Chandrasekharan, M. Nitsche, T. Welsh, and A Mazalek. 2016. Design of embodied interfaces for engaging spatial cognition. *Cognitive Research* 1, 24 (2016). DOI: http://dx.doi.org/10.1186/s41235-016-0032-5
6. Hubert L. Dreyfus and Stuart E. Dreyfus. 1999. The Challenge of Merleau-Ponty's Phenomenology of Embodiment for Cognitive Science. In *Perspectives on Embodiment: The Intersections of Nature and Culture*, Gail Weiss and Honi Fern Haber (Eds.). Routledge, 103–120.
7. Efraim Fischbein. 1987. *Intuition in Science and Mathematics: An Educational Approach*. Springer, Dordrecht, Holland.
8. Corinne Holmes, Steven A. Marchette, and Nora Newcombe. 2017. Multiple Views of Space: Continuous Visual Flow Enhances Small-Scale Spatial Learning. (02 2017).
9. Daniel Kahneman. Maps of bounded rationality: A perspective on intuitive judgment and choice. (????).
10. Robb Lindgren and Mina Johnson-Glenberg. 2013. Emboldened by Embodiment. *Educational Researcher* 42, 8 (2013), 445–452. DOI: http://dx.doi.org/10.3102/0013189X13511661
11. Robb Lindgren and J. Michael Moshell. 2011. Supporting Children's Learning with Body-based Metaphors in a Mixed Reality Environment. In *Proceedings of the 10th International Conference on Interaction Design and Children (IDC '11)*. ACM, New York, NY, USA, 177–180. DOI: http://dx.doi.org/10.1145/1999030.1999055
12. Marcia C. Linn and Anne C. Petersen. 1985. Emergence and Characterization of Sex Differences in Spatial Ability: A Meta-Analysis. *Child Development* 56, 6 (1985), 1479–1498. http://www.jstor.org/stable/1130467
13. Edward F. Melcer and Katherine Isbister. 2016. Bridging the Physical Divide: A Design Framework for Embodied Learning Games and Simulations. In *Proceedings of the 2016 CHI Conference Extended Abstracts on Human Factors in Computing Systems (CHI EA '16)*. ACM, New York, NY, USA, 2225–2233.
14. Ayelet Segal. 2011. *Do Gestural Interfaces Promote Thinking? Embodied Interaction: Congruent Gestures and Direct Touch Promote Performance in Math.* Ph.D. Dissertation. Columbia University. https://doi.org/10.7916/D8DR32GK
15. David Uttal, Nathaniel Meadow, Elizabeth Tipton, Linda Liu Hand, Alison R Alden, Christopher Warren, and Nora Newcombe. 2012b. The Malleability of Spatial Skills: A Meta-Analysis of Training Studies. 139 (06 2012).
16. David H. Uttal, Cheryl A. Cohen, Ken Forbus, Dedre Gentner, Mary Hegarty, Madeleine Keehner, Ken Koedinger, Nora Newcombe, Kay Ramey, and Uri Wilenski. 2012a. Spatial Thinking and STEM Education: When, Why, and How?
17. Helen Wauck, Ziang Xiao, Po-Tsung Chiu, and Wai-Tat Fu. 2017. Untangling the Relationship Between Spatial Skills, Game Features, and Gender in a Video Game. In *Proceedings of the 22Nd International Conference on Intelligent User Interfaces (IUI '17)*. ACM, New York, NY, USA, 125–136. DOI: http://dx.doi.org/10.1145/3025171.3025225
18. Yuan Yao, Po-Tsung Chiu, and Wai-Tat Fu. 2017. A Gestural Interface for Practicing Children's Spatial Skills. In *Proceedings of the 22Nd International Conference on Intelligent User Interfaces Companion (IUI '17 Companion)*. ACM, New York, NY, USA, 43–47. DOI: http://dx.doi.org/10.1145/3030024.3038265
19. Ting Zhang, Yu-Ting Li, and Juan P. Wachs. 2016. The Effect of Embodied Interaction in Visual-Spatial Navigation. *ACM Trans. Interact. Intell. Syst.* 7, 1, Article 3 (Dec. 2016), 36 pages. DOI: http://dx.doi.org/10.1145/2953887

Bio-adaptive Social VR to Evoke Affective Interdependence - DYNECOM

Mikko Salminen; Simo Järvelä
Aalto University School of Business
Helsinki, Finland
mikko.salminen@aalto.fi; simo.jarvela2@aalto.fi

Antti Ruonala; Janne Timonen
Helsinki Institute for Information Technology, University of Helsinki
Helsinki, Finland
antti.ruonala@aalto.fi; janne.timonen@cs.helsinki.fi

Kristiina Mannermaa
Aalto University School of Business
Helsinki, Finland
kristiina.mannermaa@aalto.fi

Niklas Ravaja
Faculty of Medicine, University of Helsinki; Aalto University School of Business
Helsinki, Finland
niklas.ravaja@helsinki.fi

Giulio Jacucci
Helsinki Institute for Information Technology, University of Helsinki
Helsinki, Finland
giulio.jacucci@helsinki.fi

ABSTRACT

The effects of bio-adaptation-based visual cues in conveying affective information was studied while conducting social meditation in a virtual reality (VR) environment. In a laboratory study, 22 dyads practiced a short duration, modified version of empathy-evoking compassion meditation. The immersive VR provided electroencephalography (EEG) -based real-time visual feedback, as changing color, on the user's brain activation; the breathing rate of the users was visualized as a movement cue. In addition, the synchronization of the feedback signals between the users was also visualized. Initial results suggest that the perceived affective interdependence, a component of social presence, was increased when both of the bio-adaptive visual feedbacks were presented to the users, compared to when there was no visual feedback. Also, the EEG-based visual feedback led to higher affective interdependence than the respiration based visual feedback. The findings suggest that affective contagion may occur by mediated adaptive cues that are based on physiological signals.

IUI'18, March 7–11, 2018, Tokyo, Japan

ACM ISBN 978-1-4503-4945-1/18/03…$15.00
https://doi.org/10.1145/3172944.3172991

Author Keywords
Neurofeedback; bio-feedback; meditation; empathy; affective contagion; virtual reality.

INTRODUCTION

Recent advances in virtual reality (VR) technology and in physiological sensors for quantified-self applications have brought these technologies available to the wider audience. Consumer grade VR sets and EEG sets are already on the market and have thus opened new possibilities to develop applications for social interaction, wellbeing, e-health, and cyber-therapy. It is thus suggested that research is needed on the new possibilities of combining VR with bio-adaptive technologies.

The topic of the current study is to examine the possibilities that bio-adaptive social VR technologies have in conveying and inducing affective states from one user to the other. Emotions serve important functions during social interaction; emotional expressions are social information that help to understand and solve ambiguous social situations, in addition, own felt emotions can help this sense-making since emotions include inferences about the existing situation [24]. Given that new and emerging technologies provide novel ways to extract, mediate, and represent emotional information, it is crucial to study how these types of information are contagious, how they are perceived and interpreted, and how they affect the behaviour of the perceiver. To examine these themes, we developed a social bio-adaptive VR environment that could be used in simplified empathy exercises. The bio-feedback functionality that encourages the users to reach a state of physiological synchrony is suggested to enhance the conducting of the empathy exercises. We suggest that a task where the users pursue physiological synchronization in the VR also evokes affective interdependence, which enables empathy.

Affective interdependence

Affective interdependence is a sub-component of social presence, and it denotes the effect that the interaction partner's affective and attitudinal state have on one's own affective and attitudinal state, and vice versa [13]. Emotions are a member of the larger family of affective processes, and can be defined as biologically based action dispositions which have an important role in determining behaviour [10, 18]. Emotions consist of three reactive systems: 1) expressive and evaluative language; 2) physiological response; and 3) behavioural response [18]. Emotional contagion is a central process by which emotions and other affective states become social [2]. The affective or emotional contagion may occur by spontaneous mimicry of others; by consciously occurring social comparison; by interpreting the other's emotions (thus considering emotions as information); or by empathy [7].

Empathy, on the other hand, is a process where the perception or imagination of the other's emotional state leads one to obtain a similar affective state, or merging of emotions or affective states with the other occurs [6, 8].

Empathy typically leads to positive outcomes, such as increased willingness to help [4]. As a psychophysiological index, frontal asymmetry of the electroencephalography (EEG), calculated as the relative difference in the activations of the frontal right and left hemispheres [1] has been utilized in previous studies on affective processes and empathy [12, 15, 5; but for sadness-related empathy, see also: 23].

Figure 1. Overview of the DYNECOM VR setting. The two illuminated statues represent the users. Color of the statues and the halos represent the empathy-related EEG frontal asymmetry.

Bio-adaptation as an index of affective state

Use of emoticons is probably the simplest form of adding emotional information to the mediated communication, but it requires actions from the users. Another approach is to automatically detect the affective state of the user (by e.g. psychophysiological measurements) and to convey this information by some type of adaptive visualizations. This approach has been studied widely in the field of affective computing [e.g., 21].

There are already some VR environments targeted for meditative exercises that are reactive to the user's psychophysiological signals, i.e. that are bio-adaptive. For example, Virtual Meditative Walk is adaptive to the user's galvanic skin response [9], and Meditation Chamber utilizes also respiration rate and blood volume pulse [20]. RelaWorld [16, 17] is one of the few bio-adaptive, immersive, VR environments that utilize the EEG, in the context of focused attention meditation. There are already some neuro-feedback brain-computer interfaces that are targeted to support emotional control [e.g., 3]. However, to the best of our knowledge, there are no previous immersive, bio- or neuro-adaptive VR environments that would be designed for the practice of empathy evoking, compassion meditation, or related exercises.

Current experiment

In the bio-adaptive VR environment presented in this paper, a novel way to extract, visualize, and mediate affective information was studied. The DYNECOM (Dyadic Neuro COMpassion) VR, designed by brainstorming between professionals in VR design and research, is a platform for inducing physiological synchronization between two or more users, with the goal to increase empathy. In the current implementation, the context is an empathy evoking exercise, bearing close resemblance to currently popular compassion meditation [e.g., 14].

Figure 2. Visual feedback of the respiration rate. Left: outbreath not initialized; middle: two tiles illuminated visualizing travelling outbreath; right: colliding tiles visualizing synchronization of the outbreaths.

DYNECOM VR

Hardware and software

The DYNECOM VR needed four computers for the current experiment: there was a pc for both of the users to run the VR (with Oculus Rift headset attached) and another pc for both users to control the amplifier (a Brain Products QuickAmp for each participant) that recorded the psychophysiological data. The recorded psychophysiological data was streamed from the BrainVision Recorder software to OpenViBE (http://openvibe.inria.fr/) for processing and calculating the required indices for the adaptations; the calculated values were further streamed to Unity-3D (https://Unity3d.com) based program used for networking and visualizations.

Design

In the DYNECOM VR the users are represented by statue-like avatars that are seated in a circle with four other statues (Fig. 1). The statues are surrounded by a forest environment and there is a soothing audio track (pink noise) that resembles the sound of wind in the leaves. The system allows no exploratory movement in the environment in the current version, and focus is directed fully to the empathy evoking exercise. The two statues, representing the users, are connected with a bridge, and a ring-like aura is reflected around the active statues. These two visual elements were included for the purpose of bio-feedback visualization.

The respiration of the users was visualized as a movement in both, the pulsating of the aura and the gradual illumination of the tiles on the bridge connecting the users (Fig. 2). The synchronization of the out-breaths of the users was visualized by colliding tiles at the middle of the connecting bridge, with an evoked highlight.

The frontal asymmetry of the users was visualized as a changing colour in three visual elements of the environment: the bridge tiles, bars at the sides, and the aura (Fig. 1). The colour representing the approach motivation related frontal asymmetry varied from green (withdrawal motivation), to yellow, orange, red, and pink (approach motivation). A glowing effect on the side bars of the bridge was shown when the users' frontal asymmetries were synchronized.

Adaptivity of the system

The values from the psychophysiological signals that controlled the visualizations were calculated using algorithms that adapted for each participant during each of the experimental conditions. The system determined and adapted the range of values for each individual separately in each condition. A 9-second moving average of the frontal asymmetry was used in the calculating the colour of the feedback visualization, using the formula ln(F4) – ln(F3) for the 8-13 Hz alpha band, as suggested by [1], since in the current setting approach motivation, rather than withdrawal motivation –related empathy was encouraged [e.g., 23; see also, 19]. A common reference montage was used. Due to the adaptive nature of the system, the synchronization between the two user's EEG frontal asymmetry levels was determined on their percentage levels, and not on the absolute values of their frontal asymmetries. This constantly adaptive feature of the feedback visualizations was selected since it handled well spiking outlier values, and it was found to be responsive and functional for most test users when pilot testing the system prior the actual data collection.

USER STUDY

A user study was designed to test the effects that two different bio-feedbacks, which encourage the users to reach a synchronized state, have on perceived affective interdependence. The working hypothesis was that the bio-feedbacks would increase physiological synchronization between the two users of the DYNECOM VR and this would lead to a subjective perception of interdependence. Given that the users are instructed to evoke a sense of empathy towards the other during the experiment conditions, it is suggested that the bio-feedbacks lead specifically to affective interdependence.

Participants

The participants were 22 dyads; of which 21 were female-female dyads, and one was a male-female dyad. We intend to collect more data and aim to recruit male-male dyads to balance the gender distribution. In the current sample the mean age was 27 years and all the participants were right-handed. The participants received two movie tickets as compensation. Written consent was obtained from all of the participants.

Procedure

Upon arrival to the laboratory, the electrodes (six EEG electrodes: F3, F4, C3, C4, P3, P4; respiration belt) were attached to the participants; the impedances were kept below 5 kΩ. Next, the participants were provided with necessary instructions on the functionality of the DYNECOM VR environment. In the experiment there were eight conditions, each consisting of a two-minute baseline measurement session (to obtain baselines for the studied physiological signals), a 6,5-minute meditation session, and answering to a self-report questionnaire. The eight conditions were presented in randomized order to minimize habituation or learning effects, and they were combinations of the sociality of the meditation (2 levels: solo, dyadic) X bio-adaptation type (4 levels: no feedback, respiration based feedback, EEG based feedback, both respiration and EEG based feedbacks). The task of the users was to evoke empathic, warm, and compassionate feelings directed to the avatar statue that represented their partner. The information provided by the bio-feedback was encouraged to be used in the exercise, with the goal to establish high experienced empathy.

Measure

Perceived affective interdependence was assessed after each experimental condition as self-reports, using a corresponding subscale from the Networked Minds Social

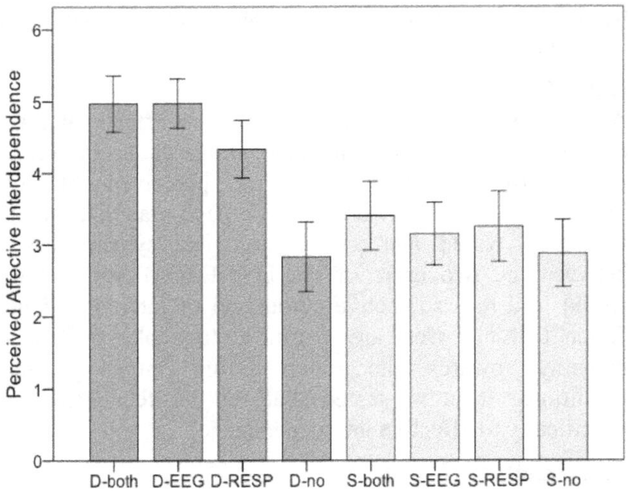

Figure 3. Perceived affective interdependence for different experiment conditions. D = dyadic meditation; S = solo meditation; both = both feedbacks (RESP & EEG) on; EEG = only EEG feedback on; RESP = only respiration feedback on; no = no bio-feedback. Error bars denote 95% confidence intervals.

Presence Measure [13]. The subscale consists of six items, rated with a scale from 1 (fully disagree) to 7 (fully agree). Exemplary items include: "I was sometimes influenced by my partner's moods", and "My feelings influenced the mood of our interaction". The internal consistency of the subscale was $\alpha = .973$ in the current sample.

RESULTS

The analyses are confined to the dyadic meditation conditions, since there was no visual feedback of the other user's bio-signals in the solo conditions. Within the dyadic conditions, the condition where both the feedbacks were on evoked higher affective interdependence than the condition where there were no adaptations, $t(1, 43) = 4.39$, $p < .001$; the same was also true for the EEG feedback, $t(1, 43) = 4.80$, $p < .001$, and the respiration feedback conditions, $t(1, 43) = 4.52$, $p < .001$. In addition, the EEG feedback condition evoked higher affective interdependence than the respiration feedback condition, $t(1,43) = 3.695$, $p = .001$ (Fig. 3).

DISCUSSION

We have presented an initial version of an immersive VR environment that adapts to the user's breathing rate and brain electrical activity. The results suggest that each of the bio-adaptive feedback visualizations (EEG-based, respiration-based, or both) led to higher perceived affective interdependence between the users than a corresponding condition without any bio-feedbacks. These findings show that emotional or affective contagion may occur also via bio-adaptive feedback visualizations in a VR environment, where the users are represented as avatars.

In addition, it was observed that the EEG-based visual feedback evoked higher affective interdependence than the respiration-based visual feedback. Thus, the visualization of the partner's EEG-based frontal asymmetry had a more pronounced effect to the perception that the user had of the partner's effect to one's own affective state. And similarly, the users considered their own visualized EEG-based frontal asymmetry to have a stronger effect to their partner's affective state, than the respiration-based visualization. That is, the EEG-feedback was possibly considered as a stronger signal of one's own and of the partner's affective state. It is possible, that the users considered the EEG-based feedback to reflect a more informative, or reliable index of the affective state of the other, and also of oneself.

Limitations of the current study include, for example, the high number of meditation conditions presented for each participant, due to the employed within-subjects design. This may have led to fatigue in the participants, and thus to diminished physiological responses. In addition, the controlling for eye-movement related artefacts by using EOG (electro-oculogram) electrodes is difficult with a head-mounted display and in future studies an integrated eye-movement camera could be employed.

Next, we will focus to analyse relationships between the collected physiological data and self-reported affective interdependence, to study whether there would be effects also on other frequency bands of the EEG, for example. In future versions of the DYNECOM VR system the adaptive algorithms could be refined to include a learning scheme to, for example, gradually increase the resting state frontal asymmetry such that it would have a beneficial effect to the user's prevailing mood [e.g., 12, 22]. Another interesting research question would be to study how sham visual feedback on user's physiological parameters could be used to manipulate his or her actual physiological and subjectively reported state.

ACKNOWLEDGEMENTS

The work was supported by The Academy of Finland (project EMOEMP: 305576 & 305577).

REFERENCES

1. John J. B. Allen, James A. Coan, and Maria Nazarian. 2004. Issues and assumptions on the road from raw signals to metrics of frontal EEG asymmetry in emotion. *Biol. Psych.* 67, 1: 183-218.
2. Sigal G. Barsade and Donald E. Gibson. 2007. Why does affect matter in organizations? *Acad. Manag. Perspect.* 21, 1: 36–59.
3. Marc Cavazza, Fred Charles, Gabor Aranyi, Julie Porteous, Stephen W. Golroy, et al. 2014. Towards emotional regulation through neurofeedback. *Proceedings of the 5th Augmented Human International Conference*. ACM Press, New York, NY, USA, Article No. 42.

4. Jay S. Coke, Daniel C. Batson, and Katherine McDavis. 1978. Empathic mediation of helping: A two-stage model. *J. Pers. Soc. Psych.* 36, 7: 752-766.
5. Richard J. Davidson. 2004. What does the prefrontal cortex "do" in affect: perspectives on the frontal EEG asymmetry research. *Biol. Psychol.* 67, 1: 219-234.
6. Frederique De Vignemont and Tania Singer. 2006. The empathic brain: how, when and why? *Trend. Cogn. Sci.* 10, 10: 435–441.
7. Hillary Anger Elfenbein. 2014. The many faces of emotional contagion. *Org. Psych. Rev.* 4, 4: 326-362.
8. Jennifer Edson Escalas and Barbara B. Stern. 2003. Sympathy and empathy: Emotional responses to advertising dramas. *J. Consum. Res.* 29, 4: 566-578.
9. Diane Gromala, Xin Tong, Amber Choo, Mehdi Karamnejad, and Chris D. Shaw. 2015. The Virtual Meditative Walk: Virtual Reality Therapy for Chronic Pain Management. *Proceedings of the 33rd Annual ACM Conference on Human Factors in Computing Systems* (2015), 521–524. http://dx.doi.org/10.1145/2702123.2702344
10. James J. Gross and Ross A. Thompson, R. A. 2007. Emotion Regulation: Conceptual Foundations. In J. J. Gross (Ed.), *Handbook of emotion regulation* (pp. 3-24). New York: Guilford Press.
11. Eddie Harmon-Jones. 2003. Clarifying the emotive functions of asymmetrical frontal cortical activity. *Psychophys.* 40, 6: 838-848.
12. Eddie Harmon-Jones and John J. B. Allen. 1997. Behavioral activation sensitivity and resting frontal EEG asymmetry: Covariation of putative indicators related to risk for mood disorders. *J. Abn. Psych.* 106, 1: 159-163.
13. Chad Harms and Frank Biocca. 2004. Internal consistency and reliability of the networked minds social presence measure. In M. Alcaniz & B. Rey (Eds.), *Seventh Annual International Workshop: Presence 2004*. Valencia: Universidad Politecnica de Valencia. Retrieved October 4, 2017 from http://cogprints.org/7026/
14. Stefan G. Hofmann, Paul Grossman, and Devon E. Hinton. 2011. Loving-kindness and compassion meditation: Potential for psychological interventions. *Clin. Psych. Rev.* 31, 7: 1126-1132.
15. Nancy Aaron Jones, Tiffany Field, Marisabel Davalos, and Sybil Hart. 2004. Greater right frontal EEG asymmetry and nonemphathic behavior are observed in children prenatally exposed to cocaine. *Int. J. Neurosci.* 114, 4: 459-480.
16. Ilkka Kosunen, Antti Ruonala, Mikko Salminen, Simo Järvelä, Niklas Ravaja, and Giulio Jacucci. 2017. Neuroadaptive Meditation in the Real World. *Proceedings of the 2017 ACM Workshop on An Application-oriented Approach to BCI out of the laboratory – BCI for Real '17.* ACM Press, New York, NY, USA, 29–33. https://doi.org/10.1145/3038439.3038443
17. Ilkka Kosunen, Mikko Salminen, Simo Järvelä, Antti Ruonala, Niklas Ravaja, and Giulio Jacucci. 2016. RelaWorld: Neuroadaptive and Immersive Virtual Reality Meditation System. *Proceedings of the 21st International Conference on Intelligent User Interfaces - IUI '16.* ACM Press, New York, New York, USA, 208–217. http://dx.doi.org/10.1145/2856767.2856796
18. Peter J. Lang. 1995. The emotion probe: Studies of motivation and attention. *Am. Psychol.* 50, 5: 372–385.
19. Christopher A. Moyer, Michael P. W. Donnelly, Jane C. Anderson, et al. 2011. Frontal electroencephalographic asymmetry associated with positive emotion is produced by very brief meditation training. *Psychol.Sci. 22*, 10: 1277-1279.
20. Chris D. Shaw, Diane Gromala and A. Fleming Seay. 2007. The meditation chamber: Enacting autonomic senses. *Proceedings of ENACTIVE/07. 4th International Conference on Enactive Interfaces.* Grenoble, France, November 19th-22nd, 2007, pp. 405-408. Retrieved October 4, 2017 from http://www.academia.edu/download/34771139/Enactive07_Proceedings-LQ.pdf#page=405
21. Jianhua Tao and Tieniu Tan. 2005. Affective Computing: A Review. In: Tao J., Tan T., Picard R.W. (eds) *Affective Computing and Intelligent Interaction. ACII 2005. Lecture Notes in Computer Science*, vol 3784. Springer, Berlin, Heidelberg. https://doi.org/10.1007/11573548_125
22. Andrew J. Tomarken, Richard J. Davidson, and Jeffrey B. Henriques. 1990. Resting frontal brain asymmetry predicts affective responses to films. *J. Pers. Soc. Psych.* 59, 4: 791-801.
23. Alexa M. Tullet, Eddie Harmon-Jones, and Michael Inzlicht. 2012. Tight frontal cortical asymmetry predicts empathic reactions: Support for a link between withdrawal motivation and empathy. *Psychophysiol. 49*, 8: 1145-1153.
24. Evert A. van Doorn, Gerben A. van Kleef, and Joop van der Pligt. (2015). Deriving meaning from others' emotions: attribution, appraisal, and the use of emotions as social information. *Front. Psychol.* 6:1077. https://dx.doi.org/10.3389%2Ffpsyg.2015.01077

Eye Gaze Controlled MFD for Military Aviation

Pradipta Biswas
Indian Institute of Science
Bangalore, India
pradipta@iisc.ac.in

Jeevithashree DV
Indian Institute of Science
Bangalore, India
jeevitha@iisc.ac.in

ABSTRACT
Multi-Function Displays (MFD) are essential part of glass cockpit of modern military and civilian aircrafts. They can display more information in less space than traditional analog displays. Interacting with MFDs is still now limited to a joystick system attached to throttle (called Target Designation System, TDS). This paper explored using gaze controlled interface for MFD and proposed two algorithms based on hotspots and adaptable zooming for improving response times in a gaze controlled interface. Three user studies confirmed gaze controlled MFD can significantly reduce response times for big peripheral buttons compared to touchscreen in a head down configuration and compared to existing TDS in a head up configuration.

General terms: Design, Human Factors, Experimentation

Keywords: Eye Gaze Tracker, Gaze Controlled Interface, MFD, HUD, Flight Simulator

1. INTRODUCTION
Multi-Function Displays (MFD) are used in aviation for showing various information ranging from primary flight information to details of airborne objects in a configurable way. A MFD is usually placed as a head down display. It is rectangular in shape, consists of a set of soft buttons on the periphery and a graphical user interface (GUI) in the middle. MFD can present data in multiple pages, rather than always being present at once like analog displays and so consumes less space in a cockpit compared to analog displays. A subset of information from the MFD is shown in head up (HUD) and head mounted displays (HMD) but due to lack of space and interaction modalities in HUD and HMD, the MFD is responsible for showing the vast amount of information required for both flying and mission control tasks.

Traditionally in military aviation platform, MFDs are operated using physical touch and Target Designation System (TDS), which is a joystick attached to the throttle [7]. Recently, voice commands [9] were also used by uttering the caption on buttons. In desktop computing environment, screen elements of a GUI do not change position unless the user manually drags them to different locations. For example, in a Windows home screen, the icons are arranged in rectangular fashion on left side or in an Android smartphone, icons are arranged at the bottom of the screen. However, the GUI part of a MFD poses new challenge for any interaction design as an airborne target may appear anywhere and in any number on the screen. Hence the inter-element spacing among different screen elements are dynamic and any interaction system needs to be accurate enough to handle the minimum value of inter-element spacing.

Existing military aircrafts have multiple MFDs and physically touching a MFD with gloves may often turn difficult for small targets [9]. The TDS can be improved by reducing the pointing time (the time needed to bring a cursor on a screen element). We cannot use any target prediction algorithm that needs apriori location of targets on screen [5] as targets may appear anywhere on the GUI part. We also have limited interaction modalities available as pilots find it difficult to take their hands away from throttle and flight stick in high G maneuvers. Direct voice input has already been tested in military aviation although the voice recognition systems are challenging for non-native English speakers and for countries having multiple language speakers [3, 9].

This paper proposes to use eye gaze control system to improve existing TDS. Eye gaze trackers as a direct controller of pointer movement has not yet been tested in military aviation environment. We tested an eye gaze controlled interface with a flight simulator and proposed a couple of adaptation algorithms for a gaze controlled MFD. Our algorithm significantly reduced pointing and selection times for bog peripheral buttons as well as improved flying performance for gaze controlled system compared to touchscreen for representative flying and pointing and selection tasks. We also explored an idea of using MFDs in head up display instead of head down display and designed a frugal eye gaze controlled head up display. Our proposed algorithms significantly reduced pointing time and improved flying performance in terms of deviation from flight envelope compared to an existing TDS. The main contributions of the paper are

1. Integrating and exploring eye gaze controlled interface for a flight simulator
2. Proposing new algorithms to improve pointing and selection times in gaze controlled interface
3. Designing and evaluating a gaze controlled head up display

The paper is organized as follows. Section 2 presents related literature on gaze controlled interface and pointing facilitation systems. Sections 3 describes our flight simulator set up followed by a couple of pilot studies involving a military

IUI'18, March 7–11, 2018, Tokyo, Japan

ACM ISBN 978-1-4503-4945-1/18/03…$15.00
https://doi.org/10.1145/3172944.3172973

aircraft and high-end third party simulator in section 4. Sections 5 to 7 present three user studies using our flight simulator set up. Section 8 presents general discussion followed by concluding remarks in section 9.

2. Related Work

Eye tracking is the process of measuring either the point of gaze (where one is looking) or the motion of an eye relative to the head. An eye tracker is a device for measuring eye positions and eye movement. Although research on eye tracking dates back to early 19th century [11] but controlling a display with gaze tracking is relatively new concept. Eye gaze controlled interfaces were mainly explored as assistive technology for people with severe motor impairment. However, using eye tracking in situational impairment poses new challenge in terms of speed and accuracy. A detailed survey on gaze controlled interface can be found in different papers [3, 4, 29]. Existing research on comparing eye gaze controlled interfaces with other modalities is mainly limited to desktop computing and except a few cases involving novice users [2], generally traditional input devices like mouse or touchscreen worked better than gaze controlled systems [27, 28]. A few recent studies on automotive user interfaces found gaze controlled interfaces worked worse [20] or similar [4] to touchscreen in terms of pointing and selection times although with higher rate of errors.

Researchers already explored different target prediction or intent recognition techniques for reducing pointing times. Most of these techniques continuously record velocity, acceleration, and bearing of cursor movement, fit different models and use that model to predict either the cursor movement or the target itself [15, 17, 21]. However, eye gaze movements are not as smooth as mouse or finger or hand movement, rather follow a 'spotlight' metaphor and so far not any next point or target prediction models are tested for gaze controlled interface. A backpropagation neural network model was used in [3], but only to differentiate between ballistic and homing movements. Farrell [6] noted that "humans use their eyes naturally as perceptive, not manipulative, body parts. Eye movement is often outside conscious thought, and it can be stressful to carefully guide eye movement as required to accurately use these target selection systems". Gaze tracking is used for zooming or accentuating part of display to help pointing by another pointing modality [12, 19, 29].

There is not much reported work in aviation domain about comparing modalities for secondary mission control tasks. However modern military aircraft supports multiple modalities including joystick (as part of TDS), touchscreen, voice activation and so on - an exhaustive list can be found in a different paper [24]. Grandt [8] compared trackball, touchscreen, speech input and mouse for an Anti-Warfare system but the experimental set up was similar to desktop computing environment with pointing and selection be the only task to be undertaken. Thomas [25] reported results from ISO 9241 task involving thumbstick, trackball, touchpad and touchscreen and found trackpad to be most accurate and argued for supporting new modalities for HOTAS Cursor Control Device (CCD). Biswas [3] reported significant reduction in reaction time for gaze controlled interface compared to HOTAS TDS for operating a simulated MFD but their study did not involve any primary flying task and was configured in a desktop computing environment.

3. Flight Simulator and Adaptive MFD Set Up

There was not any reported work on exploring gaze controlled interface with a flight simulator set up. We designed the flight simulator to conduct studies in dual task settings. Using our set up participants undertook standard flying task in parallel to representative pointing and selection tasks. This set up allowed us to measure not only pointing and selection times but also the total response time consisting of the time required to switch between primary flying to secondary mission control task. We set up the flight simulator with both head down and an interactive head up display. Existing high end simulators are meant for pilot training purpose and do not allow configuring the MFDs to explore different adaptation strategies due to software integration, time duration and security reasons. They also do not have any interactive HUD. To our knowledge, no head up displays both in automotive and aviation domain take input from users, it is only used to display primary flight information. We explored the possibility of displaying MFD at the same visual line of sight of pilots' normal seating position, so that they never need to look down for any information. Presently, Head Mounted Displays (HMD) are designed to interact with a display without losing situational awareness [7], our results on head up display can also be extended for HMD. In the following paragraphs, we described both our hardware and software set up to undertake dual task studies in military aviation settings. The experimental setup consisted of primary and secondary displays. The flight simulator was projected on a screen. The secondary task was displayed either on a LCD screen or on a projected display configured as a HUD. The projected display (fig 1) consisted of a semi-transparent 8mm Polyethylene sheet and a stand to hold it in front of the pilot with minimal occlusion of the situation in front. A support structure was developed in order to keep the thin plastic screen upright along with a support for the eye gaze tracker. The projected display system was configured so that its distance from the projector and angle of the eye tracker adjustable for individual pilot.

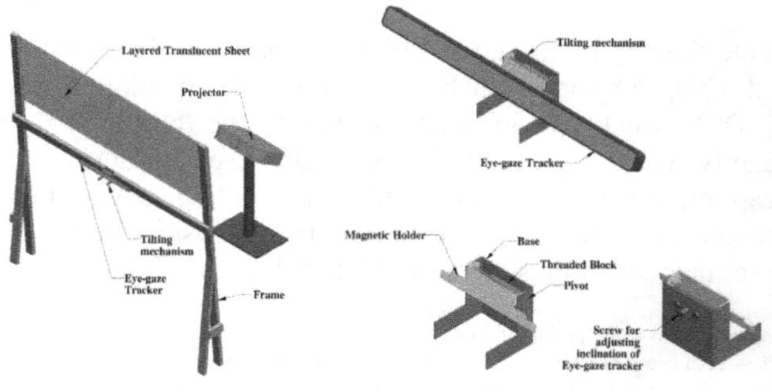

Figure 1. Projected Display used as HUD

We used either the LCD screen or the HUD but not both together (fig.2). The secondary projection display is positioned in line of sight with the primary projection display.

Table 1 below furnishes the dimensions and resolutions of all three displays.

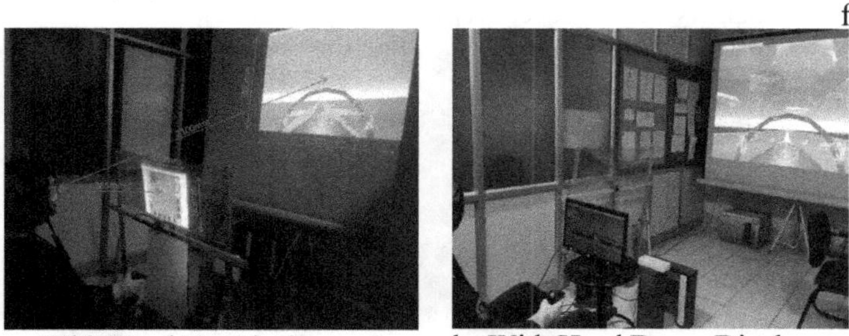

a. With Head Up Display b. With Head Down Display

Figure 2. Flight Simulator Set Up

Table 1: Specification of Displays

	Primary display	Secondary display for HUD	Secondary display for HDD
Projector / Monitor Model	*Dell 1220*	*Acer X1185G*	*Waveshare 10.1" LCD*
Resolution (pixel)	*1024x768*	*1024x768*	*1280x800*
Size of Projection / Monitor (mm)	*1200x900*	*380x295*	*250x167*
Distance from Eye (mm)	*2100*	*285*	*280*

Third-party flight simulator *YSFlight* with data logging feature was configured for this study as a *F/18 E/F Super Hornet* aircraft. The flight simulator was configured with Thrustmaster Warthog Hands On Throttle And Stick (HOTAS [10]). Both flight simulator and secondary pointing tasks were run on an Intel® Pentium® CPU G3220@3Ghz computer running Windows 7 operating system with 4GB RAM and NVidia GeForce 210 graphics card. A Tobii X3 eye gaze tracker was used for eye gaze tracking. The usefulness and suitability of this flight simulator with respect to this study was verified with senior pilots with ranks ranging from Air Marshall to Wing Commander operating fast jets for the national air force. The size of the MFD was also set up based on literature [7] and feedback from Hindustan Aeronautics Limited (HAL). During trial, participants don a helmet and pair of gloves supplied by the Hindustan Aeronautics Limited (fig.3). The big peripheral buttons were 1.7 cm square while small buttons are 0.5 cm diamonds.

Flying Task: A map was configured with a straight line drawn in the middle. Participants were instructed to fly between 1000 and 2000 feet along the straight line. The secondary task was initiated after the flight reached the designated flight envelope.

Secondary Task: In all our subsequent studies, users undertook pointing and selection tasks in the MFD while flying. Pointing and selection task involved selecting a random button on the MFD. The secondary task was initiated with an auditory cue. On hearing a beep sound, participants were instructed to undertake one button selection task on the MFD and then switch their attention back to flying until they hear the next auditory cue (beep sound).

Target Designation System (TDS): A joystick on the throttle of the HOTAS was configured as the TDS. For gaze controlled interface, the TDS was only used for selection but not for moving the pointer on the MFD.

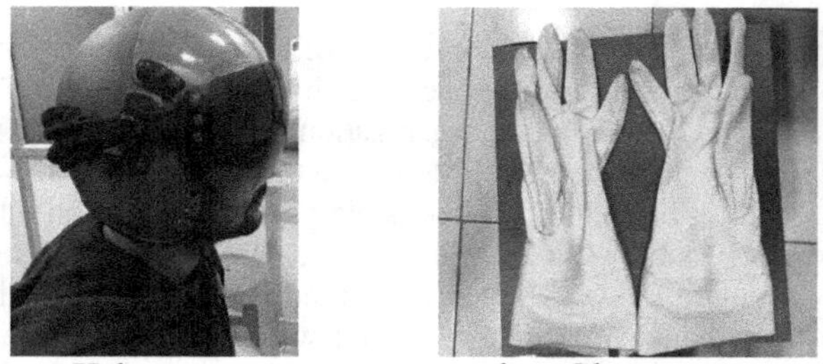

a. Helmet b. Gloves

c. Flight Stick d. Throttle

Figure 3. Instruments used in Flight Simulator

Adaptation for Big Buttons: In user studies involving gaze controlled interface, we noted that as users stare at the middle of the target, due to the inaccuracy of the tracker or their head movement, the neighboring button was occasionally selected. This probability of wrong selection increases if the buttons are closely spaced in the interface. Hence the probability of wrong selection will be reduced if we can increase the inter-button spacing. However, we cannot change the design of an interface like an existing MFD just to make a particular interaction technique working better.

We have explored the option of introducing hotspots inside each button to facilitate eye gaze tracking interaction. If we can introduce a hotspot on each button and keep them well separated, we can instruct users such that the first saccade on a button would launch on these hotspots. We hypothesize that keeping these hotspots well-separated will reduce pointing times and chances of wrong selection.

To find the best position of hotspots, we have represented an interface as a graph where each node corresponds to a target button (clickable objects) and neighboring buttons are connected by an edge. We assumed each button has a hotspot on it, which is initially located at the center of the button. The weight of each edge is equal to the Euclidian distance between the hotspots of two neighboring buttons. We explored two different algorithms to increase the distances between hotspots. We have defined the following cost function and tried to minimize it.

Cost Function = $\sum_{\forall d_{ij}} \frac{1}{d_{ij}^2}$

where d_{ij} is the distance of the hotspots between buttons *i* and *j* and is equal to the weight of the edge between nodes *i* and *j*.

We have modelled the problem of finding optimum locations of hotspots as a state space search problem. Each state corresponds to a particular organization of hotspots. A state transition occurs when any hotspot changes its position. If we consider each button has *k* possible positions and if an interface has *n* buttons, then an exhaustive search algorithm need to evaluate k^n states. Even for a moderately complex interface an exhaustive search algorithm will be computationally intensive or almost impossible. Hence we used the following two algorithms.

Greedy Algorithm: This algorithm picks up the edge with minimum weight, which means the two most closely spaced buttons. It checks the degrees of the two nodes of the minimum-weight edge and updates the hotspot of the node with higher degree. The algorithm calculates the centroid of the hotspots of neighboring nodes of the selected node and the new hotspot is calculated as the nearest point on the selected button (or node) to the centroid. While selecting the next node for updating hotspot, the algorithm checks whether the node is visited earlier and if so, it selects a different node. The algorithm is greedy in the sense that it only updates the hotspot if the overall value of the cost function is reduced from the previous value.

Simulated Annealing: This algorithm randomly selects a node and also randomly selects a point on the node as its new hotspot. If the new hotspot reduces the value of the cost function, then it is selected and updated. However even if the new hotspot increases the value of the cost function, it may still be selected based on the following condition

$e^{\frac{(oldCostFn - newCostFn)}{T}}$ > A random number between 0 and 1.

In the above equation, the value of *T* runs from 5000 to 1 and reduced by 1 in each iteration.

We have tested the algorithm on a sample multi-function display (MFD) and tested the algorithms multiple times with different initial positions of the hotspots. It may be noted that both algorithms reduced the cost function and increased the overall weight of edges (fig 4). The Simulated Annealing (SA) algorithm reduced the cost function further than the greedy algorithm. The greedy algorithm was stuck in cycle and a local optimum after visiting all nodes a couple of times. The SA algorithm never stuck in local optimum due to randomly choosing node and hotspots although we also could not conclude whether it reached the global optimum. It may be noted that the weights of edge in the final state of SA were significantly lower ($t(0,13)=3.2$, $p<0.01$) from the initial state in a paired *t*-test. Figure 5 shows example of a set of hotspots on a sample MFD, the blue dots on the buttons are obtained through the Simulated Annealing algorithm discussed above.

Adaptation for Small Buttons: The previous strategy of introducing hotspots did not work for small buttons used to indicate air-borne objects as the buttons are too small to hold a hotspot. Additionally, these buttons may appear at a higher density than the accuracy of an eye gaze tracker.

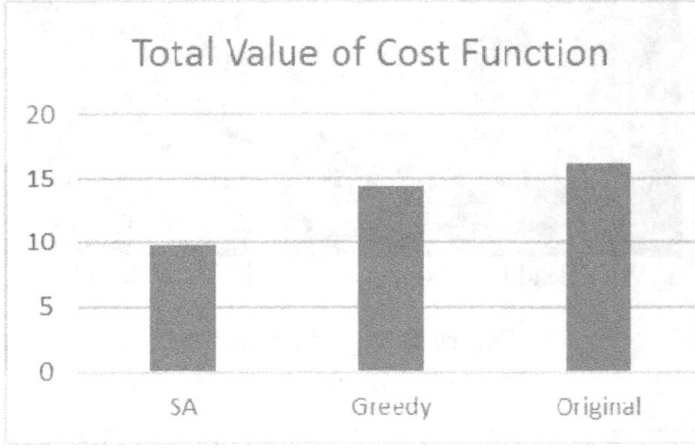

Figure 4. Comparing State Space Search Algorithms

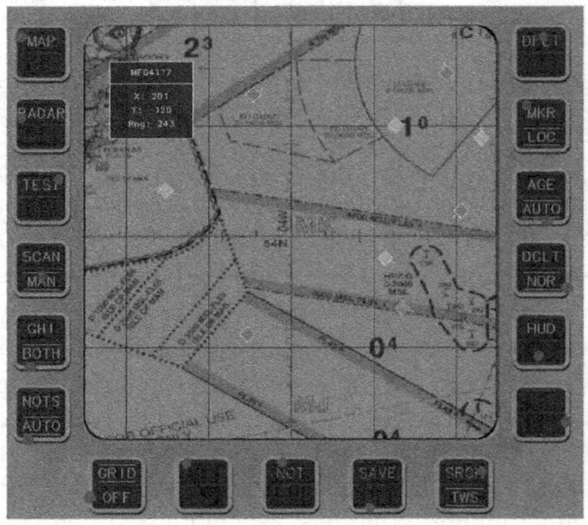

Figure 5. Hotspots for a representative MFD

We developed an adapting zooming technique to increase inter-button spacing of densely packed on-screen elements. In desktop computing, zooming a part of display for reducing pointing times has already been well explored [14] and for gaze controlled interfaces, too [1]. In our experimental set up, we used 175% zooming as it resulted inter-button spacing more than 0.4° of visual angle (fig.6), which was the accuracy of our eye gaze tracker. In actual implementation, whenever a new target appears or an existing one changes position, we calculate the pairwise distance among all pairs of targets and decide the zooming level based on the minimum distance. We implemented the following two techniques for selecting small targets in the MFD.

Adaptive 1: In this technique, if users click near a small button, a 250 × 250 pixels area around the button zoomed in. In this particular experimental set up, we hard-code the zooming percentage and zooming area, although both of them can be configured dynamically. In the zoomed in area, a nearest neighborhood predictor was implemented and users could select a target by clicking near the target.

Adaptive 2: This technique was similar to the previous technique with one more feature in the implementation of the nearest neighborhood predictor. In this technique, users only need to stare (or look at) near the target item and upon dwelling for 1 sec, the target is automatically selected. Additionally, users could also select a target by clicking near the target like the previous strategy.

In all adaptation strategies, the target button was indicated by drawing a yellow ring around it so that users need to undertake a serial search to find the target, rather it was popped out from background.

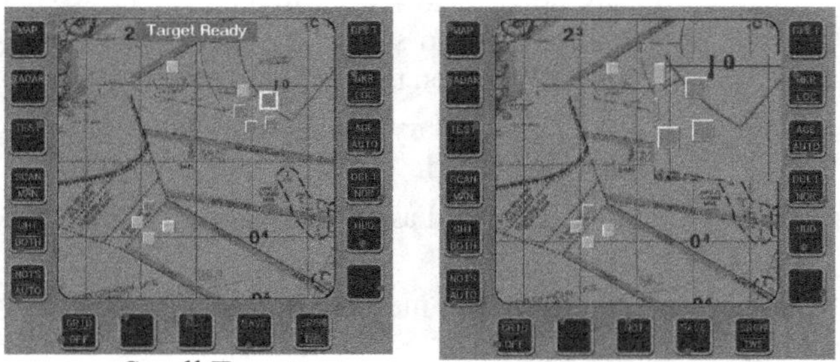

a. Small Targets b. Zoomed In Position

Figure 6. Zooming for Small Buttons

The following flow chart (fig.7) explains working of the adaptive MFD. It may be noted that the adaptation strategies are developed for a Cursor Control Device (CCD) and not for facilitating physical touch in a touchscreen. In the diagram below, the blue boxes indicate system initiated function while brown boxes indicate user initiated action.

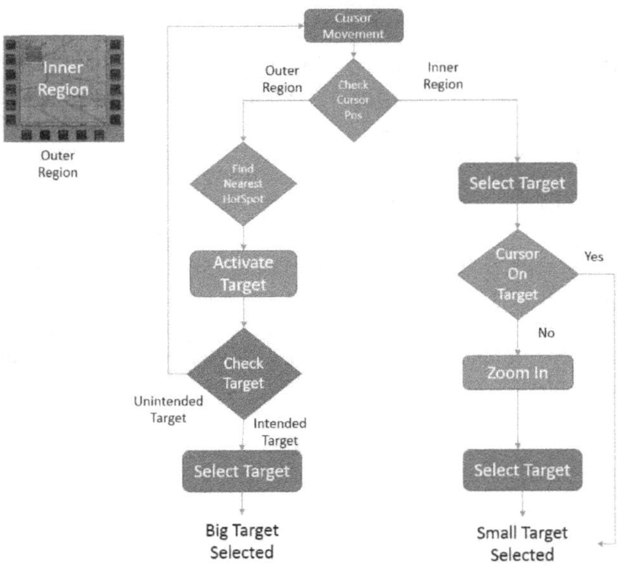

Figure 7. Flow Chart of Adaptive MFD Operation

If the cursor moves in the outer region of the MFD (marked in Fig X), the nearest neighborhood predictor finds the closest hotspot and activates one of the peripheral big buttons. Activation is indicated by changing background color and enlarging the target 1.5 times its size. The user selects target by pressing the Slew button on the throttle stick of the HOTAS.

If the cursor moves in the inner region of the MFD, users were instructed to press the Slew button when the cursor in on or near one of the small buttons. If the Slew button is pressed when the cursor is on the target, it is selected right away. If the cursor is not on the button, the neighborhood is zoomed in. The user then selects the target by bringing the cursor near the target button and then either by pressing the Slew button (Adaptive 1) or by staring in (dwelling, Adaptive 2) near the target button.

Controlling GUI through eye gaze: After developing the flight simulator, we developed the following algorithm for controlling an on-screen cursor using eye gaze. Our retinal ganglion cells only respond to change in stimuli and even we focus eye gaze at a point, microsacadic eye gaze movements always change the gaze location around the point of interest. Due to these microsacadic eye gaze movements, the raw output from any eye gaze tracker cannot be used to control an on screen pointer and it requires filtering to stabilize the cursor. Our gaze tracking system records the eye gaze positions continuously (refer point A in fig 8) and takes the median of the pixel locations in every 250 msecs to estimate the region of interest or saccadic focus points (refer point B in fig 8). The median was less susceptible to outliers than arithmetic mean in case the eye gaze tracker briefly lost signal. We simulate the eye movement using a Bezier curve that smoothers the cursor movement between two focus points as we wanted to make the cursor movement looking similar to an existing TDS. It then pushes the focus points into a stack and the Bezier curve [22] algorithm interpolates points in between two focus points (refer point B in fig 8). The pointer is drawn at each interpolated points in every 16 msecs to visualize a smooth on-screen movement (refer point C in fig 8). For adaptive conditions, it activates or enlarges the on-screen target nearest to present gaze location (refer point C in fig 8).

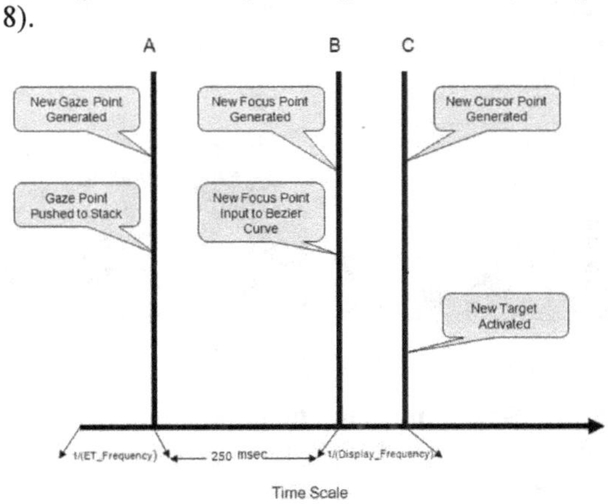

Figure 8. Cursor Control through Eye Gaze

For subsequent studies, although we used a Tobii X3 eye gaze tracker but our algorithm can also be used and tested for cheaper Tobii EyeX and 4C trackers.

4. Pilot studies for external validation

Before undertaking the trial with our flight simulator, we undertook two pilot studies for studying feasibility of putting an eye gaze tracker in a cockpit. Our testing investigated both ergonomic and engineering challenges on connecting cockpit computers to eye gaze tracker and positioning the tracker in cockpit so that the tracker can track eyes of pilots of different height. Due to time constraint and security issues we could manage to collect data from only 4 participants (height range 5'6" to 6'1", age range 24 to 34 years, 3 male, 1 female).

We tried to fit an eye gaze tracker in a BAES Hawk Trainer aircraft. We used an Intel NUC computer with *i3* processor and kept the set up on the wing of the aircraft. We hold a 10" screen fitted with an eye gaze tracker on top of existing MFDs. We tried all six MFDs of the Hawk Trainer spread over two cockpits and the tracker worked for the top most MFD of the rear cockpit (fig.9). We used similar experimental task with simulated MFD discussed above for secondary task. In our simulated MFD, participants undertook 40 pointing tasks at an average speed of 1.35 secs (stdev 1.19 sec) inside the aircraft.

Figure 9. Testing with a Hawk Trainer Aircraft

Later we also integrated an eye gaze tracker to an existing simulator (fig.10) at the National Aerospace Laboratory (NAL, India) and participants could undertake pointing and selection tasks in the MFD using our algorithm. In this set up, we installed our gaze tracking program and simulated MFD into the cockpit computer. Participants undertook 30 pointing task at an average speed of 2.4 secs (stdev 1.21 secs) in the simulator.

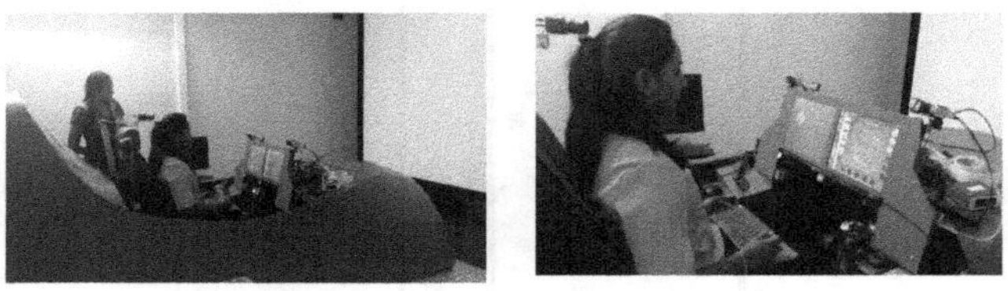

Figure 10. Testing with *XYZ* Simulator

5. Study 1 – Gaze controlled head down MFD

This study describes a dual task study using a 10" LCD display for rendering a MFD in head down configuration.

Participants: We collected data from 12 participants (10 male, 2 female, age range 25 to 35 years, average age 28.3 years). All participants volunteered for the study, did not report any problem with the experimental set up during practice session. None of them used gaze controlled interface or the particular flight simulator set up before the study.

Design: The study was designed as 3 × 2 repeated measure design with the following factors

- Modality- Touchscreen × Adaptive 1 ×Adaptive 2
- Button size- Big buttons × Small buttons

Participants required to press big and small buttons alternatively on listening the auditory cue. Each participant was instructed to press 8 big and 8 small buttons alternatively. We have measured the following dependent variables

- Flying Performance was measured by
  - Deviation from the straight line flying path
  - Deviation in altitude outside the specified envelope of 1000 and 2000 feet
- Pointing and Clicking performance is measured as
  - Response time as the time difference between the auditory cue and the time instant of the selection of the target button. This time duration adds up time to react to auditory cue, switch from primary to secondary task and the pointing and selection time in the secondary task.
  - Error in secondary task as the number of wrong buttons selected.
- Cognitive load measured as the NASA Task Load Index (TLX) score.
- Subjective preference as measured as the System Usability Score (SUS [23]).

Procedure: Initially participants were briefed about the purpose of the study. Then they were trained with the flying and pointing and selection tasks separately and undertook both tasks separately. We proceeded with the trial only when they could complete each task separately. Finally, they undertook the dual task study. In this study, we used a clear visor of the helmet while a later study separately collected data on clear and dark visors. On completion of each condition, we recorded their cognitive load and preference using TLX and SUS questionnaire.

Results: All participants could complete the trial in all conditions. In total, we recorded 580 pointing tasks although they did not select equal number of buttons in each condition. In the following graphs, error bars represent standard deviation.

For response time calculation (fig.11), initially we removed outliers by removing values which are greater than outer fence (Q3 + 3 × interquartile distance) and discarded 11 pointing tasks. For the remaining tasks, we calculated average response time for big and small buttons separately for each participant and undertook a 3 × 2 repeated measure ANOVA.

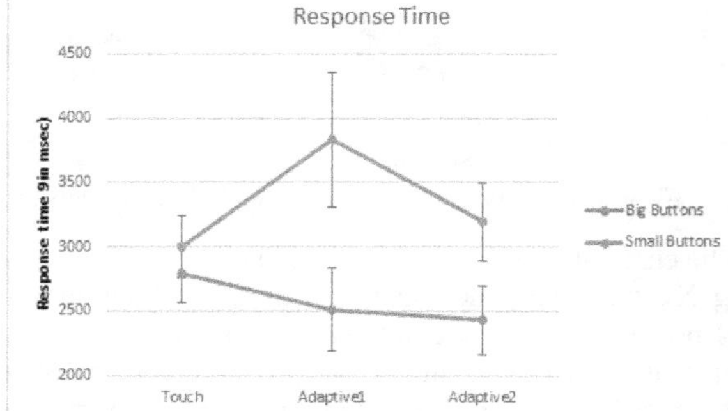

Figure 11. Comparing Response Times

The Mauchy's test confirmed no violation from sphericity assumption. We found a

- Significant main effect of button size (F(1,11)=31.84, p<0.01, η^2= 0.09] and

- Significant interaction effect between button size and modality ($F(2,22)=11.54$, $p<0.01$, $\eta^2 = 0.51$]

The main effect of modality was not significant

A set of pairwise comparisons using t-tests among different conditions only find that the response times for small button selections were significantly slower for 1st adaptive condition compared to touchscreen.

We also conducted a set of pairwise unequal variance t-tests on the response times without averaging them for individual participants and found

- A significant reduction in response time for selecting big peripheral buttons for 1st adaptive condition and considering both adaptive conditions together compared to touchscreen [$t(0,232)=2.53$, $p<0.05$ for 1st adaptive condition, not significant on 2nd condition alone, $t(0,284)=2.07$, $p<0.05$ considering both conditions as both conditions used similar technique for big buttons]
- A significant increase in response time for selecting small buttons in both adaptive conditions compared to touchscreen [$t(0,80)=3.24$,$p<0.001$ for 1st adaptive condition, $t(0,127)=2.14$,$p<0.05$ for 2nd adaptive condition]. The second adaptive condition reduced the average response time by 9% compared to the 1st adaptive condition.

Finally, we combined the response times for big and small buttons together (fig.12) and evaluated the overall response times. This analysis aims to evaluate whether increase in response times for small buttons are big enough to make a significant difference in overall response time. We did not find any significant difference in response times in a one-way ANOVA with the overall response time being lowest for the first adaptive condition and highest for 2nd adaptive condition.

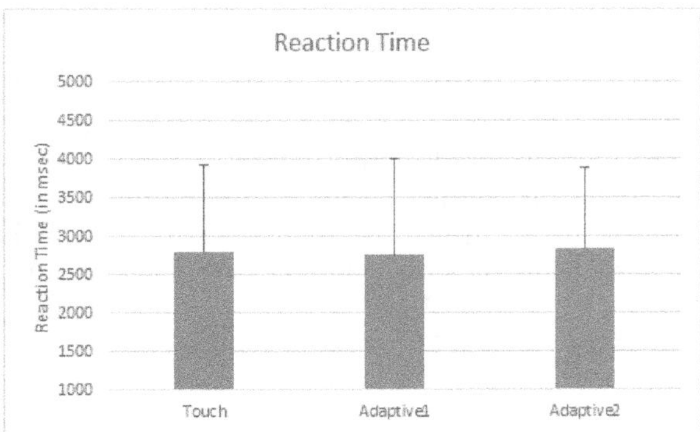

Figure 12. Comparing Response Times combining big and small buttons

There was only one instance of wrong selection for 2nd adaptive condition. However, it may be noted for small button selection in adaptive condition, participants were instructed to click anywhere near the target area to zoom in and so that click action near the area (but not exactly on the target button) was not considered as a wrong selection.

We did not find significant difference for any other dependent variables although the deviation from flight path was lowest in the 1st adaptive condition while the cognitive load was 10% lower and preference 20% higher for the 2nd adaptive system compared to touch screen (fig.13).

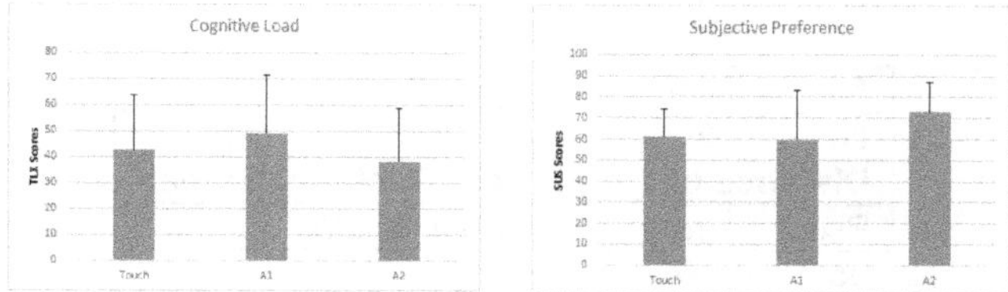

a. Cognitive Load b. Subjective Preference

Figure 13. Subjective feedback for MFD Study with HDD

Discussion: This study found that gaze controlled interface reduced response time for bigger peripheral buttons of an MFD while smaller buttons were still quicker to select using touchscreen. Use of gaze controlled interface did not degrade flying performance, rather it was best in one of the adaptive conditions and users' subjective ratings about cognitive load and preference also favored gaze controlled interface over touchscreen. The overall response time was not different across three conditions being lowest for the adaptive condition. It may also be noted that all users used touchscreen everyday while they were using gaze controlled interface for the first time. In high G environment it will be difficult to move hand but pilots will still use saccadic eye gaze movement to watch MFDs and our gaze controlled interface can leverage this gaze movement to directly control MFDs. Although users undertook significant higher response time for small buttons in the adaptive conditions, but the one with dwell time selection reduced pointing and selection time than the other adaptive condition. Future studies may adapt and optimize dwell time duration to further reduce response times. In the following studies, we explored using gaze controlled interface as a head up display.

The following two studies rendered a MFD on a projected display configured as a HUD and evaluated its performance.

6. Study 2 – ISO 9241 Pointing Task in HUD

In this study, we compared existing TDS and gaze controlled interface for a representative pointing task without any adaptation.

Participants: Participants with prior gaming experience were recruited from our university and they volunteered for the study. They were trained with the flight simulator, among which 9 participants were selected for this study based on their performance in maintaining altitude and direction in flight simulator. All participants were male with an average age of 28 years.

Design: We conducted a dual task study with the primary task consisted of take-off maneuver followed by *Straight and Level* maneuver without trim control. A pointing and selection task complying with ISO 9241-9 standard was developed as the secondary task with following target sizes and distances.

Table 2: Details on Pointing Targets

Width of Target		
Pixels	Size (in mm)	Arc Angle
40	*14.6*	*3°*
45	*18.7*	*3.4°*
55	*20.4*	*4.1°*
60	*22.3*	*4.5°*
Distance of Target from Center of Screen		
Pixels	mm	Arc Angle
65	*24.2*	*4.8°*
120	*44.6*	*9.0°*
200	*74.2*	*14.8°*
315	*116.8*	*23.2°*

The flow of the secondary task is listed below.

1. An auditory cue (beep sound) was played.
2. The participant shifted his head and gaze to the MFD, in search for the cursor. For this task, the cursor was always placed in the center of the screen on a red-button (fig.14). The eye tracker was used to determine if the pilot gazed at the button. The time taken by the participant to shift his head and gaze to the cursor on the MFD upon hearing the auditory cue was measured and logged.
3. On activation of the red-button, fourteen buttons were displayed in a circular fashion around the center of the screen, of which one button was colored odd in white referred as target and the rest were colored in blue referred as distractors (fig.14).
4. The participant recognized the target from distractor, and manipulated the cursor using the provided input modality (TDS or eye gaze) to reach the target and then selected the target, using Slew Button on the HOTAS. The time taken from the activation of the red-button to the selection of target button was measured and logged as the pointing and selection time.
5. The participant then shifted his gaze back to the flight simulator to continue with the primary task.

a. Beginning of task b. Target and distractors

Figure 14. Design of Pointing Task for ISO Study

Steps 1 to 5 were repeated with different target size and its position from the center. The task was designed in such a way to make sure that equal number of samples is logged for each Index of Difficulty (ID).

Procedure: Initially, participants were given practice session in flight-simulator and secondary task. Then, participants initiated the primary flying task. After the participant completed the take-off maneuver of the primary task, the secondary task was initiated. After completion of the secondary task, the primary task was halted. Feedback for the given modality with respect to the pointing and selection task was collected in form of NASA Task Load Index (TLX Score) and System Usability Scale (SUS Score). The same procedure was repeated for the remaining modalities.

Results: For each dependent variable, we initially compared the descriptive statistics and then undertook parametric or non-parametric statistical hypothesis test. If an ANOVA or H-test found a significant difference, we also used t-test or U-test for pairwise comparisons based on the distribution of the data set.

The deviation from flight path and altitude was both higher while participants used gaze controlled system compared to joystick although the difference was not statistically significant in signed rank test. Participants flew longer distance while they used gaze controlled system compared to joystick.

We plotted selection times with respect to indices of difficulty (fig.15) of target. The selection times were significantly less for eye gaze controlled interface compared to joystick in a paired t-test ($p<0.05$). The correlation between indices of difficulty and selection times was 0.34 for gaze controlled interface and 0.91 for joystick.

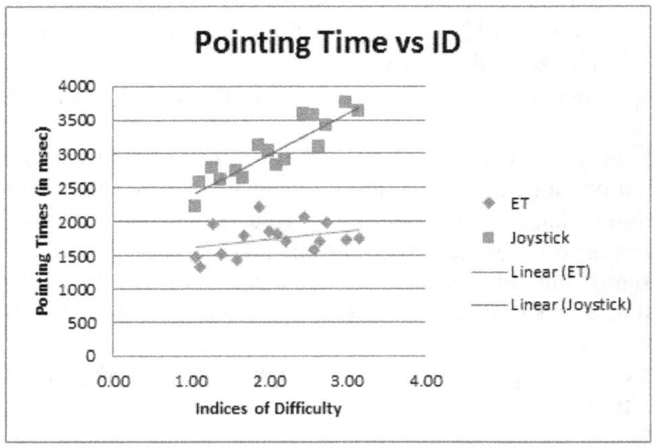

Figure 15. Comparing Pointing and Selection Times w.r.t. ID

The cognitive load (fig. 16) measured in terms of NASA TLX scores was higher for joystick than gaze controlled interface although the difference was not significant in an unequal variance t-test. The subjective preference was higher and greater than 68 for gaze controlled interface compared to joystick.

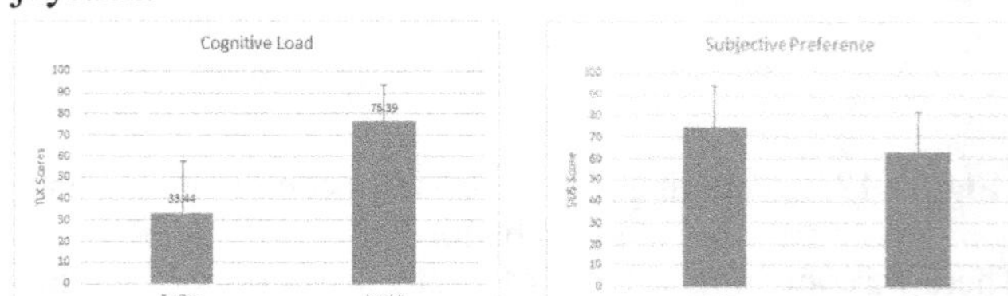

a. Cognitive Load b. Subjective Preference

Figure 16. Subjective feedback for ISO Study with HUD

Discussion: This study found that pointing and selection times can indeed be improved with eye gaze controlled interface compared to HOTAS joystick for targets as small as 1.4cm but at the expense of marginal degradation in flying performance by novice users. The cognitive load and subjective preference of users also indicated that novice participants preferred to use gaze controlled system over joystick. It may be noted that in this study, we did not use any algorithm to help in pointing like zooming or hotspots discussed before.

It may be noted that the correlation between indices of difficulty and pointing time was significant for joystick while not for gaze tracking. It may indicate that if the gaze tracker is accurate, smaller button will not significantly reduce pointing times. However, in the first study, we noted higher pointing times for small buttons. Actually, in Head Up configuration, we could increase the size of display and the minimum target size was 14 mm in this study compared to 5 mm in Head Down configuration in the first study. A future study will be designed to optimize the size of target for gaze control interface although the study may be specific to the accuracy of a particular eye gaze tracker.

A post-hoc analysis showed that participants took significantly less time to switch gaze from primary to secondary display for the gaze controlled system than joystick, which may indicate that they paid less attention to the primary flying task. One possible solution could be to further reduce pointing and selection times in secondary task so that they can quickly switch attention back to the flying task. In the next study, we used adaptation algorithms the projected display with standard multi-function displays.

7. Study 3 –HUD based MFD Task

This study undertook similar task as the first study. However, instead of analysing big and small buttons separately, we compared the gaze controlled interface with different visors of the helmet in a projected display.

Participants: We collected data from 11 participants (9 male, 2 female, age range 25 to 34 years) recruited from our university with similar sampling criteria as the 2nd study discussed above. The participants had no visual, cognitive and motor impairment and did not have any problem in using the experimental set up. None of them have used either HOTAS joystick or eye gaze tracking based interface earlier.

Design and Material: The study used similar set of material as the previous studies described before. Instead of the ISO task, we used the screenshot of figure 6 and each participant was instructed to make at least 8 selections for each condition while undertaking the flying task. We also used a helmet given to us by the local military aerospace company. The helmet had a clear and a dark visor. Since eye gaze tracker works based on reflected infra-red light, we wanted to evaluate and compare the quality of interaction with dark visor. Our study consisted of the following three conditions for pointing and selection tasks

a. Using HOTAS Joystick
b. Using eye gaze tracking with clear visor (ETC)
c. Using eye gaze tracking with dark visor (ETD)

Procedure: We followed same procedure as the first study but recorded data separately with clean and dark visor.

Results: We initially analysed the flight performance under three different conditions in terms of the standard deviation in x-axis, standard deviation in altitude when the flight was outside the envelope between 1000 and 2000 feet and total distance covered during the task. We did not find any significant difference among those parameters in one-way ANOVAs. In fact, the deviation in altitude (fig.17) was 10% less with eye gaze tracking with clear visor compared to HOTAS joystick.

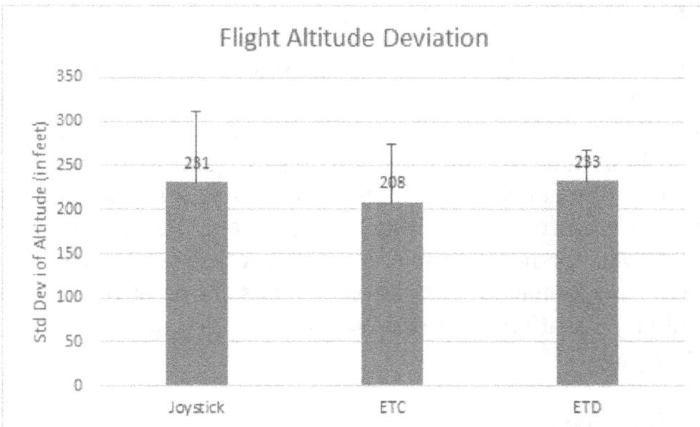

Figure 17. Quality of flying w.r.t. change in altitude

Next we analysed response times for 268 pointing tasks and found a significant difference among three different conditions [F(2,246)= 9.65, p<0.05 $\eta^2 = 0.07$]. A set of pairwise t-tests also found significant difference between the response times for gaze tracking system and HOTAS Joystick (fig.18).

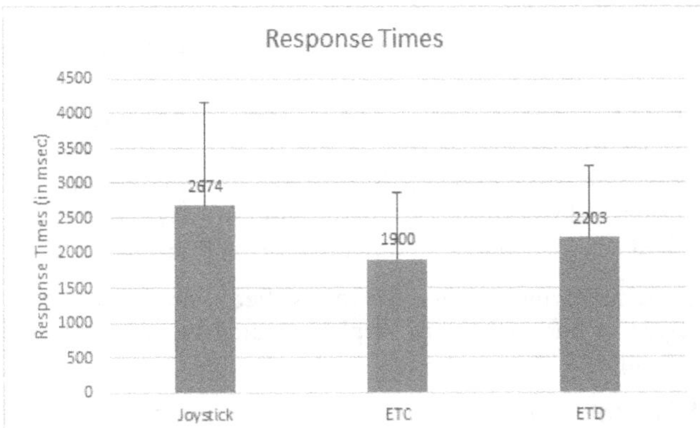

Figure 18. Analysing response times in flight simulator

The number of wrong selections was measured and reported in terms of percent error, which was lowest for Joystick and under 10% for all conditions. There were 4 wrong selections for HOTAS, 9 for eye gaze tracking with clear visor and 6 for eye gaze tracking with dark visor.

Users reported significantly less cognitive load (fig.19) for gaze controlled systems in terms of TLX scores [F(2,26)=5.04, p<0.05, $\eta^2 = 0.28$] and they also reported significantly higher preference [F(2,26)=8.78, p<0.05 $\eta^2 = 0.40$] for gaze controlled system over HOTAS joystick in terms of SUS scores.

Discussion: This study demonstrates that for standard flying task, the eye gaze controlled interface can perform better than existing HOTAS joystick both in terms of response times and subjective preference.

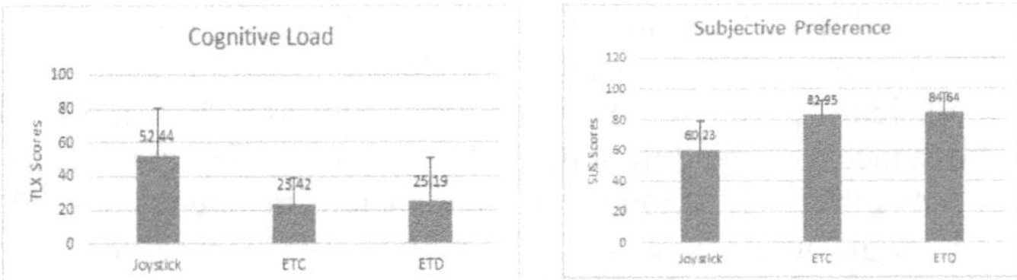

a. Cognitive Load

b. Subjective Preference

Figure 19. Subjective feedback for MFD Study with HUD

The average response time was even lower than the gaze controlled head-down display reported by Biswas [3] in a single task study. The flying performance in terms of deviation in altitude marginally improved for gaze controlled system than joystick. Users preference also significantly higher for the gaze controlled system. In summary, we can conclude that even for novice users, gaze controlled system can improve performance with secondary mission control tasks in military aviation environment without degrading primary flying task.

8. Summary

Overall, we can conclude that gaze controlled system can improve performance with secondary tasks with respect to joystick and at least for peripheral big buttons compared to a touchscreen even for first time users. The flying performance was not affected by using gaze controlled interface, rather was slightly improved in terms of deviation from flight envelope. In all three user studies, users' subjective feedback also favored gaze controlled system over touchscreen or TDS.

A video demonstration of the system can be found at https://youtu.be/j4KznPbc7n8 The video shows the simulated MFD in Head Down configuration, then the Head Up projected display and finally a snapshot of its use with third party high end simulator. In the head down configuration, the video demonstrates a small button press after zooming in and a big peripheral button press using hotspot.

In the following paragraphs we clarified a few issues about design of our studies and implementation of the adaptation techniques.

Adaptable zooming technique: The zooming technique was adaptable in the sense as the magnification ratio is selected based on the minimum distance between all pairs of targets at any point of time. It was implemented by drawing a window across the required area, which in fact occlude part of the display. However, the occlusion duration was limited by the dwell time duration and was less than or equal to 1 sec in present implementation. The zooming window disappeared as soon as a gaze location was recorded outside the zooming window. We also implemented a nearest neighborhood predictor within the zooming window so that users need not to bring the cursor exactly on target. Unlike existing work, the magnification did not occur continuously, rather initiated by pressing Slew button on the throttle. Although we did not find reduction in pointing times for small MFD buttons compared to touch screen, but use of dwell time reduced reaction times by 9% than without it. The zooming technique can also be used with other modalities and future studies will explore further adaptation options like optimizing the dwell time [16].

Selection for gaze control interface: In gaze controlled interface, selection of a target, popularized as Midas Touch problem, is not as straight forward as with other interaction techniques like touchscreen, touchpad or mouse. A previous study [3] explored hardware switch and voice command based selection while researchers on assistive technology [18] explored dwell time based selection. Considering the timing constraint, we used a button on the throttle (Slew button) for selecting target in the reported user studies while dwell time was used in one adaptive method.

Sampling strategy: Senior pilots suggested us to collect data from university students as they thought any new technology is most likely to be tested first on training platform with students with little flying knowledge rather than on an established platform with more experienced pilots. We constantly took suggestions from experienced pilots on designing the flight simulator and flying task during design of the study. We collected data from one pilot of Wing Commander rank of Indian Air Force and he could undertake 16 pointing tasks at an average duration of 3.5 secs (stdev 1.6 secs) and reported a TLX score of 23 and SUS rating of 82. The average time of selecting big buttons was 2.8 secs while that of small buttons was 4.3 secs. The low TLX and high SUS scores indicated that he did not have high cognitive load and prefer to use the system.

Data analysis strategy: We checked normality by drawing box plots and comparing mean and median for each individual dependent variable. If the data were normally distributed, we conducted parametric tests and otherwise we undertook non-parametric tests. For all graphs, the column represents average while the error bar represents standard deviation.

9. Conclusion

This paper reports three used studies on undertaking pointing and selection tasks in a simulated MFD using eye gaze in addition to flying an aircraft in straight and level maneuver and compared performance of both flying and pointing tasks with state-of-the-art interaction devices (touch screen and target designation system). We also explored possibilities of rendering an MFD at a Head Up Display (HUD) instead of traditional Head Down (HDD) configuration. For conducting the study, we designed bespoke hardware as a working prototype of a configurable HUD and designed and implemented new algorithms to control an on-screen cursor through operators' eye gaze. Using our set up that consists of helmet, gloves and HOTAS used in existing military aircraft, participants could undertake pointing and selection tasks at an average time of 2.43 secs (fig 11) for Head Down Display and 1.9 secs (fig 18) for Head Up Display. This time estimation includes context switching from primary flying to secondary pointing task and was significantly better than existing TDS (2.67 secs) and touchscreen (2.8 secs). We have already integrated our software with an existing high end simulator at the Indian National Aerospace Laboratory and also working on integrating it with an existing aviation platform. The proposed algorithms for gaze controlled interface can also be extended to other areas like automotive control and assistive technology.

References

1. Bates R., Multimodal Eye-Based Interaction for Zoomed Target Selection on a Standard Graphical User Interface. Proceedings of INTERACT 1999
2. Biswas P. and Langdon P., Eye-Gaze Tracking based Interaction in India, Elsevier Procedia Computer Science 39, pp 59-66, 2014
3. Biswas P. and Langdon P., Multimodal Intelligent Eye-Gaze Tracking System, International Journal of Human-Computer Interaction 31 (4), Taylor & Francis, Print ISSN: 1044-7318
4. Biswas P., Prabhakar G., Rajesh J., Pandit K. and Halder A., Improving Eye Gaze Controlled Car Dashboard using Simulated Annealing, Proceedings of the 31st British Human Computer Interaction Conference (HCI 17)
5. Dixon, M., Fogarty, J., and Wobbrock, J. 2012. A general-purpose target-aware pointing enhancement using pixel-level analysis of graphical interfaces. In Proceedings of the 2012 ACM Annual Conference on Human Factors in Computing Systems (CHI'12). ACM, New York, 3167--3176.
6. Farrell S., Zhai S.(2005), System and method for selectively expanding or contracting a portion of a display using eye-gaze tracking, US Patent No.: 20050047629 A1
7. Flight Manual for the package Eurofighter Typhoon Professional, Available at https://www.afs-design.de/pdf/AFS_EFpro_English.pdf, Accessed on 3/10/2017
8. Grandt M., Pfendler C., Mooshage O., Empirical Comparison of Five Input Devices for Anti-Air Warfare Operators, Available at: http://dodccrp.org/events/8th_ ICCRTS/pdf/035.pdf, Accessed on 30/11/2013
9. Hierl R., Neujhar H, Sandl P., Military Aviation in Information Ergonomics: A theoretical approach and practical experience in transportation, Springer Science & Business Media, edited by Michael Stein, Peter Sandl
10. HOTAS, Available at http://www.thrustmaster.com /products/hotas-warthog, Accessed on 12/07/2017
11. Huey, E. (1908) The Psychology and Pedagogy of Reading (Reprint). MIT Press 1968 (originally published 1908)
12. Jacob M., Hurwitz B., Kamhi G. (2013), Eye tracking based selective accentuation of portions of a display, WO Patent No.: 2013169237 A1
13. Lank, E., Cheng, Y.N., Ruiz, J. (2007). Endpoint prediction using motion kinematics. In: Proceedings of the SIGCHI conference on Human factors in computing systems (CHI '07). pp637-646. New York, NY, USA.
14. McGuffin, M.J., Balakrishnan, R. (2005), Fitts' law and expanding targets: Experimental studies and designs for user interfaces. In: ACM Transactions Computer-Human Interaction. Is. 12, vol. 4, pp. 388-422.
15. Murata, A. (1998) Improvement of Pointing Time by Predicting Targets in Pointing with a PC Mouse, International Journal of Human-Computer Interaction, 10 (1), pp.23-32.
16. Nayyar A. et al., OptiDwell: Intelligent Adjustment of Dwell Click Time, Proceedings of International Conference on Intelligent User Interfaces (IUI'17)
17. Pasqual P. and Wobbrock J., Mouse pointing endpoint prediction using kinematic template matching, CHI '14 Proceedings of the SIGCHI Conference on Human Factors in Computing Systems, pp 743-752
18. Penkar A.M., Lutteroth C. and Weber G., Designing for the Eye - Design Parameters for Dwell in Gaze Interaction, OZCHI 2012
19. Pfeuffer, K., & Gellersen, H. (2016, October). Gaze and Touch Interaction on Tablets. In Proceedings of the 29th Annual Symposium on User Interface Software and Technology (pp. 301-311). ACM.
20. Poitschke T., Laquai, F. , Stamboliev S. and Rigoll, G. (2011), Gaze-based interaction on multiple displays in an automotive environment, IEEE International Conference on Systems, Man, and Cybernetics (SMC), 2011 Page(s):543 - 548, ISSN : 1062-922X
21. Ruiz, J. and Lank, E. 2010. Speeding pointing in tiled widgets: Understanding the effects of target expansion and misprediction. In Proceedings of the 15th International Conference on Intelligent User Interfaces (IUI'10). ACM, New York, 229--238.
22. Salomon D. (2005), Curves and Surfaces for Computer Graphics, Springer Verlag, August 2005. ISBN 0-387-24196-5
23. System Usability Scale, Available at http://en.wikipedia.org/wiki/System_usability_scale, Accessed on 12/07/2014
24. Thomas P., Biswas P., Langdon P. (2015) State-of-the-Art and Future Concepts for Interaction in Aircraft Cockpits. In: Antona M., Stephanidis C. (eds) Universal Access in Human-Computer Interaction. Access to Interaction. UAHCI 2015. Lecture Notes in Computer Science, vol 9176. Springer
25. Thomas P., Performance, characteristics, and error rates of cursor control devices for aircraft cockpit interaction, In International Journal of Human-Computer Studies, Volume 109, 2018, Pages 41-53, ISSN 1071-5819,
26. Tobii Pro X3 Eye Tracker, Available at: http://www.tobii .com/xperience/, Accessed on: 31st August, 2015
27. Vertegaal R. (2008), A Fitts' Law Comparison of Eye Tracking and Manual Input in the Selection of Visual Targets, Proceedings of the International Conference of Multimodal Interaction 2008, pp 241- 248
28. Ware C. and Mikaelian H. M (1987), An Evaluation of an Eye Tracker as a Device for Computer Input, Proceedings of the ACM SIGCHI Conference on Human Factors in Computing Systems (CHI) 1987, pp 183-187
29. Zhai S., Morimoto C. and Ihde S.(1999), Manual and Gaze Input Cascaded (MAGIC) Pointing. ACM SIGCHI Conference on Human Factors in Computing System (CHI) 1999

Cubicle: An Adaptive Educational Gaming Platform for Training Spatial Visualization Skills

Ziang Xiao[1] **Helen Wauck**[1] **Zeya Peng**[2] **Hanfei Ren**[2] **Lei Zhang**[3]
Shiliang Zuo [4] **Yuqi Yao**[1] **Wai-Tat Fu**[1]
University of Illinois at Urbana-Champaign[1] Zhejiang University[2]
Shanghai Jiao Tong University[3] Tsinghua University[4]
{zxiao5,wauck2,yuqiyao2,wfu}@illinois.edu[1]
{zeyapeng,renhanfei}@zju.edu.cn[2]
rayne_@sjtu.edu.cn[3] zsl14@mails.tsinghua.edu.cn[4]

ABSTRACT
Research has demonstrated that spatial visualization skills are crucial for success in Science, technology, engineering, and mathematics (STEM) disciplines. With an increasing number of students entering STEM disciplines, the question of how to effectively train students' spatial visualization skills has become very important. While a scalable existing solution is to implement online workshops for students, the problem of how to motivate students to participate in these online workshops remains unsolved. In this study, we studied gamification as a way to motivate first year engineering students to take part in an online workshop designed to train their spatial visualization skills. Our game contains eight modules, each designed to train a different component of spatial visualization. The game records players' in-game behavior with high granularity, which allows us to provide automated, scalable feedback on players' problem-solving strategies. Ten students with different levels of spatial ability played our game and expressed a strong interest in using the game to train their spatial visualization skills in the future. In addition, our analysis of players' in-game behaviors shows the potential benefits of implementing adaptive and personalized learning guidance.

CCS Concepts
•**Applied computing** → **Interactive learning environments; Computer games;** *Computer-managed instruction;* •**Computing methodologies** → **Spatial and physical reasoning;**

Author Keywords
Spatial Visualization Skills; Education; Video Games; Game Features; STEM; Player Behavior; Learning Analytics

INTRODUCTION
Established research has demonstrated that spatial visualization skills, which refer to the ability to understand the visual and spatial relationship among objects, are crucial to reasoning and solving complex problems in Science, technology, engineering, and mathematics (STEM) disciplines [19,35,36,43,47,48].

With the increased number of students pouring into STEM disciplines, effectively evaluating and preparing students' spatial visualization skills for their future STEM coursework and careers has become a very important problem [12,35,36,43,47,48]. An established solution is the use of scalable online training workshops [12,47,48]. Xiao et al built a scalable online platform for evaluating and training first year engineering students' spatial visualization skills [48]. They hosted a semester-long workshop for training spatial visualization skills. An evaluation with over 600 engineering students showed clear training effects and a strong potential for future deployment at a larger scale. However, the major problem they reported was low retention rate, as a lot of students quit in the middle of the workshop [48]. Therefore, a new method is needed to intrinsically motivate students to train their spatial visualization skills.

A popular way of providing intrinsic motivation is through gamification [8,23,25,29,44,45]. Gamification can introduce higher levels of motivation and engagement than traditional instructional methods [8,23,25]. Instead of formal instruction, video game players learn through their actions and experiences in the game [26]. Video games allow self-directed learning via a trial-and-error approach. Meanwhile, when introducing new levels or game mechanics, video games provide tutorials and in-game assistance for players to facilitate the learning process. These properties of video games have great potential for increasing students motivation to learn [26,31,32]. Therefore, we gamified Xiao et al's online workshop into a scalable gaming platform, *Cubicle*. *Cubicle* aimed to motivate students to engage in effective spatial visualization skill training.

Cubicle is a modular educational gaming platform with multiple game modules. Such modular design allows for flexible game content and more generalizability. Although spatial visualization skills are critical for the STEM disciplines in general, different academic fields emphasize different aspects of these skills [35]. For example, mental rotation is more important for Organic Chemistry, where mental rotation is the key to visualizing and manipulating chemical modular structure, than for Mechanical Engineering, where visuliazing 3D object from 2D blue print is more important [35]. Flexible and expand-

IUI'18, March 7–11, 2018, Tokyo, Japan
© 2018 ACM. ISBN 978-1-4503-4945-1/18/03...$15.00
DOI: https://doi.org/10.1145/3172944.3172954

able game modules allow the platform to compose the most suitable learning materials for game players from different disciplines. Meanwhile, *Cubicle* also welcomes instructors to write their customized game modules and host them on our platform. Currently, *Cubicle* has eight game modules based on five major aspects of spatial visualization skills: 3D object visualization and manipulation, perspective taking, mental rotation, 2D to 3D transformation, and spatial memory.

Cubicle is designed not only to train players' spatial visualization skills, but also to help researchers or instructors acquire more insights into players' behavior and problem-solving strategies through the in-game player behavioral data [2, 13]. Our fine-grained in-game player behavior data collection allows for the possibility of implementing adaptive learning, personalized hints, error pattern analysis, and large-scale collaborative games. These learning analytic methods can give researchers and educators a better understanding of how people with different level of spatial visualization skills approach the problem and which problem-solving strategy best suits their skill level [2,4,6,13].

We evaluated *Cubicle* with ten students from three entry-level STEM engineering graphics courses. The results of our evaluation showed that all eight modules on our game platform tap into players' spatial visualization skills. Feedback from student participants revealed high levels of interest and motivation to use our platform as a tool for training their spatial skills in the future. In addition, our gaming platform shows great potential for implementing learning analytics and adaptive learning at scale.

Our work provides three major contributions to the IUI community: First, we present an approach to build an intelligent educational gaming platform to train college students' spatial visualization skills. Second, we developed a gaming platform, *Cubicle*, based on this approach and evaluated it in an empirical study, demonstrating its potential as a motivational tool for spatial skill training. Third, we provide insights and design suggestions for future learning analytics features in educational games.

RELATED WORK

Spatial Visualization Skill Training

Due to the importance of spatial visualization skills, a lot of effort has been invested in training engineering student's spatial ability. Existed research shows the spatial visulizaton skills are malleable [35,36,40]. With proper training methods, people's spatial visulization skills can be improved signifciantly in several months [10,15,36,48].The most well-known training material was developed by Sorby in 2011, and has been used at multiple universities [10,15,36,48]. However, most workshops based on these materials were organized in a face-to-face classroom environment with less than 30 people. This approach is not scalable with the large number of students who need spatial skill training [48]. There are two major obstacles hindering the scaling of the workshop approach: 1) scheduling problems and 2) lack of resources. It is very difficult to schedule a time and location that can fit a large number of students' schedules. Also, teaching and grading requires considerable amount of work from the instructors and teaching assistants in a large class. To reduce the cost of scaling, researcher moved Sorby's workshop online and showed success [48]. Therefore, in *Cubicle*, we adapted the learning materials from Sorby with focus on five major aspects of the spatial visualization skills and considered the scalbility issue.

Increasing Learning Motivation through Video Games

As insufficient spatial ability is a barrier to success in STEM coursework, it is important to motivate students to train and improve their spatial ability [19,35,36,43,48]. Video games are one potential solution since gaming is fun and enjoyable to many people, and can intrinsically motivate players to engage [12,16,35,36,43]. Existing research suggests four main characteristics of games make them engaging educational tools: challenge, fantasy, complexity and control [16, 21]. Ideally, combining difficult game tasks, an attractive backgroud story, mutiple game modes and a free exploration map can acquire most interest from game players [21]. Thomas and Macredie mentioned that the key factor that draws players into a game is that their actions have no real world repercussions [39]. Without real world consequences, players will feel more encouraged to explore all potential solving strategies, which is key for effective learning, especially for those who don't have a clear direction to solve the game task.

In our game design, we incorporated those engaging features as well to make our game modules more motivational. The player needs to escape [control] from a dungeon maze [Fantasy] by solving multiple puzzles [challenge, complexity]. And players are free to keep trying to solve a puzzle repeatedly [no consequence for exploring the solution space].

Training Spatial Skills with Video Games

Using video games as a method for training spatial visualization skills has been investigated in recent years as well. Research on commercial games has shown that a wide variety of video games can train spatial visualization skills, such as Tetris, Zaxxon, Medal of Honor, Portal 2 and Super Mario [11,14,18,33,34,38]. However, those commercial games usually only train a single aspect of spatial visualization and the content is not customizable. Wauck et al. looked into specific game features that may help improve spatial visualization skills and recommended two useful game features: 1) object rotation and 2) object alignment in 3D model construction [47]. Our designed game module specifically emphasized these features.

GAME PLATFORM DESIGN

We designed and developed an online game platform called *Cubicle* to incorporate features focused on training five aspects of spatial visualization: 3D object visualization and manipulation, perspective taking, mental rotation, 2D to 3D transformation, and spatial memory [35]. *Cubicle* contains eight modules: 1) Block Building, 2) Constructive Solid Geometry (CSG), 3) Plane Exploration, 4) View Point, 5) Transform Limitation, 6) Shape Revolving, 7) Cube Shift and 8) Flat Pattern (Table 1).

The premise of the game is that the player is trapped in a dungeon maze. To escape, the player needs to navigate through

Game Modules	*Target Spatial Skills*
Block Builder	3D Object Visualization & Manipulation 2D to 3D Transformation
Constructive Solid Geometry	3D Object visualization & manipulation Perspective Taking
View Point	Perspective Taking 2D to 3D transformation
Transform Limitation	Mental Rotation Perspective Taking 3D Object Visualization & Manipulation
Shape Revolving	Perspective Taking 2D to 3D transformation
Plane Exploration	3D object visualization & manipulation Perspective Taking
Cube Shift	Spatial Memory
Flat Pattern	Perspective Taking 2D to 3D transformation

Table 1: The eight game modules in *Cubicle* and their corresponding target spatial visualization skill(s)

the maze and unlock all the rooms. The player starts from a large center room with multiple smaller adjoining rooms. Each smaller room contains a totem, the entry to a game module. In each game module, a chain of locked rooms contains different levels in that game module. Finishing the game task in the room is the only way to unlock the door to the next room.

Game Module Design

Block Builder

The Block Builder is aimed at training the player's ability to mentally construct a 3D model from orthographic drawings (Figure 1b). We designed this module to improve the player's ability to visualize 3D objects through the process of transforming orthographic drawings into 3D models [36].

In this game, the target 3D block model is algorithmically generated for each level. The player is shown orthographic views of the target block model and asked to build the model on the 3×3 grid empty base by adding or deleting cubes. The interface also shows the 3-views of the current model next to the 3-views of the target model.The game will automatically end once all views match. The level of difficulty is controlled by the complexity of the generated 3D block model.

The interface strictly follows the rule of orthographic drawings in engineering graphics, with the front view at the bottom left, the top view at the top left, and the side view at the bottom right.

Constructive Solid Geometry

The Constructive Solid Geometry game is aimed at training player's ability to visualize 3D objects and manipulate them (Figure 1c) [28]. The main goal of the game is to construct a 3D object by performing Boolean operations, including Union, Intersection and Subtraction, on existing 3D objects. The player needs to mentally visualize what an operation would do to objects to complete this task [36].

In this game, the player is given several primitive objects (e.g., cube, cuboid, sphere, cylinder) and a complex target object generated by the primitive objects with Boolean operations. The player will perform a series of Boolean operations to create the complex target object. To emphasize the importance of mental visualization, the player is not allowed to undo any operation. As soon as the player makes a mistake, they lose the game and must reset to start over. Once the player believes their object matches the target object, they can check the result by submitting the object to the system for evaluation. The difficulty level increases with the increment number of operations needed to build the target model.

View Point

The View Point game aims to train the ability to imagine different perspectives or orientations in space, an important component in the spatial visualization skill sets (Figure 1d) [36]. The player is asked to mentally visualize a three-dimensional landscape from a two-dimensional map and determine the observation point that is being displayed. Mental rotation is needed to correctly visualize the scenes.

In the game, a variety of solid shapes are randomly generated on a circular base, with a camera randomly chosen from eight candidates, each with a different position and angle. All candidate cameras face the center of the base. The player needs to determine where the camera is based on the view of the chosen camera and the top view of the scene. The number of solids on the circular base increases with the game's difficulty.

Transform Limitation

The Transform Limitation game taps into the player's mental rotation ability (Figure 1e). In this game, the player is asked to rotate or mirror a 3D object to match a target object within a limited number of steps. In each step, the player either rotates the object 90 degrees about an axis, or mirrors the object once. Since the number of steps is limited, the player needs to mentally rotate and visualize the result before taking an action. The difficulty of the game progresses as the number of operations required increases and the number of operations allowed decreases.

Shape Revolving

The Shaping Revolving game emphasizes 2D to 3D transformation (Figure 1f). The game aims to improve players' understanding of surfaces and solids from revolution. The player needs to envision the relationship between 3D objects and 2D shapes, mentally revolve a 2D shape about an axis, and visualize the created 3D model [36, 48].

In this game, the player is shown a 2D shape as well as a 3D object. Like the section "Rotation of Objects about Axes" in Sorby's book, the goal is to identify which axis the 2D

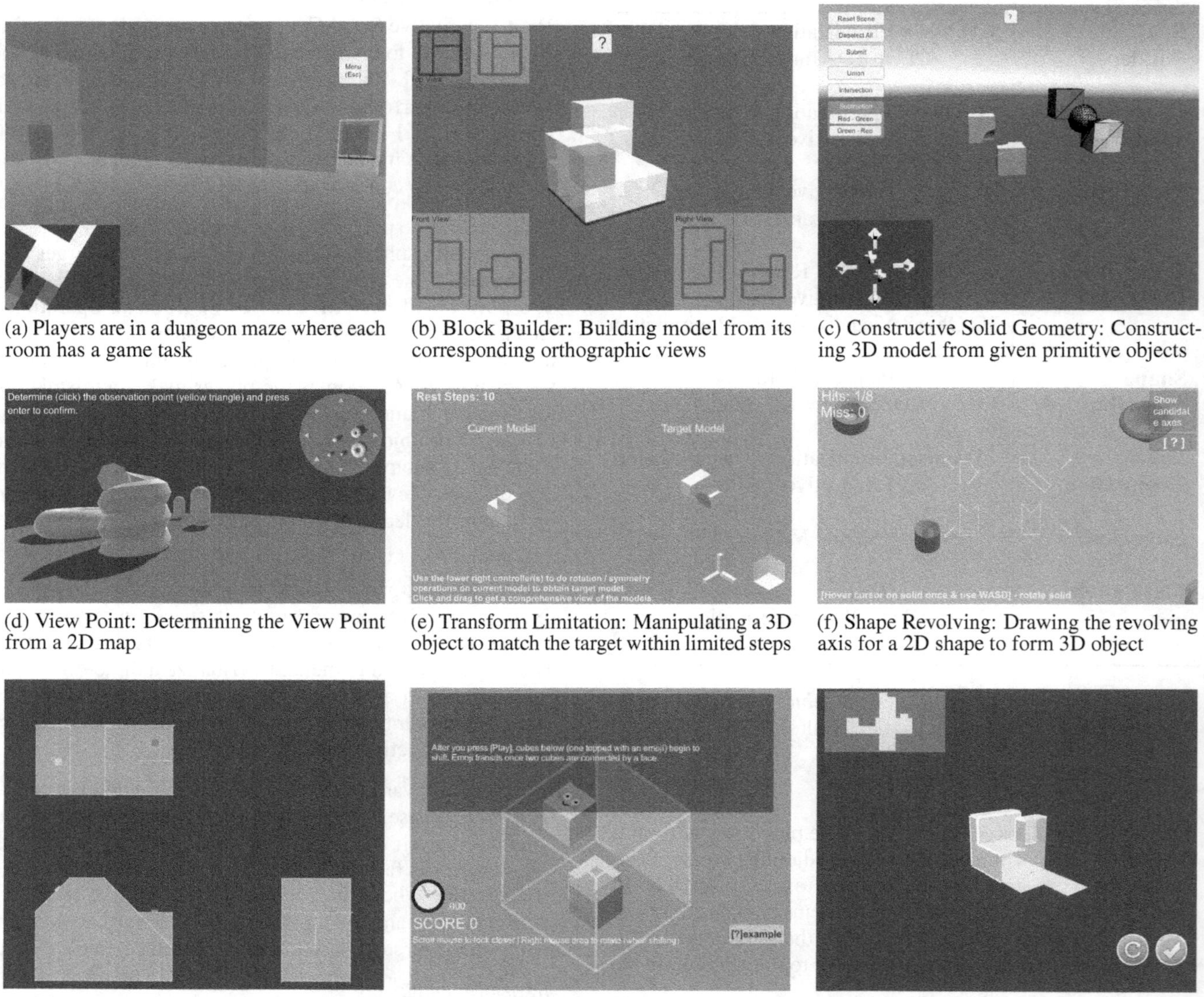

(a) Players are in a dungeon maze where each room has a game task

(b) Block Builder: Building model from its corresponding orthographic views

(c) Constructive Solid Geometry: Constructing 3D model from given primitive objects

(d) View Point: Determining the View Point from a 2D map

(e) Transform Limitation: Manipulating a 3D object to match the target within limited steps

(f) Shape Revolving: Drawing the revolving axis for a 2D shape to form 3D object

(g) Plane Exploration: Navigating on a 3D landscape with only orthographic views of the landscape

(h) Cube Shift: Keeping track of a series of cube shifting and idenfying the missing emoji

(i) Flat Pattern: Unfolding a 3D object to a target 2D pattern

Figure 1: Screenshots from the *Cubicle*. [a], The dungeon maze connects access eight game modules; [b - i], the screenshots from each game module

shape revolved around to generate the 3D model [36]. An advanced level of this game shows 4 pairs of shapes and objects simultaneously (Figure 1f). Over the course of the game, objects move gradually towards the center of the screen. The player needs to draw 8 correct axes to unlock the next level. If the player fails to draw the revolution axis before the object reaches the center, the object will disappear and one miss will be recorded. If the player missed more than 8 2D shapes, the counter for the correct answers will be reset to zero. Thus, the player must respond as fast as possible. The player completes a level once the number of successful attempts reaches a certain threshold. The game becomes steadily more difficult as the objects become more complex and their movement speed increases.

Plane Exploration

The Plane Exploration game is designed to train 3D object visualization and perspective taking (Figure 1g). Similar to "Orthographic Drawings" in Sorby's book, the player needs to understand standard orthographic drawings and mentally visualize the corresponding 3D model in order to win [36].

In this game, the player's goal is to guide a yellow square across a 3D landscape model to an orange square, with only orthographic views available. The game allows the player to climb upward or down via ramps but not stairs, so it is critical for the player to mentally visualize the 3D landscape before deciding which way to go. If the yellow square falls through a stair, the game is over.The difficulty of each level is controlled by the complexity of the 3D landscape model.

The 3D landscape models in the game come from existing spatial visualization training material, which follows the display rule of orthographic drawings in engineering graphics as well. A player's performance is measured by how long it takes for the player to reach the orange square and how many failed attempts are made.

Cube Shift

The Cube Shift game is designed to focus on spatial memory, which taps into two strong indicators of spatial abilities: working memory span and short-term memory [36] (Figure 1h). Cube Shift requires players to direct their attention to the image on a series of cubes while avoiding the distraction of their shifting movements. At the same time, players must also remember previous configurations of the cubes. The game design resembles the n-back tasks by Wayne Kirchner, where the subject is presented with a sequence of stimuli, and the task consists of indicating when the current stimulus matches the one from n steps earlier in the sequence [24]. It also resembles the Dot Memory task [22], a test of short-term memory, where the subject briefly views a 2D grid with dots shown in sequence inside of it. After the dots disappear, the subject indicates the dot locations in an answer grid.

In this game, the player sees a 3D grid with 3 (or more) cubes that shift position a specified number of times. There is an emoji on one of the cubes, which moves between cubes whenever two cubes' faces touch. Once the sequence of shifts ends, the emoji will disappear. The subject is asked to find where the emoji last appeared n steps earlier in the shift sequence. Different levels of game manipulate the factor n, the number of cubes, and the number of shifting steps to vary the difficulty level. The player wins once they successfully find the emoji five times and loses if they make more than eight mistakes.

Flat Pattern

The Flat Pattern aims to enhance students' capabilities of establishing the corresponding relationship between a 3D model and the unfolded 2D pattern (Figure 1i). This requires the ability of 2D to 3D transformation and perspective taking [36,48]. During the gameplay, the player is expected to envision the spatial relationship between faces on a 3D model.

In this game, the player is shown a 2D flat target pattern and a corresponding 3D model. The player can cut an edge to unbind the two faces that it connects, then unfold the whole model progressively. The goal is to unfold the 3D model and make it the same pattern as the 2D target pattern. The player is only allowed to undo one edge cutting; otherwise, the level needs to be reset.

Different levels are designed based on the complexity of the 3D model and the number of hints to help the students acquire the related visuospatial skills gradually. At first, hints are given by displaying icons on certain faces to help the player establish the correspondence between the 3D model and the 2D pattern. As the difficulty increases, players must establish the relationship on their own with fewer hints and more complicated models.

Modular Game Platform Design and Fine-grained Data Collection

The game platform is designed modularly, allowing for flexible content. Game modules can be added or removed easily by communicating through documented APIs. The map of the dungeon maze can be modified through a single JSON file. The game platform collects player's in-game behavior in detail, which allows for the possibility of implementing adaptive learning. The completion time for each attempt is recorded for all levels of each game. Meanwhile, in-game behaviors are logged in great detail. Every single click, action, move is recorded. Using this data, the system can infer a player's problem-solving strategy and react by adjusting game difficultly or repeating failed challenges.

METHOD

To test our game platform in the field and validate our research hypotheses, we conducted a mixed-method study, in-game behavior analysis and qualitative interview, with participants from three entry-level engineering graphics courses at a large public university. All courses focus on the various aspects of engineering drawings where the spatial visualization skills are strongly emphasized.

Iterative Design & Development Process

Before the formal evaluation, we iteratively modified and improved our design. In an eight-week period, our team met with a group of testers weekly. With their valuable feedback, we adjusted the difficulty level for each game module and implemented a detailed tutorial system.

Participants

We sent out study invitations for a spatial visualization training game via email to students in three entry-level engineering graphics courses. All three courses share two learning goals: 1) to gain familiarity with the standards and conventions of engineering design graphics and 2) to gain exposure to computer aided design techniques. 10 students agreed to join our study. Five were male and five were female, and all had Freshman standing within an engineering major. Participants were compensated with 15 dollars for their participation at the end of the study.

Procedure

Before participants started the game, we tested their spatial visualization skills using the Revised Purdue Spatial Relations Test (PSVT:R) [49]. The PSVT:R test is widely used in assessing college students' spatial visualization skills [47,48,49]. The PSVT:R consists of 30 questions in order of increasing difficulty with a 20-minute time limit [49].

After participants finished taking the PSVT:R, research assistants installed the game on the participant's computers and went through the tutorial of each game module with them to make sure they understood the game objective and the basic controls. After that, participants were asked to play the game over a 3 days period and try to complete as many levels as possible. We estimated that it would take participants about 1.5 hours to complete the entire game. Considering participants' schedule, we believed 3 days was more than enough time for everyone to complete as much of the game as they could. At the end of game-playing period, research assistants collected in-game player behavior data through a network protocol. After finishing the gameplay session, participants completed a post-game survey in which they rated how fun, boring, easy, and frustrating they found the game and their opinion about the gaming platform overall.

In-Game Player Behavior Metrics

We collected a large amount of player behavior data from our participants. Data collected for each player focused primarily on three major aspects: 1) Game Progress, 2) Completion Time, and 3) Error Rate. Each of these player behaviors help us understand how players' spatial visualization skills are associated with game difficulty, and different types of player strategies. An explanation of the metrics follows below.

Game progress. For each game module, a player's Game Progress is the percentage of levels they completed. For the overall game, the game progress is the average game progress of all eight modules.

Average Level-completion Time. Average Level-completion Time measures the time in seconds taken to complete each level. For each game module, the player's completion time is the averaged across all levels in that game module. For the overall game, the completion time is the average level-completion time of all eight modules. If the player did not successfully complete a level, the time they spend in failure attempt did not count.

Average Error Rate. The Error Rate measures how many failed attempts (resets) a player made before they successfully completed a level. Due to the difference in game mechanics across the eight modules, error rate is calculated differently for each of them:

- *Block Builder.* In this game module, the Error Rate is calculated by dividing the number of incorrect addition/deletion actions by the total number of addition/deletion actions. An incorrect addition is defined by as adding a block that is not a part of the correct model. Meanwhile, an incorrect deletion action is defined as removing a correctly added block.

- *Constructive Solid Geometry / Flat Pattern.* In the Constructive Solid Geometry (CSG) and Flat Pattern game, the Error Rate is defined by the percentage of failed submissions out of all submission attempts. "Failed submissions" here counts both the number of failed submissions and how many times the player reset the scene.

- *Plane Exploration/ View Point / Transform Limitation/Shape Revolving/ Cube Shift.* The Error Rate in these game modules is the percentage of failed attempts out of total attempts.

For each game module, the player's Average Error Rate is the average Error Rate of all completed levels. The overall game's Average Error Rate is the mean of all eight modules' Average Error Rate.

Post-Game Survey

In addition to in-game player behavior data, we are also interested in what players thought of our game and whether they are motivated to use our gaming platform as a training tool after trying it out. We had players fill out a post-game survey rating their game experience on a 1-5 Likert scale (1 not at all to 5 very much) on the following measures:

Perception of the Game Platform. The Game Perception measure contained 4 items asking how easy, boring, frustrating, and fun the game was.

Willingness To Use the Game Platform. This measure contained 2 items asking players how they liked our game overall and whether they wanted to use our game as a tool to develop their spatial visualization skills in the future.

We also asked the participants to leave any comments or suggestions in a text box.

Hypotheses

We had the following three hypotheses for this user study.

H1: Players' existing spatial visualization skills will be correlated with their in-game behavior metrics. More specifically, players with lower level of spatial visualization skills will spend more time to complete a level and make more errors.

H2: Players with higher spatial visualization skills will explore and complete more game levels than players with lower spatial visualization skills.

H3: Players will be intrinsically motivated to use our platform to train their spatial visualization skills.

RESULT

The focus of our analysis was to determine if players' spatial visualization skills were associated with their in-game player behaviors and number of completed levels, and to assess player's impressions of our game platform. We performed a hierarchical two-stage correlation analysis, starting with the aggregate in-game player behavior metrics for the game as a whole and then looking into the in-game player behavior metrics for each game module.

Spatial Visualization Skills

Participants' average PSVT:R score was 19.8 out of 30 (SD=7.8) which is similar to previous findings in a large scale assessment of college students using the PSVT:R [20]. From the distribution of PSVT:R scores, we can see players' spatial visualization skills range from 8 to 30 and are not skewed to either direction. Consistent with previous research [3,20,47], we found a significant gender difference in test scores, with males (M=24.6, SD = 6.1) scoring higher than females (M=15.0, SD = 6.4); $t = 2.41$, $p < 0.05$.

Spatial Visualization Skills and Average Game Completion Time

The time spent on each level is a good indicator of how challenging the level is to the player. We looked into the relationship between players' spatial visualization skills and how much time they used to complete each level on average. There

In-Game Player Behavior Metrics	*Mean*	*SD*	*Correlation w/ PSVT:R Score*
Block Builder			
Average Level-completion Time (in seconds)	116.8	93.48	$-.97^{**}$
Error Rate	0.27	0.12	$-.87^{**}$
Constructive Solid Geometry			
Average Level-completion Time (in seconds)	61.24	32.59	$-.95^{**}$
Error Rate	0.50	0.20	$-.91^{**}$
View Point			
Average Level-completion Time (in seconds)	32.87	32.00	$-.94^{**}$
Error Rate	0.35	0.31	$-.89^{**}$
Transform Limitation			
Average Level-completion Time (in seconds)	33.49	21.08	$-.65^{**}$
Error Rate	0.31	0.14	$-.67^{**}$
Shape Revolving			
Average Level-completion Time (in seconds)	28.88	16.95	$-.51^{**}$
Error Rate	0.55	0.14	$-.91^{**}$
Plane Exploration			
Average Level-completion Time (in seconds)	32.19	32.83	$-.65^{**}$
Error Rate	0.46	0.24	$-.91^{**}$
Cube Shift			
Average Level-completion Time (in seconds)	9.06	2.15	$-.87^{**}$
Error Rate	0.12	0.11	$-.40^{**}$
Flat Pattern			
Average Level-completion Time (in seconds)	185.37	82.87	$-.97^{**}$
Error Rate	0.64	0.20	$-.96^{**}$

Table 2: Pearson's correlation between player's spatial visualization skills (PSVT:R Score) and in-game player behavior metrics for each game module. *Note. ** indicates p < .01.*

was a significant strong negative correlation between players' PSVT:R scores and Average Level-completion Time (M = 72, SD = 36), r = -0.94, n = 10, $p < .01$. The correlation holds for all eight game modules as well (Table 2).

This result suggests that players who have higher spatial visualization skills spent less time completing each level, which supports our hypothesis that our gaming platform utilizes player's spatial visualization skills. The result also aligned with established research that when solving spatial tasks, players who are lower at spatial visualization skills take more time to mentally visualize potential solution and to find the correct problem-solving strategy [37,41,42]. However, the time used in solving such question indicates potential learning effects [7]. Therefore, players with lower spatial visualization skills may benefit from the time they spent in solving those questions.

Spatial Visualization Skills and Error Rate

Next, we analyzed players' game actions. We expect that players with lower levels of spatial visualization skills made more mistakes, as the game is designed to train spatial visualization skills. Person's correlation test revealed that spatial visualization skill was negatively correlated with Average Error Rate(M = 0.36, SD = 0.13),r = -.97, n = 10, $p < .01$). Players with lower spatial visualization ability made more mistakes than those with higher spatial ability. This relationship also holds for all eight modules (Table 2).

Without a clear solving strategy, players with lower spatial visualization explore multiple potential strategies and experience more failure attempts [37]. Learning often happens in the process of exploring potential strategies. When players experience multiple failures, they either learn from the failure or give up. Our analysis on game progress shows no significant correlation between players' spatial visualization skills and their game progress which indicates that players with lower spatial visualization skills eventually acquire the strategy that leads them in the right direction.

Spatial Visualization Skills and Game Progress

We analyzed the relationship between players' spatial visualization skills and the percentage of game they completed. The average Game Progress was 85.6 % (SD = 9.1%). Pearson's correlation test revealed a positive but not significant correlation between player's PSVT:R score and the Game Progress, $r = 0.58$, $n = 10$, $p > .05$. The result did not support our hypothesis that players with lower spatial visualization skills will complete less game content than others.

Players' Impressions of the Game

We collected player's opinions in the post-game survey immediately after they finished playing the game. Overall, player's impressions were positive. Most of the participants found our gaming platform is interesting and moderately fun to play (M = 3.3, SD = 0.5). As two of our participants explained:

> *"There are many interesting types of spatial visualization and memory that I hadn't really used before. I'm not sure how much my skills have improved, but it was fun to complete the puzzles!"* (P1)

and

> *"I really enjoyed it! There [are] a ton of cool training tools there"* (P2)

Being fun and enjoyable is the key indicator of a good game. Our goal with *Cubicle* was to combine effective spatial skill training exercises with the entertaining aspects of traditional video games. We believe, therefore, that our game can attract and motivate students to voluntarily use our platform as a tool for training spatial visualization skills.

We also asked our players how much they liked our platform in general and whether they would want to use it in the future as a training tool. Most participants reported liking our platform (M = 3.5, SD = 0.5) and wanted to use it in the future (M = 3.8, SD = 1.1) (5-point Likert Scale). After analyzing their comments further, we found that players who had lower levels of spatial visualization skills (PSVT:R score lower than 18, N = 5) all expressed strong interests in training their spatial visualization skills via our platform (M = 4.2, SD = 0.8). For example, some players said,

> *"I think overall it is useful for helping to understand visual and spatial organization, and I'm glad to have this experience to learn what I'm good and not good at."*(P3)

and

> *"I wish there were more levels to improve my spatial visualization skills."*(P4)

Through our players' impression, we can see a great potential for the gaming platform to be deployed on a larger scale.

DISCUSSION

Our results indicate that our gaming platform, *Cubicle*, tapped into players' spatial visualization skills, supporting our hypothesis **H1**. We found that players with lower spatial visualization skills tend to spend more time on each level of the game and make more errors. In addition, participants exhibited a high level of willingness and enthusiasm to use Cubicle for future training, especially those with lower level of spatial ability, supporting our hypothesis **H3**.

However, our **H2** is not supported by the result that players' spatial visualization skills does not predict how many game levels they complete. Game progress can be used to infer how engaging players find our game [27]. The game allows players to make an unlimited number of attempts on each level, and we give our participants more than enough time to play the game. Therefore, as long as players are engaged in our game, they will achieve a similar level of game progress.Thus, one way to interpret this result is players were equally engaged in our game regardless of their existed spatial visualization skills.

Although the *Cubicle* has the feature that supports learning analytics, our analysis did not reveal any clear error patterns for players with different levels of spatial visualization skills. Our small sample size is a likely cause; learning analytics requires large scale data collection. However, our evaluation results suggest a bright future for our platform once deployed on a large scale.

Future Directions and Development

Our study demonstrated the potential of our gaming platform, *Cubicle*, as a tool for training college students' spatial visualization skills at scale. The design of the platform allows fine-grained in-game player behavior collection which creates the possibility of multiple learning analytics. We envision the following future directions.

Data-Driven Adaptive Learning Trajectory

A data-driven method can be implemented to achieve adaptive learning trajectories. Adaptive learning has been researched in different contexts and has been shown to promote learning [5, 17]. However, hindering implementation of adaptive learning at large scale is the problem of how to automatically detect the student's current learning progress and what the next step should be. With the in-game behavior data collected in our platform, a learning model could be built for each player by comparing their problem-solving strategy with those of past players. For example, based on a player's in-game behaviors, the system can infer their level of spatial visualization skills and provide the most effective materials for players with the a similar level of spatial ability. As the player progresses in the game, the storyline and game modules can evolve to give the player the most effective gaming content for their skill level.

The player's problem-solving strategy can also be captured by the platform, which can analyze the player's strategy to provide personalized guidance. For example, the system can help a player who exhibits incapability in mental rotation by analyzing which specific part of the problem-solving strategy (e.g. using the wrong reference point while rotating the subject) is the issue and guide the player to the best strategy found by previous players.

Hint systems are prevalent in all kinds of games and are designed to adjust the game difficulty for individual users [46]. A good hint system could reduce a player's frustration and increase their engagement [9, 46]. In an educational game, the hint system can be designed as an instruction system that helps players learn more efficiently. The design of our game platform allows for the possibility of personalized hints. With sufficient in-game player data, our system can classify player mistakes into different categories and generate hints accordingly. If the player is stuck in the middle of a game, hints can be provided automatically and adaptively, which will help the user to gain a deeper understanding of the best problem-solving strategies and increase learning efficiency.

Comprehensive Feedback System

People learn from the feedback they receive from a game. A good feedback system can provide the player with more useful information beyond merely telling them whether what they did was right or wrong. It is even better if the feedback not only tells the player what they did wrong but also provides information on how to solve the problem. In our game platform, all in-game behavior data was stored in a large database that allows knowledge discovery. Future work could enable a comprehensive feedback system that deconstructs a player's performance and problem-solving strategies and provides a comparison with other players. With such a feedback system, the player could gain more insight about how to solve such problems in the future.

Large Scale Collaborative Game Module

Large scale collaborative learning has been examined in multiple studies as an effective way to increase player engagement and create a better learning environment [1, 30]. Our gaming platform was built using the Unity game engine, which allows us to compile it as a WebGL application. Hosting it on web allows players all over the world to use our platform to train their visualization skills. Meanwhile, with more players' in-game behavior data, our platform can better engage those learning analytic methods we mentioned above.

Because of its modular design, *Cubicle* can add more game modules designed for collaborative learning. For example, we can extend the Block Building module to allow players to collaborate and build together. This would allow players to learn from each other. With such large-scale collaborative features, we believe our future platform can benefit a wider range of audiences and promote more effective learning.

Limitations

Our current study has several limitations. First, although all current gaming modules were adapted from an existing spatial visualization workshop, we have not yet tested whether the training effects of the workshop was preserved. In addition, training spatial visualization skills is a long-term process that our short evaluation in this study could not capture. Therefore, we plan to deploy our gaming platform with more content in the future within an actual classroom environment and examine its training effectiveness. Lastly, players found several bugs while playing the game in our study. Although we fixed them as soon as possible, they may have negatively impacted players' engagement with the game.

Conclusion

Certain in-class or online workshops have been empirically shown to train spatial visualization, a set of cognitive skills tightly linked to future success in STEM disciplines. However, current methods of training students' spatial visualization skills face two main problems : scalability and engagement. In this study, we gamified an existing online platform and created a modular educational gaming platform, *Cubicle*, to train players spatial visualization skills while addressing the problems of scalability and motivation. A user study of 10 participants with varied level of spatial ability showed a strong correlation between performance in *Cubicle* game modules and players' existing spatial skills. Players reported a strong willingness and motivation to keep using our platform as a tool of training spatial visualization skills in the future. In addition, our platform is capable of implementing intelligent learning features, such as data-driven adaptive learning trajectories, a comprehensive feedback system, and large scale collaborative game modules. Therefore, we believe *Cubicle* is a great educational gaming platform with bright future potential for helping students to engage spatial visualization skills training and prepare them for STEM coursework and future careers.

ACKNOWLEDGEMENT

This work was partially funded by the Strategic Instructional Innovations Program (SIIP) at College of Engineering of the University of Illinois at Urbana-Champaign and by the NSF grants SES-1419297 and IIS-1441563.

REFERENCES

1. Alissa N Antle, Allen Bevans, Josh Tanenbaum, Katie Seaborn, and Sijie Wang. 2011. Futura: design for collaborative learning and game play on a multi-touch digital tabletop. In *Proceedings of the fifth international conference on Tangible, embedded, and embodied interaction*. ACM, 93–100.
2. Ryan Shaun Baker and Paul Salvador Inventado. 2014. Educational data mining and learning analytics. In *Learning analytics*. Springer, 61–75.
3. Michael T Battista. 1990. Spatial visualization and gender differences in high school geometry. *Journal for research in mathematics education* (1990), 47–60.
4. Matthew Berland, Ryan S Baker, and Paulo Blikstein. 2014. Educational data mining and learning analytics: Applications to constructionist research. *Technology, Knowledge and Learning* 19, 1-2 (2014), 205–220.
5. Adriana Berlanga and Francisco J Garcia. 2005. Learning technology specifications: semantic objects for adaptive learning environments. *International Journal of Learning Technology* 1, 4 (2005), 458–472.
6. Paulo Blikstein. 2011. Using learning analytics to assess students' behavior in open-ended programming tasks. In *Proceedings of the 1st international conference on learning analytics and knowledge*. ACM, 110–116.
7. Benjamin S Bloom. 1974. Time and learning. *American psychologist* 29, 9 (1974), 682.
8. Elizabeth A Boyle, Thomas M Connolly, Thomas Hainey, and James M Boyle. 2012. Engagement in digital entertainment games: A systematic review. *Computers in Human Behavior* 28, 3 (2012), 771–780.

9. Cristina Conati and Xiaohong Zhao. 2004. Building and evaluating an intelligent pedagogical agent to improve the effectiveness of an educational game. In *Proceedings of the 9th international conference on Intelligent user interfaces*. ACM, 6–13.

10. Agata K. Dean. 2017. Applied Spatial Visualization for Engineers. In *2017 ASEE Annual Conference & Exposition*. ASEE Conferences, Columbus, Ohio. https://peer.asee.org/27598.

11. Michel Dorval and Michel Pepin. 1986. Effect of playing a video game on a measure of spatial visualization. *Perceptual and motor skills* 62, 1 (1986), 159–162.

12. Lelli Van Den Einde and Nathan Delson. 2014. Using Touch Interface Technology for Spatial Visualization Training. In *2014 ASEE Annual Conference & Exposition*. ASEE Conferences, Indianapolis, Indiana. https://peer.asee.org/23284.

13. Magy Seif El-Nasr, Anders Drachen, and Alessandro Canossa. 2016. *Game analytics*. Springer.

14. Jing Feng, Ian Spence, and Jay Pratt. 2007. Playing an action video game reduces gender differences in spatial cognition. *Psychological science* 18, 10 (2007), 850–855.

15. Alex Friess, Eric L. Martin, Ivan E. Esparragoza, and Oenardi Lawanto. 2016. Improvements in Student Spatial Visualization in an Introductory Engineering Graphics Course using Open-ended Design Projects Supported by 3-D Printed Manipulatives. In *2016 ASEE Annual Conference & Exposition*. ASEE Conferences, New Orleans, Louisiana. https://peer.asee.org/25608.

16. Rosemary Garris, Robert Ahlers, and James E Driskell. 2002. Games, motivation, and learning: A research and practice model. *Simulation & gaming* 33, 4 (2002), 441–467.

17. Vicki Jones and Jun H Jo. 2004. Ubiquitous learning environment: An adaptive teaching system using ubiquitous technology. In *Beyond the comfort zone: Proceedings of the 21st ASCILITE Conference*, Vol. 468. Perth, Western Australia, 474.

18. Simone Kühn, Tobias Gleich, Robert C Lorenz, Ulman Lindenberger, and Jürgen Gallinat. 2014. Playing Super Mario induces structural brain plasticity: gray matter changes resulting from training with a commercial video game. *Molecular psychiatry* 19, 2 (2014), 265–271.

19. David Lubinski. 2010. Spatial ability and STEM: A sleeping giant for talent identification and development. *Personality and Individual Differences* 49, 4 (2010), 344âĂŞ351. DOI: http://dx.doi.org/10.1016/j.paid.2010.03.022

20. Yukiko Maeda and So Yoon Yoon. 2013. A meta-analysis on gender differences in mental rotation ability measured by the Purdue spatial visualization tests: Visualization of rotations (PSVT: R). *Educational Psychology Review* 25, 1 (2013), 69–94.

21. Thomas Malone. 1981. *What makes computer games fun?* Vol. 13. ACM.

22. Gregory McCarthy, Andrew M Blamire, Aina Puce, Anna C Nobre, Gilles Bloch, Fahmeed Hyder, Patricia Goldman-Rakic, and Robert G Shulman. 1994. Functional magnetic resonance imaging of human prefrontal cortex activation during a spatial working memory task. *Proceedings of the National Academy of Sciences* 91, 18 (1994), 8690–8694.

23. Katie Larsen McClarty, Aline Orr, Peter M Frey, Robert P Dolan, Victoria Vassileva, and Aaron McVay. 2012. A literature review of gaming in education. *Gaming in education* (2012), 1–35.

24. Akira Miyake, Naomi P Friedman, David A Rettinger, Priti Shah, and Mary Hegarty. 2001. How are visuospatial working memory, executive functioning, and spatial abilities related? A latent-variable analysis. *Journal of experimental psychology: General* 130, 4 (2001), 621.

25. Cristina Ioana Muntean. 2011. Raising engagement in e-learning through gamification. In *Proc. 6th International Conference on Virtual Learning ICVL*. 323–329.

26. Richard S Prawat and Robert E Floden. 1994. Philosophical perspectives on constructivist views of learning. *Educational Psychologist* 29, 1 (1994), 37–48.

27. Andrew K Przybylski, C Scott Rigby, and Richard M Ryan. 2010. A motivational model of video game engagement. *Review of general psychology* 14, 2 (2010), 154.

28. Aristides AG Requicha and Herbert B Voelcker. 1977. Constructive solid geometry. (1977).

29. Ganit Richter, Daphne R Raban, and Sheizaf Rafaeli. 2015. Studying gamification: the effect of rewards and incentives on motivation. In *Gamification in education and business*. Springer, 21–46.

30. Margarida Romero, Mireia Usart, Michela Ott, Jeffrey Earp, and Sara de Freitas. 2012. Learning through playing for or against each other? Promoting collaborative learning in digital game based learning. *Learning* 5, 2012 (2012), 15–2012.

31. Yigal Rosen and Gavriel Salomon. 2007. The differential learning achievements of constructivist technology-intensive learning environments as compared with traditional ones: A meta-analysis. *Journal of Educational Computing Research* 36, 1 (2007), 1–14.

32. Debra Sanders and Dorette Sugg Welk. 2005. Strategies to scaffold student learning: Applying Vygotsky's zone of proximal development. *Nurse educator* 30, 5 (2005), 203–207.

33. Valerie J Shute, Matthew Ventura, and Fengfeng Ke. 2015. The power of play: The effects of Portal 2 and Lumosity on cognitive and noncognitive skills. *Computers & Education* 80 (2015), 58–67.

34. Valerie K Sims and Richard E Mayer. 2002. Domain specificity of spatial expertise: The case of video game players. *Applied cognitive psychology* 16, 1 (2002), 97–115.

35. Sheryl A. Sorby. 2009. Educational Research in Developing 3âĂŘD Spatial Skills for Engineering Students. *International Journal of Science Education* 31, 3 (2009), 459âĂŞ480. DOI: http://dx.doi.org/10.1080/09500690802595839

36. Sheryl Ann Sorby. 2011. *Developing spatial thinking*. Delmar Cengage Learning.

37. Sheryl A Sorby and Beverly J Baartmans. 2000. The Development and Assessment of a Course for Enhancing the 3-D Spatial Visualization Skills of First Year Engineering Students. *Journal of Engineering Education* 89, 3 (2000), 301–307.

38. Melissa S Terlecki, Nora S Newcombe, and Michelle Little. 2008. Durable and generalized effects of spatial experience on mental rotation: Gender differences in growth patterns. *Applied cognitive psychology* 22, 7 (2008), 996–1013.

39. Peter Thomas and Robert Macredie. 1994. Games and the design of human-computer interfaces. *Programmed Learning and Educational Technology* 31, 2 (1994), 134–142.

40. David H Uttal, Nathaniel G Meadow, Elizabeth Tipton, Linda L Hand, Alison R Alden, Christopher Warren, and Nora S Newcombe. 2013. The malleability of spatial skills: A meta-analysis of training studies. (2013).

41. Delinda van Garderen. 2006. Spatial visualization, visual imagery, and mathematical problem solving of students with varying abilities. *Journal of learning disabilities* 39, 6 (2006), 496–506.

42. Steven G Vandenberg and Allan R Kuse. 1978. Mental rotations, a group test of three-dimensional spatial visualization. *Perceptual and motor skills* 47, 2 (1978), 599–604.

43. Norma L. Veurink and AJ Hamlin. 2011. Spatial Visualization Skills: Impact on Confidence and Success in an Engineering Curriculum. In *2011 ASEE Annual Conference & Exposition*. ASEE Conferences, Vancouver, BC. https://peer.asee.org/18591.

44. Luis Von Ahn and Laura Dabbish. 2004. Labeling images with a computer game. In *Proceedings of the SIGCHI conference on Human factors in computing systems*. ACM, 319–326.

45. Luis von Ahn and Laura Dabbish. 2008. Designing Games with a Purpose. *Commun. ACM* 51, 8 (Aug. 2008), 58–67. DOI:http://dx.doi.org/10.1145/1378704.1378719

46. Helen Wauck and Wai-Tat Fu. 2017. A Data-Driven, Multidimensional Approach to Hint Design in Video Games. In *Proceedings of the 22Nd International Conference on Intelligent User Interfaces (IUI '17)*. ACM, New York, NY, USA, 137–147. DOI: http://dx.doi.org/10.1145/3025171.3025224

47. Helen Wauck, Ziang Xiao, Po-Tsung Chiu, and Wai-Tat Fu. 2017. Untangling the Relationship Between Spatial Skills, Game Features, and Gender in a Video Game. In *Proceedings of the 22Nd International Conference on Intelligent User Interfaces (IUI '17)*. ACM, New York, NY, USA, 125–136. DOI: http://dx.doi.org/10.1145/3025171.3025225

48. Ziang Xiao, Yuqi Yao, Chi-Hsien Yen, Sanorita Dey, Helen Wauck, James M. Leake, Brian Woodard, Angela Wolters, and Wai-Tat Fu. 2017. A Scalable Online Platform for Evaluating and Training Visuospatial Skills of Engineering Students. In *2017 ASEE Annual Conference & Exposition*. ASEE Conferences, Columbus, Ohio. https://peer.asee.org/27509.

49. So Y. Yoon. 2011. Psychometric properties of the Revised Purdue Spatial Visualization Tests: Visualization of Rotations (the Revised PSVT:R). (2011). https://search.proquest.com/docview/904417099?accountid=14553

An Interactive Relevance Feedback Interface for Evidence-Based Health Care

Ivania Donoso-Guzmán
Pontificia Universidad Católica de Chile
Santiago, Chile
indonoso@uc.cl

Denis Parra
Pontificia Universidad Católica de Chile
Santiago, Chile
dparras@uc.cl

ABSTRACT
We design, implement and evaluate EpistAid, an interactive relevance feedback system to support physicians towards a more efficient citation screening process for Evidence Based Health Care (EBHC). The system combines a relevance feedback algorithm with an interactive interface inspired by Tinder-like swipe interaction. To evaluate its efficiency and effectiveness in the citation screening process we conducted a user study with real users (senior medicine students) using a large EBHC dataset (Epistemonikos), with around 400,000 documents. We compared two relevance feedback algorithms, Rocchio and BM25-based. The combination of Rocchio relevance feedback with the document visualization yielded the best recall and F-1 scores, which are the most important metrics for EBHC document screening. In terms of cognitive demand and effort, BM25 relevance feedback without visualization was perceived as needing more physical and cognitive effort. EpistAid has the potential of improving the process for answering clinical questions by reducing the time needed to classify documents, as well as promoting user interaction. Our results can inform the development of intelligent user interfaces for screening research articles in the clinical domain and beyond.

CCS Concepts
•**Information systems → Search interfaces;**
•**Human-centered computing → Empirical studies in interaction design;** *Empirical studies in visualization;*

Author Keywords
Evidence-Based Health Care; Intelligent User Interfaces; Information Filtering; Visualization; Human in the Loop.

INTRODUCTION
Evidence-Based Health Care (EBHC) is a medical practice approach that emphasizes the use of research evidence to justify a medical treatment. Sackett et al. defined it as *"the conscientious, explicit, and judicious use of current best evidence in making decisions about the care of individual patients"* [51]. EBHC has produced a large impact in the practice of medicine, since applying the knowledge gained from large clinical trials to patient care promotes consistency of treatment and optimal outcomes, in contrast to solely relying on anecdotal cases [50].

Clinicians have established a process to practice evidence based health care [28] which can be summarized as follows: (i) first they pose a question, then (ii) seek studies related to it, (iii) select documents which are relevant to the question, (iv) evaluate the selected documents according to a their methodological quality, (v) next they perform a meta-analysis, (vi) to finally answer the initial clinical question. Despite its growing importance in health care, the process of finding articles which answer a medical question is currently very time consuming and can take several months [4, 5, 12, 17, 37]. This situation can be problematic because in practice, many health-care related decisions must be made quickly [54]. Moreover, with the explosion of scientific knowledge being published, it is difficult for clinicians to stay updated on the latest best medical practices [12, 17]. Another issue in this area is that the cost of not having all the relevant documents for a given question is very high. Missing a few documents could mean that the answer of the medical question can be wrong, and in consequence, clinicians could treat patients with outdated protocols.

In order to solve the aforementioned issues, some researchers have tried to reduce the time spent in this task using automatic machine learning techniques [41]. However, these algorithms still produce several false positives and negatives, and since the cost of not including a relevant document is high, this task is still performed by clinicians and requires further research to be fully automated [14]. Nowadays, there are some systems designed to support clinicians in the process of collecting, organizing, and searching for scientific evidence such as Embase [18], Covidence [1], and *Epistemonikos* [49]. These systems serve mostly as search engines, but they do not provide advanced functionalities to reduce the workload of the article screening process.

In this context, the main objectives of this research are to design, implement and evaluate a more efficient way to find and screen documents for answering a medical question. We propose *EpistAid*, a system which combines well-established relevance feedback algorithms with a Tinder-like user interface designed to find articles relevant to a medical question, using *Epistemonikos*' database as ground truth.

IUI'18, March 7–11, 2018, Tokyo, Japan

ISBN 978-1-4503-4945-1/18/03...$15.00
DOI: https://doi.org/10.1145/3172944.3172953

By identifying our main task as *citation screening to efficiently classify relevant articles for a clinical question*, we aim to answer the following research questions:

RQ1. Can we expect large differences in performance between relevance feedback algorithms? We answer this question with an off-line analysis over a dataset of close to 400,000 documents.

RQ2. Does an interface in combination with an algorithm perform better than the algorithm alone? We design, implement and evaluate with a user study an interactive Tinder-like user interface which allows physicians to find documents related to a clinical question.

RQ3. Can a document corpus visualization improve the task's outcome? We investigate whether a 2D visualization of the corpus related to a clinical question improves the document screening process.

RQ4. Are there other factors that can affect the task's outcome, such as user expertise or familiarity with visualization? We analyze if there are other factors such as reading skills in English or expertise in EBCH that could affect the citation screening performance.

Contributions. We contribute to the area of intelligent user interfaces applied to Evidence Based Health Care (EBHC) by (i) introducing an interactive interface which supports clinicians in classifying documents for EBHC, (ii) presenting an off-line evaluation of algorithms to classify documents using a real EBHC database; (iii) performing a user study with actual medicine students, not only an off-line evaluation, as much previous research has reported. We found that Rocchio combined with a 2D visualization yielded the best performance in terms of recall, and that previous expertise on EBHC and sufficient command in the documents' language has also a significant effect.

THE PROCESS TO ANSWER CLINICAL QUESTIONS

EBHC requires collecting a list of articles which provide the evidence to answer a clinical question such as "Is there a relationship between vaccines with thimerosal and autism?" The two main types of articles used are systematic reviews (SR) and primary studies (PS). PS is an umbrella term that includes any study design, qualitative or quantitative, where data is collected from individuals or groups of people. On the other side, the main objective of a SR is to synthesize primary studies. Collecting articles to answer a clinical question is iterative, since it involves the manual process of curating documents. The process starts by selecting a seed SR, based on a clinical question. If the seed SR has been digitalized, the screening process checks the cited PS (PS_{cited}), and then continues with other SR which cited documents in PS_{cited}. In summary:

The problem. Find a list a papers relevant to a clinical question by: (i) Identifying a seed SR and PS_{cited}, next (ii) removing cited papers PS_{cited} not related to the clinical question, and then (iii) adding new SR and PS strongly related to the clinical question. This process can take several months, especially (iii), since it involves physicians manually searching and screening papers in several databases without clear guidelines for building queries.

Our solution. We call our solution *EpistAid.* We propose a series of methods combined with an interactive user interface with the aim of reducing the effort of document search and screening. Our solution involves investigating relevance feedback algorithms such as Rocchio and BM25, [35], as well as visualizing documents via dimensionality reduction over the text of the articles [13].

RELATED WORK

Citation screening

Several approaches have been proposed to reduce the workload associated with the task of citation screening in EBHC. Automatic classification has been explored by several authors [3, 4, 10, 11, 23, 29, 32, 33, 38, 57, 62]. They have compared known classifiers (Naive Bayes, Support Vector Machines, K-Nearest Neighbors) with different sets of features (title, abstract, and MESH [1] terms). Their results were promising, but there were large differences in performance depending on the dataset.

There is also research in active learning [37, 58, 60, 61]. These studies have used certainty and uncertainty approaches to select what documents should be shown to the user. Like automatic classification, they have used different sets of features and also sampling techniques to improve results. These authors only performed off-line evaluations and used a few medical questions. The datasets in these studies have 3,000 to 10,000 documents, which is unrealistically small, considering that only Epistemonikos has close to 400,000 documents. In the area of information retrieval, relevance feedback was used in [23, 27] to classify documents. Data Visualization was also used to do citation screening. A visual text mining tool was presented in [21, 22], which used both text and the citation network as input.

To the best of our knowledge, there are two software that include tools to help filter documents for a systematic review. Wallace et al. introduced *Abstrack* in [59] a system that uses active learning and a simple interface to classify documents. Recently, *SWIFT-Review* was presented in [26]. This is a software that ranks documents according to a set of documents previously classified. Both systems require users to enter a reduced list of papers to be screened.

A common characteristic among the works surveyed, is that most research on this topic has been done using small datasets. Olorisade et al. [42] analyzed the quality of the research made in the area and states that *"More than half of the studies used a corpus size of below 1,000 documents for their experiments while corpus size for around 80% of the studies was 3,000 or fewer documents"*. Using these small datasets does not seem appropriate in this area because they are not comparable to the size of current medical databases[2].

In our research, we use *Epistemonikos*' database which has nearly 400,000 documents. For this reason, this is the first

[1] https://www.ncbi.nlm.nih.gov/mesh

[2] https://www.nlm.nih.gov/bsd/index_stats_comp.html

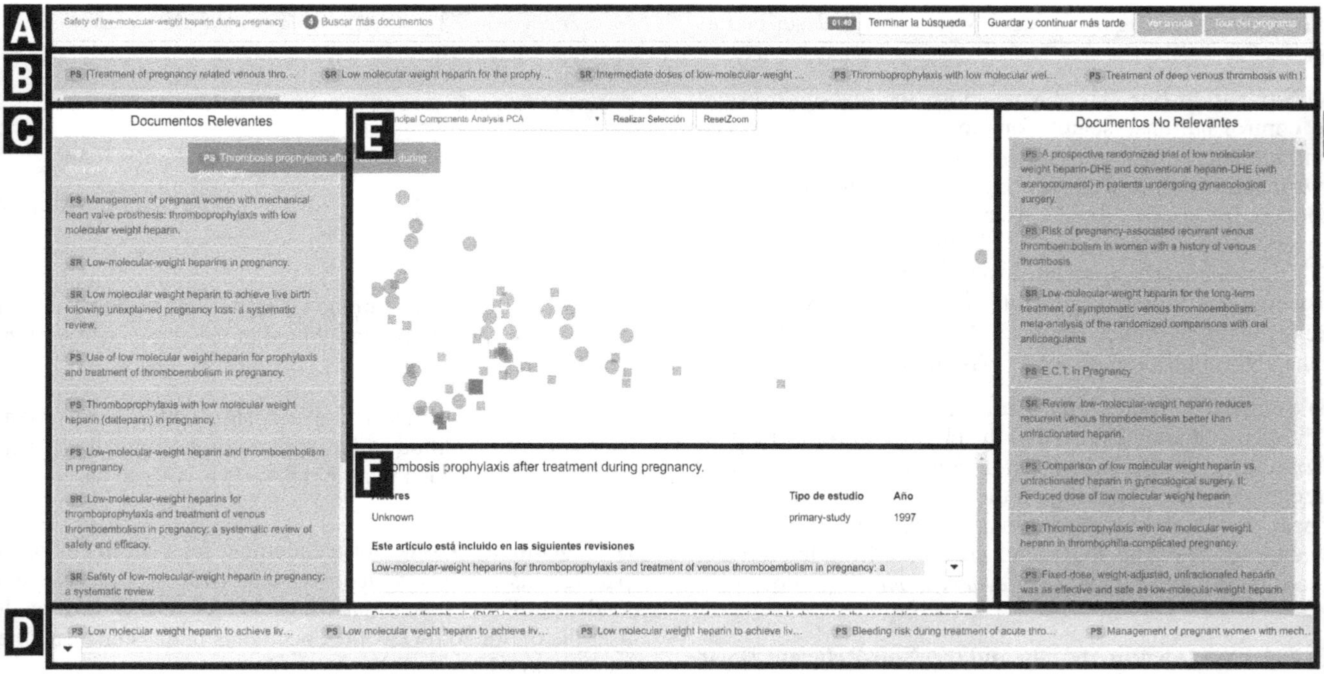

Figure 1: *EpistAid* document screening interface. (A) Navigation Bar shows information about the session and provides buttons to control it. (B) Suggested Documents' Bin contains the documents the algorithm deems relevant. (C) Relevant Documents' Bin and (G) Non-Relevant Documents' Bin contains the documents classified as relevant or non-relevant by the user. (E) Documents Visualization area shows documents as figures in a 2D chart. (F) Document Detail shows document meta-data. (D) Actions Timeline shows the actions performed by the user sorted by time.

research in the area made on a real, large and noisy database. With respect to filtering and classification techniques, for our research we chose relevance feedback over active learning, since the former mimics the actions done by users when they search for documents: users look for documents, see whether they are relevant or not, reformulate the search query and so on, until they think they have found all related evidence.

Controllable User interfaces

Ideally, we would like to create an automatic system to solve the problem of finding relevant research articles for answering clinical questions. However, domain experts usually like to have more control than non-experts on systems supported by intelligent algorithms [31, 44]. This is the case for physicians looking for papers to answer a medical question. Research has shown that controllable interfaces increase satisfaction in recommender and search systems, because they increase transparency and trust [8, 25, 30, 45, 24, 56, 2]. This type of interface also increases user engagement and leads to better user experience [44].

Following these previous works, some authors have created interfaces that support information filtering. For instance, di Sciascio et al. [15] proposed a new interface to present search results. In this interface all results can be ranked according to words present in the documents. Users can assign a weight to each word they select and the documents will be re-ranked accordingly. More recently, Peltonen et al. [47] presented an interface to support relevance feedback that has a visualization of topics and keywords. Users can give positive feedback as well as negative feedback. They found that for certain types of difficult information seeking tasks, negative feedback could benefit an exploratory system even when a good deal of positive feedback is available. Beltran et al. [6] presented a new interface with swipe gestures (Tinder-like) that allows users to classify documents in two groups. This intelligent system creates bins in each group that allow users to justify their classification without needing to write. One common feature of these systems is having a human-in-the-loop (HITL) aspect in the process, that is, they require human interaction to achieve the goal. In EBHC users need to find articles in a way they can understand and trust the results. For this reason we propose a controllable and transparent information filtering system designed for the practice of EBHC, inspired by controllable recommender system interfaces.

EPISTAID

EpistAid evolves from an initial design [16], which was introduced but never evaluated. Here we present *EpistAid* in detail focusing on three aspects: (i) User interface, layout and visual components, (ii) Interactions, where we describe our design based on Schneidermann's visual Information-Seeking mantra [53], and (iii) Algorithms, which support the intelligence behind the filtering process.

User interface

EpistAid is implemented as a web application. The user interface was developed using D3.js [9], dragula.js (`https://bevacqua.github.io/dragula/`) and Bootstrap [43]. The GUI layout, shown in Figure 1, has 7 views and is described as follows:

(A) Navigation Bar. The navbar shows the search's title and the control buttons: search for more documents, save and continue later, finish the search and get help. It also shows how much time the user has left for document screening – functionality needed for the user study. Users do not input a query in the search process. They simply start by picking a *systematic review* related to the clinical question to be answered, and *EpistAid* generates the initial and subsequent queries using relevance feedback. More details are presented in the algorithms coming section **Algorithms**.

(B) Suggested Documents' Bin. The system will look for additional documents related to the clinical question and will display them in this bin. Each document is represented by a rectangle. When clicking on the document, its details will appear on **(F)** and its related mark in visualization **(E)** will increase its size. The documents are sorted from left to right according to their score in the *relevance model* of the document set.

(C) Relevant Documents' Bin and (G) Non-Relevant Documents' Bin. These bins have the documents that have already been classified by the user as relevant or non-relevant. Documents inside the bins don't have any particular order and users can simply place documents on them by drag-and-drop from the (B) panel.

(E) Documents Visualization. This area shows the documents as figures in a 2D chart. Its purpose is to provide an overview of the documents that are in any of the bins (suggested, relevant and non-relevant), and to let the user explore the content based on proximity among documents. Since we represent this set of documents as a document-term matrix (DTM) using a vector space model [35], we perform dimensionality reduction over this DTM to represent each document with a low-rank vector of two dimensions. %delvania: aca hay solo 4 metodos We chose 5 different dimensionality reduction algorithms: Principal Components Analysis (PCA), Linear Discriminant Analysis (LDA), Latent Semantic Analysis (LDA), Multidimensional Scaling (MDS) [19] and the recent t-distributed Stochastic Neighbor Embedding (t-SNE) [34]. Users can choose the type of dimensionality reduction they prefer in order to eventually visualize the documents in the two dimensional (2D) chart.

In the 2D chart, primary studies (PS) are represented by squares (■, ■, ■) and systematic reviews (SR) by circles (●, ● , ●). The color is used to discriminate the current status of the document: relevant (■, ●), non-relevant (■, ●) or unknown (■, ●). We decided to use these colors (teal, orange, and purple) in order to provide a colorblind safe pallete.

For selecting a subset of documents for more detailed exploration, the user can draw a *brush*. The brushing interaction enables the user to navigate through all the documents by subsetting them based on their positions in the 2D projections. The selected documents are highlighted in all bins (relevant, non-relevant, suggested) and in the *Actions Timeline*. It is also possible to zoom in and out on the visualization.

Figure 2: Brush applied in the visualization. It shows how the selected documents are highlighted in the corresponding bins.

(D) Actions Timeline. This panel shows all the documents the user has classified so far, sorted chronologically by time of user labeling. Each item in this view is colored based on its labeled class.

(F) Document Detail. For a document selected in any of the panels, this area shows its meta-data (title, abstract, type of study, publication year and authors). Its goal is to offer the user the option to review the documents in the same way they usually do with a traditional interface.

Justifying the design choices

To justify the visualization we use the framework introduced by Tamara Munzner in [39]. This framework has three layers: *why* is the task being performed, *what* data is shown in the views, and *how* is the visualization idiom constructed in terms of design choices.

Why. The interface allows users to *explore* the set of documents and *identify* documents of certain types (SR or PS), which could be relevant or not. Users have to *analyze* to *produce annotations* on each document. The annotation is the relevance they assign to the document, given the clinical question. In the visualization, users explore without a specific *target* (document) or a pre-defined corpus hierarchy.

What. This visualization is showing document objects which are initially represented in a tabular format, where each document is a row and each column is a word of the corpus. Each cell contains the frequency of that word in the document. After performing dimensionality reduction, each document is represented with a 2D vector, which allows us to display it in the corresponding view. In the visualization, the document's relative positions provide users more information about the document they want to classify. For example, if a document is surrounded by relevant documents, it is very likely that the document is relevant. For this reason, including non-relevant documents was important, since it allowed users to see how close the unknown documents are to the non-relevant ones.

How. We *encoded* all items (documents) using color *hue* for relevance, *shape* for different types of publication and *size* to identify what is being selected. Users can *filter* the data by *selecting* documents using a brush, as seen in Figure 2. Also, users can *change* the position of documents using a dimensionality reduction algorithm and *navigate* using the pan and zoom features. The position channel is given by the result of the dimensionality reduction, so a document will not have the same position given different dimensionality reduction algorithms.

Interactions

Our interaction design is based on the visual Information-Seeking Mantra: overview first, zoom and filter, then details-on-demand [53].

Overview first. We implement the *overview-first* functionality with the *Documents Visualization* where users can see a summary of the documents that are in any of the bins in the 2D projection resultant from a dimensionality reduction over the term-document matrix. Users can also see both bins: relevant and non-relevant documents already classified.

Zoom and Filter: selecting documents. The *brush* tool described in the previous section allows users to subset documents from the 2D *Documents Visualization*. These documents will be highlighted in all panels, so the user can see their titles, as seen in Figure 2. Users can also zoom in the visualization to look a small quantity of papers and select them by clicking on them or using the brush tool.

Details on demand. When users click a document from any of the bins, *Actions Timeline* or *Documents Visualization* the system provides additional details displayed in *Document Detail*.

The *Tinder*-like inspiration of the interface is implemented in a way that users drag/swipe items to the left if they think they are relevant and to the right if they want to classify as non-relevant.

Algorithms

The application back-end was programmed in Python 3 using Scikit-Learn [46], Pandas [36] and Scipy & Numpy [55]. The code is available at `https://github.com/indonoso/EpisteAid`, a public repository. The documents were represented using a bag-of-words model [35], where the term weights used were based on Term-Frequency.

The main aspect of our "human-in-the-loop" algorithmic procedure starts with modeling the medical question as a *query*, which is updated iteratively when users provide feedback of relevant and non-relevant documents with respect to the clinical question being answered. We tested two algorithms: Rocchio [52], that computes a new query by weighing the words in relevant and non-relevant documents, and BM25, which scores each document based on the frequency of its words in the document and query, as well as based on some global parameters [35].

For both models we define a query q_i as a vector of words, as $\overrightarrow{q_i} = \{w_1, w_2, \ldots, w_n\}$ where n is the number of words in the corpus and w_j is the frequency of the word j. In our system the initial query q_0 is made from the words in the title and abstract from an initial document which represents the source for searching documents relevant to the clinical question. Since this document is a chosen systematic review, we call it *Seed SR*.

For replicability, we disclose the parameters of our algorithms. In Rocchio relevance feedback, parameters were $\alpha = \beta = \delta =$ 0.25 and $\gamma = 0.5$. For BM25, parameters used were $k_1 = 1.7$, $k_2 = 1.2$ and $i = 25$.

Type of publication	Articles in database
Primary Study (PS)	277, 967
Systematic Review (SR)	73,040
Overview	1, 229
Structured Summary of PS	1,351
Structured Summary of SR	37,779

Table 1: Statistics of Epistemonikos' document database.

Epistemonikos Documents Dataset

Epistemonikos is a collaborative database which stores research articles that provide the best evidence according to the EBHC principles [49]. Since the evidence comes from scientific literature, this information is collected from specialized online sites such as PubMed and Cochrane, among other 24 sources of scientific information [20]. In this research, we used a dump of their database by December 2016. The database contains around 390,000 documents of five types. Table 1 shows the number of items per publication type. For simplification, anything which is not a PS (excepting for the structured summary of PS), is considered a Systematic Review (SR).

In the Epistemonikos dataset, clinical questions and documents are related through *evidence matrices*, the basic information unit in *Epistemonikos*. Although it is basically a list of research papers, it is called a matrix because it is shown to users in a matrix format, where the rows are Systematic Reviews (SR) and the columns are Primary Studies (PS) cited within those SR. According to data collected by Epistemonikos between 2010 and 2016, physicians require 2-6 months to get from an initial matrix version M_0 to a final revised M_f. They remove non-related articles from the list and then manually search for other articles until convergence. In our experiments, an Epistemonikos' evidence matrix corresponds to a medical question with its relevant documents. All documents that are not listed in the matrix are considered non relevant. The content of the seed systematic review (Seed SR) is used to form the initial query q_0. Epistemonikos currently has over 1,500 evidence matrices in their database, created using Epistemonikos' current document screening process.

Text processing. Each document was represented by the words in its title and abstract. Tokenization was performed by splitting the text by non alphanumeric characters (spaces, tabs, etc.). We then removed all English stopwords in the NLTK package [7]. Many articles used acronyms of medical concepts with less than three characters, and the same acronym is used in different medical domains with different meanings. For this reason we removed any word that had less than three characters. All words were stemmed using *Porter Stemmer* from the same package. This process resulted in a final corpus of 158,457 words. We removed all documents that did not have tokens of the corpus, resulting in 391,364 documents.

	Question	Specialty	Context	Relevant docs.
1	Echinacea for common cold	General Medicine	Echineacea is a flower. There are some web sites that say that it is useful for common cold.	54
2	Safety of Low-Molecular-Weight heparin during pregnancy	Internal Medicine	Low-molecular-weight heparin is anticoagulant medication. This question inquires whether it is safe to use during pregnancy, because of the possible risk to the baby.	112

Table 2: Detail of medical questions used in the user study, with their respective number of relevant documents.

EVALUATION METHODOLOGY

We conducted two types of evaluations. The first one, an offline evaluation to compare the performance of both relevance feedback algorithms. The second one, a user study to investigate whether differences in algorithms would be equally reflected in a user interface, or could be moderated by the effect of visualization and interaction.

Offline Evaluation Protocol

We split the document dataset in train (70%) and test (30%) randomly. The train set was used to tune the parameters of each relevance feedback algorithm (Rocchio and BM25), while the test was used to double check for potential problems in the models, such as overfitting. The experiment consisted of a simulation of the relevance feedback process. We selected $1,067$ clinical questions for which we knew the respective seed SR as well as all the relevant documents. For each clinical question, using the seed SR we issued an initial query q_0, using the words present on its title and abstract, and for the documents returned by the algorithms we assumed having a *simulated expert* able to exactly tell relevant from non-relevant documents. The relevance feedback algorithm then would re-issue queries $q_1, q_2, \ldots$ based on the feedback of the simulated expert, so for each query attempt we calculated recall and AP (average precision), two well known metrics in information retrieval [35]. In this way, we could see how much to expect on average for the physicians in the user study, and we could also have a better idea of the performance of Rocchio and BM25 before conducting the user study.

User Study Protocol

We conducted a user study to compare performance of users considering four conditions, based on the relevance feedback algorithm (Rocchio vs. BM25) and on the interface (with and without 2D visualization of documents, i.e., box E in Figure 1). We designed a 2x2 mixed-subjects experiment, where each user had to screen documents in two out of four conditions (For instance, BM25 with visualization and then Rocchio without visualization). The conditions and their sequence were counterbalanced in order to have similar number of users on each one. The user study sequence for every user was:

1. Answer a pre-study survey with questions related to their previous knowledge on the topics (see Table 2), their experience with EBHC, with reading research in English language, and with data visualizations.
2. In the assigned condition, find documents related to one medical question (shown in Table 2). They could obtain documents to label by clicking on the button "search for more documents". In each iteration, users had to provide *relevance feedback* to at least 5 documents to be able to search for more documents.
3. Answer a post-study survey with questions related their satisfaction with the system. Moreover, we measured cognitive effort using the NASA-TLX survey.
4. repeat points 2. and 3. with another assigned *interface-algorithm* condition.

To evaluate the algorithm we paid special attention to recall [48] because in EBCH, having all the relevant documents for a research question is more important that having high precision [41]. However, since we could not afford the participation of physicians in our study for more than two weeks, we made a compromise by studying how much recall they could get by using *EpistAid* for 30 minutes over a period of 10 days.

RESULTS

Offline Evaluation Results

Both models have a similar behavior on how they respond to parameters, but overall Rocchio performs clearly better than BM25. Rocchio shows close to 30% better recall than BM25 under different values of the parameter *feedback items* (for how many items the simulated expert provides feedback). Both algorithms show a similar behavior result in terms of Mean Average Precision.

Recall. Figure 4 shows the results of accumulated recall for Rocchio and BM25, respectively. Results were averaged over the clinical questions in the test set. We see a similar trend in both algorithms, where increasing the number of items for which feedback is given in each query attempt (*feedback items:* 10, 20, 30), improves significantly the maximum recall obtained. Other common pattern between these algorithms is that the top accumulated recall is reached after 5-6 query attempts. After that, no significant improvement in recall is observed. With respect to differences, Rocchio clearly outperforms BM25. Based on this offline evaluation, having an expert user labeling the documents we can expect recall values close to 0.4 with Rocchio, while only close to 0.3 in the case of BM25. Considering these results, and since in this area recall is more important than precision [41], we decided to show 30 documents for obtaining user feedback in the user study.

Mean Average Precision@k. Results of Mean Average Precision are shown in Figures 3 (a) for Rocchio and (b) for BM25. We evaluated Average Precision (AP) on each query attempt, and by averaging over all clinical questions, we obtained Mean AP (MAP) at different values of the variable *query attempts* (x-axis in the aforementioned figures). It is important to notice

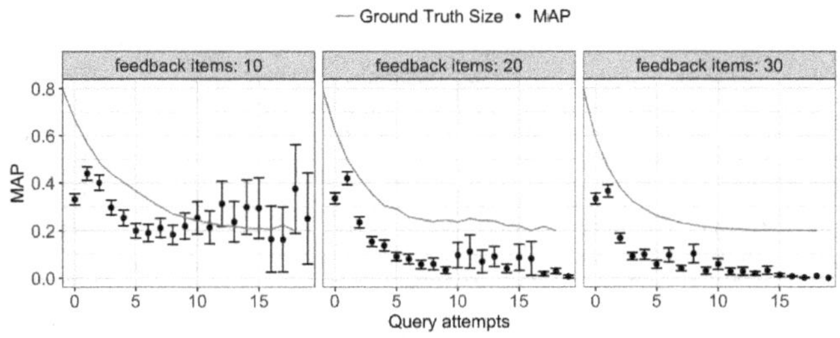

(a) Rocchio

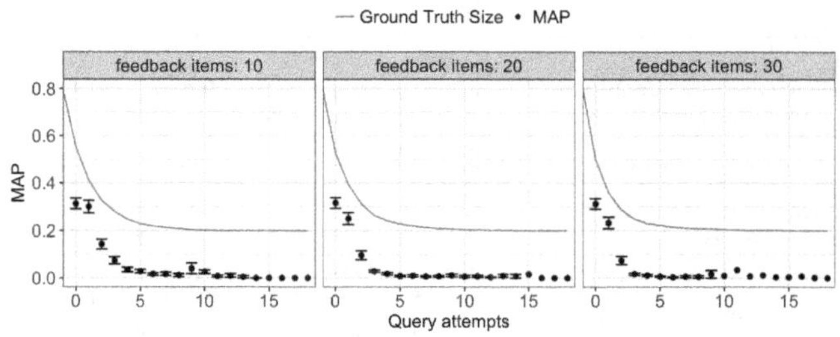

(b) BM25

Figure 3: Offline evaluation. MAP@k for (a) Rocchio and (b) BM25 where *feedback items* is the amount of documents with relevance feedback in each query attempt. The red line shows the percentage of relevant documents left in the ground truth after each query attempt.

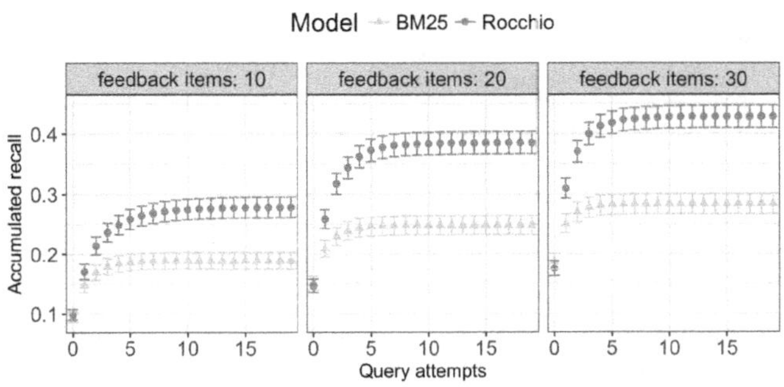

Figure 4: Offline evaluation. Accumulated recall for BM25 and Rocchio, where *feedback items* is the amount of documents the simulation gave feedback in each iteration.

that after each query, when relevant items are identified, we decrease the size of the ground truth. This effect is presented as a decreasing red curve in each plot of Figure 3. In this way we represent the fact that when a relevant document is already found, the probability of finding other relevant documents in subsequent queries diminishes, and is likely to obtain smaller values of MAP.

We observe that MAP yields their maximum values (0.35-0.42) between the first two queries, and then it falls significantly after the second query attempt, probably indicating that after the second query it becomes significantly more difficult to find relevant documents. This observation is supported by the quick drop of the ground truth size (the red line in Figure 3) especially with number of *feedback items* = 30, which indicates that within the first five queries the users find most of the relevant documents they could potentially find by these relevance feedback methods.

User Study Results

Demographics. The study had a total of $N = 22$ subjects, 19 of them were students in their latest year of the medicine program at PUC Chile, and the other 3 user subjects were professors. In terms of experience, 19 of them had never written a systematic review. Moreover, with the exception of one subject, all subjects had created at least one *evidence matrix* (list of papers which answer a clinical question), and 16 had created at least two. Finally, 86% reported being able to read in English language without problems.

Model / Interface	Time (in secs.)	Docs. class. p/query	Docs. class. p/session	Nbr. of queries
BM25 / Non-Vis	1443.9 ± 107.2	21.2 ± 1.3	107.9 ± 17.7	5.1 ± 1.2
BM25 / Vis	1280.1 ± 117.2	20.4 ± 1.5	100.4 ± 16.7	4.9 ± 0.7
Rocchio / Non-Vis	1115.7 ± 80.3	19.8 ± 1.6	88.1 ± 11.9	4.5 ± 0.8
Rocchio / Vis	1267.7 ± 87.7	26.3 ± 0.9	116.3 ± 22.6	4.4 ± 0.9

Table 3: Interaction statistics in each condition studied (mean ± SE). *Docs. class.* stands for *Documents Classified.*

			Seen documents			Ground Truth
Model	Interface	N	Recall	Precision	F-1 score	Recall
BM25	Non-Vis	12	.66 ± .08	.52 ± .06	.58 ± .07	.20 ± .04
BM25	Vis	11	.71 ± .06	.64 ± .04	.64 ± .03	.18 ± .02
Rocchio	Non-Vis	11	.65 ± .08	.73 ± .02	.65 ± .05	.21 ± .04
Rocchio	Vis	12	.77 ± .06	.67 ± .01	.70 ± .03	.23 ± .03

Table 4: Mean (± SE) recall, precision and F-1 score (per user) considering only documents seen by users in the session, and recall considering all documents in the ground truth.

Engagement and interaction statistics. In order to measure user interaction and engagement between the four conditions, we compared four metrics which results are displayed in Table 3: time spent on the interface (Time), average number of documents classified per query (Docs. class. p/query), average number of documents classified per session (Docs. class. p/session), and average number of queries issued per session (Nbr. of queries).

We observe that in terms of time, users spent more on the conditions with BM25 ($M = 1443.91$ and $M = 1280.1$) than on the conditions with Rocchio ($M = 1115.7$ and $M = 1267.67$). In terms of queries issued, people also issued more queries on average in the BM25 conditions ($M = 5.1$ and $M = 4.9$) compared to Rocchio ($M = 4.5$ and $M = 4.4$). However, in terms of number of papers classified, list-wise and session-wise, people were more productive in the Rocchio condition with visualization ($M = 116.3$ session-wise and $M = 26.33$ list-wise). The condition with the fewest interactions was Rocchio without 2D document visualization ($M = 88.1$ session-wise and $M = 19.8$ list-wise). Another interesting metric is that in

Question	Model	Interface	M	SE	SD
The suggested documents were relevant	BM25	Non-vis	3.42	0.34	1.16
	BM25	Vis	3.60	0.34	1.07
	Rocchio	Non-vis	4.20	0.13	0.42
	Rocchio	Vis	3.25	0.35	1.22
The suggested documents were diverse	BM25	Non-vis	4.25	0.13	0.45
	BM25	Vis	4.00	0.45	1.41
	Rocchio	Non-vis	4.60	0.22	0.70
	Rocchio	Vis	4.33	0.14	0.49
I understood why the documents were recommended	BM25	Non-vis	3.50	0.36	1.24
	BM25	Vis	3.80	0.42	1.32
	Rocchio	Non-vis	4.40	0.22	0.70
	Rocchio	Vis	3.50	0.31	1.09
The system didn't miss any relevant documents	BM25	Non-vis	2.67	0.31	1.07
	BM25	Vis	3.40	0.45	1.43
	Rocchio	Non-vis	4.00	0.42	1.33
	Rocchio	Vis	3.42	0.34	1.16
I would use the system again	BM25	Non-vis	3.50	0.38	1.31
	BM25	Vis	3.60	0.37	1.17
	Rocchio	Non-vis	4.20	0.20	0.63
	Rocchio	Vis	3.75	0.28	0.97
The system was easy to use	BM25	Non-vis	**4.33***	0.26	0.89
	BM25	Vis	3.90	0.38	1.20
	Rocchio	Non-vis	**4.70***	0.15	0.48
	Rocchio	Vis	3.50	0.31	1.09
I believe the system needs a recommender system	BM25	Non-vis	3.67	0.26	0.89
	BM25	Vis	3.30	0.42	1.34
	Rocchio	Non-vis	3.70	0.26	0.82
	Rocchio	Vis	3.92	0.19	0.67
I didn't realize how the time passed	BM25	Non-vis	3.75	0.33	1.14
	BM25	Vis	3.50	0.34	1.08
	Rocchio	Non-vis	3.70	0.33	1.06
	Rocchio	Vis	3.25	0.30	1.06
I would recommend the system to a collegue	BM25	Non-vis	3.33	0.38	1.30
	BM25	Vis	3.40	0.37	1.17
	Rocchio	Non-vis	3.90	0.23	0.74
	Rocchio	Vis	3.42	0.31	1.08

Table 5: Post-session survey. The only significant difference was found in the question *the system was easy to use*

most experiments (91%), users reported they used at least title or abstract to classify the articles.

Performance Metrics. Table 4 presents the results of recall, precision and F-1 score [35] at the end of the session, averaged per user. These metrics are calculated based on the documents presented to the users during the session. We also calculated recall considering the actual items in the ground truth (112 relevant documents for evidence matrix A and 54 relevant documents for evidence matrix B). Considering all the metrics, the best combination of interface and algorithm was the use of 2D document visualization with the Rocchio relevance feedback algorithm, since it has the best F-1 score considering the items seen during the session ($M = 0.7$) and the best recall with respect to the ground truth, the evidence matrices ($M = 0.23$). The interface that seemed to have the worst general performance was BM25 without visualization, specially in terms of precision, and in terms of recall considering the whole ground truth.

Post-Session Survey. Results of the post-session survey are presented in Table 5. We conducted 2x2 between subjects ANOVA over each of the 9 questions and we only found one statistically significant result. This result was over the question *The system was easy to use*. We found no significant interaction effect, $p = .19$, but we found an effect of the interface variable. Conducting a Tukey HSD post-hoc analysis,

	BM25		Rocchio	
Variable	Non-Vis	Vis	Non-Vis	Vis
Effort	48.9 ± 6.8	31.8 ± 6.0	27.6 ± 5.1	31.7 ± 5.1
Frustration	**46.3*** ± 6.2	**32.8*** ± 6.4	18.0 ± 5.1	27.2 ± 6.4
Mental Demand	47.8 ± 5.2	36.6 ± 9.1	28.1 ± 6.4	41.8 ± 5.3
Performance	55.3 ± 5.5	57.3 ± 9.9	72.5 ± 6.3	63.7 ± 6.9
Physical Demand	32.8 ± 6.3	17.3 ± 7.8	18.4 ± 6.4	31.3 ± 7.9
Temporal Demand	30.3 ± 5.3	25.7 ± 8.3	21.1 ± 4.5	30.8 ± 5.6

Table 6: NASA-TLX results grouped by algorithm and interface. BM25 model was significantly more frustrating.

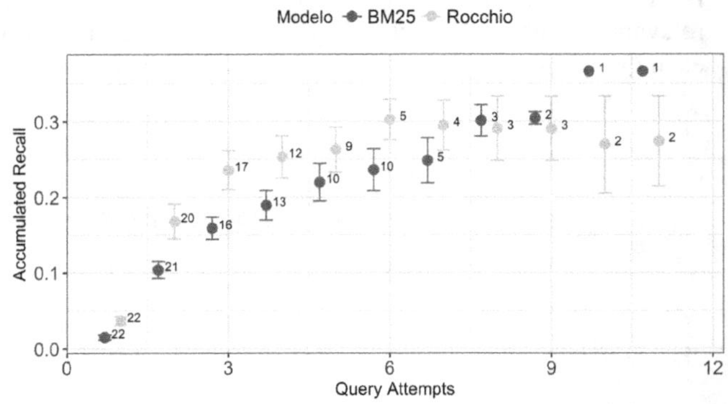

Figure 5: User study. Accumulated recall at different query attemps. Error bar depicts standard error.

we found that interface with no visualization ($M = 4.5$) was perceived as significantly easier than using an interface with visualization ($M = 3.7$), $p = .007$.

Perception of Effort. We used the NASA TLX to measure the perception of effort, results are presented in Table 6. Among the six variables measured, by conducting a 2x2 between subjects ANOVA we found a significant result on *Frustration*. We found no interaction effect between algorithm (BM25, Rocchio) and interface (vis, non-vis), $p = .07$, but we found a significant effect of the algorithm model. In particular, BM25 ($M = 39.6$) produced significantly more frustration than Rocchio ($M = 22.6$), $p = .008$.

DISCUSSION

In the following section, we answer the research questions stated in the introduction.

RQ1. Can we expect large differences in performance between relevance feedback algorithms?

The offline evaluation showed Rocchio clearly outperforming BM25 in both recall and MAP. We observed a similar behavior during the user study, but the difference was not as large as in the offline evaluation. For understanding this behavior, one aspect to consider is how much feedback people needed to provide in order to receive relevant documents. During the user study, Rocchio yields high recall faster than BM25 (Figure 5). After the second query attempt, the mean accumulated recall reached by Rocchio is significantly better than BM25, but the difference decreases as more query attempts are made. Then if the users are persistent, they can reach good results with either

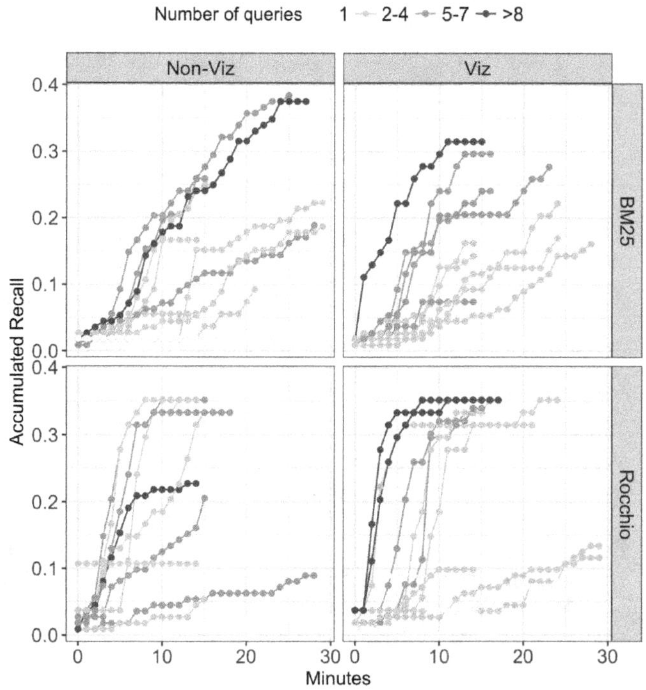

Figure 6: Accumulated recall at different minutes of the session. Each line represents a user. Rocchio achieves higher recall faster than BM25.

method, but if they try no more than 6 queries, they will more likely obtain better results with Rocchio.

Another perspective can be seen by analyzing the recall at different algorithm and interface (with an without visualization), as a function of session time, what we show in Figure 6. The plot indicates that many users under the Rocchio algorithm can reach their top recall within 5 minutes, meanwhile users under BM25 achieve it not before than 10-15 minutes. However, this results also in shorter sessions for Rocchio users, they feel satisfied with their result and stop exploring, while many users under BM25 keep exploring, even reaching recall levels close to 0.4. The results indicate that persistent users can leverage the interface to improve the weak offline results of BM25, compared to Rocchio users.

RQ2. Does an interface in combination with an algorithm perform better than the algorithm alone?

The offline evaluation showed that Rocchio reached more than 30% of the recall of BM25 (Figure 4). The important decrease of this difference during the user study indicates an effect of the interface. To dig deeper into this result, we performed the same offline experiment only considering the two clinical questions in the user study. We see, in Figure 7, that BM25 is clearly outperformed by Rocchio and even more, in question 1 it yields a $recall = 0$ since it never returns a relevant document.

One explanation we have for this result is that in the offline evaluation, the simulated user judges documents simply as relevant or not, without considering levels of relevancy. On the other side, in the user study, the *human in the loop* can infer

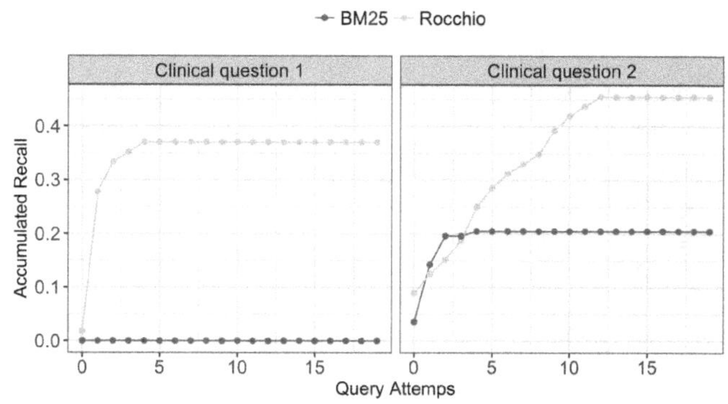

Figure 7: Offline evaluation conducted on the two questions of the user study. Accumulated recall at different query attemps. BM25 does not find relevant documents for question 1. Rocchio performs two times better than BM25 in question 2.

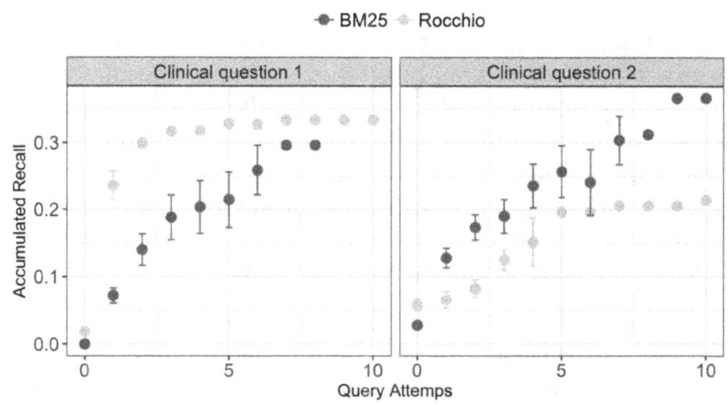

Figure 8: Accumulated recall in the user study, split by clinical question.

degrees or relevance, labeling a "barely relevant document" as relevant in order to diversify the results for the upcoming iteration until an actual relevant document is found. In summary, the use of an interactive interface favors BM25 making the difference with Rocchio smaller in terms of performance metrics. We then split results of the user study according to the clinical questions and we analyzed the actual user performance in Figure 8. Unlike the offline evaluation (Figure 7), for clinical question 1 Rocchio yields similar results, but BM25 users obtained $recall > 0$, and those who issued 6 or more queries can reach up to Rocchio level. In clinical question 2, people using BM25 actually reach better recall then Rocchio, specially users using 7 or more queries.

RQ3. Can a visualization of the documents increase performance or engagement?

Our results shown in the previous section, specially those in Table 3 and Table 4, show a trend towards better recall in visualization conditions when considering the documents seen by users during the session. However, this trend is not the same in terms of precision. Results shown in Table 4 indicate that the top levels of precision are found with Rocchio algorithm in an interface without visualization.

Since the success of the task of document screening depends more on recall than on precision, we focus on this aspect. To

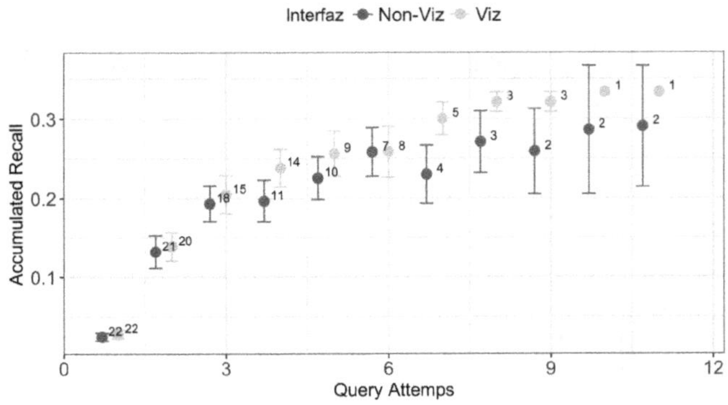

Figure 9: Accumulated recall at different query attempts. Error bar depicts standard error. The number by the circle indicates number of users N.

get a deeper understanding on the effect of visualization in terms of recall, we analyzed the average accumulated recall by query attempt and by interface, shown in Figure 9. We see that in conditions with visualization, after the 6th query attempt, the accumulated recall significantly improves over non-visualization conditions. After the 9th query attempt the difference disappears, but only 3 users reach that number so no statistical tests are valid at that point.

One possible explanation for this is that visualization helps users see relations between more documents holistically, which decreases the chances of missing documents. It happens specially at further query attempts because in each iteration more documents are added to the system, so there is more information to improve the discriminative utility of the visualization. Some comments of users support this explanation: a user said *"The visualization was useful to find similar studies"*, and another user stated *"I used the visualization to estimate how useful a study could be"*. The visualization does not significantly reduce cognitive load (Table 6) but it also promotes engagement. More users stayed longer than 15 minutes when using the visualization (Figure 6).

RQ4. Are there other factors that can affect performance?

To better understand the differences in user performance for the task of document screening, we split users in three groups based on their results on recall: *best*, *middle* and *worst*. These groups were separated by maintaining the same number of experiment sessions in each group. The thresholds were: (i) *worst*: less than 0.12 recall, (ii) *middle*: more than 0.12 and less than 0.30 recall, and (iii) *best*: more than 0.30 recall. There were 14 sessions in groups *worst* and *middle*, and 16 sessions within *best*.

During the pre-study survey, the experience of the users was measured in three topics: general academic experience, experience working in Evidence Based Health Care, as well as experience with data visualizations. In this latest aspect we found no differences among groups. Having the ability to read research in English (as opposed to reading any kind of text in English language) does affect recall. Users who strongly agreed with the statement *"I can read research in English"*, had significantly ($p < .01$) better performance than those who did not.

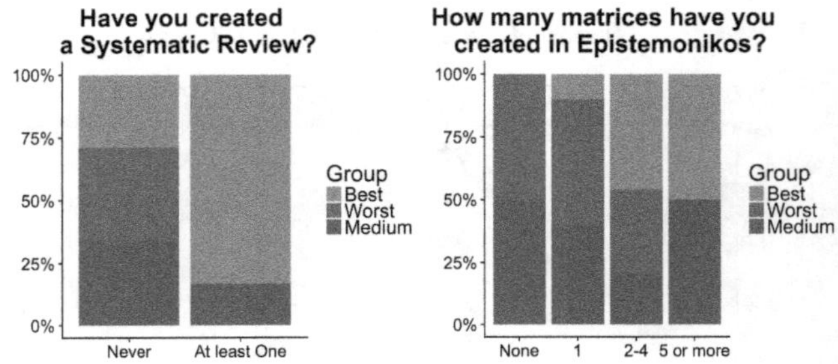

Figure 10: Experience with Evidence Based Health Care.

With respect to experience with EBHC, Figure 10 shows the experience among the aforementioned recall-performance groups. Having worked in the creation of a Systematic Review helped to get better results ($p < .05$). Users that had created two o more evidence matrices had better recall than those who had never created one or had only created one matrix ($M = 0.23$ vs. $M = 0.13$, $p < .01$).

CONCLUSION

In this article we have investigated whether an interactive relevance feedback user interface could help physicians in the process of screening documents to answer a medical question. We have introduced *EpistAid*, our proposed solution, and we have evaluated it with an offline simulation, as well as with a user study considering a large dataset and real users of a EBHC system, medical doctors and medicine students.

We found that the algorithm used in the process is not only relevant for performance metrics, but also for perception of cognitive demand. Rocchio relevance feedback combined with a visualization of documents was found to be better than the other conditions in terms of recall and F-1 score for medical document screening. We also discovered that a good command on reading research in English language was an important factor. This finding might seem negligible, but it supports the current efforts by Epistemonikos on translating articles into different languages. Experience with working in EBHC was also found to be an important variable, which supports the need for training physicians in this type of research activity.

In future work it would be interesting to test other style of algorithms, in particular active and reinforcement learning. The current system and evaluation had the limitation of making physicians work independently, so a system which promotes collaborative work for answering clinical questions could be of great help. Finally, we also think that adding explanations [40] to justify why a document is recommended as relevant is an important idea for research considering that we will continue working with a *human in the loop* paradigm.

Acknowledgments

We acknowledge the help of Gabriel Rada and Daniel Perez from Epistemonikos foundation. Authors were supported by the Chilean research agency Conicyt, Fondecyt grant#11150783.

REFERENCES

1. Clive E. Adams, Stefanie Polzmacher, and Annabelle Wolff. 2013. Systematic reviews: Work that needs to be done and not to be done. *Journal of Evidence-Based Medicine* 6, 4 (2013), 232–235. DOI: http://dx.doi.org/10.1111/jebm.12072
2. Ivana Andjelkovic, Denis Parra, and John O'Donovan. 2016. Moodplay: Interactive Mood-based Music Discovery and Recommendation. In *Proceedings of the 2016 Conference on User Modeling Adaptation and Personalization (UMAP '16)*. ACM, New York, NY, USA, 275–279. DOI:http://dx.doi.org/10.1145/2930238.2930280
3. Tanja Bekhuis and Dina Demner-Fushman. 2010. Towards automating the initial screening phase of a systematic review. *Studies in Health Technology and Informatics* 160, PART 1 (2010), 146–150. DOI: http://dx.doi.org/10.3233/978-1-60750-588-4-146
4. Tanja Bekhuis, Eugene Tseytlin, Kevin J. Mitchell, and Dina Demner-Fushman. 2014. Feature engineering and a proposed decision-support system for systematic reviewers of medical evidence. *PLoS ONE* 9, 1 (2014), 1–10. DOI: http://dx.doi.org/10.1371/journal.pone.0086277
5. Elaine M Beller, Joyce Kee-Hsin Chen, Una Li-Hsiang Wang, and Paul P Glasziou. 2013. Are systematic reviews up-to-date at the time of publication? *Syst Rev* 2 (2013), 36. DOI: http://dx.doi.org/10.1186/2046-4053-2-36
6. Juan Felipe Beltran, Ziqi Huang, Azza Abouzied, and Arnab Nandi. 2017. Don'T Just Swipe Left, Tell Me Why: Enhancing Gesture-based Feedback with Reason Bins. In *Proceedings of the 22Nd International Conference on Intelligent User Interfaces (IUI '17)*. ACM, New York, NY, USA, 469–480. DOI: http://dx.doi.org/10.1145/3025171.3025212
7. Steven Bird, Ewan Klein, and Edward Loper. 2009. *Natural Language Processing with Python* (1st ed.). O'Reilly Media, Inc.
8. Svetlin Bostandjiev, John O'Donovan, and Tobias Höllerer. 2012. TasteWeights: A Visual Interactive Hybrid Recommender System. In *Proceedings of the Sixth ACM Conference on Recommender Systems (RecSys '12)*. ACM, New York, NY, USA, 35–42. DOI: http://dx.doi.org/10.1145/2365952.2365964
9. Michael Bostock, Vadim Ogievetsky, and Jeffrey Heer. 2011. D3 Data-Driven Documents. *IEEE Transactions on Visualization and Computer Graphics* 17, 12 (Dec. 2011), 2301–2309. DOI: http://dx.doi.org/10.1109/TVCG.2011.185
10. Sungbin Choi, Borim Ryu, Sooyoung Yoo, and Jinwook Choi. 2012. Combining relevancy and methodological quality into a single ranking for evidence-based medicine. *Information Sciences* 214 (2012), 76–90. DOI:http://dx.doi.org/10.1016/j.ins.2012.05.027
11. Aaron M Cohen. 2006. An effective general purpose approach for automated biomedical document classification. *AMIA ... Annual Symposium proceedings / AMIA Symposium. AMIA Symposium* (2006), 161–165.
12. Aaron M Cohen, Clive E Adams, John M Davis, Clement Yu, Philip S Yu, Weiyi Meng, Lorna Duggan, Marian McDonagh, and Neil R Smalheiser. 2010. Evidence-based medicine, the essential role of systematic reviews, and the need for automated text mining tools. *Proceedings of the ACM international conference on Health informatics - IHI '10* (2010), 376. DOI: http://dx.doi.org/10.1145/1882992.1883046
13. Steven P Crain, Ke Zhou, Shuang-Hong Yang, and Hongyuan Zha. 2012. Dimensionality reduction and topic modeling: From latent semantic indexing to latent dirichlet allocation and beyond. In *Mining text data*. Springer, 129–161.
14. V Dhar. 2016. When to trust robots with decisions, and when not to. *Harvard Business Review* (2016).
15. Cecilia di Sciascio, Vedran Sabol, and Eduardo E. Veas. 2016. Rank As You Go: User-Driven Exploration of Search Results. In *Proceedings of the 21st International Conference on Intelligent User Interfaces (IUI '16)*. ACM, New York, NY, USA, 118–129. DOI: http://dx.doi.org/10.1145/2856767.2856797
16. Ivania Donoso-Guzmán. 2017. EpistAid: An Interactive Intelligent System for Evidence-based Health Care. In *Proceedings of the 22Nd International Conference on Intelligent User Interfaces Companion (IUI '17 Companion)*. ACM, New York, NY, USA, 177–180. DOI: http://dx.doi.org/10.1145/3030024.3038281
17. Julian H. Elliott, Tari Turner, Ornella Clavisi, James Thomas, Julian P. T. Higgins, Chris Mavergames, and Russell L. Gruen. 2014. Living Systematic Reviews: An Emerging Opportunity to Narrow the Evidence-Practice Gap. *PLoS Medicine* 11, 2 (2014), e1001603. DOI: http://dx.doi.org/10.1371/journal.pmed.1001603
18. Elsevier. 2016. *Embase, Biomedical evidence is essential.* http://store.elsevier.com/embase
19. Daniel Engel, Lars Hüttenberger, and Bernd Hamann. 2012. A survey of dimension reduction methods for high-dimensional data analysis and visualization. In *OASIcs-OpenAccess Series in Informatics*, Vol. 27. Schloss Dagstuhl-Leibniz-Zentrum fuer Informatik.
20. Epistemonikos. 2016. *Epistemonikos database methods.* http://www.epistemonikos.org/en/about_us/methods
21. Katia R. Felizardo, Gabriel F. Andery, Fernando V. Paulovich, Rosane Minghim, and Jose C. Maldonado. 2012. A visual analysis approach to validate the selection review of primary studies in systematic reviews. *Information and Software Technology* 54, 10 (2012), 1079–1091. DOI: http://dx.doi.org/10.1016/j.infsof.2012.04.003
22. Katia Romero Felizardo, Simone R S Souza, and José Carlos Maldonado. 2013. The use of visual text mining to support the study selection activity in systematic literature reviews: A replication study. In *Proceedings - 2013 3rd International Workshop on Replication in Empirical Software Engineering Research, RESER 2013*. DOI: http://dx.doi.org/10.1109/RESER.2013.9
23. J. J. García Adeva, J. M. Pikatza Atxa, M. Ubeda Carrillo, and E. Ansuategi Zengotitabengoa. 2014. Automatic text classification to support systematic reviews in medicine. *Expert Systems with Applications* 41, 4 PART 1 (2014), 1498–1508. DOI: http://dx.doi.org/10.1016/j.eswa.2013.08.047
24. Shuguang Han, Daqing He, Jiepu Jiang, and Zhen Yue. 2013. Supporting Exploratory People Search: A Study of Factor Transparency and User Control. In *Proceedings of the 22Nd ACM International Conference on Information & Knowledge Management (CIKM '13)*. ACM, New York, NY, USA, 449–458. DOI: http://dx.doi.org/10.1145/2505515.2505684
25. Yoshinori Hijikata, Yuki Kai, and Shogo Nishida. 2012. The relation between user intervention and user satisfaction for information recommendation. In *Proceedings of the 27th Annual ACM Symposium on Applied Computing*. ACM, 2002–2007.
26. Brian E Howard, Jason Phillips, Kyle Miller, Arpit Tandon, Deepak Mav, Mihir R Shah, Stephanie Holmgren, Katherine E Pelch, Vickie Walker, Andrew A Rooney, Malcolm Macleod, Ruchir R Shah, and Kristina Thayer. 2016. SWIFT-Review: a text-mining workbench for systematic review. *Systematic reviews* 5 (2016), 87. DOI: http://dx.doi.org/10.1186/s13643-016-0263-z
27. Siddhartha Jonnalagadda and Diana Petitti. 2013. A new iterative method to reduce workload in systematic review process. *International journal of computational biology and drug design* 6, 1-2 (2013), 5–17. DOI:http://dx.doi.org/10.1504/IJCBDD.2013.052198
28. Khalid S Khan, Regina Kunz, Jos Kleijnen, and Gerd Antes. 2003. Five steps to conducting a systematic review. *Journal of the Royal Society of Medicine* 96, 3 (2003), 118–121. DOI: http://dx.doi.org/10.1258/jrsm.96.3.118
29. Halil Kilicoglu, Dina Demner-Fushman, Thomas C. Rindflesch, Nancy L. Wilczynski, and R. Brian Haynes. 2009. Towards Automatic Recognition of Scientifically Rigorous Clinical Research Evidence. *Journal of the American Medical Informatics Association* 16, 1 (2009), 25–31. DOI:http://dx.doi.org/10.1197/jamia.M2996
30. Bart P. Knijnenburg, Svetlin Bostandjiev, John O'Donovan, and Alfred Kobsa. 2012. Inspectability and Control in Social Recommenders. In *Proceedings of the Sixth ACM Conference on Recommender Systems (RecSys '12)*. ACM, New York, NY, USA, 43–50. DOI: http://dx.doi.org/10.1145/2365952.2365966

31. Bart P Knijnenburg and Martijn C Willemsen. 2011. Each to His Own : How Different Users Call for Different Interaction Methods in Recommender Systems. *Proceedings of the 5th ACM conference on Recommender systems - RecSys '11* (2011), 141–148. DOI: http://dx.doi.org/10.1145/2043932.2043960

32. Alexandre Kouznetsov and Nathalie Japkowicz. 2010. *Using Classifier Performance Visualization to Improve Collective Ranking Techniques for Biomedical Abstracts Classification.* Springer Berlin Heidelberg, Berlin, Heidelberg, 299–303. DOI: http://dx.doi.org/10.1007/978-3-642-13059-5_33

33. Alexandre Kouznetsov, Stan Matwin, Diana Inkpen, Amir H Razavi, Oana Frunza, Morvarid Sehatkar, Leanne Seaward, and Peter O'Blenis. 2009. *Classifying Biomedical Abstracts Using Committees of Classifiers and Collective Ranking Techniques.* Springer Berlin Heidelberg, Berlin, Heidelberg, 224–228. DOI: http://dx.doi.org/10.1007/978-3-642-01818-3_29

34. Laurens van der Maaten and Geoffrey Hinton. 2008. Visualizing data using t-SNE. *Journal of Machine Learning Research* 9, Nov (2008), 2579–2605.

35. Christopher D. Manning, Prabhakar Raghavan, and Hinrich Schütze. 2008. *Introduction to Information Retrieval.* Cambridge University Press, New York, NY, USA.

36. Wes McKinney. 2010. Data Structures for Statistical Computing in Python. In *Proceedings of the 9th Python in Science Conference*, Stéfan van der Walt and Jarrod Millman (Eds.). 51–56.

37. Makoto Miwa, James Thomas, Alison O'Mara-Eves, and Sophia Ananiadou. 2014. Reducing systematic review workload through certainty-based screening. *Journal of Biomedical Informatics* 51 (2014), 242–253. DOI:http://dx.doi.org/10.1016/j.jbi.2014.06.005

38. Yuanhan Mo, Georgios Kontonatsios, and Sophia Ananiadou. 2015. Supporting systematic reviews using LDA-based document representations. *Systematic Reviews* 4, 1 (2015), 172. DOI: http://dx.doi.org/10.1186/s13643-015-0117-0

39. Tamara Munzner and Eamonn Maguire. 2015. *Visualization analysis and design.* CRC Press, Boca Raton, FL. https://cds.cern.ch/record/2001992

40. Ingrid Nunes and Dietmar Jannach. 2017. A systematic review and taxonomy of explanations in decision support and recommender systems. *User Modeling and User-Adapted Interaction* 27, 3-5 (2017), 393–444.

41. Alison O Mara-Eves, James Thomas, John McNaught, Makoto Miwa, and Sophia Ananiadou. 2015. Using text mining for study identification in systematic reviews: a systematic review of current approaches. *Systematic reviews* 4, 1 (2015), 5. DOI: http://dx.doi.org/10.1186/2046-4053-4-5

42. Babatunde K. Olorisade, Ed de Quincey, Pearl Brereton, and Peter Andras. 2016. A Critical Analysis of Studies That Address the Use of Text Mining for Citation Screening in Systematic Reviews. In *Proceedings of the 20th International Conference on Evaluation and Assessment in Software Engineering (EASE '16).* ACM, New York, NY, USA, Article 14, 11 pages. DOI: http://dx.doi.org/10.1145/2915970.2915982

43. Mark Otto and Jacob Thornton. 2016. *Bootstrap.* http://getbootstrap.com/

44. Denis Parra and Peter Brusilovsky. 2015. User-controllable Personalization. *Int. J. Hum.-Comput. Stud.* 78, C (June 2015), 43–67. DOI:http://dx.doi.org/10.1016/j.ijhcs.2015.01.007

45. Denis Parra, Peter Brusilovsky, and Christoph Trattner. 2014. See What You Want to See: Visual User-Driven Approach for Hybrid Recommendation. In *Proceedings of the 19th international conference on Intelligent User Interfaces.* ACM, 235–240.

46. F. Pedregosa, G. Varoquaux, A. Gramfort, V. Michel, B. Thirion, O. Grisel, M. Blondel, P. Prettenhofer, R. Weiss, V. Dubourg, J. Vanderplas, A. Passos, D. Cournapeau, M. Brucher, M. Perrot, and E. Duchesnay. 2011. Scikit-learn: Machine Learning in Python. *Journal of Machine Learning Research* 12 (2011), 2825–2830.

47. Jaakko Peltonen, Jonathan Strahl, and Patrik Floréen. 2017. Negative Relevance Feedback for Exploratory Search with Visual Interactive Intent Modeling. In *Proceedings of the 22Nd International Conference on Intelligent User Interfaces (IUI '17).* ACM, New York, NY, USA, 149–159. DOI:http://dx.doi.org/10.1145/3025171.3025222

48. David Martin Powers. 2011. Evaluation: from precision, recall and F-measure to ROC, informedness, markedness and correlation. (2011).

49. Gabriel Rada, Daniel Perez, and Daniel Capurro. 2013. Epistemonikos: a free, relational, collaborative, multilingual database of health evidence. *Studies in health technology and informatics* 192 (2013), 486–490. DOI: http://dx.doi.org/10.3233/978-1-61499-289-9-486

50. David L Sackett and William MC Rosenberg. 1995. The need for evidence-based medicine. *Journal of the Royal Society of Medicine* 88, 11 (1995), 620–624.

51. David L Sackett, William MC Rosenberg, JA Muir Gray, R Brian Haynes, and W Scott Richardson. 1996. Evidence based medicine: what it is and what it isn't. *Bmj* 312, 7023 (1996), 71–72.

52. G. Salton. 1971. *The SMART Retrieval System—Experiments in Automatic Document Processing.* Prentice-Hall, Inc., Upper Saddle River, NJ, USA.

53. B. Shneiderman. 1996. The eyes have it: a task by data type taxonomy for informatio nvisualizations. *Proceedings 1996 IEEE Symposium on Visual Languages* (1996), 336–343. DOI: http://dx.doi.org/10.1109/VL.1996.545307

54. James Thomas, John McNaught, and Sophia Ananiadou. 2011. Applications of text mining within systematic reviews. *Research Synthesis Methods* 2, 1 (2011), 1–14. DOI: http://dx.doi.org/10.1002/jrsm.27

55. S. van der Walt, S. C. Colbert, and G. Varoquaux. 2011. The NumPy Array: A Structure for Efficient Numerical Computation. *Computing in Science Engineering* 13, 2 (March 2011), 22–30. DOI: http://dx.doi.org/10.1109/MCSE.2011.37

56. Katrien Verbert, Denis Parra, Peter Brusilovsky, and Erik Duval. 2013. Visualizing recommendations to support exploration, transparency and controllability. In *Proceedings of the 2013 international conference on Intelligent user interfaces.* ACM, 351–362.

57. Byron C. Wallace, Kevin Small, Carla E. Brodley, Joseph Lau, Christopher H. Schmid, Lars Bertram, Christina M. Lill, Joshua T. Cohen, and Thomas A. Trikalinos. 2012b. Toward modernizing the systematic review pipeline in genetics: efficient updating via data mining. *Genetics in Medicine* 14, 7 (2012), 663–669. DOI: http://dx.doi.org/10.1038/gim.2012.7

58. Byron C Wallace, Kevin Small, Carla E Brodley, Joseph Lau, and Thomas a Trikalinos. 2010. Modeling Annotation Time to Reduce Workload in Comparative Effectiveness Reviews Categories and Subject Descriptors Active Learning to Mitigate Workload. *Proceedings of the 1st ACM International Health Informatics Symposium. ACM,* (2010), 28–35. DOI:http://dx.doi.org/10.1145/1882992.1882999

59. Byron C. Wallace, Kevin Small, Carla E. Brodley, Joseph Lau, and Thomas A. Trikalinos. 2012a. Deploying an Interactive Machine Learning System in an Evidence-based Practice Center: Abstrackr. In *Proceedings of the 2Nd ACM SIGHIT International Health Informatics Symposium (IHI '12).* ACM, New York, NY, USA, 819–824. DOI: http://dx.doi.org/10.1145/2110363.2110464

60. BC C Wallace, K Small, CE E Brodley, and TA A Trikalinos. 2011. Who Should Label What? Instance Allocation in Multiple Expert Active Learning. *Sdm* (2011), 176–187. DOI: http://dx.doi.org/10.1137/1.9781611972818.16

61. Byron C Wallace, Thomas a Trikalinos, Joseph Lau, Carla Brodley, and Christopher H Schmid. 2010. Semi-automated screening of biomedical citations for systematic reviews. *BMC bioinformatics* 11, 55 (2010), 55. DOI:http://dx.doi.org/10.1186/1471-2105-11-55

62. Wei Yu, Melinda Clyne, Siobhan M Dolan, Ajay Yesupriya, Anja Wulf, Tiebin Liu, Muin J Khoury, and Marta Gwinn. 2008. GAPscreener: An automatic tool for screening human genetic association literature in PubMed using the support vector machine technique. *BMC Bioinformatics* 9 (2008), 205. DOI: http://dx.doi.org/10.1186/1471-2105-9-205

Modality Switching for Mitigation of Sensory Adaptation and Habituation in Personal Navigation Systems

Kyle Kotowick
Massachusetts Institute of Technology
Department of Aeronautics and Astronautics
Computer Science and Artificial Intelligence Laboratory
Cambridge, MA, USA
kotowick@mit.edu

Julie Shah
Massachusetts Institute of Technology
Department of Aeronautics and Astronautics
Computer Science and Artificial Intelligence Laboratory
Cambridge, MA, USA
julie_a_shah@csail.mit.edu

ABSTRACT
When humans need to navigate across terrain accurately and quickly, they often use portable electronic navigation systems for directional guidance. Prior work in this field has focused on selecting either the visual or haptic sensory modality for providing such guidance and has indicated that either option may be preferable depending on the user's specific goals. However, basing the selection of visual or haptic guidance on static criteria of this type discounts important time-varying effects, primarily stimulus-specific adaptation (SSA) and habituation. Here, we propose a navigation system design that mitigates these detrimental effects by periodically switching between visual and haptic navigation guidance. While this is likely to incur an undesirable switching cost, we hypothesize that the long-term benefits of counteracting SSA and habituation will outweigh this cost. In this paper, we describe the design and results of a human-participant study intended to evaluate this hypothesis. Our findings indicate that modality switching results in a transient cost to performance, but also that switching modalities lessens the SSA and habituation effects over time as compared with single-modality systems. The results support the hypothesis that an alternating-modality system would outperform a single-modality system for long-duration navigation tasks.

Author Keywords
Multimodal; Sensory Modality; Navigation; Habituation; Adaptation.

INTRODUCTION
Assisting humans with navigational tasks is one of the most common uses for portable electronic devices. In particular, users in extreme environments — such as emergency first responders or military infantry on patrol — often make use of devices that aid them in locating and navigating to emergency scenes, victims, or enemy targets. For such users, high performance is of paramount importance and it is critical that these navigational devices provide directional guidance in the most effective manner possible.

Historically, navigation systems have been based on visual displays. For millennia, maps and compasses — both of which require visual attention from the user — were the primary navigational tools. In the last few decades, with the development of computerized audio systems, auditory directional guidance (i.e., verbalized directions) has also become available on many devices. Only in recent years, however, has a third major sensory modality been actively investigated for directional guidance: haptic feedback.[1]

Investigation into the use of haptic feedback for navigation systems began in the early 2000s, primarily within the military community. Multiple studies and research programs have demonstrated the merits of a haptic navigation belt: a belt with vibrating motors placed throughout which vibrate in the direction the user needs to move [11, 13, 19, 18, 17, 14]. One of the main outcomes of this prior work was determination of the relative advantages and disadvantages of visual vs. haptic directional guidance. Each performs better under specific circumstances; for example, in one study by the U.S. Army Research Laboratory, a visual GPS display allowed significantly faster traversal over terrain by a soldier with no other tasks to complete, while a haptic navigation system allowed a soldier to pay significantly more attention to visual search tasks, detection and avoidance of obstacles, and weapon control [13]. In related work to date, these advantages and disadvantages have formed the sole basis for selecting one modality over another: the optimal modality is that which is most compatible with the user's specific goals. These relative merits, however, are of a static nature: they only consider the present circumstances and do not allow for time-varying effects. We believe there are additional important, dynamic effects that must be consid-

IUI'18, March 7–11, 2018, Tokyo, Japan

ISBN 978-1-4503-4945-1/18/03...$15.00

DOI: https://doi.org/10.1145/3172944.3172980

[1]Throughout related literature, the terms "haptic" and "tactile" are used interchangeably. Specifically, "haptic" refers to the overall sense of touch including kinesthetic (the sense of position and movement of muscles, tendons, and joints) and tactile (the sense of touch or vibration in the fingers or on the surface of the skin) sensory input. We use "haptic" throughout this paper for simplicity and consistency.

ered during modality selection: specifically, stimulus-specific adaptation and habituation.

Stimulus-specific adaptation (SSA) and habituation — physiological and behavioural (respectively) detrimental effects that result in decreased sensitivity to continuous stimulation over time [21, 48] — are likely to reduce a navigation system's effectiveness over time if it continues to incorporate a single directional guidance modality, regardless of whether the chosen modality is that which is most compatible with the user's specific goals. As the user continues to receive directional guidance in the same modality, he or she is naturally less likely to notice and respond to it. Both of these effects, however, can be "reset" by changing the modality of the stimulus, causing the user to regain full sensitivity to it [59, 48]. We hypothesize that by regularly changing the modality in which directional guidance is presented, we can counteract the effects of SSA and habituation in order to provide greater performance stability over long-duration navigation tasks.

In this paper, we describe the design and results of a 32-participant experiment intended to determine the impact of SSA and habituation on a visual/haptic navigation system, as well as to investigate whether that impact can be mitigated trough periodic switching between modalities. We conducted the experiment according to a within-participants design, with the navigation feedback modality as the controlled independent variable. The data was analyzed with linear mixed-effects models; the main and interaction effects of various factors on multiple performance metrics are presented and discussed here.

RELATED WORK

Haptic Navigation

Following from extensive prior research into use of the haptic modality to convey information in general, research into haptic directional guidance became quite active in the mid-2000s for both civilian and military applications.

Research for civilian applications of haptic directional guidance has been conducted independently by numerous research groups. A study by Tsukada and Yasumura examined the feasibility of a prototype haptic navigation belt, finding that it was able to assist users in accurately navigating through waypoints [57]. Pielot and Boll conducted similar work by comparing the effectiveness of their prototype haptic navigation belt with conventional visual navigation systems, finding that the haptic system required less attention but was not as effective in helping the user reach the waypoint [42]. That same research group conducted another study to evaluate the use of haptic vibration patterns on a mobile phone to convey navigation information, finding that it required less attention while having no significant navigation performance differences compared to a visual system [43]; they then incorporated these results into a prototype haptic navigation system and conducted a large-scale study of its use in an urban environment and confirmed these results [44]. Several studies have investigated the design and use of haptic directional guidance for blind users, all showing encouraging results [1, 34, 67, 45]. Many additional, similar studies on haptic directional guidance for pedestrian use have demonstrated positive effects [36, 30, 33, 47].

Research for military applications has been conducted primarily by the U.S. Army Research Laboratory. This research program included four major experiments on the use of haptic directional guidance for soldiers in the field using a "personal tactile navigator" (PTN), i.e. a haptic belt that vibrates in the direction the soldier needs to move. A series of four experiments all demonstrated potential benefits and detriments of haptic guidance compared to visual guidance: the visual modality allowed faster navigation when there were no additional tasks, while the haptic modality was less likely to interfere with secondary visual-based tasks such as target identification [16, 11, 13, 14]. Other publications have included details of improvements to the navigation system [15] and a summary of the first three experiments [18].

Overall, prior work on haptic directional guidance has demonstrated that it is a worthwhile technology to develop and integrate into modern navigation systems, thereby motivating the research described in this paper.

Modality Switching Cost

One of the potential disadvantages of any system that switches between modalities for conveying information, as would be the case with this proposed navigation system, is that an effect known as "switching cost" may be introduced. Switching cost is when a user experiences a worsened response time or sensitivity to a stimulus due to having to switch attention from one sensory modality to another. The specific type of switching cost that is relevant to this study is known as a "within-task switching cost."

A within-task switching cost occurs when information from a given source/task is presented to the user in a sensory modality other than the one it was expected in, e.g. if a user expects an alert to be provided auditorily as an alarm, but instead it is presented visually as a warning light. While the body of research assessing this effect is smaller than that of other types of switching cost, numerous studies have shown its influence to be significant. In a study by Klein, participants exhibited slower response time when they received a simple stimulus in a modality different from that which they expected [32]. A later, similar study by Spence *et al.* yielded the same result for the detection of target locations [52]. Post and Chapman demonstrated that participants responded less quickly to simple stimuli when they did not know which modality to expect them in or when they expected them in the incorrect modality, compared to when their expectations were correct [46]. The results of these studies suggest that navigation performance while using a navigation device which switches between different modalities would drop after each switch before recovering as the user becomes accustomed to the new modality.

Sensory Adaptation

Sensory adaptation, also referred to as neural adaptation, is a physiological effect where continuous exposure to a stimulus causes changes in the response properties of the activated neurons, usually resulting in decreased sensitivity to that stimulus over time [64]. The body of work investigating this effect is extensive, beginning with research conducted by Herman von Helmholtz in the 19th century who investigated visual and auditory adaptation to abnormal stimuli [27]. Similar work was conducted in the field of psychology later that century [53]. In more recent years, research has focused on the specific mechanisms that cause this effect and the evolutionary process that lead to them. Various reasons for the evolution of this trait have been proposed, such as efficient coding of neurological signals (similar to a form of digital compression) and allowing for heightened response to rare or changing stimuli [35, 63, 12].

Stimulus-Specific Adaptation

Stimulus-specific adaptation (SSA) is sub-category of sensory adaptation and relates to adaptation to the history of a stimulus. As the neurological system receives the same stimulus continuously for an extended duration — or receives a brief stimulus frequently — the neural response to that stimulus decreases over time [3, 21]. SSA is most widely known for its relevance to the concept of change detection [23].

Although much of the research on this topic has been conducted on rats or primates due to the invasive procedures required to obtain measurements, the effect has also been found to exist in humans for both visual [39, 5, 8, 50, 38, 49, 51] and auditory [59, 58, 2, 37, 4, 54, 41, 40] stimuli. SSA has been shown to exist for stimuli with durations of 200ms (the same duration as the vibration pulses used in the Army Research Laboratory's haptic directional guidance experiments) and after only one occurrence of a stimulus [62]. Prior work has suggested that SSA may end after the stimulus has not been received for ~2 seconds [59]. Unfortunately, research into this phenomenon appears to have focused exclusively on visual or auditory stimuli and provides little information regarding how SSA relates to haptic stimuli. However, study results have indicated that auditory SSA occurs in the thalamus [2], and that the thalamus is also involved in the perception of touch [9]. It is likely, then, that SSA exists for haptic stimuli as well; if this is the case, repeated pulses of vibration used for haptic directional guidance (even if limited to a duration of 200 ms) may become less noticeable to the user over time.

The presence of this effect supports the idea that switching between modalities within a navigation system would yield a beneficial effect. Every time the modality (i.e., the stimulus) changes, the user would not be adapted to this new modality and should therefore not suffer from the detrimental effects of SSA.

Habituation

Habituation, although similar to sensory adaptation, is a behavioural learning effect (as opposed to a physiological one). While adaptation is a passive effect — i.e., a person has no direct control over it — habituation is an active effort by the brain to filter out background stimuli in order to allow more attention to be paid to irregular stimuli. Specifically, habituation is defined as "a behavioural response decrement that results from repeated stimulation and that does not involve sensory adaptation/sensory fatigue or motor fatigue" [48].

Research into habituation has a rich and extensive history. The term was already in widespread use by the beginning of the 20th century [31, 24], with a number of related terms used to describe the same concept, including "acclimatization" and "accommodation" [29]. Initially, habituation and adaptation were not clearly distinguished as separate effects. A landmark paper published in 1966 by Thompson and Spencer, however, reviewed definitive evidence that the decrease in sensitivity to repeated stimuli could not be entirely attributed to sensory adaptation, and that a separate effect must be present [56]. Further work by Groves and Thompson developed a more concrete theory of habituation [22].

Two elements of habituation are of particular importance in the context of this paper: *dishabituation* and *spontaneous recovery*, which are two of the characteristics of habituation originally specified by Thompson and Spencer [56] and later revised by Rankin *et al.* [48]. *Dishabituation* refers to a characteristic wherein "presentation of a different stimulus results in an increase of the decremented response to the original stimulus" [48]. In other words, if a person is habituated to a stimulus and therefore experiencing decreased sensitivity to it, providing him or her with an alternative stimulus will result in increased sensitivity to subsequent presentations of the original. *Spontaneous recovery* refers to a circumstance wherein "if the stimulus is withheld after response decrement, the response recovers at least partially over the observation time" [48]. This means that if a person is habituated to a stimulus and experiencing decreased sensitivity to it, withholding that stimulus for a duration of time will result in increased sensitivity to it upon its reintroduction. Results from various studies have indicated that the time required for spontaneous recovery can range from seconds to weeks depending on multiple factors [56, 65, 61, 68, 10, 20].

Both dishabituation and spontaneous recovery provide motivation for a navigation system that switches between modalities over time. If a user has become habituated to stimuli from a given directional guidance modality, be it visual or haptic, switching to the alternative modality would improve performance in multiple ways. This alternate modality would represent a new type of stimulus, thereby dishabituating the user from the prior modality and improving his or her sensitivity to it when it is reintroduced later. Switching to a new modality would also provide a break from the stimulus that the user has become habituated to, creating an opportunity for spontaneous recovery to occur.

HYPOTHESES

Our experiment evaluated a navigation system able to provide directional guidance in visual-only, haptic-only, or visual/haptic switching modes. Based on prior work regarding modality switching costs, SSA, and habituation, we designed this experiment to investigate the following two hypotheses:

Hypothesis 1: Switching directional guidance modalities during a navigation task will result in an immediate decrease in performance due to the associated modality switching cost, but performance will gradually recover over time. Specifically, this will be represented as a positive coefficent for the main effect of the amount of time since the last modality change on the

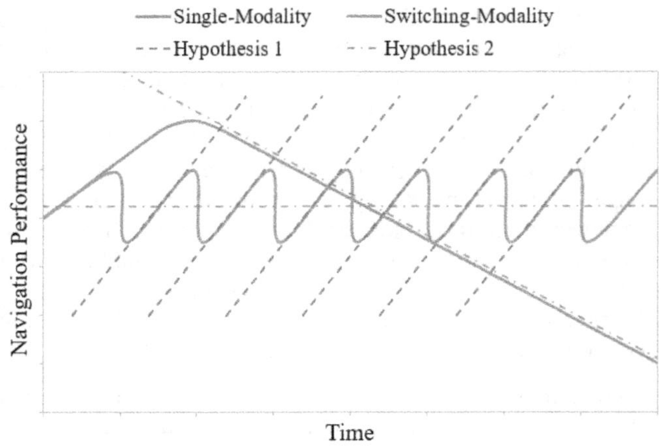

Figure 1. A graphical representation of the hypotheses. After the user becomes familiar with a single-modality navigation system, the performance gradually decreases over time due to SSA and habituation. For a switching-modality system, there is a decrease in performance after each switch, but no long-term SSA or habituation effects.

dependent performance variable (i.e. performance improves with time after each modality change).

Hypothesis 2: Switching directional guidance modalities periodically over the course of a navigation task will result in improved long-term navigation performance compared with visual- or haptic-only navigation systems by counteracting the effects of SSA and habituation. Specifically, this will be represented as a negative coefficient for the interaction effect between visual- or haptic-only modes (with the switching mode as the reference category) and the time since the navigation task began on the dependent performance variable (i.e., performance in visual- or haptic-only modes decreases with time compared with the switching–modality mode).

Figure 1 depicts a visual representation of the hypotheses. These hypotheses relate to overall navigation performance (the ability to reach a waypoint quickly); however, it is possible that individual components of performance may be affected differently. Therefore, we tested effects across multiple metrics including navigation speed, deviation from the shortest path (bearing error), and workload.

EXPERIMENTAL DESIGN

The experiment, conducted according to a within-participants design, consisted of a navigation task performed on a desktop computer, with the navigation system "mode" (*visual*, *haptic*, or *switching*) serving as the controlled independent variable.

Equipment

We conducted the experiment using the ARMA 3 simulation software [7] on a custom-built computer.[2] ARMA 3 was selected due to its in-game scripting language that allows for programming of the experiment task, its open-world environment, and its external C++ extension callback capability for operating the haptic device and recording data to an external database. A custom-built wearable device consisting of an elastic belt containing eight tactors, evenly distributed around the waist, was used to convey information to the participant in the haptic modality. The tactors were C-2 models from Engineering Acoustics, Inc. Figure 2 depicts the experiment setup.

Figure 2. Experiment Setup

Navigation Task

The participant's only task during each experiment trial was to move his or her in-game avatar from its current position to a given waypoint. The participant controlled the avatar's movement using the "W" (forward), "A" (left strafe), "S" (backward), "D" (right strafe), and "SHIFT" (sprint) keys, while controlling the avatar's direction via the mouse. Participants received directional guidance through either a visual or haptic system, as described below. When participants reached the waypoint they would hear a chime and would be assigned a new waypoint. Trials lasted 8 minutes each, with participants continuing to receive new waypoints until time ran out.

Visual Navigation

When the navigation system was operating under the visual modality, participants were able to see a device attached to their avatar's chest that closely resembled a commercial GPS navigation display. The chest-mounted location was chosen in order to emulate the vest-mounted, flip-down GPS pouch utilized by the US Army as part of the Nett Warrior program (see Figure 3). The display showed a map centered on the avatar's current location and oriented such that the top of the map corresponded to the direction the avatar was presently facing. The display also included an arrow at the center that always pointed toward the current waypoint; to face directly toward the waypoint, the participant would turn the avatar until the arrow on the display pointed directly forward. The waypoint itself was not marked on the display, only the direction toward it — this was so that the visual modality would not provide additional information that was not also available

[2]**OS:** Windows 10; **CPU:** Intel Core i7 6700K; **Memory:** 64GB Corsair DDR4-3200; **Motherboard:** ASUS Z170; **SSD:** 1TB Intel 600p M.2; **VGA:** 2x NVIDIA Titan X in SLI; **Audio:** Sennheiser HD 202 II headphones; **Mouse:** Logitech M500; **Keyboard:** Logitech G710+

Figure 3. Flip-down GPS pouch used by the US Army. Image reproduced from [60].

Figure 4. In-simulation visual navigation display.

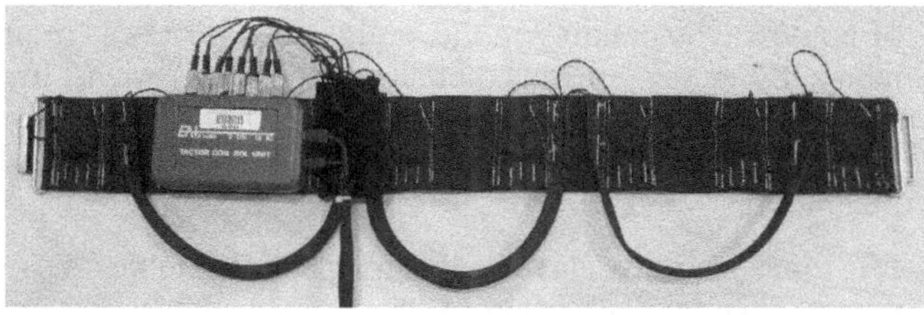

(a) Outside

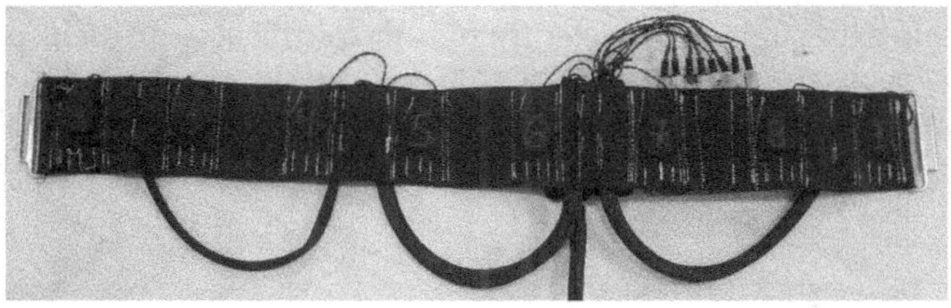

(b) Inside

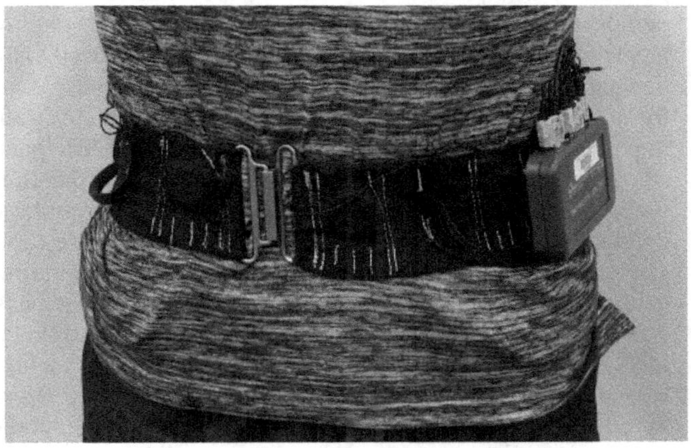

(c) As worn by participants

Figure 5. Custom-built haptic navigation belt.

in the haptic modality. Figure 4 depicts the visual navigation display.

Haptic Navigation

When the navigation system was operating under the haptic modality, the GPS display was hidden, with directional guidance instead conveyed through the haptic belt around the participant's waist. The eight tactors in the belt were evenly spaced at the 0°, 45°, 90°, 135°, 180°, 225°, 270°, and 315° positions with corresponding IDs of 1 – 8 respectively (the 0° position was located directly underneath the participant's navel). Figure 5 shows the haptic belt. The two tactors closest to the actual bearing of the waypoint relative to the avatar's current direction were vibrated at 250 Hz, with the gain of each tactor relative to its proportional representation of the actual bearing, according to the following equations:

$$G_{\lfloor B/45 \rfloor + 1} = ((45 - (B \bmod 45))/45)^{0.75} \quad (1)$$

$$G_{\lfloor B/45 \rfloor + 2} = ((B \bmod 45)/45)^{0.75} \quad (2)$$

G_x is the gain level (0 to 1) of the tactor with ID equal to x and B is the bearing, in degrees, of the current waypoint relative to the avatar's current direction. For example, if the direction to the waypoint was at 80° relative to the avatar's current direction, the tactors at the 45° (ID = 1) and 90° (ID = 2) positions would vibrate with gain levels of 0.32 and 0.83, respectively. These non-linear equations were selected via pilot testing with the intention of providing an equal sensation of vibration strength regardless of direction.

Scoring

Participants received financial compensation based on a competitive structure, with the two highest-performing participants receiving bonus monetary prizes, as described in the Compensation section below. Therefore, it was necessary to implement a scoring system to motivate participants to maximize their performance. Every time a participant successfully reached a waypoint with his or her avatar, he or she received a number of points corresponding to the straight-line distance (in meters) between the last waypoint and the one that had just been reached. At the end of the trial, additional points were awarded for any progress made toward the final waypoint when time ran out.

Due to the open-world environment represented in the trials, it was possible for participants to cause their avatars to fall from heights or into open water. In order to prevent such behaviour — and the associated noise in the resulting data due to difficulty in extricating their avatar from its predicament — participants received a score penalty of -200 points if their avatar fell from a substantial height or into open water. Following such a fall, their avatar was then reset to its location 10 seconds prior to the event.

Procedure

The entire experiment took approximately 2 hours per participant. Participants began with a questionnaire to collect demographic information and ensure they met the requirements to participate, and were then gradually introduced to the navigation task, the visual and haptic navigation systems, and the scoring mechanisms through a training phase. This training also acted as a screening process, identifying participants who were unable to complete any individual task and therefore ineligible to continue. Upon completing the training phase, participants received three opportunities to complete a test trial and achieve the minimum overall performance level required to continue, which was set at the 25th percentile following a pilot study involving 11 participants. As the hypotheses tested in this experiment related to users in environments where a high level of performance is critical, this minimum threshold served to reduce the potential for low-performance outliers that did not represent the population the results would be applied to.

Participants who met the minimum performance level then began the main phase after a brief rest period. The participants completed eight trials, each of a different type, as shown in Table 1. Each trial took place in one of two environments: urban (Figure 6b) or jungle (Figure 6a). Within each environment, one trial was conducted in each of the following four navigation modes (depicted in Table 2):

- **Visual-only**: The entire trial is conducted using only the visual modality for directional guidance.
- **Haptic-only, continuous**: The entire trial is conducted using only the haptic modality for directional guidance, with the haptic belt providing continuous vibrations.[3]
- **Haptic-only, pulsed**: The entire trial is conducted using only the haptic modality for directional guidance, with the haptic belt providing 200 ms pulses of vibration with 800 ms pauses in between.
- **Switching**: The initial directional guidance modality alternatesx between visual and pulsed haptic at 60-second intervals (the modality used at the start of the trial is randomly selected).

[3]The "haptic-only, continuous" mode was included to simultaneously collect data for evaluating a hypothesis unrelated to this paper, and was not used in the analysis presented here.

(a) Jungle

(b) Urban

Figure 6. The two environments used throughout the experiment.

The order in which the trials were conducted was balanced between participants using a full Latin square design in order to compensate for learning effects. Four different Latin squares of eight rows each were concatenated to allow for balancing between all 32 participants. After each trial, participants responded to a NASA-TLX workload scale [26]. Following the first four trials, participants received a brief rest period. Upon completing the final four trials, the participants responded to an exit questionnaire in which they provided subjective opinions about which modes they felt allowed for the best performance, as well as which they preferred. Participants were also able to provide open-ended feedback regarding several aspects of the experiment.

Compensation

All participants who completed the training phase received $5 compensation; participants who met the minimum performance level after the training and completed the remainder of the experiment received an additional $15. In order to motivate participants to remain focused on the task and perform as well as possible, we also implemented a competitive score-based incentive structure as previously described, wherein the participants who achieved the highest and second-highest scores (as defined in the Scoring section above) received additional $85 and $40 prizes, respectively.

Trial Type	Environment	Navigation Mode
1	Urban	Visual
2	Urban	Haptic (Continuous)
3	Urban	Haptic (Pulsed)
4	Urban	Switching
5	Jungle	Visual
6	Jungle	Haptic (Continuous)
7	Jungle	Haptic (Pulsed)
8	Jungle	Switching

Table 1. The trial types completed by each participant.

Time	Navigation Mode			
	Visual	Haptic (C)	Haptic (P)	Switching
0 - 60	V	HC	HP	V
60 - 120	V	HC	HP	HP
120 - 180	V	HC	HP	V
180 - 240	V	HC	HP	HP
240 - 300	V	HC	HP	V
300 - 360	V	HC	HP	HP
360 - 420	V	HC	HP	V
420 - 480	V	HC	HP	HP

Table 2. The directional guidance modalities used for each navigation mode.

Data Collection

The experiment began with a questionnaire designed to determine whether participants were eligible to complete the experiment (see the Participant Demographics section below), as well as to collect the following demographic information:

- The participant's age
- The participant's physiological birth sex
- Hours per day of computer use
- Hours per day of video game use
- Whether the participant had served in any first-responder role (military, police, fire, EMS)
- Whether the participant was a student

Over the course of each trial, the status of the participant's avatar and objective — including avatar position, waypoint position, avatar direction, and avatar speed — were recorded at 50 Hz. This, combined with the NASA-TLX workload scale conducted upon the completion of each trial, allowed for analysis of the following dependent variables:

- **Navigation Speed:** The rate, in meters per second, at which the participant's avatar progressed toward the waypoint. Note that this is different from the avatar's speed, as it only incorporates the component of the avatar's velocity vector occurring in the direction of the waypoint.
- **Bearing Error:** The difference between the bearing from the avatar's position to the waypoint and the avatar's current direction.
- **Workload:** This value was calculated according to the standard NASA-TLX workload scale instructions [26]. We analyzed the standard weighted single-value workload, as well as the individual "raw" rating scales (described in [25] and shown to potentially be more accurate in [6, 28]).

Participant Demographics

Recruitment was limited to people between the ages of 18 and 50 years with a waist circumference between 71.1 cm (28in) and 101.6 cm (40in), which was the range compatible with the haptic belt. All participants were required to have vision in both eyes, hearing in both ears, and no disability that would prevent them from feeling vibrations from the haptic belt or interacting with the computer mouse and keyboard.

Thirty-two participants completed the primary experiment, including 20 men and 12 women. These participants ranged in age from 18 to 34 years (mean, 21.8 years; median, 21 years). Twenty-seven of the participants were students at the Massachusetts Institute of Technology, three were students at other universities, and two were not students.

Five additional participants began the experiment, but failed to meet the minimum performance level following training and were therefore excluded. Note that although the minimum overall performance level was set as the 25th percentile of post-training performance in the pilot study, suggesting that 25% of all participants in the main study should have failed to meet that minimum, the threshold was calculated using only the first post-training trial per pilot participant. In the main study, each participant was allowed three attempts to meet that threshold in order to accommodate those who took longer for the learning effect to subside, resulting in a much lower exclusion rate. Four additional participants voluntarily ended the experiment early for various reasons.

RESULTS

We conducted all modeling and analysis in MATLAB 2017b [55] using MATLAB's native linear mixed effects modeling capability (`fitlme`). Each model was either data point-based (incorporating individual data points collected at 50 Hz during the trials) or trial-based (incorporating aggregate data specific to a single trial). The models used the following independent variables:

- **Age:** The participant's age in years. Prior to analysis, **Age** values were centered using the mean age of all participants in order for the models' intercept values to represent the expected values at the average participant age.
- **Sex:** The participant's physiological sex. In the models, *female* was the reference category and *male* was the indicator variable.
- **Computer Use:** The average number of hours per day that the participant reported using computers.
- **Game Use:** The average number of hours per day that the participant reported playing video games.
- **Environment:** The simulated environment in which the trial was conducted. In the models, *jungle* was the reference category and *urban* was the indicator variable.
- **Trial Time:** The time, in minutes, since the start of the trial (only applicable for data point-based models).

- **Current Modality:** The directional guidance modality in use at the time the data point was recorded (only applicable for data point-based models). In the models, *Haptic* was the reference category and *Visual* was the indicator variable.
- **Modality Time:** The time, in minutes, since the last directional guidance modality switch (only applicable for data point-based models using the *switching* mode).
- **Mode:** The mode used for the given trial (*Visual*, *Haptic* (pulsed) or *Switching*). In the models, *Switching* was the reference category and *Haptic* and *Visual* were indicator variables.
- **Participant:** A unique ID number assigned to the participant.
- **Trial:** The chronological number of the trial for the given participant (i.e. 1 through 8, only applicable for data point-based models). Note that the trial number does not correlate with the trial environment or mode, as the order of trial types differed between participants according to the Latin square design.

Hypothesis 1

In order to determine whether there was a significant switching cost associated with changing directional guidance modality mid-task, we fit linear mixed-effects models to the set of all data points collected across all trials conducted in the *switching* mode. The models were formulated according to the following equation in Wilkinson notation [66]:

$$DV \sim Age + Sex + GameUse + ComputerUse + Environment + TrialTime + CurrentModality + ModalityTime + (1 \mid Participant) + (1 \mid Participant : Trial)$$

DV is the dependent variable in question. We fit this model for both the **Navigation Speed** and **Bearing Error** dependent variables. In order to test Hypothesis 1, we specifically evaluated the effect of *Modality Time* on the dependent variables.

Random Effects

Each of the linear mixed effects models testing Hypothesis 1 was fit using *Participant* as a grouping variable with a random intercept (baseline performance for each participant), as well as *Trial* as a nested grouping variable within *Participant* with a random intercept (baseline performance on each trial).

Analysis

The results of the Hypothesis 1 models are presented in Table 3. This table depicts the effect estimate for each factor on each dependent variable as as a percentage of the estimate for the model's intercept. As the intercept indicates a baseline value, representing each factor's effect size as a proportion of the intercept value allows for easier understanding of its relative size. The table also indicates which effects were statistically significant.

Hypothesis 2

In order to determine whether periodically switching directional guidance modalities prevented SSA and habituation, we fit linear mixed-effects models to the set of all data points collected across all trials. The models were formulated according to the following equation in Wilkinson notation [66]:

	Navigation Speed	Bearing Error
(Intercept)	100%**	100%**
Age	0.452%	-0.834%
Sex (Male)	6.61%	-14.6%*
Computer Use	-2.00%*	2.82%
Game Use	4.64%*	-10.2%*
Environment (Urban)	-9.83%**	47.3%**
Trial Time	1.29%**	-3.14%**
Modality (Visual)	-1.57%**	-0.300%
Modality Time	6.52%**	-9.81%**

Table 3. Effects for Hypothesis 1 models. Blue cells indicate improved performance, red cells indicate reduced performance. $*p < 0.05$, $**p < 0.001$.

$$DV \sim Age + Sex + GameUse + ComputerUse + Environment + TrialTime * Mode + (1 \mid Participant) + (1 \mid Participant : Trial)$$

DV is the dependent variable in question. We fit this model for both the **Navigation Speed** and **Bearing Error** dependent variables. In addition to the main effects of each independent variable, we also included a two-way interaction effect between *Trial Time* and *Mode*, as determining the effect of this interaction term (and whether the effect is significant) is necessary in order to test Hypothesis 2.

Random Effects

As with the modelling for Hypothesis 1, each of the linear mixed effects models testing Hypothesis 2 was fit using *Participant* as a grouping variable with a random intercept (baseline performance for each participant), as well as *Trial* as a nested grouping variable within *Participant*, also with a random intercept (baseline performance on each trial).

Analysis

The results of the Hypothesis 2 models for performance-based dependent variables are presented in Table 4. As with the results for Analysis, this table depicts the effect estimate for each factor on each dependent variable as a percentage of the estimate for the model's intercept, as well as which effects were statistically significant.

Subjective Workload

In order to determine whether periodically switching directional guidance modalities affected subjective workload levels, we fit linear mixed-effects models to the set of aggregate trial data (as workload values were only collected once per trial). The models were formulated according to the following equation in Wilkinson notation [66]:

$$DV \sim Age + Sex + GameUse + ComputerUse + Environment + Mode + (1 \mid Participant)$$

Again, *DV* represents the dependent variable in question. We fit this model for overall weighted workload, as well as individual ratings for each workload type.

	Navigation Speed	Bearing Error
(Intercept)	100%**	100%**
Age	-0.030%	-0.131%
Sex (Male)	9.13%*	-18.9%*
Computer Use	-1.65%*	2.04%
Game Use	3.43%*	-8.16%*
Environment (Urban)	-10.7%**	52.1%**
Trial Time	1.39%**	-3.31%**
Mode (Visual)	7.75%**	-14.9%**
Mode (Haptic)	8.86%**	-14.3%**
Trial Time : Mode (Visual)	-2.61%**	4.17%**
Trial Time : Mode (Haptic)	-1.53%**	3.09%**

Table 4. Effects for Hypothesis 2 models. Blue cells indicate improved performance, red cells indicate reduced performance. $^*p < 0.05$, $^{**}p < 0.001$.

Random Effects

Each of the linear mixed effects models testing Hypothesis 2 was fit using *Participant* as a grouping variable with a random intercept (baseline performance for each participant). Since workload values were only recorded once per trial, it was not necessary to include *Trial* as a nested grouping variable within *Participant*.

Analysis

The results of the Hypothesis 2 models for workload dependent variables are presented in Table 5. As with the results for Hypothesis 1, this table depicts the effect estimate for each factor on each dependent variable as a percentage of the estimate for the model's intercept, as well as which effects were statistically significant.

DISCUSSION

In this section, we present the evidence supporting our hypotheses, as well as the effects of other factors such as participant demographics. The names of dependent variables are bolded and the names of factors are italicized for clarity. "Significant" refers to $p < 0.05$, and "highly significant" refers to $p < 0.001$.

Hypothesis 1

In order for Hypothesis 1 to be true, the *Modality Time* factor must have a coefficient corresponding with improved performance. In other words, performance should improve with the amount of time since the modality last switched (as performance recovers after decreasing due to switching cost). As indicated by the data in Table 3, we found this hypothesized effect to be highly significant for **Navigation Speed** and **Bearing Error**, with per-minute effect sizes equivalent to approximately 6.5% and 9.8% of the model's intercept value, respectively. This model suggests that in our experiment, where the modality was switched every minute, there was a ~6.5% reduction in **Navigation Speed** and a ~9.8% increase in **Bearing Error** immediately following a modality switch. As hypothesized, participants suffered a significant switching cost when the directional guidance modality was changed.

Hypothesis 2

In order for Hypothesis 2 to be true, the interaction effect between the *Trial Time* and *Mode* factors must have a coefficient corresponding with reduced performance for both the *Mode (Visual)* and *Mode (Haptic)* indicator variables. In other words, performance should drop over time when using either of the single-modality modes compared with the switching-modality mode. As the data in Table 4 indicates, we found this hypothesized effect to also be highly significant. While using the *haptic-only* or *visual-only* modes had highly significant effects on **Navigation Speed** and **Bearing Error** — suggesting that they allowed better average performance over the course of the entire trial compared to the *switching* mode — the *Trial Time : Mode (Visual)* and *Trial Time : Mode (Haptic)* interaction effects were both highly significant in the direction of reduced performance regarding the same dependent variables. The model had a crossover point (the *Trial Time* at which the expected performance of the *switching* mode exceeded that of the single-modality modes) of ~3 minutes (visual) and ~5.8 minutes (haptic) for **Navigation Speed**, and ~3.6 minutes (visual) and ~4.6 minutes (haptic) for **Bearing Error**. These results suggest that single-modality modes allow for better performance in the early stages of a navigation task, but performance in these modes will steadily decrease over time compared with the *switching* mode. As hypothesized, periodically switching modalities provides a more stable level of performance for long-duration navigation tasks.

Subjective Workload

Although not related to either of our initial hypotheses, we also evaluated the relative subjective workload levels associated with the *switching* mode compared with the single-modality modes. As shown in Table 5, we found that the *switching* mode did not result in significantly higher workload than either of the single-modality modes, i.e. neither the *Mode (Visual)* nor *Mode (Haptic)* indicator variables differed significantly from the *Mode (Switching)* reference category.

Other Factors

The effects of other factors not related to our hypotheses were evaluated with the same linear mixed models used for Hypothesis 2 (shown in Table 4), as those models included data from all trials and were not restricted to the *switching* mode alone.

Age

Age did not have a significant effect on any dependent variables in any analysis. We believe this is likely due to the relatively small age range of the study's participants (18 – 34 years).

Sex

All models were fit using "female" as the reference category and "male" as the indicator variable. *Sex (Male)* had a significant beneficial effect on **Navigation Speed** and **Bearing Error** over all trials, and also resulted in a significantly lower **Workload (Performance)** rating. These results suggest that men performed better in the navigation task than women, and that they had a higher self-evaluation of their performance.

	Overall	Mental	Physical	Temporal	Performance	Effort	Frustration
(Intercept)	100%**	100%*	100%	100%*	100%*	100%*	100%*
Age	0.897%	0.535%	-1.24%	1.01%	-0.851%	2.92%	4.98%
Sex (Male)	-11.6%	19.5%	14.0%	5.80%	-49.1%*	-7.36%	-19.8%
Computer Use	0.614%	1.19%	9.27%	-3.11%	7.80%	-2.39%	2.27%
Game Use	6.32%	-4.95%	42.4%	15.3%	-7.39%	10.2%	27.5%*
Environment (Urban)	7.01%*	27.5%**	-11.4%	9.68%*	4.51%	8.32%*	3.18%
Mode (Visual)	-1.34%	4.05%	-13.7%	-3.01%	3.89%	-1.26%	11.1%
Mode (Haptic)	-5.99%	-10.3%	-4.57%	-0.940%	-7.43%	-9.26%	-15.3%

Table 5. Effects for workload models. Blue cells indicate reduced workload, red cells indicate increased workload. $*p < 0.05$, $**p < 0.001$.

Computer Use

Computer use was self-reported by participants as the number of hours per day that they used computers. Increased computer use had a significant detrimental effect on **Navigation Speed**, for which we can offer no definitive explanation.

Game Use

Game use was self-reported by participants as the number of hours per day that they played video games. Increased game use had a significant beneficial effect on **Navigation Speed** and **Bearing Error**, as would be expected (more experienced video game players performed better within the experiment's video game environment). Additionally, participants who played video games more often exhibited significantly higher **Workload (Frustration)**, suggesting that they were accustomed to different or easier tasks in video games and were more frustrated by the experiment task.

Environment

All models were fit using "jungle" as the reference category and "urban" as the indicator variable. *Environment (Urban)* had a highly significant detrimental effect on **Navigation Speed** and **Bearing Error**, which was to be expected due to the requirement to navigate around large obstacles. *Environment (Urban)* also had a significant detrimental effect on **Workload (Overall)**, **Workload (Mental)**, **Workload (Temporal)**, and **Workload (Effort)**, likely due to the same reason.

Design Implications

The various significant effects observed throughout this study suggest a number of interesting design implications for personal navigation systems. As hypothesized, periodically switching the directional guidance modality of a navigation system results in a transient modality switching cost that dominates short-duration navigation tasks. However, it also appears to mitigate the detrimental effects of SSA and habituation associated with long-duration use of single-modality navigation systems. Together, these results suggest that if a navigation task is expected to have a short duration (less than ~5 minutes) before the user is expected to perform a different task, a single-modality navigation system is more appropriate. For longer navigation tasks that are unlikely to be interrupted, a switching-modality system will likely provide greater overall performance.

Limitations and Future Work

Due to limitations in how long participants were willing to engage in a study of this nature, combined with the numerous trial types that we asked each participant to complete, we were restricted to relatively short trials of 8 minutes each. Longer trials would have allowed us to better examine the effects of SSA and habituation on long-duration navigation tasks. Additionally, the experiment was carefully designed to maximize internal validity, which came at the cost of ecological validity. Participants had no additional tasks to complete while navigating, which is rarely the case in real-world applications. Further research is required to address these two limitations through the use of longer navigation tasks and additional secondary tasks.

CONCLUSION

In this paper, we describe the design and results of an experiment evaluating the effects of periodically switching the directional guidance modality of a personal navigation system in comparison to single-modality systems. Based on prior work across multiple fields, we hypothesized that periodically switching modalities would incur a transient switching cost to performance, but would also mitigate the potential stimulus-specific adaptation and habituation effects associated with a single-modality system. Linear mixed effects modelling of the results for the 32-participant experiment indicates that both these hypotheses are true, and that periodically switching directional guidance modalities over the course of a long-duration navigation task will lead to improved stability of navigation performance.

ACKNOWLEDGEMENTS

This work was funded in part by the Natural Sciences and Engineering Research Council of Canada. The authors would like to thank Pravina Samaratunga for her contributions to the project.

REFERENCES

1. Tomohiro Amemiya and Hisashi Sugiyama. 2008. Design of a haptic direction indicator for visually impaired people in emergency situations. In *Proceedings of the International Conference on Computers for Handicapped Persons*. Springer, Linz, Austria, 1141–1144.
2. Lucy A Anderson, G Björn Christianson, and Jennifer F Linden. 2009. Stimulus-specific adaptation occurs in the auditory thalamus. *Journal of Neuroscience* 29, 22 (2009), 7359–7363.
3. Flora M Antunes and Manuel S Malmierca. 2014. An overview of stimulus-specific adaptation in the auditory thalamus. *Brain topography* 27, 4 (2014), 480–499.
4. Flora M Antunes, Israel Nelken, Ellen Covey, and Manuel S Malmierca. 2010. Stimulus-specific adaptation in the auditory thalamus of the anesthetized rat. *PLoS One* 5, 11 (2010), e14071.
5. GC Baylis and ET Rolls. 1987. Responses of neurons in the inferior temporal cortex in short term and serial recognition memory tasks. *Experimental brain research* 65, 3 (1987), 614–622.
6. Alvah C Bittner, James C Byers, Susan G Hill, Allen L Zaklad, and Richard E Christ. 1989. Generic workload ratings of a mobile air defense system (LOS-FH). In *Proceedings of the Human Factors and Ergonomics Society Annual Meeting*, Vol. 33. SAGE Publications, Denver, CO, 1476–1480.
7. Bohemia Interactive Studio. 2013. Arma 3. (Sept. 2013). `http://arma3.com/`
8. MW Brown, FAW Wilson, and IP Riches. 1987. Neuronal evidence that inferomedial temporal cortex is more important than hippocampus in certain processes underlying recognition memory. *Brain research* 409, 1 (1987), 158–162.
9. Karen D Davis, Chun L Kwan, Adrian P Crawley, and David J Mikulis. 1998. Functional MRI study of thalamic and cortical activations evoked by cutaneous heat, cold, and tactile stimuli. *Journal of Neurophysiology* 80, 3 (1998), 1533–1546.
10. Shu Dong and David F Clayton. 2009. Habituation in songbirds. *Neurobiology of learning and memory* 92, 2 (2009), 183–188.
11. M Duistermaat. 2005. *Tactile Land Navigation in Night Operations*. Technical Report. DTIC Document.
12. David M Eagleman and Vani Pariyadath. 2009. Is subjective duration a signature of coding efficiency? *Philosophical Transactions of the Royal Society of London B: Biological Sciences* 364, 1525 (2009), 1841–1851.
13. Linda R Elliott, Maaike Duistermaat, Elizabeth S Redden, and Jan Van Erp. 2007. *Multimodal guidance for land navigation*. Technical Report. DTIC Document.
14. Linda R Elliott, Bruce Mortimer, Gina Hartnett-Pomranky, Gary Zets, and Greg Mort. 2015. Augmenting soldier situation awareness and navigation through tactile cueing. In *Proceedings of the International Conference on Human Interface and the Management of Information*, Vol. 17. Springer, Los Angeles, USA, 345–353.
15. Linda R Elliott, Bruce JP Mortimer, Roger W Cholewiak, Greg R Mort, Gary A Zets, and Rodney Pittman. 2013. Development of dual tactor capability for a soldier multisensory navigation and communication system. In *Proceedings of the International Conference on Human Interface and the Management of Information*, Vol. 15. Springer, LAs Vegas, USA, 46–55.
16. Linda R Elliott, Elizabeth S Redden, Rodger A Pettitt, Christian B Carstens, Jan van Erp, and Maaike Duistermaat. 2006. *Tactile guidance for land navigation*. Technical Report. DTIC Document.
17. Linda R Elliott, Elmar T Schmeisser, and Elizabeth S Redden. 2011. Development of tactile and haptic systems for US infantry navigation and communication. In *Symposium on Human Interface*. Springer, Orlando, USA, 399–407.
18. Linda R Elliott, Jan BF Van Erp, Elizabeth S Redden, and Maaike Duistermaat. 2010. Field-based validation of a tactile navigation device. *Haptics, IEEE Transactions on* 3, 2 (2010), 78–87.
19. Richard D Gilson, Elizabeth S Redden, and Linda R Elliott. 2007. *Remote tactile displays for future soldiers*. Technical Report. DTIC Document.
20. David L Glanzman. 2009. Habituation in Aplysia: the Cheshire cat of neurobiology. *Neurobiology of learning and memory* 92, 2 (2009), 147–154.
21. Kalanit Grill-Spector, Richard Henson, and Alex Martin. 2006. Repetition and the brain: neural models of stimulus-specific effects. *Trends in cognitive sciences* 10, 1 (2006), 14–23.
22. Philip M Groves and Richard F Thompson. 1970. Habituation: a dual-process theory. *Psychological review* 77, 5 (1970), 419.
23. Yoram Gutfreund. 2012. Stimulus-specific adaptation, habituation and change detection in the gaze control system. *Biological cybernetics* 106, 11-12 (2012), 1–12.
24. J Donald Harris. 1943. Habituatory response decrement in the intact organism. *Psychological Bulletin* 40, 6 (1943), 385.
25. Sandra G Hart. 2006. NASA-task load index (NASA-TLX); 20 years later. In *Proceedings of the human factors and ergonomics society annual meeting*, Vol. 50. Sage Publications, San Francisco, CA, 904–908.
26. Sandra G Hart and Lowell E Staveland. 1988. Development of NASA-TLX (Task Load Index): Results of empirical and theoretical research. *Advances in psychology* 52 (1988), 139–183.

27. Hermann von Helmholtz and Russell Kahl. 1971. *Selected writings of Hermann von Helmholtz*. Wesleyan University Press, Middletown, CT, USA.
28. Keith C Hendy, Kevin M Hamilton, and Lois N Landry. 1993. Measuring subjective workload: when is one scale better than many? *Human Factors: The Journal of the Human Factors and Ergonomics Society* 35, 4 (1993), 579–601.
29. George Humphrey. 1933. *The nature of learning: in its relation to the living system*. Vol. 4. Psychology Press, Abingdon, United Kingdom.
30. Ricky Jacob, Peter Mooney, and Adam C Winstanley. 2011. Guided by touch: Tactile pedestrian navigation. In *Proceedings of the international workshop on Mobile location-based service*, Vol. 1. ACM, Beijing, China, 11–20.
31. Herbert Spencer Jennings. 1906. *Behavior of the lower organisms*. Vol. 10. Columbia University Press, The Macmillan Company, agents, Charleston, SC, USA.
32. Raymond M Klein. 1977. Attention and visual dominance: a chronometric analysis. *Journal of Experimental Psychology: Human Perception and Performance* 3, 3 (1977), 365.
33. Rebecca L Koslover, Brian T Gleeson, Joshua T De Bever, and William R Provancher. 2012. Mobile navigation using haptic, audio, and visual direction cues with a handheld test platform. *IEEE transactions on haptics* 5, 1 (2012), 33–38.
34. Orly Lahav and David Mioduser. 2008. Haptic-feedback support for cognitive mapping of unknown spaces by people who are blind. *International Journal of Human-Computer Studies* 66, 1 (2008), 23–35.
35. Simon B Laughlin. 1989. The role of sensory adaptation in the retina. *Journal of Experimental Biology* 146, 1 (1989), 39–62.
36. Ming-Wei Lin, Yun-Maw Cheng, and Wai Yu. 2008. Using tactons to provide navigation cues in pedestrian situations. In *Proceedings of the Nordic conference on Human-computer interaction: building bridges*, Vol. 5. ACM, Lund, Sweden, 507–510.
37. Manuel S Malmierca, Salvatore Cristaudo, David Pérez-González, and Ellen Covey. 2009. Stimulus-specific adaptation in the inferior colliculus of the anesthetized rat. *Journal of Neuroscience* 29, 17 (2009), 5483–5493.
38. Earl K Miller, Lin Li, and Robert Desimone. 1991. A neural mechanism for working and recognition memory in inferior temporal cortex. *Science* 254, 5036 (1991), 1377.
39. J Anthony Movshon and Peter Lennie. 1979. Pattern-selective adaptation in visual cortical neurones. *Nature* 278, 5707 (1979), 850–852.
40. Israel Nelken. 2014. Stimulus-specific adaptation and deviance detection in the auditory system: experiments and models. *Biological cybernetics* 108, 5 (2014), 655–663.
41. Israel Nelken, Amit Yaron, Ana Polterovich, and Itai Hershenhoren. 2013. Stimulus-specific adaptation beyond pure tones. In *Basic Aspects of Hearing*. Springer, New York, NY, USA, 411–418.
42. Martin Pielot and Susanne Boll. 2010. Tactile Wayfinder: comparison of tactile waypoint navigation with commercial pedestrian navigation systems. In *Proceedings of the International conference on pervasive computing*, Vol. 8. Springer, Helsinki, Finland, 76–93.
43. Martin Pielot, Benjamin Poppinga, Wilko Heuten, and Susanne Boll. 2011. A tactile compass for eyes-free pedestrian navigation. In *Proceedings of the IFIP Conference on Human-Computer Interaction*, Vol. 13. Springer, Lisbon, Portugal, 640–656.
44. Martin Pielot, Benjamin Poppinga, Wilko Heuten, and Susanne Boll. 2012. PocketNavigator: studying tactile navigation systems in-situ. In *Proceedings of the SIGCHI Conference on Human Factors in Computing Systems*, Vol. 30. ACM, Austin, Texas, USA, 3131–3140.
45. Seth Polsley, Vijay Rajanna, Larry Powell, Kodi Tapie, and Tracy Hammond. 2016. CANE: A Wearable Computer-Assisted Navigation Engine for the Visually Impaired. In *Proceedings of the ACM Workshop on Smart Connected and Wearable Things*, Vol. 1. ACM, Sonoma, CA, USA, 13–19.
46. LJ Post and CE Chapman. 1991. The effects of cross-modal manipulations of attention on the detection of vibrotactile stimuli in humans. *Somatosensory & motor research* 8, 2 (1991), 149–157.
47. Manoj Prasad, Paul Taele, Ayo Olubeko, and Tracy Hammond. 2014. HaptiGo: A navigational 'tap on the shoulder'. In *Proceedings of the IEEE Haptics Symposium*. IEEE, Houston, TX, USA, 339–345.
48. Catharine H Rankin, Thomas Abrams, Robert J Barry, Seema Bhatnagar, David F Clayton, John Colombo, Gianluca Coppola, Mark A Geyer, David L Glanzman, and Stephen Marsland. 2009. Habituation revisited: an updated and revised description of the behavioral characteristics of habituation. *Neurobiology of learning and memory* 92, 2 (2009), 135–138.
49. IP Riches, FA Wilson, and Malcolm W Brown. 1991. The effects of visual stimulation and memory on neurons of the hippocampal formation and the neighboring parahippocampal gyrus and inferior temporal cortex of the primate. *Journal of Neuroscience* 11, 6 (1991), 1763–1779.
50. Edmund T Rolls, GC Baylis, ME Hasselmo, and V Nalwa. 1989. The effect of learning on the face selective responses of neurons in the cortex in the superior temporal sulcus of the monkey. *Experimental Brain Research* 76, 1 (1989), 153–164.

51. Stanislaw Sobotka and James L Ringo. 1994. Stimulus specific adaptation in excited but not in inhibited cells in inferotemporal cortex of macaque. *Brain research* 646, 1 (1994), 95–99.

52. Charles Spence, Michael ER Nicholls, and Jon Driver. 2001. The cost of expecting events in the wrong sensory modality. *Perception & Psychophysics* 63, 2 (2001), 330–336.

53. George M Stratton. 1896. Some preliminary experiments on vision without inversion of the retinal image. *Psychological review* 3, 6 (1896), 611.

54. Nevo Taaseh, Amit Yaron, and Israel Nelken. 2011. Stimulus-specific adaptation and deviance detection in the rat auditory cortex. *PLoS One* 6, 8 (2011), e23369.

55. The MathWorks, Inc. 2017. MATLAB. (Sept. 2017). https://www.mathworks.com/products/matlab/

56. Richard F Thompson and William A Spencer. 1966. Habituation: a model phenomenon for the study of neuronal substrates of behavior. *Psychological review* 73, 1 (1966), 16.

57. Koji Tsukada and Michiaki Yasumura. 2004. Activebelt: Belt-type wearable tactile display for directional navigation. In *Proceedings of the International Conference on Ubiquitous Computing*, Vol. 6. Springer, Nottingham, England, 384–399.

58. Nachum Ulanovsky, Liora Las, Dina Farkas, and Israel Nelken. 2004. Multiple time scales of adaptation in auditory cortex neurons. *Journal of Neuroscience* 24, 46 (2004), 10440–10453.

59. Nachum Ulanovsky, Liora Las, and Israel Nelken. 2003. Processing of low-probability sounds by cortical neurons. *Nature neuroscience* 6, 4 (2003), 391–398.

60. U.S. Army Acquisition Support Center. 2016. Nett Warrior (NW). (2016). http://asc.army.mil/web/portfolio-item/soldier-nw/

61. Verónica S Valentinuzzi and Elenice AM Ferrari. 1997. Habituation to sound during morning and night sessions in pigeons (Columba livia). *Physiology & behavior* 62, 6 (1997), 1203–1209.

62. Miranda van Turennout, Timothy Ellmore, and Alex Martin. 2000. Long-lasting cortical plasticity in the object naming system. *Nature neuroscience* 3, 12 (2000), 1329–1334.

63. Barry Wark, Brian Nils Lundstrom, and Adrienne Fairhall. 2007. Sensory adaptation. *Current opinion in neurobiology* 17, 4 (2007), 423–429.

64. Michael A Webster. 2012. Evolving concepts of sensory adaptation. *F1000 Biology Reports* 4, 21 (2012), 1–7.

65. Norman M Weinberger, Terrence D Oleson, and John H Ashe. 1975. Sensory system neural activity during habituation of the pupillary orienting reflex. *Behavioral biology* 15, 3 (1975), 283–301.

66. GN Wilkinson and CE Rogers. 1973. Symbolic description of factorial models for analysis of variance. *Journal of the Royal Statistical Society. Series C (Applied Statistics)* 22, 3 (1973), 392–399.

67. John S Zelek. 2005. Seeing by touch (haptics) for wayfinding. *International Congress Series* 1282 (2005), 1108–1112.

68. Heinz Zimmer. 2006. Habituation of the orienting response as reflected by the skin conductance response and by endogenous event-related brain potentials. *International journal of psychophysiology* 60, 1 (2006), 44–58.

Touch-Supported Voice Recording to Facilitate Forced Alignment of Text and Speech in an E-Reading Interface

Benett Axtell[1], Cosmin Munteanu[1, 2], Carrie DEMMANS EPP[1, 3], Yomna Aly[1], Frank Rudzicz[4]

[1] TAGlab, University of Toronto
Toronto, Canada
{benett, cosmin, yomna}@taglab.ca

[2] Institute of Communication, Culture, Information and Technology, University of Toronto Mississauga
Mississauga, Canada

[3] Learning Research and Development Center,
University of Pittsburgh
Pittsburgh, United States
cdemmans@pitt.edu

[4] Toronto Rehabilitation Institute,
Toronto, Canada
frank@spoclab.ca

ABSTRACT
Reading a book together with a family member who has impaired vision or other difficulties reading is an important social bonding activity. However, for the person being read to, there is little support in making these experiences repeatable. While audio can easily be recorded, synchronizing it with the text for later playback requires the use of forced alignment algorithms, which do not perform well on amateur read-aloud speech. We propose a human-in-the-loop approach to augmenting such algorithms, in the form of touch metaphors during collocated read-aloud sessions using tablet e-readers. The metaphor is implemented as a finger-follows-text tracker. We explore how this could better handle the variability of amateur reading, which poses accuracy challenges for existing forced alignment techniques. Data collected from users reading aloud as assisted by touch metaphors show increases in the accuracy of forced alignment algorithms and reveal opportunities for how to better support reading aloud.

Author Keywords
Assistive technology; multi-modal interfaces; forced alignment; natural language and speech processing;

INTRODUCTION
Many assistive applications need to synchronize audio and text, such as closed captioning [27]. For many of these, the aim is purely to address an impairment, but there are many other applications where the ability to synchronize audio and text will enhance both the accessibility of the application and user experience. One such application is collocated family reading, which is an enjoyable social activity among family members, especially when one has impaired vision, limited literacy, or other difficulties reading. Reading aloud is a skill that is common in many professions, like lecturing, but for casual readers, such as within a family, it can be an unfamiliar or even uncomfortable activity.

IUI'18, March 7–11, 2018, Tokyo, Japan

ACM ISBN 978-1-4503-4945-1/18/03...$15.00
https://doi.org/10.1145/3172944.3172984

Alignment of text with speech has been shown to benefit marginalized users (such as low-literacy adults) trying to read e-texts, especially when accompanied by a moving prompt that shows the synchronization of text and speech [30,31]. The audience for casual read-alouds, however, is also more accepting of errors such as mispronounced words or filled pauses (e.g., "um", in English). Additionally, recordings of these readings, while easy to create, are likely of a lower quality than those of professional readings (e.g., lectures or audio books) because of substandard recording conditions and equipment [24]. Due to these factors, forced alignment and available tools to align speech to text are unsuited for these settings.

To aid the alignment of text and speech, this research investigates how a classic forced alignment (FA) algorithm can be enhanced by using a human-in-the-loop approach with assistive touch metaphors. The motivation for this is to move towards options that better suit casually read-aloud speech. Human-in-the-loop approaches can aid in the development and use of adaptive systems [29] and other technologies [37]. This approach combines system and human efforts to provide the individualized support readers need. The system learns from the people who interact with it by deferring part of the decision process to those users [29,34]. Improving adaptive systems with similar systems has previously supported underrepresented users [29,36]. As such, we explore a human-in-the-loop system in this casual reading setting, using a family member to support those with various reading difficulties.

We explore and analyze the effects of these interaction metaphors and their text to speech alignment on the assessment of speech. We use measures of reading time and accuracy, and analyze how these measures change over the course of reading a text. We expand on these findings by building on a classic FA algorithm to create a new algorithm that accounts for the less precise nature of the expected speech. Our Touch-Enabled Forced Alignment algorithm (TFA) proposes improvements to classic FA by accounting for expected human behaviours in casually read-aloud speech, which limits outlier data found in classic FA. These expected reading behaviours include interruptions, out of sync speech and touch, and variations in readers' timing of interaction, while also incorporating data from assistive touch interaction. We compare these to parallel results using a classic FA algorithm and human-aligned speech to text.

This paper contributes to the evaluation of intelligent user interfaces by demonstrating that touch interaction support for forced alignment more accurately aligns text to speech. We show that these alignment results better represent the accuracy of reading aloud for amateur readers by accounting for their normal variations is reading. We also explore opportunities to augment forced alignment in order to better support casually read-aloud data.

RELATED WORK

Previous research on forced alignment showed that, although such speech processing algorithms have greatly improved recently, there are significant shortcomings in the application of forced alignment to several application areas. Assisted reading research, especially when providing support to various marginalized groups of readers, commonly encounters some of these difficulties of aligning speech to text. The intersection of these areas reveals various possible approaches to address these shortcomings in order to better meet the needs of a wide range of readers.

Assisted Reading

Audio-books and e-readers have been proposed as alternatives to interacting with text for members of groups who have limited access to text-based information. This lack of access may be due to low literacy or impaired vision [31,32]. Professionally created audio books are expensive and time consuming to create [45]. Synthetic speech, which has been used to read to adults with vision impairments [39], is still found to be unnatural [21,38,42] and sometimes difficult to understand [12,18]. There are also few available texts that are properly formatted to be read aloud completely by commercial e-readers [1,3,32], and current accessibility features (e.g. screen readers) have limitations, such as navigation within a long text [5]. Other solutions allow people to record their own reading for children (e.g., http://explore.hallmark.com/recordable-storybooks) and adults [13], though these can take significant effort from the reader.

Alignment of text and recorded speech has been shown to benefit marginalized users [31] and to aid users in reading e-texts by using tools such as prompts that move along the text [13]. This alignment should enable access to those who cannot read on their own, but this is blocked by technical barriers [11]. Additionally, the variability of human reading behaviours, including self-correction and filled pauses, are a major factor in the high error rates found with standard options for alignment [11,15].

Speech to Text Alignment

There are several different methods to align long audio to text depending on the context [8,17,20,28]. Forced alignment is one such method of speech recognition that uses a transcription of what was expected to have been said and attempts to align the speech to the given transcript. It then produces time segments corresponding to particular words in the transcript. This information can be used to analyze speech data, including correctness through measures like Word Error Rate (WER). Since a transcript is provided, it is a logical approach when what is going to be said is known ahead of time, such as when a book is being read aloud. Classic FA is commonly used to align speech from a variety of settings such as lectures or other public speeches [16] or broadcast media subtitles [27]. It is also employed in the production of synchronized materials for students learning the pronunciation of a foreign language [4,40].

In some cases, the performance of FA is measured by the time differential of various anchors (e.g., words or sentences) between the gold standard manual alignment and some test data. This is useful for very long audio recordings [28] or when it is important to improve alignment of small phonetic units [19]. However, as found by Hazen, the role of FA is often to support "downstream" applications [16], including when the original text is known, such as for forced alignment of audio books with their corresponding texts [8], and even for medium-length audio recordings of broadcast news [27]. As our work is similar to these examples, we too use WER.

There are several examples of recent improvements to accuracy of forced alignment including those done in the areas of real time forced alignment [26] and precision requirements for different settings and ease of use [14]. Other work has looked at the shortcomings of forced alignment and how to improve upon them. Zhang et al [44] found that their system for scoring reading quality avoided known disadvantages of forced alignment by switching to large vocabulary continuous speech recognition (LVCSR). LVCSR was able to recognize more miscues (mistakes in reading) than forced alignment.

Anguera et al [1] argued that improving alignment accuracy and speech recognition will enable more effective synchronization of speech to texts. However, many challenges remain as speech recognition and alignment must account for human errors that make up 15% of speech [15]. These errors and human behaviours include mispronunciations [43] and added or off-script speech [6,23], including re-reading [29]. Other work further demonstrated the limitations of forced alignment [21,29,41], including inadequate miscue detection. All of this contributes to the at least 19% error rate of standard alignment methods [11], which interferes with the effectiveness of assistive tools and metaphors for reading on assessment.

Alignment of Assisted Reading

Much of the existing research into the assessment of read-aloud speech is focused on children or language learning [9,22]. One project not focusing on these groups investigated a more accurate alignment option for large amounts of coherent text, such as audio books [8], and supports that forced alignment, on its own, is not ideal for large read-aloud recordings. More recent work improves on long text speech recognition by improving the recognition of types of pauses including inhalations, which are more common in longer, casual readings [7]. Other research has explored the use of multimodal books for language learning [4] by developing a system that uses synchronized reading to aid language-learner spelling. This system plays the audio for a given text while a cursor follows, pointing at the current phoneme. Their preliminary findings show that spelling can be improved with the bimodal approach of audio and visuals. The bimodal interaction from this work is similar to the interaction that produced the data used in this paper.

THE ALLT PROJECT

For this work, our researchers were given access to the data from a study assessing the usability of assistive touch metaphors within the ALLT e-book reader (Figure 1) [13]. The ALLT (Accessible, Large-print Listening and Talking) e-book tablet reader uses a bimodal touch and speech interface and provides assistive interfaces for users to read aloud and record books that can be played back by other family members. ALLT is intended to support collocated reading between an older adult (likely with some vision impairment) and an adult grandchild (e.g. university-aged). A grandchild can record a read-aloud text with some level of

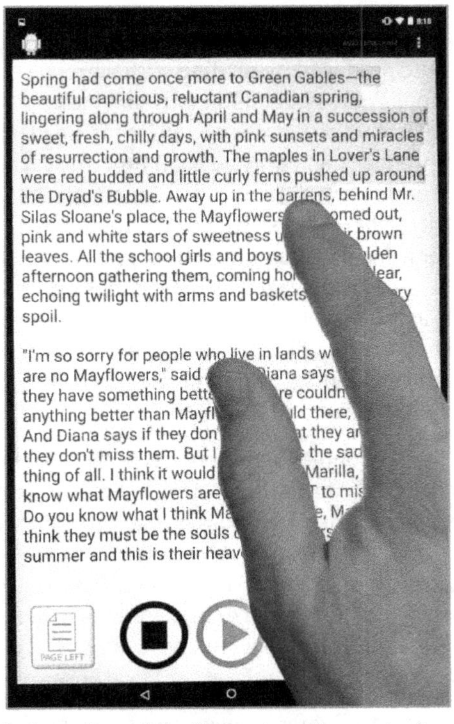

Figure 1. A version of the finger-tracking metaphor used to augment recording. The user is currently reading *barrens*.

tracking and a grandparent can later listen and follow (read) along while hearing the familiar voice of the grandchild. While recording, the user is presented with a karaoke-style reading prompt, based on the tracked position of the user's finger under the text they are reading. This prompt advances as the text is read aloud, as described below. As we have shown in [13], this assisted tracking can guide a user through audio content production. It is also expected to ease reading for low-vision older adults by highlighting each sentence as it is read [2,25]. This metaphor is grounded in prior work on finger-tracking of text to support reading [10,33].

Assistive Touch Metaphors

The ALLT e-book reader offers four assistive touch metaphors, which were tested empirically against a control condition (no touch interaction). The metaphors use touch interaction (F: finger) to highlight either the current word (W) or sentence (S) as the user reads through the text. Each level can either be advanced manually (M), or can use timer (T) to advance the highlighting automatically based on the user's initial reading speed. The four modes are:

- FSM – sentence level, manual highlight advance
- FST – sentence level, advance highlight with timer
- FWM – word level, manual highlight advance
- FWT – word level, advance highlight with timer

These touch metaphors help to align text to speech as the user interacts with the text and is expected to better support forced alignment for this data.

Initial ALLT Study and Observations of Reading

For the initial user study, users read sections of *Anne of Green Gables* aloud using an Android Nexus 7 tablet, with the different assistive modes that ALLT provides through touch interactions. This book was selected because it is publicly available. The assistive modes allowed the user to track what they were currently reading aloud using touch metaphors at the sentence or word level. Basic timing information from this input could be used to advance the tracking automatically after a certain amount of manual use.

The font size was approximately the size of a large-text print book to mimic the books most likely used by low-vision older adults. Users were not able to change the font size, and touch error was not measured in the original experiment. No participant's performance was noticably affected by touch error and none commented on font size as an issue.

The audio was recorded for each sentence separately based on a user's touch interaction. However, there were observed differences in how participants used this interaction. For example, at the sentence level, some users tapped exactly as they began to read, some paused their reading as they tapped and then began again, and others tapped after they began each sentence. As such, speech associated with a particular sentence may actually be captured in the audio recording for the next or previous sentence. Occurrences of disfluencies and mispronunciations are also not uncommon in this data due to the outdated nature of the language and the uncommon nature of the activity. Additionally, during the study, users occasionally interrupted themselves to comment on their activity or to ask questions without first pausing the recording (as they had been instructed to do). This likely mimics the reality of casually recording reading, as readers may be interrupted while recording or may make comments themselves without pausing the recording. Forced alignment cannot currently account for these digressions from the expected text.

AUGMENTED FORCED ALIGNMENT FOR READING

Typically, forced alignment uses the Viterbi algorithm and a pre-trained language model with a pronunciation dictionary to extract speech features from the provided audio and force its alignment to the given script [16,35]. The Viterbi algorithm, commonly used to find the most likely path through hidden states, is used to provide the optimal alignment for the sounds in the audio file by using the transcription as a state machine (in this case, a sequence of words). Our proposed algorithm (TFA) augments the classic forced alignment algorithm, implemented here by the CMUSphinx tool (https://cmusphinx.github.io/), to measure the alignment and timings for a sentence of a read-aloud text with multimodal interaction.

To incorporate the different timings of users' touch inputs, this measure of alignment accounts for audio files that correspond to the sentences immediately preceding and following. It also disregards speech that is not part of the intended reading by skipping many concurrent insertions. This produces the following outputs: individual alignments for each word within a sentence, a measure of accuracy for each sentence (Word Error Rate - WER), and an adjusted total time for each sentence.

Modifications to Classic Forced Alignment

All use of forced alignment for both TFA and classic FA uses CMUSphinx's implementation of forced alignment with three minor changes: allowing for alignment of one-word sentences, allowing alignment to exclude a given number of milliseconds from the start of an audio file, and adding a standard count of substitutions (used for the WER measure described later). The original code only included deletions and insertions. Substitutions are defined as adjacent insertions and deletions, regardless of order.

Additionally, there were minor changes made to the pronunciation dictionary to include words in the read texts missing from the provided CMU Sphinx English language pronunciation dictionary (Table 1). It is not unexpected that some words would need to be added because of the source's use of regional language. These added words were either names (e.g., *Avonlea*) or already present in the dictionary as another part of speech (e.g., *bewitching* from *bewitch*; *marillas* from *marilla*; *scornfully* from *scornful*). The phoneme transcriptions were derived using a grapheme to phoneme tool within CMU Sphinx.

Word in text	Phoneme transcription
airily	EH R IH L IY
avonlea	AE V AH N L IY
bashfully	B AE SH F AH L IY
betaken	B IH T EY K AH N
bewitching	B IH W IH CH IH NG
birches	B ER CH IH Z
bootjack	B UW T JH AE K
budded	B AH D IH D
creakily	K R IY K IH L IY
dizzily	D IH Z IH L IY
dreamily	D R IY M IH L IY
dryads	D R AY AE D Z
heedlessness	HH IY D L AH S N AH S
marillas	M AA R IH L AH Z
mayflowers	M EY F L AW ER Z
mossy	M AA S IY
resignedly	R IH Z AY N IH D L IY
scornfully	S K AO R N F AH L IY
sloanes	S L OW N Z
sloped	S L OW P T
smilelessly	S M AY L L AH S L IY
starrier	S T AA R IY ER
unobservant	AH N AH B Z ER V AH N T
unvarying	AH N V EH R IY IH NG
upspringing	AH P S P R IH NG IH NG
woodbox	W UH D B AA K S
woodsy	W UH D Z IY

Table 1: Words added to the provided CMU Sphinx pronunciation dictionary and their phoneme transcriptions (using CMUBET phoneme codes)

Description of TFA

Because of how people interacted with the text being read, any audio file produced by reading with various touch-based assistive modes may not contain only and exactly the speech of the sentence that was expected to be read. The TFA algorithm produces an adjusted total time for each sentence representing the actual time spent reading the sentence, disregarding when users spoke off the script (e.g., to comment or ask a question of the researchers), and including the time spent reading the sentence before or after the associated audio file. If an audio file contains only exactly the speech corresponding to the expected sentence, this adjusted time would be the same as the total time of the original audio file.

Ideally, the chronologically-ordered speech files each correspond exactly to the text of one sentence in the same order. This is the case that classic FA algorithms expect; a provided text corresponds precisely to some provided speech. In this work, classic FA is modified to account for the case when the start or end of a sentence is in the preceding or following audio file, respectively.

When describing TFA, the terms "previous audio" and "previous sentence" refer respectively to the audio file from the previous round of alignment and the sentence of text that the audio is expected to contain. Likewise, "current audio" and "current sentence" are the audio and sentence for the current round, and "next audio" and "next sentence" are those for the next round. This algorithm is applied to each audio file from a reading of a text in the recorded order and consists of three main steps:

1. If there was unaligned audio at the end of the previous sentence, align this sentence to that remaining audio.
2. Align the expected sentence to this audio. This excludes any text that was just aligned in step one and excludes any audio that was aligned to the end of the previous sentence in the last round's step three.
3. If there is unaligned text at the end of this sentence, align that remaining text to the next audio file. Compare this alignment with the next sentence's standard alignment. Use the alignment with the better (lower) resulting WER.

```
FOR EACH audio file for text by participant:
  //1: align missing audio from last round to
  this sentence
  IF previous audio had unaligned audio at end:
    Align current sentence to remaining
    unaligned previous audio
    Update adjusted time and WER for this
    sentence
  END IF

  //2: base alignment of current sentence to
  this audio
  // (exclude audio aligned in step 1 or the
  previous round's step 3)
  IF step 1 unaligned words left in this
  sentence:
    Align current unaligned sentence to this
    audio
    Update adjusted time and WER for this
    sentence
  END IF
  IF end of this alignment does not include the
  end of the audio:
    Set the time that unaligned starts for
    next round's step 1
    Remove this time from this sentence's
    adjusted time

  //3: align remaining text to next audio
  ELSE IF final alignment does not include end
  of sentence text:
    Align remaining expected sentence to next
    audio
    Align next sentence to next audio file
    IF remaining WER is lower (more accurate):
      Use this alignment
      Update adjusted time and WER for this
      sentence
    ELSE:
      Use next sentence alignment instead
    END IF
  END IF
END FOR EACH audio file
```

Figure 2: Pseudocode for the TFA algorithm, which accounts for amateur reading behaviours

The comparison in step 3 is to prevent the remaining alignment from using the entirety of the next audio that should truly be aligned to the next sentence. For example, if both the remaining text and the next sentence contain a common word, there is no way to know if the remaining alignment has correctly found the remaining audio or the next sentence's audio. To protect against this, both alignments are compared and the more accurate is used. This is not a perfect approach, but it should cover the majority of cases.

In order to handle off-script speech, insertions are excluded from WER calculations if there is a section at least two seconds long that contains only concurrent insertions. This is because it is unlikely that text would be incorrectly read in a manner that would produce a long series of insertions when the user is reading along with a provided text. In the case where many seconds worth of insertions are detected, it is most likely the user is no longer reading the text. The adjusted time for this sentence also excludes this time.

TFA is expected to improve upon classic FA to better suit the work of aligning amateur read-aloud text especially in a multimodal, assistive setting. See Figure 2 for a pseudocode explanation of TFA.

METHODS

Data

TFA was assessed using the data resulting from a previous study into touch-assisted casual reading [13]. This included speech data from 22 English-speaking participants. Each participant read the same five 2-page texts on the assistive ALLT tablet using a different touch interaction for each text or a control condition without touch interaction. This resulted in over 2,500 audio files each corresponding to either a sentence in a text (when using a touch metaphor) or the whole text (when in the control condition). The speech was recorded in separate audio files for each sentence based on the interaction from the reader. Recording for each sentence began when a user tapped on it or when a user's finger highlighted the first word, depending on the condition.

The data presented in this paper consist of Word Error Rate (WER) scores and durations of each sentence read by each participant as measured from three sources:

1) Classic FA algorithm as offered by CMU Sphinx
2) The augmented algorithm proposed in this paper (TFA)
3) Human alignment completed by a researcher not involved in this project

WER is a simple and standard measure of correctness in speech, which is regularly used to assess FA results, especially when the text is known ahead of time [8,16]. It assesses how correct speech is compared to a text by

	FSM		FST		FWM		FWT		Control	
	Mean	(SD)	Mean	(SD)	Mean	(SD)	Mean	(SD)	Mean	(SD)
Classic FA	30.26	(10.85)	44.69	(15.11)	41.32	(13.22)	42.42	(12.68)	47.97	(22.24)
TFA	32.14	(9.96)	45.22	(15.07)	41.16	(12.34)	41.11	(10.02)	44.93	(19.61)
Human	3.28	(2.54)	14.45	(14.78)	7.36	(6.37)	3.09	(2.58)	1.56	(1.09)

Table 2: WER scores per participant across assessment methods and touch metaphors

	FSM		FST		FWM		FWT		Control	
	Mean	(SD)	Mean	(SD)	Mean	(SD)	Mean	(SD)	Mean	(SD)
Classic FA	358.39	(51.10)	283.05	(70.65)	353.42	(72.15)	372.73	(61.11)	340.49	(67.99)
TFA	340.73	(47.18)	310.87	(59.27)	322.96	(53.43)	362.38	(52.98)	336.20	(67.83)

Table 3: Reading time per participant across assessment methods and touch metaphors

measuring the number of deletions (D), insertions (I), and substitutions (S). A visual representation of how such errors are relevant to forced alignment is given by [28, Figure 2]. A deletion is a word that is expected to be said but was missing, an insertion is a word that was spoken that does not correspond to a word in the script, and a substitution is a replaced word. WER is defined as (D + I + S) / N where N is the number of words in the script. A WER of 0 represents a perfectly read sentence, and higher values are less correct. There is no upper bound on WER as there is no limit to how many insertions may be present. For example, a five-word sentence where nothing is read will have a score of 100 (N = 5, D = 5, I = 0, S = 0) as will that same sentence where each word is incorrect (S = 5), but the same sentence read correctly with a ten-word diversion in the middle will have a score of 200 (N = 5, D = 0, I = 10, S = 0).

Reading time was measured as (duration of the sentence reading in milliseconds / number of words in sentence). This was done to normalize times across the large variety in sentence lengths (1 to 53 words). Higher values of reading time indicate the user is reading at a slower pace (more time spent on each word) and vice versa. There is no human measure of reading time because of the nature of the audio files – the audio for individual sentences was split between different files, making it difficult to accurately measure manually.

We also analyze how WER and reading time changed over the course of reading a text. This is measured as the slope of the trendline for all the WERs or reading times for each sentence from a text as read by one participant. In order to compare trends in WER and reading times to each other, we scale all trends to be between -100 and 100. These trends can show how the effect of an assistive mode may change over the course of a session. For example, readers may become more comfortable with an interaction or may be rushed by the timer if it continues to get ahead of them.

RESULTS

Since WER measures insertions, deletions, and substitutions between a reference text and the automatic transcript of an audio recording, it is sensitive to the alignment between the reference text and the audio recording. As such, differences in alignment are expected to yield different WERs. We thus analyze the data between the three alignment methods tested in our investigation (classic FA, TFA, and human) as these are expected to measure WER in different ways. Beside these accuracy comparisons, we also analyze data that is relevant to the user's experience, such as reading time for the two automated alignments. We measure changes in WER and reading time over the course of a reading session for each of the assistive modes. This is not possible for the control sessions as there is no subdivision of the speech data. A summary of WER and reading time measures are provided in Tables 2 and 3, respectively.

Supporting Classic FA with Touch Metaphors

We discuss here the performance of the classic FA according to the measures stated above. It should be noted that, while we did not modify the classic FA, its performance has already benefitted from the assistive touch metaphors. This is in the form of intrinsic alignment of speech to text through the human-in-the-loop approach used during the touch-enabled assisted reading sessions from which data was collected. This further highlights the usefulness of a human-in-the-loop approach to intrinsically capture the start time of each audio segment from the users' touch interaction as it corresponds to each sentence. Additionally, we have labelled this baseline "classic" as this algorithm was not modified from the standard. This or similar algorithms have been previously employed both with segmented audio [8] and with unsegmented medium-length recordings [27,28].

WER and Reading Time

In classic FA, only the sentence-level metaphor (FSM) significantly improved WER scores over the control scores, as shown by a Wilcoxon Signed-rank test ($W = 237$, $Z = 3.59$, $p < 0.001$, $r = 0.77$). Reading time for the sentence-level with timer mode (FST) was significantly faster than for the control case ($W = 202$, $Z = 2.45$, $p < 0.014$, $r = 0.52$).

Using Spearman's correlation, the only significant correlation between WER and reading time was in the FST mode. WER was strongly negatively correlated with reading time ($r_s = -0.73$, $p < 0.001$). This could reflect two situations; either WER increases as reading time per word decreases (i.e., pace of reading increases), or WER increases as more insertions are introduced, both cases demonstrate that faster reading in this mode leads to more errors.

	FSM	FWT	FWM
r_s	0.75	0.73	0.505
p	< 0.001	< 0.001	0.019

Table 4: Correlation scores for reading times compared to the control case

There was, however, positive correlations for reading time between all other modes (FSM, FWT, FWM) and the control case (see Table 4). This shows that participants who read slower during the control case also read slower during other modes (with the exception of FST) and vise versa.

There was a significant positive correlation between WERs between the control case and FSM ($r_s = 0.52, p = 0.012$). This shows that if a participant's reading was more accurate in the control case, it would be better in FSM as well. This parallels the reading time correlation, but only in this mode.

Trends in WER and Reading Time

Trends in how WER and reading time changed over the course of reading show how the different metaphors affect reading. Using classic FA, three modes (FSM, FST, and FWT) had significantly higher trends in WER than in reading time (see Table 5). These modes also had negative correlations between the trend of the WER over the course of reading and the reading time (see Table 6). This demonstrates that, at the sentence level and when using a timed mode, readers either slowed their reading pace and decreased their error rate over the course of a reading, or sped up their reading and increased their error rate. When using a timer, this was likely caused by the timer getting ahead of the reader without the reader adjusting the timer. In FSM, it is likely users adjusted their speed to be slower as they were reading as accuracy was best in this mode and users had full control over their reading speed.

	FSM	FST	FWT
W	200	241	207
Z	2.39	3.72	2.61
p	0.017	< 0.001	0.009
r	0.51	0.79	0.56

Table 5: Wilcoxon test results for trends in reading time and WER over time

	FSM	FST	FWT
r_s	-0.62	-0.70	-0.50
p	0.002	< 0.001	0.019

Table 6: Correlation scores for trends in reading times and WERs

Touch-Enhanced FA

Results from TFA largely correspond to classic FA, which was already partially optimized for amateur reader speech through the assistive metaphors. FST is also the least accurate mode, and FSM is the most (see Table 1). TFA did not see significant improvements in WER across the assistive modes as compared to classic FA. The standard deviations for all modes are lower in TFA. This is because TFA detects human variations in reading and interaction, which are outliers in the data, and normalizes them to more realistically represent casually reading aloud. This shows that TFA handles the irregularities of casual reading aloud better than classic FA, even if not resulting in lower WERs.

Parallels and Differences Between Algorithms

Just as was found with classic FA, the WER for FSM shows significant improvement ($W = 210, Z = 2.71, p = 0.007, r = 0.58$) over the control case. There was also the same negative correlation between WER and reading time for FST ($r_s = -0.62$, $p = 0.002$), but TFA revealed a weak negative correlation in the FSM mode ($r_s = -0.43, p = 0.046$).

Similar changes are seen in the trends over WER and reading time. As in the results with classic FA, FST and FWT are found to have significantly higher trends in WER than reading time (FST: $W = 237, Z = 3.59, p < 0.001, r = 0.77$; FWT: $W = 189, Z = 2.03, p = 0.043, r = 0.43$), and a negative correlation between the WER trend and that of the reading time is found for FST ($r_s = -0.49$, $p = 0.024$), but this is no longer found for FWT. TFA also finds a similar negative correlation for FSM ($r_s = -0.43$, $p = 0.048$), but no longer finds a significant difference for this condition. So, both sentence-level conditions, but not the word-level ones, show correlations between faster reading and lower accuracy, and slower reading and higher accuracy. This also finds that FSM, in which readers have complete control over the interaction, has no correlation between reading speed and accuracy.

TFA also finds a positive correlation between the reading times for FSM and the control case ($r_s = 0.63, p = 002.$), and between WERs for the same conditions ($r_s = 0.56, p = 0.007$). However, there is no correlation in reading time with the control case for either FWM or FWT, which was found in classic FA.

Effects on WER and Reading Time

WER with TFA has a significant positive correlation with WER in classic FA for each mode. This is also true for reading time between the algorithms. The strengths of these correlations show how these measures have been changed by TFA. The two sets of reading times for the control case are nearly perfectly correlated, showing there was very little change in that data. This can be seen in Figure 3; the data for the control case are nearly all on the diagonal. Reading times for FWT are the least correlated. The spread of FWT data points in Figure 3 compared to that of the control demonstrate this. All other modes have similarly strong correlations (see Table 7 and Figure 3).

The control case also has a very strong correlation for WER. The strongest correlation for WER, though, is in FST, the least accurate mode, and the weakest correlation is found in the most accurate mode (FSM). The WERs for the word-level conditions are similarly correlated between algorithms, and are more correlated than the reading time correlations for

	FSM		FST		FWM		FWT		Control	
	r_s	p	r_s	p	r_s	p	r_s	p	r_s	p
WER	0.66	< 0.001	0.95	< 0.001	0.85	< 0.001	0.90	< 0.001	0.90	< 0.001
Reading time	0.74	< 0.001	0.76	< 0.001	0.72	< 0.001	0.53	< 0.001	0.99	< 0.001

Table 7: WER and reading time correlations between algorithms

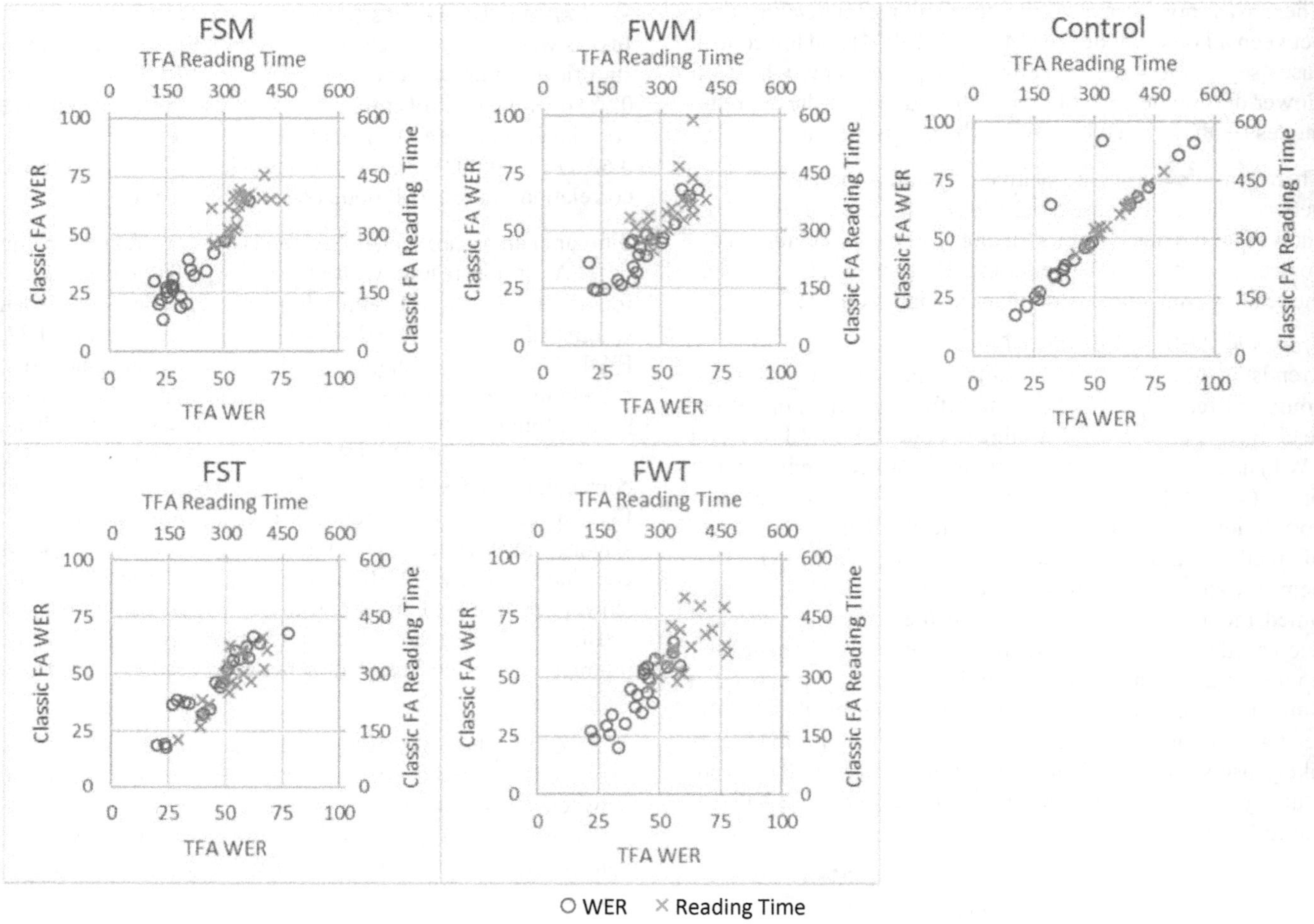

Figure 3: Mappings of WER and reading time between algorithms. Blue circles are WER, orange X's (diagonal crosshairs) are reading time.

the same modes. The more varied correlations across modes in reading time suggest that the changes to the algorithm had more of an effect on the time measures than the WERs.

Human Scoring

Unlike both algorithms, the human-scored WERs were significantly better in the control case than in any of the assistive modes (see Table 8). This is not unexpected since the assistive metaphors were new to the readers and the

	FSM	FST	FWM	FWT
W	221	249	252	220
Z	3.07	3.98	4.07	3.04
p	0.002	< 0.001	< 0.001	0.002
r	0.65	0.85	0.87	0.65

Table 8: Wilcoxon test results for the human measured WER in each assistive mode compared to the control case

technical division of files caused some audio to be lost. Since the human scores showed so much improvement over classic FA and TFA, it is difficult to explore these differences meaningfully.

WER Between Algorithms

The human scoring confirms the general findings of both algorithms; FST was found to be least accurate, and FSM the most accurate (see Table 2). However, both algorithms were far more inaccurate than the human aligned data. This is expected as classic FA has been shown to have around a 19% WER in ideal settings [11]. For our study, the speech was recorded on commercially available tablets using the built-in microphone, so quality of audio is much lower than in professional recording settings. As this setting is conducive to even higher WERs for machine alignments as compared to humans' (gold standard), the pairwise differences between the versions of machine alignment tend to not be significant.

DISCUSSION

The significantly lower WER scores for the FSM mode show that using a human-in-the-loop approach can improve accuracy in both classic FA and TFA. The manual tracking of the current sentence by an active reader aligned the speech to text at the sentence level, which simplifies the work of forced alignment after the fact. However, while some assistive reading modes clearly improve accuracy (FSM), others (like FST) seem to decrease it.

FST and FWT, metaphors that employed timers, caused users to speed up their reading over the course of a session and as reading time sped up, reading accuracy decreased. This suggests the auto-advancing function of the timed modes is going too fast for users and causing them to create more errors. Reading faster may also decrease the accuracy of alignment algorithms as readers will speak less clearly when rushed.

Though FSM has the same correlation between reading time and reading accuracy, this condition's higher rates of accuracy shows that this correlation can be interpreted in the other direction than the timed modes. That is, readers slowed their speed over the course of reading and increased accuracy. Readers were able to follow their own pace and minimize errors by not being rushed. As they were not rushed, their speech was likely clearer and therefore easier to align correctly.

TFA showed many of the same findings as classic FA. This is encouraging as TFA was designed to build on classic FA and the human-in-the-loop interactions to compensate for the differences in casual read-alouds. There were no clear and significant improvements in alignment, but the more normalized data, demonstrated by the lower standard deviations in each mode and the control case, show that some aspects of TFA work as intended. By checking neighbouring files for missing words and excluding off-text speech or sounds, TFA avoids large numbers of deletions or insertions that were not errors by the readers but natural variations in casual reading. This process seems to allow the data to more closely reflect the realities of casually reading aloud, and demonstrates how TFA handles differences in casually read-aloud speech better than classic FA. Overall, this suggests that leveraging touch interaction (where available) shows potential to improve on classic FA algorithms and better serve applications that are more natural and richer in an interaction context.

Where the classic FA results suggested that the timer negatively affected reading speed and WER over the course of a reading session, TFA only finds this to be true at the sentence level (FST). This shows that the word level conditions have little effect on reader behaviour and on the alignment of text to speech for forced alignment.

TFA also finds stronger evidence for FSM as the best metaphor for supporting reading as that is the only mode showing positive correlations with the control case in both WER and reading time. So, a reader using this mode can interact with the text and read similarly to how they would in the control case. Classic FA had shown similar correlations in reading time for word level modes as well. The changes implemented in TFA better interpreted outlier data in reading speed. These outliers may have implied a correlation with the control in classic FA that was not there.

The high correlations between reading time and WER in FST found for both algorithms demonstrate that readers using this condition made more errors and did not have as many acceptable variations in their reading, such as repeated insertions. Acceptable variations would have been recognized by TFA and weakened the WER and reading time correlation. The negative correlation between trends in WER and reading time for FST, also in both algorithms, showed that readers were rushed by the timer and accuracy decreased as they sped up. These findings together provide strong evidence that the poor accuracy in this mode is because of reader error and not because of the anticipated and acceptable reading differences that TFA accounts for.

The same high correlations between trends in reading time and WER are also present in both algorithms for FSM. However, this correlation can be interpreted in the opposite direction as FST since FSM was the most accurate mode and the only mode to show significant improvement. That is, the lower WERs support that readers slowed their speed over the course of reading and improved accuracy. The manual interaction of this condition allowed readers to follow their own reading pace, easily adjust is as they preferred, and aided them in reading the text correctly and clearly.

With the exception of FSM, TFA did not have a very strong effect on WER across the modes of interaction, as shown by the similarly high correlation between the algorithms. However, this same comparison for reading time had weaker correlations across modes than for the control, which had practically no change between algorithms. This suggests the changes in TFA successfully adjusted reading times to account for overlaps in the audio files before or after a given sentence. FWT has an even lower correlation than the other modes, implying that the overlaps in audio files were more extreme in this mode. Generally, these correlations between algorithms for all metaphors and their variation demonstrate how these interactions can affect alignment of speech data, positively or negatively.

While there are some improvements, TFA did not significantly improve WER accuracy in any of the assistive modes as compared to the base algorithm. We suspect this is due to the limitations of speech recognition when audio quality is lower. Even with the changes made specifically for this kind of speech, low audio quality and clipped words may have prevented TFA from reaping the benefits of the changes.

The human alignment, unsurprisingly, showed far more accurate WER scores than either algorithm. It does support the main findings of the effect of the assistive touch metaphors: FST is the least accurate across all three methods of WER scoring, and FSM has higher accuracy. Beyond this general support, as these results were significantly different than either of the forced alignment algorithms, the pairwise differences between the two machine algorithms were much smaller compared to the human scores. This is another example of the need for improvements in forced alignment and how there is still much work to be done in these spaces.

Limitations

The technology of the ALLT tablet has limitations in how the audio files are divided into sentence segments on the fly. This resulted in some missing or clipped audio data and may have generally affected the accuracy of any alignment and scoring. While this is not ideal, it is not uncommon for non-professionally recorded data to have inconsistencies.

Future Work

TFA is proposed as an initial exploration into the potential for adjusting existing tools to better suit amateur readers, and to raise awareness of the lack of alignment tools for this type of speech data. As such, it has not been designed with performance in mind. As TFA applies forced alignment multiple times for each file, there is clearly a performance cost. Future work should look to develop a stand-alone algorithm or variation on forced alignment building off the work done here, to create a better performing option.

In the future, the considerations for amateur readers presented here should be explored in a broader context than with the results of one study. Of particular interest will be whether the general changes of ignoring repeated insertions and accepting speech slightly off the given alignment (in this case, found in adjacent audio files) can generalize to other sources of amateur read-aloud speech.

CONCLUSION

The analysis presented here, shows that touch interaction can support the alignment of text to speech, especially for amateur readers in casual settings. This resulting alignment supports assessment using tools like forced alignment. A human-in-the-loop approach, where a human can track their current sentence (FSM), provides the best improvement to forced alignment algorithms. This is done by providing some initial alignment of text to speech from the reader's manual tracking interaction that also supported their reading accuracy.

We show the changes in TFA, that were designed to improve classic FA, account for the variability of amateur read-alouds, limit outlier data compared to classic FA, and build on assistive touch metaphors by demonstrating how these interactions affect reading in both quality and pace. As such, this work expands on the sources of speech that can be meaningfully assessed using existing methods of alignment, by incorporating the support of assistive touch metaphors to provide text and speech alignment.

ACKNOWLEDGEMENTS

This work was supported by AGE-WELL NCE Inc., a member of the Networks of Centres of Excellence (NCE), a Government of Canada program supporting research, networking, commercialization, knowledge mobilization and capacity building activities in technology and ageing to improve the quality of lives of Canadians. The authors also wish to acknowledge the sacred lands on which the University of Toronto operates. These lands are the traditional territories of the Huron-Wendat and Petun First Nations, the Seneca, the Haudenosaunee, and most recently, the Mississaugas of the Credit River. Today, the meeting place of Tkaronto is still the home to many Indigenous people from across Turtle Island, and we are grateful to have the opportunity to work in the community, on this territory.

REFERENCES

1. Xavier Anguera, Jordi Luque, and Ciro Gracia. 2014. Audio-to-text alignment for speech recognition with very limited resources. In *Fifteenth Annual Conference of the International Speech Communication Association.*
2. Abbas Attarwala, Cosmin Munteanu, and Ronald Baecker. 2013. An accessible, large-print, listening and talking e-book to support families reading together. In *Proceedings of the 15th international conference on Human-computer interaction with mobile devices and services*, 440–443.
3. Jill Attewell and Carol Savill-Smith. 2004. Mobile learning and social inclusion: focusing on learners and learning. *Learning with mobile devices: research and development*: 3–11.
4. Gérard Bailly and William-Seamus Barbour. 2011. Synchronous reading: learning French orthography by audiovisual training. In *12th Annual Conference of the International Speech Communication Association (Interspeech 2011)*, 1153–1156.
5. Valentina Bartalesi and Barbara Leporini. 2015. An Enriched ePub eBook for Screen Reader Users. In *International Conference on Universal Access in Human-Computer Interaction*, 375–386.
6. Joseph E. Beck and June Sison. 2006. Using knowledge tracing in a noisy environment to measure student reading proficiencies. *International Journal of Artificial Intelligence in Education* 16, 2: 129–143.
7. Norbert Braunschweiler and Langzhou Chen. 2013. Automatic detection of inhalation breath pauses for improved pause modelling in HMM-TTS. In *Eighth ISCA Workshop on Speech Synthesis.*
8. Norbert Braunschweiler, Mark JF Gales, and Sabine Buchholz. 2010. Lightly supervised recognition for automatic alignment of large coherent speech recordings. In *Eleventh Annual Conference of the International Speech Communication Association.*

9. Leen Cleuren, Jacques Duchateau, Alain Sips, Pol Ghesquière, and Hugo Van Hamme. 2006. Developing an automatic assessment tool for children's oral reading. In *Ninth International Conference on Spoken Language Processing.*
10. Luca Colombo, Monica Landoni, and Elisa Rubegni. 2012. Understanding reading experience to inform the design of ebooks for children. In *Proceedings of the 11th International Conference on Interaction Design and Children*, 272–275.
11. Rasmus Dali, Sandrine Brognaux, Korin Richmond, Cassia Valentini-Botinhao, Gustav Eje Henter, Julia Hirschberg, Junichi Yamagishi, and Simon King. 2016. Testing the consistency assumption: Pronunciation variant forced alignment in read and spontaneous speech synthesis. In *Acoustics, Speech and Signal Processing (ICASSP), 2016 IEEE International Conference on*, 5155–5159.
12. Kathryn DR Drager and Joe E. Reichle. 2001. Effects of Discourse Context on the Intelligibility of Synthesized Speech for Young Adult and Older Adult ListenersApplications for AAC. *Journal of Speech, Language, and Hearing Research* 44, 5: 1052–1057.
13. Carrie Demmans Epp, Cosmin Munteanu, Benett Axtell, Keerthika Ravinthiran, Yomna Aly, and Elman Mansimov. 2017. Finger tracking: facilitating non-commercial content production for mobile e-reading applications. In *Proceedings of the 19th International Conference on Human-Computer Interaction with Mobile Devices and Services*, 34.
14. Jean-Philippe Goldman. 2011. EasyAlign: an automatic phonetic alignment tool under Praat.
15. Sharon Goldwater, Dan Jurafsky, and Christopher D. Manning. 2010. Which words are hard to recognize? Prosodic, lexical, and disfluency factors that increase speech recognition error rates. *Speech Communication* 52, 3: 181–200.
16. Timothy J. Hazen. 2006. Automatic alignment and error correction of human generated transcripts for long speech recordings. In *Ninth International Conference on Spoken Language Processing.*
17. Athanasios Katsamanis, Matthew Black, Panayiotis G. Georgiou, Louis Goldstein, and S. Narayanan. 2011. SailAlign: Robust long speech-text alignment. In *Proc. of Workshop on New Tools and Methods for Very-Large Scale Phonetics Research.*
18. Simon King. 2014. Measuring a decade of progress in text-to-speech. *Loquens* 1, 1: 006.
19. Thea Knowles, Meghan Clayards, Morgan Sonderegger, Michael Wagner, Aparna Nadig, and Kristine H. Onishi. 2015. Automatic forced alignment on child speech: Directions for improvement. In *Proceedings of Meetings on Acoustics 170ASA*, 060001.
20. Benjamin Lecouteux, Georges Linares, Pascal Nocéra, and Jean-François Bonastre. 2006. Imperfect transcript driven speech recognition. In *InterSpeech.*
21. Nat Lertwongkhanakoola, Natthawut Kertkeidkachornb, Proadpran Punyabukkanac, and Atiwong Suchatod. 2014. An Automatic Real-time Synchronization of Live Speech with Its Transcription Approach. *ENGINEERING JOURNAL* 19, 5. Retrieved May 8, 2017 from http://engj.org/index.php/ej/article/view/703
22. Xiaolong Li, Li Deng, Yun-Cheng Ju, and Alex Acero. 2008. Automatic children's reading tutor on hand-held devices. In *Ninth Annual Conference of the International Speech Communication Association.*
23. Yan-Hua Long and Hong Ye. 2015. Filled Pause Refinement Based on the Pronunciation Probability for Lecture Speech. *PloS one* 10, 4: e0123466.
24. Yoshitaka Mamiya, Adriana Stan, Junichi Yamagishi, Peter Bell, Oliver Watts, Robert AJ Clark, and Simon King. 2013. Using Adaptation to Improve Speech Transcription Alignment in Noisy and Reverberant Environments. In *Eighth ISCA Workshop on Speech Synthesis.*
25. Michael Massimi, Rachelle Campigotto, Abbas Attarwala, and Ronald Baecker. 2013. Reading together as a Leisure Activity: Implications for E-reading. In *14th International Conference on Human-Computer Interaction (INTERACT)*, 19–36.
26. Petr Mizera, Petr Pollak, Alice Kolman, and Mirjam Ernestus. 2014. Impact of irregular pronunciation on phonetic segmentation of nijmegen corpus of casual czech. In *International Conference on Text, Speech, and Dialogue*, 499–506.
27. Pedro J. Moreno and Christopher Alberti. 2009. A factor automaton approach for the forced alignment of long speech recordings. In *Acoustics, Speech and Signal Processing, 2009. ICASSP 2009. IEEE International Conference on*, 4869–4872.
28. Pedro J. Moreno, Chris Joerg, Jean-Manuel Van Thong, and Oren Glickman. 1998. A recursive algorithm for the forced alignment of very long audio segments. In *Fifth International Conference on Spoken Language Processing.*
29. Jack Mostow. 2012. Why and how our automated reading tutor listens. In *Proceedings of the International Symposium on Automatic Detection of Errors in Pronunciation Training (ISADEPT)*, 43–52.
30. Cosmin Munteanu, Joanna Lumsden, Hélène Fournier, Rock Leung, Danny D'Amours, Daniel McDonald, and Julie Maitland. 2010. ALEX: mobile language assistant for low-literacy adults. In *Proceedings of the 12th international conference on Human computer interaction with mobile devices and services*, 427–430.
31. Cosmin Munteanu, Heather Molyneaux, Julie Maitland, Daniel McDonald, Rock Leung, Hélène Fournier, and Joanna Lumsden. 2014. Hidden in plain sight: low-literacy adults in a developed country overcoming social and educational challenges through mobile learning support tools. *Personal and ubiquitous computing* 18, 6: 1455–1469.

32. Emma Murphy, Ravi Kuber, Graham McAllister, Philip Strain, and Wai Yu. 2008. An empirical investigation into the difficulties experienced by visually impaired Internet users. *Universal Access in the Information Society* 7, 1–2: 79–91.
33. Susan B. Neuman and David K. Dickinson. 2003. *Handbook of early literacy research.* Guilford Press.
34. Andrea Passerini and Michele Sebag. 2015. 4.2 Learning and Optimization with the Human in the Loop. *Constraints, Optimization and Data*: 21.
35. Kishore Prahallad and Alan W. Black. 2011. Segmentation of monologues in audio books for building synthetic voices. *IEEE Transactions on Audio, Speech, and Language Processing* 19, 5: 1444–1449.
36. Frank Rudzicz, Rosalie Wang, Momotaz Begum, and Alex Mihailidis. 2014. Speech recognition in Alzheimer's disease with personal assistive robots. In *Proceedings of the 5th Workshop on Speech and Language Processing for Assistive Technologies (SLPAT)*, 20–28.
37. Nithya Sambasivan, Ed Cutrell, Kentaro Toyama, and Bonnie Nardi. 2010. Intermediated technology use in developing communities. In *Proceedings of the SIGCHI Conference on Human Factors in Computing Systems*, 2583–2592.
38. Kei Sawada, Shinji Takaki, Kei Hashimoto, Keiichiro Oura, and Keiichi Tokuda. 2014. Overview of NITECH HMM-based text-to-speech system for Blizzard Challenge 2014. In *Blizzard Challenge Workshop.*
39. Roy Shilkrot, Jochen Huber, Wong Meng Ee, Pattie Maes, and Suranga Chandima Nanayakkara. 2015. FingerReader: a wearable device to explore printed text on the go. In *Proceedings of the 33rd Annual ACM Conference on Human Factors in Computing Systems*, 2363–2372.
40. Ronanki Srikanth and Li Bo2 James Salsman. 2012. Automatic pronunciation evaluation and mispronunciation detection using CMUSphinx. In *24th International Conference on Computational Linguistics*, 61.
41. Richard K. Wagner, Andrea E. Muse, and Kendra R. Tannenbaum. 2007. *Vocabulary acquisition: Implications for reading comprehension.* Guilford Press.
42. Mirjam Wester, Matthew Aylett, Marcus Tomalin, and Rasmus Dall. 2015. Artificial personality and disfluency. In *Sixteenth Annual Conference of the International Speech Communication Association.*
43. Silke M. Witt. 2012. Automatic error detection in pronunciation training: Where we are and where we need to go. In *International Symposium on Automatic Detection of Errors in Pronunciation Training, Stockholm, Sweden.*
44. Junbo Zhang, Fuping Pan, and Yonghong Yan. 2012. An LVCSR based automatic scoring method in English reading tests. In *Intelligent Human-Machine Systems and Cybernetics (IHMSC), 2012 4th International Conference on*, 34–37.
45. LibriVox | free public domain audiobooks. Retrieved October 4, 2017 from https://librivox.org/

Comparing Speech and Text Input in Interactive Narratives

Diego Gonzalez
Williams College
Williamstown, Massachusetts, USA
drg4@williams.edu

Andrew S. Gordon
University of Southern California
Los Angeles, California, USA
gordon@ict.usc.edu

ABSTRACT
Intelligent user interfaces are finding new applications in interactive narratives, where players take on the role of a character in a fictional storyline. A recent example is the interactive audio narrative "Traveler", in which a combination of technologies for speech recognition and unsupervised text classification allow players to navigate a branching storyline via open-vocabulary spoken input. We hypothesize that the affordances of audio-based interaction in interactive narratives are different than text-based interaction, and that these differences change the player experience and their understanding of their fictional role. To test this hypothesis, we conducted a controlled experiment (n=39) to compare player interaction in "Traveler" with a text-only variant of the same storyline. We found significant differences in the types of input provided by players, suggesting that interaction modality impacts how players conceive of their relation to narrators of fictional storylines.

ACM Classification Keywords
Human-centered computing: Natural language interfaces

Author Keywords
Interactive Narratives; Natural Language Interfaces; Speech Interaction

USER INTERFACES FOR INTERACTIVE NARRATIVES
Artificial Intelligence (AI) research routinely finds application in computer games and other forms of interactive entertainment, e.g. to control autonomous virtual characters, adjust the difficulty of gameplay, and to procedurally generate content in virtual worlds. In game user interfaces, AI has helped enable new types of game controllers, e.g. motion sensing input devices [13, 5], which may qualitatively change the player's sense of agency in a virtual world. This effect on sense of agency can be seen in computer-based interactive narratives, where AI advances are beginning to enable natural language interfaces that eschew multiple-choice lists or simple verb-object commands in favor of more natural input using text [7, 14] and speech [11, 2, 15].

IUI 2018, March 7–11, 2018, Tokyo, Japan.

ACM ISBN 978-1-4503-4945-1/18/03 ...$15.00.
http://dx.doi.org/10.1145/3172944.3172999

One example is the Data-driven Interactive Narrative Engine (DINE) [1], a web-based authoring and deployment platform for free-text interactive fiction. After reading a passage of scenario content, players of DINE scenario are presented with a free-text input box to articulate, in natural language, what they would do in the fictional situation. The system analyzes this input, and responds with an outcome that moves the storyline forward. Authors of DINE scenarios design these experiences as static branching storylines, in a style reminiscent of early Choose-Your-Own-Adventure books [12]. The task of interpreting player input is left to the underlying DINE engine, which selects the most appropriate outcome at a given branch point using an unsupervised text classification algorithm that compares statistical word embeddings [8] of player input to the first ten words written for each available outcome.

While DINE's natural language interface can greatly increase players' sense of agency compared to choice-based branching storylines, the success of this approach is highly dependent on the author's ability to anticipate the breadth of actions that players will take in a given situation, as well as the algorithm's ability to route a player's natural language input to the most appropriate outcome. Cychosz et al. [4] describes a series of user studies to identify effective designs for DINE scenarios, focusing on the effect of storyline structure and narrative style on the coherence of the interaction. Most notably, the author's choice of style in presenting character dialogue was a significant predictor of players' coherence ratings. Players were likely to match the author's dialogue style (direct or indirect speech) and tense in their own input, and mirroring direct speech had a negative effect on the classification accuracy of the algorithm. In free-text interfaces for interactive narratives, the success of the technology is dependent on the contributions of both interacting parties (the author and the player).

The interactive digital artwork "Traveler" [16] further explores the use of natural language interfaces in interactive narratives by incorporating speech recognition and by presenting story content as produced audio clips rather than as text. In this piece, players take on the role of Dr. Ramon Pineda, an American physician returning from an international conference in Germany. His homecoming takes a turn for the worse when passing through immigration at LAX airport, where he is whisked away by border agents for questioning and held alongside other travelers affected by increased border security measures. "Traveler" uses interactive narrative to expose players to the dystopian consequences of racial profiling and warrantless border searches, and challenges them to consider what their own actions might be in similar situations. "Traveler" was constructed as a four-scene interactive audio drama. In each scene, the player hears Dr. Pineda describe part of his experience, and is prompted (with a bell sound) to say what they would have Dr. Pineda do next. Player speech is processed using the large-vocabulary speech recognition engine built into recent versions of the Google Chrome web browser, results of which are then passed to an underlying algorithm that selects among four to seven outcomes for a given scene. "Traveler" uses the same unsupervised text classification algorithm as DINE [1] for selecting outcomes, comparing player input to the first ten words of textual representations of the outcome audio clips. In each scene, players are repeatedly prompted for input until the algorithm selects the specific one that transitions the story to the next scene, or to the ending audio clip in the case of the fourth scene.

We hypothesized that the use of audio interaction instead of text interaction in "Traveler" effects the content of player input, which in turn effects the ability of underlying algorithm to route player input to appropriate outcomes. Following the results of Cychosz et al. [4], we expect that players are more likely to mirror the characteristics of the presentation modality in their spoken inputs, e.g. by voicing speech that is directed to other storyline characters, rather than voicing storyline narration. We further hypothesized that this effect, combined with speech recognition errors, will degrade the classification accuracy compared to text-based interaction.

EXPERIMENT

To test these hypotheses, we conducted a human-subjects experiment to compare players' interaction with "Traveler" to a text-only version of the same interactive narrative, where players typed their input rather than speaking.

We recruited 39 English-speaking participants consisting of undergraduate and graduate students enrolled in colleges and universities across the United States, each of whom was completing an academic summer internship at *institution withheld during blind review.* Each participant was randomly assigned to either the text or speech condition. Total participation time was no more than 30 minutes, including the completion of a post-experiment questionnaire.

In the speech condition, 19 of 39 participants interacted with "Traveler" as it was originally conceived as an interactive audio narrative. Sitting at a desktop computer, participants listened to the produced audio clips of this audio drama, and spoke their inputs into the computer's microphone when prompted by a bell sound. In addition, a second microphone was used to record each interaction in the speech condition, which was later transcribed to evaluate the effect of errors in automated speech recognition on the unsupervised text classification algorithm used by "Traveler". An example audio-only interaction in this condition is as follows:

SICK WOMAN: *Help me, please! I'm very sick.* (coughing)

BORDER AGENT: *Not my problem right now.*

NARRATOR: *I couldn't believe what was happening. A sick woman was crying for help but this agent kept yelling at her. That's when I decided I had to do something.* [bell prompt]

`>hey this woman needs help`

NARRATOR: *I waited for someone to help the woman.*

SICK WOMAN: (coughs uncontrollably)

WOMAN TRAVELER: *Hey, aren't you a doctor?* [...]

In the text condition, 20 of 39 participants interacted with a new variation of "Traveler" that we authored specifically for this experiment. Sitting at a desktop computer, participants read textual narrative passages that ended in text input boxes, where participants typed their free-text inputs. This text-only version mirrored the content of the audio version, but was modified to read more as an interactive novel than as a script for an audio play. Starting from the script of the audio version, we converted character dialogue lines to narrated quoted speech. The lines of the "narrator" in the audio version (Dr. Pineda) were expanded slightly to convey events and information evident from sound effects and actors' performances in the audio version. The following interaction illustrates how the text version differed from the original audio version:

I could see the sick woman approach a nearby armed officer.

"Help me, please!" she pleaded him, "I'm very sick. I have a fever and severe pain, I need to leave!"

"Not my problem right now." He said, brushing her off, "So just shut up and sit down!"

I couldn't believe what was happening. A sick woman was crying for help but this agent kept yelling at her. That's when I decided I had to do something.

`> I pleaded with the agent to help her`

I waited for someone to help the sick woman. It wasn't long before I heard her go back into one of her coughing fits.

"Hey, aren't you a doctor?" asked the woman standing next to me. [...]

In both conditions, the underlying branching storyline structure remained the same. Overall, "Traveler" is structured around four "pages" corresponding to scenes of the narrative: meeting border security agents, an initial interrogation, waiting with other detainees, and a final interrogation. Associated with each scene are four to seven "outcomes" that are presented to the participant in response to their input, selected automatically by comparing the input (text or recognized speech) to the first ten words of each outcome, using the "MaxAvgMaxSim_{10}" algorithm described by [1]. Only outcomes not previously presented to participants are ranked, guaranteeing that participants eventually select the single outcome on each page that advances the storyline to the next page, or to the end in the case of the fourth page.

Table 1 lists the number of outcomes possible on each of the four pages ("outcomes" column), along with the number of inputs collected in both the text and speech conditions ("inputs" column). The number of inputs varied by both page and condition, with means just above two inputs per page in both conditions. A total of 179 inputs were collected from the

20 participants in the text condition, and 230 inputs from the 19 participants in the speech condition.

RESULTS

Our hypothesis was that the modality of interaction would effect the content of participants input, and that differences would subsequently effect the accuracy of the algorithm used to select outcomes. To explore these hypotheses, we conducted a series of three analyses using the 409 interactions collected in our experiment.

Classification accuracy across conditions

First, we investigated whether there was evidence that the classification algorithm performed differently across conditions. To make this comparison, we hand-annotated each of the participants' inputs, noting both whether there existed at least one appropriate outcome on the page and, if so, the most appropriate outcome. For the speech condition, these gold-standard annotations were made on transcriptions of the participants' spoken words (rather than the recognized words), as heard by the annotator in the audio recordings of the participants' interactions.

Table 1 lists the number of inputs for each page that had at least one appropriate outcome available ("supported" column). Overall, inputs in the text condition were more supported by the available outcomes on each page, with 81.6% of inputs supported compared to 68.3% for the voice condition.

Considering only the supported inputs, we used the gold-standard annotations to compute both the percent agreement ("acc." column) and chance-corrected agreement using Cohen's Kappa statistic ("κ" column). Here, chance agreement was simply estimated to be 1 over the number of outcomes on the page, affording comparison of classification performance across pages with different numbers of outcomes. Although performance varied widely across pages and conditions, mean accuracy scores favored the text condition by over ten percent.

Effect of ASR errors on accuracy

Second, we investigated the role that errors in automated speech recognition (ASR) had in degrading the accuracy of the classification algorithm in speech condition. "Traveler" uses the large-vocabulary ASR engine built into recent desktop versions of Google's Chrome browser, backed by state-of-the-art cloud-based ASR models. We computed the Word Error Rate (WER) by comparing the annotator's transcriptions of speech input with the output of ASR, finding a WER of 13.6%, such that 37.6% of speech inputs contained ASR errors. The observed error rate is similar to that seen in previous interactive dialogue systems [10].

We subsequently computed what the classification accuracy of the speech condition would have been given perfect ASR performance ("corrected speech" in Table 1). Percent agreement and chance-corrected agreement improved substantially across each of the four pages, but made up for less than half of the difference in mean accuracy scores as compared to the text condition.

Comparison of input types

Third, we investigated whether there were qualitative differences in the types of inputs provided by participants across conditions. When creating gold-standard annotations to compute classification accuracy, we observed a wide variety of relationships between the participants' input and the various voices and perspectives of characters in the story. Sometimes participants would enter words as if they were speaking directly to storyline characters, e.g. the border agent or the sick woman. Other times, participants adopted the voice of the narrator (Dr. Pineda), describing their intended actions as a continuation of his own past-tense narration. Some participants mirrored the input conventions of traditional interactive fiction [9] by issuing commands to Dr. Pineda, while others spoke directly to Dr. Pineda as if listening to his story.

To investigate whether there were systematic differences across conditions, we categorized all 409 participant inputs across both conditions into five distinguishing categories:

Narrate story: The participant continues the narration of the the narrator, in the past tense. Example: *"I opened the door"*

Speak to narrator: The participant converses directly with the narrator (or the computer), in the present tense, about the situation. Examples: *"You should to open the door," "I'd like to open the door," "I open the door?"*

Speak to character: The participant converses directly with storyline characters, e.g. in response to questions posed to the protagonist. Example: (Character says, "Do you want to open the door?") *"Yes I do."*

Command: The participant issues a command to the protagonist, as if using their input to control an avatar. Example: *"Open the door"*

Meta comment: The participant provides an input that is to be interpreted above the diegetic level of the story, as if speaking to the computer (or experimenter) about the interaction. Examples: *"How do I tell it that I want to open the door?" "I'm not sure why he would open the door."*

Figure 1 graphs the percentage of per-user interactions assigned to each of these five categories across text and speech conditions. Two significant differences were observed ($p < 0.05$, two-tailed t-test). Participants were significantly more likely to narrate the story (in the narrative voice of Dr. Peneda) in the text condition than in the speech condition. In contrast, participants were significantly more likely to speak directly to the narrator (Dr. Peneda) in the speech condition. Smaller differences seen in other input categories were not significant.

In post-experiment questionnaires, we specifically asked participants to indicate (on Likert scales) how much they felt they were interacting with a computer, the narrator, the protagonist, other characters, or the author of the story. Despite observed differences in the distributions of input types, no statistically significant differences were found in the participants questionnaire responses. In both conditions, participants most felt that they were interacting with the author of the story. Despite observed differences in classification performance, there was not a significant difference in participants ratings of the coherence

		text condition (n=20)				**speech condition** (n=19)				**corrected speech**	
page	*outcomes*	*inputs*	*supported*	*acc.*	*κ*	*inputs*	*supported*	*acc.*	*κ*	*acc.*	*κ*
1	4	48	38	.526	.368	28	21	.810	.746	.857	.810
2	7	56	45	.711	.663	69	57	.474	.386	.509	.427
3	3	40	32	.469	.203	41	37	.108	-.338	.135	-.297
4	7	35	31	.742	.699	46	42	.595	.528	.643	.583
mean	5.25	44.75	36.5	.612	.483	46	39.25	.497	.330	.536	.381

Table 1. Comparison of input classification accuracy

of the experience, or the believability of the fictional storyline events. Only one significant difference in subjective experience was evident across conditions: participants in the text condition more strongly agreed with the statement, "I found it easy to come up with responses" ($p < 0.05$).

Figure 1. Comparison of input type, p < 0.05 (*)

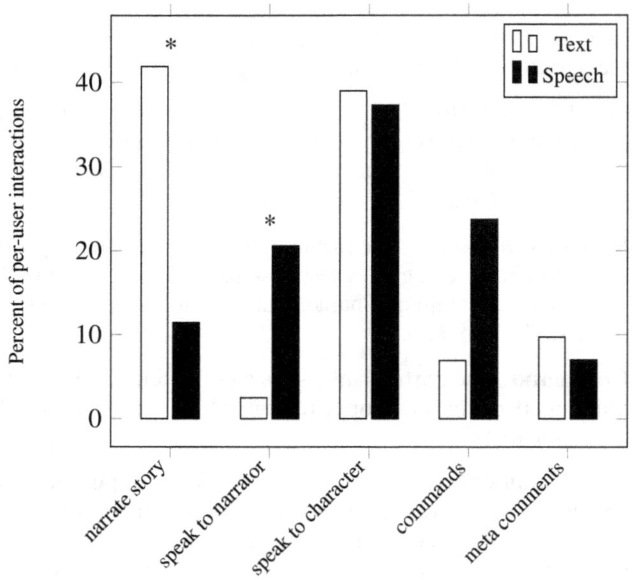

DISCUSSION

The affordances of text versus speech input have been compared in prior studies [6] and in various interactive applications, such as the tagging of smartphone photographs [3]. The contribution our study is to explore how these affordances are changed by the unique features of interactive narrative. One of the interesting features of interactive narrative, in general, is that there is a wide range of roles that the participant can play in the interaction. As seen in "Traveler," the participants may alternatively see themselves as the protagonist in the storyline, the narrator of this storyline, or as an audience member in the telling of the story. Our third analysis provides evidence that each interaction modality promotes some roles over others. In the speech condition, participants are less likely to adopt the role of the narrator, and more likely to address the narrator directly as a storyteller. In the speech condition, the "voice" of the narrator is, literally, that of another person – a professional voice actor, in this case. In contrast, the "voice" of the narrator in written fiction is that of the reader, either imagined when reading silently or vocalized when reading out loud. When a participant narrates the story using text, they are continuing a monologue already begun through the process of reading. When a participant narrates the story using speech, they are interrupting someone else's telling of a story.

The affordances of each interaction modality shape the distribution of input types provided by participants, with consequences for classification accuracy. In the text condition, roughly 80% of the inputs are either narration or direct speech to storyline characters, and roughly 80% of inputs were supported by one of the available outcomes on each page. Given that nearly all of the authored outcomes in "Traveler" consist of narration or the direct speech of storyline characters, these categories of inputs are more likely to invoke coherent outcomes at correspondent levels of discourse. Furthermore, this parity in interaction supports the underlying classification algorithm, which relies on the similarity of word-level embeddings between inputs and outcomes. The relative diversity of input types in the voice condition make it more difficult for authors to anticipate the breadth of inputs, resulting in fewer inputs that can be supported by authored outcomes. As participants move further afield from narration and direct speech, the similarity-based classification algorithm suffers in performance.

While these results favor text interaction given the technology, we believe that these results also chart a path forward for interactive audio narratives. To facilitate both the ability of authors to cover the input space and the algorithm's ability to select appropriate outcomes, future interactive audio narratives should strive to reduce the diversity of participant input categories, either through instruction or design. While tutorial "how-to-play" instruction might suffice, we hypothesize that removing the voice of the narrator from the audio production would inhibit participants from speaking above the diegetic level of discourse. By moving the genre closer to that of an interactive radio drama than an audio book, some scenario design innovations will be necessary to allow for player agency beyond conversational speech acts, e.g. by designing scenarios where the topic of conversation is which actions to take in the given situations.

ACKNOWLEDGMENTS

This material is based upon work supported by the National Science Foundation under Grant No. 1560426. The projects or efforts depicted were or are sponsored by the U. S. Army. The content or information presented does not necessarily reflect the position or the policy of the Government, and no official endorsement should be inferred.

REFERENCES

1. Jenna Bellassai, Andrew S. Gordon, Melissa Roemmele, Margaret Cychosz, Obiageli Odimegwu, and Olivia Connolly. 2017. Unsupervised Text Classification for Natural Language Interactive Narratives. In *Proceedings of the 10th International Workshop on Intelligent Narrative Technologies, Snowbird, Utah, October 5-6, 2017.*

2. Marc Cavazza, Jean-Luc Lugrin, David Pizzi, and Fred Charles. 2007. Madame Bovary on the Holodeck: Immersive Interactive Storytelling. In *Proceedings of the 15th ACM International Conference on Multimedia.* 651–660.

3. Mauro Cherubini, Xavier Anguera, Nuria Oliver, and Rodrigo de Oliveira. 2009. Text versus Speech: A Comparison of Tagging Input Modalities for Camera Phones. In *Proceedings of the 11th Conference on Human-Computer Interaction with Mobile Devices and Services, Mobile HCI 2009, Bonn, Germany, September 15-18, 2009.*

4. Margaret Cychosz, Andrew S. Gordon, Obiageli Odimegwu, Olivia Connolly, Jenna Bellassai, and Melissa Roemmele. 2017. Effective Scenario Designs for Free-text Interactive Fiction. In *Proceedings of the 10th International Conference on Interactive Digital Storytelling, Madeira, Portugal, November 14-17, 2017.*

5. Felix Kistler, Elisabeth André, Samuel Mascarenhas, André Silva, Ana Paiva, Nick Degens, Gert Jan Hofstede, Eva Krumhuber, Arvid Kappas, and Ruth Aylett. 2013. *Traveller: An Interactive Cultural Training System Controlled by User-Defined Body Gestures.* 697–704.

6. Gale L. Martin. 1989. The utility of speech input in user-computer interfaces. *International Journal of Man-Machine Studies* 30, 4 (1989), 355 – 375.

7. Michael Mateas and Andrew Stern. 2003. Integrating Plot, Character and Natural Language Processing in the Interactive Drama Facade. In *Proceedings of Technologies for Interactive Digital Storytelling and Entertainment (TIDSE), Darmstadt, Germany.*

8. Tomas Mikolov, Ilya Sutskever, Kai Chen, Greg Corrado, and Jeffrey Dean. 2013. Distributed Representations of Words and Phrases and Their Compositionality. In *Proceedings of the 26th International Conference on Neural Information Processing Systems (NIPS'13).* Curran Associates Inc., USA, 3111–3119.

9. Nick Montfort. 2003. *Twisty Little Passages: An Approach to Interactive Fiction.* Cambridge, MA: MIT Press.

10. Fabrizio Morbini, Kartik Audhkhasi, Kenji Sagae, Ron Artstein, Dogan Can, Panayiotis G Georgiou, Shrikanth S Narayanan, Anton Leuski, and David R Traum. 2013. Which ASR should I choose for my dialogue system?. In *Proceedings of the 14th annual SIGdial Meeting on Discourse and Dialogue, Aug 22-24, 2013, Metz, France.* 394–403.

11. Jeff Orkin and Deb K. Roy. 2014. Understanding speech in interactive narratives with crowd sourced data. In *Proceedings of the 8th AAAI Conference on Artificial Intelligence and Interactive Digital Entertainment, AIIDE 2012.*

12. Edward Packard. 1979. *The Cave of Time.* New York: Bantum Books.

13. Daniel Shapiro, Josh McCoy, April Grow, Ben Samuel, Andrew Stern, Reid Swanson, Mike Treanor, and Michael Mateas. 2013. Creating Playable Social Experiences through Whole-Body Interaction with Virtual Characters. In *Ninth Artificial Intelligence and Interactive Digital Entertainment Conference.*

14. Reid Swanson and Andrew S. Gordon. 2012. Say Anything: Using Textual Case-Based Reasoning to Enable Open-Domain Interactive Storytelling. *ACM Trans. Interact. Intell. Syst.* 2, 3, Article 16 (Sept. 2012), 35 pages.

15. David Traum, Andrew Jones, Kia Hays, Heather Maio, Oleg Alexander, Ron Artstein, Paul Debevec, Alesia Gainer, Kallirroi Georgila, Kathleen Haase, Karen Jungblut, Anton Leuski, Stephen Smith, and William Swartout. 2015. New Dimensions in Testimony: Digitally Preserving a Holocaust Survivor's Interactive Storytelling. In *Proceedings of the 8th International Conference on Interactive Digital Storytelling (ICIDS), Copenhagen, Denmark.*

16. Mike Treanor, Nicholas Warren, Mason Reed, Adam Smith, Pablo Ortiz, Laurel Carney, Loren Sherman, Elizabeth Carré, Nadya Vivatvisha, D. Harrell, Paola Mardo, Andrew Gordon, Joris Dormans, Barrie Robison, Spencer Gomez, Samantha Heck, Landon Wright, and Terence Soule. 2017. Playable Experiences at AIIDE 2017. In *Proceedings of the 13th AAAI Conference on Artificial Intelligence and Interactive Digital Entertainment (AIIDE'17), Snowbird, Utah, October 5-9, 2017.*

Eye Gaze-driven Prediction of Cognitive Differences during Graphical Password Composition

Christina Katsini[1,2], Christos Fidas[3], George E. Raptis[1,2], Marios Belk[4,5], George Samaras[5], Nikolaos Avouris[2]
[1]Human Opsis, Patras, Greece, [2]HCI Group, University of Patras, Greece,
[3]Dept. of Cultural Heritage Management and New Technologies, University of Patras, Greece,
[4]Cognitive UX GmbH, Heidelberg, Germany,
[5]Dept. of Computer Science, University of Cyprus, Nicosia, Cyprus
katsinic@upnet.gr, fidas@upatras.gr, raptisg@upnet.gr, belk@cognitiveux.de, cssamara@cs.ucy.ac.cy, avouris@upatras.gr

ABSTRACT
Evidence suggests that individual cognitive differences affect users' memorability, visual behavior, and graphical passwords' security. Such knowledge denotes the added value of personalizing graphical password schemes towards the unique cognitive characteristics of the users. However, real-time and accurate cognition-based predictive user models are necessary to reach such a break-through. In this paper, we present the results of such an attempt, where an in-lab eye-tracking study was conducted with 36 participants who completed a recall-based graphical password composition task. We adopted a credible cognitive style theory, and investigated a variety of eye-tracking metrics to predict participants' cognitive styles. Results' analysis reveals that inferring individual cognitive differences in real-time during graphical password composition is feasible within a few seconds and that specific eye-tracking metrics correlate stronger with certain cognitive style groups. The findings further support the vision of incorporating real-time adaptive mechanisms in graphical password schemes for the benefit of service providers and end-users.

Author Keywords
Graphical User Authentication; Eye-Tracking; Human Cognitive Differences; User Modeling; Classification.

ACM Classification Keywords
• Human-centered computing ~ Human computer interaction (HCI) • Security and privacy ~ Human and societal aspects of security and privacy

INTRODUCTION
Graphical user authentication (GUA) is a widely deployed alternative to traditional text-based authentication. There are two types of GUA schemes: *recall-based* (i.e., users draw a graphical password) and *recognition-based* (i.e., users select a set of images to form a password). Despite that GUA was proposed as a possible solution for the memorability and security issues associated with textual passwords [19], recent research revealed that people make predictable choices in GUA too, affecting both the memorability and the security of passwords [2,6,12,14].

Predictable password choices are affected, among others, by cognitive characteristics [2,6,12], and when they are related to visual behavior, such as the Field Dependence-Independence (FD-I) theory [36], they affect password composition [14,15] and login [3] in GUA. FD-I suggests that individuals have different approaches in retrieving, recalling, processing, and storing visual information, and characterizes individuals either as *field dependent (FD)* or *field independent (FI)*, based on their ability to process visual information and identify details in complex scenes.

Despite that research results raise the need for providing assistive and/or adaptive mechanisms in the GUA domain, this is currently impractical since elicitation of FD-I style is achieved through time-consuming in-lab tools. Hence, this work aims to investigate whether user's FD-I style can be predicted implicitly in real-time during graphical password composition, using eye-tracking data, given that FD-I is related to visual behavior [18,21,24]. We envisage that this will enable GUA scheme designers to predict the users' cognitive characteristics, include a time-related predictive model to the GUA schemes, and provide design solutions catered for the users' cognitive characteristics during registration and/or login. This is of major importance considering that the users' cognitive characteristics have been associated with performance differences in terms of memorability and security, and such knowledge could be used to provide GUA schemes adjusted to users who share common cognitive characteristics to assist them during GUA tasks.

RELATED WORK
Several research attempts have been made to infer cognitive styles and abilities in varying domains. Frias-Martinez et al. [7] showed that the Holistic-Analytic cognitive style can be inferred when users are engaged in information seeking tasks in a digital library (accuracy over 75%). Clewey et al. [4]

IUI'18, March 7–11, 2018, Tokyo, Japan

ACM ISBN 978-1-4503-4945-1/18/03…$15.00
https://doi.org/10.1145/3172944.3172996

revealed that the Holism-Serialism cognitive style can be inferred when users are engaged in content exploration tasks within web-based instruction environments (accuracy over 79%). Similar findings were revealed for the FD-I cognitive style [5]. Hochberg et al. [10] revealed that the automatic annotation of Analytic-Intuitive cognitive style can be achieved when users are engaged with an image-based clinical reasoning task (accuracy over 84%). Wang et al. [34] revealed that Adaptive/Innovative and Analytic/Intuitive cognitive styles can be inferred from user-generated social media content (accuracy over 65%).

Focusing on eye-gaze based elicitation, Raptis et al. [26] revealed that FD-I cognitive style can be inferred from visual search and visual decision-making tasks (accuracy over 75%). Regarding elementary cognitive attributes (i.e., skills and abilities), Steichen et al. [29,30] performed classification experiments to classify users according to their perceptual speed, verbal and visual working memory when performing information visualization tasks; Yelizarov and Gamayunov [37] developed a mechanism to detect the users' cognitive overload and adapt the content quantity.

The discussed research endeavors lie under diverse application domains and do not consider time as a classification factor. Focusing on the user authentication domain, to the knowledge of the authors, no attempt has been made to classify users based on their cognitive characteristics using their eye-gaze data in real-time. Given existing effects of FD-I in GUA [2,14], we stress the importance of providing assistive/adaptive mechanisms in the GUA domain, and consider this work as a first step towards this vision.

USER STUDY

Research Questions

Q1: Is it feasible to use real-time eye-gaze data to elicit the FD-I style when users are engaged in a graphical password composition task?

Q2: Which eye-gaze metrics are most predictive for FIs and which metrics are most predictive for FDs?

Study Instruments and Metrics

Graphical User Authentication Scheme

We used *Windows™ Picture Gesture Authentication* [13], a popular and widely-used recall-based GUA scheme. The users choose a background picture and draw three gestures on it. The gestures can be any combination of circles, lines, and/or taps. The combination, the size, the position, and the direction of the drawn gestures constitute the graphical password.

Equipment

The participants created their password using a Samsung Galaxy Tab S2 (9.7" screen size with 2048x1536 pixels resolution). Their eye movements were captured using Tobii Pro Glasses 2 (50Hz). Fixations were extracted using a velocity threshold identification (I-VT) algorithm [17], based on the I-VT algorithm provided by Tobii.

Cognitive Style Elicitation Test

To elicit the participants' FD-I style, we used *Group Embedded Figures Test* (GEFT) [23], a credible and validated time-administered tool [16]. GEFT consists of 18 pattern-recognition tasks, where the users are asked to identify and outline a given pattern within a complex context, in a given amount of time. The GEFT score is the number of the correctly identified patterns; thus, the GEFT score ranges between 0 and 18. The higher the score, the more field-independent the individual is.

Eye-Gaze Metrics

Following common practice, we selected *fixation count* and *fixation duration* as suggested in [25], and *saccade length* as suggested in [8], which could provide trends in user attention patterns. For each of these basic measures, we included computed features, as discussed in [33]. For fixation count, we calculated the total number of fixations and the fixation rate. For fixation duration, we calculated the sum, mean, max, and std. deviation. For saccade length, we calculated the sum, mean, max, and std. deviation.

Classification Setup

To investigate whether it is possible to elicit FD-I in real-time, we performed a classification experiment with the discussed eye-gaze metrics. Following Toker's et al. [32] approach, we divided the activity time in time-slots of *1 second.* The time-slots start from the first second of the user's engagement with the password composition task and last until the mean time required to complete the task. In each time-slot, the users were classified either as FD or FI for each of the gaze-based metrics and their combination, and an accuracy rate (in relation to the ground-truth GEFT classification) was calculated. We also compared the classification results with those of the baseline model (i.e., all participants are classified as FDs in each time-slot according to ZeroR classifier).

Since classifications are done in consecutively increasing time-slots within the password composition task, there are cases where users complete the task in less than the mean time. We remove these users from our dataset at those time-slots, to ensure that the results are not biased, given that some metrics are correlated with time (e.g., fixation duration). Moreover, the baseline, which is based on the ZeroR classifier, is re-calculated in each time-slot.

Participants

We recruited 36 individuals (16 females) with an age range between 22 and 38 years (m=31.7; sd=6.1), of varying educational and professional background. Participants had no vision problems, had never taken a GEFT test before, and had no prior experience with GUA schemes (to avoid familiarity effects). The participants' GEFT scores were normally distributed (m=11.27, sd=3.51, p=.085). To classify each user as either FD or FI, we set the GEFT cut-off score at 12, a score that is widely used in the literature [1,27]. 17 participants were classified as FD (score: 0-11), and 19 were classified as FI (score: 12-18).

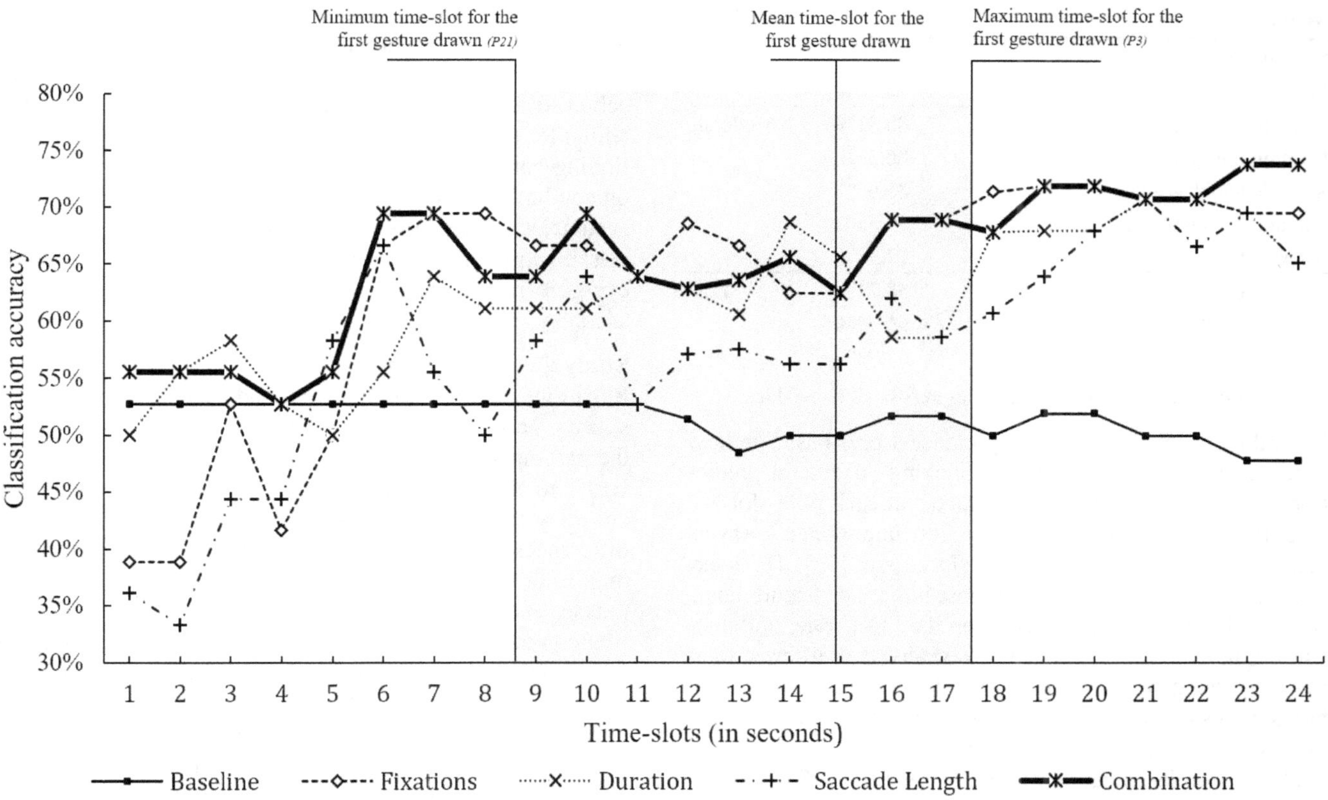

Figure 1: Classification accuracy across time-slots based on eye-gaze metrics.

Study Procedure

The study was conducted in a quiet room in our lab in one-to-one sessions and involved the following steps: *i)* the participants were introduced to the task and familiarized with the eye-tracking equipment, *ii)* we calibrated the eye-tracker following the process described in [31], *iii)* the participants used a provided background picture and drew a graphical password on it, *iv)* they completed GEFT, *v)* we asked them to log-in using their credentials to ensure they did not create the passwords randomly, and *vi)* we performed the classification experiment using the collected and calculated eye-gaze data.

RESULTS

To investigate our research questions we used WEKA software [9], following a 10-fold classification approach, mainly due to our small sample size. Regarding **Q**$_1$, we tested several classifiers (Logistic Regression, Naïve Bayes, k-Nearest Neighbors, Classification and Regression Trees, and Support Vector Machines), towards the percentage of the correctly classified instances, with Logistic Regression (LR) providing the best results.

The results revealed that the peak accuracy was achieved towards the last time-slots (e.g., 72% accuracy for fixation count at the 19th and the 20th second). We should note that the high accuracies achieved towards the last time-slots could be due to some users completing the task in previous time-slots (e.g., the first user created the password at the 13th time-slot). Nonetheless, there was an upward trend of the combined model after the 4th second (Figure 1, Table 1).

Early prediction capabilities are of major importance for the present work, considering that the aim is to identify the user's cognitive style at the early stages of the password composition task. This will enable the delivery of suitable assistive and/or adaptive mechanisms during registration which could influence the users' decisions towards more secure and memorable passwords. Moving towards this direction, the LR classifier achieved maximum accuracies (over 63%) between the 6th and 10th time-slot and performed better than the baseline in all time-slots (apart from the 4th). The LR classifier provided the best results, regarding classification accuracy, when all the eye-gaze metrics were considered (Table 1).

Metric	Time-slot	FD	FI	Overall
Fixation count	6	12/17	12/19	66.67%
	7	12/17	13/19	69.44%
	8	11/17	14/19	69.44%
Fixation duration	7	13/17	10/19	63.89%
Saccade length	6	14/17	10/19	66.67%
Combined metrics	6	12/17	13/19	69.44%
	7	11/17	14/19	69.44%
	10	11/17	14/19	69.44%

Table 1: Maximum early prediction accuracies.

Metric	Importance	Imp. Level
Saccade length – total	100.00%	High
Fixation rate	90.30%	
Fixation duration – mean	88.81%	Moderate
Fixation duration – total	86.57%	
Saccade length – mean	85.07%	
Fixation duration – max	84.33%	
Saccade length – max	73.13%	
Fixation count – total	58.21%	Low
Saccade length – std	56.72%	
Fixation duration – std	53.73%	

Table 2: Most predictive metrics across all time-slots.

Regarding **Q_2**, we report the importance scores based on how much each metric contributes to making successful predictions. Since the classifier is constructed at each time-slot, we determine the features with the highest importance by averaging their scores across all time-slots, as in [32]. The averages are normalized so that the most important feature has a score of 100 (Table 2). Focusing on the FD-I style, our analysis on the accuracy of each class revealed that different metrics performed best for classifying the FDs and the FIs in terms of F-measure. For the classification of the FDs, the most effective metric was the saccade length (F = .795), while for the classification of the FIs, the most effective metric was the fixation count (F = .767). This could be attributed to the visual behavior differences between the FD and the FI individuals in terms of fixations and saccades, as FDs tend to produce more fixations than FIs [20,25], and they search in a more unarticulated and disoriented way [22,35], visually scanning different areas, producing saccades of larger length.

DISCUSSION

We explored the feasibility of building a classifier that identifies the user's FD-I cognitive style after collecting a few seconds of eye-gaze data during a graphical password composition task. Our classifier was based on the Logistic Regression model and outperformed the baseline classifier providing higher accuracy rates across time-slots. Focusing on the early time-slots (before the user drew the first gesture), the classifier achieved comparably similar accuracy with the accuracy towards the last time-slots.

Considering that studies have revealed effects of FD-I on password security [14] and usability [3], the classifier could be used to provide adaptive and/or assistive mechanisms for GUA schemes, such as the one described in [15], based on the individual cognitive styles elicited in real time. This could be used in combination with adaptive policies [28] to provide appropriate mechanisms for password composition and/or login. For example, given the less analytic nature of FDs, mechanisms that draw attention to overlooked areas of the background image could be used. On the other hand, given that FIs tend to pay attention to details, images could be blurred to deemphasize details and enable FIs to have a more holistic view of the image.

The results indicated that different eye-gaze metrics performed better for the FDs and the FIs, in terms of F-measure (precision and recall). Higher classification accuracy was achieved for the FDs when using the saccade length metric, whilst for the FIs when using the fixation count metric. This finding could drive the development of a mechanism based on combined classifiers, which could possibly achieve higher accuracies towards the FD-I classification. Furthermore, the classification mechanism could be complemented with more eye-gaze metrics and other interaction features to improve accuracy.

Study Validity and Limitations

Regarding internal validity, the study environment and the study procedure and instruments remained the same for all the participants. Focusing on the study instruments, we used GEFT to classify an individual as either FD or FI based on a cut-off score. Given that the GEFT test highlights cognitive differences along a continuum scale, the use of a cut-off might not classify correctly individuals that fall in between the two endpoints. However, the sample's mean GEFT score was comparable to general public scores across populations with varying demographics [1,11,16]. Regarding classification, further work towards selecting task-specific areas of interest could improve the classification accuracy. Regarding the external validity of the study, given that our approach is based mainly on eye-gaze metrics gathered and calculated in real time within a visual search task (i.e., password composition), we are positive that reasonably accurate predictions could be achieved for other visual search activities in GUA (e.g., recognition-based schemes) and other domains (e.g., gaming, automotive).

CONCLUSIONS

In this paper we investigated the feasibility of classifying users in real-time based on their FD-I style, using eye-tracking data during a graphical password composition task. Results revealed that classification is possible at the early stages of the task. Identifying the user's FD-I style early during graphical password composition could be used to introduce assistive mechanisms to help users make better password choices. The results are encouraging for further investigating various experimental designs for improving the accuracy of real-time cognitive style classifiers. A multi-level classification approach based on the combination of the FD-I most predictive metrics could be adopted during graphical password composition, to predict the users' FD-I style more accurately and assist them to create stronger and more memorable passwords.

ACKNOWLEDGMENTS

This paper was partially supported by the project ADVisE, in the frame of the University of Cyprus' internal funded research projects; the project SUCCESS, funded by the EU Active and Assisted Living Programme (KOINA/AAL/0216/10); the General Secretariat for Research and Technology (GSRT) and the Hellenic Foundation for Research and Innovation (H.F.R.I.) – 1st Proclamation of Scholarships for PhD Candidates / Code: 617.

REFERENCES

1. Charoula Angeli, Nicos Valanides, & Paul Kirschner. 2009. Field dependence–independence and instructional-design effects on learners' performance with a computer-modeling tool. *Computers in Human Behavior* 25, 6: 1355–1366. https://doi.org/10.1016/j.chb.2009.05.010
2. Marios Belk, Christos Fidas, Panagiotis Germanakos, and George Samaras. 2017. The Interplay between Humans, Technology and User Authentication: A Cognitive Processing Perspective. *Computers in Human Behavior*. https://doi.org/10.1016/j.chb.2017.06.042
3. Marios Belk, Christos Fidas, Christina Katsini, & George Avouris Nikolaos Samaras. 2017. *Effects of human cognitive differences on interaction and visual behavior in graphical user authentication.* https://doi.org/10.1007/978-3-319-67687-6_19
4. Natalie Clewley, Sherry Y. Chen, and Xiaohui Liu. 2009. Cognitive styles and web-based instruction: Field dependent/independent vs. Holist/Serialist. In *2009 IEEE International Conference on Systems, Man and Cybernetics*, 2074–2079. https://doi.org/10.1109/ICSMC.2009.5346314
5. Natalie Clewley, Sherry Y. Chen, and Xiaohui Liu. 2010. Cognitive styles and search engine preferences. *Journal of Documentation* 66, 4: 585–603. https://doi.org/10.1108/00220411011052966
6. Katherine M. Everitt, Tanya Bragin, James Fogarty, and Tadayoshi Kohno. 2009. A comprehensive study of frequency, interference, and training of multiple graphical passwords. In *Proceedings of the 27th international conference on Human factors in computing systems - CHI 09*, 889. https://doi.org/10.1145/1518701.1518837
7. Enrique Frias-Martinez, Sherry Y. Chen, and Xiaohui Liu. 2007. Automatic cognitive style identification of digital library users for personalization. *Journal of the American Society for Information Science and Technology* 58, 2: 237–251. https://doi.org/10.1002/asi.20477
8. Joseph H. Goldberg and Jonathan I. Helfman. 2010. Comparing information graphics. In *Proceedings of the 3rd BELIV'10 Workshop on BEyond time and errors: novel evaLuation methods for Information Visualization - BELIV '10*, 71–78. https://doi.org/10.1145/2110192.2110203
9. Mark Hall, Eibe Frank, Geoffrey Holmes, Bernhard Pfahringer, Peter Reutemann, and Ian H. Witten. 2009. The WEKA data mining software. *ACM SIGKDD Explorations Newsletter* 11, 1: 10. https://doi.org/10.1145/1656274.1656278
10. Limor Hochberg, Cecilia Ovesdotter Alm, Esa M Rantanen, Qi Yu, Caroline M Delong, Anne Haake, and Cecilia O Alm. 2014. Towards Automatic Annotation of Clinical Decision-Making Style. *Proceedings of LAW VIII - The 8th Linguistic Annotation Workshop*: 129–138.
11. Jon Chao Hong, Ming Yueh Hwang, Ker Ping Tam, Yi Hsuan Lai, and Li Chun Liu. 2012. Effects of cognitive style on digital jigsaw puzzle performance: A GridWare analysis. *Computers in Human Behavior* 28, 3: 920–928. https://doi.org/10.1016/j.chb.2011.12.012
12. L. Huestegge and L. Pimenidis. 2014. Visual Search in Authentication Systems Based on Memorized Faces: Effects of Memory Load and Retention Interval. *International Journal of Human-Computer Interaction* 30, 7: 604–611. https://doi.org/10.1080/10447318.2014.907464
13. Jeffrey Jay Johnson, Steve Seixeiro, Zachary Pace, Giles van der Bogert, Sean Gilmour, Levi Siebens, and Kenneth Tubbs. 2014. Picture Gesture Authentication.
14. Christina Katsini, Christos Fidas, Marios Belk, Nikolaos Avouris, & George Samaras. 2017. Influences of Users' Cognitive Strategies on Graphical Password Composition. In *Proceedings of the 2017 CHI Conference Extended Abstracts on Human Factors in Computing Systems - CHI EA '17*, 2698–2705. https://doi.org/10.1145/3027063.3053217
15. Christina Katsini, Christos Fidas, George E Raptis, Marios Belk, George Samaras, and Nikolaos Avouris. 2018. Influences of Human Cognition and Visual Behavior on Password Security during Picture Password Composition. In *CHI 2018: CHI Conference on Human Factors in Computing.* https://doi.org/10.1145/3173574.3173661
16. Mohammad Khatib and Rasoul Mohammad Hosseinpur. 2011. On the Validity of the Group Embedded Figure Test (GEFT). *Journal of Language Teaching and Research* 2, 3. https://doi.org/10.4304/jltr.2.3.640-648
17. Oleg V Komogortsev, Denise V Gobert, Sampath Jayarathna, Do Hyong Koh, and Sandeep M Gowda. 2010. Standardization of Automated Analyses of Oculomotor Fixation and Saccadic Behaviors. *IEEE Transactions on Biomedical Engineering* 57, 11: 2635–2645. https://doi.org/10.1109/TBME.2010.2057429
18. Franco Mawad, Marcela Trías, Ana Giménez, Alejandro Maiche, and Gastón Ares. 2015. Influence of cognitive style on information processing and selection of yogurt labels: Insights from an eye-tracking study. *Food Research International* 74: 1–9. https://doi.org/10.1016/j.foodres.2015.04.023
19. William Melicher, Michelle L. Mazurek, Darya Kurilova, Sean M. Segreti, Pranshu Kalvani, Richard Shay, Blase Ur, Lujo Bauer, Nicolas Christin, and Lorrie Faith Cranor. 2016. Usability and Security of Text Passwords on Mobile Devices. In *Proceedings of the 2016 CHI Conference on Human Factors in Computing Systems - CHI '16*, 527–539. https://doi.org/10.1145/2858036.2858384

20. Efi A. Nisiforou and Andrew Laghos. 2013. Do the eyes have it? Using eye tracking to assess students cognitive dimensions. *Educational Media International* 50, 4: 247–265. https://doi.org/10.1080/09523987.2013.862363
21. Efi A. Nisiforou, Eleni Michailidou, and Andrew Laghos. 2014. Using Eye Tracking to Understand the Impact of Cognitive Abilities on Search Tasks. . 46–57. https://doi.org/10.1007/978-3-319-07509-9_5
22. Efi Nisiforou and Andrew Laghos. 2016. Field Dependence–Independence and Eye Movement Patterns: Investigating Users' Differences Through an Eye Tracking Study. *Interacting with Computers* 28, 4: 407–420. https://doi.org/10.1093/iwc/iwv015
23. Philip K Oltman, Evelyn Raskin, and Herman A. Witkin. 1971. *Group Embedded Figures Test*. Consulting Psychologists Press, Palo Alto CA, USA.
24. George E. Raptis, Christos A. Fidas, and Nikolaos M. Avouris. 2016. Differences of Field Dependent / Independent Gamers on Cultural Heritage Playing : Preliminary Findings of an Eye – Tracking Study. . Springer International Publishing, 1–8. https://doi.org/10.1007/978-3-319-48974-2_22
25. George E. Raptis, Christos A. Fidas, and Nikolaos M. Avouris. 2016. Using Eye Tracking to Identify Cognitive Differences. *Proceedings of the 20th Pan-Hellenic Conference on Informatics - PCI '16*: 1–6. https://doi.org/10.1145/3003733.3003762
26. George E. Raptis, Christina Katsini, Marios Belk, Christos Fidas, George Samaras, and Nikolaos Avouris. 2017. Using Eye Gaze Data and Visual Activities to Infer Human Cognitive Styles: Method and Feasibility Studies. In *Proceedings of the 25th Conference on User Modeling, Adaptation and Personalization - UMAP '17*, 164–173. https://doi.org/10.1145/3079628.3079690
27. George E Raptis, Christos A Fidas, and Nikolaos M Avouris. 2016. Do Field Dependence-Independence Differences of Game Players Affect Performance and Behaviour in Cultural Heritage Games? In *Proceedings of the 2016 Annual Symposium on Computer-Human Interaction in Play - CHI PLAY '16*, 38–43. https://doi.org/10.1145/2967934.2968107
28. Sean M. Segreti, William Melicher, Saranga Komanduri, Darya Melicher, Richard Shay, Blase Ur, Lujo Bauer, Nicolas Christin, Lorrie Faith Cranor, and Michelle L. Mazurek. 2017. Diversify to Survive: Making Passwords Stronger with Adaptive Policies. *The Proceedings of the Thirteenth Symposium on Usable Privacy and Security (SOUPS 2017)*: 1–12.
29. Ben Steichen, Giuseppe Carenini, and Cristina Conati. 2013. User-adaptive information visualization. In *Proceedings of the 2013 international conference on Intelligent user interfaces - IUI '13*, 317. https://doi.org/10.1145/2449396.2449439
30. Ben Steichen, Michael M a Wu, Dereck Toker, Cristina Conati, and Giuseppe Carenini. 2014. Te,Te,Hi,Hi: Eye gaze sequence analysis for informing user-adaptive information visualizations. *Lecture Notes in Computer Science (including subseries Lecture Notes in Artificial Intelligence and Lecture Notes in Bioinformatics)* 8538: 183–194. https://doi.org/10.1007/978-3-319-08786-3_16
31. Tobii AB. Tobii Pro Glasses Analyzer User's Manual.
32. Dereck Toker, Sébastien Lallé, and Cristina Conati. 2017. Pupillometry and Head Distance to the Screen to Predict Skill Acquisition During Information Visualization Tasks. In *Proceedings of the 22nd International Conference on Intelligent User Interfaces - IUI '17*, 221–231. https://doi.org/10.1145/3025171.3025187
33. Dereck Toker, Ben Steichen, Matthew Gingerich, Cristina Conati, and Giuseppe Carenini. 2014. Towards facilitating user skill acquisition. In *Proceedings of the 19th international conference on Intelligent User Interfaces - IUI '14*, 105–114. https://doi.org/10.1145/2557500.2557524
34. Yi Wang, Jalal Mahmud, Taikun Liu, I B M Research-almaden, Harry Road, and San Jose. 2016. Understanding Cognitive Styles from User-Generated Social Media Content. In *Proceedings of the Tenth International AAAI Conference on Web and Social Media (ICWSM 2016)*.
35. James L. C. Wijnen and Cees J. Groot. 1984. An eye movement analysis system (EMAS) for the identification of cognitive processes on figural tasks. *Behavior Research Methods, Instruments, & Computers* 16, 3: 277–281. https://doi.org/10.3758/BF03202402
36. Herman. A. Witkin, Carol A. Moore, Donald R. Goodenough, and Patricia W. Cox. 1975. Field-Dependent and Field-Independent Cognitive Styles and their Educational Implications. *ETS Research Bulletin Series* 1975, 2: 1–64. https://doi.org/10.1002/j.2333-8504.1975.tb01065.x
37. Anatoly Yelizarov and Dennis Gamayunov. 2014. Adaptive Visualization Interface That Manages User's Cognitive Load Based on Interaction Characteristics. In *Proceedings of the 7th International Symposium on Visual Information Communication and Interaction - VINCI '14*, 1–8. https://doi.org/10.1145/2636240.2636844

Detecting Low Rapport During Natural Interactions in Small Groups from Non-Verbal Behaviour

Philipp Müller
Max Planck Institute for Informatics, Saarland Informatics Campus
pmueller@mpi-inf.mpg.de

Michael Xuelin Huang
Max Planck Institute for Informatics, Saarland Informatics Campus
mhuang@mpi-inf.mpg.de

Andreas Bulling
Max Planck Institute for Informatics, Saarland Informatics Campus
bulling@mpi-inf.mpg.de

ABSTRACT
Rapport, the close and harmonious relationship in which interaction partners are "in sync" with each other, was shown to result in smoother social interactions, improved collaboration, and improved interpersonal outcomes. In this work, we are first to investigate automatic prediction of low rapport during natural interactions within small groups. This task is challenging given that rapport only manifests in subtle non-verbal signals that are, in addition, subject to influences of group dynamics as well as inter-personal idiosyncrasies. We record videos of unscripted discussions of three to four people using a multi-view camera system and microphones. We analyse a rich set of non-verbal signals for rapport detection, namely facial expressions, hand motion, gaze, speaker turns, and speech prosody. Using facial features, we can detect low rapport with an average precision of 0.7 (chance level at 0.25), while incorporating prior knowledge of participants' personalities can even achieve early prediction without a drop in performance. We further provide a detailed analysis of different feature sets and the amount of information contained in different temporal segments of the interactions.

Author Keywords
Social Signal Processing; Affective Computing; Facial Expressions; Body Posture; Speech Prosody; Personality Traits; Leadership; Dominance

INTRODUCTION
Inter-personal conflicts are pervasive and can happen in a variety of social settings, from festivals, to family gatherings, to a bar or the classroom. Many of these conflicts are the result of low rapport between interaction or conversation partners, or more specifically, the failure of a person to establish good rapport. While a precise definition is difficult, rapport refers to the close and harmonious relationship in which interaction partners are "in sync" and can interact naturally and smoothly with each other. Failure to build rapport can lead to mutual

IUI'18, March 7–11, 2018, Tokyo, Japan

ISBN 978-1-4503-4945-1/18/03...$15.00

DOI: https://doi.org/10.1145/3172944.3172969

Figure 1. Example images of natural behaviours from the dataset.

feelings of disharmony or, in the worst case, even verbal or physical hostility. The fundamental importance of rapport for social interactions underlines the significant potential of developing intelligent user interfaces that are able to detect low rapport and to reduce or even avoid inter-personal conflicts.

While several previous works in social signal processing and affective computing investigated automatic detection of rapport during *dyadic* (person-person or person-machine) interactions from verbal and non-verbal behaviour [10, 20, 46, 48], few works studied the link between non-verbal behaviour and rapport in larger groups [29]. No attempt has so far been made to automatically detect low rapport in *multi-person* interaction settings. This is despite the fact that much of our social life takes place in groups larger than two people, e.g. in business meetings or friend gatherings. Detecting low rapport and performing an early intervention to avoid social conflicts can therefore have a significant and practical impact.

We present the first study on detecting the failure to establish rapport in natural multi-person interactions with a small number of people. Given that no dataset exists that comprises small group interactions as well as annotations of felt rapport, we record a new dataset (see Figure 1 for example images). Based on this dataset, we then develop a multimodal approach to automatically detect low rapport from non-verbal behaviour. Our approach is based on state-of-the-art methods to analyse facial expression and posture, as well as speech activities and prosodic features. We further propose new features that exploit the mirroring effect by accounting for behaviour synchronisation among group members as well as cross-modal features that delineate simultaneous actions from different modalities. Our results show that while facial features perform best when the full interaction is observed, prior information about participants' personalities can boost facial features to achieve the same performance while observing only the first third of the whole interaction.

The specific contributions of our work are three-fold: 1) We collect the first dataset for small group interactions with informative audio-visual signals and rich annotations, including *felt rapport*, perceived leadership, dominance, competence and liking of the dyads in the group. 2) We propose a multimodal approach to low rapport detection that exploits both dyadic audiovisual information, such as facial action units and speech prosody, as well as group information, such as cross-modal features and mirroring effects, and potential prior knowledge of the participants' personalities. 3) We provide an in-depth performance evaluation of our method and identify key features and time segments that are most important for rapport detection in this setting.

RELATED WORK

We first summarise prior works that aimed to predict social aspects in multi-person interactions. We then focus on rapport as a particularly important social aspect, followed by computational methods to predict rapport in dyadic interactions.

Automatic Analysis of Multi-Person Interactions

While a major part of research in social signal processing and affective computing focuses on the analysis of dyadic interactions [8, 33, 38], a growing body of work on multi-person interactions has developed in recent years. Among the social concepts that have been studied in multi-person interactions from a computational perspective are turn-taking [6, 30, 39], laughter [32], general interest level of the group [18], and engagement of individuals inside the group [36]. Cohesion is one of the more abstract concepts and describes the tendency of group members to create social bonds and stay united as a group. Cohesion is commonly understood as a global measure given by each interactant to the whole group. In contrast, rapport can be measured for each pair of people within a group and can thus provide a more detailed picture of intra-group relations. Hung and Gatica-Perez analysed audio, visual and audio-visual cues to predict cohesion levels in small groups using annotations from external observers [24]. More recently, Nanninga et al. specifically focused on the connection between group mimicry and task cohesion [34]. Other works focused on leadership and listener behaviour. Automatic recognition of emergent leaders is particularly relevant given that those leaders emerge from the interaction among group members (as opposed to designated leaders). The prediction of perceived leadership alongside dominance, competence and liking in groups of three to four people was also studied using information on speaking activity and speech prosody as well as activity of the body and head [5, 41]. Other works aimed to differentiate instructed considerate from authoritarian leadership styles [17] or, more recently, naturally emerging autocratic or democratic behaviour [5]. Classification of group members into attentive listeners, side participants, and bystanders was studied in [35].

In summary, while a number of works studied different prediction tasks in multi-person interactions, some of which are related to rapport, to the best of our knowledge we are first to predict rapport in a multi-person setting.

Rapport

Among the different concepts of social interactions, rapport is arguably one of the most fundamental and thus important. Failure to build rapport can result in poor social interactions, decreased collaboration, and worse interpersonal outcomes [7, 28, 44]. In an early work, Tickle-Degnen and Rosenthal identified three components that are important for rapport: attention, positivity, and coordination [43]. The importance of these components can change over the course of a relationship as can the expression of components of rapport. For example, insults can help build rapport in later stages of a relationship [37]. Izard hypothesised connections between personality traits and the ability to build rapport [25]. For example, people with high extraversion were deemed to find it easier to build rapport given that they might more easily focus their attention on others. Furthermore, people with a tendency towards negative emotions might not be able to express the positivity component of rapport strongly enough.

Research on the link between dyadic rapport and non-verbal behaviour is extensive, so we only discuss two representative works. Harrigan, Oxman and Rosenthal analysed rapport ratings for physicians obtained from nurses [21]. They found that physicians sitting with uncrossed legs and arms in symmetrical side-by-side positions directly facing the patient received higher rapport ratings. Bernieri et al. conducted an important analysis on dyad rapport and its judgement across different situations [4]. When comparing subjective rapport ratings with ratings by external observers they found that observers had a hard time rating rapport consistently with the participants who experienced the situation. Further analyses showed that while observer judgements were mainly based on the amount of expressiveness, self-ratings were adapted to the specific situation at hand. These results indicate that observer ratings of rapport are not adapted to the specific situation. We therefore opted to use self-reported rapport ratings in this work.

Predicting Rapport in Dyadic Interactions

Computational approaches to rapport prediction focused on dyadic interactions, typically with the motivation to develop artificial agents that are able to build rapport with users. The first line of work investigated non-verbal cues for rapport prediction. For example, Wang and Gratch used selected facial action units (AU) to predict felt rapport in human-human and human-agent interactions [46]. They found that felt rapport was encoded in the absence of AUs encoding negative emotions rather than in the presence of AUs indicating positive emotions. Hagad et al. used participants' postures and their congruences to predict rapport in dyadic interactions [20]. Other works used verbal cues or mixtures of non-verbal and verbal cues for rapport prediction. A recent study by Cerekovic et al. focused on predicting self-reported and observer-rated rapport between humans and virtual agents using verbal and non-verbal cues [10]. The results showed that self-reported rapport is rather weakly correlated with observer-judged rapport, and also harder to predict than the latter. Zhao et al. applied temporal pattern mining to extract rules for rapport management in dyads of peer-tutoring strangers and friends [47, 48]. An example of such a rule indicative of high rapport in friend dyads is the verbal violation of a social norm by one interactant while in parallel her friend is smiling. Finally, bonding is a concept related to rapport and has recently been studied in the context of dyadic human-human and human-agent interactions [27], also depending on personality [26].

A DATASET OF SMALL-GROUP INTERACTIONS

Given the lack of suitable datasets for the development and evaluation of algorithms for rapport detection, we designed a human study to collect audio-visual non-verbal behaviour data and rapport ratings during small group interactions. Our dataset consists of 22 group discussions in German, each involving either three or four participants and each lasting about 20 minutes, resulting in a total of more than 440 minutes of audio-visual data.

Recording Setup

The data recording took place in a quiet office in which a larger area was cleared of existing furniture. The office was not used by anybody else during the recordings. To capture rich visual information and allow for natural bodily expressions, we used a 4DV camera system to record frame-synchronised video from eight ambient cameras. Specifically, two cameras were placed behind each participant and with a position slightly higher than the head of the participant (see the green indicators in Figure 2). With this configuration a near-frontal view of the face of each participant could be captured throughout the experiment, even if participants turned their head while interacting with each other. In addition, we used four Behringer B5 microphones with omnidirectional capsules for recording audio. To record high-quality audio data and avoid occlusion of the faces, we placed the microphones in front of but slightly above participants (see the blue indicators in Figure 2). To synchronise the audio and video streams, we clapped our hands before and after every recording session.

Recording Procedure

We recruited 78 German-speaking participants (43 female, aged between 18 and 38 years) from a German university campus, resulting in 12 group interactions with four participants, and 10 interactions with three participants. During the group forming process, we ensured that participants in the same group did not know each other prior to the study. To prevent learning effects, every participant took part in only one interaction.

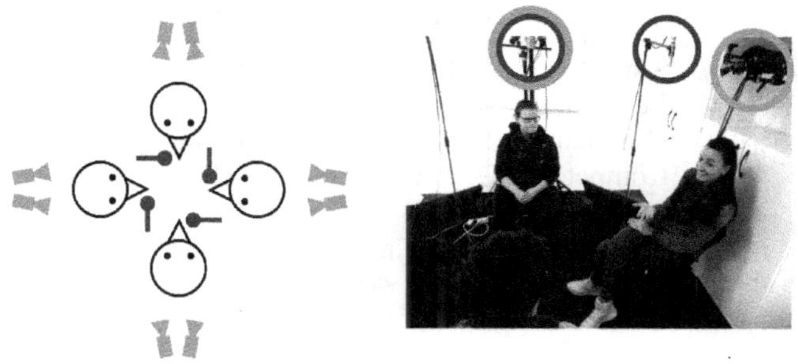

Figure 2. Illustration of camera and microphone positions during a recording session with four participants. Cameras are shown in green, and microphones in blue. Please note all the equipment was placed slightly above the participants to avoid occlusion for video recording.

Preceding each group interaction, we told the participants that first personal encounters could result in various artifacts that we were not interested in. As a result, we would first do a pilot discussion for them to get to know each other, followed by the actual recording. We intentionally misled the participant to believe that the recording system would be turned on only *after* the pilot discussion, so that they would behave naturally. In fact, however, the recording system was running from the beginning and there was no follow-up recording. To increase engagement, we prepared a list of potential discussion topics and asked each group to choose the topic that was most controversial among group members. Afterwards, the experimenter left the room and came back about 20 minutes later to end the discussion. Participants were then asked to complete several questionnaires about the other groups members as described below. Finally, participants were debriefed, in particular about the deceit, and gave free and informed consent to their data being used and published for research purposes.

Data Annotation Using Questionnaires

Although in this work we were only interested in detection of low rapport, with a view to potential other future uses of our dataset, participants were asked to complete three questionnaires about different social aspects relevant for small group interactions. All questionnaires were given in German to increase comprehension of the questions and, in turn, obtain more reliable scores.

- *Rapport:* Since rapport is a subjective feeling that is hard to gauge through any existing equipment, we followed previous practice using an 18-item-questionnaire [4] to measure rapport from self reports. Responses were recorded on seven point Likert scales. Each participant rated each item for other individuals in the group, yielding two rapport scores for each dyad inside the larger group.

- *Leadership, Dominance, Competence, and Liking:* We were also interested in the correlation between rapport and other well-studied aspects in small group interactions. We thus asked participants to complete the questionnaire used in [41] that consists of 12 questions about four different sub-scales (leadership, dominance, competence, and liking) which we recorded using seven-point Likert scales.

	Means	Standard Deviations
Rapport	5.41	0.46
Leadership	3.71	0.94
Dominance	4.14	0.96
Competence	5.22	0.87
Liking	5.81	0.56

Table 1. Means and standard deviations of the aggregated annotations obtained from seven-point Likert scales.

- *Personality:* Finally, each participant also completed the well-established NEO-FFI questionnaire to assess personality traits, including openness to experience, conscientiousness, extraversion, agreeableness, and neuroticism [13].

Given that we were mainly interested in the overall degree to which a participant is able to build rapport with others, we aggregated the rapport scores for a target participant by averaging those given to him by the other participants in the group. Consequently, a low rapport score indicates that a particular participant did not evoke the feeling of rapport in general for the other participants. We processed the other annotations in the same way (leadership, dominance, competence and liking).

Dataset Statistics

Table 1 summarises the means and standard deviations of the questionnaire responses over all participants. Especially for liking, competence and rapport we can observe a tendency towards higher ratings. A more fine-grained depiction of the distribution of rapport scores is shown in Figure 3, which shows a tendency towards a left-skewed distribution with a peak at 5.6 and most scores between 5.0 and 6.0. The bias towards higher values in questionnaires which involve a potentially more hurtful evaluation of others (liking, competence and rapport in contrast to leadership and dominance) might be due to a general social desirability bias [31]. Given that we were particularly interested in low rapport, we grouped the data with the lower 25% percentile of rapport scores as "low rapport" and the rest as "high rapport". This results in 11 interactions without a low-rapport participant (seven of them are three-participant interactions), four interactions with a single low-rapport participant (two three-participant interactions), six interactions with two low-rapport participants (one three-participant interaction), and one interaction with three low-rapport participants (four-participant interaction).

The diversity of the dataset in terms of participants' behaviour can be illustrated, for example, by the portion of time they spoke and smiled. Figure 4 shows the histogram of the portion of speaking time (blue bars). While most participants spoke around 10% to 40% of the time per discussion, several participants spoke less than 10% or more than 50% of the time. Moreover, the amount of smiling is highly diverse across participants (see Figure 4, transparent green bars). While some participants hardly smiled at all, others smiled almost constantly. Table 2 shows the average activation AUs across participants. Inspecting the standard deviations, we can see that there is substantial variability in participants' average level of AU activations.

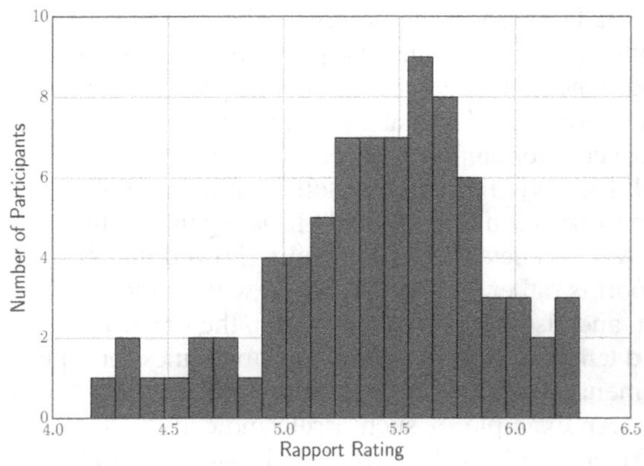

Figure 3. Histogram of the number of participants (y-axis) against the average received rapport ratings from other participants in an interaction (x-axis).

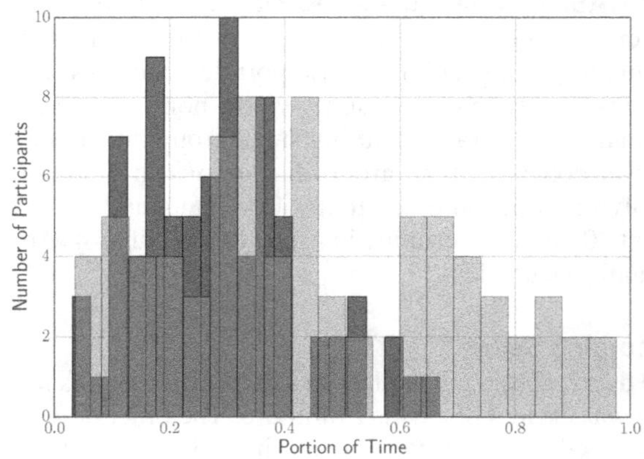

Figure 4. Histogram of the number of participants (y-axis) against the portion of time that participants are speaking (blue bars) and smiling (transparent green bars; detected by AU12) during the interactions.

MULTIMODAL METHOD WITH NON-VERBAL FEATURES

Our multimodal approach to detecting low rapport relies on non-verbal features only, rather than word-related features. Specifically, it considers facial expression, hand motion, speech activity, and prosodic features. In addition, we also exploit synchronisation features and cross-modal features. The following subsections discuss each of these feature sets.

Non-Verbal Features

Speech Activity Features

Turn-taking is an important attribute in conversations, and there may be a potential link between the turn-taking behaviour in group discussion and felt rapport, for example via reflecting aspects of the coordination component of rapport [43]. To extract speech activity features, we annotate speaking turns from all recordings. Based on this information, we compute several features that encode the duration and frequency with which participants speak, and also different characteristics of turn-taking (see Table 3).

AU	1	2	4	5	6	7	9	10	12	14	15	17	20	23	25	26	45
μ	0.18	0.25	0.36	0.53	0.34	0.43	0.07	0.70	0.44	0.59	0.27	0.39	0.20	0.47	0.20	0.15	0.21
σ	0.08	0.10	0.26	0.25	0.26	0.27	0.06	0.24	0.25	0.26	0.10	0.12	0.10	0.22	0.08	0.07	0.07

Table 2. Statistics for average AU activations of all extracted AUs when the participant is not speaking.

Modalities	Notation	Feature Description
Speech Activity	$TimeSpeak$	The portion of time the target participant speaks
	$TimeTurn$	The average length of speaking turns
	$RateTurn$	The number of speaking turns per minute
	$ProbTurn \mid TurnTrans$	Probability of taking the turn at turn transition
Prosody	$PRSx$	Set of 768 prosodic features based on IS09 challenge feature set from [16]
Face	$PosiFace^{\mu/\sigma}$	Mean and stddev of facial positivity indicator
	$PosiFace_{200s}^{\mu/\sigma}$	Mean and stddev of facial positivity indicator during the beginning 200 seconds
	$PosiFace^{sync}$	Amount of synchronisation of facial positivity indicator with other participants
	$Facing$	How much other participants are facing the target participant
	$MutualFacing$	Amount of mutual facing with other participants
	AUx	Mean intensity of AUx
	AUx_{200s}	Mean intensity of AUx during the beginning 200 seconds
	AUx^{sync}	Amount of synchronisation of intensity of AUx with other participants
	AU^{sync}	Average amount of synchronisation of all AU intensities
	$ProbAUx$	Probability of AUx being active
	$ProbAUx_{200s}$	Probability of AUx being active during the beginning 200 seconds
	$ProbAUx^{sync}$	Amount of synchronisation of AUx activation with other participants
	$ProbAU^{sync}$	Average amount of synchronisation of all AU activations
Face and Speech Activity	$AUx_{target \mid targetSpeak}$	Mean intensity of AUx of target participant when he/she is speaking
	$AUx_{target \mid targetNotSpeak}$	Mean intensity of AUx of target participant when he/she is not speaking
	$AUx_{other \mid targetSpeak}$	Average mean intensity of AUx of other participants when target participant is speaking
	$AUx_{target \mid otherSpeak}$	Average mean intensity of AUx of target participant when another participant is speaking
	$ProbAUx_{target \mid targetSpeak}$	Probability of AUx of target participant being active when he/she is speaking
	$ProbAUx_{target \mid targetNotSpeak}$	Probability of AUx of target participant being active when he/she is not speaking
	$ProbAUx_{other \mid targetSpeak}$	Average probability of AUx being active in other participants when target participant is speaking
	$ProbAUx_{target \mid otherSpeak}$	Average probability of AUx being active in target participants when another participant is speaking
Hand Motion	$VelHand$	Average velocity of hands
	$VelHand^{sync}$	Amount of synchronisation of hand velocity with other participants
Hand Motion and Speech Activity	$VelHand_{target \mid targetSpeak}$	Average hand velocity of target participant when he/she is speaking

Table 3. Feature notations and descriptions of different modalities.

Prosodic Speech Features

Apart from the speech activity features, we extract a set of prosodic speech features using openSmile [16]. We choose the feature set used for the IS09 emotion challenge, as it is a rather small feature set (384 features) and we assume effective features for emotion recognition might also be helpful for rapport detection. The features are extracted from individual segments when the participant speaks, and then aggregated over all segments of a speaker by taking the mean and the standard deviation, resulting in 768 features.

Facial Features

Facial expressions convey informative visual cues of emotions, and they are an important non-verbal channel to express one's feelings and views. Therefore, we include facial expression as one of our main features for rapport detection.

Our facial features include head orientations as well as the activation/intensity of facial action units (AUs), and additionally some higher-level facial features built on top of these basic concepts. For example, we incorporate features encoding aspects of all three components of rapport suggested by Tickle-Degnen and Rosenthal [43]. They include 1) the amount of positivity, 2) interpersonal synchronisation/coordination, and 3) mutual attention reflected by head orientations. An overview of the facial features is given in Table 3.

In practice, we used OpenFace [2]. It is an automatic tool for facial expression analysis that identifies facial landmarks, head pose, and the activation/intensity level of the 17 facial AUs displayed in Table 2 from a video. As there are four cameras that cover the face of each participant from different angles, we extract the facial information from all four videos. Based on the confidence scores given by OpenFace, we selected the best view for each frame and use the facial AUs in this view for further analysis and recognition. This procedure results in high OpenFace confidence scores (>0.8 on a scale from 0 to 1) in almost all frames (97%).

Facial positivity is computed following previous practice [11]. The facial positivity indicator *PosiFace* for the target participant is set to 1, if AU12 is active, and -1 if AU15 is active in conjunction with at least one of AU1 and AU4 [11]. *PosiFace* is set to 0, when none of the above holds, or when both the positivity (AU12) and negativity AUs (AU1, AU4, AU15) are active. To reflect the intuition that the first minutes of a discussion are special, as the participants are just getting to know each other, we include additional versions of the above features that only take into account the first 200 seconds of the interaction (e.g. AUx_{200s}). Face orientation features (*Facing* and *MutualFacing*) are constructed by thresholding of the face orientation estimated from the frontal view of the target participant. Additionally, we extract various features to describe the synchronisation of facial expressions among participants. The general approach to computing synchronisation of features between participants is detailed below.

Synchronisation Features

Inspired by the findings that 1) mirroring is an important phenomenon that can reflect rapport and facilitate the building of rapport [3] and that 2) synchronisation/coordination is one of three basic components of rapport [43], we build features to delineate the amount of behavioural synchronisation between participants. To measure the feature synchronisation of two participants, we compute the distance between the pair of feature signals using Dynamic Time Warping (DTW) with a Sakoe-Chiba band of five seconds [40, 11]. We then compute the amount of synchronisation of a target participant i with all other participants in the interaction, by averaging the DTW distances of the target participant to others. In other words, for a feature signal F_i, the resulting average synchronisation is $\sum_{j\in N\setminus\{i\}} \mathrm{DTW}(F_i, F_j)$, where N is the set of all participants in the interaction where the target participant i takes part, and DTW denotes the DTW function.

Hand Motion Features

Body posture and its coordination among people can be indicative of rapport [3]. Since in our study setup all the participants were sitting, we focuse on hand motion. We use the multi-person pose estimation method OpenPose [9] to extract poses from videos. OpenPose extracts the joint locations of the human body from the 2D video data. Based on the frames in which both hands are detected (on average 77%), we compute several features, such as the total amount of hand movement for each participant as well as the synchronisation of hand movements between participants (see Table 3 for details).

Cross-Modal Features

In addition to the unimodal features described above, prior research pointed out that the coordination between different modalities, such as gaze-hand coordination, can reflect human mental states [23]. Moreover, cross-modal features have been applied in the context of leadership prediction [5].

We design a number of cross-modal features, specifically to encode participants' evaluation of each other by analysing their facial expressions while others are speaking, and also to compensate for the influence on AU detection during speaking. These features include 1) AU activations and intensities while the participant is speaking or not speaking, 2) average AU activations and intensities of all other participants while the target participant is speaking, and 3) AU activations and intensities of the target participant while other participants are speaking. Apart from AUs, we combine hand motion information with speech activity into a feature that measures the amount of hand movement while the participant is speaking. This feature is intended to encode how much a participant is gesticulating during speaking.

Learning Low Rapport Using an Ensemble of SVMs

We train Support Vector Machines (SVM) with radial basis function kernels to classify participants' received rapport ratings into low versus medium-to-high rapport. The cost parameter C of SVM is tuned in a nested inner validation loop. We use a leave-one-interaction-out cross-validation scheme to evaluate the performance of our models. As a performance metric, we choose average precision (AP), which is common for detection problems, as it is better suited to measure the performance of models on data with class imbalances than, for example, accuracy. The necessary ranking of test examples is obtained by using probability estimates of the SVM. To marginalise out any fluctuations due to random initializations of the SVM optimisation method, we train 1,000 SVMs, from which we extract ensemble predictions by averaging.

EXPERIMENTAL RESULTS

In the experimental evaluation of our proposed approach to low rapport detection, we quantify the contribution of different feature sets and individual features, as well as the amount of information that can be exploited from different temporal segments of an interaction. Finally, we show additional results concerning the relation of rapport to other previously investigated concepts in small groups.

Identifying Important Feature Sets

To understand the contribution of different modalities to recognition of low rapport, we evaluate our approach with different subsets of features. Figure 5 shows the performance comparison. The x-axis presents different feature sets. Bars with different colour represent the performances of models using different temporal segments for feature extraction, i.e. from the whole interaction (blue), and the first (yellow), middle

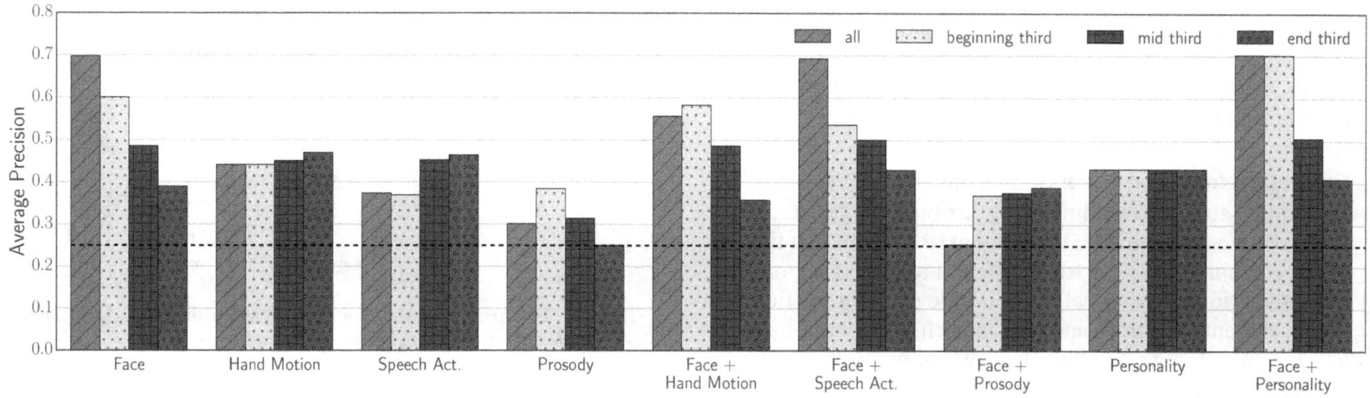

Figure 5. Performance of different feature sets (groups along x-axis) across temporal segments for feature extraction (colour). From left to right, the first four groups indicate the performances using unimodal feature sets, followed by three groups of performances using two modalities, and another two using personality and with facial features. The dotted line indicates the performance of a random predictor.

(red), and last (purple) third of the interaction. Since we define the 25 percentile of our data with the lowest score as low rapport, the baseline method (dashed line) that ranks the test data randomly results in 0.25 AP.

In this subsection, we focus on results on full interaction data only (blue bars), for which the overall highest performance is achieved by facial features (0.7 AP). They perform significantly better than the other unimodal feature sets (see the first four groups in Figure 5). However, hand motion, speech activity and prosodic feature sets can also outperform the baseline (0.37, 0.44, 0.30 AP, respectively), indicating that each modality carries a certain amount of useful information for low rapport detection.

Surprisingly, adding additional features to the facial features does not further improve the performance for whole-interaction data. Specifically, adding speech activity and cross-modal combinations of speech activity and facial features (Face + Speech Act.) achieves a comparable result (0.69) to Face alone (0.7). The combination of face and hand motion features (Face + Hand Motion) produces an AP of 0.56, whereas combining face and speech activity (Face + Speech Act.) or prosodic features (Face + Prosody) yields a baseline performance. All possible further combinations of feature sets fail to improve performance. This result implies that facial features play an important role for rapport detection in group interactions.

To further understand which types of facial features lead to good performance, we perform an ablation analysis (see Figure 6). Firstly, we split face features into four groups: 1) synchronisation features, 2) non-synchronisation features, 3) without using facial features extracted in the beginning 200s of each interaction, and 4) using only those features that were extracted in the first 200s of an interaction. Surprisingly, it turns out that facial features without synchronisation even outperform Face (comprising both sync and non-sync features), though with a marginal improvement (0.72 AP). In contrast, facial features with synchronisation only result in 0.53 AP. Thus, although facial synchronisation features carry a certain amount of information about rapport, the mirroring and behavioural

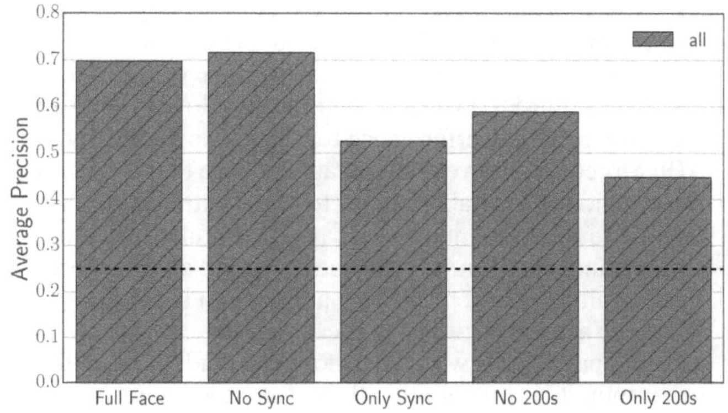

Figure 6. Results of ablation studies on facial feature set. From left to right: full set of facial features, without synchronisation features, only synchronisation features, without features extracted from the beginning 200s, only features extracted from the beginning 200s.

coordination effects encoded in them are not indicative enough to improve over the basic facial features. Still, it could be possible that mirroring of particular member(s), or at particular points in time in the interaction (e.g. while speaking), may have a stronger indication of rapport, which needs further investigation. We also see that including the features extracted from the beginning 200s contribute to an improvement (Face vs. No 200s), though using these features alone has a low AP (0.45). This indicates that features extracted at the beginning of an interaction have a special relation to rapport, complementary to features extracted from the full interaction.

Finally, we study how well low rapport can be predicted from personality scores, a factor that can be measured without observing the actual interaction. To this end, we train a SVM on NEO-FFI scores of the target participants, which leads to an AP of 0.43. Although training on personality scores alone does not give a high rapport recognition performance, it can clearly outperform the baseline (0.25), and even speech activity (0.37) and prosodic features (0.30), and yields a comparable result with that of hand motion (0.44) from the actual interaction. This finding is interesting, as it indicates that if an intelligent user interface can gather information on personal traits, e.g. from a personal device, there is a high chance that it can make a correct prediction of rapport in a future group interaction even without access to the actual interaction signals.

Prediction from Temporal Segments

In addition to understanding the contribution of different feature sets, we also evaluate the amount of information that our method is able to exploit from different temporal segments of the interactions. Specifically, we divide each interaction into three segments and train and test on each segment of the interactions only. Figure 5 shows the average precisions achieved in these three cases (yellow, red, and purple bars).

For our best-performing feature set on full recordings, facial features without synchronisation features, we can observe a clear trend that the amount of useful information diminishes over the time of the interaction. This indicates that rapport is encoded in facial behaviour especially at the beginning of an interaction. However, other parts of the interaction carry complementary information, as the performance of facial features for the first third (0.60 AP) is significantly lower compared to the corresponding performance for the whole interaction (0.70 AP). Moreover, it is very encouraging to see that if personality information is available, facial features extracted only from the first third of the interaction can successfully reach the best performance that can be achieved using the entire interaction. This result implies a promising application scenario, since it indicates a prior personality measurement can help to make accurate predictions with only short observations of additional behaviour. This potentially allows for effective interventions to support group interactions at an early stage.

Identifying Important Features

This section extends the previous evaluation to a finer granularity, by investigating the contribution of individual features on the best-performing feature set (facial features without synchronisation features). The presented results are obtained from whole interaction data. To identify how well individual features can discriminate between low and high rapport we compute t-scores for each feature separately. T-scores measure the linear dependency between features and the target (in our case: low vs. medium-to-high rapport). The higher the absolute value of a t-score, the more likely it is that a linear dependence exists in the population. In addition, the sign of the t-score indicates the direction of the dependency, making them straightforward to interpret. It is important to note that our trained SVMs might also use nonlinear dependencies in the data, which cannot be reflected in t-scores. A list of features with the highest absolute t-scores is given in Table 4.

Feature	t-score
$AU09$	2.19
$AU23$	2.04
$AU02_{before200}$	1.78
$MutualFacing$	1.77
$ProbAU25$	1.75
$AU25$	1.50
$AU14$	1.41
$PosiFace^{\sigma}$	-1.93

Table 4. Features from the face feature set with the highest absolute t-scores for discriminating between low and high rapport.

According to these results, low rapport is especially associated with the average intensities of AU9 (nose wrinkler), AU23 (lip tightener), AU2 (outer brow raiser) during the beginning 200s, AU25 (lips part) and AU14 (dimpler), as well as the probability of AU25 being active. AU9 is often seen in disgust or anger, AU23 in sadness, and AU2 in surprise, fear, disgust or anger [19]. This is in line with prior work finding that low rapport is encoded in the presence of facial AUs associated with negative emotions [46]. AU25 on the other hand indicates speaking, meaning that a large amount of talking is indicative of low rapport. This is confirmed by the strong dependency between the amount of speaking and low rapport (t=2.9). A bit surprisingly, AU14 seems to be indicative of low rapport although this AU is often present in facial displays of happiness [19]. Moreover, our results show that a lot of mutual facing is indicative of low rapport. As mutual facing can be seen as a proxy for attention, this result seems to contradict the theory put forward by Tickle-Degnen and Rosenthal [43] who postulated that a high degree of mutual attention is indicative of high rapport. The most likely reason for the negative connection observed in our interaction context is that mutual facing is more frequent in participants who speak a lot, resulting from the social convention of facing the current speaker. A lot of speaking, in turn, seems to be related to low rapport. As such, this finding underlines the strong context dependency of the connection between nonverbal behaviour and rapport.

Understanding Correlations Among Group Attributes

As we are the first to propose the detection of low rapport in a multiparty conversation setting where all participants rate each other, it is important to investigate how this concept of rapport is related to the existing concepts that have been studied in multiparty conversations in the literature.

In particular, the attributes (leadership, dominance, competence, and liking) proposed by Sanchez-Cortes et al. [41] are relevant to our work and are measured via the same paradigm as ours. That is, every participant rates every other participant within the group. Moreover, especially the PLike scale suggested in their work [41] seems conceptually close to rapport. In contrast, it is difficult to directly compare with cohesion, as it is a group-level attribute [12]. To investigate the association between rapport and other group interaction attributes, we compute the aggregated score in the same way as we process rapport. Specifically, we average all ratings a participant received from other participants. We then calculate the Pearson correlation coefficient between the resulting scores.

Table 5 gives the correlations between different interaction attributes. It is interesting to see that rapport shows a strong correlation with competence (0.70), an obvious correlation with dominance (0.52) and liking (0.52), and a moderate correlation with leadership (0.39). The correlation analysis also reveals that although rapport is highly associated with competence, they are rather different with respect to their correlation

	Lead	Dom	Com	Like	Rap
Lead		**0.80**	**0.41**	0.01	**0.39**
Dom			**0.50**	0.08	**0.52**
Com				**0.31**	**0.70**
Like					**0.52**
O	0.01	0.10	0.21	0.02	0.15
C	-0.09	-0.13	-0.06	-0.04	-0.13
E	0.12	0.12	-0.00	0.17	0.16
A	-0.22	-0.11	-0.07	**0.30**	0.04
N	**-0.25**	**-0.32**	-0.18	0.10	-0.21

Table 5. Pearson correlations coefficients between interaction attributes. The lower part of the Table shows correlations between personality scores and the rest interaction attributes. Bold coefficients indicate statistical significance at $\alpha = 0.05$, two-tailed.

with liking (rapport: 0.52; competence: 0.31). This implies that rapport is a complex construct associated with multiple different interaction attributes.

Finally, we computed Pearson correlation coefficients between personality scores and rapport (see Table 5). Although not significant in a two-tailed test, the small negative correlation of rapport with neuroticism and the small positive correlation with extraversion is in line with hypotheses on the connection between rapport and personality found in prior work [25]. As with our previous feature analysis, it is important to keep in mind that the SVM might exploit nonlinear dependencies which are not reflected in the correlations.

In general, the correlations between rapport and different interaction attributes corroborate our hypothesis that rapport is a concept pertinent to but considerably distinct from the existing attributes proposed in previous studies [13, 41].

DISCUSSION

In this work we proposed a multimodal approach for detecting low rapport in small group interactions. To the best of our knowledge, we are the first to conduct such an investigation, taking into consideration individual behavioural features from separate modalities (e.g. facial expression and speech activity), cross-modal features (e.g. hand motion while speaking), as well as high-level interaction signals (e.g. behavioural mirroring). Evaluations on a novel 78-participant dataset, the first of its kind, showed that facial expressions are, in general, the most powerful signal for low rapport detection. We further demonstrated that incorporating participants' personality into our pipeline could improve performance for early prediction. This is encouraging, as recent years have seen an increase of methods to automatically predict personality traits of an individual user [45], e.g. using mobile phones [15] or eye movement analysis [22]. These methods could help improve early rapport prediction without requiring additional explicit user input in the from of personality questionnaires.

The possibility to predict low rapport early and accurately enables next-generation ambient intelligent systems with the ability to support users if they fail to establish rapport with each other. Such systems could, for example, use ambient displays to encourage or amplify behaviour known to improve rapport [1]. Advice for the whole group could involve proposing different interaction strategies or even socialising games to increase rapport, or encourage other people to take over or lead the discussion. Individual advice could be provided on personal screens or head-mounted displays [14, 42]. Beyond the small group setting, we believe automatic detection of low rapport also has potential for applications in autism spectrum disorders, e.g. by supporting people with this disorder in properly interpreting rapport in interactions with others or even helping them to notice low rapport at all. To execute effective support strategies in these settings, it will be particularly important to detect low rapport at an early stage of the interaction. Encouragingly, our approach is able to achieve this goal when incorporating prior knowledge of personality. In addition, our results showed that facial features alone can achieve high performance given information on the entire interaction. As cameras and microphones become pervasive in personal devices, low rapport detection could become a key component in many intelligent user interfaces that aim to positively influence daily social interactions, reduce stress, avoid conflicts, and thus lead to harmonious computer-mediated interactions.

Our results also suggest that a prediction performance above chance can still be reached if certain modalities are unavailable. This implies the ability of low rapport detection to adapt to diverse interaction settings. In practice, our method therefore can suggest an alternative modality combination in case the best modality is temporarily inaccessible. Even when there is no data from the actual interaction at all, an educated guess can be made based on the prior knowledge of personality scores in order to support those who are most likely to fail in establishing rapport with others. Given all this, our method has significant potential to pave the way for rapport-aware computer-meditated communication.

Despite these promising results, there are some limitations that we plan to address in future work. Our results showed that facial expressions are the most indicative modality. However, analysing multimodal signals using a more sophisticated model, such as a neural network, might allow use of information from multiple modalities more efficiently and achieve an even higher recognition accuracy. Furthermore, the present study was conducted in a controlled laboratory environment. While this is in line with prior works on rapport during dyadic interactions and beneficial for experimental control, it will be interesting to investigate how our findings can generalise to in-the-wild situations, e.g. interactions at home, and combining the analysis of rapport with other personal or social signals that can be captured using mobile devices or on-body sensors.

CONCLUSION

This work proposed the first audio-visual multimodal approach to low rapport detection in small group interactions. We evaluated our method on a novel 78-participant dataset consisting of 22 three- and four- person discussions. We studied a diverse set of non-verbal behaviours, including facial expressions and orientations, hand motion, speech activities, and prosodic features as well as higher-level interaction signals, e.g. reflecting mirroring effects. Our results showed that facial features in general are most indicative to detect failure in establishing rapport in group interactions. Moreover, adding personality traits allows us to predict low rapport early on in the interaction. As such, our study advances the understanding of non-verbal behaviour and rapport establishment, pointing the way towards new intelligent user interfaces that incorporate low rapport detection to prevent disharmony in social interactions on the fly.

ACKNOWLEDGMENTS

This work was supported, in part, by the Cluster of Excellence on Multimodal Computing and Interaction at Saarland University, Germany, as well as a JST CREST research grant (JPMJCR14E1), Japan.

REFERENCES

1. Madeline Balaam, Geraldine Fitzpatrick, Judith Good, and Eric Harris. 2011. Enhancing Interactional Synchrony with an Ambient Display. In *Proc. of the ACM Conference on Human Factors in Computing Systems*. 867–876.
2. Tadas Baltrušaitis, Peter Robinson, and Louis-Philippe Morency. 2016. OpenFace: an open source facial behavior analysis toolkit. In *Proc. of the IEEE Winter Conference on Applications of Computer Vision*. 1–10.
3. Frank J Bernieri. 1988. Coordinated movement and rapport in teacher-student interactions. *Journal of Nonverbal Behavior* 12, 2 (1988), 120–138.
4. Frank J Bernieri, John S Gillis, Janet M Davis, and Jon E Grahe. 1996. Dyad rapport and the accuracy of its judgment across situations: A lens model analysis. *Journal of Personality and Social Psychology* 71, 1 (1996), 110–129.
5. Cigdem Beyan, Francesca Capozzi, Cristina Becchio, and Vittorio Murino. 2017. Prediction of the Leadership Style of an Emergent Leader Using Audio and Visual Nonverbal Features. *IEEE Transactions on Multimedia* (2017).
6. Dan Bohus and Eric Horvitz. 2011. Multiparty Turn Taking in Situated Dialog: Study, Lessons, and Directions. In *Proc. of the Annual SIGdial Meeting on Discourse and Dialogue*. 98–109.
7. Michael Burns. 1984. Rapport and relationships: The basis of child care. *Journal of Child Care* 2, 2 (1984), 47–57.
8. Angelo Cafaro, Johannes Wagner, Tobias Baur, Soumia Dermouche, Mercedes Torres Torres, Catherine Pelachaud, Elisabeth André, and Michel Valstar. 2017. The NoXi Database: Multimodal Recordings of Mediated Novice-expert Interactions. In *Proc. of the ACM International Conference on Multimodal Interaction*. 350–359.
9. Zhe Cao, Tomas Simon, Shih-En Wei, and Yaser Sheikh. 2017. Realtime Multi-Person 2D Pose Estimation using Part Affinity Fields. In *Proc. of the IEEE Conference on Computer Vision and Pattern Recognition*. 7291–7299.
10. Aleksandra Cerekovic, Oya Aran, and Daniel Gatica-Perez. 2016. Rapport with Virtual Agents: What Do Human Social Cues and Personality Explain? *IEEE Transactions on Affective Computing* 8, 3 (2016), 382–395.
11. Prerna Chikersal, Maria Tomprou, Young Ji Kim, Anita Williams Woolley, and Laura Dabbish. 2017. Deep Structures of Collaboration: Physiological Correlates of Collective Intelligence and Group Satisfaction. In *Proc. of the International Conference on Computer-Supported Collaborative Work*. 873–888.
12. Wynne W Chin, Wm David Salisbury, Allison W Pearson, and Matthew J Stollak. 1999. Perceived Cohesion in Small Groups: Adapting and Testing the Perceived Cohesion Scale in a Small-Group Setting. *Small group research* 30, 6 (1999), 751–766.
13. Paul T Costa and Robert R MacCrae. 1992. *Revised NEO personality inventory (NEO PI-R) and NEO five-factor inventory (NEO-FFI): Professional manual.*
14. Ionut Damian, Chiew Seng Sean Tan, Tobias Baur, Johannes Schöning, Kris Luyten, and Elisabeth André. 2015. Augmenting Social Interactions: Realtime Behavioural Feedback using Social Signal Processing Techniques. In *Proc. of the ACM Conference on Human Factors in Computing Systems*. 565–574.
15. Yves-Alexandre de Montjoye, Jordi Quoidbach, Florent Robic, and Alex Pentland. 2013. Predicting Personality Using Novel Mobile Phone-Based Metrics. In *Proc. of the International Conference on Social Computing, Behavioral-Cultural Modeling and Prediction*. 48–55.
16. Florian Eyben, Felix Weninger, Florian Gross, and Björn Schuller. 2013. Recent Developments in openSMILE, the Munich Open-Source Multimedia Feature Extractor. In *Proc. of the ACM International Conference on Multimedia*. 835–838.
17. Sebastian Feese, Amir Muaremi, Bert Arnrich, Gerhard Troster, Bertolt Meyer, and Klaus Jonas. 2011. Discriminating Individually Considerate and Authoritarian Leaders by Speech Activity Cues. In *Proc. of the IEEE International Conference on Privacy, Security, Risk and Trust and IEEE International Confernece on Social Computing*. 1460–1465.
18. Daniel Gatica-Perez, L McCowan, Dong Zhang, and Samy Bengio. 2005. Detecting Group Interest-Level in Meetings. In *Proc. IEEE International Conference on Acoustics, Speech, and Signal Processing*, Vol. 1. 489–492.
19. Mehdi Ghayoumi and Arvind K Bansal. 2016. Unifying Geometric Features and Facial Action Units for Improved Performance of Facial Expression Analysis. *arXiv preprint arXiv:1606.00822* (2016).
20. Juan Lorenzo Hagad, Roberto Legaspi, Masayuki Numao, and Merlin Suarez. 2011. Predicting Levels of Rapport in Dyadic Interactions through Automatic Detection of Posture and Posture Congruence. In *Proc. of the IEEE International Conference on Social Computing*. 613–616.

21. Jinni A Harrigan, Thomas E Oxman, and Robert Rosenthal. 1985. Rapport expressed through nonverbal behavior. *Journal of Nonverbal Behavior* 9, 2 (1985), 95–110.
22. Sabrina Hoppe, Tobias Loetscher, Stephanie Morey, and Andreas Bulling. 2015. Recognition of Curiosity Using Eye Movement Analysis. In *Adj. Proc. ACM International Joint Conference on Pervasive and Ubiquitous Computing*. 185–188.
23. Michael Xuelin Huang, Jiajia Li, Grace Ngai, and Hong Va Leong. 2016. StressClick: Sensing Stress from Gaze-Click Patterns. In *Proc. of the ACM Conference on Multimedia*. 1395–1404.
24. Hayley Hung and Daniel Gatica-Perez. 2010. Estimating Cohesion in Small Groups Using Audio-Visual Nonverbal Behavior. *IEEE Transactions on Multimedia* 12, 6 (2010), 563–575.
25. Carroll E Izard. 1990. Personality, Emotion Expressions, and Rapport. *Psychological Inquiry* 1, 4 (1990), 315–317.
26. Natasha Jaques, Yoo Lim Kim, and Rosalind Picard. 2016a. Personality, Attitudes, and Bonding in Conversations. In *Proc. of the International Conference on Intelligent Virtual Agents*. 378–382.
27. Natasha Jaques, Daniel McDuff, Yoo Lim Kim, and Rosalind Picard. 2016b. Understanding and Predicting Bonding in Conversations Using Thin Slices of Facial Expressions and Body Language. In *Proc. of the International Conference on Intelligent Virtual Agents*. 64–74.
28. John M Kelley, Gordon Kraft-Todd, Lidia Schapira, Joe Kossowsky, and Helen Riess. 2014. The Influence of the Patient-Clinician Relationship on Healthcare Outcomes: A Systematic Review and Meta-Analysis of Randomized Controlled Trials. *PloS one* 9, 4 (2014), e94207.
29. Marianne LaFrance and Maida Broadbent. 1976. Group Rapport: Posture Sharing as a Nonverbal Indicator. *Group & Organization Studies* 1, 3 (1976), 328–333.
30. Kornel Laskowski. 2010. Modeling Norms of Turn-Taking in Multi-Party Conversation. In *Proc. of the 48th Annual Meeting of the Association for Computational Linguistics*. 999–1008.
31. Paul J Lavrakas. 2008. *Encyclopedia of survey research methods*.
32. Gary McKeown, William Curran, Johannes Wagner, Florian Lingenfelser, and Elisabeth André. 2015. The Belfast storytelling database: A spontaneous social interaction database with laughter focused annotation. In *Proc. of the International Conference on Affective Computing and Intelligent Interaction*. 166–172.
33. Philipp M Müller, Sikandar Amin, Prateek Verma, Mykhaylo Andriluka, and Andreas Bulling. 2015. Emotion recognition from embedded bodily expressions and speech during dyadic interactions. In *Proc. of the International Conference on Affective Computing and Intelligent Interaction*. 663–669.
34. Marjolein Nanninga, Yanxia Zhang, Nale Lehmann-Willenbrock, Zoltán Szlávik, and Hayley Hung. 2017. Estimating Verbal Expressions of Task and Social Cohesion in Meetings by Quantifying Paralinguistic Mimicry. In *Proc. of the ACM International Conference on Multimedia Interaction*. 206–215.
35. Catharine Oertel, Kenneth A Funes Mora, Joakim Gustafson, and Jean-Marc Odobez. 2015. Deciphering the Silent Participant: On the Use of Audio-Visual Cues for the Classification of Listener Categories in Group Discussions. In *Proc. of the ACM on International Conference on Multimodal Interaction*. 107–114.
36. Catharine Oertel and Giampiero Salvi. 2013. A Gaze-based Method for Relating Group Involvement to Individual Engagement in Multimodal Multiparty Dialogue. In *Proc. of the ACM International Conference on Multimodal Interaction*. 99–106.
37. Amy Ogan, Samantha L Finkelstein, Erin Walker, Ryan Carlson, and Justine Cassell. 2012. Rudeness and Rapport: Insults and Learning Gains in Peer Tutoring.. In *Proc. of the International Conference on Intelligent Tutoring Systems*. 11–21.
38. Fabien Ringeval, Andreas Sonderegger, Juergen Sauer, and Denis Lalanne. 2013. Introducing the RECOLA multimodal corpus of remote collaborative and affective interactions. In *Proc. of the IEEE International Conference and Workshops on Automatic Face and Gesture Recognition (FG)*. 1–8.
39. Christoph Rühlemann and Stefan Gries. 2015. Turn order and turn distribution in multi-party storytelling. *Journal of Pragmatics* 87 (2015), 171–191.
40. Hiroaki Sakoe and Seibi Chiba. 1978. Dynamic Programming Algorithm Optimization for Spoken Word Recognition. *IEEE Transactions on Acoustics, Speech, and Signal Processing* 26, 1 (1978), 43–49.
41. Dairazalia Sanchez-Cortes, Oya Aran, Marianne Schmid Mast, and Daniel Gatica-Perez. 2012. A Nonverbal Behavior Approach to Identify Emergent Leaders in Small Groups. *IEEE Transactions on Multimedia* 14, 3 (2012), 816–832.
42. Gianluca Schiavo, Alessandro Cappelletti, Eleonora Mencarini, Oliviero Stock, and Massimo Zancanaro. 2014. Overt or Subtle? Supporting Group Conversations with Automatically Targeted Directives. In *Proc. of the ACM International Conference on Intelligent User Interfaces*. 225–234.
43. Linda Tickle-Degnen and Robert Rosenthal. 1990. The Nature of Rapport and Its Nonverbal Correlates. *Psychological Inquiry* 1, 4 (1990), 285–293.
44. Philip Tsui and Gail L Schultz. 1985. Failure of rapport: Why psychotherapeutic engagement fails in the treatment of Asian clients. *American Journal of Orthopsychiatry* 55, 4 (1985), 561–569.

45. Alessandro Vinciarelli and Gelareh Mohammadi. 2014. A Survey of Personality Computing. *IEEE Transactions on Affective Computing* 5, 3 (2014), 273–291.

46. Ning Wang and Jonathan Gratch. 2009. Rapport and Facial Expression. In *Proc. of the International Conference on Affective Computing and Intelligent Interaction Workshops*. 1–6.

47. Ran Zhao, Alexandros Papangelis, and Justine Cassell. 2014. Towards a Dyadic Computational Model of Rapport Management for Human-Virtual Agent Interaction. In *Proc. of the International Conference on Intelligent Virtual Agents*. 514–527.

48. Ran Zhao, Tanmay Sinha, Alan W Black, and Justine Cassell. 2016. Socially-Aware Virtual Agents: Automatically Assessing Dyadic Rapport from Temporal Patterns of Behavior. In *Proc. of the International Conference on Intelligent Virtual Agents*. 218–233.

A Data-Driven Approach to Developing IoT Privacy-Setting Interfaces

Paritosh Bahirat*, Yangyang He*, Abhilash Menon*, Bart Knijnenburg
Clemson University School of Computing
Clemson, USA
{pbahira,yyhe,abhilas,bartk}@clemson.edu

ABSTRACT

User testing is often used to inform the development of user interfaces (UIs). But what if an interface needs to be developed for a system that does not yet exist? In that case, existing datasets can provide valuable input for UI development. We apply a data-driven approach to the development of a privacy-setting interface for Internet-of-Things (IoT) devices. Applying machine learning techniques to an existing dataset of users' sharing preferences in IoT scenarios, we develop a set of "smart" default profiles. Our resulting interface asks users to choose among these profiles, which capture their preferences with an accuracy of 82%—a 14% improvement over a naive default setting and a 12% improvement over a single smart default setting for all users.

Author Keywords

Data-driven design; Internet of Things; Privacy settings; Machine learning

INTRODUCTION

Under the moniker of 'Internet of Things' (IoT), smart connected devices are revolutionizing our everyday life, just like smartphones did for cellphones. Smartphones, however, have shown to increase users' privacy concerns [4], and the same may be true for IoT. Like smartphones, IoT devices collect and store personal information to personalize the user experience, share it across other devices, and/or sell it to third parties. Consequently, preserving users' privacy is a big concern that limits the adoption of IoT devices [10].

Privacy is an inherent trade-off in IoT, because IoT devices cannot provide their services without collecting data. Preserving users' privacy therefore means giving them control over this trade-off, by allowing them to decide what information can be collected about them. Outside the home environment, people have little control over the data IoT devices collect. Researchers at Intel are working on a framework that allows people to be notified about surrounding IoT devices collecting personal information, and to control these collection practices [5].

Smartphones give users control over their privacy settings in the form of prompts that ask whether the user allows or denies a certain app access to a certain type of information. Such prompts are problematic for IoT, because IoT devices are supposed to operate in the background. Moreover, as the penetration of IoT devices in our environment continues to increase, prompts would become a constant noise which users will soon start to ignore, like software EULAs [8] or privacy policies [12].

A better solution would be to regulate privacy with global settings. But research has shown that users are highly concerned about their privacy, but find it difficult to implement privacy settings [1, 9, 19]. Indeed, the vast number of encounters people have with a myriad of different IoT devices makes chosing adequate privacy settings a very challenging task that is likely to result in information and choice overload [28].

Data-driven design

What design process allows us to develop a usable privacy-setting interface for IoT? The development of usable privacy interfaces commonly relies on user studies with existing systems. However, this method is not possible in our IoT control scenario, because the Intel control framework has yet to be implemented [5]. We therefore develop and employ a *data-driven design* methodology, leveraging an existing dataset collected by Lee and Kobsa [16], who asked users whether they would allow or deny IoT devices in their environment to collect information about them. We use this dataset in two phases.

In our first phase, we develop a "layered" settings interface, where users make a decision on a less granular level (e.g., whether a certain recipient is allowed to collect their personal information or not), and only move to a more granular decision (e.g., what types of information this recipient is allowed to collect) when they desire more detailed control. This reduces the complexity of the decisions users have to make, without reducing the

*: These authors contributed equally.

IUI 2018, March 7–11, 2018, Tokyo, Japan.

http://dx.doi.org/10.1145/3172944.3172982

amount of control available to them. We use statistical analysis of the Lee and Kobsa dataset to decide which aspect should be presented at the highest layer of our IoT privacy-setting interface, and which aspects are relegated to subsequently lower layers.

In our second phase, we develop a "smart" default setting, which preempts the need for many users to manually change their settings [26]. However, since people differ extensively in their privacy preferences [20], it is not possible to achieve an optimal default that is the same for everyone. Instead, different people may require different settings. Outside the field of IoT, researchers have been able to establish distinct clusters or "profiles" based on user behavioral data [14, 20, 29]. We perform machine learning analysis on the Lee and Kobsa dataset to create a similar set of "smart profiles" for our IoT privacy-setting interface.

The remainder of this paper is structured as follows: We first summarize previous work on privacy in IoT scenarios, and describe the structure of the Lee and Kobsa [16] dataset. We then *inspect* users' behaviors using statistical analysis. Next, we *predict* users' behaviors using machine learning methods. We subsequently present a set of prototypes for an IoT privacy-setting interface. Finally, we conclude with a summary of our proposed procedure and the results of our analysis.

APPROACH AND RELATED WORK

Our goal is to develop intuitive interfaces for IoT privacy settings, using a data-driven approach. In this section we therefore discuss existing research on privacy-setting interfaces and on privacy prediction.

Privacy-Setting Interfaces

The most basic privacy-setting interface is the "access control matrix", which allows users to indicate who gets to see what [25]. This can be simplified by grouping recipients into categories, such as Google+'s *circles* [27]. Taking a step further, Raber et al. [22] proposed *Privacy Wedges*, which allow users to make privacy decisions using a combination of categorization (the wedges) and inter-personal distance (the position of a person on the wedge). Users can decide who gets to see their posts or personal information by "coloring" parts of each wedge.

These wedges have been tested on limited numbers of friends, and in the case of IoT they are likely insufficient, due to the complexity of the decision space. To wit, IoT privacy decisions involve a large selection of devices, each with various sensors that collect data for a range of different purposes. This makes it complicated to design an interface that covers every possible setting [28]. A wedge-based interface will arguably not be able to succinctly represent such complexity without a significant amount of information and choice overload.

We propose a data-driven approach to solve this problem: statistical analysis informs the construction of a layered settings interface, while machine learning-based privacy prediction helps us find smart privacy profiles.

Privacy Prediction

Several researchers have proposed privacy prediction as a solution to the privacy settings complexity problem. Sadeh et al. used a k-nearest neighbor algorithm and a random forest algorithm to predict users' privacy preferences in a location-sharing system [24], based on the type of recipient and the time and location of the request. They demonstrated that users had difficulties setting their privacy preferences, and that the applied machine learning techniques can help users to choose more accurate disclosure preferences. Similarly, Pallapa et al. [21] present a system which can determine the required privacy level in new situations based on the history of interaction between users. Their system can efficiently deal with the rise of privacy concerns and help users in a pervasive system full of dynamic interactions.

Dong et al. [6] use a binary classification algorithms to give users personalized advice regarding their privacy decision-making practices on online social networks. They found that J48 decision trees provided the best results. Li and et al. [17] similarly use J48 to demonstrate that taking the user's cultural background into account when making privacy predictions improves the prediction accuracy. Our data stems from a culturally homogeneous population (U.S. Mechanical Turk workers), so cultural variables are outside the scope of our study. We do however follow these previous works in using J48 decision trees in our prediction approach.

We further extend our approach using *clustering* to find several smart default policies ("profiles"). This is in line with Fang et al. [7], who present an active learning algorithm that comes up with privacy profiles for users in real time. Since our approach is based on an existing dataset, our algorithm does not classify users in real time, but instead creates a static set of profiles 'offline', from which users can subsequently choose. This avoids cold start problems, and does not rely on the availability of continuous real-time behaviors. This is beneficial for IoT settings, because users often specify their settings in these systems in a "single shot", leaving the settings interface alone afterwards.

Ravichandran et al. [23] employ an approach similar to ours, using k-means clustering on users' contextualized location sharing decisions to come up with several default policies. They showed that a small number of default policies could accurately reflect a large part of the location sharing preferences. We extend their approach to find the best profiles based on various novel clustering approaches, and take the additional step of designing user interfaces that incorporate the best solutions.

We apply our procedure to a dataset by Lee and Kobsa [16], who presented users with a total of 2800 IoT usage scenarios that were systemstically manipulated along five dimensions. Lee and Kobsa observed that the scenarios can be grouped into four clusters in terms of privacy risks. Their clusters differ substantially along several dimensions, most notably regarding the inquirer ('who') and data type ('what'). The dominance of the 'who' parameter is also reflected in a study in a ubiquitous computing environment by Lederer et al. [15]. Extending upon Lee and Kobsa, our clustering procedure is performed at the *user* level rather than the *scenario* level. This allows us to create privacy profiles.

DATASET

This study is based on a dataset collected by Lee and Kobsa [16]. A total of 2800 scenarios were presented to 200 participants (100 male, 99 female, 1 undisclosed) through Amazon Mechanical Turk. Four participants were aged between 18 and 20, 75 aged 20–30, 68 aged 30–40, 31 aged 40–50, 20 aged 50–60, and 2 aged > 60.

Each participant was presented with 14 scenarios describing a situation where an IoT device would collect information about the participant. Each scenario was a combination of five contextual parameters (Table 1), manipulated at several levels using a mixed fractional factorial design that allowed us to test main effects and two-way interactions between all parameters.

For every scenario, participants were asked a total of 9 questions. Our study focuses on the **allow/reject** question: "If you had a choice to allow/reject this, what would you choose?", with options "I would allow it" and "I would reject it". We also used participants' answers to three attitudinal questions regarding the scenario:

- **Risk:** How risky or safe is this situation? (7pt scale from "very risky" to "very safe")
- **Comfort:** How comfortable or uncomfortable do you feel about this situation? (7pt scale)
- **Appropriateness:** How appropriate do you consider this situation? (7pt scale)

INSPECTING USERS' BEHAVIORS

In this section we analyze how users' behavioral intentions to allow or reject the information collection described in the scenario are influenced by the scenario parameters. In line with classic attitude-behavior models [2], we also investigate whether users' attitudes regarding the scenario—their judgment of risk, comfort, and appropriateness—mediate these effects. This mediation analysis [3] involves the following test:

- **Test 1:** The effect of the scenario parameters (who, what, where, reason, persistence) on participants' attitudes (risk, comfort, appropriateness).
- **Test 2:** The effect of participants' attitudes on their behavioral intentions (the allow/reject decision).
- **Test 3:** The effect of the parameters on behavioral intentions, controlling for attitudes.

Table 1: Parameters used in the experiment. Example scenarios:
"A device of a friend records your video to detect your presence. This happens continuously, while you are at someone else's place, for your safety."
"A government device reads your phone ID to detect your identity. This happens once, while you are in a public place (e.g. on the street), for health-related purposes."

Parameter	Levels
Who *The entity collecting the data*	1. Unknown 2. Colleague 3. Friend 4. Own device 5. Business 6. Employer 7. Government
What *The type of data collected and (optionally) the knowledge extracted from this data*	1. PhoneID 2. PhoneID>identity 3. Location 4. Location>presence 5. Voice 6. Voice>gender 7. Voice> age 8. Voice>identity 9. Voice>presence 10. Voice>mood 11. Photo 12. Photo>gender 13. Photo>age 14. Photo>identity 15. Photo>presence 16. Photo>mood 17. Video 18. Video>gender 19. Video>age 20. Video>presence 21. Video>mood 22. Video>looking at 23. Gaze 24. Gaze>looking at
Where *The location of the data collection*	1. Your place 2. Someone else's place 3. Semi-public place (e.g. restaurant) 4. Public space (e.g. street)
Reason *The reason for collecting this data*	1. Safety 2. Commercial 3. Social-related 4. Convenience 5. Health-related 6. None
Persistence *Whether data is collected once or continuously*	1. Once 2. Continuously

Table 2: Effect of scenario on attitudes. Each model builds upon and is tested against the previous.

Model	χ^2	*df*	*p*-value
risk ~ (1|*sid*)			
+who	315.37	6	< .0001
+what	67.74	23	< .0001
+reason	15.65	5	.0079
+persistence	9.95	1	.0016
+where	7.47	3	.0586
+who:what	166.47	138	.0050
Model	χ^2	*df*	*p*-value
comfort ~ (1|*sid*)			
+who	334.06	6	< .0001
+what	83.24	23	< .0001
+reason	18.68	5	.0022
+persistence	14.73	1	.0001
+where	3.25	3	.3544
+who:what	195.07	138	.0001
Model	χ^2	*df*	*p*-value
appropriateness ~ (1|*sid*)			
+who	315.77	6	< .0001
+what	72.87	23	< .0001
+reason	23.27	5	.0003
+persistence	8.97	1	.0027
+where	5.46	3	.1411
+who:what	214.61	138	< .0001

If tests 1 and 2 are significant, and test 3 reveals a substantial reduction in conditional direct effect (compared to the marginal effect), then we can say that the effects of the scenario parameters on participants' behavioral intention are mediated by their attitudes. Moreover, if the conditional direct effect is (close to) zero, then the effects are fully (rather than partially) mediated.

Scenario Parameters and Attitude

ANOVA Test of Main Effects

To understand the effect of the scenario parameters on participants' attitudes, we created a separate *linear mixed effects regression* (*lmer*) model with a random intercept (to account for repeated measures on the same participant) for each dependent variable (risk, comfort, appropriateness), using the scenario parameters as independent variables. We employed a forward stepwise procedure, adding the strongest remaining parameter into the model at each step and comparing it against the previous model. Table 2 shows that all parameters except **where** have a significant effect on each of the attitudes.

Post-hoc Comparisons

We also conducted Tukey post hoc analyses to better understand how the various values of each parameter influenced the attitudes. **Where** was excluded from these analyses, as it did not have an overall significant effect. Some key findings of these post hoc analyses are:

Who: Participants perceive more *risk* when the recipient of the information is 'unknown' than for any other recipient (d range = [0.640, 1.450] and all $ps < .001$, except for 'government': $d = 0.286$, $p < .05$). 'Government' is the next most risky recipient (d range = [0.440, 1.190], all $ps < .001$). Participants consider their 'own device' the least risky (d range = [0.510, 1.450], all $ps < .001$). Similar patterns were found for *comfort* and *appropriateness.*

Reason: Participants were more *comfortable* disclosing information for the purpose of 'safety' than for any other reason except 'health' (d range = [0.230, 0.355], all $ps < .05$). They also believe that disclosing information for the purpose of 'health' or 'safety' is more *appropriate* than for 'social' or 'commercial' purposes (d range = [0.270, 0.310], all $ps < .05$).

Persistence: Participants were more *comfortable*, found it more *appropriate*, and less *risky* to disclose their information 'once' rather than 'continuously' ($d = 0.146$, $p < .01$).

What: This parameter has a large number of values, so we decided to selectively test planned contrasts instead of post-hoc tests. We first compared different mediums (voice, photo, video) regardless of what is being inferred:

- Participants were significantly more *comfortable* with 'voice' than 'video' ($d = 0.260$, $p = .005$), and found 'voice' less *risky* ($d = -0.239$, $p = .005$) and more *appropriate* ($d = 0.217$, $p = .015$) than 'video'.
- Participants were significantly more *comfortable* with 'voice' than 'photo' ($d = 0.201$, $p = .007$) and found 'voice' more *appropriate* than 'photo' ($d = 0.157$, $p = .028$). There was no significant difference in terms of *risk* ($p = .118$).
- No differences were found between 'photo' and 'video' in terms of *risk* ($p = .24$), *comfort* ($p = .35$) and *appropriateness* ($p = .26$).

We also compared different inferences (e.g. age, gender, mood, identity) across mediums. The following planned contrasts were significant (all others were not):

- Participants were significantly more *comfortable* ($d = 0.363$, $p = .028$) and found it more *appropriate* ($d = 0.371$, $p = .018$) to reveal their 'age' rather than their 'identity'.
- Participants were significantly more *comfortable* ($d = 0.363$, $p = .008$) and found it more *appropriate* ($d = 0.308$, $p = .024$) to reveal their 'presence' rather than their 'identity'.

Interaction effects

We also checked for two-way interactions between the scenario parameters. The only significant interaction effect observed was between **who** and **what.** The last line of each section in Table 2 shows the results of adding this interaction to the model. Due to space concerns, we choose not to address the post-hoc analysis of the $7 * 24 = 168$ specific combinations of who and what.

Table 3: Effect of attitudes and scenario on allow/reject.

Model	OR	χ^2	*df*	*p*-value
allow $\sim$ (1|*sid*)				
+risk	0.25	1005.24	1	< .0001
+comfort	5.04	723.27	1	< .0001
+appropriateness	3.47	128.17	1	< .0001
+who		8.80	6	.1851
+what		26.07	23	.2976
+reason		19.33	5	.0017
+persistence		12.69	1	.0004

Table 4: Effect of scenario on allow/reject, *not* controlling for attitudes.

Model	χ^2	*df*	*p*-value
allow $\sim$ (1|*sid*)			
+who	221.36	6	< .0001
+what	78.55	23	< .0001
+reason	21.95	5	.0005
+persistence	20.64	1	< .0001

Attitude and Behavioral intention

To test the effects of participants' attitudes on their allow/reject decision, we ran a *generalized linear mixed effects regression* (*glmer*) with a random intercept and a logit link function to account for the binary dependent variable. We found significant effects of all the three attitudes on participants' allow/reject decision (see Table 3). Each 1-point increase in **risk** results in a 4.04-fold decrease in the odds that the scenario will be allowed ($p < .0001$). Each 1-point increase in **comfort** results in a 5.04-fold increase ($p < .0001$), and each 1-point increase in **appropriateness** results in a 3.47-fold increase ($p < .0001$).

Mediation Analysis

The bottom half of Table 3 shows the *conditional* effects of the significant parameters (who, what, reason, persistance) on participants' allow/reject decision, controlling for attitude. **Who** and **what** are no longer significant; these effects are thus fully mediated by attitude. The effects of **reason** and **persistance** are still significant, but smaller than the marginal effects (i.e., without controlling for attitude, see Table 4)—their χ^2s are reduced by 12% and 39%, respectively. This means that the mediation effect was substantial in all cases. The final mediation model is displayed in Figure 1.

Discussion of Statistical Results

Our statistical results show several patterns that can inform the development of an IoT privacy-setting interface. We find that **who** is the most important scenario parameter, and should thus end up at the top layer of our interface. People are generally concerned about IoT scenarios involving unknown and government devices, but less concerned about about data collected by their own devices. Mistrust of government data collection is in line with Li et al.'s finding regarding US audiences [17].

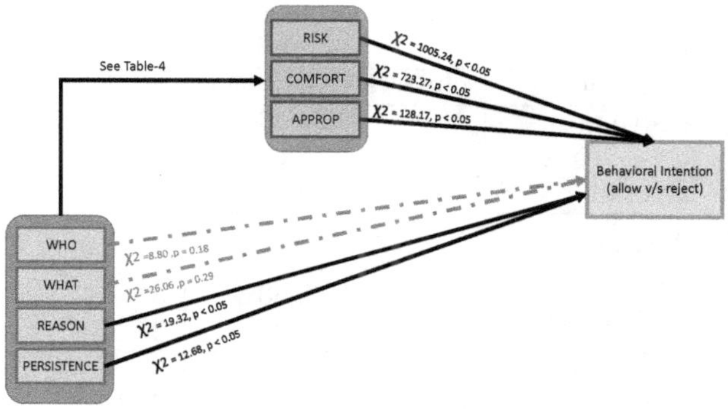

Figure 1: Mediation model of the effect of scenario parameters on participants' intention to allow/reject the scenario, mediated by attitudinal factors

What is the next most important scenario parameter, and its significant interaction with **who** suggests that some users may want to allow/reject the collection of different types of data by different types of recipients. Privacy concerns are higher for photo and video than for voice, arguably because photos and videos are more likely to reveal the identity of a person. Moreover, people are less concerned with revealing their age and presence, and most concerned with revealing their identity.

The **reason** for the data collection may be used as the next layer in the interface. Health and safety are generally seen as acceptable reasons. **Persistence** is less important, although one-time collection is more acceptable than continuous collection. **Where** the data is being collected does not influence intention at all. This could be an artifact of the dataset: location is arguably less prominent when reading a scenario than it is in real life.

Finally, participants' attitudes significantly (and in some cases fully) mediated the effect of scenario parameters on behavioral intentions. This means that these attitudes may be used as a valuable source for classifying people into distinct groups. Such attitudinal clustering could capture a significant amount of the variation in participants in terms of their preferred privacy settings, espcially with respect to the **who** and **what** dimensions.

PREDICTING USERS' BEHAVIORS

In this section we predict participants' allow/reject decision using machine learning methods. Our goal is to find suitable *default settings* for an IoT privacy-setting interface. Consequently, we do not attempt to find the best possible solution; instead we make a conscious tradeoff between parsimony and prediction accuracy. Accuracy is important to ensure that users' privacy preferences are accurately captured and/or need only few manual adjustments. Parsimony, on the other hand, prevents overfitting and promotes fairness: we noticed that more complex models tended to increase overall accuracy by predicting a few users' preferences more accurately, with no effect on other users. Parsimony also makes the associated default setting easier to understand for the user.

Table 5: Comparison of clustering approaches

Approach	clusters	Accuracy	# of profiles
Naive classification	1	28.33%	1 (all 'yes')
	1	71.67%	1 (all 'no')
Overall	1	73.10%	1
Attitude-based clustering	2	75.28%	2
	3	75.17%	3
	4	75.60%	3
	5	75.25%	3
Fit-based clustering	2	77.99%	2
	3	81.54%	3
Agglomerative clustering	200	78.13%	4
	200	78.27%	5

Our prediction target is the participants' decision to allow or reject the data collection described in each scenario, classifying a scenario as either 'yes' or 'no'. The scenario parameters serve as input attributes. These are nominal variables, making decision tree algorithms such as ID3 and J48 a suitable prediction approach. Unlike ID3, J48 uses gain ratio as the root node selection metric, which is not biased towards input attributes with many values. We therefore use J48 throughout our analysis.

We discuss progressively sophisticated methods for predicting participants' decisions. After discussing naive solutions, we first present a cross-validated tree learning solution that results in a single "smart default" setting that is the same for everyone. Subsequently, we discuss three different procedures that create a number of "smart profiles" by clustering the participants and creating a separate cross-validated tree for each cluster. For each procedure, we try various numbers of clusters. Accuracies of the resulting solutions are reported in Table 5.

Naive Prediction Methods

We start with naive or "information-less" predictions. Our dataset contains 793 'yes'es and 2007 'no's. Therefore, predicting 'yes' for every scenario gives us a 28.33% prediction accuracy, while making a 'no' prediction gives us an accuracy of 71.67%. In other words, if we disallow all information collection by default, users will on average be happy with this default for 71.67% of the settings.

Overall Prediction

We next create a "smart default" by predicting the allow/reject decision with the scenario parameters using J48 with Weka's [11] default settings. The resulting tree (Figure 2) has an accuracy of 73.10%. The confusion matrix (Table 6) shows that this model results in overly conservative settings; only 208 'yes'es are predicted.

Figure 2 shows that this model predicts 'no' for every recipient (**who**) except 'Own device'. For this value, the default setting depends on **what** is being collected (see Table 7). For some levels of **what**, there is a further drill down based on **where**, **persistence** and **reason**.

Table 6: Confusion matrix for the overall prediction

Observed	Prediction: Yes	Prediction: No	Total
Yes	124 (TP)	669 (FN)	793
No	84 (FP)	1923 (TN)	2007
Total	208	2592	2800

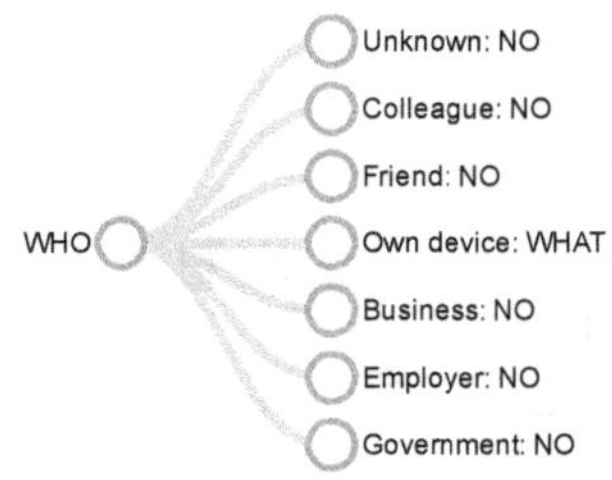

Figure 2: The Overall Prediction decision tree. Further drill down for **who** = 'Own device' is provided in Table 7

We can use this tree to create a "smart default" setting; in that case, users would on average be content with 73.10% of these settings—a 2% improvement over the naive "no to everything" default setting.

Given that people differ substantially in their privacy preferences, it is not unsurprising that this "one size fits all" default setting is not very accurate. A better solution would cluster participants by their privacy preferences, and then fit a separate tree for each cluster. These trees could then be used to create "smart profiles" that new users may choose from. Subsequent sections discuss several ways of creating such profiles.

Attitude-Based Clustering

Our first "smart profile" solution uses the attitudes (comfort, risk, appropriateness) participants expressed for each scenario on a 7-point scale. We averaged the values per attitude across each participant's 14 answers, and ran k-means clustering on that data with 2, 3, 4 and 5 clusters. We then added participants' cluster assignments to our original dataset, and ran the J48 decision tree learner on the dataset with the additional **cluster** attribute. Accuracies of the resulting solutions are reported in Table 5 under "attitude-based clustering".

All of the resulting trees had **cluster** as the root node. This indicates that this parameter is a very effective parameter for predicting users' decisions. This also allows us to split the trees at the root node, and create separate default settings for each cluster.

The 2-cluster solution (Figure 3) has a 75.28% accuracy — a 3.0% improvement over the "smart default". This solution results in one profile with 'no' for everything, while for the other profile the decision depends on the recipient (**who**). This profile allows any collection involving the user's 'Own device', and may allow collection by a 'Friend' or an 'Employer/School', depending on **what** is being collected.

Table 7: Drill down of the Overall Prediction tree for **who** = 'Own device'

What	Decision		
PhoneID	Yes		
PhoneID>identity	Yes		
Location	No		
Location>presence	Reason	Safety	Yes
		Commercial	Yes
		Social-related	No
		Convenience	No
		Health-related	Yes
		None	Yes
Voice	No		
Voice>gender	Where	Your place	No
		Someone else	No
		Semi-public	No
		Public	Yes
Voice> age	No		
Voice>identity	Yes		
Voice>presence	Yes		
Voice>mood	Yes		
Photo	No		
Photo>gender	No		
Photo>age	No		
Photo>identity	Yes		
Photo>presence	No		
Photo>mood	No		
Video	No		
Video>gender	No		
Video>age	No		
Video>presence	No		
Video>mood	Yes		
Video>looking at	Persistence	Once	Yes
		Continuous	No
Gaze	No		
Gaze>looking at	Reason	Safety	Yes
		Commercial	No
		Social-related	No
		Convenience	Yes
		Health-related	Yes
		None	Yes

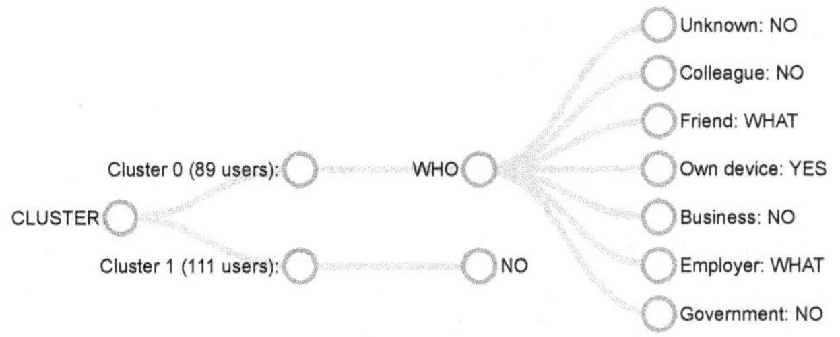

Figure 3: Attitude-based clustering: 2-cluster tree. Further drill down for **who** = 'Friend' or 'Employer/School' in Cluster 0 is hidden for space reasons.

The 3-cluster solution has a slightly lower accuracy of 75.17%, but is more parsimonious than the 2-cluster solution. There is one profile with 'no' for everything, one profile that allows collection by the user's 'Own device' only, and one profile that allows any collection except when the recipient is 'Unknown' or the 'Government'. The 4- and 5-cluster solutions have several clusters with the same sub-tree, and therefore reduce to a 3-cluster solution with 75.60% and 75.25% accuracy, respectively.

Fit-based clustering

Our fit-based clustering approach clusters participants without using any additional information. It instead uses the fit of the tree models to bootstrap the process of sorting participants into clusters. Like many bootstrapping methods, ours uses *random starts* and *iterative improvements* to find the optimal solution.

Random starts: We randomly divide particpants over N separate groups, and learn a tree for each group. This is repeated until a non-trivial starting solution (i.e., with distinctly different trees per cluster) is found.

Iterative improvements: Once each of the N groups has a unique decision tree, we evaluate for each participant which of the trees best represents their 14 decisions. If this is the tree of a different group, we switch the participant to this group. Once all participants are evaluated and put in the group of their best-fitting tree, the tree in each group is re-learned with the data of the new group members. This then prompts another round of evaluations, and this process continues until no further switches are performed.

Since this process is influenced by random chance, it is repeated in its entirety to find the optimal solution. Cross-validation is performed in the final step to prevent over-fitting. Accuracies of the 2- and 3-cluster solutions are reported in Table 5 under "fit-based clustering". We were not able to converge on a higher number of clusters.

The 2-cluster solution has a 77.99% accuracy—a 6.7% improvement over the "smart default". One profile has 'no' for everything, while the settings in the other profile depends on **who**: it allows any collection by the user's 'Own device', and may allow collection by a 'Friend's device' or an 'Employer', depending on **what** is collected.

The 3-cluster solution (Figure 4) has a 81.54% accuracy — an 11.5% improvement over the "smart default". We find one profile with 'no' for everything; one profile that may allow collection by the user's 'Own device', depending on **what** is being collected; and one profile that allows any collection except when the recipient (**who**) is 'Unknown', the 'Government', or a 'Colleague', with settings for the latter depending on the **reason**.

Agglomerative clustering

Our final method for finding "smart profiles" follows a hierarchical bottom-up (or agglomerative) approach. It

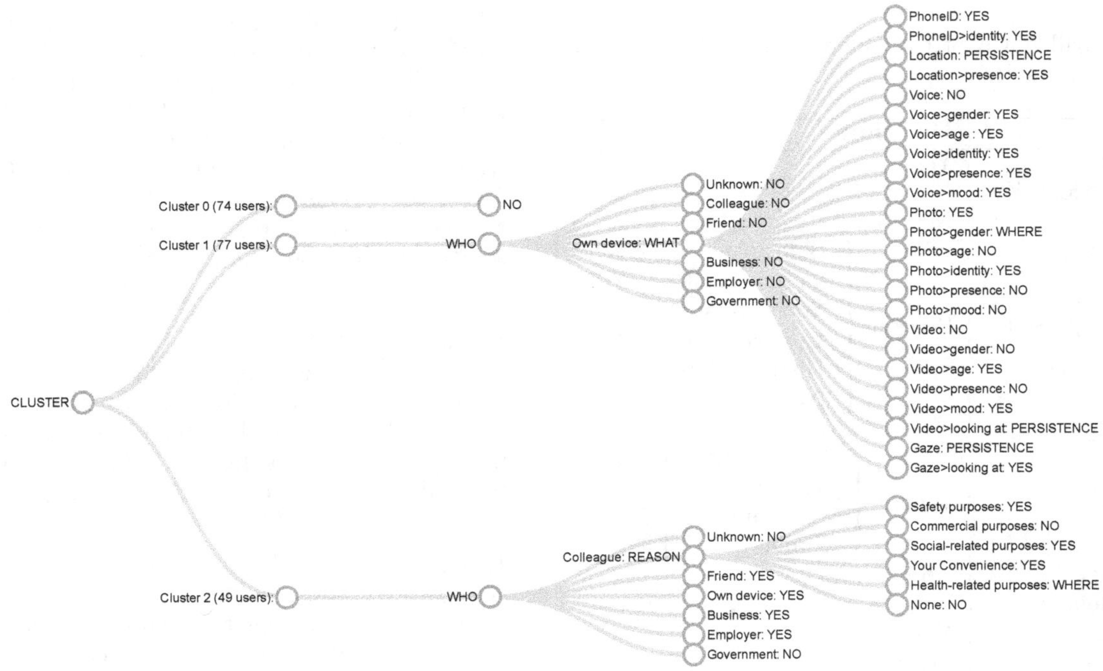

Figure 4: Fit-based clustering: 3-cluster tree. Further drill down is hidden for space reasons.

first fits a separate tree for each participant, and then iteratively merges them based on similarity. 156 of the initial 200 trees predict "no for everything" and 34 of them predict "yes for everything"—these are merged first. For every possible pair of the remaining 10 trees, the accuracy of the pair is compared with the mean accuracy the individual trees, and the pair with the smallest reduction in accuracy is merged. This process is repeated until we reach the predefined number of clusters.

We were able to reach a 5- and 4-cluster solution. The 3-cluster solution collapsed down into a 2-cluster solution with one profile of all 'yes'es and one profile of all 'no's (a somewhat trivial solution with a relatively bad fit). Accuracies of the 4- and 5-cluster (Table 5, "agglomerative clustering") are 78.13% and 78.27% respectively. For the 4-cluster solution, we find one profile with 'no' for everything, one profile with 'yes' for everything, one profile that depends on **who**, and another that depends on **what**. The latter two profiles drill down even further on specific values of **who** and **what**, respectively.

Discussion of Machine Learning Results

Figure 5 shows a comparison of the presented approaches. Compared to a naive default setting (all 'no'), a "smart default" makes a 2.0% improvement. The fit-based 2-cluster solution results in two "smart profiles" that make another 6.7% improvement over the "smart default", while the three "smart profiles" of the fit-based 3-cluster solution make an 11.5% improvement. If we let users choose the best option among these three profiles, they will on average be content with 81.54% of the settings. This rivals the accuracy of some of the "active tracking" machine learning approaches (cf. [24]).

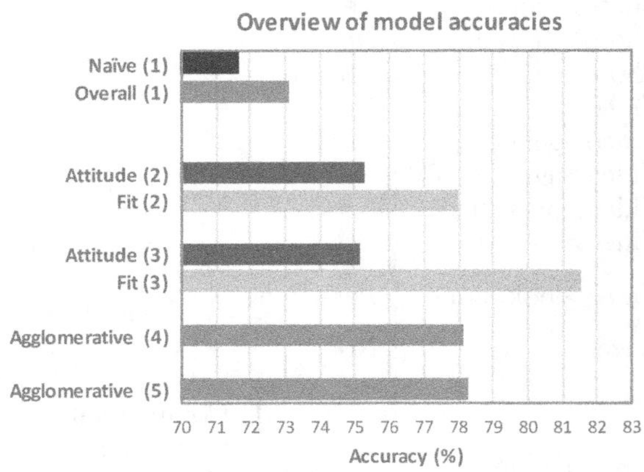

Figure 5: Accuracy of our clustering approaches

In line with our statistical results, the factor **who** seems to be the most prominent parameter, followed by **what**. In some cases the settings are more complex, depending on a combination of **who** and **what**. This is in line with the interaction effect observed in our statistical results.

Even our most accurate solution is not without fault, and its accuracy depends most on the **who** parameter. Specifically, the solution is most accurate for the user's own device, the device of a friend, and when the recipient is unknown. It is however less accurate when the recipient is a colleague, a nearby business, an employer, or the government. In these scenarios, more misclassifications tend to happen, so it would be useful to 'guide' users to specifically have a look at these default settings, should they opt to make any manual overrides.

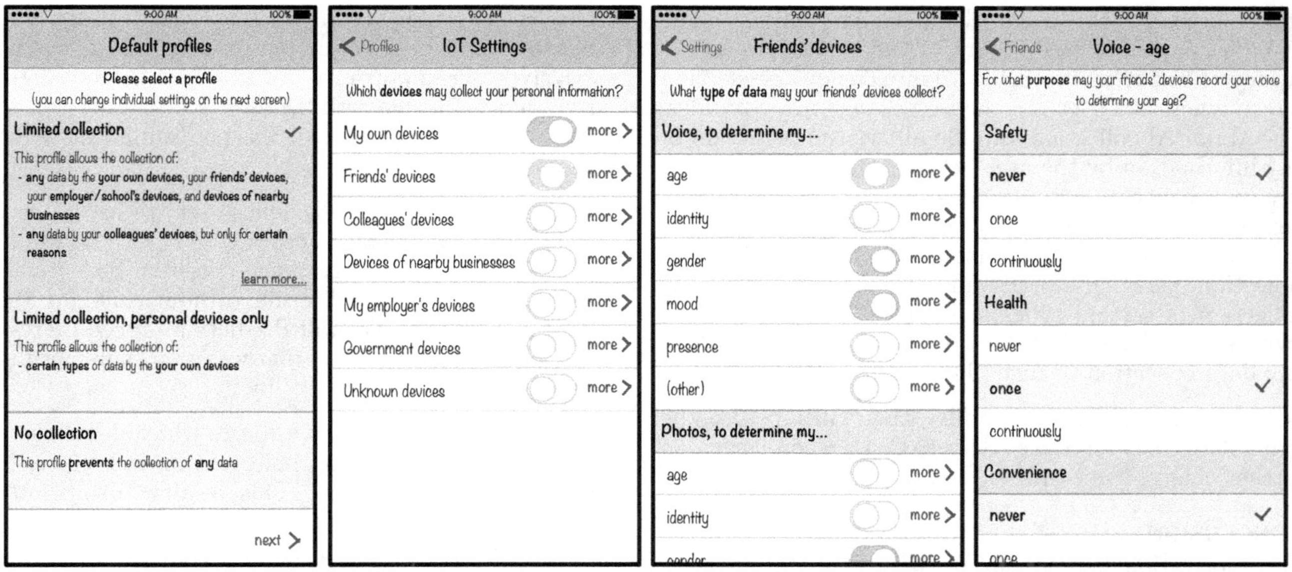

Figure 6: From Left, Screen 1 shows three default settings, Screen 2,3 and 4 shows layered interface

PRIVACY-SETTING PROTOTYPES

Designers of IoT privacy-setting interfaces face a difficult challenge. Since there currently exists no system for setting one's privacy preferences for public IoT scenarios, designers must rely on existing data such as the Lee and Kobsa [16] dataset to inform the design of these interfaces. Moreover, even for the simplified scenarios in this dataset, a privacy-setting interface will likely be complex, as it requires users to navigate settings for 7 types of recipients (**who**), 24 types of information (**what**), 4 different locations (**where**), 6 purposes (**reason**), and decide whether they want to allow the collection once or continuously (**persistence**). In this section we employ our data-driven design methodology to develop a prototype for an IoT privacy-setting interface based on the results of our statistical and machine learning analyses.

Manual Settings

The first challenge is to design an interface that users can navigate manually. Using the results of our statistical analyses, we design a "layered" settings interface: users can make a decision based on a single parameter only, and choose 'yes', 'no', or 'it depends' for each parameter value. If they choose 'it depends', they move to a next layer, where the decision for that parameter value is broken down by another parameter.

The manual interface is shown in Screens 2-4 of Figure 6. At the top layer of this interface should be the scenario parameter that is most influential in our dataset. Our statistical results inform us that this is the **who** parameter. Screen 2 shows how users can allow/reject data collection for each of the 7 types of recipients. Users can choose "more", which brings them to the second-most important scenario parameter, i.e. the **what** parameter. Screen 3 shows the data type options for when the user clicks on "more" for "Friends' devices". We have conveniently grouped the options by collection medium. Users can turn the collection of various data types by their friends' devices on or off. If only some types of data are allowed, the toggle at the higher level gets a yellow color and turns to a middle option, indicating that it is not completely 'on' (see "Friends' devices" in Screen 2).

Screen 4 shows how users can drill down even further to specify **reasons** for which collection is allowed, and the allowed **persistence** (we combined these two parameters in a single screen to reduce the "depth" of our interface). Since **reason** and **persistence** explain relatively little variance in behavioral intention, we expect that only a few users will go this deep into the interface for a small number of their settings. We leave out **where** altogether, because our statistical results deemed this parameter to be non-significant.

Smart Default Setting

The next challenge is to decide on a default setting, so that users only have to make minimal adjustments to their settings. We can use a simple "yes to everything" or "no to everything" default, but these are on average only accurate 28.33% and 71.67% of the time, respectively.

Using the results from our Overall Prediction (see Figure 2), we can create a "smart default" setting that is 73.10% accurate on average. In this version, the IoT settings for all devices are set to 'off', except for 'My own device', which will be set to the middle option. Table 7 shows the default settings at deeper levels. As this default setting is on average only 73.10% accurate, we expect users to still change some of their settings. They can do this by navigating the manual settings interface.

Smart Profiles

To improve the accuracy of the default setting, we can instead build two "smart profiles", and allow the user to choose among them. Using the 3-cluster solution of the fit-based approach (see Figure 4), we can attain an accuracy of 81.54%. Screen 1 in Figure 6 shows a selection screen where the user can choose between these profiles. The "Limited collection" profile allows the collection of any information by the user's own devices, their friends' devices, their employer/school's devices, and devices of nearby businesses. Devices of colleagues are only allowed to collect information for certain reasons. The "Limited collection, personal devices only" profile only allows the collection of certain types of information by the user's own devices. The "No collection" profile does not allow any data collection to take place by default.

Once the user chooses a profile, they will move to the manual settings interface (Screens 2–4), where they can further change some of their settings.

CONCLUSION

The motivation behind our research was the information and choice overload associated with the plethora of choices that users might face while setting their privacy settings in an IoT environment. We have made use of statistical analyses and machine learning algorithms to provide a data-driven design for an IoT privacy-setting interface. We summarize this procedure as follows:

- Using statistical analysis, uncover the relative importance of the parameters that influence users' privacy decisions. Develop a "layered interface" in which these parameters are presented in decreasing order of importance.
- Using a tree-learning algorithm, create a decision tree that best predicts participants' choices based on the parameters. Use this tree to create a "smart default" setting.
- Using a combination of clustering and tree-learning algorithms, create a set of N decision trees that best predict participants' choices. Use the trees to create N "smart profiles".
- Develop a prototype for an IoT privacy-setting interface that integrates the layered interface with the smart default or the smart profiles.

We demonstrated this procedure by applying it to a dataset collected by Lee and Kobsa [16]. In the process, we made a number of interesting observations.

The statistical and machine learning results both indicated that recipient of the information (**who**) is the most significant parameter in users' decision to allow or reject IoT-based information collection. This parameter therefore features at the forefront in our layered settings interface, and plays an important role in our smart profiles.

The **what** parameter was the second-most important decision parameter, and interacted significantly with the **who** parameter. This parameter therefore features at the second level of our settings interface, and further qualifies some of the settings in our smart profiles.

Our layered interface allows a further drill-down to the **reason** and **persistence** parameters, but given the relatively lesser importance of these parameters, we expect few users to engage with the interface at this level. Moreover, the **where** parameter was not significant, so we left it out of the interface.

While a naive ('no' to all) default setting in our interface would have provided an accuracy of 71.67%, it would not have allowed users to reap the potential benefits associated with IoT data collection without changing the default setting. Our Overall Prediction procedure resulted in a smart default setting that was a bit more permissive, and increased the accuracy by 2%.

The fit-based clustering approach, which iteratively clusters users and fits an optimal tree in each cluster, provided the best solution. This resulted in an interface where users can choose from 3 profiles, which increases the accuracy by another 11.5%.

Our analysis allowed us to use *data-driven design* to bootstrap the development of a privacy-setting interface, but a future user experiment could investigate whether users are comfortable with the layered interface, and whether they prefer a single "smart default" setting or a choice among "smart profiles".

The scenario-based method presented in this paper is particularly suited for novel domains where few real interaction exist. We note, though, that this novelty may hamper our approach: users' decisions are inherently limited by the knowledge they have about IoT. Lee and Kobsa [16] made sure to educate users about the presented scenarios, hence their data is arguably better in this regard than data from "live" systems. However, as the adaptation of IoT becomes more widespread, the mindset and knowledge regarding such technologies—and thus their privacy preferences—might change. Our "smart profiles" may thus eventually have to be updated in future work, but for now, our current profiles can at least help users make make better privacy decisions in their initial stages of usage.

Future work could also apply the proposed procedure to other privacy-setting domains. In using scenarios, the procedure avoids typical decision externalities such as default effects, framing effects, and decision-context effects that tend to obfuscate users' behaviors in more naturalistic studies. Moreover, the scenarios can inform the creation of privacy-setting interfaces for novel or currently non-existent technologies. As such we imagine that the procedure could be applied in new domains, such as household IoT ("smart home") privacy, drone privacy, and nano-tech privacy. In some of these domains, fully "adaptive" privacy mechanisms that use "active tracking" (cf. [13, 18]) are more suitable, while other domains could benefit from our static, profile-based approach.

ACKNOWLEDGEMENT

This work was supported by NSF award no. 1640664.

REFERENCES

1. Acquisti, A., and Gross, R. Imagined communities: Awareness, information sharing, and privacy on the facebook. In *International workshop on privacy enhancing technologies* (2006), Springer, pp. 36–58.
2. Ajzen, I., and Fishbein, M. Attitude-behavior relations: A theoretical analysis and review of empirical research. *Psychological bulletin 84*, 5 (1977).
3. Baron, R. M., and Kenny, D. A. The moderator–mediator variable distinction in social psychological research: Conceptual, strategic, and statistical considerations. *Journal of personality and social psychology 51*, 6 (1986), 1173.
4. Boyles, J. L., Smith, A., and Madden, M. Privacy and Data Management on Mobile Devices. Tech. rep., Pew Internet & American Life Project, 2012.
5. Chow, R., Egelman, S., Kannavara, R., Lee, H., Misra, S., and Wang, E. HCI in Business: A Collaboration with Academia in IoT Privacy. In *HCI in Business*, F. F.-H. Nah and C.-H. Tan, Eds., no. 9191 in Lecture Notes in Computer Science. Springer International Publishing, 2015.
6. Dong, C., Jin, H., and Knijnenburg, B. P. Ppm: A privacy prediction model for online social networks. In *International Conference on Social Informatics* (2016), Springer, pp. 400–420.
7. Fang, L., and LeFevre, K. Privacy wizards for social networking sites. In *Proceedings of the 19th international conference on World wide web* (2010), ACM, pp. 351–360.
8. Good, N., Dhamija, R., Grossklags, J., Thaw, D., Aronowitz, S., Mulligan, D., and Konstan, J. Stopping Spyware at the Gate: A User Study of Privacy, Notice and Spyware. In *Proceedings of the 2005 Symposium on Usable Privacy and Security* (2005), ACM, pp. 43–52.
9. Gross, R., and Acquisti, A. Information revelation and privacy in online social networks. In *Proceedings of the 2005 ACM workshop on Privacy in the electronic society* (2005), ACM, pp. 71–80.
10. Gubbi, J., Buyya, R., Marusic, S., and Palaniswami, M. Internet of things (iot): A vision, architectural elements, and future directions. *Future generation computer systems 29*, 7 (2013), 1645–1660.
11. Hall, M., Frank, E., Holmes, G., Pfahringer, B., Reutemann, P., and Witten, I. H. The weka data mining software: an update. *ACM SIGKDD explorations newsletter 11*, 1 (2009), 10–18.
12. Jensen, C., and Potts, C. Privacy Policies as Decision-Making Tools: An Evaluation of Online Privacy Notices. In *2004 Conference on Human Factors in Computing Systems* (2004), pp. 471–478.
13. Knijnenburg, B. P. *A user-tailored approach to privacy decision support.* Ph.D. Thesis, University of California, Irvine, Irvine, CA, 2015.
14. Knijnenburg, B. P., Kobsa, A., and Jin, H. Dimensionality of information disclosure behavior. *International Journal of Human-Computer Studies 71*, 12 (2013), 1144–1162.
15. Lederer, S., Mankoff, J., and Dey, A. K. Who wants to know what when? privacy preference determinants in ubiquitous computing. In *CHI'03 extended abstracts on Human factors in computing systems* (2003), ACM, pp. 724–725.
16. Lee, H., and Kobsa, A. Understanding user privacy in internet of things environments. *Internet of Things (WF-IoT)* (2016).
17. Li, Y., Kobsa, A., Knijnenburg, B. P., and Nguyen, M. C. Cross-cultural privacy prediction. *Proceedings on Privacy Enhancing Technologies 2* (2017), 93–112.
18. Liu, B., Andersen, M. S., Schaub, F., Almuhimedi, H., Zhang, S. A., Sadeh, N., Agarwal, Y., and Acquisti, A. Follow My Recommendations: A Personalized Privacy Assistant for Mobile App Permissions. In *Proceedings of the 2016 Symposium on Usable Privacy and Security* (2016).
19. Madejski, M., Johnson, M., and Bellovin, S. M. A study of privacy settings errors in an online social network. In *IEEE International Conference on Pervasive Computing and Communications Workshops* (2012), IEEE, pp. 340–345.
20. Olson, J. S., Grudin, J., and Horvitz, E. A study of preferences for sharing and privacy. In *CHI'05 extended abstracts on Human factors in computing systems* (2005), ACM, pp. 1985–1988.
21. Pallapa, G., Das, S. K., Di Francesco, M., and Aura, T. Adaptive and context-aware privacy preservation exploiting user interactions in smart environments. *Pervasive and Mobile Computing 12* (2014), 232–243.
22. Raber, F., Luca, A. D., and Graus, M. Privacy wedges: Area-based audience selection for social network posts. In *Proceedings of the 2016 Symposium on Usable Privacy and Security* (2016).
23. Ravichandran, R., Benisch, M., Kelley, P. G., and Sadeh, N. M. Capturing social networking privacy preferences. In *Proceedings of the 2009 Symposium on Usable Privacy and Security* (2009), Springer, pp. 1–18.

24. Sadeh, N., Hong, J., Cranor, L., Fette, I., Kelley, P., Prabaker, M., and Rao, J. Understanding and capturing people's privacy policies in a mobile social networking application. *Personal and Ubiquitous Computing 13*, 6 (2009), 401–412.

25. Sandhu, R. S., and Samarati, P. Access control: principle and practice. *IEEE Communications Magazine 32*, 9 (1994), 40–48.

26. Smith, N. C., Goldstein, D. G., and Johnson, E. J. Choice Without Awareness: Ethical and Policy Implications of Defaults. *Journal of Public Policy & Marketing 32*, 2 (2013), 159–172.

27. Watson, J., Besmer, A., and Lipford, H. R. +Your circles: sharing behavior on Google+. In *Proceedings of the 8th Symposium on Usable Privacy and Security* (2012), ACM, pp. 12:1–12:10.

28. Williams, M., Nurse, J. R., and Creese, S. The perfect storm: The privacy paradox and the internet-of-things. In *Availability, Reliability and Security (ARES), 2016 11th International Conference on* (2016), IEEE, pp. 644–652.

29. Wisniewski, P. J., Knijnenburg, B. P., and Lipford, H. R. Making privacy personal: Profiling social network users to inform privacy education and nudging. *International Journal of Human-Computer Studies 98* (2017), 95–108.

To Draw or Not to Draw: Recognizing Stroke-Hover Intent in Non-instrumented Gesture-free Mid-Air Sketching

Umema Bohari
Texas A & M University
umemabohari_123@tamu.edu

Ting-Ju Chen
Texas A & M University
carol0712@tamu.edu

Vinayak
Texas A & M University
vinayak@tamu.edu

ABSTRACT

Drawing curves in mid-air with fingers is a fundamental task with applications to 3D sketching, geometric modeling, handwriting recognition, and authentication. Mid-air curve input is most commonly accomplished through explicit user input; akin to click-and-drag, the user may use a hand posture (e.g. pinch) or a button-press on an instrumented controller to express the intention to start and stop sketching. In this paper, we present a novel approach to recognize the user's intention to draw or not to draw in a mid-air sketching task without the use of postures or controllers. For every new point recorded in the user's finger trajectory, the idea is to simply classify this point as either hover or stroke. Our work is motivated by a behavioral study that demonstrates the need for such an approach due to the lack of robustness and intuitiveness while using hand postures and instrumented devices. We captured sketch data from users using a haptics device and trained multiple binary classifiers using feature vectors based on the local geometric and motion profile of the trajectory. We present a systematic comparison of these classifiers and discuss the advantages of our approach to spatial curve input applications.

Author Keywords

Mid-air interactions; 3D Sketching; Random forest; Intent recognition; Curve Modeling

MOTIVATION

The ability to draw curves in air using hand and arm movements is fundamental to spatial (mid-air) interactions with applications in 3D sketching [5, 30], geometric modeling [8], hand-writing [26, 34, 1], and spatial authentication [6]. Recently, there has been significant interest in techniques for recognizing symbols within curves drawn in the air [34, 32]. Most, if not all, of these works focus on determining the semantic content in a curve input (*what the user wanted to express through the curve input*). Our goal in this paper is to investigate a complementary yet fundamental problem in mid-air sketching task: determining when users actually intend to draw in mid-air.

IUI'18, March 7–11, 2018, Tokyo, Japan

 ISBN 978-1-4503-4945-1/18/03...$15.00

DOI: https://doi.org/10.1145/3172944.3172985

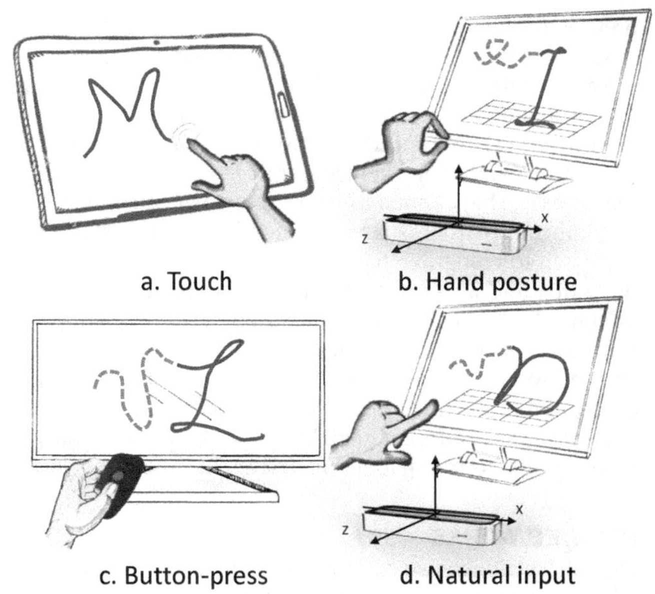

Figure 1. Different mid-air input modalities.

When sketching on a desktop or a tablet, the distinction between a stroke (*what the user actually intends to draw*) and a hover (*all other movements that are not intentional to the drawing task*) is trivially accomplished through explicit events such as mouse button down or touch down (Figure 1(a)). In mid-air interaction, such explicit *interrupts* can either be provided with some specific hand posture (Figure 1(b)) or with a hand-held device with buttons (Figure 1(c)). Most existing approaches embody this requirement in their hardware setup and use events that (such as pen up, pen down, hand posture, etc.) segment the hover points from stroke points for performing further analysis for the stroke segments of the curve. With this in view, the following questions motivate our work:

1. How do users draw in mid-air to express general shapes? What is the effect of spatial input devices or hand postures on the intuitiveness of mid-air sketch input?

2. For processing and recognition of symbols and alphanumeric patterns, a library of pre-defined canonical shapes is needed. How do we approach recognition of sketches that represent known objects but may not be composed of individually recognizable strokes (such as design sketches)?

3. Does the movement of the hand while mid-air sketching posses inherent geometric and temporal structure that can be used to identify when the user intends to draw in mid-air?

Motivated by these questions, our intention was to study how users move during mid-air sketching, develop qualitative insights regarding such movements, and consequently implement a computational approach to determine when the user intends to draw in mid-air without the use of an explicit mechanism (such as an instrumented controller or a specified hand-posture). In doing so, we make two contributions. First, we present an observational study wherein we characterize hand trajectories generated by users in mid-air sketching tasks with three sketching interfaces. This study helped us gain a better understanding of the quantitative aspects of spatial user input in terms of relative speeds of stroke and hover, intuitiveness of postures and instrumented controllers for sketching, and the types of shapes such as characters, shape primitives, and general multi-stroke shapes. Secondly, we present a novel approach to recognize the user's intention to draw or not to draw in a mid-air sketching task without the use of postures or controllers. Given a sequence of points in the user's finger trajectory, we trained a binary classifier to learn the relationship between the motion profile and geometric features of each point in the trajectory with its true classification (hover or stroke). The resulting model allows for the classification of points on the user's spatial trajectory.

RELATED WORKS

Digital sketching is an extensively studied area of research. In contrast to 3D geometric models, sketches are rough, ambiguous, and vague by nature. As a result there has been significant prior work [23, 24, 11] on segmenting sketches into meaningful objects or components. Curve inputs, in general, have also been used as *gestures* by several approaches in multi-touch devices [7, 2, 3, 37, 33]. However, these techniques are not always scalable to spatial inputs due to the additional uncertainty added by the third dimension: the intended planarity of strokes is not guaranteed.

With the increasing availability of interactive devices such as Wii Remote, Microsoft's Kinect, and Leap Motion, there has been rising interest in techniques for mid-air curve input for gesture recognition [32, 29, 4, 36], hand-writing [26, 34, 1], and sketching [5, 8, 30]. These works are focused on the identification of the curve drawn by the user as some known symbol from an existing list (e.g. alphanumeric symbols) and subsequent analysis of that known symbol. There are also hand-posture based approaches [21, 27, 31, 25] for spatial curve input for detecting user intent for creating mid-air strokes. Despite the significant advances, hand pose estimation and skeleton tracking still lack the required robustness for simple tasks such as sketching. Further, posture recognition is not scalable for interactions with large displays [22, 9, 20], making it difficult to use multiple body skeleton tracking controllers to identify the user intent. Special devices have also been proposed for curve creation, especially for design applications. Grosman et al. [14, 13] propose a physical tape drawing metaphor for automotive curve design, and this approach involves using robust hand trackers for hand skeleton detection. 3D input techniques for large displays as described in [19] make use of infrared trackers and Wiimotes for improved robustness of the interactions.

Our work aims at enabling future interfaces that will be able to eliminate the need for a prescribed set of gestures/postures or controllers to allow users to express 3D artifacts. There are three observations in relation to the previous works that motivate our problem and approach. First, as Taranta et al. [32] note, the particular effectiveness of such recognizers for segmentation and recognition of curve inputs on touch surfaces have not been particularly successful in higher dimensional spaces. Second, in order to expand the scope of intelligent user interfaces beyond symbol recognition to free-form design interfaces, there is a need for methods that do not rely on comparing user input with canonical shapes in a repository. Most techniques are developed and evaluated using segmented data, rather than considering a continuous time-stamped data sequence of 3D points [25, 10]. To address this issue, Krishnan et al. [18] develop and evaluate a sliding window based approach to perform activity recognition with streaming sensor data. The approach adopted in JackKnife [32] proposes implementation of dynamic time warping for continuous dynamic identification of gestures. While JackKnife [32] treats each gesture as a time series representation of direction vectors and then classifies with regard to all templates stored in a database, our work processes mid-air curve input as sequential points which have individual set of feature vectors, and performs the classification on each point as and when new points are recorded. Finally, unlike sketching on a tablet with a finger or stylus, using a spatial device or a hand posture is not necessarily natural [8]. Works such as Data Miming [15] and grasp-based virtual pottery [35] have demonstrated that for continuous and free-form tasks such as design, users' movements are guided by their interactions with the physical world rather than actions prescribed by the interface designer. We draw from these latter approaches and present a method that encapsulates human movement patterns during mid-air sketching within an intelligent framework for sketch intent recognition.

MID-AIR SKETCHING: OBSERVATIONAL STUDY

To better motivate the need for our approach, we conducted an observational study where our intention was to observe how users specifically react to known spatial input conditions (such as constraining the sketch on a canvas or using a specific gesture) in comparison to a completely rule-free scenario (how one might describe an object through spatial movement without a computer interface at all). For this, we implemented three interfaces using the Leap Motion Controller to record the trajectory of the user's hand skeleton while drawing a given curve. Based on the recorded hand position, the following rules were applied for detecting whether the recorded point is stroke or hover:

I1 *Proximal Plane:* We consider a trajectory point as a stroke point if the palm is in proximity to a pre-defined sketching plane within a threshold (Figure 2 (a)). The interface recognizes the user's intention to sketch when the palm is within a certain threshold of the front facing plane on the screen. Even though this method is agnostic to any specific pose of the hand, we asked users to assume a pointing posture while sketching to maintain a natural way of providing input.

I2 *Pinch Posture:* We consider a trajectory point as a stroke point if the hand assumes the pinching posture (Figure 2 (b)). Our choice of the pinch posture is motivated from the way one holds a pen while sketching on a piece of paper. We recognize a pinch based on the Euclidean distance between the thumb and index finger is within a pre-defined threshold.

I3 *Unrestricted:* In the third interface, we simply asked users to describe a curve in the air without any restrictions on their hand movement or posture. Here, there was no explicit distinction between hover and stroke for the recorded data (i.e. all points were stroke points).

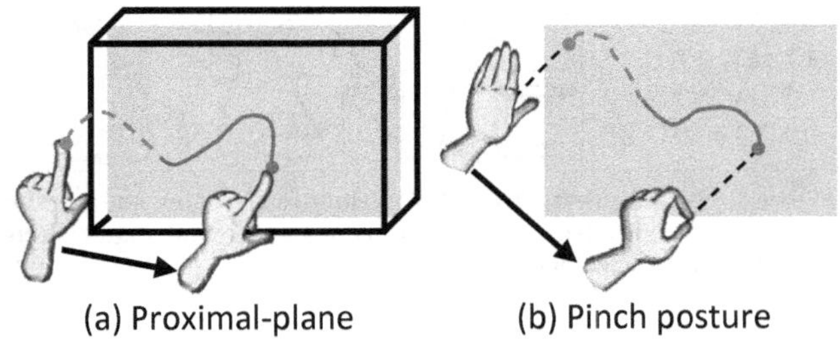

Figure 2. Illustration of the plane-proximity and pinch gesture mechanisms used in Leap Motion interfaces I1 and I2 for the observational study.

Participants

We recruited 10 engineering students (5 female) within the age range of 19-30 years. Except one participant, none of these participants had prior experiences with motion tracking devices such as Wii and Kinect or mid-air sketching.

Procedure

The total time taken during the experiment varied between 30 and 35 minutes and the three interfaces were randomized across the participants. After describing the setup, the purpose of the study, we described the features of the first sketching interface and practically demonstrated its usage. For each participant and task **T3**, we recorded a video of the task, the completion time, and the time-stamped 3D coordinates of the trajectories generated by the users for each sketched shape. Each participant performed the following tasks:

T1 *Unrestricted Sketch*: Participants were asked to draw primitive shapes a square in mid-air without restrictions on their hand posture or movement. The participants' responses were video recorded for observational exploration.

T2 *Posture-preference*: Participants were then asked to repeat the primitive sketching, but with one or more hand postures of their choice from a list of pointing, two-finger pinch, open palm, and pen-holding posture. In addition to video recording, we also recorded the reasons for these choices.

P *Practice*: To familiarize themselves with the interaction of their hand postures with the corresponding three interfaces, the participants were given a brief demonstration of the software and its functions, and were allowed to practice for 5 minutes on each interface. They were allowed to ask questions and were provided guidance when required.

T3 *Sketching with I1 & I2*: Participants were asked to sketch on the planar-proximity and pinch based interfaces in a randomized manner. For each of these interfaces, every participant sketched at least two primitives (Figure 3). Although the duration of time for each interface was set to five minutes, we allowed the participants to sketch more shapes with their aspirations. The canvas was cleared after completion of each primitive.

Q *Questionnaire*: Finally, each participant answered a series of questions regarding their perception of each of the interfaces in terms of ease of use, intuitiveness, and robustness. We also collected open-ended comments regarding the tasks.

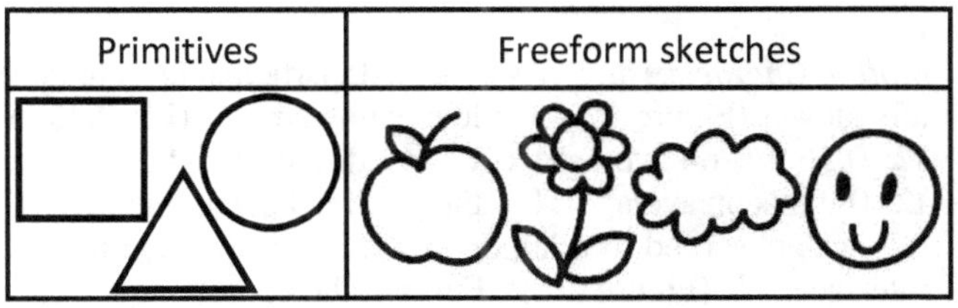

Figure 3. Primitives and free-form multi-stroke sketches drawn by users during the observational study.

Findings

With each participant drawing 6 sketches, a total of 106670 points (55919 *stroke*, 60751 *hover*) were recorded.

Posture Comparison: As expected, nine out of ten participants used index finger to draw single-stroke primitives in the unrestricted sketch interface (**I3**). However, in the posture-preference task (**T2**), three out of these nine participants who used the pointing posture in **I3**, changed their preference to the pinching posture. One user stated: *"It is more like using pen and paper"*. Another user stated: *"Pinching can help me deal with more complex, detailed drawings"*. This indicates that (a) there is a natural *default* hand posture and body movement that manifests commonly across users during mid-air curve input and (b) the way users move while sketching in air is dependent on the nature of the artifact itself that they are trying to draw.

Interface Comparison: We further observed that the order of interfaces affected ease of adopting different hand postures in mid-air sketching. A participant who completed sketching tasks with **I1** and **I2** before **I3**, stated: *"It is difficult to turn it on and off, people normally do not change their hand posture despite it is a stroke or a hover"*. Nine participants out of ten also preferred **I3** over the other two even though I3 did not have any visual cue that distinguished hover from stroke. They stated: *"The normal interface was easiest"* and *"I do not need to worry about gestures and everything was detected with the normal interface"*.

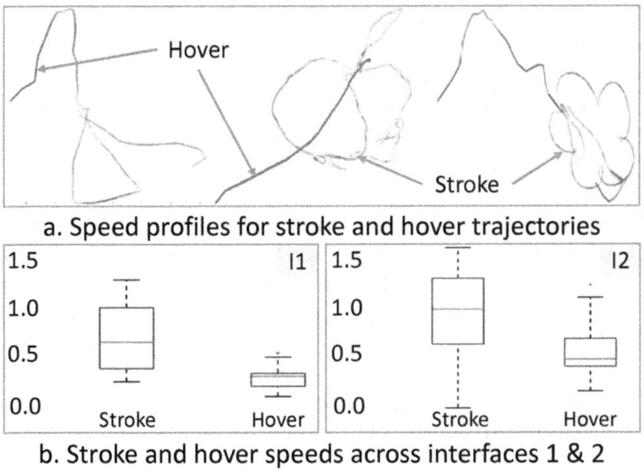

Figure 4. The speed profile (top) shows a near-constant speed for hover that is greater than stroke speeds. The avaerage hover and stroke speeds were greater for the pinch-posture interface (I2) in comparison to proximal plane (I1)

Motion Characteristics: As expected, participants were generally slower (Figure 4(a)) while creating strokes (**I1:** 0.35 m/s, **I2:** 0.56 m/s on average) as opposed to hover (**I1:** 0.66 m/s, **I2:** 0.9 m/s on average). For the proximal plane interface (**I1**), this was observed to a larger extent in comparison to pinch interface (**I2**) (Figure 4(b)). Further, the uncertainty of users' trajectory increased as they reached closer to the instance of transitioning from hover to stroke. This was observed in terms of large straight hover trajectories followed by short zigzag ones while transitioning from hover to stroke.

Shape Type: There were significant differences in how participants approached different types of primitives. They spent time in refining details for multi-stroke shapes. The distribution of hover and stroke regions trajectories for drawing single-stroke primitives were common across users when compared with general multi-stroke shapes. This strongly indicated that for arbitrary sketches, there is a need for a general computational strategy for segmenting and recognizing meaningful parts of the users' trajectory.

STROKE-HOVER RECOGNITION METHODOLOGY

The lack of robust finger tracking was a major concern for our pinch-posture interface (**I2**). As a result, stroke points were intermittently lost due to incorrect prediction of the pinch posture. One of the participants, who had experience in motion tracking devices such as Wii and VR, stated: *"The software interface with hardware probably had some minor issues with detection of fingers...It couldn't follow the movement of my hand and veered off course many times"*. In contrast to our behavioral study, we used the GeoMagic Touch device for data acquisition. Here, users specified their intent to sketch through the use of buttons on the device stylus (similar to a mouse click-and-drag). Our choice of hardware was directly a result of the lack of robustness observed in our behavioral studies with the Leap Motion wherein capturing user intent was prohibitively difficult.

Participants

We recruited 21 engineering students (11 female) within the age range of 19-30 years. None of these participants had prior experience with using the GeoMagic Touch device.

Sketching tasks and assumptions

Each participant was asked to draw 47 different sketches comprising of symbols, 2D and 3D primitives, and free-form sketches in mid-air (Figure 5). The participants were instructed to sketch the curves as naturally as they could (i.e. as fast or as slow as they would if there were no interface). We assume that the 2D data sketched by users is primarily planar, and can be drawn using single strokes or multi-strokes; while the 3-dimensional primitives recorded are multi-planar and multi-stroke sketches.

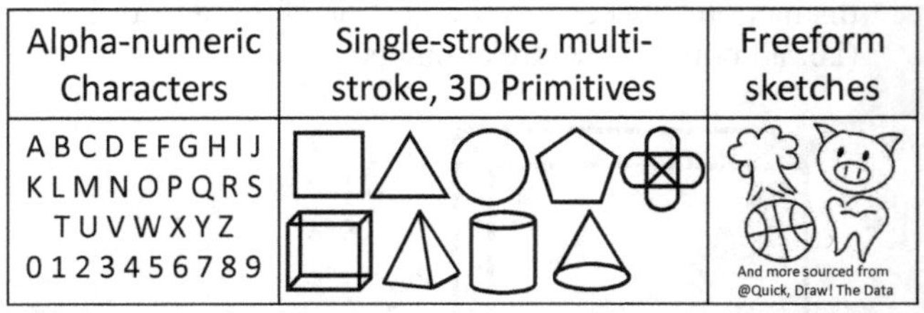

Figure 5. Symbols (left), 2D and 3D primitives (center), and free-form 2D sketches (right) drawn by users during 3D sketching data collection using the GeoMagic Touch device.

Recorded Data

We developed a simple interface that allows the participants to sketch in 3D using the GeoMagic Touch stylus (Figure 6). For every curve drawn, the interface records a continuous sequence of 3D coordinates of the stylus tip trajectory $P_{x,y,z}$, and the classification of that point as being *stroke*(1), or *hover*(0). While writing on a piece of paper, or sketching on tablet surfaces, velocity of the traversal trajectories between two successive strokes is much faster than the stroke trajectories themselves. As noted by Johnson et al.[16], time data is generally used for segmenting strokes in different sketch recognition algorithms. Speed profiles of the data recorded in the observational studies (Figure 4), also point towards a similar distinguishing factor between *stroke* and *hover* curves. Therefore, along with the curve coordinates and classification status, we record the time stamp in milliseconds t of all drawn points.

Features

Based on the motion profiles and local geometric properties of the recorded 3D temporal data, to train and test our classifiers, we construct a feature list comprising of the following:

1. **Motion profile** For every given point i on the trajectory, we calculate its speed (s_i), acceleration (a_i), and jerk (j_i) relative to the $(i-1)^{th}$ point.

$$s_i = \|P_i - P_{i-1}\|, a_i = \frac{s_i - s_{i-1}}{t_i - t_{i-1}}, j_i = \frac{a_i - a_{i-1}}{t_i - t_{i-1}}$$

Based on the motion characteristics of the 3D data recorded in the observational study (figure 4), we note that at the *stroke-hover* transition, there is an abrupt shift in the local

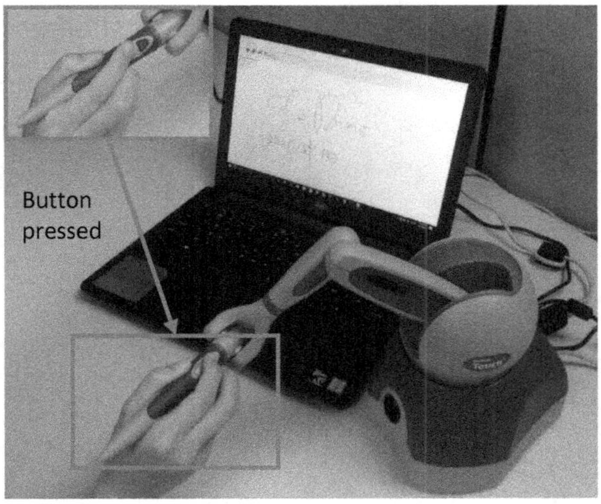

Figure 6. GeoMagic Touch 3D sketching data recording setup. Inset: Stylus button that needs to be pressed by the user to draw an intended *stroke* curve.

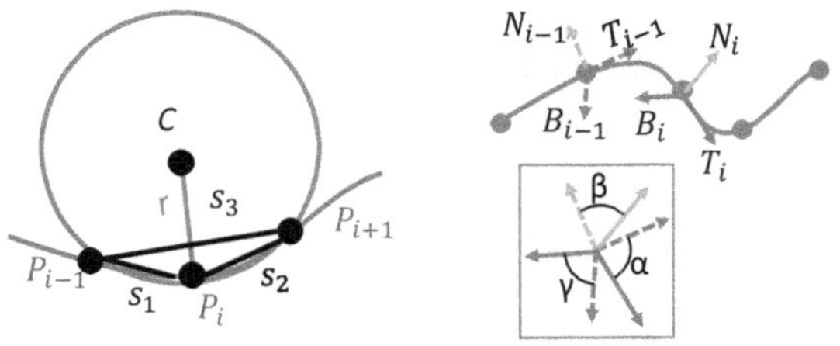

a. Curvature Estimate b. Frenet frame rotation

Figure 7. Estimated curvature and discrete Frenet frames of the recorded curve.

curve speed. To capture this shift, we calculate the relative speed ratio (S_r) at a given point, as:

$$S_r = \frac{s_i}{s_{i-1}}$$

2. **Curvature** Recorded curve trajectories from the Leap Motion observational study, and GeoMagic Touch data collection study are suggestive of the fact that *hover* trajectories have a higher degree of flatness, whereas *stroke* trajectories have a higher curvature. This measure of flatness of the curve at the $(i)^{th}$ point is captured by estimating the Menger curvature (c_i) at that point (Figure 7 (a)). For a given triangle formed by P_i, P_{i-1}, P_{i+1}, the curvature is given by:

$$c_i = \frac{1}{r} = \frac{4A}{s_1 s_2 s_3}$$

where A is the area of $\triangle P_{i-1}P_iP_{i+1}$, and s_1, s_2, and s_3 are lengths of the triangle's sides.

3. **Rate of change of Frenet frame** We associate discrete Frenet frames for every edge forming the curve (Figure 7 (b)). The three orthogonal components of each Frenet frame (tangent t_i, normal n_i, binormal b_i) are computed as:

$$t_i = \frac{P_i - P_{i-1}}{||P_i - P_{i-1}||}, b_i = t_{i-1} \times t_i, n_i = b_i \times t_i$$

As the user draws the *stroke* and *hover* curves, the change in planarity is estimated by calculating the rate of change of angles between the consecutive Frenet frame components. These angular velocities (ω_α, ω_β, ω_γ) form the last three components of our training and testing feature vector:

$$\omega_\alpha = \frac{\alpha_i - \alpha_{i-1}}{t_i - t_{i-1}}, \omega_\beta = \frac{\beta_i - \beta_{i-1}}{t_i - t_{i-1}}, \omega_\gamma = \frac{\gamma_i - \gamma_{i-1}}{t_i - t_{i-1}}$$

Training and Testing

Of the total data recorded from 21 participants, data from 2 participants had to be discarded, due to misrepresentation of visual cues that hinted towards it being a plane drawing task instead of mid-air sketching task. Of the remaining data, we used 50000 points (22923 *stroke*, 27078 *hover*) for training the model, while the remaining 50000 points (24292 *stroke*, 25708 *hover*) were used to test and cross-validate the data. While training, the feature vectors were randomly sampled from the available pool to eliminate any kind of over-fitting of the trained model due to adjacent data points. For testing, sequences of points belonging to a given shape were sampled. We used MATLAB's implementations of different binary classifiers. With mid-air sketches essentially being a series of alternating *stroke* and *hover* curves, we believe that the status of a given point on the curve is dependent on that of its neighbors. To test this, we train a *k*-Nearest Neighbor binary classifier. We ensure there is an equal mix of *stroke* and *hover* features in the training list to eliminate model bias towards the over-represented class. Since Support Vector Machines (SVM) find utility in multiple gesture recognition tasks, we also train a binary SVM classifier. Training and testing data is uniformly scaled for accurate implementation of SVM. Finally, we explore random forest classifiers, and discuss different tuning parameters for accurate predictions.

RESULTS

In this section, we discuss the prediction accuracies of the 3 classifiers, and identify the optimum model for *stroke-hover* classification. Next, we perform a parametric optimization for the random forest model, and discuss its prediction results, and limitations.

Classifier Comparison

To compare the classification accuracies (η) across the 3 models, we sample and predict symbols, 2D and 3D primitives, and free-form sketches from the testing feature list.

After performing parametric optimization, with 27 closest neighbors, and *correlation* distance metric, the *k*-NN model predicts with an average accuracy of $\eta = 57.11\%$ at a 0.04 seconds per point prediction rate. For cross-validated two-class SVM models using both radial basis function, and Gaussian kernels, the average prediction accuracy is $\eta = 51.44\%$ at a 0.02 seconds per point prediction rate. It is observed that while the *k*-NN model shows some trends of segmenting the stroke-hover data (Figure 8 (1a),(2a),(3a),(4a)), the SVM model classifies every point as being *stroke* (high false positive) (Figure 8 (2b), (3b),(4b)). The random forest model, on the other hand, exhibits good demarcation between *stroke* and

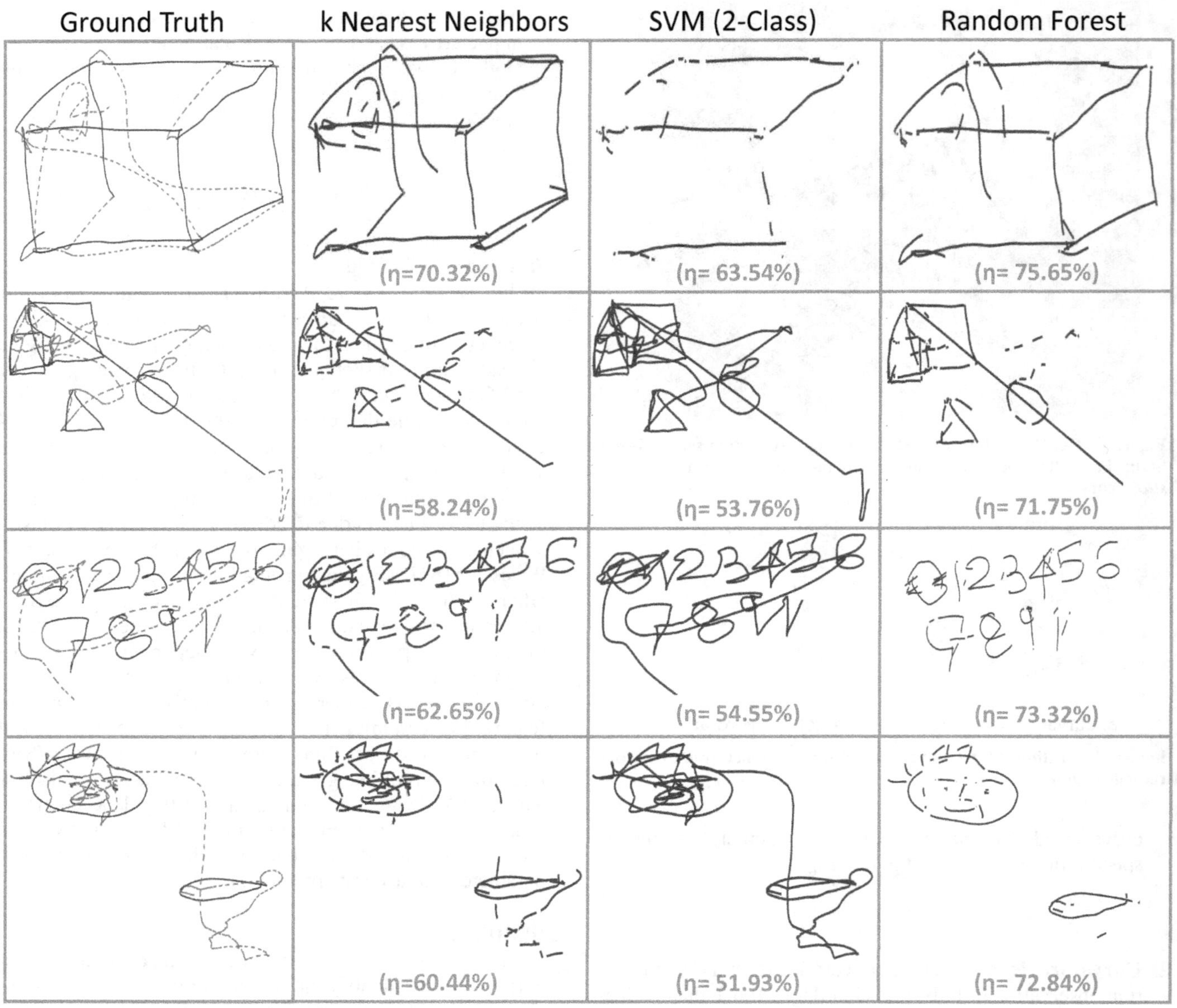

Figure 8. Sampled prediction results with accuracies (η) for *k*-NN, SVM, and Random Forest binary classifiers. *k*-NN and SVM models show high false positives.

hover curves, and classifies them with an average accuracy of $\eta = 71.63\%$ at 0.03 seconds per point prediction rate.

Random Forest

We explore the random forest classifier to further improve its accuracy, by training different models using the following feature list:

$$F_i = \begin{bmatrix} s_i & a_i & j_i & c_i & S_r & \omega_\alpha & \omega_\beta & \omega_\gamma \end{bmatrix} \quad (1)$$

Two main tuning parameters – maximum node splits per decision tree N_s, and number of trees per forest, N_t, are used to control the prediction accuracy. The depth of every decision tree is controlled by N_s. We begin with the default values of $N_s = 7$ and $N_t = 10$, and perform a grid search to identify optimum parameters. Based on this analysis, the model with $N_s = 779$ and $N_t = 40$ performs best with a prediction accuracy of $\eta = 82\%$ for 50000 points (Figure 9).

As in the case of SVM, we explore the effect of scaling 3D data coordinates as well as processed features, on the model prediction accuracy. It is observed that the model with no scaling performs with the best accuracy. Speed (s_i), Speed ratio (S_r), local curvature (c_i), and ω_α are found to be the dominating features, and we retrain the final random forest model using only these parameters.

Instrumented Controller Predictions:

The optimum random forest model is tested using symbols, 2D and 3D primitives, and free-form shapes from the testing feature list. Higher prediction accuracy is observed in case of

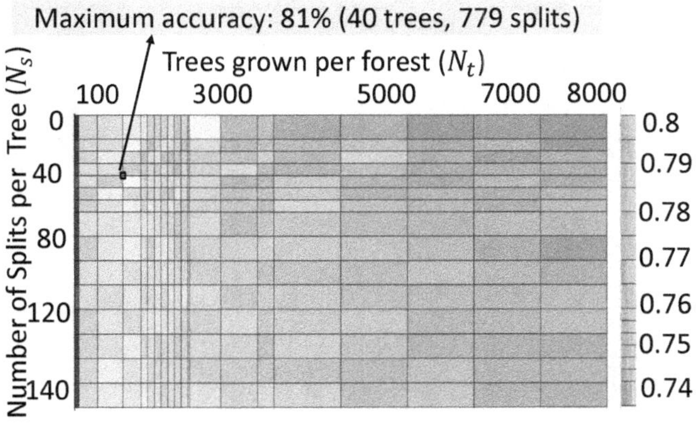

Figure 9. Variation in random forest model accuracy (η) with changes in number of individual tree splits (N_s) and number of trees per forest (N_t).

primitives and free-form shapes $\eta = 85.75\%$ (Figure 11, 10), as compared to symbols $\eta = 78.75\%$ (Figure 10 (a)). This can be explained in a couple of ways. First, during the data collection study, it was observed that due to familiarity with symbols, participants sketched them at a much faster rate. On the other hand, the participants were found to be cautious while sketching multi-stroke free-form sketches and 3D primitives. This had a direct effect on our hypothesis that *hover* trajectories should essentially be traversed faster as compared to *stroke*, in the sense that, this was followed for the multi-stroke shapes, but was not reflected for the recorded symbols data. Second, from a close analysis of the data collection video, it was observed that symbol sketches were primarily restricted to a single plane, while multi-stroke primitives and free-form sketches spanned multiple planes. While the multi-planarity was effectively captured for the shapes using the three Frenet frame vectors, the same cannot be guaranteed for symbols.

Interesting results are observed for free-form 2D sketches and 3D primitives (Figure 11). A majority of these sketches are multi-stroke, involving constant shifts between *hover* and *stroke* curves. The 3D primitives also involve frequent movements between different planes. Despite this fact, the classifier is able to segment such curves with a high accuracy without consulting an existing database to identify the nature of the drawn sketches. In other words, the model is able to classify a given point based on its local properties, rather than classifying it based on the nature of the entire sketch as a whole.

Bare Hand Predictions:
We measured the performance of the model by predicting 3D sketching data recorded in the Unrestricted Interface **I3** using the Leap Motion controller (Figure 12). The predicted results have two characteristics: discontinuity in predictions (Figure 12 (a)), and high false positive rates (hover misclassification) (Figure 12 (b)). These characteristics can be attributed to the different ways in which the training and testing data sets are recorded on the GeoMagoc Touch and Leap motion interfaces, respectively. On one hand, while the GeoMagic Touch based interface recorded data with accurate sketch-hover demarcation, it ultimately is a tethered device, with limited work volume availability. On the other hand, with the Leap interface, users had comparatively more freedom with respect to workspace availability, and were able to draw curves at a much faster rate. However, it is worth noting that the model was able to classify sufficient points without geometrically pre-processing the recorded data using techniques like corner detection.

Limitations
The primary reason for using the haptics device for 3D sketching data collection was to ensure accurately recording the *stroke-hover* data of the drawn points. However, the device itself posed certain limitations due to its physical manipulation capacities, offering roughly an interaction space of 16 in x 12 in x 10 in. Also, since it was primarily tethered to the computer, the user did not have much freedom in terms of moving away from the computer and sketching. It was also observed that participants experienced high resistance from the stylus pivot while traversing wavy curves like the tree crown (Figure 11). This resulted in the user dwelling for much longer time while drawing *stroke* curves. Restricted motion about the stylus pivot also resulted in wavy hover trajectories, resulting in high curvature *hover* curves. In future, we plan to eliminate these limitations by conducting a similar study using a non-tethered instrumented controller. Further, mid-air curve input speed is dependent on some other factors like the type of curves, preciseness with which they are drawn, and the application for the 3D curve. In future studies, we plan to record and develop a model on variety of mid-air 3D curves.

DISCUSSION

Design Implications
At its core, our approach offers a different perspective for mid-air sketching, that is, considering intentional strokes as *anomalies* within a continuous hover activity. The ability to detect this anomaly changes the way we design mid-air interfaces. The validation of this model opens up new vistas in the domain of mid-air interactions in context of design ideation, and early stage concept design. With an on-the-fly implementation of our approach, designers will be able to naturally construct 3D concepts through consecutive curve descriptions without the need for specific gestures or instrumented controllers. The classified *stroke* data can then be recognized using standard sketch recognition techniques. In collaborative design ideation setups, coupling this approach with semantic data may lead to the development of intelligent mixed-initiative interfaces.

Application to 3D Modeling
Our approach can be considered complementary to existing segmentation and recognition applications. It is interesting to consider the implications of this model in context of 3-dimensional sketching applications like Tilt Brush [12] and Gravity Sketch [28], that use augmented reality and instrumented controllers for enabling mid-air sketching. Participant feedback from the behavioral study is indicative of the fact that sketching in mid-air without specifying explicit gestures, or using instrumented controllers, is both natural, as well as intuitive. Our work shows that both aspects are relevant and related. One of the major problems associated with using

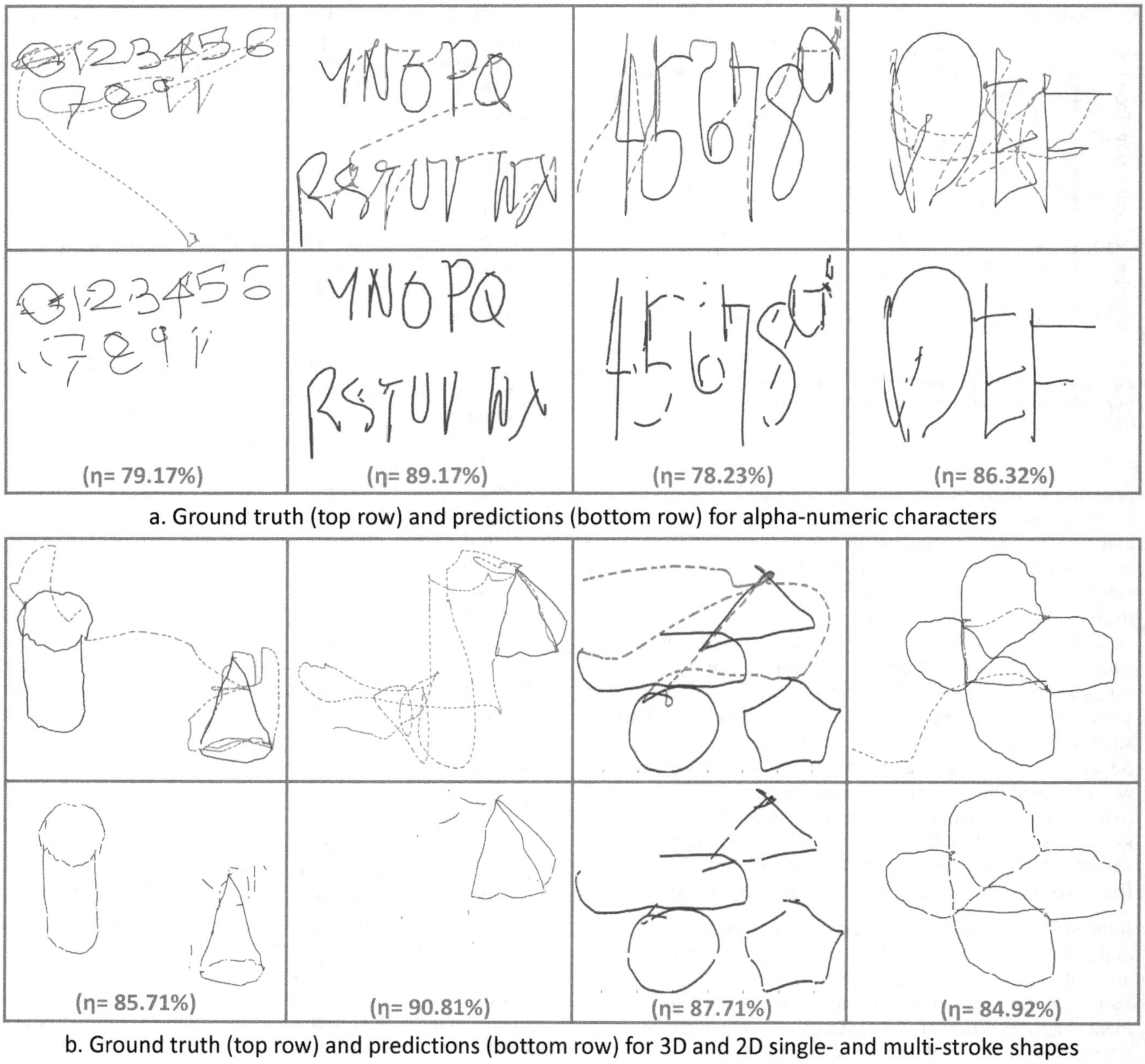

Figure 10. Random Forest model prediction accuracies (η) for symbols (first two rows) and 3D/2D primitives (bottom two rows) sketch data recorded using GeoMagic Touch.

freehand 3D data in geometric modeling applications is the lack of controllability[17]. Scaling our approach and modeling geometric shape controllability using the *sketch-hover* analogy may lead to the development of mid-air curve input based 3D modeling applications.

Scalability across different interaction volumes

In order for mid-air interactions to scale, we must have different levels of details for recognizing when a user wants to affect the state of an interactive system - specifically in setups involving large displays. In this context, we offer a possibility of bypassing hand skeletal tracking by simply analyzing body-level activity (that can be robustly tracked by most available algorithms) to identify user intent for curve drawing [13]. This will further allow for implementation of novel and richer interfaces for large displays and interaction spaces enabling collaborative design experiences.

CONCLUSIONS & FUTURE DIRECTIONS

In this paper, we presented an approach for capturing user intent for creating strokes using spatial input. Our idea was based on a simple premise that the user's intention to draw in mid-air is inherently present in the motion and geometric characteristics of user-generated hand trajectory. With the

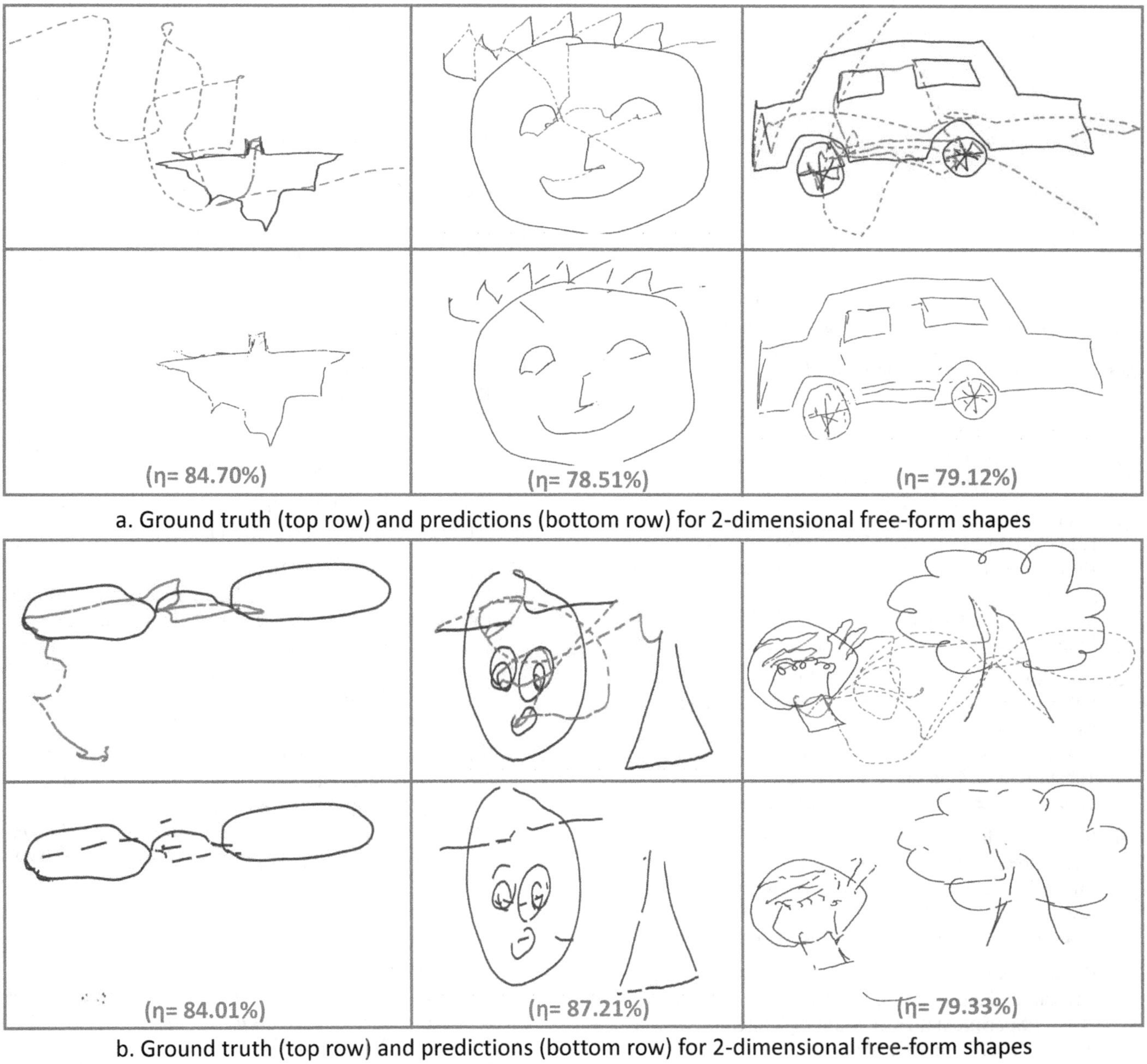

Figure 11. Random Forest model prediction accuracies (η) for multi-stroke free-form sketch data recorded using GeoMagic Touch.

current accuracy of our classification algorithms, we believe it is possible to create interesting applications such as interactive art, especially for large displays with multiple users. However, for more precise applications such as 3D design, our approach needs improvements in overall accuracy. We intend to collect a richer and more extensive dataset that can be used for training classifiers based on neural networks (especially recurrent neural networks that can capture the time-series nature of the underlying data). Further, we plan to investigate how our approach could be utilized as an intermediate step toward improving known frameworks for recognition of spatial symbols and gestures. In the broader domain of mid-air curve input, our work opens a new problem context that can potentially lead to novel approaches for enabling users to express visual ideas through spatial interactions.

ACKNOWLEDGMENTS

We thank the reviewers for their valuable feedback and comments. This work was supported by the Texas A&M University start-up fund and the Department of Mechanical Engineering at Texas A&M University.

REFERENCES

1. Chelsi Agarwal, Debi Prosad Dogra, Rajkumar Saini, and Partha Pratim Roy. 2015. Segmentation and recognition

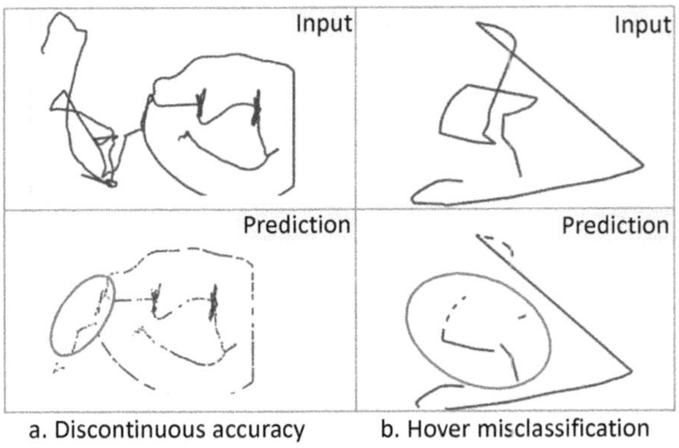

Figure 12. Random Forest model prediction results for 3D sketch data recorded using Leap Motion. Discontinuity in predictions (left), and false positives (right) observed during predictions.

of text written in 3d using leap motion interface. In *Pattern Recognition (ACPR), 2015 3rd IAPR Asian Conference on*. IEEE, 539–543.

2. Lisa Anthony and Jacob O. Wobbrock. 2010. A Lightweight Multistroke Recognizer for User Interface Prototypes. In *Proceedings of Graphics Interface 2010 (GI '10)*. Canadian Information Processing Society, Toronto, Ont., Canada, Canada, 245–252. http://dl.acm.org/citation.cfm?id=1839214.1839258

3. Lisa Anthony and Jacob O. Wobbrock. 2012. $N-protractor: A Fast and Accurate Multistroke Recognizer. In *Proceedings of Graphics Interface 2012 (GI '12)*. Canadian Information Processing Society, Toronto, Ont., Canada, Canada, 117–120. http://dl.acm.org/citation.cfm?id=2305276.2305296

4. Relja ArandjeloviÄĞ and Tevfik Metin Sezgin. 2011. Sketch recognition by fusion of temporal and image-based features. *Pattern Recognition* 44, 6 (2011), 1225 – 1234. DOI:http://dx.doi.org/https://doi.org/10.1016/j.patcog.2010.11.006

5. Rahul Arora, Rubaiat Habib Kazi, Fraser Anderson, Tovi Grossman, Karan Singh, and George W Fitzmaurice. 2017. Experimental Evaluation of Sketching on Surfaces in VR.. In *CHI*. 5643–5654.

6. Ilhan Aslan, Andreas Uhl, Alexander Meschtscherjakov, and Manfred Tscheligi. 2014. Mid-air authentication gestures: an exploration of authentication based on palm and finger motions. In *Proceedings of the 16th International Conference on Multimodal Interaction*. ACM, New York, NY, USA, 311–318.

7. Seok-Hyung Bae, Ravin Balakrishnan, and Karan Singh. 2008. ILoveSketch: As-natural-as-possible Sketching System for Creating 3D Curve Models. In *Proceedings of the 21st Annual ACM Symposium on User Interface Software and Technology (UIST '08)*. ACM, New York, NY, USA, 151–160. DOI: http://dx.doi.org/10.1145/1449715.1449740

8. Yu Chen, Jianzhuang Liu, and Xiaoou Tang. 2008. Sketching in the air: a vision-based system for 3d object design. In *Computer Vision and Pattern Recognition, 2008. CVPR 2008. IEEE Conference on*. IEEE, 1–6.

9. Mary Czerwinski, George Robertson, Brian Meyers, Greg Smith, Daniel Robbins, and Desney Tan. 2006. Large Display Research Overview. In *CHI '06 Extended Abstracts on Human Factors in Computing Systems (CHI EA '06)*. ACM, New York, NY, USA, 69–74. DOI: http://dx.doi.org/10.1145/1125451.1125471

10. Fabio Dominio, Mauro Donadeo, and Pietro Zanuttigh. 2014. Combining Multiple Depth-based Descriptors for Hand Gesture Recognition. *Pattern Recogn. Lett.* 50, C (Dec. 2014), 101–111. DOI: http://dx.doi.org/10.1016/j.patrec.2013.10.010

11. Martin Field, Sam Gordon, Eric Peterson, Raquel Robinson, Thomas Stahovich, and Christine Alvarado. 2010. The effect of task on classification accuracy: Using gesture recognition techniques in free-sketch recognition. *Computers & Graphics* 34, 5 (2010), 499–512.

12. Google. 2017. Tilt Brush. https://www.tiltbrush.com/. (2017). [Online; accessed 01-October-2017].

13. Tovi Grossman, Ravin Balakrishnan, Gordon Kurtenbach, George Fitzmaurice, Azam Khan, and Bill Buxton. 2001. Interaction Techniques for 3D Modeling on Large Displays. In *Proceedings of the 2001 Symposium on Interactive 3D Graphics (I3D '01)*. ACM, New York, NY, USA, 17–23. DOI: http://dx.doi.org/10.1145/364338.364341

14. Tovi Grossman, Ravin Balakrishnan, Gordon Kurtenbach, George Fitzmaurice, Azam Khan, and Bill Buxton. 2002. Creating Principal 3D Curves with Digital Tape Drawing. In *Proceedings of the SIGCHI Conference on Human Factors in Computing Systems (CHI '02)*. ACM, New York, NY, USA, 121–128. DOI: http://dx.doi.org/10.1145/503376.503398

15. Christian Holz and Andrew Wilson. 2011. Data Miming: Inferring Spatial Object Descriptions from Human Gesture. In *Proceedings of the SIGCHI Conference on Human Factors in Computing Systems (CHI '11)*. ACM, New York, NY, USA, 811–820. DOI: http://dx.doi.org/10.1145/1978942.1979060

16. Gabe Johnson, Mark D. Gross, Jason Hong, and Ellen Yi-Luen Do. 2009. Computational Support for Sketching in Design: A Review. *Found. Trends Hum.-Comput. Interact.* 2, 1 (Jan. 2009), 1–93. DOI: http://dx.doi.org/10.1561/1100000013

17. D. Keefe, R. Zeleznik, and D. Laidlaw. 2007. Drawing on Air: Input Techniques for Controlled 3D Line Illustration. *IEEE Transactions on Visualization and Computer Graphics* 13, 5 (Sept 2007), 1067–1081. DOI: http://dx.doi.org/10.1109/TVCG.2007.1060

18. Narayanan C. Krishnan and Diane J. Cook. 2014. Activity Recognition on Streaming Sensor Data. *Pervasive Mob. Comput.* 10 (Feb. 2014), 138–154. DOI: http://dx.doi.org/10.1016/j.pmcj.2012.07.003

19. Beverley Laundry, Masood Masoodian, and Bill Rogers. 2010. Interaction with 3D Models on Large Displays Using 3D Input Techniques. In *Proceedings of the 11th International Conference of the NZ Chapter of the ACM Special Interest Group on Human-Computer Interaction (CHINZ '10)*. ACM, New York, NY, USA, 49–56. DOI: http://dx.doi.org/10.1145/1832838.1832847

20. Lars Lischke, Jürgen Grüninger, Khalil Klouche, Albrecht Schmidt, Philipp Slusallek, and Giulio Jacucci. 2015. Interaction Techniques for Wall-Sized Screens. In *Proceedings of the 2015 International Conference on Interactive Tabletops & Surfaces (ITS '15)*. ACM, New York, NY, USA, 501–504. DOI: http://dx.doi.org/10.1145/2817721.2835071

21. Stan Melax, Leonid Keselman, and Sterling Orsten. 2013. Dynamics Based 3D Skeletal Hand Tracking. In *Proceedings of Graphics Interface 2013 (GI '13)*. Canadian Information Processing Society, Toronto, Ont., Canada, Canada, 63–70. http://dl.acm.org/citation.cfm?id=2532129.2532141

22. Tao Ni, Greg S. Schmidt, Oliver G. Staadt, Mark A. Livingston, Robert Ball, and Richard May. 2006. A Survey of Large High-Resolution Display Technologies, Techniques, and Applications. In *Proceedings of the IEEE Conference on Virtual Reality (VR '06)*. IEEE Computer Society, Washington, DC, USA, 223–236. DOI: http://dx.doi.org/10.1109/VR.2006.20

23. G. Noris, D. Sýkora, A. Shamir, S. Coros, B. Whited, M. Simmons, A. Hornung, M. Gross, and R. Sumner. 2012. Smart Scribbles for Sketch Segmentation. *Comput. Graph. Forum* 31, 8 (Dec. 2012), 2516–2527. DOI: http://dx.doi.org/10.1111/j.1467-8659.2012.03224.x

24. Brandon Paulson and Tracy Hammond. 2008. PaleoSketch: Accurate Primitive Sketch Recognition and Beautification. In *Proceedings of the 13th International Conference on Intelligent User Interfaces (IUI '08)*. ACM, New York, NY, USA, 1–10.

25. Z. Ren, J. Meng, and J. Yuan. 2011. Depth camera based hand gesture recognition and its applications in Human-Computer-Interaction. In *2011 8th International Conference on Information, Communications Signal Processing*. IEEE, 1–5. DOI: http://dx.doi.org/10.1109/ICICS.2011.6173545

26. Alexander Schick, Daniel Morlock, Christoph Amma, Tanja Schultz, and Rainer Stiefelhagen. 2012. Vision-based handwriting recognition for unrestricted text input in mid-air. In *Proceedings of the 14th ACM international conference on Multimodal interaction*. ACM, 217–220.

27. Toby Sharp, Cem Keskin, Duncan Robertson, Jonathan Taylor, Jamie Shotton, David Kim, Christoph Rhemann, Ido Leichter, Alon Vinnikov, Yichen Wei, Daniel Freedman, Pushmeet Kohli, Eyal Krupka, Andrew Fitzgibbon, and Shahram Izadi. 2015. Accurate, Robust, and Flexible Real-time Hand Tracking. In *Proceedings of the 33rd Annual ACM Conference on Human Factors in Computing Systems (CHI '15)*. ACM, New York, NY, USA, 3633–3642. DOI: http://dx.doi.org/10.1145/2702123.2702179

28. Gravity Sketch. 2017. Gravity Sketch. https://www.gravitysketch.com/. (2017). [Online; accessed 01-October-2017].

29. Poonam Suryanarayan, Anbumani Subramanian, and Dinesh Mandalapu. 2010. Dynamic Hand Pose Recognition Using Depth Data. In *Proceedings of the 2010 20th International Conference on Pattern Recognition (ICPR '10)*. IEEE Computer Society, Washington, DC, USA, 3105–3108. DOI: http://dx.doi.org/10.1109/ICPR.2010.760

30. Paul Taele. 2014. Intelligent sketching interfaces for richer mid-air drawing interactions. In *CHI'14 Extended Abstracts on Human Factors in Computing Systems*. ACM, New York, NY, USA, 339–342.

31. Andrea Tagliasacchi, Matthias Schröder, Anastasia Tkach, Sofien Bouaziz, Mario Botsch, and Mark Pauly. 2015. Robust articulated-ICP for Real-time Hand Tracking. In *Proceedings of the Eurographics Symposium on Geometry Processing (SGP '15)*. Eurographics Association, Aire-la-Ville, Switzerland, Switzerland, 101–114. DOI: http://dx.doi.org/10.1111/cgf.12700

32. Eugene M. Taranta II, Amirreza Samiei, Mehran Maghoumi, Pooya Khaloo, Corey R. Pittman, and Joseph J. LaViola Jr. 2017. Jackknife: A Reliable Recognizer with Few Samples and Many Modalities. In *Proceedings of the 2017 CHI Conference on Human Factors in Computing Systems (CHI '17)*. ACM, New York, NY, USA, 5850–5861. DOI: http://dx.doi.org/10.1145/3025453.3026002

33. Radu-Daniel Vatavu, Lisa Anthony, and Jacob O. Wobbrock. 2012. Gestures As Point Clouds: A $P Recognizer for User Interface Prototypes. In *Proceedings of the 14th ACM International Conference on Multimodal Interaction (ICMI '12)*. ACM, New York, NY, USA, 273–280. DOI: http://dx.doi.org/10.1145/2388676.2388732

34. Sharad Vikram, Lei Li, and Stuart Russell. 2013. Writing and sketching in the air, recognizing and controlling on the fly. In *CHI'13 Extended Abstracts on Human Factors in Computing Systems*. ACM, 1179–1184.

35. Vinayak and Karthik Ramani. 2015. A gesture-free geometric approach for mid-air expression of design intent in 3D virtual pottery. *Computer-Aided Design* 69 (2015), 11 – 24.

36. Don Willems, Ralph Niels, Marcel van Gerven, and Louis Vuurpijl. 2009. Iconic and multi-stroke gesture recognition. *Pattern Recognition* 42, 12 (2009), 3303 – 3312. DOI: http://dx.doi.org/https://doi.org/10.1016/j.patcog.2009.01.030 New Frontiers in Handwriting Recognition.

37. Jacob O. Wobbrock, Andrew D. Wilson, and Yang Li. 2007. Gestures Without Libraries, Toolkits or Training: A $1 Recognizer for User Interface Prototypes. In *Proceedings of the 20th Annual ACM Symposium on User Interface Software and Technology (UIST '07)*. ACM, New York, NY, USA, 159–168. DOI: http://dx.doi.org/10.1145/1294211.1294238

Webcam-based Attention Tracking in Online Learning: A Feasibility Study

Tarmo Robal
Department of Computer Systems
Tallinn University of Technology
Tallinn, Estonia
tarmo.robal@ttu.ee

Yue Zhao, Christoph Lofi and Claudia Hauff
Web Information Systems
Delft University of Technology
Delft, Netherlands
{y.zhao-1, c.lofi, c.hauff}@tudelft.nl

ABSTRACT

A main weakness of the open online learning movement is retention: a small minority of learners (on average $5-10\%$, in extreme cases $< 1\%$) that start a so-called Massive Open Online Course (MOOC) complete it successfully. There are many reasons why learners are unsuccessful, among the most important ones is the lack of *self-regulation*: learners are often not able to self-regulate their learning behavior. Designing tools that provide learners with a greater awareness of their learning is vital to the future success of MOOC environments. Detecting learners' loss of focus during learning is particularly important, as this can allow us to intervene and return the learners' attention to the learning materials. One technological affordance to detect such loss of focus are webcams—ubiquitous pieces of hardware available in almost all laptops today. In recent years, researchers have begun to exploit eye tracking and gaze data generated from webcams as part of complex machine learning solutions to detect inattention or loss of focus. Those approaches however tend to have a high detection lag, can be inaccurate, and are complex to design and maintain. In contrast, in this paper, we explore the possibility of a simple alternative—the presence or absence of a face—to detect a loss of focus in the online learning setting. To this end, we evaluate the performance of three consumer and professional eye/face-tracking frameworks using a benchmark suite we designed specifically for this purpose: it contains a set of common xMOOC user activities and behaviours. The results of our study show that even this basic approach poses a significant challenge to current hardware and software-based tracking solutions.

ACM Classification Keywords

H.5 Human-centered computing: Human computer interaction; Empirical studies in HCI

Author Keywords

Eye tracking; Face detection; Online learning; MOOCs

IUI'18, March 7–11, 2018, Tokyo, Japan

DOI: https://doi.org/10.1145/3172944.3172987

INTRODUCTION

MOOCs have gained a lot of popularity over the past years and are now being offered to millions of learners on various platforms such as `Coursera`, `Udacity` and `edX`, among others. A major motivation behind MOOCs is the provision of ubiquitous learning to learners of all walks of life across the globe. Yet, despite their popularity, MOOCs suffer from low levels of learner engagement and learner retention, as only a very small percentage of learners who start a course actually complete it successfully; on average $5-10\%$ of learners succeed, in extreme cases this metric can drop below 1% [9].

One reason why learners fail to complete MOOCs can be found in the design of the platforms. They tend to be rather basic (as a large amount of effort goes towards platform maintenance and scalability) and thus the delivery of course content does not always follow the latest educational findings. This setup contributes to the lack of self-regulation (in planning, motivation, goal setting) learners tend to exhibit, especially those without a higher education background [6]. In the MOOC context, loss of focus (during video watching, quiz submissions, etc.) is a core challenge, as it can have disastrous effects on learning efficiency [22]. Therefore, technological interventions which can detect a learner's loss of attention and can subsequently guide the learner's focus back to the course content could be of great value.

In recent years, a number of works have investigated inattention prediction based on various signals, including heart-rate data [28], EEG data [29], skin conductance and temperature [4] as well as computer mouse pressure data [27]. While insightful, none of these approaches can be applied at scale in an online learning environment in the near future and thus, most of the existing research on inattention detection relies on eye-tracking data, including [1, 2, 3, 13, 17, 21, 30]. Here, the eye-mind link [18] is exploited as the eye gaze usually correlates well with a person's focus.

A major issue of existing eye tracking based inattention detection approaches is the lack of *real-time* detection capabilities (thirty to sixty second delays are common) [30]. An additional point of concern in our setting are the privacy requirements of MOOC environments—to ensure a learner's privacy all necessary computations should be conducted within the learner's *browser environment* (the alternative approach of streaming a learner's webcam data to a high-performant server has severe privacy implications, while requiring the installation of dedicated software packages hampers usability)[1].

In this paper, we explore a significantly simpler alternative approach towards detecting a loss of focus whilst learning in a MOOC environment: we use the departure of a user's face from the webcam's viewport as a proxy for learner inattention—a user whose face is not aimed at the screen is unlikely to pay attention to a video playing on it. It turns out, that even this deceptively simple detection task is challenging in a MOOC environment where we have to consider widely varying consumer-grade hardware and browser software. In this paper we conduct an extensive study involving two open-source browser-based software frameworks for gaze and face detection, `WebGazer.js` and `tracking.js`, as well as a third hardware-based solution (a Tobii eye tracker) to determine an upper performance bound. Both software-based frameworks can be integrated into current MOOC environments, and perform all their processing on the user's computer without the need for a server infrastructure or additional browser plugins. We benchmark the ability of the three frameworks to reliably detect a user's focus towards the screen content (using the presence/abscence of a face as proxy) across a variety of common MOOC user activities such as watching a MOOC video whilst leaning on one's hand, checking the weather report on a smart-phone or drinking coffee.

We address the following research questions in our work:

RQ1 *Which activities—that lead to different face positions in front of the screen—are typical for MOOC learners?* To this end, we compile a benchmark suite of fifty typical MOOC learner activities, partitioned into activities that are indicative of (i) focus, (ii) certain loss of focus and (iii) likely loss of focus.

RQ2 *How reliable can current software frameworks detect the presence or absence of a face under typical MOOC conditions?* We conduct an extensive lab study involving `tracking.js` and `WebGazer.js` as well as a professional eye tracker (our upper bound in terms of performance). A total of twenty study participants execute the benchmark suite of activities in a controlled environment.

We find that in our setup, `tracking.js` performs significantly better than `WebGazer.js`, achieving a median detection accuracy of 62% across all fifty tasks (for the most difficult task detection accuracy was 17%), with the professional hardware-based eye tracker achieving a median accuracy of 72.5% (the most difficult task resulted in 27% accuracy). The observed detection delay is below two seconds for `tracking.js`, making it a viable choice for webcam-based attention detection (using face detection as a proxy). At the same time, the reported accuracy numbers suggest that current software and hardware solutions still struggle to provide a consistently high detection quality across all tasks.

[1]In order to investigate to what extent current MOOC learners are technologically able and willing to allow the MOOC platform to access their webcam feed (a necessity to make our vision of webcam-based attention tracking a reality) we conducted a preliminary study: we developed a working privacy-aware webcam intervention (i.e. none of the webcam data leaves a learner's computer) and deployed it to more than 800 learners in an engineering MOOC offered by TU Delft on the edX platform; we found 78% of learners had the technological capabilities (hardware, including a webcam, of sufficient quality) to run the intervention and 31% enabled it as learning support technology. Among those learners not enabling the intervention, about a quarter had privacy concerns, indicating that our vision is realistic for a significant number of MOOC learners.

RELATED WORK: ATTENTION LOSS IN LEARNING

Different data collection methods have been used to study the loss of attention or focus of students in traditional classrooms since the 1960s, such as the observation of inattention behaviors [8], the retention of course content [12], using direct probes in class [23, 10] and relying on self-reports from students [5]. A common belief was that learners' attention may decrease considerably after 10-15 minutes of the lecture, which was supported by [23]. However, Wilson and Korn [26] later challenged this claim and argued that more research is needed. In a recent study, Bunce et al. [5] asked learners to report their attention loss voluntarily during 9-12 minute course segments. Three buttons were placed in front of each learner, representing attention lapses of 1 minute or less, of 2-3 minutes and of 5 minutes or more. During the lectures, the learners were asked to report their loss of attention by pressing one of three buttons once they *noticed* their attention loss. This led Bunce et al. [5] to conclude that learners start losing their attention early on in the lecture and may cycle through several attention states within the 9-12 minute course segments.

In online learning environments, attention loss may be even more frequent. Risko et al. [19] used three one hour video-recorded lectures with different topics (psychology, economics, and classics) in their experiments. While watching the videos, participants were probed four times throughout each video. The attention-loss frequency among the participants was found to be 43%. Additionally, Risko et al. [19] found a significant negative correlation between test performance and loss of attention. Szpunar et al. [24] investigated the impact of interpolated tests on learners' loss of attention within online lectures. The study participants were asked to watch a 21-minute video lecture (4 segments with 5.5 minutes per segment) and report their loss of attention in response to random probes (one probe per segment). In their experiments, the loss of attention frequency was about 40%. Loh et al. [11] also employed probes to measure learners' loss of attention and found a positive correlation between media multitasking activity and learners' loss of attention (average frequency of 32%) whilst watching video lectures. Based on these considerably high loss of attention frequencies we conclude that reducing loss of attention in online learning is an important approach to improve learning outcomes.

In a typical in-class setting a teacher has the ability to detect and re-gain learner attention through various pedagogical approaches. This is not applicable in MOOC environments due to the nature of online learning. Various technological approaches have been explored to detect and record signals of user (in)attention in the past besides eye tracking, including heart-rate tracking through mobile cameras [28], brain activities through EEG analysis [29], skin conductance and temperature [4], posture and body pressure sensing and pressure applied on a computer mouse [27]. As already implied, most of the existing research though focuses on either face or eye-gaze detection [1, 2, 3, 13, 17, 21, 30].

Inspired by the eye-mind link effect [18], a number of previous studies [2, 3, 13] focused on the automatic detection of learners' loss of attention by means of gaze data. In [2, 3], Bixler and D'Mello investigated the detection of learners' loss of attention during computerized reading. To generate the ground truth, the study participants were asked to manually report their loss of attention when an auditory probe (i.e. a beep) was triggered. Based on those reports, the loss of attention frequency ranged from 24.3% to 30.1%. During the experiment, gaze data was collected using a dedicated eye tracker. In [13], Mills et al. asked the study participants to watch a 32 minute, non-educational movie and self-report their loss of attention. In order to detect loss of attention automatically, statistical features and the relationship between gaze and video content were considered. In contrast to [2, 3], the authors mainly focused on the relationship between a participant's gaze and areas of interest, i.e. specific areas in the video a participant should be interested in. In [30], Zhao et al. presented a method for detecting inattention similar to the studies in [13], but adapted and optimized for the MOOC setting.

All mentioned approaches relying on the eye-mind link share two common issues: they are usually unable to provide real-time feedback as they are trained on eye-gaze recordings with sparse manually provided labels (e.g., most approaches have a label frequency of 30-60 seconds, which directly translates into a detection delay of similar length), and the reported accuracy is too low for practical application (e.g., [30] reports detection accuracies of 14%-35% depending on training and video). As a result, we choose a different approach as discussed in the following sections.

EYE AND FACE TRACKING FRAMEWORKS

Recall that we employ face presence and absence as proxies of learner attention and inattention respectively. Next to explicit face tracking software frameworks, eye-tracking frameworks are suitable for our work as well, as in the absence of a face, no eye tracking is possible.

In order to determine an upper performance bound, we use the professional high-end hardware eye tracker Tobii X2-30 Compact[2]. `Tobii` uses its own proprietary analytic software Tobii Studio to analyze the gathered eye tracking data.

Although there exist a number of different eye and face tracking software solutions, our choice is limited by the typical MOOC environment (which runs within the browser, and thus we require browser-based software frameworks), privacy aspects (all computations have to be performed on the user's device) and the variety of hardware capabilities we can expect MOOC learners' devices to have (the computations should not require too many resources). Evidently, JavaScript-based solutions fit the task description. Libraries such as `CCV.js`, `clmtrackr`, `headtrackr`, `ObjectDetect`, `tracking.js`, and `WebGazer.js` are thus potential candidates. After an initial testing phase of all mentioned frameworks we settled on two suitable ones: `WebGazer.js` [15][3] and `tracking.js`[4].

WebGazer.js

`WebGazer.js` is an open-source eye tracking library written in JavaScript that is able to infer eye-gaze locations in real-time. Use-case specific extensions, e.g. to track users' web search behaviour [16] exist as well. `WebGazer.js` can be configured with different components to track gaze, pupils, or faces. We used the `clmtrackr` component[5], a face fitting library (referred to as `CLM` in the following), which has previously been used among others in works on camera-based emotion detection [20], and intelligent public displays in city environments [14]. `CLM` tracks a face and the coordinate positions of a face model, as shown in Figure 1. Using this face model, Webgazer can extrapolate the user's gaze (i.e., the point of the screen on which a user's gaze focuses) by estimating the face's distance and orientation from the screen. A weakness of `CLM` is its "agressive" face-fitting algorithm that often attempts to fit a model even when no face is present. This leads to many potential problems where random background elements (like posters, plants, furniture) are mistaken for faces, and sometimes even preferred over a real user's face clearly visible in the camera's viewport.

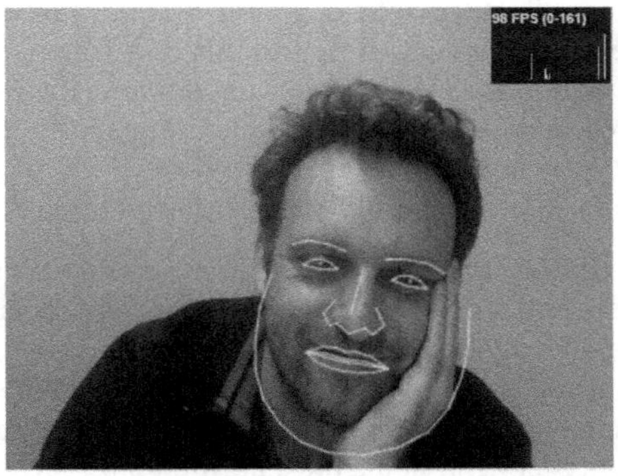

Figure 1. Face fitting model generated by CLM. This example shows a common face fitting error due to hand positioning.

tracking.js

`tracking.js` is a JavaScript-based face tracking library (`TJS` in the following), which has been employed, among others, in security systems for identity verification [7] and object recognition tasks [25]. With respect to eye and face tracking, this library offers a significantly less powerful feature set than both `Tobii` and `CLM`, as it can only detect the presence and location of the boundary box of an object—in our case the face—in a video stream (see Figure 2). While it can also be employed to track the eyes' locations (but not the gaze), we do not use that feature in this study. We hypothesize that the

[2] https://www.tobiipro.com/product-listing/tobii-pro-x2-30/

[3] https://webgazer.cs.brown.edu

[4] https://trackingjs.com

[5] https://github.com/auduno/clmtrackr

simplicity of TJS leads to more reliable face presence and face absence detection.

Figure 2. Face Boundary Box detected by tracking.js

Detecting Face-miss events

We define a face-miss event to be an event of a user's face turning or moving away from the computer screen. The differences in the three evaluated frameworks (Tobii, CLM, TJS) leads to different heuristics for detecting a face-miss:

- Tobii: A face-miss event is detected if the proprietary Tobii Studio software cannot determine gaze point coordinates. This usually represents a problem with detecting the users' eyes by the tracker hardware (e.g., they are not within the camera viewport, they are closed, or obstructed by an object). At times, while the eyes can be found by Tobii, no gaze coordinates can be determined as the gaze direction is unclear. We cannot distinguish this case from a case where there is no face at all. In our experience, the presence of gaze coordinates is a very reliable proxy for the presence of a face (low false positive rate), while the lack of coordinates does not necessarily imply the absence of a face.
- CLM: Similar to Tobii, we define a face-miss event as the software's inability to fix exact gaze coordinates, which also means a failure in reliable face detection in case of CLM. In contrast to Tobii, due to the aggressiveness of the face fitting algorithm, CLM is is quite prone to detect faces where in reality there are none present (high false positive rate).
- TJS: We define a face-miss event as the library's inability to fix a face boundary box in the webcam's video stream. We do not try to track eyes or gaze.

The video or eye tracker stream is continuously processed while it is recorded. The Tobii system relies on dedicated hardware support for this task (which partially contributes to its high retail price), and is thus able to guarantee a sampling rate of 30 samples per second mostly independent of the computer hardware. For the webcam-based solutions, image processing of the video stream needs to be handled by the system's CPU and within the browser's environment. As a result, only low sampling rates are possible without overwhelming low-end computer systems. For this reason, we fix the sampling rate to 4 samples per second. However, due to the unreliability of the JavaScript timer events under high system loads, the standard deviation of the targeted sampling time of 250ms is 48ms in our experiments (described further in Section User Study). Furthermore, we have extreme cases where the sampling times increased up to 1157ms, i.e., less than one sample per second. Therefore, Tobii should be able to react with significantly lower delays than the webcam-based frameworks.

USER STUDY

In order to evaluate the suitability of the chosen webcam toolkits for face and gaze tracking, we developed a **benchmark set of tasks**, which we argue represent common behaviours of online learners in front of their laptops. For each of the tasks we define the desired behaviour: the eye-tracking devices should either report the loss of the face/gaze (in the case of face-miss tasks) or keep detecting the face/gaze (in the case of face-hit tasks). We exclude mobile learners from these tasks as desktop learners are still the vast majority of learners in today's MOOC environments[6].

We designed a total of fifty tasks together with a small sample of regular MOOC learners (graduate students in our research lab). These tasks are—to some extent—abstract versions of the behaviour MOOC learners exhibit when watching lecture videos, one of the most common activities in so-called xMOOCs (i.e. MOOCs that are heavily relying on video lectures to convey knowledge, in contrast to cMOOCs which rely on learners' self-formed communities and peer teaching). The task descriptions we developed are shown in Table 3. They fall under three broad categories:

- face-miss tasks describe those user behaviours that *should* result in the loss of a detected face/gaze. Twenty-one tasks belong to this category; examples include *Take a sip from the cup [next to you] while turning away from the camera* or *Look straight up to the ceiling for 8 seconds.*
- likely-face-miss tasks should result in our frameworks reporting a mix of face hit and face miss samples. Two examples among the fourteen tasks in this category are *Lean back and put your hands behind your neck for 5 seconds* and *Draw a square on the paper.*
- Lastly, face-hit tasks describe user behaviours that should not influence our frameworks' ability to detect the face, though they may influence gaze detection. Fifteen tasks belong to this category, for example *Reposition yourself in the chair* and *Stare at the camera for 3 seconds.*

We developed a dedicated Web application as testing ground. The fifty tasks are presented as virtual "cue cards" to study participants and both TJS and CLM are included as webcam-based eye tracking solutions. The design of the application is modular, additional frameworks can easily be evaluated as well. We have open-sourced our application at **https://github.com/trx350/xMOOC_benchmark**.

The opening screen of the application is shown in Figure 3; an example task cue card is shown in Figure 4. The task order is randomized. The procedure for each task Q_i is the same: the task description is shown and five seconds later a bell sound

[6]Concretely, based on a sample of twenty edX MOOCs offered at TU Delft, fewer than 20% of learners accessed the course content via mobile devices.

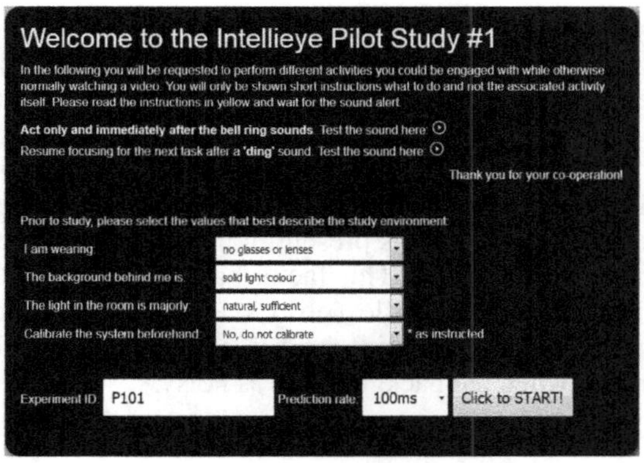

Figure 3. Opening screen of the user study

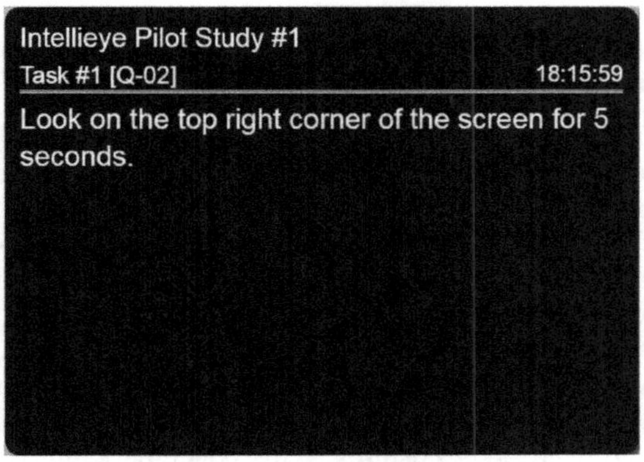

Figure 4. Example task "cue card" of the user study.

indicates the start of the task at time t_{start}^{Qi}: at the sound of the bell the participant is expected to perform the task. Another bell sound (different to the one indicating the start) indicates to the participant when the task has been finished at time t_{end}^{Qi}, and this is followed by the next task description. Task durations differ, depending on the specific task, e.g. Q31 requires a participant to look at a certain angle for 5 seconds while Q39 asks a participant to check his or her phone for 10 seconds.

Study setup

We conducted all our experiments on a Dell Inspiron 5759 laptop (with built-in webcam situated in the center of the top screen bezel) with a 17-inch screen and a 1920 × 1080 resolution running Windows 10. The `Tobii` eye tracker was placed on the lower screen bezel.

The study was conducted across a one week period: twenty participants were recruited among TU Delft's graduate students and staff members via email lists. The participants did not receive compensation and spent less than an hour on this study. Among the twenty participants, nine wore glasses and two had contact lenses. In ten of the sessions the background behind the test subject had a uniform (light) color, in another 10 cases a poster or photographic background was observed. We recorded these settings in our study as we had conducted preliminary experiments which indicated that eye trackers (especially the software-based ones) can be mislead by noisy backgrounds.

As this is a controlled study, in order to facilitate the proper execution of the tasks, the participants were provided with the necessary tools to perform all necessary behaviours, including a sheet of paper and a pen (required for Q22, Q24 & Q25), a cup (Q41 & Q42) and a phone (Q39).

The `Tobii` requires a calibration step which participants concluded at the start of the study. The `CLM` framework can also be calibrated in a light-weight manner: five red dots are shown on the screen that have to be clicked one after the other. To test the effect of the calibration we randomly switched on the calibration step for eight of the twenty learners.

To prepare the participants for the tasks, each participant was trained on two tasks before the start of the actual study. The participants were reminded repeatedly to only start executing a task's required behaviour after the sound of the bell and to keep executing the behaviour until the ending sound occurred.

Detection accuracy

For every task and participant, we determine the eye trackers' `face-hit/face-miss` predictions from the collected logs between the t_{start}^{Qi} and t_{end}^{Qi} timestamps. As the eye trackers vary in their sampling rate they all produce a differing amount of labels (face-hit, face-miss) for each sample interval. We evaluate the accuracy of the produced labels by computing the percentage of correct predictions (as defined by the type of task) in the task interval. For example, in a five second task slot the webcam-based approach takes a sample once every 250ms (on average), and thus we collect approximately 20 predictions. For a `face-miss` task, if 14 of the 20 predictions are a miss, the detection accuracy will be 70%. Lastly, we average the accuracy for each task across all participants.

Table 1. `Tobii`'s delay between the start of a face-miss/likely-face-miss task and the first face-miss event. The data is averaged across all participants of a single task.

Delay	% of tasks
1 sec	53%
2 sec	28%
3 sec	6%
4 sec	3%
5+ sec	9%

Table 2. Overview of the impact of the participants' background on `TJS`'s and `Tobii`'s accuracy.

		Accuracy in %	
Background	#	TJS	Tobii
Solid light	10	61.5	68.6
Poster/photo	10	55.7	67.8

RESULTS

In this section we report the outcomes of our user study along three dimensions: (i) accuracy across tasks, (ii) reaction times and (iii) the influence of the participants' background on the accuracy levels.

Accuracy

The first question we consider is the accuracy of the three eye trackers under investigation across the fifty tasks of our benchmark suite. Table 3 lists the detection accuracy for each task, aggregated across the twenty study participants. As expected, Tobii achieves the highest accuracy, with an average of 68.2% across all tasks. Among the two software solutions, TJS clearly outperforms CLM, achieving an average accuracy of 58.6% compared to CLM's 35.4%. If we were only to focus on the tasks where face misses and likely face misses form the ground truth, CLM's accuracy would drop to 9.6%. The reason for this poor performance is CLM's approach to face and gaze detection: it will try to match anything in the video frame to a potential face area, a separate face detection phase is not performed. This also explains its high accuracies in the face hits tasks. Note that the calibration step performed by some of our participants for CLM did not result in a different outcome.

The comparison between Tobii and TJS shows a relatively small performance gap between the Webcam-based eye tracker and the high-end device. While Tobii outperforms TJS in 39 of the 50 tasks, in many instances the difference in accuracies is rather small. Using Tobii as a reference point, TJS is able to conform with 77.8% of Tobii's detected labels.

Due to the clear performance differences between TJS and CLM, in further analyses we focus exclusively on TJS and its performance compared to Tobii.

Reaction Times

As one of the potential reasons for TJS's lag in performance compared to Tobii we investigated the reaction times of both users and frameworks. More specifically, we measured the delay between the *instructed* start time of the task (i.e., the timestamp $t_{start}^{Q_i}$) and the first time a framework detects a face-miss. This time delta of course consists of both the user delay (i.e., the time it took for the study participant to finally start performing the task, which for some tasks—e.g. Q23 & Q46—showed a considerable delay) and the actual detection delay imposed by the framework. We averaged the delays of all participants for a task and report the percentage of tasks whose average delay is up to 1 second, up to 2 seconds, etc. in Table 1. For the majority of tasks, Tobii is able to detect the first face-miss within a second of the start of the task.

The Tobii eye tracker runs with a very high fixed sampling rate of 30 samples per second, and is mostly unaffected by the current CPU load of the host machine. Therefore, we make the assumption that the delays in Table 1 represent the user delay. In contrast, TJS and CLM can have very low sampling rates depending on the current system load (we aim at 4 samples per second, but we also experienced significantly lower rates). By comparing the times of detecting the first face-miss of both TJS and CLM with Tobii, we can obtain an intuition of the delays imposed by those frameworks. For TJS, this resulted in a delay of 0.6 ± 1.1 seconds, and for CLM in 1.3 ± 1.0 seconds. While these detection delays are not instantaneous, the delays are short enough for practical applications.

Background as an Influencing Factor

As we conducted the user study in different rooms on different times of the day, we also recorded our participants with various backgrounds. In Table 2 we partitioned our participants according to the background they sat in front of during the study. All participants reported their background to be either of a solid light color (as present in many offices) or contain a poster and/or photo. This factor had an impact on the eye trackers' accuracy: while Tobii's accuracy remained unaffected by the background, the TJS eye tracker considerably degraded when the background was noisy.

SUMMARY AND DISCUSSION

In this paper, we have introduced the presence or absence of a face in a learner's webcam viewport as a simple proxy of learner attention or inattention in order to enable real-time attention tracking in a standard MOOC environment. This in turn will stimulate and support self-regulated learning.

We compared three potential technical solutions for this task: using the high-end professional Tobii X2-30 Compact hardware eye tracker, and using two software-based solutions that analyze the video stream of a consumer-grade webcam. We conducted a lab study with twenty participants, who had to perform a controlled benchmark suite of fifty realistic tasks, which introduced several challenging factors such as body movement, partially covering the face, noisy backgrounds, and crooked body postures. This benchmark suite and the accompanying Web application allows for a standardized and fair comparison of different approaches for face-hit and face-miss detection, and we provide it under an open-source license to foster future research.

Our experiments showed that the professional dedicated hardware solution outperforms the open-source software-based solutions both in respect to detection performance and processing speed, but is of course unsuitable for a large-scale deployment outside of a controlled lab setting. For the software-based solutions which can indeed run on typical hardware used by MOOC learners, the complicated CLM gaze tracking as employed by WebGazer.js introduces many complications, resulting in poor detection performance both for the presence and absence of a user's face. In contrast, the face tracking library TJS shows significantly higher performance for nearly all benchmark tasks. Additionally, both software libraries incur an additional time delay of around 1-2 seconds over the nearly instantaneous detection response of the hardware solution. With careful design, this delay should be easily manageable in a future MOOC learner attention detection component.

In our future work, we plan an implementation of an attention tracker suitable for a large-scale MOOC deployment on the basis of the TJS framework. Beyond purely technical or methodical challenges, this allows us to tackle additional interesting research questions: Would MOOC learners be willing to accept and use such an attention detection tool? What are the reasons why they would like/or refuse to use such technology? And of course finally, if learners accept the use of such tools, does this indeed positively impact their learning outcomes?

Acknowledgments
This research has been co-financed by the EU Widening Twinning project TUTORIAL and the Leiden-Delft-Erasmus Centre for Education and Learning.

REFERENCES

1. Stylianos Asteriadis, Kostas Karpouzis, and Stefanos Kollias. 2014. Visual Focus of Attention in Non-calibrated Environments using Gaze Estimation. *International Journal of Computer Vision* 107, 3 (2014), 293–316.
2. Robert Bixler and Sidney D'Mello. 2014. Toward fully automated person-independent detection of mind wandering. In *UMAP '14*. 37–48.
3. Robert Bixler and Sidney D'Mello. 2016. Automatic gaze-based user-independent detection of mind wandering during computerized reading. *User Modeling and User-Adapted Interaction* 26, 1 (2016), 33–68.
4. Nathaniel Blanchard, Robert Bixler, Tera Joyce, and Sidney D'Mello. 2014. *Automated Physiological-Based Detection of Mind Wandering during Learning*. Springer International Publishing, Cham, 55–60.
5. Diane M Bunce, Elizabeth A Flens, and Kelly Y Neiles. 2010. How long can students pay attention in class? A study of student attention decline using clickers. *Journal of Chemical Education* 87, 12 (2010), 1438–1443.
6. Dan Davis, Ioana Jivet, René F. Kizilcec, Guanliang Chen, Claudia Hauff, and Geert-Jan Houben. 2017. Follow the Successful Crowd: Raising MOOC Completion Rates Through Social Comparison at Scale. In *LAK '17*. 454–463.
7. Barbara Hauer. 2016. Continuous Supervision: A Novel Concept for Enhancing Data Leakage Prevention. In *European Conference on Cyber Warfare and Security*. Academic Conferences International Limited, 342–349.
8. Alex H Johnstone and Frederick Percival. 1976. Attention breaks in lectures. *Education in Chemistry* 13, 2 (1976), 49–50.
9. Katy Jordan. 2014. Initial trends in enrolment and completion of massive open online courses. *The International Review of Research in Open and Distributed Learning* 15, 1 (2014).
10. Sophie I Lindquist and John P McLean. 2011. Daydreaming and its correlates in an educational environment. *Learning and Individual Differences* 21, 2 (2011), 158–167.
11. Kep Kee Loh, Benjamin Zhi Hui Tan, and Stephen Wee Hun Lim. 2016. Media multitasking predicts video-recorded lecture learning performance through mind wandering tendencies. *Computers in Human Behavior* 63 (2016), 943–947.
12. John McLeish. 1968. *The lecture method*. Cambridge Institute of Education.
13. Caitlin Mills, Robert Bixler, Xinyi Wang, and Sidney K D'Mello. 2016. Automatic Gaze-Based Detection of Mind Wandering during Narrative Film Comprehension. In *EDM '16*. 30–37.
14. Masaki Ogawa, Takuro Yonezawa, Jin Nakazawa, and Hideyuki Tokuda. 2015. Exploring user model of the city by using interactive public display application. In *UbiComp/ISWC '15 Adjunct*. 1595–1598.
15. Alexandra Papoutsaki, Nediyana Daskalova, Patsorn Sangkloy, Jeff Huang, James Laskey, and James Hays. 2016. WebGazer: scalable webcam eye tracking using user interactions. In *IJCAI '16*. 3839–3845.
16. Alexandra Papoutsaki, James Laskey, and Jeff Huang. 2017. SearchGazer: Webcam Eye Tracking for Remote Studies of Web Search. In *Proceedings of the 2017 Conference on Conference Human Information Interaction and Retrieval*. ACM, 17–26.
17. Matthieu Perreira Da Silva, Vincent Courboulay, Armelle Prigent, and Pascal Estraillier. 2008. Real-Time Face Tracking for Attention Aware Adaptive Games. In *ICVS '08*. 99–108.
18. Keith Rayner. 1998. Eye movements in reading and information processing: 20 years of research. *Psychological bulletin* 124, 3 (1998), 372–422.
19. Evan F Risko, Nicola Anderson, Amara Sarwal, Megan Engelhardt, and Alan Kingstone. 2012. Everyday attention: variation in mind wandering and memory in a lecture. *Applied Cognitive Psychology* 26, 2 (2012), 234–242.
20. Filipe Santos, Ana Almeida, Constantino Martins, Paulo Moura de Oliveira, and Ramiro Gonçalves. 2017. Hybrid Tourism Recommendation System Based on Functionality/Accessibility Levels. In *International Conference on Practical Applications of Agents and Multi-Agent Systems*. Springer, 221–228.
21. Kshitij Sharma, Patrick Jermann, and Pierre Dillenbourg. 2014. How Students Learn using MOOCs: An Eye-tracking Insight. In *EMOOCs*. 147–154.
22. Jonathan Smallwood, Daniel J Fishman, and Jonathan W Schooler. 2007. Counting the cost of an absent mind: Mind wandering as an underrecognized influence on educational performance. *Psychonomic Bulletin & Review* 14, 2 (2007), 230–236.
23. John Stuart and RJD Rutherford. 1978. Medical student concentration during lectures. *The Lancet* 312, 8088 (1978), 514–516.
24. Karl K Szpunar, Novall Y Khan, and Daniel L Schacter. 2013. Interpolated memory tests reduce mind wandering and improve learning of online lectures. *Proceedings of the National Academy of Sciences* 110, 16 (2013), 6313–6317.
25. Sajjad Taheri, Alexander Veidenbaum, Alexandru Nicolau, and Mohammad R Haghighat. 2017. *OpenCV.js: Computer Vision Processing for the Web*. Technical Report. University of California, Irvine.

26. Karen Wilson and James H Korn. 2007. Attention during lectures: Beyond ten minutes. *Teaching of Psychology* 34, 2 (2007), 85–89.

27. Beverly Woolf, Winslow Burleson, Ivon Arroyo, Toby Dragon, David Cooper, and Rosalind Picard. 2009. Affect-aware tutors: recognising and responding to student affect. *International Journal of Learning Technology* 4, 3-4 (2009), 129–164.

28. Xiang Xiao and Jingtao Wang. 2017. Understanding and Detecting Divided Attention in Mobile MOOC Learning. In *CHI '17*. 2411–2415.

29. Thorsten O Zander, Christian Kothe, Sabine Jatzev, and Matti Gaertner. 2010. Enhancing human-computer interaction with input from active and passive brain-computer interfaces. In *Brain-computer interfaces*. 181–199.

30. Yue Zhao, Christoph Lofi, and Claudia Hauff. 2017. Scalable Mind-Wandering Detection for MOOCs: A Webcam-Based Approach. In *ECTEL '17*. 330–344.

Table 3. Overview of all fifty benchmark tasks, and the accuracy (in %) of `CLM`, `TJS` and `Tobii` averaged across the 20 participants in our user study. For "(LIKELY) FACE MISS" tasks we report the percentage of detected face misses, i.e. the eye tracker flags frames as not containing a face. For "FACE HIT" tasks we report the percentage of detected face hits. A higher percentage indicate a better performance. The best performance per task is shown in bold. [‡] Note that for tasks Q1 and Q2 Tobii's camera was not covered and the detection reflects participants' hand moving through Tobii's camera viewport to cover the webcam on the top bezel of the experimental laptop; for task Q43 there was no gaze to detect for Tobii.

QID	Task	Accuracy in %		
		CLM	TJS	Tobii
	FACE MISS Tasks			
Q1	Cover the camera for 2 seconds	12	**45**	7[‡]
Q2	Cover the camera for 5 seconds	28	**73**	17[‡]
Q3	Cover your face with both hands for 5 seconds	17	67	**75**
Q4	Look what is under your table (3 sec)	3	64	**81**
Q5	Stand up for 5 seconds	10	68	**71**
Q20	Tilt your head to the right for 3 seconds	15	**59**	38
Q21	Check if there is a HDMI port on the laptop	12	56	**77**
Q26	Look straight up to the ceiling for 8 seconds	12	72	**92**
Q27	Tilt your head back for 5 seconds (face ceiling)	10	68	**84**
Q28	Tilt your head back for 2 seconds (face ceiling)	5	51	**66**
Q29	Look down for 3 seconds	4	35	**78**
Q32	Look left for 2 seconds	7	50	**72**
Q33	Look left for 8 seconds	14	69	**88**
Q35	Look over your right shoulder	13	50	**72**
Q36	Look right for 10 seconds	13	77	**90**
Q37	Look right for 3 seconds	14	64	**79**
Q38	Look right for 5 seconds	7	63	**83**
Q39	Check your phone for 10 seconds	7	42	**89**
Q40	Check your phone, return after the ding	13	37	**87**
Q42	Take a sip from the cup while turning away from the camera, return after the ding	5	40	**51**
Q47	Look up and return immediately	8	49	**68**
	LIKELY FACE MISS Tasks			
Q6	Lean back and put your hands behind your neck for 5 seconds	2	**67**	63
Q7	Lean closer to the screen and immediately back	3	17	**27**
Q13	Rapidly lean back and forth until the ding sounds	6	37	**57**
Q18	Tilt your body to the left and stay for 3 seconds	13	50	**57**
Q19	Tilt your body to the right and return immediately	6	41	**55**
Q22	Draw a square on the paper	9	45	**67**
Q23	Write down 5 keys left from letter A, focus back to the screen only after the ding	4	19	**61**
Q24	Write down a sentence about weather	15	47	**73**
Q25	Write down *I love Intellieye!*	10	45	**78**
Q30	Look half-left and return	7	36	**64**
Q31	Look half-right and stay for about 5 seconds	7	42	**77**
Q41	Face the camera and take a sip from the cup until you hear the ding	8	30	**35**
Q46	Cover the left side of your face with left hand over cheek and eye	8	38	**43**
Q48	Look around in the room to every direction	10	63	**82**
	FACE HIT Tasks			
Q8	Open browser and navigate to www.weather.com. Return after the ding. (15sec)	94	**97**	80
Q9	Open new browser tab and return to this after the ding	**95**	89	87
Q10	Open some program window (e.g. My computer) on top of study window and return after the ding	**99**	87	94
Q11	Feeling sleepy? Yawn and cover your mouth with a hand. (3 sec)	**94**	66	64
Q12	Grab the tip of your nose for 3 seconds	**100**	64	71
Q14	Reposition yourself in the chair	**98**	77	61
Q15	Scratch the top of your head (or nape) for 3 seconds	**94**	69	85
Q16	Scratch the lower part of your left leg for 2 seconds	**93**	79	64
Q17	Slowly lean back and stay for about 2 seconds	**96**	32	38
Q34	Look on the top right corner of your screen for 5 seconds	95	86	**96**
Q43	Rest your eyes for 5 seconds (close them)	**95**	84	14[‡]
Q44	Scratch your left cheek for 3 seconds	**95**	74	89
Q45	Sit still and face the camera for 5 seconds	**94**	87	90
Q49	Grab your ears with both of your hands for 3 seconds	**95**	76	85
Q50	Stare at the camera for 3 seconds	**95**	89	88

User-adaptive Support for Processing Magazine Style Narrative Visualizations: Identifying User Characteristics that Matter

Dereck Toker, Cristina Conati, Giuseppe Carenini
Department of Computer Science
University of British Columbia, Vancouver, Canada
{dtoker, conati, carenini}@cs.ubc.ca

ABSTRACT
In this paper we present results from an exploratory user study to uncover which user characteristics (e.g., perceptual speed, verbal working memory, etc.) play a role in how users process textual documents with embedded visualizations (i.e., *Magazine Style Narrative Visualizations*). We present our findings as a step toward developing user-adaptive support, and provide suggestions on how our results can be leveraged for creating a set of meaningful interventions for future evaluation.

Author Keywords
User study; Narrative visualization; Individual differences; User characteristics; User-adaptation; Personalization.

INTRODUCTION
As digital information continues to accumulate in our lives, information visualizations have become an increasingly relevant tool for discovering trends and shaping stories from this overabundance of data (e.g., Infographics [26], Timelines [6]). However, visualizations are typically designed and evaluated following a one size-fits-all approach, meaning they do not take into account the potential needs of individual users. There is mounting evidence that user characteristics such as cognitive abilities, personality traits, and learning abilities, can significantly influence user experience during information visualization tasks (e.g., [25,33,38,41]). These findings have prompted researchers to investigate user-adaptive information visualizations, i.e., visualizations that aim to recognize and adapt to each user's specific needs. Whereas existing work has been mostly limited to tasks involving just visualizations, the aim of our research is to broaden this work to include scenarios where users interact with visualizations embedded in narrative text, known as *Magazine Style Narrative Visualization* [35], or MSNV for short (e.g., Figure 1).

IUI'18, March 7-11, 2018, Tokyo, Japan

ACM ISBN 978-1-4503-4945-1/18/03…$15.00
https://doi.org/10.1145/3172944.3173009

Research has shown that text and graphical modalities are well suited information channels to combine (e.g., [44]). Moreover, the *multimedia principle* states that "users learn more deeply from words and pictures than from words alone." [29]. However, an established problem arising from combined modalities is the *split-attention effect*. Split-attention occurs when users are required to split their attention between two information sources (e.g., text and visualization), which can increase cognitive load and can negatively impact learning [2]. This problem is exacerbated in MSNVs where often there is more than one visual task specified through the narrative text. Multiple visual tasks in MSNVs are captured by *references*, namely segments of text that specifies a visual task in on an accompanying visualization. An example of a reference is shown in Figure 1, it includes the sentence *"An overwhelming majority of chaplains who responded to these questions say that inmates' requests for religious texts (82%) and for meetings with spiritual leaders of their faith (71%) are usually approved."* plus the two bars outlined in orange. Typically, references are used to support arguments or statements being made in the document text by providing added details or interpretations to an accompanying visualization. As a user reads through a MSNV, they will often encounter a variety of references in the text, each soliciting attention to different aspects of the accompanying visualization. Since visualizations cannot be designed to favor the performance of any particular reference (because favoring one task may hinder the others) it has been proposed by Carenini et al. [8] to address this problem by providing *user-adaptive* support: highlighting interventions would be provided to relevant aspects of the visualization depending on what part of the text the user is reading and depending on the *user's characteristics* that may impact MSNV processing.

In this paper we present a first step toward understanding how to provide this adaptive support, by focusing specifically on identifying which user characteristics impact MSNV processing and thus warrant personalization. We conducted an exploratory user study to evaluate a set of 9 different user characteristics that could potentially influence MSNV performance. These include characteristics that were previously found to impact visualization processing (e.g., perceptual speed, spatial memory), plus some that are related to text processing (e.g., reading proficiency, verbal

IQ). Results from our user study identified five user characteristics that could be suitable targets for providing adaptive support. In the remainder of the paper we discuss related work, followed by a description of the user study. We then report results, and wrap up with the conclusion.

RELATED WORK

A growing amount of work has linked several user characteristics to performance and preference with various information visualizations. For instance, the cognitive ability *perceptual speed* has been shown to correlate negatively with time on task [9,10,41], and can also influence visualization suitability [1,12]. Users with high *visual working memory* were found to have a stronger preference for radar charts [38], and were shown to prefer deviation charts over maps [24]. Findings for other cognitive traits include: *disembedding* on task accuracy [41], *verbal working memory* on response time [9,10], and *spatial memory* on performance [12,41] and usability [24]. *Locus of control*, a personality trait, has also been shown to play a significant role in determining which type of visualization a user performs best with [20,33,43].

There are several works that have demonstrated the value of employing user-adaptive strategies in visualization systems. For instance, Gotz & Wen [17] reported a significant reduction in task time and task error-rate, by recommending an appropriate visualization to users based on patterns detected in the sequence of actions they performed while carrying out search and comparison tasks. Grawemeyer [18] also reported improved task performance with a series of database queries, by tracking users' evolving knowledge of the task domain and recommending visual representations accordingly. Nazemi et al. [32] improved the performance of searching bibliographic entries, by tracking users' interactions and adapting the size, color, and order of the entries shown across several visualizations. Carenini et al. [9] evaluated several forms of dynamic highlighting to guide attention to relevant datapoints within grouped bar charts, and they reported a significant improvement in task performance when compared to using no interventions. Outside of visualization, work has been done on providing user-adaptive support to text reading/comprehension. For instance, Lobodoa et al. [27] examined the feasibility of using eye tracking to infer word relevance during reading tasks, so that the informational needs of users could be assessed unobtrusively. Some work in intelligent user interfaces has looked at automatic generation of text and graphical presentations [19], but to the best of our knowledge, no one has focused on designing user-adaptive support to help users process them.

USER STUDY

Study Procedure

56 subjects (32 female) ranging in age from 19 to 69, participated in the study. 60% of participants were university students, and the others were from a variety of backgrounds (e.g., retail manager, restaurant server, retired). The experiment was a within-subjects repeated measures design, lasting at most 115 minutes. Participants were given the task of reading over a MSNV, and would signal they were done by clicking 'next'. They were then presented with a set of questions designed to elicit their opinion and to test their comprehension of relevant concepts discussed in the document. Participants were required to carry out this task for 15 different MSNVs (described in the next subsection). Users were not given a time-limit to read the MSNVs, but we told them that speed and accuracy would be factors in determining their performance. Standard tests were used to assess user characteristics (see Table 1). To reduce fatigue, we split up the user characteristic tests so that some were done at home the night before the experiment, and the rest were

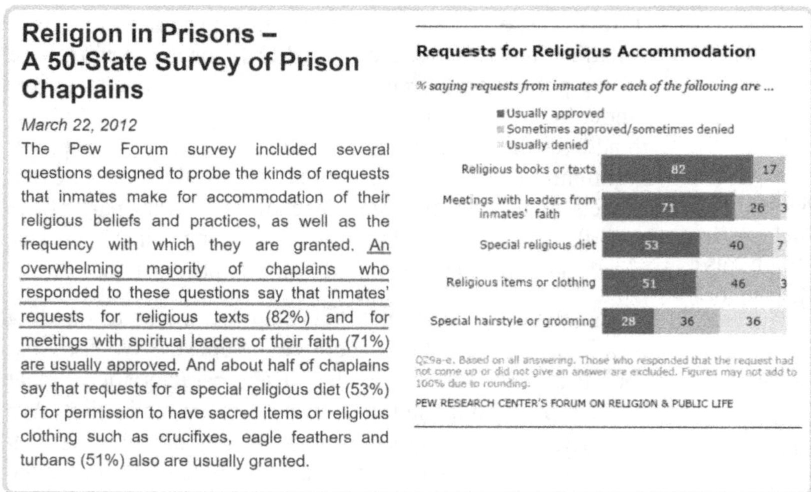

Figure 1. One of 15 MSNVs administered in the user study.
*Note: Orange highlighting is shown to illustrate the concept of a *reference*. Highlighting was not provided to users in the study.

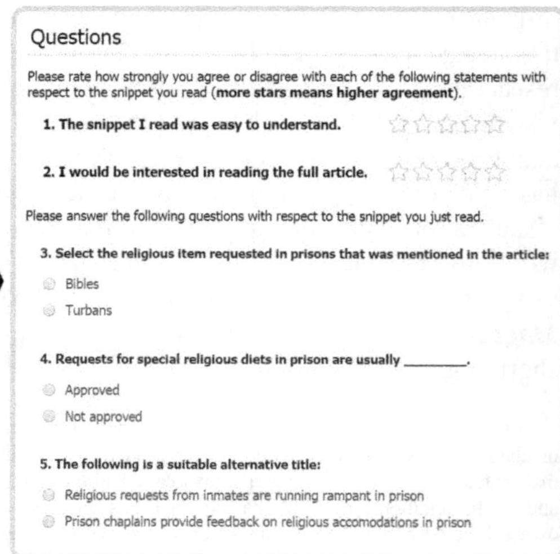

Figure 2. Comprehension questions presented to users after reading each MSNV.

administered in the lab before and after the set of 15 MSNV tasks[1]. Each participant was compensated $45 for the study. We further incentivized users by offering a $50 bonus to the top three participants with the best performance, so that users would be more inclined to put in effort with the tasks.

Study tasks

As we mentioned in the introduction, salient processing points in a MSNV are solicited by *references*, namely segments of text that specify a visual task on an accompanying visualization. The 15 MSNVs we used for the study tasks were derived from an existing dataset of magazine style documents by Kong et al. where the *references* in each document were identified via a rigorous coding process indicating which data points in each visualization correspond to each reference sentence [23]. All documents in the dataset were extracted from real-world sources including *Pew Research*, *The Guardian*, and *The Economist*. The 15 MSNVs in our study were self-contained excerpts from longer articles, selected to include one visualization each, and one body of narrative text ranging between 42 and 228 words (avg. = 91), and 1 to 7 *references*[2] (avg. = 2.6). Number of words and references were varied to account for the potential influence that these factors of complexity might have on MSNV processing. All the visualizations we selected were an assortment of bar charts (e.g., simple, stacked, grouped [31]).We focused on one class of visualizations to keep the complexity of study manageable, and we chose bar-graphs because they are one of the most popular and effective visualizations.

The aim of our study is to evaluate the impact of user characteristics on users' experience with MSNVs, where experience comprises of both task performance and subjective measures. These measures were assessed for each MSNV via a set of questions (see Figure 2) shown to the user after they read each document. Two *subjective* questions measured, respectively, perceived ease-of-understanding and interest (see top two questions in Figure 2), based on work by Waddell et al. [42]. The remaining questions measured task performance in terms of document comprehension, based on the work by Dyson & Haselgrove [13]. They included:

- One *title question* which asks to select a suitable alternative title for the MSNV (see question 5, bottom of Figure 2), and provides a simple way to ensure that the user had a grasp of the general document narrative.
- One or two (depending on document length) *recognition questions* asking to recall specific information from the MSNV: either a *named entity* discussed in the text (e.g., question 3 in Figure 2), or the *magnitude/directionality* of two named entities (e.g., question 4 in Figure 2).

[1] In the future, we plan to predict user characteristics in real-time by using classifiers based on eye tracking data, as done in [11,39].

[2] We also varied the *type* of references included in the documents, e.g., references that identify specific datapoints in the visualization; and references that emphasize comparisons among groups of datapoints.

User Characteristics Explored in the Study

The nine user characteristics we investigated in the study are shown in Table 1. The first seven characteristics consist of cognitive abilities and traits that we selected because previous research has shown that they play a significant role in user experience with visualizations (e.g., [9,10,12,24,38,41]). In addition, we included two user characteristics relating to reading abilities, to account for the fact that the MSNVs each contain a body of narrative text. All of the user characteristics were measured with standard tests in psychology (refer to Table 1 for citations).

Characteristic	Definition + Test Source
NEED FOR COGNITION	Extent to which individuals are inclined towards effortful cognitive activities [7].
BAR CHART LITERACY	Ability to use a bar chart to translate questions specified in the data domain into visual queries in the visual domain, as well as interpret visual patterns in the visual domain as properties in the data domain [5].
VISUAL WORKING MEMORY	Part of the working memory responsible for temporary storage and manipulation of visual and spatial information [16,28].
SPATIAL MEMORY	Ability to remember the configuration, location, and orientation of figural material [14].
VERBAL WORKING MEMORY	Part of the working memory responsible for temporary maintenance and manipulation of verbal information [3,40].
PERCEPTUAL SPEED	Speed in scanning/comparing figures or symbols, or carrying out other very simple tasks involving visual perception [14].
DISEMBEDDING	Ability to hold a given visual percept or configuration in mind so as to disembed it from other well defined perceptual material [14].
READING PROFICIENCY	Vocabulary size and reading comprehension ability in English [30].
VERBAL IQ	Overall verbal intellectual abilities that measures acquired knowledge, verbal reasoning, and attention to verbal materials [4,36].

Table 1. User characteristics measured in the study.

RESULTS

To assess the impact of the tested user characteristics on MSNV processing, we looked at 4 dependent measures:

- *MSNV Speed:* time in seconds that users spent looking at the document ($M = 57.2$, $SD = 32.9$).
- *MSNV Accuracy:* combined score of the objective comprehension questions ($M = 0.69$, $SD = 0.30$).
- *MSNV Ease-of-Understanding:* subjective rating on a 5-point Likert Scale ($M = 3.9$, $SD = 1.0$).
- *MSNV Interest:* subjective rating on a 5-point Likert Scale ($M = 3.3$, $SD = 1.3$).

To account for possible redundancies, we carried out a preliminary check for correlations within the user characteristics as well as within the dependent measures

(Pearson correlation). For both groups, no correlations were high enough to justify removal. We then ran one path analysis model[3] on each of the 4 dependent measures of user experience using the *lavaan* software package in R [34]. Each path model included the set of 9 user characteristics as covariates, as well as 5 factors to account for document complexity (e.g., number of words in the text, amount of references, number of datapoints in the visualization). We adjusted for multiple comparison error using a Bonferroni correction of $m = 4$ [15]. In terms of model fit, all four path models yielded a Tucker-Lewis Index (TLI) = 1.0, which is the best fit possible, and is well above the minimum acceptable threshold of 0.9 [21]. Due to space limitations, we report only the statistically significant findings for which there are obvious implications for adaptive support.

Main Effect of User Characteristic	MSNV Speed	MSNV Accuracy	MSNV Understanding	MSNV Interest
Disembedding	$p = .002$, $\beta = -0.12$	-	-	-
Verbal WM	$p < .0001$, $\beta = -0.22$	-	-	-
Reading Proficiency	$p < .0001$, $\beta = -0.15$	-	-	-
Need for Cognition	$p < .0001$, $\beta = 0.12$	-	$p < .0001$, $\beta = 0.21$	$p < .0001$, $\beta = 0.14$
Spatial Memory	$p < .0001$, $\beta = 0.19$	-	$p < .0001$, $\beta = 0.13$	-
Bar Chart Literacy	$p < .0001$, $\beta = 0.20$	-	-	-

Table 2. Significant results from our path model analyses. Beta values reported indicate size and directionality of standardized regression coefficient.

We found main effects for six user characteristics on MSNV Speed, but no main effects on MSNV Accuracy (see Table 2), which indicates that all users were similarly accurate though some of them likely needed more time to achieve comparable accuracy. If we look at the results in more detail, the main effects can be clustered into three rather different groups.

The first group includes user characteristics (*Disembedding*, *Verbal WM*, and *Reading Proficiency*) that display a *negative directionality* with MSNV Speed (i.e., users with **low** abilities spend more time looking at the MSNV). This is not surprising, as *Disembedding* relates to visualization processing, and *Verbal WM* and *Reading Proficiency* relate to text processing, and having low abilities for these characteristics are plausible causes of slower performance.

The second group of main effects includes user characteristics (*Need for Cognition* and *Spatial Memory*) that have *positive directionality* with MSNV Speed (i.e., users with **high** abilities are the ones spending more time looking at the MSNVs). This would seem counterintuitive, if we had not also found that for these same two characteristics there are main effects on the subjective measures of MSNV Understanding and/or Interest (see last two columns of Table 2), indicating that these users with **high** abilities are also rating the documents more favorably. What appears to be happening for this group of users, is that longer time on task does not translate into higher accuracy, but it does improve their overall experience, and this could be beneficial depending on the goals of the system or user.

The third group only includes only *Bar Chart Literacy*, for which we also found *positive directionality* with MSNV Speed, but no results with the subjective measures. A possible explanation is that these users linger on the document because they are more inclined to explore extra details in the visualizations (i.e., bar charts), but this unfortunately does not generate any improvement in either accuracy or user experience.

Discussion

Although our results are quite preliminary, the first two groups of main effects can viably inform some adaptation strategies. We have identified characteristics where users with *low abilities* were taking longer to achieve comparable accuracy as their counterparts. Such users could be supported in completing the task faster by providing interventions to facilitate visualization processing for users with low *Disembedding*, or facilitating text processing for users with low *Verbal WM* or *Reading Proficiency*. In the second group of main effects, we have identified characteristics (*Need for Cognition* and *Spatial Memory*) where users with *high abilities* were spending more time on task, with no improvement in objective accuracy, but with higher subjective ratings of document understanding and document interest. For these characteristics, it may make sense to focus on engaging users with low abilities to spend more meaningful time with the MSNVs, which may consequently improve their attitude towards the documents.

CONCLUSION

In this paper, we conducted an exploratory user study to investigate which user characteristics play a role in user experience with Magazine Style Narrative Visualizations (MSNVs). Results from our analysis identified several significant main effects of user characteristics that can inform possible strategies for adaptation. As a next step, we plan to analyze eye tracking data that we collected in our study, which can support and further clarify our results in an objective way. For instance, we expect that users with low *Reading Proficiency* spend more time processing the text in the MSNVs compared to their counterparts. Using gaze analysis methodology described in [37], we can verify if our expectation is true, plus we can further evaluate where within the text users are having difficulty (e.g., possibly while they are processing the *references*).

[3] Path analysis is a more sophisticated model that will facilitate mediation analysis for future work, but at this stage is equivalent to using multiple regression analysis [22].

REFERENCES

1. Bryce Allen. 2000. Individual differences and the conundrums of user-centered design: Two experiments. *Journal of the American society for information science* 51, 6: 508–520.
2. P Ayres and G Cierniak. 2012. Split-Attention Effect. In *Encyclopedia of the Sciences of Learning, ed. Norbet M. Seel*. Springer, 3172–3175.
3. Alan D. Baddeley. 1986. *Working memory*. Clarendon Press ; Oxford University Press, Oxford [Oxfordshire] : New York.
4. Jennifer R. Blair and Otfried Spreen. 1989. Predicting premorbid IQ: A revision of the national adult reading test. *Clinical Neuropsychologist* 3, 2: 129–136. https://doi.org/10.1080/13854048908403285
5. J. Boy, R.A. Rensink, E. Bertini, and J.-D. Fekete. 2014. A Principled Way of Assessing Visualization Literacy. *IEEE Transactions on Visualization and Computer Graphics* 20, 12: 1963–1972. https://doi.org/10.1109/TVCG.2014.2346984
6. Matthew Brehmer, Bongshin Lee, Benjamin Bach, Nathalie Henry Riche, and Tamara Munzner. 2016. Timelines Revisited: A Design Space and Considerations for Expressive Storytelling. *IEEE Transactions on Visualization and Computer Graphics*: 1–1. https://doi.org/10.1109/TVCG.2016.2614803
7. John T. Cacioppo, Richard E. Petty, and Chuan Feng Kao. 1984. The Efficient Assessment of Need for Cognition. *Journal of Personality Assessment* 48, 3: 306–307. https://doi.org/10.1207/s15327752jpa4803_13
8. Giuseppe Carenini, Cristina Conati, Enamul Hoque, and Ben Steichen. 2013. User Task Adaptation in Multimedia Presentations. In *Proceedings of the 1st International Workshop on User-Adaptive Information Visualization (WUAV 2013), in conjunction with the 21st conference on User Modeling, Adaptation and Personalization (UMAP 2013)*.
9. Giuseppe Carenini, Cristina Conati, Enamul Hoque, Ben Steichen, Dereck Toker, and James T. Enns. 2014. Highlighting Interventions and User Differences: Informing Adaptive Information Visualization Support. In *Proceedings of the SIGCHI Conference on Human Factors in Computing Systems*, 1835–1844. https://doi.org/https://doi.org/10.1145/2556288.2557141
10. Conati Conati, Giuseppe Carenini, Enamul Hoque, Ben Steichen, and Dereck Toker. 2014. Evaluating the impact of user characteristics and different layouts on an interactive visualization for decision making. In *Computer Graphics Forum*, 371–380. https://doi.org/10.1111/cgf.12393
11. Cristina Conati, Sébastien Lallé, Md. Abed Rahman, and Dereck Toker. 2017. Further Results on Predicting Cognitive Abilities for Adaptive Visualizations. In *Proceedings of the 26th International Joint Conference on Artificial Intelligence*.
12. Cristina Conati and Heather Maclaren. 2008. Exploring the role of individual differences in information visualization. In *Proceedings of the working conference on Advanced visual interfaces*, 199–206. https://doi.org/10.1145/1385569.1385602
13. Mary C. Dyson and Mark Haselgrove. 2001. The influence of reading speed and line length on the effectiveness of reading from screen. *International Journal of Human-Computer Studies* 54, 4: 585–612. https://doi.org/10.1006/ijhc.2001.0458
14. Ruth B. Ekstrom, John W. French, Harry H. Harman, and Diran Dermen. 1976. *Manual for kit of factor referenced cognitive tests*. Educational Testing Service Princeton, NJ.
15. Andy P. Field. 2003. *How to design and report experiments*. Sage publications Ltd.
16. Keisuke Fukuda and Edward K. Vogel. 2009. Human Variation in Overriding Attentional Capture. *The Journal of Neuroscience* 29, 27: 8726–8733. https://doi.org/10.1523/JNEUROSCI.2145-09.2009
17. David Gotz and Zhen Wen. 2009. Behavior-driven visualization recommendation. In *Proceedings of the 14th international conference on Intelligent user interfaces*, 315–324. https://doi.org/10.1145/1502650.1502695
18. Beate Grawemeyer. 2006. Evaluation of ERST: an external representation selection tutor. In *Proceedings of the 4th international conference on Diagrammatic Representation and Inference* (Diagrams'06), 154–167. https://doi.org/10.1007/11783183_21
19. Nancy L Green, Giuseppe Carenini, Stephan Kerpedjiev, Joe Mattis, Johanna D Moore, and Steven F Roth. 2004. AutoBrief: an experimental system for the automatic generation of briefings in integrated text and information graphics. *International Journal of Human-Computer Studies* 61, 1: 32–70. https://doi.org/10.1016/j.ijhcs.2003.10.007
20. Tear Marie Green and Brian Fisher. 2010. Towards the Personal Equation of Interaction: The impact of personality factors on visual analytics interface interaction. In *2010 IEEE Symposium on Visual Analytics Science and Technology (VAST)*, 203–210. https://doi.org/10.1109/VAST.2010.5653587
21. Li-tze Hu and Peter M. Bentler. 1999. Cutoff criteria for fit indexes in covariance structure analysis: Conventional criteria versus new alternatives. *Structural Equation Modeling: A Multidisciplinary Journal* 6, 1: 1–55. https://doi.org/10.1080/10705519909540118
22. Rex B. Kline. 2016. *Principles and practice of structural equation modeling*. The Guilford Press, New York.
23. Nicholas Kong, Marti A. Hearst, and Maneesh Agrawala. 2014. Extracting references between text and charts via crowdsourcing. In *Proceedings of the*

SIGCHI conference on Human Factors in Computing Systems, 31–40. https://doi.org/10.1145/2556288.2557241
24. Sébastien Lallé, Cristina Conati, and Giuseppe Carenini. 2017. Impact of Individual Differences on User Experience with a Visualization Interface for Public Engagement. In *Adjunct Publication of the 25th Conference on User Modeling, Adaptation and Personalization* (UMAP '17), 247–252. https://doi.org/10.1145/3099023.3099055
25. Sébastien Lallé, Dereck Toker, Cristina Conati, and Giuseppe Carenini. 2015. Prediction of Users' Learning Curves for Adaptation while Using an Information Visualization. In *Proceedings of the 20th International Conference on Intelligent User Interfaces*, 357–368. https://doi.org/https://doi.org/10.1145/2678025.2701376
26. Jason Lankow, Josh Ritchie, and Ross Crooks. 2012. *Infographics: the power of visual storytelling*. John Wiley & Sons, Inc, Hoboken, N.J.
27. Tomasz D. Loboda, Peter Brusilovsky, and Jöerg Brunstein. 2011. Inferring word relevance from eye-movements of readers. 175. https://doi.org/10.1145/1943403.1943431
28. Robert H. Logie. 2009. *Visuo-spatial working memory*. Psychology Press, Hove.
29. Richard E. Mayer. 2009. *Multimedia learning*. Cambridge University Press, Cambridge ; New York.
30. Paul Meara. 1992. *EFL vocabulary tests, second edition 2010*. Lognostics, Swansea: Wales.
31. Tamara Munzner. 2015. *Visualization analysis and design*. CRC Press, Taylor & Francis Group, CRC Press is an imprint of the Taylor & Francis Group, an informa business, Boca Raton.
32. Kawa Nazemi, Reimond Retz, Jürgen Bernard, Jörn Kohlhammer, and Dieter Fellner. 2013. Adaptive Semantic Visualization for Bibliographic Entries. In *Advances in Visual Computing* (Lecture Notes in Computer Science), 13–24. https://doi.org/10.1007/978-3-642-41939-3_2
33. Alvitta Ottley, Huahai Yang, and Remco Chang. 2015. Personality as a Predictor of User Strategy: How Locus of Control Affects Search Strategies on Tree Visualizations. 3251–3254. https://doi.org/10.1145/2702123.2702590
34. Yves Rosseel. 2012. lavaan: An R Package for Structural Equation Modeling. *Journal of Statistical Software* 48, 2. https://doi.org/10.18637/jss.v048.i02
35. E Segel and J Heer. 2010. Narrative Visualization: Telling Stories with Data. *IEEE Transactions on Visualization and Computer Graphics* 16, 6: 1139–1148. https://doi.org/10.1109/TVCG.2010.179
36. Esther Strauss, Elisabeth M. S. Sherman, Otfried Spreen, and Otfried Spreen. 2006. *A compendium of neuropsychological tests: administration, norms, and commentary*. Oxford University Press, Oxford ; New York.
37. Dereck Toker and Cristina Conati. 2014. Eye tracking to understand user differences in visualization processing with highlighting interventions. In *Proceedings of the 22nd international conference on User Modeling, Adaptation, and Personalization* (UMAP'14). https://doi.org/https://doi.org/10.1007/978-3-319-08786-3_19
38. Dereck Toker, Cristina Conati, Giuseppe Carenini, and Mona Haraty. 2012. Towards adaptive information visualization: on the influence of user characteristics. In *Proceedings of the 20th international conference on User Modeling, Adaptation, and Personalization* (UMAP'12), 274–285. https://doi.org/10.1007/978-3-642-31454-4_23
39. Dereck Toker, Sébastien Lallé, and Cristina Conati. 2017. Pupillometry and Head Distance to the Screen to Predict Skill Acquisition During Information Visualization Tasks. In *In Proceedings of the 22nd International Conference on Intelligent User Interfaces*, 221–231. https://doi.org/10.1145/3025171.3025187
40. Marilyn L Turner and Randall W Engle. 1989. Is working memory capacity task dependent? *Journal of Memory and Language* 28, 2: 127–154. https://doi.org/10.1016/0749-596X(89)90040-5
41. Maria C. Velez, Deborah Silver, and Marilyn Tremaine. 2005. Understanding visualization through spatial ability differences. In *Proceedings of the IEEE Conference on Visualization*, 511–518. https://doi.org/10.1109/VISUAL.2005.1532836
42. T. Franklin Waddell, Joshua R. Auriemma, and S. Shyam Sundar. 2016. Make it Simple, or Force Users to Read?: Paraphrased Design Improves Comprehension of End User License Agreements. In *Proceedings of the SIGCHI Conference on Human Factors in Computing Systems* (CHI'16), 5252–5256. https://doi.org/10.1145/2858036.2858149
43. Caroline Ziemkiewicz, R. Jordan Crouser, Ashley Rye Yauilla, Sara L. Su, William Ribarsky, and Remeo Chang. 2011. How locus of control influences compatibility with visualization style. In *Proceedings of the IEEE Conference on Visual Analytics Science and Technology*, 81–90. https://doi.org/10.1109/VAST.2011.6102445
44. 2008. *Human Factors (HF); Guidelines on the multimodality of icons, symbols and pictograms*. European Telecommunications Standards Institute.

Detecting Memory-Based Interaction Obstacles with a Recurrent Neural Model of User Behavior

Felix Putze*
University of Bremen
Bremen, Germany
felix.putze@uni-bremen.de

Mazen Salous
University of Bremen
Bremen, Germany
mazen.salous@uni-bremen.de

Tanja Schultz
University of Bremen
Bremen, Germany
tanja.schultz@uni-bremen.de

ABSTRACT
A memory-based interaction obstacle is a condition which impedes human memory during Human-Computer Interaction, for example a memory-loading secondary task. In this paper, we present an approach to detect the presence of such memory-based interaction obstacles from logged user behavior during system use. For this purpose, we use a recurrent neural network which models the resulting temporal sequences. To acquire a sufficient number of training episodes, we employ a cognitive user simulation. We evaluate the approach with data from a user test and on which we outperform a non-sequential baseline by up to 42% relative.

CCS Concepts
•**Human-centered computing** → **User models;**

Author Keywords
Classification of user behavior; memory; interaction obstacles; LSTMs

INTRODUCTION
When humans interact with computers, they may face interaction obstacles which constrain their ability to successfully complete their tasks. Interaction obstacles occur in various forms, related to perceptual, cognitive, or motor challenges. For an adaptive interaction system, modeling such interaction obstacles is important to provide individual support targeting these interaction obstacles. One of the central human cognitive functions is working memory. Working memory is strongly correlated to general intelligence [4] and determines performance in most non-trivial HCI tasks. If working memory of the user is impeded, an intelligent system could for example adapt by reducing its own memory load [25].

Existing approaches (see Section 2) for dynamically detecting memory-based interaction obstacles online make use of one or more sensors to classify the cognitive state of the user. In many situations however, using sensors may not be feasible due to cost, convenience, or privacy considerations. In this paper, we present an approach for detecting a memory-loading secondary task as an interaction obstacle purely by exploiting behavioral patterns from interaction features without any additional sensors. To this end, we employ Long Short Term Memory (LSTM) networks, which are a special type of recurrent neural networks to model temporal relationships in the sequence of behavioral patterns.

For analyzing this approach, we investigate data recorded during the play of a game of matching pairs. Matching pairs is a stand-in for a complex interaction task with a strong memory component. Matching pairs is also a relevant study subject in its own right as it is used for the activation of people suffering from dementia [6], which is a condition that strongly affects memory. In this work, our goal is to identify the presence of memory-based interaction obstacles in the form of a memory-loading secondary task by classifying sequences of user behavior data, recorded as interaction features. We expect players to behave differently based on whether their memory is distracted by a secondary task, e.g., by missing opportunities to collect previously revealed pairs of cards or revealing the same card multiple times. We will show that, by using a sequential classification model of human behavioral data, we are able to discriminate between game play situations with and without secondary task.

Our two main contributions in this paper are: First, we present a novel LSTM-based approach for the detection of memory-based interaction obstacles from sequential behavioral data. Second, for dealing with data sparseness in modeling user behavior from real data, we present a novel approach for the cognitively motivated simulation of user behavior to generate enough training sequences.

RELATED WORK
As working memory is such an important cognitive construct influencing many HCI tasks, there exists a large body of research which aims at measuring working memory load [21], which is usually modulated through memory-loading secondary tasks. Actual measurement of working memory load then takes place by classifying features from various sensors. Most prominently, researchers investigate signals from neural sources, for example recorded from electroencephalography (EEG): Berka et al. [3] showed the feasibility of classifying working memory load from frequency features at different electrode sides using an unobtrusive EEG headset. Baldwin

*Partially funded by DFG grant PU 613/1-1: Detection of Interaction Competencies and Obstacles (DINCO).

IUI'18, March 7–11, 2018, Tokyo, Japan

ISBN 978-1-4503-4945-1/18/03...$15.00
DOI: 10.1145/3172944.3173006

and Penaranda [2] used a classifier based on Neural Networks to discriminate two difficulty levels across three different memory tasks. Ke et al. [16] showed that a memory load classifier based on a broad range of frequency features could be transferred from a simple n-back task to the more complex Multi-Attribute Task battery. Herff et al. [13] showed how a hybrid classifier (combining EEG and fNIRS measurement) was able to reliably discriminate pairs of difficulty levels in a sequential memory task. Mühl et al. [18] used Common Spatial Patterns on different frequency ranges to generate features for classification of workload under different stress conditions. Heger et al. [12] showed that adapting the behavior of a system to workload measured from EEG in a multitasking situation helped users to improve efficiency and effectiveness in the main task. Brain activity is not the only modality which carries information on memory load; eye tracking data can also be used for this purpose: Rozado and Dünser [22] demonstrated that EEG-based load estimation can be combined with pupillometry data for increased accuracy. Katidioti et al. [15] used pupillometry-based load estimation to create a task-independent interruption management system.

All of the presented approaches have in common that they only regard relatively short segments of sensor data without resorting to a larger temporal context. Recurrent neural networks as sequential classification models allow to take such information into account. An LSTM network is a type of recurrent neural network which uses designated memory cells to model long-range dependencies within sequential data. For example, Gers et al. [8] showed that LSTMs were able to successfully learn the rules encoded in context-free and context-dependent formal languages. Schaul and Schmidhuber [23] investigated the use of LSTMs for modeling playing strategies in complex games and the ability of the model to generalize from small to larger game boards. Graves et al. [10] used bidirectional LSTMs for recognition of unconstrained, connected handwriting. Eck and Schmidhuber [5] showed that LSTMs were able to discover and reproduce the temporal structure of complex pieces of music due to their ability in detecting long-range dependencies. While LSTM has been established as a powerful modeling tool, it has to our best knowledge never been applied to behavioral data in the HCI context.

DATA COLLECTION

The well-known matching pairs game, constitutes a complex HCI task which relies on working memory. In this game, a player in one turn reveals two cards from a display of face-down cards. If the revealed cards match (i.e., show the same picture), they are removed from the game, otherwise, they are turned face-down again. The goal of the game is to clear the display with as few turns as possible, by memorizing the location of already revealed cards. How people approach this task carries a lot of information about their working memory status. The game used in our data collection experiments consists of randomly shuffled fourteen cards (seven pairs) and was presented on an Android tablet, see Figure 1. Participants played a single-player variant of the game in which they had the goal of clearing the display as fast as possible. The game application records log files of interaction features, such as position and identity of selected cards.

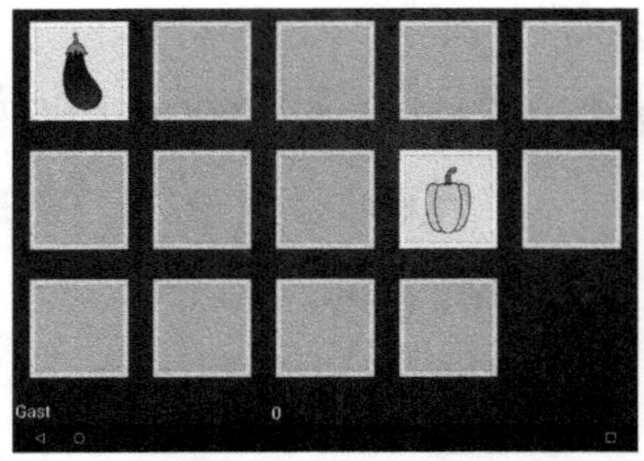

Figure 1. Matching Pairs Game

To create a memory-related interaction obstacle, we introduced a secondary task to the matching pairs game. Participants were asked to play the game two times with and without secondary task, in randomized order:

- Only Matching Pairs (MP): The participants are asked to play the game without any parallel secondary task.
- Matching Pairs with Cumulative Sum (MP+CS): Whenever the participant reveals a card, a random number between 1 and 9 will be spoken by the synthesized voice. The participant is asked to calculate and memorize the sum of all spoken numbers throughout the game.

In total, 31 people participated in our experiments. 22 participants were male and the other 9 participants were female. The ages range from 19 till 48, most of the participants were students or university employees. All participants gave their informed written consent. They were compensated with 10€ for their participation. The data collection was approved by the ethics committee of the University of Bremen. For a subset of 24 participants, we conducted the Memory Update Test (MU) [17] in order to enable further evaluation of our paradigm in comparison to a standard working memory test. For the same subset of participants, we also recorded EEG data, but this data is not evaluated in the current paper.

CLASSIFICATION SETUP

In this section, we will introduce the classification setup which we implemented for the detection of memory-based interaction obstacles. We treat the recorded data as a binary classification task, where the output label is either MP or MP+CS. For this purpose, we compare two classification models: A sequential neural model based on LSTMs [14] and a static baseline model based on Linear Discriminant Analysis (LDA). As the number of available training episodes is very limited (each session yields two episodes, one of each class), we generate additional training data from a cognitive user simulation. We train the classifier from data of 15 participants. For each participant, we generate 1,000 episodes, resulting in a total of 15,000 training episodes.

The overall system consists of two main components: The Cognitive Memory Model (CMM) [19], which is used to simulate plausible additional training episodes, and the classifier which is trained to label given game sequences (or prefixes thereof) as either MP or MP+CS. The following subsections explain the role of both parts.

CMM-based User Simulation

A challenge of generating additional training sequences for training of a sequential classification model is that the sequences have to maintain plausible temporal relationships between time slices. While traditional oversampling approaches, such as ADASYN [11], do not consider the temporal structure of sequences, recent approaches, such as [9], aim at capturing this temporal structure to generate plausible sequential data.

The Cognitive Memory Model [19] (CMM) is a general computational cognitive model of human memory inspired by the ACT-R theory [1]. It has been successfully employed to model games of matching pairs, revealing different playing strategies and levels of memory performance. In this work, the CMM acts as a simulator to generate additional training episodes for the classifier to detect memory-based interaction obstacles. The CMM is based on a decay-based forgetting mechanism to realistically simulate non-perfect human memory. For each item in memory (cards in our use case), the CMM maintains an activation value from which the likelihood of retrieval can be calculated. In general, the activation of an item depends on the frequency and recency of stimulations of said item. Based on the retrieval likelihood for all individual cards in a given game state, we execute a specific strategy to select which cards to reveal. This strategy balances exploration (revealing cards which are unknown to the player or not remembered) and exploitation (revealing pairs when position of both corresponding cards is remembered with high enough probability). By repeatedly executing this strategy and updating the game state, artificial sequences of game play can be generated. See the work by Putze et al. [20] for details on how to model the game of matching pairs using the CMM.

The CMM has a number of free parameters, such as the degree of memory decay, which determine its predictions of memory performance. Those parameters can be optimized by a genetic optimization algorithm in CMM to best fit the empirical training data. The genetic optimizer maintains a population of CMM configurations consisting of all free parameters. The population is initialized randomly and then iteratively updated according to the standard operations of genetic optimization, mutation and selection [7]. For selection, we employ two different similarity metrics, the so-called matching-pairs and exploiting-punishment measures, to compare a set of generated game sessions to real game sessions. The matching-pairs measure counts the number of removed card pairs for each turn. The exploiting-punishment measure counts the number of card pairs which have both been revealed at some point of the game but have not been removed by the player (presumably, because the location of one or both of the cards to that pair have been forgotten by the player). A CMM configuration is then selected more likely if it generates game sessions which are close to the real data according to the specified similarity metrics. As we are comparing sequences, the similarity measures are also defined per game turn and distance between two game sessions is measured as the Root Mean Squared Error (RMSE) between the two turn-wise sequences.

Playing behavior in the game of matching pairs varies between individual players, for example depending on working memory capacity and differences in playing strategy. To achieve enough variance in the training data, we do not pool all available real sessions together to optimize a global parameter set; instead, we repeat the process for each session individually and only pool the resulting simulated sessions together to form a richer, more varied corpus of simulated sessions.

Classifiers

LSTMs are a special form of recurrent neural network which are designed to model sequential data. LSTMs consist of so-called LSTM cells which explicitly store, retain, or forget information from previous time steps. This approach is chosen to battle the challenge of vanishing gradient in traditional recurrent neural networks. The network for our approach is shown in Figure 2. It starts with an LSTM layer with 32 LSTM

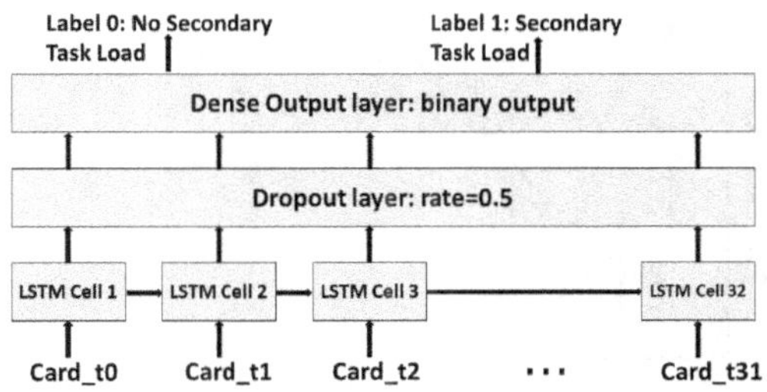

Figure 2. Prediction model bottom-up topology

cells as input layer to handle the training data sequences. The LSTM is followed by a Dropout layer with rate of 0.5 acting as a regularization technique that avoids over-fitting by randomly ignoring neurons during training [24]. The output layer is a fully connected dense layer that uses soft-max activation and outputs a binary label. To fit the model, we perform 500 epochs of Stochastic Gradient Decent (SGD) which has been used with adaptive learning rate $lr = \frac{0.1}{\#epoch}$. The input sequences consist of the ordered consecutive chosen cards, each card represented by two features: The first one encodes its position in the revealing order of motives (from 1 to 7, since the game has 14 cards, i.e., 7 pairs), while the second feature encodes the card's position in the corresponding pair (1 or 2). After 500 training epochs on simulated data, we retrain the resulting model with the original 15 real training sessions.

In contrast to the LSTM model, the LDA model considers a whole game at once. For this purpose, we need to manually define the features which are expected to differ between classes. The following features summarize for a game prefix how efficient and close-to-optimal a player performed: 1) Number of cards left in the game, 2) Number of never revealed cards in the game, 3) Maximum number of times revealing the same card, and 4) Number of turns since game completion ($= 0$ if game not yet completed). From these features, we train an LDA model to classify logged games into MP and MP+CS.

EVALUATION

Before analyzing the trained classifiers, we check the behavioral differences between classes MP and MP+CS. Figure 3 shows the matching-pairs statistic for both classes. We see a difference between the two conditions, although standard deviation is high. This implies that the secondary task deteriorates MP performance but its presence cannot immediately detected from simple behavioral measurements[1]. We also compared performance in MP for participants with above-median and below-median memory capacity according to the MU test and saw a significant difference in game completion time. This confirms that the MP task is actually memory-dependant.

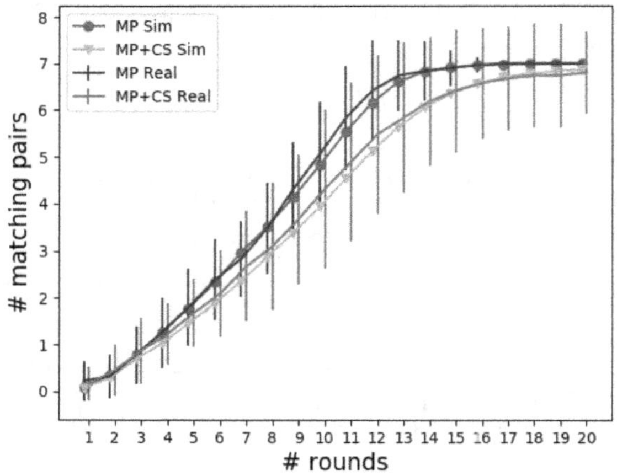

Figure 3. Mean matching-pairs statistic for MP and MP+CS conditions of real data (*MP Real* and *MP+CS Real*) and simulated data (*MP Sim* and *MP+CS Sim*). For real data, whiskers show standard deviation.

As a next step, we compare the simulated sessions to the real ones. Figure 3 also presents the mean matching-pairs metric of all generated sessions. The evident similarity can also be quantified by calculating turn-wise RMSE between curves for corresponding real and simulated curves. Simulated data from class MP yields an RMSE of 0.12 to the real data from class MP and an RMSE of 0.41 from class MP+CS. Distance is similarly large for simulated data from class MP+CS (RMSE of 0.67 to real MP and 0.21 to real MP+CS).

For evaluating the classifiers, we repeatedly split the available 31 playing sessions randomly into training and testing sets, of size 15 and 16, respectively. For each split, we again performed multiple "inner" iterations with different randomly generated sets of 15000 training sessions. In this setting, we used 20 splits with 20 inner iterations each. Training and testing data is balanced for classes MP and MP+CS. We test the trained classification model on the testing data of the respective split, as well as on 3000 newly generated sessions which are disjoint from the training sessions. We perform the analysis for game prefixes of different fixed lengths. Since our matching pairs game has 7 pairs of cards, the minimum game length is 7 turns. In addition, all participants' logs show that the participants finish the game in 10 to 15 game turns.

[1]the matching-pairs statistic corresponds to the first LDA feature.

Length	*LSTM Sim*	*LDA Sim*	*LSTM Real*	*LDA Real*
7	58.2 (0.9)	52.6 (0.9)	62.6 (1.1)	43.9 (1.3)
10	59.3 (0.8)	50.0 (0.1)	66.1 (0.5)	56.2 (0.0)
15	60.1 (0.5)	56.8 (0.8)	65.1 (1.3)	57.9 (2.3)

Table 1. Average accuracy (and standard error) for LSTM and and LDA classification models on simulated and real testing data for game prefixes of different lengths.

Therefore, we look at game prefixes of length 7, 10, and 15. As performance metric, we report classification accuracy, summarized in Table 1.

These results show that the LSTM model outperforms the LDA model. The improvement is statistically significant for all results on simulated and real data ($p < 0.05$, calculated using a paired t-test on the result of individual iterations). The LSTM model outperforms the LDA baseline by more than 42% relative for 7 game turns, 17% relative for 10 game turnes and more than 12% relative for 15 game turns. Such results show high advantages of using LSTM over LDA especially for short behavioural sequences (7 game turns). While the manual defined LDA features require relatively long game prefixes to estimate reliable game statistics, the LSTM exploits temporal dependencies also from shorter game prefixes. However, the model is still in-progress and these results can be further improved by tuning the hyper-parameters and generating more training data.

DISCUSSION

In this paper, we have demonstrated the feasibility of detecting memory-based interaction obstacles without resorting to additional sensors by modeling time series of user behavior with sequential LSTMs. For generating additional training episodes, we employed a novel, cognitively inspired simulation and showed their similarity to the real data. We showed that the simulation was able to generate plausible training sessions and that the sequential LSTM-based model outperformed a static LDA-based baseline by up to 42% relative. Although classification needs to be further improved to be reliable enough for adaptive HCI systems, the approach is promising to be helpful for a large variety of scenarios: Cognitive architectures such as ACT-R, which is the main source for the employed simulation, aim at modeling general human behavior. Therefore, we assume that the approach for classifying sequences of human behavior data can be transferred to other tasks by adjusting the simulation. For this purpose, it is also relevant that it is not necessary to engineer features for the LSTM which works with the raw sequence of user behavior. Next steps will focus on the exploitation of the additional data recorded in this study: 1) We will investigate the recorded EEG data for the detection of memory-based interaction obstacles from combined neural and behavioral features. 2) We will use the data from the MU test to investigate memory-based interaction obstacles which result from limited working memory capacity (in contrast to memory-loading secondary tasks).

REFERENCES

1. John R. Anderson, Daniel Bothell, Michael D. Byrne, Scott Douglass, Christian Lebiere, and Yulin Qin. 2004.

An Integrated Theory of the Mind. *Psychological Review* 111, 4 (2004), 1036–1060.

2. Carryl L Baldwin and BN Penaranda. 2012. Adaptive training using an artificial neural network and EEG metrics for within-and cross-task workload classification. *NeuroImage* 59, 1 (2012), 48–56.
3. Chris Berka, Daniel J. Levendowski, Michelle N. Lumicao, Alan Yau, Gene Davis, Vladimir T. Zivkovic, Richard E. Olmstead, Patrice D. Tremoulet, and Patrick L. Craven. 2007. EEG Correlates of Task Engagement and Mental Workload in Vigilance, Learning, and Memory Tasks. *Aviation, Space, and Environmental Medicine* 78 (2007), B231–B244.
4. Andrew RA Conway, Michael J Kane, and Randall W Engle. 2003. Working memory capacity and its relation to general intelligence. *Trends in cognitive sciences* 7, 12 (2003), 547–552.
5. Douglas Eck and Juergen Schmidhuber. 2002. Finding temporal structure in music: Blues improvisation with LSTM recurrent networks. In *Neural Networks for Signal Processing, 2002. Proceedings of the 2002 12th IEEE Workshop on*. IEEE, 747–756.
6. S Ehret, F Putze, H Miller-Teynor, A Kruse, and T Schultz. 2017. Technique-based game for daycare visitors with and without dementia: Effects, heuristics and correlates. *Zeitschrift fur Gerontologie und Geriatrie* 50, 1 (2017), 35–44.
7. David B Fogel. 1994. An introduction to simulated evolutionary optimization. *IEEE transactions on neural networks* 5, 1 (1994), 3–14.
8. Felix A Gers, Jrgen Schmidhuber, and Fred Cummins. 2000. Learning to forget: Continual prediction with LSTM. *Neural computation* 12, 10 (2000), 2451–2471.
9. Zhichen Gong and Huanhuan Chen. 2016. Model-Based Oversampling for Imbalanced Sequence Classification. In *Proceedings of the 25th ACM International on Conference on Information and Knowledge Management.* ACM, 1009–1018.
10. Alex Graves, Marcus Liwicki, Santiago Fernndez, Roman Bertolami, Horst Bunke, and Jrgen Schmidhuber. 2009. A novel connectionist system for unconstrained handwriting recognition. *IEEE transactions on pattern analysis and machine intelligence* 31, 5 (2009), 855–868.
11. Haibo He, Yang Bai, E. A. Garcia, and Shutao Li. 2008. ADASYN: Adaptive synthetic sampling approach for imbalanced learning. In *2008 IEEE International Joint Conference on Neural Networks (IEEE World Congress on Computational Intelligence)*. 1322–1328.
12. Dominic Heger, Felix Putze, and Tanja Schultz. 2010. An adaptive information system for an empathic robot using EEG data. In *Social Robotics*. Springer, 151–160.
13. C. Herff, O. Fortmann, Chun-Yu Tse, Xiaoqin Cheng, F. Putze, D. Heger, and T. Schultz. 2015. Hybrid fNIRS-EEG based discrimination of 5 levels of memory load. In *2015 7th International IEEE/EMBS Conference on Neural Engineering (NER)*. 5–8.
14. Sepp Hochreiter and Jürgen Schmidhuber. 1997. Long short-term memory. *Neural computation* 9, 8 (1997), 1735–1780.
15. Ioanna Katidioti, Jelmer P Borst, Douwe J Bierens de Haan, Tamara Pepping, Marieke K van Vugt, and Niels A Taatgen. 2016. Interrupted by Your Pupil: An Interruption Management System Based on Pupil Dilation. *International Journal of Human–Computer Interaction* 32, 10 (2016), 791–801.
16. Yufeng Ke, Hongzhi Qi, Feng He, Shuang Liu, Xin Zhao, Peng Zhou, Lixin Zhang, and Dong Ming. 2014. An EEG-based mental workload estimator trained on working memory task can work well under simulated multi-attribute task. *Frontiers in human neuroscience* 8 (2014).
17. Stephan Lewandowsky, Klaus Oberauer, Lee-Xieng Yang, and Ullrich KH Ecker. 2010. A working memory test battery for MATLAB. *Behavior Research Methods* 42, 2 (2010), 571–585.
18. Christian Mühl, Camille Jeunet, and Fabien Lotte. 2014. EEG-based workload estimation across affective contexts. *Frontiers in neuroscience* 8 (2014).
19. Robert Pröpper, Felix Putze, and Tanja Schultz. 2011. JAM: Java-based Associative Memory. In *Proceedings of the Paralinguistic Information and its Integration in Spoken Dialogue Systems Workshop*. Springer, 143–155.
20. Felix Putze, Sonja Ehret, Heike Miller-Teynor, Andreas Kruse, and Tanja Schultz. 2015. Model-based Evaluation of Playing Strategies in a Memo Game for Elderly Users. In *Proceedings of IEEE International Conference on Systems, Man and Cybernetics*. Hongkong, China.
21. Felix Putze and Tanja Schultz. 2014. Adaptive cognitive technical systems. *Journal of neuroscience methods* 234 (2014), 108–115.
22. David Rozado, Andreas Duenser, and Ben Howell. 2015. Improving the performance of an EEG-based motor imagery brain computer interface using task evoked changes in pupil diameter. *PloS one* 10, 3 (2015), e0121262.
23. Tom Schaul and Jürgen Schmidhuber. 2009. Scalable Neural Networks for Board Games. In *Artificial Neural Networks ICANN 2009*. 1005–1014.
24. Nitish Srivastava, Geoffrey Hinton, Alex Krizhevsky, Ilya Sutskever, and Ruslan Salakhutdinov. 2014. Dropout: A Simple Way to Prevent Neural Networks from Overfitting. *Journal of Machine Learning Research* 15 (2014), 1929–1958.
25. Maria Wolters, Kallirroi Georgila, Johanna D Moore, Robert H Logie, Sarah E MacPherson, and Matthew Watson. 2009. Reducing working memory load in spoken dialogue systems. *Interacting with Computers* 21, 4 (2009), 276–287.

Bringing Transparency Design into Practice

Malin Eiband[1], Hanna Schneider[1], Mark Bilandzic[3], Julian Fazekas-Con[2], Mareike Haug[2], Heinrich Hussmann[1]

[1] {malin.eiband, hanna.schneider, hussmann}@ifi.lmu.de
[2] {julian.fazekas-con, mareike.haug}@campus.lmu.de
[3]mark@freeletics.com

[1,2]LMU Munich, [3]Freeletics GmbH, Munich, Germany

ABSTRACT

Intelligent systems, which are on their way to becoming mainstream in everyday products, make recommendations and decisions for users based on complex computations. Researchers and policy makers increasingly raise concerns regarding the lack of transparency and comprehensibility of these computations from the user perspective. Our aim is to advance existing UI guidelines for more transparency in complex real-world design scenarios involving multiple stakeholders. To this end, we contribute a stage-based participatory process for designing transparent interfaces incorporating perspectives of users, designers, and providers, which we developed and validated with a commercial intelligent fitness coach. With our work, we hope to provide guidance to practitioners and to pave the way for a pragmatic approach to transparency in intelligent systems.

Author Keywords

Transparency; explanation interfaces; participatory design; mental models; intelligibility; scrutability; intelligent systems.

INTRODUCTION

Intelligent systems are becoming increasingly pervasive in everyday life: Voice-commanded virtual assistants, product recommenders, spam filtering applications, smart-home devices, and personalized news feeds are already state of the art and support users in various tasks. Intelligent systems track and process user and usage data, from which they learn and derive their decisions and predictions. How these decisions and predictions have come into place is often hidden from users, which has been shown to negatively impact user acceptance of system reasoning [7], and satisfaction with recommendations and predictions [15, 22, 25]. Moreover, trust in the system and its predictions is diminished in opaque systems [11, 29].

Over the last 30 years, researchers therefore have repeatedly called for more *transparency* in intelligent systems, and have presented design guidelines and exemplary prototypes for such explanations (e.g., [21, 27]). Yet, to date, these learnings have barely been taken up by industry and practitioners. A notable exception is the widely adopted use of labels in recommender systems [37]. Beyond that, the inner workings of most commercial intelligent systems, such as Facebook's news feed, the Google search, or the fitness app presented in this paper, remain opaque.

There are several possible reasons for the industry's lack of enthusiasm to make their applications transparent:

(1) Proposed guidelines are not easy to integrate into complex real-world scenarios since they partly remain on a very abstract level (as we will see later in this paper);
(2) they come with requirements conflicting with real-world conditions, such as the need for extensive screen estate to integrate explanations [21];
(3) work on how to integrate transparency into *existing* UIs is, to the best of our knowledge, still missing; and
(4) companies might use algorithms that, by nature, may only be made transparent to a certain extent, such as neural networks and deep learning.

Hence, industry might not have seen clear additional benefit that would justify the investment necessary to develop transparent interfaces. However, this situation will soon be changing tremendously: European Union's General Data Protection Regulation will become enforceable on 25 May 2018. It includes a "right to explanation" of algorithmic decisions [33] as well as a right to opt-out of such decision making altogether [34]. Furthermore, the need for transparency in intelligent systems has recently been expressed in the *Joint Statement on Algorithmic Transparency and Accountability* by the ACM U.S. Public Policy Council and the ACM Europe Policy Committee [5]. Hence, big and small companies will be faced with increasing pressure to make their systems transparent.

The aim of this paper is to provide structured support in this task, in which the complexity and challenges of real-world applications and the needs of different stakeholders have to be met: Users might want to understand the system's reasoning, but do not want to be overwhelmed by information. Companies might want to meet the regulations on transparency without unveiling the details of the underlying algorithm, and thus their intellectual property. Designers might be faced with constraints that come with corporate design guidelines, limited screen estate, or system-specific user flows, and might need to solve conflicting needs between users and companies.

IUI'18, March 7–11, 2018, Tokyo, Japan

ISBN 978-1-4503-4945-1/18/03...15.00

DOI: https://doi.org/10.1145/3172944.3172961

Hence, guidance in the form of *processes* which can be adapted to the setting at hand instead of abstract design guidelines might be a better support for designers. As the industry partner for this research confirms, there is a serious need for a structured process to develop intelligent interfaces to meet the new regulations. However, such processes have not yet been defined in prior work.

In this paper, we contribute a stage-based participatory process for integrating transparency into real-world applications, which focuses on the improvement of users' *mental models* when working with the system.The process has been developed and validated with the Freeletics Bodyweight Coach [12], a commercial intelligent fitness app that computes personalized workouts for its users. We developed it in an iterative and user-centered style in co-operation with the main stakeholders with the aim of practically applying the outcome of the process to the app. We suggest exemplary participatory methods along with each stage to facilitate the application of the process.

The process is divided into two parts. The first part defines the *content* of an explanation (*what to explain*), the second focuses on the *presentation format* of the explanation (*how to explain*). The following stages emerged during the six months we spent working on integrating transparency into the system:

(A) What to Explain: Expert Mental Model
The *key components* of the algorithm are summarized in a hypothetical, "optimal" version of a *user mental model*.

(B) What to Explain: User Mental Model
The users' current mental model is elicited, and any differences and matches with the *expert mental model* are recorded.

(C) What to Explain: Synthesis – Target Mental Model
Based on the *differences* between the *expert mental model* and the *user mental model*, users select the *key components* from the *expert mental model* that are most relevant to them in their preferred level of detail. These *key components* are added to the *target mental model* and determine the focus of the prototype design.

(D) How to Explain: Iterative Prototyping
Based on corporate design guidelines and the user flow of the system, possible visualizations of the *key components* in the *target mental model* are explored.

(E) How to Explain: Design Evaluation
Differences and matches between the *user mental model* and the *target mental model* are investigated in order to evaluate the prototype design.

With our work, we aim at making transparency design more applicable in real-world scenarios, and argue that a pragmatic view on transparency in intelligent systems and case-by-case learning are feasible and promising approaches towards the emergence of best practices.

BACKGROUND

In the following sections, we first introduce the specific problems at hand with the Freeletics Bodyweight Coach before presenting existing findings and approaches of related work with regard to transparency that might help tackle these problems by introducing transparency. As we will demonstrate, previous learnings are difficult to apply to the specific requirements brought by the Freeletics Bodyweight Coach, and thus partially lack practical guidance for the case at hand.

Introducing the Freeletics Bodyweight Coach

The Freeletics Bodyweight Coach is a personal fitness application that offers users personalized body exercising via their mobile phone. Users get new training plans on a weekly basis, consisting of different types of workouts. The training plans are the result of an AI calculation based on, for example, each individual user's profile (height, weight, BMI), goals (loose weight, gain muscle, etc.), preferences (training days per week) and fitness level.

However, the rationale of the AI is currently[1] hidden from users. This lack of transparency became problematic as some users imagined real human coaches assembling their workout and requested the "human" coaches to better adapt the workouts to their preferences through the customer service hotline. The expectations that come with imagining real coaches assembling workouts are likely not met and may possibly lead to a negative user experience. On the other hand, when the coaching algorithm actually selected shorter workouts for regeneration, some users amended the training regime and performed workouts for two or three days in one session – a potentially dangerous misuse not intended by the application that can lead to overtraining and injury.

In summary, the current UI of the Freeletics Bodyweight Coach does not optimally support the underlying AI concepts. The aim of this project was to integrate transparency in order to help users to better understand the exercising suggestions.

Improving Mental Models through Transparency

In scientific terms, the above mentioned flaws in comprehensibility are called erroneous *mental models* [6] of the fitness coach. Mental models emerged as a concept in psychology and cognitive science, and have since been widely used also in HCI [32]. When we interact with our environment, we build internal conceptualizations of the objects, systems or processes around us that allow us to explain and predict their workings [31]. This applies to less complex systems, for example, light switches, just as much as to more complex systems such as smartphones. Our beliefs and conceptions about how a system behaves and reacts guide our future interaction [32], that is, mental models evolve as users interact with the system. Individuals have different experiences and backgrounds, and thus also develop individual mental models of a system in the course of their interaction. However, most mental models are simplified representations of the actual system workings [32, 45] – which is sufficient if it allows users to comprise the majority of observed system behavior [30]. For example, users do not have to know how electric circuits work in order to successfully use a light switch. However, if mental models are erroneous, or do not adequately reflect the complexity of a system, users may experience difficulty in predicting and explaining the system behavior [31]. Mental models may therefore indicate usability problems.

[1] This work is based on the mid 2017 version of the Freeletics Bodyweight Coach, which is under continuous development.

Making an intelligent system and its underlying design decisions *transparent*, i.e., explaining how the system works, has been shown to improve users' mental models of that system [22, 23]. In opaque systems, in contrast, users are more likely to build flawed mental models [32]. Improved mental models contribute positively to user satisfaction and perceived control [22] as well as to overall trust in the system [29] and its decisions and recommendations [7, 40].

However, improving mental models comes with several challenges: Mental models are characterized, among others, by their persistence (they tend to be robust to change even if they conflict with actual system behavior) [30], incompleteness (they represent only part of the system functions in an abstracted way), and instability (users forget details about the system over time) [32].

Increasing Transparency with Explanation Interfaces

To increase system transparency and to allow users to build better mental models, a commonly used approach are so-called *explanation interfaces*. Explanation interfaces originated as decision-aids in expert systems [13], and have successfully supported users in building useful mental models in, among others, context-aware systems [28], recommenders [15, 35], and interactive machine learning [21, 22].

The usefulness of explanation interfaces depends highly on their design [15, 22]. Two main design decisions have to be made [15]: (1) "What exactly do we explain?" (content of an explanation), which we will refer to as *what to explain*, and (2) "In what manner?" (presentations format of an explanation), which we will refer to as *how to explain*. In our case study – and we suspect this to hold true for many other products – both questions are not easily answered. For example, the UI could indicate that age and gender, past workout times and a model of a training cycle (including high intensity and recovery workouts) are used to narrow down the set of workouts. Alternatively, it could indicate the machine learning algorithms and data sets that are used. Integrating all information in a high degree of detail would require a tremendous amount of screen space and likely overwhelm or annoy users who prefer a simple UI to get their main aim – performing a workout – done. To determine (1) *what to explain* and (2) *how to explain*, we therefore reviewed prior work for guidelines applicable to our case:

What to Explain?

A basic question when designing for transparency is whether to aim for complete transparency, or whether to select information that is most important or useful for users to understand. On the one hand, several scholars have argued for completeness [21, 24]. Kulesza et al. [21] found that completeness was positively correlated with improved mental models, and did not impair user experience or task load. They define more complete explanations as including more of Lim and Dey's [25] intelligibility types. These intelligibility types include possible questions that users might have about the system model (Why did the system behave in a certain way? Why did it not behave in an expected way? How does the system work? What would happen if a specific interaction took place? What else can the system do?), as well as the system certainty about a calculated decision, and inputs and outputs. Similarly, Kulesza et al. [21, 24] argue that explanations should be "as sound as practically possible", meaning that they should not give the impression of a simpler system logic than actually used. This claim is supported by Tullio et al.'s [45] observation that users are able to form a lay, but surprisingly accurate mental model of machine learning concepts. At the same time, Kulesza et al. [21] acknowledge that explanations should remain comprehensible and that soundness and completeness have to be balanced against a possibly overwhelming amount of information.

The latter point has been stressed by researchers who recommend not to aim for completeness, but to select relevant and important information. Herlocker et al. [15] found that explanations that are too complex might lead to decreased acceptance of a system. Lim and Dey [25] have argued that implementing all intelligibility types is "excessive and may even be detrimental". This view is shared by Schaffer et al. [40] who found that full explanation of a recommender's reasoning had a negative impact on user confidence and enjoyment, which is in line with early work on explanations [13]. Instead, they suggest to "carefully explain the search strategy of a recommender to users when this is appropriate". Dourish et al. [9] argue on the same lines that systems unveiling their underlying logic should do so by disclosing features deemed relevant and hiding unnecessary details. Bellotti and Edwards [1] call for appropriate abstraction from the system model when informing users about the underlying calculations. The necessity for abstraction has also been highlighted by Tullio et al. [45] who distinguish between low-level (e.g., information about system input) and high-level explanations (e.g., information about how system input is related). According to them, high-level explanations allow users to modify their prior beliefs about a system more easily, and are suitable to address the challenge of persistent mental models.

Conclusion: To this date, there is no agreement in prior work whether to include all details of system logic in explanation interfaces. Moreover, there might not be a universal answer to this question, but it might rather depend on the product domain, user groups, and the context of use. For example, Pu and Chen [35] found that the preferred level of detail of explanations in recommenders was dependent on the perceived risk associated with the product domain: Users were satisfied with a short explanation for recommended books or movies, but preferred a more detailed explanation for products like cars and houses. Similarly, Schaffer et al. [40] as well as Gregor and Benbasat [13] highlight the importance of considering the user group or individual differences between users when thinking about *what to explain*: Explanations turned out to be more useful when tailored to the interest of a specific user group, and may even reduce user satisfaction if not [7].

Reviewing guidelines and recommendations on *what to explain* did thus not reveal an agreed-upon answer, but rather highlighted the need to determine the necessary amount of information on a case-by-case basis. As this challenge will be faced by many designers of IUIs, there is a need for methods and processes that help designers to answer these questions for their specific case.

(2) How to explain?
Once it has been decided what to explain, designers need to integrate explanations into the existing UI and user flow. To the best of our knowledge, concrete guidelines for the presentation format of explanations are still sparse: Prior work differentiates roughly between text-based and multimedia [13] and suggests that "general rules for interface design are at present the best guide available for choice of presentation method". Pu and Chen [35] claim that text-based explanations should make use of conversational language. Lim and Dey recommend to "augment" explanations with visualizations [25]. Herlocker et al. [15] explored a variety of explanation types and presentation formats; their results suggest that simpler graphs are more appealing to users. Kouki et al. [20] investigated user preferences for visualizations of explanations in recommenders, and found that Venn diagrams performed best in comparison to other visual interfaces, but were restricted by the number of information items presented. However, their findings also suggest that plain text explanations may perform similarly well. Lim and Dey [26] presented a toolkit for automatically creating standardized explanations in context-aware systems. However, when the authors applied the toolkit in a later study, they concluded that it was difficult to translate the automatically generated explanations into textual descriptions [27].

Several scholars agree that providing explanations should be done in a way that reduces users' cognitive effort [13, 21]. From their literature review, Gregor and Benbasat [13] conclude that low cognitive effort is expected, for example, for case-specific rather than generic explanations. Kulesza et al. [21, 22] claim that in situ explanations during interaction are necessary to support the formation of useful mental models. They further assume that helping users might be most effective if explanations can be evoked on-demand and come in "concise, easily consumable 'bites' of information", supporting a continuous, iterative learning process.

Conclusion: Recommendations on *how to explain* currently remain on a rather abstract level and largely rely on designers to interpret and apply them to a specific case. To date, there is no consensus as to when to use text-based explanations or visualizations, and in which form. Again, the answer is likely dependent on the specific requirements of a particular scenario.

Open Questions
Designing explanations in intelligent systems is a challenging task, and there is already considerable and very valuable work which may be taken into account when designing for increased transparency and improved mental models. Yet, we experienced difficulties when we tried to apply prior learnings to the concrete case at hand since many open questions remain:

(1) As shown in the last sections, opinions and guidelines about the design of explanations and *what to explain* differ or even disagree in crucial aspects, such as the level of detail and abstraction of an explanation. Also, advice is often given in a very general way, leaving much room for interpretation with regard to a concrete case.
(2) There is little guidance yet with respect to the *presentation form* of explanations. There are currently no best practices for visualizations or text-based explanations. Moreover, prior work does not take into account real-world needs influencing *how to explain*, such as company-specific style guidelines or corporate identities.
(3) Although research has presented various prototypes for explanation interfaces (e.g., [21, 23, 27, 35]), there is no work on how to integrate transparency into *existing* applications yet. For example, one important question as part of *how to explain* would be *where exactly* to display explanations on the interface. Also, many prototypes and guidelines do not take into account interface restrictions found in real-world situations, such as limited screen estate (except for [35]).
(4) In addition, designing for transparency comes with the challenge of meeting the different needs of the stakeholders involved in a real-world scenario. In our case, the project took place in a corporate environment, where design decisions in the product need to be aligned with several stakeholders in the company: management, marketing and branding, as well as the product design and engineering teams that consist of experts from sport science, psychology, computer science, machine learning, and UX/UI design.

We therefore argue that designing for transparency in complex real-world scenarios calls for individual solutions based on participatory design. Hence, the aim of this paper is not to formulate another set of guidelines adapted to a complex design scenario, but rather to suggest a *design process*, along with exemplary participatory methods. Designers can use this process as a guide in different scenarios that all come with different challenges to build appropriate explanations tailored to the target user group, while keeping the interface usable and in line with the existing interface elements and style guidelines. This is in agreement with calls for context-specific design solutions for explanations [13, 15, 35, 40] using a participatory approach [15, 25].

A STAGE-BASED PARTICIPATORY PROCESS FOR TRANSPARENCY DESIGN
In the following sections, we will present a stage-based participatory design process for integrating transparency into intelligent systems (see figure 1). The stages of this process are the result of six months work on a weekly basis in an eight-person team consisting of four external researchers from the university and company employees (two UX designers, one product manager, and one sports scientist). They are each guided by several central underlying questions that should be answered in the course of the stage. In line with prior work (e.g., [23]), mental models are a core aspect of our process.

The first three stages aim at clarifying the content of an explanation, that is, *what to explain*, the last two focus on the presentation, that is, *how to explain*. To answer the guiding questions in each stage, we suggest exemplary participatory methods that are established practice in participatory design, or are adopted from prior work on mental models. These suggestions are based on literature review and on the experiences made during our project, and are meant to facilitate the application of our process, but should not be taken as the only methods possible – other methods from the plethora of participatory design research methods [38, 46] might be equally appropriate.

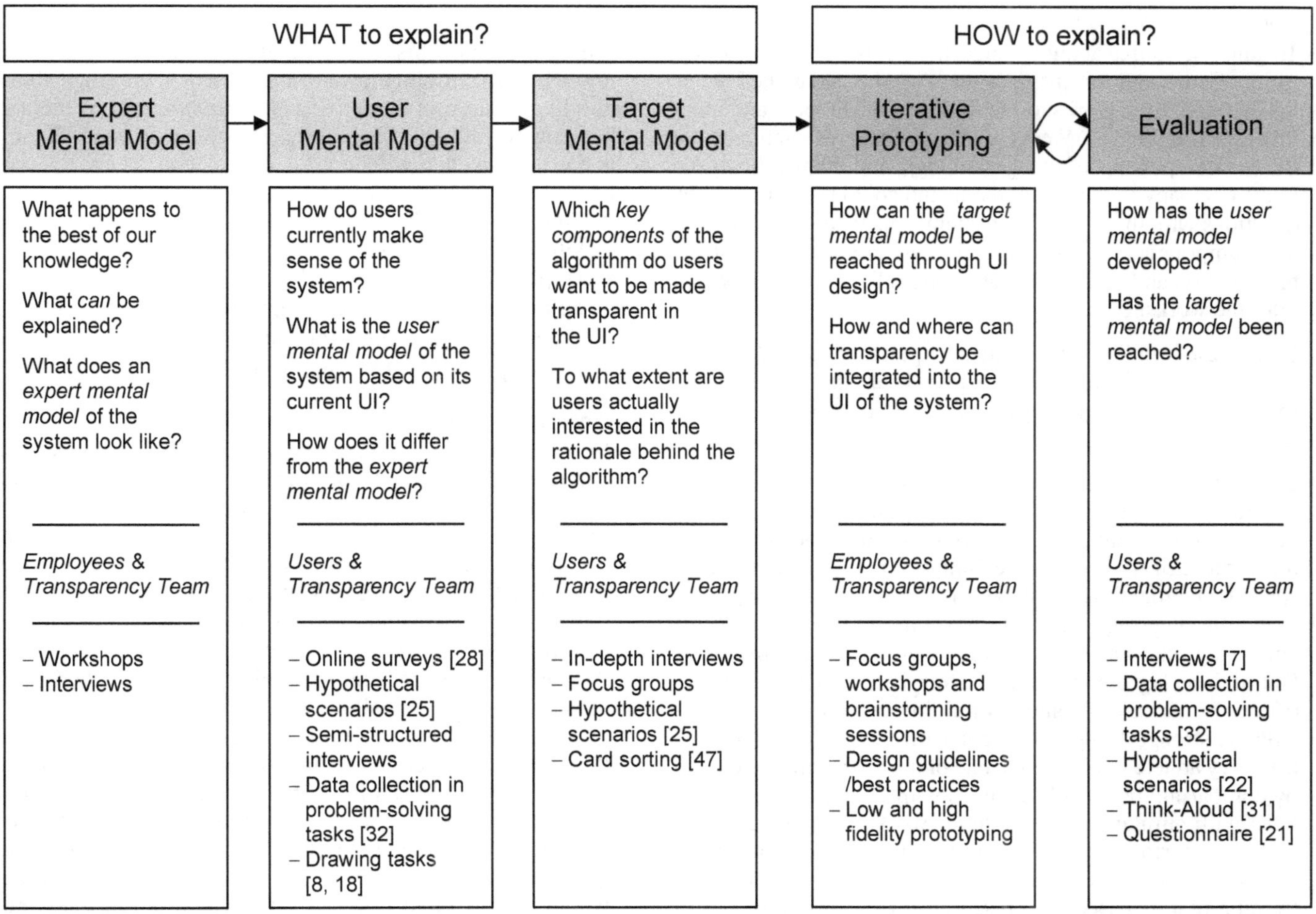

Figure 1. Our stage-based participatory design process for the integration of transparency in intelligent systems. The first three stages focus on *what to explain* in the system (content of an explanation) the last two on *how to explain* (presentation format). The stages are each guided by central underlying questions and involve different stakeholders. We also suggest exemplary methods for each stage that are either established in participatory design or have been used in prior work on eliciting and improving mental models.

Each stage may involve several stakeholders: members of the team responsible for the integration of transparency, other members of the company, and different user groups. We will distinguish between these stakeholders as *transparency team*, *employees* and *users* in the remainder of this section.

We will furthermore refer to central aspects of the algorithm, be it input items, output items, the relation between those items, or calculation steps, as *key components* of the algorithm.

Complementary material as to the application of the process in the Freeletics project can be found under the following link: medien.ifi.lmu.de/team/malin.eiband/transparencydesign.

What to Explain: (A) Expert Mental Model

The first stage serves two purposes: (1) The *transparency team* acquires knowledge about the system logic through communication and exchange with *employees*. (2) From this knowledge, the *transparency team* extracts the *key components* used in the calculation of the algorithm to build what we call an *expert mental model*, a hypothetical version of a user mental model that includes all *key components*. This is likely to require a certain level of abstraction from the system logic, and may take into account intellectual property protection.

Guiding Questions

What happens to the best of our knowledge? What *can* be explained? What does an *expert mental model* of the system look like?

Why is this Important?

The *expert mental model* serves as a reference for eliciting users' mental models in the next stages.

Outcome

The outcome of this stage should be twofold: (1) A *shared understanding* of the data collection and processing methods in place among all members of the *transparency team*, as well as a common language when talking about the algorithms. (2) An *expert mental model* that specifies all *key components* used by the algorithm, as far as possible.

Exemplary Methods

– Workshops with *employees* (approach taken)
– Interviews with *employees*

Application to our Case

To gain knowledge about the algorithm of the Freeletics Bodyweight Coach, our transparency team was invited to the Freeletics facilities for a workshop with the AI developers and other Freeletics employees. We were first given a presentation about the key components of the system logic and the wording used in the company to talk about them, and could then discuss any questions with the present staff members. We wrote down the key components, but we were also given a summary of the presentation and complementary material about the algorithm after the workshop.

From these insights, we created an expert mental model which we discussed in the transparency team in another meeting. The resulting version of the expert mental model was then sent to the developers for corrections.

The final expert mental model specifies five types of data that the AI uses to personalize users' training plans, namely athlete profiles (e.g., gender, BMI), user feedback (e.g., self-assessment of the workout technique), fitness level (e.g., results of an initial fitness test, performance class), training cycle (e.g., muscle group, day and week within the training cycle), and situational variables (physical limitations, equipment). Out of these key components, the transparency team identified (a) performance class and (b) training cycle as components with the strongest impact on personalization of training plans: (a) Every athlete is assigned to one of nine performance classes by comparing their workout times with workout times of athletes with similar profiles. Better workout times lead to a higher performance class and in turn to more difficult workouts in the workout selection process. (b) Every athlete's training plan is based on a research-informed twelve weeks training cycle. The training cycle is designed to improve the overall training results by alternating the training intensity and volume and incorporating breaks for regeneration. Based on insights in sports science, it is assumed that training success depends on the athlete following workouts and breaks as suggested.

What to Explain: (B) User Mental Model

The second stage focuses on user research and consists of two steps: (1) The *transparency team* elicits the mental models of *users*, based on the current UI of the system, and condenses them into one overarching *user mental model* representing the mental model of the target user group. (2) The *transparency team* then compares the *user mental model* to the *expert mental model*, and identifies any differences and matches with regard to the *key components* (missing, erroneous and correct *key components*).

Guiding Questions

How do users currently make sense of the system? What is the *user mental model* of the system based on its current UI? How does it differ from the *expert mental model*?

Why is this Important?

Users' current beliefs about the system logic are used to indicate the status quo of the current system transparency. This might depend on the target group and vary within different user groups of a system [13, 40].

Outcome

The outcome of this stage is again twofold: (1) The mental model *users* currently have of the system's workings, that is, the items that users identify as *key components* of the algorithm. (2) A list of differences and matches in comparison to the *expert mental model*.

Exemplary Methods

- Online surveys [28]
- Hypothetical scenarios [25]
- Semi-structured interviews (approach taken)
- Data collection in problem-solving tasks [32]
- Drawing tasks [8, 18] (approach taken)

Application to our Case

We conducted semi-structured interviews to investigate users' current mental models of the Freeletics app. Questions focused on (1) users' awareness of different key components of the AI, and (2) their idea of how these key components are used to generate their personal workout. The interview also included a drawing task, which has been used by other scholars to elicit mental models about privacy [18] and the web [8]. We also collected general feedback on app usage. All interviews were audio-recorded. These methods were selected because they allowed us to investigate users' mental models as they emerge through long-term product use while the algorithm processes their *own* data as input (in contrast to hypothetical scenarios [25]) and to generate in-depth qualitative data (in contrast to online surveys [28]). The interview was conducted with 14 active Freeletics users, ten men and four women between 20 and 42 (M=30.3 years), whom we recruited in a city park which is known to be a popular workout spot.

We used Thematic Analysis [3] to analyze the collected data. After transcribing the audio files of the interviews, we reviewed the data, searched for patterns, and then clustered answers and statements. From our data, we extracted the key components of users' current mental model of the Freeletics Bodyweight Coach. We found that the mental model already correctly included a part of the algorithmic key components, namely those that were explicitly shown in the current UI. For example, most participants suspected that their age and gender as well as past workout times might influence the training plan somehow. However, they had no understanding of the connections and relations between these components. For example, all participants were unaware that workout times of the last six months were used to calculate the performance class, which was then in turn used to calculate their training plan. Understanding this mechanism might show users that they need to improve their workout times consistently over a longer time to receive more challenging workouts in the future and that an unusually slow workout would not immediately impact their training plan. Hence, it might have an impact on users' expectations, patience, persistence, and ultimately, the user experience. Moreover, participants were unaware that their training plans follow a twelve weeks training cycle. Low intensity workouts (intended to incorporate recovery times) led some users to question the quality of the training plan and thus to train more than suggested. Revealing underlying principles from sports science in the UI might therefore convince users to adhere to the suggested program and to incorporate appropriate recovery times.

What to Explain: (C) Synthesis – Target Mental Model

In this stage, (1) users' explicit opinion of and interest in the *key components* of the AI is investigated and (2) the *transparency team* finalizes *what to explain* in the system logic: First, the *transparency team* uses the missing or erroneous *key components* (in comparison to the *expert mental model*) in the *user mental model* as a basis to investigate whether and in what degree of detail users are actually interested in knowing and understanding these components. When investigating users' explicit opinions, the *transparency team* can either use a within-group design (involving the same *users* as in stage B), or a between-groups design (involving different but comparable *users* than in stage B). The *key components* identified as important and valuable by *users* or the *transparency team* are then combined with the already correct *key components* in the *user mental model* to form the *target mental model*. This means that users either explicitly expressed their interest in this information or the *transparency team* has reason to believe that incorporating the information would improve the user experience.

The *target mental model* specifies which *key components* of the AI to focus on in the prototype design.

Guiding Questions

Which *key components* of the algorithm do users want to be made transparent in the UI? To what extent are users actually interested in the rationale behind the algorithm?

Why is this Important?

Since screen estate is limited, the *transparency team* is faced with the trade-off between displaying more information (higher transparency) and visual clutter or cognitive load for *users*. Moreover, it is likely that not all information about the system logic is perceived as relevant or helpful by *users*. While stage A and B provide useful insights into what can be made transparent, we argue that it is also important to elicit and acknowledge users' explicit opinion and interest in *key components* before jumping into the redesign of the UI design.

Outcome

The outcome of this stage is a *target mental model*. The *key components* from the *target mental model* that are still missing or erroneous in the current *user mental model* will be implemented in the prototype.

Exemplary Methods

- In-depth interviews
- Focus groups
- Hypothetical scenarios [25]
- Card sorting [47] (approach taken)

Application to our Case

We decided to let participants do card sorting [47] to find the key components most relevant to them. In the transparency team, we prepared 19 cards with text statements about key components in the target mental model in two levels of detail and conversational language, thus following Tullio et al.'s [45] and Pu and Chen's [35] recommendation. Cards with low level of detail only mentioned *that* a specific key component has an impact on the selection of workouts. Cards with higher level of detail explained *how* a specific key component influences the selection of workouts. Text-based explanations on cards allowed us to illustrate how each of the key components could be explained while avoiding that specifics of their visualization and implementation in a prototype influence users' reactions.

We recruited eleven participants in total, four women and seven men between 24 and 60 (M=33.5 years). They were a mixture of active long- and short-term Freeletics users, former Freeletics users, and people who had not used Freeletics before. Because we could not recruit the same set of users as in stage B, we incorporated some questions to elicit participants' current mental model (from stage B). Participants were then introduced to explanations on cards and instructed to sort them with respect to what would interest them most and help them to understand why a specific workout was recommended by the app while thinking aloud. They were also allowed to leave cards aside if the information seemed unnecessary or irrelevant. For each participant, we took a photo of the final card sorting and audio-recorded their verbalized thoughts.

For the analysis, cards were categorized as high-rated, medium-rated, and low-rated depending on how often they appeared in the participants' sorting. Additionally, audio-recordings were transcribed and analyzed with Thematic Analysis. In this procedure, four cards were categorized as high-rated: detailed explanations of performance class, detailed explanations of the influence of training focus (strength or cardio), detailed explanations of the influence of workout times, and detailed explanations of the influence of training cycles. Hence, the corresponding key components were added to the already correct key components in the user mental model from stage B to build the target mental model.

How to Explain: (D) Iterative Prototyping

Based on the *key components* from the *target mental model*, the *transparency team* and *employees* are co-designing prototype versions of the new UI. This stage is likely to take several iterations. (1) The *transparency team* and *employees* first identify possible locations for explanations in the current UI and the user flow. (2) The *transparency team* explores visualization possibilities for the explanations. These visualizations take the current UI design, the screen estate, corporate and system design guidelines as well as best practices in UI design into account.

Guiding Questions

How can the *target mental model* be reached through UI design? How and where can transparency be integrated into the UI of the system?

Why is this Important?

Since each system has a different UI design and a different user flow, we argue that is important to find visualizations that integrate explanations according to the look-and-feel of the UI in place and the available screen estate. Moreover, there are currently few guidelines in prior work and no best practices concerning the presentation format of explanations yet (see Background section), so that companies have to explore a way to visualize explanations.

Outcome
The outcome of this stage should be one or – ideally – several prototypes that explore possibilities of integrating explanations into the existing UI.

Exemplary Methods
- Focus groups, workshops and brainstorming sessions in the *transparency team* and with *employees* (approach taken)
- Design guidelines and best practices in UI design (approach taken)
- Low and high fidelity prototyping (approach taken)

Application to our Case
The first step in the iterative prototype design was a "How might we" brainstorming session [10] based on the target mental model in the transparency team and with other employees. In this process, all team members quietly sketched out ideas how and when key components of the target mental model could be visualized in the current UI and user flow and subsequently explained their ideas to the rest of the team. To select the most promising ideas, all team members then voted for five ideas perceived as most promising followed by a short discussion of pros and cons. The workshops allowed the transparency team to generate a list of promising implementation ideas, while leveraging the expertise of employees and adhering to the the design requirements and guidelines of Freeletics.

Next, we implemented two of the most promising ideas in a series of low and high fidelity prototypes. For this purpose, Freeletics had provided us with the necessary documents about the current user flow in the app. Within this user flow, we identified suitable locations for the integration of transparency into the Freeletics Bodyweight Coach UI.

The prototypes were evaluated and subsequently refined in several informal user testings (with only one or two participants), design workshops and expert reviews with the UI design experts within the transparency team and with other employees. As a result, we designed and developed two high-fidelity click prototypes that followed the corporate design guidelines of Freeletics and best practices in UI design. These click prototypes simulated the normal user flow as far as necessary in order to integrate the new transparency design concepts. Explanations were embedded in the user flow following an on-demand approach recommended by prior work [21, 22]: Users were first presented with an explanation of low detail and could get more detailed information in another screen if they wanted to know more.

How to Explain: (E) Design Evaluation
This stage completes the design process and aims at evaluating the effectiveness of the prototype(s) developed in stage D. Effectiveness is measured in terms of the differences between the *user mental model* and the *target mental model*. An effective prototype will reduce the differences between the *user mental model* and the *target mental model*.

(1) The *transparency team* elicits the *user mental model* based on the new UI. Again, the *transparency team* needs to decide whether to recruit the same or different users as in stage B (within-group or between-groups experimental design) according to resources and constraints. However, in this stage, the user group should not be the same as in stage C, where the *target mental model* was elicited, as these participants have been exposed to explanations before. For the same reason, if multiple prototypes have been developed (as in our project), it is sensible to recruit different user groups for each prototype to investigate the effect of the different design solutions on users' mental models (in contrast to the general recommendation to show users more than one prototype to elicit their opinion [44]). (2) The *key components* of the new *user mental model* are compared to those of the *target mental model*. The *transparency team* may decide to go back to stage D if the prototype is not effective enough, that is, if *user mental model* and *target mental model* do not match.

Guiding Questions
How has the *user mental model* developed? Has the *target mental model* been reached?

Why is this Important?
The final stage tests whether the prototype design has reached the intended goal of improving users' mental models.

Outcome
The outcome of this stage are the learnings from the evaluation of the prototype(s) that describe which design changes improved users' mental models and should therefore be integrated into the working system.

Exemplary Methods
- Interviews [7] (approach taken)
- Data collection in problem-solving tasks [32] (approach taken)
- Hypothetical scenarios [22]
- Think-Aloud [31] (approach taken)
- Questionnaire [21]

Application to our Case
Our prototypes were evaluated with seven and nine active Freeletics users, respectively, six women and nine men between 19 and 47 (M=30.7 years). Participants were randomly assigned to one of the two prototypes and guided through the prototype by the user flow that they knew from using the app. We encouraged them to explore the prototypes and think-aloud (1) what they saw on each screen, (2) what they thought could be done, and (3) where they would tap next.

Participants were then asked a set of comprehension questions about the key components explained in the prototype in a semi-structured interview, for example, "May some of your workouts be longer or more intense compared to other Freeletics users of the same sex and age? If so, why?", or "What influence do better or worse workout times have?". We also wanted to know whether participants perceived the explanations as useful and interesting, and whether they liked the level of detail or had rather wanted more or less information. We audio-recorded all answers and used screen-recording to capture their behavior while interacting with the prototypes. In the last part of the study, participants filled out the System Usability Scale [4] for the prototype they had tested.

Answers to the semi-structured interview questions were transcribed and then compared to model answers we had prepared beforehand. We rated given answers as "correct", "rather correct", "rather wrong", and "wrong". We found that overall, participants' answers indicated "correct" or "rather correct" understanding of the training cycles (15 participants), workout times (all participants) and performance classes (14 participants). For example, they could explain the purpose of training cycles and knew where they could get information about how intense and long workouts in the next week will be in the prototype. Moreover, 14 participants perceived the explanations as interesting and informative and only two participants stated that they were rather not interested in the reasoning of the system. The prototypes reached an overall score of 89.6 and 82.0, respectively, on the System Usability Scale, which corresponds to "excellent" usability [4].

While this indicates the effectiveness of our prototypes in terms of the *target mental model*, we found room for improvement regarding the location of the explanations. For example, screen-recordings showed that buttons and links that would have led to more detailed on-demand explanations were completely overlooked by several participants.

In summary, the evaluation in this stage allowed us to demonstrate the effectiveness of the developed prototypes to all stakeholders while also highlighting directions for future work and opportunities for improvement.

LIMITATIONS

The presented process evolved over six months and has proven successful in the Freeletics design scenario. Yet, we acknowledge that it is certainly not the only, but a promising way to address the complexity of designing for transparency in real-world design settings. We will further elaborate on this point in the discussion section of this paper. Moreover, the presented methods are based on those used in the reviewed literature and should facilitate application of our process. They served well in answering the guiding questions in each process stage in our project – however, other participatory methods may be equally suitable.

Moreover, our process inherits the limitations that come with investigating mental models in general. Researchers' opinions are divided when it comes to the elicitation of mental models: While Norman [32], for example, claims that asking users about their mental model is less reliable than collecting data in problem-solving tasks, Nielsen [31] states that methods like card sorting or think-aloud are valid approaches to elicit users' mental models.

DISCUSSION AND FUTURE WORK

We have presented a stage-based design process to facilitate the integration of transparency in complex real-world design scenarios, which was developed and tested in an exemplary case with the Freeletics Bodyweight Coach. In the following sections, we reflect on our process and different views on the design of transparent systems.

Validity and Universality of our Process

Our process successfully addressed the challenges of the Freeletics project, met the different needs of the stakeholders involved, and improved users' mental model of the Freeletics Bodyweight Coach. These points strongly indicate the validity of the process in the given scenario. Moreover, mental models as a system-indepentent concept have been used in prior work as a way to approach the design of transparent intelligent systems in different contexts [22, 23, 24]. We therefore assume that our process is valid beyond the scope of our case and universal in the sense that it is applicable to other, similarly complex scenarios involving other types of systems, yet concrete enough to serve practitioners as a starting point for their work. However, this needs further evaluation in comparable real-world settings, and we acknowledge that variants of the process may exist that are better suited for specific scenarios. We therefore invite other researchers to validate and build on our process in the future.

Possible Improvements

We acknowledge that even though our process aims at facilitating the integration of transparency, it still requires more effort in terms of cost and time than automatically generating explanations, which not all companies might be willing to invest. However, evaluation of the prototypes showed that users were able to improve their mental models based on the explanations resulting from our process. This strongly suggests that explanations tailored to the users' interests may add to the value of an application by supporting appropriate usage while taking the companies' needs into account. A point worth investigating in this context would therefore be whether the stages of our process could be fully or partially automated in the future to reduce the effort necessary to generate suitable explanations.

While prior work argues that both communications from the systems to the user and from the user to the system are important, for example for correcting system mistakes [7], the focus in our case, the Freeletics project, was on transparency of the system only. Although considering user-to-system communication was out of scope of the presented project, it is an important aspect for shaping interaction with intelligent systems in the future. We assume that our process might be equally helpful for designing for this direction of the communication between system and user, since the setting does not change and the resulting difficulties as well as the importance of mental models therefore might be comparable. However, this assumption needs to be validated in future work.

Another concept closely linked to transparency is trust in an intelligent system [41], which is of crucial importance for safety-related systems, for example, airplanes [29], but does also influence user satisfaction with systems such as recommenders [43]. Trust was not assessed during our project, but future work might investigate how our process and improved mental models affect trust, using frameworks such as [17].

Transparency Normativism vs Pragmatism

Transparency in HCI is a fuzzy and multi-facetted concept which spans a variety of research areas. Explaining how a system works might enable users to correct system decisions through feedback (as in [21, 23]), might improve understanding of the system recommendations and thus foster efficient or effective use [35, 36], prevent mis- and disuse of a system through increased trust [39] or protect users' privacy [19] , to mention a few exemplary purposes. When following the call for transparency in intelligent systems, one therefore has to wonder what the standard for transparency should look like – what is a "genuinely" transparent system? Some underlying algorithms such as decision trees and Naive Bayes might fairly well be made transparent, while others, such as neural networks, are black-boxes by nature, and inherently not interpretable even by their developers. Hildebrandt [16] argues that "decisions that seriously affect individuals' capabilities must be constructed in ways that are comprehensible as well as contestable. If that is not possible, [...] such decisions are unlawful". As a consequence, she claims that intelligent algorithms that cannot explain themselves to users must not be deployed. However, this view would imply that undoubtedly useful machine learning algorithms, in particular deep learning algorithms, such as used in computer vision and self-driving cars, were not to be applied in practice as researchers are still working on ways to make their decisions explainable [2]. A normative view on transparency might also imply that any kind of abstraction from the algorithms' reasoning is not consistent with the principle of transparency. This might nudge companies to present users with extensive legal declarations, similar to End User License Agreements [14], and thus undermine the "right to explanation" emerging through EU's GDPR [33] with information that requires a lot of effort to process.

In this discussion, we follow a pragmatic view on transparency that sees transparency as a trade-off between practical applicability and literal transparency – transparency "as good as possible". We argue that transparency should be designed in a way that benefits users most while taking requirements of other stakeholders into account.

A pragmatic view also acknowledges that users might not be interested in *all* of the systems underlying reasoning [25], and that they find some pieces of information more interesting than others [25] (as it was the case in our project with Freeletics). Based on our learnings in this case study, we hypothesize that users might follow the principle of *satisficing* [42] also in the context of transparency: Transparency satisfices users if it allows them to build mental models good enough to predict and explain the observed system behavior, even though the given explanations might not include all factors relevant for the workings of the algorithm. In this paper, we presented a process that aims at balancing conflicting influencing factors when designing for transparency and, hence, to help designing for satisficing. Once this approach has been applied to a variety of scenarios, future work might be able to extract general patterns or guidelines for transparency satisficing.

Establishing Best Practices for Transparency Design

Our work raises the questions if it is possible to establish best practices for transparency design similar to best practices in the design of UIs or user interaction, and if so, how they can emerge. These questions will become more urgent as companies need to fulfill the legal requirements of the European Union's General Data Protection Regulation. Gregor and Benbasat [13], for example, claim that the design of explanations in intelligent systems should be theory-based instead of bottom-up. From our experience with the Freeletics case however, where we faced considerable difficulty of working top-down from existing guidelines, we argue that this top-down approach needs to be complemented with a bottom-up approach that focuses on extracting learnings on a case-by-case basis. These learnings from practice could then be condensed into higher-level guidelines, or design patterns, which might possibly focus on specific product domains that share similar characteristics and challenges, or similar goals.

CONCLUSION

In this paper, we suggested a stage-based, participatory design process to help designers to integrate transparency into applications in complex real-world scenarios involving multiple stakeholders. This process was developed and validated during a six months project in cooperation with Freeletics, in which we worked on integrating transparency into the Freeletics Bodyweight Coach, an intelligent fitness application whose AI calculates personalized exercising plans for the users. The process makes use of transparency as a means to improve users' mental models. Our approach follows a pragmatic view on transparency, where transparency is implemented based on (1) what can generally be made transparent of the underlying algorithm, and (2) the information that is interesting and relevant to users. We argue that designing UIs for transparency may greatly benefit from case-by-case learning, and hope that our process can pave the way for more transparency in similarly complex design settings.

ACKNOWLEDGMENTS

We are greatly indebted to Natalia Patiño Pérez, Renato Pereira and Peter Just, who were an amazing help during discussion, prototype design and user research. We also thank Laith Alkurdi for the workshop on the AI of the Freeletics Bodyweight Coach, and Robert Schmidt and Tobias Seitz as well as the anonymous reviewers for their helpful comments on earlier versions of this manuscript.

REFERENCES

1. Victoria Bellotti and Keith Edwards. 2001. Intelligibility and Accountability: Human Considerations in Context-Aware Systems. *Human–Computer Interaction* 16, 2-4 (2001), 193–212.

2. Mariusz Bojarski, Philip Yeres, Anna Choromanska, Krzysztof Choromanski, Bernhard Firner, Lawrence D. Jackel, and Urs Muller. 2017. Explaining How a Deep Neural Network Trained with End-to-End Learning Steers a Car. *CoRR* abs/1704.07911 (2017). http://arxiv.org/abs/1704.07911

3. Virginia Braun and Victoria Clarke. 2006. Using Thematic Analysis in Psychology. *Qualitative Research in Psychology* 3, 2 (2006), 77–101. DOI: http://dx.doi.org/10.1191/1478088706qp063oa

4. John Brooke and others. 1996. SUS – A Quick and Dirty Usability Scale. *Usability Evaluation in Industry* 189, 194 (1996), 4–7.

5. ACM U.S. Public Policy Council and ACM Europe Policy Committee. 2017. Statement on Algorithmic Transparency and Accountability. (2017). https://www.acm.org/binaries/content/assets/public-policy/2017_joint_statement_algorithms.pdf

6. Kenneth James Williams Craik. 1967. *The Nature of Explanation*. Vol. 445. CUP Archive.

7. Henriette Cramer, Vanessa Evers, Satyan Ramlal, Maarten van Someren, Lloyd Rutledge, Natalia Stash, Lora Aroyo, and Bob Wielinga. 2008. The Effects of Transparency on Trust in and Acceptance of a Content-Based Art Recommender. *User Modeling and User-Adapted Interaction* 18, 5 (20 Aug 2008), 455. DOI: http://dx.doi.org/10.1007/s11257-008-9051-3

8. Jérôme Dinet and Muneo Kitajima. 2011. "Draw Me the Web": Impact of Mental Model of the Web on Information Search Performance of Young Users. In *Proceedings of the 23rd Conference on L'Interaction Homme-Machine (IHM '11)*. ACM, New York, NY, USA, Article 3, 7 pages. DOI: http://dx.doi.org/10.1145/2044354.2044358

9. Paul Dourish, Annette Adler, and Brian Cantwell Smith. 1996. Organising User Interfaces around Reflective Accounts. *Reflection, San Francisco, CA* (1996).

10. Stanford d.school. 2017. "How Might We" Questions. (2017). Retrieved 07 October 2017 from https://dschool.stanford.edu/resources/how-might-we-questions

11. Mary T. Dzindolet, Scott A. Peterson, Regina A. Pomranky, Linda G. Pierce, and Hall P. Beck. 2003. The Role of Trust in Automation Reliance. *International Journal of Human-Computer Studies* 58, 6 (2003), 697–718.

12. Freeletics. 2017. Freeletics Bodyweight Coach. (2017). Retrieved 20 December 2017 from freeletics.com/en/bodyweight/coach/get

13. Shirley Gregor and Izak Benbasat. 1999. Explanations from Intelligent Systems: Theoretical Foundations and Implications for Practice. *MIS Quarterly* (1999), 497–530.

14. Jens Grossklags and Nathan Good. 2007. Empirical Studies on Software Notices to Inform Policy Makers and Usability Designers. *Financial Cryptography and Data Security* (2007), 341–355.

15. Jonathan L. Herlocker, Joseph A. Konstan, and John Riedl. 2000. Explaining Collaborative Filtering Recommendations. In *Proceedings of the 2000 ACM Conference on Computer Supported Cooperative Work (CSCW '00)*. ACM, New York, NY, USA, 241–250. DOI: http://dx.doi.org/10.1145/358916.358995

16. Mireille Hildebrandt. 2016. *The New Imbroglio. Living with Machine Algorithms*. Amsterdam University Press, 55–60.

17. Kimberly F. Jackson, Zahar Prasov, Emily C. Vincent, and Eric M. Jones. 2016. A Heuristic Based Framework for Improving Design of Unmanned Systems by Quantifying and Assessing Operator Trust. *Proceedings of the Human Factors and Ergonomics Society Annual Meeting* 60, 1 (2016), 1696–1700. DOI: http://dx.doi.org/10.1177/1541931213601390

18. Ruogu Kang, Laura Dabbish, Nathaniel Fruchter, and Sara Kiesler. 2015. "My Data Just Goes Everywhere:" User Mental Models of the Internet and Implications for Privacy and Security. In *Eleventh Symposium On Usable Privacy and Security (SOUPS 2015)*. USENIX Association, Ottawa, 39–52. https://www.usenix.org/conference/soups2015/proceedings/presentation/kang

19. Judy Kay and Bob Kummerfeld. 2013. Creating Personalized Systems That People Can Scrutinize and Control: Drivers, Principles and Experience. *ACM Trans. Interact. Intell. Syst.* 2, 4, Article 24 (Jan. 2013), 42 pages. DOI: http://dx.doi.org/10.1145/2395123.2395129

20. Pigi Kouki, James Schaffer, Jay Pujara, John O'Donovan, and Lise Getoor. 2017. User Preferences for Hybrid Explanations. In *Proceedings of the Eleventh ACM Conference on Recommender Systems (RecSys '17)*. ACM, New York, NY, USA, 84–88. DOI: http://dx.doi.org/10.1145/3109859.3109915

21. Todd Kulesza, Margaret Burnett, Weng-Keen Wong, and Simone Stumpf. 2015. Principles of Explanatory Debugging to Personalize Interactive Machine Learning. In *Proceedings of the 20th International Conference on Intelligent User Interfaces (IUI '15)*. ACM, New York, NY, USA, 126–137. DOI: http://dx.doi.org/10.1145/2678025.2701399

22. Todd Kulesza, Simone Stumpf, Margaret Burnett, and Irwin Kwan. 2012. Tell Me More? The Effects of Mental Model Soundness on Personalizing an Intelligent Agent. In *Proceedings of the SIGCHI Conference on Human Factors in Computing Systems (CHI '12)*. ACM, New York, NY, USA, 1–10. DOI: http://dx.doi.org/10.1145/2207676.2207678

23. Todd Kulesza, Simone Stumpf, Margaret Burnett, Weng-Keen Wong, Yann Riche, Travis Moore, Ian Oberst, Amber Shinsel, and Kevin McIntosh. 2010. Explanatory Debugging: Supporting End-User Debugging of Machine-Learned Programs. In *Proceedings of the 2010 IEEE Symposium on Visual Languages and Human-Centric Computing (VLHCC '10)*. IEEE Computer Society, Washington, DC, USA, 41–48. DOI: http://dx.doi.org/10.1109/VLHCC.2010.15

24. Todd Kulesza, Simone Stumpf, Margaret Burnett, Sherry Yang, Irwin Kwan, and Weng-Keen Wong. 2013. Too Much, Too Little, or Just Right? Ways Explanations Impact End Users' Mental Models. In *2013 IEEE Symposium on Visual Languages and Human Centric Computing*. 3–10. DOI: http://dx.doi.org/10.1109/VLHCC.2013.6645235

25. Brian Y. Lim and Anind K. Dey. 2009. Assessing Demand for Intelligibility in Context-aware Applications. In *Proceedings of the 11th International Conference on Ubiquitous Computing (UbiComp '09)*. ACM, New York, NY, USA, 195–204. DOI: http://dx.doi.org/10.1145/1620545.1620576

26. Brian Y. Lim and Anind K. Dey. 2010. Toolkit to Support Intelligibility in Context-aware Applications. In *Proceedings of the 12th ACM International Conference on Ubiquitous Computing (UbiComp '10)*. ACM, New York, NY, USA, 13–22. DOI: http://dx.doi.org/10.1145/1864349.1864353

27. Brian Y. Lim and Anind K. Dey. 2011. Design of an Intelligible Mobile Context-aware Application. In *Proceedings of the 13th International Conference on Human Computer Interaction with Mobile Devices and Services (MobileHCI '11)*. ACM, New York, NY, USA, 157–166. DOI: http://dx.doi.org/10.1145/2037373.2037399

28. Brian Y. Lim, Anind K. Dey, and Daniel Avrahami. 2009. Why and Why Not Explanations Improve the Intelligibility of Context-aware Intelligent Systems. In *Proceedings of the SIGCHI Conference on Human Factors in Computing Systems (CHI '09)*. ACM, New York, NY, USA, 2119–2128. DOI: http://dx.doi.org/10.1145/1518701.1519023

29. Joseph B. Lyons, Garrett G. Sadler, Kolina Koltai, Henri Battiste, Nhut T. Ho, Lauren C. Hoffmann, David Smith, Walter Johnson, and Robert Shively. 2017. Shaping Trust through Transparent Design: Theoretical and Experimental Guidelines. In *Advances in Human Factors in Robots and Unmanned Systems*. Springer, 127–136.

30. Neville Moray. 1987. Intelligent Aids, Mental Models, and the Theory of Machines. *International Journal of Man-Machine Studies* 27, 5 (1987), 619 – 629. DOI: http://dx.doi.org/https://doi.org/10.1016/S0020-7373(87)80020-2

31. Jakob Nielsen. 2010. Mental Models. (2010). Retrieved 04 October 2017 from www.nngroup.com/articles/mental-models/

32. Donald A. Norman. 1983. Some Observations on Mental Models. *Mental Models* 7, 112 (1983), 7–14.

33. PrivacyPlan. 2017a. Article 13 EU GDPR "Information to be Provided where Personal Data are Collected from the Data Subject". (2017). Retrieved 27 September 2017 from http://www.privacy-regulation.eu/en/13.htm

34. PrivacyPlan. 2017b. Article 22 EU GDPR "Automated Individual Decision Making, Including Profiling". (2017). Retrieved 27 September 2017 from http://www.privacy-regulation.eu/en/22.htm

35. Pearl Pu and Li Chen. 2006. Trust Building with Explanation Interfaces. In *Proceedings of the 11th International Conference on Intelligent User Interfaces (IUI '06)*. ACM, New York, NY, USA, 93–100. DOI: http://dx.doi.org/10.1145/1111449.1111475

36. Pearl Pu and Li Chen. 2007. Trust-Inspiring Explanation Interfaces for Recommender Systems. *Knowledge-Based Systems* 20, 6 (2007), 542 – 556. DOI: http://dx.doi.org/https://doi.org/10.1016/j.knosys.2007.04.004 Special Issue On Intelligent User Interfaces.

37. Pearl Pu, Li Chen, and Rong Hu. 2012. Evaluating Recommender Systems from the User's Perspective: Survey of the State of the Art. *User Modeling and User-Adapted Interaction* 22, 4 (01 Oct 2012), 317–355. DOI: http://dx.doi.org/10.1007/s11257-011-9115-7

38. Virpi Roto, Heli Väätäjä, Satu Jumisko-Pyykkö, and Kaisa Väänänen-Vainio-Mattila. 2011. Best Practices for Capturing Context in User Experience Studies in the Wild. In *Proceedings of the 15th International Academic MindTrek Conference: Envisioning Future Media Environments*. ACM, 91–98.

39. Garrett Sadler, Henri Battiste, Nhut Ho, Lauren Hoffmann, Walter Johnson, Robert Shively, Joseph Lyons, and David Smith. 2016. Effects of Transparency on Pilot Trust and Agreement in the Autonomous Constrained Flight Planner. In *2016 IEEE/AIAA 35th Digital Avionics Systems Conference (DASC)*. 1–9. DOI: http://dx.doi.org/10.1109/DASC.2016.7777998

40. James Schaffer, Prasanna Giridhar, Debra Jones, Tobias Höllerer, Tarek Abdelzaher, and John O'Donovan. 2015. Getting the Message? A Study of Explanation Interfaces for Microblog Data Analysis. In *Proceedings of the 20th International Conference on Intelligent User Interfaces (IUI '15)*. ACM, New York, NY, USA, 345–356. DOI: http://dx.doi.org/10.1145/2678025.2701406

41. Thomas B. Sheridan. 1992. *Telerobotics, Automation, and Human Supervisory Control*. MIT press.

42. Herbert A. Simon. 1955. A Behavioral Model of Rational Choice. *The Quarterly Journal of Economics* 69, 1 (1955), 99–118. DOI: http://dx.doi.org/10.2307/1884852

43. Rashmi Sinha and Kirsten Swearingen. 2002. The Role of Transparency in Recommender Systems. In *CHI '02 Extended Abstracts on Human Factors in Computing Systems (CHI EA '02)*. ACM, New York, NY, USA, 830–831. DOI: http://dx.doi.org/10.1145/506443.506619

44. Maryam Tohidi, William Buxton, Ronald Baecker, and Abigail Sellen. 2006. Getting the Right Design and the Design Right. In *Proceedings of the SIGCHI Conference on Human Factors in Computing Systems (CHI '06)*. ACM, New York, NY, USA, 1243–1252. DOI: http://dx.doi.org/10.1145/1124772.1124960

45. Joe Tullio, Anind K. Dey, Jason Chalecki, and James Fogarty. 2007. How It Works: A Field Study of Non-technical Users Interacting with an Intelligent System. In *Proceedings of the SIGCHI Conference on Human Factors in Computing Systems (CHI '07)*. ACM, New York, NY, USA, 31–40. DOI: http://dx.doi.org/10.1145/1240624.1240630

46. Arnold P. O. S. Vermeeren, Effie L-C. Law, Virpi Roto, Marianna Obrist, Jettie Hoonhout, and Kaisa Väänänen-Vainio-Mattila. 2010. User Experience Evaluation Methods: Current State and Development Needs. In *Proceedings of the 6th Nordic Conference on Human-Computer Interaction: Extending Boundaries*. ACM, 521–530.

47. Jed R. Wood and Larry E. Wood. 2008. Card Sorting: Current Practices and Beyond. *Journal of Usability Studies* 4, 1 (Nov. 2008), 1–6. http://dl.acm.org/citation.cfm?id=2835577.2835578

Toward Foraging for Understanding of StarCraft Agents: An Empirical Study

Sean Penney, Jonathan Dodge, Claudia Hilderbrand,
Andrew Anderson, Logan Simpson, Margaret Burnett
Oregon State University, Corvallis, OR, 97331 USA
{ penneys, dodgej, minic, anderan2, burnett }@eecs.oregonstate.edu

ABSTRACT
Assessing and understanding intelligent agents is a difficult task for users that lack an AI background. A relatively new area, called "Explainable AI," is emerging to help address this problem, but little is known about how users would forage through information an explanation system might offer. To inform the development of Explainable AI systems, we conducted a formative study — using the lens of Information Foraging Theory — into how experienced users foraged in the domain of StarCraft to assess an agent. Our results showed that participants faced difficult foraging problems. These foraging problems caused participants to entirely miss events that were important to them, reluctantly choose to ignore actions they did not want to ignore, and bear high cognitive, navigation, and information costs to access the information they needed.

CCS Concepts
•**Human-centered computing** → **User studies;**
•**Computing methodologies** → *Intelligent agents;*

Author Keywords
Intelligent Agents; Explainable AI; Intelligibility; Content Analysis; Video Games; StarCraft; Information Foraging

INTRODUCTION
Real-time strategy (RTS) games are a popular test bed for artificial intelligence (AI) research, and platforms supporting such research continue to improve (e.g., [41]). The RTS domain is challenging for AI due to real-time adversarial planning requirements within sequential, dynamic, and partially observable environments [30]. Since these constraints transfer to the real world, improvements in RTS agents can be applied to other domains, for example, mission planning and execution for AI systems trained to control a fleet of unmanned aerial vehicles (UAVs) in simulated environments [38]. However, the intersection of two complex domains, such as AI and flight, poses challenges: who is qualified to assess behaviors of such a system? For example, how can a domain expert, such as a flight specialist, assess whether the system is making its decisions *for the right reasons*?

If a domain expert making such assessments is not an expert in the complex AI models the system is using, there is a gap between the knowledge they need to make such assessments vs. the knowledge they have in the domain. To close this gap, a growing area known as "Explainable AI" aims to enable domain experts to understand complex AI systems by requesting explanations. Prior work has shown that such explanations can improve mental models [17, 19], user satisfaction [15], and users' ability to effectively control the system [1, 3, 18].

However, little is known about what an RTS domain expert's information needs are – what they need to have explained, in what sequence, and at what cognitive and time costs. Therefore, to inform explanation systems in this area, we conducted a formative study of how experienced RTS players would go about trying to understand and assess an intelligent agent playing the RTS game of StarCraft.

Our setting was StarCraft replay files. A StarCraft replay file contains an action history of a game, but no information about the players (i.e., no pictures of players and no voice audio). This anonymized set-up enabled us to tell our participants that one of the players was an AI agent. (We detail this design further in the Methodology section.) In addition, the

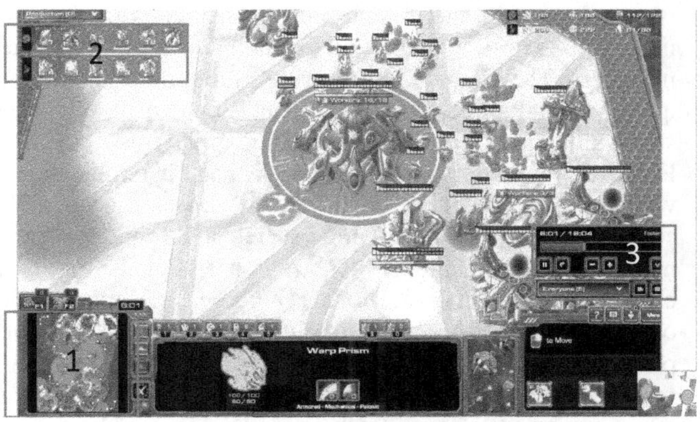

Figure 1. A screenshot from our study, with participants anonymized (bottom right corner). Superimposed red boxes point out: (1, bottom left) the *Minimap*, a birds-eye view enabling participants navigate around the game map; (2: top left) a drop-down menu to display the *Production tab* for a summary of build actions in progress; (3, middle right) *Time Controls* to rewind/forward or change speed.

IUI 2018, March 7–11, 2018, Tokyo, Japan.

http://dx.doi.org/10.1145/3172944.3172946

participants had functionality to seek additional information about the replay, such as navigating around the game map, drilling down into production information, pausing, rewinding, fast-forwarding, and so on (Figure 1).

However, we wanted a higher level of abstraction than features specific to StarCraft. Specifically, we aimed for (1) applicability to other RTS environments, and (2) connection with other research about humans seeking information. To that end, we turned to Information Foraging Theory (IFT).

IFT has a long history of revealing useful and usable information functionalities in other information-rich domains, especially web environments (e.g., [34]) and software development environments (e.g., [9, 32]). Originally based on classic predator-prey models in the wild, its basic constructs are the *predator* (information seekers like our participants) seeking *prey* (information goals) along pathways marked by *cues* (signposts) in an *information environment* (such as the StarCraft replay environment). The predator decides which paths to navigate by weighing the expected cost of navigating the path against the expected value of the location to which it leads.

Drawing from this theory, we investigated how people would assess a (purported) intelligent agent, via the following research questions (RQs):

RQ1 *The Prey*: What kind of information do domain experts seek, how do they ask about it, and for what reasons?

RQ2 *The Foraging Paths*: What paths do domain experts follow in seeking their prey, why, and at what cost?

RQ3 *The Decisions and the Cues*: What decision points do domain experts consider to be most critical, and what cues lead them astray from these decision points?

BACKGROUND AND RELATED WORK

When assessing whether an AI agent is making its decisions for the right reasons, humans automatically develop mental models of the system [29]. Mental models, defined as "internal representations that people build based on their experiences in the real world," enable users to predict system behavior [29].

Ideally, mental models of a system would help people gain the understanding they need to assess an AI agent, but this is not always the case. Tullio et al. [39] examined mental models for a system that predicted the interruptibility of their managers. They found that the overall structure of their participants' mental models was largely unchanged over the 6 week study, although they did discount some initial misconceptions. However, their study did not deeply engage in explanation; it was mostly visualization. In other work, Bostandjiev et al. [3] studied a music recommendation system and found that explanation led to a remarkable increase in user-satisfaction. In an effort to improve mental models by increasing transparency of a machine learning system, Kulesza et al. [17] identified principles for explaining (in a "white box" fashion) how a machine learning based system makes its predictions more transparent to the user. In their study, participants using a prototype following the principles observed an improvement of their mental model quality by up to 52%.

Several studies have also found that explanations have been able to improve users' ability to actually *control* the system. Stumpf et al. [37] investigated how users responded to explanations of machine learning predictions, finding that participants were willing to provide a wide range of feedback in an effort to improve the system. Kulesza et al. [18] found that the participants who were best able to customize recommendations were the ones who had adjusted their mental models the most in response to explanations about the recommender system. Further, those same participants found debugging more worthwhile and engaging. Kapoor et al. [15] found that interacting with explanations enabled users to construct classifiers that were more aligned with target preferences, alongside increased satisfaction. Beltran et al. [1] presented a novel gestural approach to querying text databases, allowing users to refine queries by providing reasons why the result was correct or incorrect. Their results indicated that action explanation allowed for more efficient query refinement.

However, in the domain of intelligent agents in RTS games, although there is research into AI approaches [30], there is only a little research investigating what *humans* need or want explained. Cheung et al. [5] studied how people watch the RTS genre, creating personas for various types of viewers. Metoyer et al. [26] studied how experienced players explained the RTS domain to novice users while demonstrating how to play the game. Finally, McGregor et al.'s [25] work is also pertinent, describing support for testing and debugging in settings with thousands of decisions being made sequentially. The work most similar to our own is Kim et al.'s [16] study of intelligent agent assessment in StarCraft. Their study invited experienced players to assess skill levels and overall performance of AI bots by playing against them. They observed that the humans' ranking differed from an empirical ranking based on the bots' win rate at AI competitions. Our study differs from theirs in that our participants did not play, but instead strove to *understand and explain* by interacting with a game replay.

In everyday conversation, people obtain explanations by asking questions. Drawing upon this point, Lim et al. [23] have categorized questions people ask about AI systems in terms of "intelligibility types." In their work, they investigated participants' information demands about context-aware intelligent systems powered by decision trees, determining which explanation types provided the most benefit to users. They found the most often demanded questions were `Why` and `Why not` (Why did or didn't the system do X?). We provide more details of that work and build upon it in when we discuss RQ1 results.

In recognition of the particular importance of these two types of questions, researchers have been working on `Why` and `Why not` explanations in domains such as database queries [2, 14], robotics [13, 24, 35], email classification [20], and pervasive computing [40]. These types of explanations have also attracted attention from the social sciences, which seek to help ground AI researchers' efforts in cognitive theories [27]. Other research has demonstrated that the intelligibility type(s) the system supported impact which aspects of users' attitudes are affected. For example, Cotter et al. [7] found that justifying *why* an algorithm works the way it does (but not *how* it works) increased users' confidence (blind faith) in the system — but not for improving their *trust* (beliefs which inform a full cost-benefit analysis) in the system. Further, it seems that the relative importance of the intelligibility types may vary from one domain to another. For example, Castelli et al. [4] found that in the smart homes domain, users showed a strong interest in `What` questions, but few of the other intelligibility types.

We drew upon Information Foraging Theory (IFT) to investigate the information that people would seek in the RTS domain. In IFT terms, when deciding where to forage for information, predators (our participants) make cost/benefit estimates, weighing the information value per time cost of staying in the current *patch* (location on the game map or tab with supplemental information) versus navigating to another patch [34]. However, predators are not omniscient: they decide based on their *perceptions* of the cost and value of the available options. Predators form these perceptions using their prior experience with similar patches [32] and the *cues* (signposts in their information environment like links and indicators) that point toward various patches. Of course, predators' perceived values and costs are often inaccurate [33].

IFT constructs have been used to understand humans' information-seeking behavior in other domains, particularly web navigation [6, 10], debugging [9, 21, 32], and other software development tasks [28, 31, 33, 36]. However, to our knowledge, it has not been used in RTS environments like StarCraft. Our paper aims to help fill this gap.

METHODOLOGY

We conducted a pair think-aloud study, where participants worked to understand and explain the behavior of an intelligent agent playing StarCraft II, a real-time strategy (RTS) game. We brought participants in as pairs to keep them talking, by leveraging the social convention of discussing a shared task.

StarCraft II is a popular RTS game [30] that has been used for AI research [41]. We chose a match from a top level tournament, featuring professional players[1]. The replay we chose to analyze was a representative sample in terms of game flow, e.g., initially building up economy, some scouting, transitioning to increasing combat [30].

Because we were interested in how participants would go about understanding an intelligent agent's behaviors, we hid the players' names and told participants that one of the players was under AI control — even though that was untrue.

Instead of using deception to simulate an intelligent agent with a human player, an alternative design might use a replay of a game with an intelligent agent playing. However, we needed replay files with both interactive replay instrumentation and high-quality game-play. We were unable to locate an intelligent agent in the RTS domain with high enough quality for our investigation, i.e., without limitations like exploiting "a strategy only successful against AI bots but not humans" [16].

[1]We used game 3 of the match between professional players *ByuL* (displayed as "CPU1") and *Stats* (displayed as "Human") during the *IEM Season XI - Gyeonggi* tournament. The IEM tournament series is denoted as a "Premier Tournament," by TeamLiquid, a multi-regional eSports organization that takes a keen interest in professional StarCraft II. The replay file is public at: `http://lotv.spawningtool.com/23979/`

Participant: Age, Gender, Major			*SC2 Hours*		*RTS Hours*	
			Casual	*Comp.*	*Casual*	*Comp.*
Pair1-P1	41 M	EE[1]	200	100	500	300
Pair1-P2	20 M	ECE[2]	50	20	30	30
Pair2-P3	23 M	CE[3]	10	5	25	55
Pair2-P4	23 M	ME[4]	100	200	50	0
Pair3-P5	21 M	EE	50	0	150	12
Pair3-P6	27 M	CE	15	2	150	10
Pair4-P7	23 M	CE	40	20	20	30
Pair4-P8	28 F	EnvE[5]	200	100	300	30
Pair5-P9	21 M	BE[6]	40	40	100	0
Pair5-P10	19 M	ECE	700	300	50	0
Pair6-P11	22 M	BE	100	2	160	100
Pair6-P12	22 F	EnvE	0	70	0	0
Pair7-P13	22 M	CE	15	60	100	50
Pair7-P14	20 M	BE	35	3	40	0
Pair8-P15	23 M	CE	10	0	100	5
Pair8-P16	22 M	BE[7]	16	1	15	0
Pair9-P17	21 M	PS[8]	90	5	500	80
Pair9-P18	19 M	ME	100	0	20	0
Pair10-P19	24 F	FA[9]	5	5	0	0
Pair10-P20	23 M	EdEn[10]	80	15	50	0

Table 1. Participant demographics and their casual vs. competitive (Comp.) experience. SC2 is StarCraft II, and RTS is any other Real-Time Strategy game.

[1] Electrical Engr. [2] Electrical & Computer Engr. [3] Chemical Engr. [4] Mechanical Engr. [5] Environmental Engr. [6] Biological Engr. [7] Business Entrepreneurship [8] Political Science [9] Fine Arts [10] Education & English

However, for us to obtain data on how people assess AI agents, our participants needed only to *believe* that a player was an AI. Fortunately, participants were generally convinced of the deception. For example, Pair5-P10 speculated about implementation, "*he must have been programmed to spam*", and Pair10-P20 decided "*...the AI <is> trying to act like a human.*"

Participants

We wanted participants familiar with the StarCraft user interface and basic game elements, but without knowledge of machine learning or AI concepts, so we recruited StarCraft players at Oregon State University with at least 10 hours of experience – but excluding computer science students. Also, to avoid language difficulties interfering with the think-aloud data, we accepted only participants with English as their primary language. As per these criteria, 20 undergraduate students participated (3 females and 17 males), with ages ranging from 19–41, whom we paired based on availability. Participants had an average of 93 hours of casual StarCraft experience and 47 hours of competitive StarCraft experience (Table 1).

Procedures

Main Task's Procedures

For the main task, each pair of participants interacted with a 16-minute StarCraft II replay while we video-recorded them. The interactive replay instrumentation, shown in Figure 1, allowed participants to actively forage for information within the replay, and we gave them a short tutorial of its capabilities. Examples of ways they could forage in this environment were to move around the game map, move forward or backward in time, find out how many units each player possessed, and drill down into specific buildings or units.

When a participant paused the replay...
- What about that point in time made you stop there?
- Did you consider stopping on that object at any other point in time?
When a participant navigated to a patch...
- What about that part of the game interface/map made you click there?
- Did you consider clicking anywhere else on the game interface/map?
When a participant navigated away from a patch (or unpaused)...
- Did you find what you expected to find?
- What did you learn from that click/pause?
- Did you have a different goal for what to learn next?

Table 2. Interview questions (drawn from prior IFT research [33]), and the triggers that caused us to ask them.

Participants watched and foraged together as a pair to try to make sense of the agent's decisions. One participant controlled the keyboard and mouse for the first half of the task, and the other participant took control for the second half. To help them focus on the decisions, we asked them to write down *key decision points*, defined for them as, "an event which is critically important to the outcome of the game." Whenever they encountered what they thought was a key decision point, they were instructed to fill out a form with the decision's time stamp, a note about it, and which player(s) effected it.

Retrospective Interview's Procedures

After the main task, we conducted a multi-stage interview based on the actions the participants took during the main task. To add context to what participants wrote down during the main task, we played parts of our recording of their main task session, pausing along the way to ask why they chose the decision points they did. The wording we used was: *"In what way(s) is this an important decision point in the game?"*

We went through the main task recording again, pausing at their navigations to ask the questions in Table 2. Since there were too many to ask about them all, we sampled pre-determined time intervals to enable covering several instances of each type of navigation (e.g. temporal, spatial, UI) for all participant pairs.

Analysis Methods

To answer RQ1, we qualitatively coded instances in the main task where participants asked a question out loud, regardless of whether they were discussing the human or the intelligent agent, using the code set outlined later in Table 3. Our researchers had used this code set on a different corpus [8] in which they independently coded 34% of the corpus and achieved 80% inter-rater reliability (IRR). In this study, the same researchers who achieved this IRR split up the coding of the current data.

To answer RQ2, we qualitatively analyzed the participants' responses to the retrospective interview questions. To develop a code set to answer the question *"Why was the participant seeking information?"* we started with affinity diagramming to generate groups of answers, which was performed by a group of four researchers. The affinity diagram led to the following codes: *Monitoring State*, *Updating Game State*, *Obsolete Domain*, and *New Event*, as shown later in Table 5. Two researchers then individually qualitatively coded the participants' responses using this code set on 20% of the data. Given that our IRR on this portion was 80%, one researcher then completed the rest of the coding alone.

Intelligibility Type	*Freq*
`What`: What the player did or anything about game state. -Pair3-P5: *"So he just killed a scout right?"*	148
`What-could-happen`: What the player could have done or what will happen. -Pair5-P10: *"What's he gonna do in response?"*	16
`Why-did`: Why the player performed an action. -Pair10-P20: *"What was the point of that?"*	14
`How-to`: Explaining rules, directives, audience tips, high level strategies. -Pair3-P5: *"You have to build a cybernetics core [structure that unlocks new units], right?"*	9
*`How-good/bad-was-that-action`: Evaluation of player actions. -Pair10-P19: *"Like, clearly it didn't work the first time, is it worth it to waste four units the second time?"*	8
`Why-didn't`: Why the player did not perform an action. -Pair10-P20: *"Why aren't they attacking the base?"*	7

Table 3. Intelligibility type code set, frequency data, and examples. The code set is slightly modified (denoted by the asterisk) from the schema proposed by Lim & Dey: We added `How-good/bad-was-that-action` because the users wanted an evaluation of agent actions.

To answer RQ3, we qualitatively coded the decision point forms the participants used during the main task. Here again, we developed a code set using affinity diagramming. The four higher level codes we used were building/producing, scouting, moving, and fighting. We coded 24% of the 228 identified decision points according to this code set, and reached IRR of 80%, at which point one researcher coded the rest of the data.

RESULTS

RQ1: The Prey

To understand how predators seek prey in the RTS domain, we analyzed questions participants asked during the main task. To situate our investigation in the literature of humans trying to understand AI, we coded the utterances using the Lim & Dey intelligibility types [22] (Table 3).

The results were surprising. Although prior research has reported `Why` questions to be much in demand [22, 23], only 10% of our participants' questions fell into the `Why did` and `Why didn't` categories combined (Table 4). Over 70% of our participants' questions pertained to `What`.

To get a sense of how representative our participants' questions were, we turned to the experts — namely, professional explainers in this domain, known as "shoutcasters." Because we were interested in the very best explainers in this domain, we restricted our search for shoutcaster videos to those that fit the description in the Methodology (top level tournament, professional players). From this pool, we used the same code set as Table 3 to analyze two professionally explained games: Byun vs. Iasonu[2] and Nerchio vs. Elazer[3].

Consistent with our participants' questions, the shoutcasters' explanations were dominated by answers to `What` questions. In the Nerchio vs. Elazer game, shoutcasters answered `What` questions 54% of the time, and in Byun vs. Iasonu they

[2]Game 2 of *Byun* vs. *Iasonu* in the *2016 IEM Gyeonggi* tournament, available at: `https://sc2casts.com/cast20681-Byun-vs-Iasonu-BO3-in-1-video-2016-IEM-Gyeonggi-Group-Stage`

[3]Game 2 of *Nerchio* vs. *Elazer* in the *2016 WCS Global Finals* tournament, available at: `https://sc2casts.com/cast20439-Nerchio-vs-Elazer-BO3-in-1-video-2016-WCS-Global-Finals-Group-Stage`

Question	*Total*	*Pair 1*	*Pair 2*	*Pair 3*	*Pair 4*	*Pair 5*	*Pair 6*	*Pair 7*	*Pair 8*	*Pair 9*	*Pair 10*
What	148	2	3	41	1	6	14	10	1	8	62
What-could-happen	16		1	1		3	1	1		2	7
Why-did	14			2			3	1			8
How-to	9	1		3							5
How-good/bad-was-that-action	8			3		3					2
Why-didn't	7	1		1							5
Total	202	4	4	51	1	12	18	12	1	10	89

Table 4. Frequency of Lim & Dey questions participants asked each other, by session. Note how often What questions were asked, both by the population of participants as a whole, and by few individual pairs, where it was particularly prevalent.

provided What answers 48% of the time. Since shoutcasters are hired to provide what game audiences want to know, their consistency with our participants' questions suggest that this distribution of questions was typical for the domain.

The many flavors of "What" prey

Why such a difference from prior research results? One hypothesis is that, in this kind of situation, participants' prey was simply "play-by-play" information. However, this hypothesis is not well supported by the data. Although participants did seek *some* play-by-play information (Pair3-P5: "*...so he just killed a scout, right?*"), several common prey patterns in their What questions went beyond play-by-play. Three of these patterns accounted for about one-third of the What questions.

The "drill-down What" of current state: One common question type participants asked when pursuing prey were questions that involved drilling down to find the desired information. Half of the pairs asked drill-down What questions about the game players' unit production or composition. There were 21 instances of this type of What question alone, accounting for almost 15% of the total What questions. For example, the following question required the participants to drill down into several structures on the map to answer it:

> Pair3-P6: "*Is the human building any new stuff now?*"

Navigating in pursuit of this kind of prey was often costly. The least expensive way was navigating via a drop-down menu (2 clicks) in region 2 of Figure 1, but participants instead often foraged in other ways. For example, to find the answer to a question (like Pair3-P6's earlier) participants sometimes navigated to several unit producing structures on the map, into a structure, and then on to the next. For example, Pair 3 made seven navigations to answer their question about "building new stuff."

Shoutcasters' comments closely matched the participants' interest in drilling down: 18% of shoutcasters' What comments answered drill-down questions, compared to the 15% of our participants' drill-down Whats. As an example of the match to shoutcasters' comments, Pair6-P12's drill-down question about unit composition: "*I think, well, we have a varied composition, besides roaches [ground military unit], and what are these?*" would be well-matched to shoutcaster explanations such as these:

> Shoutcaster for Byun v Iasonu: "*[the player has] 41 zerglings [cheap military unit] at the moment.*"

> Shoutcaster for Nerchio v Elazer: "*And 12 [zerglings] as well, [and] that's just a few more [zerglings] than you normally see.*"

This suggests using shoutcasters as a possible content model for future explanation systems, given that shoutcasters' "supply" of explanations seem to match well with participants' "demand" for explanations of this type.

The "temporal What" of past states: A second common prey pattern, used by almost half (4 of the 10) participant pairs, was asking What questions to fill in gaps regarding past states. These accounted for 15 instances (about 10%) of their Whats.

> Pair3-P6: "*When did he start building [a] robotics facility [unit producing structure]?*"

As in the drill-down pattern, the participants' demand for temporal Whats matched well with the shoutcasters' supply: about 10% of the shoutcasters' What explanations reminded listeners of some past event pertinent to current game state. For example:

> Shoutcaster for Byun v Iasonu: "*...the +1 carapace [defensive unit upgrade] early upgrade ...[is] paying off.*"

The "higher-level What": The third common prey pattern was at a higher level of abstraction than the specific units or events, aiming instead toward more general understanding of what was going on in the game. These What questions arose 12 times (about 8%) across all instances. For example, Pair10-P20 asked, "*What's going on over there?*" in which "there" referred to a location on the map with military units that could have been gearing up for combat. The shoutcasters seemed enthusiastic about providing this kind of information[4], perhaps because it provided opportunities to add nuance and insight to their commentary. For example:

> Shoutcaster for Byun v Iasonu: "*This is about to get crazy because [of] this drop coming into the main base [and] the banelings [suicide bomber unit] trying to get some connections in the middle.*"

> Shoutcaster for Nerchio v Elazer: "*I like Elazer's position; he's bringing in other units in from the back...*"

Questioning the unexpected

Lim & Dey's reported that when a system behaved in unexpected ways, users' demand to know Why increased [22]. Consistent with this, when our participants saw what they expected to see, they did not ask Why or Why-didn't questions. For example, Pair 4 and Pair 5 did not ask any Why or Why didn't questions at all. Instead, they made remarks like:

> Pair4-P7: "*the Zerg is doing what they normally do.*"

> Pair4-P8: "*[The agent is] kind of doing the standard things.*"

> Pair5-P10: "*This is a standard build.*"

[4]We did not count the number of shoutcaster comments that answered this question because we could not narrow them down in this way. That is, although many of their comments *could* be said to be applicable to this type of question, the same comments were also applicable to more specific questions.

However, in cases of the unexpected, a fourth What prey pattern arose, in which participants questioned the phenomena before them. We counted 9 What questions of this type:

> Pair9-P17: "*...interesting that it's not even using those.*"
> Pair10-P19: "*I don't get it, is he expanding?*"
> Pair10-P19: "*Wow, what is happening? This is a weird little dance we're doing.*"
> Pair10-P20: "*<when tracking military units> What the hell was that?*"

The unexpected also produced Why questions. About half of the participants' Why and Why-didn't questions came from seeing something they had not expected or *not* seeing something they had expected. For example:

> Pair1-P1: "*<noticing a large group of units sitting in a corner> Why didn't they send the big army they had?*"

Implications for a Future Interactive Explanation System

Using the Lim & Dey intelligibility types (What, Why, etc.) to categorize the kinds of prey our participants sought produced implications for shoutcasters as possible "gold standards" for informing the design of a future automated explanation system in this domain. For example, the high rate of What questions from participants matched reasonably well with a high rate of What answers from shoutcasters. Drawing explanation system design ideas from these expert explainers may help inform the needed triggers and content of the system's What explanations.

Also, the dominance of What questions point to participants' prioritizing of state information in this domain. Drill-down Whats were about state information they hadn't yet seen, temporal Whats were about past states they either hadn't seen or had forgotten, and higher-level Whats were about understanding the purpose of a current or emerging state. Further, the shoutcasters matched and sometimes exceeded the participants' rate of Whats in each of these categories with their explanations. This suggests that in the RTS domain, an explanation system's most sought-after explanations may be its explanations relating to state.

Also, as noted in prior research, unexpected behaviors (or omissions of expected behaviors) led to increases in questions of both the What and the Why intelligibility types [22]. If an explanation system can recognize unexpected behavior, it could then better predict when users will want Why and What explanations to understand the deviation from typical behavior.

Finally, the cost of navigating to some of the prey at times became expensive, which points to the need for explanation systems to keep an eye on the cost to users of obtaining that information. In this section, this came out in the form of navigation actions. The next section will point to costs to human cognition as well.

RQ2: The Foraging Paths

Various cognitive costs were incurred by participants by following paths to find prey. As an information environment, RTS games have foraging characteristics that set them apart from other information environments that have previously been studied from an IFT perspective, such as web sites [34]

Reasons for participants' path choices code set	*Freq*
Monitoring State: Continuous game state monitoring, such as watching a fight. -Pair4-P7: "*I wanted to see how the fight was going.*"	65
New Event: Attending to a new event for which participant wished to satisfy curiosity about. -Pair2-P4: "*I saw there was a new building.*"	36
Update Game State: Updating potentially stale game information that the participant explicitly stated prior knowledge about. -Pair1-P2: "*I was mainly looking at the army composition, seeing how it had changed from the last fight.*"	29
Obsolete Domain: Explicitly using domain info that may not be current, such as game rules (e.g., what buildings can produce). -Pair3-P6: "*I mainly clicked on the adept because I'm more familiar with [a previous version of the game].*"	11

Table 5. Reasons for participants' path choices code set, with examples and frequency data, to answer the question "Why was the participant seeking that information?"

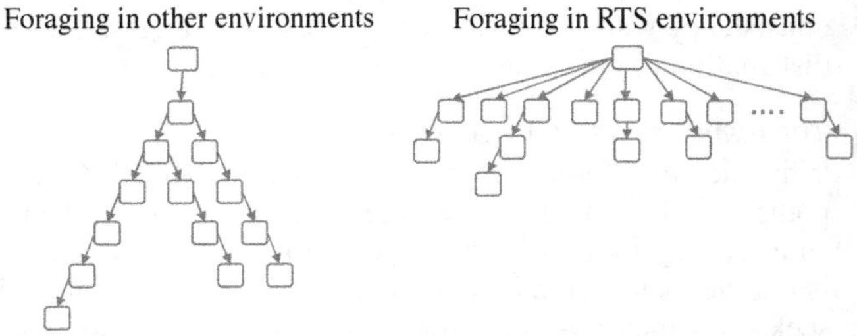

Figure 2. Conceptual drawing of foraging in the RTS domain vs. previously studied foraging. (Left): Information environments in prior IFT literature: the predator considers few paths, but the paths are sometimes very deep. This figure inspired by an IDE foraging situation in [[33] Fig. 5]. (Right): Foraging in RTS, where most navigation paths are shallow, but with numerous paths to choose from at the top level.

and programming IDEs [33]. These previously studied domains are relatively static, with most changes occurring over longer periods. In contrast, an RTS information environment changes rapidly and continually, driven by actions that do not originate from the foragers themselves. As we will see, this caused participants to spend some time monitoring the overall game state, waiting for a suitable cue to appear for them to investigate further.

The *number* of paths a forager might follow in an RTS information environment increases with the complexity of the game state, but path *lengths* tend to be short. This is conceptualized in Figure 2. This means that most questions are answered within a few navigations. However, in foraging environments like IDEs, there might only be a few interesting links from any one information patch, but some can lead to lengthy sequences of navigations (e.g., the "Endless Paths" problem [33]).

Foraging in the RTS domain

Interestingly, there was hardly any difference between RTS foraging and other environments at first. During the early stages of a game, there are very few units, buildings, or explored regions for users to navigate to, so foraging is relatively straightforward. As one participant put it:

> Pair7-P14: "*There is only so many places to click on at this point.*"

As long as this remained the case, each relevant path could potentially be carefully pursued, similarly to an IDE. Four participant pairs (2, 4, 7, 9) paused the replay for an average of 90 seconds within the first 1:30. They studied individual objects and actions with a great deal of scrutiny, which was surprising considering the sparse environment. In contrast, later on in the game, when 50 of the same unit existed, they received much less attention than when there was just one.

Choosing among many available paths created cognitive challenges for participants. Participants needed to keep track of an increasing amount of information as the match progressed. Each time a player performed an action, which added information, the participants could forage for this new information. If the participant did so, we coded their navigation as a *New Event*, which accounted for 26% of our interviewed navigations (Table 5). For example:

> Pair10-P19: "*...noticed movement in the Minimap, and that the Zerg troops were mobilizing in some fashion. So I guess I just preemptively clicked...*"

The rate of path creation exacerbated the "many paths" problem. Professional StarCraft players regularly exceed several hundred actions per minute (APM) [43]. This meant that players performed rapid actions that changed the game state. Each of these actions not only potentially created new paths; they potentially updated the existing ones. This caused the knowledge the participants had about paths that had not been recently checked to become stale, which in turn led to a strong prevalence of two behaviors. *Update Game State* was very common in our data set, indicating that participants often needed to check on paths that may have been updated (21% of interviewed navigations, Table 5).

> Pair8-P15: "*...there's a big force again. Just checking it out to see if anything has progressed from earlier.*"
> Pair1-P2: "*I was mainly just looking at the army composition, seeing how it had changed from the last fight, see if they had made any serious changes ...*"

Note that this is slightly different from our second behavior, *Monitoring State*, which is like updating game state, but with a nonspecific goal. *Monitoring State* was the most common reason for interviewed navigations (46% of navigations were for the purpose of monitoring, Table 5), for example:

> Pair5-P9: "*I noticed like the large mass of units on the map and I wanted to know what the player was doing with them.*"
> Pair8-P16: "*I was just kinda checking on things. Sort of due diligence keeping an eye on the different happenings that the AI was doing at the time.*"

Since each event and its corresponding cues were only visible for a limited time, paths not chosen right away by our participants quickly disappeared. Further, paths are numerous, and frequently updated. Thus, there is a large risk for paths of inquiry to be forgotten or going unnoticed as the game proceeds, as in these examples:

> Pair7-P14: "*Oh my gosh, I didn't even notice he was making an ultralisk den.*"
> Pair3-P6: "*I didn't notice they canceled the assimilator [mining structure]*"

Many Rapidly Updating Paths: Coping Mechanisms

Our participants responded to this issue in several ways. First, some participants chose a path and stuck to it, ignoring the others. Note that this required paying an information cost, because contextual information that may have been very important for future decisions could be discarded in the process. This strategy was exclusively followed by 3 pairs (2,7,8), who made barely any temporal navigations during the study, as described in Table 6. These participants analyzed the replay using not much more time than shoutcasters spend. However, achieving this speed of analysis required participants to *ignore* many game events.

For example, when asked about desire to click anywhere else, one participant volunteered:

> Pair10-P19: "*Mmm, if I had multiple, like, different screens yeah. But no, that seemed to be where the action was gonna be.*"

In this fashion, participants chose to triage game events based on some priority order. In both of the following examples, the participants navigated away from the conclusion of a fight:

> Pair6-P11: "*I wanted to check on his production that one time, because he just lost most of his army, and he still had some [enemies] to deal with.*"
> Pair3-P5: "*I was trying to see what units they were building, after the fight, see if they were replenishing, or getting ready for another fight.*"

The second method our participants used to manage the complexity of paths was to use the time controls to slow down, stop, or rewind the replay. Although pausing to assess the state was fairly common in all groups, rewind behavior yielded more information. Pairs 3 and 10 rewound the most often (Table 6), and paid higher *navigation* costs to do so, but they viewed these navigations as worthwhile to providing necessary information:

> Pair6-P11: "*I looped back to the beginning of the final fight ... to see if there was anything significant that we had missed the first time around.*"

However, the cost of doing so was more than just time, because the more paths they monitored, the greater the cognitive load:

> Pair10-P19: "*There's just so much happening all at once; I can't keep track of all of it!*"

Implications for a Future Interactive Explanation System

Assessing an agent required considering a great *many* paths, and choosing one (or few), though most paths followed were not particularly *long*. Note that this contrasts with previous literature in software engineering, which is characterized by "miles of methods [33]," such as a long sequence of methods in the stack trace. Thus, rapid evaluation and pruning of paths is critical in the RTS domain, but less so in software engineering, where the options to consider are fewer and time pressure is lighter. One solution could be a recommender system to help the user triage which path to follow next.

During assessment, participants' often forgot about or otherwise interrupted their paths of inquiry. For example, if a new important path appeared, such as a critical battle, either that

	Task Time	*Real-Time Ratio*	*Rewinds*	*Timestamp Rewinds*	*Context Notes*
Pair 1	20:48	1.3	3	1	Rewatched 1 fight
Pair 2	20:40	1.3			Extensive pause around 1:00 to evaluate game state
Pair 3	55:08	3.4	12	9	Rewatched fights and fight setup. Slowed down replay during 1 combat.
Pair 4	32:16	2.0	2		Rewatched opening build sequence and evaluated information available to the agent at a key moment. Many pauses to explain game state.
Pair 5	24:23	1.5	5		Rewatched unit positioning, AI reaction to events, and scouting effectiveness.
Pair 6	31:56	2.0	4	2	Rewatched 2 fights.
Pair 7	29:49	1.9			Made no use of time controls other than pausing to write down decision points.
Pair 8	21:27	1.3			Made no use of time controls other than pausing to write down decision points.
Pair 9	39:17	2.4	2	1	Rewatched 1 fight. Slowed down replay for the entire task.
Pair 10	61:14	3.8	Lots	Some	Rewound extensively, in a nested fashion. Changed replay speed many times.

Table 6. Participant task time (33:42±14:18 minutes) and time control usage information. Note that the replay file was just over 16:04, so dividing each pair's time by 16 yields the third column, *"Real-Time Ratio"* (2.1±0.89). Some of times participants rewound the replay were because we requested timestamps for events, shown in the fourth column, *"Timestamp Rewinds."* The last column provides any additional context in which replay and pause controls were used.

path or the current path had to be dropped. In another domain (spreadsheet debugging), participants faced with branching paths with multiple desirable directions became more effective when the environment supported a strategy they call "to-do listing" [12]. Because to-do listing was supported on its own or in composition of other problem-solving approaches, it could also act as a strategy enhancer. Perhaps in the RTS domain, a similar strategy could enable users to carry on with their current path uninterrupted — but also keep track of the critical battle to come back to later.

Code	*Total*	*Pair 1*	*Pair 2*	*Pair 3*	*Pair 4*	*Pair 5*	*Pair 6*	*Pair 7*	*Pair 8*	*Pair 9*	*Pair 10*
Expansion	52	7	7	8	8	-	6	3	-	7	6
Building - Rest	69	6	4	7	15	1	7	11	2	12	4
Building - All	114	13	11	15	21	1	12	12	2	18	9
Fighting - All	98	8	4	11	8	4	10	6	8	11	28
Moving - All	26	3	1	5	1	2	2	2	2	3	5
Scouting - All	23	1	2	1	5	1	1	3	-	3	6
Total	228	34	20	40	45	11	31	39	16	42	65

Table 7. Summary of decision points identified by our participants. Sums may exceed totals, since each decision point could have multiple labels. Note how prevalent *Expansion* was within the *Building* category.

RQ3: The Decisions and the Cues

When participants were not heading down the "right" path, what cues did they instead follow toward some other path? Also, what did they consider the "right" cues to follow?

In the RTS domain, players and intelligent agents make thousands of sequential decisions, and there is a paucity of literature that considers humans trying to understand AI decisions in such a setting. (A notable exception is McGregor et al. [25].) There is, however, literature that starts with the AI's perspective: instances of its decision-making system components (i.e., neurons) that are interpretable by humans [44, 45]. In contrast, here we wanted to start with the human's perspective and the foraging paths that result from it: namely, how participants would identify behaviors that were not only potentially human interpretable, but also of interest.

Thus, we asked participants to write down what they thought were the important game events. We defined the term *key decision points* to our participants as "an event which is critically important to the outcome of the game," to give participants leeway to apply their own meaning. Since all participant pairs were examining the same replay file, we were then able to compare the decision points the different participants selected. That is, the cues in the information environment were the same for all the participants — whether they noticed them or not.

Key decision points fell into four main categories: *building/producing*, *fighting*, *moving*, and *scouting*. The participants were in emphatic agreement about the most important types of decision points to pursue. Of the 228 total decision points participants identified, *Fighting* and *Building* made up 85% (Table 7).

In fact, participants showed remarkable consistency about the importance of the *Expansion* subcategory of *Building*.

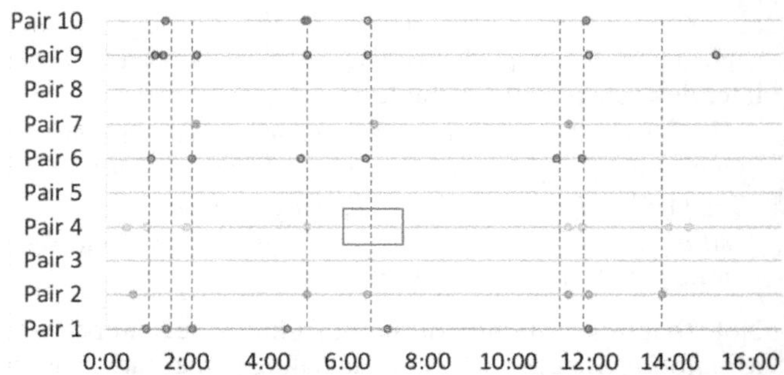

Figure 3. Dots show the *Building-Expansion* decision points each participant pair (y-axis) identified over time (x-axis). Red lines show when *Expansion* events actually occurred. (Participants noticed most of them.) The red box shows where Pair 4 failed to notice an event they likely wanted to note, based on their previous and subsequent behavior.

Eight of the ten participant pairs identified *Expansion* decision points, when a player chooses to build a new resource-producing base (Table 7). Extra resources from expanding allowed a player to gain an economic advantage over their opponent because they could build more units:

> Pair1-P2: "*Of course, if you have a stronger economy you will likely win in the end.*"

Moreover, because those that identified any *Expansion* found at least three, *Expansions* seemed to be considered important throughout the duration of the game.

> Pair6-P11: "... *the third base is important for the same reason the first one was, because it was just more production and map presence.*"

Even so, they missed some of the cues pointing out expansion decisions. The event logs in the replay file reveal that new bases were constructed at roughly {1:00, 1:30, 2:00, 5:00,

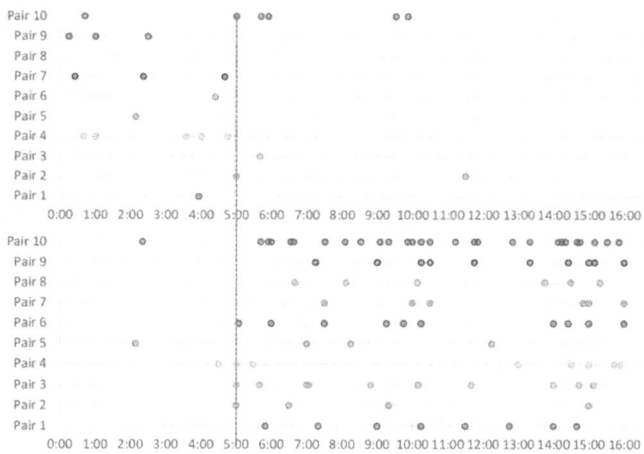

Figure 4. (Top:) The *Scouting* decision points identified by our participant pairs (y-axis), with game time on the x-axis. (Bottom:) The *Fighting* decision points identified, plotted on the same axes. After *Fighting* events begin (red line), *Scouting* decision points are no longer noticed often — despite important *Scouting* actions continuing to occur.

6:30, 11:20, 12:00, and 13:45}, each of which is marked with a red line on Figure 3. Only Pair 3 identified decision points for all 8 of these, and 7 pairs omitted at least one[5], with one example highlighted with a red box in Figure 3.

Since *Expansion* decisions were so important to our participants, why did they miss some? Some cues in the information environment led participants *away* from desirable prey[6]. We term such cues "distractor cues." Participants were so distracted by cues that provided an alluring scent, albeit to low-value information, they did not notice the other cues that pointed toward the "Expansion" decisions.

Distractor cues led participants astray from *Expansion* in nine cases, and eight of them involved units in combat or potentially entering combat. (The ninth involved being distracted by a scouting unit.) For example, Pair 7 missed the expansion at the 13:45 minute mark, instead choosing to track various groups of army units, which turned out to be unimportant to them:

Pair7-P14: *"These zerglings are still just chilling."*

Interestingly, participants had trouble with distractor cues even when the number of events competing for their attention was very low. For example, in the early stages of the game, players were focused on building economies and scouting. There was little to no fighting yet, so it was not the source of distracting cues. We were not surprised that the *Expansion* event at 13:45, when the game state had hundreds of objects and events, was the most often missed (5 instances). However, we were surprised that even when the game state was fairly simple — such as at 1:30 where the game had only 13 objects — participants missed the Expansion events. The extent of distractibility the partipants showed even when so little was going on was beyond what we expected.

So if decision points went unnoticed in simple game states, what did they notice in complex ones? *Fighting*. All participants agreed *Fighting* was key, identifying at least one decision point of that type (Table 7). The ubiquity of *Fighting* codes is consistent with Kim et al. [16], who found that combat ratings were the most important to the participant's perception score. *Fighting* provided such a strong scent that it was able to mask most other sources of scent, even those which participants prioritized very highly.

Scouting offers an example of *Fighting* leading participants away from other important patches. *Scouting* decision points occurred in the first half of the game, but died out once *Fighting* decision points started to occur in the second half of the game. As Figure 4 shows, the start of *Fighting* decision points coincides with the time that *Scouting* decision points vanish — despite the fact that scouting occurred throughout the game, and that participants believed scouting information mattered:

Pair4-P8: *"But it's important just to know what they're up to and good scouting is critical to know who you are going to fight."*

Implications for a Future Interactive Explanation System

Participants had a tendency toward following cues that were interesting or eye-catching, at the expense of those that were important but more mundane. In this domain, the "eye-catching" cues were combat-oriented, whereas the "mundane" cues were scouting oriented. Other domains may have similar phenomena, wherein certain aspects of the agent's behaviors distract from other important views due to triggering an emotional response in the viewer. Thus, supporting users' attending to actions that are important but mundane is a design challenge for future interactive explanation systems.

THREATS TO VALIDITY

Every study has threats to validity [42]. This paper presents the first study of information foraging either in the area of explainable AI or in the domain of RTS games, so its results cannot yet be compared or validated by other studies by other researchers. Thus, we must be conscious of its limitations.

Aspects of our study may have influenced our participants to ask less questions in general, such as not asking a question of their partner if they did not expect their partner to be able to answer it. Also, participants took different amounts of time to do the task, ranging from 20 minutes to an hour. Thus, certain participant pairs talked more than others in the main task, creating a form of sampling bias. Threats like these can be addressed only by additional empirical studies across a spectrum of study designs, types of intelligent interfaces, and intelligent agents.

DISCUSSION: WHAT IFT CAN OFFER EXPLAINABLE AI

The Implications sections along the way have discussed detailed implications of IFT on XAI explanation design. Here, we turn to how IFT allows us to "connect the dots" between our work and other work done from an IFT perspective.

[5] Table 7 shows Pair 4 also finding eight *Expansion* decision points, but one of those is about the *commitment* to expand, based on building other structures to protect the base, rather than the action of building the base itself.

[6] Reminder: Cues are signposts in the *environment* that the predator observes, such as rabbit tracks. Scent is what predators make of cues in their *heads*, such as thinking that rabbit tracks will lead to rabbits.

IFT allows abstracting above game objects like "assimilators" to the IFT constructs of *prey* (RQ1), foraging *paths* (RQ2), and following *cues* (RQ3). The IFT lens revealed that participants faced difficult foraging problems – some of which are new to IFT research – and faced high foraging costs. For example, failure to follow the "right" paths resulted in a high *information cost* being paid, but finding a reasonable path needed to be done quickly due to the ever-changing game environment (at a high *cognitive cost*). Although the user could relax the real-time pressure by pausing the replay, excessive rewinding incurred not only a high *navigation cost* for rewind-positioning and pausing, but also an additional *cognitive cost* of remembering more context.

Participants had to make trade offs between two types of these costs, navigational and informational, and their triaging to manage such trade-offs led to even more cognitive cost. Each path participants followed incurred a navigational cost, so following more paths led to higher cumulative costs. However, reducing the number of paths they followed incurred the information cost of missing out on potentially important information. Worse, the information cost paid by adhering to a single path compounded over time. For example, if participants made a bad path choice early in the game, and repeated that mistake throughout the game, then later in the game they may be confused by an event that they did not expect — due to lacking appropriate context. One cause for making a bad choice was "distractor cues," where, in order to curtail their current navigation direction and move to another, participants paid the high information cost of missing information important to them, often unwittingly.

The IFT perspective also connects some of the problems our participants faced to known problems of foraging in other domains. One open problem in IFT is the Prey in Pieces problem[7] [33]. Our participants encountered this problem because they had to piece together bits of evidence of the agent's decisions in order to assess the agent. In doing so, participants were sometimes uncertain about what each of these decisions meant about the competencies and strategies of the agent. When aggregating multiple sources of uncertain data like this, prior research has shown that computational assistance can increase user confidence, although manual comparison is still preferred in high-stakes situations [11]. This seems to suggest that a recommender may be helpful to help users select and aggregate agent actions for explanation, though manual comparison may still be necessary at times.

Another open problem in IFT is the Scaling Up problem [33]. This problem was revealed in the domain of IDEs, in which foragers (developers) had great difficulty accurately predicting the cost and value of going to patches more than one link away. The problem that the developers faced was a *depth* problem (recall Figure 2). In contrast, in our domain, participants faced a *breadth* Scaling Up foraging problem: constantly having to choose which of many paths to follow. The Scaling Up problem as a depth problem is still open; so too is the breadth version of it identified here.

In both cases, users foraging for information want to maximize value per cost. In the IDE case, this is accomplished by pruning low value paths unrelated to the bug. For example, if a developer is fixing a UI bug, they can potentially ignore database code. However, in RTS, any action could be important, so many paths need to stay on the table. Further, the rapid rate of change in the environment limits the user's planning depth, which decreases accuracy of predictions of cost/value. Thus, the Scaling Up problem is different in the RTS domain. In depth domains like IDEs, the problem is predicting cost/value in far-distant patches, whereas in the RTS domain, the difficulty is rapidly choosing at the top level among the many, many available paths.

CONCLUSION

In this paper, we presented the first theory-based investigation into how people forage for information about an intelligent agent in an RTS environment and the implications for Explainable AI. Our results suggest that people's information seeking in this domain is far from straightforward. We saw evidence of this from multiple perspectives:

RQ1 *The Prey*: Participants favored `What` information over the `Whys` reported by most previous research, and their `Whats` were nuanced, complex, and sometimes expensive.

RQ2 *The Paths*: The dynamically changing RTS environment and the breadth-oriented structure of its information paths caused unique information foraging problems in deciding which paths to traverse. These problems led not only to navigation costs, but also to information and cognitive costs.

RQ3 *The Decisions and the Cues*: These costs rendered it infeasible for participants to investigate all of the decision points they wanted. This problem was exacerbated by "distractor cues," which drew participants' attention elsewhere with interesting-looking cues (like signs of fighting), at the expense of information that was often important to participants (like scouting or expansion).

Perhaps most importantly, our results point to the benefits of investigating humans' understanding of intelligent agents through the lens of Information Foraging Theory. For example, the IFT lens enabled us to abstract beyond StarCraft, to reveal phenomena – such as the frequent need to trade off cognitive foraging costs against navigation foraging costs against information costs – that are widely relevant to the RTS domain. As we have noted in the "Implications" sections along the way, these theory-based results reveal opportunities for future Explainable AI systems to enable domain experts to find the information they need to understand, assess, and ultimately decide how much to trust their intelligent agents.

ACKNOWLEDGMENTS

This work was supported by DARPA #N66001-17-2-4030 and NSF #1314384. Any opinions, findings and conclusions or recommendations expressed are those of the authors and do not necessarily reflect the views of NSF, DARPA, the Army Research Office, or the US government.

[7] "Prey in Pieces" is analogous to buying a coffeemaker one piece at a time [33]. The cost of going to every store must be paid plus the cost of piecing things together at the end, rather than the cost of going to one store that has a preassembled coffeemaker.

REFERENCES

1. Juan Felipe Beltran, Ziqi Huang, Azza Abouzied, and Arnab Nandi. 2017. Don't just swipe left, tell me why: Enhancing gesture-based feedback with reason bins. In *Proceedings of the 22nd International Conference on Intelligent User Interfaces*. ACM, 469–480.
2. Sourav S Bhowmick, Aixin Sun, and Ba Quan Truong. 2013. Why Not, WINE?: Towards answering why-not questions in social image search. In *Proceedings of the 21st ACM International Conference on Multimedia*. ACM, 917–926.
3. Svetlin Bostandjiev, John O'Donovan, and Tobias Höllerer. 2012. TasteWeights: a visual interactive hybrid recommender system. In *Proceedings of the Sixth ACM Conference on Recommender Systems*. ACM, 35–42.
4. Nico Castelli, Corinna Ogonowski, Timo Jakobi, Martin Stein, Gunnar Stevens, and Volker Wulf. 2017. What Happened in my home? An end-user development approach for smart home data visualization. In *Proceedings of the 2017 CHI Conference on Human Factors in Computing Systems*. ACM, 853–866.
5. Gifford Cheung and Jeff Huang. 2011. Starcraft from the Stands: Understanding the Game Spectator. In *Proceedings of the SIGCHI Conference on Human Factors in Computing Systems (CHI '11)*. ACM, New York, NY, USA, 763–772. DOI: http://dx.doi.org/10.1145/1978942.1979053
6. Ed H Chi, Peter Pirolli, Kim Chen, and James Pitkow. 2001. Using information scent to model user information needs and actions and the web. In *Proceedings of the SIGCHI Conference on Human Factors in Computing Systems*. ACM, 490–497.
7. Kelley Cotter, Janghee Cho, and Emilee Rader. 2017. Explaining the News Feed Algorithm: An Analysis of the "News Feed FYI" Blog. In *Proceedings of the 2017 CHI Conference Extended Abstracts on Human Factors in Computing Systems*. ACM, 1553–1560.
8. Jonathan Dodge, Sean Penney, Claudia Hilderbrand, Andrew Anderson, and Margaret Burnett. 2018. How the experts do it: Assessing and explaining agent behaviors in real-time strategy games. In *ACM Conference on Human Factors in Computing Systems*. ACM.
9. Scott D. Fleming, Chris Scaffidi, David Piorkowski, Margaret Burnett, Rachel Bellamy, Joseph Lawrance, and Irwin Kwan. 2013. An information foraging theory perspective on tools for debugging, refactoring, and reuse tasks. *ACM Transactions on Software Engineering and Methodology (TOSEM)* 22, 2 (2013), 14.
10. Wai-Tat Fu and Peter Pirolli. 2007. SNIF-ACT: A cognitive model of user navigation on the world wide web. *Human-Computer Interaction* 22, 4 (2007), 355–412.
11. Miriam Greis, Emre Avci, Albrecht Schmidt, and Tonja Machulla. 2017. Increasing users' confidence in uncertain data by aggregating data from multiple sources. In *Proceedings of the 2017 CHI Conference on Human Factors in Computing Systems (CHI '17)*. ACM, New York, NY, USA, 828–840. DOI: http://dx.doi.org/10.1145/3025453.3025998
12. Valentina I Grigoreanu, Margaret M Burnett, and George G Robertson. 2010. A strategy-centric approach to the design of end-user debugging tools. In *Proceedings of the SIGCHI Conference on Human Factors in Computing Systems*. ACM, 713–722.
13. Bradley Hayes and Julie A Shah. 2017. Improving robot controller transparency through autonomous policy explanation. In *Proceedings of the 2017 ACM/IEEE International Conference on Human-Robot Interaction*. ACM, 303–312.
14. Zhian He and Eric Lo. 2014. Answering why-not questions on top-k queries. *IEEE Transactions on Knowledge and Data Engineering* 26, 6 (2014), 1300–1315.
15. Ashish Kapoor, Bongshin Lee, Desney Tan, and Eric Horvitz. 2010. Interactive optimization for steering machine classification. In *Proceedings of the SIGCHI Conference on Human Factors in Computing Systems*. ACM, 1343–1352.
16. Man-Je Kim, Kyung-Joong Kim, SeungJun Kim, and Anind K Dey. 2016. Evaluation of StarCraft Artificial Intelligence Competition Bots by Experienced Human Players. In *Proceedings of the 2016 CHI Conference Extended Abstracts on Human Factors in Computing Systems*. ACM, 1915–1921.
17. Todd Kulesza, Margaret Burnett, Weng-Keen Wong, and Simone Stumpf. 2015. Principles of explanatory debugging to personalize interactive machine learning. In *Proceedings of the 20th International Conference on Intelligent User Interfaces*. ACM, 126–137.
18. Todd Kulesza, Simone Stumpf, Margaret Burnett, and Irwin Kwan. 2012. Tell me more? The effects of mental model soundness on personalizing an intelligent agent. In *Proceedings of the SIGCHI Conference on Human Factors in Computing Systems*. ACM, 1–10.
19. Todd Kulesza, Simone Stumpf, Margaret Burnett, Weng-Keen Wong, Yann Riche, Travis Moore, Ian Oberst, Amber Shinsel, and Kevin McIntosh. 2010. Explanatory debugging: Supporting end-user debugging of machine-learned programs. In *Visual Languages and Human-Centric Computing (VL/HCC), 2010 IEEE Symposium on*. IEEE, 41–48.
20. Todd Kulesza, Simone Stumpf, Weng-Keen Wong, Margaret M Burnett, Stephen Perona, Andrew Ko, and Ian Oberst. 2011. Why-oriented end-user debugging of naive Bayes text classification. *ACM Transactions on Interactive Intelligent Systems (TiiS)* 1, 1 (2011), 2.
21. Sandeep Kaur Kuttal, Anita Sarma, and Gregg Rothermel. 2013. Predator behavior in the wild web world of bugs: An information foraging theory perspective. In *Visual Languages and Human-Centric Computing (VL/HCC), 2013 IEEE Symposium on*. IEEE, 59–66.

22. Brian Y Lim and Anind K Dey. 2009. Assessing demand for intelligibility in context-aware applications. In *Proceedings of the 11th International Conference on Ubiquitous Computing*. ACM, 195–204.

23. Brian Y. Lim, Anind K. Dey, and Daniel Avrahami. 2009. Why and why not explanations improve the intelligibility of context-aware intelligent systems. In *Proceedings of the SIGCHI Conference on Human Factors in Computing Systems*. ACM, 2119–2128.

24. M. Lomas, R. Chevalier, E. V. Cross, R. C. Garrett, J. Hoare, and M. Kopack. 2012. Explaining robot actions. In *2012 7th ACM/IEEE International Conference on Human-Robot Interaction (HRI)*. 187–188. DOI: http://dx.doi.org/10.1145/2157689.2157748

25. S. McGregor, H. Buckingham, T. G. Dietterich, R. Houtman, C. Montgomery, and R. Metoyer. 2015. Facilitating testing and debugging of Markov Decision Processes with interactive visualization. In *2015 IEEE Symposium on Visual Languages and Human-Centric Computing (VL/HCC)*. 53–61. DOI: http://dx.doi.org/10.1109/VLHCC.2015.7357198

26. Ronald Metoyer, Simone Stumpf, Christoph Neumann, Jonathan Dodge, Jill Cao, and Aaron Schnabel. 2010. Explaining how to play real-time strategy games. *Knowledge-Based Systems* 23, 4 (2010), 295–301.

27. Tim Miller. 2017. Explanation in Artificial Intelligence: Insights from the Social Sciences. *CoRR* abs/1706.07269 (2017). http://arxiv.org/abs/1706.07269

28. Nan Niu, Anas Mahmoud, Zhangji Chen, and Gary Bradshaw. 2013. Departures from optimality: Understanding human analyst's information foraging in assisted requirements tracing. In *Proceedings of the 2013 International Conference on Software Engineering*. IEEE Press, 572–581.

29. Donald A Norman. 1983. Some observations on mental models. *Mental Models* 7, 112 (1983), 7–14.

30. S. Ontañón, G. Synnaeve, A. Uriarte, F. Richoux, D. Churchill, and M. Preuss. 2013. A Survey of Real-Time Strategy Game AI Research and Competition in StarCraft. *IEEE Transactions on Computational Intelligence and AI in Games* 5, 4 (Dec 2013), 293–311. DOI: http://dx.doi.org/10.1109/TCIAIG.2013.2286295

31. Alexandre Perez and Rui Abreu. 2014. A diagnosis-based approach to software comprehension. In *Proceedings of the 22nd International Conference on Program Comprehension*. ACM, 37–47.

32. David Piorkowski, Scott D. Fleming, Christopher Scaffidi, Margaret Burnett, Irwin Kwan, Austin Z Henley, Jamie Macbeth, Charles Hill, and Amber Horvath. 2015. To fix or to learn? How production bias affects developers' information foraging during debugging. In *Software Maintenance and Evolution (ICSME), 2015 IEEE International Conference on*. IEEE, 11–20.

33. David Piorkowski, Austin Z Henley, Tahmid Nabi, Scott D Fleming, Christopher Scaffidi, and Margaret Burnett. 2016. Foraging and navigations, fundamentally: developers' predictions of value and cost. In *Proceedings of the 2016 24th ACM SIGSOFT International Symposium on Foundations of Software Engineering*. ACM, 97–108.

34. Peter Pirolli. 2007. *Information Foraging Theory: Adaptive Interaction with Information*. Oxford University Press.

35. Stephanie Rosenthal, Sai P. Selvaraj, and Manuela Veloso. 2016. Verbalization: Narration of autonomous robot experience. In *Proceedings of the Twenty-Fifth International Joint Conference on Artificial Intelligence (IJCAI'16)*. AAAI Press, 862–868. http://dl.acm.org/citation.cfm?id=3060621.3060741

36. Sruti Srinivasa Ragavan, Sandeep Kaur Kuttal, Charles Hill, Anita Sarma, David Piorkowski, and Margaret Burnett. 2016. Foraging among an overabundance of similar variants. In *Proceedings of the 2016 CHI Conference on Human Factors in Computing Systems*. ACM, 3509–3521.

37. Simone Stumpf, Vidya Rajaram, Lida Li, Margaret Burnett, Thomas Dietterich, Erin Sullivan, Russell Drummond, and Jonathan Herlocker. 2007. Toward harnessing user feedback for machine learning. In *Proceedings of the 12th International Conference on Intelligent user interfaces*. ACM, 82–91.

38. Katia Sycara, Christian Lebiere, Yulong Pei, Donald Morrison, and Michael Lewis. 2015. Abstraction of analytical models from cognitive models of human control of robotic swarms. In *International Conference on Cognitive Modeling*. University of Pittsburgh.

39. Joe Tullio, Anind K Dey, Jason Chalecki, and James Fogarty. 2007. How it works: A field study of non-technical users interacting with an intelligent system. In *Proceedings of the SIGCHI Conference on Human Factors in Computing Systems*. ACM, 31–40.

40. Jo Vermeulen, Geert Vanderhulst, Kris Luyten, and Karin Coninx. 2010. PervasiveCrystal: Asking and answering why and why not questions about pervasive computing applications. In *Intelligent Environments (IE), 2010 Sixth International Conference on*. IEEE, 271–276.

41. Oriol Vinyals et al. 2017. StarCraft II: A New Challenge for Reinforcement Learning. Tech Report. (2017). Retrieved December 22, 2017 from https://deepmind.com/documents/110/sc2le.pdf.

42. Claes Wohlin, Per Runeson, Martin Höst, Magnus C. Ohlsson, Bjöorn Regnell, and Anders Wesslén. 2000. *Experimentation in Software Engineering: An Introduction*. Kluwer Academic Publishers, Norwell, MA, USA.

43. Kevin Wong. 2016. StarCraft 2 and the quest for the highest APM. (Jul 2016). https://www.engadget.com/2014/10/24/starcraft-2-and-the-quest-for-the-highest-apm/

44. Tom Zahavy, Nir Ben Zrihem, and Shie Mannor. 2016. Graying the black box: Understanding DQNs. In *Proceedings of the 33rd International Conference on International Conference on Machine Learning - Volume 48 (ICML'16)*. JMLR.org, 1899–1908. http://dl.acm.org/citation.cfm?id=3045390.3045591

45. Matthew D. Zeiler and Rob Fergus. 2014. *Visualizing and understanding convolutional networks*. Springer International Publishing, Cham, 818–833. DOI: http://dx.doi.org/10.1007/978-3-319-10590-1_53

Beyond the Ranked List: User-Driven Exploration and Diversification of Social Recommendation

Chun-Hua Tsai
University of Pittsburgh
Pittsburgh, USA
cht77@pitt.edu

Peter Brusilovsky
University of Pittsburgh
Pittsburgh, USA
peterb@pitt.edu

ABSTRACT
The beyond-relevance objectives of recommender systems have been drawing more and more attention. For example, a diversity-enhanced interface has been shown to associate positively with overall levels of user satisfaction. However, little is known about how users adopt diversity-enhanced interfaces to accomplish various real-world tasks. In this paper, we present two attempts at creating a visual diversity-enhanced interface that presents recommendations beyond a simple ranked list. Our goal was to design a recommender system interface to help users explore the different relevance prospects of recommended items in parallel and to stress their diversity. Two within-subject user studies in the context of social recommendation at academic conferences were conducted to compare our visual interfaces. Results from our user study show that the visual interfaces significantly reduced the exploration efforts required for given tasks and helped users to perceive the recommendation diversity. We show that the users examined a diverse set of recommended items while experiencing an improvement in overall user satisfaction. Also, the users' subjective evaluations show significant improvement in many user-centric metrics. Experiences are discussed that shed light on avenues for future interface designs.

Author Keywords
Social Recommendation; User Interface; User-Driven Exploration; Diversification; Diversity

INTRODUCTION
Recommending *people* within a social system is a challenging task. A traditional approach for offering recommendations is generating a single ranked list of relevant people that is adapted to the profile of the user requesting information. However, users may look for other people for a range of reasons; for example, they may wish to re-connect with an acquaintance or to find new friends with similar interests [6]. This diversity in user needs makes it difficult to generate a static ranked list that fits all cases.

IUI'18, March 7–11, 2018, Tokyo, Japan

ISBN 978-1-4503-4945-1/18/03...$15.00

DOI: https://doi.org/10.1145/3172944.3172959

A particular instance in which a single ranked list might not work well is in a parallel hybrid-recommendation system that fuses several recommendation sources. In this case, different sources might be preferred for various needs (i.e., social similarity could work best for finding known friends while content-based similarity could be used to find people with similar interests [6]). Several authors have argued that the best approach in this situation is to offer users the ability to control the fusion by choosing the contribution of various algorithms [6, 10] or data sources [3]. Providing a visual interface that makes the process of fusion more transparent - for example, by showing recommended sources and their overlaps as set diagrams [29, 44] - could further address this problem. However, the set-based approach that has previously been applied to visualize the results of controlled source fusion has limited applicability, since it ignores the strength of relevance within each of the sources (which is a continuous variable). In this paper, we attempt to overcome the limitations of set-based visual fusion by exploring two visual fusion approaches that reflect the continuously varying strength of relevance within each source while keeping the fusion process transparent.

When selecting a visual design for the transparent fusion of recommendation sources, we focused on better-informing users about the *diversity* of the recommended results. It has been previously demonstrated that a proper user interface could promote diversity in information exploration. For example, a diversity-enhancing interface evaluated in [15] led to higher user satisfaction than a simple ranked list interface. Several attempts to design a diversity-focused interface using a dimension reduction technique to present opinion similarity by latent distance have been presented in [46, 11, 35]. However, the clustering distance was not easily interpreted, and as a result, users were unable to make personalized judgments. It remains challenging to design a recommender interface in which the user can both perceive the diversity and be able to control the interface to filter the recommended items.

The project presented in this paper reports our experience with two different visual recommender interfaces. First, we proposed a recommender interface that explores the value of a two-dimensional scatter-plot visualization to present recommendations with several dimensions of relevance. In our context, the scatter plot interface was used to help users combine different aspects of relevance for recommended items, while providing inspectability to the users. Second, we proposed a recommender interface that enhances the fusion control function within a ranked list with meaningful visual encoding for multiple dimensions of relevance. The users can adjust the relevance weightings to customize the recommendation results, which provides the user with a greater level of control over their results.

The two interfaces were designed to explore the value of user-controllable and diversity-aware interfaces in a social recommender system. Each of the interfaces has been evaluated in a controlled field study in the target context. The results show that the new visual interfaces reduce exploration efforts for a set of realistic tasks, and also make the users more aware of the diversity of recommended items. Also, the users' subjective evaluation shows a significant improvement in many user-centric metrics. We further discussed the effects of the proposed interfaces on the users' experience with a diversity-enhanced social recommender system.

The main contribution of this paper is threefold. 1) we propose two interfaces that support the continuously controlled fusion of several relevance aspects with inspectability and controllability. 2) we provide evidence that the diversity-aware interface not only helps the user to perceive diversity but also helps the user to improve usability in the real world beyond simple relevance tasks. 3) finally, we discuss the user experience effects on proposed interfaces through a structural equation model analysis.

BACKGROUND

Users access a hybrid social recommender system for different reasons. A static ranked list may not be suitable for all scenarios, which creates the challenge of increasing system's controllability as well as making diversity in the recommendation items more evident [40]. However, not every user equally values diversity [1]. The level of diversity-seeking is an existing individual difference. The findings of [23] indicated the individual differences in the information-seeking process and the needs of designing a customized interface to fit different users. [4] argues for considering a "diverse conceptions of democracy" when we develop a diversity-enhancing tool or application. Furthermore, to only present different information may not cause users to interact with diverse content. If a user feels threatened by unfamiliar information, a reinforcing effect may happen to cause users to avoid interacting with the various content [21, 11]. Hence, a diversity-aware recommender system should consider aspects of both item and user diversity, but not decrease the overall levels of user satisfaction and system usability [36].

Many scholars have suggested different explanation functions to increase the inspectability of recommender system. The function provides the transparency that let users realize how the system works [37, 14]. The exposure of the recommendation process through visual interfaces can also increase the inspectability of the system [20]. Many different types of research have been done on this subject. For example, [42] provides recommendation visualization to increase the transparency of the recommender system. [44] provides a set-based visualization to let the user explore the desired recommendation items. Other researchers further indicated that the value of explaining interfaces could enhance user experiences. The explanation interface was associated with the perception of recommendation quality [37], gaining trust in the system [7] and experiencing the competence of the system [45]. The studies of [13, 27, 26] have all mentioned that providing a controllable interface in the social recommender system can increase overall user satisfaction. The authors adopted an interactive graphical interface to present a social recommender that enables control on an item or user-level preference in a collaborative recommender system.

Some previous studies have been conducted to solve issues of recommendation diversity through interface design. For example, adopting a visual discovery interface can increase the click-through rate (CTR) across different item categories in an e-commerce website [35]. The user can explore new or relevant products without the need for search queries. The key factor of the interface is to provide the user with the ability to control the filtering of the recommendation contents. [32, 46] proposed a user-controllable interface for users to interactively change the ranking or feature weighting for a better-personalized ranking. [15, 11] proposed interfaces to show the various recommendation results that promote the users' perception of the diversity of recommendations. The study of [41] demonstrated a more diverse exploration pattern when the user was adopting a two-dimensional interface, versus a standard ranked list.

There are studies tried to enhance the recommendation diversity through exploratory search interfaces. For instance, [28] introduced an interface for interactive search, which uses overlaying graphs representing different information sources. The studies [18, 19] proposed interfaces which can present multi-faceted information on map or touch screen to diversify and explore the generated recommendations. The studies of [46] adopted dimensionality-reduction techniques to project the multidimensional data in two or three dimensions for the purposes of visualization. SciNet interface [31, 12] recommends keywords spatially in an interactive visualization to help diversification in exploratory search. However, the nature of each item is expressed in polar coordinates rather by two independent axes.

FIRST ATTEMPT: SCATTER VIZ

In a hybrid recommendation context with multiple types of relevance, the traditional ranked list makes it hard for the user to recognize how different relevance aspects are correlated. A typical example of this situation is recommending other attendees to meet at a research conference. Here a range of similarity functions (social, past publications, current interest, location) could indicate a person worth to meet. To help conference attendees in their conference networking, we propose a dual social recommender interface, **Scatter Viz**, which includes a ranked list and visual scatter plot components. The ranked list was selected as a traditional way of presenting recommended results in a single dimension, listed from high to low relevance. The scatter plot was chosen as an intuitive way to present multidimensional data [17]. We hoped that the ability to view recommended items in two dimensions could reveal the overall diversity of results and help to correlate multiple types of relevance among the social recommendations.

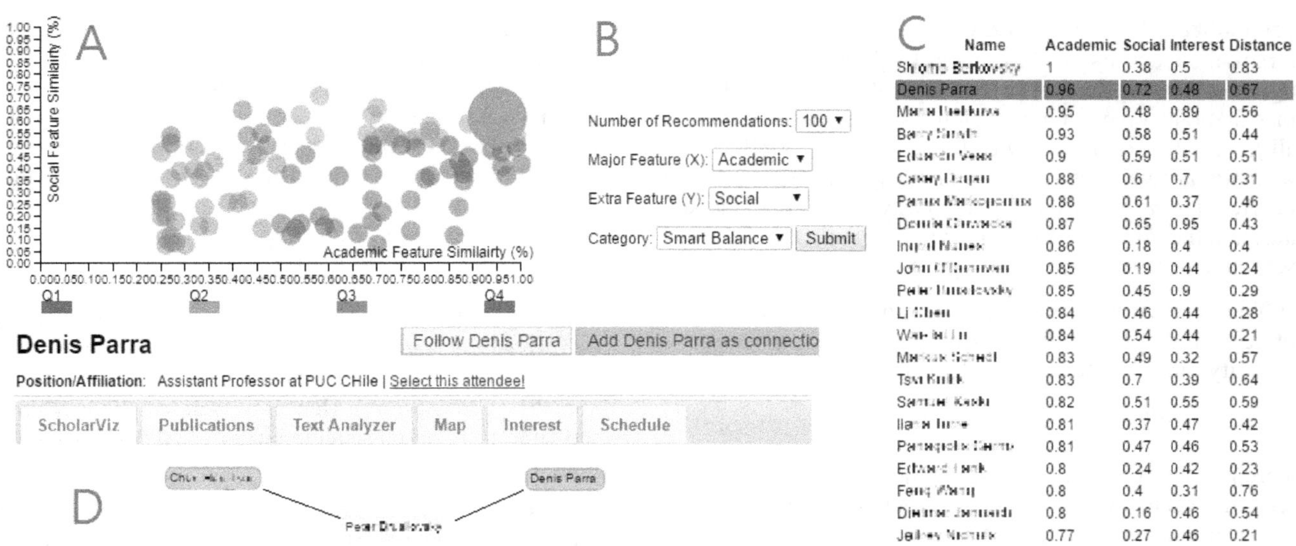

Figure 1. The design of Scatter Viz: (A) Scatter Plot; (B) Control Panel; (C) Ranked List; (D) User Profile Page. The interface supports exploration of recommended items in Section A or C and detail inspection in section D. (The scholar names have been pixelated for privacy protection.)

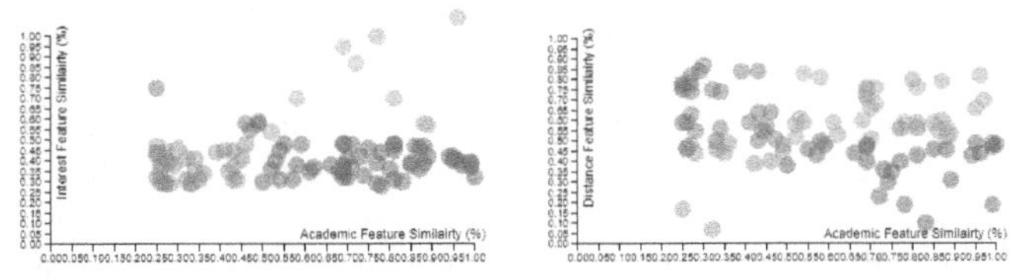

Figure 2. Scatter plot layouts: the layout would adjust, based on the selected *Major* and *Extra* features (Section B in Figure 1). Here is an example that presents the sane items presented in Academic/Interest and Academic/Distance feature coordinates. The nodes are colored using four quadrants if the Category "Smart Balance."

Visual Design

Figure 1 illustrates the design of the dual interface. **Section A** is the scatter plot. The interface presents each item (a conference attendee) as a circle on the canvas in two selected dimensions. The user can move the mouse over the circle to highlight the selection. **Section B** shows the control panel, with which the user can interact. The user can select the number of recommendations to display and choose the *major feature* and the *extra feature* to visualize the recommendations on the scatter plot. The major feature is used to rank the results along the X-axis and in the ranked list (section C), while the extra feature shows the diversity of results in the selected aspect along the Y-axis. To further investigate the diversity of the displayed recommendations, the user can also use another data aspect as a *category* to color-code the results. The default category was *Smart Balance*, which highlights four quadrants of the displayed data with a 0.5 ratio. Figure 2 presents a sample scatter plot layout combining "Academic" and "Interest/Distance" relevance features and color-coded using the Smart Balance Category.

Section C is the standard ranked list. More precisely, it is a combination of four ranked lists produced by four recommender engines, as explained below. To make the four dimensions more comprehensive, the model normalized relevance scores from 0-1 of each user to the target user, generated by each recommender engine. All the relevance scores are shown on the right side of the ranked list. The user can hover over each row to highlight the location in the scatter plot or click for a more detailed user profile. **Section D** presents more detailed information about the person who has been selected in either the visualization or the ranked list. Among other aspects, four of the six tabs visually explain how each recommender engine calculates the relevance of the selected user to the target user. Due to the page limitation, the details of each explanation tabs are omitted. The design detail of the explanation functions can be found in the work of [42].

The visual encoding affects the way users process the information. Pre-attentive processing let users absorb and precept the enormous amount of information in a short period [9]. The proposed interface helps to present the recommendation results in two kinds of visual encoding. First, the interface displays the recommendation relevance in two dimensions. The visual encoding helps the user to *spot* the item in different dimensions. It helps the user to make a decision beyond single or combined relevance, which is more realistic in many real-world scenarios. For example, a user may be interested in a scholar who whose research area is highly relevant to their research and who is also affiliated with nearby cities. The scatter interface helps to filter a group of recommended items with the two desired relevance features. Second, the node is color-coded in different categorical features; for example, in Smart Balance mode, the node is color-coded by the four quadrants between two dimensions of features. The user can perceive the tendencies of the recommendation item, based on their coloring, and the user can also update the layout with different Category features, including the meta-data of the recommended scholar's title, position, and home country. In addition, both the node and table row are highlighted synchronously while the user moves over the recommended items (see example in Figure 1). As a result, the scatter plot interface can be used for recommended item selection or just as a diversity-oriented recommendation explanation.

Personalized Relevance Model

To rank the recommended attendees by their relevance to the target user, the system uses four separate recommender engines that rank other attendees along four dimensions that we call *features*: text similarity of their *academic* publications, *social* similarity through the co-authorship network, similarity of current *interests* measured as similarity of their bookmarked talks, and the *distance* of their place of affiliation to the target user. Each of these features is defined below.

(1) The Academic feature is determined by the degree of publication similarity between two attendees using cosine similarity [43]. The function is defined as:

$$Sim_{Academic}(x,y) = (t_x \cdot t_y)/\|t_x\|\|t_y\| \quad (1)$$

where t is word vectors for user x and y. We used tf-idf to create the vector with a word frequency upper bound of 0.5 and lower bound of 0.01 to eliminate both common and rarely used words.

(2) The Social feature approximates the social similarity between the target and recommended users by combining co-authorship network distance and common neighbor similarity from publication data. We adopted the depth-first search (DFS) method to calculate the shortest path p [34] and common neighborhood (CN) [24] for the number n of coauthors overlapping in two degrees for user x and y.

$$Sim_{Social}(x,y) = p + n \quad (2)$$

(3) The Interest feature is determined by the the number of co-bookmarked papers and co-connected authors within the experimental social system [5]. The function is defined as

$$Sim_{Interest}(x,y) = (b_x) \cap (b_y) + (c_x) \cap (c_y) \quad (3)$$

where b_x, b_y represent the paper bookmarking of user x and y; c_x, c_y represents the friend connection of user x and y.

(4) The Distance feature is a measure of geographic distance between attendees. We retrieve longitude and latitude data based on attendees' affiliation information. We used the Haversine formula to compute the geographic distance between any pair of attendees [43].

$$Sim_{Distance}(x,y) = Haversine(Geo_x, Geo_y) \quad (4)$$

where *Geo* are pairs of latitude and longitude coordinates for user x and y.

Diversity Navigation Model

The Personalized Relevance Model determines the combined relevance score for each conference attendee, i.e., instead of ranking the recommended people using a static ensemble fusion of relevance aspects, the system allows the user to rank and visualize items using on different aspects of relevance through our proposed interface. We can measure the user's selection diversity with two diversification models.

(1) Feature Diversification: the user can select any two pairs of proposed features and spot the recommended items from the intersection of their relevance. All of the proposed features were calculated on a different scale. For example, the distance feature is the physical distance in miles, while the academic feature is calculated as a percentage. To enable the comparison of diverse features, we adopted a standard Z-score to normalize all the features to the same scale, from 0 to 1. The function was defined as:

$$ZScore = \frac{x_i - u_j}{\sigma_j} \quad (5)$$

where x_i is the ith recommended item and j represents the corresponding feature with its average u and variance σ. Then, we use a standard Z-table to convert the *ZScore* to the corresponding percentile p_{ij}. Hence, we can list all the features on the same scale for presentation in a ranked list and scatter plot diagram.

(2) Category Diversification: it is a model of diversifying the different categories [16]. In the scatter plot, we color-code the items from different categories, such as title, position, and country. In the ranked list, we listed the category as one column for a user to access.

(3) Selection Diversity: we can then measure the user selection/exploration diversity, based on the two diversification models. We observe the user's interaction with items from different "quadrants" (feature intersections) [38], such as high academic and high social features, or high academic and low social features. The extent of diversity is measured by *Shannon Entropy*:

$$Entropy: d_u = -\sum_{i=1}^{4} p_i log_4 p_i \quad (6)$$

where p_i is the probability for a particular quadrant (feature or category) and the proportion of all of the user's selections [22]. Based on the definition, we can measure the diversity in the different aspects of the relevance dimension. We can compare the combinations of all the proposed features. For example, in a recommendation system fused with $four$ features. We can measure the entropy difference among the $4*(4-1) = 12$ pair of dimensions.

STUDY 1: RANKED LIST V.S. SCATTER VIZ

Data and Participants

The recommendations produced by all four engines are mostly based on data collected by the Conference Navigator 3 (CN3) system [5]. The system has been used to support 38 conferences at the time of writing this paper and has data on approximately 6,398 articles presented at these conferences; 11,939 authors; 6,500 users (attendees of these conferences); 28,590 bookmarks; and 1,336 social connections. We used the Aminer dataset [33] to mediate the cold-start issue for academic and social engines that occurs when users have no publications or co-authorship information [39].

A total of 25 participants (13 female) were recruited for the user study. All of the participants were attendees at the 2017 Intelligent User Interfaces Conference (IUI 2017). Since the primary goal of our system was to help junior scholars connect with other people in the field, we specifically selected junior scholars, such as graduate students or research assistants. The participants came from 15 different countries; their ages ranged from 20 to 50 (M=37, SE=7.07). All of them could be considered as knowledgeable in the area of the intelligent interface for at least one academic publication from IUI 2017. To control for any prior experience with the recommender system, we included a question about in the background questionnaire. The average answer score was (M=3.28, SE=1.13) on a five-point scale.

Experiment Design and Procedure

To assess the value of the proposed interface, we compared the dual interface with the scatter plot and the ranked list (SCATTER) with a baseline interface using only a ranked list (RANK) with Section A (in Figure 1) removed. The study used a within-subjects design. All participants were asked to use each interface for three following tasks and to fill out a post-stage questionnaire at the end of their work with each interface. At the end of the study, participants were asked to compare interfaces regarding their explicit preference. The order of using interfaces was randomized to control for the effect of ordering. In other words, half of the participants started the study with the SCATTER interface. To minimize the learning effect (becoming familiar with data), we used data from two years of the same conference: the SCATTER interface used papers and attendees from IUI 2017, while the RANK interface used the corresponding data from IUI 2016.

Participants were given the same three tasks for each interface. The tasks were explicitly designed as diverse but realistic tasks that could be naturally pursued by attendees at research conferences. **Task 1:** Your Ph.D. adviser has asked you to find four Committee Member candidates for your dissertation defense. You need to find candidates with expertise close to your research field while trying to lower their travel cost to your defense. **Task 2:** Your adviser has asked you to meet four attending scholars, preferably from different regions across the world, who have a close connection to your research group. **Task 3:** You want to find four junior scholars (not yet faculty members) with reasonably similar interests among the conference attendees to establish networking.

The participants were asked to pick suitable candidates among conference attendees, based on their best judgment in each task. When designing the tasks, we attempted to make them realistic, yet focused on multiple aspects of relevance, as many real tasks are. We consider that task 1 is relevance-oriented and that tasks 2& 3 are diversity-oriented. For a relevance-oriented task, we expect to see if the proposed interface helps the user to coordinate different relevance aspects of the desired target efficiently. In contrast, for the diversity-oriented task, we expect the system to help to recognize the diversity of recommended items, as compared to the baseline interface.

Action Analysis

Table 1 shows the system usage for two interfaces. The data indicate that participants extensively used both the control panel and explanation tabs to complete the tasks. The participants usually required more actions on the first task to familiarize themselves with the system. There is no significant difference on the action of change control panel and the click on the explanation tab between the interfaces in three tasks; although, in the SCATTER interface, the users tended to click the explanation functions less. The click frequency presented a significant difference between the two interfaces. This finding is not surprising because the RANK interface lacks the visualization information that pushes the participant to click more on the user profile page to inspect the necessary information. It is interesting to see that not every user clicked on the scatter plot. This data hints that some participants treated the scatter plot visualization as an explanation function rather than an interactive exploration interface. At the same time, we found no significant difference in the time spent on the tasks. The data hints that each action taken in the SCATTER interface delivered more interesting information with which to engage.

		RANK		SCATTER		P
Task	Action	M (SE)	User Count	M (SE)	User Count	
T1	Control Panel	3.88 (2.40)	24	4.12 (2.02)	25	
	Explanation Tab	34.28 (29.50)	25	7.96 (7.48)	19	
	Click - Rank	26.28 (29.50)	25	4.92 (6.75)	15	*
	Click - Scatter	-	-	3.04 (5.45)	13	*
	Time Spent	345.44 (209.86)	25	389.12 (235.29)	25	
T2	Control Panel	2.88 (1.64)	24	2.88 (1.12)	25	
	Explanation Tab	19.96 (17.47)	25	9.16 (6.28)	25	
	Click - Rank	16.96 (17.47)	25	2.68 (4.69)	15	*
	Click - Scatter	-	-	3.48 (5.41)	13	*
	Time Spent	216.6 (144.95)	25	190.84 (115.33)	25	
T3	Control Panel	2.56 (1.04)	24	2.84 (1.10)	25	
	Explanation Tab	20.08 (20.29)	25	6.4 (7.22)	19	
	Click - Rank	19.08 (20.29)	25	3.48 (7.80)	9	*
	Click - Scatter	-	-	2.92 (2.95)	15	*
	Time Spent	345.95 (156.39)	25	369.2 (169.77)	25	

Table 1. User action summary of study 1: the table shows the user interaction statistics while performing each of the three tasks using two interfaces. (Statistical significance level: (*) $p < 0.05$.)

User Feedback Analysis

To compare subjective feedback, we analyzed the responses of the post-stage questions using paired sample t-tests. Figure 3 shows the result of this analysis. We compared the twelve aspects of subjective feedback from the participants; among them, the SCATTER interface received a significantly higher rating for six aspects: Trust (Q4), Supportiveness (Q5), Interest (Q6), Satisfaction (Q8), Intention to Reuse (Q9), and Enjoyable (Q11). In two questions, facilitation (Q7) and the Reversed Benefit Question (Q12), the SCATTER interface scored higher, but not significantly so. It is interesting to see

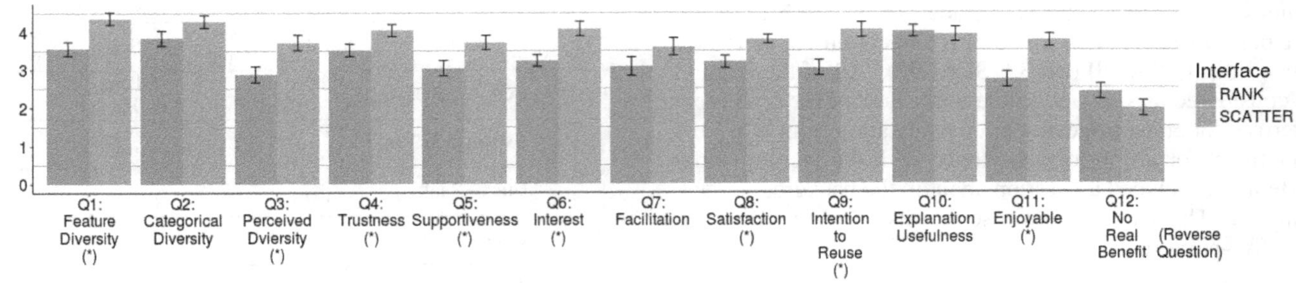

Figure 3. User feedback analysis results for Study 1 shows that the SCATTER interface received a significantly higher rating for six aspects. (A cut-off value was set at 3.5 on the 5 point scale. Statistical significance level: (*) $p < 0.05$.)

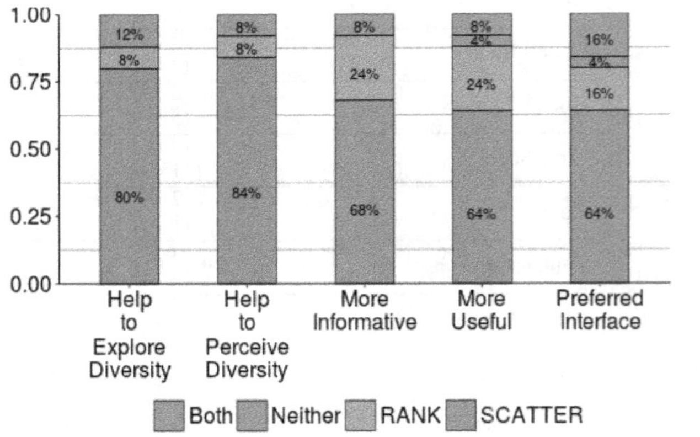

Figure 4. User preference analysis in study 1 (the preferences were collected after the users experienced both interfaces). The result shows the SCATTER interface was preferred by the users in all aspects.

		RANK	SCATTER	P
Task	Dimensions	M (SE)	M (SE)	
T1	Academic + Social	0.14 (0.06)	0.11 (0.03)	*
	Academic + Interest	0.16 (0.09)	0.13 (0.08)	
	Academic + Distance	0.13 (0.07)	0.12 (0.04)	
	Social + Interest	0.27 (0.13)	0.21 (0.09)	*
	Social + Distance	0.27 (0.12)	0.24 (0.08)	
	Interest + Distance	0.26 (0.13)	0.25 (0.13)	
	Title	0.17 (0.12)	0.22 (0.07)	*
	Position	0.26 (0.12)	0.23 (0.10)	
	Country	0.49 (0.25)	0.46 (0.15)	
T2	Academic + Social	0.14 (0.06)	0.13 (0.04)	
	Academic + Interest	0.14 (0.09)	0.14 (0.08)	
	Academic + Distance	0.12 (0.07)	0.14 (0.04)	
	Social + Interest	0.25 (0.13)	0.24 (0.11)	
	Social + Distance	0.26 (0.13)	0.28 (0.10)	
	Interest + Distance	0.23 (0.14)	0.27 (0.13)	-
	Title	0.17 (0.14)	0.31 (0.12)	*
	Position	0.29 (0.17)	0.25 (0.14)	
	Country	0.46 (0.31)	0.68 (0.26)	*
T3	Academic + Social	0.14 (0.06)	0.13 (0.03)	
	Academic + Interest	0.12 (0.07)	0.12 (0.08)	
	Academic + Distance	0.14 (0.07)	0.16 (0.04)	
	Social + Interest	0.22 (0.12)	0.22 (0.14)	
	Social + Distance	0.24 (0.11)	0.31 (0.10)	*
	Interest + Distance	0.21 (0.14)	0.23 (0.11)	
	Title	0.17 (0.16)	0.32 (0.10)	*
	Position	0.19 (0.14)	0.15 (0.08)	
	Country	0.44 (0.26)	0.66 (0.26)	*

Table 2. Diversity analysis for study 1: the table shows selection diversity for three tasks in the feature and category dimensions. The result shows that the SCATTER interface can help users to explore a more diverse set of recommendation in diversity-oriented tasks (T2 & T3). (Statistical significance level: (*) $p < 0.05$; (-) $p < 0.1$.)

that the RANK interface scored a bit higher (though not significantly so) on explanation usefulness, which hints that the lack of visualization made explanations more important in the RANK interface. In the final preference test, the SCATTER interface received much stronger support than the RANK interface in the user preference feedback (Figure 4). Most importantly, a majority of users (84%) considered the SCATTER interface to be a better system for recommending attendees and a better help in diversity-oriented tasks, as well as a better system for recommending.

Diversity Analysis

Table 2 shows the diversity analysis for each task and interface. The result shows the users' responses to the tasks with a different pattern of exploration, which caused a variance of diversity and coverage measurements. All three tasks are shown a least one significance between two interfaces but in the different aspects of features. For the SCATTER interface, task 1 (relevance-oriented) shows significance statically on less difference between academic/social & social/interest features, but more coverage on the title category. Tasks 2 & 3 (diversity-oriented) show higher selection diversity in the interest/distance and social/distance features, respectively, as well as higher selection coverage in the title & country category features. The data supports the finding that the SCATTER interface helped the participants to accurately filter the attendees in the relevance-oriented task, as well as extend the selection diversity in the diversity-oriented tasks.

Discussion

In study 1, we evaluated a dual visual interface for recommending attendees at a research conference. A research conference context introduces several dimensions of attendee relevance, such as social, academic, interest, and distance similarities. Due to these factors, a traditional ensemble ranked list makes it difficult to express the diversity of recommended items (attendees). By spreading rankings over two dimensions, the suggested interface helps users to explore recommendations and recognize their diversity in several aspects. To assess the visual approach, we conducted a user study in a real conference environment to compare our interface (SCATTER) with a traditional ranked list (RANK) in three practical tasks. Our experimental result shows a tangible incremental impact on the metrics of system usage, efficiency, and diversity.

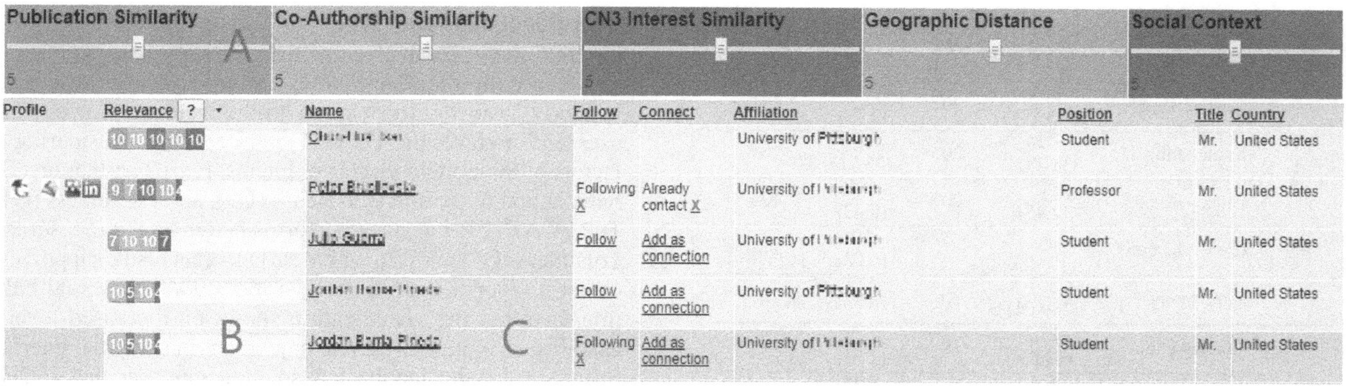

Figure 5. The design of the Relevance Tuner: (a) Relevance Sliders; (B) Stackable Score Bar; (C) User Profiles. The interface enables the user to adjust the feature weighting on-the-fly for retrieving a customized recommendation list. The user can examine the relevant aspects of the recommended item through the multicolored score bar. (The Name and Affiliation entities have been pixelated for privacy protection.)

We found that the **Scatter Viz** interface can improve user inspection on recommendations with multi-relevance, which leads to a higher selection diversity in the given tasks. However, we also noticed that some of the experiment participants still stick to the familiar ranked list, even when an enhanced visualization was provided. This finding helps us to realize a user preference on adopting the interface with lower learning efforts. Besides, the scatter visualization requires additional space to present, which may not be feasible in many real-world rank-based recommender systems. These findings lead to our second attempt at extending the ranked list with multi-aspect awareness, controllability, and diversity-aware designs.

SECOND ATTEMPT: RELEVANCE TUNER

The ranked list is widely applied to recommender systems for presenting recommendations to users. Even in visual recommender systems, a basic ranked list is still essential for user interactions [44, 29, 40]. A qualified recommender system usually ranks the recommended items from high to low relevance, which may reduce the users' cognitive decision loading [2]. However, in a context with multiple relevance aspects, a statically ensembled ranked list makes it more difficult for the user to recognize the impact of different aspects and to adjust the recommendations to different needs. In addition, the persuasive design of the ranked list causes users to pay more attention to items on top of the list [8], which may cause the low selection diversity and the fitter bubble effect [25].

According to the first study, we knew the users were able to correlate the multiple relevances in a two-dimensional scatter plot visualization, but that this ability came with a high learning curve. In our second attempt, we would like to see if the user can still correlate the multi-relevance within a ranked list extended with a controllable tuner and stackable color bars. We proposed the **Relevance Tuner** - a visual interface with user-driven control function and meaningful visual encoding. This design aims to help the users to inspect and filter recommendations of multi-relevance from a ranked list, which may facilitate the exploration of diversity-oriented tasks. The interface is extensible to various types of recommender systems without the limitation of dual interfaces. This design reduces the user's difficulties in getting familiar with the interface.

Visual Design

The design of the Relevance Tuner is shown in Figure 5. **Section A** contains five controllable sliders with the different colors representing the features of the Personalized Relevance Model. The scale of the slider ranges from 0 to 10. The user can change the weighting on the fly to re-rank the ranked list below. It provides controllability for the user to adjust the ranking to different recommendation needs and preferences. The interface also adds one new feature: Social Context. This feature computes the Google search result based on the scholar's name and affiliation information; that is, the text similarity of the homepage and other related search results. **Section B** shows the stackable relevance score bar of each recommended item in the ranked list. The color corresponds to the features in section A. It would adaptively adjust the bar score (length) from 0 to 20, based on the weighting percentage of the sliders. A stackable color bar interface is known for its ability to enhance controllability and transparency in a multi-aspect ranking [9]. In our system, the stackable color bars help the user to see how different relevant aspects of a recommended item are coordinated while adding transparency to the multi-aspect recommendation process. **Section C** shows the recommended scholar's meta-data, including name, social connection, affiliation, position, title, and country. The user can sort the ranked list by clicking the head of each column, or can inspect the explanation tabs (same as Section C in Figure 1) by clicking the name entities.

STUDY 2: SCATTER VIZ V.S. RELEVANCE TUNER

Data and Participants

Study 2 was conducted through the Conference Navigator 3 (CN3) system. The data was extended from Study 1 to a new conference: the 25th Conference on User Modeling, Adaptation, and Personalization (UMAP 2017). A total of 20 participants (7 female) were recruited for the user study. All of the participants were attendees at the UMAP 2017 conference. They were from 15 different countries; their ages ranged from 20 to 40 (M=31.19, SE=4.97). All of them had at least one publication from UMAP 2017. The background knowledge of recommender systems score was (M=3.85, SE=0.79) on a five-point scale.

Task	Action	TUNER M (SE)	TUNER User Count	SCATTER M (SE)	SCATTER User Count	P
T1	Control Panel	38.4 (37.71)	20	2.85 (2.23)	18	
	Explanation Tab	9.35 (8.28)	20	22.95 (23.71)	20	*
	Click - Rank	5.05 (2.45)	20	9.8 (8.43)	17	*
	Click - Scatter	-	-	4.1 (6.03)	11	
	Time Spent	357 (289.04)	20	537 (596.98)	20	
T2	Control Panel	15.2 (13.63)	19	2 (1.71)	17	*
	Explanation Tab	6.5 (8.74)	20	8.45 (6.79)	20	
	Click - Rank	4.3 (1.21)	20	5.2 (3.76)	18	
	Click - Scatter	-	-	1.8 (2.94)	8	*
	Time Spent	201 (235.43)	20	294 (470.78)	20	
T3	Control Panel	12.2 (11.67)	17	2.25 (1.80)	19	*
	Explanation Tab	9.25 (8.75)	20	12.9 (14.38)	20	
	Click - Rank	5.15 (2.51)	20	10.2 (16.93)	17	
	Click - Scatter	-	-	2.05 (3.13)	10	*
	Time Spent	153 (92.28)	20	285 (470.78)	20	

Table 3. User action summary of study 2: the table shows the statistics of user interaction while solving each of the three tasks using each interface. (Statistical significance level: (*) $p < 0.05$.)

Experiment Design and Procedure

In Study 2, we compared the interface of the ranked list plus the relevance tuner (TUNER) with a baseline of the scatter plot plus ranked list (SCATTER). The experiment design and procedure repeat the setting of Study 1. We manipulated the new proposed interface and adapted data from different conferences: the SCATTER interface used papers and attendees from UMAP 2017, while the TUNER interface used the same data from UMAP 2016, to minimize the learning effect between the two manipulations.

Action Analysis

Table 3 shows the system usage for the two interfaces of Study 2. In TUNER interface, the control panel usage is defined as each time the user moves the sliders. The data supports the users interacting more frequently (it shows significance in all three tasks) with the control panel in TUNER than in SCATTER. Conversely, the users clicked more on explanation tabs in SCATTER than in TUNER. The data implies that the information listed on the table was sufficient for the users to inspect and make decisions in three proposed tasks. In task 1, the SCATTER has a significantly higher clicking frequency and longer time spent (not significant) than the TUNER interface. The same pattern repeats in task 2 & 3, which shows that the users took more time to get familiar with the SCATTER interface. The users were gaining familiar with the TUNER interface more rapidly than with the SCATTER interface.

User Feedback Analysis

Figure 6 shows the analysis of the post-stage survey. The high rating in both interfaces shows the positive user acceptance in Study 2 (no significance on all the factors). However, the user tends to favor the TUNER interface when considering the factors of Supportiveness (Q5), Interest (Q6), Facilitation (Q7), Satisfaction (Q8), Intend to Reuse (Q9), and Usefulness (Q10). The SCATTER interface performs better on the measures of Trustiness (Q4) and Enjoyable (Q11). This result supports the users in favor of rank-based list more than the visual-based interface, but the visualization shows an increased level of usability on gaining trust and enjoyment in using the interface. Surprisingly, the feedback also indicates that the TUNER interface would be better for the user to fulfill the task on the feature diversity (Q1) and category diversity (Q2), but that the SCATTER interface is outperformed on the ability to Perceive Diversity (Q3).

This result shows that a user tends to use the ranked list with better controllability and transparency to conduct diversity-oriented tasks. The scatter visualization would play the role of helping the users to perceive diversity in multiple areas of relevance. The final preference result in Figure 7 also confirms this conclusion. About half of the users select the TUNER interface as the one with an advantage at helping to explore diversity, providing more informative information, being more useful, and fitting their preference - but the users also agree that the SCATTER interface could better help to perceive diversity after they finished the three tasks on two interfaces.

Diversity Analysis

Table 4 shows the diversity analysis of Study 2. In task 1 (relevance-oriented), there is no significant difference between the two interfaces on the diversity measurement, showing both of the interfaces can support the user to fulfill a relevance-oriented task. However, in the diversity-oriented tasks 2&3, we found the TUNER group could achieve higher entropy than the SCATTER group. This finding hints that even with a ranked-list interface the user can achieve a good level of selection diversity if controllability and transparency for each considered dimension of relevance is available. At the same time, the SCATTER interface performed slightly (but not significantly) better than the TUNER interface in the *category* diversity metrics. This finding helps to highlight the value of color-coding data in the SCATTER interface, a feature not supported by TUNER. The diversity analysis of Social Context is omitted due to the page limitation.

Discussion

In Study 2, we presented a new rank-based interface for recommender attendees at a research conference. A total of five dimensions of relevance were proposed from the Personalized Relevance Model. We conducted a user study in a real conference environment to compare the two interfaces of an enhanced ranked list (TUNER) and the visualization interface (SCATTER). Our experimental results suggested the different suitable scenarios for the two interfaces. We found that, even in diversity tasks with multi-relevance settings, the users were still able to fulfill the diversity task with a rank-based interface, but it required the support of interface controllability

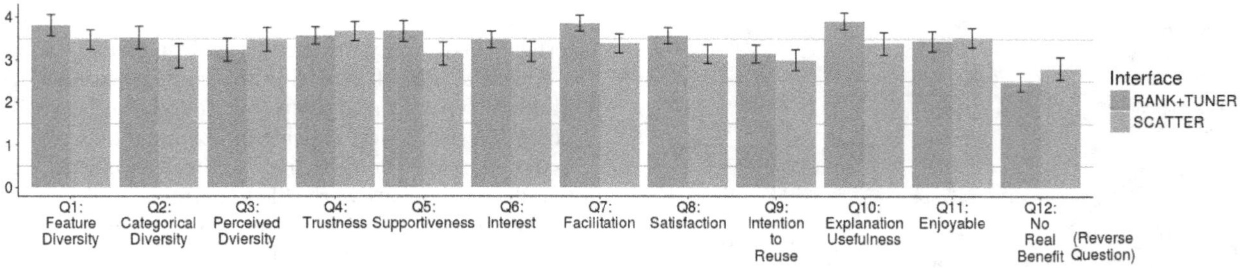

Figure 6. User feedback analysis results for study 2: we did not find significant difference in all aspects, which indicates that the usability of two interfaces was comparable. (A cut-off value was set at 3.5 on the 5 point scale. Statistical significance level: (*) $p < 0.05$.)

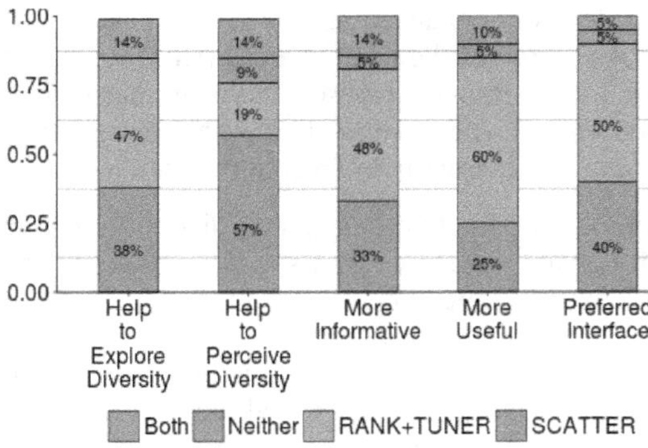

Figure 7. User preferences for study 2 collected after the users experienced both interfaces. The result shows that the TUNER interface was preferred by users in all aspects except perceived diversity.

		TUNER	SCATTER	P
Task	Dimensions	M (SE)	M (SE)	
T 1	Academic + Social	0.12 (0.05)	0.12 (0.05)	
	Academic + Interest	0.17 (0.10)	0.16 (0.07)	
	Academic + Distance	0.13 (0.06)	0.12 (0.04)	
	Social + Interest	0.23 (0.11)	0.23 (0.10)	
	Social + Distance	0.23 (0.10)	0.22 (0.09)	
	Interest + Distance	0.24 (0.16)	0.29 (0.12)	
	Title	0.12 (0.04)	0.16 (0.13)	
	Position	0.29 (0.15)	0.27 (0.12)	
	Country	0.35 (0.20)	0.57 (0.29)	*
T 2	Academic + Social	0.15 (0.02)	0.12 (0.04)	*
	Academic + Interest	0.17 (0.07)	0.13 (0.07)	*
	Academic + Distance	0.16 (0.06)	0.12 (0.05)	*
	Social + Interest	0.25 (0.07)	0.19 (0.08)	*
	Social + Distance	0.28 (0.07)	0.22 (0.10)	*
	Interest + Distance	0.31 (0.15)	0.24 (0.13)	*
	Title	0.15 (0.02)	0.17 (0.12)	
	Position	0.28 (0.12)	0.32 (0.15)	
	Country	0.41 (0.24)	0.58 (0.22)	*
T 3	Academic + Social	0.16 (0.03)	0.13 (0.05)	
	Academic + Interest	0.14 (0.07)	0.14 (0.06)	
	Academic + Distance	0.17 (0.05)	0.14 (0.05)	*
	Social + Interest	0.32 (0.09)	0.26 (0.16)	
	Social + Distance	0.32 (0.08)	0.26 (0.09)	*
	Interest + Distance	0.28 (0.12)	0.26 (0.13)	
	Title	0.15 (0.02)	0.14 (0.05)	
	Position	0.16 (0.07)	0.22 (0.16)	
	Country	0.48 (0.19)	0.54 (0.32)	

Table 4. Diversity analysis for study 2: the table shows selection diversity for three tasks for each feature combination and category dimensions. The result indicates that the TUNER interface enabled users to explore a more diverse set of recommendation in diversity-oriented tasks T2 & T3. (Statistical significance level: (*) $p < 0.05$.)

and transparency through visual encoding. Besides, while we found that the user would better perceive the diversity in the SCATTER interface, the user would prefer to adopt the TUNER interface to fulfill the diversity tasks.

Furthermore, when the user was interacting with the TUNER interface, the user spends more time on inspecting the information on each row, instead of checking the explanation functions. This result shows that the higher level of diversity exploration was not triggered by the diversity-enhanced visualization or explanation (fewer clicks on the explanation tabs), but was instead contributed by the intention of the user reaction to the simulated diversity-oriented tasks. In the SCATTER interface, the user relies more on the explanation function and multi-relevance visualization to explore diversity-oriented tasks. Although the result showed lower entropy measurement when the user adapted to the SCATTER interface, the SCATTER interface can better help the user to perceive the diversity among multiple-relevance dimensions, based on the user feedback analysis through post-study questionnaires.

USER-CENTRIC EVALUATION

To better understand the mediation effects across the two interfaces, we conducted a structural equation model (SEM) analysis [20] to inspect the effects of the proposed interfaces on the user experiences. We used the logged data and questionnaire feedback from the two studies. There are two conditions and five summarized factors in the model (as shown in Figure 8). In objective system aspects (OSA), there are two manipulations based on the proposed interfaces. In subjective system aspects (SSA) and user experience (EXP), we proposed four factors based on the classification by [30] and our post-experiment questions. In interaction (INT), we listed the entropy of the participant's selection diversity (average of Task 2&3 that shown in Table 2 and 4). The model fit the statistics of $\chi^2(96) = 234.68$, $p < 0.01$, $RMSEA = 0.18$, $90\%CI: [0.152, 0.211]$, $CFI = 0.941$, $TLI = 0.922$.

The model shows that the two manipulations have different positive effects on the system. The TUNER condition has a positive effect on the Perceived Usefulness and Perceived Diversity factors. It supports providing controllability and transparency on the ranked list, which helps the users to perceive the variety of recommendation results and increase the overall usefulness rating. The SCATTER condition only affects the Trust factor, which supports the argument for providing multi-relevance visualization to help the user to gain trust in the interface, but not mediates to the ratings of satisfaction or

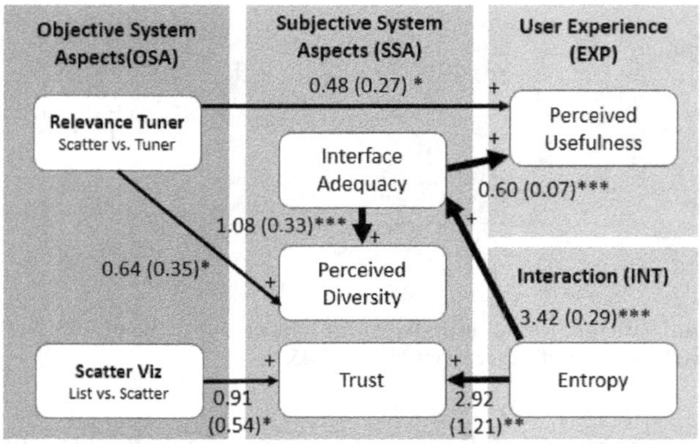

Figure 8. The structural equation model of the experiments. The number (thickness) on the arrows represents the β coefficients and standard error of the effect. Significance: *** $p < 0.01$, ** $p < 0.05$, * $p < 0.1$.

usefulness. We also found the effect between Interface Adequacy and Perceived Diversity, which supports a better design interface that helps the user to perceive the recommendation diversity. Furthermore, a positive impact on Interface Adequacy to Perceived Usefulness implied that the usefulness is contributed by the rating of the interface design. The Entropy value mediates the additional effect of the two interfaces. We found that the Entropy factor has a positive impact on Interface Adequacy and Trust; that is, the users who can achieve higher selection diversity through the given interfaces gain more trust and interface adequacy ratings in the system. This finding explains why the rank-based interface, with a lower learning curve, is preferred by the participants on the proposed tasks. In other words, it also supports the multi-relevance visualization that is appreciated by the users only when they are capable of taking full advantage of the interface.

CONCLUSION

In this paper, we presented experiments on three different interfaces: RANK, TUNER, and SCATTER. We first showed that providing a scatter plot (SCATTER) can help the user to better fulfill the diversity-related tasks, as compared to a simple ranked list (RANK). However, despite the benefits of the new two-dimensional presentation, the users still extensively use the ranked list component of the interface. Based on the results of the first study, we attempted to integrate the ability to coordinate multiple aspects of relevance within the ranked list rather than offering it in a separate component as in SCATTER. To compensate for the biasing nature of the ranked list, we also provided controllable fusion of relevance aspects. The resulting TUNER interface offered both controllability and visual encoding of multiple relevance aspects. We showed that the users could adopt a rank-based list to fulfill diversity-oriented tasks with higher selection diversity. The usability analysis reveals that both SCATTER and TUNER were ranked by the conference users with high subjective ratings. However, TUNER requires less learning effort. We also discussed the mediation effects of the proposed interfaces on the user experience. The analysis helps to describe the benefits of the two proposed interfaces in social recommender systems.

We aim to understand how the user adopts the recommender interfaces to diversity-oriented tasks. The given tasks indicated a concrete goal of exploring the conference attendees with multiple types of relevance. We found that both of the proposed interfaces were capable of helping the user to fulfill the assigned tasks. The experimental result supported the finding that the participants were able to correlate multiple aspects of relevance using two dimensions of visualization in SCATTER and the controllable ranked list with multi-aspect visualization in TUNER. We found that an extension of a traditional ranked list was better than a separate visualization component in the sense of on getting familiar with the new interface, which led to a higher rating on the user preference. In other words, a separate diversity-enhanced visualization can also achieve the goal, but it came at the cost of a steeper learning curve for the user. However, once the users were familiar with the interface, it brought an advantage of helping the users to perceive diversity and gain trust in the recommendations.

The findings shed light on designing diversity-enhanced and diversity-aware interfaces in a social recommender system. In a diversity-enhanced system, the target users would have a concrete goal of exploring the recommendation results. A similar scenario was reported in this paper; that is, the conference attendees explore the social recommendation within a particular conference. The user has specific goals on the exploration from multiple aspects of relevance. However, the users may not have specific goals when interacting with the recommender system. For example, when accessing news article on social media, the user may not have a strong desire to read the news article from a different perspective. In this case, we need a diversity-aware interface to help the user to perceive the prospect diversity, which may be a solution to help to solve the filter-bubble effect [36]. In this paper, we find that the effects of usability and perceived diversity are additive. The best user experience may happen when the users can take advantages from both of the proposed interfaces. It remains an open question as to how to design an interface to reflect the needs of users better.

LIMITATIONS AND FUTURE WORK

Our study has some limitations. First, the within-subject user study was conducted using consecutive years of the same conference series. Some well-known and senior domain experts may appear in the recommendation list for both conferences. This repetition may cause bias in our user studies. Second, the data sparsity and cold-start problem may hurt the recommendation performance; for example, the Interest feature is less useful for users who never bookmarked any talks with CN3. We tried our best to send out emails both before and during the conference to improve interest-based recommendations. Third, the scale of reported user studies is relatively small. It may decrease the statistical power of the findings. Fourth, the experiment was conducted at mid-size conferences, so we were not able to explore scaling issues which might occur at conferences with much larger number of attendees or in a different recommendation context with a large set of items to explore. We hope to address some of these limitations in our future work.

REFERENCES

1. Jisun An, Daniele Quercia, and Jon Crowcroft. 2013. Why individuals seek diverse opinions (or why they don't). In *Proceedings of the 5th Annual ACM Web Science Conference*. ACM, 15–18.
2. Dirk Bollen, Bart P Knijnenburg, Martijn C Willemsen, and Mark Graus. 2010. Understanding choice overload in recommender systems. In *Proceedings of the fourth ACM conference on Recommender systems*. ACM, 63–70.
3. Svetlin Bostandjiev, John O'Donovan, and Tobias Höllerer. 2012. TasteWeights: a visual interactive hybrid recommender system. In *Proceedings of the sixth ACM conference on Recommender systems*. ACM, 35–42.
4. Engin Bozdag and Jeroen van den Hoven. 2015. Breaking the filter bubble: democracy and design. *Ethics and Information Technology* 17, 4 (2015), 249–265.
5. Peter Brusilovsky, Jung Sun Oh, Claudia López, Denis Parra, and Wei Jeng. 2016. Linking information and people in a social system for academic conferences. *New Review of Hypermedia and Multimedia* (2016), 1–31.
6. Jilin Chen, Werner Geyer, Casey Dugan, Michael Muller, and Ido Guy. 2009. Make new friends, but keep the old: recommending people on social networking sites. In *Proceedings of the SIGCHI Conference on Human Factors in Computing Systems*. ACM, 201–210.
7. Henriette Cramer, Vanessa Evers, Satyan Ramlal, Maarten Van Someren, Lloyd Rutledge, Natalia Stash, Lora Aroyo, and Bob Wielinga. 2008. The effects of transparency on trust in and acceptance of a content-based art recommender. *User Modeling and User-Adapted Interaction* 18, 5 (2008), 455.
8. Paolo Cremonesi, Franca Garzotto, and Roberto Turrin. 2012. Investigating the persuasion potential of recommender systems from a quality perspective: An empirical study. *ACM Transactions on Interactive Intelligent Systems (TiiS)* 2, 2 (2012), 11.
9. Cecilia di Sciascio, Vedran Sabol, and Eduardo E Veas. 2016. Rank As You Go: User-Driven Exploration of Search Results. In *Proceedings of the 21st International Conference on Intelligent User Interfaces*. ACM, 118–129.
10. Michael D Ekstrand, Daniel Kluver, F Maxwell Harper, and Joseph A Konstan. 2015. Letting users choose recommender algorithms: An experimental study. In *Proceedings of the 9th ACM Conference on Recommender Systems*. ACM, 11–18.
11. Siamak Faridani, Ephrat Bitton, Kimiko Ryokai, and Ken Goldberg. 2010. Opinion space: a scalable tool for browsing online comments. In *Proceedings of the SIGCHI Conference on Human Factors in Computing Systems*. ACM, 1175–1184.
12. Dorota Glowacka, Tuukka Ruotsalo, Ksenia Konuyshkova, Samuel Kaski, Giulio Jacucci, and others. 2013. Directing exploratory search: Reinforcement learning from user interactions with keywords. In *Proceedings of the 2013 international conference on Intelligent user interfaces*. ACM, 117–128.
13. Brynjar Gretarsson, John O'Donovan, Svetlin Bostandjiev, Christopher Hall, and Tobias Höllerer. 2010. Smallworlds: visualizing social recommendations. In *Computer Graphics Forum*, Vol. 29. Wiley Online Library, 833–842.
14. Jonathan L Herlocker, Joseph A Konstan, and John Riedl. 2000. Explaining collaborative filtering recommendations. In *Proceedings of the 2000 ACM conference on Computer supported cooperative work*. ACM, 241–250.
15. Rong Hu and Pearl Pu. 2011. Helping Users Perceive Recommendation Diversity.. In *DiveRS@ RecSys*. 43–50.
16. Marius Kaminskas and Derek Bridge. 2016. Diversity, Serendipity, Novelty, and Coverage: A Survey and Empirical Analysis of Beyond-Accuracy Objectives in Recommender Systems. *ACM Transactions on Interactive Intelligent Systems (TiiS)* 7, 1 (2016), 2.
17. Hannah Kim, Jaegul Choo, Haesun Park, and Alex Endert. 2016. Interaxis: Steering scatterplot axes via observation-level interaction. *IEEE transactions on visualization and computer graphics* 22, 1 (2016), 131–140.
18. Khalil Klouche, Tuukka Ruotsalo, Diogo Cabral, Salvatore Andolina, Andrea Bellucci, and Giulio Jacucci. 2015. Designing for exploratory search on touch devices. In *Proceedings of the 33rd Annual ACM Conference on Human Factors in Computing Systems*. ACM, 4189–4198.
19. Khalil Klouche, Tuukka Ruotsalo, Luana Micallef, Salvatore Andolina, and Giulio Jacucci. 2017. Visual Re-Ranking for Multi-Aspect Information Retrieval. In *Proceedings of the 2017 Conference on Conference Human Information Interaction and Retrieval*. ACM, 57–66.
20. Bart P. Knijnenburg, Svetlin Bostandjiev, John O'Donovan, and Alfred Kobsa. 2012. Inspectability and Control in Social Recommenders. In *6th ACM Conference on Recommender System*. 43–50.
21. Q Vera Liao and Wai-Tat Fu. 2013. Beyond the filter bubble: interactive effects of perceived threat and topic involvement on selective exposure to information. In *Proceedings of the SIGCHI conference on human factors in computing systems*. ACM, 2359–2368.
22. Jennifer Moody and David H Glass. 2016. A Novel Classification Framework for Evaluating Individual and Aggregate Diversity in Top-N Recommendations. *ACM Transactions on Intelligent Systems and Technology (TIST)* 7, 3 (2016), 42.
23. Sean A Munson and Paul Resnick. 2010. Presenting diverse political opinions: how and how much. In *Proceedings of the SIGCHI conference on human factors in computing systems*. ACM, 1457–1466.

24. Mark EJ Newman. 2001. Clustering and preferential attachment in growing networks. *Physical Review E* 64, 2 (2001), 025102.

25. Tien T Nguyen, Pik-Mai Hui, F Maxwell Harper, Loren Terveen, and Joseph A Konstan. 2014. Exploring the filter bubble: the effect of using recommender systems on content diversity. In *Proceedings of the 23rd international conference on World wide web*. ACM, 677–686.

26. John O'Donovan, Brynjar Gretarsson, Svetlin Bostandjiev, Tobias Hollerer, and Barry Smyth. 2009. A visual interface for social information filtering. In *Computational Science and Engineering, 2009. CSE'09. International Conference on*, Vol. 4. IEEE, 74–81.

27. John O'Donovan, Barry Smyth, Brynjar Gretarsson, Svetlin Bostandjiev, and Tobias Höllerer. 2008. PeerChooser: visual interactive recommendation. In *Proceedings of the SIGCHI Conference on Human Factors in Computing Systems*. ACM, 1085–1088.

28. Valeria Orso, Tuukka Ruotsalo, Jukka Leino, Luciano Gamberini, and Giulio Jacucci. 2017. Overlaying social information: The effects on usersâĂŹ search and information-selection behavior. *Information Processing & Management* 53, 6 (2017), 1269–1286.

29. Denis Parra and Peter Brusilovsky. 2015. User-controllable personalization: A case study with SetFusion. *International Journal of Human-Computer Studies* 78 (2015), 43–67.

30. Pearl Pu, Li Chen, and Rong Hu. 2011. A user-centric evaluation framework for recommender systems. In *Proceedings of the fifth ACM conference on Recommender systems*. ACM, 157–164.

31. Tuukka Ruotsalo, Jaakko Peltonen, Manuel Eugster, Dorota Głowacka, Ksenia Konyushkova, Kumaripaba Athukorala, Ilkka Kosunen, Aki Reijonen, Petri Myllymäki, Giulio Jacucci, and others. 2013. Directing exploratory search with interactive intent modeling. In *Proceedings of the 22nd ACM international conference on Conference on information & knowledge management*. ACM, 1759–1764.

32. J Ben Schafer, Joseph A Konstan, and John Riedl. 2002. Meta-recommendation systems: user-controlled integration of diverse recommendations. In *Proceedings of the eleventh international conference on Information and knowledge management*. ACM, 43–51.

33. Jie Tang, Jing Zhang, Limin Yao, Juanzi Li, Li Zhang, and Zhong Su. 2008. Arnetminer: extraction and mining of academic social networks. In *Proceedings of the 14th ACM SIGKDD international conference on Knowledge discovery and data mining*. ACM, 990–998.

34. Robert Tarjan. 1972. Depth-first search and linear graph algorithms. *SIAM journal on computing* 1, 2 (1972), 146–160.

35. Choon Hui Teo, Houssam Nassif, Daniel Hill, Sriram Srinivasan, Mitchell Goodman, Vijai Mohan, and SVN Vishwanathan. 2016. Adaptive, Personalized Diversity for Visual Discovery. In *Proceedings of the 10th ACM Conference on Recommender Systems*. ACM, 35–38.

36. Nina Tintarev. 2017. Presenting Diversity Aware Recommendations: Making Challenging News Acceptable. (2017).

37. Nava Tintarev and Judith Masthoff. 2012. Evaluating the effectiveness of explanations for recommender systems. *User Modeling and User-Adapted Interaction* 22, 4-5 (1 Oct. 2012), 399–439.

38. Chun-Hua Tsai. 2017. An Interactive and Interpretable Interface for Diversity in Recommender Systems. In *Proceedings of the 22Nd International Conference on Intelligent User Interfaces Companion (IUI '17 Companion)*. ACM, New York, NY, USA, 225–228.

39. Chun-Hua Tsai and Peter Brusilovsky. 2016. A personalized people recommender system using global search approach. *IConference 2016 Proceedings* (2016).

40. Chun-Hua Tsai and Peter Brusilovsky. 2017a. Enhancing Recommendation Diversity Through a Dual Recommendation Interface. In *Workshop on Interfaces and Human Decision Making for Recommender Systems*.

41. Chun-Hua Tsai and Peter Brusilovsky. 2017b. Leveraging Interfaces to Improve Recommendation Diversity. In *Adjunct Publication of the 25th Conference on User Modeling, Adaptation and Personalization*. ACM, 65–70.

42. Chun-Hua Tsai and Peter Brusilovsky. 2017c. Providing Control and Transparency in a Social Recommender System for Academic Conferences. In *Proceedings of the 25th Conference on User Modeling, Adaptation and Personalization*. ACM, 313–317.

43. Chun-Hua Tsai and Yu-Ru Lin. 2016. Tracing and Predicting Collaboration for Junior Scholars. In *Proceedings of the 25th International Conference Companion on World Wide Web*. International World Wide Web Conferences Steering Committee, 375–380.

44. Katrien Verbert, Denis Parra, Peter Brusilovsky, and Erik Duval. 2013. Visualizing recommendations to support exploration, transparency and controllability. In *Proceedings of the 2013 international conference on Intelligent user interfaces*. ACM, 351–362.

45. Weiquan Wang and Izak Benbasat. 2007. Recommendation agents for electronic commerce: Effects of explanation facilities on trusting beliefs. *Journal of Management Information Systems* 23, 4 (2007), 217–246.

46. David Wong, Siamak Faridani, Ephrat Bitton, Björn Hartmann, and Ken Goldberg. 2011. The diversity donut: enabling participant control over the diversity of recommended responses. In *CHI'11 Extended Abstracts on Human Factors in Computing Systems*. ACM, 1471–1476.

Opportunity Team Builder for Sales Teams

Oznur Alkan
IBM Research
Dublin, Ireland
oalkan2@ie.ibm.com

Elizabeth M. Daly
IBM Research
Dublin, Ireland
elizabeth.daly@ibm.com

Inge Vejsbjerg
IBM Research
Dublin, Ireland
ingevejs@ie.ibm.com

ABSTRACT
Sellers work together as a team on sales opportunities, using their expertise in different roles to increase the probability of a win. These roles include managing the relationship with the client, overall architecture support or deep knowledge of a particular product depending on the seller's expertise, and the current opportunity requirements. Forming the right team for an incoming opportunity is vital and depends on several factors including understanding the required roles for the opportunity and assigning the right person to fulfil these roles, taking into consideration the seller's social network. In this paper, we present the Opportunity Team Builder solution, which supports sellers in this work by dividing the process into the following sub-tasks; identifying the required roles for the opportunity based on the products that the client is interested in, recommending the best people to fulfil these roles, and providing a win probability figure to guide users in team formation. This supports the sellers in forming the best-fitting team for current opportunity dynamics. Each task in the solution is implemented as a model using historical data from previous sales opportunities. Models work in coordination with each other to ultimately maximize the probability of win over loss. The solution not only recommends the best person to join a team taking into account a combination of inferred skills and social relationships, but also the predicted impact the person can have on the overall performance of the team. We present how the whole solution is realized with an intelligent user interface enabling interaction with the user throughout the team formation process. Substantial experiments with real world data show that win/loss prediction is performed accurately and the Opportunity Team Builder solution can recommend teams that achieve a higher win probability.

Author Keywords
Team recommendation; explanation interfaces; prediction model

INTRODUCTION
In organisations, understanding who to reach out for different knowledge based tasks and roles is something that tends to come with experience. Over time people either build up their personal view of the others they interact with, or they understand whose opinion they trust and therefore who to solicit for advice when they don't know which person to reach out to. As a result, institutional knowledge is embedded in the people inside the organisation, and an organization's intranet enables a way to exchange and share this knowledge so as to facilitate collaboration between them. Expert recommendation systems are developed in order to fullfill this need by identifying employees who can perform a specific task or fulfill the requirements of a role based on their knowledge, skills and experience [18].

Different approaches have been proposed for expert recommendation systems that utilize collaborative and content-based filtering as well as hybrid solutions so as to uncover people-task associations to return a list of tasks that a person is knowledgeable about [7]. Depending on the requirements of the domain and possible sparsity of the data, expert recommendation can be a complex task and the validity of the proposed solution is difficult to assess.

In this paper we focus on team recommendation, where our aim is to recommend not a single expert but a team of experts that best fit a given task. This is a very common real-life scenario with more challenges than expert recommendation, since in team recommendation, the aim is not only to identify best fitting experts for specific roles, but also to balance and distribute the expertise on different areas over a number of people. In addition, the proposed solution aims to recommend the team that maximizes the probability of success over failure for the team on the given task. Our solution, namely, Opportunity Team Builder (OTB), focuses specifically on sales teams that come together and work on opportunities with the goal of successfully selling a product or collection of products to a client. Although the proposed solution is developed in the sales domain where the aim is at the end to recommend seller-teams, the presented approach can easily be extended to support other domains such that, the aim is to form a team of people to maximize a success metric and historical data about previous such cases are available. We deployed our solution on top of a real-world system and enabled it to be interactively used by the sellers.

OTB divides team formation into three main subtasks:

- Determine which team roles are required to most successfully win a sales opportunity
- Recommend a list of experts based on their skill set and experience that can fulfil each role

IUI'18, March 7–11, 2018, Tokyo, Japan

DOI: https://doi.org/10.1145/3172944.3172968

Figure 1. Role Recommender

- Predict the impact that adding a given person to the opportunity will have on the potential success of the opportunity

The user is involved throughout the whole team formation process to both increase solution accuracy and user satisfaction and trust with the system. In particular, we make the following contributions to the state of the art:

- We introduce a novel team recommendation solution that analyses sales data in order to provide recommendations to build a team that maximizes the win probability of an opportunity. The solution involves three models that works in cooperation to provide the result.
- An intelligent interface is presented which enables user interaction with these models to analyse the resulting roles and team recommendation, make changes based on the results and see the immediate effect of these changes on the updated model.
- We introduce a novel way of assessing individual seller expertise considering a specific opportunity and using these individual scores to build up a team confidence score. We define a methodology to evaluate a team for a new opportunity and at the end decide the best team that will lead to win with high probability.
- We formally represent the problem space. The problem formulation and solution presented can be applied to any other domain to evaluate a team of people assigned on a specific task, when the historical data about previous tasks that the members tackled before is available.
- We analyse the relative importance of our features and the whole model using a real world dataset.

The rest of the paper is organized as follows: we first give a summary of the works from state of art. Then, we present OTB in detail by describing the components of the solution and how they interact so as to fullfil requirements from user perspective aiming for high accuracy and better user satisfaction. Next, we present the evaluation framework and metrics used to assess the system's performance. We discuss the results and present the feedback collected from an initial user study. Finally, we conclude the paper in the last section and propose next directions of research.

BACKGROUND

OTB project builds on previous work in the area of expert recommender systems and team recommender systems.

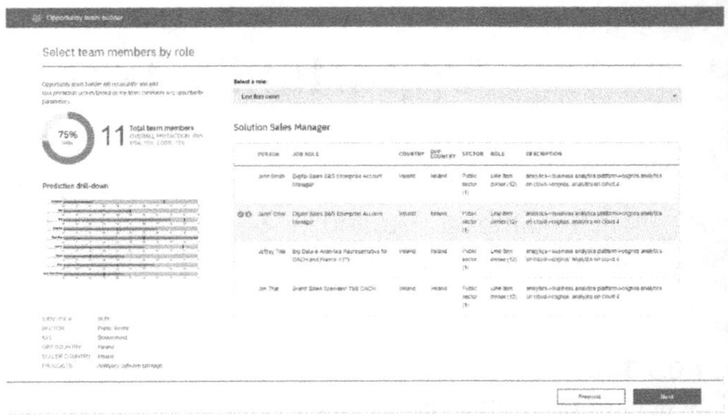

Figure 2. Team Builder

Expert recommender systems

Understanding who to reach out to in an organisation can represent a challenge particularly in a large organisation.

McDonald and Ackermann proposed that expert finding consists of two main tasks; *expert identification*, finding people who are likely to have the required expertise, and *expert selection*, selecting which of the potential experts to approach [15].

Expert identification requires assessing the knowledge of an individual which can be self reported [12], inferred [17] or a combination of both [11].

Earlier expert recommender systems relied on database systems, which allowed people to add keywords to their own profiles. Reichling et al. proposed an information retrieval solution, which mines data from documents associated with a person to determine their expertise level, using techniques that allow users to search based on keywords [17].

More recently, expert recommender systems have been used in software project management to more efficiently staff projects, from a top-down human resources perspective or a developer collaboration point of view. Gerogiannis et al. explore the allocation of human resources to development tasks in software projects. They consider skill relationships for technical and task-related skills using a group-based fuzzy multi-criteria approach, which makes use of the fuzzy linguistic 2-tuple model to create an evaluation and selection approach for developers [9]. By considering skill relationships, they can better indicate the most appropriate person for the task. However, these projects are based on finding the best expert, rather than the best expert who will work well for the current team profile. Surian et al. examine software development collaborations with information from Source Forge, attempting to find a list of the most compatible experts by considering if the input developer and the experts have ever worked together before, their past projects, and skill profiles [19]. This is accomplished with a random walk with restart. In addition, frequent pattern mining is employed to find frequent patterns of collaboration on software projects. The proposed solution in this paper, OTB, also mines professional relationships rather than social relationships, however OTB considers the role of the actors, the success of previous opportunities, and the current team profile when producing a list of recommendations.

Team recommender systems

The team recommendation problem has been viewed as a generalization of the expert recommendation problem, where a team needs to be formed to carry out a task requiring multiple skills from multiple experts [5]. Aral et al. showed an inverted U-shaped relationship between mutual information of team members and team productivity [2]. They mention that, if team members have no overlapping knowledge, communication is difficult and this as a result negatively affects the performance. On the other hand if the team members know too much of the same information, then individual team members bring little to the team. As a result, team recommendation also present an interesting challenge, where cohesive communities and teams foster communication, but overly similar collaborators can reduce creativity and performance [3]. Therefore, team recommendations need to balance not only skill requirements, but also address social factors and balance the knowledge and expertise distribution throughout the team.

Multidisciplinary team search and recommendation was demonstrated by the T-RecS project, where the skills of the actors within the context of their social interactions are examined [5]. In addition, as discussed in [6], team recommendation problem can also be solved by dividing the recommendation solution into a number of smaller sub-systems, such as, expertise identification, identification of relations, and graph mining . Crespo and Antunes examined prediction of team results in the context of prediction of student performance, by using decision trees to model team results from social network analysis [4]. They suggest that, predicting students' results when teamwork is present, is more difficult than predicting individual scores which may lead to lower accuracy values. They address this in their project, named *educare team advisor*, where students query recommendations about the best team to join, rather than the student themselves being profiled as the best fit for that team.

Much of the research regarding evaluating recommendation systems has focussed on making the algorithms as accurate as possible. McNee et al. state that *being accurate is not enough*, and that recommender systems should looked at from a more user-centric perspective, as the most accurate recommendations may not be those that are most useful to the user [16]. In our case we don't seek to replicate the decisions made by users but to make recommendations that maximise the probability of a specific goal to win a sales opportunity.

OPPORTUNITY TEAM BUILDER

The primary focus of any sales organization is to convert opportunities into successful deals. During this process, sellers go through different phases, one of which is building an opportunity team. The aim of the proposed Opportunity Team Builder (OTB) solution is to provide a framework to guide sellers throughout this process. We intentionally include sellers in the various stages of incrementally building the team, given their personal knowledge will have a follow-on effect on the team that is being built.

To understand the problem and underlying use case we dealt with, consider the following example scenario where a new seller with few experience in the company would like to build a team for a sales opportunity that will maximize success. The seller in this scenario is the *identifier* of the opportunity, which is one of the key roles and reflects the fact that, the opportunity is first discovered by that seller. First task for the seller is to start the OTB process through identifying the roles needed to handle this opportunity. Except for some roles which are predetermined and exist in every opportunity, like the *identifier*, OTB recommends a set of roles aiming to maximize success probability through the *role recommender task*. However, the user is also enabled to interact with the system at this stage through selecting the roles that seller thinks are most appropriate considering her expertise. This enables sellers to bring their own prioritization into the decision flow. Figure 1 shows a sample interface of this use case, where the seller is displayed with a set of roles. The seller enters herself as the identifier and selects the roles of "Line Item Owner", and "Brand Specialist" from the recommendations.

Once the user confirms which roles to include, next step is to select team members for each role recommended, and this is performed in an iterative role-by-role manner. During each iteration, one role is fulfilled, and the recommended sellers on the next iteration for a role depends on selected sellers on previous iterations. Although recommender task suggests a set of sellers towards maximizing win probability, the system suggests top k sellers, and users are involved in process by accepting or rejecting the suggested team members. Any modification on the team causes team profile to change, and seller recommendations are recalculated to take into account the changing team profile. Figure 2 shows an example interface, where the user decides who to work with on an opportunity by selecting members from recommended list.

Evidence on why an expert has been recommended is presented using the prediction model, such as experience with the product, the sector or the social connectivity of the candidate team member to the existing team. This enables sellers to bring their own priorities to bear on the process and influence further team member recommendations. For instance, for some sales opportunities it may be more important to have a team member with a high level of technical expertise in the product than to work with an expert that the user has a previous connection with.

As the team grows, the user can view the calculated success prediction and also the drill down into which factors are contributing to the predicted success of that team, as part of the team recommender interface. A focused example of the drill-down chart is given in Figure 3, where the screen in the background corresponds to a drilldown of the opportunity features of an actual team, and the foreground screen displays the changed confidence values after adding a new team member. The chart shows team confidence scores corresponding to different opportunity features, such as customer, country, etc., which are significant features linked to win probability. As team members are added, the team confidence values change, with the goal of increasing the predicted win probabil-

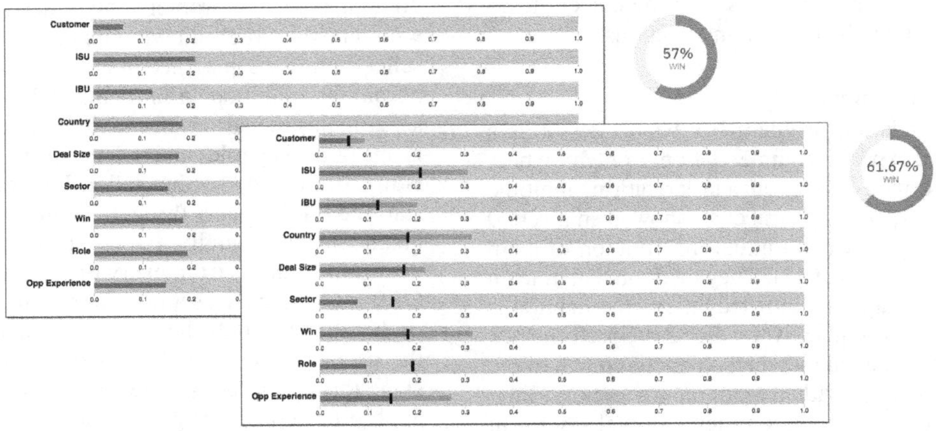

Figure 3. Drill down of the probability score, 4.67% increase in win probability when seller accepts the recommmended team

Table 1. Opportunity Dataset Features

categorical	dealsize, ibu, isu, country, sector, stage, team, customer
numerical	amount
date	dc (closing date), do (opening date)

ity. In Figure 3, the updated scores are shown after the user accepts the recommended team members. For instance, the isu confidence is increased from 20.90% to 30.60% whereas the sector confidence is decreased from 15.14% to 7.85%. The win prediction score is increased by 4.67% as shown in the foreground.

Solution Overview

OTB solution involves four main tasks, namely, *data processing* so as to analyse opportunity and seller data, *role recommendation, team recommendation*, and *opportunity output prediction* to realize the scenario described in the previous section. *User interface (UI)* of the OTB is the main module that exposes the whole functionality to the user in order to enable the user to integrate their expertise to the whole team formation process. The components of the solution are displayed in Figure 4.

OTB is based on data taken from a sales database, which is processed and analysed so as to extract information about sellers to form seller expertise metrics and their social connections to build a network graph. The team building process is initiated by *team role recommendation*, which recommends the required roles to handle a current opportunity. Once the required roles are determined, *team recommender* iteratively enables sellers to construct a seller team through recommending sellers to roles. The recommender uses the *win/loss prediction task* which gives a prediction for the result of the opportunity considering both the opportunity characteristics and the team dynamics. This task is used by the recommender to select the best candidate sellers among the others so as to maximize the probability of success.

In the following paragraphs, detailed descriptions of the solution components are presented.

Data Processing

The input to OTB is sales data which contains historical opportunity records. The data includes information about *opportunity signature, seller data* and the *sales team*, where opportunity signature and seller data represents features of an opportunity and seller, respectively. *Sales team*, on the other hand, represents the team members that handled the opportunity together with their associated roles.

Opportunity Analysis

Opportunity signature represents the features of an opportunity, which are, *dealsize, country, amount, stage, customer, isu, sector, ibu, date of opening* and *date of completion* as provided in Table 1. *Isu* stands for Industry Solution Unit, and *ibu* represents Industry Business Unit. All features except amount, *date of opening* and *date of completion* are categorical. *Amount* is numerical, and date of opening and completion are date fields representing the opportunity enterance and completion times.

The set of opportunities are denoted as $O = \{o_1, o_2, ..., o_n\}$ where each opportunity record o_i is represented as an ordered list of values, $o_i =< customer, do, dc, dealSize, amount, ibu, isu, country, sector, stage, team >$, which, except for the *team* field, correspond to relevant fields of the opportunity signature. Each feature f of an opportunity o can be denoted as o_f.

Opportunity *stage* stores the current status of the opportunity which can take three values, namely, {*won, loss, open.*} Once the opportunity is entered into the system, its stage is set to *open*. The stage does not change until the opportunity is finalized. $team_o = \{s_1, s_2, ..., s_m\}$ represents the *team* of an opportunity o of m sellers, where each seller s_i includes the role of the seller associated with o, denoted by $o_{s_i^{role}}$. More than one seller can share the same role and each seller can be assigned to different roles on an opportunity.

Seller Expertise Analysis

Seller metrics aim to reflect each individual seller's expertise on areas represented by opportunity feature values. Formally, each seller is represented by a vector of confidence values parametrized over *feature and time*. Time parametrization is

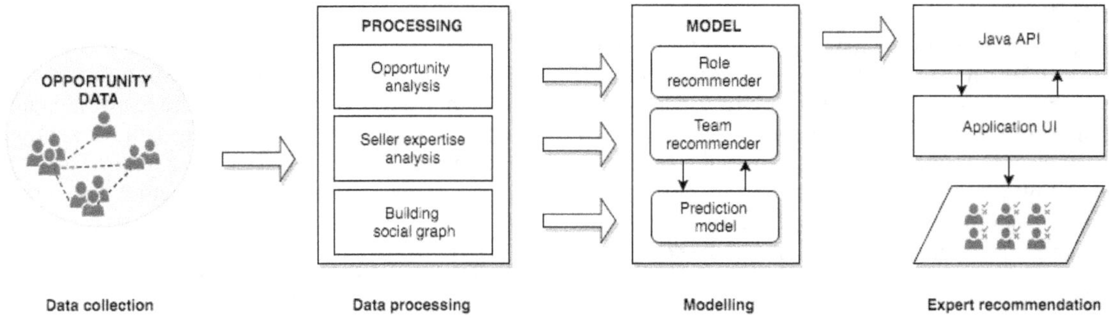

Figure 4. Solution Components

needed so as to have dynamic seller profiles that are updated each time a seller's experience is enhanced. In addition, this enables OTB to have more accurate seller profiling, which at the end leads to higher accuracy throughout the whole recommendation pipeline. Confidence scores are calculated using Equation 1:

$$conf_s(f,t) = ws(W_{s,f,t}, L_{s,f,t}) \quad (1)$$

where *ws* function in the equation stands for the lower bound of Wilson score confidence [1] interval for a Bernoulli parameter. $conf_s(f,t)$ reflects the confidence of seller s on feature f at time t, considering all the opportunities having f that s has dealt with and that have been closed before t. The motivation behind using Wilson score confidence interval is the following: we assume that, using the ratio of the number of opportunities that are won over lost considering a specific feature may not be accurate when we want to assess the expertise of the sellers. Considering the ratio may be problematic for a sample scenario including two sellers, one of whom has dealt with quite many opportunities and the other is a new seller with little opportunity experience, and their win/loss ratios happen to be the same. Therefore, using lower bound of Wilson score interval, we want to balance the proportion of wins with the uncertainty of a small number of opportunities dealt with so far.

$W_{s,f,t}$ and $L_{s,f,t}$ in Equation 1 represents the number of opportunities that are won and lost considering the feature f and time limit t, respectively, which are calculated as shown in Equation 2.

$$W_{s,f,t} = |O_{s,f}| \quad (2)$$

where

$$\forall o \in O_{s,f} | \{o_{dc} < t \quad \text{and} \quad s \in o_{team} \quad \text{and} \quad o_f = f \quad \text{and} \quad o_{stage} = won\} \quad (3)$$

where $O_{s,f}$ is the set of all opportunities having f that seller s has taken a role in and o_{dc} refers to the closing date of o. For the sake of keeping discussion short, $L_{s,f,t}$ calculation is omitted, however, it is calculated using the same equation given for calculating $W_{s,f,t}$, except for the change of controlling the stage as loss instead of won in the last conditional phrase.

For each seller existing in the system, confidence scores are calculated based on the opening date of each opportunity. In other words, for each opportunity o and seller s, where $o \in O$ and $s \in o_{team}$, $conf_s(f, o_{do})$ is calculated for predicting the stage of the opportunity o at time o_{do}, so as to consider the expertise of each seller by looking back all the opportunities the seller has dealt with prior to current opportunity. This enables us to accurately and exactly model seller profiles during training the model and the whole evaluation process, where each data point corresponds to an opportunity instance. Therefore, each opportunity's opening date establishes a timepoint in the model where a prediction is to be made.

As a result of confidence score calculations, each seller s according to an opportunity o is represented as given in Definition 4, where *role* corresponds to $o_{s_{role}}$:

$$s_o =< conf_s(f, o_{do}) | f \in \{customer, dealSize, ibu, isu, country, sector, stage, role\} > \quad (4)$$

Team Scoring

Constructing team related features involves two steps: *constructing seller metrics*, and *forming team scores*. The former is described in the previous section and in the following discussion, forming team confidence metrics out of individual team members' scores, that is the seller features, are described.

After confidence scores of the features for each team member within the sales team of an opportunity are calculated, a team score of each feature is assessed using Equation 5. Here, φ represents the function that calculates team score using individual scores. We evaluated $\varphi = max$ and $\varphi = avg$ so as to evaluate two hypotheses. First, we want to evaluate whether the confidence score of the team for a feature is dominated by the highest scored team member for that feature, which is realized by $\varphi = max$. Second, we experiment on setting the team score as the average score of all team members.

$$conf(o_{team}, f, o_{do}) = \forall s \in o_{team} \{\varphi(conf(s, f, o_{od}))\} \quad (5)$$

Building Social Graph

Opportunity teams are used to construct a social network of sellers, which is later on used by the team recommender during candidate seller ranking. In order to build the network, sellers are considered as nodes, and an edge is added between two sellers if they work together on a team of the same opportunity. Each link is enhanced with the number of won and lost opportunities, and this information is later on used by the recommender to rank sellers that are in closer connection in the social network.

The graph is constructed in two iterations, where the first iteration processes all the teams in O and added sellers to the network while constructing relations between them. The next iteration processes only the newly added ones so as to extend the graph with new relations and sellers.

Role Recommender

One of the first tasks that should be accomplished for team formation is to determine which roles are needed to handle the current opportunity. The roles may differ considering the customer, sector, or amount of the opportunity that is under consideration, which are part of the opportunity signature. The *role recommender* aims to assist sellers at this step, through identifying necessary job roles to be assigned to an opportunity considering the opportunity signature and previous similar opportunities.

The role recommender takes as input the opportunity dataset O, and the current opportunity oc, and it outputs a list of roles to be fulfilled for oc to maximize success probability. The whole process involves two steps, namely, *weighted similarity based opportunity ranking*, and *extracting frequent roles*.

First, the opportunities are ranked on a weighted basis to determine the most similar opportunities to the current opportunity signature. Here, to find the most similar opportunity items, a normalized feature weighted scheme is used, such that, for every feature $f \in \{customer, isu, country, sector, dollaramount\}$, w_f represents the weight of f for similarity based ranking. $|w_f|$ vector is determined according to both the user feedback taken during discussions with the sellers and the cardinality of the feature within the data, so as to normalize towards features that have high cardinality in comparison with the ones having low cardinality. The result of this process is a set of k opportunities, O^k_{oc} that are most similar to our current opportunity based on $|w_f|$. For similarity scoring, only the opportunities having $o_{stage} = won$ are considered.

After similar opportunities are determined, frequent roles within O^k_{oc} are extracted. To do so, o_{team} for each $o \in O^k_{oc}$ are considered as itemsets to find frequent co-occurring roles in opportunities that are most similar to oc. Once the frequent role sets are determined, they are ranked based on a voting scheme such that, the roles existing with high occurrence within the whole frequent sets are ranked at the top of the resulting role recommendation list.

Team Recommender

The aim of the proposed solution is to form the team that maximizes the win probability of the current opportunity entered into the sales database. Once the team roles necessary to assign an opportunity are identified, the next step is to find out the sellers who will best fit these roles. This is accomplished by the *team recommender* task, and the underlying algorithm is given in Algorithm 1.

Algorithm 1: Team Recommender Algorithm

Data: R: roles needed to be fulfilled , oc: current opportunity, O: opportunity dataset

Result: rec_team: recommended team for oc, $max\_winprob$: recommended team's predicted win probability score

```
1  rec_team ← {}
2  rec_team_metrics ←<>
3  seller_metrics ←<>
4  foreach role ∈ R do
5      candidates ← FindBestCandidates(oc,role)
6      foreach seller ∈ candidates do
7          sm ← SellerMetrics(seller, oc_do)
8          add sm to seller_metrics
9      end
10     team_score_vec ← TeamScore(rec_team_metrics)
11     current_winprob ← PredictionModel(team_score_vec)
12     display current_winprob to user
13     best_seller ←
         UserSelectBestCandidate(candidates,role)
14     modify rec_team, rec_team_metrics using
         seller_metrics, best_seller
15     team_score_vec ← TeamScore(rec_team_metrics)
16     max_winprob ← PredictionModel(team_score_vec)
17 end
18 return max_winprob, rec_team
```

The team recommender algorithm takes as input, a list of roles, R, which contains the roles identified by the *role recommender* for the opportunity oc to be fulfilled, and it returns the recommended list of sellers, *rec_team*, to fulfil these roles that best fit the opportunity oc, together with the team's predicted win probability, *max_winprob*.

The algorithm iteratively determines the best seller to fulfil a role (Lines 4-17). For each role, it first selects the best candidates using the *FindBestCandidate* method, which examines the current opportunity signature and seller metrics to find the candidate sellers that best fit the role (Line 5). Sellers that are in close connection with the members of the *rec_team* ranked higher than the other existing candidates identified by similarity ranking.

After candidate sellers are determined, and their metrics are added to be used later to *seller_metrics* (Lines 7,8), current team score and win probability is calculated (Lines 10,11). The user is shown the ranked list of sellers along with the ability to view the evidence and the predicted impact adding the seller will have on the win probability, and the key metrics that have been determined to influence a win (Line 12). After *UserSelectBestCandidate* (Line 13), the seller is added to the

Table 2. Prediction model parameters

opportunity related	o_amount, o_cust, o_ibu, o_isu, o_sector,o_country, o_dealsize
team related	t_custconf, t_ibuconf, t_isuconf, t_sectorconf, t_countryconf, t_dealsizeconf,t_oppexp, t_winconf, t_roleconf

recommendation. Selecting best candidate results in updating *rec_team* and *rec_team_metrics* accordingly (Line 14), and recalculating the team score and win probability (Lines 15,16). The process continues until all roles in R are covered.

Prediction Model

The *Prediction model* is created so as to assess and evaluate the probability of the outcome of current opportunity considering its signature and the team assigned. The success of a seller team assigned to an opportunity can depend on: 1. current opportunity dynamics, 2. expertise and properties of the team assigned to deal with it. To realize this, we built the prediction model on top of two different sets of features, namely, current *opportunity related* and *team related*, as listed in Table 2.

Opportunity related parameters reflect the current opportunity properties regardless of the team assigned. *Team related* parameters, on the other hand, reflect the team dynamics. In other words, they represent combined team performance considering expertise of the sellers on different features of the opportunity, such as country, sector or the deal-size. For instance, for a medium-sized opportunity in the communication sector, the probability of win will be higher if the seller team has members who have experience in that sector and has also dealt with a significant number of medium-sized opportunities that were won. We reflect these both in the seller metrics and team metrics construction, as described in data description.

The dataset was imbalanced in the number of instances in prediction classes. We used SMOTE [13] resampling method, which proceeds by oversampling the minority class by creating synthetic instances. Using SMOTE, the size of the original dataset was changed, leading to the same number of won and lost opportunities. After data is preprocessed through balancing and discretization, the prediction model is built using the *Extra-Trees classifier* package of scikit [1], which uses the results of *RandomForest algorithm* and the *Extra-Trees method*, and the prediction of the ensemble is calculated by averaging the prediction of the individual classifiers.

Assessing the Effect of Frequent Sub Teams

In addition to evaluating team performance using individual seller scores, we want to evaluate the effect of combined expertise of the team members on an opportunity. To measure team cooperation and overall combined expertise, we identify sub groups of sellers who worked together on different opportunities by using *FPClose algorithm* [10] from SPMF library [8]. To apply FPClose, we consider each seller team as an itemset and resulting frequent itemsets from the algorithm are frequent closed seller teams considering the provided support parameter.

Algorithm 2: Frequent Sub Team Based Team Score Calculation

Data: *FMT*: list of frequent teams, O: opportunity dataset
Result: team confidence scores

```
1  foreach o ∈ O do
2      newteam ← {}
3      foreach ft ∈ FMT do
4          if o_team has ft as sub team then
5              add ft to newteam
6          end
7      end
8      if newteam is not empty then
9          o_team ← newteam
10     end
11 end
12 foreach o ∈ O do
13     foreach s ∈ o_team do
14         calculateSellerMetric(s, o_do)
15     end
16 end
17 foreach o ∈ O do
18     calculateTeamMetric(o)
19 end
```

The frequent sub team based team score calculation is illustrated in Algorithm 2. After frequent closed teams are identified, each opportunity record is examined to find out, whether it involves any of the frequent teams as a sub team [Lines 1-11]. The calculation is performed in the same way as individual seller scores are calculated, where we consider a frequent sub team as one seller. In other words, we consider the opportunities that they tackled with together while we are calculating seller metrics. The motivation behind is to assess the influence of team collaboration on the prediction accuracy through considering a frequent team as one seller. If a seller team includes a frequent team as a sub team, that frequent subteam is added as a single seller to the team of the opportunity [Lines 4-6]. After each opportunity record is processed, team metrics are recalculated to be used with the recommender and prediction tasks [Lines 12-19].

Contribution of the User Interface

UI of OTB is a very essential part of the whole framework as it enables the user to be involved in team formation in an intelligent way during decision making points to both increase the system accuracy and achieve higher user satisfaction. In other words, with the UI, users can be involved in decision points like, selecting roles and revising team recommendations through adding/removing sellers. UI is designed such that, users can observe the impact of their changes immediately. As a result, their decisions become a part of the team formation algorithm whose benefit is two-fold: increased user satisfaction and better accuracy of the solution.

[1] http://scikit-learn.org/stable/modules/generated/sklearn.ensemble.ExtraTreesClassifier.html

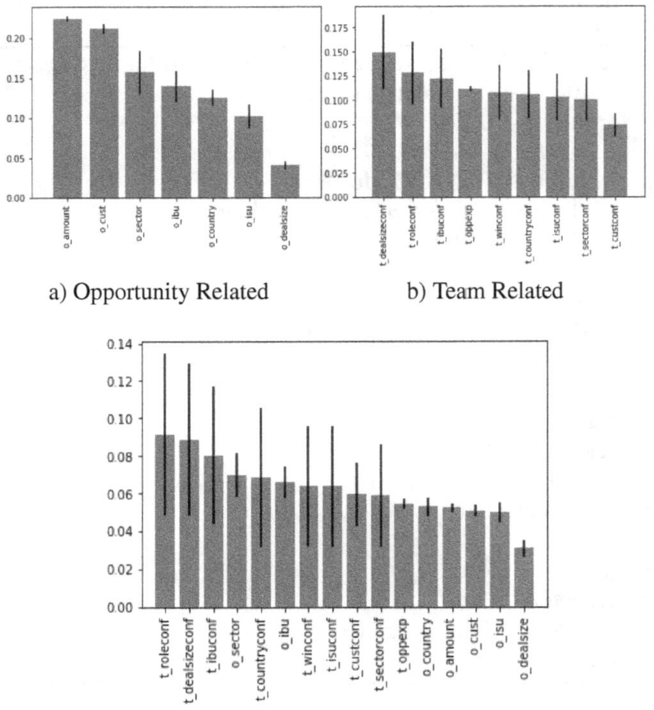

a) Opportunity Related b) Team Related

c) Combined

Figure 5. Feature Importance Distributions

EXPERIMENTS

In this section, experiments for the evaluation of OTB solution is given. In order to evaluate the proposed system in an exhaustive manner, we experiment with the prediction model and the whole OTB pipeline separately so as to analyse their standalone performances and the overall system performance. In addition, we conducted an initial user study with real sellers to assess an evaluation of the proposed system from end-user perspective. OTB user interface, role and team recommender tasks are implemented in Java and the prediction model is implemented in Python.

Dataset Characteristics

Data used during evaluation is taken from a real sales database spanning two years of sales records. The dataset includes *331K* opportunities and *40K* sellers. The number of opportunities a seller dealt with ranges between *1* to *54K*, where *37%* of the sellers dealt with more than *10* opportunities and *8.87%* of whole seller population has more than *100* opportunity experience.

Evaluation of Prediction Module

All the opportunities within the dataset are utilized to construct first the seller and then the team features. The evaluation of the prediction model uses only the finalized opportunities who are set to either win or lost, which makes around 251K opportunities.After resampling with SMOTE, we end up with an even distribution of the two prediction classes.

Methodology and Metrics

We divide the dataset on 80-20% basis to training and test sets respectively in a random manner. We evaluated six different variants of the prediction model in order to assess the effect of opportunity-related and team-related features and selecting either the average confidence score of the whole team or the dominant score within the team as the final team confidence value during team metric calculation.

We used precision, recall and F1 metrics to evaluate the model. We reported the evaluation results of each class separately to discuss the classification accuracy with respect to different opportunity outcomes.

Results

The results of the evaluation are given in Table 3. *PMOppMax*, *PMOppAvg* refers to the model using only the opportunity related features with $\varphi = max$ and $\varphi = avg$, respectively. *PMTeamMax*, *PMTeamAvg* uses only team related scores and *PMCombMax*, *PMCombAvg* uses both opportunity and team related features with φ set to *max* and *avg* as part of team metric calculation. p_win, p_loss, p_avg represents precision, r_win, r_loss, r_avg represents recall, and $f1\_win$, $f1\_loss$, $f1\_avg$ represents $f1$ values for wins, losses and average value over both prediction classes.

The results show that, the model has a higher accuracy in predicting losses in comparison with wins for all the variants. The overall accuracy is 75% when the model uses only the opportunity related features for both of the φ settings. We observe that φ setting results in different accuracies for both prediction classes, when only team related features are used, which is reasonable. Since using opportunity related features, we end up with same feature values to use in the model, as values are team-independent. However, φ setting makes a difference when we use only team features and combination of both feature classes, as selecting the dominant or average confidence score ends up with different feature values. Moreover, the results reveal the fact that, team related features increase the overall system performance and best performance is achieved when we use the combination of opportunity and team related features.

Figure 5 shows the Gini-importance values distribution of the features used during the prediction, where the importance of each feature is assesed by the normalized total reduction of the criterion brought by that feature. Both values of φ results in same distribution for different feature combination settings. As can be observed from the figures, the distribution of features change when the features are used individually and in combination. For opportunity related features on its own, the most important determiner is the amount of the opportunity, o_{amount}, whereas $t_{dealsizeconf}$ is the first in ranking for only team related features' setting. However these two determiners are similar in the sense that, they both reveal the importance of the size of the opportunity. On the other hand, for the combined version, we observe that, opportunity and team related features are mixed in the ranking and role confidence of the team appears to be the best determiner.

Table 3. Prediction Model Results

	p_win	p_loss	p_avg	r_win	r_loss	r_avg	f1_win	f1_loss	f1_avg
PMOppMax	0.57	0.82	0.75	0.48	0.86	0.76	0.52	0.84	0.75
PMOppAvg	0.57	0.82	0.75	0.48	0.86	0.76	0.52	0.84	0.75
PMTeamMax	0.58	0.87	0.79	0.67	0.82	0.78	0.62	0.84	0.78
PMTeamAvg	0.54	0.88	0.79	0.70	0.78	0.76	0.61	0.83	0.77
PMCombMax	0.66	0.86	0.80	0.60	0.88	0.81	0.63	0.87	0.80
PMCombAvg	0.65	0.86	0.80	0.61	0.88	0.80	0.63	0.87	0.80

Table 4. Frequent Team Based Prediction Model Results

	p_win	p_loss	p_avg	r_win	r_loss	r_avg	f1_win	f1_loss	f1_avg
PMCombinedMax	0.66	0.82	0.77	0.61	0.85	0.77	0.63	0.83	0.77
PMCombinedFTMax	0.68	0.81	0.78	0.62	0.85	0.77	0.65	0.82	0.78

Evaluation of Frequent Team Based Prediction

Frequent teams are built by setting the support parameter to *2*. Only the teams having at most *10* members are used, since we assume that, larger teams may lack the assumption of behaving like one seller. We select the first *10K* opportunities that have the earliest date of entry into the system. Within this set, we include only the wins and losses in evaluation. Seller teams recorded on these opportunities are processed to find out whether they have any of the extracted frequent subteams; and if so, metrics of those subteams considering the opening date of that opportunity are constructed. The dataset is divided to training and test sets in a random 80-20% manner.

The results of the evaluation are displayed in Table 4, where *PMCombinedFTMax* refers to the variant of the model that uses frequent teams. Both variants use combined features and $\varphi = max$. As it is observed from the results, frequent team based technique has not improved the overall accuracy significantly. It results in a 2% increased accuracy for wins, and 1% decrease in losses. This may be due to the fact that, many teams involve few people and those people have similar histories in terms of dealt opportunities. Since we examine a shorter time period by considering 10K opportunities, this may lead to having same metric values as features for both individuals and frequent teams. Our future work is planned to elaborate this approach towards including a longer time period and increasing the support value to better differentiate the cohesion in frequent teams from individual seller scores.

Evaluation of OTB

In order to evaluate our complete team recommender solution we selected 2000 real sales opportunities.

We compared the predicted win ratio of the sales teams based on three scenarios:

- Actual Team: Here we measure the win probability of the real world sales team taking into account the sellers expertise and the opportunity features as described in the previous section.
- Recommended *FindBestCandidate* Team: Here we evaluate the baseline recommender strategy that does not take into account the predicted impact adding an individual seller to the team will have. The real world opportunity features were extracted along with the roles that were required to fulfil the opportunity. The Opportunity Identifier was kept the same in order to simulate a seller creating a new opportunity and building a team from scratch. For each role on the opportunity the Team recommender was queried to provide the selection of candidate experts. In this case we simply selected the highest ranked seller and added them to the opportunity before moving on to the next available role. This is because each new team member can influence the following team recommendations.
- Recommended Expert with Win Prediction: Similar to the previous scenario team recommender is queried to return the top-*k* experts for a given role. However instead of selecting the highest ranking seller, the win/lose prediction model is called in order to assess the impact of the seller. The seller with the highest predicted impact is added, filling the roles in an incremental process.

We evaluate the two recommender strategies based on the predicted improvement in win probability with a value of *k*=10. The results of the evaluation are presented in Table 5.

When evaluating the scenarios where OTB increases the win probability the average increase was in the order of 1-2% with a maximum of 12% increase. Although the overall increase was modest, it should be noted that in general we created teams as good if not better than those created by sellers meaning our system can assist users new to a the role to find experts to join their team without seeking recommendations and assistance from others. When evaluating the rank in the returned candidate sellers list that was eventually added to the team using the MaxWinPredCandidate strategy, 80% were in the top 4 suggesting increasing the value of *k* would have limited impact. This could be because of the similarity of the sellers returned. As a result, a candidate seller recommendation strategy that increased diversity of skills could have an impact on further improving results.

User Study Results

In order to validate the continued development and changes to the application, informal in-person interviews were carried out with sellers. The participants of the user study were sellers of a company who are at various stages of their career ranging from 5 months to 30+ years' experience. The participants were selected from different sales departments and a list of questions were asked about the interviewee's previous team formation experience, and a short demonstration of the system allowed the sellers to understand the aims of the project and give general feedback on their experience of the system. The interviews were directed to attempt to uncover if the quality of the recommendations could be validated by finding out if the list of experts suggested made sense to the user and also their experience of the overall system and what they would see as possible aids to the team formation process. A number of themes emerged:

Current tools and solutions: All interviewees reported leveraging their personal networks to build the team for the opportunities and asking more experienced sellers for recommendations. When asked about their use of existing internal tools that could be used to aid in the task of opportunity team formation, options listed included the internal company directory of self-reported skills. This solution was reported by multiple interviewees as not being able to provide an accurate assessment of individuals' expertise. Interest was shown in the evidence-based UI which could help solve this issue.

The value of Team Recommendations: Of particular interest were the responses of the sellers who had less than one years' experience with the company, but several years of sales experience outside of the company. *"The biggest challenge is to know who to talk to internally"*, having a team member who understands who to navigate internal processes was perceived as very important to achieve a successful sale. OTB was seen as a potential solution to this problem through providing evidence based recommendations.

Validation of recommendations: Test scenarios were presented to the respondents based on the product and sectors that they worked in. The respondents largely agreed with the roles suggested by the system for a successful opportunity based on the opportunity parameters provided. Some of the lower-ranked roles were suggested as being unnecessary. An experienced seller who was an expert in their product area validated the recommendations by stating that he would be happy to work with 7 or 8 of the 10 recommendations shown for each of the repeated scenarios as we built the team.

User control: As previous studies have shown, the interviewees responded well to being able to inspect and control the interactions, [14]; by filling in the parameters and being afforded the option to accept and reject sellers and see the evidential explanations for the basis of the recommendations.

An issue which came to light was the differing opinions between interviewees in their opinions on what were the important factors in picking team members. Some stated that a previous relationship with the client was considered just as important as ensuring that the salesperson was a technical expert in that particular product. This was reported differently in the Cloud sales and services division where it was reported that sellers needed to be extremely technically competent. This supports the design decision of separating out the two tasks of expert identification and expert selection, where the user is able to influence the incremental team formation taking into account their own knowledge and preferences. Future work could go further by giving the user the ability to influence the overall weighting of parameters in the expert identification process or by learning these preferences.

Table 5. OTB Recommender Results: Impact on Win Probability

	decrease	neutral	increase
BestCandidate	36%	37%	27%
MaxWinPredCandidate	6.27%	24.12%	69.6%

Time in role: One issue which came up in the interviews with experienced sellers was that of predicted adoption of the technology. Experienced sellers would be less likely to use the tool as they already know the network of people in their field that they would ask. *"Now it isn't a problem, I know who to ask but that is something you learn. I have established my network of people which took at least a year to get a feeling of who to ask."* It was perceived as being more helpful when they would be called upon to work with people from other branches in the company, in different countries and experts from the delivery side.

CONCLUSION AND FUTURE WORK

In this paper, we formalized the problem of team formation in sales and proposed a novel solution, OTB, that utilizes a set of models to assist sellers during their team formation process to handle opportunities. The whole process involves determining the roles that is needed to handle an opportunity and later on assigning people to the roles that best fit their expertise. This pipeline at the end aims to maximize the probability of win by using role recommender, team recommender and prediction models, where these models work in coordination with each other. There does not exist many related work that dealt with team recommendation problem, and the problem solved by OTB is different in the sense that, it involves selecting both the roles and the people to assign to these roles to maximize the win probability. To do so, it has to select the most appropriate set of roles and the corresponding sellers to fulfil them, which will at the end aim to result in success. Although the problem is applied to sales domain, it can easily be extended to handle team recommendation in another domain with a similar data setting.

Substantial experiments performed on both the prediction model and the team recommender showed that, the model can successfully predict the outcome of the opportunities and the overall team recommendation increases the win probability of the opportunities through assigning roles and sellers that better fit the opportunity requirements. An initial user study has been conducted, however, we plan to extend the user study towards collecting more data around their satisfaction for the whole solution and the model reasoning provided. In addition, we plan to eloborate the frequent team effect further by conducting experiments on a larger volume of the data and experimenting on the support parameter.

ACKNOWLEDGMENTS

We would like to acknowledge the support and collaboration of the CAO team: Alice Chang, Claire Tian, Casey Klippel, Ben J Dubiel, and Chen Xu; for their valuable insights into the realm of digital sellers.

REFERENCES

1. Alan and Brent A. Coull. 1998. Approximate is Better than Exact for Interval Estimation of Binomial Proportions. *The American Statistician* 52 (1998), 119–126.
2. Sinan Aral, Erik Brynjolfsson, and Marshall W Van Alstyne. 2008. Antecedents and Consequences of Mutual Knowledge in Teams. (2008).
3. Ronald S Burt. 2004. Structural holes and good ideas. *American journal of sociology* 110, 2 (2004), 349–399.
4. Pedro Terras Crespo and ClÃąudia Antunes. 2015. Predicting teamwork results from social network analysis. *Expert Systems* 32, 2 (2015), 312 – 325.
5. Anwitaman Datta, Jackson Tan Teck Yong, and Anthony Ventresque. 2011. T-RecS: Team Recommendation System Through Expertise and Cohesiveness. In *Proceedings of the 20th International Conference Companion on World Wide Web (WWW '11)*. ACM, New York, NY, USA, 201–204. DOI: http://dx.doi.org/10.1145/1963192.1963289
6. Anwitaman Datta, Jackson Tan Teck Yong, and Stefano Braghin. 2014. The zen of multidisciplinary team recommendation. *Journal of the Association for Information Science and Technology* 65, 12 (2014), 2518 – 2533. http://search.ebscohost.com.ucd.idm.oclc.org/login.aspx?direct=true&db=bth&AN=99454639&site=ehost-live
7. Elnaz Davoodi, Keivan Kianmehr, and Mohsen Afsharchi. 2013. A semantic social network-based expert recommender system. *Applied Intelligence* 39, 1 (01 Jul 2013), 1–13.
8. Lin C.W. Gomariz A. Gueniche T. Soltani A. Deng Z. Lam H. T. Fournier-Viger, P. 2016. The SPMF Open-Source Data Mining Library Version 2.. In *Proc. 19th European Conference on Principles of Data Mining and Knowledge Discovery (PKDD 2016)*. Springer LNCS 9853, 36–40.
9. Vassilis C. Gerogiannis, Elli Rapti, Anthony Karageorgos, and Panos Fitsilis. 2015. On Using Fuzzy Linguistic 2-tuples for the Evaluation of Human Resource Suitability in Software Development Tasks. *Adv. Soft. Eng.* 2015, Article 1 (Jan. 2015), 1 pages. DOI: http://dx.doi.org/10.1155/2015/695873
10. Gosta Grahne and Jianfei Zhu. 2005. Fast Algorithms for Frequent Itemset Mining Using FP-Trees. *IEEE Trans. on Knowl. and Data Eng.* 17, 10 (Oct. 2005), 1347–1362. DOI: http://dx.doi.org/10.1109/TKDE.2005.166
11. Ido Guy, Inbal Ronen, and Eric Wilcox. 2009. Do you know?: recommending people to invite into your social network. In *Proceedings of the 14th international conference on Intelligent user interfaces*. ACM, 77–86.
12. Jungpil Hahn and Mani R Subramani. 2000. A framework of knowledge management systems: issues and challenges for theory and practice. In *Proceedings of the twenty first international conference on Information systems*. Association for Information Systems, 302–312.
13. N.V. Chawla K.W. Bowyer L.O. Hall W.P. Kegelmeyer. 2002. SMOTE: Synthetic Minority Over-Sampling Technique. *J. Artificial Intelligence Research* 16 (2002), 321–357.
14. Bart P Knijnenburg, Svetlin Bostandjiev, John O'Donovan, and Alfred Kobsa. 2012. Inspectability and control in social recommenders. In *Proceedings of the sixth ACM conference on Recommender systems*. ACM, 43–50.
15. David W McDonald and Mark S Ackerman. 2000. Expertise recommender: a flexible recommendation system and architecture. In *Proceedings of the 2000 ACM conference on Computer supported cooperative work*. ACM, 231–240.
16. Sean M. McNee, John Riedl, and Joseph A. Konstan. 2006. Being Accurate is Not Enough: How Accuracy Metrics Have Hurt Recommender Systems. In *CHI '06 Extended Abstracts on Human Factors in Computing Systems (CHI EA '06)*. ACM, New York, NY, USA, 1097–1101. DOI: http://dx.doi.org/10.1145/1125451.1125659
17. Tim Reichling, Michael Veith, and Volker Wulf. 2007. Expert Recommender: Designing for a Network Organization. *Computer Supported Cooperative Work (CSCW)* 16, 4 (01 Oct 2007), 431–465. DOI: http://dx.doi.org/10.1007/s10606-007-9055-2
18. Tim Reichling and Volker Wulf. 2009. Expert Recommender Systems in Practice: Evaluating Semi-automatic Profile Generation. In *Proceedings of the SIGCHI Conference on Human Factors in Computing Systems (CHI '09)*. ACM, New York, NY, USA, 59–68. DOI: http://dx.doi.org/10.1145/1518701.1518712
19. D. Surian, N. Liu, D. Lo, H. Tong, E. P. Lim, and C. Faloutsos. 2011. Recommending People in Developers' Collaboration Network. In *2011 18th Working Conference on Reverse Engineering*. 379–388. DOI: http://dx.doi.org/10.1109/WCRE.2011.53

Combining Brain-Computer Interface and Eye Tracking for High-Speed Text Entry in Virtual Reality

Xinyao Ma, Zhaolin Yao, Yijun Wang, Weihua Pei, Hongda Chen
Institute of Semiconductors, Chinese Academy of Sciences, Beijing, China
University of Chinese Academy of Sciences, Beijing, China
Center for Excellence in Brain Science and Intelligence Technology, Chinese Academy of Sciences, Shanghai, China
mxy1108@gmail.com; {yaozhaolin, wangyj, peiwh, hdchen}@semi.ac.cn

ABSTRACT

Gaze interaction provides an efficient way for users to communicate and control in virtual reality (VR) presented by head-mounted displays. In gaze-based text-entry systems, eye tracking and brain-computer interface (BCI) are the two most commonly used approaches. This paper presents a hybrid BCI system for text entry in VR by combining steady-state visual evoked potentials (SSVEP) and eye tracking. The user interface in VR designed a 40-target virtual keyboard using a joint frequency-phase modulation method for SSVEP. Eye position was measured by an eye-tracking accessory in the VR headset. Target-related gaze direction was detected by combining simultaneously recorded SSVEP and eye position data. Offline and online experiments indicate that the proposed system can type at a speed around 10 words per minute, leading to an information transfer rate (ITR) of 270 bits per minute. The results further demonstrate the superiority of the hybrid method over single-modality methods for VR applications.

Author Keywords

Brain-computer interface; steady-state visual evoked potentials; eye tracking; virtual reality; text entry

ACM Classification Keywords

Multi-modal interfaces; Intelligent wearable, mobile and ubiquitous interfaces

INTRODUCTION

Gaze interaction is one of the most common ways for people with motor disabilities to navigate and control their computer with their eyes [18]. Gaze interaction only requires the movement of the eyes without any need for other additional muscle control, which makes it a perfect solution for those with disabilities such as spinal cord injury (SCI), repetitive strain injury (RSI), and amyotrophic lateral sclerosis (ALS) to communicate with their environments. Gaze interaction approaches including eye tracking, electrooculogram (EOG), and brain-computer interface (BCI) have been widely used in augmentative and alternative communication (AAC) systems [5].

Eye tracking is the predominant method used for gaze interaction nowadays. Eye-tracking devices detect eye positions by processing visible light or infrared images of the eyes captured by a camera. Towards different applications, desktop-mounted and head-mounted eye trackers have been developed by eye-tracking companies such as Tobii [19]. Eye tracking based text entry techniques have been well established and an eye typing system can be implemented by combining an eye tracker with a virtual keyboard interface on the computer screen [10]. In general, eye tracking based typing speed ranges from 5-10 words per minute (wpm) [11]. Although high-performance eye trackers can detect eye movements with high accuracy and precision, current applications of eye tracking are still limited because the system is always expensive and the tracking performance is sensitive to environmental factors such as light condition.

BCIs provide a very promising technique for interaction with computers by establishing a direct link between human brain and computer [20]. Using frequency or time domain coding methods, gaze detection can be realized by visual BCIs based on visual evoked potentials (VEPs) and P300 potentials recorded by scalp electroencephalogram (EEG) [4]. In BCI based text-entry systems, steady-state visual evoked potentials (SSVEP) have shown high performance and usability. For example, Chen et al. [2] developed an SSVEP-based BCI speller with a typing speed around 10 wpm, which was comparable to the eye-tracking approach. Furthermore, combining BCIs with other assistive technologies have received increasing attention in recent years [12]. A hybrid BCI system that combines a traditional BCI with other physiological signals has shown great advantages in BCI performance and system flexibility [16, 13]. For example, eye tracking and BCI methods have been combined to develop hybrid BCIs [8, 9].

Recently, with the proliferation of virtual reality (VR) headsets such as HTC Vive and Oculus Rift, human-computer interface design in VR opens a new frontier, as

IUI'18, March 7–11, 2018, Tokyo, Japan

ACM ISBN 978-1-4503-4945-1/18/03...$15.00
https://doi.org/10.1145/3172944.3172988

the traditional mouse-keyboard configuration is no longer the best interaction method inside VR environments. HTC Vive [15] uses active motion-tracked handheld controllers with input buttons and triggers to interact with the environment, which is reliable but not intuitive and may cause fatigue. Alternatively, gaze input provides an efficient way for interaction in VR applications because of its intuitive and immersive style. On one hand, eye-tracking accessories in VR head-mounted displays (VRHMD) have been proposed and developed [17]. On the other hand, gaze control has been realized in recent VR-based BCI studies [6]. Technically, for applications such as text entry in VRHMDs, eye tracking and BCI methods can be easily combined towards improved accuracy and precision. However, to our knowledge, gaze-based text entry in consumer VR headsets has not been reported yet.

In this paper, we designed and implemented a hybrid gaze-based text-entry system in VR for high-speed typing. The system combined an SSVEP-based BCI with a low-cost eye-tracking module in VRHMD. With a virtual keyboard, gaze direction was detected by combining simultaneously recorded SSVEP and eye position data. To evaluate system performance, this study designed offline and online experiments to simulate text entry tasks. In addition, classification results corresponding to the hybrid method and the single-modality methods were estimated separately for comparison. The contributions of this paper include: a) a viable solution for robust and intuitive high-speed gaze interaction in VR, b) a hybrid method to combine SSVEP BCIs and low-cost eye-tracking devices, and c) a general experimental platform for VR-based BCI research [7, 1].

METHODS

System Design

This study designed a hybrid gaze-based text-entry system using an HTC Vive VR platform. Figure 1 shows the system architecture with closed-loop data flow. EEG data were acquired using a Synamps2 system from Neuroscan (https://compumedicsneuroscan.com/). Eye positions were measured with an embedded infrared eye-tracking module: aGlass DKI from 7invensun (https://www.7invensun.com). All software programs ran on a computer (with an Intel core i7 processor and an NVIDIA GTX1080 graphic card) supporting the HTC Vive platform. The VRHMD used two screens (one per eye) and each screen had a resolution of 1080×1200 pixels. The text-entry software was written in C# in Unity 3D engine and SteamVR platform, which rendered 3D scene inside HMD to give the user an immersive 3D perception at a 90Hz refresh rate. The software included programs for stimulus presentation, data communication, data analysis, and feedback presentation. Eye position data were collected using aGlass SDK in real time. A separate computer was used to record and transfer real-time EEG data to the VR computer through TCP/IP. Event triggers (i.e., stimulus onset) from the VR computer were sent to the EEG system through a parallel port for synchronizing event and EEG data.

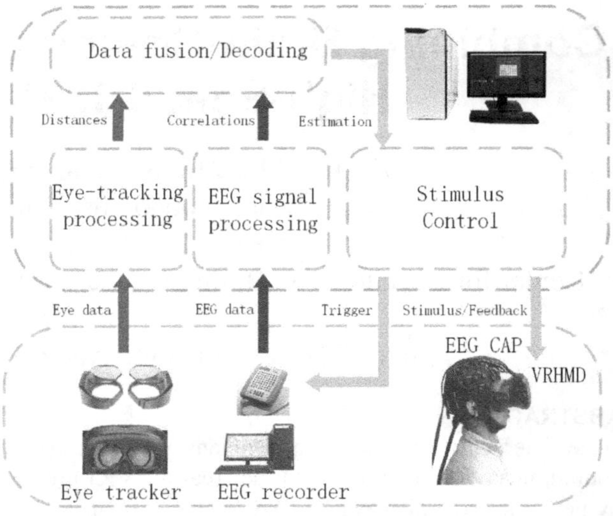

Figure 1. Diagram of the hybrid text entry system. EEG and eye position data are measured and processed simultaneously to detect gaze direction for text entry in VRHMD.

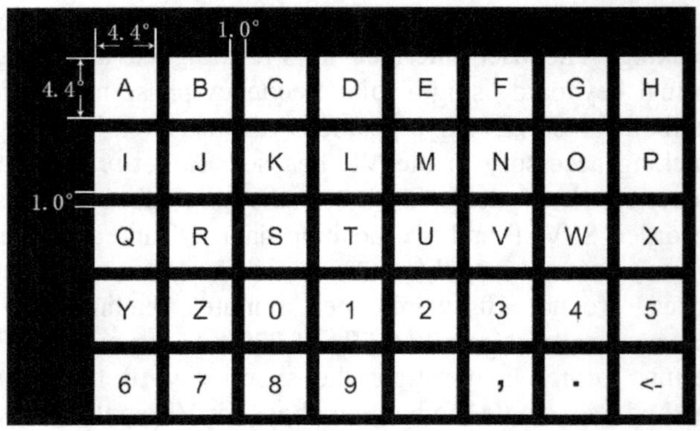

Figure 2. Layout of the virtual keyboard in VR.

As shown in Figure 2, the stimulus program adopted a 40-target virtual keyboard designed for an SSVEP BCI speller [2], which was a 5×8 matrix containing 40 characters (26 English alphabet letters, 10 digits, and 4 other symbols). For multi-target SSVEP coding, 40 characters were tagged differently using a joint frequency-phase modulation (JFPM) method (frequency range: 8-15.8Hz with an interval of 0.2Hz, phase interval between two adjacent frequencies: 0.35π) [2]. As shown in Figure 2, the width and height of each character were 4.4° and the horizontal and vertical distances between two neighbors were 1.0°. The virtual keyboard seen in VRHMD corresponded to the actual situation where a person sat at a distance of 60cm in front of a 22-inch computer monitor.

For data communication, EEG data and eye-tracking data were received and recorded separately by the stimulus program. For offline analysis, data files were saved for further analysis using Matlab (Mathworks, Inc.). For online analysis, an online data processing program was developed in an Anaconda Python environment. EEG data transferred by TCP/IP were directly thrown into the online processing program. Eye-tracking data were saved to files by the stimulus program, and loaded automatically into the online processing program. The online processing program further performed a hybrid data fusion algorithm for target identification, and returned the results to the stimulus program for feedback presentation.

Experiment Design

Eleven healthy subjects (2 females and 9 males, aged 19-29 years) with normal or corrected to normal vision participated in the experiment. The subject first wore EEG cap and then fixed the HMD as shown in Figure 1. Nine electrodes over the parietal and occipital areas (Pz, PO5, PO3, POz, PO4, PO6, O1, Oz, O2) were used to record SSVEPs at a sampling rate of 1000Hz. Eye position data were recorded by the eye-tracking module with a monocular (right eye) mode at a sampling rate of 120Hz. For each subject, eye tracking was calibrated through pupil alignment and a 9-points calibration procedure.

This study designed separate offline and online experiments to evaluate system performance using a cue-guided target selection task [2]. All subjects took part in the offline experiment, and two of them (S1 and S5) joined in the online experiment on a different day. In the offline experiment, all participants were asked to accomplish eight blocks of target selection. In each block, all 40 characters were cued sequentially in a random order. Each trial lasted 1.8 seconds in total. At the beginning of each trial, a red square appeared as the target cue for 0.8 seconds. Subjects were asked to direct their gaze to the target as soon as possible. After the cue, all stimuli started to flicker for 1 second. Subjects were asked to avoid blinks during stimulation. EEG and eye-tracking data were saved for offline analysis. In the online experiment, stimulation duration was reduced to 0.3 seconds towards high information transfer rates (ITRs) [14]. After an 8-blocks training procedure, the subjects performed an online 4-blocks test with algorithms trained from the training data. A blue square at the target location flashed for 0.2 seconds as feedback after online data analysis.

EEG Data Analysis

Data epochs for the nine-channel SSVEP signals were extracted according to event triggers generated by the stimulus program and then down-sampled to 250Hz. A filter bank method [3] with the frequency range of 8-88Hz was used to decompose SSVEP signals into seven sub-band components to cover multiple harmonics of SSVEPs.

For SSVEP detection, this study employed the task-related component analysis (TRCA) algorithm [14] to design spatial filters for SSVEP, and then implemented a template-matching based target identification method. After spatial filtering, the correlation coefficient between the projections of single-trial test data $\boldsymbol{X}$ and an individual template $\overline{\boldsymbol{X}}_k$ for the k-th visual stimulus was calculated as:

$$\rho_k = \rho(\boldsymbol{X}^T\boldsymbol{W}, \overline{\boldsymbol{X}}_k^T\boldsymbol{W})$$

where $\boldsymbol{W}$ consisted of spatial filters corresponding to all N_f stimulus frequencies:

$$\boldsymbol{W} = \left[\boldsymbol{w}_1\ \boldsymbol{w}_2\ \dots\ \boldsymbol{w}_{N_f}\right].$$

The stimulus frequency with the maximal correlation coefficient was selected as the target frequency. For each trial, the correlation coefficient vector was used for data fusion with eye-tracking data.

Eye Tracking Data Analysis

Eye positions were tracked in combination with head attitude measured by the HMD. A 9-points calibration was performed to map the gaze points onto the 2D keyboard plane within a normalized coordinate system. The whole virtual keyboard was visible and trackable in the coordinate system. Eye tracking analysis was performed by two methods. The first method was based on the prediction of coordinate values according to calibration. The mean coordinates of the gaze point from a certain period after the visual cue was used to calculate Euclidean distance to all 40 characters. The character with the minimal distance was chosen as the target. The second method was a template-matching method in which the gaze point was estimated by comparing with the training data. The template coordinates for 40 eye-gaze points corresponding to the 40 characters were calculated by averaging across all training trials. The distances between the test gaze point and the template coordinates were calculated. The character with the minimal distance was then selected as the target.

In addition to target detection, this study also evaluated accuracy and precision of the eye-tracking module [18]. Across eight trials for each character, eye-tracking points of each trial were averaged, and then the tracking accuracy and precision were calculated for each character.

Hybrid Data Fusion

To combine information from SSVEP and eye tracking, a hybrid data fusion method was developed to enhance target detection. The hybrid decision model was defined as:

$$R_{hybrid} = R_{EEG} \times ACC_{EEG}^2 + \frac{1}{D_{EYE}} \times ACC_{EYE}^2$$

where R_{EEG} was the correlation coefficients between SSVEP and individual templates, D_{EYE} was the distances between gaze coordinates and trained templates, ACC_{EEG} and ACC_{EYE} were the weights obtained by calculating the averaged classification accuracy of the EEG and eye-tracking methods. Both R_{EEG} and $\frac{1}{D_{EYE}}$ were normalized to zero mean and unit variance. To estimate ACC_{EEG} and ACC_{EYE}, leave-one-out cross-validation was performed with the training data to calculate the averaged classification accuracy corresponding to EEG and eye tracking separately. The hybrid method chose the k-th character with the maximal R_k as the target character.

RESULTS AND DISCUSSION

Performance of SSVEP BCI

This study employed the TRCA-based method to detect SSVEP. The offline classification accuracy and ITR (in bits per minute, bpm) [20] were estimated using a leave-one-out cross-validation method. Table 1 lists the classification accuracy and ITR with a data length of 0.3 seconds. The

Subject	Eye-calibrated		Eye-template		EEG-template		Hybrid	
Metrics	Acc	ITR	Acc	ITR	Acc	ITR	Acc	ITR
S1	60	123	80	194	89	234	**97**	272
S2	65	140	92	247	43	72	**95**	261
S3	47	84	71	160	**96**	268	95	263
S4	77	182	98	277	**99**	287	**99**	287
S5	50	94	87	225	90	235	**96**	270
S6	49	90	84	211	70	156	**91**	243
S7	80	194	99	283	70	157	**99**	287
S8	80	196	97	273	85	217	**99**	285
S9	35	51	91	244	75	176	**95**	260
S10	66	144	83	208	**97**	272	**97**	272
S11	70	156	87	224	89	233	**96**	266
Mean	62	132	88	232	82	210	96	270
Std	14	46	8	36	15	60	2	12

Table 1. Accuracy (%) and ITRs (bpm) for all subjects using a data length of 0.3 seconds. Results for the eye tracking, EEG, and hybrid methods were calculated separately for comparison. Values in bold indicate the best accuracy.

averaged accuracy across all subjects is 82 ± 15%, while the averaged ITR is 210 ± 60bpm. Figure 3 illustrates the classification results using different data lengths. The accuracy increases when data length increases. After around 0.3 seconds, the accuracy for EEG becomes comparable to the eye-tracking method. ITR peaks around 0.35 seconds. These results are consistent with previous studies using LCD monitors as stimulus platforms [2, 14], demonstrating the efficiency of SSVEP BCIs in VR environments.

Performance of Eye Tracking

This study calculates two types of accuracy for the eye tracking system. As shown in Table 1, the eye-calibrated method obtained averaged accuracy of 62±14%. The low classification accuracy was caused by the relatively low tracking accuracy of the low-cost eye-tracking module. The supervised eye-template method achieved significantly higher classification accuracy of 88±8%. The tracking accuracy for the experiment setting in this study was roughly estimated as 3.1±2.7 degrees and the tracking precision was 1.8±1.5 degrees. The tracking precision was higher for targets with small viewing angles (i.e., central areas in the keyboard). As shown in Figure 3, eye tracking could reach stable classification accuracy within a very short time window around 50ms. Different from SSVEP, longer data length doesn't improve the classification accuracy for eye tracking. This is due to the fact that accuracy and precision of eye tracking is time invariant.

Performance of the Hybrid System

The hybrid method achieved higher performance than the single-modality methods. As shown in Table 1, the averaged classification accuracy is 96±2% and the ITR is 270±12bpm. One-way repeated-measures analysis of variance (ANOVA) shows that there is significant difference of accuracy between the four different methods ($F(3, 43)=16.45$, $p<10^{-5}$). Bonferroni corrected post-hoc pairwise comparisons using paired t-tests indicate the improvements of accuracy for the hybrid method are significant (vs. eye-calibrated: $p<10^{-5}$, vs. eye-template: $p<0.05$, vs. EEG-template: $p<0.05$). As shown

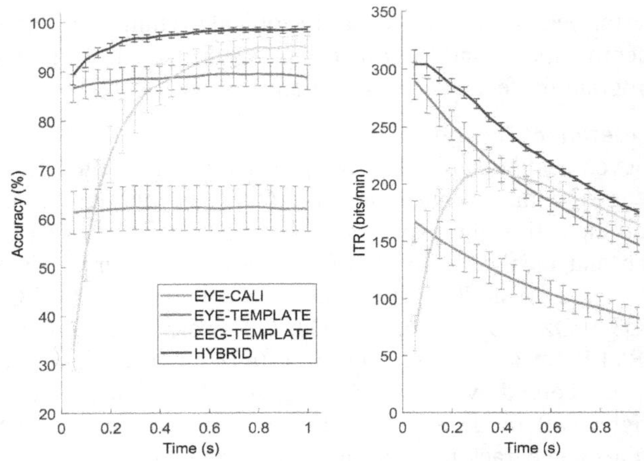

Figure 3. Classification accuracy and ITRs using different data lengths (from 50ms to 1000ms with a step of 50ms). The error bars represent standard errors.

in Figure 3, the hybrid method showed very consistent improvements of accuracy and ITRs at all data lengths compared with the single-modality methods. Furthermore, the hybrid accuracy is significantly higher than the method in which the single modality with higher performance was chosen for each subject (96% vs. 93%, $p<0.01$).

Online Validation

Two subjects (S1, S5) participated in the online experiment. The online processing program took about 16ms to implement the hybrid algorithm. For S1, accuracies for EEG and eye tracking were 88% and 93% respectively, and the hybrid method achieved accuracy of 97%. For S5, accuracies for EEG, eye tracking, and the hybrid method were 89%, 92%, and 98%. Hybrid classification results in the online test were consistent to those in the offline analysis (S1: 97%, S5: 96%), which proved the feasibility of the proposed method for online applications.

CONCLUSION

This study presents a hybrid BCI for high-speed text entry in VRHMD by combining SSVEP and eye tracking. A 40-target virtual keyboard was designed for eliciting SSVEPs and tracking gaze at the same time. A hybrid decision model was proposed for gaze detection. With a cue-guided target selection task, both offline and online experiments indicate that the proposed system can input text at a speed around 10wpm (1.1s per character), leading to an averaged ITR of 270bpm, which is comparable to the highest ITR reported in BCI studies [2]. The results also demonstrate the superiority of the hybrid method over the single-modality methods. Future work will focus on improvement of eye tracking and data fusion methods, as well as the implementation of real text-entry applications in VR environments.

ACKNOWLEDGEMENTS

This work is supported in part by the National Key Research and Development Plan (2017YFA0205903), the National Natural Science Foundation of China (61671424, 61335010, and 61634006), National Science Foundation of China (AWS16J028), Thousand Youth Talents Plan, and Beijing S&T planning task (Z161100002616019).

RFERENCES

1. Jessica D. Bayliss and Dana H. Ballard. 2000. A virtual reality testbed for brain-computer interface research. *IEEE Transactions on Rehabilitation Engineering* 8, 2: 188-190.
2. Xiaogang Chen, Yijun Wang, Masaki Nakanishi, Xiaorong Gao, Tzyy-Ping Jung, and Shangkai Gao. 2015. High-speed spelling with a noninvasive brain-computer interface. *Proceedings of the National Academy of Sciences* 112, 44: E6058-E6067.
3. Xiaogang Chen, Yijun Wang, Shangkai Gao, Tzyy-Ping Jung, and Xiaorong Gao. 2015. Filter bank canonical correlation analysis for implementing a high-speed SSVEP-based brain-computer interface. *Journal of Neural Engineering* 12, 4, 046008.
4. Shangkai Gao, Yijun Wang, Xiaorong Gao, and Bo Hong. 2014. Visual and Auditory Brain-Computer Interfaces. *IEEE Transactions on Biomedical Engineering* 61, 5: 1436-1447.
5. Ivo Käthner, Andrea Kübler and Sebastian Halder. 2015. Comparison of eye tracking, electrooculography and an auditory brain-computer interface for binary communication: a case study with a participant in the locked-in state. *Journal of Neuroengineering and Rehabilitation* 12, 76.
6. Bonkon Koo, Hwan-Gon Lee, Yunjun Nam, and Seungjin Choi. 2015. Immersive BCI with SSVEP in VR head-mounted display. *2015 37th Annual International Conference of the IEEE Engineering in Medicine and Biology Society* (EMBC).
7. Anatole Lecuyer, Fabien Lotte, Richard B. Reilly, Robert Leeb, Michitaka Hirose, and Mel Slater. 2008. Brain-Computer Interfaces, Virtual Reality, and Videogames. *Computer* 41, 10: 66-72.
8. Eui Chul Lee, Jin Cheol Woo, Jong Hwa Kim, Mincheol Whang, and Kang Ryoung Park. 2010. A brain-computer interface method combined with eye tracking for 3D interaction. *Journal of Neuroscience Methods* 190, 2: 289-298.
9. Jeong-Hwan Lim, Jun-Hak Lee, Han-Jeong Hwang, Dong Hwan Kim, and Chang-Hwan Im. 2015. Development of a hybrid mental spelling system combining SSVEP-based brain-computer interface and webcam-based eye tracking. *Biomedical Signal Processing and Control* 21: 99-104.
10. Päivi Majaranta and Kari-Jouko Räihä. 2002. Twenty years of eye typing: systems and design issues. *Proceedings of the 2002 symposium on Eye tracking research & applications* (ETRA '02): 15-22.
11. Päivi Majaranta and Kari-Jouko Räihä.2007 Text entry by gaze: Utilizing eye-tracking. In *Text entry systems: Mobility, accessibility, universality*, I. Scott MacKenzie and Kumiko Tanaka-Ishii (eds.). Morgan Kaufmann, San Francisco, 175-187.
12. José del R. Millán, Rüdiger Rupp, Gernot Müller-Putz, Roderick Murray-Smith, Claudio Giugliemma, Michael Tangermann, C. Vidaurre, Febo Cincotti, Andrea Kübler, Robert Leeb, Christa Neuper, Klaus-Robert Müller and Donatella Mattia. 2010. Combining brain-computer interfaces and assistive technologies: state-of-the-art and challenges. *Frontiers in Neuroscience* 4, 161.
13. Gernot Müller-Putz, Robert Leeb, Michael Tangermann, Johannes Höhne, Andrea Kübler, Febo Cincotti, Donatella Mattia, Rüdiger Rupp, Klaus-Robert Müller, and José del R. Millán. 2015. Towards Noninvasive Hybrid Brain-Computer Interfaces: Framework, Practice, Clinical Application, and Beyond. *Proceedings of the IEEE* 103, 6: 926-943.
14. Masaki Nakanishi, Yijun Wang, Xiaogang Chen, Yu-Te Wang, Xiaorong Gao, and Tzyy-Ping Jung. 2018. Enhancing Detection of SSVEPs for a High-Speed Brain Speller Using Task-Related Component Analysis. *IEEE Transactions on Biomedical Engineering*, 65, 1: 104-112.
15. Diederick C. Niehorster, Li Li, and Markus Lappe. 2017. The Accuracy and Precision of Position and Orientation Tracking in the HTC Vive Virtual Reality System for Scientific Research. *i-Perception* 8, 3: 1-23.
16. Gert Pfurtscheller, Brendan Z. Allison, Clemens Brunner, Gunther Bauernfeind, Teodoro Solis-Escalante. 2010. The hybrid BCI. *Frontiers in Neuroscience* 4, 30.
17. Thorsten Roth, Martin Weier, Andre Hinkenjann, Yongmin Li, and Philipp Slusallek. 2016. An analysis of eye-tracking data in foveated ray tracing. *2016 IEEE Second Workshop on Eye Tracking and Visualization (ETVIS)*: 69-73.
18. Kelly Tai, Stefanie Blain, and Tom Chau. 2008. A Review of Emerging Access Technologies for Individuals With Severe Motor Impairments. *Assistive Technology* 20, 4: 204-221.
19. Tobii Pro Accuracy and precision test method for remote eye trackers: https://www.tobiipro.com/siteassets/tobii-pro/accuracy-and-precision-tests/tobii-accuracy-and-precisiontest-method-version-2-1-1.pdf
20. Jonathan R. Wolpaw, Niels Birbaumer, Dennis J. Mcfarland, Gert Pfurtscheller, and Theresa M. Vaughan. 2002. Brain-computer interfaces for communication and control. *Clinical Neurophysiology* 113, 6: 767-791.

AnchorViz: Facilitating Classifier Error Discovery through Interactive Semantic Data Exploration

Nan-Chen Chen[1], Jina Suh[2], Johan Verwey[2], Gonzalo Ramos[2], Steven Drucker[2], Patrice Simard[2]
[1] University of Washington, Seattle, WA, USA
[2] Microsoft Research, Redmond, WA, USA
nanchen@uw.edu, {jinsuh, joverwey, goramos, sdrucker, patrice}@microsoft.com

ABSTRACT

When building a classifier in interactive machine learning, human knowledge about the target class can be a powerful reference to make the classifier robust to unseen items. The main challenge lies in finding unlabeled items that can either help discover or refine concepts for which the current classifier has no corresponding features (i.e., it has *feature blindness*). Yet it is unrealistic to ask humans to come up with an exhaustive list of items, especially for rare concepts that are hard to recall. This paper presents *AnchorViz*, an interactive visualization that facilitates error discovery through semantic data exploration. By creating example-based anchors, users create a topology to spread data based on their similarity to the anchors and examine the inconsistencies between data points that are semantically related. The results from our user study show that AnchorViz helps users discover more prediction errors than stratified random and uncertainty sampling methods.

Author Keywords

interactive machine learning; visualization; error discovery; semantic data exploration; unlabeled data

INTRODUCTION

Interactive machine learning (iML) is a growing field in machine learning (ML) that emphasizes building models with humans in the loop. Unlike traditional ML's sequential development workflows, model developers in iML iteratively explore and label data, add features to fix errors, and modify models to enhance performance. As models constantly get feedback from humans, their evolving directions can align with the model developers' goals better. Since data are labeled on the fly in iML, there is no way to tell how the current model performs on the unlabeled set until these data points (hereafter, we refer to a data point as an "item") are labeled. As it is undesirable to label the whole dataset in iML, it becomes critical to efficiently locate unlabeled items that the current model will predict incorrectly (i.e., *errors in unlabeled items*).

One common approach in iML for selecting unlabeled items is sampling based on uncertainty (e.g., items with prediction scores near a decision boundary) or uniform distribution (i.e., items uniformly sampled based on the prediction score distribution). Although these sampling methods can help pull out errors, often the selected items are ambiguous or random errors. Errors with high prediction confidence are not likely to be selected by these sampling algorithms. Hence, model developers may not even be aware of such defects in their models. Furthermore, these sampling methods do not fully leverage the value of human-in-the-loop. They treat humans as oracles and cause humans to feel annoyed, lose track of teaching progress, or lose interest [2]. As the discovered errors are mostly uncertain or random, it can be challenging for humans to make sense of the errors to provide useful inputs.

Past discussions have pointed out the benefits of semantic models – models that have semantically meaningful feature representations [11]. Semantic models are useful in helping humans make sense of the model behaviors and ensure their predictions are not based on problematic associations. Specifically in classification problems, humans usually possess knowledge about the target class; they can come up with hypotheses on what underlying "concepts" (i.e., abstract notions that altogether represent the target class) are challenging to the model, and try to fix the errors by providing more labeled items or adding features. However, it is costly and unrealistic to ask humans to provide an exhaustive list of concepts and items, especially for rare cases that are hard to recall. Therefore, careful design is required to efficiently utilize human efforts and maximize the value of each interaction.

In this work, we extend the idea of building semantic models to include semantic exploration on unlabeled dataset for error discovery and propose a polar-coordinate-based interactive visualization, *AnchorViz*, to facilitate this semantic exploration process. Through the visualization, users can create example-based anchors to spread items based on pair-wise similarity. Since users can understand the meaning of the chosen items, they can associate and contrast items' relations to the anchors. Hence, they can tease apart concepts and find items whose predictions do not align with the corresponding concepts.

We evaluated AnchorViz with 16 participants to examine the users' exploration strategies and the use of anchors in the tool in building a binary classifier. Our results show that items highlighted through anchors are more likely to be errors for which the current classifier has no corresponding features (hereafter referred to as "feature blindness errors"). In addition, our participants used a variety of strategies to explore the dataset and distill positive and negative concepts of the target class through creating anchors.

IUI'18, March 07–11, 2018, Tokyo, Japan

ISBN 978-1-4503-4945-1/18/03...$15.00
DOI: https://doi.org/10.1145/3172944.3172950

The contributions of this work are three-fold: First, we highlight the opportunity for leveraging semantic data exploration to locate classifier errors in unlabeled items. Second, we design and build AnchorViz to support such exploration through interactive visualization. Third, we evaluate AnchorViz with users and analyze users' intentions and exploration strategies to show that AnchorViz opens a new research space for semantic interactions with an iML classifier.

Motivating Scenario

Discovering an error in a large dataset is like finding a needle in a haystack, and in some cases, one cannot even tell whether a needle is in the haystack. Sifting through the haystack haphazardly is an inefficient method to find the needle. Using a magnet to pull the needle would be a fine solution. However, one needs many different magnets to find all kinds of needles, each representing a missing concept in the model. In addition, as these needles are unknown, it can be tough to create corresponding magnets to pull them out.

In this work, we leverage this magnet analogy, but instead of creating magnets that aim to pull needles directly, we propose to use semantic magnets, called "anchors" in this paper, to decompose the dataset semantically and highlight prediction inconsistency in items that are neighbors in the semantic space. In other words, anchors are representations of concepts in the dataset. An anchor can *spread* the dataset based on the items' semantic similarity to different concepts. If one expects to see items of a certain type of prediction near an anchor, any item with a different prediction from its neighbors or the nearby anchor can be an error or a seed to discover new concepts.

To illustrate how one can create and use anchors in a classification task, we provide the following scenario: A food blog writer wants to build a binary classifier for finding recipe webpages. The writer already considers restaurant menu pages as negative, so the writer uses existing restaurant menu pages to create a *restaurant menu* anchor to see other items similar to the concept of restaurant menus. Among the items similar to restaurant menu concept, the writer notices that some items are being predicted as positive. Upon inspection of those predicted positive items, the writer discovers catering webpages. The writer considers catering webpages as not belonging to recipes, labels the discovered catering webpages as negative, and creates a *catering* anchor. With both *restaurant menu* and *catering* anchors, the writer can see if there are other similar items being predicted incorrectly.

BACKGROUND AND RELATED WORK

In a supervised iML setting, humans build models by providing training items and features in a quick, iterative and continuous loop [9]. This model building approach has shown its success in building a decent model using fewer features [30]. In addition, it provides meaningful interactions to improve the user's trust and understanding of the system [27]. This interaction between humans and machines goes beyond simply treating humans as label oracles and requires thoughtful design and careful user studies [2]. However, like traditional supervised ML, supervised iML also needs to find items to which the current model is blind for better generalization performance in the real world, which is the focus of this paper.

Unknown Unknowns and Prediction Errors

Attenberg et al. [3] and Lakkaraju et al. [13] use a model's confidence score to categorize prediction errors into known unknowns and unknown unknowns. Known unknowns are errors for which the model has low confidence, and correcting such errors are useful for fine-tuning the system. Unknown unknowns are errors for which the model has high confidence, and such errors can be potentially disastrous depending on the problem domain.

Another approach is to characterize prediction errors as feature blindness, ignorance, mislabeling, or learner errors [17]. Feature blindness errors arise because the model does not have the appropriate feature representation to learn from the training items. In contrast, ignorance errors will be correctly classified if they are added to the training set as the model already has the appropriate feature representation. Mislabeling errors come from mislabeled items, whereas learner errors refer to issues caused by the configurations of the learning algorithms. In our work, we focus on finding *feature blindness* errors since these errors represents missing concepts in the current model.

Searching for Items to Label

There are two types of strategies for searching items to label: Machine-initiated and human-initiated approaches. The machine-initiated or algorithmic approach uses learning algorithms to suggest items for humans to label so that the model needs fewer training items to perform better [22]. Uncertainty sampling is one of the most commonly used active learning strategies. In binary classification, this strategy samples items whose confidence scores are near the decision boundary [16, 15]. Active learning strategies are not suitable for finding unknown unknowns or feature blindness errors because they often rely on the model's current training results, which cannot overcome the model's blind spots [3, 13, 17].

Recently, Lakkaraju et al. introduced an algorithmic approach to find unknown unknowns directly [13]. Their approach leverages systematic biases that are concentrated on specific places in the feature space. Their explore-exploit strategy partitions a dataset based on similarities in feature space and confidence scores, and searches for partitions with high concentration of items with high confidence. The underlying assumption for their system is that any unknown unknowns introduced to the algorithm can be characterized by the automatically extracted features (e.g., bag-of-words (BoW)), but using such features for training can have undesired consequences of losing interpretability [11]. In our work, we aim to preserve semantic meanings during exploration to maximize interpretability.

The human-initiated approach allows the humans to find the items that the model should learn. Attenberg et al. introduced the notion of *guided learning* [4] and implemented *Beat the Machine* (BTM), where crowd workers are tasked to find items from the open world [3]. Their results showed that BTM found more unknown unknowns compared to a stratified random sampler. Guided learning puts a significant load on users to find adversarial items since recalling is difficult, but when combined with other active learning strategies, this method can help the model learn quickly, especially on skewed datasets. One unique characteristic of BTM is that it leverages the open world as a search space, rather than a closed and biased sample set used in traditional settings. However, this approach does not keep the concepts or structures created and leveraged by users during the search process, so it has limited support for subsequent searches.

In AnchorViz, humans do not play a passive role as labelers of items presented by algorithmic techniques, but take advantage of algorithmic techniques. For example, AnchorViz uses hierarchical clustering (HC) [25] to reduce the user's search space, but ultimately, it is the user that chooses to label the item. The system also computes the similarity between sets of items in the BoW feature space and presents the results for users to take actions. In addition, we allow the users to externalize their concepts or structures so that they can decompose the target class, reuse previously defined concepts, or redefine and evolve their search strategies as they explore the dataset.

Visualization for ML

Visualization is one key approach to facilitating model development. Prior work that supports specific ML tasks usually contains a form of interactive visualization. For example, Talbot et al. designed *EsembleMatrix* for creating and tuning ensemble classifiers [28]. Lee et al. visualized topic models and allowed users to modify the models through their interface [14]. Ren et al. used a parallel coordinate style of visualization to help examine classification errors [21]. However, existing work mostly focuses on discovering errors in the labeled set with little attention to finding errors in unlabeled items.

In AnchorViz, we focus on locating errors in unlabeled items by using visualization to spread out items in a semantic manner. Our design is inspired by VIBE [19] and Dust and Magnet (D&M) [26]. D&M uses magnet metaphor to attract similar items using pre-defined dimensions of the data. However, the existing dimensions in our iML scenario (i.e., features) may not have any connections with unlabeled items to *attract* them. Similar to Adaptive VIBE [1], we allow the users to create and refine "anchors" as our version of magnets. We explain the anchors in further details in the next section.

Semantic Memory and Concept Decomposition

In psychology, semantic memory is a type of human memory that stores general knowledge, such as facts and concepts [29, 20]. Network models are commonly used to describe semantic memory; the theory of hierarchical network models [5] points out that a concept can be decomposed into smaller concepts to store in memory. In ML, concept decomposition is a learning method that leverages clustering [6, 7, 8]; the goal is to divide a concept into smaller concepts so that the algorithm can learn easily. Our work is inspired by these two similar ideas, and we put focus on semantic exploration and decomposition of the dataset through anchors.

ANCHORVIZ

In this section, we introduce the design of *AnchorViz*, an interactive visualization to help model developers locate classifier errors. Our design is based on the following design objectives that we came up with based on the motivating scenario:

DO1. Let users define concepts of the target class and unrelated classes

DO2. Spread the dataset based on concepts

DO3. Show how user-defined concepts impact the positions of items

DO4. Provide information about the model's current prediction along the user's labels

DO5. Optimize for efficient reviewing process

Interface and System Design

The interface for AnchorViz (Figure 1) contains a RadViz-based visualization that shows both labeled and unlabeled items (Figure 1C) as well as anchors that represent concepts (Figure 1D). When users click an item, the thumbnail view (1B) will switch to show its content, and users can inspect the item to provide a label. This gives users a quick way to check if the item is an error and provide correct label (DO5).

Define Concepts with Example-Based Anchors

In this work, we let users define a concept via examples (DO1), which is a common view of how a concept is stored in brain [18]. Thus, these anchors are "example-based" anchors. We leave exploring other types of anchors as future work. To create an anchor, users can drag an item to the outer circle (Figure 1D). Users can also drag an item to an existing anchor to modify the corresponding concept. When a user clicks on an anchor to reveal the anchor detail view, users can provide a meaningful name for the anchor, view the list of items that belong to the anchor, and remove items that no longer belong to the anchor. In addition, users can hide an anchor from the visualization. The hidden anchors sit inside the "Anchor Repository" at the bottom drawer of the left pane (Figure 1F) where users can restore the anchors to the visualization.

Manipulate Topology and Layout

Once a concept is defined, the user should be able to see the correlation between the concept and the items (DO2; e.g., this webpage is more like "catering") as well as the relationship between several concepts with respect to the items (DO3; e.g., this webpage is more like "catering" and less like "restaurant menu" while that webpage is unrelated to both concepts). We map the relative similarity of the items to the concepts to the position of items in a non-orthogonal coordinate system in a circle; the center point of the outer circle to each anchor forms a set of axes on a 2D surface. Namely, an axis k is a vector with the length of the outer circle's radius r and an angle θ to the corresponding anchor (Eq 1).

$$\vec{V_k} = (r \cdot cos\theta, r \cdot sin\theta) \tag{1}$$

An item along an axis forms a vector with an angle identical to that of the axis and a magnitude of the cosine similarity in the BoW space between the item and the items in the anchor. The final position of an item in the visualization is the sum of the vectors to each anchor (Eq 2).

$$Position(i) = (x_i, y_i) = \sum_k \frac{value_k(i)}{\sum_j value_j(i)} \cdot \vec{V_k} \tag{2}$$

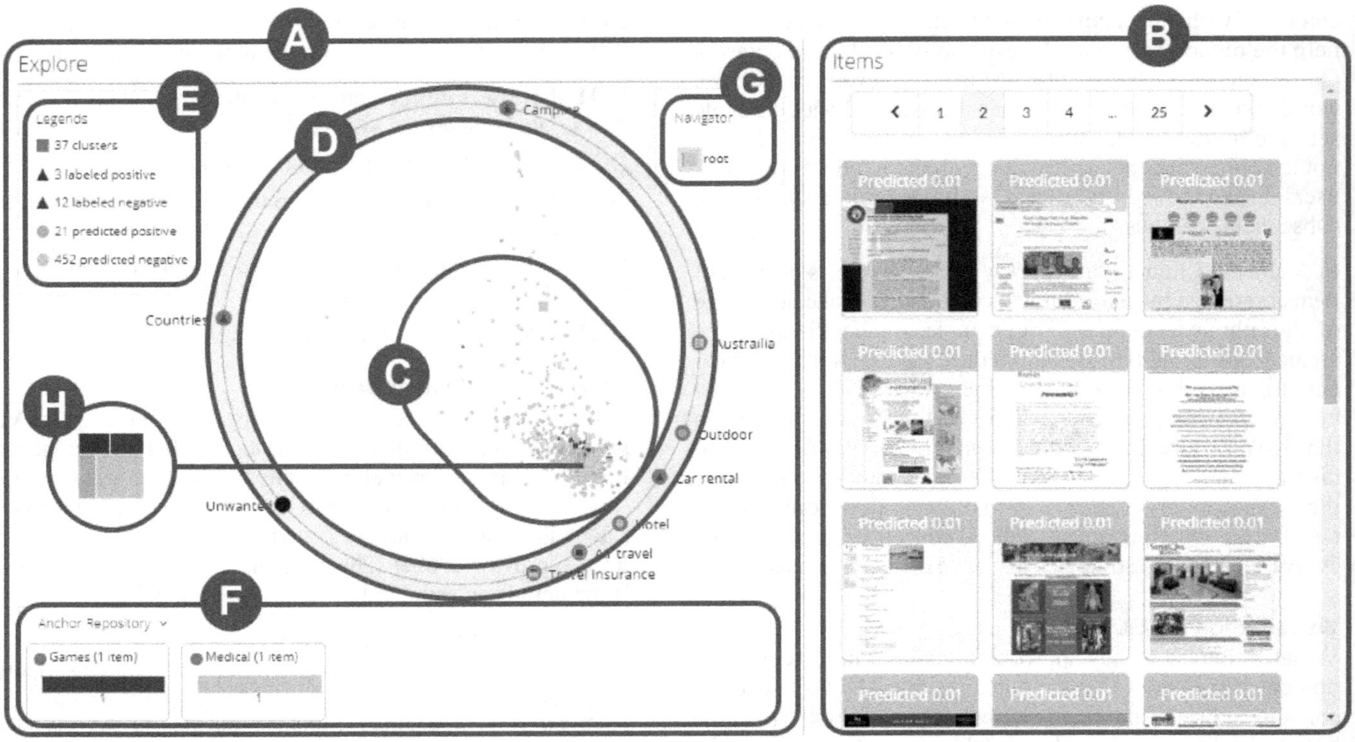

Figure 1. Overview of AnchorViz interface. The interface has Explore pane (A) that includes the visualization and Items pane (B) which shows a paginated grid of thumbnails of all currently visible items in the left pane. The visualization shows data points (C) within the outer circle (D) where anchors are positioned. The legend for data points (E) also acts as filters. Anchor repository (F) contains unused anchors. The navigator (G) shows which cluster the visualization is displaying in the current navigation stack. Clusters are represented as treemap-style squares (H).

Thus, the items that are closer to an anchor are more similar to the items in the anchor. The items that are affected by moving the anchor will move along with it, whereas items that do not share any similarity will remain still (DO3). In addition, since we want to ensure all items sit within the outer circle, an item's value on an axis is normalized by the sum of all its values on all the axes. This normalization follows the typical normalization used in RadViz [10]. In this way, the users are effectively creating a topology in the semantic space defined by the anchors. We have considered multiple visualization techniques for defining this topology, but ultimately chose RadViz because of its support for arbitrary number of axes and its flexibility in positioning of axes while preserving the relative independence of the axes [23]; we leave other visualization options for future work.

Contrast Model Predictions with Concepts

Semantic data exploration alone does not address our goal of finding errors of a classifier if the model is not involved in the exploration process. By surfacing the model predictions and the labels on the semantic topology created by anchors, the user should be able to contrast the predictions with concepts (DO4) to look for potential inconsistencies in two different ways. First, the user can look for items that are predicted to be in the opposite class as the class expected to be close to an anchor. For example, restaurant menus should be treated as a negative concept for the recipe class. If an item near a restaurant menu anchor is predicted as positive, then the item is a potential prediction error. Second, if an item is predicted or labeled as positive in a sea of negatively predicted or labeled items, that item is an outlier worth inspecting. We encode model predictions and user labels into color and shape of items as illustrated in Figure 1E. Users can also click on the categories in the legend to filter items based on their types.

Inspect Groups of Items

Manipulation of the concept topology defined by anchors and efficient visual encoding of model predictions still leaves the user with hundreds of items to inspect in order to arrive at an error worth labeling and adding to the training set. We pre-process the dataset by grouping similar items using HC algorithm; this helps reduce the search space by limiting the number of visible data points and allowing users to review groups of similar items rather than individual items. Note that the clusters do not change when anchors vary since the goal is to group similar semantic items, not merely visually close points.

In our clustering algorithm, the distance between any two items is their cosine similarity in the BoW space. The distance between clusters (C_a and C_b), including single point clusters, is the average distance between pairs among two clusters (Eq 3).

$$distance(C_a, C_b) = \frac{\sum_i \sum_j distance(C_{ai}, C_{bj})}{|C_a||C_b|} \quad (3)$$

In each step of HC, the algorithm selects a pair with the shortest distance and merges the two as a new cluster. The step is repeated until there is only one cluster left. We reorganize the result of HC, which is a binary tree, into a n-ary tree from the top tree node and expand the tree in a breath-first order. At any given node of the n-ary tree, it can contain leaves (items) or sub-trees (clusters) which can further divide into sub-trees and leaves. For our user study, we used $n = 500$ which is neither too cluttered nor sparse. We leave choosing an optimal value of n for future work.

These pre-processed groups of similar items (hereafter, we refer to a group of similar items as a *cluster*), are displayed as treemap-style squares (Figure 1H) in the visualization, and the size of the square is a function of the number of items inside the cluster. Namely, each square is also a single-level treemap [24] representing the composition of items in four categories (labeled positive, labeled negative, predicted positive and predicted negative). With treemaps, we aim to provide an at-a-glance understanding of the distribution of items within so that users can make a quick decision to navigate into the cluster. For example, if the cluster contains predicted negative items and labeled positive items, there may be potential inconsistencies between the clustering, the classifier, or the labels that need to be investigated and resolved. We display the same treemap for each anchor as a way to visualize their item composition as well as their class association along with the descriptive name.

Each square representing a cluster is positioned in the visualization based on the average similarity of all the leaf items inside the cluster. Clusters move along with the anchors that they are most similar to just like any individual items. When users click on a cluster, they can navigate into the cluster and the visualization will update to show the items and clusters belonging to the cluster. The navigator on the top right (Figure 1F) shows which cluster the visualization is displaying in the current navigation stack. The "root" cluster at the top of the stack represents the entire dataset. Users can navigate back to a previous level through the navigator or double click on the white space in the Explore pane.

Implementation

Our system has two components – a self-hosted web service and a web application. We implemented the web service using .NET, ASP.NET Core and the Nancy framework; we implemented the web application using Typescript, React, and D3. All relevant data, including the exploration dataset, training data, client states, and classifier configurations, are persisted to disk on the web server to support browser refreshes and for evaluation of the study results.

EVALUATION

We conducted a user study to evaluate our visualization and its effectiveness in helping users discover classifier errors. To the best of our knowledge, AnchorViz is the only visualization tool for error discovery that allows interactive exploration with the users' explicit semantic formulations, so there is no baseline to compare purely on its contribution to facilitating data exploration. Thus, the focus of our study is to understand the different strategies people use to explore the dataset and observe people's interactions with the anchors while all other conditions (e.g., features, distribution of positives) are fixed. This section describes the design of the user study and data collection, and we introduce definitions of several metrics that can be used for analysis and comparison in the future.

User Study

Participants

We recruited 20 participants from a large software company. Initially, we designed a controlled experiment comparing the visualization to an uncertainty sampler for effectiveness in discovering errors. However, the pilot study with the first four participants revealed that learning the tool and the target class took significant amount of time. Since our goal is not to test the ease of learning of the tool, we changed our study design to evaluate the visualization in depth. Our analysis is only based on the remaining 16 participants (7 females/9 males, ages 25-55) who completed the study.

We categorized our participants into four groups according to their ML background. Four participants have taken some courses in ML (P1-4), four occasionally build ML models in practice (P5-8), three frequently build ML models (P9-11), and five have a doctoral degree in ML-related fields (P12-16). Our participants' professional roles in the company are that of applied data scientist (9), program manager (2), researcher (1), financial manager (1), and software engineer (3). Six participants have a doctoral or professional degree, nine have a master's degree, and one has a bachelor's degree.

Background Scenario and Tasks

To evaluate the visualization, we provided the participants with a specific scenario. The premise for the user study is that the participant is developing a binary classifier using an iML tool (i.e., iteratively sampling for items, labeling the items, adding features, and debugging the target classifier). Through this iterative process, the participant has achieved almost 100% accuracy on the training set. Despite high training accuracy, the classifier performs poorly on a held-out test set, and the participant cannot recall any items or features where the classifier could be making a mistake. Therefore, the participant switches to explore a large unlabeled dataset to find potential sources of errors.

Based on the above scenario, we asked participants to (1) find items where the classifier is making a mistake, (2) find a set of items that are diverse from each other, and (3) try to understand the dataset and classifier performance in the process.

Dataset, Classifier, and Setup

To set up the user study according to the scenario above, we built a binary classifier whose training accuracy is 100% in an iML tool. The binary classifier outputs prediction scores from 0 to 1 and uses 0.5 to be the decision threshold. For our dataset, we took webpages and categories from the Open Directory Project (`http://www.dmoz.org/`) where the webpages were voluntarily organized into hierarchical categories by the community editors. After rendering the webpages, we discarded the webpage markup and retained only rendered and visible text tokens for each webpage. Following the categorization descriptions provided by the dataset, we built binary classifiers for several hours in an iterative model-building loop using logistic regression as the learning algorithm, text search and uncertainty sampling for item selection, and human-generated dictionaries (single weight for a group of n-grams) as features. Out of nine binary classifiers, we picked a classifier for predicting cooking-related webpages which had the highest train accuracy (97.5%) with 674 labeled items and 37 human-generated features. The choice of the learning algorithm is independent of the problem of discovering errors and is out of scope for this paper.

To control for the ratio between the labeled set and the unlabeled set, we uniformly sampled for 4000 items from the full dataset (50% positive for cooking) and 400 items in the labeled items such that approximately 8-10% of the dataset was labeled. To simulate blindness to concepts within positive and negative classes of cooking, we removed 25 features related to cooking (e.g., appliances, seasoning), and we left only one n-gram in each feature to degrade its test accuracy further. After training the classifier, we subsequently removed incorrect items in order to achieve 100% training accuracy. The final cooking classifier had 309 labeled items (130 positive), 12 features, 100% train accuracy and 75.8% test accuracy. For participants to practice, we also picked a travel-related binary classifier to use throughout the tutorial. This classifier only appeared during the practice round.

A limitation of the current interface design is that the visualization requires at least one anchor to be present to begin the exploration process. In an ideal case, we would provide the users with ways to bootstrap the visualization such as selecting items based on keyword search or choosing a set of labeled items to seed an example-based anchor. Evaluating the cold-start scenario is out of scope for this study, and therefore, we bootstrapped the visualization with one pre-defined anchor containing a positively labeled item and another containing a negatively labeled item.

Procedure

We conducted our study through video conferencing where participants shared their screens and thought aloud during the study, and we audio and screen-recorded the entire session. The user study consisted of four parts: The first part (20 minutes) involved an introduction to basic ML knowledge such as classification, errors, precision and recall, description of the data set, overview of the study interface, and introduction of the "travel" class (webpages about traveling and tourism). The second part (10-20 minutes) was a practice round using the travel class as a reference to get familiar with the interface, followed by an introduction of the "cooking" class (webpages about home cooking) which is used for the actual task. The third part was the actual task (20 minutes) where we asked the participants to use AnchorViz to find and label a diverse set of items where the participants disagree with the classifier's predictions. At the end of the study (5+ minutes), we asked participants to complete a quick survey to assess their satisfaction and collect open-ended feedback. Each study was a 70-90 minute session with a $30 gift card compensation.

Quantitative and Qualitative Data Analysis

We focused our analysis on the items that the participants discovered and the circumstances and the behaviors surrounding their discovery. These items should represent concepts which the model is blind to and the users could not think about in isolation. We captured the participants' interaction and behavior through recordings of their conversation and usage of the tools, and we instrumented the web application for user behavior to replay their interactions with anchors or items.

Qualitative Coding

We used the recordings in depth to understand the behavior of the participants. Since the participants followed the think aloud protocol, we were able to replay the recording to interpret the context of their actions. We coded their actions (e.g., click cluster, move anchor), the motivations for their actions (e.g., inspect prediction inconsistencies, see how items move), and the reactions to the actions they performed (e.g., whole cluster is positive, anchor is not very good). We used the results of the qualitative analysis to catalog different exploration strategies used by the participants and insights they obtained.

Error Categorization and Generalization

We evaluated the effectiveness of our visualization on discovering prediction errors in two ways. First, we computed the number of prediction errors that the participants discovered. Then we examined whether these errors are feature blindness errors by individually retraining the classifier with every item and see if that item is still a prediction error. Second, we looked at the score distribution of the discovered items to see how many high confidence errors the participants were able to find. We computed the magnitude of error as the absolute difference between the prediction score and 0.5. For comparison, we computed the same metrics with other samplers (e.g., uncertainty, stratified random samplers) given a fixed number of items comparable to that of the participants.

We also measured the quality of items by evaluating a classifier trained with the discovered items against a held-out test set. There are several challenges here. One is in simulating a human's featuring ability which is required in an iML loop that we operate in. Another is that the test set may not include a representative item for a concept that the participant discovered. For example, there is not a single item with reference to "insect recipes" in the test set which can be found during exploration of the unlabeled set. Fully acknowledging the challenges in evaluating the classifier's generalization performance, we computed the classifier's accuracy on the held-out test set using the original feature set (37 features). Our justification is that comparing two classifiers with or without the discovered items on a fixed feature set would provide us with a glimpse into the quality of the items added.

Anchor Effectiveness

To measure the effective of anchors on discovering errors, we define two metrics: *anchor error precision* (AEP) and *anchor error recall* (AER). The two metrics have similar concepts as the common precision and recall metrics in ML, but instead of measuring based on the target classes (positive/negative), AEP and AER look at whether items are errors or not.

Before further defining AEP and AER, we first define "contrasted items". Contrasted items aim to capture items that become salient through anchors. The steps to determine whether an item is a contrasted item are:

1. Collect neighbor anchors: Given an item, take up to three of its nearest neighbor anchors. Note that an anchor must be within $r/2$ range of an item to be its neighbor.

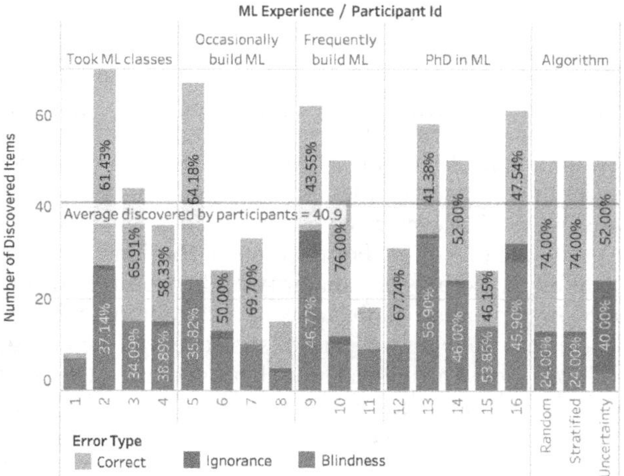

Figure 2. Distribution of errors across participants and algorithmic samplers. Text in each bar shows the percentage of errors in different categories. All participants except for P10 discovered feature blindness errors at a rate higher than any algorithmic samplers.

2. Determine the class label for each neighbor anchor: For every neighbor anchor, we determine its label based on majority voting from its items' ground truth labels. That is, if an anchor has three items, with two of their ground truth labels are positive and the other is negative, then the label of this anchor is positive.
3. Determine the contrasted base label: The contrasted base label is determined by majority voting from all the neighbor anchors' labels. The contrasted base label is unsure in a tie.
4. Determine if the item is a contrasted item: If the item's predicted label is opposite to the contrasted base label (not including unsure), then the item is a contrasted item.

Then we can define AEP and AER as follows:

$$AEP = \frac{\#\text{ true errors in contrasted items}}{\#\text{ contrasted items}} \quad (4)$$

$$AER = \frac{\#\text{ true errors in contrasted items}}{\text{total }\#\text{ true errors}} \quad (5)$$

An intuitive explanation of these two metrics is that they help examine how many error items a setup of anchors can bring into attention. Note that we calculated these two metrics based on all the contrasted items given the whole layout of anchors and points at a time, not merely a single anchor. We also consider all items by their spread-out positions, not their clusters' positions, as our goal of the two metrics is to measure the anchors' effectiveness, not the clustering algorithm.

We calculated AEP and AER for all active anchor settings of each participant over time. By active anchor settings, we refer to the layout of anchors and items when participants actively interact with items, which include: creating an anchor, adding/removing items in an anchor, navigating into a cluster, viewing an item, and labeling an item. Thus, if a participant interacts with 10 items, the participant will have 10 measurements for AEP and AER.

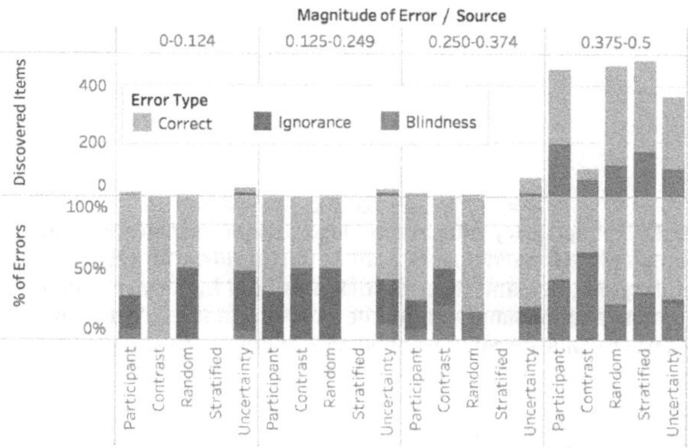

Figure 3. Distribution of discovered items (top) and the magnitude of errors (bottom) across participants and algorithmic samplers. The items are skewed towards high magnitude errors, but items discovered by participants and contrasted items higher chance of getting high magnitude items than algorithmic samplers.

RESULTS

Discovered Items

For the analysis of the items discovered by the participants, we used the ground truth labels provided by the original dataset as well as 4000 exploration candidate items (50% positive) and 1600 test items (50% positive).

Error Analysis

On average, participants discovered 40.9 errors (SD=19.6). We looked at the percentage, instead of the count, of errors in the total number of discovered items because of high variability in the number of discovered items. We also looked at the first 50 (mean number of items for PhD in ML group) items returned from algorithmic samplers. Of the unlabeled items (3691 items), the initial cooking classifier made prediction errors on 943 or 25.5% of the items and feature blindness errors on 886 or 24.0% of the items. Except for P10 who discovered errors at a rate of 24%, all participants discovered errors at a higher rate than the total error distribution, random, stratified random, or uncertainty sampler. The uncertainty sampler selected errors at 47.8% but only 8.7% of the sampled items were feature blindness errors. Again, except for P10, all participants discovered feature blindness errors at a rate higher than any algorithmic samplers. Figure 2 shows the distribution of errors among discovered items across participants.

Figure 3 shows the distribution of the magnitude of errors across different samplers. Here, we looked at all the unique items discovered by the participants (n=493) and contrasted items among the discovered (n=111), and we selected the first 493 items from each of the algorithmic samplers. According to the distribution of discovered items, the dataset is skewed towards high confidence scores and high magnitude of error. However, the percentage of errors indicates that the participants and contrasted group had a higher chance of discovering errors than algorithmic samplers. As expected, the uncertainty sampler selects more ignorance errors than any other samplers.

Test Accuracy

Assuming that the features were fixed to the original set of 37 features, we compared the classifier accuracy on the held-out test set before and after the discovered items were added to

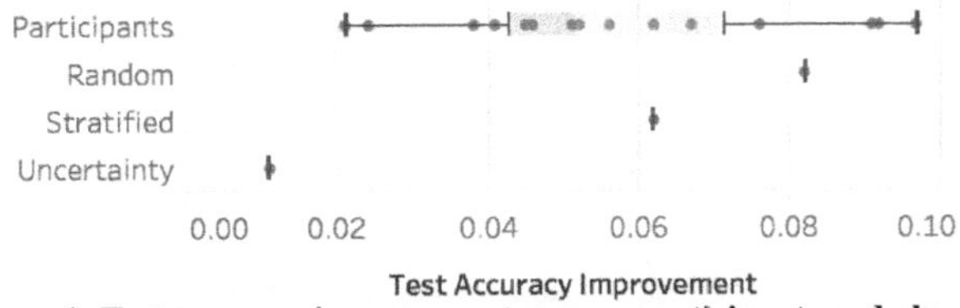

Figure 4. Test accuracy improvements across participants and algorithmic samplers. All participants built better performing classifiers than uncertainty sampler, and three participants built better performing classifiers than random samplers. While random samplers performed well on the test set, they discover less feature blindness errors as indicated by Figure 3

the training set. As before, we selected first 50 items from algorithmic samplers for comparison. Figure 4 shows that all participants made test accuracy improvements, and their classifiers performed better than the uncertainty sampler. Because the dataset is skewed towards high confidence scores, random samplers were able to select high magnitude error items and improved test accuracy. However, random samplers discovered less feature blindness errors as indicated by Figure 3, and three of our participants (P9, P13, P16) had classifiers with higher test accuracy than the ones created by random samplers.

Anchor Effectiveness

Figure 5 shows the average AEP and AER of each participant. The reference line "Random" of AEP shows the baseline for AEP to be 0.255, the error rate in the dataset. This baseline is how likely an item is an error if randomly selected by a user. As the figure shows, 12 out of 16 participants had an average AEP greater than random. This indicates that contrasted items are likely to pull errors to attention.

For AER, we plotted the average across participants as a reference line since the same analogy in random is 1 (all the errors are in the dataset). The average AER ($= 0.1321$) indicates that only about 13% of the errors are the contrasted items. However, the goal of our tool is not to find all errors, but to find errors that are critical. We further analyzed the types of errors in contrasted items and found most errors in contrasted items have a higher chance to find feature blindness errors than other approaches, including the algorithmic samplers, as we described in the error analysis section.

User Behavior

In this section, we outline different exploration strategies that the participants used when interacting with the visualization tool from qualitative analysis. We focus on three key aspects of the participants' use: (1) their reasons for creating anchors, (2) their exploration strategies, and (3) their understanding of classifier performance.

Reasons for Creating Anchors

All participants created anchors when they discovered a concept that could be useful for defining positive or negative classes (e.g., desserts, biography, Turkish cuisine). Anchors were also used to capture items that could potentially be confusing to the classifier. For example, P16 found a webpage containing a recipe, but a majority of the webpage was dedicated to explaining the benefits of a certain ingredient. P3 found a personal blog webpage of someone who enjoys eating food, but the webpage was not about cooking. One participant (P8) created anchors to group the items based on the confusion categories (i.e., false positive, false negative, true positive, true negative). P14 created an anchor from an entire cluster of items from a single recipe site to create a good recipe anchor. One participant (P1) tried to create anchors to differentiate webpages with recipes that did not have typical recipe headers (e.g., ingredients, instructions, prep time) from webpages with prototypical recipe structures. Some participants (P11, P13, P14) created anchors to capture or filter potential issues with the dataset. For example, there were webpages with recipes translated into two languages, webpages written only in one foreign language and are still cooking related, and webpages written in foreign languages and are not cooking related. Some participants created anchors to validate their hypothesis formed from exploration. For example, P9 discovered that the classifier was making a mistake on a webpage with lists of recipes and suspected that a lot of webpages with lists of recipes would be errors. He created an anchor to look at similar items around the anchor and said, "*basically pages that index a lot of recipes is not [correct].*"

Exploration Strategies

Participants used various aspects of the visualization to explore the dataset, and different strategies were used to meet their needs and at different points in time. Below, we enumerate an exhaustive list of how the participants explored the dataset.

Participants leveraged the visual encoding (i.e., position, color) to look for discrepancies or items that stood out. All participants looked at outliers in color (e.g., labeled positive in the sea of predicted negatives) or outliers in position (e.g., an item positioned away from the cloud of items in the middle. One participant (P1) looked at discrepancies between the global distribution and the local cluster distribution. Some participants used the cluster treemap to search for a specific cluster distribution (e.g., cluster with mixed predictions).

All participants, at some point, used the placement of anchors to define and modify the exploration topology. Most participants placed positively associated anchors on one side and negatively associated anchors on the other side of the visualization. P13 spread out the anchors to see items better. Some participants overlaid anchors on top of each other to combine concepts or to strengthen their effects (P7, P11, P12, P16). One participant (P3) removed anchors because he was not making any forward progress, and another participant (P16) removed anchors because he did not understand their meanings. One participant with a good understanding of BoW similarity (P9)

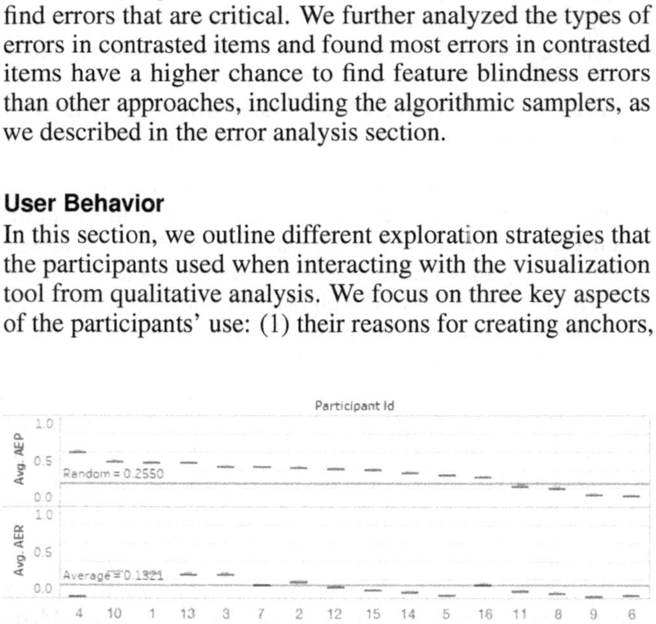

Figure 5. Average anchor effectiveness metrics (AEP/AER) for each participant. Most participants have better AEP than random.

inspected words in items both close to the anchors and far away from the anchors.

Participants used the anchors to pull or push items of specific prediction class, label class, or concept from the cloud of items. As mentioned earlier, some participants used the anchors to validate that there were a lot of non-English webpages in the dataset. Some participants used the labeled items as a way to validate that the anchors were pulling correct items. Some participants moved the anchors to create a parallax effect to see which items were impacted by the anchor or to determine the effectiveness of anchors they created. Most of the time, the participants were using the anchors to look for items near the anchors that were predicted in the opposite class from the labels of the items in the anchors.

As participants are interacting with anchors, they refined the anchors to make them more effective. P11 added similar items to an existing anchor to make the anchor stronger. P9 and P11 removed items from an anchor because the definition of the anchor had deviated from its initial intent P4 renamed the anchor from "cucumber" to "vegetables" because the anchor's representative concept evolved over time. Most participants added items of a similar concept to existing anchors. When the participants discovered an item and they could not decide on its label, they added the item to an anchor as a way to collect similar items and to defer the decision until a later point (P12 - "*Cook book can be negative in my opinion, but I'm not sure. It's about cooking and maybe it's related to cooking. Let's treat it as positive for now.*").

All the participants navigated into a cluster at some point, but the intentions varied across participants and contexts. Some participants (P7, P13) went into clusters of a specific prediction or label class to look for good items for creating anchors. Some participants (P1) looked for clusters with discrepancies between different sources of truths (clusters, the classifier, and labels). Others (P5, P9) used the clusters to reduce the search space or to evaluate items in bulk. Once anchors were created, some others (P3, P15) navigated up and down the cluster hierarchy to see the anchor's effects at various levels.

Some participants developed a repeatable process for exploration. The process for P11 was to find negatives around positive anchors, look at the clusters of mixed predictions near positive anchors, create appropriate anchors and to repeat the steps. When the participants reached a saturation point for exploration in the current view, P9 went back to the root cluster to start over, and P3 removed anchors to reset the topology.

Classifier Performance

Throughout the process of exploration, some participants were able to comment on the classifier's performance. In general, participants could discover an error or a concept, explore similar items using anchors, find a whole group of errors (P9 - "*Most of the same webpage [in this cluster]. This whole cluster seems to be false negative.*"), or make general statements about the concept (P2 - "*I guess we're doing nice for sushi*"). P9 said, "*I looked first at predicted positives. They all looked to be reasonable. There's no pattern there. I concluded there's mostly likely not bad precision problem. Most likely recall problem. Looking at the negatives, indeed, it seems to be a lot of missed use cases. I found two main categories of false negatives, mostly the lists of recipes and the more instructional pages that has a lot of words in them.*"

Although our visualization did not provide any debugging support, participants were able to come up with some explanations for the classifier's mistakes. For example, P14 commented that "*cooking blogs are easy to mis-predict*" because they share a lot of words with non-cooking blogs. P10 found an item with "*poems and other mixed things*" about cooking and called it a "*grayish area.*" P4 found webpages that contain words with multiple meanings, such as "squash" (a food and a sport), could be confused with cooking. Some understandings about how the classifier is learning from tokens was also used. For example, P11 said, "*I think there are few words. That's why it's not able to classify it as recipe.*"

DISCUSSION AND FUTURE WORK

Concept Evolution and Feature Discovery

Our evaluation reveals that AnchorViz not only helps users to find prediction errors, but also supports them in performing other necessary classifier building tasks. In particular, we observed that the participants used the anchors to facilitate concept evolution, which is "the labeler's process of defining and refining a concept in their minds [12]." Several participants used the anchors to collect items that they were unsure about (e.g., cookbooks, recipe links), deferred the decision for class assignment, and bulked label the items at a later point. P13 said the interface is "*great for concept discovery and dynamic labeling.*" This interface can also be used for managing discovered concepts and "*creat[ing] new concepts that can be shared across people (P12),*" and for "*hierarchically expressible classification tasks (P16).*" In contrast to previous approaches to find unknown unknowns, our visualization also facilitates feature blindness discovery, as P2 commented that this interface is useful for "*finding features I didn't know about and finding instance that can represent some useful concepts.*" P13 said, "*it was also really useful for discovering items that were out of scope (e.g., foreign language).*"

Anchor Types and Manipulation

In our current design, we explore the use of example items and determine their similarity in the BoW space. However, creating an anchor with example items is only one way to define its corresponding concept. We envision to use other types of anchors and distance metrics in AnchorViz. For example, instead of creating anchors based on items that users encounter, the tool can support search to enable direct access to specific items, and create an anchor based on all items with the given search terms. This is similar to P10's suggestion: "*keyword search through the data to find tougher items from intuition and see where they lie on the interface.*" In addition, the tool can let users specify a set of keywords to compute prevalence of the keywords or allow defining any arbitrary function that outputs a normalized score given any item. Furthermore, the current design treats all anchors equally. It is possible to add weights to anchors so that users can express their levels of interests on different concepts. We leave all these directions for future research.

Integration into Interactive Model Building Loop

A typical iML loop involves selection and labeling of items, featuring, and training the model in an iterative loop. The evaluation in this paper is focused on the selection step of finding errors that are worth labeling because selecting right examples is critical to efficient model building process. Though we leave the evaluation of AnchorViz in iterative iML loop for future works, we discuss below how such a tool can be incorporated into all stages of iML.

Once an error is discovered through the tool, labeled and added to the training set, a new model reclassifies the dataset; the user could continue to select the next item if there are no additional training errors or address new training errors by modifying features or adding new labeled items. For example, a positive label on a webpage about an edible flower recipe could be classified as negative even after retraining a model if the model does not have the appropriate feature representation for it (i.e., feature blindness error). The system would prompt the user to provide a feature to fix the error, and upon adding an "edible flower" feature, the model is finally retrained to correctly classify the webpage as positive. In addition, the tool could be useful for bulk labeling of items within an anchor or items co-located in a topology created by many anchors. Since the tool supports capturing concepts in the form of anchors, another use of the tool is for the evaluation of the model performance at the concept level by looking at the error rate within the anchor or around the anchor.

Some participants also wanted support for feature debugging. During the study, participants were making best guesses as to why the classifier was making a mistake (P16 - "*I think there are few words. That's why it's not able to classify it as recipe.*"). Providing feedback about the model's current feature set and additional anchor types could remedy this issue. For example, the user could create an anchor representing the number of tokens in an item to see if it is indeed true that low token count correlates with negative prediction.

Furthermore, the anchors contain rich information that could be used for suggesting useful features or highlighting the discrepancies among an anchor's items in the current model's feature space. After any model-changing action (featuring or labeling), a new model is trained to reclassify the entire dataset for the user to evaluate whether the action led to an expected outcome (e.g., better performance, discovery of new errors).

Interface Improvements

When we asked the participants what they liked about the interface, participants commented that the interface supported exploration in an intuitive and fun way. P4 said, "*visual inspection of outliers is intuitive,*" and P6 said that the interface is "*very intuitive when the anchors are meaningful.*" P13 liked the "*visualization and self-organization of item space.*" P14 commented during the study, "*I play too happily with it!*"

However, many improvements could be made: P7 wanted to see a "*succinct summary*" of the items instead of thumbnails when she was looking at items around the anchor to see if there were any obvious errors. Several participants wanted the ability to select multiple items for bulk labeling or adding to anchors. Several participants wanted to overlay additional data into the visualization. For example, a user would search for keywords and see the highlighted search results against the current anchor configuration. Instead of using the predicted label, actual prediction score could be used as color. In addition to the current filters, participants wanted to filter based on a range of scores such that they could focus on items around the decision boundary or with high prediction confidence.

Further Evaluation

So far, we have evaluated the interface for a binary classification scenario and a fixed dataset. Further investigation into how the visualization will be used in different contexts is necessary. While we observed that the visualization can be useful for general data exploration, it would be helpful to understand when to promote the interface to people who are less familiar with ML through evaluating the visualization at different model building stages (i.e., cold start, ready to deploy) and with models of different performance characteristics (i.e., recall, precision, error distribution). Varying the distribution of positive items or labeled items in the exploration set could also potentially change the effectiveness of the visualization. One participant suggested that this tool could be useful for exploring an image dataset with model features as anchors; another wished to extend the visualization for multiclass scenarios. There is an opportunity to extend the application of the visualization to different ML problems or data types.

Finding a baseline tool to compare against is a challenge due to many confounding and complex variables such as choice of samplers, choice of workflow, and variability in the user's abilities (e.g., the ability to feature and debug the model). Nevertheless, further investigation into comparing the visualization against a baseline is necessary to quantify the benefits of tool.

CONCLUSION

This paper presents AnchorViz, an interactive visualization tool for semantic data exploration and error discovery in iML. Our user study shows that AnchorViz helps users discover more prediction errors than stratified random sampling and uncertainty sampling. We have enumerated various exploration strategies used by the participants and discovered that the participants used AnchorViz beyond its intended usage with potentials for facilitating concept evolution and feature discovery. AnchorViz can be extended to support features, models, and active learning algorithms which opens several possibilities for future research.

ACKNOWLEDGEMENT

We acknowledge all the reviewers for their valuable feedback and the participants for their time, as well as the Machine Teaching group at Microsoft Research for their support.

REFERENCES

1. Jae-wook Ahn and Peter Brusilovsky. 2009. Adaptive visualization of search results: Bringing user models to visual analytics. *Information Visualization* 8, 3 (2009), 167–179.

2. Saleema Amershi, Maya Cakmak, William Bradley Knox, and Todd Kulesza. 2014. Power to the people: The role of humans in interactive machine learning. *AI Magazine* 35, 4 (2014), 105–120.

3. Joshua Attenberg, Panos Ipeirotis, and Foster Provost. 2015. Beat the Machine: Challenging Humans to Find a Predictive Model's "Unknown Unknowns". *Journal of Data and Information Quality (JDIQ)* 6, 1 (2015), 1.

4. Josh Attenberg and Foster Provost. 2010. Why label when you can search?: alternatives to active learning for applying human resources to build classification models under extreme class imbalance. In *Proceedings of the 16th ACM SIGKDD international conference on Knowledge discovery and data mining*. ACM, 423–432.

5. Allan M Collins and M Ross Quillian. 1969. Retrieval time from semantic memory. *Journal of verbal learning and verbal behavior* 8, 2 (1969), 240–247.

6. Inderjit S Dhillon and Dharmendra S Modha. 2001. Concept decompositions for large sparse text data using clustering. *Machine learning* 42, 1 (2001), 143–175.

7. Inderjit Singh Dhillon and Dharmendra Shantilal Modha. 2003. Concept decomposition using clustering. (May 6 2003). US Patent 6,560,597.

8. Jasminka Dobsa and BJ Basic. 2003. Concept decomposition by fuzzy k-means algorithm. In *Web Intelligence, 2003. WI 2003. Proceedings. IEEE/WIC International Conference on*. IEEE, 684–688.

9. Jerry Alan Fails and Dan R. Olsen, Jr. 2003. Interactive Machine Learning. In *Proceedings of the 8th International Conference on Intelligent User Interfaces (IUI '03)*. ACM, New York, NY, USA, 39–45. DOI: http://dx.doi.org/10.1145/604045.604056

10. Patrick E Hoffman. *Table visualizations: a formal model and its applications*. Ph.D. Dissertation. University of Massachusetts. Lowell.

11. Camille Jandot, Patrice Simard, Max Chickering, David Grangier, and Jina Suh. 2016. Interactive Semantic Featuring for Text Classification. *arXiv preprint arXiv:1606.07545* (2016).

12. Todd Kulesza, Saleema Amershi, Rich Caruana, Danyel Fisher, and Denis Charles. 2014. Structured labeling for facilitating concept evolution in machine learning. In *Proceedings of the SIGCHI Conference on Human Factors in Computing Systems*. ACM, 3075–3084.

13. Himabindu Lakkaraju, Ece Kamar, Rich Caruana, and Eric Horvitz. 2017. Identifying Unknown Unknowns in the Open World: Representations and Policies for Guided Exploration. In *AAAI*. 2124–2132.

14. Hanseung Lee, Jaeyeon Kihm, Jaegul Choo, John Stasko, and Haesun Park. 2012. iVisClustering: An Interactive Visual Document Clustering via Topic Modeling. *Computer Graphics Forum* 31, 3pt3 (June 2012), 1155–1164. DOI: http://dx.doi.org/10.1111/j.1467-8659.2012.03108.x 00041.

15. David D Lewis and Jason Catlett. 1994. Heterogeneous uncertainty sampling for supervised learning. In *Proceedings of the eleventh international conference on machine learning*. 148–156.

16. David D Lewis and William A Gale. 1994. A sequential algorithm for training text classifiers. In *Proceedings of the 17th annual international ACM SIGIR conference on Research and development in information retrieval*. Springer-Verlag New York, Inc., 3–12.

17. Christopher Meek. 2016. A Characterization of Prediction Errors. *CoRR* abs/1611.05955 (2016). http://arxiv.org/abs/1611.05955

18. R M Nosofsky. 1986. Attention, similarity, and the identification-categorization relationship. *Journal of experimental psychology. General* 115 1 (1986), 39–61.

19. Kai A Olsen, James G Williams, Kenneth M Sochats, and Stephen C Hirtle. 1992. Ideation through visualization: the VIBE system. *Multimedia Review* 3 (1992), 48–48.

20. Daniel Reisberg. 2013. *The Oxford handbook of cognitive psychology*. Oxford University Press.

21. D. Ren, S. Amershi, B. Lee, J. Suh, and J. D. Williams. 2017. Squares: Supporting Interactive Performance Analysis for Multiclass Classifiers. *IEEE Transactions on Visualization and Computer Graphics* 23, 1 (Jan. 2017), 61–70. DOI: http://dx.doi.org/10.1109/TVCG.2016.2598828 00000.

22. Burr Settles. 2012. Active learning. *Synthesis Lectures on Artificial Intelligence and Machine Learning* 6, 1 (2012), 1–114.

23. John Sharko, Georges Grinstein, and Kenneth A Marx. 2008. Vectorized radviz and its application to multiple cluster datasets. *IEEE transactions on Visualization and Computer Graphics* 14, 6 (2008).

24. Ben Shneiderman. 1992. Tree Visualization with Tree-maps: 2-d Space-filling Approach. *ACM Trans. Graph.* 11, 1 (Jan. 1992), 92–99. DOI: http://dx.doi.org/10.1145/102377.115768

25. Robert R Sokal. 1958. A statistical method for evaluating systematic relationship. *University of Kansas science bulletin* 28 (1958), 1409–1438.

26. Ji Soo Yi, Rachel Melton, John Stasko, and Julie A Jacko. 2005. Dust & magnet: multivariate information visualization using a magnet metaphor. *Information visualization* 4, 4 (2005), 239–256.

27. Simone Stumpf, Vidya Rajaram, Lida Li, Weng-Keen Wong, Margaret Burnett, Thomas Dietterich, Erin Sullivan, and Jonathan Herlocker. 2009. Interacting meaningfully with machine learning systems: Three experiments. *International Journal of Human-Computer Studies* 67, 8 (2009), 639–662.

28. Justin Talbot, Bongshin Lee, Ashish Kapoor, and Desney S. Tan. 2009. EnsembleMatrix: Interactive Visualization to Support Machine Learning with Multiple Classifiers. In *Proceedings of the SIGCHI Conference on Human Factors in Computing Systems (CHI '09)*. ACM, New York, NY, USA, 1283–1292. DOI: http://dx.doi.org/10.1145/1518701.1518895 00097.

29. Endel Tulving and others. 1972. Episodic and semantic memory. *Organization of memory* 1 (1972), 381–403.

30. Malcolm Ware, Eibe Frank, Geoffrey Holmes, Mark Hall, and Ian H Witten. 2001. Interactive machine learning: letting users build classifiers. *International Journal of Human-Computer Studies* 55, 3 (2001), 281–292.

Interactive Document Clustering Revisited: A Visual Analytics Approach

Ehsan Sherkat
Dalhousie University
Halifax, Canada
ehsansherkat@dal.ca

Seyednaser Nourashrafeddin
Dalhousie University
Halifax, Canada
nourashr@cs.dal.ca

Evangelos E. Milios
Dalhousie University
Halifax, Canada
eem@cs.dal.ca

Rosane Minghim
Universidade de São Paulo
São Paulo, Brazil
rminghim@icmc.usp.br

ABSTRACT
UPDATED—December 29, 2017. Document clustering is an efficient way to get insight into large text collections. Due to the personalized nature of document clustering, even the best fully automatic algorithms cannot create clusters that accurately reflect the user's perspectives. To incorporate the user's perspective in the clustering process and, at the same time, effectively visualize document collections to enhance user's sense-making of data, we propose a novel visual analytics system for interactive document clustering. We built our system on top of clustering algorithms that can adapt to user's feedback. First, the initial clustering is created based on the user-defined number of clusters and the selected clustering algorithm. Second, the clustering result is visualized to the user. A collection of coordinated visualization modules and document projection is designed to guide the user towards a better insight into the document collection and clusters. The user changes clusters and key-terms iteratively as a feedback to the clustering algorithm until the result is satisfactory. In key-term based interaction, the user assigns a set of key-terms to each target cluster to guide the clustering algorithm. A set of quantitative experiments, a use case, and a user study have been conducted to show the advantages of the approach for document analytics based on clustering.

Author Keywords
Interactive document clustering; key-term; visualization; document projection; user study; text.

INTRODUCTION
A huge amount of text documents are produced each day, resulting in the generation of many documents per subject. One of the most effective solutions to manage and get insight into this huge amount of data is by automatically clustering them into meaningful clusters. There exist several clustering algorithms for document clustering, which try to group similar documents together with the help of different similarity measures. However, it is not always possible to automatically create the clustering that best matches the user's point of view or the application's goals, even with state-of-the-art clustering algorithms. A sensible solution for this problem is involving the human in the loop of clustering. In this approach, it is possible to generate clusters close to the user's perspectives, while in the process supporting the human in making sense of the document collection [23, 18, 5, 4].

There are several semi-supervised clustering algorithms that use a few labeled instances to improve the quality of their results [6, 39]. Some other algorithms exploit the user's feedback in terms of the split or merge signals [4]. In that case, the user only asks to merge two clusters or split a cluster without specifying how to split the cluster. Most of these approaches have been tested in theory, but not used in everyday activities. In practice, an interactive clustering algorithm that gives the user an intuitive way of interaction and is feasible in terms of user effort would be more appropriate. On the other hand, the constrained clustering algorithms assume that the constraints or the user feedback are known before clustering starts, and they do not support, in their set up, interaction during clustering or progressive clustering improvement by the user.

Topic modeling, sometimes viewed as soft clustering of documents, is a different way of categorizing similar content by extracting meaningful topics from the document collection. In reality it is sometimes hard to know how separated the topics generated with topic modeling are, which makes it difficult for user interactions. A few research papers have proposed interactive topic modeling systems for the end user by providing different visualization modules [23, 14]. In spite of these progresses, there is still a need to propose more effective visualization and interaction components to bring better insight into a document collection for the user.

IUI'18, March 7–11, 2018, Tokyo, Japan

DOI: https://doi.org/10.1145/3172944.3172964

We propose a practical solution for interactive document clustering by combining an interactive clustering algorithm with a visual interface. We have chosen key-term based interaction because it has been demonstrated that not only is it effective in improving the results but it is more intuitive for the user to interact with the clustering algorithm [7, 29, 25, 31]. In our key-term based interaction method, the user only assigns a short list of key-terms (less than five) to the desired cluster to guide the clustering algorithm. Ability to interact with the clustering algorithm with a very short list of key-terms distinguishes the proposed method from other key-term based interactive systems. Additionally, interactions are convertible to each other. For example, document based interaction can be achieved easily by assigning top key terms of the selected document(s) to a cluster as opposed to just directly linking the document(s) to a cluster.

Lexical Double Clustering (LDC) [30] and a novel KMeans style interactive clustering algorithm called iKMeans are incorporated in our proposed system. We have select document clustering algorithms instead of topic modeling ones to avoid problems of inconsistency after several runs, empirical convergence criteria and difficulty to interact with their complicated formula and algorithm. LDC has shown better performance compared to state-of-the-art topic modeling algorithms such as Latent Dirichlet Allocation (LDA) [9] and Non-negative Matrix Factorization (NMF) [32] on several standard document clustering datasets. Both LDC and iKMeans are deterministic in each interaction and generate similar results for the same key-term based user feedback. Because of the simple nature of KMeans-like algorithms, it is easy to incorporate user feedback and scale the algorithm to very large datasets with a short running time, which is hard to achieve in topic modeling algorithms.

In the proposed system, it is possible to switch between the LDC and iKMeans algorithms on demand. Interactively switching algorithms during clustering is not used in any other interactive clustering system. For example, the user can start with the LDC algorithm which is robust to outliers and when the user gets sufficiently familiar with the dataset, switch to iKMeans to generate highly customized clusters. The ability to alternate between different clustering algorithms demonstrates the independence of our system of the specific clustering algorithm, which means it can incorporate any other key-term based interactive clustering algorithm.

We have designed a visual interface to integrate the key-term based user interactions with the clustering algorithms as well as to allow the users to explore the data set and the relationships between documents and clusters. Several visual components are developed to guide the user for more effective interaction with the clustering algorithm and give the user better insight into the document collection. We combined the t-distributed stochastic neighbor embedding (t-SNE) [27] with the Force-directed placement [16] in a novel way to better improve cluttering typical of such embeddings and provide a better distinction among clusters. We have conducted various experiments using real-world datasets including a use case and a user study to demonstrate the effectiveness of the proposed system. All the datasets and code developed or used in this paper are available on Github[1].

RELATED WORK

Each interactive clustering system consists of two integrated parts: an interactive clustering algorithm and a visual interface. The main focus of some research papers is in the clustering algorithm, some in the visualization part and others focus on the integration of both. In the following we targeted these three types of related work.

Constrained Clustering Algorithms

Semi-supervised clustering algorithms use labeled data to guide the clustering process. Two semi-supervised clustering algorithms, Seeded-KMeans and Constrained-KMeans, inspired by the KMeans algorithm, were introduced in [6]. In Seeded-KMeans, instead of randomly initializing the KMeans, the labeled data points are used to initiate the clustering. Constrained-KMeans is similar to the seeded one but it keeps the label of seeds unchanged in every iteration of the algorithm. These two algorithms are modeled based on the Expectation-Maximization (EM) algorithm on a mixture of k (number of clusters) Gaussians. Each data point has k possible conditional distributions and the initial supervision is to determine these conditional distributions for seed points. These two algorithms showed better performance in comparison to COP-KMeans [39]. The supervision in COP-KMeans is in terms of *must-link* (two data points must be in the same cluster) and *cannot-link* (two data points cannot be in the same cluster) constraint. In each step of KMeans, partitions are generated in a way that satisfies all the given constraint. The problem with these algorithms is that they assume that all the constrains are known in advance, hence they are not designed for interactive use.

Interactive Clustering Algorithms

A class of interactive clustering algorithms captures all the necessary interactions between the user and the clustering algorithm as cluster *split* and *merge* queries [5]. The user sends a Merge request if two clusters are a subset of a target cluster and a split request if a cluster contains data points belonging to distinct targeted clusters. The user does not enter how to split or point out possible mistakes in the have led to the request. Several different merge and split operations are introduced by Awasthi et al. [4] to reduce the number of merge and split requests. We believe that for textual data the user should not only be able to send the split request but also to specify how to split the cluster by providing some key-terms, aiming to reduce the number of split and merge requests. These algorithms have not been equipped with visualization or tested by end users.

Constrained Topic Modeling

Latent Dirichlet Allocation (LDA) [9] has been widely used for topic modeling. LDA models topics as distributions over words and documents as distributions over topics. One can consider the most probable topic of a document as a document cluster label. LDA has been extended to incorporate domain knowledge into the topic modeling through must-link

[1] https://github.com/ehsansherkat/IDC

and cannot-link constraints over terms [3]. The *must-link* constraint between two terms indicates that they tend to be generated by the same topic, while the cannot-link constraint says that two terms tend to be generated by different topics. The *Dirichlet forest prior* is used to encode must-link and cannot-link constraints in which the prior is a mixture of Dirichlet tree distributions. The must-link constraints only were used as a supervision to the LDA in [41]. They used a collection of tree-structured (based on *must-link* terms) multinomial distributions instead of multinomial distributions over words. Must-link and cannot-link constraints over documents were incorporated in the LDA model by changing the Gibbs sampling of the original LDA [41]. Contrary to the original LDA, the document topic distribution prior is updated in every iteration based on user feedback. They applied this system to improve topic model stability after adding new documents to the model.

A supervised version of LDA that incorporates labeled documents in the model has been proposed by [34]. In this model, the user can improve the quality of LDA by providing some topics for documents. These algorithms are not designed to obtain the user feedback in an interactive way. One of the major problems of topic modeling algorithms is inconsistency of results after each iteration which makes them difficult to use interactively. Algorithms described in this subsection have not been tested by the end user with the help of a visualization.

Interactive Topic Modeling Systems

iVisClustering is an interactive clustering system that introduced a visual interface on top of the LDA algorithm to involve the user in the loop [23]. The interaction with the LDA is performed only by changing terms' weights. This system has several different visualization modules called views. The *Graph View* using force-directed layout shows the general view of the document collection. The summary of clusters with their top terms are depicted in rectangle shaped boxes called *Cluster Summary View* beside the hierarchical style visualization of clusters (*Cluster View*). The user hands over a cluster in *Cluster Summary View* and the system shows document grids with the color spectrum which depicts their relatedness to the cluster. By clicking on a grid, the relatedness of that document to other clusters will be shown in a *Parallel Coordinates View* plus the content of documents in a *Document View*. The list of top terms of each cluster is in the *Term-Weight View* in which the user can change the weight of each term and impact the result of clustering. Because of the complicated nature of LDA formulas the interaction with this algorithm is not straightforward so changing term weights may confuse the user. In our system, the user only needs to define a set of key-terms without any need to assign a weight to them. Relative importance of terms is given by their order, without having to assing values. In addition to their lack of intuitiveness, topic modeling algorithms suffer from inconsistency in the results after each interaction. In contrast to *iVisClustering*, in our proposed system, all the visualization modules are coordinated with each other.

UTOPIAN [14] is an interactive topic modeling system, which is based on Non-negative Matrix Factorization (NMF) [32] instead of LDA. The interaction with NMF is based on changing term weights. Author´s used Graph View, Document View, and Term-Weight View as supporting visualizations. In the Graph View, the location of nodes is assigned by t-SNE [27]. The t-SNE algorithm is a method for dimensionality reduction mostly used for 2D and 3D projection of data points. UTOPIAN is developed by the same group of developers of iVisClustering system. In this system, they used NMF instead of LDA to handle the inconsistency problem of LDA algorithms. UTOPIAN still suffers from the empirical convergence problem and difficulty to meaningfully interact because of their complicated formula and algorithm. Unlike our proposed system, neither UTOPIAN nor iVisClustering were evaluated by end users. The overall differences between the key-term based document clustering systems and the UTOPIAN and the iVisClustering is described in more details in [31].

Interactive Document clustering Systems

An active learning scheme for selecting seed documents to be labeled by the user is presented in [19]. These seed documents will be used as an input to a semi-supervised KMeans algorithm. To facilitate the process of finding seed documents, a visualization is designed, which contains a *Term Cloud View* of each document and cluster, *Document View*, and *Pie Visualization* of clusters. In the *Pie Visualization*, each slice is a cluster and in the middle of the pie, there is a circle which contains all unlabeled documents. The user can assign these unlabeled documents to a desired cluster. *TopicPanorama* has also used a pie visualization for topics. All these topics are sub-topics of a few major topics determined by the user. Topics are linked together based on graph matching techniques in this system. This sub-topic graph structure is inside a hollow circle named *Radial Icicle Plot* in which for each major topic there is a color-coded arc. The user can zoom in on a topic by changing the length of the arc. Subtopics more similar to the major topics are near its arc and the common sub-topics are in the middle of the circle. In our proposed system, we used key-term based interactions, which is easier and more effective than document based interactions [31].

In our proposed system, we focus on key-term based interaction, which has been argued to be more effective and intuitive for the user than document based interaction or hybrid interaction in our previous work [31]. Novel contributions of this paper over [31] are the following: a flexible framework for key-term based document clustering, where users can interact based on key-terms with more than one word (e.g. bigrams); a new key-term based clustering algorithm, which shows how to combine a key-term interaction with document supervision; improved document projection by combining t-SNE with Force-directed placement in order to better visually distinguish groups of documents; and a user study that evaluates both the effectiveness of this type of interface for supervised clustering and the overall interactive document clustering approach.

OVERVIEW OF THE PROPOSED SYSTEM

The proposed system is a web-based user-centered document clustering system that integrates key-term based clustering algorithms with an interactive visualization. First, the user uploads documents, which the system preprocess and provides an initial fully automatic clustering. Second, the user obtains insight into the document collection by inspecting the visual components including the document projection. Third, the user provides key-term based feedback to the clustering algorithm to guide the result of clustering. In the following, each component of the system is described.

Document Preprocessing

In the first step, we extract the plain text of each documents after removing punctuations and numbers. In the next step, we remove useless terms from the document collection dictionary. Even a few documents can lead to several thousand unique terms. This will cause a negative impact on the quality of document clustering [24] and increases the clustering time which is very crucial for interactive systems. In order to tackle this problem, we used an unsupervised feature selection method based on terms *tf-idf* score. This score shows the discriminative power of a term over each document [28]. Let D be the set of documents and d a document in D, the tf-idf score of the term w is as Equation 1.

$$tf\_idf(w,d,D) = f(w,d) \times log\frac{|D|}{|d \in D : w \in d|} + 1. \quad (1)$$

The $f(w,d)$ is the frequency of term w in document d. Now each document has a vector of terms' tf-idf score. We normalize each document vector based on the *Euclidean (L2) norm.* For each term, the *mean-tf-idf* score is calculated based on Equation 2.

$$mean\_tf\_idf(w,D) = \frac{1}{|D|} \times \sum_{d \in D} tf\_idf(w,d,D). \quad (2)$$

All terms with the mean-tf-idf score above the average mean-tf-idf of all terms are selected to shape the final document-term matrix. Approaches based on term frequency are reported [26, 42] to be as effective as more complicated methods while having linear time complexity for unsupervised feature selection in textual datasets.

Document Clustering

In this system, we used two document key-term based clustering algorithms, LDC and iKMeans. The user can switch between these algorithms in each iteration.

The LDC Algorithm

LDC contains two steps, the first step is term clustering and the second step is using term clusters to create a distilled set of terms to guide the assignment of documents to each term cluster. The *Fuzzy C-means* algorithm [8] is used for term clustering. This algorithm allows a term to belong to more than one cluster (soft clustering). The goal of Fuzzy C-means (FCM) is to optimize the objective function in Eq. 3.

$$FCM = \sum_{i=1}^{|W|}\sum_{j=1}^{k} u_{ij}^{m} cosineSim(w_i, c_j), \quad 1 < m < \infty \quad (3)$$

The w_i ($w \in W$: W=set of terms) is the ith column of the document-term matrix which is a $|D|$ dimensional vector of tf-idf scores. The c_j is a $|D|$ dimensional vector of the jth (k=*number of clusters*) cluster center. The *cosine distance* is used to calculate the similarity between each term and term clusters center. The membership matrix of u is recalculated in every iteration of FCM to optimize the objective function shown in Eq. 3. In the first iteration, all the values in matrix u are assigned randomly. In case there exist user feedback, the matrix u will be initialized based on user's feedback instead of random initialization. LDC distills the term clusters and then assigns documents to the closest term cluster after several steps.

Algorithm 1: *iKMeans* algorithm

```
input  : K=Number of clusters;document-term
         matrix^{|D|×|W|};F=User defined seed
         term;Confidence(%)
output : Doc_clusters

if firstIteration then
    termClusters ← FCM(document-term
      matrix,K,m=1.1,maxIter=50);
    foreach termCluster ∈ termClusters do
        termCluster ← getTopTerms(Default=5)
else
    termClusters ← F
end
termClustersCenter ← CC(termClusters);
for i ← 1 to K do                          // Expand key-terms
    while counter_1 < α × |W| × 2^(2 − Confidence/25) do
        termClusters_i +=                  // Cosine Sim.
          nextSimilar(term∈W,termClustersCenter_i);
        counter_1 ← counter_1 + 1
    end
end
termToDocCenter ← CC(termClusters^T);
for i ← 1 to K do                          // Find seed docs
    while counter_2 < β × |D| × 2^(2 − Confidence/25) do
        SeedDocs_i +=                      // Cosine Sim.
          nextSimilar(doc∈D,termToDocCenter_i);
        counter_2 ← counter_2 + 1
    end
end
SeedDocsCenter ← CC(SeedDocs);
Doc_clusters ← KMeans(document-term
  matrix,K,SeedDocsCenter);
Function CC(M^{I×J}):                      // Calculate Center
    for i ← 1 to I do
        Center_{M_i} ← (Σ_{j=1}^{|M_i|} (M_ij=[m_1,m_2,...,m_n])) / |M_i|
    end
```

iKMeans Algorithm

To demonstrate that our proposed system is independent of the clustering algorithm, we proposed an extension of Seeded-KMeans [6] algorithm based on *seed term* interaction. The main contribution of this algorithm is the way it converts key-term seeds to document seeds because the Seeded-KMeans only designed to work with documents seeds. The same procedure could be applied to other document supervised clusters and be subject to the same interface as our framework.

The first step of the algorithm is term clustering (lines 2-4 of Algorithm 1). Fuzzy C-means is used to find top terms (the top 5) for each cluster. In term clustering, we cluster the columns of the document-term matrix which represent a term as a vector of documents. This step is only for the first iteration of the algorithm; in the next iterations the top terms are determined by the user (lines 1-7 of Algorithm 1). This property represents the interactivity of the algorithm.

The center of these top term is calculated to extend the list of top terms for each cluster (line 8 of Algorithm 1). The center is the average *entry-wise* sum of each term vector (column of document-term matrix). A term vector is the representation of a term in the vector space defined by the documents. Terms that co-occur often in the same documents will have similar term vectors. As the number of top terms increases, the result of document clustering will be more biased to the top terms indicated by the user. The user can determine his/her confidence percentile in every interaction. The user confidence level regulates the number of top terms to be extended. Based on user confidence, the number of extension of top terms is calculated from the equation in line 10 of Algorithm 1 (Default $\alpha = 0.2$). A term is assigned to the list of top terms of a term cluster if it is more similar to its center according to *Cosine similarity*.

Each term cluster contains a list of terms in which one could imagine that all these terms may belong to a single imaginary document. The average tf-idf score of these terms in all documents is considered as the tf-idf score of terms in this imaginary document (line 11 of Algorithm 1). This imaginary document is now the center of document cluster. Several documents are assigned to each document cluster center based on Cosine similarity. The number of assigned documents for each document center is related to the user confidence level (line 17 of Algorithm 1). The KMeans algorithm uses these seed documents to initialize the document clusters and then assigns all the remaining documents to each cluster. Based on our experiments in Section 4.1, KMeans can produce promising results by having good seed documents.

Document Projection

Projecting all documents in a 2D space gives the user a global view of the document clusters with their internal and external relations. Principal Component Analysis (PCA) [40] and t-Distributed Stochastic Neighborhood Embedding (t-SNE) [27] are among the most popular approaches for projection of documents. The t-SNE algorithm demonstrates better performance in visualizing clusters of data points than the PCA [27]. The t-SNE and PCA algorithms use the bag of words representation of documents to calculate the pairwise similarity between documents. In t-SNE, there is a chance that data points are loosely grouped and consequently, there may be many overlaps between data points from different clusters which makes it difficult for the user to fully understand the structure of clusters. The UTOPIAN [14] and TopicLens [21] systems tried to tackle this problem by multiplying the pairwise distance of data points belonging to the same cluster by a particular factor. In this way, data points belonging to the same cluster are grouped together which results in a clearer view of clusters. The problem with this approach is that, by changing the pairwise distance between data points, the positions of nodes are no longer as meaningful and the user cannot easily find similar documents belonging to different clusters on the visualization.

Extended t-SNE: In order to tackle the cluttering problem and avoid the pitfall of perturbing original similarities with bias towards cluster assignment, we combine Force-directed placement [16] with t-SNE. First, t-SNE is calculated in the conventional way for nodes; then, starting from the current location of nodes, Force-directed placement is applied. Force algorithms try to improve proximity of similar data point and increase separation for dissimilar data points. By starting from a favorable position, such as that calculated by t-SNE, new improved positions are obtained that may correct possible imprecise positioning in the embedding. The projection of 489 documents belonging to BBC sport dataset [17] based on original t-SNE is displayed in Fig. 1a. After labeling nodes based on their clusters, it becomes clearer that some nodes overlap (Fig. 1b). After some iterations of force directed algorithm, it is evident that segregation is improved (Figs. 1c, 1e, 1d). As the goal of Force-directed placement is reducing the number of cross-links, before applying the Force-directed forces, we add links to nodes. The links are added according to the cosine similarity between the bag of words vector representation of documents (nodes). The two nodes will have a link if they are similar above a certain threshold. After applying a few Force-directed steps the overlaps between nodes decrease significantly while still preserving the meaning of nodes location (based on t-SNE) (Fig. 1d). If the number of Force-directed iterations increases, the result of extended t-SNE will be similar to the original Force-directed layout (Fig. 1e).

Projecting documents based on Force-directed approach will place documents with similar cluster labels together while placing the isolated nodes far from the center (Fig. 1e). The problem with Force-directed placement is that the location of nodes is not directly related to their pairwise similarity (contrary to t-SNE). This means that two nodes placed near each other are not necessarily similar to each other unless there exists a link between them. In addition to the augmented t-SNE with the Force-directed projection of documents, we also provide the user of the document with the layout based exclusively on Force-directed, with flexible threshold for the links. If the user selects a node in one of these layouts, that node will be highlighted in the other layouts as well.

Visual Components

The implemented web-based user-centered system is depicted in Fig. 2. The system contains several visual components called *views*. The name of each component is given in its header. The size and the location of each view are designed as a result of our user study due to their importance and usage frequency (see Section 4.3). The *Graph view* is the most frequently used component, and views on its right part are more frequently used than the ones on the left. The user has the freedom of resizing and relocating every component of the system. The components are coordinated and changing a

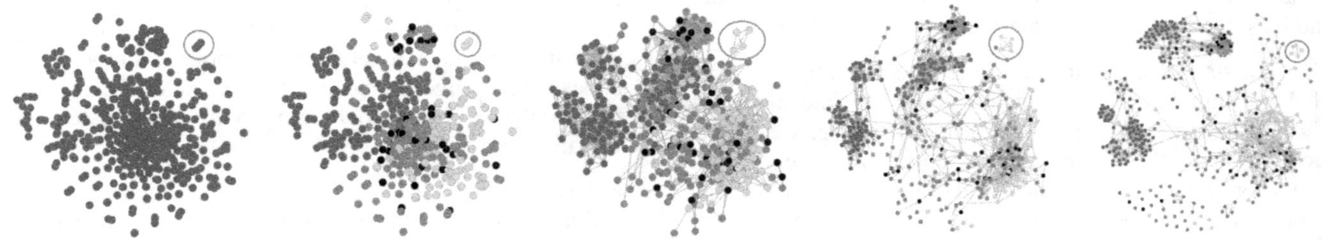

(a) The original t-SNE (b) Cluster labels added (c) 2 Force-directed ticks plus adding edges (d) 10 Force-directed ticks (e) 100 Force-directed ticks

Figure 1. The comparative result of t-SNE (a, b) and the t-SNE combined with Force-directed (c, d, e). Cluster labels are based on clustering algorithm. Even with applying a few Force-directed iterations a clearer projection of documents is producing (d). If the number of Force-directed iterations increases, the result of t-SNE will be similar to the Force-directed layout (e). A subset of 490 randomly chosen documents of *BBC sport* data set is used in these figures.

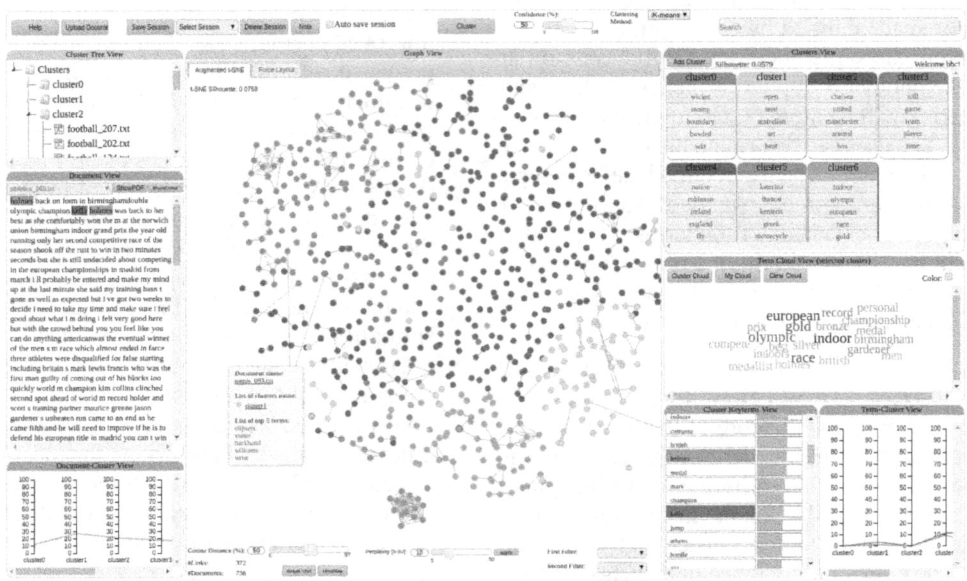

Figure 2. The visual interface of the proposed system. In the middle, the projection of 737 documents of the *BBC Sport* dataset is depicted (*Graph view*). On the left, we see the *Cluster tree view* for a hierarchical display of clusters and documents, the *Document view* for showing the plain text of documents, and the *Document-cluster view* to depict the relatedness of the selected document to each cluster. The name of each visual component is given in its header. On the right, we see the *Clusters view*, which demonstrates top terms of clusters, the *Term cloud view* for highlighting top terms of a selected cluster or set of documents, the *Cluster key-terms view* for listing top terms of a selected cluster with their level of importance (bar charts), and beside it the *Term-cluster view* to depict relatedness of a selected term(s) in *Cluster key-terms view* to each cluster. The views with colored header are all related to the selected cluster in the *Clusters view*. The selected cluster has a red margin and the same header color. The user can add, remove, rename or recolor a cluster or merge two clusters in *Clusters view*. The feedback to the clustering process by changing the number of clusters or adding/removing terms in *Clusters view*, as well as adding or removing cluster. The user can send changes made by pressing the *cluster* button on the top of the *Graph view*.

parameter in one could impact the other components as well. For example, the components with the similar color header are sharing information about the selected cluster with the same color (the one with red color margin in the picture) in the *Cluster view*, in Fig. 2. The user gains insights into the document collection and provides feedback to the clustering algorithm through the views. The feedback is in terms of adding, removing, and reordering of the clusters' top terms or adding a new cluster or removing a cluster (which change the number of clusters) in *Cluster view*. The user can iteratively interact with the clustering algorithm and in each iteration can apply a different clustering algorithm. The clustering result can be saved in each iteration so the user can roll back to previous results, and pursue different clustering directions.

The document's glyph in Graph view (the circles) contains information such as document cluster(s) color, document's name, and a list of top terms based on the documents' tf-idf score. The user can find the location of the selected document in the Document view by the red color stroke of a glyph, or load the textual content of a node in Document view by clicking on the name of a cluster in the node's tool-tip. If a document belongs to more than one cluster, its inner color turns to black. This is more convenient for the user to spot such documents than using Pie Visualization when there are many documents. The user can zoom in and out in the Graph view. The glyphs are connected according to Cosine similarity exceeding a threshold. If the user changes the threshold, links will be added/removed from graph view in real time. By setting the Cosine distance threshold to zero, only duplicate documents will still have a link. Two documents are duplicate if they share exactly the same textual content with different file names. If the user clicks on a glyph, that glyph and its neighbors will be highlighted in both augmented t-SNE and Force-directed layouts (the second tab in Graph view). It is possible to attach and select more nodes to the selected nodes (*keep function*) or deselect a node from the selected nodes (*un-keep function*). The user can view the summary of selected nodes in *Term cloud view*. Let G be a set of selected glyphs (documents), and $M^{|G|\times|W|}$ a subset of document-term matrix containing selected documents. The score (its level of importance) of a term t belonging to the selected documents is defined as Equation 4.

$$Score(t_i) = \frac{1}{|G|}\sum_{j\in G} M_{ji} \quad (4)$$

In the *Term cloud view*, a term with higher score has a larger font size and darker color. The black and white term representation helps the user to spot the important terms faster than the color version of it. It is possible to switch between black and white to the colored versions, for instance in case of better spotting of *bigram* terms.

Selecting terms in *Cluster key-term view* highlights all documents containing those terms in the *Graph view*, and the Document view. This will help the user to understand the discriminative power of selected terms, which is related to visualizing the tf-idf score of selected terms. We chose the gray-scale color for highlighting the selected terms in the *Cluster key-term view*, and the Document view to differentiate them from the clusters' color. The user can search a term in document collection and directly add it to the list of top terms of a cluster. The document relatedness in Document-cluster view and term relatedness in *Term-cluster view* are calculated by the Chi-squared statistic (χ^2) using assigned clusters labeled by the clustering algorithm as the classes in the typical use of the Chi-squared statistic in supervised feature selection.

EXPERIMENTS

In this section, a quantitative evaluation, a case study and a user study are reported to examine the quality and effectiveness of the proposed system. The back end of the proposed web-based system is implemented in Python, while the front end in JavaScript, jQuery, HTML, and D3 [10]. The result of document clustering can be saved as a Zip file of clustered documents, as a Mind Map [1], or in VNA graph format [2]. The following datasets are used in our experiments.

NG5: This dataset is a subset of 20 *Newsgroups*[2] dataset including 5 categories with 80 randomly chosen documents for each category. *Newsgroups* dataset consists of nearly 20,000 messages of Internet news articles with 20 categories collected by Ken Lang [22].

R8: A subset of *Reuters-21578* dataset containing 8 categories with 2,189 test and 5,485 training documents (7,674 documents together) [12]. Reuters-21578 is a popular dataset for text classification from Reuters newswire in 1987 assembled by David Lewis [35].

[2] www.qwone.com/~jason/20Newsgroups/

Table 1. The comparison result of clustering algorithms with random initialization (The average 200 runs for each algorithm). Adjusted Random Score (ARS), Adjusted Mutual Information (AMI), Homogeneity (H), and Average Silhouette (S) are used as a metric.

Dataset Name	Metric	Fuzzy C-means	LDC	KMeans	iKMeans
NG5 (400 doc. 4 classes)	ARS	0.521	0.501	0.201	0.628
	AMI	0.614	0.577	0.297	0.710
	H	0.619	0.582	0.306	0.714
	S	0.090	0.074	0.034	0.087
R8 (2189 doc. 8 classes)	ARS	0.353	0.440	0.195	0.305
	AMI	0.438	0.481	0.387	0.447
	H	0.637	0.659	0.473	0.592
	S	0.092	0.083	0.077	0.092
WebKB (4199 doc. 4 classes)	ARS	0.310	0.324	0.265	0.320
	AMI	0.337	0.326	0.281	0.311
	H	0.354	0.337	0.283	0.314
	S	0.027	0.025	0.024	0.022

Table 2. The role of seeds (documents) quality in the result of document clustering. The *NG5* dataset is used in this experiment. Bad seeds are assigning 3 seed document with similar label to each cluster. Good seeds are assigning 5 correctly labeled seeds to each of cluster. Semi-bad and -good are between bad and good seeds.

Seed Type	Evaluation metric	Fuzzy C-means	Seeded KMeans
Bad seeds	Adjusted Random Score	0.558	0.006
	Adjusted Mutual Info	0.647	0.006
	Homogeneity	0.651	0.051
	Average Silhouette	0.104	0.010
Semi-bad seeds	Adjusted Random Score	0.486	0.067
	Adjusted Mutual Info	0.588	0.198
	Homogeneity	0.593	0.208
	Average Silhouette	0.102	0.052
Semi-good seeds	Adjusted Random Score	0.548	0.305
	Adjusted Mutual Info	0.641	0.414
	Homogeneity	0.646	0.422
	Average Silhouette	0.103	0.048
Good seeds	Adjusted Random Score	0.545	0.637
	Adjusted Mutual Info	0.639	0.711
	Homogeneity	0.644	0.715
	Average Silhouette	0.103	0.088

NewsSeparate: This dataset contains 381 news feeds manually categorized into 13 categories [33]. In the user study (Section 4.3), we randomly selected 100 documents belonging to 4 categories from this dataset.

WebKB: This dataset is 4199 faculty, student, project, and course web sites crawled from the computer science faculty website of four universities in January 1997 [15].

Yahoo Answers: A collection of 189,467 questions and answers extracted from Yahoo! answers website with 20 top-level and 280 sub-categories [13]. In the user study, we used 6 sub-categories containing general questions about *Computer*, *Education*, *Music*, *Food Receipts*, *General Health*, and *Society*. For each category we randomly selected 100 question and answer pairs.

BBC Sport: Introduced by Greene and Cunningham [17] which contains 737 news articles about 5 sport categories extracted from BBC website from 2004-2005.

Quantitative Evaluation

In our experiments we employed *Adjusted Random Score* (ARS), *Adjusted Mutual Information* (AMI), *Homogeneity* (H), and *Average Silhouette* (S) (the average of all documents' *Silhouette* score). ARS is a measure of similarity between the ground truth clustering and the clustering algorithm [20]. ARS is between 0 and 1, where value near 0 reflects random clustering. ARS is penalized by the number of false positive and false negative predictions. AMI is an adjusted version of *Mutual Information* to reduce the effect of the agreement by chance and it is 0 in random clustering [38]. Homogeneity is between 0 and 1. A clustering has a higher *Homogeneity* score if its clusters contain more documents which are members of a single class [36]. *Silhouette* is an unsupervised metric for evaluation of the document clustering algorithm and helping the user to find the optimum number of clusters [37]. The Silhouette is between -1 and 1, where the higher positive value for a document shows it is more similar to the assigned cluster than the other clusters.

We compared different clustering algorithms implemented within our proposed framework without the user interactions in Table 1. The experiments are a result of using unigrams with mean-tf-idf as feature selection, and algorithms are initialized randomly. First, iKMeans (Algorithm 1) receives the top 5 terms for each cluster from the output of the Fuzzy C-means algorithm, then it provides seed documents for the KMeans algorithm. In all of the datasets iKMeans performed better than KMeans which demonstrates the effectiveness of our proposed framework. Comparing iKMeans with LDC and Fuzzy C-means algorithms shows that there is no clear winner. What algorithm performs best is dependent on the dataset.

In the next experiment, the interactivity of the KMeans algorithm, which is called Seeded KMeans in Table 2 is evaluated. In this experiment, the documents' labels are provided as supervision to the algorithm so instead of random initialization it has been initialized based on these document labels. This is somehow simulating lines 1-21 of Algorithm 1 by directly providing the seed documents to the KMeans clustering algorithm. We provided four different sets of seed documents.

- *Bad Seeds*: In the case of Bad Seeds, 3 seed documents are assigned to each cluster where all of these seed documents have a similar label.
- *Semi Bad Seeds*: If the number of seed documents per cluster is reduced to 1, Semi Bad Seeds situation will occur.
- *Good Seeds*: For clustering with Good Seeds, 5 seed documents are assigned to each cluster, where each cluster's seeds are labeled to a single correct label different from other clusters' seeds.
- *Semi Good Seeds*: Reducing the number of seed documents to 1 results in a Semi Good Seeds setting.

The results in Table 2 demonstrate that by providing a few good labeled documents KMeans performance increases significantly. On the other hand, the Fuzzy C-means performance did not change with this number of documents and more seeds are needed to see a positive impact. From the user's point of view, the algorithm which could be improved with a smaller number of interactions is preferable.

Table 3. The improvement of the Avg. Silhouette after each interaction.

Avg. Silhouette	Interaction 1	Interaction 2	Interaction 3
t-SNE	0.3493	0.3533	0.3544
Clustering	0.1267	0.1382	0.1530

Use Case

We asked a computer science researcher with good knowledge of document clustering to cluster the *Yahoo Answers* dataset without mentioning the subject of the dataset to her. The use case took 40 minutes including 20 minutes for system introduction. We recorded the user interactions and report the summary of them in this paragraph. First, the user asked the clustering algorithm to generate 4 clusters, shown in Fig. 3a. Second, the user checked the Term Cloud of clusters to know their topic and by looking at the Graph view, she noticed that there were two dense groups of documents in the cluster with the topics *Cancer*, *Syndrome*, and *Lymphoma*. Third, the user selected several nodes related to one of these groups of documents in the Graph view with the help of the Keep function. She noticed that these nodes were about *education* and *university* (the blue Term Cloud in Fig. 3a), so she selected the top three terms from Term Cloud and created the new cluster. The new clustering result after adding a new cluster is shown in Fig. 3b. The new cluster (blue color) now had two dense sets of nodes. Fourth, the user found out that terms such as *Education* were common between these two sets of documents with the help of Term-cluster view. On the other hand, one of the sets of documents was more about *Language*, *French*, and *Spanish* so she decided to create a new cluster. The user also removed the term *Education* from the blue color cluster to help the clustering algorithm separate these two sets of documents. The result of clustering after the third interaction of the user is in Fig. 3c. The improvement in the Silhouette score after each interaction (see Table 3), gave the user more confidence about the usefulness of the feedback to the clustering algorithm.

User Study

We invited 18 participants (9 female) for a user study. The participants were computer science students with at least acceptable knowledge of document clustering and strong English comprehension skills. The study was in an office with a single monitor with 1920x1200 resolution. In this study, we had two research questions: 1) evaluate the impact of users' interactions on the quality of document clustering. 2) determine if the visualization assists the users in obtaining better insight into the document collection and in improving the clustering result. To find the answer to these questions we designed two separate tasks. For each user, 20 minutes were allocated for training and 50 minutes were allocated to finish both tasks of the study.

Task 1. Interactive clustering.

In the first task, we gave each of the 18 participants 30 minutes to cluster the *Yahoo Answers*. Each document in this dataset was renamed to prevent the user from finding the correct cluster label of documents by their name. We did not provide any

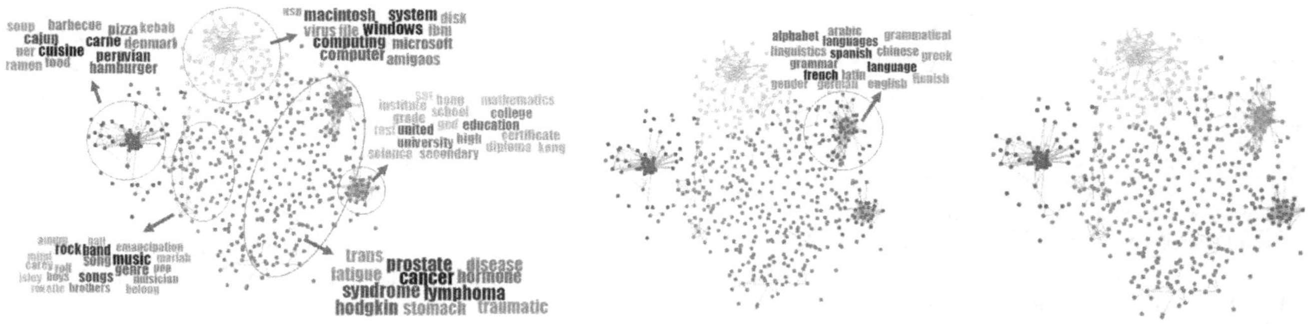

Figure 3. The screen-shots of different interaction rounds conducted by the user. The *Yahoo Answers* dataset and the iKMeans algorithm is used in this use case.

Table 4. Statistics about the study. The left table shows users' vote for visualization modules. The middle table is average number of important users' interactions in the first task. The right table highlights the most frequent users' operations and the name of its parent module.

Module name	# Votes
Document-cluster & Document view	4
key-terms view & Term-cluster view	6
Cluster view	5
Term cloud view	6
Graph view	14

Action name	Avg. Count
Re-clustering	7.17 ± 4.78
Add term	25.39 ± 26.42
Remove term	5.61 ± 5.77
Add cluster	4.22 ± 2.05
Remove cluster	0.33 ± 0.77

Operation description	Module name	Percent
Highlight documents containing the selected term	Graph view	11.45%
Click on a cluster to load its information on views	Cluster view	10.95%
Mouse over a node to see its information (tool-tip)	Graph view	7.56%
Creating terms cloud	Term Cloud view	6.86%
Click term in key-term view & load Term-cluster view	key-terms view & Term-cluster view	6.69%

information about the topics of the dataset or its number of clusters. To provide similar conditions for each user, each one started with the result of random initialization of the clustering algorithm with 3 clusters. We recorded every operation that users conducted during this task. The average frequency of five important actions of the term-based interactive clustering that users conducted is in the middle section of Table 4. The following is a summary of findings in the first task.

- The high standard deviation for the number of *Add term*, indicates that some users generated a longer list of key terms as the supervision to the clustering algorithm. There is a +0.42 (Pearson) correlation between the number of *Add term* and the Homogeneity score of the final clustering result after users' interactions.
- The users categorized this dataset to 5.7 ± 1.3 clusters in average which is close to the actual number of classes in this dataset.
- The most frequent operations users did during this task is summarized in the right section of Table 4.
- The users were asked in the post-task questionnaires to vote for each module of the system (multiple votes were allowed). The level of popularity and the importance of the Graph view by the users is displayed in left part of Table 4.

In order to investigate the impact of users' interactions on the quality of the final clustering result, we compared the initial clustering and the clustering after user interactions in the first task. The evaluation metrics are Adjusted Random Score (ARS), Adjusted Mutual Information (AMI), Homogeneity (H), and Average Silhouette (S) (See Fig. 4). Results demonstrate that user supervision significantly improved the result of clustering. During the study, four participants misunderstood the instructions and were not able to complete the task properly. A higher improvement with lower Standard Deviation was achieved after removing these participants (Final2 bar charts in Fig. 4).

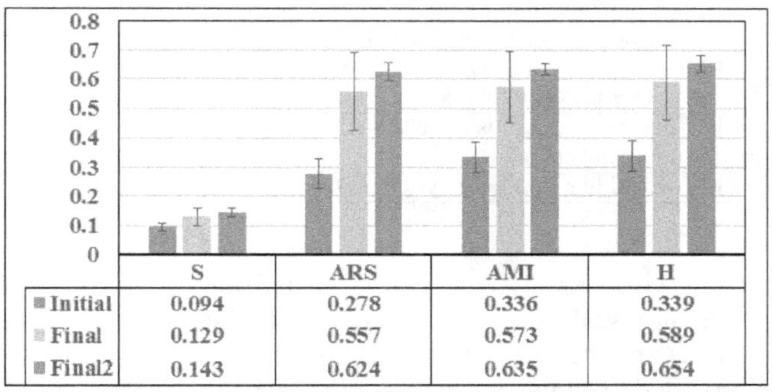

Figure 4. The comparison between the initial clustering and the final clustering after user interactions. The final2 is after removing outliers.

Task 2. Obtaining insight on a document collection.

In the second task, we studied the impact of the user interface on helping the user obtain better insight into the document collection. The *NewsSeparate* dataset with 3 initial clusters is used in this task. The users were unfamiliar with the content of the dataset prior to the experiments. After the user performed the task, a questionnaire was provided to each user, who had 10 minutes to complete it (See Table 5). We asked the user to answer these questions twice (two modes); once with and

Table 5. Comparing the result (number of correct answers) of the system with (Vis.) and without (Base) visualization and their significance differences based on Wilcoxon signed-rank test with $p < 0.05$.

Question	Base	Vis.	P-value
1-Provide a title for each cluster	14/18	16/18	0.2119
2-Give the names of two clusters with most similar topics	4/18	9/18	0.0184
3-For each cluster, provide at least 1 term belong to other clusters as well	2/18	9/18	0.0054
Overall (for all questions)	**20**	**34**	**0.0023**

Table 6. The Post-task questionnaire. Questions 1-10 are from the Software Usability Scale (SUS) questionnaire. All answers are in 5-point Likert scale agreement scores (1: strongly disagree, 2: disagree, 3: neither agree nor disagree, 4: agree, 5: strongly agree).

Statement	Avg.
1-I think that I would like to use this system frequently	4.28±0.83
2-I found the system unnecessarily complex	2.28±0.83
3-I thought the system was easy to use	4.22±0.65
4-I think that I would need the support of a technical person to be able to use this system	2.22±1.06
5-I found the various functions in this system were well integrated	4.61±0.50
6-I found there was too much inconsistency in this system	1.44±0.62
7-I would imagine that most people would learn to use this system very quickly	4.17±0.92
8-I found the system very cumbersome to use	2.17±1.04
9-I felt very confident using the system	4.28±0.75
10-I needed to learn a lot of things before I could get going with this system	2.28±1.13
11-It is more meaningful to use phrases instead of single words to determining the clusters topics	3.89±0.83
12-Term based visualization and term labeling is a useful way in generating desired cluster topics	4.67±0.69
13-The user interface is a useful tool for document clustering in general	4.67±0.59
14-I would like to use the system in the future	4.61±0.70

once without (base mode) the visualization. In the mode without visualization, the ordered list of the top terms of each cluster and the folder of documents related to each cluster was provided. The users used the Windows file explorer and the Notepad++ text editor to dig into the clustering result in this mode. These are common tools for users to inspect automatic clustering results without the visualization. We randomly divided the participants into two halves. For the first half of the participants the clustering results with and for the second half without visualization was provided first. For the first question, the users were able to answer it properly in both modes. We believe the reason is that the ordered list of the top terms for each cluster is a good description of each cluster and it was easily accessible in both modes. For the next two questions, the result of the visualization mode is statistically significantly better, which shows the effectiveness of the visualization. The order of providing the visualization or the base mode at first did not have a statistically significant impact on the quality of users' answers. We did not inform the users that in both modes they were answering the same questions about the same dataset. The overall comparison result in Table 5 demonstrates that the visualization is significantly better than the base mode.

Three more questions were asked from users to test the *ease of use* and the *learnability* of the visualization. The first question asked which cluster has the highest number of documents and 83% of participants answered correctly. The second question was about the number of repetitive documents in the collection and 45% of participants were able to answer this question correctly. For the third question, participants needed to give the number of documents with more than one cluster labels. 67% of the participants answered this question correctly. The correct answer rate for the complicated questions such as the second question indicates that near a half of users were able to learn the very detail of the system only after 20 minutes of training.

The result of the post-task questionnaire is in Table 6. The goal of these questions was to get the users experience and opinion during the user study. The first 10 questions of Table 6 are selected from the Software Usability Scale (SUS) questionnaire [11]. The result of participants answers to the questions of Table 6 demonstrates the effectiveness and usefulness of the proposed system for interactive document clustering.

CONCLUSION AND FUTURE WORK

We introduced a novel solution for interactive document clustering. First, the proposed solution was evaluated in real world datasets by end users, demonstrating significant improvement in the quality of the clusters over fully automatic clustering. We built our system based on key-term interaction because of its intuitiveness for the user. Second, we introduced an interactive version of KMeans called iKMeans. The proposed method for iKMeans could be applied to other clustering algorithms and consequently could be employed in the proposed system. Third, we have combined the t-SNE algorithm with force directed display for improved projection of documents. The evaluation result demonstrates the effectiveness of the proposed system on improving the clustering result.

In the future, we intend to add a visualization module for better depicting the clusters' change during user' interactions. Incorporating the feedback obtained as a result of the user study to extend the functionality and usability of the system for better visualization and clustering of document collection is in the list of our future work. We would like to further extend our system for datasets with temporal aspect, in that case user can interact with the clustering algorithm to improve the result of the clustering for only a specific time frame.

ACKNOWLEDGMENTS

The authors thank all participants in the user study. The research was partially funded by the Natural Sciences and Engineering Research Council of Canada, the Boeing Company (Canada), CNPq and FAPESP (Brazil), and the International Development Research Center, Ottawa, Canada.

REFERENCES

1. Accessed: 2017-10-07. Mind Map file format Description. `http://http://freemind.sourceforge.net`. (Accessed: 2017-10-07).

2. Accessed: 2017-10-07. VNA file format Description. `https://gephi.org/users/supported-graph-formats/netdraw-vna-format/`. (Accessed: 2017-10-07).

3. David Andrzejewski, Xiaojin Zhu, and Mark Craven. 2009. Incorporating Domain Knowledge into Topic Modeling via Dirichlet Forest Priors. In *Proceedings of the 26th Annual International Conference on Machine Learning (ICML '09)*. ACM, New York, NY, USA, 25–32. DOI:http://dx.doi.org/10.1145/1553374.1553378

4. Pranjal Awasthi, Maria-Florina Balcan, and Konstantin Voevodski. 2014. Local Algorithms for Interactive Clustering. In *Proceedings of the 31st International Conference on International Conference on Machine Learning - Volume 32 (ICML'14)*. JMLR.org, II–550–II–558. http://dl.acm.org/citation.cfm?id=3044805.3044954

5. Maria-Florina Balcan and Avrim Blum. 2008. Clustering with Interactive Feedback. In *Proceedings of the 19th International Conference on Algorithmic Learning Theory (ALT '08)*. Springer-Verlag, Berlin, Heidelberg, 316–328. DOI: http://dx.doi.org/10.1007/978-3-540-87987-9_27

6. Sugato Basu, Arindam Banerjee, and Raymond J. Mooney. 2002. Semi-supervised Clustering by Seeding. In *Proceedings of the Nineteenth International Conference on Machine Learning (ICML '02)*. Morgan Kaufmann Publishers Inc., San Francisco, CA, USA, 27–34. http://dl.acm.org/citation.cfm?id=645531.656012

7. Ron Bekkerman, Hema Raghavan, James Allan, and Koji Eguchi. 2007. Interactive Clustering of Text Collections According to a User-specified Criterion. In *Proceedings of the 20th International Joint Conference on Artifical Intelligence (IJCAI'07)*. Morgan Kaufmann Publishers Inc., San Francisco, CA, USA, 684–689. http://dl.acm.org/citation.cfm?id=1625275.1625385

8. James C. Bezdek. 1981. *Pattern Recognition with Fuzzy Objective Function Algorithms*. Kluwer Academic Publishers, Norwell, MA, USA.

9. David M Blei, Andrew Y Ng, and Michael I Jordan. 2003. Latent dirichlet allocation. *Journal of machine Learning research* 3, Jan (2003), 993–1022.

10. Michael Bostock, Vadim Ogievetsky, and Jeffrey Heer. 2011. D3 Data-Driven Documents. *IEEE Transactions on Visualization and Computer Graphics* 17, 12 (Dec. 2011), 2301–2309. DOI: http://dx.doi.org/10.1109/TVCG.2011.185

11. John Brooke and others. 1996. SUS-A quick and dirty usability scale. *Usability evaluation in industry* 189, 194 (1996), 4–7.

12. Ana Cardoso-Cachopo. 2007. Improving Methods for Single-label Text Categorization. PdD Thesis, Instituto Superior Tecnico, Universidade Tecnica de Lisboa. (2007).

13. M. Chang, L. Ratinov, D. Roth, and V. Srikumar. 2008. Importance of Semantic Representation: Dataless Classification. In *AAAI*. http://cogcomp.cs.illinois.edu/papers/CRRS08.pdf

14. Jaegul Choo, Changhyun Lee, Chandan K. Reddy, and Haesun Park. 2013. UTOPIAN: User-Driven Topic Modeling Based on Interactive Nonnegative Matrix Factorization. *IEEE Transactions on Visualization and Computer Graphics* 19, 12 (Dec. 2013), 1992–2001. DOI: http://dx.doi.org/10.1109/TVCG.2013.212

15. Mark Craven, Dan DiPasquo, Dayne Freitag, Andrew McCallum, Tom Mitchell, Kamal Nigam, and Seán Slattery. 1998. Learning to Extract Symbolic Knowledge from the World Wide Web. In *Proceedings of the Fifteenth National/Tenth Conference on Artificial Intelligence/Innovative Applications of Artificial Intelligence (AAAI '98/IAAI '98)*. American Association for Artificial Intelligence, Menlo Park, CA, USA, 509–516. http://dl.acm.org/citation.cfm?id=295240.295725

16. Thomas M. J. Fruchterman and Edward M. Reingold. 1991. Graph drawing by force-directed placement. *Software: Practice and Experience* 21, 11 (1991), 1129–1164. DOI: http://dx.doi.org/10.1002/spe.4380211102

17. Derek Greene and Pádraig Cunningham. 2005. Producing Accurate Interpretable Clusters from High-dimensional Data. In *Proceedings of the 9th European Conference on Principles and Practice of Knowledge Discovery in Databases (PKDD'05)*. Springer-Verlag, Berlin, Heidelberg, 486–494. DOI: http://dx.doi.org/10.1007/11564126_49

18. Yuening Hu, Jordan Boyd-Graber, and Brianna Satinoff. 2011. Interactive Topic Modeling. In *Proceedings of the 49th Annual Meeting of the Association for Computational Linguistics: Human Language Technologies - Volume 1 (HLT '11)*. Association for Computational Linguistics, Stroudsburg, PA, USA, 248–257. http://dl.acm.org/citation.cfm?id=2002472.2002505

19. Yeming Hu, Evangelos E. Milios, James Blustein, and Shali Liu. 2012. Personalized Document Clustering with Dual Supervision. In *Proceedings of the 2012 ACM Symposium on Document Engineering (DocEng '12)*. ACM, New York, NY, USA, 161–170. DOI: http://dx.doi.org/10.1145/2361354.2361393

20. Lawrence Hubert and Phipps Arabie. 1985. Comparing partitions. *Journal of Classification* 2, 1 (1985), 193–218. DOI:http://dx.doi.org/10.1007/BF01908075

21. M. Kim, K. Kang, D. Park, J. Choo, and N. Elmqvist. 2017. TopicLens: Efficient Multi-Level Visual Topic Exploration of Large-Scale Document Collections. *IEEE Transactions on Visualization and Computer Graphics* 23, 1 (Jan 2017), 151–160. DOI: http://dx.doi.org/10.1109/TVCG.2016.2598445

22. Ken Lang. 1995. Newsweeder: Learning to filter netnews. In *Proceedings of the Twelfth International Conference on Machine Learning*. 331–339.

23. Hanseung Lee, Jaeyeon Kihm, Jaegul Choo, John Stasko, and Haesun Park. 2012. iVisClustering: An Interactive Visual Document Clustering via Topic Modeling. *Computer Graphics Forum* 31, 3pt3 (2012), 1155–1164. DOI: http://dx.doi.org/10.1111/j.1467-8659.2012.03108.x

24. Y. Li, C. Luo, and S. M. Chung. 2008. Text Clustering with Feature Selection by Using Statistical Data. *IEEE Transactions on Knowledge and Data Engineering* 20, 5 (May 2008), 641–652. DOI: http://dx.doi.org/10.1109/TKDE.2007.190740

25. Bing Liu, Xiaoli Li, Wee Sun Lee, and Philip S. Yu. 2004. Text Classification by Labeling Words. In *Proceedings of the 19th National Conference on Artifical Intelligence (AAAI'04)*. AAAI Press, 425–430. http://dl.acm.org/citation.cfm?id=1597148.1597218

26. Tao Liu, Shengping Liu, Zheng Chen, and Wei-Ying Ma. 2003. An Evaluation on Feature Selection for Text Clustering. In *Proceedings of the Twentieth International Conference on International Conference on Machine Learning (ICML'03)*. AAAI Press, 488–495. http://dl.acm.org/citation.cfm?id=3041838.3041900

27. Laurens van der Maaten and Geoffrey Hinton. 2008. Visualizing data using t-SNE. *Journal of Machine Learning Research* 9, Nov (2008), 2579–2605.

28. Christopher D. Manning, Prabhakar Raghavan, and Hinrich Schütze. 2008. *Introduction to Information Retrieval*. Cambridge University Press, New York, NY, USA.

29. Seyednaser Nourashrafeddin, Evangelos Milios, and Dirk Arnold. 2013. Interactive Text Document Clustering Using Feature Labeling. In *Proceedings of the 2013 ACM Symposium on Document Engineering (DocEng '13)*. ACM, New York, NY, USA, 61–70. DOI: http://dx.doi.org/10.1145/2494266.2494279

30. Seyednaser Nourashrafeddin, Evangelos Milios, and Drik V. Arnold. 2014. An Ensemble Approach for Text Document Clustering Using Wikipedia Concepts. In *Proceedings of the 2014 ACM Symposium on Document Engineering (DocEng '14)*. ACM, New York, NY, USA, 107–116. DOI: http://dx.doi.org/10.1145/2644866.2644868

31. Seyednaser Nourashrafeddin, Ehsan Sherkat, Rosane Minghim, and Evangelos Milios. in press. A Visual Approach for Interactive Keyterm-based Clustering. *ACM Transactions on Interactive Intelligent Systems* (in press).

32. Pentti Paatero and Unto Tapper. 1994. Positive matrix factorization: A non-negative factor model with optimal utilization of error estimates of data values. *Environmetrics* 5, 2 (1994), 111–126. DOI: http://dx.doi.org/10.1002/env.3170050203

33. F. V. Paulovich, L. G. Nonato, R. Minghim, and H. Levkowitz. 2008. Least Square Projection: A Fast High-Precision Multidimensional Projection Technique and Its Application to Document Mapping. *IEEE Transactions on Visualization and Computer Graphics* 14, 3 (May 2008), 564–575. DOI: http://dx.doi.org/10.1109/TVCG.2007.70443

34. Daniel Ramage, David Hall, Ramesh Nallapati, and Christopher D. Manning. 2009. Labeled LDA: A Supervised Topic Model for Credit Attribution in Multi-labeled Corpora. In *Proceedings of the 2009 Conference on Empirical Methods in Natural Language Processing: Volume 1 - Volume 1 (EMNLP '09)*. Association for Computational Linguistics, Stroudsburg, PA, USA, 248–256. http://dl.acm.org/citation.cfm?id=1699510.1699543

35. Tony Rose, Mark Stevenson, and Miles Whitehead. 2002. The Reuters Corpus Volume 1-from Yesterday's News to Tomorrow's Language Resources.. In *LREC*, Vol. 2. 827–832.

36. Andrew Rosenberg and Julia Hirschberg. 2007. V-Measure: A Conditional Entropy-Based External Cluster Evaluation Measure.. In *EMNLP-CoNLL*, Vol. 7. 410–420.

37. Peter Rousseeuw. 1987. Silhouettes: A Graphical Aid to the Interpretation and Validation of Cluster Analysis. *J. Comput. Appl. Math.* 20, 1 (Nov. 1987), 53–65. DOI: http://dx.doi.org/10.1016/0377-0427(87)90125-7

38. Nguyen Xuan Vinh, Julien Epps, and James Bailey. 2010. Information Theoretic Measures for Clusterings Comparison: Variants, Properties, Normalization and Correction for Chance. *J. Mach. Learn. Res.* 11 (Dec. 2010), 2837–2854. http://dl.acm.org/citation.cfm?id=1756006.1953024

39. Kiri Wagstaff, Claire Cardie, Seth Rogers, and Stefan Schrödl. 2001. Constrained K-means Clustering with Background Knowledge. In *Proceedings of the Eighteenth International Conference on Machine Learning (ICML '01)*. Morgan Kaufmann Publishers Inc., San Francisco, CA, USA, 577–584. http://dl.acm.org/citation.cfm?id=645530.655669

40. Svante Wold, Kim Esbensen, and Paul Geladi. 1987. Principal component analysis. *Chemometrics and intelligent laboratory systems* 2, 1-3 (1987), 37–52.

41. Yi Yang, Shimei Pan, Yangqiu Song, Jie Lu, and Mercan Topkara. 2015. User-directed Non-Disruptive Topic Model Update for Effective Exploration of Dynamic Content. In *Proceedings of the 20th International Conference on Intelligent User Interfaces (IUI '15)*. ACM, New York, NY, USA, 158–168. DOI: http://dx.doi.org/10.1145/2678025.2701396

42. Yiming Yang and Jan O. Pedersen. 1997. A Comparative Study on Feature Selection in Text Categorization. In *Proceedings of the Fourteenth International Conference on Machine Learning (ICML '97)*. Morgan Kaufmann Publishers Inc., San Francisco, CA, USA, 412–420. http://dl.acm.org/citation.cfm?id=645526.657137

Closing the Loop: User-Centered Design and Evaluation of a Human-in-the-Loop Topic Modeling System

Alison Smith
University of Maryland
Computer Science
College Park, Maryland, USA
amsmit@umd.edu

Varun Kumar
University of Maryland
Computer Science
College Park, Maryland, USA
varunk@cs.umd.edu

Jordan Boyd-Graber
University of Maryland
CS, iSchool, UMIACS, LSC
College Park, Maryland, USA
jbg@umiacs.umd.edu

Kevin Seppi
Brigham Young University
Computer Science
Provo, Utah, USA
kseppi@byu.edu

Leah Findlater
University of Washington
Human Centered Design and Engineering
Seattle, Washington, USA
leahkf@uw.edu

ABSTRACT
Human-in-the-loop topic modeling allows users to guide the creation of topic models and to improve model quality without having to be experts in topic modeling algorithms. Prior work in this area has focused either on algorithmic implementation without understanding how users actually wish to improve the model or on user needs but without the context of a fully interactive system. To address this disconnect, we implemented a set of model refinements requested by users in prior work and conducted a study with twelve non-expert participants to examine how end users are affected by issues that arise with a fully interactive, user-centered system. As these issues mirror those identified in interactive machine learning more broadly, such as unpredictability, latency, and trust, we also examined interactive machine learning challenges with non-expert end users through the lens of human-in-the-loop topic modeling. We found that although users experience unpredictability, their reactions vary from positive to negative, and, surprisingly, we did not find any cases of distrust, but instead noted instances where users perhaps trusted the system too much or had too little confidence in themselves.

INTRODUCTION
Topic modeling helps users understand vast document collections when there are too many documents or too little time to read individual documents: a journalist processing the reports surrounding breaking news or a legal team finding interesting e-mails during discovery. Topic modeling automatically discovers the themes (topics) in large corpora of unstructured text [7] by modeling the intuition that groups of words that form a common theme appear more often together than not; the discovered topics are sets of words (e.g., "football, touchdown, NFL, ..."), and each document can contain multiple topics. However, traditional topic models can include poor quality topics [30] or can be misaligned with a domain expert's understanding of the corpus [23]. Pre-processing techniques and parameter tuning [36] can improve model quality, but typically require many time-consuming iterations and can only be performed by an algorithm expert. Human-in-the-loop topic modeling (HL-TM) aims to solve these problems by allowing end users who are not experts with topic modeling algorithms to directly refine the model (e.g., changing which words are included in a topic, or merging or splitting topics).

HL-TM has largely implemented topic model refinements based on what algorithm developers *assume* users want, as well as algorithm concerns, such as which refinements are the most straightforward to implement [23, 10, 21, 26]. In contrast, Lee et al. [27] employed a user-centered approach to identify a set of topic refinement operations that users expect to have in a HL-TM system. However, because no existing implementation supported the set of refinement operations (e.g., add a topic word, change word order, merge topics), they used Wizard-of-Oz refinements: the resulting topics were updated superficially—not as the output of a data-driven statistical model (the goal of topic models). Thus, this study is limited, as it ignores the common interactive machine learning issues that arise in a fully interactive system—such as, unpredictability, latency, and complexity—that can affect user experience and impact how users interact with a HL-TM system.

To address these limitations we implemented a broad set of refinements operations [27, 31] in a single system: *add word*, *remove word*, *remove document*, *change word order*, *split topic*, *merge topics*, and *add to stop words*. Unlike in Lee et al. [27], where refinements were immediately applied only in the interface and were not saved to the backing model, in our study

IUI 2018, March 7–11, 2018, Tokyo, Japan.

ACM ISBN 978-1-4503-4945-1/18/03 ...$15.00.
https://doi.org/10.1145/3172944.3172965

participants chose when to "save" and update the backing model with their refinements. We evaluated this fully interactive, user-centered HL-TM system with 12 participants who were not experts in topic modeling. This system is also fast enough to support (and study) interactive use of fine-grained topic modifications, unlike prior systems [21, 10, 23] (e.g., early HL-TM systems took $5-50$ seconds for each update [23], whereas ours took $.09-.63$ seconds to update after saving during the user study). In addition to observing how participants employed the refinements to improve a topic model, we qualitatively assessed overall experience and the potential impacts of common interactive machine learning challenges, such as unpredictability and latency.

Participants subjectively and objectively improved topic model quality using the given refinements. Similar to Lee et al. [27], simple refinements, such as *remove word* and *change word order* were most common, however, unlike Lee et al. [27], usage did not align perfectly with perceived utility, as participants found *change word order* to be one of the least useful refinements. Our fully interactive system also exposed previously hidden issues: unexpected results from using refinements and an inability to track model changes. Participants also varied in when and why they saved their local updates to the underlying model. Additionally, participants who had more trust in the system (or perhaps less confidence in themselves) were not as frustrated by unpredictability as others.

This work makes the following contributions: (1) efficient asymmetric prior-based implementation of a broader set of user-centered refinement operations than has been previously implemented in a single system; (2) extension of a previous, limited HL-TM user study [27] to this fully interactive system; (3) understanding of how interactive machine learning issues such as unpredictability, trust, and lack of control impact HL-TM usage and design; and (4) design principles for user-centered HL-TM systems.

BACKGROUND

Topic modeling automatically identifies the themes or topics that occur in a collection of documents. A common approach is Latent Dirichlet Allocation (LDA) [4], which is a generative statistical model that models each document as a distribution of topics and each topic as a distribution of words. Here, we provide a brief background of LDA and existing HL-TM systems. We also discuss design challenges for interactive machine learning systems more generally.

Latent Dirichlet Allocation

LDA [4] is a generative model, which assumes that each document d is generated from a fixed set of k topics. Each topic is a multinomial distribution, ϕ_z, over the vocabulary, V. Each instance of a word, or token, w_i, is generated by sampling a topic assignment z_i from the document's topic distribution θ_d, followed by sampling the selected topic's distribution ϕ_{z_i}, to generate a token w_i.

The multinomial distributions θ_d and ϕ_z are drawn from Dirichlet distributions that encode sparsity—how many words you expect to see in a topic or how many topics in a document—and can also incorporate expert knowledge from users. Below, we show how to adjust the Dirichlet hyperparameters, α and β, to encode user information about documents (α) and topics (β).

Given this model, we need to find the distribution that best explains our observed documents. Griffiths and Steyvers [17] propose a collapsed Gibbs sampling based method. In collapsed Gibbs sampling, the probability of a topic assignment $z=t$ in document d given an observed token, w_i, and the other topic assignments, z_{-}, is

$$P(z=t\,|\,z_{-},w) \propto (n_{d,t}+\alpha)\frac{n_{w,t}+\beta}{n_t+V\beta}. \quad (1)$$

Here, z_{-} are the topic assignments of all other tokens, $n_{d,t}$ is the number of times topic t is used in document d, $n_{w,t}$ is the number of times token w is used in topic t, and n_t is the marginal count of the number of tokens assigned to topic t. For traditional topic models, the Gibbs sampler assigns latent topics Z for all tokens in the corpus, going over all the documents in the corpus repeatedly until the algorithm converges.

The state of the sampler represents the algorithm's best guess of the topic assignments for every token. Adding a human in the loop requires the user to be able to inject their knowledge and expertise into the sampling equation to guide the algorithm to better topics.

Human-in-the-loop Topic Modeling

Compared to traditional tools that visualize static topic models [15, 13, 9], HL-TM provides mechanisms to allow end users to refine *changing* topic models. Numerous tools have been designed around this concept, each implementing a variety of refinements, but without extensive user studies on real world-tasks to show the refinement implementations match user expectations. Andrzejewski et al. [3], building on Boyd-Graber et al. [6], introduced a statistical framework for users to specify pairs of words that should or should not belong to the same topic through "must-link" and "cannot-link" constraints. This framework has been extended by numerous HL-TM tools [23, 11, 33]; however, this approach limits the possible set of refinements that can be supported and does not match users expectations in that end users typically do not think of specifying model refinements as pairwise word correlations [27].

Other HL-TM tools take alternative approaches, such as UTOPIAN [10], which uses nonnegative matrix factorization and supports creating, splitting, and merging topics, in addition to changing word weights. Lund et al. [28] also uses a fast matrix-factorization approach but only supports a limited set of interactions. ConVisIT [21] uses fragment quotation graphs and supports splitting and merging topics. Finally, Distillery [31] uses informative priors to support merging and removing topics, as well as adding and removing topic words and adding to stop words. However, no prior implementation supports the complete set of refinement operations requested by users [27].

Interactive Machine Learning Design Challenges

Interactive machine learning—also known as mixed-initiative or human-in-the-loop systems—incorporate human input to produce an output or a decision. Designers of these must account for challenges inherent in machine learning, which deviates from traditional user interface design. While user interfaces should provide immediate updates [29], be predictable [18], ensure the user feels in control, and reduce short term memory load [34], interactive machine learning systems are commonly slow, unpredictable, share control between user and system, and are complex [2, 19].

Prior work has examined how predictability, control, and accuracy affect the user experience. Gajos et al. [14] showed that increasing predictability and accuracy lead to improved satisfaction, while Kangasraasio et al. [24] showed that allowing users to see the predicted effects of an action before committing to it can improve task performance and acceptance. Similarly, users of PeerFinder—a tool that recommends similar students based on academic profiles—were more confident and engaged when given more control even with the negative effect of added complexity [12]. In this work, we explore how users are affected by complexity, unpredictability and lack of control in HL-TM.

REFINEMENT IMPLEMENTATION

Prior work [27, 31] identified a set of refinements that users expected to be able to use in a HL-TM system. There is no implementation for the broad set of user preferred refinements, so Lee et al. [27] simulated refinements using a Wizard-of-Oz method. To truly evaluate user experience with a fully functional HL-TM system, we implemented seven refinements requested by users: *add word*, *remove word*, *change word order*, *remove document*, *split topic*, *merge topic*, and *add to stop words*.

These refinements include the six top refinements identified, but not implemented, by Lee et al. [27], except for *merge words*. *Merge words* was discussed in that study as a means for organizing topic words in the interface rather than a deeper specification that should be implemented in the model. We also included two refinements that were not suggested by users in Lee et al. [27], perhaps due to that study's method: *merge topics* did not arise because users only refined individual topics and *add to stop words* may have been overlooked because the study used a generic corpus with a well-curated stop words list.

Refinement Implementation

When a user provides feedback to a topic model, we view this as correcting an error the model made. We can thus divide this feedback into two broad classes: *forgetting* bad things the model learned and *injecting* new knowledge into the model. Forgetting is accomplished by invalidating the topic-word assignments for targeted word types. This is equivalent to the model seeing that word for the very first time, allowing it to make better decisions. In tandem with forgetting, injecting provides hints that encourage the algorithm to make better decisions going forward.

Injecting information happens through modifying the Dirichlet parameters for each document, α, and each topic, β.[1] Recall the Gibbs sampling conditional probability $P(z=t\,|\,z\_, w)$ (1), which has two parts: how much a document likes a topic—$(n_{d,t}+\alpha_{d,t})$—and how much a topic likes a word—$(n_{w,t}+\beta_{w,t})$. The priors are added to the topic assignment counts; thanks to the conjugacy of multinomial and Dirichlet distributions, these priors are sometimes called "pseudocounts". Our HL-TM takes advantage of this by creating pseudocounts to encourage the changes users want to see in the topic.

The refinement operations are:

1. *Add word*: to add the word w to topic t we forget w from all other topics and encourage the Gibbs sampler to assign topic t for all of the word's tokens, w_i. For the former, we forget the tokens' topic assignments. For the latter, we increase the prior of w in t by the difference between the topic-word counts of w and topic's top word w' in topic t (i.e., $n_{w',t} - n_{w,t}$).
2. *Remove word*: to remove the word w from topic t we need to forget all the word's tokens w_i from t and discourage the Gibbs sampler from reassigning t to the word w. To discourage the sampler from assigning w to t with a high probability, we assign a very small prior,[2] ε, to w in t.
3. *Change word order*: to reorder word w_2 to appear before word w_1 in topic t we need to ensure that w_2 is ranked higher than w_1 in the topic t. To enforce this, we increase the prior of w_2 in t by the difference between the topic-word counts (i.e. $n_{w_1,t} - n_{w_2,t}$). Intuitively, this operation resembles providing supplemental counts to w_2 so that it ranks higher than w_1 in the topic.
4. *Remove document*: in LDA, each document can be represented as a probability distribution over topics. To remove the document d from topic t, we forget the topic assignment for all words in the document d and assign a very small prior,[2] ε, to the topic t in α_d.
5. *Merge topic*: merging topics t_1 and t_2 means the model will have a combined topic that represents both t_1 and t_2. We assign t_1 to all tokens that were previously assigned to t_2. This effectively deletes t_2 from the model and decrements the number of topics.
6. *Split topic*: to split topic t the user provides a subset of the topic's words, or seed words, which need to be moved from the original topic, t, to a new topic, t_n. To implement this, we invalidate the original topic assignment of all seed words, create a new topic by incrementing the number of topics, and assign a large prior for each of the seed words, w_s, in the new topic, t_n. The Gibbs sampler's job is to sort which words land in which of the new child topics.
7. *Add to stop words*: adding the word w to global stop words removes w from *all* topics. We exclude that w from the vocabulary, V. This ensures that the Gibbs sampler will ignore all occurrences of w in the corpus.

[1] To implement these refinement operations, we make use of the vector interpretation (rather than scalar) of these priors. Thus, α_d is a K dimensional vector for each document d and ϕ_k is a V dimensional vector for each topic k.

[2] We use $\varepsilon = 0.000001$ for our experiments.

Interface

The HL-TM user interface (Figure 1) represents a topic model as a list of topics on the left panel, each displayed as their first three words. Selecting any topic in the list shows the full topic view in the right panel, which consists of the top 20 topic words and snippets of the top 40 topic documents. Documents are ordered by their probability for the topic t given the document d, or $p(t \mid d)$. Each word, w, is ordered and sized by its probability for the topic t, or $p(w \mid t)$; this simple word list representation provides users a quick topic understanding [1, 35]. Hovering or clicking on topic words highlights the word in the displayed document snippets.

Users refine the topic model using simple interactive mechanisms. We require users to click "save" to incorporate their specified refinements instead of applying them immediately because the system does not support reverting the model after an update (we discuss batch vs. immediate refinements in Discussion and Future Work). Instead, the interface displays intermediate feedback, such as bold and italicized words, representing users' specified refinements before saving, and any or all of the outstanding refinements can be undone. When users press "save", their specifications are incorporated into the model (Refinement Implementation).

QUALITATIVE EVALUATION OF A HL-TM SYSTEM

Our fully interactive user-centered HL-TM system focuses on topic model novices. Participants explored and refined a model built from a Twitter corpus of complaints about airlines, followed by a semi-structured interview. The study focused on a broad set of operations in a fully interactive system (compared to [27]), as well as understanding how interactive machine learning challenges–predictability, complexity, and latency–complicate topic modeling. For refinements in HL-TM, we divide predictability into *control* and *stability*, where *control* is how much the user's refinement is reflected after the model updates (e.g., a specified word is added to the topic), and *stability* is how many other changes not specified by the user appear in the model (e.g., other unspecified words are added). Instability, in particular, is a concern with HL-TM: small changes to the model can propagate in unexpected ways.

Method

The study protocol included a training task to familiarize users with topic modeling, a test task to refine a topic model, and a semi-structured interview on the experience.

Participants

We recruited twelve participants (five male, seven female) from campus e-mail lists. They were on average 30.5 years old ($SD = 10.3$) and fluent English speakers. Educational backgrounds included human-computer Interaction (5), information management (2), education (1), mechanical engineering (1), computer science (1), psychology (1), and international government (1). Experience with topic modeling varied (nine with no experience, three with limited) as did experience with data science or machine learning (seven with no experience, three limited, two significant). Each participant got a \$15 Amazon gift card. We refer to participants as P1–P12.

Dataset and Topic Model

We used a separate dataset and model for the training and test tasks. For *training* we generated a model with 10 topics from a dataset of 2,225 BBC news articles corresponding to stories in five topical areas (business, entertainment, politics, sports, tech) from 2004 – 2005 [16]. For the *test* we used the Twitter US Airline Sentiment dataset from Kaggle,[3] which includes 14,485 total tweets from February 2015 directed to six popular airlines (American, Delta, Southwest, United, US Airways, Virgin America). The dataset includes manually applied labels organizing the tweets into "positive" (2,363 tweets), "neutral" (3,099 tweets), and "negative" (9,178 tweets) sentiment categories. We modeled the 9,178 negative sentiment tweets with 10 topics using a standard stop words list[4] and 300 Gibbs sampling iterations. For each subsequent update during the task, 30 Gibbs sampling iterations were run. Table 1 shows the initial set of topics (henceforth T1–T10). We automatically computed topic quality for each topic using a topic coherence metric based on Normalized Pointwise Mutual Information [5, NPMI] with Wikipedia as the reference corpus [25].

Procedure

Sessions were designed to take one hour, but in practice took up to 90 minutes, and they were conducted remotely with audio and screen-capture recording. We introduced participants to topic modeling and to the HL-TM tool using the *training topic model*. The interviewer described each refinement operation and asked the participant to practice sample operations.

Participants then reviewed the raw tweets of the *test* dataset in a csv file and were told to imagine they had been asked to organize these tweets to identify different classes of airline complaints. They then opened the HL-TM tool with the *test topic model* (Figure 1) and were instructed that an initial model of 10 topics had been generated to help summarize the tweets, but that they may notice flaws and may need to refine the model. The interviewer asked a few introductory questions about the model and the tool, then instructed participants to think aloud while refining the model using the tool until they felt it best categorized the tweets into types of complaints. Participants were given a maximum of 20 minutes for the task, and afterwards they answered semi-structured interview questions about the task, model, and tool.

Data and Analysis

We logged user interaction with the HL-TM tool, including the state of the model at each iteration, when the user pressed "save", and refinement usage. The task audio was also transcribed and coded along with the responses for the post-task interview. Coding followed a thematic analysis approach [8] to uncover the overarching themes represented by more specific codes within the data. The codebook was organized into five themes containing a total of 40 codes: challenges (10 codes), tool requests (10), refinement requests (8), save strategies (6), and refinement strategies (6). To determine agreement, two researchers independently coded transcripts for a random participant. Of 21 instances, the researchers agreed on the codes for 12 and disagreed on nine. Disagreements were resolved

[3] https://www.kaggle.com/crowdflower/twitter-airline-sentiment

[4] https://raw.githubusercontent.com/mimno/Mallet/master/stoplists/en.t

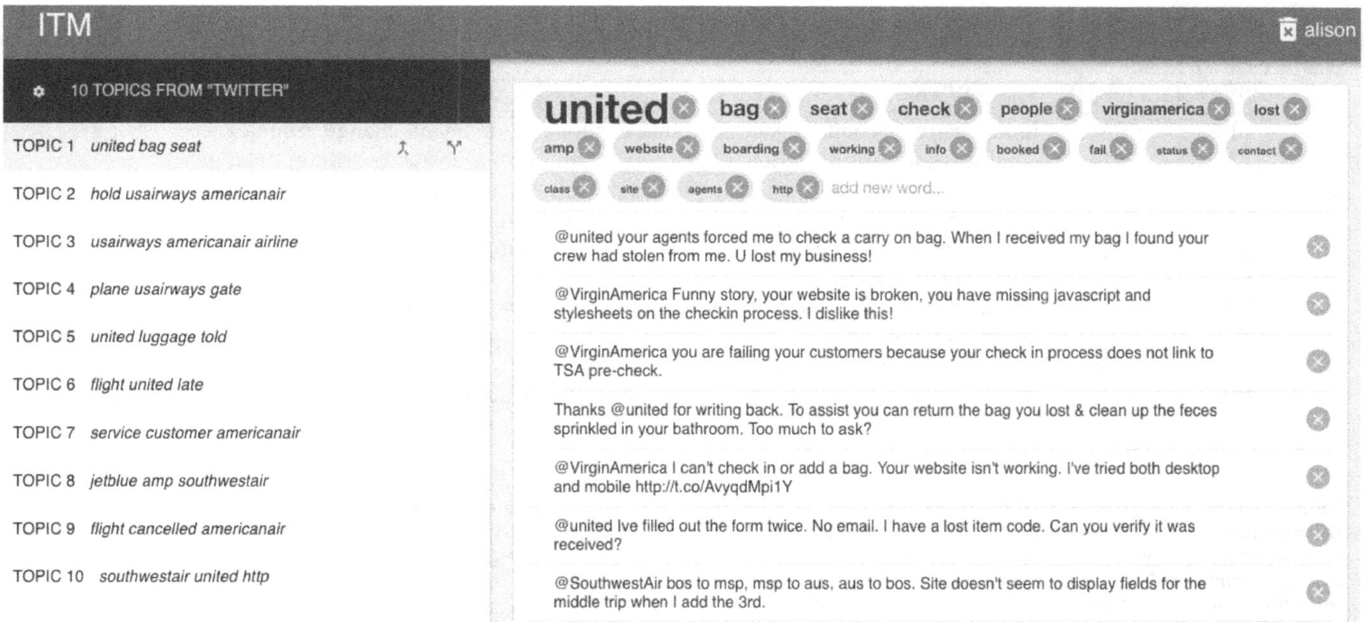

Figure 1. User interface for the HL-TM tool. A list of topics (left) are represented by topics' first three topic words. Selecting a topic reveals more detail (right): the top 20 words and top 40 documents. Hovering or clicking on a word highlights it within the documents. Users can refine the model using simple mechanisms: click "x" next to words or documents to remove them, select and drag words to re-order them, type new words from the vocabulary into the input box and press "enter" to add them, select a word and click the trash can to add it to the stop words list, or click "split" and "merge" (to the right of the topic words) to enter into split and merge modes.

and codes clarified through discussion, and a second round of coding on transcripts for a different random participant achieved better agreement (researchers agreed on codes for 14 of 15 instances). One researcher then coded the remaining transcripts.

Findings: Simplicity and Improvement

We discuss findings related to refinement and save strategies, ability to improve the topic model, and challenges faced in using a fully functional HL-TM system.

Users prefer simple refinements

Like Lee et al. [27], simple refinements, such as *remove word*, *change word order*, and *add word to stop words* were the most commonly used. While perceived utility aligned with usage in Lee et al. [27], which is not surprising as refinements did not affect the model, there were two misaligned cases in our study: *change word order* and *add word* (Table 2). *Change word order* was the second most common refinement, yet only two of the 10 participants who used it in the task thought it was one of the most useful; alternatively, *add word* was only the fourth most common refinement, yet all six participants who used it thought it one of the most useful. These refinements provide varied control; we discuss this discrepancy in Discussion and Future Work.

Detailed refinements usage and strategies

We recorded which refinements participants used. The most common refinement, *remove word*, was used by 11 participants a total of 270 times, followed by *change word order* (10 participants, 136 times), *add to stop words* (seven participants, 90 times), and *add word* (six participants, 41 times). Other refinement operations were used by only three or fewer participants (Table 2).

When we asked participants the strategies they used, we got similar answers: *remove irrelevant words* (9 participants), *remove typos* (2), *skip bad topics* (2), *group common words* (2), *change word order to name* (2), *move irrelevant words to the end of the list* (1) , and *pinpoint refine* (1). To remove irrelevant words, participants were not consistent, instead employing both *remove word* and *add to stop words*. For example, P6 described that he would, *"first remove all similar words (e.g., make/makes) in each topic and then put all generic words in the stop words list."* Two participants described using *change word order* not only to fix the relative importance of words, but to name a topic, which they did by dragging three descriptive words to the front of the word list (each topic was represented by its top three words in the topic list on the left of the interface). A more expected usage of *change word order* came from P4, who said, *"I reordered the airline names to go to the end as I was not interested in what airlines attracted complaints."* For dealing with poor quality topics, two participants described their strategy to ignore bad topics, while one participant described a pinpoint refinement strategy in which she would choose a single topic word from a seemingly random topic and then use *add word* and *remove word* to make the topic more about that single word. Finally, we also noted cases of participants using refinements to explore the model. For example, P10 used the *add word* refinement to see if words showed up in the topic's documents, by first adding a word and then hovering over it to see it highlighted in the documents. P10 would then undo the added word if it did not appear in any of the top documents.

Table 1. Initial *test topic model* of 10 topics generated for the negative tweets from the airline Twitter corpus. Topics are represented by their top words. Observed topic coherence calculated by NPMI, which deems topics to be of higher quality if they contain words that appear more frequently together than apart in a reference corpus.

Topic ID	NPMI	Topic Words
T1	.031	hold, usairways, americanair, call, back, phone, hours, wait, change, minutes
T2	.014	southwestair, virginamerica, ticket, united, amp, fly, website, boarding, time, guys
T3	.024	flight, usairways, delayed, hrs, hours, late, miss, made, delay, connection
T4	.045	united, bag, bags, luggage, lost, baggage, check, find, airport, time
T5	.015	jetblue, http, time, united, email, long, jfk, give, amp, guys
T6	.029	americanair, usairways, people, weather, due, day, airport, hotel, issue, issues
T7	.022	united, plane, gate, waiting, hour, seat, sitting, crew, delay, min
T8	.009	usairways, americanair, make, problems, days, travel, refund, miles, told, booking
T9	.030	service, customer, united, usairways, worst, airline, experience, agents, staff, flying
T10	.025	flight, cancelled, southwestair, flightled, americanair, flights, today, flighted, late, tomorrow

Table 2. List of refinements ordered by in-task usage with count of participants that selected the specified refinement as one of the most useful or least useful refinements. Simple, word-level refinements are both the most commonly used and judged to be most useful (except for change word order: only two of the 10 participants who used it found it to be most useful).

Refinement	Most Useful	Least Useful	Used By	Total Usage
Remove word	5	1	11	270
Change word order	2	1	10	136
Add to stop words	3	0	7	90
Add word	6	1	6	41
Remove document	0	3	3	20
Merge topic	2	3	2	5
Split topic	1	5	1	1

Table 3. Save strategies described by participants and the number of times each participant saved during the task, ordered from most to least iterations. There was no dominant strategy: save usage and strategy varied across participants.

Participant	Iterations	Save Strategy
P8	42	After each refinement
P9	28	When sure
P12	19	After a batch of refinements
P2	19	After each topic modified
P7	18	After a batch of refinements
P10	16	After each refinement
P11	15	When sure
P4	9	After each topic modified
P5	8	After each refinement
P1	3	Forgot to save
P6	1	Forgot to save
P3	0	Afraid to save

When and why do users choose to save their changes?

Users refine the topic model by applying refinements and then separately clicking "save". Before saving, users can undo some or all of their changes. To understand when participants choose to save and because the HL-TM system does not support undo after saving, the system did not enforce a particular save strategy, such as after every refinement or a set number of refinements. Instead, participants could specify a series of local refinements, but these would only be applied to the model once they clicked "save", which they could do at any time. Save usage varied substantially ($min = 0$, $max = 42$, $avg = 14$, $SD = 12$); see Table 3.

Users were asked about strategies for when to click "save": *after each refinement* (4 participants), *after each topic modified* (2), *after a batch of refinements* (2), *when sure* (2). These varied strategies suggest that HL-TM should allow users to choose when to save their refinements. Additionally, two participants *forgot to save*, and another was *afraid to save*, which suggests that systems should remind users to save and support undo. "Save" counts and strategy feedback (Table 3).

P8 saved the most frequently (42 times) and described his strategy as saving after each refinement, saying, *"I always press the save button when I make any refinements."* P9 saved 28 times, saying, *"only when I am very sure about the result, I would press the save button."* In contrast, P6 and P1 reported that they forgot to save, and four other participants stated that remembering to save was one of the main challenges of using the tool. P12 wondered, *"if moving the [save] button over from the side would have helped me remember [to save]."* Finally, P3 was afraid to save, saying, *"I didn't want to start from scratch."* She suggested that having a history of refinements that could have been rolled back might mitigate timidity.

Did users improve the model?

To determine if participants improved the initial topic model using the HL-TM tool, we measured the quality of the initial topic model and the final topic models using qualitative and quantitative methods.

All participants started with the same model. We computed topic quality for the initial model and final models using a topic coherence metric based on NPMI [25]. The average topic coherence for the 10 topics of the initial model was .024 ($min = .01$, $max = .04$, $SD = .01$) (per-topic coherence shown in Table 1). The average topic coherence for the final model for each participant ranged from .021 to .037 ($M = .027$, $SD = .005$), which a paired t-test showed a significant improvement from the refinement process, $t(10) = 2.89$, $p = .037$.

Participants gave their satisfaction with the topic model before and after the task on a scale from one to seven, with one being not at all satisfied and seven being very satisfied. The average subjective model satisfaction increased from 4.7 ($SD = 1.29$) before the task to 5.2 ($SD = 0.83$) after the task. While this increase was not statistically significant by a Wilcoxen signed rank test ($Z = -1.04$, $p = .15$), six of the 12 participants commented unprompted after the task that their final model provided a good organization of the complaints. For example, P5 said, *"I'm overall happy with the [final] model and I like that I can use the tool to make the changes that I want."*

Participants gave the best and worst topics in the initial model (Table 1). Most participants agreed the best topics were T4 (4 participants), T3 (3), T1 (3), and T9 (3) and the worst topics were T5 (8), T6 (3), and T8 (2), which correlates with the observed topic coherence. The three best topics by NPMI are T4 (NPMI=.045), T1 (.031), and T9 (.030), while the three worst topics are T8 (.009), T2 (.014), and T5 (.015).

What challenges do users face?

To understand how general interactive machine learning challenges affect users of HL-TM, we coded four common challenges—tracking complex changes, instability, lack of control, latency—and identified challenges with our system. Participants also stated which challenges were most and least frustrating during the task. Of the four common challenges, tracking complex changes was the most frustrating, followed by instability, lack of control, and latency was the least frustrating challenge.

Tracking complex changes

When users click "save", the algorithm updates the model, and the resulting model may have substantial changes. To explore whether participants could track these changes, they rated their agreement with the statement, *"I was able to remember what the model looked like before my updates"* on a scale from one, meaning no agreement, to seven, meaning complete agreement (Figure 2, D) and discussed how this affected them. The average response was 3.7 out of 7 ($SD = 1.7$), and four of the 12 participants said this was the most frustrating challenge while one said it was the least.

Five participants said not being able to remember what the model looked like hurt their performance. For example, P9 said, *"a moment ago, I was satisfied with this topic, but now it's gone, and I don't think I am, but I can't remember,"* and P3 and P8 felt the lack of "undo" intensified this challenge. P3 said, *"I think this is a big issue–I'd like to know if I'm capturing the true data–and be able to step back to early versions of the model before saving,"* and P8 said, *"I don't know what I have done sometimes, and there are no ways to go back ... "*. Four participants mentioned a similar challenge, that it was hard to tell what changed in the model after an update, such as P10, who *"had to brush through all the words to confirm if [his specified] change occurred,"* and P5, who *"did not understand it at first, that the model actually changes, as there was no feedback or indication."* Finally, three participants requested a long-term history view of the model, such as P3, who suggested *"having a history of refinements."*

Stability

A user interface should be predictable to support user confidence and understanding [18]; however, interactive machine learning often violates this principle [2] as these systems combine hidden knowledge—such as previously learned models or data—with users' instructions. We describe system predictability as a combination of stability (no changes other than those specified occur) and control (the change occurs as specified).

We asked if participants agreed with the statement, *"no changes other than the refinements I made occurred when I clicked update"* on a scale from one, or no agreement, to seven, or complete agreement (Figure 2, C). The average response was 4.1 out of seven ($SD = 2.0$), and three of 12 participants said instability was the most frustrating challenge while no participants said it was the least.

There was a large variance for not only whether users perceived instability but also their reactions to it. After the task, eight of 12 participants mentioned they had perceived instability. Of those, two participants found this to be positive. For example, P6 observed an unspecified change when *"new words were added on to the list to replace the ones I removed. It made the model better."* P2 noted that after removing some words from a topic there was *"some slight surprise at seeing words that I had not chosen show up, but I was pretty satisfied on looking at the results."* Three participants felt neutral about the instability. For example, P7 said, *"[instability] did not impact"* his ability to perform the task, and P4 said, *"when I removed some keywords, other keywords came up. I wasn't paying enough attention to this to determine if it helped or harmed."* Finally, three participants had negative reactions, such as P9, who was unsure of what had changed in the model after an update, but stated, *"... but I remember being happy with the topic and when that changed it made me unhappy."* This participant also requested the ability to *freeze a topic*, meaning it would not be changed as other refinements were made.

Control

Similar to the challenge of instability, users should always be in control of user interfaces [34]; however, interactive machine learning is by definition a *collaboration* between algorithm and user [19]. In this collaboration, we define "control" as whether the user's refinements are incorporated into the model as expected. For example, if a user removes a word from a topic, the word should not be in the topic after the update.

To explore whether participants felt in control of the system, they stated on a seven-point scale whether they agreed with the statement, *"the refinements I made were applied as expected when I clicked update"* from not agreeing at all to completely agreeing (Figure 2, B) and discussed how this affected their task. The average response was 5.6 out of seven ($SD = 1.0$), meaning overall users found the system to be fairly controllable. One of the 12 participants said lack of control was the most frustrating challenge and one said it was the least.

However, during the task seven participants noted frustration with the lack of control with the interface, and five participants

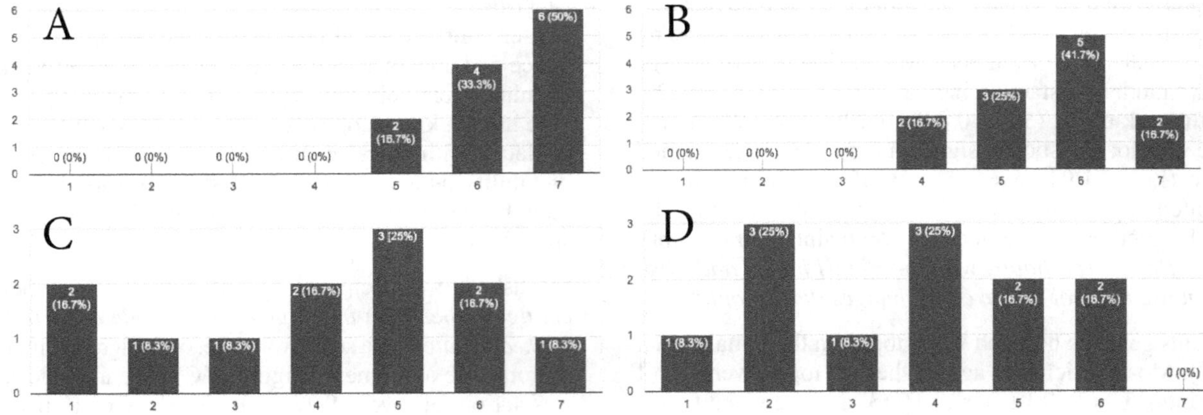

Figure 2. Counts for responses on a scale from one to seven for participants' agreement with statements related to latency (A), lack of control (B), instability (C), and tracking complex changes (D), with seven meaning they did not experience it and one that they did. Most participants found that the system updated quickly and refinements were applied as expected, while there was substantial variance for if participants could remember what the model looked like before updating or if they felt the updated model included other changes than those specified.

specifically observed that *change word order* was uncontrollable. P4 tried to drag important words to the front of the topic list and stated that, *"the reordering didn't always get accepted,"* and P8 tried to drag unimportant words to the end of the list and said, *"I tried to move this word and it just goes back up."*

Latency

Prior work in interactive machine learning calls for rapid interaction cycles [2] to minimize attention loss [22] and reduce short-term memory load [34]. However, many interactive systems do not provide real-time updates: this latency—the user has to wait while the algorithm is performing an update—is typically related to the size of the data and complexity of the computation. For example, an early HL-TM implementation [23] took 5 to 50 seconds to update the model based on refinement operations.

Our refinement implementation is efficient by design, and the data set used in this user study was relatively small (both in document size and length), therefore the algorithm updated almost instantaneously during the task (.09 – .63 seconds). No participant said that latency was the most frustrating challenge while two participants said it was the least frustrating, and the average response was 6.3 out of seven ($SD = 0.8$) for participants agreement with the statement, *"after clicking the update button, the model updated quickly"* (Figure 2, A).

However, for a more realistic corpus size or alternative refinement implementation, latency becomes a challenge. We asked participants to describe how their ability to perform the task would be affected had the wait time been 10 seconds, 30 seconds, two minutes, or 10 minutes. Most participants felt 10 seconds would be an acceptable time to wait: five participants felt that waiting 10 seconds would have no effect on the task and two participants felt that this longer wait time would have a positive effect, for example, P5 stated that waiting longer *"would be better for me to realize that the tweets have changed."* For a 30 second wait time, two participants felt this would be an acceptable wait time without any changes to the interface, whereas four participants said that changes to the interface would be required for this longer wait time. P7 worried this wait would further hinder the ability to remember what the model looked like before updating, and P3 thought this would further affect save strategy, suggesting that it would instead be *"better to not 'save' changes, but to have highlights to show what it 'might' look like once saved."* Most participants felt that both two minutes and 10 minutes would be unacceptable wait times.

Trust and confidence

Trust is a primary design challenge for intelligent systems [32, 20]. An entire sub-field of machine learning focuses on interpretability to build trust and promote adoption of these systems. Surprisingly, we did not see participants mistrusting the HL-TM system. While users are quick to distrust a classification system that produces easily identifiable, incorrect classifications, topic models have less obvious *incorrect* answers.

However, participants sometimes put too much trust in the system or lacked self-confidence. For example, P10 was confused about a topic word, saying, *"if the system coughed it up, there must be a reason for it, right?"* Some participants lacked confidence in their refinements: P7 said that *remove document* is the least useful refinement, because, *"I don't feel comfortable removing a document."* And when P5 added words to a topic, she said, *"it's putting my words on top . . . I've added too many words, which have gone to the top of the list, so either the algorithm thinks it's important or it's because I've added them,"* followed by, *"I don't think that it should always give more importance [to my added words], because I could be wrong!"* This challenge has a direct connection to the issues of instability and lack of control, which we discuss in more detail in Discussion and Future Work.

What other requests do users have for the system?

Many participants wanted a better understanding of the model and the data. For example, two participants requested a better model overview, such as P7, who wanted to *"see the entire list of the top 20 words for each topic on one screen to allow for making bulk, faster changes."* Additionally, three participants wanted to view words or documents across topics, such as P12 who suggested, *"a note or color to indicate that a certain term appears only in this topic and not in the others."* Two participants requested enhancing the word in context feature, such as by scrolling to the selected word or filtering to only documents containing the word. Three participants wanted to view more documents than the 40 shown, and two participants wanted to view the total number of documents for a topic.

Similar to the *merge word* operation identified by Lee et al. [27], six participants requested a refinement to add phrases (instead of just single words), and four participants requested a refinement to group synonyms and plurals. As anticipated, participants used the *add to stop words* refinement, and two participants requested an enhancement to the stop words functionality, such as being able to view the stop words list and remove words that have been added to it. However, seven participants noted confusion between the *add to stop words* and *remove word* refinements, which should be clarified in future interface design. For example, P5 said, *"removing a word feature is similar to the delete feature, which got me a bit confused,"* and P9 said, *"I got confused between removing keywords from a particular [topic] and the overall [topics], so I made mistakes in the beginning."* To help better organize the view, three participants wanted to name topics, noting that it would be a useful way to remember what the topics are about, and two participants wanted to reorder topics in the list. Finally, two participants wanted to delete a topic if it was particularly bad.

Summary

Participants were frustrated by their inability to track how the model changed throughout the refinement process. While participants perceived system instability, they had varied reactions (positive and negative). On the other hand, users did not experience substantial latency or lack of control. We did not find any cases where users distrusted the system, but users perhaps trusted the system too much or had too little confidence in themselves. Participants specifically requested the ability to undo changes after saving and to curate the topic model view, such as by re-ordering the topic list, removing poor quality topics, and naming topics. Participants also requested multi-word refinements, such as adding phrases and grouping synonyms.

DISCUSSION AND FUTURE WORK

We outline implications for future HL-TM system design, discuss open questions related to interactive machine learning, and provide a reflection on our HL-TM implementation.

Design Recommendations

Provide richer history: Participants voiced concerns with their inability to remember the history of the model, and four of 12 participants said they were unable to tell how the model has changed after an update. HL-TM interfaces should strive to support visualization of short term and long term model changes; users want to track how the model changed throughout the refinement process. This was the most consistent and most frustrating issue in the study.

Support undo: When possible, HL-TM should support reverting to prior states of the model: some noted that this made them afraid to save during the task, while others specifically requested an undo functionality.

Allow users to choose when to save, but remind them to do so: We had anticipated needing a separate save action to allow users to confirm refinements (lacking undo) and to counteract latency, but we also noted users who created refinements as a data exploration tool without the intent of having them update the model. Thus, HL-TM systems should allow users to choose when to save their refinements to the model instead of forcing a save. However, because users forget to save, additional information should be provided in the interface to remind users, such as a more prominent count of outstanding refinement operations or a visual cue that displays if they have not saved recently.

Freeze topics to protect from instability: Users complained of instability when topics that were once high quality or about a particular thing had changed. A process, such as freezing a topic, suggested by one participant as a mechanism to hold a particular topic constant during subsequent updates, is a promising solution to this problem and should be incorporated in future design.

Support multi-word refinements: Participants requested the ability to add phrases and group synonyms. Group synonyms could be implemented as the merge word refinement discussed in Lee et al. [27], not as an update to the underlying model, but as a way of organizing words in the interface. On the other hand, add phrases should be implemented in the interface as an extension to *add word* (as requested by participants), but would likely require a more complex modeling approach that supports n-grams as opposed to single tokens.

Clarify difference between adding a word to stop words and removing it from a single topic: Future design should explicitly delineate between removing a word from all topics (and the modeling process entirely), *add to stop words*, and removing a word from a single topic, *remove word*, as many participants confused the two operations during the task.

Support user-curated model view: Three participants requested named topics. Two other participants used *change word order* for *ad hoc* topic naming. As this operation is not always applied as expected, providing a controllable topic naming functionality will improve user experience. Participants also requested other techniques for curating their model view, which should be incorporated in the design of future systems, such as the ability to re-order the topic list and to remove poor quality topics entirely.

Open Questions

This is the first system to efficiently implement a full suite of refinements desired by users in prior work [27, 31], enabling the study of true human-in-the-loop interactions of a comprehensive HL-TM system. We enumerate open questions about HL-TM design that follow from our findings.

Trust vs. instability and control: Users were not bothered by instability or lack of control either because they trusted the system or had little confidence in themselves. Specifically, users with limited confidence blamed *themselves* for creating poor refinements (i.e., when the change did not happen as anticipated). If system builders do not want novice users to feel like the "junior partner" in the human-machine collaboration, future work should explore whether ensuring users understand the teaming aspect of these systems can improve their experience and make unpredictability more acceptable (and sometimes welcome, as it can drive discovery).

Trust, control, and refinement: Lee et al. [27] studied refinement usage without a refinement implementation, meaning users did not see the full effect of their refinements on the model. In that study, *remove document* was a commonly used refinement, however, that is not the case in our study. Before the study participants worried that it may take too long to determine which documents to remove, while afterwards noted they lacked confidence to remove a document. Although Lee et al. [27] considered that refinements that take too long would hurt usage, lack of trust or confidence in HL-TM is a new challenge to consider.

Change word order was commonly used, but frustrating to users, while *add word* was used less, yet all participants who used it thought it was useful. This discrepancy highlights the difference in control of the two refinements: *change word order* was unpredictable and thus frustrating, but *add word* always worked on the first try.

Save strategy and instability: When users save after a batch of refinements (as opposed to a single requirement) their intentions are clearer. This in turn minimizes instability as the system has more information to incorporate into the model. On the other hand, each refinement may have cascading effects, and a batch of refinements could therefore appear to be more unstable than a single refinement. We did not find a relationship between users' described save strategies and their perceived system instability. Future work should explore the relationship with a specific focus on how much information users provide to the system and whether this information affects the system's stability and how users react.

Algorithm Reflection

This work proposes an asymmetric prior-based HL-TM implementation. We implemented seven refinement operations using the proposed algorithm, which can be easily extended to other refinements, such as creating a new topic using seed words or deleting a topic. One limitation of this algorithm is the difficulty to specify word order constraints. For example, if a user wants to change a word's position from rank eight to two in the word list, the algorithm cannot reliably maintain the exact user provided word order. We argue that topic models are probabilistic models and during parameter estimation they can ignore user provided feedback if the underlying data does not support the user's hypothesis. For example, if a user wants to add a word to a topic that only shows up a few times in the corpus, the model might not put that word in the list of top ranked words for that topic. Another limitation of our algorithm is with the *split topic* refinement; our proposed implementation cannot reliably generate a good quality topic if the user provides only very few or unrelated seed words.

CONCLUSION

Prior work in HL-TM either implemented refinement operations without first understanding the needs of end users [23, 21, 10] or identified the refinement operations that users wish to do [27], but did not implement them. This work is the first to examine user experience with a fully-functional HL-TM system that contains the refinements users want. Specifically, we validate prior results, such as refinement usage and effectiveness, and explore how these and user experience are affected by previously hidden issues, such as unpredictability, trust, and lack of control. We also present suggestions, such as the need to visualize complex model changes and support undo. Non-expert end users used the system to refine a topic model and we explored how these users perceived and were affected by common challenges in interactive machine learning, such as latency, unpredictability, and trust. Participants improved a topic model using the tool and identified additional refinement and tool suggestions that should guide HL-TM development.

Acknowledgments

This work was supported by the collaborative NSF Grant IIS-1409287 (UMD) and IIS-1409739 (BYU). Boyd-Graber is also supported by NSF grant IIS-1652666 and IIS-1748663. Any opinions, findings, conclusions, or recommendations expressed here are those of the authors and do not necessarily reflect the view of the sponsor.

REFERENCES

1. Eric Alexander and Michael Gleicher. 2016. Assessing Topic Representations for Gist-Forming. In *Proceedings of the International Working Conference on Advanced Visual Interfaces*. 100–107. DOI: http://dx.doi.org/10.1145/2909132.2909252
2. Saleema Amershi, Maya Cakmak, William Bradley Knox, and Todd Kulesza. 2014. Power to the People: The Role of Humans in Interactive Machine Learning. (2014). DOI: http://dx.doi.org/10.1609/aimag.v35i4.2513
3. David Andrzejewski, Xiaojin Zhu, and Mark Craven. 2009. Incorporating Domain Knowledge into Topic Modeling via Dirichlet Forest Priors.. In *Proceedings of the International Conference on Machine Learning*, Vol. 382. 25–32. DOI: http://dx.doi.org/10.1145/1553374.1553378
4. David M. Blei, Andrew Y. Ng, and Michael I. Jordan. 2003. Latent Dirichlet Allocation. *The Journal of Machine Learning Research* 3, 1 (2003), 993–1022. DOI: http://dx.doi.org/10.1162/jmlr.2003.3.4-5.993
5. G. Bouma. 2009. Normalized (Pointwise) Mutual Information in Collocation Extraction. In *Proceedings of the Biennial GSCL Conference*. Tübingen, 31–40.
6. Jordan Boyd-Graber, David M. Blei, and Xiaojin Zhu. 2007. A Topic Model for Word Sense Disambiguation.
7. Jordan Boyd-Graber, Yuening Hu, and David Mimno. 2017. *Applications of Topic Models*. Foundations and Trends in Information Retrieval, Vol. 11. NOW Publishers. http://www.nowpublishers.com/article/Details/INR-030

8. Virginia Braun and Victoria Clarke. 2006. Using Thematic Analysis in Psychology. *Qualitative Research in Psychology* 3, 2 (1 2006), 77–101. DOI: http://dx.doi.org/10.1191/1478088706qp063oa

9. Allison June-Barlow Chaney and David M. Blei. 2012. Visualizing Topic Models. In *Proceedings of the International Conference on Weblogs and Social Media.* 419–422.

10. Jaegul Choo, Changhyun Lee, Chandan K. Reddy, and Haesun Park. 2013. UTOPIAN: User-Driven Topic Modeling Based on Interactive Nonnegative Matrix Factorization. *IEEE Transactions on Visualization and Computer Graphics* 19, 12 (2013), 1992–2001. DOI: http://dx.doi.org/10.1109/TVCG.2013.212

11. Jason Chuang, Yuening Hu, Ashley Jin, John D. Wilkerson, Daniel A. McFarland, Christopher D. Manning, and Jeffrey Heer. 2013. Document Exploration with Topic Modeling: Designing Interactive Visualizations to Support Effective Analysis Workflows. In *Conference on Neural Information Processing Systems (NIPS) Workshop on Topic Models: Computation, Application, and Evaluation.* 1–4.

12. Fan Du, Catherine Plaisant, Neil Spring, and Ben Shneiderman. 2017. Finding Similar People to Guide Life Choices: Challenge, Design, and Evaluation. In *Proceedings of the SIGCHI Conference on Human Factors in Computing Systems.* DOI: http://dx.doi.org/10.1145/3025453.3025777

13. Jacob Eisenstein, Duen Horng Chau, Aniket Kittur, and Eric Xing. 2012. TopicViz: Interactive Topic Exploration in Document Collections. In *Proceedings of the ACM annual conference extended abstracts on Human Factors in Computing Systems Extended Abstracts.* 2177–2182. DOI:http://dx.doi.org/10.1145/2212776.2223772

14. Krzysztof Z. Gajos, Katherine Everitt, Desney S. Tan, Mary Czerwinski, and Daniel S. Weld. 2008. Predictability and Accuracy in Adaptive User Interfaces. In *Proceeding of the SIGCHI conference on Human Factors in Computing systems.* 1271–1274. DOI: http://dx.doi.org/10.1145/1357054.1357252

15. Matthew J. Gardner, Joshua Lutes, Jeff Lund, Josh Hansen, Dan Walker, Eric Ringger, and Kevin Seppi. 2010. The Topic Browser: An Interactive Tool for Browsing Topic Models. In *Proceedings of the Workshop on Challenges of Data Visualization, held in conjunction with the 24th Annual Conference on Neural Information Processing Systems.* 1–9. http://cseweb.ucsd.edu/~lvdmaaten/workshops/nips2010/papers/gardner.pdf

16. Derek Greene and Padraig Cunningham. 2006. Practical Solutions to the Problem of Diagonal Dominance in Kernel Document Clustering. In *Proceedings of the International Conference on Machine Learning.* 377–384. DOI:http://dx.doi.org/10.1145/1143844.1143892

17. Thomas L Griffiths and Mark Steyvers. 2004. Finding scientific topics. In *Proceedings of the National Academy of Sciences of the United States of America*, Vol. 101. 5228–35. DOI: http://dx.doi.org/10.1073/pnas.0307752101

18. Robert Hoekman. 2007. *Designing the Obvious: A Common Sense Approach to Web Application Design.* Vol. 48. 255 pages. http://www.worldcat.org/isbn/032145345X

19. Lars Erik Holmqvist. 2017. Intelligence on tap: artificial intelligence as a new design material. *Interactions* (2017), 28–33. DOI: http://dx.doi.org/https://doi.org/10.1145/3085571

20. K. Höök. 2000. Steps to take before intelligent user interfaces become real. *Interacting with Computers* 12, 4 (2000), 409–426. DOI: http://dx.doi.org/10.1016/S0953-5438(99)00006-5

21. Enamul Hoque and Giuseppe Carenini. 2015. ConVisIT: Interactive Topic Modeling for Exploring Asynchronous Online Conversations. In *Proceedings of the International Conference on Intelligent User Interfaces.* ACM, New York, 169–180. DOI: http://dx.doi.org/10.1145/2678025.2701370

22. Eric Horvitz. 1999. Principles of Mixed-Initiative User Interfaces. In *Proceeding of the SIGCHI conference on Human Factors in Computing Systems.* ACM, New York, 159–166. DOI:http://dx.doi.org/10.1145/302979.303030

23. Yuening Hu, Jordan Boyd-Graber, Brianna Satinoff, and Alison Smith. 2014. Interactive Topic Modeling. *Machine Learning* 95, 3 (6 2014), 423–469. DOI: http://dx.doi.org/10.1007/s10994-013-5413-0

24. Antti Kangasrääsiö, Dorota Głowacka, and Samuel Kaski. 2015. Improving Controllability and Predictability of Interactive Recommendation Interfaces for Exploratory Search. In *Proceedings of the International Conference on Intelligent User Interfaces.* 247–251. DOI: http://dx.doi.org/10.1145/2678025.2701371

25. Jey Han Lau, David Newman, and Timothy Baldwin. 2014. Machine Reading Tea Leaves : Automatically Evaluating Topic Coherence and Topic Model Quality. In *Proceedings of the Conference of the European Chapter of the Association for Computational Linguistics.* 530–539. http://www.aclweb.org/anthology/E14-1056

26. Hanseung Lee, Jaeyeon Kihm, Jaegul Choo, John Stasko, and Haesun Park. 2012. iVisClustering: An Interactive Visual Document Clustering via Topic Modeling. *Computer Graphics Forum* 31, 3pt3 (2012), 1155–1164. DOI: http://dx.doi.org/10.1111/j.1467-8659.2012.03108.x

27. Tak Yeon Lee, Alison Smith, Kevin Seppi, Niklas Elmqvist, Jordan Boyd-Graber, and Leah Findlater. 2017. The Human Touch: How Non-ExpertUusers Perceive, Interpret, and Fix Topic Models. *International Journal of Human Computer Studies* 105 (2017), 28–42. DOI: http://dx.doi.org/10.1016/j.ijhcs.2017.03.007

28. Jeff Lund, Connor Cook, Kevin Seppi, and Jordan Boyd-Graber. 2017. Tandem Anchoring: A Multiword Anchor Approach for Interactive Topic Modeling. In *Association for Computational Linguistics*.

29. Theo Mandel. 1997. *The Elements of User Interface Design*. 440 pages. http://books.google.com/books?id=H-ZQAAAAMAAJ&pgis=1

30. David Mimno, Hanna M Wallach, Edmund Talley, Miriam Leenders, and Andrew McCallum. 2011. Optimizing Semantic Coherence in Topic Models. In *Proceedings of the Conference on Empirical Methods in Natural Language Processing*. 262–272.

31. Chris Musialek, Philip Resnik, and Andrew S. Stavisky. 2016. Using Text Analytic Techniques to Create Efficiencies in Analyzing Qualitative Data : A Comparison between Traditional Content Analysis and a Topic Modeling Approach. In *AAPOR Conference*.

32. Donald A Norman. 1994. How might people interact with agents. *Commun. ACM* 37, 7 (1994), 68–71. DOI: http://dx.doi.org/10.1145/176789.176796

33. Amir M. Saeidi, Jurriaan Hage, Ravi Khadka, and Slinger Jansen. 2015. ITMViz: Interactive Topic Modeling for Source Code Analysis. In *Proceedings of the IEEE International Conference on Program Comprehension*. 295–298. DOI:http://dx.doi.org/10.1109/ICPC.2015.44

34. Ben Shneiderman, Catherine Plaisant, Maxine Cohen, and Steven Jacobs. 2009. *Designing the User Interface: Strategies for Effective Human-Computer Interaction*. Vol. 25. 624 pages.

35. Alison Smith, Tak Yeon Lee, Forough Poursabzi-Sangdeh, Jordan Boyd-Graber, Niklas Elmqvist, and Leah Findlater. 2017. Evaluating Visual Representations for Topic Understanding and Their Effects on Manually Generated Topic Labels. *Transactions of the Association for Computational Linguistics* 5 (2017), 1–15.

36. Hanna M Wallach, David Mimno, and Andrew Mccallum. 2009. Rethinking LDA : Why Priors Matter. *Advances in Neural Information Processing Systems 22* 22, 2 (2009), 1973–1981. DOI: http://dx.doi.org/10.1007/s10708-008-9161-9

User Modelling for Avoiding Overfitting in Interactive Knowledge Elicitation for Prediction

Pedram Daee[†], **Tomi Peltola**[†], **Aki Vehtari, Samuel Kaski**
Helsinki Institute for Information Technology HIIT
Department of Computer Science
Aalto University, Espoo, Finland
firstname.lastname@aalto.fi
[†]Authors contributed equally.

ABSTRACT
In human-in-the-loop machine learning, the user provides information beyond that in the training data. Many algorithms and user interfaces have been designed to optimize and facilitate this human–machine interaction; however, fewer studies have addressed the potential defects the designs can cause. Effective interaction often requires exposing the user to the training data or its statistics. The design of the system is then critical, as this can lead to double use of data and overfitting, if the user reinforces noisy patterns in the data. We propose a user modelling methodology, by assuming simple rational behaviour, to correct the problem. We show, in a user study with 48 participants, that the method improves predictive performance in a sparse linear regression sentiment analysis task, where graded user knowledge on feature relevance is elicited. We believe that the key idea of inferring user knowledge with probabilistic user models has general applicability in guarding against overfitting and improving interactive machine learning.

Author Keywords
Interactive machine learning; probabilistic modelling; Bayesian inference; overfitting; expert prior elicitation; human-in-the-loop machine learning;

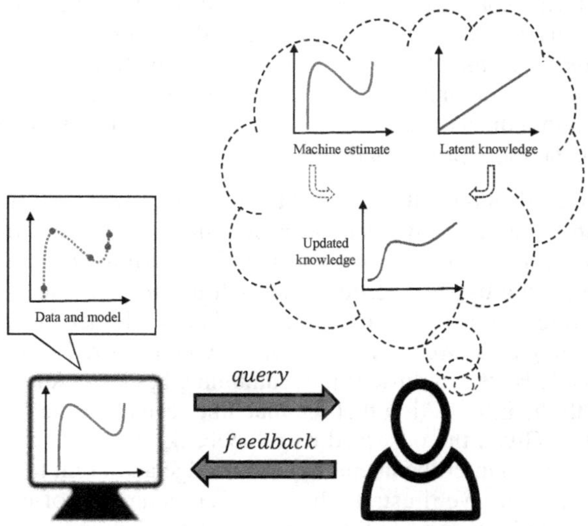

Figure 1. A schematic example of overfitting in human-in-the-loop machine learning. The machine and user are collaborating to improve a regression problem. The machine fits a regression model to the training data (green dots) and employs it to interact with the user (here by visualizing the trained model). Through the interaction, the user learns aspects of the training data and considers them to update her latent knowledge and to form her feedback. This creates a dependency between the feedback and training data that needs to be accounted for in the model to avoid double use of data and overfitting.

INTRODUCTION
Interactive and human-in-the-loop machine learning (and the related field of visual analytics) exploits the complementary knowledge and skills of humans and machines to improve performance over automatic training-data-based machine learning and to extend the reach of machine learning systems [1, 2, 3, 8, 13, 17]. However, the study of how to optimally combine the strengths of humans and machines is still in its early phase, and many possible issues arising from the interaction have not been thoroughly considered yet.

IUI'18, March 7–11, 2018, Tokyo, Japan

ACM ISBN 978-1-4503-4945-1/18/03... $15.00
DOI: https://doi.org/10.1145/3172944.3172989

Overfitting, that is, the model fitting to idiosyncrasies in the training data and hence not generalizing to new data, is a thoroughly studied topic in automatic machine learning. Subtle issues with regard to overfitting can arise when introducing a human into the loop. Yet the risk of overfitting seems little discussed in the interactive machine learning literature, although many methods combine user interaction with training-data-based machine learning models. For example, many methods visualize statistics of training data or machine output directly for the user [1, 10, 11, 18, 13, 14, 21, 23] or use the training data to select informative queries to present for the user (e.g., active learning) [3, 19, 20]. Some methods use *validation* datasets in addition to the training set to evaluate the performance. This can help to alleviate overfitting, but if the user can interact with the model based on the results on the validation, the validation set is effectively only another training dataset. A parallel line of research into controlling for overfitting has spawned in adaptive data analysis [4, 16], which has a related but different goal from interactive machine learning, of exploring the data for interesting hypotheses.

In interactive machine learning, we note that, in particular, the following three steps can lead to overfitting and hence decrease in the performance of the model, as they violate the assumption of independence of the feedback and the training data: (1) showing the training data or some of its statistics to the user, (2) querying the user for feedback, and (3) inputting the feedback back to the model as independent data (a common assumption in machine learning models). Figure 1 illustrates the induced user behaviour producing a dependency between the feedback and training data. Overfitting can also happen if the user controls some preferences (e.g., cost function weighting or regularization) in the model based on the training or validation data, since the effected improvement in the fit to the training or validation data will not necessarily generalize. The more freedom the user has (or, in this sense, the richer the feedback is), the more problematic this can be.

Rather than tying the hands of the user, improved performance can be attained by accounting for the risk of overfitting in the design of the interactive machine learning system. We propose a user modelling approach in probabilistic models to infer the user's knowledge that is complementary to the training data. We assume that the user behaves rationally, in a simple Bayesian sense [6], in combining her latent knowledge with the information that the machine reveals of the training data. Given the observed user feedback, we then invert the process to infer the latent user knowledge and use it to update the model. We illustrate the approach in a proof-of-concept user study in a sparse linear regression prediction task, where graded feature relevance knowledge is elicited from the users.

METHOD

Overview

We consider human–machine interaction in probabilistic models. In particular, we consider a situation, where the machine estimates a probabilistic model from training data, and then asks the user for feedback for the learned model. The feedback is included as further data in the model. This procedure can be iterated, although in the specific implementation here, we only consider a single round.

The setup is as follows. The machine has a probabilistic model for a prediction task and a set of training data that it uses to fit the parameters of the model. The machine assumes that the user has knowledge about some aspect of the task and elicits user knowledge by displaying the result of learning from the training data and asking for feedback. This kind of interaction is common in interactive machine learning. If the system naively uses this user feedback to update the model, for example, including it as an observation that is assumed independent of the training data, it risks double use of the data and overfitting, because such assumption could be easily violated. On the other hand, building a feedback model that would adequately describe the dependency of the feedback on the training data can be difficult.

We instead propose to infer the latent (unobserved) user knowledge, representing information that the user has beyond that of the training data, from the observed user feedback. This inferred knowledge can then be used to update the machine's model without double use of the training data. To make this feasible, we assume that the user behaves rationally, using the Bayes theorem, in integrating the information sources (her knowledge beyond training data and the information the machine provided). We then invert the process to infer the latent user knowledge.

General Mathematical Formulation

Let the observation model of a training dataset $\mathscr{D}$ be $p(\mathscr{D} \mid \boldsymbol{\theta})$, where $\boldsymbol{\theta}$ is a vector containing the model parameters, and $p(\boldsymbol{\theta})$ be their prior distribution. Given the model and the training dataset, the machine computes the posterior distribution $p(\boldsymbol{\theta} \mid \mathscr{D})$ of the parameters using the Bayes theorem. We assume the user has knowledge about some parameter or statistic ϕ, which is an element in $\boldsymbol{\theta}$ or, more generally, a function of $\boldsymbol{\theta}$. The machine provides the user with information on ϕ, for example, its posterior distribution $p(\phi \mid \mathscr{D})$ and asks the user to provide feedback on it.

Let f be the latent (unobserved) user knowledge. Our goal is to infer from the observed feedback a latent feedback likelihood function $p(f \mid \phi)$ that can be used to update the model to $p(\boldsymbol{\theta} \mid \mathscr{D}, f)$. By the assumption of a rational user, the observed feedback is based on the posterior distribution

$$p(\phi \mid \mathscr{D}, f) = \frac{p(f \mid \phi)p(\phi \mid \mathscr{D})}{p(f \mid \mathscr{D})}, \tag{1}$$

where $p(f \mid \mathscr{D}) = \int p(f \mid \phi)p(\phi \mid \mathscr{D})d\phi$ is the normalization constant. The technical details on how to invert this to learn $p(f \mid \phi)$ are case-specific. In the next section, we will show how to do this in eliciting feature relevance for sparse linear regression.

Feature Relevance Elicitation in Sparse Linear Regression

We apply the approach to infer user knowledge on feature relevance in sparse linear regression. We use a probabilistic sparse linear regression model described in [3], which formulates a linear model to predict the target variable y given a vector of features $\boldsymbol{x}$ and uses a spike-and-slab prior to model whether features are included or excluded from the regression:

$$\begin{aligned} y_i &\sim \mathrm{N}(\boldsymbol{x}_i^{\mathrm{T}}\boldsymbol{w}, \sigma^2), \\ \sigma^{-2} &\sim \mathrm{Gamma}(\alpha_\sigma, \beta_\sigma), \\ w_j &\sim \gamma_j \mathrm{N}(0, \tau^2) + (1 - \gamma_j)\delta_0, \\ \gamma_j &\sim \mathrm{Ber}(\rho), \end{aligned}$$

where $i = 1, \ldots, N$ runs over N training samples $(y_i, \boldsymbol{x}_i) \in \mathscr{D}$, $j = 1, \ldots, M$ runs over M features, σ^2 is a residual variance parameter, the w_j are regression weights, and the γ_j are binary variables indicating whether feature j is included in the regression ($\gamma_j = 1$: w_j is a priori normally distributed with variance τ^2) or excluded ($\gamma_j = 0$: $w_j = 0$ via the point mass δ_0). The parameter ρ is the prior expected proportion of included variables. The probabilistic parameters of the model are $\boldsymbol{\theta} = (\boldsymbol{w}, \sigma^2, \boldsymbol{\gamma})$; here, α_σ, β_σ, τ^2, and ρ are fixed hyperparameters.

To elicit feedback on feature relevance, we show the marginal posterior probability $p(\gamma_j = 1 \mid \mathscr{D})$ to the user and ask her to provide as feedback her estimate of the probability of the feature being relevant for the prediction. To infer the latent user knowledge, we assume that the user is rational in integrating her latent knowledge f_j and the information (i.e., $p(\gamma_j = 1 \mid \mathscr{D})$) revealed of the training data. In particular, we assume that the user's observed feedback is the posterior probability

$$p(\gamma_j = 1 \mid \mathscr{D}, f_j) = \frac{p(f_j \mid \gamma_j = 1) p(\gamma_j = 1 \mid \mathscr{D})}{Z}, \quad (2)$$

where Z is the normalization constant and the latent feedback likelihood, representing the latent user knowledge, is

$$p(f_j \mid \gamma_j) = A_{f_j} \gamma_j + B_{f_j}(1 - \gamma_j),$$

where A_{f_j} is the likelihood for the latent f_j when $\gamma_j = 1$ and B_{f_j} when $\gamma_j = 0$. Without loss of generality (for using the likelihoods for updating the model later), we can set $A_{f_j} + B_{f_j} = 1$, with $A_{f_j} \in (0,1)$ and $B_{f_j} \in (0,1)$.

We infer A_{f_j} (and, consequently, $B_{f_j} = 1 - A_{f_j}$) by solving from the Bayes theorem in Equation 2:

$$A_{f_j} \propto \frac{p(\gamma_j = 1 \mid \mathscr{D}, f_j)}{p(\gamma_j = 1 \mid \mathscr{D})},$$

where the numerator is the observed feedback given by the user and the denominator is the machine's posterior probability that was shown to the user.

Given a set of observed feedbacks $\mathscr{F}$ from the user (consisting of a set of $p(\gamma_j = 1 \mid \mathscr{D}, f_j)$ values), we update the model to $p(\boldsymbol{\theta} \mid \mathscr{D}, \mathscr{F})$, where $\boldsymbol{\theta}$ denotes all parameters of the model. This is done by updating $p(\boldsymbol{\theta} \mid \mathscr{D})$ using the Bayes theorem with the inferred likelihood functions $p(f_j \mid \gamma_j)$ for each feature j with observed feedback.

Computation of the posterior distribution is intractable. Expectation propagation is used to approximate it (see [3]).

EXPERIMENT AND RESULTS

Sentiment Analysis Task

We considered the problem of rating prediction from user reviews on Amazon kitchen products. The task and data were previously studied in [3, 7]. The data consist of review texts, represented as bag-of-words with 824 distinct unigram and bigram keywords, and their corresponding 1–5 star ratings. The machine learning system aims to predict the ratings of new reviews (test data), given some training data and external expert knowledge. To make the prediction challenging, the data set was randomly partitioned in 500 training data and 4649 test data (the number of training data is smaller than the number of dimensions).

The goal of the experiment was introduced to the participants as eliciting domain knowledge from people to help in designing better predictors of product ratings. However, the real research question was to investigate the efficiency of the user model and user interaction in different scenarios. We listed 70 keywords from the reviews and asked the participants to judge the probability of relevance of each keyword in predicting the product rating. The participants could provide feedback by adjusting the probability value between 0 (not-relevant at all) to 1 (absolutely relevant) by moving a slider. The feedback was only recorded after the slider was moved. The participants could skip giving feedback to keywords that they were very uncertain about. The task description provided example keywords *must buy*, *disaster*, and *is* and explained that the first two provide useful information about the product rating, and therefore, they are relevant while the latter is uninformative for rating prediction.

	Test MSE ± STD		
Condition	*No feedback*	*User feedback*	*User model*
Baseline	1.835	1.749 ± 0.050	NA
IE	1.835	1.744 ± 0.045	1.705 ± 0.038

Table 1. Mean and standard deviation (STD) of MSE on test data for the two systems in different conditions.

Two systems were implemented, a baseline system where no information about the training data is revealed to the user and the initial positions of the sliders were set to the default value 0, and an interactive elicitation (IE) system where the initial positions were set by the machine to the posterior inclusion probabilities $p(\gamma_j = 1 \mid \mathscr{D})$ based on the training data. The participants were informed about the initialization method. Both systems use the prediction model and the feedback likelihoods introduced in the previous section with the difference that IE can infer the latent user knowledge based on the proposed user model while the baseline directly applies the user feedback in the model. Following [3], the model hyperparameters were set as $\alpha_\sigma = 1$, $\beta_\sigma = 1$, $\rho = 0.3$, and $\tau^2 = 0.01$. Mean squared error (MSE) on test data is used as the performance measure. The codes, data, and experiment forms can be found in https://github.com/HIIT/human-overfitting-in-IML.

Results

48 university students and researchers participated in the user study, 3 were excluded since they either left more than 2/3 of the questions unanswered or they finished the study in less than 3 minutes (it was unrealistic to go through the form in less than 3 minutes). 23 participants used the baseline and the remaining 22 the IE system.

Table 1 shows the average test MSE for participants of the two systems before and after receiving feedback and also after the correction done by the proposed user model in IE. The feedback improved the predictive performance in both systems (p-value= 3×10^{-8} in baseline and p-value= 5×10^{-9} in IE without user model, using paired-sample t-test between participants before considering any feedback and after directly using the feedbacks). This shows, as analogously claimed in [3], that the participants, on average, have the necessary knowledge to improve the prediction. More prominently, the predictive performance further improved in the IE system after inferring the latent user knowledge using the user model (p-

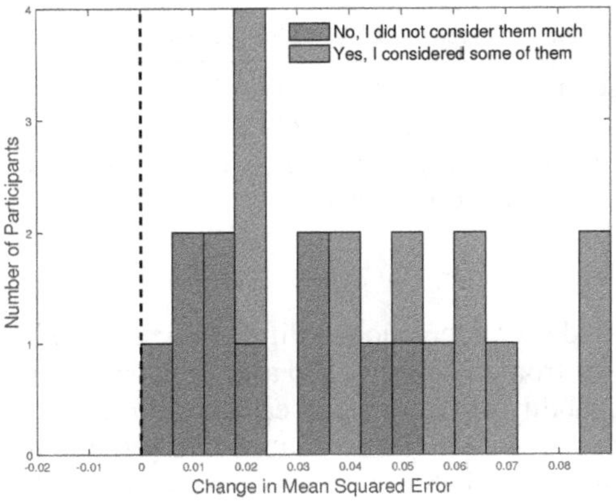

Figure 2. Stacked histogram of MSE change (the difference between MSE after directly using the feedbacks and MSE after the correction done by the propose user model) for 22 participants in IE system. The participants are grouped based on their answer to the question on whether they found the machine estimates useful or not. User modelling has improved MSE values for all participants.

value$= 7 \times 10^{-7}$ in paired-sample t-test between directly using the feedbacks and after employing the user model). Moreover, the user model improved the predictions for each individual user (Figure 2). In a post-questionnaire, we asked the participants of the IE system about the usefulness of the machine estimates: 12 participants answered that they considered them when giving some of the answers and the remaining 10 responded that they did not consider machine estimates that much. On average, the predictions of the former group improved more with the user model (Figure 2).

The feedback the participants gave to the keywords differed between the two systems in several aspects. Table 2 lists average feedback values and machine estimates for 10 keywords with the lowest nominal p-values (two-sample t-test without assuming equal variances between the two systems), showing the keywords that were the most different between the systems. The average correlation to machine estimates for users in IE system was 0.46 (0.33 for the baseline system) and the average variance of feedbacks on keywords was 0.043 (0.060 for the baseline system). These support the hypothesis that the participants considered the machine estimates in the IE system. In the IE system, the average correlation to machine estimates after the correction done by the user model declined to -0.017 which suggests that the user model was successful in reducing the dependency to the training data.

Keyword	*Machine*	*IE*	*Baseline*	*P-value*
best	0.89	0.90	0.80	0.014
great	1.00	0.95	0.83	0.031
disappointed	0.99	0.96	0.85	0.038
heavy	0.20	0.36	0.52	0.038
buy this	0.70	0.77	0.63	0.053
steel	0.19	0.12	0.24	0.073
line	0.34	0.15	0.06	0.088
don't	0.47	0.54	0.38	0.090
recommend	0.16	0.74	0.84	0.102
good	0.26	0.71	0.81	0.115

Table 2. Difference between user feedback in the baseline and IE systems (without user model).

DISCUSSION AND CONCLUSION

We described a user modelling methodology in probabilistic models for disentangling latent user knowledge from observed user feedback that was given in response to machine revealing information from the training data. We used this to guard against double use of the training data and overfitting in interactive machine learning. The proof-of-concept user study in interactive knowledge elicitation of feature relevance information in sparse linear regression showed the potential of the approach for improving prediction performance.

Our approach is based on a simple rationality assumption of the user. It is, however, unreasonable to assume that users would in general behave completely rationally. In particular, the amount information and the way it is presented to the user are important factors that should be considered in designing interactive machine learning systems and user models. In our experiment, the interaction was based on reporting probability values through sliders. Such probability elicitation can be prone to the anchoring effect [5, 22]. Arguably, similar psychological mechanisms will appear in many interactive machine learning applications, since the machine often needs to guide the user for efficient interaction. This paper demonstrates that as long as the user modelling is able to capture the main sources of defects in the interaction, it would be expected to improve the results.

We believe that, as the field of interactive machine learning matures, more consideration will be put into the possible defects in the human–machine interaction. In particular, better user modelling will allow the user to behave naturally in providing feedback to the machine, while the machine (that is, the design of the machine learning system and models) will account for the inevitable human factors and biases [2, 5, 9, 12, 15, 17, 22, 24] to optimally combine the complementary knowledge and skills of the user and the machine. Our work is a step towards this with regard to overfitting in the interaction.

ACKNOWLEDGMENTS

This work was financially supported by the Academy of Finland (Finnish Center of Excellence in Computational Inference Research COIN; Grants 295503, 294238, 292334, and 284642), Re:Know funded by TEKES. We acknowledge the computational resources provided by the Aalto Science-IT Project. We thank Marta Soare for collaboration and helpful comments in early stage of the project.

REFERENCES

1. Homayun Afrabandpey, Tomi Peltola, and Samuel Kaski. 2017. Interactive Prior Elicitation of Feature Similarities for Small Sample Size Prediction. In *Proceedings of the 25th Conference on User Modeling, Adaptation and Personalization (UMAP '17)*. ACM, New York, NY, USA, 265–269. DOI: http://dx.doi.org/10.1145/3079628.3079698

2. Saleema Amershi, Maya Cakmak, William Bradley Knox, and Todd Kulesza. 2014. Power to the people: The role of humans in interactive machine learning. *AI Magazine* 35, 4 (2014), 105–120.

3. Pedram Daee, Tomi Peltola, Marta Soare, and Samuel Kaski. 2017. Knowledge elicitation via sequential probabilistic inference for high-dimensional prediction. *Machine Learning* 106, 9 (2017), 1599–1620. DOI: http://dx.doi.org/10.1007/s10994-017-5651-7

4. Cynthia Dwork, Vitaly Feldman, Moritz Hardt, Toniann Pitassi, Omer Reingold, and Aaron Roth. 2015. The reusable holdout: Preserving validity in adaptive data analysis. *Science* 349, 6248 (2015), 636–638.

5. Paul H Garthwaite, Joseph B Kadane, and Anthony O'Hagan. 2005. Statistical Methods for Eliciting Probability Distributions. *J. Amer. Statist. Assoc.* 100, 470 (2005), 680–701. DOI: http://dx.doi.org/10.1198/016214505000000105

6. Samuel J Gershman, Eric J Horvitz, and Joshua B Tenenbaum. 2015. Computational rationality: A converging paradigm for intelligence in brains, minds, and machines. *Science* 349, 6245 (2015), 273–278.

7. José Miguel Hernández-Lobato, Daniel Hernández-Lobato, and Alberto Suárez. 2015. Expectation propagation in linear regression models with spike-and-slab priors. *Machine Learning* 99, 3 (01 Jun 2015), 437–487. DOI: http://dx.doi.org/10.1007/s10994-014-5475-7

8. Andreas Holzinger. 2016. Interactive machine learning for health informatics: when do we need the human-in-the-loop? *Brain Informatics* 3, 2 (01 Jun 2016), 119–131. DOI: http://dx.doi.org/10.1007/s40708-016-0042-6

9. Tzu-Kuo Huang, Lihong Li, Ara Vartanian, Saleema Amershi, and Xiaojin Zhu. 2016. Active Learning with Oracle Epiphany. In *Advances in Neural Information Processing Systems 29*, D. D. Lee, M. Sugiyama, U. V. Luxburg, I. Guyon, and R. Garnett (Eds.). Curran Associates, Inc., 2820–2828. http://papers.nips.cc/paper/6155-active-learning-with-oracle-epiphany.pdf

10. Ashish Kapoor, Bongshin Lee, Desney Tan, and Eric Horvitz. 2010. Interactive Optimization for Steering Machine Classification. In *Proceedings of the SIGCHI Conference on Human Factors in Computing Systems (CHI '10)*. ACM, New York, NY, USA, 1343–1352. DOI: http://dx.doi.org/10.1145/1753326.1753529

11. Josua Krause, Adam Perer, and Enrico Bertini. 2014. INFUSE: interactive feature selection for predictive modeling of high dimensional data. *IEEE Transactions on Visualization and Computer Graphics* 20, 12 (2014), 1614–1623.

12. Todd Kulesza, Saleema Amershi, Rich Caruana, Danyel Fisher, and Denis Charles. 2014. Structured Labeling for Facilitating Concept Evolution in Machine Learning. In *Proceedings of the 32nd Annual ACM Conference on Human Factors in Computing Systems (CHI '14)*. ACM, New York, NY, USA, 3075–3084. DOI: http://dx.doi.org/10.1145/2556288.2557238

13. Luana Micallef, Iiris Sundin, Pekka Marttinen, Muhammad Ammad-ud din, Tomi Peltola, Marta Soare, Giulio Jacucci, and Samuel Kaski. 2017. Interactive Elicitation of Knowledge on Feature Relevance Improves Predictions in Small Data Sets. In *Proceedings of the 22nd International Conference on Intelligent User Interfaces (IUI '17)*. ACM, New York, NY, USA, 547–552. DOI: http://dx.doi.org/10.1145/3025171.3025181

14. Thomas Mühlbacher and Harald Piringer. 2013. A partition-based framework for building and validating regression models. *IEEE Transactions on Visualization and Computer Graphics* 19, 12 (2013), 1962–1971.

15. Edward Newell and Derek Ruths. 2016. How One Microtask Affects Another. In *Proceedings of the 2016 CHI Conference on Human Factors in Computing Systems (CHI '16)*. ACM, New York, NY, USA, 3155–3166. DOI: http://dx.doi.org/10.1145/2858036.2858490

16. Daniel Russo and James Zou. 2016. Controlling bias in adaptive data analysis using information theory. In *Proceedings of the 19th International Conference on Artificial Intelligence and Statistics*, Vol. PMLR 51. 1232–1240.

17. Dominik Sacha, Michael Sedlmair, Leishi Zhang, John A Lee, Jaakko Peltonen, Daniel Weiskopf, Stephen C North, and Daniel A Keim. 2017. What you see is what you can change: Human-centered machine learning by interactive visualization. *Neurocomputing* 268 (2017), 164–175.

18. Advait Sarkar, Mateja Jamnik, Alan F Blackwell, and Martin Spott. 2015. Interactive visual machine learning in spreadsheets. In *Visual Languages and Human-Centric Computing (VL/HCC), 2015 IEEE Symposium on*. IEEE, 159–163. DOI: http://dx.doi.org/10.1109/VLHCC.2015.7357211

19. Burr Settles. 2010. *Active learning literature survey.* Computer sciences technical report 1648. University of Wisconsin, Madison.

20. Iiris Sundin, Tomi Peltola, Muntasir Mamun Majumder, Pedram Daee, Marta Soare, Homayun Afrabandpey, Caroline Heckman, Samuel Kaski, and Pekka Marttinen. 2017. Improving drug sensitivity predictions in precision medicine through active expert knowledge elicitation. *arXiv preprint arXiv:1705.03290* (2017).

21. Justin Talbot, Bongshin Lee, Ashish Kapoor, and Desney S. Tan. 2009. EnsembleMatrix: Interactive Visualization to Support Machine Learning with Multiple Classifiers. In *Proceedings of the SIGCHI Conference on Human Factors in Computing Systems (CHI '09)*. ACM, New York, NY, USA, 1283–1292. DOI: http://dx.doi.org/10.1145/1518701.1518895

22. Amos Tversky and Daniel Kahneman. 1974. Judgment under Uncertainty: Heuristics and Biases. *Science* 185, 4157 (1974), 1124–1131. DOI: http://dx.doi.org/10.1126/science.185.4157.1124

23. Stef Van Den Elzen and Jarke J van Wijk. 2011. BaobabView: Interactive construction and analysis of decision trees. In *Proceedings of IEEE Symposium on Visual Analytics Science and Technology (VAST)*. IEEE, 151–160.

24. Emily Wall, Leslie M Blaha, Lyndsey Franklin, and Alex Endert. 2017. Warning, bias may occur: A proposed approach to detecting cognitive bias in interactive visual analytics. In *IEEE Conference on Visual Analytics Science and Technology (VAST)*.

Who is the Hero, the Villain, and the Victim? Detection of Roles in News Articles using Natural Language Techniques

Diego Gomez-Zara
Northwestern University
Intelligent Information Lab
Evanston, Illinois, USA
dgomezara@u.northwestern.edu

Miriam Boon
Northwestern University
Intelligent Information Lab
Evanston, Illinois, USA
MiriamBoon2012@u.northwestern.edu

Larry Birnbaum
Northwestern University
Intelligent Information Lab
Evanston, Illinois, USA
l-birnbaum@northwestern.edu

ABSTRACT
News articles often use narrative frames to present people, organizations, and facts. These narrative frames follow cultural archetypes, enabling readers to associate each of the presented elements with familiar stereotypes, well-known characters, and recognizable outcomes. In this way, authors can cast real people or organizations as heroes, villains, or victims. We present a system that identifies the main entities of a news article, and determines which is being cast as a hero, a villain, or a victim. As currently implemented, this system interacts directly with news consumers through a browser extension. Our hope is that by informing readers when an entity is cast in one of these roles, we can make implicit bias explicit, and thereby assist readers in applying their media literacy skills. This approach can also be used to identify roles in well-understood event sequences in a more prosaic manner, e.g., for information extraction.

Author Keywords
Computational journalism; entity recognition; information extraction; role detection; contextual information; sentiment analysis.

ACM Classification Keywords
• **Computing methodologies~Natural language processing** • *Human-centered computing~Natural language interfaces*

INTRODUCTION
A frequent problem in understanding news lies in comprehending the broader context of the particular news story or other informational content at hand. One important mechanism that the media may use to shape public opinion is by *framing* people, events, and issues in particular ways. By using common narrative structures and cultural references, framing enables a communication source to present and define an issue within a "field of meaning" [5]. Framing helps to contextualize events by connecting with readers' prior knowledge, cultural narratives, and moral values [8]. It can present the agents involved in a story as heroes, villains, or victims, so that readers can more easily anticipate and comprehend the attitudes, beliefs, decisions, and actions of these agents as characters. Narrative frames are widespread throughout media, be it films, literature, or news. Their use reflects pervasive cultural models for structuring the presentation of political discourse and identities [10, 12]. As a key element of popular culture storytelling, they use emotionality to unambiguously distinguish between good and evil through clear depictions of victimization, heroism, and villainy [2]. Frames tend to use positive terms to describe heroes, and negative terms for victims and villains [7, 13]. Culturally, heroes embody courage, outstanding achievements, or other noble qualities, whereas villains embody evil intentions, plotting, and other negative qualities. In sum, narrative frames are critical to how readers understand new situations in terms of previous ones, and thereby make sense of the causes, events, and consequences reported by news articles [4].

IUI'18, March 7–11, 2018, Tokyo, Japan

ACM ISBN 978-1-4503-4945-1/18/03...$15.00
https://doi.org/10.1145/3172944.3172993

We present a system that detects how the main characters of a news article are framed as heroes, victims, or villains. As currently implemented, this system interacts with news consumers directly through a browser extension. This approach can also be used to identify roles in well-understood event sequences in a more prosaic manner, e.g., for information extraction.

A MODEL FOR ROLE DETECTION
A standard approach to recognizing narrative frames is to analyze the semantic relations among the different entities in the narrative, and with respect to the events it describes [1, 11]. However, determining these relations—understanding the events in a narrative, and the roles that the entities in that narrative play in those events—is a complex, difficult, and indeed, unsolved, computational challenge. Moreover, to the extent that we do understand how to address this challenge, the techniques involved can be quite expensive computationally. Using standard coreference resolution packages, for example, our system can take more than 20 seconds to analyze a single sentence. Users simply will not wait that long to see the classification results for an entire news article.

We propose a different approach: Rather than determining the specific events and event types described in the narrative, and the semantic relations among the entities involved in those events, in detail, we suggest analyzing the entities at a much higher level of abstraction—specifically, in terms of whether they possess the qualities of heroes, victims, or villains, as conveyed by the terms used to describe them. This approach suggests a relatively simple computational realization, in which the terms closest to each entity are assessed with respect to their similarity to the terms typically used in connection with heroes, villains, or victims. News articles, in particular, facilitate this approach given their use of consistent styles. We provide a simple, computationally cheap, and reasonably (although not perfectly) accurate role classifier.

More specifically, we seek to classify entities involved in narratives into the semantic / thematic categories "heroes," "victims," and "villains"—categories which are highly abstract and thus broadly applicable, and yet are also likely to be comprehensible to typical users. To accomplish this, we have developed a framework and platform for role detection that comprises the following core procedures:

1. Recognize and rank the main entities present in the news article based on prominence.
2. Identify the terms closest to these entities.
3. Use sentiment analysis to determine the polarity of these terms.
4. Calculate the similarity of these terms to those typically used to describe heroes, villains, and victims, using standard term sets or dictionaries.
5. Classify the main entities, as determined in step 1, according to the proposed semantic categories, using the analyses provided by steps 3 and 4.

Entity recognition

The system starts by identifying the main characters involved in a news story. Taking the news article's headline and text as inputs, it analyzes them for relevant entities using standard (and actually somewhat basic) entity recognition methods, for example those provided by the Natural Language Toolkit (NLTK) [3]. For each entity, the system saves the relevant terms and relations and tracks all the possible name forms to establish their connections later. For example, a person could be called "John Smith" and also be mentioned in the article as "Mr. Smith," "Smith," or just "John." The system tracks all these references, and reduces and merges them in a later step. Entities may be a *Person*, an *Organization*, *Geopolitical Entity* (GPE), or only a *Position* (such as "the witness" or "the police officer"). Since news articles have consistent narrative styles, we used standard grammatical forms to detect entities and their relations. The relations associated with *Persons* and *Organizations* are demonyms (e.g., "The *French* president..."), countries (e.g., "The president of *Spain*..."), organizations (e.g., "The CEO of *Google*..."), and positions (e.g., "*Judge* Mark..."). We assume that heroes, villains, and villains are *Persons*, *Organizations*, *GPE*, or *Positions* identified in this way.

Because of their significance, the system uses the headline first to detect the main characters of a story. Headlines present an optimal context for interpretation since the heroes, victims, or villains are often highlighted [6]. The system next analyzes the entities in the text, sentence by sentence, saving their locations in a list using the indices of their corresponding sentences. During this process, the system establishes the connection between the headline entities and those mentioned in the news article's body. This generates a list of several entities with their respective name forms and locations in the text.

One difficulty in applying entity detection in this context is that news articles often involve previously unreferenced names that *a priori* are novel for knowledge databases (e.g., the name of a victim) as well as using generic words to refer to these entities (e.g., "A *woman* was killed..."). To address this challenge, entity recognition incorporates a search for proper nouns as well as generic terms (i.e., "man," "woman," "boy," etc.). All these entities are classified as *Person*. According to the gender and role detected, the system then associates the most frequently mentioned entity in the text with the most relevant generic word found in the text. For example, if "Mrs. Smith" is the most mentioned "victim" in the text, and "*woman*" is often used to refer a victim, we merge these entities.

Entity cut-off

Once the system recognizes all the entities, it must detect and merge the multiple references to a given entity and select the most relevant entities in the article for role assignment. First, the system merges different references to the same entity and selects the longest entity that has proper nouns as the canonical form (e.g., the best results for "Mr. Smith," "John Smith," and "Smith," would be "John Smith"). During this process, the system counts the number of times that each entity is mentioned in the text. It then calculates the relevance score of each merged entity as:

$$r_i = \alpha h_i + \frac{n_i}{\|s\| f_i}$$

where r_i is the relevance score of the merged entity i, h_i is a dummy variable where 1 means that the merged entity was mentioned in the headline (0 otherwise), n_i is the number of times that the merged entity is mentioned in the body of the text, $\|s\|$ is the total number of sentences in the text, and f_i is the first location where the merged entity is mentioned in the text. In other words, we assume that entities that (a) appear in the headline, (b) are frequently mentioned in the article, and (c) are located near the beginning of the text are more relevant. The coefficient α is to weight the impact of a mention in the news article's headline.

Finally, the system takes all the entities found in the headline, and the three entities from the body with the highest relevance score, and assesses the role of each. We use both sets to ensure that all entities in the headline are included; and to compare the results as described below.

Role dictionaries

To determine the roles that these entities play in the narrative frame, the system checks the terms related to each entity and calculates their similarity with terms that typically describe heroes, villains, and victims. For each role, we created a term set or dictionary D_j, where j belongs to the set {"hero," "villain," "victim"}. The terms in each set were manually selected from news articles and blogs, as well as synonyms and antonyms. In total, each role dictionary comprises approximately 200 words.

Our intention with this step is to calculate how similar the terms related to each entity are to each role's dictionary. The system calculates the similarity of each term-pair by using WordNet, a lexical database of English [9] (also contained in NLTK). Specifically, we use the built-in methods for calculating Wu-Palmer Similarity [14]. This method returns a score denoting how similar two words are, based on the depth of the two senses in the taxonomy and that of their most specific ancestor node.

Sentiment analysis

One problem this approach faces is the similarity of opposite words that are closely related. For example, using Wu-Palmer, "*love*" is more similar to "*hate*" than to "*romance*." Since archetypal characters are frequently assessed in emotional terms—positive for heroes and negative for victims and villains—the system leverages this property by filtering the terms used for the similarity comparisons based on sentiment. The program calculates and saves the sentiment score of the terms closest to the relevant entities. If the term is positive or neutral, the system calculates its similarity with the hero dictionary. Equally, if the analyzed word is negative or neutral, the system checks its similarity to the victim and villain dictionaries. We calculate sentiment for each term using standard toolkits, in the current implementation *TextBlob*[1], yielding a polarity for each term, ranging from -1.0 (very negative) to 1.0 (very positive).

Role detection

We assume that the terms used to describe entities are usually closer to their respective characters in the text. Based on this assumption, the system calculates for each relevant entity its distance to other terms present in the sentence, and then prioritizes the similarity scores of the closest terms. More specifically, we define $S_i \in \{1, 2, \ldots, K\}$ as the set of K sentences where the entity i is mentioned. Each element of S_k has a list of terms $\{w_{k,1}, w_{k,2}, \ldots, w_{k,n}\}$, where n is the total length of the kth sentence. The system calculates the similarity of a term w with respect to a role j by calculating the average of the similarities between that term w and each term d from the dictionary D_j, as follows:

$$sim(w, j) = \sum_{d \in D_j} \frac{s(w, d)}{\|D_j\|}$$

To calculate the similarity that entity i has with role j in sentence k, we sum the similarity scores for each term in the sentence. To implement our proximity assumption, we apply a decay factor f according to the distance between the entity i and each term analyzed. Additionally, to take into account active vs. passive roles—heroes and villains are assumed to be more active, victims more passive—the system analyzes whether the entity i is the subject of the sentence (i.e., the entity that performs the action) or the object of the sentence (i.e., the entity that receives the action). In the first case, the words identified in the hero and villain dictionaries receive an additional score. If the entity is the object of the sentence, the words related to the victim dictionary receive an additional score. In summary, we calculate the score of the merged entity i for role j in sentence k as:

$$ro_{i,j,k} = \sum_{w \in S_k} \big(sim(w, j) + a(i, j, w)\big)(1 - f)^{d(i,w)}$$

where f is the decay factor between 0 and 1, $d(i, w)$ is the distance between the entity i and the term w of the sentence k, and $a(i, j, w)$ is the additional score that the role j receives according to the positions of the term w and the entity i in the sentence k. Finally, the system calculates the overall role scores for each entity by averaging all the scores computed using sentences in which they occur. The results are role scores for each relevant entity of the news article's headline and body.

The final step is to assign the hero, villain, and victim of the story, if any of these roles exist. To establish a baseline, we use the headline as a reference to compare the role scores assigned by the system. First, the system places the headline's entities in descending order according to their assigned role scores. Next, the system takes the highest value achieved by any entity on these three roles and classifies the entity according to that role. The system continues this selection process by picking the next highest role score from the remaining entities and classifies the next entity according to that role, and so on. Finally, the system performs the same ranking procedure for the relevant entities from the body. As a result, the system establishes a role classification of the headline's entities, and of the body's entities, which are then compared. If they differ, the role assignment based on the text is preferred.

INTERFACE AND EXAMPLES

Using the method described above, we have developed a Google Chrome extension that determines which entities are the hero, villain, or victim, for any article being displayed. To better contextualize these results, the system also presents the most relevant terms that explain each classification, based on similarity with the assigned role's dictionary and proximity to the respective entity.

[1] http://textblob.readthedocs.io/en/dev/

Figure 1. The system detects President Trump as villain, President Macron as the hero, and France as the victim.

Figure 2. President Trump is detected as the hero, his friend Jim as the victim, and Paris as the villain.

We will illustrate the system's operation using two examples that show how the tool distinguishes the coverage by two different news organizations of the same news event. Figure 1 shows the system's results given an article from The New York Times entitled "Emmanuel Macron to welcome Trump, an unlikely partner, to France" (July 12, 2017). In his visit to France, the NYT focused on President Trump's relationship with the France's president Emmanuel Macron. Based on the article's body, the story's results indicate "Macron" as the hero, "Trump" as the villain, and "France" as the victim. On the other hand, Fox News covered this same visit focusing in Trump's friend Jim, who did not attend because—according to the president—Paris has been infiltrated by foreign extremists. This article was published the same day and entitled "Trump visits Paris without his friend, the mysterious Jim" (Figure 2). Initially, the system assigns Paris as the victim because it is included in the subject of the headline. Ultimately, however, it classifies Paris as the villain because is associated with the words "ruined," "terrorism," and "infiltrated." Additionally, the system classifies President Trump as the hero and his friend "Jim" as the victim of this story.

CONCLUSIONS

Our current implementation leverages standard entity recognition, sentiment analysis, and the use of term sets or dictionaries, which as a starting point have yielded promising results. During development, we iteratively improved our original results by incorporating a variety of disambiguation techniques and putting more weight on headlines. However, because it utilizes simple proximity, this approach cannot handle situations in which the article presents complex grammar structures such as use of passive voice. Moreover, the system clearly requires more testing to establish a reasonable threshold for assigning the roles: Sometimes, articles do not present clear heroes, victims, or villains, suggesting that a cut-off score is needed.

Moving forward, it will be critical to conduct a serious evaluation aimed at proving and quantifying the performance of the role detection process described here. We must develop performance indicators based on either user evaluation or a comparison with an annotated ground truth. As we conduct such an evaluation, and develop data that can be used to make reasoned choices, we expect to incorporate more up-to-date packages and technologies to improve the system's performance.

We have described an architecture for abstract or thematic role detection in news articles, instantiated in a browser extension. Rather than identifying entities in narratives as serving event- or topic-specific roles, such as buyer (or seller), inventor, thief, author, etc., we aim to identify them as serving highly abstract narrative or thematic roles, as either "hero," "villain," or "victim." From a computational perspective, we believe that these abstract thematic roles may be significantly easier to identify than topic-specific roles involving more fine-grained semantic analysis. Moreover, in many instances we believe that abstract role identification might be useful in determining these more specific roles. For example, if a story is about a kidnapping, and we identify an entity in that story as the villain, then he or she is probably the kidnapper.

We expect to release the tool and the code shortly for use by others to develop and perform experiments related to the consumption and diffusion of news articles. From a user perspective, we believe that these role identifications can ultimately help reveal bias in news articles and improve "media literate" information consumption. For example, this tool could be used to highlight and explain the differences in framing of a specific news event covered by different media sources. Similarly, it could be used to study polarization in media. Finally, since the system is able to identify the emotional words related to the main characters of an article, we may be able to use its results to modify the article to present a more neutral version of events.

ACKNOWLEDGMENTS

Our work at the Intelligent Information Lab (InfoLab) at Northwestern University has been supported in part by Google. Miriam Boon has also been supported by Northwestern University's program in Technology and Social Behavior. We thank Jason Cohn and Victor Bursztyn for many useful discussions.

REFERENCES

1. Gabor Angeli, Julie Tibshirani, Jean Wu and Christopher D Manning. 2014. Combining Distant and Partial Supervision for Relation Extraction. in *EMNLP*, 1556-1567.
2. Elisabeth Anker. 2005. Villains, victims and heroes: Melodrama, media, and September 11. *Journal of Communication*, 55 (1). 22-37.
3. Steven Bird, Ewan Klein and Edward Loper. 2009. *Natural language processing with Python: analyzing text with the natural language toolkit.* " O'Reilly Media, Inc.".
4. Miriam L Boon. 2017. Augmenting Media Literacy with Automatic Characterization of News along Pragmatic Dimensions. in *Companion of the 2017 ACM Conference on Computer Supported Cooperative Work and Social Computing*, ACM, 49-52.
5. Claes H De Vreese. 2005. News framing: Theory and typology. *Information Design Journal & Document Design*, 13 (1).
6. Daniel Dor. 2003. On newspaper headlines as relevance optimizers. *Journal of Pragmatics*, 35 (5). 695-721. https://doi.org/10.1016/S0378-2166(02)00134-0
7. Jeff Goodwin, James M Jasper and Francesca Polletta. 2009. *Passionate politics: Emotions and social movements*. University of Chicago Press.
8. Melanie C Green. 2004. Transportation into narrative worlds: The role of prior knowledge and perceived realism. *Discourse processes*, 38 (2). 247-266.
9. George A. Miller. 1995. WordNet: a lexical database for English. *Commun. ACM*, 38 (11). 39-41. 10.1145/219717.219748
10. Zhongdang Pan and Gerald M Kosicki. 1993. Framing analysis: An approach to news discourse. *Political communication*, 10 (1). 55-75.
11. Karthik Raghunathan, Heeyoung Lee, Sudarshan Rangarajan, Nathanael Chambers, Mihai Surdeanu, Dan Jurafsky and Christopher Manning. 2010. A multi-pass sieve for coreference resolution. in *Proceedings of the 2010 Conference on Empirical Methods in Natural Language Processing*, Association for Computational Linguistics, 492-501.
12. Dietram A Scheufele. 1999. Framing as a theory of media effects. *Journal of communication*, 49 (1). 103-122.
13. Stefan Stieglitz and Linh Dang-Xuan. 2013. Emotions and Information Diffusion in Social Media-Sentiment of Microblogs and Sharing Behavior. *Journal of Management Information Systems*, 29 (4). 217-248. 10.2753/MIS0742-1222290408
14. Zhibiao Wu and Martha Palmer. 1994. Verbs semantics and lexical selection. in *Proceedings of the 32nd annual meeting on Association for Computational Linguistics*, Association for Computational Linguistics, 133-138.

Cloud Menus, a Circular Adaptive Menu for Small Screens

Jean Vanderdonckt[1], Sara Bouzit[2,3], Gaëlle Calvary[3], Denis Chêne[2]
[1]Université catholique de Louvain, [2]Orange Labs, [3]Université Grenoble Alpes
jean.vanderdonckt@uclouvain.be, {sara.bouzit, gaelle calvary}@imag.fr, denis.chene@orange.com

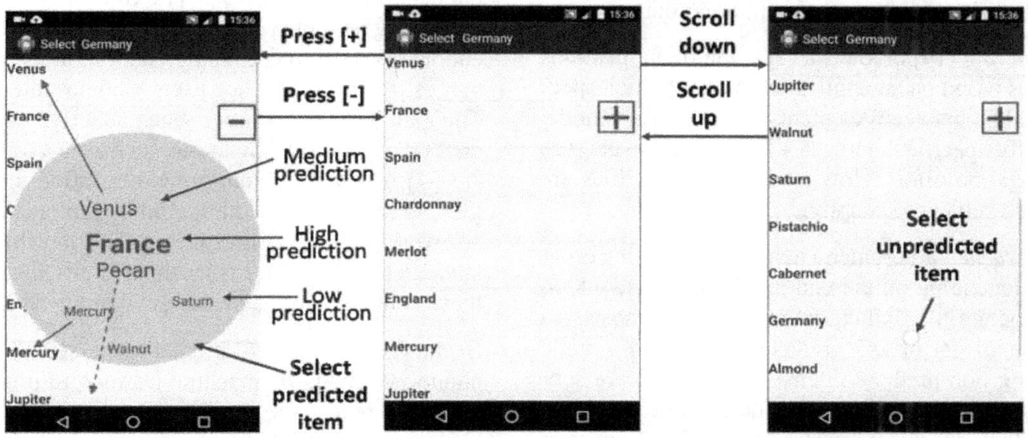

Figure 1. The Cloud Menus: a circular adaptive cloud contains predicted items that can be made (in)visible by pressing [+], [–].

ABSTRACT
This paper presents Cloud Menus, a split adaptive menu for small screens where the predicted menu items are arranged in a circular tag cloud with a location consistent with their corresponding position in the static menu and a font size depending on their prediction level. This layout results from a 3-step design process: (i) defining an initial design space on Bertin's 8 visual variables and 4 quality properties, (ii) identifying the most preferred layout based on agreement rate, and (iii) implementing it into Cloud Menus, a new widget for Android with circular layout. An empirical study suggests that cloud menus reduce item selection time and error rate when prediction is correct without penalizing it when prediction is incorrect, compared to two baselines: a non-adaptive static menu and an adaptive linear menu. From this study, design guidelines for cloud menus are elaborated.

Author Keywords
Adaptive menu, prediction window, split menu, tag cloud.

ACM CLASSIFICATION KEYWORDS
• **Human-centered computing ~ Human computer interaction (HCI).**

INTRODUCTION
Split Adaptive Interfaces [11] reproduce a limited part of the User Interface (UI) elements (e.g., a menu [30], a toolbar [15], icons [19,26], a help system [1]) that are predicted to be of immediate use to preserve stability [13]. Split adaptive menus typically present the end user with predicted menu items for improving feature findability [13], speeding up the item selection [9] without searching for them in deep and wide menus. Since selecting a menu item requires a navigation time and a visual search time that depend on the number of items displayed, small screens are particularly affected and the risk of not benefiting from the adaptivity advantages is real. UI adaptation remains essential to ensure the user experience and to introduce the right UI changes at the right time [20]. The quality of adaptation is proportional to the quality of prediction [14,32]: if the prediction is accurate enough, adaptation brings its earnings by accelerating and facilitating user interaction. Since the quality of prediction can never be guaranteed, the following questions are stated: what do we win when the prediction is accurate?, how to avoid penalizing interaction when prediction is wrong?, how to prevent user from errors induced by a wrong prediction? In order to address these challenges, this paper proposes *Cloud Menus* (Fig. 1), a split adaptive menu for small screens with a prediction window displayed as a word cloud and demonstrates that it accelerates interaction when prediction is correct without slowing it down when prediction is incorrect. Also important is to assess to what extent increasing the amount of predicted items impacts the interaction.

The remainder of this paper is structured as follows: Section 2 reviews works related to adaptive menus for small screens. Section 3 discusses the 3-step design process that leads to defining and implementing Cloud Menus. Section 4 reports on a controlled study performed to test Cloud Menus (with adaptivity) against a static menu (without any adaptivity) and a linear menu (with adaptivity, but without the cloud layout). Section 5 concludes the paper, by presenting some future avenues to this paper.

IUI 2018, March 7–11, 2018, Tokyo, Japan.
© 2018 ACM ISBN 978-1-4503-4945-1/18/03...$15.00.
https://doi.org/10.1145/3172944.3172975

RELATED WORK

There is a rich background [2,3] of designing interaction techniques for menu selection, which is understood as one of the most frequently used interaction style in UIs. While a great deal of this work focuses on the interaction techniques themselves, prior work also investigates how a menu could be made adaptive depending on different data sources.

Adaptive Prompting [19] predicts a selection of applications and related files based on an application model (which specifies relationships between elements) and a user model (which manually specifies the user's experience level, etc.) to reduce navigation effort. How applications and files are presented is also subject to adaptivity.

Frequency-based menus sort menu items by decreasing order of frequency, depending on the end user's actions [2]. *Split menus* [30] separate a graphical menu into a topmost area promoting a small list of 2-3 predicted items and a static menu containing non-predicted items. Split menus are subject to instability [9,13]: end users oscillate between the two areas because they are unsure where to find the menu item they want. To preserve this stability, *Split menus with replication* leaves the adaptive part as stated before and the second part remains unaltered, thus enabling end users to always refer to the menu as they know it. *Adaptive Activation-Area Menu* (AAMU) [33] is an adaptive morphing menu containing an enlarged activation area for predicted items which dynamically resizes itself providing a broader steering path for menu navigation. Predicted items can be emphasized by highlighting [1], bolding [24], coloring or underlying [21], changing font size [33], moving them [23] to a comfort zone [25], by shortcut [7], and animation [10,26].

Ephemeral menus [10] is an adaptive temporal menu where the gradual onset was used in order to display non-predicted items. At opening the menu, user finds predicted items and after a delay of 500ms remaining items appear gradually. When the prediction accuracy is relatively high (79%), ephemeral adaptation significantly offers better performance and user satisfaction over static menus, and a performance benefit over a graphical adaptation technique. Obtaining high prediction accuracy of menu items is crucial to the success of adaptive menus. However, there still lacks an effective prediction method of menu items. *In-Context Disappearing* (ICD) are smartphone menus [5]: at opening the initial menu, the full list of items is superimposed with a window prompting predicted items. This latter contains three items and disappears gradually. *Out-of-Context Disappearing (OCD)* approach is the inverse: at opening, the prediction window is immediately displayed with the predicted items; after a delay of 500 msec [10], the complete menu is gradually displayed from the back, thus replacing the prediction window.

The perceived efficiency of three split menus is measured [9]: a static menu with top four items remaining constant, an adaptable menu where top four items can be changed by the end user, and an adaptive menu where top four items in the split menu are predicted according to user's recently and frequently used items. Static menus are found efficient compared to both adaptable and adaptive menus. However, overall participants tend to prefer adaptable menus.

Split Adaptive Interfaces exhibit a certain amount of potential benefits at a certain cost [14,20]. The gain expected from promoting predicted items should be counter-balanced by the end user's need to constantly adapt to the altered menu layout, especially for novice users who hesitate between areas. The gain becomes positive when adaptivity significantly reduces the menu selection time, such as in a hierarchical menu [13,34] or when limited screen resolution induces scrolling [32]. Other potential shortcomings are: adaptive menus do not work well with short menus [27] or when the end user alternates between an amount of items that is larger than those contained in the prediction window [13].

Bridle & McCreath [6] predict menu selection on a mobile phone by relying on machine learning to improve usability: it helps to reduce the number of key presses. While Xie *et al.* [35] predict menu items on a mobile phone based on a Markov Chain, Fukazawa *et al.* [12] prefer Support Vector Machine (SVM): the system ranks both frequently and rarely used functions based on user operation history. While accessibility of these menu items is improved, this system may cause significant performance loss [12]. Asthana *et al.* [2] study the adverse impact of adaptive voice menu on experienced users. They also propose strategies to lower the negative effect of adaptivity on familiar users. Gajos & Chauncey [15] demonstrate systematic individual differences in the utilization of the adaptivity, which correlate with the stable user traits of Need for Cognition and Extraversion.

Stability can be further refined based on Bertin's height *visual variables* [4] conveying an adaptation scheme [5]: *position* (e.g., change in the *x*, *y*, *z* location), *size* (e.g., change in length, area, or repetition), *shape* (e.g., change by shape), *value* (e.g., change from light to dark), *orientation* (e.g., change in alignment, angle), *color* (e.g., change in hue at a given value), *texture* (e.g., change in pattern), and *motion* (e.g., animated transition or visual effect). Four properties can be defined for comparing adaptive menu [5]:

1. *Spatial stability*: the ability of an adaptive menu to preserve its spatial layout after adaptivity, thus keeping position and orientation constant.
2. *Physical stability*: the ability of an adaptive menu to preserve its physical configuration after adaptivity, thus keeping size and shape constant.
3. *Format stability*: the ability of an adaptive menu to preserve the format of its layout after adaptivity, thus keeping value, color, and texture constant.
4. *Temporal stability*: the ability of an adaptive menu to preserve its layout over time while being adapted, thus keeping motion constant.

For example, ephemeral adaptation [10] preserves spatial, physical, and format stability, but not temporal stability.

In conclusion, several adaptive menus have been researched for pull-down menus displayed on desktop [34]. Transposing these techniques to small screens is not straightforward because all items cannot be displayed on a single screen [27] and because they require interaction techniques that small screens are not able to afford [18]. These adaptive menus are always presented at once, which is not the case on small screens: any predicted item located on a subsequent screen requires a cognitive effort to explore the whole set of items.

There are not many adaptive menus tailored to small screens. Either menus are adaptive, but not tailored to small screens or menus are tailored for these devices, but pursue different goals, such as information display optimization [21], reducing number of taps [27], increasing efficiency [27]. The amount of predicted items in the aforementioned menus is usually limited to 2-3 items [10,14]. Increasing this amount has never been explored before and the presentation of the prediction window remains very similar to the initial menu.

THE CLOUD MENU DESIGN PROCESS

An exploratory session was organized by an Internet Service Provider with ten participants, two UI designers, one Human Factors expert and one experienced developer. From a focus group, five requirements were elicited for a new adaptive menu for smartphones: **(R1)** provide an adaptive menu that accelerates user interaction when item prediction is accurate without decelerating it when prediction is inaccurate, **(R2)** address constraints imposed by small screen devices, **(R3)** display more than 3 predicted items if possible (as opposed to other adaptive menus), **(R4)** maintain spatial stability, and **(R5)** rely on physical, format, and temporal coding. Then, a 3-step design process has been conducted in order to progressively define and investigate a design space.

Step 1: Define a Design Space of Prediction Window

The goal of this design space is to define how the prediction window could be laid out by theoretically exploring design alternatives. Bertin's visual variables offer eight dimensions for choosing the layout of the presentation window, but have a varying ability to be *selective* (is a change enough to allow us to select it from a group) and/or *ordered* (are changes according to this variable perceived as ordered?) (Table 1). Fig. 2 sorts coding schemes by decreasing order of precision: in the last column for nominal values (we hereby assume that menu items are neither quantitatively sorted nor ordered), position is the most precise coding scheme, length and surface coming later, the other ones have not been retained.

	Bertin's visual variable [3]	Select	Order
1	Position	●	●
2	Size	●	●
3	Shape	◑	○
4	Value	●	●
5	Color	◑	○
6	Orientation	●	○
7	Texture	●	○
8	Motion	◑	○

Table 1. Level of support of Bertin's visual variables expressed according to Harvey's Balls.

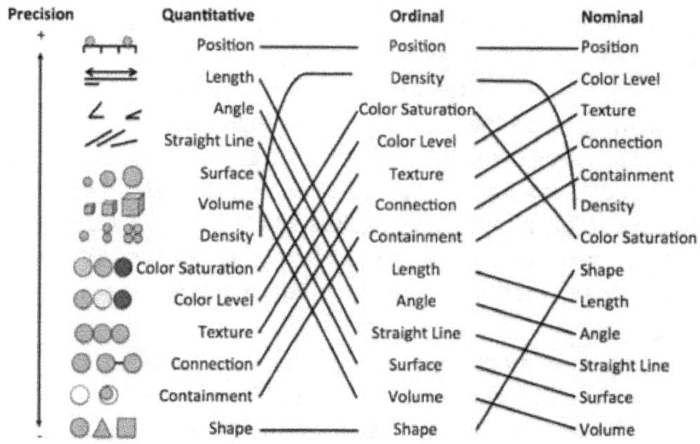

Figure 2. Coding schemes sorted by order of precision.

The Cloud Layout for Prediction Window

Addressing R5, while respecting R4, means that the prediction window should not necessarily be embedded in the initial menu, but could be presented in another way, such as by superimposition, but not far away. Therefore, the driving principle of the prediction window layout consists in displaying a *modal word-cloud based* [17] *prediction window* overlapping the full initial menu and enabling the user to control the prediction window on-demand. The general cloud layout was initially motivated by the following reasons.

A *tag cloud*, or *Wordle* [8], is a visual representation of text data, typically used to depict keyword metadata (*tags*) on any textual document or collection of documents (e.g., a report, a web site, a set of papers, a digital library) [22]. Tags are usually single words whose importance is shown is depicted through one or many visual variables [4], typically font size or color. These coding schemes are useful for quickly perceiving the most prominent terms and for locating them to determine their relative prominence. Tag clouds are extensively researched and used in many areas [8,16,17,22,28,31], except for menu selection: for *indexing* (e.g., for faster term discriminativeness), for *searching* (e.g., semantic expansions for web search, personalized search), for *generating a taxonomy* (e.g., for generating a taxonomy of terms selected in a domain), for *clustering and classification* (e.g., classifying blog entries and general web objects), for *social interest discovery* (e.g., user profiling, end user's topics of interest), and *browsing* (e.g., when terms are hyperlinked to items associated with the tag). *Word clouds* [17] emerge as a usable [28], straightforward and visually appealing [31] method for emphasizing important terms in a textual document or a collection of documents. They are used in various contexts as a means to provide an overview by drilling down text to those terms that appear with the highest frequency. The word cloud layout has an impact on its perceived usability [22,31].

Halvey & Keane [16] examine the time for selecting a country a list of all countries presented in 6 varying formats: alphabetical horizontal list (μ=2.88 sec), alphabetical vertical list (μ=2.89 sec), alphabetical cloud (μ=2.94 sec), horizontal list (μ=3.19 sec), vertical list (μ=3.24 sec), and normal cloud (μ=3.40 sec). The cloud is slower than both lists because items in the lists are ordered alphabetically (which is faster with westernized reading) as opposed to distance from the center (which is faster when scanning). When the font size of items in the cloud is larger, the cloud reaches to μ=2.74 sec. These results suggest that a cloud-based representation for a menu, where items are not necessarily sorted by alphabetical order, may be appropriate since it does not decrease the performance with respect to lists. The question of which cloud layout then arises for the prediction window.

Findlater test

In order to explore cloud representations based on Bertin's visual variables, the menu considered by Findlater *et al.* [10] for their experiment on *ephemeral adaptation* was considered: the full menu contains 4 groups of 4 related items (i.e., England, France, Germany, Spain – Venus, Mercury, Jupiter, Saturn – Cabernet, Chardonnay, Merlot, Shiraz – Almond, Pecan, Pistachio, Walnut) and the prediction was defined as follows: Venus=80%, Spain, Shiraz=70%, Pecan, Cabernet, Pistachio=60%, all other items having the same normal probability to be selected. This configuration is in line with other research in this area [5,34] both in terms of prediction probabilities and in terms of prediction level [14]. We will refer to this list as the *Findlater test*.

Initial prototypes for Cloud Menus

Based on Findlater test, initial prototypes for Cloud Menu layouts were developed in Adobe Flash V27.0 for Bertin's variables: *size* (1D vertical vs 1D horizontal vs 2D – Fig. 3), *shape* (rectangle, circle, oval – Fig. 4), *value* (highlighting of current item, zooming in, zooming in with rotation in case of a vertical label – Fig. 5), *color* (Fig. 6a), *font size* (Fig. 6b), *orientation* by changing label angle (horizontal, vertical, angular – Fig. 7), *texture* by changing font family (regular, bold, italic, or combined – Fig. 6b), and *motion* by animation (without vs with animation of non-horizontal items – Fig. 8).

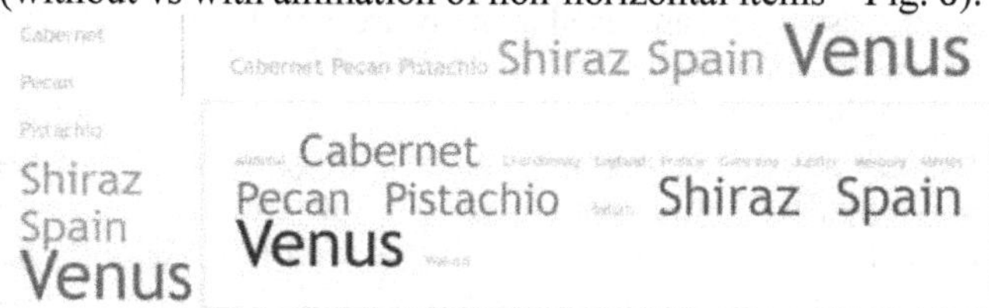

Figure 3. 1D vertical, 1D horizontal, 2D layouts.

Figure 4. Rectangle, circle, oval layouts.

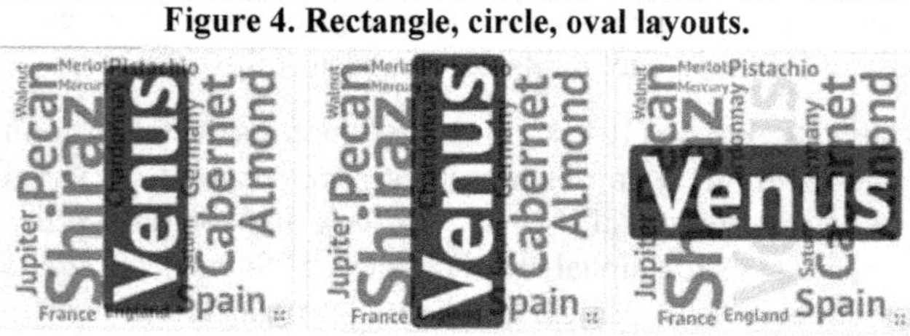

Figure 5. Layout with highlighting, zooming in, zooming in with rotation of vertical label.

Figure 6. Layouts with colors (a), different fonts (b).

Figure 7. Horizontal, vertical, bidirectional, angular layouts.

Figure 8. Layouts with animation of non-horizontal items, without or with zoom of selected item, with adjustable speed.

Step 2: Exploratory Study of Prediction Window Layouts

Similarly to the procedure by Ponsard *et al.* [26], who prototyped various techniques for ephemeral adaptation of icons, we performed an exploratory user study to evaluate people's reactions with respect to the various layouts generated (Fig. 3-8). We were interested in what people would think of the different adaptations conveyed by the different layouts of the prediction window and which they would prefer.

Procedure of the Exploratory Study

Each participant performed the task in a controlled environment. Prior to the task each participant was welcomed, had the process explained to them (including signing a consent form) and filled in a short questionnaire on their background. After the questionnaire was completed, the researcher demonstrated the initial prototypes for Cloud Menus. The participants were given 5 min. to familiarize themselves with the software and ask any questions. If desired, the participant could finish this part early. The participants were then given 15 min. to use a small program where each referent can be tested. The instructions were to select each referent one after another and experiment the corresponding layout. During this experiencing time, the researcher sat next to the participant and observed them. The participant then rated each layout using a five point Likert scale on the layout effectiveness in preserving the meaning: one was strongly disagree through to five being strongly agree. Then they were asked to rank the layouts in order from most preferred to least preferred. After reviewing the referents, the participant was asked for any recommendations on which layout could be selected for conveying the prediction window. This then concluded the user study.

Analysis

After each participant, the questionnaire, ratings and ranking data was added into an MS Excel spreadsheet. The data was entered in an anonymous format so the participants could not be identified.

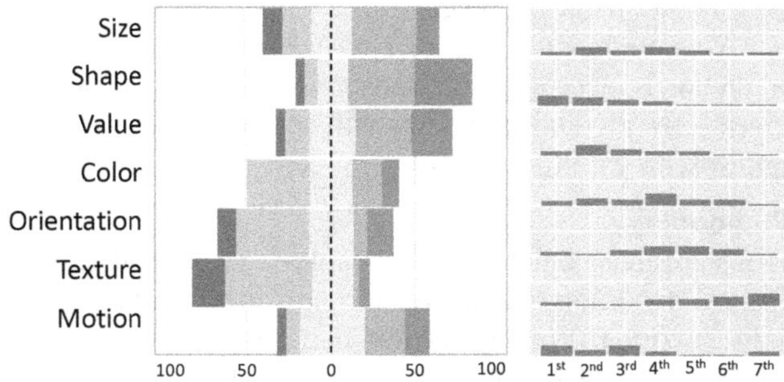

Figure 9. Participants' rating and ranking for each variable.

Results and Discussion

A total of thirty participants (μ=32.3 years, SD=6.2 y.) participated in this experiment. All participants were regular computer users and recruited in our organization through a mailing list. They have different backgrounds such as: accounting, finance, information systems, management, marketing, and human resources. They were all volunteers: they were not given any remuneration (financial or otherwise). Fig. 9 shows the correspondence between the distribution of layout appropriateness in terms of percentage (represented as a divergent horizontal stacked bar based on a Likert R package - http://jason.bryer.org/likert/) and the distribution of ranking (represented as vertical bars). The coding scheme is as follows: red=strongly disagree, orange=disagree, yellow= neutral, light green=agree, dark green= strongly agree). The yellow neutral part is divided into two equal parts in Fig. 9.The preferred variables for layout appropriateness are respectively: shape (82% of the 30 participants), value (71%), size (66%), motion (61%), color (46%), orientation (40%), and texture (22%). Shape was also ranked first followed by motion. Value was ranked second the most frequently, followed by shape. Motion was ranked third the most frequently, followed by shape. With seventh rank most frequently assigned, texture was judged the least appropriate variable on which we can play for conveying adaptivity because of its questionable legibility. For these reasons, shape was selected as the variable to indicate adaptivity.

In order to fulfill (R1)-(R5) requirements, a circular cloud layout was finally adopted, where font size and distance to the center represent the importance of a menu item, but where distance between the items does not represent their similarity (such as in document semantic tagging [17]) or adjacency in the initial menu (although this option could be further investigated). The rationale behind the choice is justified by the following findings and motivations:

- Among all referents (Fig. 2-7), the most preferred word cloud was a 2D circular (for its distinctiveness with the rectangular are of the initial menu) shape with horizontal items (in order not to reduce item legibility), without any animation (because it is hard to control and lengthy [9]), without any color or font effect apart from font size.
- Circular layouts have additionally shown to be most effective to spot high frequency terms in word clouds [22]: layouts generated by these algorithms are compact and clear, reduce unused white space and may feature arbitrary convex polygons as boundaries (which is not really usable for menu, though). The results of the user study and the technical evaluation enable designers to devise a combination of algorithm and parameters which produces satisfying word cloud layouts for many application scenarios [28].
- Users prefer a less extensive menu hierarchy on a small screen device and that item category classification and item labelling influence item selection performance [27].
- Small screens do not display more than 15 items simultaneously as opposed to dozens on desktop, thus providing an opportunity for applying this finding: provide a direct access to menu items that are the most predicted, since there is no room enough for displaying them all [27].
- For a small list with emphasized items, ocular saccades should be easier to perform than on linear list [6,21].

Step 3: Final Implemented Design of Cloud Menus

The final design of cloud menus is developed as a widget in Java for Eclipse based on Android Software Development Kit. The Cloud Menu consists of a linear list for the static menu superimposed by a prediction window materialized as a circular word cloud with three prediction levels (Fig. 1): (1) any item with high prediction (probability ≥ 80%) is located in the center of the circle highlighted with large font size; (2) any item with medium prediction (60% ≤ probability ≤ 80%) is presented in the periphery with a decreasing size font and a larger distance from the center depending on the probability (the lower the prediction, the more far and the smaller the item becomes) ; (3) any item with low prediction (probability ≤ 60%) is displayed only in the static menu.

The Cloud Menu for Findlater test is depicted in Fig. 1: the France item with high prediction is presented in the center with the largest font size; Venus and Pecan with medium prediction are presented afterwards on a position indicating the original position of item in the static menu; Mercury, Walnut and Saturn with low prediction are located in the periphery with an increasing distance from the center and a decreasing size font. Note that the Pecan item is located on an imaginary line indicating an off-screen location. When prediction is correct, the user selects the item directly from the Cloud Menu. When prediction is incorrect, the user makes the cloud menu disappearing by pressing the [–] button and selects the item from the static menu after scrolling down/up.

CONTROLLED EXPERIMENT

A controlled experiment was conducted based on two conditions: a *Control condition* (or baseline), which presents the Findlater test in a static menu without any adaptation and prediction and a *Cloud Menu*, which presents the Findlater test as a Cloud Menu with 6 items in the prediction window. In order to test the influence of the circular layout of the Cloud Menu, a third condition was developed: the *Linear Menu*, where both prediction window and full list of items are presented as superimposed linear lists (Figure 4), but without any cloud. In order to backward and forward prediction window, the two [–] and [+] pushbuttons are also added.

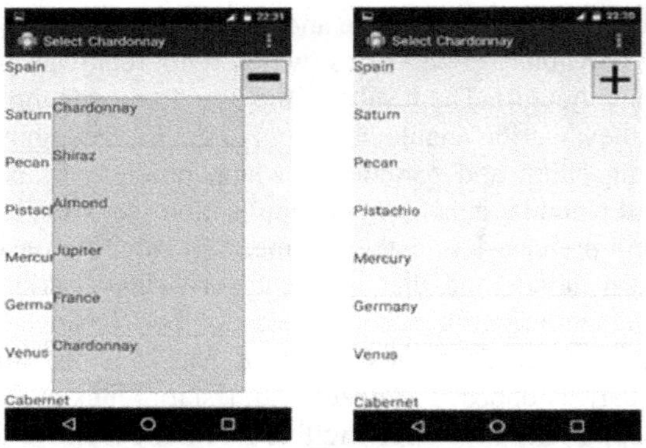

Figure 10. Linear Menu: a linear list with 6 predicted items.

Hypotheses. We made the following assumptions:

Speed with high prediction

H_{11}=*The Cloud Menu and the Linear Menu will be faster than Control condition.* When prediction is correct, the user finds the target item among 6 predicted items in the Cloud Menu and in the Linear Menu more quickly than in Control condition where the target belongs to a list of 16 items.

H_{21}=*The Cloud Menu will be faster than the Linear Menu.* The circular layout of the 6 predicted items with different font sizes and positions is faster than a linear list without any visual distinction between predicted items, as said in [29].

H_{31}=*A target item located in the center of the Cloud Menu will be selected faster than when located in its periphery.* Indeed, a target item located in the center is considered easy to find because it is emphasized with a large font size (thus inducing a larger activation area as in AAMU [33]), contrarily to a target item located in another part of the cloud menu.

Speed with low prediction

H_{41}=*The Cloud Menu and the Linear Menu will not be worse than Control condition.* Cloud and Linear adaptive menus will not be worse than the static menu as they avoid penalizing interaction when prediction is incorrect. The ⊟ button should enable the end user to escape from the Cloud Menu and Linear menu in case of an incorrect prediction.

H_{51}=*The Cloud Menus will be faster than the Linear Menu.* Exploration of predicted items will be easier in the Cloud Menu, where items are highlighted with different font sizes and positions, than in the Linear Menu.

H_{61}=*In all conditions (Cloud Menu, Linear menu and Control condition), the target item will be selected faster when located on the first interaction screen than on the second.* Accessing a target item on the first screen will be faster and easier than on the second screen requiring vertical scrolling.

Error rate with high prediction

H_{71}=*The error rate of the Cloud Menu is similar to the Linear Menu.* When the target item is one of the 6 predicted items in Cloud and Linear Menu, the visual search time and selection time are reduced, which also reduces error rate.

H_{81}=*When target item is located in the center of the cloud, errors will be less frequent than when target is in its periphery.* User attention will be attracted to the center where an item is displayed with a larger font size compared to items in other parts of the cloud, thus facilitating the item selection.

Error rate with low prediction

H_{91}=*No significant difference between all conditions.* When prediction is incorrect in both adaptive conditions (Cloud and Linear), the prediction window will not be used and will disappear with ⊟, thus generating the same error rate.

Methodology

There are three independent variables: (1) the MENU TYPE: Control condition, Cloud Menu, and Linear Menu, (2) the TARGET LOCATION: in the center, in its periphery, or outside, (3) the LEVEL OF PREDICTION: low, high. Two levels of prediction were decided to test the performance when prediction algorithm works well and bad, they were selected randomly. Each menu is divided into two screens of 8 items, all coming from Findlater test [10]. Predicted items appearing in the Cloud Menu and Linear Menu are controlled. The target item can be located either on the prediction window or on the static menu and its distribution is controlled. The target item in Cloud condition was controlled randomly between three locations: in the center, in its periphery, or outside in case of incorrect prediction. Accurate prediction level is when prediction is correct and target item is inside the Cloud Menu without any restriction. Inaccurate prediction level is when prediction is incorrect and target item is outside the Cloud Menu. The same behavior occurs in the Linear Menu where the target item was also controlled randomly between two prediction accuracy levels. High prediction level is when prediction is correct and target is one of the six predicted items presented on the prediction window. Low prediction level is when prediction is wrong and target is outside the prediction window. For both high and low prediction levels, the target item always appears in the static menu.

Task

A between-subjects design was decided to avoid any carryover effects such as practice (learning effect) and fatigue: two independent groups of participants were asked to perform a sequence of item selections. Participants of the first group tested Cloud Menu and Control condition, while the second group tested Linear Menu and Control Condition. Participants were divided into two groups using *matched-group design*, through which the subjects were matched according to their age and then allocated into group. For each condition, first, a message appeared indicating the target item to select. Then a list of items appeared and the target item was displayed at the screen top as a reminder. In Cloud Menu, participants selected the target item from the Cloud of predicted items and/or from the static menu. In Linear Menu, participants selected the target item from the prediction window and/or full list of items. In Control condition, participants selected target items from the main list on the first or on the next screen. When the selected item matched the requested target item, a new message appeared indicating next target item until the test was complete. When the selected item did not match the requested target item, an error message prompted the participant to select the right target before moving to the next target. When the test was complete, a "thank you" message was displayed.

Selections were performed by finger touch on the touchable surface of the smartphone, no stylus or pen were used. Generally, participants were holding the smartphone in their left hand and had to point with right hand (index finger). In each menu, order and position of items were controlled and changed randomly after ten selections in order to avoid learning effect. Selection sequence (target selection) was also randomly controlled. Target position on first screen or on second screen and prediction accuracy level were also controlled. Each participant had to execute 20 item selections in the Control condition, 20 item selections in the Cloud+High prediction condition and 20 item selections in the Cloud+ Low prediction condition, 20 item selections in the Linear +High prediction condition and 20 items selections in the Linear+Low prediction condition. Selections in the Cloud and Linear conditions were mixed in order to avoid any learning effect induced by a repetitive usage of a task.

Quantitative and Qualitative Measures. The dependent variables measured were: 1) menu item selection time (in seconds), which was measured as the time taken from opening the menu until final selection of requested target, and 2) error rate (in percentage %).

Apparatus. Android-based Google Nexus smartphones were used, with 2 Gb LPDDR3 RAM, 16 Gb of storage and a 1920 x 1080 pixel screen resolution (423 ppi).

Participants. Two independent groups of nineteen subjects each participated in this experiment. All participants were regular smartphone users and they were recruited in our organization through a mailing list.

Procedure. Before starting the test, the principle of each condition (Cloud Menu, Linear Menu and Control) was explained to participants but prediction levels were not. Each participant trained with a pre-test composed of ten targets. A different item list was used in the pre-test than the one used in the test. Both groups selected 60 target items as follows:

Group 1: **40** target items for Cloud Menu (20 with high prediction and 20 with low prediction) = 20 items when prediction is correct (10 located in the center of the Cloud Menu and 10 when target is in the periphery) + 20 items when prediction is wrong (items are all outside the Cloud Menu: 10 located on the first screen and 10 on the second screen). There were also **20** items for Control condition: 10 items located on the first screen and 10 on the second screen.

Group 2: **40** targets for Linear Menu = 20 items when prediction is correct and 20 items when prediction is wrong (target is outside the prediction window: 10 located on the first screen and 10 on the second screen). Similarly to group 1, there were also **20** items for Control condition: 10 items located on the first screen and 10 on the second screen.

In summary, the design was as follows:
19 participants ×
2 groups ×
60 targets ×
= 2280 menu item selections in total.

Group	Menu	Selection time (sec.)			Error rate (%)		
		μ	σ	W/Z	μ	σ	W/Z
G1 G2	Control Control	3.40 3.04	1.07 1.07	0.93	0.17 0.33	0.29 0.62	0.22
G1 G2	Cloud (P+) Linear (P+)	1.76 4.12	0.61 3.08	3.08 ***	0.95 1.93	1.20 2.12	1.47
G1 G1	Cloud (P+) Control	1.76 3.40	0.61 1.07	4.11 ***	0.95 0.17	1.20 0.29	3.04 **
G1 G2	Cloud (P-) Linear (P-)	5.60 3.40	1.65 2.84	3.08 **	0.74 2.66	1.74 2.79	1.47
G1 G1	Cloud (P-) Control	5.60 3.40	1.65 1.07	4.17 ***	0.74 0.17	1.74 0.29	1.22
G2 G2	Linear (P+) Control	4.12 3.04	3.08 1.07	2.04 *	1.20 0.33	2.11 0.62	2.54 *
G2 G2	Linear (P-) Control	3.40 3.04	2.84 1.07	0.20	2.66 0.33	2.79 0.62	3.54 **

Table 2. Results: P+=high prediction, P–=low prediction – No significance= p>.05, *= p≤ .05, **= p≤ .01, ***=p≤ .001

Results and Discussion

Levene's test was applied to verify homogeneity of variance between the two independent samples. Since this later was partially determined, non-parametric Mann-Whitney Comparison test was used for analysis between independent samples (groups), and Wilcoxon Signed Ranks test was applied in the case of within-subjects conditions (Table 2). Data were submitted to a Bonferroni Type I correction before handling.

Selection time

Selection time for all conditions is reported in the third column of Table 2 and graphically depicted in Fig. 11 with a 95% confidence interval for difference between normal means (α=.05). First of all, according to **row 1** in Table 2, there is no significant difference (Z=.93, p=.35) in Control condition between group G1 who tested the cloud menu (μ=3.40, σ=1.07) and group G2 (μ=3.04, σ=1.07), which allows us to properly compare these two independent groups.

According to **row 3**, Cloud condition with high prediction (P+: μ=1.76, σ=0.61) is significantly faster (W(22)=4.11, p= .00004) than Control condition (μ=3.40, σ=1.07). Similarly, Cloud condition with high prediction (P+: μ=1.76, σ=0.61) is significantly faster (Z=3.08, p=.002) than Linear condition in both cases as indicated in **row 2**: when target is in the center of the Cloud (μ=1.19, σ=0.54) and when it is in the periphery (μ=2.35, σ=1.04). Interestingly, when target is located in the center of the Cloud, participants are also significantly faster (W(23)=3.71, p=.0002) than when it is located in the periphery. Usually, corner locations are faster to reach.

Row 6 suggests that Control condition (μ=3.04, σ=1.07) is faster (W(14)=2.04, p=.05) than Linear condition when prediction is high (P+: μ=4.12, σ=3.08). In addition in **row 4**, when prediction is low, users are significantly faster (Z=3.08, p=.002) in Linear condition (P–: μ=3.40, σ=2.84) than in Cloud condition (P–: μ=5.60, σ= 1.65). In **row 5**, we observe that users are also significantly faster (W(22)=4.17, p=.0003) in Control condition (μ=3.40, σ= 1.07) than in Cloud condition with low prediction (P–: μ=5.60, σ=1.65).

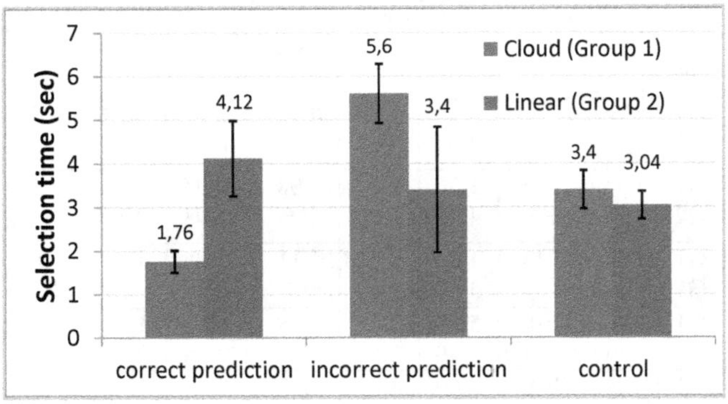

Figure 11. Selection time for all conditions (normal mean, α=.05).

More detailed results further suggest that:

1. Cloud with low prediction and target on first screen of the main list (P–: μ=4.98, σ=1.76) is significantly faster (W(22)=4.14, p=.00003) than Control with target on first screen (μ=2.42, σ=0.83)
2. Cloud with low prediction and target on second screen of the main list (μ=6.24, σ=1.63) is significantly faster (W(22)=3.56, p=.0003) than Control with target on second screen (μ=4.40, σ=1.78).
3. In Control condition, users are also significantly faster (W(22)=4.14, p=.00003) when the target is on the first screen (μ=2.42, σ=0.83) than when it is located on the second screen (μ=4.40, σ=1.78).

However, **row 7** reveals that there is no significant difference (W(14)=0.20, p=.84) between Control condition (μ=3.04, σ=1.07) and Linear condition when prediction is low (P–: μ=3.40, σ=2.84). More detailed results further suggest the following absences of significance:

1. No significance (W(14)=0.91, p=.36) between Linear with low prediction and target on first screen of the main list (P–: μ=3.55, σ=3.42), Control with target on first screen (μ=2.11, σ=0.53).
2. No significance (W(14)=1.14, p=.25) between Linear with low prediction and target on second screen of the main list (μ=3.25, σ=2.35) and Control with target on second screen (μ=3.97, σ=0.86).

However, users belonging to the Control condition are significantly faster (W(14)=3.40, p=.0006) when the target is in the first screen (μ=2.11, σ=0.53) than when it is located on the second screen (μ=3.97, σ=0.86), which is of course normal since any navigation to the second screen will inevitably increase the selection time. Fig. 12 depicts the item selection time by participant in the two groups by condition.

***H_{11}* is supported.** When prediction is high, end users find the target item among the 6 predicted items in the Cloud Menu and the Linear Menu faster than in Control condition when the target belongs to a list of 16 items, which somewhat normal since item selection is operated with a smaller amount of time included in a smaller surface, which is in line with [30].

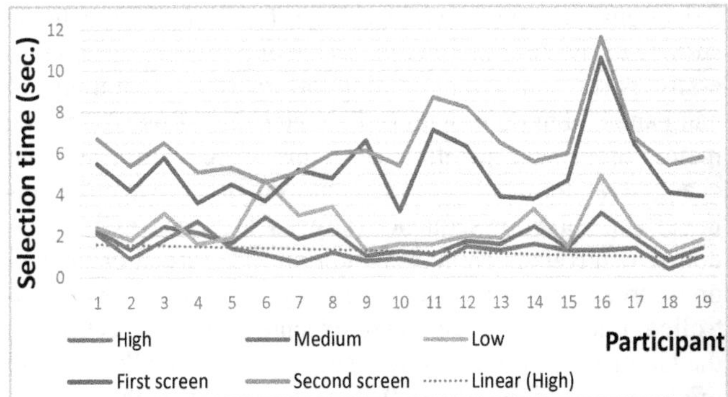

Figure 12. Selection time by participant.

***H_{21}* is supported.** When prediction is high, users are faster in Cloud menu than in Linear condition. This result can be justified by the fact that circular form of the Cloud facilitates exploration of a number of predicted items assigned to 6, which is higher than the typical 3 items found in other Split Adaptive menus. The user attention is distributed to different sides of the Cloud in contrary to the Linear condition when the user has to browse all items one by one. Consequently, by transitivity, Cloud Menu is faster than Linear menu, which is in turn faster than Control condition, which is the most important conclusion that demonstrates the effectiveness and efficiency of Cloud Menus.

***H_{31}* is supported.** This is justified by the fact that user attention is often attracted by the item in the center of the Cloud Menu because it is consistently located and it is always emphasized by a larger font size compared to other predicted items in the Cloud, which is consistent with [22]. Therefore, the central item is always the most pre-eminent among all menu items and its position is very predictable, even it requires some scanning. Suggested conclusions are:

1) Prediction step is crucial, it reduces navigation time and visual search time especially when menus are long.
2) Increasing the amount of predicted items is not penalizing the interaction because it is still better than the non-adaptive menu provided that this amount is not prohibitive, which may require another study to determine the threshold beyond which the positive effect no longer occurs.
3) The presentation of the prediction window as a circular word cloud may be an important factor making the Cloud Menu efficient. The results suggest that the Cloud Menu is better than the Linear Menu because of its impact on user perception [21] and usability of word clouds [22,32].
4) Linear menu is competitive to scan items (one eye fixation, one column), but becomes surpassed by a cloud menu (many eye fixations, multiple directions) when too many items increase the length of the split area.

***H_{41}* and *H_{51}* are partially supported.** Results showed that, overall when prediction is low, Control condition is faster than Cloud Menu and no significant difference is detected between the Linear and Control conditions. This result can be justified by the fact that being sure that the target is not one of the predicted items is easiest in the case of a linear list than in the Cloud. In this latter, the human perception is going in all directions and the user scans the Cloud several times in order not to miss any item. In Linear Menu, the user is often sure not to miss the target item since the whole menu is browsed sequentially. But as in the Cloud Menu, six predicted items are conveyed to the end user, thus implying that there is a higher probability to present the item of interest to the end user than when three predicted items are presented.

***H_{61}* is supported.** Users can have direct access to target when this latter is on first screen contrary to when it is on the second screen, in this case scrolling is required that can justify the fact that selection time is shorter on first screen than on second screen.

Error Rate

Error rate for all conditions is reported in the fourth large column of Table 2 and graphically depicted in Fig. 13 with a 95% confidence interval for difference between normal means (α=.05). Error rates are assessed as equivalent (Z= 0.22, p=.82) in Control condition both in G1 (μ=0.17, σ= 0.29) and G2 (μ=0.33, σ=0.62) as reported in **row 1** of Table 2. Overall, there is no significant difference observed (Z=1.47, p=.14) in terms of errors between the Cloud condition (μ=0.95, σ=1.20) and Linear condition (μ=1.93, σ=2.12) as indicated in **row 2**. In Cloud Menu, when prediction is high and item target is located in the center of the Cloud (P+: μ=0.04, σ=0.21), errors are less frequent ($W(22)$=3.44, p=.0005) than when the target is located in the periphery (μ=1.87, σ=2.40). In **row 3**, we observe that errors are significantly less frequent ($W(22)$=3.04, p=.002) in Control condition (μ=0.17, σ= 0.29) than in Cloud Menu (μ=0.96, σ=1.20), which may be due to tally errors in the periphery of the Cloud. When prediction is low in Cloud Menu (P–: μ=0.74, σ=1.74), there is no significant difference ($W(22)$= 1.22, p=.22) with respect to the Control condition (μ=0.17, σ=0.29) as reported in **row 5**. Similarly, errors are less frequent ($W(14)$=2.54, p=.01) in Control condition (μ=0.33, σ=0.62) than in Linear condition (μ=1.20, σ=2.11) as reported in **row 6** when prediction is high. When prediction is low in **row 7**, it is even more significant: errors are less frequent ($W(14)$=3.54; p=.007) in Control Condition than in Linear case with low prediction.

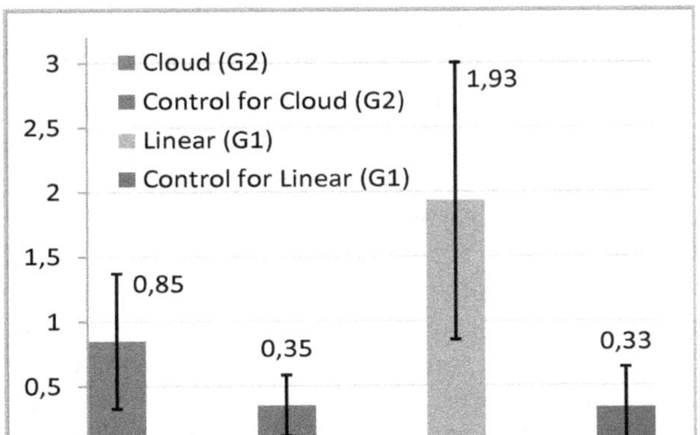

Figure 13. Error rate for all conditions.

***H_{71}* is supported.** When target is one of the 6 predicted items in Cloud and Linear Menu, the visual search time and selection time are reduced which reduce errors number.

***H_{81}* is supported.** In the periphery, some items can be close together, which suggests that a large number of tally errors can be generated. Contrarily to a target located in the center, locations, directions, and font size are factors minimizing tally errors. Items predicted inside the cloud can be laid out in a more optimized way by calculating the distance between items and the center, and distributing them, e.g., by considering their semantic relation. Further investigation is required to improve this aspect, by laying these items out depending on their position in the static menu.

***H_{91}* is supported.** In the case of low prediction, participants did not rely on the Cloud Menu and used the ⊟ button to make it disappear. The target is in the static menu, like in Control condition, which suggests that there is no difference between Cloud Menu and Control condition.

Experiment overview

The experiment conducted on the cloud menu corroborates several findings from Lohmann *et al.* [22]:

- *Item font size*: items with a large font size attract more user attention than with a small font size (an effect influenced by other parameters, such as item length, item position, and item neighboring). According to this study, recognition for items with a larger font size was significantly higher than items with a smaller font size: 83%, 73%, and 59% respectively for the three first font sizes. This also confirms the effect observed in Adaptive Activation-Area Menus [33], where a large selection area attracts more user attention than with a small area. AAMUs are spatially and physically instable, but preserve format and temporal stabilities. Conversely, Cloud Menus leave untouched the initial (static) menu.
- *Scanning*: cloud menus have been proved as an efficient adaptive split menu for small screens because participants tend to scan menu items rather than reading them, which accelerates their processing time. Concentrating this scanning into a designated area fosters this focus as opposed to distribute predicted items or to move the split area into another location, which is feasible for desktop, but not for small screens.
- *Centering*: menu items located in the middle of the cloud attract more user attention than tags near the borders, an effect influenced by radial layout like in pie menus. *H_{31}* and *H_{81}* are two supported hypotheses that confirm this finding.
- *Position*: the upper left quadrant receives more user attention than the others, but we did not exploit this effect since menu items are positioned so that they can point to their original position in the static menu, even when they are off-screen. This facility is optional and we did not identify any significant difference between a location-dependent item positioning and a location-independent one.

DESIGN GUIDELINES FOR CLOUD MENUS

A cloud menu represents a split adaptive menu for which the following design guidelines can be devised.

G1. A cloud menu should be used for a substantive static menu. The main idea behind using a tag cloud in information retrieval is that the relevance of a document must be determined with respect to a set of documents before this document actually appears. Similarly, the main idea behind using a tag cloud as an adaptive split menu is that the probability of selecting a menu item among other items in that menu should appear before the menu is entirely browsed and displayed. It does not make sense to produce an adaptive split menu such as the cloud menu for an initial (static) menu containing only a few items, even on a small screen. In our experiment, the half of the menu is visible: 8 items among 16.

G2. A cloud menu should not hold more than 6 items. So far, split adaptive menus have been mainly explored for large screens (e.g., laptop, desktop, large monitors, wall screens). Even under these conditions, 3 to 4 items were recommended [9,10] as the maximum threshold. The results of the experiment conducted suggest that this threshold could be upgraded up to 6, even on a small screens. Another study could conduct the same experiment on a large screen to determine to what extent the benefit is more important.

G3. A cloud menu should not exceed 3 levels of prediction. Beyond this threshold, the end user is likely to be no longer able to make any difference between the three levels. This is somewhat consistent with the 3 levels of highlighting recommended in usability guidelines. Other coding schemes could augment this representation, but may also increase the cognitive load as opposed to reinforcing the same data.

G4. A cloud menu should be located as close as possible to the static original menu. When a split adaptive menu is located too far away from its original menu, there is a risk of losing the semantic or physical relationship between the static and the predicted parts. This is consistent with the recommendation from [29,30] to minimize visual displacement between the various regions.

G5. The items of a cloud menu should be located as much as possible to point to their corresponding (static) items. When both are on the same display, they should be positioned on the same line (plain red arrow in Fig. 1). When a predicted item refers to an off-screen location, it should also be positioned to indicate this situation (dotted red arrow in Fig. 1). This guideline is applicable to any adaptive split menu, but is even more important for desktop applications.

G6. A cloud menu on a small screen can be superimposed. While large screens can accommodate another (close) location for displaying the prediction window, a small screen is unable to satisfy the same constraint. Thus, a superposition avoids creating another parallel menu like in the traditional split menu, with the risk of oscillating between the two. It also preserves spatial, physical, and format stability (since the static menu is left untouched), but not temporal stability.

G7. A cloud menu should optimize its circular layout. Since shape was elicited in the focus group as the first variable to manipulate for materializing a cloud, other parameters, like color, texture, animation should be left out. Instead, the circular layout could be optimized based on [29], with only one item per line and only one background and foreground color. We did not play with transparency like alpha blending.

CONCLUSION AND FUTURE WORK

This paper presented Cloud Menus, a new type of adaptive split menu in which predicted menu items are arranged in a circular word cloud superimposed on the static menu. Menu items adhere to a series of seven design guidelines that have been devised. Through a controlled study, the cloud menu has been shown as a promising interaction technique for accelerating interaction with menus on small screens (e.g., watches, mobile phones, smartphones): due to its adaptivity, it exhibits a faster and more reliable behavior than a static (non-adaptive) menu, whether the prediction is correct or not. The circular layout was demonstrated to be superior to the Linear Menu, in which the adaptivity is identical, but the prediction window is presented as a linear menu instead.

Although tag clouds and word clouds (as used in this adaptive split menu) are becoming more popular and ubiquitous, especially after they have been offered as free widgets in many environments like jQuery, WordPress, Joomla!, and even Unity, we only know a little about usability of word clouds, apart from [22]. This paper contributes to a better understanding of their usability when applied as a cloud menu, but much remains to be done to examine its full potential. 3D clouds are also becoming popular and, yet, their usability is even less known. Their usability is likely to be largely affected by the visibility of the items which are subject to animation without any user control. In our preliminary experiment, motion came in the fourth position, but only for a 2D cloud menu. Studying a 3D cloud menu is another thing: items are floating around, thus generating occlusion.

In principle, the font size of a word in a word cloud is determined by its incidence. For smaller frequencies one can specify font sizes directly, from one to whatever the maximum font size. For larger values, a scaling should be made. Since the amount of predicted items is limited, it does not make sense to devote computational time for calculating the font size dynamically with respect to all levels of prediction.

In future work, we will investigate the impact of the cloud layout on menu selection, namely based on alternate prototypes (Fig. 2) so as to better study the distance of an item to the center of the Cloud as a function of accuracy level of this item. Also studying and improving presentation of predicted items allows us to minimize the number of errors, namely by a systematic analysis of Bertin's visual variables, either for one visual variable at a time or for a combination of them. Throughout this paper, we hope to open and encourage exploring other directions in split adaptive interface. We hope that both researchers and practitioners will benefit from this new form of split adaptive menu.

REFERENCES

[1] L. Antwarg, T. Lavie, L. Rokach, B. Shapira, J. Meyer. 2013. Highlighting items as means of adaptive assistance. *Behaviour & Information Technology*, 32, 8, 761–777. http://dx.doi.org/10.1080/0144929X.2011.650710

[2] S. Asthana, P. Singh, A. Singh. 2013. Exploring adverse effects of adaptive voice menu. In *Proc. of CHI EA'2013*, 775–780. https://doi.org/10.1145/2468356.2468494

[3] G. Bailly, E. Lecolinet, L. Nigay. 2016. Visual Menu Techniques. *ACM Computing Surveys* 49, 4, article #40. http://dx.doi.org/10.1145/3002171

[4] J. Bertin, *Sémiologie graphique*. Paris, Mouton/Gauthier-Villars, 1967.

[5] S. Bouzit, G. Calvary, D. Chêne, J. Vanderdonckt. 2016. A design space for engineering graphical adaptive menus. In *Proc. of EICS'2016*, 239–244. https://doi.org/10.1145/2933242.2935874

[6] R. Bridle, E. McCreath. 2005. Predictive Menu Selection on a Mobile Phone. In *Proc. of Workshop W7 on mining spatio-temporal data* (ECML/PKDD'2005). Retrieved Aug. 24th, 2017 from https://cs.anu.edu.au/~Eric.McCreath/papers/mining05.pdf

[7] R. Bridle, E. McCreath. 2006. Inducing shortcuts on a mobile phone interface. In *Proc. of IUI'2006*, 327–329. https://doi.org/10.1145/1111449.1111526

[8] J. Feinberg. 2010. Wordle. In *Beautiful Visualization: Looking at Data through the Eyes of Experts*, J. Steele, N. Iliinsky (eds.). O'Reilly, Sebastopol. 37–58.

[9] L. Findlater, J. McGrenere. 2004. A comparison of static, adaptive and adaptable menus. In *Proc. of CHI'2004*, 89–96. http://dx.doi.org/10.1145/985692.985704

[10] L. Findlater, K. Moffatt, J. McGrenere, J. Dawson. 2009. Ephemeral Adaptation: The Use of Gradual Onset to Improve Menu Selection Performance. In *Proc. of CHI'2009*, 1655–1664. http://dx.doi.org/10.1145/1518701.1518956

[11] L. Findlater, K.Z. Gajos. 2009. Design Space and Evaluation Challenges of Adaptive Graphical User Interfaces. *AI Magazine* 30, 4, 68–73. https://doi.org/10.1609/aimag.v30i4.2268

[12] Y. Fukazawa, M. Hara, M. Onogi, H. Ueno. 2009. Automatic mobile menu customization based on user operation history. In *Proc. of MobileHCI'2009*. Article #50. https://doi.org/10.1145/1613858.1613921

[13] K.Z. Gajos, M. Czerwinski, D.S. Tan, D. Weld. 2006. Exploring the Design Space for Adaptive Graphical User Interfaces. In *Proc. of AVI'2006*, 201–208. http://dx.doi.org/10.1145/1133265.1133306

[14] K.Z. Gajos, K. Everitt, D.S. Tan, M. Czerwinski, D.S. Weld. 2008. Predictability and accuracy in adaptive user interfaces. In *Proc. of CHI'2008*, 1271–127. https://doi.org/10.1145/1357054.1357252

[15] K.Z. Gajos, K. Chauncey. 2017. The Influence of Personality Traits and Cognitive Load on the Use of Adaptive User Interfaces. In *Proc. of IUI'2017*, 301–306. https://doi.org/10.1145/3025171.3025192

[16] M. Halvey, M.T. Keane (2007). An Assessment of Tag Presentation Techniques. In *Proc. of WWW'2007*, 1313–1314. http://dx.doi.org/10.1145/1242572.1242826

[17] F. Heimerl, S. Lohmann, S. Lange, T. Ertl. 2014. Word Cloud Explorer: Text Analytics based on Word Clouds. In *Proc. of HICSS'2014*, 1833–1842. http://dx.doi.org/10.1109/HICSS.2014.231

[18] S.C. Huang, I-F. Chou, R.G. Bias. 2006. Empirical evaluation of a popular cellular phone's menu system: theory meets practice. *Journal of Usability Studies* 1, 2, 91–108. http://uxpajournal.org/empirical-evaluation-of-a-popular-cellular-phones-menu-system-theory-meets-practice/

[19] T. Kühme, U. Malinowski, J.D. Foley. 1993. Facilitating interactive tool selection by adaptive prompting. In *Proc. of InterCHI'93*, 149-150. https://doi.org/10.1145/259964.260160

[20] T. Lavie, J. Meyer. 2010. Benefits and costs of adaptive user interfaces. *Int. J. of Human-Comp. Studies* 68, 8, 508–524. http://dx.doi.org/10.1016/j.ijhcs.2010.01.004

[21] W. Liu, G. Bailly, A. Howes. 2017. Effects of Frequency Distribution on Linear Menu Performance. In *Proc. of CHI'2017*, 1307–1312. https://doi.org/10.1145/3025453.3025707

[22] S. Lohmann, J. Ziegler, L. Tetzlaff. 2009. Comparison of Tag Cloud Layouts: Task-Related Performance and Visual Exploration. In *Proc. of INTERACT'2009*, 392–404. http://dx.doi.org/10.1007/978-3-642-03655-2_43

[23] L. Norrie, R. Murray-Smith. July 2016. Investigating UI Displacements in an Adaptive Mobile Homescreen. *Int. J. of Mobile Human Computer Interaction*, 8, 3, 1–17. https://doi.org/10.4018/IJMHCI.2016070101.oa

[24] J. Park, S.H. Han, Y.S. Park, Y. Cho. 2007. Usability of Adaptable and Adaptive Menus. In *Proc. of 2nd Int. Conf. on Usability and Internationalization* (UI-HCII'2007), LNCS 4559, 405–411. http://dx.doi.org/10.1007/978-3-540-73287-7_49

[25] M. Pielot, A. Kazakova, T. Hesselmann, W. Heuten, S. Boll. 2012. PocketMenu: nonvisual menus for touch screen devices. In *Proc. of MobileHCI'2012*, 327–330.

[26] A. Ponsard, K. Ardekani, K. Zhang, F. Ren, M. Negulescu, J. McGrenere. 2015. Twist and Pulse: Ephemeral Adaptation to Improve Icon Selection on Smartphones. In *Proc. of GI'2015*, 219–222. https://dl.acm.org/citation.cfm?id=2788929

[27] D. Raptis, N. Tselio, J. Kjeldskov, M.B. Skov. 2013. Does size matter?: investigating the impact of mobile phone screen size on users' perceived usability, effectiveness and efficiency. In *Proc. of MobileHCI'2013*, 137–136. http://dx.doi.org/10.1145/2493190.2493204

[28] A.W. Rivadeneira, D.M. Gruen, M.J. Muller, D.R. Millen. 2007. Getting Our Head in the Clouds: Toward

Evaluation Studies of Tagclouds. In *Proc. of CHI'2007*, 995–998. http://dx.doi.org/10.1145/1240624.1240775

[29] K. Samp, S. Decker. 2011. Visual Search in Radial Menus. In *Proc. of Interact'2011*, 248–255. http://dx.doi.org/10.1007/978-3-642-23768-3_21

[30] A. Sears, B. Shneiderman. 1994. Split menus: Effectively using selection frequency to organize menus. *ACM Trans. on Comp.-Human Interaction* 1, 1, 27–51. http://dx.doi.org/10.1145/174630.174632

[31] C. Seifert, B. Kump, W. Kienreich, G. Granitzer, M. Granitzer. On the beauty and usability of tag clouds. In *Proc. of IV'2008*, 17–25. http://dx.doi.org/10.1109/IV.2008.89

[32] Ch. Shin, J.-H. Hong, A.K. Dey. 2012. Understanding and Prediction of Mobile Application Usage for Smart Phones. In *Proc. of UbiComp'2012*. 173–182. http://dx.doi.org/10.1145/2370216.2370243

[33] E. Tanvir, J. Cullen, P. Irani, A. Cockburn. 2008. AAMU: Adaptive Activation Area Menus for Improving Selection in Cascading Pull-Down Menus. In *Proc. of CHI'2008*. 1381–1384. http://dx.doi.org/10.1145/1357054.1357270

[34] T. Tsandilas, M.C. Schraefel. 2005. An empirical assessment of adaptation techniques. In *Proc. of CHI'2005 Extended Abstracts*, 2009–2012. http://dx.doi.org/10.1145/1056808.1057079

[35] T. Xie, T. Lin, Y. Zhu, R. Chen. 2015. Modeling Human Behavior to Reduce Navigation Time of Menu Items: Menu Item Prediction Based on Markov Chain. In *Human Behavior, Psychology, and Social Interaction in the Digital Era*. Chapter 8, IGI Global. http://dx.doi.org/10.4018/978-1-4666-8450-8.ch008

Creative Writing with a Machine in the Loop: Case Studies on Slogans and Stories

Elizabeth Clark[1], **Anne Spencer Ross**[1], **Chenhao Tan**[2], **Yangfeng Ji**[1], **& Noah A. Smith**[1]
[1]Paul G. Allen School for Computer Science & Engineering, University of Washington, Seattle, WA, USA
[2]Department of Computer Science, University of Colorado Boulder, Boulder, CO, USA
eaclark7@cs.washington.edu, ansross@cs.washington.edu, chenhao@chenhaot.com,
yangfeng@cs.washington.edu, nasmith@cs.washington.edu

ABSTRACT
As the quality of natural language generated by artificial intelligence systems improves, writing interfaces can support interventions beyond grammar-checking and spell-checking, such as suggesting content to spark new ideas. To explore the possibility of machine-in-the-loop creative writing, we performed two case studies using two system prototypes, one for short story writing and one for slogan writing. Participants in our studies were asked to write with a machine in the loop or alone (control condition). They assessed their writing and experience through surveys and an open-ended interview. We collected additional assessments of the writing from Amazon Mechanical Turk crowdworkers. Our findings indicate that participants found the process fun and helpful and could envision use cases for future systems. At the same time, machine suggestions do not necessarily lead to better written artifacts. We therefore suggest novel natural language models and design choices that may better support creative writing.

Author Keywords
natural language processing; machine in the loop; creative writing

CCS Concepts
•Human-centered computing → **Natural language interfaces;** **•Computing methodologies** → *Natural language generation;*

INTRODUCTION
Researchers have made significant progress in advancing artificial intelligence since Turing famously asked "Can machines think?" [32]. Although the focus of artificial intelligence has been on improving the capabilities of machines, e.g., through the use of machine learning, we propose a *machine-in-the-loop* framework, where the goal is to improve the ability of humans, with the machine playing a supporting role.[1] Humans are the central actor and have full agency in deciding what to do with machine outputs. Accordingly, machine learning models should be designed to assist humans.

This paper explores the possibility of incorporating a machine in the loop of creative writing. The motivation is twofold. First, writers often experience "cognitive inertia," a phenomenon known in the writing domain as "writer's block" [11]. A collaborator who provides suggestions and points out new directions might help alleviate writer's block. The new combination of a writer's own ideas with suggested ideas is a form of psychological creativity [3]. Second, recent studies show that machines outperform humans in some tasks [15, 24, 31], including identifying which message will be retweeted more on Twitter. Perhaps a machine-learned algorithm can provide valuable suggestions to writers. We explore the space of designing machine-in-the-loop systems for creative writing and learn insights from user studies that can inform future interface design and research on natural language processing models.

Machines can support writers as they edit, structure, and refine their work, as demonstrated by word processors, grammar and spell checkers, version control, or even language or style analysis tools (such as the Hemingway Editor[2]). We focus on systems that assist people by suggesting content as they write and that are designed to inspire creativity throughout the writing process while still leaving writers in control of the final written artifact. In particular, we investigate the following questions:

- How can we design machine-in-the-loop systems to support diverse writing tasks and processes?
- What effect do these systems have on people's writing, both as perceived by the writer and by other people?
- What do people want to see in machine-generated suggestions and creative writing support systems?

To answer these questions, we developed two prototype systems to help writers enhance their creativity in two tasks:

IUI'18, March 7–11, 2018, Tokyo, Japan

ISBN 978-1-4503-4945-1/18/03... $15.00
DOI: https://doi.org/10.1145/3172944.3172983

[1]In contrast, human-in-the-loop machine learning actively includes humans in the process of training machine learning models by asking humans to provide feedback such as labeling difficult examples or suggesting new features [4, 6, 9, 20].

[2]http://www.hemingwayapp.com

story writing and slogan writing. These two creative tasks have different goals and require different writing styles. Thus, the systems that assist in these tasks should provide different types of help. We built two system prototypes that use two different models to generate suggestions. We had study participants write with these prototypes and compared their experiences and the quality of their writing to that of participants who did not receive suggestions. This paper discusses the current capabilities of machine-in-the-loop writing systems and suggests improvements both for system interfaces and models.

Although providing helpful suggestions is important in a machine-in-the-loop writing system, we leave writers with complete editorial control and the freedom to disregard any unwanted suggestions. Our goal is *not* to replace human creativity or automate creative writing; rather, we seek to amplify people's creativity by providing suggestions that are most useful to them. By offering suggestions as a person writes, the writing process has elements of both collaborative writing and constrained writing tasks. It also provides a versatile setup; a machine-in-the-loop writing system could be used as an educational tool, a writer's tool, or for entertainment.

MACHINE-IN-THE-LOOP SYSTEM CHARACTERISTICS

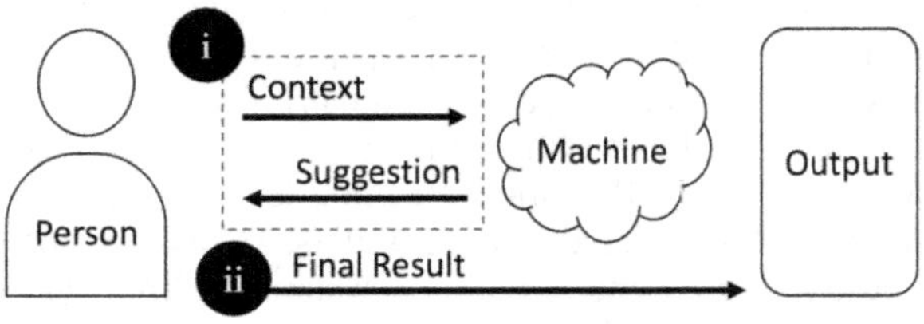

Figure 1: Machine-in-the-loop system structure: the loop (i) is initiated with the person providing context and the machine responding with a suggestion. The person always has control over the final result (ii).

This paper considers machine-in-the-loop (MIL) systems that are composed of a person and a machine working together to create output (Figure 1). The person and machine are in a loop in which the person provides context and the machine responds with suggestions (Figure 1 i). The person controls the final output (Figure 1 ii).[3] Different creative writing tasks have different demands for MIL systems. We consider the following three characteristics for designing MIL systems: interaction structure, interaction initiation, and interaction intrusiveness. We use our story and slogan writing tasks as examples to explain each aspect, as summarized in Table 1.

Interaction Structure

Interaction structure can be *iterative*, where a writer works with the help of a machine to refine a single idea, or *additive*, where the writer and machine work to add multiple ideas

[3] The setup this paper explores does not represent all possible configurations for writing with a machine. More complex setups might involve the person and the machine working in parallel or the machine directly altering the output in a mixed-initiative fashion.

	Story writing	Slogan writing
interaction structure	additive	iterative
interaction initiation	push	pull
interaction intrusiveness	high	low

Table 1: Characteristics of MIL systems for our story and slogan writing tasks.

together. This can be represented as how many times the loop of the person and machine exchanging context and suggestions (see section "i" in Figure 1) is repeated before the person commits to a final result. For example, story writing is additive because as a story unfolds, writers (and machines) need to introduce new ideas, and these ideas are combined into a final story. Slogan writing, by contrast, is a highly iterative process: the loop is repeated for a single phrase or sentence until a final slogan is decided upon.

Interaction Initiation

Interaction initiation refers to how the context-suggestion loop (see section "i" in Figure 1) is triggered. It can follow a *push* (automatically initiated) or *pull* (person-initiated) method of initiation, or a combination of the two. To have breadth of exploration, we implemented the story writing system as a push-style system. At every other sentence, the machine presents a suggestion to the writer. The slogan system uses the pull method for retrieving suggestions. Writers provide a slogan-in-progress and keywords and prompt from the system whenever they want new suggestions.

Interaction Intrusiveness

Interaction intrusiveness describes the extent to which computer-generated suggestions are ignorable. Although writers can always edit or reject suggestions, some require more attention than others. We designed the story writing system's suggestions to be highly intrusive. They appear directly in the text box where the person is writing, and the writer must interact with the suggestion (even if only to delete it entirely) before moving on in the writing process (see Figure 2). In the slogan writing system, suggestions have low intrusiveness. Suggestions appear in a separate column from the writing space and require no interaction once they are retrieved (see Figure 4).

RELATED WORK

We propose "machine-in-the-loop" in contrast with "human-in-the-loop" machine learning. This concept resonates with "mixed-initiative user interfaces" [17]. Although Horvitz emphasizes the development of user interfaces in settings where both the human and the computer can drive towards a shared goal (as opposed to our human-driven setup), many of the principles he considers are relevant to this work, including the timing of machine contributions, providing editing capabilities, and understanding the social expectations of collaborators [17]. As in mixed-initiative interface work, the goal of our work is to explore interaction paradigms and to combine human and computational strengths to enhance human ability [1]. The mixed-initiative setup has been used for creative tasks such as game design [34], and adapting our systems to a more complex mixed-initiative setup (e.g., dynamically deciding when to offer suggestions and what format of suggestion would be most helpful) is a promising future direction.

Several tools have been developed to provide suggestions to assist people in writing, both within the research community [30, 26] and as personal projects [27]. Swanson and Gordon's "Say Anything" [30] provides suggestions for writing short stories by prompting writers with full sentences retrieved from a database of stories scraped from the web after every turn of writing. In "Creative Help" [26], writers are offered suggestions as they write stories, but only when they explicitly request them (i.e., a pull method of interaction). While these systems retrieve their sentences from existing stories, we use natural language generation to provide suggestions.

Author Robin Sloan created a sentence completion story-writing assistant tool that suggests the end to a partially-written sentence when prompted by the writer [27]. The focus of Sloan's project is on how to provide suggestions to the writer. Our work focuses on the role these suggestions play in the writing process, the interface, and people's interaction with the system. Past collaborative creativity research has also looked at other related writing tasks include headlines for newspaper articles [12] and lines for poetry [14], and other artistic domains like music [16] and dance [18].

Finally, there is work on collaborative writing systems that bring together a group of people to write collaboratively. For example, "Ensemble" was a system that had multiple participants work together to write a single story [21]. Each story had a lead author and contributors who submitted alternate versions of a scene and voted on alternatives they liked. The lead author ultimately had the authority to choose the winning scene. The person in our work plays a similar role to the lead author in Ensemble; they control the direction of the story and decide how to incorporate the external (system) input. Similarly, Soylent [2] uses crowdsourcing to provide assistance to writers. However, Soylent assists in shortening text and editing grammar rather than providing content and new ideas.

STORY WRITING SYSTEM

Our first system explores writing to expand a visual prompt into a story. The setup is inspired by *Exquisite Corpse*, a game played by Surrealist artists in which people take turns contributing to a drawing [5]. The portions of the drawing that were completed in previous turns are partially or completely hidden from the current artist, resulting in silly and bizarre drawings. A parallel version of the game exists in literature, where each player writes a sentence of a story, folds the paper over to hide all but the most recent round of writing, and then passes it to the next player. With only two players (as in our setting), hiding earlier rounds has no effect (every sentence was written or seen by the person).

We use the turn-taking aspect of the Exquisite Corpse game to help foster creativity while writing. We provide people with machine suggestions to encourage stories that are unexpected, unusual, and novel, all of which are characteristics of creativity [29]. These machine suggestions may surprise writers, sway them to change their own ideas about the direction of the story, and include ideas they may not have thought of.

User Study Task

For our story system user study, the participant is prompted to write a ten sentence story based on an unlabeled, single-panel cartoon from *The New Yorker* caption contest[4] (in the space indicated in Figure 2, section a). The task was either done alone (solo condition) or partnered with machine suggestions (MIL condition). Both versions were done through a web interface, presented in Figure 2. Participants entered the story sentence by sentence (Figure 2, section c). Once submitted, a sentence could not be edited. The complete story, along with the number of sentences completed, appeared at the bottom of interface (Figure 2, section d).

In the solo case, no additional prompting or interactions were provided beyond the image. In the MIL condition, the participant began by writing the first sentence. Once the sentence was submitted, the next sentence would be generated by the machine and "pushed" to the participant, appearing directly in the submission box (Figure 2, section c). Full sentences were used based on a preliminary study showing that people liked full-sentence suggestions as much or more than partial sentences or keywords when writing stories. The person was free to edit the machine-suggested sentence to any extent, including deleting it entirely, before submitting it. The third sentence was again written by the participant alone. This turn-taking continued until the story was 10 sentences long. Our demo system is available at http://bit.ly/iui-story-demo.

Computational Model for Suggestions

Our computational model for suggesting a sentence given preceding text is built on a neural language model. Neural language models have been used for various natural language generation tasks, including image captioning [33], conversational modeling [28], and poetry generation [13]. To make the generated sentences fluent and coherent in context, our language model uses contextual information both within and across sentence boundaries.

Neural language models are effective at predicting words that fit well in a context locally, thereby generating coherent sentences. A sentence-level language model [23] defines the probability distribution over the next word, from within a predefined vocabulary, conditioned on the left context (i.e., the context of the generated sentence so far). Figure 3 shows an example of next-word probabilities given "He arrived in the". To complete this sentence, the model's generation process randomly picks the next word based on its probability. In the example, the word "car" will have a higher chance of being generated than the other eight words. It is not a coincidence that the generation process tends to pick a word that fits well into the left context both syntactically and semantically. Language models are able to learn some syntactic and semantic patterns automatically from the data. The language model for our story writing system was trained on 390 adventure novels (about 400 million words) from the

[4] https://contest.newyorker.com

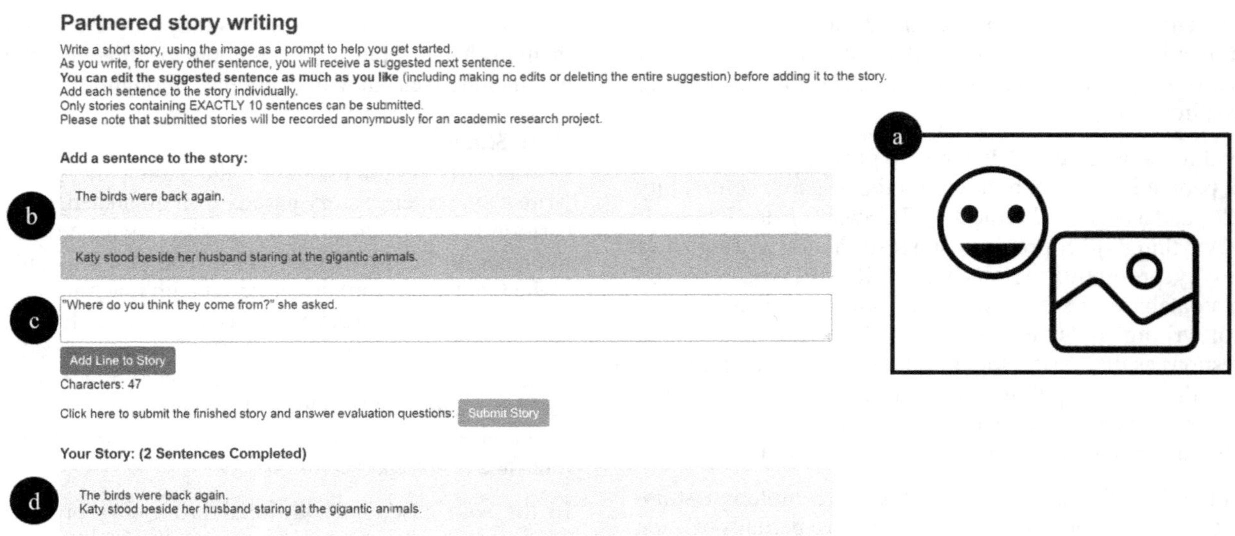

Figure 2: The MIL story writing interface: (a) an image prompt from the New Yorker (actual image: [8]) (b) the story so far, dark colored sentence boxes were turns written with machine suggestions, (c) entry box for next sentence, the machine suggestions appeared here, (d) the full story so far. The solo condition interface was the same except no machine suggestions appeared.

Figure 3: The probability distribution over words to follow "He arrived in the". The x-axis shows a small sample of the vocabulary. The full vocabulary includes more than 35,000 words extracted from adventure novels.

Toronto Book Corpus [35]. Although the model generates one word at each step, people writing with the system only see complete generated sentences.

Standard language models only use the left context within a sentence to compute the probability distribution for the next word; they ignore earlier sentences. To overcome this limitation, we adapted a neural language model that takes account of left context from both the current sentence and the previous sentence [19].

SLOGAN WRITING SYSTEM

Slogans present a challenge to writers distinct from that of writing a story: to generate a concise, memorable, and powerful statement that is representative of the object, organization, or idea it promotes and matches the intention of the authors. Slogans are used in a variety of settings, ranging from organizing a social movement to promoting a product. The process of condensing information into a memorable and informative phrase used to create slogans is paralleled in other tasks, such as writing headlines, titling papers, and naming products. Therefore, a system that supports slogan writing could likely be extended to related tasks that prioritize catchy and succinct language.

User Study Task

For the slogan writing task, participants were asked to write a slogan for three distinct scenarios: a food packaging tool, the movie *Her*[5], and a social cause that protests animal testing for cosmetic products. The prompts included descriptions and images, from which the participant had to invent an original slogan. Like in the story writing case, the task was either done alone or partnered with a machine in the loop. In the MIL condition, participants used a web interface (see Figure 4). Participants in the solo case worked in a blank Google Doc.

When writing with the web interface, the writer must provide a few keywords and write an initial version of the slogan (Figure 4, section a). The writer can then "pull" machine suggestions at will (Figure 4, section b). Based on the writer's input, the system suggests alternative slogans (Figure 4, section c), and the history of the retrieved suggestions is tracked for future reference (Figure 4, section d). The system provides at most three suggestions in response to each request. The writer's input is on the left, and machine suggestions are on the right, reducing the intrusiveness of the suggestions. A demo system is available at http://tremoloop.com.

Computational Model for Suggestions

We developed a constrained language model that was inspired by the BRAINSUP system of Ozbal et al. [25]. First, we extract existing syntactic patterns to improve the grammaticality of the generated suggestions. Specifically,

[5] http://www.imdb.com/title/tt1798709/

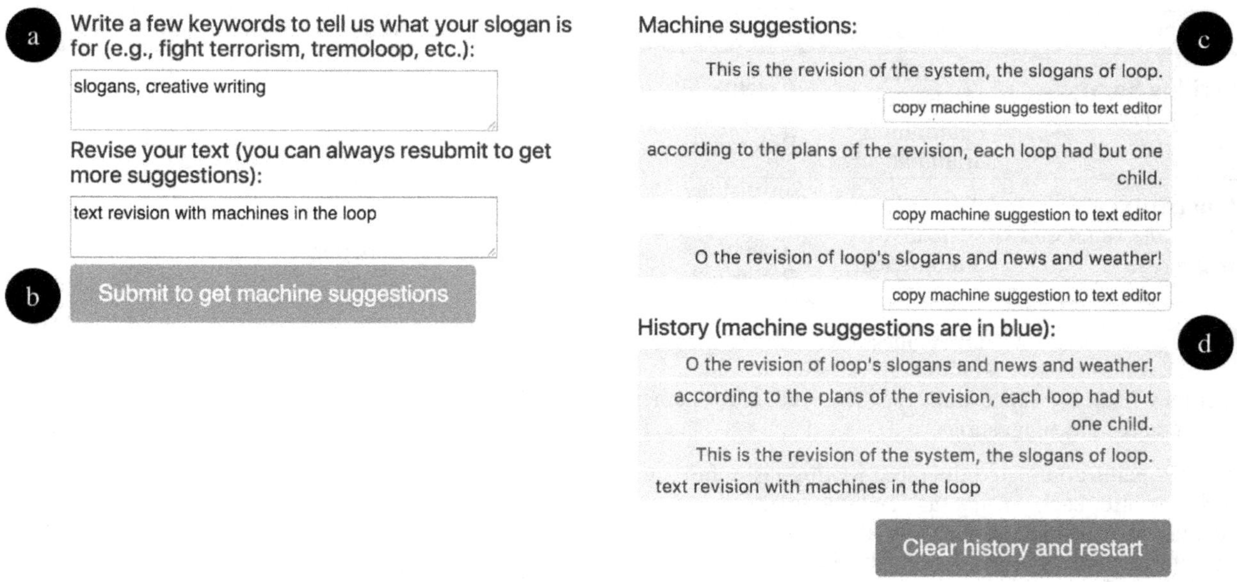

Figure 4: The MIL slogan writing interface: (a) the person can provide keywords and the slogan, (b) a button to "pull" suggestions, (c) the current round of suggestions, (d) the history of all slogan submissions and corresponding suggestions.

DT	JJ	NNS	VBP	RBR	JJ	IN	DT	NN	.
Some	Human-AI	interactions	are	more	profound	than	a	movie	.
Some	*	*	are	more	*	than	a	*	.

Figure 5: A slogan and its resulting skeleton. The top row shows the corresponding part-of-speech tags. This slogan was written about the movie *Her* with a machine in the loop.

we start from quotations from Wikiquotes[6] and replace all content words with a wildcard symbol. These patterns become *skeletons* for our generation system. Figure 5 shows an example; the skeleton is shown at the bottom. Because the skeletons all come from real quotations, their structures are grammatically plausible, as long as the slots are filled with appropriate words. Which words are appropriate (individually or together) is a matter of linguistic judgment.

Information from the writer's input (see Figure 4, section a) and the extracted skeletons are combined to generate slogan suggestions. To make sure that generated suggestions contain keywords from the writer's input, we randomly sample content words from the input and treat them as target words. We identify skeletons that have empty slots that match the part-of-speech tags of the target words and choose three candidate skeletons. Given a skeleton, we follow Ozbal et al.'s approach [25] and use beam search to fill in slots with words that approximately maximize a scoring function. The scoring function gives high scores if the target words are used to fill in slots. In addition, the scoring function factors in language model probability scores to encourage grammaticality and a word diversity score to avoid repetition.

[6]https://en.wikiquote.org/wiki/Main_Page. Ideally, we would use a slogan dataset. Given that there is no public slogan database, we believe that quotations and slogans share some similar characteristics, such as memorability and pithiness.

USER STUDY SETUP

To explore how people will interact with machine-in-the-loop writing, we had people write with or without a machine in the loop. We obtained third-party reviews of the final written pieces. This gave us insight into what types of interactions and suggestions people are interested in and find most useful when writing with a machine in the loop.

Task Setup

For both the story writing task and slogan writing task, we assigned half of the participants to write with the machine-in-the-loop system prototype (the MIL condition) and half without it (the solo condition). Half of the participants in each condition (solo and MIL) were asked to write three stories and the other half wrote three slogans, based on three different prompts. The order of the prompts was balanced across participants. In both the solo and MIL tasks, after each story or slogan was complete, the participant completed a survey consisting of seven-point Likert scale questions about the final piece of writing. Table 2 lists the exact questions for each task under "Writing Survey." Surveys for both tasks additionally asked how satisfied participants were with the final piece of writing.

After three rounds of writing and evaluation, participants completed a final survey. All participants were asked a seven-point Likert scale question on how enjoyable they found the writing process. They were then asked open-response questions on the interface design, the difficulty of the task, and what improvements could be made to the tool. The solo case participants were also asked to describe any tools that could have helped their creative process. The MIL participants were additionally asked a four-choice question on how likely they were to use the system again and Likert scale questions about the quality of the suggestions the prototype system provided (see the exact questions under "Final Survey" in Table 2),

	Story Task	Slogan Task
Writing Survey *"Is the final product:"*	Creative? Coherent? Entertaining? Grammatical?	Creative? Catchy? Relevant?
Final Survey *"Were the suggested sentences:"*	Surprising? Creative? Grammatical?	Surprising? Creative? Catchy? Relevant?

Table 2: Survey questions

whether they liked the suggestions they received, and whether they appreciated the suggestions.

After participants completed the three writing tasks and four surveys (one after each writing task and one final survey), we conducted an open-ended interview about their experience with the task, their creative writing background, and their thoughts about future improvements and uses for the tool.

Although participant enjoyment and personal perception of their own success are important measures of the prototypes, we also wanted to know how third-party evaluators perceived the writing done alone versus with a machine in the loop. Amazon Mechanical Turkers evaluated the writing that participants produced along the same dimensions as the participants who wrote them ("Writing Survey" in Table 2).

Analysis Methods

The first two authors created an interview coding scheme [22] based on the Likert scale prompts and other areas of interest. The first two authors independently coded two interviews, compared coding, resolved conflicts, and revised the coding scheme. The final codes covered insights on: interface, machine suggestions, writing process, writing background, collaboration, use cases, and writing prompt. They then independently coded four more interviews, one from each of the study conditions. These codings were compared, and disparities were discussed. The first two authors then each independently coded separate halves of the remaining interviews, evenly distributed between conditions. The coders then came together to compile results.

Participant Demographics

We had 36 participants complete the writing tasks, 9 in each of the 4 task categories: solo story writing, MIL story writing, solo slogan writing, and MIL slogan writing. Participants were compensated with a $20 Amazon gift card. We categorized participant writing experience into none, some, or a lot. Participants with a lot of experience included professional creative writers and passionate hobbyists who wrote frequently. Participants with some experience included those that wrote occasionally or had formal creative writing education in their past. Participants with no experience included those who had not done creative writing since primary school. Table 3 shows the breakdown of experience by task condition. Participants were randomly assigned to conditions regardless of experience; there were more expert writers in the solo conditions than

Condition	None	Some	A Lot
Solo Story	3	2	3
MIL Story	5	4	0
Solo Slogan	3	1	5
MIL Slogan	4	4	1

Table 3: Number of participants in each condition with a given level of writing experience.

Jim slouched in the corner, feeling sorry for the patient in front of him.
["This is ridiculous," said Duke.]
"Yesterday I felt fine, and now you're telling me I'm at death's door?!"
["We'll take care of Furble tomorrow,"] the doctor said.
"You've named my tumor?!" Duke shrieked.
["Yeah,]" replied the doctor coolly, "we've found that anthropomorphizing tumors helps people in your position come to terms with their condition more easily."
Jim watched as Duke's eyes got even wider, and he wondered if it was because of the doctor's casual tone or the fact that the tumor had such a ridiculous name as "Furble".
~~[Lance yells over the speakers "no sudden hammering"]~~
"Anyway, we feel that Furble will most likely be gone within a month," the doctor said.
Jim grew more concerned about Duke's eyes, they seemed impossibly large now and if he wasn't careful Furble might not be the man's only medical concern.
["You're joking right], ["] Duke said.

Figure 6: Sample story written with the story writing system by participant MST65. The computer suggestions are in color and brackets; struck out text indicates rejected submissions. (Image prompt: [7]).

the MIL conditions, which should be kept in mind when comparing solo and MIL results.

Amazon Mechanical Turkers evaluated the final writing samples, with 9 evaluations collected for each of the 108 writing samples (3 per participant). Turkers were paid $0.15 for each evaluation they completed. To qualify, Turkers had to have completed over 1,000 tasks, have over a 95% task acceptance rate, and be from the United States.

EXPERIMENT RESULTS

Due to differences in the system designs and goals, as described in the above sections, we describe results for each system separately. The participant IDs indicate task and condition: MST (MIL story writing), SST (solo story writing), MSL (MIL slogan writing), and SSL (solo slogan writing).

Story Writing

We present insights from the story writing system from participants and third-party evaluators. Some participant insights did not depend on condition, such as enjoyment, interface suggestions, and opinions about story writing. Other comments from the MIL condition were more focused on the strengths and weaknesses of the machine suggestions.

Enjoyment

Overall, people found the story writing task fun. Two participants liked that it was a low-stakes, non-judgmental experience. Participants in both the MIL and the solo condition rated the task as highly enjoyable (both averaged 6.0).[7]

Participants who wrote in the solo condition had higher average satisfaction with their final stories than those in the MIL condition (average rating of 5.03 versus 4.59, p=0.27)[8], and solo condition participants thought their stories were more creative (5.30 versus 4.30, p=0.01). However, as seen in Figure 7, the MIL condition did have one more positive vote ($\geq$5 on the Likert scale) for satisfaction than the solo condition.

When Help is Useful

Of the participants who found the suggestions helpful in directing their stories, three said the suggestions were most useful early in their story; they were more able to incorporate new elements from the suggestions before they had an established vision of the story. MST79 said, "By the time I'm hitting sentence 5, 6, 7, 8, I've developed so much of the story in my head already, most of the time suggestions are so far and away from anything I want to consider." This is seen in Figure 6; earlier suggestions were incorporated, while a later suggestion was deleted entirely. Five participants liked having the suggestions throughout the writing process to help if they got writer's block. One participant thought it would have been helpful toward the end of his writing to be prompted to start wrapping up the story.

Suggestion Usefulness

When asked what they considered when evaluating the creativity of their final stories, most participants emphasized unexpectedness or deviation from the obvious as key aspects. In the MIL condition, there were mixed reactions to the usefulness of the suggestions in enhancing creativity. All participants said that the suggestions were very random. For eight participants, this meant they disregarded most suggestions, but two participants said that the randomness of the suggestions inspired them to write sillier stories or that incorporating those suggestions lead to more odd and creative writing; "when I took the AI into account and tried to incorporate that, it got a lot more creative because, again, it was just so spontaneous and much more random than I normally write" (MST65). Eight participants said the suggestions did or could have influenced the direction of the story. However, six participants said they did not find the suggestions helpful once they had a clear direction for the story. This is reflected in the ratings participants gave the suggestions; the mean score of how much participants appreciated the suggestions is 3.78, but there was high variation between participants, with answers ranging between 2 and 6.

[7]Due to the subjectiveness of evaluating writing and the varied participant background, both the self-evaluations and the Turk scores highly varied, often covering the full Likert scale (1-7).

[8]p-values are calculated using independent two-sample t-tests. Although we report p-values, we encourage caution in drawing firm conclusions from these calculations because of the small sample size (27 for each condition in both self-evaluations and third-party evaluations) and the imbalance across conditions in author expertise.

Use Condition	Story	Slogan
I'd use it, exactly as it is now.	2	0
I'd use it, but only if the suggestions were better.	4	5
I'd use it, but only if the writing set-up changed.	0	1
I wouldn't use it.	3	3

Table 4: Responses to "Would you use this system again?"

Participants found some elements of the suggestions more helpful than others. One participant liked using snippets of suggested dialogue, while a different participant found dialogue-heavy suggestions unhelpful. One participant mentioned taking the tone of the suggestions, and another participant appreciated a plot suggestion, although they didn't incorporate it as it would have required more context. Characters were a divisive element; some appreciated getting suggestions with new character names, while six others found suggestions that introduced new character names hurt the relevance of the suggestions. Consider the example in Figure 6. Although the character names in early suggestions are all used, a later suggestion that references "Lance" is deleted as all of the characters in the story have already been introduced. Timing may also affect the usefulness of new characters because characters are often introduced in the beginning of a story, as can be seen in the example stories in Table 5.

When asked what type of help they would like to receive as they wrote, eight MIL participants mentioned the machine could contribute by suggesting plot points, tone, or keywords. One participant from the solo condition envisioned a system where the computer took the role of a character in the story and provided dialogue. Other MIL participants appreciated the idea of receiving full sentences, especially if the suggestions had been more relevant. Four participants felt more back-and-forth iterations were needed to treat the machine as a viable collaborator and would appreciate feedback on their writing, such as encouragement, agreement, or advice.

Interaction

Three MIL condition participants found the every-other-sentence injection into their workspace disruptive. Participant MST65 wrote, "The 'partner' [MIL system] often made no sense, so it was difficult to incorporate their responses and often I just deleted the entire suggestion but it was a disruption." Four participants would have liked the ability to edit already submitted sentences, especially professional writers who were not able to follow their normal writing process. However, six participants enjoyed the constrained, non-editable, sentence-by-sentence structure as it kept them moving forward. Participant SST17 wrote, "Even when I got stuck, I eventually could tell myself, 'Just write one sentence!' and then move on. ... it forced me to keep moving forward instead of getting bogged down in getting all the details just right and trying to overhaul the whole thing when I didn't like one little thing."

Use Cases

Most people who wrote with the story writing system would use it again in some capacity, with the most frequent response being they would use it again if suggestions were better, as seen in Table 4. Of the people who said they wouldn't use the system again, one wrote that they might actually use it for fun or ungraded work, one said they didn't need help creating story ideas, and the third expressed skepticism at the general idea of writing technologies.

Of the participants who would use the story writing tool again, two of the participants envisioned "just for fun" applications, such as a game to play with children or a short, fun activity that pops up on Facebook. Four participants saw it as a way to practice writing or a low-stake activity to become motivated to write. Three participants envisioned using the system for outlining, story boarding, or other early idea generation, while two people indicated interest in using the tool to directly write a final product.

As for types of suggestions that may be useful, three participants wanted editorial feedback on grammar, syntax, and sentence structure. One participant envisioned feedback from the machine that more directly influenced the content of the story. When describing experiences with human collaborators, participants said that back-and-forth iteration was a key component that they wanted machines to mimic. Other characteristics of good past human collaborators included trust and like-mindedness.

Third-party Evaluations

There was no statistically significant difference in the Amazon Mechanical Turk third-party evaluation ratings between the solo and MIL conditions. For creativity, the average score for the solo condition was 4.87 and was 4.84 for the MIL condition (p=0.88). Story coherence scores had an average of 5.05 for solo and 4.77 for MIL (p=0.21).

It is important to note that most of the third-party scores did not correlate with the scores writers assigned their own work. The average Turker score and the self-evaluation score had Pearson correlation coefficients of 0.08, 0.07, and 0.04 for how creative the story was, how entertaining it was, and how much they liked it, respectively. The correlations for coherence and grammaticality were slightly better (0.31 and 0.41, respectively) but still weak.

Slogan Writing

As with story writing, some topics from the slogan tasks were mentioned by participants regardless of condition. However, because the solo case participants did not have suggestions nor the interface, MIL participants provided some unique insights.

Enjoyment

Five participants found writing slogans to be very difficult. One participant said they found it demoralizing because they felt so bad at it. Two participants expressed that writing something both succinct and informative was challenging; the top-rated slogans tended to be shorter than the lowest-rated slogans, as seen in the examples in Table 5. Four participants enjoyed the task and found it fun.

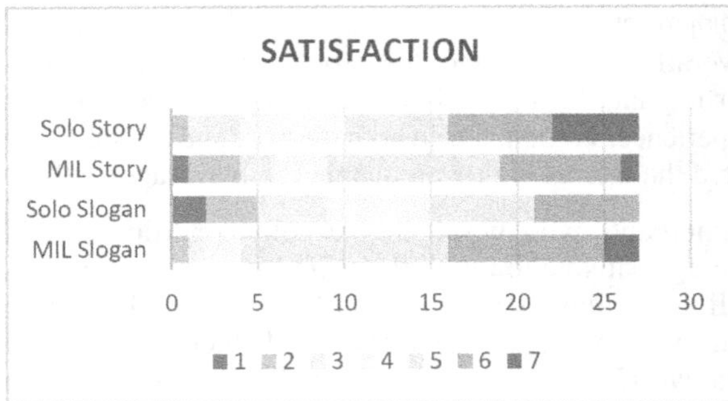

Figure 7: Slogan writers in the MIL condition were generally more satisfied with their final product than the solo slogan writers. More MIL story writers were positively satisfied with their final story, but only by one story.

Participant self-evaluation of the final slogans was generally higher in the MIL condition than the solo condition, even though the scores for the slogan suggestions were low. For example, the mean score for final slogans from the MIL condition was higher than in the solo case for both satisfaction (5.22 vs. 4.07, $p<0.01$) and creativity (4.48 vs. 3.93, p=0.15).

Suggestion Usefulness

Slogan participants in the MIL condition felt the suggestions did not introduce enough novelty. Three participants expressed frustration with suggestions that had just reorganized their input slogan words. These suggestions were too close to the original slogan and therefore not creative enough to be helpful. This frustration is reflected in low average scores for how much participants liked the suggestions (2.00) and appreciated the suggestions (2.78). Similar to the story writing task, appreciation varied greatly between participants, with scores ranging from 1 to 6. When participants used the provided suggestions, it was mainly to incorporate novel, relevant words or structural elements.

Seven MIL condition participants noted they would have preferred words instead of full sentences as suggestions; the system could act as a thesaurus to bring relevant but creative words and ideas. Participants also envisioned machine contributions such as searching the web for more information on a product, or finding similar, popular slogans as seed ideas. One participant found the machine had a different impact, "it impacted my overall thought process and creativity rather than actual words" (MSL87). Participants mentioned word play, use of literary devices (like alliteration or puns), cleverness, and catchiness as elements of creative slogans that they were looking for in suggestions.

Four participants described productive collaborations as bouncing ideas off someone else, building and iterating on good ideas, and coming to a feeling of "we found it!" Five participants thought the machine was a good collaborator, "it seemed like kind of having another pair of eyes in the room to give me some feedback and the fact that it was in real time was great and wouldn't argue with you over coffee was great" (MSL87). One participant felt the interaction with the system was not as conducive to enhancing creativity. One

	Highest-rated	Lowest-rated
Solo Slogan	Compassion is Always in Style	"Be Beautiful: End Animal Testing! Sign our petition today to show Neutrogena animal testing is unnecessary, unkind, and needs to stop now."
MIL Slogan	The real animals are the ones who test chemicals on living things.	"Stop animal research testing now! Studies confirm ther [sic] is no need for such testing, and msot [sic] adults are opposed to this practice."
Solo Story	Norman walked into the doctor's office just before his last appointment; Norman flicked his cigarette into the cold, winter night behind him as he walked into the building. The pretty blonde receptionist greeted Norman but Norman had no time for flirtation or romance; he was about to find the murderer of Trystan Lee and the doctor was key to this plan.	A middle aged male is meeting with a dentist. This gentleman is so stressed that he looks like his eyes are popping out of his face. This meeting is part of an investigation about a crime so that's why this meeting includes an investigator who looks creepy.
MIL Story	The nervous doctor cleared his throat, "Thank you...eh-hem...Mr. Collin, for coming into the office on such short notice." Craig slicked back his hair, listening to his wife's voice echoing in his head, reminding him that all of those late night trips to McDonalds would catch up with his heart eventually. "You see, we've found some...unusual...results from your recent stress test, and I thought it prudent to bring you in as soon as possible."	"Hey Docta Don, dis is da kat we wuz talkin' about last night, whachu wan' me to do wit 'im?" Fabin said through his cold eyes shaded by his pitch black sunglasses. He tapped his finger on the trigger and shook his head, Docta Don was never happy with how excited Fabin was to get into trouble; he was a good man, but followed all orders without ever thinking things through for himself.

Table 5: Highest and lowest rated slogans and stories for a given prompt. Slogans are for an animal rights cause. Only the first few lines of each story are shown.

challenge five participants described was that the suggestions were not aware enough of context and therefore were not working on the same idea, just with the same words. MSL33C said, "they weren't understanding my keywords correctly, I think, so I could say something like 'end animal harm' and it would suggest harming animals ... so I don't think it was quite interpreting my intentions very well." Three participants also were interested in non-content-based interactions such as feedback on whether an idea was good, reminders if a slogan was too close to an older discarded slogan, or an expression of closure upon deciding on a final slogan.

Interaction

Two participants liked having the history of suggestions in order to refer back to previous slogans. Another found the history distracting and wanted to curate the list to only keep good recommendations. For the physical placement of suggestions, two participants liked that the suggestions were out of the way and not intrusive. For four others, the suggestions were too far out of the way and required effort to check. These participants would have preferred a more condensed interface. One participant would have liked the ability to have more brainstorming space, either as a free form writing space or to iterate on multiple slogans at the same time.

Use Cases

Like the story writing case, most people who wrote with the slogan writing system would use it again in some capacity, especially if the suggestions were better (see Table 4). The people who said they would not use the system again wrote that they received suggestions that were too far from what they wanted to motivate them to use the system again.

The participants who said they would use the system again drew parallels between writing slogans and tasks such as naming courses or products, writing headlines, and writing titles. One participant said he might use a system like this to write emails in order to be reminded to be pithy and catchy. One participant did not think they would use the tool for any regular activities and would just use it for slogans.

Third-party Evaluations

The Amazon Mechanical Turk third-party evaluations rated the slogans written in the MIL condition as slightly less creative than the slogans from the solo condition, giving an average score of 3.84 and 4.37 (p=0.03), respectively. There was no statistically significant difference in any of the other scores, with relevance scoring the closest between the solo (average 5.98) and MIL (average 5.93) conditions (p=0.76).

Like in the story case, most of the third-party scores did not correlate with the scores writers assigned their own work. The average Turker score and the self-evaluation score had a Pearson correlation coefficient of 0.13 and 0.10, for how creative the slogan was and how much they liked it, respectively. The correlation for catchiness and relevance were slightly better (0.39 and 0.22, respectively) but still weak.

DISCUSSION

We found that people generally enjoyed writing with the help of suggestions and were enthusiastic about the concept of writing with a "collaborator," especially once natural language generation capabilities improve. Though some professional authors hesitated at the idea of using computer-generated suggestions when writing a final product, participants envisioned the usefulness of this system as a writing warm-up or game and for difficult processes that are often collaborative (naming products or papers, writing headlines, etc.).

Another advantage of writing with a machine in the loop that participants observed was that writing with these systems allowed them to write in a judgment-free setting. Although collaborative writing is useful, it can be intimidating for less experienced writers to brainstorm or write with the pressure of a human collaborator. Writing with a machine in the loop can be a low-cost, easy way to provide new ideas and support to writers, particularly in the early stages of writing.

For machine-in-the-loop writing systems, we recommend a high level of writer control over the interaction. This will allow systems to cater to a wider range of writers and to adapt to changing writer needs at different points of the writing process. We also recommend carefully considering the interaction design choices (especially along the characteristics we describe) and how they may affect both the enjoyment of the task and the quality of the final product. Systems with low intrusiveness and a pull method of interaction initiation allow people to write more closely to their normal writing process. However, these characteristics also mean that suggestions are more easily ignored and may never be requested. If the goal is to encourage interaction with the machine or a more structured interaction, a higher intrusiveness and push method system may be better. A careful introduction and framing of the system is also necessary to encourage the desired level of interaction with the machine in the loop.

For story writing and other tasks that expand on a prompt and have an additive interaction structure, systems may benefit from an interface that supports outlining or non-linear writing. For example, Flower and Hayes [10] describe the hierarchical nature of the creative writing process; future system designs could reflect knowledge about the cognitive processes of writing to better support the writing process. The slogan writing task, along with other condensing writing tasks that have an iterative structure, may benefit from an interface that provides more space for brainstorming and drafting slogans.

We recommend using models that strike a balance between generating coherent suggestions and surprising suggestions. An element of randomness provides new ideas and directions for a writer, but suggestions too far away from the writer's ideas may be unhelpful and ignored. We recommend pushing towards surprising suggestions for tasks that use a pull method of initiation and have a low level of intrusiveness because when writers decide to initiate a suggestion loop, it generally means they are stuck or at least open to new ideas. Although surprising suggestions run the risk of being irrelevant, a less intrusive system means unhelpful suggestions can be easily ignored and minimally interrupt the writing process. Coherence should be a bigger priority for push method, high-intrusiveness interactions, as high levels of randomness in suggestions may distract writers.

For the story writing task, we found that participants wanted more coherent suggestions from the model. For similar tasks, we recommend working towards incorporating more context into the suggestion-generating models. Characters may be an important aspect of the context to consider, as suggestions with incorrect pronouns or that lack references to existing characters are difficult to work into a story. Models would also benefit from the ability to play with the content type of its suggestions, such as choosing to offer lines of dialogue, action-driven sentences, or descriptive lines.

Models for writing slogans should provide more variety in their suggestions, particularly on a lexical level, as diverse language is important for an iterative task. Models that can generate related keywords, synonyms, and alliterative words when given a person's ideas would be useful for this type of task.

We noted that there is little to no correlation between the ratings that writers gave themselves and the ratings that Amazon Mechanical Turker workers gave them. This observation echoed the finding in Tan et al. [31] that it is hard for humans to evaluate the quality of writing. Therefore, machine-in-the-loop writing systems that aim to improve a writer's work should measure the system's success not only as perceived by the writer but also by third-party evaluators.

CONCLUSION

By analyzing people's experiences and results from writing with two different machine-in-the-loop systems, we find that participants enjoyed collaborating with a machine and would use systems like ours again, particularly as the quality of suggestions the system can generate improves. Participants who wrote with a machine in the loop were more satisfied (in the slogan case) or comparably satisfied (in the story case) to solo writers with their final written artifacts. The writing completed with machine-generated suggestions has yet to surpass that of the participants who wrote alone, as judged by third-party evaluators.

We recommend several directions of research towards improving these suggestions, including improving the ability to control the amount of unexpectedness in suggestions and considering different generation formats (including higher-level ideas or keywords) based on the characteristics and the goal of the system. Furthermore, we recommend choosing the interaction structure, initiation, and intrusiveness of the system design thoughtfully according to the nature of the task and the desired level of interaction. We, along with the participants in our study, envision many possible applications in which machine-in-the-loop support would be helpful, including related writing tasks (like writing headlines or poetry), education, and entertainment.

Acknowledgments. This research was supported in part by NSF graduate research fellowships, the DARPA CwC program through ARO (W911NF-15-1-0543), NSF IIS-1702751, a Samsung GRO award, and a UW Innovation award. Yejin Choi, Michael Ernst, James Fogarty, and Lillian Lee gave early feedback. Emily Furst, Lucy Lin, Kelvin Luu, and Maarten Sap contributed to preliminary work. The authors also thank the anonymous reviewers and the participants who took part in our study.

REFERENCES

1. James F. Allen, Curry I. Guinn, and Eric Horvitz. 1999. Mixed-initiative interaction. *IEEE Intelligent Systems* 14, 5 (Sept. 1999), 14–23.
2. Michael S. Bernstein, Greg Little, Robert C. Miller, Björn Hartmann, Mark S. Ackerman, David R. Karger, David Crowell, and Katrina Panovich. 2010. Soylent: a word processor with a crowd inside. In *Proceedings of UIST.*
3. Margaret A. Boden. 2004. *The Creative Mind: Myths and Mechanisms.* Routledge, London; New York.
4. Steve Branson, Catherine Wah, Florian Schroff, Boris Babenko, Peter Welinder, Pietro Perona, and Serge Belongie. 2010. Visual recognition with humans in the loop. In *Proceedings of ECCV.*
5. Alastair Brotchie and Mel Gooding (Eds.). 1995. *A Book of Surrealist Games: Including the Little Surrealist Dictionary.* Shambhala Redstone Editions, distributed in the United States by Random House, Boston.
6. Justin Cheng and Michael S. Bernstein. 2015. Flock: hybrid crowd-machine learning classifiers. In *Proceedings of CSCW.*
7. Leo Cullum. 2005. Doctor talking to patient in his office as a man. *The New Yorker* 81, 39 (5 Dec. 2005). `http://archives.newyorker.com/?i=2005-12-05`
8. Liza Donnelly. 2014. A man and woman look at three very large birds. *The New Yorker* 90, 22 (4 Aug. 2014). `http://archives.newyorker.com/?i=2014-08-04`
9. Jerry Alan Fails and Dan R. Olsen Jr. 2003. Interactive machine learning. In *Proceedings of IUI.*
10. Linda Flower and John R. Hayes. 1981. A cognitive process theory of writing. *College Composition and Communication* 32, 4 (1981), 365–387.
11. Monica J. Garfield. 2008. Creativity support systems. In *Handbook on Decision Support Systems 2.* Springer, Berlin, Heidelberg, 745–758.
12. Lorenzo Gatti, Gözde Özbal, Marco Guerini, Oliviero Stock, and Carlo Strapparava. 2016. Heady-Lines: a creative generator of newspaper headlines. In *Companion Publication of the 21st International Conference on Intelligent User Interfaces.* 79–83.
13. Marjan Ghazvininejad, Xing Shi, Yejin Choi, and Kevin Knight. 2016. Generating topical poetry. In *Proceedings of ACL.* 1183–1191.
14. Marjan Ghazvininejad, Xing Shi, Jay Priyadarshi, and Kevin Knight. 2017. Hafez: an interactive poetry generation system. In *Proceedings of ACL (system demonstrations).* 43–48.
15. Kaiming He, Xiangyu Zhang, Shaoqing Ren, and Jian Sun. 2015. Delving deep into rectifiers: surpassing human-level performance on ImageNet classification. In *Proceedings of ICCV.*
16. Guy Hoffman and Gil Weinberg. 2011. Interactive improvisation with a robotic marimba player. *Autonomous Robouts* 31, 2–3 (October 2011), 133–153.
17. Eric Horvitz. 1999. Principles of mixed-initiative user interfaces. In *Proceedings of CHI.*
18. Mikhail Jacob and Brian Magerko. 2015. Viewpoints AI. In *Proceedings of the 2015 ACM SIGCHI Conference on Creativity and Cognition.* ACM, New York, NY, 361–362.
19. Yangfeng Ji, Trevor Cohn, Lingpeng Kong, Chris Dyer, and Jacob Eisenstein. 2016. Document context language models. In *Proceedings of the 4th International Conference on Learning Representations (Workshop Track).*
20. Thorsten Joachims, Adith Swaminathan, and Tobias Schnabel. 2017. Unbiased learning-to-rank with biased feedback. In *Proceedings of WSDM.*
21. Joy Kim, Justin Cheng, and Michael S. Bernstein. 2014. Ensemble: exploring complementary strengths of leaders and crowds in creative collaboration. In *Proceedings of CSCW.*
22. Jonathan Lazar. 2017. In *Research Methods in Human Computer Interaction* (2nd edition ed.). Elsevier, Cambridge, MA, Chapter 11.
23. Tomáš Mikolov, Martin Karafiát, Lukáš Burget, Jan Černocký, and Sanjeev Khudanpur. 2010. Recurrent neural network based language model. In *Proceedings of Interspeech.*
24. Myle Ott, Yejin Choi, Claire Cardie, and Jeffrey T. Hancock. 2011. Finding deceptive opinion spam by any stretch of the imagination. In *Proceedings of ACL.*
25. Gözde Özbal, Daniele Pighin, and Carlo Strapparava. 2013. BRAINSUP: brainstorming support for creative sentence generation. In *Proceedings of ACL.*
26. Melissa Roemmele and Andrew S. Gordon. 2015. Creative Help: a story writing assistant. In *Proceedings of ICIDS.*
27. Robin Sloan. 2016. Writing with the machine. (2016). `https://www.robinsloan.com/notes/writing-with-the-machine/`
28. Alessandro Sordoni, Michel Galley, Michael Auli, Chris Brockett, Yangfeng Ji, Margaret Mitchell, Jian-Yun Nie, Jianfeng Gao, and Bill Dolan. 2015. A neural netowrk approach to context-sensitive generation of conversational responses. In *Proceedings of ACL.* 196–205.
29. Robert J. Sternberg. 2005. Creativity or creativities? *International Journal of Human-Computer Studies* 63, 4-5 (Oct. 2005), 370–382.
30. Reid Swanson and Andrew S. Gordon. 2008. Say Anything: a massively collaborative open domain story writing companion. In *Proceedings of ICIDS.*

31. Chenhao Tan, Lillian Lee, and Bo Pang. 2014. The effect of wording on message propagation: Topic- and author-controlled natural experiments on Twitter. In *Proceedings of ACL*.

32. Alan M. Turing. 1950. Computing machinery and intelligence. *Mind* 59, 236 (1950), 433–460.

33. Oriol Vinyals, Alexander Toshev, Samy Bengio, and Dumitru Erhan. 2015. Show and tell: a neural image caption generator. In *Proceedings of the IEEE Conference on Computer Vision and Pattern Recognition*. 3156–3164.

34. Georgios N. Yannakakis, Antonios Liapis, and Constantine Alexopoulos. 2014. Mixed-initiative co-creativity. In *Proceedings of FDG*.

35. Yukun Zhu, Ryan Kiros, Rich Zemel, Ruslan Salakhutdinov, Raquel Urtasun, Antonio Torralba, and Sanja Fidler. 2015. Aligning books and movies: Towards story-like visual explanations by watching movies and reading books. In *Proceedings of ICCV*. 19–27.

Session-based Suggestion of Topics for Geographic Exploratory Search

Noemi Mauro
Computer Science Dept., University of Turin
Torino, Italy
noemi.mauro@unito.it

Liliana Ardissono
Computer Science Dept., University of Turin
Torino, Italy
liliana.ardissono@unito.it

ABSTRACT

Exploratory information search can challenge users in the formulation of efficacious search queries. Moreover, complex information spaces, such as those managed by Geographical Information Systems, can disorient people, making it difficult to find relevant data. In order to address these issues, we developed a session-based suggestion model that proposes concepts as a *"you might also be interested in"* function, by taking the user's previous queries into account. Our model can be applied to incrementally generate suggestions in interactive search. It can be used for query expansion, and in general to guide users in the exploration of possibly complex spaces of data categories.

Our model is based on a concept co-occurrence graph that describes how frequently concepts are searched together in search sessions. Starting from an ontological domain representation, we generated the graph by analyzing the query log of a major search engine. Moreover, we identified clusters of ontology concepts which frequently co-occur in the sessions of the log via community detection on the graph. The evaluation of our model provided satisfactory accuracy results.

CCS Concepts

•Information systems → Information retrieval; Query log analysis; Query suggestion; Query reformulation;

Author Keywords

Geographical Information Retrieval; Session-based Concept Suggestion; Query Expansion.

INTRODUCTION

During an information search task, various issues challenge the specification of efficacious queries. Firstly, as discussed by Belkin in [8], users are often unable to use the appropriate keywords because they are looking for data they do not know about. Secondly, complex information spaces, organized in several topic categories, can overload and disorient people, preventing them from finding the information they need; e.g., see [36]. In order to address these issues, several systems present lists, or hierarchies, of information categories to search for. However, in this way they expose users to possibly large sets of options to choose from.

Our work focuses on exploratory search, which is affected by the above issues because the users' information goals are ill-defined; see [29, 47]. We aim at helping users orientate themselves by suggesting relevant topics (concepts) to be explored, given their observed search behavior. More specifically, we aim at guiding data exploration by proposing a small set of concepts that the user might be interested in, given the search context, as a *"you might also be interested in"* function that helps her/him complete the search. We adopt an associative information retrieval model [15]: our hypothesis is that, by analyzing the first query(ies) of a search session, and by taking into account which types of data are often searched together by people, the system can help the user identify further topics he or she might be interested in, by suggesting terms for query expansion. E.g., if the user looks for kindergartens in a town, he or she might also be interested in play and sports areas, as well as in other data related with children activities. Our work aims at supporting the suggestion of such concepts. Specifically, we aim at answering the following research question:

H1: Can the data about the concepts frequently searched together by people within a search session be exploited to help the user explore the portions of an information space relevant to her/his information needs?

This is particularly useful in Geographic Information Retrieval [24, 6], where several queries are aimed at finding the available items, per category, within a geographical area. Guiding the user towards the exploration of information, such as in the above examples, enables her or him to quickly generate custom maps reflecting individual information needs.

In order to answer our research question, we developed a session-based concept suggestion model which, starting from the queries submitted by the user, proposes a set of possibly relevant data categories, complementing the types of information that he or she has focused on. Our model is based on an ontological representation of the information space, and on a Natural Language approach to the interpretation of search queries that identifies the referred concepts in a flexible way, by considering synonyms and by applying Word Sense Disambiguation to resolve the meaning of words. For the development of our model, we analyzed the log of a major search

IUI 2018, March 7–11, 2018, Tokyo, Japan.

ACM ISBN 978-1-4503-4945-1/18/03 ...$15.00.
https://doi.org/10.1145/3172944.3172957

AnonID	Query	QueryTime	ItemRank	ClickURL
67910	las vegas sports teams	2006-04-30 18:14:57	1.0	http://www.vegas.com
67910	las vegas transportation	2006-04-30 18:19:59	1.0	http://www.vegas.com
67910	mccarran international airport	2006-04-30 18:22:30	3.0	http://en.wikipedia.org
67910	mccarran international airport	2006-04-30 18:22:30	1.0	http://www.mccarran.com
67910	hub airports in the united states	2006-04-30 18:25:28	9.0	http://www.airportcodes.us
67910	hub airports in the united states	2006-04-30 18:25:28	9.0	http://www.airportcodes.us
67910	black las vegas itineraries	2006-04-30 18:30:03		
67910	educational facilities in las vegas	2006-04-30 18:30:53		
67910	medical facilities in las vegas nv	2006-04-30 18:31:44	1.0	http://lasvegas.citysearch.com
67910	medical facilities in las vegas nv	2006-04-30 18:31:44	3.0	http://www.lasvegasnevada.gov
67910	medical facilities in las vegas nv	2006-04-30 18:31:44	9.0	http://www.lasvegasrelocating.com
67910	unique architecture in las vegas nv	2006-04-30 18:35:02	10.0	http://www.guggenheim.org
67910	unique architecture in las vegas nv	2006-04-30 18:35:02	2.0	http://travel.yahoo.com
67910	architecture in las vegas nv	2006-04-30 18:40:28	4.0	http://lasvegas.citysearch.com
67910	architecture in las vegas nv	2006-04-30 18:40:28	2.0	http://www.library.unlv.edu
67910	architecture in las vegas nv	2006-04-30 18:40:28	3.0	http://local.yahoo.com
67910	religious sites in lasvegas	2006-04-30 18:50:35	1.0	http://www.lasvegas.worldweb.com
67910	religious sites in lasvegas	2006-04-30 18:50:35	2.0	http://www.lasvegas.worldweb.com
67910	religious sites in lasvegas	2006-04-30 18:56:09	12.0	http://travel2.nytimes.com
67910	religious sites in lasvegas	2006-04-30 18:56:09	12.0	http://travel2.nytimes.com

Table 1. Sample session from the AOL log.

engine and we generated a weighted co-occurrence graph that represents how often concepts are searched together in the sessions of the log. Then, we extracted the clusters of concepts that most frequently co-occur by applying a community detection algorithm to the graph. Those clusters are the basis for query expansion, starting from the concepts referred by the user in the observed part of the search session. We defined a few heuristics for recommending relevant types of information and we tested them on the log, achieving satisfactory accuracy results.

The main contributions of our work are: (i) a session-based query expansion model that suggests complementary concepts for satisfying the user's information needs in geographic exploratory search, and (ii) evaluation results of the model.

The following section positions our work in the related research. Section DATASET describes the dataset we used for our experiments. Section IDENTIFYING CLUSTERS OF FREQUENTLY OCCURRING CONCEPTS describes the approach we adopted to identify the co-occurrences of concepts in search sessions. Section SESSION-BASED QUERY EXPANSION proposes some query expansion strategies and the subsequent section evaluates the strategies. The last section concludes the paper and outlines some future work.

RELATED WORK

Various semantic information retrieval models employ concept networks to identify the meaning of queries and propose query expansions aimed at finding information, regardless of the terminology used by the user. E.g., both [35] and [19] use a local thesaurus inferred from the source pool of documents to identify the concepts referred by the queries. Moreover, [28] shows that the integration of different types of thesauri (linguistic, domain specific, etc.) improves the performance of query expansion techniques. The co-occurrence of word phrases in documents is also mined in [22] and [20] to automatically generate associative conceptual spaces, and in [25] and [1] for term suggestion based on the documents returned by search engines. Differently, Wang et al. [44] classify queries in patterns according to their syntactic components and match them to a knowledge base to generate the answers. Finally, a knowledge-based approach is adopted in [43] for concept interpretation, and in [13] to enhance information retrieval in the Semantic Web. On a different perspective, [32] proposes domain-specific ontologies for the interpretation of queries, assuming that users find it easier to specify what they want to do, rather than the concepts they are interested in.

Similarly, we use an ontology, and linguistic information, to interpret search queries at the conceptual level. However, we offer a *"you can also be interested in"* function to propose complementary concepts, i.e., topics, for expanding queries in order to satisfy the user's information needs, in a serendipitous way. For this purpose, we propose an associative information retrieval model [15] based on the observation of concepts co-occurrence in search sessions. Our work is related to the contextual query suggestion model by Cao et al. [11], who suggest queries on the basis of the context provided by the user's recent search history. However, we mine *ontology concepts* from a linguistic interpretation of search queries, while the concepts defined in [11] are clusters of queries associated to similar sets of click results selected by users.

Our model also relates to session-based term suggestion approaches such as the one by Huang et al. [21], and with term suggestion models used for web site advertisement, e.g., see Chen et al. [12]. However, it differs from those works because we look for *concept co-occurrence*, which abstracts from the specific words used to refer to concepts, while they observe *term co-occurrence* for query expansion.

Some recent work on information filtering and in recommender systems attempts to acquire relations among information items from the observation of users' behavior, and is complementary to our work. E.g., Google search engine manages the Knowledge Graph [16] to relate facts, concepts and entities depending on their co-occurrence in queries. Moreover, Oramas et al. [33] use a knowledge graph for personalized item recommendation in the music domain. Furthermore, CoSeNa [10] employs keyword co-occurrence in the corpus of documents to be retrieved, and ontological knowledge about the domain concepts, to support the exploration of text collections using a keywords-by-concepts graph. Our work differs from the above mentioned ones because we exploit a knowledge graph to predict further concepts that the user might be interested in, i.e., we suggest topics, not individual items.

Working at the conceptual level, our work is also complementary to the research on exploration vs. exploitation in information retrieval, which provides models to recognize the type of search that the user is performing, and/or to adapt the search results accordingly; e.g., [34, 5, 31].

DATASET

We defined our concept suggestion model, and evaluated its accuracy, by using as a dataset the AOL query log.[1] The log is composed of 10 files; however, we excluded one of them because it seemed to be corrupted by queries likely performed by a bot: that file included a session spawning over 6 days and included more than 20000 queries, or click through, submitted by the same user.

Each line of the AOL log represents either a query, or a click-through event (in which the user clicks on one of the search results of the previously submitted query). The lines contain the following fields:

- *AnonID*: ID that represents a user in an anonymous way.
- *Query*: search query submitted by the user.
- *QueryTime*: date and hour when the query was submitted.
- *ItemRank*: given the list of results (links to web pages) returned by the search engine, this field represents the relative position of the link on which the user has clicked. If the user has not selected any search results, this field is empty.
- *ClickURL*: URL of the search result selected by the user. Similar to field *ItemRank*, this field can be empty.

Table 1 shows a session from the AOL log. It can be noticed that the user looks for various types of information, concerning sports, transportation, medical facilities, and others. This substantiates the need for a suggestion model that helps her/him by proposing different topics for exploration.

Since we aim at developing an intelligent search support function for Geographical Information Systems, we selected an example system for our experiments, i.e., OnToMap [3, 4], and

rdfs:label	"Kindergarten"@en
rdfs:comment	"An educational institution for young children, usually before they go to primary school."@en
:keywords	"child"@en, "educational"@en, "young"@en
:lemma	"kindergarten"@en
:synonyms	"0th_grade"@en, "all-day_kindergarten"@en, "didactics"@en, "childcare"@en, "educability"@en, "education_program"@en, "education_system"@en, "junior_kindergarten"@en, "kindergarden"@en, "nursery"@en, "pre-primary"@en, "pre-school"@en, "preschoolar"@en

Table 2. Ontology definition of concept "Kintergarden". Values are tagged with the reference language (@en, for English).

we pre-processed the AOL log to work on a smaller dataset, focused on the search sessions relevant to geographical information. The ultimate goal is to train a query expansion model suitable for improving information search in OnToMap.

In order to build the dataset of our experiments, we first identified the search sessions from the log: we aggregated the queries performed by the same user according to their temporal proximity, following the widely applied rule that two consecutive queries belong to different sessions if the time interval between them exceeds half an hour; see [46]. Then, we selected the sessions including at least one query that refers to the concepts of the OnToMap ontology.[2] For this purpose, our main task was the identification of the concepts referred by the terms of the queries, which we carried out using the approach described in [2, 30]. Concept identification is a particularly important task: as reported in [44], the analysis of the log of a major search engine proved that about the 62% of the queries contain at least one conceptual class term.

Reference Ontology

The OnToMap ontology describes concepts by merging linguistic, encyclopedic and technical knowledge, focusing on concepts that are typical of Participatory Processes; see [2, 42]. Each concept has a textual description, and a set of lemmatized synonyms and keywords extracted from the description. E.g., Table 2 shows the specification of concept "Kintergarden". It reports the concept name (rdfs:label), its textual description (rdfs:comment), a few lemmatized keywords (:keywords), the lemma of the concept (:lemma), and a set of lemmatized synonyms of the terms occurring in the description (:synonyms).

Creation of the Dataset for the Experiments

We identified the AOL queries relevant to our experiments by matching the knowledge about concepts (i.e., the lemmatized synonyms and keywords extracted from the textual description

[1] We retrieved the AOL query log in June 2016 from http://www.cim.mcgill.ca/dudek/206/Logs/AOL-user-ct-collection/. Currently, the log is available at https://archive.org/details/AOL_search_data_leak_2006.

[2] We did not consider any broader ontologies, such as WordNet [48] or ProBase [49], because we aimed at obtaining a focused dataset to be analyzed.

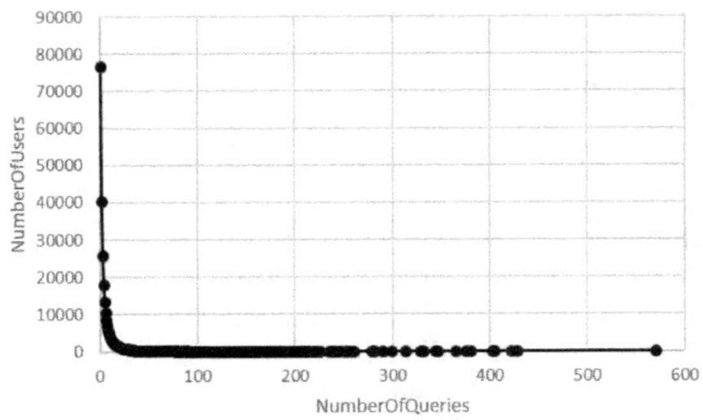

Figure 1. Distribution of the number of queries per user.

Minimum number of queries per user	1
Maximum number of queries per user	428
Mean number of queries per user	6.38
Median number of queries per user	3
Standard Deviation	11.37

Table 3. Measures about the distribution of the queries per user.

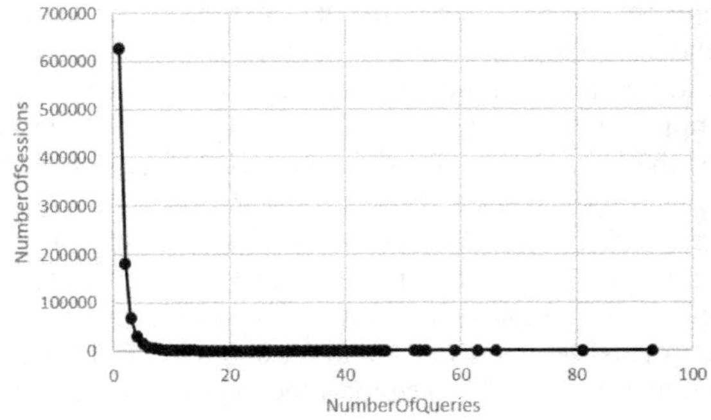

Figure 2. Distribution of queries in sessions.

Minimum number of queries per session	1
Maximum number of queries per session	93
Mean number of queries per session	1.67
Median number of queries per session	1
Standard Deviation	1.45

Table 4. Measures about the length of the search sessions.

of the ontology concepts) to the lemmatized words that compose the queries. If there was at least one match between a concept and a query, we considered the query as relevant, and we included the session to which it belonged in our dataset.

Each query can refer to one or more ontology concepts: the mean number of concepts per query of AOL-reduced is 1.502. This is due to the following reasons:

- The query might refer to independent concepts, each one identified in an unambiguous way. For instance, in a sample query like "public school and transportation in New York" the identified concepts would be *School* and *Local Public Transportation*. Notice that, similar to the findings reported in [7], most queries of the AOL log are short and refer to a single concept, as in the examples of Table 1.
- Because of ambiguity issues, more than one concept could be identified. For instance, given query "missouri child support" from the AOL log, the concepts identified from word "child" are *Childcare Service*, *Play Area* and *Kindergarten*, both including term "child" in their descriptions. As the query is short, it is difficult to understand which topic is the most probable one. Therefore, we assume that the query matches all concepts, with uncertainty.
  In the analysis of the log, we could not exploit the search results selected by users to disambiguate the queries, because we found out that, in most cases, they refer to the root pages of large web sites (e.g., see the URLs in Table 1), or they are obsolete (e.g., the link reported as a search result of query "missouri child support", http://www.dss.state.mo.us). Thus, they help in few cases.

Characteristics of the Dataset

The dataset obtained after the pre-processing phase, henceforth denoted as *AOL-reduced*, is composed of 1581817 queries submitted by 247868 users. The chart in Figure 1 shows the distribution of users with respect to the number of queries they specified. It can be noticed that the distribution follows a Power Law: most users submitted a very small set of queries, whereas a small group of users submitted several queries. As shown in Table 3, the mean number of queries per user is 6, but the distribution differs from this value for about 11 queries (standard deviation).

The dataset includes 945945 sessions, on which we performed two types of analyses:

- Firstly, we analyzed the distribution of sessions w.r.t. the number of queries they include. Table 4 shows the measures related to the length of sessions considering the number of queries. The mean length of a session is 1.67. The distribution follows a Power Law, as shown in Figure 2.
- Secondly, we analyzed the distribution of sessions with respect to users in order to compute the mean number of sessions that the users started; see Figure 3. We found out that users engaged in a mean number of about 3.82 sessions (median = 2). Moreover, the distribution follows a Power Law, with several people engaging in few search sessions, and a small number of users starting a larger number of sessions.

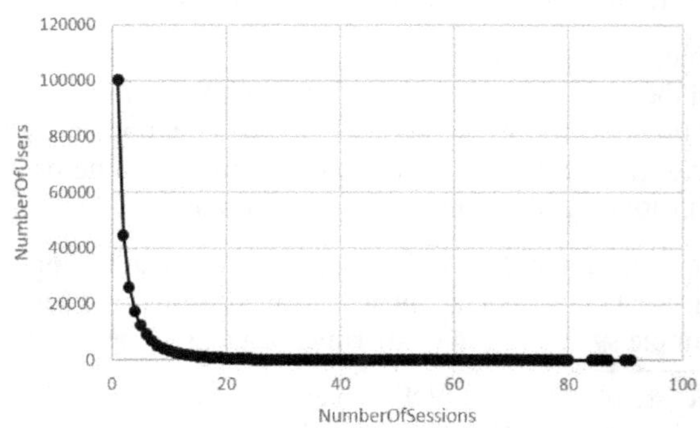

Figure 3. Distribution of sessions per users.

IDENTIFYING CLUSTERS OF FREQUENTLY CO-OCCURRING CONCEPTS

As described in the introduction, starting from the interpretation of the search queries that the user submits, we aim at suggesting further concepts which could be relevant to her/his needs. The idea is to provide an adaptive list of pointers to the types of information provided by the system, which are useful in the context of the user's search. We did this by identifying, from the concepts referred by the queries of the AOL-reduced dataset, other concepts that are related to the former from the viewpoint of commonly shared interests.

Step 1: Creation of the Concept Co-occurrence Graph

Starting from the AOL-reduced dataset, we built a graph that represents concepts co-occurrence in search sessions. By co-occurrence we mean the fact that two or more concepts are referred by the queries belonging to the same session. The graph is composed as follows:

- Each node represents a concept;
- Each edge represents the co-occurrence weight of the two connected concepts. This weight is computed by summing up the evidence of co-occurrence observed in all the sessions of the dataset.

The idea is that, each time two concepts are identified within the same session, the weight of the edge connecting them must increase, in order to capture and reinforce the hypothesis that people frequently search these concepts together.

Given two concepts c_i and c_j, the weight of the edge that connects them is defined as:

$$w_{c_i c_j} = \sum_{S=1}^{nSessions} Freqs_{S_{ij}} \tag{1}$$

where $Freqs_{S_{ij}}$ represents the contribution provided by session S to the co-occurrence frequency of c_i and c_j.

The contribution of the sessions to the weights of the co-occurrence graph (CG) is represented by a local weighted graph created by interpreting the queries of S. Specifically, $Freqs_{S_{ij}}$ is obtained by considering the evidence of co-occurrence provided by the queries that compose S. However, within a session, we avoid summing up the evidence provided by multiple occurrences of the same concepts, because they could derive from a query reformulation [37] or from the repetition of the queries in click-through events; see Table 1.

Given $S = \{Q_1, \ldots, Q_n\}$, $Freqs_{S_{ij}}$ is thus computed as follows:

$$Freqs_{S_{ij}} = Max_{k=1}^{n}(Freq_{ij_{Q_k}}, ev_{ij_{Q_{k-1}}}) \tag{2}$$

where $Freq_{ij_{Q_k}}$ is the co-occurrence evidence of concepts c_i and c_j provided by query Q_k, and $ev_{ij_{Q_{k-1}}}$ is the one estimated during the interpretation of queries $Q_1, \ldots, Q_{k-1}$.

Finally, the contribution of a query Q is computed as follows:

- If Q contains n terms ($n >= 0$), each one identifying a non-ambiguous concept: $T_1 \Rightarrow c_1$, $T_2 \Rightarrow c_2$, ..., $T_n \Rightarrow c_n$, then, Q generates nodes $c_1, \ldots, c_n$ of the local graph (if they do not exist yet). For all pairs of concepts c_a and c_b referred by Q, $Freq_{ab_Q} = 1$. Moreover, $Freq_{vw_Q} = 1$ for all the edges connecting c_a, or c_b, to some non-ambiguous concept of the local graph. $Freq_{vw_Q} = 0$ for the other edges of the graph.

  For instance, suppose that Q ="public school and transportation in New York" is the first query of a session. The terms and concepts referred by Q are:

  - school $\Rightarrow$ *School* - denoted as concept x;
  - transportation $\Rightarrow$ *Local Public Transportation* - denoted as concept y.

  Then, the local graph is composed of the x and y nodes. Moreover, $Freq_{xy_Q} = 1$.

- If Q contains a term t that refers to m concepts $\{c_1, \ldots, c_m\}$, the interpretation is ambiguous. Therefore, the evidence brought by t to the concepts is $\frac{1}{m}$, in order to take into account the possible interpretations of the query, and spread the weight to the ambiguous concepts. Thus, for each pair c_a, c_b in $\{c_1, \ldots, c_m\}$, $Freq_{ab_Q} = \frac{1}{m}$. $Freq_{vw_Q} = 1/m$ for all the edges connecting c_a, or c_b, to the other concepts of the local graph. Finally, $Freq_{vw_Q} = 0$ for all the edges of the local graph that are not outgoing arcs of c_a or c_b.

  For example, if $Q =$ "missouri child support" is the first query of a session:

  - The concepts identified from word "child" are: *Childcare Services* - denoted as x, *Play Areas* - y, and *Kindergartens* - z.
  - Then, the local graph is composed of the x, y and z nodes. Moreover, $Freq_{xy_Q} = Freq_{xz_Q} = Freq_{yz_Q} = \frac{1}{3}$.

We now sketch the generation of the local co-occurrence graph for a sample search session S. We recall that the contribution of multiple sessions to the overall co-occurrence graph (GC) is incremental: i.e., we sum up the weights provided by the individual sessions. Let's suppose that the terms of S refer to the following concepts:

$Q_1 : t1 \Rightarrow c_1$
$Q_2 : t2 \Rightarrow c_2$
$Q_3 : t3 \Rightarrow c_3, c_4$
$Q_4 : t4 \Rightarrow c_2$
$Q_5 : t5 \Rightarrow c_3$

Figure 4 shows the local co-occurrence graph generated by S.

- Q_1 adds node c_1 to the local graph.
- Q_2 adds c_2 and assigns a weight = 1 to the edge between c_1 and c_2, because there is no ambiguity: $Max(Freq_{c_1 c_{2Q_2}}, ev_{c_1 c_{2Q_1}}) = Max(1, 0) = 1$.
- Q_3 adds c_3 and c_4. Moreover, it assigns a weight = $\frac{1}{2}$ to the edge connecting c_3 and c_4 (the ambiguity concerns two concepts). Furthermore, it assigns the same weight to the edges connecting c_3, and c_4, to the concepts of the previous queries (i.e., the edges between c_3 and c_1, c_3 and c_2, c_4 and c_1, c_4 and c_2).

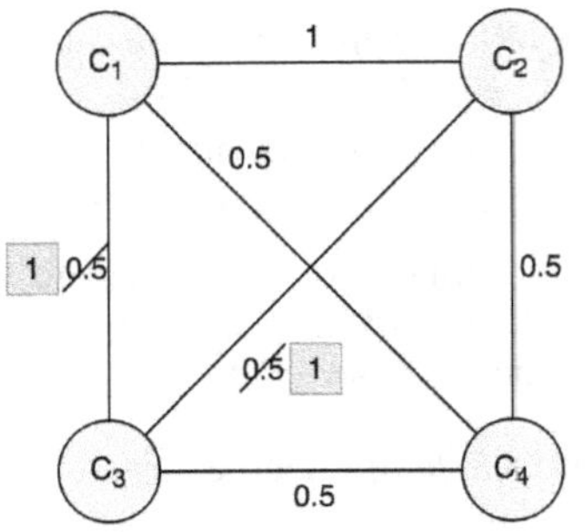

Figure 4. Construction of the graph describing the concepts co-occurrence frequency for a session.

- Q_4 does not add any nodes, nor does it modify the weights in the local graph because the evidence of c_2 doesn't solve the ambiguity between c_3 and c_4:
$Max(Freq_{c_2c_{3Q_4}}, ev_{c_2c_{3Q_3}}) = Max(0.5, 0.5) = 0.5$
$Max(Freq_{c_2c_{4Q_4}}, ev_{c_2c_{4Q_3}}) = Max(0.5, 0.5) = 0.5$
$Max(Freq_{c_1c_{2Q_4}}, ev_{c_1c_{2Q_3}}) = Max(1, 1) = 1.$

- Q_5 does not add any nodes, but it solves the ambiguity between c_3 and c_1, and c_3 and c_2, respectively, because it provides a non ambiguous evidence of c_3. Thus, the respective weights of the local graph are updated:
$Max(Freq_{c_1c_{3Q_5}}, ev_{c_1c_{3Q_4}}) = Max(1, 0.5) = 1.$
$Max(Freq_{c_2c_{3Q_5}}, ev_{c_2c_{3Q_4}}) = Max(1, 0.5) = 1.$
Notice that we maintain the ambiguity between c_3 and c_4 (in a conservative approach) because, in general, we cannot assume that Q_5 is a reformulation of Q_3. Thus, we do not use it to exclude c_4 from the interpretation of Q_3.

Step 2: Pruning the Graph

The co-occurrence graph of the AOL-reduced dataset is strongly connected: almost all of the ontology concepts are linked to each other by an edge whose weight is > 0. We thus decided to analyze the distribution of weights in the graph, in order to understand the strength of the correlation between concepts. Figure 5 shows this distribution: the x-axis represents the edges, and the y-axis represents their weights, which take values in [0, 68707.5].

The distribution highlights the fact that there is a large number of weakly connected concepts, i.e., of candidate items for query expansion. As, different from keyword suggestion in search engines, we aim at proposing few concepts, we decided to delete the edges having low weight, assuming that they represent weak associations between concepts, and that they capture less commonly shared interests.

Figure 5. Distribution of the weight of edges in the co-occurrence graph.

We selected a threshold for pruning the graph in order to optimize the prediction accuracy of the resulting concept co-occurrence clusters; i.e., the degree of matching between the set of concepts composing the clusters and the concepts identified in the sessions of AOL-reduced. The selected threshold is 2200. Details about the evaluation of accuracy follow.

Step 3: Creation of the Concept Co-occurrence Clusters

Starting from a co-occurrence graph (*CG*) pruned with a threshold, the clusters are created by applying a community detection algorithm which identifies the sets of strictly correlated concepts. Our hypothesis is that they correspond to sets of concepts that are frequently searched together.

For the identification of clusters we analyzed various algorithms. We selected COPRA [18], which works on weighted graphs and detects overlapping communities. In this way, a concept can belong to different clusters at the same time. Our idea was that, within a session, the user might focus on more than one set of highly correlated concepts, and that, starting from the same query, (s)he might explore different paths of the information space.

The COPRA algorithm, applied to the concept co-occurrence graph pruned with threshold 2200, returned 23 clusters having a minimum and maximum number of concepts equal to 1 and 6, respectively.

Three sample clusters are:

1. {Play Area, Sport Area, Kindergarten, Law Enforcement, Hospital}.
2. {National Park, Provincial Park, Regional Park, Urban Park, Furnished Green}.
3. {Play Area, Sport Area, Library, Childcare service, Law Enforcement, School}.

Step 4: Validation of the Clusters

We tested the clusters returned by COPRA on different versions of the pruned graph (using different weight thresholds) in order to estimate how close they reflected user behavior in the AOL-reduced dataset. We considered the AOL-reduced sessions as the ground-truth and we computed standard accuracy measures for the evaluation.

We treated the clusters as unordered sets and we did not care about the observed order of exploration of concepts in the sessions. The reason for this is the fact that, after each search query, we plan to suggest concepts as a set of selectable items, in a multi-choice box. This set is a projection on the information categories managed by the system, based on the search context.

For each threshold, we tested the accuracy of the clusters by applying 10-fold cross-validation, after having randomly distributed the sessions of the dataset on folders. We used 90% of the sessions as learning set and 10% as test set.

Given a session $S = \{c_{s_1}, \ldots, c_{s_n}\}$, and a cluster $CL = \{c_{cl_1}, \ldots, c_{cl_m}\}$, we evaluated the following measures:

- Precision, describing the rate of concepts of CL that also occur in S. These concepts represent correct predictions if CL is used for query expansion:

$$precision = \frac{|\{c_{s_1}, \ldots, c_{s_n}\} \cap \{c_{cl_1}, \ldots, c_{cl_m}\}|}{|\{c_{cl_1}, \ldots, c_{cl_m}\}|} \quad (3)$$

- Recall, representing the rate of relevant concepts of S which CL contains, and thus can suggest, if used for query expansion:

$$recall = \frac{|\{c_{s_1}, \ldots, c_{s_n}\} \cap \{c_{cl_1}, \ldots, c_{cl_m}\}|}{|\{c_{s_1}, \ldots, c_{s_n}\}|} \quad (4)$$

- F1 score, computed as:

$$2 * \frac{precision * recall}{precision + recall} \quad (5)$$

Moreover, we considered two types of evaluation:

- Eval1: accuracy of the clusters that best represent search behavior within a session. The aim of this test was to measure the optimal adherence of the clusters to users behavior, assuming to be able to identify the best cluster from the observed queries. In this case, for each session S, we computed the precision, recall and F1 score of all the clusters. Then, we selected the accuracy of the best performing one as the representative value for S. Finally, we computed the mean accuracy of such best clusters.
- Eval2: mean accuracy of the clusters that include at least one concept referred in the search session. In this case, we aimed at testing the accuracy of a broader set of clusters, related to search sessions in a looser way. As above, we computed the mean precision, recall and F1 score.

Table 5 reports the accuracy values we obtained using the threshold that maximizes the mean F1 (*threshold* = 2200) for pruning the concept co-occurrence graph:

- The precision values show that, during the search sessions, users refer to a substantial portion of the concepts included in the clusters. However, the clusters contain some concepts that are not explored: by using all the clusters that have at least one concept in common with the session, we obtain a precision of about 0.626.
- The recall shows that the suggested clusters largely cover the search sessions: in both evaluations, the recall is about 0.794. Thus, the clusters help propose relevant concepts.

	Eval1	**Eval2**
Precision	0.659	0.626
Recall	0.794	0.794
F1	0.720	0.700

Table 5. Evaluation of the clusters accuracy.

Overall, we can say that, by selecting clusters that have some concepts in common with those referred in the observed portion of a search session, we have good chances to suggest types of information that the user will be interested in. These results helped us in the identification of the query expansion strategies described in the following section.

In the computation of these measures, we did not take into account the occurrence of ambiguities in the interpretation of search queries. Basically, we considered all the concepts referred (either ambiguously or non ambiguously) in the queries as concepts belonging to the search sessions. This might introduce some noise in the evaluation results (e.g., it could increment the number of concepts relevant to the search sessions, reducing the precision results). However, we could not retrieve more precise information about the search interests of the AOL users because, as already discussed, most queries of the dataset are short, and the dataset provides little information to disambiguate them.

SESSION-BASED QUERY EXPANSION

Let's consider a search session $S = \{Q_1, \ldots, Q_i, \ldots, Q_n\}$, and suppose that we have observed the first i queries of S. We denote the sequence $\{Q_1, \ldots, Q_i\}$ as $S@i$, and the set of concepts identified by interpreting the queries of $S@i$ as: $C@i = \{c1, \ldots, \{c_{k_1}, \ldots, c_{k_m}\}, \ldots, \{c_{t_1}, \ldots, c_{t_s}\}, \ldots, c_n\}$.
In $C@i$, the ambiguities in concept identification are represented by including the tuples of ambiguous concepts in subsets of $C@i$. For instance, in the above example, $\{c_{k_1}, \ldots, c_{k_m}\}$ and, respectively, $\{c_{t_1}, \ldots, c_{t_s}\}$ are ambiguous. In the following, we will refer to the tuples of ambiguous concepts as *ambiguity sets*.

We consider three concepts suggestion strategies, which differ from each other in the method for selecting the clusters to be used for query expansion. We assume that they could be applied immediately after the interpretation of the first query of a session, or incrementally, in order to support interactive information search.

- **SLACK:**
  1. Select a set of clusters $\{CL_{x_1}, \ldots, CL_{x_y}\}$ that contain *at least* one concept c such that $c \in C@i$; i.e., c has been referenced in the observed portion of the search session, $S@i$, either ambiguously or unambiguously.
  2. Propose the concepts that belong to at least one of the selected clusters, and the user has not yet explored. For each cluster CL_{x_j}, we denote the set of concepts included in CL_{x_j} as $Sugg_{x_j}$. The set of concepts to be suggested is computed as follows: $Sugg@i = \{Sugg_{x_1} \cup \cdots \cup Sugg_{x_y}\} - C@i$.

  For instance, given $C@i = \{c_1, \{c_3, c_4\}\}$, and two selected clusters, $CL_1 = \{c_1, c_7\}$ and $CL_2 = \{c_2, c_3, c_5, c_8\}$, $Sugg@i = \{c_2, c_5, c_7, c_8\}$.

- **SLACK-selective:** Same as SLACK, but only the clusters that best match $C@i$ are used to compute $Sugg@i$. For our experiments, we selected the best matching cluster. The evaluation of the concept suggestion strategies, described

Indicator	SLACK	SLACK-selective	STRICT
Min number of candidate clusters	0	0	0
Max number of candidate clusters	**2**	N=1	2
Mean number of candidate clusters	**1.192**	1	1.188
Min number of suggested concepts	0	0	0
Max number of suggested concepts	**7**	5	**7**
Mean number of suggested concepts	**2.688**	2.309	2.681
Precision	0.614	**0.621**	0.615
Recall	**0.791**	0.783	0.790
F1	**0.692**	**0.692**	**0.692**
Success rate (%)	**51.5**	51.2	**51.5**

Table 6. Statistical measures of concept suggestion strategies applied to the first query of the search sessions ($S@1$).

Indicator	SLACK	SLACK-selective	STRICT
Min number of candidate clusters	0	0	0
Max number of candidate clusters	**2**	N=1	2
Mean number of candidate clusters	**1.223**	1	1.192
Min number of suggested concepts	0	0	0
Max number of suggested concepts	**7**	5	**7**
Mean number of suggested concepts	**2.861**	2.446	2.799
Precision	0.594	**0.598**	0.596
Recall	**0.819**	0.801	0.818
F1	**0.689**	0.685	**0.689**
Success rate (%)	**39.7**	39.2	39.6

Table 7. Statistical measures of concept suggestion strategies applied to the first two queries of the search sessions ($S@2$).

later on, provided satisfactory accuracy results for this setting of the strategy.

We compute the degree of matching between a cluster CL and $C@i$ as the cardinality of $CL \cap C@i$ (i.e., the number of concepts they have in common), taking the ambiguity in $C@i$ into account. Specifically:

- Each concept c occurring both in CL and, as a non-ambiguous element, in $C@i$, contributes to the computation of the degree of matching with a value = 1.
- Each concept c that occurs in CL, and is part of an ambiguity set AMB in $C@i$, contributes to the computation with $\frac{1}{|AMB|}$; i.e., the cardinality of the ambiguity set mitigates its contribution to the computation of the degree of matching.

For instance, given $C@i = \{c_1, \{c_3, c_4\}, c_5\}$, the degree of matching with cluster $CL_1 = \{c_1, c_7\}$ is 1 and the one with $CL_2 = \{c_2, c_3, c_5, c_8\}$ is 1.5.

- **STRICT:**
  1. Select the set of clusters $\{CL_{x_1}, \ldots, CL_{x_y}\}$ containing *all* of the concepts c such that $c \in C@i$. These are the clusters covering the whole portion of the search session observed so far (regardless of the fact that the concepts are ambiguous or not).
  2. As above, the set of concepts suggested for query expansion is: $Sugg@i = \{Sugg_{x_1} \cup \cdots \cup Sugg_{x_y}\} - C@i$.

We did not propose a STRICT-selective strategy because STRICT generates very small candidate sets.

EVALUATION OF CONCEPT SUGGESTION STRATEGIES

We tested the accuracy of our strategies by applying 10-fold cross-validation on the AOL-reduced dataset, after having randomly distributed the sessions on folders. For the evaluation, we compared the concepts suggested by the strategies to those explored by users in the search sessions (ground-truth). Specifically, for each search session, we tested the strategies after having interpreted the first query alone ($S@1$), the first two queries ($S@2$), and so forth. In each case, we computed the mean precision, recall and F1 score of the strategies by comparing the concepts of the suggested clusters to the concepts referred in the remainder of the sessions.

Evaluation Results

Table 6 summarizes the results that we obtained in the suggestion of concepts immediately after having interpreted the first query of the search sessions ($S@1$):

- SLACK: the minimum, mean, and maximum number of candidate clusters identified by this strategy are 0, 1.192, and 2, respectively. The mean number of concepts suggested for query expansion is about 2.688. This number goes up to 7 in some sessions.
- SLACK-selective with number of best matching clusters N=1. The minimum, mean and maximum number of selected clusters are 0, 1 and N=1, respectively. The strategy suggests a lower mean number of concepts: about 2.309, and it proposes at most 5 concepts.
- The STRICT strategy proposes a maximum of 2 candidate clusters per session, with about 1.188 clusters in average, and it generates at most 7 concept suggestions, with a mean value of about 2.681 concepts.

The three strategies have almost the same accuracy (see Table 6): the F1 measure can be approximated to 0.692 in all the cases. However, they differ from each other if we look at finer-grained measures:

- Precision: SLACK-selective outperforms the other two, i.e., it suggest the highest number of concepts that users are observed to explore in the remainder of the search session. The lower precision of SLACK can be explained with the fact that it selects a superset of the clusters picked by

SLACK-selective, and thus can introduce more noise in the suggestions. Similarly, STRICT can select more than one cluster (covering all the concepts referred in the first query), thus incrementing noise in some cases.

- Recall: the best strategy is SLACK, which outperforms SLACK-selective because it selects a larger pool of clusters and thus has better chances to guess the concepts explored by users. Interestingly, however, STRICT achieves almost the same recall, having a stricter cluster selection policy. We explain this finding with the fact that, by selecting all the clusters that cover the observed query, the strategy has good chances to guess the user's exploration path, among the possible ones (remember that the concept co-occurrence clusters mirrored common search behavior in a fairly accurate way).

- Success rate: as proposed by Huang et al. in [21], this metric measures the percentage of sessions for which our strategies propose at least one concept that is referred in the portion of the search session to be observed. Looking at the table, we can see that all of the strategies are successful in more than 50% of cases. However, the best performing ones are SLACK and STRICT. In other words, SLACK is as good as STRICT if we aim at suggesting at least one relevant concept.
  We compared our strategies to the Huang et al.'s term suggestion model, which is the most similar one among those available in the literature. As that model achieves 23% success rate, we can say that our approach definitely outperforms it.

Table 7 shows the evaluation results after the interpretation of the first two queries of the search sessions. It can be seen that, for all the strategies, the minimum, mean and maximum number of selected clusters are constant. Moreover, the minimum, mean and maximum number of suggested concepts are constant or increase.
Regarding accuracy, we notice that for all the three strategies, the recall increases, while the precision and F1 scores decrease to about 0.6, but the SLACK-selective strategy is the most precise one. SLACK has the best recall and STRICT a rather similar one; as result, both strategies have the best F1 value. The higher recall of these strategies suggests that the selection of a single cluster, best representing the observed portion of search session, is not general enough to cover all the possible developments of the search session. Thus, a less restrictive approach, that makes it possible to consider more than one development of a search session (as the one adopted in both SLACK and STRICT) achieves better results.

We measured the trend for longer portions of search sessions and we discovered that it is consistent, i.e., the precision decreases, and the recall increases, when more queries are interpreted. See Figures 6 and 7, which report the values of these measures after the interpretation of 1 to 5 queries.[3] However, the three strategies behave slightly differently:

[3]We did not consider any longer sequences because very few search sessions are composed of more than 5 queries.

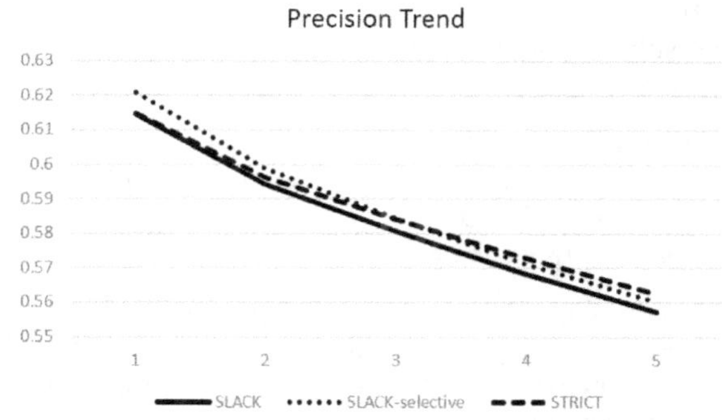

Figure 6. Precision of the concept suggestion strategies in function of the number of interpreted queries ($S@i$).

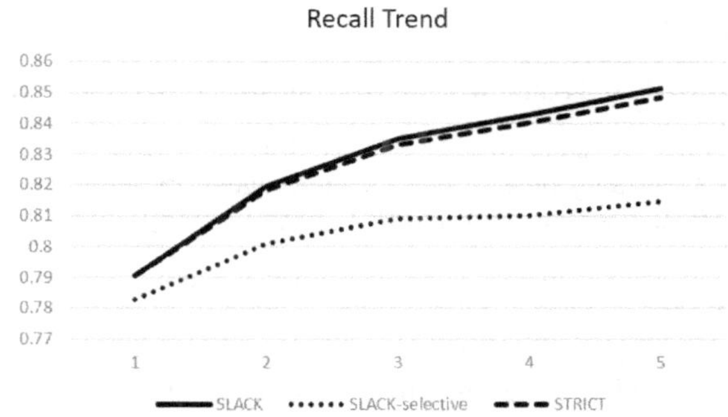

Figure 7. Recall of the concept suggestion strategies in function of the number of interpreted queries ($S@i$)

- SLACK-selective is the most precise strategy when observing the first two queries, and is always better than SLACK, but it is outperformed by STRICT after the observation of 3 queries. We explain this with the fact that, when more information about the search context is available, STRICT is able to select the clusters that best represent the user's search interests, and thus to mirror her/his behavior.

- Regarding recall, we believe that it increases when more information about a search session is available because, if more concepts are identified from the search queries, there are more chances to select good candidates and thus to propose relevant concepts. However, the improvement of this accuracy measure varies depending on the selectivity of the strategy:
  - SLACK selects the highest number of clusters, and thus suggest a larger set of concepts. This increases the chances that the suggested concepts are identified in the session.
  - SLACK-selective chooses a single cluster that best matches the search session, at the expense of recall.
  - STRICT selects the clusters matching the whole portion of session observed so far. These are the best representative of the session and thus have very good changes to predict correct concepts, being used together for concept prediction.

Discussion

The results of our experiments enable us to positively answer our research question:

H1: Can the data about the concepts frequently searched together by people within a search session be exploited to help the user explore the portions of an information space relevant to her/his information needs?

The results show that our concept suggestion strategies have high recall, i.e., they are able to suggest most of the concepts that the users explore in the AOL-reduced dataset. However, their accuracy differs:

- The SLACK-selective strategy is the best one from the viewpoint of precision, at least when the first queries of a session are analyzed in order to suggest concepts for query expansion.
- The SLACK and the STRICT ones achieve the best recall.

Looking at these findings, we believe that the decision of which strategy best suits concept suggestion depends on the way how we want to implement this function:

- If we can suggest a larger number of concepts, then the SLACK strategy is the best one, because (i) it achieves better recall and (ii) the mean number of suggested concepts is just a bit higher than that of the other two.
- Differently, if we aim at precision, SLACK-selective is the preferred one at the beginning of a search session, while STRICT is more suitable for concept suggestion after the first queries.

For our current work, SLACK is the most convenient strategy because it is fairly precise and, at the same time, it suggests more relevant concepts than the other ones. Specifically, we aim at providing the user with an overview of the sets of concepts to choose from, given the search context provided by the previous queries. As the user will be enabled to choose relevant concepts in a multiple-choice box, the presence of very few irrelevant concepts, as is the case of SLACK, is not a problem.

It should be noticed that other strategies might be considered. For instance, the past search history of the individual user might be analyzed to identify the concepts he or she most frequently searched for, assuming that these represent interesting types of information. Then, this might be used to select candidate clusters for query expansion. In this paper, we left these strategies apart for two main reasons:

- Firstly, as discussed by Greenstein et al. in [17], session-based recommendation is of primary importance because users frequently interact with systems in an anonymous way, or there might be privacy or technical reasons for avoiding the tracking of their identities. Therefore, we decided to focus on this function before exploring other scenarios.
- Secondly, the introduction of historic information about user behavior deserves a separate research; e.g., see [45, 40, 39]. Specifically, [9] showed that historic information about the search behavior of an individual user helps re-ranking of search results at the beginning of a search session, while local information about the session is more effective later on, because it provides information about the actual context of search. As we deal with concept suggestion, these results cannot be immediately transferred to our case. We will thus carry out this type of analysis in a broader perspective of ontology-based personalized search support and ontology-based user models; e.g., see [41, 23, 38, 14, 27, 26].

CONCLUSION

We described a session-based concept suggestion model that supports information search by proposing concepts for query expansion, given the context provided by the observed portions of the search sessions. We focus on presenting types of information that the user might also be interested in, given the data he or she is searching for, at the conceptual level. We aim at supporting the exploration of information spaces including rather different types of data, such as those managed by Geographical Information Systems.

Our model is based on an analysis of search behavior, that we carried out by studying the AOL query log. Specifically, our model is based on (i) the identification of clusters of concepts that frequently co-occur in search sessions, and (ii) the definition of strategies that select the clusters for concept suggestion by taking the search context that emerges from the first queries of the sessions. The evaluation of our model has provided satisfactory results about its prediction accuracy.

Having performed off-line experiments, we could not test the serendipity of the concept suggestions, as we relied on data about the types of information that users autonomously explored in the search sessions. Our future work includes (i) analyzing users' past behavior for improving concept suggestion, and (ii) studying the impact of our model on the serendipity of suggestions by testing it in an online experiment with users.

ACKNOWLEDGMENTS

We thank the anonymous reviewers for their fruitful comments and suggestions. This work is partially funded by project MIMOSA (MultIModal Ontology-driven query system for the heterogeneous data of a SmArtcity, "Progetto di Ateneo Torino_call2014_L2_157", 2015-17) and by projects "Ricerca Locale" and "Ricerca Autofinanziata" of the University of Turin.

REFERENCES

1. M. Akaishi, K. Satoh, and Y. Tanaka. 2004. *An Associative Information Retrieval Based on the Dependency of Term Co-occurrence*. Springer Berlin Heidelberg, Berlin, Heidelberg, 195–206.
2. L. Ardissono, M. Lucenteforte, N. Mauro, A. Savoca, A. Voghera, and L. La Riccia. 2016. Exploration of Cultural Heritage Information via Textual Search Queries. In *MobileHCI '16 Proceedings of the 18th Int. Conf. on Human-Computer Interaction with Mobile Devices and Services Adjunct*. ACM, 992–1001.
3. L. Ardissono, M. Lucenteforte, N. Mauro, A. Savoca, A. Voghera, and L. La Riccia. 2017a. Semantic

Interpretation of Search Queries for Personalization. In *Proc. of UMAP 2017 Adjunct*. ACM, 101–102.

4. L. Ardissono, M. Lucenteforte, N. Mauro, A. Savoca, A. Voghera, and L. La Riccia. 2017b. OnToMap - Semantic Community Maps for knowledge sharing. In *Proceedings of Hypertext 2017*. ACM, 317–318.
5. L. Athukorala, A. Medlar, A. Oulasvirta, G. Jacucci, and D. Glowacka. 2016. Beyond relevance: adapting exploration/exploitation in information retrieval. In *Proc. of the 21st Int. Conf. on Intelligent User Interfaces (IUI'16)*. ACM, Sonoma, California, USA, 359–369.
6. A. Ballatore, W. Kuhn, M. Hegarty, and E. Parsons. 2016. Spatial approaches to information search. *Spatial Cognition & Computation* 16, 4 (2016), 1–16.
7. S.M. Beitzel, E.C. Jensen, O. Frieder, D.D. Lewis, A. Chowdhury, and A. Kolcz. 2005. Improving automatic query classification via semi-supervised learning. In *Proc. of the Fifth IEEE Int. Conf. on Data Mining (ICDM '05)*. IEEE Computer Society, Washington, DC, USA, 42–49.
8. N.J. Belkin. 1980. Anomalous states of knowledge as a basis for information retrieval. *Canadian Journal of Information Science* 5 (1980), 133–143.
9. P.N. Bennett, R.W. White, W. Chu, S.T. Dumais, P. Bailey, F. Borisyuk, and X. Cui. 2012. Modeling the impact of short- and long-term behavior on search personalization. In *Proc. of the 35th Int. ACM SIGIR Conf. on Research and Development in Information Retrieval (SIGIR '12)*. ACM, New York, NY, USA, 185–194.
10. K.S. Candan, M. Cataldi, L. Di Caro, M.L. Sapino, and C. Schifanella. 2009. CoSeNa: a context-based search and navigation system. In *MEDES '09 Int. Conf. on Management of Emergent Digital EcoSystems*. Chia Laguna, Italy, Art. 33.
11. H. Cao, D. Jiang, J. Pei, Q. He andZ. Liao, E. Chen, and H. Li. 2008. Context-aware query suggestion by mining click-through and session data. In *Proc. of the 14th ACM SIGKDD Int. Conf. on Knowledge Discovery and Data Mining (KDD '08)*. ACM, New York, NY, USA, 875–883.
12. Y. Chen, G-R Xue, and Y. Yu. 2008. Advertising Keyword Suggestion Based on Concept Hierarchy. In *Proc. of the 2008 Int. Conf. on Web Search and Data Mining (WSDM '08)*. ACM, New York, NY, USA, 251–260.
13. M. Fernández, I. Cantador, V. López, D. Vallet, P. Castells, and E. Motta. 2011. Semantically enhanced information retrieval: an ontology-based approach. *Web Semantics: Science, Services and Agents on the World Wide Web* 9, 4 (2011), 434–452.
14. S. Gauch, J. Chaffee, and A. Pretschner. 2003. Ontology-based personalized search and browsing. *Web Intelli. and Agent Sys.* 1, 3-4 (2003), 219–234.
15. V.E. Giuliano and P.E. Jones. 1962. *Linear Associative Information Retrieval*. Technical Report ESD-TR-62-294. ASTIA.
16. Google. 2017. Knowledge Graph. https://www.google.com/intl/it_it/insidesearch/features/search/knowledge.html.
17. A. Greenstein-Messica, L. Rokach, and M. Friedman. 2017. Session-based recommendations using item embedding. In *Proc. of the 22nd Int. Conf. on Intelligent User Interfaces (IUI '17)*. ACM, New York, NY, USA, 629–633.
18. S. Gregory. 2010. Finding overlapping communities in networks by label propagation. *New Journal of Physics* 12, 103018 (2010).
19. F.A. Grootjem and T.P. van der Weide. 2006. Conceptual query expansion. *Data & Knowledge Engineering* 56 (2006), 174–193.
20. O. Hoeber, XD. Yang, and Y. Yao. 2005. Conceptual query expansion. In *Advances in Web Intelligence. AWIC 2005, Lecture Notes in Computer Science, vol 3528.* Lodz, Poland, 190–196.
21. C.-K. Huang, L.-F. Chien, and Y.-J. Oyang. 2003. Relevant term suggestion in interactive web search based on contextual in formation in query session logs. *Journal of the American Society for Information Science and Technology* 54, 7 (2003), 638–649.
22. J. Van Den Berg and M. Schuemie. 1999. Information retrieval systems using an associative conceptual space. In *In Proc. of the 7th European Symposium on Artificial Neural Networks (ESANN'99)*. 351–356.
23. X. Jiang and A.-H. Tan. 2009. Learning and inferencing in user ontology for personalized Semantic Web search. *Information Sciences* 179 (2009), 2794–2808.
24. C.B. Jones and R.S. Purves. 2008. Geographical Information Retrieval. *Int. Journal of Geographical Information Science* 22, 3 (2008), 219–228.
25. A. Joshi and R. Motwani. 2006. Keyword Generation for Search Engine Advertising. In *6th IEEE Int. Conf. on Data Mining - Workshops (ICDMW'06)*. ACM, New York, NY, USA, 490–496.
26. K.W-T Leung and Dik D.L. Lee. 2010. Deriving concept-based user profiles from search engine logs. *IEEE Trans. on Knowl. and Data Eng.* 22, 7 (July 2010), 969–982.
27. F. Liu, C. Yu, and W. Meng. 2002. Personalized web search by mapping user query to categories. In *Proc. CIKM'02*. McLean, Virginia, USA.
28. R. Mandala, T. Tokunaga, and H. Tanaka. 1999. Combining multiple evidence from different types of thesaurus for query expansion. In *Proc. of the 22nd Annual Int. ACM SIGIR Conf. on Research and Development in Information Retrieval (SIGIR '99)*. ACM, New York, NY, USA, 191–197.
29. G. Marchiorini. 2006. Exploratory search: from finding to understanding. *Commun. ACM* 49, 4 (2006), 41–46.

30. N. Mauro and L. Ardissono. 2017. Concept-aware Geographic Information Retrieval. In *Proceedings of 2017 IEEE/WIC/ACM Int. Conf. on Web Intelligence (WI)*. ACM, Leipzig, Germany.

31. A. Medlar, J. Pyykkö, and D. Glowacka. 2017. Towards fine-grained adaptation of exploration/exploitation in Information Retrieval. In *Proc. of the 22nd Int. Conf. on Intelligent User Interfaces (IUI '17)*. ACM, New York, NY, USA, 623–627.

32. M. Molina and S. Bayarri. 2011. A multinational SDI-based system to facilitate disaster risk management in the Andean community. *Computers & Geosciences* 18 (2011), 1501–1510.

33. S. Oramas, V.C. Ostuni, T. Di Noia, X. Serra, and E. Di Sciascio. 2016. Sound and music recommendation with knowledge graphs. *ACM Transactions on Intelligent Systems and Technology* 8, 2 (2016), Art. 21.

34. R. Porrini, M. Palmonari, and G. Vizzari. 2014. Composite match autocompletion (COMMA): a semantic result-oriented autocompletion technique for e-marketplaces. *Web Intelligence and Agent Systems: an international journal* 12 (2014), 35–49.

35. Y. Qiu and H.P Frei. 1993. Concept based query expansion. In *Proc. of the 16th Annual Int. ACM SIGIR Conf. on Research and Development in Information Retrieval (SIGIR '93)*. ACM, New York, NY, USA, 160–169.

36. L. Ratzan. 2004. *Understanding information systems: what they do and why we need them.* American Library Association, Chicago, USA.

37. S.Y. Rieh and H. I Xie. 2006. Analysis of multiple query reformulations on the web: the interactive information retrieval context. *Information processing and management* 42 (2006), 751–768.

38. A. Sieg, B. Mobasher, and R. Burke. 2010. Ontology-based collaborative recommendation. *Computing* (2010).

39. B. Smyth, E. Balfe, J. Freine, P. Briggs, M. Coyle, and O. Boydell. 2005. Exploiting query repetition and regularity in an adaptive community-based web search engine. *USER MODELING AND USER-ADAPTED INTERACTION - The Journal of Personalization Research* 14, 5 (2005), 383–423.

40. D. Sontag, K. Collins-Thompson, P.N. Bennett, R.W. White, S. Dumais, and B. Billerbeck. 2012. Probabilistic Models for Personalizing Web Search. In *Proc. of the 5th ACM Int. Conf. on Web Search and Data Mining (WSDM '12)*. ACM, New York, NY, USA, 433–442.

41. J. Teevan, S.T. Dumais, and E. Horvitz. 2005. Personalizing Search via Automated Analysis of Interests and Activities. In *Proc. of the 28th Annual Int. ACM SIGIR Conf. on Research and Development in Information Retrieval (SIGIR '05)*. ACM, New York, NY, USA, 449–456.

42. A. Voghera, R. Crivello, L.Ardissono, M. Lucenteforte, A. Savoca, and L. La Riccia. 2016. Production of spatial representations through collaborative mapping. An experiment. In *Proc. of 9th Int. Conf. on Innovation in Urban and Regional Planning (INPUT 2016)*. 356–361.

43. Y. Wang, H. Huang, and C. Feng. 2017. Query expansion based on a feedback concept model for microblog retrieval. In *Proc. of the 26th Int. Conf. on World Wide Web (WWW '17)*. International World Wide Web Conferences Steering Committee, Republic and Canton of Geneva, Switzerland, 559–568.

44. Y. Wang, H. Li, H. Wang, and K.Q. Zhu. 2012. Concept-based web search. In *Conceptual Modeling. ER 2012. Lecture Notes in Computer Science, vol 7532*, P. Atzeni and D. Cheung (Eds.). Springer, Berlin, Heidelberg, 449–462.

45. R.W. White, P.N. Bennett, and S.T. Dumais. 2010. Predicting short-term interests using activity-based search context. In *Proc. of the 19th ACM Int. Conf. on Information and Knowledge Management (CIKM '10)*. ACM, New York, NY, USA, 1009–1018.

46. R.W. White, M. Bilenko, and S. Cucerzan. 2007. Studying the use of popular destinations to enhance web search interaction. In *Proc. of the 30th Annual Int. ACM SIGIR Conf. on Research and Development in Information Retrieval (SIGIR '07)*. ACM, New York, NY, USA, 159–166.

47. R.W. White and R.A. Roth. 2006. Supporting exploratory search. *Commun. ACM* 49, 4 (2006), 36–39.

48. WordNet. 2017. WordNet - a lexical database for English. https://wordnet.princeton.edu/.

49. W. Wu, H. Li, H. Wang, and K.Q Zhu. 2012. Probase: A Probabilistic Taxonomy for Text Understanding. In *Proc. of the 2012 ACM SIGMOD Int. Conf. on Management of Data*. ACM, New York, NY, USA, 481–492.

A Study on User-Controllable Social Exploratory Search

Cecilia di Sciascio
Know-Center GmbH
Graz, Austria
cdisciascio@know-center.at

Peter Brusilovsky
University of Pittsburgh
Pittsburgh, USA
peterb@pitt.edu

Eduardo Veas
Know-Center GmbH
Graz, Austria
eveas@know-center.at

ABSTRACT
Information-seeking tasks with learning or investigative purposes are usually referred to as exploratory search. Exploratory search unfolds as a dynamic process where the user, amidst navigation, trial-and-error and on-the-fly selections, gathers and organizes information (resources). A range of innovative interfaces with increased user control have been developed to support exploratory search process. In this work we present our attempt to increase the power of exploratory search interfaces by using ideas of *social search*, i.e., leveraging information left by past users of information systems. Social search technologies are highly popular nowadays, especially for improving ranking. However, current approaches to social ranking do not allow users to decide to what extent *social* information should be taken into account for result ranking. This paper presents an interface that integrates social search functionality into an exploratory search system in a user-controlled way that is consistent with the nature of exploratory search. The interface incorporates control features that allow the user to (i) express information needs by selecting keywords and (ii) to express preferences for incorporating *social wisdom* based on tag matching and user similarity. The interface promotes search transparency through color-coded stacked bars and rich tooltips. In an online study investigating system accuracy and subjective aspects with a structural model we found that, when users actively interacted with all its control features, the hybrid system outperformed a baseline content-based-only tool and users were more satisfied.

Author Keywords
exploratory search; social search; information filtering; preference elicitation, hybrid ranking

INTRODUCTION
Learning and investigative tasks entail a combination of querying and browsing actions occurring as part of a dynamic process often called exploratory search [27]. Acquiring knowledge about a new topic is rarely fulfilled with a single query. Conversely, each bit of new knowledge triggers changes in information needs. In other words, learning is the result of a discovery cycle of several queries intermingled with the analysis of retrieved resources, where facts from a large volume of information fall in a conceptual representation [33].

IUI'18, March 7–11, 2018, Tokyo, Japan

DOI: https://doi.org/10.1145/3172944.3172986

It has been long acknowledged that exploratory search process can benefit from the "collective wisdom" of many people who can explicitly or implicitly collaborate in the search process [32]. Yet, almost all work on collaborative exploratory search focuses on explicit synchronous collaboration context [32, 41], with almost no studies of exploratory search interfaces based on "implicit collaboration" where future users can leverage information left by past users of information systems. This forms a sharp contrast with general stream of research on information retrieval where "implicit collaboration" known also as social search [16, 4] has emerged into a broad stream of research. In this paper we attempt to bridge this gap by investigating the value of two social search approaches (one based on the use of social tags and another on collaborative user matching) in the context of exploratory search.

Our approach to support social exploratory search is to allow the user to filter documents by controlling the influence of search terms, as well to fuse traditional query-based document relevance with relevance produced by two "social" sources. To visualize this multi-source relevance, our interface uses visual cues to augment the ranked list, whereby relevance is not represented as a single score, but instead as the contribution of multiple dimensions, i.e. search terms and social sources. Intuitively, adding on control and transparency at multiple levels could possibly turn out into an overly complex system. Hence, our interest is to unveil whether interacting with a social exploratory search system based on multi-source relevance, like the one here proposed, can yield measurable benefits for users conducting exploratory search, in contrast to other simpler (but still interactive) systems.

In summary, the contributions of this paper are: (i) an interactive exploratory search system, with a user interface designed to maximize transparency and controllability at multiple dimensions (search terms and relevance sources); (ii) a hybrid social ranking algorithm that accounts for fast changes in user needs and produces decomposable scores to facilitate representations in the UI; and (iii) a user study revealing that active users that control the system obtain more accurate results, are able to appreciate transparency features and are more satisfied.

RELATED WORK

Exploratory Search
Information seeking is a widely studied phenomenon [36, 20], as finding and organizing pieces of information occupies a

large portion of our daily productive time. Information retrieval (IR) systems have grown as the preferred solution for contextualized search due to their ability to narrow down the number of entries to be inspected at a time. However, this kind of system requires precise user-generated queries. As the user learns about certain topic, queries have to be iteratively reformulated to express evolving information needs. Formulating queries has proven to be more complicated for humans than plainly recognizing information in a visual manner [20], which is why the combination of IR with HCI techniques has led towards a shift in the way users search. Browsing search strategies, which rely on on-the-fly selections, navigation and trial-and-error, are associated with the term that Marchionini et al. [27] coined "exploratory search". By definition, exploratory search is open-ended, i.e. the user starts the search with some initial query in mind and discovers the next query terms along the way, as she finds and scrapes new information.

Over the last decades, several approaches attempted to foster deeper exploration and sensemaking of search results or large document collections. Ranked lists have prevailed as the paradigm for presenting results, due to their familiar format and because users know where to start inspecting items. Although ranked lists alone are regarded as opaque and underinformative [19], Shani et al. [35] suggest that: (i) explaining relevance scores encourages users to explore beyond the first two results, and (ii) users prefer bars over numbers or the absence of graphical explanations. In addition, the use of visualizations has been favored due to their capacity to convey document relevance by exploiting pre-attentive patterns. For example, tile bars [19] encode relative frequency of query terms with compact shaded blocks, whereas other approaches complement lists with visual metaphors [29], similarity-preserving layouts [17] or POI-based visualizations [30].

The trend in modern search systems seems to go in the direction of highly interactive UIs supported by ever-growing artificial intelligence methods. A few examples include task models [3], categorized overviews [39], adaptive visualizations [1] and intention modeling [34]. In this context, our work follows a recent trend in the area of interactive UIs for exploratory search, which extends the popular faceted search approach [40] to a context with no hierarchical metadata. In this group of UIs, the original query is used to produce not only a list of results, but also a list of most important information entities covered by the retrieved results - from simple unigrams [12, 22] to named entities [2] and user-specified keywords [34]. These entities uncover the *aboutness* of the results and serve as interactors for further exploration of the generated ranked list.

More specifically about the uRank interactive ranking approach [12], we replicate features which allow the user to manipulate the weights of the selected entities to adjust the original ranking to their emerging needs. This system extracts keywords from titles and abstracts and displays them in the UI as interactors. As the user selects (or types) keywords of interest, a document ranking visualization is re-sorted in real-time, thus promoting a *search-by-browsing* information access paradigm. di Sciascio et al. found that search-by-browsing supported by this kind of adaptive system incurs in lower cognitive load without hindering user performance, compared to conventional list-based UIs [13].

After several users have conducted exploratory search with a system, they leave traces behind that provide hints as to what combinations of terms were fruitful in their searches, or which documents were preferred by users with similar information needs. This kind of traces are the means to support future users, by complementing exploratory search with social wisdom.

Social Search & Interactive Fusion of Relevance Sources

Social search is the common name for a group of information retrieval approaches that use traces left by past users of information systems to help future users in the search process [16, 15]. The traces of past users can be obtained from multiple sources, such as search logs, social tagging systems, Web site logs, and various social media systems. In turn, this information could be obtained to assist users in different stages of their search including query formulation [6], matching and ranking of results [7], and augmentation of results [4]. The most popular target of social search techniques is ranking of search results. The idea of social ranking is to combine traditional content-based relevance of search results with relevance measures obtained from social sources. For example, documents that are frequently selected in response to similar queries as well as results that have been recognized by target users by bookmarking, tweeting, or other kinds of sharing in social systems have high social relevance and have to be promoted in the list of search results. Traditionally, the fusion of content-based and social relevance is done automatically by learning the weights of different sources using learning-to-rank or similar data-driven approaches [23]. The automatic fusion, however, does not fit well to the nature of exploratory search where the user might want to decide to what extent social information should be considered to rank results of a particular query. In our paper, we suggest an interactive controllable fusion of content-based and social relevance judgment and present an interface that allows users to control this fusion in a way that is consistent with modern information exploration interfaces.

Interactive fusion of relevance sources is not an entirely new topic in the field of information access and intelligent interfaces. Most research on this topic, however, has been performed in the area of hybrid recommender systems (RS) [9]. In the context of so-called parallel hybridization, a RS has to fuse relevance judgment obtained from difference sources or approaches. Just like in the case of social search, the traditional approach to source fusion in hybrid systems is automatic, where the influence of each component is determined using some machine learning approach and stays the same. This, however, does not allow for accommodating to real-life context where the importance of each source could depend on the varying user needs. For example, a movie recommendation could be a hybrid of personal collaborative filtering and social recommendation collected through social connections. When watching alone, a user may put more emphasis on the personal part, while when selecting a movie to watch with friends, the social part should be more valuable. User-controlled source fusion is considered to be a part of a broader stream of work

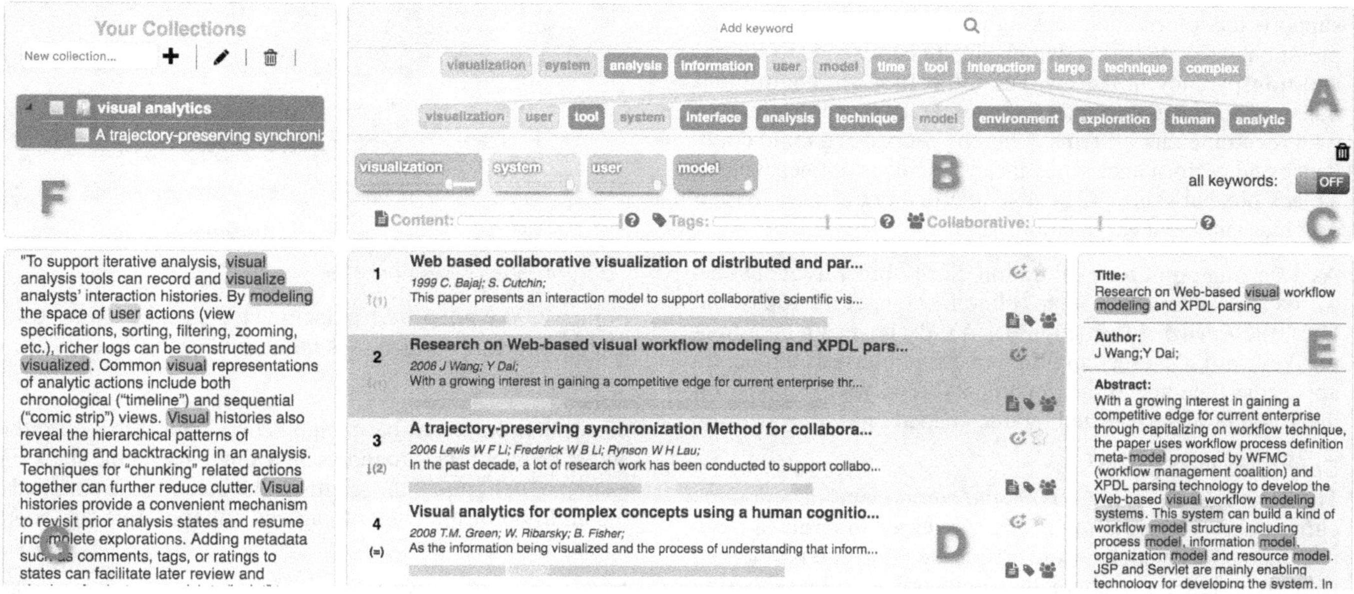

Figure 1: The UI of the social exploratory search system provides features to control a hybrid ranking model and graphic explanations of the information source provenance.

on controllability for RS. A range of user studies on interactive and controllable RS indicates that when users are given the chance, they do make use of their ability to control the system [14] and are more satisfied [8]. For example, *TasteWeights* [8] generates music recommendations from multiple sources and presents them in a visually rich interface that allows the user to interactively change the contribution of each individual source to the ranked list. *SetFusion* [31] allows to control the contribution of three sources in a hybrid RS for research talks and indicates which sources were used to recommend each item with color-coding. For further details, He et al. [18] elaborated a comprehensive survey of interactive RS, including visualization, presentation and interaction aspects.

Within the area of information retrieval, the idea of interactive fusion attracted much less attention, since the presence of several independent relevance sources is less typical. Also, extensive exploration with an interactive source-fusion interface is not natural in most search contexts. One exception is the work on personalized search, whereby each search result has two relevance scores - relevance to the query and to the user profile. Traditionally, personalized search systems perform automatic fusion of query-based and profile-based relevance rating to offer personalized ranking [28]. However, Ahn et al. [3] demonstrated that allowing users to choose how to combine these two ratings across individual queries can increase all performance aspects.

Social exploratory search offers an excellent opportunity to apply interactive fusion of relevance sources outside of the typical recommendation context. On one hand, the social search approach provides several relevance sources beyond regular query-based relevance (each type of socially collected information could be used for independent relevance ranking). On the other hand, the context of exploratory search makes interactive exploration of results with user involvement into ranking quite natural. In this paper we investigate the value of user-controllable ranking to combine a traditional query-based relevance with two "social" relevance sources - one based on user-approved tags, and one based on collaborative matching between the current and past users. The next sections describe control and transparency features implemented in the UI and the ranking model supporting the user task.

SYSTEM OVERVIEW

In order to blend exploratory and social search, we replicate features of an adaptive system designed for exploratory search (ES) of textual documents [13]. The basic system promotes a search-by-browsing information access paradigm, using keywords extracted form search results as interactors to refine a document ranking upon evolving information needs.

As the user interact with extracted keywords and bookmarks resources, our system can learn about the importance of certain keywords and their connection to documents. As a result, the social-enhanced ES system incorporates collaborative and tag-based filtering methods into a hybrid ranking model, whereby (i) tagging data used for training purposes is implicitly generated from bookmarking behavior, and (ii) the interface allows the user to weigh the fusion between content information and *social wisdom* in the resulting ranking. In the remainder of this section we briefly describe the features of the user interface (Section 3.1) and the elements of the system that enable social search functionalities alongside exploratory search.

The User Interface

Exploratory search is often motivated by a complex information problem where the user has little understanding of terminology or information space structure [38]. Our tool supports the information seeking process with features for exploration and explanation, which largely correspond to control and transparency in the UI. The motivation for control and transparency features comes from research on user experience with recommender systems, whereby users can gain in confidence and performance when the system does not behave like a black box but is instead flexible to users' preferences [8] and provides sufficient explanations [21].

As a starting point for exploration, the 12 most frequent keywords appear arranged in an inline fashion, at the top of the UI in the *Keyword Box* (Figure 1.A). By hovering on a first-row keyword, the user can discover other keywords frequently appearing together in the documents' text, which appear on the second row (connected by tree-shaped links).

Controlling the System

The *Query Box* (Figure 1.B) is the component that captures current user's information needs, expressed in terms of iterative interactions with keywords. Possible interactions inherited from the original system include keyword addition (either by selection ot manually typing), deletion and weighting. We extended these options with filtering functionalities, so that users can also: (i) filter individual keywords, so that bearing documents remain in focus and the rest are dimmed (▼ button visible on mouse over); and (ii) enable the "all keywords" filter (toggle button on the right side of the *Query Box*). The latter switches to a strict bearing criterion (from "or" to "and"), so that the ranking includes only documents where all selected keywords appear in the text.

The main addition in the UI is the possibility for the user to tell the hybrid model the desired impact of content-based and social relevance in the ranking. Sliders in Figure 1.C adjust the weights of the three methods in the hybrid ranking model:

- Content: It ranks documents based on terms contained in their titles and abstracts
- Tags: based on selected keywords matching tags associated to documents by bookmarking actions of past users.
- Collaborative: brings documents previously bookmarked by other users with similar interests.

Transparency in the UI

A highly controllable UI could be cumbersome if users cannot perceive the effect of their actions. Therefore, we rely on graphical explanations to convey system decisions and mitigate the complexity of multiple control features. Taking into account that the tool allows for tuning both keywords and model parameters, we had limited options for the use of color to convey score contributions. We decided to use a categorical color palette to represent keywords and thus maximize the amount of information encoded with color. Color-coded keywords are visual cues that pop out from their surroundings, enabling the user to pre-attentively recognize them in the text and perceive their general context prior to conscious reading.

Color-coded stacked bars embedded in the *Document Ranking* (Figure 1.D) indicate document scores. The overall width is the total score, while single bars in the stack denote individual keyword contributions. This means that the score produced by each method in the ranking model is broken down into its

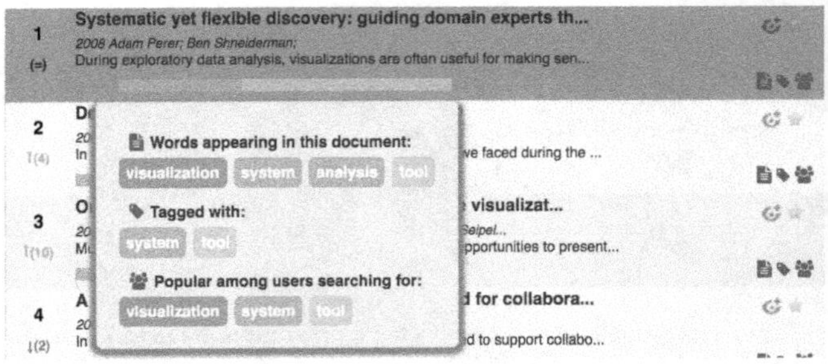

Figure 2: Hovering over a document's stacked bars shows a tooltip informing which tags influenced each RS.

constituent keyword-based sub-scores. Sub-scores are then added keyword-wise to represent a single bar in the stack. For example, in Figure 2 the length of the green bar is obtained as the addition of the content, tag and collaborative sub-scores for the keyword "tool".

In turn, icon hints at the bottom-right corner of individual items in the *Document Ranking* reveal at a glance which methods ranked a given document. The icons match the labels in the model parameter controls (Figure 1.C). Visualizing the overlap between keywords and information source is possible by hovering over the stacked bars. The tooltip in Figure 2 explains which keywords appear in the document, which ones have been used to tag the document and which ones are popular among users with similar interests.

When the user clicks on a list item, the *DocumentInfo Panel* displays the available text and metadata information for the selected document. Terms matching selected keywords in the *Query Box* are highlighted in matching colors, enabling the user to readily spot them in the text prior to conscious reading. The same principle is applied for the notepad in Figure 1.G. As the user saves a document into a collection, this piece of text is augmented with colored terms, highlighting the parts of the text related to bookmarked resources.

Generating Tagging Data

Text-mining or topic-modeling methods generate machine-based content descriptions, often referred to as keywords or key phrases (in the case of unigrams and n-grams, respectively). Conversely, tags are regarded as human-generated descriptors given by one or more users. Social tagging data is the space where relationships between users, resources and tags are captured. Unlike a typical social tagging system that serves as a platform for users to tag resources, our system is designed for users to search and explore documents. Hence, our approach to incorporate social information does not work with social tagging data in the strict sense, as users do not explicitly assign tags to documents at any time. Instead, we leverage bookmarking behavior to infer human-approved content descriptors, which we treat as (so-called) tags, i.e. tags are not generated but rather approved by humans.

As the user explores search results by selecting extracted keywords from the *Keyword Box*, they save relevant documents along the way as bookmarks. Bookmarking actions provide useful information in a twofold manner: *i)* the user establishes an explicit preference for a given document, and *ii)* the user implicitly considers that the document is relevant for their current information needs, which are expressed by the selected terms present in the *Query Box* at the moment of the bookmark event. We can assume that a user regards the currently selected terms as good content descriptors for the bookmarked document, and hence refer to them as tags in our tagging space. One reason to treat human-approved content descriptors as tags is that humans largely tend to generate keyphrases that already appear in the text [11]. For clarification, in the remainder of this paper we refer to keywords or terms as automatically extracted unigrams, and recall tags as terms used to implicitly tag bookmarked documents. Therefore, a document is tagged with *tags* $t_1, \cdots, t_n$ if a user bookmarks the document after selecting a set of *terms* $t_1, \cdots, t_n$ in the UI.

Formally, B is the set of all bookmarks, where a single bookmark is represented by a tuple of the form $(u,d,Q) \in B$. Thus, a bookmark entry denotes that user u saved a document d and implicitly tagged it with selected terms $Q = \{t_1, \cdots, t_n\}$. Hereby, we define the folksonomy $\mathcal{F} = \langle U, D, T, A \rangle$, where U is the set of all users, D the set of all documents, T the set of all tags and A (Formula 1) is a function mapping a bookmark $b \in B$ into a set of $|Q|$ triples of the three entity types, (u,d,t).

$$A = \{ \ (u,d,t) \mid u \in U, \ d \in D, \ t \in Q \subseteq T, \ \exists \ (u,d,Q) \in B \ \} \tag{1}$$

Triples mapped by A conform the tagging space that represents ternary relationships between users, documents and tags. We break down ternary relationships into the following 3 matrices:

- $R \in \mathbb{N}^{|U| \times |D|}$ is similar to the user-item matrix employed in CF. Unlike rating data, where values typically range from 1 to 5, in this context user preference for an item is binary, thus $r_{u,d} = 1$ if user u bookmarked document d, 0 otherwise.
- $P \in \mathbb{N}^{|D| \times |T|}$ is the document-tag matrix, such that the ith row represents the profile vector for the ith document, in terms of tags associated to it at the moment it was bookmarked.
- $M \in \mathbb{N}^{|U| \times |T|}$ is the user-tag matrix, such that $m_{u,t}$ indicates the number of documents bookmarked by user u after selecting term t (and implicitly using t as a tag).

In a nutshell, we extract explicit and implicit information contained in bookmarking behavior to generate tagging data, which is then employed to train the social-based ranking methods described in the next section.

Ranking Model

As user u adds a set of terms $Q = \{t_1, \cdots t_n\}$ to the *Query Box*, the system computes independent document scores with three different models and ranks them according to an overall hybrid score. The content-based model produces scores based on textual information from documents' titles and abstracts. This is the ranking method in the original system. The tag-based and collaborative models are incorporated to extend the original system and support social exploratory search. In this section we describe the three models and the hybridization of the final score. Interaction and presentation factors steered the design and implementation of these methods, namely:

1. For the system to adapt to sudden changes in information needs and provide a sense of real-time response, each method has to compute new document scores on-demand.
2. Then for presentation purposes, they should generate decomposable scores that can be graphically explained, i.e. calculate separate scores for each selected term $t \in Q$.

Content-based (CB)

CB ranks documents by the relative frequency at which the selected tags (keywords) appear in titles and abstracts. We build a vector space model and compute document-query similarity as the weighted cosine similarity (Formula 2).

$$s_{cb}(d,Q) = \frac{1}{|Q|} \sum_{t \in Q} \frac{tfidf(t,d) \ \cdot \ w_{u,t} \cdot \Gamma(d,Q)}{\| \ d \ \| \cdot \| \ Q \ \|} \tag{2}$$

, where $tfidf(t,d)$ is the tf-idf score for term t in document d, $w_{u,t}$ is the weight assigned to term t by user u in the UI, while $|| \ d \ ||$ and $|| \ Q \ ||$ are the Euclidean norms for vectors d and Q, respectively. Lastly, $\Gamma(d,Q) = exp(\alpha \ (|d \cap Q| - |Q|))$ is a decay function that penalizes documents not containing all selected keywords. We set the α parameter to 0.25 to soften the decay rate.

Tag-based (TB)

This model measures the strength between the target user's selected terms Q and a document d in the social tagging space. In other words, the model expresses to what extent terms Q are good content descriptors of d from the perspective of other users that bookmarked (and implicitly tagged) d in the past.

Given the document-tag matrix P, the similarity between term t and document d, $sim(t,d)$ is computed as the conditional probability of d to be bookmarked given t, which in Formula 3 is represented as the ratio between the tagging frequency of d under t and the tagging frequency for t across all documents. s_{tb} is then the probability of t and d occurring together, i.e. $p(t) \cdot p(d \mid t) = p(t \cap d)$.

$$s_{tb}(u,d,Q) = \sum_{t \in Q} w_{u,t} \cdot \frac{p_{t,d}}{\sum\limits_{d' \in D} p_{t,d'}} \tag{3}$$

User-based (UB)

The nature of this model resembles that of a collaborative filtering recommender, except that traditional CF was conceived to learn a model from rating data, whereas ratings in the case of bookmarks is binary. i.e. a document is either bookmarked or not. The UB model estimates the likelihood for a document d to be bookmarked by target user u based on the strength between u's neighborhood V and d. Since u's tag preferences are frequently updated through the UI, similarity between two users is in this case agnostic of u's past search interests. Instead, v is similar to u if v has bookmarked any document with selected terms Q in the past.

Given the user-tag matrix M, we calculate the similarity between u and v as the weighted ratio between the times v used t and the total times t was used by any user to bookmark any document, as denoted in Formula 4.

$$sim(u,v) = \sum_{t \in Q} w_{u,t} \cdot \frac{m_{v,t}}{\sum_{v' \in V} m_{v',t}} \quad (4)$$

The neighborhood for u, V is formed as the union set of the neighborhood for each $t \in Q$, V_t (Formula 5), such that, V_t is the set of users that implicitly tagged any document with term t. V is then trimmed to the k top neighbors ($k = 10$ by default).

$$V = \bigcup_{t \in Q} V_t \mid v \in V_t \; if \; m^{\intercal}_{t,v} > 0 \quad (5)$$

The user-item matrix R is extended into $\tilde{R} \in \mathbb{R}^{|U| \times |D|}$, such that the preference of user v for document d is 1 if v bookmarked d, $sim_J(v,d)$ otherwise, where $sim_J(v,d)$ is the Jaccard coefficient between v's user profile and the d's document vector. The final s_{ub} score is obtained as shown in Formula 6 by averaging the product of user-neighbor and neighbor-document similarities across all neighbors in V.

$$s_{ub}(u,Q,d) = \frac{1}{|V|} \sum_{v \in V} sim(u,v) \cdot r_{v,d} \quad (6)$$

Hybrid Overall Score

Relative ranking weights can be interactively adjusted in the $[0,1]$ range and are represented by vector W. W is balanced with the softmax function, so that $\sum_{i \in |W|} W_i = 1$. The outputs of the three models are first min-max normalized to avoid that higher scores from one method undermine the contribution of the others. Then, the hybrid score for d is the linear combination shown in Formula 7, where $\hat{s}_{cb}$, $\hat{s}_{tb}$ and $\hat{s}_{ub}$ are the normalized values for the corresponding scores.

$$s(u,Q,d) = W_{cb}\,\hat{s}_{cb}(d,Q) + W_{tb}\,\hat{s}_{tb}(u,d,Q) + W_{ub}\,\hat{s}_{ub}(u,d,Q) \quad (7)$$

To allow for explanations of individual keyword contributions, all methods calculate separate scores for each $t \in Q$, which are then fused and represented as color-coded bars in the UI. In the next section we analyze objective and subjective implications of fusing the three sources of relevance.

USER STUDY

We conducted an online user study to assess the worth of *user-controllable social exploratory search* (SES) in contrast to pure ES. Note that we do not aim to compare SES against basic systems without support for exploration. Instead we assess social exploratory search when users are aware and able to control it, compared to an ES system that already outperforms a traditional list-based UI (c.f., [13]). While developing the hybrid tool with numerous controllable and explanatory features, we expected these additions to positively influence system accuracy and user experience. However, the complexity of the UI could result in a system that is too difficult to use and understand. In this study we address such concerns in detail.

Evaluation Methodology

The study used a between-subject design with conditions ES and SES. As the social search system requires training data to produce document scores, we split the study execution in two stages: (i) with baseline ES condition, (ii) with hybrid SES condition, after training social models with bookmarks collected in (i). Participants of both conditions performed the same task. Figure 3 illustrates the sequence of executed steps.

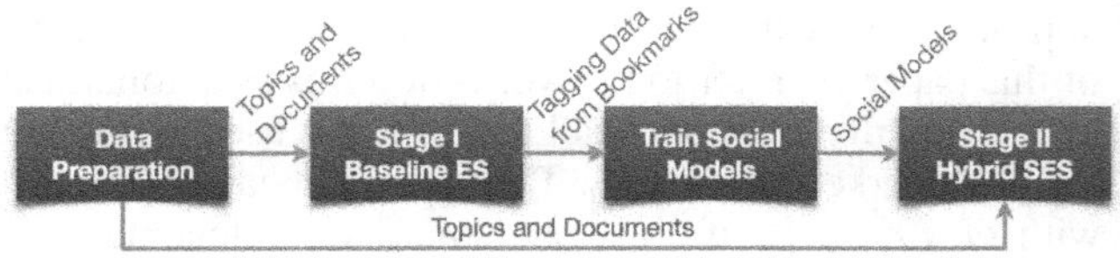

Figure 3: Stages in User Study

Baseline System

For the ES condition, we opted for a system that already supports exploratory search, but lacks social search capabilities. We used the base version of our system with the ranking computed solely on the CB model. The interface in ES resembles that of the hybrid system, as shown in Figure 4, except for the absence of sliders to control the hybrid model and explanatory hints and tooltip described in Section 3.1.2. As a result the baseline system includes most features of the hybrid system, but is inherently less complex. In other words, the user only needs to care about selecting keywords to refine information needs, without concerning about model parameters.

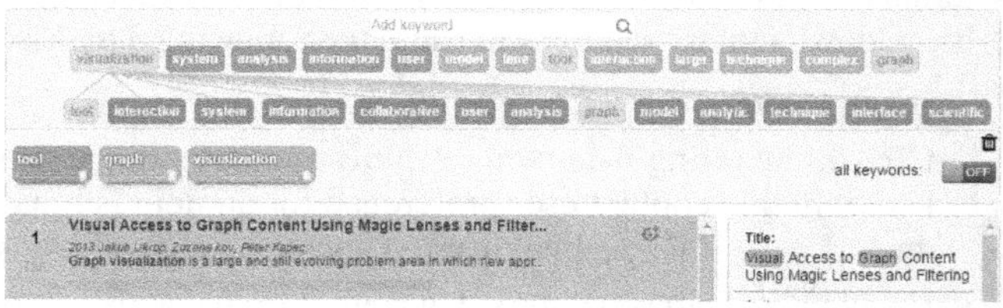

Figure 4: UI of baseline system employed in the user study. Documents are ranked solely by the CB method.

Data Preparation

The need to collect training data imposed a constraint on the number of topics used in the study. Therefore we chose 5 topics from the Computer Science field: *Augmented Reality*, *Visual Analytics*, *Recommender Systems*, *Deep Learning* and *Human-Computer Interaction*. With the help of three researchers with experience in the chosen topics, we prepared topic descriptions by selecting 2 or 3 paragraphs from known literature and removed all references from the text. We then generated datasets with a script that performed several queries to Mendeley's API[1] and manually added other documents suggested by the experts. Each dataset contained over 800 document surrogates.

After the first stage concluded, we had collected 1395 bookmarks. We further enlarged the training pool by asking the experts to perform the same tasks as regular participants, though without filling the survey. Before starting the second stage,

[1] http://dev.mendeley.com/

we trained the tag- and user-based models with the generated tagging data.

Task and Procedure

First, participants completed a step-by-step tutorial introducing the main features of the system. They had to perform interactions, e.g. keyword selection and weighting, adjusting ranking model parameters, bookmarking and collection management. The tutorial also covered explanatory features such as color-coded bars and ranking-type icons (in hybrid UI).

After the tutorial, participants were presented with a view prompting them to sort the five topics by familiarity. The least familiar topic (i.e. at the bottom) was automatically picked. The task consisted in organizing and collecting resources for the given topic. We asked participants to imagine they had to write an essay about the assigned topic. We provided the corresponding topic description, which served as the introduction section. Participants had to read it and find relevant concepts that helped them define subsequent sections of the fictitious essay. Then they had to work with the assigned tool and find relevant documents for each section. To fulfill the task, participants had to create at least 3 collections (one per section) and bookmark at least 5 documents per collection, i.e. at least 15 in total. Upon completion, the participant had to click on "Done" and fill a survey for subjective feedback.

Participants

We recruited participants through the crowd-sourced platform Prolific[2] and from mailing lists of colleagues in the field. In the case of Prolific, the eligibility requirement was that candidates had to hold at least a Bachelor degree in Computer Science. Since the tasks required dealing with scientific content, it was crucial to address users with the appropriate background. As for the field of expertise, the intention was to match the topics covered in the prepared datasets. A total of 79 people took part in the study, from which 43 worked with the baseline system and the remaining 36 with the hybrid UI. 10 participants were recruited via e-mail, while the other 69 completed the study on Prolific. Demographic information is summarized as follows:

- *Age*: 1 $[<20]$ years old, 66 $[20-29]$, 12 $[30-39]$.
- *Gender*: 62 male, 17 female.
- *Country of birth*: India (18), USA (15), UK (9), other (37).
- *Highest level of education*: 39 Bachelor (BSc), 23 Master (MSc or similar), 17 other.
- *Proficiency in English language*: 6 basic, 9 intermediate, 30 advanced, 34 native speaker.
- *Familiarity with search interfaces, e.g. Google* ($-3=$not at all familiar, $3=$very familiar): $mean = 2.65$, $sd = 0.78$.

Measurements

User Behavior. The two systems collected action logs for keyword manipulations, document clicks, bookmarks (and their position in the list). For the hybrid tool, we also logged manipulations of model parameter sliders.

System Accuracy. We computed *Discounted Cumulative Gain* (*DCG*) for each document d, defined as $DCG_d = \frac{2^{rel_d}-1}{\log(rank_d+1)}$. rel_d can take either 1 (if bookmarked) or 0 (otherwise). The final score per user, *aDCG*, was obtained by averaging *DCG* across all bookmarks performed by the user.

UX Scale for Subjective Feedback. We created a user experience (UX) scale adjusted to our task scenario, instead of using a standard but too generic questionnaire, e.g. SUS. Latent constructs, e.g. "satisfaction", cannot be directly measured and are instead inferred from a number of observed indicators, e.g. survey questions. The survey comprised 28 questions covering different UX dimensions. Answers were recorded on a 7-point Likert scale (-3 = strongly disagree, 3 = strongly agree), with some questions worded in negative tone (reverted for the analysis). We therefore built the model shown in Figure 5 in a two-step approach [5]: first we fitted a measurement model (to calculate factor loadings) and then a structural model (measurement model plus causal relationships, see Section 4.1.6). UX concepts and directionality of causal effects are partly grounded on the framework proposed by Knijnenburg et al. [26] to model the user experience with recommender systems.

We first planned for 5 latent constructs: 3 subjective system aspects (*SSA*) (perceived control, transparency and result quality) and 2 experience (*EXP*) (choice satisfaction and satisfaction with the system). "Choice satisfaction" and "satisfaction with the system" had poor discriminant validity (inter-factor correlation = .97), which means that users did not distinguish them from one another and perceived the two constructs as the same one. Since they both measure "satisfaction" aspects, we merged them into a single factor[3] and named it as such. In total 8 survey items were excluded from the analysis due to low communality or high cross-loading. In particular, all 4 items for "perceived result quality" had to be excluded as 2 of them had low communality[4]. The final three factors listed below showed good convergent validity (*AVE*), internal consistency reliability (Cronbach's α)[5] and discriminant validity[6].

- *Perceived Control* (SSA) ($AVE = .62$, $\alpha = .82$): 3 items, e.g. "The system allowed me to easily refine my search terms".
- *Perceived Transparency* (SSA) ($AVE = .62$, $\alpha = .82$) 3 items, e.g. "The system gave me a sense of transparency".
- *Satisfaction* (EXP) ($AVE = .59$, $\alpha = .93$) 9 items, e.g. "I'm satisfied with the documents I bookmarked", "I see a potential benefit in using the system for research tasks".
- The item "Are you familiar with search user interfaces?" is a single personal characteristic (PC) observed indicator.

Confirmatory factor analysis with a mean- and variance-adjusted weighted least squares estimator yielded admissible model fit[7], $\chi^2(87) = 105.68$, $p = .08$; $CFI = .994$; $TLI = .993$; $RMSEA = .051$ with $90\%CI = [0, .083]$.

[2] www.prolific.ac

[3] In practice, some respecification of the measurement model is necessary. It is acceptable as long as it is not grounded in statistical considerations alone but in conjunction with theory and content [5].

[4] Using less than 3 indicators per factor is not advisable

[5] $AVE > .5$ shows convergent validity. $\alpha > .8$ is good, $> .9$ excellent

[6] Inter-factor correlations should be $< .85$

[7] χ^2 test should be non-significant. Acceptable cut-off values: $CFI > .96$, $TLI > .95$, $RMSEA < .05$ with $90\%CI$ upper-bound $< .10$

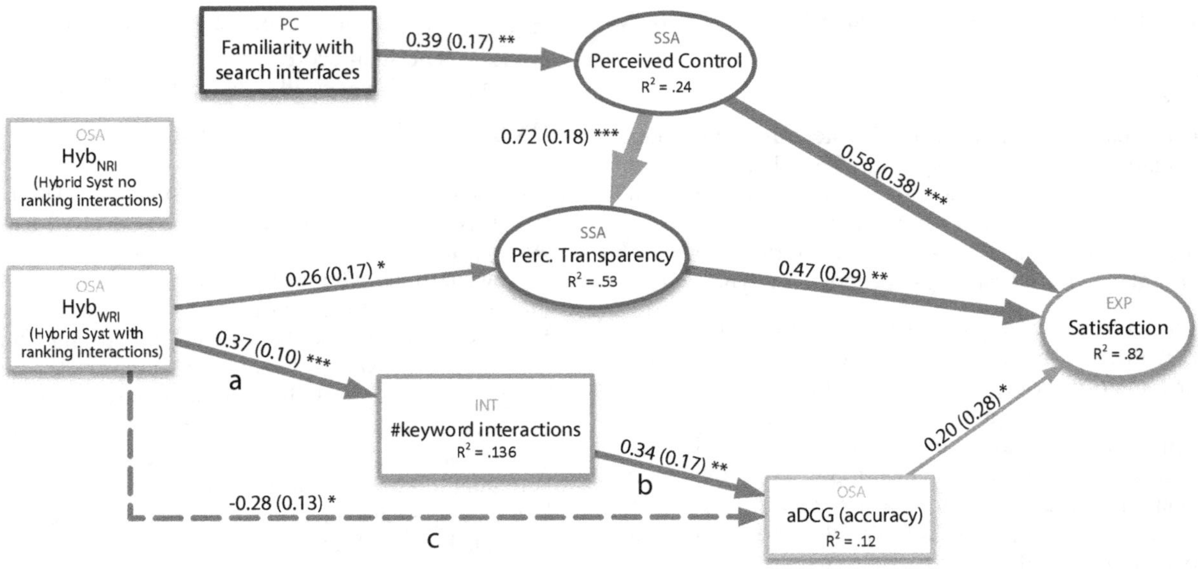

Figure 5: Structural model of system accuracy and user experience. Model Elements: Objective (*OSA*) and Subjective System Aspects (*SSA*), Personal Characteristics (*PC*), Interactions (*INT*) and Experience (*EXP*). Pathways represent significant causal relationships, with numbers and thickness indicating regression coefficients (with robust SE). Factors are scaled with variances set to 1. Full standardized solution is reported , i.e. path coefficients indicate increments in SD units. Full (dashed) lines indicate significant positive (negative) coefficients. Significance: *** $p < .001$, ** $p < .01$, * $p < .05$.

Hypotheses in Structural Model

Intuitively, the hybrid system requires several fine-tuning actions to adjust for user information needs accordingly. We then expected to observe differences in system performance and user satisfaction when users actively controlled the system via keyword interactions (*#kw.int* for short) and weighing of model parameters. Also, the only difference in control features between the two systems is the absence of model weight sliders in the baseline. Clearly, only those participants that manipulated the ranking weights in the hybrid tool were able to "appreciate" any difference with respect to the baseline (not consciously though due to the between-subject setup).

Consequently, we split participants of the hybrid system into 2 sub-groups: participants that performed at least one interaction with the ranking model, or "ranking interactions" for short, (Hyb_{WRI}, $N = 22$) and those that did not (Hyb_{NRI}, $N = 14$). Participants in the first group accumulated 5.05 ranking interactions on average ($sd = 5.19$, 17 of them with more than one). The two sub-groups represent manipulated variations, noted as objective system aspects (*OSA*) in the model diagram. Pathways originating from these nodes indicate comparisons *against the baseline* ($N = 43$). We then built the structural model in Figure 5 based on the following hypotheses:

H1: The hybrid system will be significantly more accurate than the baseline (*OSA*). As we highlighted the importance of interactions for the system to understand user needs and thus be more accurate, we hypothesized higher system performance for the hybrid tool with ranking interactions, though influenced (at least to some extent) by the amount of keyword interactions ($Hyb_{WRI} \rightarrow$ *#kw.int* $\rightarrow$ *aDCG*, where *#kw.int* is an observed behavior or interaction (*INT*)).

H2: Participants will perceive higher degree of control and transparency with the hybrid system (*SSA*): The hybrid system provides features for enhanced control (model sliders in Figure 1.C) and transparency (tooltip and hint icons in Figure 2). At least users of the Hyb_{WRI} sub-group should perceive more control over the system and transparency provided by graphic explanations. Although at first we assumed that perceived result quality would mediate the effect of perceived control and transparency on satisfaction ($Perc.Control + Perc.Transp \rightarrow Perc.Res.Quality \rightarrow Satisfaction$), the fact that the latter had to be excluded from the model does not prevent us from measuring the direct effect ($Perc.Control + Perc.Transp \rightarrow Satisfaction$).

H3: Expertise will influence users' perception of the system (*PC*): Personal characteristics of a user are known to influence their experience with a system, but cannot be accounted for by the system itself [10, 25, 24]. As such, our assumption is that, regardless of the tool employed by a user, their level of familiarity with search interfaces will contribute to how controllable and transparent they perceive the system.

H4: The hybrid system will produce higher user satisfaction (*EXP*) Ultimately, we expected that objective (*OSA*) and subjective aspects (*SSA*) of the system would lead to higher user satisfaction (*EXP*). Although the direct link between system accuracy (*OSA*) and user experience (*EXP*) is often not evident or weak, Knijnenburg et al.'s framework [26] allows to model user experience as a result of how the user perceives the characteristics of the system (*OSA* $\rightarrow$ *SSA* $\rightarrow$ *EXP*).

Results

We applied structural equation modeling to analyze causal and mediated effects in behavioral and subjective data all together.

The model in Figure 5 is the cornerstone to validate our hypotheses with respect to performance and user experience. The model obtained excellent goodness-of-fit, $\chi^2(141) = 146.55$, $p = .36$, $CFI = .998$, $TLI = .998$, $RMSEA = .022$ with 90% $CI = [0, 0.058]$. Regression pathways report standardized coefficients (β) and robust standard errors.

System Performance

We found no difference in performance (*aDCG*) between the sub-group of hybrid system users with no ranking interactions and the baseline condition, $\beta = 0.06$, $SE = 0.11$, *ns* (denoted by the absence of links originating from the Hyb_{NRI} node). Conversely, when hybrid system participants interacted with ranking sliders, they performed significantly more keyword interactions (*#kw.int*), as it can be observed in the density distribution in Figure 6. In turn, more keyword interactions had a positive effect on system accuracy. Regression paths denote two types of effect of Hyb_{WRI} on *aDCG*: *(i)* a direct negative effect (path *c* in Figure 5), and *(ii)* an indirect positive effect through *#kw.int* (pathways *a* and *b*). Coefficients for indirect and direct effects with opposite signs indicate the possibility that the mediator (*#kw.int*) acts as a suppressor.

To measure the amount of mediation of Hyb_{WRI} on *aDCG* due to *#kw.int*, we first computed estimates for the indirect effect (product of *a* and *b*) and the total effect ($c + a * b$). Then we applied bootstrap[8] with 20,000 draws to obtain standard errors and 95% confidence intervals. We found a significant indirect effect, $\beta = 0.11$, $SE = 0.060$, $CI = [0.030, 0.277]$ (CI does not include 0, i.e. $p < .05$), while the total effect turned out non significant, $\beta = -0.16$, $SE = 0.106$, $CI = [-0.368, 0.051]$. A significant indirect effect that reduces the total effect to 0 indicates complete mediation. In other words, pathway *c* connecting Hyb_{WRI} with *aDCG* in Figure 5 is broken, and thus the entire effect of the independent variable (Hyb_{WRI}) on the dependent variable (*aDCG*) is transmitted through the mediator (*#kw.int*). This evidence supports **H1**.

Considering the caveat of careless interactions, we corroborated that *#kw.int* correlates with overall session time ($r = .5$, $p < .001$). Participants of the hybrid system with full interactions opened more document abstracts per bookmark (0.85 vs. 0.54), although not statistically significant ($U = 400$, $p = .08$). For visual assessment, Figure 7 plots the temporal progression of *aDCG* scores (with SE intervals) for the first 15 minutes of an average session of the 3 groups (baseline, Hyb_{NRI} and Hyb_{WRI}). Mean accuracy does not differ significantly, but it remains higher for Hyb_{WRI} throughout the average session ($M = 10'39''$, $SD = 5'53''$). To sum up, the evidence suggests that the hybrid system outperforms the baseline, *provided that users actively make use of control features*, i.e. interactions with keyword tags and ranking model sliders.

Perceived Control and Transparency

Participants did not perceive a significant difference in the *level of control* between the two systems, which could be attributed to the baseline having similar features to interactively control the document ranking (except for ranking sliders). In turn, the hybrid tool with ranking interactions (Hyb_{WRI}) had a direct positive effect on users' perception of *transparency*. Although both systems convey keyword contribution to overall scores (through stacked-colored bars), only the hybrid one provides explanations about the methods used to compute the ranking. These results partially support **H2**. In short, the SES system influenced the perception of transparency but not of control. Moreover, we found no difference between the baseline and participants without ranking interactions (Hyb_{NRI}), which supports our initial assumption that the user should fully leverage control features of the hybrid system to appreciate the benefit of combining social and exploratory search.

[8]Bootstrap is a non-parametric technique based on resampling with replacement, often used for testing significance of indirect and total effects in mediation analysis [37].

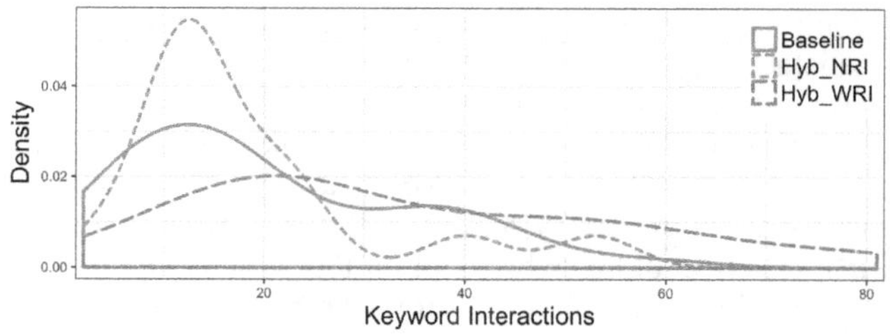

Figure 6: Density distribution of keyword interactions for the 3 groups analyzed in the user study.

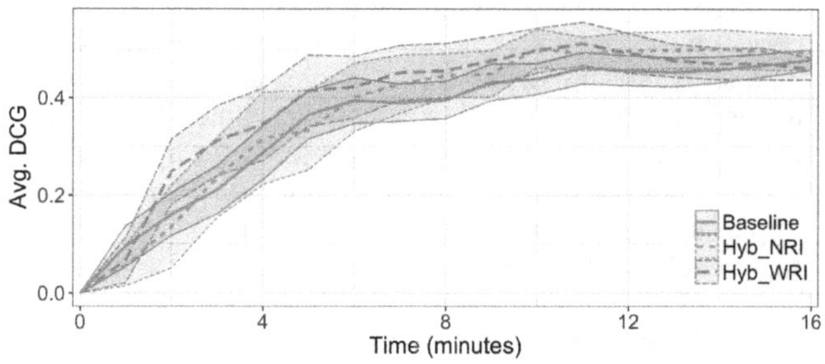

Figure 7: Temporal evolution of cumulative *aDCG*.

Expertise

Regardless of the used system, users acknowledging high familiarity with search interfaces perceived a greater level of control. It is likely the case that experienced users understood these features better, as it has been observed that users perceive more control when they understand the system [24]. The model also reveals a large effect of perceived control on transparency. More specifically, perceiving a system as transparent seems to be greatly influenced by how controllable it is regarded by the user and indirectly by their search expertise, which provides evidence supporting **H3**.

User Satisfaction

Although sometimes the effect of system accuracy cannot be directly assessed in the experience (*EXP*), but through subjective perception of system aspects [10], in this case we found evidence of a direct effect. We modeled "satisfaction" as the final output of multiple objective and subjective variables. From the statistical evidence we can corroborate that higher satisfaction is a result of not only a good-performing system but also interaction and presentation aspects in the UI. Perceived control and transparency had each a positive effect on user satisfaction. Familiarity with search interfaces contributes to user satisfaction because experienced participants felt more control over the system. This can be linked to previous findings reporting that domain experts are more satisfied when they can control the system [25]. It is important to highlight that the effect of the hybrid tool for the Hyb_{WRI} group on user satisfaction is not direct but transferable through perceived transparency (*SSA*) and system accuracy (*OSA*) (mediated by keyword interactions), thus supporting **H4**.

Discussion and Limitations

In this study we assessed system performance and user experience for a social exploratory search system contrasting it with a system supporting exploratory search alone. Allowing the user to control not only keywords (a rather familiar action for any Web user), but also parameters of a hybrid ranking model, entails a higher level of complexity. Nevertheless, an important contribution of this study is that social exploratory search achieved better system performance, as long as users exploited its full potential to refine both, keywords of interest and ranking parameters. Another key finding is that system accuracy contributed directly to higher user satisfaction.

As for perceived system traits, people who felt more in control also understood better the system's logic ($Perc.Control \rightarrow Perc.Transparency$). That is to say, the system is able to explain itself by way of interactions and visual explanations. However, the model attributes a higher perception of control to users' personal traits rather than to the incremental customization in the hybrid system. The positive effect of perceived control and transparency is directly transferred to user satisfaction. This result aligns to research in social recommender systems [8, 24], though it had not been previously analyzed in exploratory search contexts.

It is worth noting that, despite higher complexity, the hybrid system was still as engaging as the exploratory search baseline. Users in SES condition that did not adjust the hybrid model (fusion of content and social features), perceived similar levels of control and transparency, and were as satisfied as the baseline users. This is denoted by the absence of pathways originating from Hyb_{NRI} in the structural model. In other words, the extra complexity was not detrimental to user experience. We expect that novice users would be able to learn to exploit the advanced features with better initial guidance and after spending more time (beyond a single session).

As for shortcomings, the online nature of our study is at the same time an advantage and a limitation. On one hand, we believe the physical presence of an observer can lead to (intuitively positive) opinion bias. Moreover, through the crowdsourced platform we managed to recruit more participants than we would have been able in a controlled in-lab study. On the other hand, we lacked the opportunity to make our own observations and interview the participants. The participants' background in Computer Science can also be considered a limitation, arguably unavoidable since the social and collaborative models needed as much training data as possible on related topics. Generalizing to all backgrounds is not trivial but from our past experience with students from life sciences [13] and the influence of experience with search interfaces, we expect that any user habituated to research tasks should be able to understand the system after some trial and error.

Finally, we need to acknowledge that the proposed model is one among infinite possibilities. This limitation is extrinsic and in general extends to the structural equation modeling methodology. Our hypotheses, although grounded in existing theories and common sense, reflect our own conceptualization of the user experience in a specific context. Thus, we do not claim that our model is absolute but a valid alternative.

CONCLUSIONS AND FUTURE WORK

In this paper we introduced an user-controlled approach for social exploratory search. Exploratory search was extended with social search capabilities by leveraging information left by past users, in this case bookmarking behavior. In turn, control and transparency, important features in recommender systems but less exploited in exploratory search systems, allowed for fusing the social component in a consistent way. On one hand, the user is empowered to shape their information needs and decide to what extent social information should be taken into account and, on the other hand, the system effectively communicates the effect of the user's decisions.

An empirical user study reported evidence of the benefits of user-controllable fusion of content-based and social components of exploratory search (in the form of a hybrid interactive system). More specifically, the proposed structural model suggests that social exploratory search produces more accurate results, as long as the user actively "tells" the system how their information needs evolve and the right blend of content and social information. In turn, the system was perceived as transparent due to explanatory nature of the UI. Conversely, the perception of control is mostly attributed to the users' own traits rather than differences among the two systems. Together, system accuracy and perceived control and transparency promoted higher user satisfaction.

Based on this evidence, the challenge for the near future is to further exploit the interactive features to learn task models and improve ranking accuracy. An open question is whether simpler or fewer features would produce similar results in system performance and user experience. More importantly, our next goal is to investigate whether an adaptive system that personalizes the amount of advanced features exposed to a particular user (based on expertise and background) has similar effects to the ones observed in this work. Moreover, a longitudinal evaluation is necessary to validate the observed results in a more realistic context, for example with students performing search-to-learn activities with technology-enhanced learning systems or intelligent tutors.

ACKNOWLEDGMENTS

The first author was funded by the Austrian Marshall Plan Foundation. This work is supported by the European Union's Horizon 2020 Research and Innovation Programme (INSO-4-2015), MOVING project under Grant No. 693092. Know-Center GmbH is funded by the Austrian COMET Program – managed by the Austrian Research Promotion Agency (FFG). We also thank David Strohmaier for his implementation effort.

REFERENCES

1. J-w. Ahn and P. Brusilovsky. 2013. Adaptive visualization for exploratory information retrieval. *Inf. Process. Manag.* 49, 5 (2013), 1139–1164.
2. J-w. Ahn, P. Brusilovsky, J. Grady, D. He, and R. Florian. 2010. Semantic Annotation Based Exploratory Search for Information Analysts. *Inf. Process. Manag.* 46, 4 (2010), 383–402.
3. J-w. Ahn, P. Brusilovsky, D. He, J. Grady, and Q. Li. 2008. Personalized Web Exploration with Task Models. In *Proc. WWW '08*. ACM, 1–10.
4. J-w. Ahn, R. Farzan, and P. Brusilovsky. 2006. Social search in the context of social navigation. *Journal of the Korean Society for Information Management* 23, 2 (2006), 147–165.
5. J. C. Anderson and D. W. Gerbing. 1988. Structural Equation Modeling in Practice: A Review and Recommended Two-Step Approach. *Psychological Bulletin* 103, 3 (5 1988), 411–423.
6. R. Baeza-Yates, C. Hurtado, and M. Mendoza. 2004. Query Recommendation Using Query Logs in Search Engines. In *Proc. EDBT '04*. Springer-Verlag, 588–596.
7. S. Bao, G. Xue, X. Wu, Y. Yu, B. Fei, and Z. Su. 2007. Optimizing web search using social annotations. In *Proc. WWW '07*. ACM, 501–510.
8. S. Bostandjiev, J. O'Donovan, and T. Höllerer. 2012. TasteWeights: A Visual Interactive Hybrid Recommender System. In *Proc. RecSys '12*. ACM, 35–42.
9. R. Burke. 2002. Hybrid Recommender Systems: Survey and Experiments. *User Model. User-adapt. Interact.* 12, 4 (Nov. 2002), 331–370.
10. D. N. Chin. 2001. Empirical Evaluation of User Models and User-Adapted Systems. *User Model. User-adapt. Interact.* 11, 1-2 (March 2001), 181–194.
11. J. Chuang, C. D. Manning, and J. Heer. 2012. "Without the Clutter of Unimportant Words": Descriptive Keyphrases for Text Visualization. *ACM Trans. Comput.-Hum. Interact.* 19, 3, Article 19 (Oct. 2012), 29 pages.
12. C. di Sciascio, V. Sabol, and E. E. Veas. 2015. uRank: Exploring Document Recommendations through an Interactive User-Driven Approach. In *Proc. RecSys '15 workshop IntRS*, Vol. 1438. 29–36.
13. C. di Sciascio, V. Sabol, and E. E. Veas. 2016. Rank As You Go: User-Driven Exploration of Search Results. In *Proc. IUI '16*. ACM, 118–129.
14. M. D. Ekstrand, D. Kluver, F. M. Harper, and J. A. Konstan. 2015. Letting Users Choose Recommender Algorithms : An Experimental Study. In *Proc. RecSys '15*. 11–18.
15. B. M. Evans and E. H. Chi. 2010. An elaborated model of social search. *Inf. Process. Manag.* 46, 6 (2010), 656–678.
16. J. Freyne and B. Smyth. 2004. An experiment in social search. In *Adaptive Hypermedia and Adaptive Web-Based Systems*. Springer, 95–103.
17. E. Gomez-Nieto, F. San Roman, P. Pagliosa, W. Casaca, E. S Helou, M. C. F de Oliveira, and L. G. Nonato. 2014. Similarity preserving snippet-based visualization of web search results. *IEEE Trans. Vis. Comput. Graph.* 20, 3 (2014), 457–70.
18. C. He, D. Parra, and K. Verbert. 2016. Interactive Recommender Systems. *Expert Syst. Appl.* 56, C (Sept. 2016), 9–27.
19. M. A. Hearst. 1995. TileBars: Visualization of Term Distribution Information in Full Text Information Access. In *Proc. CHI '95*. ACM Press, 59–66.
20. M. A. Hearst. 2009. *Search User Interfaces* (1st ed.). Cambridge University Press.
21. J. L. Herlocker, J. A. Konstan, and J. Riedl. 2000. Explaining collaborative filtering recommendations. In *Proc. CSCW '00*. 241–250.
22. O. Hoeber and X. D. Yang. 2008. Evaluating WordBars in exploratory Web search scenarios. *Inf. Process. Manag.* 44, 2 (2008), 485–510.
23. T. Joachims and F. Radlinski. 2007. Search Engines That Learn from Implicit Feedback. *Computer* 40, 8 (Aug. 2007), 34–40.
24. B. P. Knijnenburg, S. Bostandjiev, J. O'Donovan, and A. Kobsa. 2012. Inspectability and Control in Social Recommenders. In *Proc. RecSys '12*. ACM, 43–50.
25. B. P. Knijnenburg, N. J. M. Reijmer, and M. C. Willemsen. 2011. Each to His Own: How Different Users Call for Different Interaction Methods in Recommender Systems. In *Proc. RecSys '11*. ACM, 141–148.
26. B. P. Knijnenburg, M. C. Willemsen, Z. Gantner, H. Soncu, and C. Newell. 2012. Explaining the user experience of recommender systems. *User Model. User-adapt. Interact.* 22, 4-5 (2012), 441–504.
27. G. Marchionini. 2006. Exploratory search: from finding to understanding. *Commun. ACM* 49, 4 (2006), 41.
28. A. Micarelli, F. Gasparetti, F. Sciarrone, and S. Gauch. 2007. *Personalized search on the World Wide Web*. Lecture Notes in Computer Science, Vol. 4321. Springer-Verlag, Berlin Heidelberg New York, 195–230.
29. T. N. Nguyen and J. Zhang. 2006. A novel visualization model for web search results. *IEEE Trans. Vis. Comput. Graph.* 12, 5 (2006), 981–8.
30. K. A. Olsen, R. R. Korfhage, K. M. Sochats, M. B. Spring, and J. G. Williams. 1993. Visualization of a document collection: The vibe system. *Inf. Process. Manag.* 29, 1 (1993), 69–81.
31. D. Parra, P. Brusilovsky, and C. Trattner. 2014. See what you want to see: Visual User-Driven Approach for Hybrid Recommendation. In *Proc. IUI '14*. ACM, 235–240.

32. J. Pickens, G. Golovchinsky, C. Shah, P. Qvarfordt, and M. Back. 2008. Algorithmic Mediation for Collaborative Exploratory Search. In *Proc. SIGIR '08*. ACM, New York, NY, USA, 315–322.

33. P. Pirolli and S. Card. 2005. The sensemaking process and leverage points for analyst technology as identified through cognitive task analysis. In *Proc. International Conference on Intelligence Analysis*, Vol. 5. 2–4.

34. T. Ruotsalo, J. Peltonen, M. Eugster, D. Glowacka, K. Konyushkova, K. Athukorala, I. Kosunen, A. Reijonen, P. Myllymäki, G. Jacucci, and S. Kaski. 2013. Directing exploratory search with interactive intent modeling. In *Proc. CIKM '13*. 1759—-1764.

35. G. Shani and N. Tractinsky. 2013. Displaying Relevance Scores for Search Results. In *Proc. SIGIR '13*. ACM, New York, NY, USA, 901–904.

36. B. Shneiderman, D. Byrd, and W. B. Croft. 1998. Sorting out Searching: A User-interface Framework for Text Searches. *Commun. ACM* 41, 4 (1998), 95–98.

37. P. E. Shrout and N. Bolger. 2002. Mediation in experimental and nonexperimental studies: New procedures and recommendations. *Psychological Methods* 7, 4 (2002), 422–445.

38. R. W. White, B. Kules, S. M. Drucker, and others. 2006. Supporting exploratory search. *Commun. ACM* 49, 4 (2006), 36–39.

39. M. L. Wilson, b. Kules, M. C. Schraefel, and B. Shneiderman. 2010. From Keyword Search to Exploration: Designing Future Search Interfaces for the Web. *Foundations and Trends in Web Science* 2, 1 (2010), 1–97.

40. K-P. Yee, K. Swearingen, K. Li, and M. A. Hearst. 2003. Faceted metadata for image search and browsing. In *Proc. CHI '03*. ACM Press, 401–408.

41. Z. Yue, S. Han, and D. He. 2014. Modeling Search Processes Using Hidden States in Collaborative Exploratory Web Search. In *Proc. CSCW '14*. ACM, 820–830.

Towards an Optimal Dialog Strategy for Information Retrieval Using Both Open- and Close-Ended Questions

Yunfeng Zhang, Q. Vera Liao, and Biplav Srivastava
IBM Research
Yorktown Heights, New York, USA
zhangyun@us.ibm.com, vera.liao@ibm.com, biplavs@us.ibm.com

ABSTRACT

The emerging paradigm of dialogue interfaces for information retrieval systems opens new opportunities for interactively narrowing down users' information query and improving search results. Prior research has largely focused on methods that use a set of close-ended questions, such as decision tree, to learn about the user's search target. However, when there is a myriad of documents or items to search, solely relying on close-ended questions can lead to long and undesirable dialogues. We propose an adaptive dialogue strategy framework that incorporates open-ended questions at the optimal timing to reduce the length of the dialogue. We propose a method to estimate the information gain of open-ended questions, and in each dialog turn, we compare it with that of close-ended questions to decide which question to ask. We present experiments using several synthetic datasets designed to explore the behavior of such an adaptive dialogue strategy under different environments, and compare the system's performance with that of a close-ended-questions-only strategy.

Author Keywords

question asking; decision-tree induction; interactive information retrieval; dialog systems

INTRODUCTION

We frequently engage in conversations to collaboratively narrow down information queries, for example, when a career consultant works with a client to identify the ideal job, when a salesperson helps a customer find a product, or when we discuss what kind of movie to watch together. We use diverse questioning strategies to make the conversation efficient and engaging. For example, the consultant may ask specifically "*what industry do you want to work in?*" because that would efficiently narrow down the choices. He or she may also ask open-ended questions like "*tell me what you care about work?*", in the hope of starting a reflective conversation where the client would reveal many preferences.

IUI'18, March 7–11, 2018, Tokyo, Japan

ACM ISBN 978-1-4503-4945-1/18/03...$15.00
https://doi.org/10.1145/3172944.3172998

There is a growing interest in adopting dialogue interfaces for information retrieval (IR) systems to take advantage of the interactivity that can improve the precision of information querying processes. In the simplest form, systems like Google Allo suggest query expansions for the next turn. Recent research (e.g., [7, 5, 9]) explored reasoning algorithms to ask follow-up questions, often by confirming additional features to use to narrow down the information query. While such a method is effective in improving IR results, it is inadequate for systems that aim to exhibit realistically human-like conversational behaviors. For example, to build a conversational agent taking the role of career consultant, the system should aim to identify one or a small number of candidate jobs for the user, instead of suggesting a long ranked list like conventional IR systems do. Relying solely on asking close-ended questions to confirm one feature at a time may also lead to long and boring dialogues from which the user is likely to drop out.

Towards building efficient and engaging conversational IR systems that adopt diverse questioning strategies like humans do, we propose an adaptive IR questioning strategy framework that alternates between asking close-ended and open-ended questions for feature elicitation, with the goal of minimizing dialogue length for identifying the user's target document or item. We present simulation experiments to compare the performance of the adaptive strategy to that of a baseline strategy that asks only close-ended questions. The simulations are set up to explore the performance of the adaptive strategy in several kinds of conditions characterized by (a) different user behaviors in answering open-ended questions, (b) different accuracies of the natural language processing system, and (c) different traits of the item-feature dataset (such as different mean values of features and correlations between features).

BACKGROUND AND RELATED WORK

With the recent development in NLP and conversational agents, conversational IR systems (e.g., search, recommender) are an emerging area of research drawing attention from both academia and industry [11]. Research has generally focused on two aspects. One is to develop methods to extract information from natural dialogue scripts to update queries or user models [2]. The other is to generate and manage the dialogues for information querying, e.g. [7]. A conversational interface is considered especially suitable for feature or preference elicitation for at least two reasons [1]. First, it is naturally interactive and thus users are likely more willing to provide additional information. Moreover, it can pro-actively and dynamically channel the information querying process in desired directions. For example, to narrow down users' queries, previous work explored asking confirmatory (Yes/No) clarification questions such as *"are you asking about topic X?"* [5], and eliciting values for a feature by direct inquiry (e.g., *"What VALUE would you like for FEATURE X?"*) or multi-choice questions (e.g.*"choices for FEATURE X are VALUE 1... VALUE N"*) [3]. However, most existing work focused on system-initiative dialogues by asking close-ended questions. While it is intuitively efficient to obtain targeted information, it fails to consider the benefit of open-ended question such as *"what do you care about work?"* in eliciting a larger quantity of information, sometimes key preferences that the speaker is eager to provide.

IR QUESTIONING DIALOGUE STRATEGY FRAMEWORK

Our framework is based on a few assumptions about the IR dialog system. Firstly, we assume that there are at least hundreds of items to be searched with a large number of features. Smaller search spaces may not require a dynamic or lengthy dialog to identify the queried item. Secondly, we assume that when answering open-ended questions, users describe item features in natural language, and those features are extracted by a natural language processing (NLP) system. This means that the features are binary—they are either identified or not, but systems can accommodate features that have multiple values by converting them into multiple binary features. For example, the feature "color" can be converted into binary features that describe individual colors such as red, blue, etc. This mechanism is suitable for today's dialog systems that rely heavily on NLP techniques to extract relevant information.

The core idea of our framework is a question selector that optimally chooses between asking a close-ended question to inquire about a single feature and asking an open-ended question for which the user has a chance to report multiple features. The selector decides by maximizing the expected information gain (*IG*). While IG based approach has been explored in previous work [10] to decide what features to inquire about with closed ended-questions, we extend the consideration to open-ended questions. That is, at each dialog turn, the selector asks an open-ended question if the estimated IG_{open} of user answering an open-ended question is larger than the *IG*s of any close-ended question confirming a single feature.

The equation for calculating *IG* of a close-ended question for a given feature *F* is:

$$IG(F) = -\sum_{i=1}^{n} P(I_i) log P(I_i) + \sum_{i=1}^{n} \sum_{v=0,1} P(I_i) log P(I_i|F=v) \quad (1)$$

where n is the number of candidate items in the current state, $P(I_i)$ is the *a priori* probability that the item being queried is the *i*th item, and $P(I_i|F=v)$ is the conditional probability of I_i after knowing F's value. The *IG*s need to be estimated after every dialog turn for each unknown feature, because after filtering the candidate items by the feature(s) known from the last turn, the quantities in the above equations would change.

The above calculation of *IG* is similar to the one used by the ID3 decision tree learning algorithm in [10], which is only applicable to close-ended questions. To estimate the *IG* of open-ended questions, there are many factors to consider: the expected number of features that the user would report in answering the question λ_{NF} (a higher number represents a more cooperative user), the recall rate of the NLP system R_{nlp}, each unknown feature's information gain *IG* and likelihood to be reported *L*, and the correlations between features ρ. In situations where features have high degrees of correlation, ρ needs to be considered to avoid over-estimating the advantage of open-ended questions as the combined *IG* of multiple reported features would decrease. For simplicity, in this paper, we omit the consideration of ρ and leave it for future work. In the experiment, we will show that this omission does not have a huge impact if only a few features are correlated.

Given the above considerations, we propose that:

$$IG_{open} = R_{nlp} \lambda_{NF} \sum_{j=1}^{m} L_j IG(F_j) \quad (2)$$

Essentially, this equation states that the information gain of open-ended questions can be estimated as the weighted sum of the *IG* of all the m unknown features, multiplied by the expected number of features that would be reported and the NLP system's extraction rate.

Besides *IG*, all other parameters of Equation 2 can be either individually estimated from the data or jointly learned. For example, R_{nlp} can be measured by submitting testing data to the NLP system; λ_{NF} can be estimated by having human experts to count from historical data of user answers; and *L* can be learned from historical data by counting the report frequency of each feature. Reinforcement learning algorithms such as the one described by [8] can also be used to optimally allocate a number of open-ended questions to estimate the joint quantity of $R_{nlp} * \lambda_{NF}$. In this paper, however, we will not focus on the methods for estimating these parameters. Rather, we will assume that these estimations already have a reasonable degree of accuracy, and our primary goal is to explore the behavior of the adaptive strategy and compare its performance to a close-ended-questions-only dialog strategy.

SIMULATION EXPERIMENTS

We use a simulation approach to compare the performance of our adaptive IR questioning strategy with that of a baseline strategy asking only close-ended questions. Compared to running user studies, this approach allows us to quickly explore the behavior of the system in a wide range of conditions.

Setting up the Query Items Dataset

For the experiments, we simulate a user querying about one item out of n items with m features, where the goal of the dialog system is to elicit from the user the values of these features for the targeted item. We fix n to 1000 and m to 200 as they have little impact on the dialog strategy selection as accounted for by Equations 1 and 2.

The characteristics of the dataset that would most likely cause varying system behaviors are (a) the distribution of *IG* across features, and (b) the correlations between features. The distribution of *IG* would change how close the weighted average *IG* component in Equation 2 is to the highest *IG* of individual features, and hence alter how often the adaptive strategy chooses open-ended questions. For correlation, high correlation between two features would reduce the combined IG of two features, which causes Equation 2 to overestimate IG_{open} since it assumes features are independent.

To vary the distribution of IG and the correlations across features, we went through three steps to generate the feature values of an item. Firstly, to determine Feature j's probability of being associated with an item, $P(F_j = 1)$ or $P(F_j)$ for short, we sampled a normal distribution $\mathcal{N}$ truncated to (0, 1) with mean μ and standard deviation σ. μ is fixed to a small value 0.05 to reflect the fact that each NLP-extracted concept or keyword tend to be associated with only a small portion of the items. σ changes the spread of $P(F_j)$ across features and hence the spread of IG (the closer $P(F_j)$ is to 0.5, the higher the IG), and we varied it between two values 0.3 and 0.9.

The second step of generating the feature values was to sample an m-dimensional multivariate-normal distribution $\mathcal{N}_m$ with feature dimension j's mean set to $P(F_j)$ and its standard deviation set to $\sqrt{P(F_j)(1-P(F_j))}$ (to mimic the binary Bernoulli distribution). By changing the covariance matrix of $\mathcal{N}_m$, we could vary the correlations between features. We used the hub-Toeplitz procedure (cf. [4]) to generate the correlation matrix. This procedure generates correlations that decrease from the maximum correlation ρ_{max} to the minimum correlation ρ_{min} at a specified rate γ. We set ρ_{min} to 0 and γ to 0.03 for all simulations such that only a few correlations are high and others are close to 0. We then varied the ρ_{max} between 0 (fully independent), 0.5, and 0.9 to explore the impact of feature correlations. After sampling $\mathcal{N}_m$, the last step was to convert the real-number feature values to binary by setting those below 0.5 to 0 (not associated with an item) and others to 1 (associated with an item). The above three-step procedure was then repeated n times to generate n items.

The Dialog Simulation Procedure

Besides the parameters for generating the query items, four other parameters impact the simulation. Three of them were about users' behavioral patterns: how likely they query each item $P(I_i)$, how likely they report each feature $L(F_j)$, and on average how many features they tend to report in answering open-ended questions λ_{NF}. Given a lack of user data to learn these reporting patterns, for $P(I_i)$ and $L(F_j)$, we explored a simple assumption where all features and items were equally likely to be reported and queried. For λ_{NF}, we explored a range of values between 1 and 3. Note that λ_{NF} used in Equation 2 is the expected mean value. When simulating the user, variations happen in each turn and occasionally the user can fail to report any feature existing in the system feature space. We simulated it through sampling the number of feature reported in a specific turn from a Poisson distribution with mean value of λ_{NF}. The one remaining parameter was the recall rate of the NLP system R_{nlp}, which was varied from low (0.2) to high (0.7). All parameters are summarized in Table 1.

As seen in Table 1, four parameters were varied: σ, ρ_{max}, R_{nlp}, and λ_{NF}. We ran one simulation experiment for each combination of their settings for a total of $2 \times 3 \times 3 \times 3 = 54$ experiments. Within each experiment, we ran 1000 trials, each querying about an item randomly drawn from the item dataset.

Name	*Description*	*Values*
n	Number of items	1000
m	Number of features	200
μ	Mean of $\mathcal{N}$ used to sample a feature's probability of being associated with an item	.05
σ	Standard deviation of $\mathcal{N}$	.3, .9
ρ_{max}	The maximum correlation used in the hub-Topelitz procedure	0, .5, .9
$P(I_i)$	Prob. of Item i being queried	uniform
$L(F_j)$	Prob. of Feature j being reported	uniform
R_{nlp}	NLP's feature extraction rate	.2, .5, .8
λ_{NF}	Mean of Poisson distrib. for generating the number of features reported in an answer to an open-ended question	1, 2, 3

Table 1. Summary of the simulation parameters.

Each trial went through many dialog turns until the target item was found. At each turn, the adaptive strategy picked the question with the maximum IG to ask, which could be an open-ended question if IG_{open} is larger than IG of any close-ended question. Next, we generated the simulated user answer. If the question was close-ended about Feature j, the feature value F_{ij} was taken as the answer, where i was the index of the target query item. If the question was open-ended, the simulated user first determined how many features it would report, N_r, by sampling a Poisson distribution with a mean of λ_{NF}. Then it randomly chose N_r features associated with Item i (feature value = 1) to report (to reflect the tendency that people report an item has a feature rather than lacks a feature). For open-ended questions, the answers were further passed through the simulated NLP system, where it sampled a Bernoulli distribution with a success rate of R_{nlp} to decide whether a feature would be extracted. The extracted features were then added to the known feature set to filter the candidate items for the next dialogue turn.

The Baseline Strategy and Performance Measures

We compared the adaptive strategy with a close-ended-questions-only baseline strategy. The questions of the baseline strategy were decided by SciPy's entropy-based decision tree classifier [6], which has the same performance as our proposed strategy when it only asks close-ended questions because both used the maximum information gain decision criterion. We considered two outcome measures from the simulation: the number of open- and close-ended questions asked in each trial. Next section compares the results of the two different strategies under the 54 different experimental settings.

Experimental Results

Figure 1 shows the results of the simulation. The bar length represents the mean of the total number of questions asked by the adaptive strategy in each trial. The green portion of the bar represents the number of open-ended questions asked, while the red portion close-ended. The horizontal line represents the number of questions asked by the baseline strategy, which remained at 10 across all conditions.

The results show that as λ_{NF} increased, i.e., users reporting higher number of features in answering open-ended question, the adaptive strategy asked more open-ended questions but

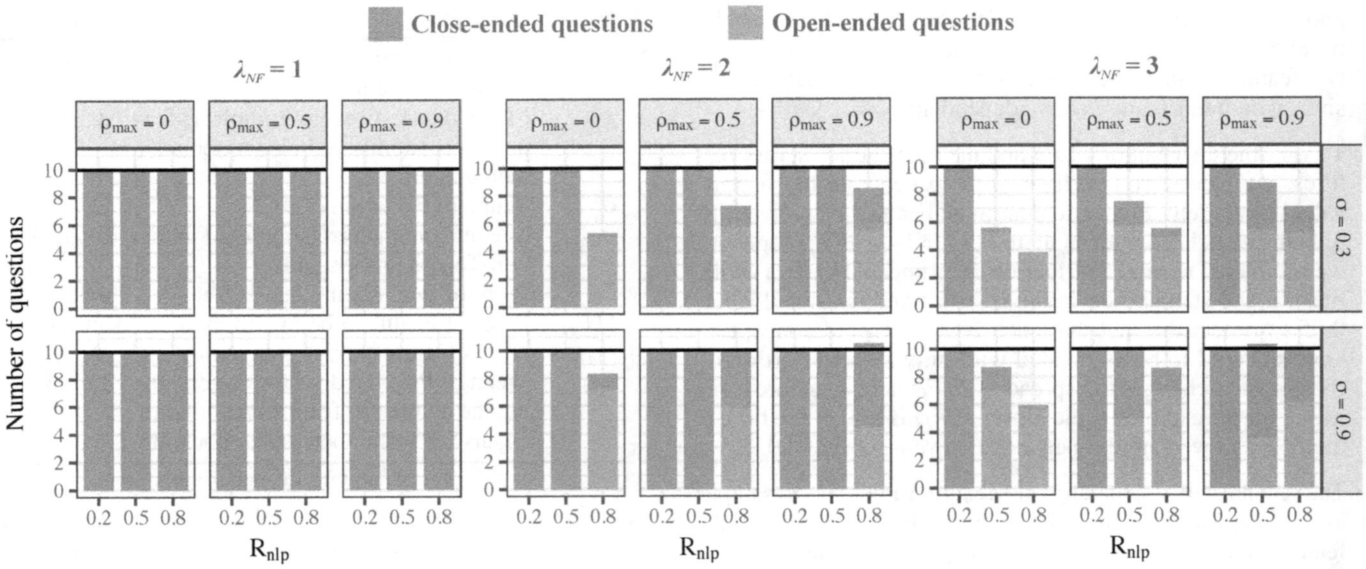

Figure 1. The average number of questions asked by the adaptive questioning strategy across the 54 experiments. The numbers are divided into close-ended (red) and open-ended (green) questions. The horizontal line at 11 of each panel represents the performance of the baseline strategy. Fewer questions, i.e. shorter bars, are better as they indicate fewer conversational turns are needed to determine the user's information need.

fewer questions in total. At $\lambda_{NF} = 1$, the adaptive strategy exclusively used close-ended questions, which resulted in similar performance to that of the baseline strategy. The adaptive strategy started to ask open-ended questions at $\lambda_{NF} = 2$ when the R_{nlp} is high, and at $\lambda_{NF} = 3$ when the R_{nlp} is medium or high. When open-ended questions were used, the total number of questions was reduced compared to that of the baseline strategy, demonstrating the effectiveness of our adaptive question selector. There are a couple of exceptions when $\sigma = 0.9$ and $\rho_{max} = 0.9$, and we will explore the reasons below.

The effects of σ and ρ_{max}, two parameters that affect the interrelations between features, are also clear from Figure 1. Comparing the first row and second row, we can see that as σ increased, the ratio of close-ended questions (red portion) increased. This is because high σ means more dispersed *IG*s across individual features, causing the maximum *IG* for close-ended questions more likely to be higher than the average *IG* used to derive IG_{open}. Therefore the adaptive strategy would shift to asking close-ended questions more often. Comparing the columns, we can see that as ρ_{max} increased, the total number of questions asked increased. This is because high ρ_{max} means high correlation between features, which would cause Equation 2 to overestimate the combined *IG* of multiple features, and hence overestimate IG_{open}. Due to this overestimation, the adaptive strategy would sometimes make suboptimal decisions and ask more questions in total. At the extreme conditions when ρ_{max} and σ were both high, the adaptive strategy even asked slightly more questions than the baseline strategy, as can be seen in Figure 1 where two bars exceeded the horizontal line.

DISCUSSION AND CONCLUSION

The simulation results suggest that under most conditions, because of the ability to exploit open-ended questions, the adaptive strategy would need to ask fewer questions than the decision-tree-based, close-ended-questions-only strategy. The results suggest that in ideal conditions such as when the users are cooperative in describing multiple features in answering open-ended questions, and when the accuracy of the NLP system is high, the adaptive strategy could slash the number of questions by half or even two-thirds. Since the number of dialog turns highly affects user satisfaction [12], our proposal could substantially increase the usability of a dialog system.

Several limitations of this study need to be addressed in future research. Firstly, to apply the adaptive strategy in conditions where the correlations between features are high, we need to improve Equation 2. Potential methods include calculating and averaging the *IG*s of all possible λ_{NF}-feature combinations. This however may be computationally intractable when there is a large number of features or when λ_{NF} is high. Secondly, as suggested previously, integrating a reinforcement learning algorithm in our adaptive strategy could help learn the expected number of features extracted by the NLP system from the historical data. Lastly, the same or similar learning mechanisms would also be useful for learning the probability that each item is to be queried and that each feature is to be reported. Knowing these parameters would further optimize the performance of our proposed system.

In conclusion, we showed that our method of including open-ended questions in an IR dialog system can substantially increase the efficiency of a dialog and our proposed method for estimating the information gain of open-ended questions can account for many critical factors, which helps our adaptive strategy make near optimal decisions about when to ask open-ended questions and when close-ended.

ACKNOWLEDGMENTS

We are indebted to Stefan Liesche for his enthusiastic support of this research, to Matthew Davis for his leadership of the overall project, and to Rachel Bellamy for her comments and feedback on the manuscript.

REFERENCES

1. Susan E Brennan. 1990. Conversation as direct manipulation: An iconoclastic view. (1990).
2. Konstantina Christakopoulou, Filip Radlinski, and Katja Hofmann. 2016. Towards Conversational Recommender Systems.. In *KDD*. 815–824.
3. Jennifer Chu-Carroll. 2000. MIMIC: An adaptive mixed initiative spoken dialogue system for information queries. In *Proceedings of the sixth conference on Applied natural language processing*. Association for Computational Linguistics, 97–104.
4. Johanna Hardin, Stephan Ramon Garcia, and David Golan. 2013. A method for generating realistic correlation matrices. *The Annals of Applied Statistics* 7, 3 (sep 2013), 1733–1762. DOI: http://dx.doi.org/10.1214/13-AOAS638
5. Eric Horvitz and Tim Paek. 1999. A computational architecture for conversation. In *UM99 User Modeling*. Springer, 201–210.
6. Eric Jones, Travis Oliphant, Pearu Peterson, and others. 2001. SciPy: Open source scientific tools for Python. (2001). http://www.scipy.org/
7. Kazunori Komatani, Tatsuya Kawahara, Ryosuke Ito, and Hiroshi G. Okuno. 2002. Efficient dialogue strategy to find users' intended items from information query results. In *Proceedings of the 19th international conference on Computational linguistics*, Vol. 1. Association for Computational Linguistics, Morristown, NJ, USA, 1–7. DOI:http://dx.doi.org/10.3115/1072228.1072380
8. T.L Lai and Herbert Robbins. 1985. Asymptotically efficient adaptive allocation rules. *Advances in Applied Mathematics* 6, 1 (mar 1985), 4–22. DOI: http://dx.doi.org/10.1016/0196-8858(85)90002-8
9. Alexander Miller, Adam Fisch, Jesse Dodge, Amir-Hossein Karimi, Antoine Bordes, and Jason Weston. 2016. Key-value memory networks for directly reading documents. *arXiv preprint arXiv:1606.03126* (2016).
10. J.R. Quinlan and J. R. 1986. Induction of Decision Trees. *Machine Learning* 1, 1 (1986), 81–106. DOI: http://dx.doi.org/10.1023/A:1022643204877
11. Filip Radlinski and Nick Craswell. 2017. A theoretical framework for conversational search. In *Proceedings of the 2017 Conference on Conference Human Information Interaction and Retrieval*. ACM, 117–126.
12. M A Walker, D Litman, C A Kamm, and A Abella. 1997. PARADISE: A general framework for evaluating spoken dialogue agents. *Proceedings of the 35th Annual Meeting of the Association for Computational Linguistics, ACL/EACL 97* (1997), 271–280. DOI: http://dx.doi.org/10.3115/979617.979652

Burst Your Bubble! An Intelligent System for Improving Awareness of Diverse Social Opinions

Mingkun Gao, Hyo Jin Do, Wai-Tat Fu
Department of Computer Science, University of Illinois at Urbana-Champaign
Urbana, USA
{mgao19, hjdo2, wfu}@illinois.edu

ABSTRACT
Social media users are overloaded with diverse opinions by people with opposing stances. Previous research shows that people often look for opinions that reinforce their pre-existing beliefs and stances, which may lead to social polarization. Traditional social media present opinions in a linear list format, which not only lacks structures for people to explore diverse viewpoints but also aggravates their selective exposure to agreeable opinions. To address this problem, we designed an intelligent system that improves awareness of diverse social opinions by providing visual hints and recommendations of opinions (e.g. news articles and comments) on different sides with different indicators. We evaluated our system with news articles about Obamacare repeal issue and their corresponding user comments from Facebook. Results demonstrate that our system could increase people's awareness of their stances and opinion selection preferences, which mitigates selective exposure and thereby leads to a more balanced perception of social opinions.

Author Keywords
Intelligent System; Social Opinion; Selective Exposure;

INTRODUCTION
Social media have been playing an increasingly important role in spreading and shaping social opinions. Pew research [28] showed that, in 2016, 62% of U.S. adults get news from social media. Contrary to the expectation that people are exposed to more diverse opinions, some research has shown that social media may have the opposite effect, i.e., they may play a role in encouraging people to be more selective in their information consumption – a phenomenon often referred to as *selective exposure* [21, 22, 23]. Selective exposure to information may not only prevent people from receiving diverse opinions but also cause polarization of social opinions. This effect may be exacerbated by implicit personalization algorithms that selectively guess what information users would like based on their history of information selection, a process that may keep users separated from information that is inconsistent with their beliefs or attitudes. Users are often not aware of this "filter bubble" [50], which may have a negative consequence on social opinions. For example, the lack of awareness has raised some concerns over how selective exposure to "fake news" on social media has influenced the US presidential election. The goal of the current paper is to investigate strategies for designing intelligent features that may mitigate this type of implicit behavioral tendencies.

IUI'18, March 7–11, 2018, Tokyo, Japan
© 2018 ACM. ISBN 978-1-4503-4945-1/18/03...$15.00
DOI: https://doi.org/10.1145/3172944.3172970

When people are selectively exposed to information, they may not be fully aware that their attitudes are influencing their selection [30]. Some people may have traces of past experiences that mediate their favorable or unfavorable feelings about certain social issues, and these feelings may influence their information selection behavior that they may not be aware of. For example, when people are asked whether they support or oppose the repeal of Obamacare, they may think that they are neutral. However, when they encounter information related to various perspectives of the issue, their experiences or beliefs (e.g., their general beliefs about the role of the government) may lead to varying level of behavioral dispositions that mediate their behavior (e.g., more likely selecting information favoring the repeal) in ways that they are not aware of. Such behavioral dispositions may be magnified as people become selectively exposed, as their beliefs are reinforced by attitude-consistent information, leading to an *echo chamber* effect.

Online interface design often simply presents social opinions (e.g. news article comments) in a linear format. There is a general lack of structure that helps improve people's awareness of their behavioral dispositions and opinion selection preferences. In fact, research shows that the lack of sensitivity to people's attitudes towards different social issues in the design of social information interfaces may aggravate selective exposure, as people have a natural tendency to process information that they agree with.

To address this problem, we proposed a novel intelligent system consisting of design features that aim to improve people's awareness of their stances and selection preferences by encouraging them to attend to more diverse opinions. To be more specific, our system provides people with novel visual hints, including showing a trace of people's stances based on previously read news articles, as well as highlighting visually on the interface when people are selectively exposed to one side of opinions. In addition, our system recommends attitude-inconsistent and attitude-consistent comments according to people's stances with different priority and different recommendation indicators. When recommending attitude-inconsistent opinions to people at first, the system will label these opinions as "Recommended". Later, when recommending attitude-consistent opinions, these opinions will be labelled as "Not Recommended". We expect that the recommendation mechanism and the indicators could *nudge* people to attend to the connection between the indicator and the stance expressed in the recommended comments so that they could realize their stances and the existence of the "filter bubble". For example, people may be accustomed to being recommended attitude-consistent opinions by personalization algorithms on social network. We hope the mismatch of the indicator and stances expressed in recommended opinions in our system could motivate people to inspect their own stances, as well as exposing diverse opinions to people.

To summarize, we proposed the following research questions:

- RQ1: Can our system help people become more aware of their stances and social opinion selection preferences?
- RQ2: Can our system mitigate selective exposure when people use it to read social opinions?

RELATED WORK

Unconscious Bias and Awareness of Stance

Previous research [30, 41, 46, 47] shows that unconscious bias is common. It has been shown that sometimes people do not realize that they have implicit attitudes towards social issues, certain organizations, or groups of people. Unconscious bias could affect people's social behaviors. For example, [12, 41, 46] showed that unconscious bias influenced people's social behaviors in various scenarios, such as recruiting people from different races and evaluating public sector performance. In addition to unconscious bias, sometimes people are not aware of their own stances. The lack of awareness of implicit attitudes imply that people are often not aware of what and why certain information is recommended by a personalization algorithm such as the news aggregators from Google or Facebook. Given that how these algorithms work is often not transparent, people are also not aware how the information is selected. As a result, users may often form an inaccurate impression on other people's opinions. In order to mitigate implicit bias in information selection, we designed novel visual hints to improve people's awareness of their own stances.

Selective Exposure to Information

The current design of social media stacks opinions using syntactic features without considering their stances. Researchers [21, 22, 23] found that such interface design of social opinions may aggravate the selective exposure tendency of users who seek for attitude-consistent opinions while avoiding attitude-inconsistent ones. Zaller [57] also showed that people often show a biased assimilation [45] of information, which refers to a tendency of accepting attitude-consistent messages more than attitude-challenging messages. These effects often lead to other undesirable consequences, such as the echo chamber effect [43, 53], a creation of filter bubbles that arise from social homophily and personalization algorithms [11], and false consensus bias [16, 17, 40, 52], in which people estimate their values are more common than others who hold opposite values. These effects are considered undesirable because they may lead to polarization of opinions in the society.

Researchers have been trying to understand the selective exposure effect in various ways [31, 48, 49]. For instance, [31] argued that selective exposure behavior can be mitigated by exposing users to weak ties and visualizing the common ground facts. Many researchers attempted to mitigate the effect of selective exposure at the interface level. For instance, Liao, et al. [44] investigated the effect of aspect indicators on moderating selective exposure in the medical decision-making process. The results showed that aspect indicators facilitated users to seek other aspects, thus mitigating selective exposure. In [43], they studied whether the presence of source expertise indicators could influence participants' selective exposure. In addition, Garimella and his colleagues [27] attempted to bridge echo chambers using algorithmic techniques with endorsement graph and random-walk controversy score [26]. In our study, we designed a system with novel visual hints and recommendation mechanism to mitigate selective exposure.

Interface Design for Social Opinions

A torrent of research has presented novel interface designs to help users to get balanced and global insight from inundating social opinions online. Hoque and his colleagues [35, 36, 37] presented an interactive text analytic system to help people gain insight from long conversations in blogs by using topic segmentation [24] and topic labeling [59] on Fragment Quotation Graph [39]. Zhang, et al. [58] presented a system that helps readers or editors to effectively break a large-scale discussion down into subtopics using a summary tree. Faridani, et al. [20] proposed Opinion Space that automatically highlights insightful opinions from a range of perspectives.

Among these design features, sentiment is one of the most frequently utilized features in interfaces for social opinions. Many customer websites such as Amazon or IMDB leverage sentiments from feedback to gain better insights. Moreover, many social interfaces utilize sentiments or emotions to organize and visualize user-generated comments. For instance, Gao, et al.[25] presented an intelligent interface that organizes comments from Reddit based on their stances and emotions, and found that the interface helped people to get global insight about controversial topics. In our study, in addition to reminding people of their stances and opinions selection preference with visual features, we deploy sentiment analysis technique [54] to detect users' stances and propose a novel recommendation mechanism to mitigate selective exposure.

Sentiment Analysis

Despite the difficulty in sentiment classification for social media text, mining sentiment on such platforms can be practically useful to gain insights of a huge volume of opinionated information. Companies can organize consumer reviews of their products and services using sentiment analysis and therefore improve their marketing strategies [29]. Governments can observe public sentiments for rapid policy-making [14]. Do, et al. [19] used sentiment classification to investigate the trend of public opinions during the Middle East Respiratory Syndrome (MERS) outbreak in the Republic of Korea. Bollen, et al. [13] used sentiment to predict the stock market. Many recent works attempt to analyze sentiment in non-English texts, such as Japanese [55], Chinese [54] and Korean [18]. Similar to sentiment analysis, there have been a surge of studies in stance and reason classification [10, 32]. In our paper, we crawled Facebook comments and reactions to build a sentiment analysis model specifically attuned to social media domain. We leveraged this model to identify users' stances from their comments about the news article, thus, can recommend attitude-consistent or attitude-inconsistent information.

SYSTEM DESIGN AND IMPLEMENTATION

Data

Facebook allows users to select emoticons, among *Like*, *Love*, *Haha*, *Wow*, *Sad* and *Angry*, to express their emotions to the articles. Many Facebook users not only write their comments to articles but also select the emoticons to express their emotional reactions. This gives us cues to know users' emotions when they write their comments. We intended to categorize emotions into positive and negative sentiments. We found that the *Like* emoticon is so general that many Facebook users always selected the *Like* emoticon regardless of the emotions expressed in their comments. In addition, the *Haha* and *Wow* emoticons are too ambiguous. Some of the comments with the *Haha* emoticon expressed the emotion of jeer whereas others may express the emotion of happiness. The *Wow* emoticon is for the feeling of surprise. However, the sentiment of surprise could be either negative or positive. On the contrary, comments with emoticons of *Love*, *Sad* and *Angry* express relatively consistent emotions with their labels in most cases. Thus, in our study, the *Love* emoticon represents positive sentiment whereas the *Sad* or *Angry* emoticons denotes negative sentiment.

We selected the Obamacare repeal issue as a controversial topic in our study. In order to implement the system and mitigate the bias caused by different news sources, we collected CNN[1] and FoxNews[2] news articles with comments from Facebook[3] using Facebook API[4]. We crawled most recent 100 CNN news articles published from May 8th 2017 to August 10th 2017 and 100 FoxNews articles published from May 1st 2017 to August 16th 2017 from Facebook. Note that the time coverage is slightly different because we were not able to collect the same number of articles in the same period of time. But we tried to remove the potential bias stemmed from different collection times by crawling articles in overlapping periods that the median dates are similar. All these articles we collected have the keywords "health care" in their Facebook news messages. We analyzed people's sentiment (positive vs. negative) towards these articles by comparing how many people selected the *Love* emoticon and how many people selected the *Sad* or *Angry* emoticons. On average, the comparison between being positive and being negative is 40.03% vs. 59.97% for CNN news articles and 45.57% vs. 54.43% for FoxNews articles. This suggested that Obamacare repeal issue is a typical controversial topic on social network so that we select this as a representative in our study.

In order to train the sentiment classifier and build our system, for each article, we also collected the corresponding Facebook comments. Thus, unlike previous sentiment analysis studies where researchers collected data first and then recruited external annotators to add sentiment labels to their data [42, 55], we only collected Facebook comments provided by people who also selected one or more emoticons to indicate their emotions. For each comment we collected, there could be one or more emotion labels selected by comment providers. We labelled comments with the *Love* emoticon as positive sentiment whereas those with the *Sad* or *Angry* emoticons as negative sentiment. These positive and negative labels are treated as gold standard sentiment labels.

Data for Sentiment Analysis

We randomly selected 4,000 positive comments and 4,000 negative comments from our dataset to train and test the sentiment classifier. To further evaluate the classifier, we randomly selected extra 200 comments from each side. These extra 400 comments are used as test data for the comparison of performance between our classifier and human annotators (e.g. online crowd-workers).

Data for System Implementation

To implement the system prototype, we selected four CNN news articles [1, 2, 3, 5] that oppose to repeal Obamacare and four FoxNews articles [4, 6, 7, 8] that support to repeal Obamacare from our article pool. For each selected article, we picked eight comments that support this article and eight comments that oppose this article to obtain diverse opinions.

Sentiment and Stance Analysis

We trained a classifier to predict people's sentiment to an article from their comments. We worked on the corpus where there are 4,000 comments on each side. We preprocessed the comment texts by stemming and removing stop words, and we converted comments into unigram feature vectors. Since different terms have different levels of importance when used to decide the sentiment, we adopted χ^2 statistic (*CHI*) test [54, 56] on each unique term in the training set of the corpus. The *CHI* statistic measures the degree of association between the term and the sentiment category. The definition of *CHI* statistics between term t and sentiment category c_i is:

$$\chi^2(t,c_i) = \frac{N \times (AD - CB)^2}{(A+C) \times (B+D) \times (A+B) \times (C+D)} \quad (1)$$

where A is the number of times t and c_i co-occur, B is the number of times t occurs without c_i, C is the number of times c_i occurs without t, D is the number of times neither t nor c_i occurs and N is the total number of comments. If t and c_i are independent, the value of the χ^2 statistic is zero. For each

[1]http://www.cnn.com/

[2]http://www.foxnews.com/

[3]https://www.facebook.com/

[4]https://developers.facebook.com/

	Positive	Negative
Precision	0.742	0.683
Recall	0.638	0.778
F_1 score	0.686	0.727

Table 1: 10-fold cross validation result of sentiment classifier.

unique term t, we calculated the χ^2 statistic for each sentiment category and finally we assigned the weight, which shows the importance of the term, to each unique term t with:

$$\chi^2_{max}(t) = \max_{i=1}^{m}\{\chi^2(t, c_i)\} \quad (2)$$

where m is the total number of categories. In our case, m equals 2 since we have two sentiment categories (positive vs. negative).

In the feature vector of each comment, the normalized weight $Weight(t,D)$ of a unique term t in comment D is calculated based on:

$$Weight(t,D) = \frac{tf(t,D) \times \chi^2_{max}(t)}{Total\_Weight(D)} \quad (3)$$

where $tf(t,D)$ is the term frequency of the unique term t in comment D and $Total\_Weight(D)$ is the total weight of all terms in comment D ($Total\_Weight(D) = \sum_{t \in D} tf(t,D) \times \chi^2_{max}(t)$).

We trained a Random Forest classifier [33, 34] on feature vectors using Python scikit-learn package[5]. We evaluated our sentiment classifier via 10-fold cross validation using the corpus. We calculated the precision, recall and F_1 score for both positive and negative sentiment categories and results are shown in Table 1.

Furthermore, we compared the performance between our classifier and human annotators on the extra test set which included 200 randomly selected comments in each sentiment category. To evaluate the performance of human annotators, we recruited Turkers on Amazon Mechanical Turk platform (AMT)[6] to annotate sentiment labels (positive vs. negative) to each comment. In each Human Intelligent Task (HIT), we presented 20 comments and we asked Turkers to identify the sentiment expressed in each comment. For each comment, we collected five sentiment labels and used majority vote to determine final sentiment. Ultimately, 100 Turkers participated into our study with a reimbursement of $1.00 per HIT on September 30th 2017. Among the 400 testing comments, 102 comments received either two positive votes and three negative votes or three positive votes and two negative votes from Turkers. This result suggested that among the 400 testing comments, about 25% of them are ambiguous. We compared model-predicted and human-annotated labels with the gold standard respectively and calculated the precision, recall and

[5]http://scikit-learn.org/

[6]https://www.mturk.com

		Positive	Negative
Random Forest	Precicion	0.734	0.678
	Recall	0.635	0.770
	F_1 score	0.681	0.721
Human Annotator	Precision	0.791	0.671
	Recall	0.585	0.845
	F_1 score	0.673	0.748

Table 2: Comparison of performance between our classifier and human annotators.

F_1 score for both methods. Results are shown in Table 2. We found that our classifier's performance is comparable to human annotators' performance on this difficult task.

With the predicted sentiment label of the comment to an article, we could predict comment providers' stances as we know the stance of these articles in our study. Here, stance means the opinion (support vs. oppose) towards an issue. For example, if the sentiment classifier predicted a comment to be negative to an article which opposes to repeal Obamacare, we would predict the comment provider's stance as supporting Obamacare repeal.

System Design Principle

Our system aims to improve people's awareness of their own stances and social opinion selection preferences, and mitigate selective exposure. Based on previous studies about nudging the bias of selection using various visualization techniques [25, 51] and recommendation systems [9, 15], we propose the design principles as below:

1. **Highlight visual difference when opinion selection bias is detected:** The system should provide highlighted difference visually when social opinion selection bias is detected. We expect that visually salient hint is effective to remind people that they may be selectively exposed to a specific side of opinions.

2. **Show the trace of people's stances:** When the system detects stances of users, it should provide explicit feedback to improve users' awareness of their stances. We expect that this feature not only will help them realize their own stances, but also be more conscious of the stances of other people's opinions relative to their own stances.

3. **Recommend social opinions from an opposite stance with positive indicators:** People who are biased towards one side of the opinions may intentionally avoid opinions on the other side, or they may be unintentionally kept in a filter bubble by personalization algorithms. In our study, we investigate whether recommending opinions opposite to a user's stance would help increase the diversity of exposure to social opinions, thereby raising their awareness of their own stances. In the current design, the system will recommend attitude-inconsistent opinions with a positive indicator (i.e. labelling these opinions as "Recommended")

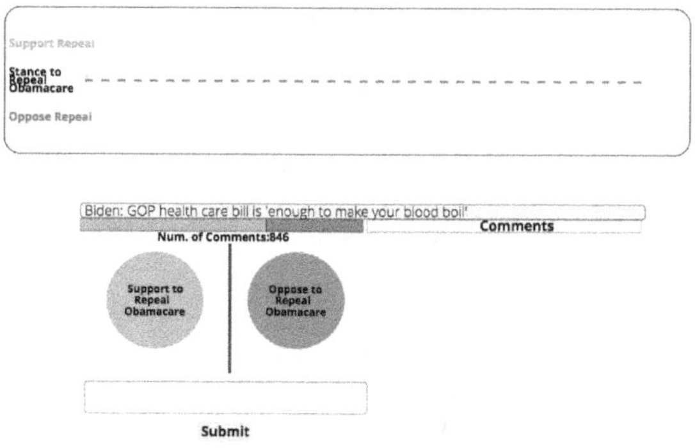

Figure 1: An overview of our new interface.

to encourage people to attend to these opinions – i.e., we expect that this will help burst the filter bubble.

4. **Recommend social opinions in the same stance with negative indicators:** If the system only recommends attitude-inconsistent opinions to people, people may leave the platform when they feel dissatisfied with the recommended information. In the current design, we investigate whether recommending attitude-consistent opinions will fulfill the implicit information needs of users. However, to avoid the effect of a filter bubble, we will provide a negative indicator to the opinions (i.e. labelling these opinions as "Not Recommended"). The negative indicator may also stimulate people's curiosity about why the system shows opinions which are not recommended. By nudging people to figure out the connection between the indicator and the stances expressed in the opinions, our system may help people realize their stances.

Visual Encoding and Implementation

To achieve our design goals, our system incorporates visual hints and opinion recommendations. There are four articles (two FoxNews articles and two CNN news articles) in our system. The system only shows people one article at a time and recommends the next article based on people's stances to the previous one. Figure 1 shows the overview of our new interface. On the top of the article title, there's a panel to trace people's stances on previous articles. The color bar under the article title indicates how controversial the article may be. The length of the green bar indicates the proportion of comments which support to repeal Obamacare and the length of the purple bar indicates the proportion of comments on the other side. There are two round clickable stance labels under the color bar. Green stance label represents comments which support to repeal Obamacare and purple stance label represents comments in the opposite stance. There's a text entry field under the stance labels where people could write their own comments. For each article, we selected eight comments on both sides respectively. We split comments on each side into two groups and each group has four comments. On each side, the first group of the comments will be presented when people click the corresponding stance label to read comments. The second group of comments will be used as recommended

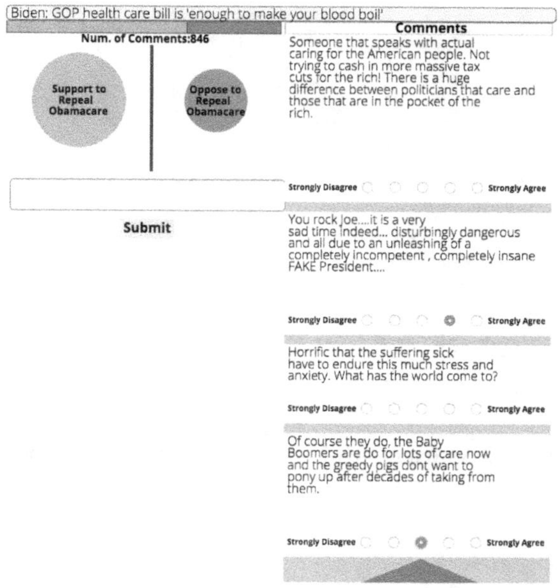

Figure 2: An example of size changeable stance labels.

comments when the system makes recommendations based on people's stances.

Visual Hints (DP-1, DP-2)

Our system provides various visual hints to help people realize their opinion selection bias and stances.

The interface highlights the visual difference in terms of the stance label size (*DP-1*). Figure 2 shows an example that after a user clicked a stance label to read comments on that side, the stance label became smaller. This could improve the user's awareness of their social opinion selection preference. Under each comment, the interface allows the user to rate the degree of (dis)agreement on the comment in a 5 Point Likert scale ranging from strongly disagree to strongly agree. If necessary, these ratings could be used to evaluate the user's stance after submitted by the user.

Figure 3 shows that after the user wrote and submitted a comment, our system predicted the user's stance on the Obamacare repeal issue. In case of inaccurate classification, our system gives the user a chance to correct the predicted stance label and confirm. Previous research [38] shows that most people are willing to correct the prediction mistakes caused by auto-systems.

Figure 4 shows an example of the function of stance record panel. After submitting the ratings to comments which were selected to read and confirming the stance for the first article, the user moved on to next article. The stance record panel showed the trace of the user's stances on previous article(s) to improve the self-awareness of his/her own stance (*DP-2*). The dashed line in the middle represents the neutral stance. The small round purple label below the dashed line is a user stance indicator showing the user's confirmed stance (oppose the repeal). If the user confirmed the stance as "support to repeal

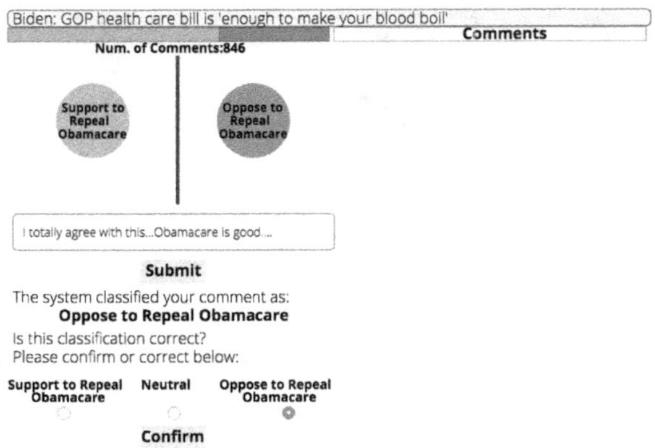

Figure 3: An example of our new interface after people write and submit a comment.

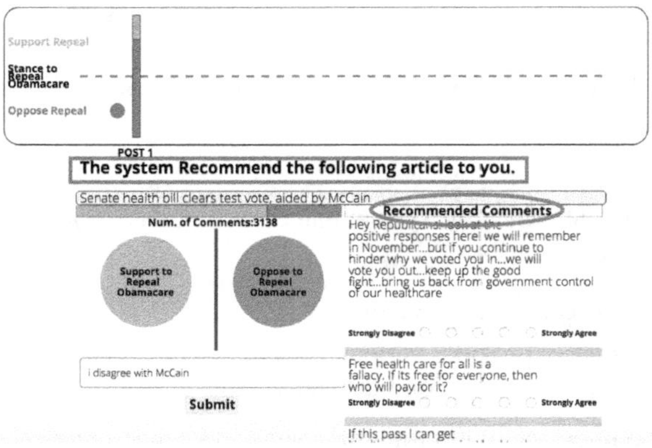

Figure 4: An example of our new interface after people move on to the next article and the system conducts *Type 1* article recommendation and *Type 1* comment recommendation.

Obamacare", there would be a green user stance indicator above the dashed line. For neutral stance confirmation, a grey user stance indicator would appear on the dashed line. There is a bar colored with green and purple on the right of the user stance indicator. The length of the green part indicates the mean of ratings given to comments which support to repeal Obamacare while the length the purple part indicates the mean of ratings given to comments on the other side. The ratio between the lengths of these two parts indicates the ratio between the average ratings for comments on each side. In the example shown in Figure 4, the purple part exceeds the dashed line, which means the user rated comments which oppose to repeal Obamacare higher than comments on the other side.

Social Opinion Recommendation (DP-3,DP-4)

Our system recommends diverse social opinions to mitigate selective exposure. Before recommending articles or comments, the system needs to detect people's stances. If a user confirmed a non-neutral stance expressed in his/her own comment, the user's stance would be the same as the confirmed one. If the user didn't confirm or confirmed a neutral stance

Type	Recommendation Mechanism
Type 1	Recommend attitude-inconsistent opinions with a positive indicator (*DP-3*)
Type 2	Recommend attitude-consistent opinions with a negative indicator (*DP-4*)

Table 3: Two types of recommendations.

and the mean of his/her ratings given to each side of comments are different, the user's stance would follow the stance of the side with higher average rating. Furthermore, the user's stance would be neutral if he/she confirmed neutral stance and the average rating for comments on each side is the same. If the user confirmed a neutral stance and only rated comments on one side, the user's stance label will be chosen based on the mean of ratings given to the comments on that side. If the mean value was higher than three, the user's stance would be the same as the stance of this side. Otherwise, if the mean value was lower than three, the user's stance would be opposite to the stance of this side. If it's three, the user's stance would be considered as neutral.

In order to recommend diverse opinions to users, our system provides two types of recommendations (*Type 1* vs. *Type 2*; See Table 3) at both the article and comment level. For both article and comment level recommendations, *Type 1* recommendation has higher priority than *Type 2* recommendation since attitude-inconsistent opinions could make people be conscious of the existence of opinions with different stances, which could mitigate selective exposure. In our system, as long as there are attitude-inconsistent opinions available, our system will conduct *Type 1* recommendation. *Type 2* recommendation will be conducted after all attitude-inconsistent opinions (e.g. articles and comments) have been recommended.

Figure 4 shows an example of *Type 1* article recommendation. Based on the user's ratings to comments and stance confirmation, our system determined his/her stance as opposing to repeal Obamacare. Since there were articles with an opposite stance available in our article database, the system conducted *Type 1* recommendation by recommending an article expressing an opposite stance with a positive indicator "The system Recommend the following article to you" (See the red rectangle in Figure 4). However, if at this moment, there were only articles with the same stance available in the system, the system would conduct *Type 2* recommendation by recommending the same-stance article with a negative indicator "The system Doesn't Recommend the following article to you".

Comment recommendation is conducted in the same way as the article recommendation. Figure 4 also shows an example of *Type 1* comment recommendation. The user confirmed the stance as opposing to repeal Obamacare. The system recommended four comments which support to repeal Obamacare with a positive indicator "Recommended Comments" (See the red circle in Figure 4). After the user clicked the "readmore" button (the upside-down blue triangle at the bottom of the comment list), the system conducted *Type 2* recommendation by presenting four agreeable comments with a negative indicator "Not Recommended Comments" to the user. Last but not least, if the system determines the user's stance as neutral, there's no recommendation for articles and comments. The system will randomly select articles and comments for the user to read.

USER STUDY

We conducted a user study to evaluate how our system could improve users' awareness of their stances and selection preferences of social opinions. In addition, we examined how our interface could mitigate selective exposure effect and encourage users to read more diverse opinions.

Participant

In this study, 12 subjects (age range from 18 to 64, 6 females) from the Midwest of the U.S. were recruited via email. They all reported that they have considerable knowledge about the Obamacare issues. When they were asked about their stances on the Obamacare repeal issue prior to the user study, four of them reported neutral and eight of them reported opposing to repeal Obamacare.

Experimental Design and Task

As shown in Figure 5, the control interface shows 16 comments in a linear list format for each article. These comments are shown in a randomized order. To compare our new interface (system) with the control interface, we designed a within-subject study where the interface is the within-subject factor. To avoid potential carry-over effect caused by the order of exposure to specific interface and group of articles, we first split eight selected news articles into two groups where each group had two CNN news articles and two FoxNews articles. Then, we changed the order of the interfaces and the article groups.

In the beginning of the user study, participants took a background survey about their demographic information and their experience in reading controversial topics. Then, participants did the following tasks for each interface: 1) Participants watched a tutorial video about how to use the interface; 2) Participants were asked to read each article, rate comments they were interested in and to write a comment to the article; 3) After finishing the task, participants worked on a two-part in-study survey. The first part asked about how the interface could help them realize their stances and comment selection preferences, and whether the interface could help them discover diverse opinions easily. The second part asked about usability of the interface, which focused on the following measures: 1) *Usefulness*: "I found this interface to be useful for reading controversial issues"; 2) *Ease of use*: "This interface is easy to use when reading controversial topics"; 3) *Enjoyable*:"I found this interface enjoyable to use"; 4) *Effective*: "The interface is effective in helping me complete the tasks"; 5) *Overall Satisfaction*: "Overall, I am satisfied with this system." All the questions in the in-study survey were measured on a 5 Point Likert scale. Then, after finishing the tasks and in-study surveys for both interfaces, participants were asked to finish a post-study questionnaire about the usefulness of each design feature in our system and their perception of how the system recommends articles to them. Finally, we conducted a short interview. The user study lasted about 1 hour and 20 minutes with a payment of $12.

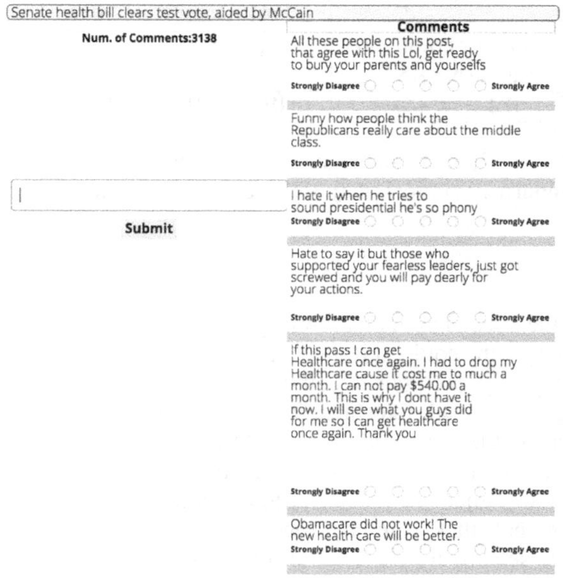

Figure 5: An overview of the control interface.

RESULTS

Improving Awareness of Diverse Opinions (RQ1,RQ2)

Figure 6 shows the comparison between two interfaces for the first part of the in-study survey. We performed Wilcoxon Signed Ranks Test to each measure and found that our new interface is significantly more helpful than the control interface in terms of helping people realize their stances ($Z = -2.859$, $p < 0.01$) and their selection preferences in comments ($Z = -1.982$, $p < 0.05$). Furthermore, results indicated that our new interface is significantly more helpful for users to discover diverse opinions than the control interface ($Z = -2.214$, $p < 0.05$).

Since participants' interface usage behaviors (e.g. which comments they rated, what rating they gave to each comment, participants' stances) were recorded, we conducted analysis

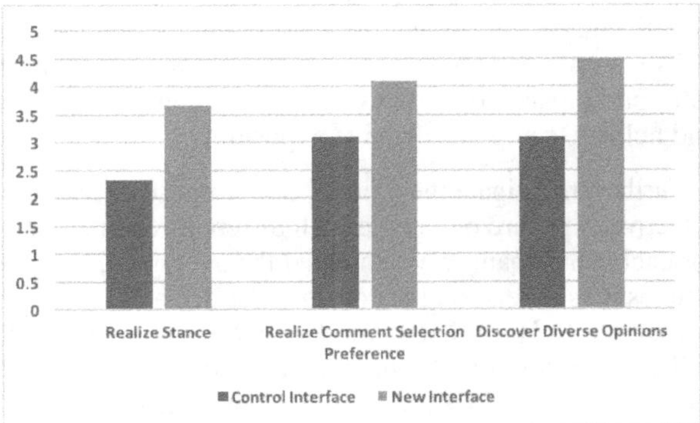

Figure 6: Comparison of average ratings between two interfaces in terms of whether the interface could help users realize their stance, comment selection preference and discover diverse opinions.

	New Interface	Control Interface
Number of comments rated (n = 48)	12.33 (± 3.49)	6.50 (± 2.61)
SEI (n = 48)	0.49 (± 0.08)	0.57 (± 0.21)

Table 4: For both interfaces, we calculated the mean and the standard deviation of the numbers of comments rated and SEIs.

on their social opinion browsing behaviors to evaluate whether our system could mitigate selective exposure. During the user study, each participant was asked to read four different articles on each interface. The system recorded which comment(s) they selected to rate with corresponding ratings and their stances to Obamacare repeal issue after reading each article. Since we asked participants to only select and rate comments they were interested in, we could evaluate how they were selectively exposed to attitude-consistent opinions by comparing the number of comments they selected on different sides. To measure selective exposure effect, we defined Selective Exposure Index (SEI) for an article as:

$$SEI = \frac{N_{consistent}}{N_{consistent} + N_{inconsistent}} \quad (4)$$

where $N_{consistent}/N_{inconsistent}$ is the number of selected comments which are consistent/inconsistent with participants' stances respectively. An SEI higher than 0.50 means the participant tends to be selectively exposed to agreeable social opinions.

We counted the total number of comments participants selected for each article and calculated the SEI for each article in both interfaces. Since every participant read four articles using each interface, in total, for each interface, we have 48 data entries collected from 12 participants for each measure. The results of comparison between these two interfaces for each measure are shown in Table 4. A two-tailed paired-sample t-test was conducted on each of these measures. The result showed that participants read more comments on our new interface than the control interface and the difference is significant ($t(47) = 12.717$, $p < 0.001$). In addition, the SEI of our new interface is significantly lower than that of the control interface ($t(47) = -2.280$, $p < 0.05$), which suggests that our new interface motivates participants to read more attitude-inconsistent comments and helps to mitigate selective exposure.

To further investigate the efficacy of our interface in mitigating selective exposure on people with different reading behaviors, for each participant, we calculated the average SEI of all four articles he/she read on the control interface and separated participants into High SEI group (with 9 participants) and Low SEI group (with 3 participants). High SEI group participants have an average SEI higher than 0.50 and Low SEI group participants have an average SEI lower than 0.50. We evaluated the effect of our new interface on different groups of participants and Table 5 shows the mean and standard deviation of SEIs on different groups and interfaces. A two-tailed paired-sample t-test showed that there is a significant difference between two interfaces ($t(35) = -2.621$, $p < 0.05$) for High

	New Interface	Control Interface
High SEI group (n = 36)	0.50 (± 0.08)	0.61 (± 0.23)
Low SEI group (n = 12)	0.47 (± 0.05)	0.45 (± 0.12)

Table 5: For both High and Low SEI groups, we calculated the mean and the standard deviation of SEIs for both interfaces.

SEI group. Meanwhile, no significant difference is found for Low SEI group ($t(11) = 0.457$, $p = 0.657$). This result indicated that High SEI group participants have more balanced comment selection behaviors when using our interface. However, there's no significant difference in comment selection behaviors for Low SEI group participants when using different interfaces.

These results show that our new interface (system) improves people's awareness of their stances and social opinion selection preferences (RQ-1), and mitigates selective exposure (RQ-2).

Usability Improvement

Figure 7 shows the comparison between two interfaces for the second part of the in-study survey. We conducted Wilcoxon Signed Ranks Test on each measure of usability (Table 6) and found that for the measures of *EaseofUse*, *Enjoyable*, *Effective* and *Overall Satisfaction*, our new interface are rated better than the control interface with a significant difference. However, we only found marginal significant difference in the *Usefulness* measure when comparing our new interface with the control interface.

Evaluation of System Features

In the post-study questionnaire, we asked participants how system features (e.g. size-changeable stance labels, stance recorder panel, *Type 1*/*Type 2* recommendations of articles/comments) help them realize their stances and comment selection preferences.

Figures 8a and 8b show participants' evaluation about these system features. Based on the result, we found that the stance

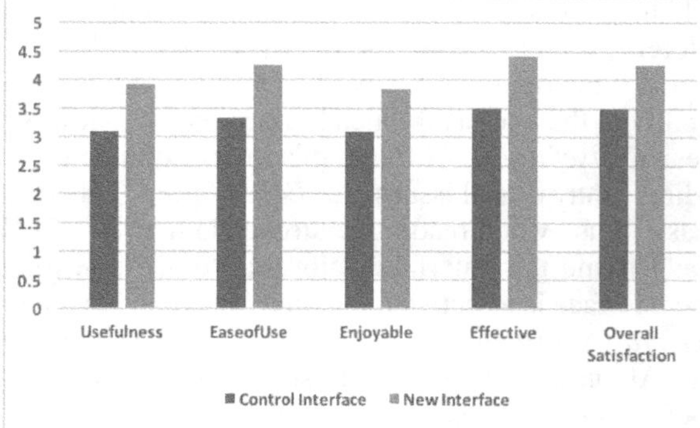

Figure 7: Comparison of average ratings between two interfaces in terms of usability measures: Usefulness, EaseofUse, Enjoyable, Effective and Overall Satisfaction. Higher rating means better interface efficacy.

Measures	New Interface vs. Control Interface
Usefulness	Z = -1.831; p = 0.067
EaseofUse	Z = -2.598; p <0.01
Enjoyable	Z = -2.460; p <0.05
Effective	Z = -2.428; p <0.05
Overall Satisfaction	Z = -2.165; p <0.05

Table 6: Wilcoxon Signed Ranks Test on Usefulness, EaseofUse, Enjoyable, Effective and Overall Satisfaction.

	SEI (Mean ± SD)
Control Interface	0.57 (± 0.21)
Stance Label Comments	0.50 (± 0.14)
Recommended Comments	0.48 (± 0.11)

Table 7: We calculated the mean and the standard deviation of SEIs in each comment browsing scenario.

recorder panel is the most important feature to help participants realize both of their stances and opinion selection preferences with an agreement rate of 9/12 and 11/12 respectively. In addition, all other features have an agreement rate equal to or higher than 50%, which means participants found the proposed features useful in general.

Unlike the control interface where all comments are shown together at once, there are two types of comments in our interface: stance label comments (comments which are presented after people click the corresponding stance label) and recommended comments (comments which are recommended by both *Type 1* and *Type 2* recommendations). We compared participants' comment selection behaviors in the measure of SEI among different comment browsing scenarios: 1) browsing comments on control interface; 2) browsing stance label comments on our interface and 3) browsing recommended comments on our interface. Table 7 shows the mean and standard deviation of SEIs in each scenario. A repeated measures ANOVA (with Greenhouse-Geisser correction for sphericity) found that the SEI differs significantly between scenarios ($F(1.708, 80.280) = 4.176$, $p < 0.05$). Post-hoc tests using the Bonferroni correction indicated that there's a significant difference between scenario 1) and 3) ($p < 0.05$) but no significant difference between 2) vs. 3) ($p = 0.968$) and 1) vs. 2) ($p = 0.242$). This result indicates that recommendation feature mitigates selective exposure more effectively than the size-changeable stance label feature when comparing with the control interface.

Qualitative Analysis

We asked participants about their perception of how the system recommends articles to them. Specifically, we asked 1) whether they could figure out why sometimes the system showed a "Recommended" article but sometimes showed a "Not Recommended" article, 2) whether they thought the recommendation was related to their stances, and 3) how the system recommended articles to them. As a result, 10 out of 12 participants agreed to the first question, saying that they could figure out how the system made recommendations. For the second question, 8 out of 12 participants agreed, which illustrates that most of the users thought the recommendations were made based on their stances. For the third question, 6 out of 12 participants correctly described how the system made recommendations. For example, participant *U7* reported "I think that the recommended articles are trying to get you to see different perspectives on the issue" and participant *U12* reported "The counter-recommendation mechanism is there to provide an opportunity to 'burst your bubble' so the reader is exposed to opposing points of view...This whole mechanism that was implemented is interesting considering the buzz around the whole notion of being trapped in a bubble of one's own opinions: as in everyone they talk to or read from agrees with them and only reinforces their beliefs." These results show that our recommendation mechanism nudged participants to figure out the connection between the indicator and stance expressed in recommended opinions, which improved self-awareness of their own stances. However, the other 6 participants couldn't accurately describe the recommendation mechanism, which suggests that people's perception of how the system made recommendations may vary. In addition, all participants showed an overall preference to our system and 11 out of 12 participants agreed our system helped them to get global insight across different opinions during our short interview.

DISCUSSION

Past research has pointed out the need to design informational structures or personalization algorithms for the vast amount of user-generated contents on online social media platforms. These informational structures or algorithms often focus on helping users find and select information they desire. There is, however, a general lack of attention to how these structures may lead to undesirable effects, such as selective exposure to information and social polarization. The design goal of our system is different from these approaches: Instead of *only* helping users find information they desire, our system *also* aims to help user correctly perceive and understand different perspectives expressed by other users. In this paper, we showed how the general techniques of sentiment analysis and opinion recommendation can be repurposed to satisfy this design goal.

Analyzing People's Sentiments for Controversial Topics

Sentiment analysis technique is typically used to find emotional reactions to a topic. However, we utilized the technique to infer people's stances, whether they support or oppose a controversial topic. Specifically, in our study, we wanted to infer people's stances on Obamacare issue using a classifier that predicts sentiment labels of people's comments about Obamacare issue. We conducted feature engineering with the χ^2 statistic test on each unique term. We found some terms, such as "president", "Trump" and "McCain" were assigned a very high weight. These terms are highly related to the topic of the issue and people's stereotypes of political figures related to the issue. However, they are not the common terms people use to express sentiments. This indicates that when analyzing people's sentiments on controversial issues, we should consider not only their emotional expressions but also their stereotypes of the topic and people related to the issue.

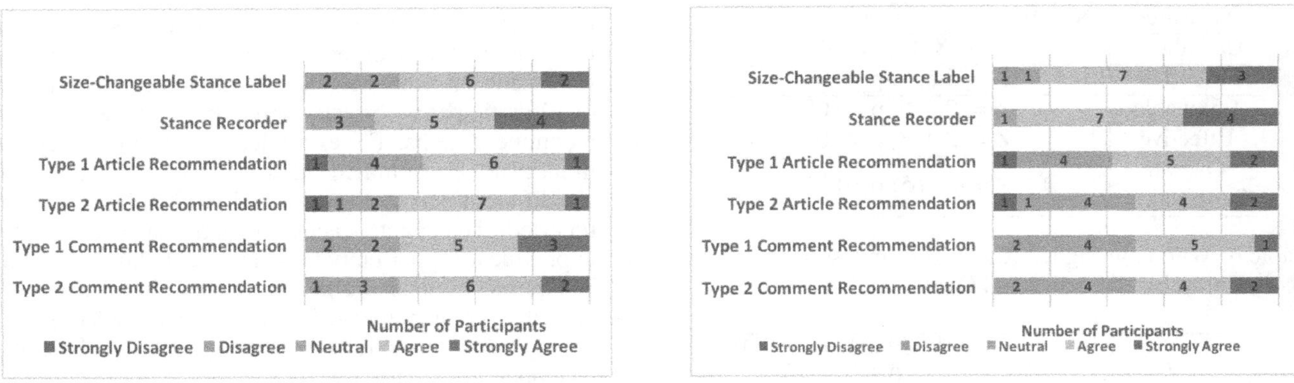

(a) (b)

Figure 8: (a) Evaluation for specific system features in helping participants realize their stances. (b) Evaluation for specific system features in helping participants realize their comment selection preferences.

Social Opinion Recommendation

Traditional personalized recommendation systems select and recommend agreeable information or opinions to people based on their records of information selection. This mechanism aims to increase people's satisfaction with the system but it often separates people from attitude-inconsistent information and may further aggravate the selective exposure effect. We designed our recommendation mechanism differently. Although our system recommends opinions on both sides, the system recommends attitude-consistent opinions (*Type 2* recommendation) after the attitude-inconsistent opinions (*Type 1* recommendation). We found that our new recommendation mechanism could mitigate selective exposure. We should point out that, in more realistic situations where there are a large amount of opinions on each side, the system may need to use an appropriate ratio between *Type 1* recommendation and *Type 2* recommendation. We believe that the question of how to set this ratio will be an interesting research topic in the future.

Limitations

In our study, we tested user behavior using only four articles and a limited number of comments on Obamacare topic. In the future, we plan to investigate people's social opinion browsing behavior with more articles and comments on other controversial topics over a longer period of time in a larger-scale user study. This would generate a richer set of data to achieve more comprehensive evaluation and inform better design of such interfaces.

In addition, we only considered positive and negative sentiments when designing and implementing the system. However, people may have other types of emotions when browsing social opinions. Also, people may get a better understanding of comments by checking scores or ratings about sentiments. We plan to improve the sentiment classifier to support multi-category emotion classification as well as generating numeric sentiment scores in the future.

Lastly, although users could be motivated to inspect both stances at the same time, we decided to present opposite viewpoints asynchronously for the sake of testing our design ideas more effectively and conveniently. However, we will consider this alternative design in our future studies.

CONCLUSION

In this paper, we presented an interactive intelligent system that organizes social opinions using a combination of novel visual cues and recommendation mechanisms to increase self-awareness of users' stances and to mitigate effects of selective exposure. Compared to a control interface in which opinions are organized in a linear format, the new system was found to help users become more aware of their own stances and their selection preferences of opinions. We also found that users attended to more diverse opinions and showed less selective exposure to attitude-consistent information in the new interface. We concluded that the proposed new system is promising in raising users' awareness of their own stances and preferences, as well as mitigating selective exposure to information.

ACKNOWLEDGMENTS

This research was supported by the NSF SES grant #1419297 and the NSF IIS grant #1441563. We would like to thank Yang Du for her help to this project and all the reviewers for their valuable feedback.

REFERENCES

1. 2017a. Bernie Sanders: Every state should have a public option. CNN Facebook. (30 July 2017).

2. 2017b. Bernie Sanders to headline 'Don't Take Our Health Care' tour. CNN Facebook. (24 June 2017).

3. 2017c. Biden: GOP health care bill is 'enough to make your blood boil'. CNN Facebook. (18 July 2017).

4. 2017a. He Must Be 'Clairvoyant': Huckabee Blasts Schumer for Immediate Rebuttal of Health Care Bill. FoxNews Facebook. (25 June 2017).

5. 2017d. Obama on Senate bill: It's 'not a health care bill'. CNN Facebook. (23 June 2017).

6. 2017b. ObamaCare replacement bill approved in House. FoxNews Facebook. (4 May 2017).
7. 2017c. Pro-Trump group launches $1M ad campaign against Sen. Heller over ObamaCare stance. FoxNews Facebook. (23 June 2017).
8. 2017d. Senate health bill clears test vote, aided by McCain. FoxNews Facebook. (25 July 2017).
9. Gediminas Adomavicius and Alexander Tuzhilin. 2005. Toward the next generation of recommender systems: A survey of the state-of-the-art and possible extensions. *IEEE transactions on knowledge and data engineering* 17, 6 (2005), 734–749.
10. Isabelle Augenstein, Tim Rocktäschel, Andreas Vlachos, and Kalina Bontcheva. 2016. Stance Detection with Bidirectional Conditional Encoding. In *Proceedings of the 2016 Conference on Empirical Methods in Natural Language Processing*. Association for Computational Linguistics, Austin, Texas, 876–885. https://aclweb.org/anthology/D16-1084
11. Eytan Bakshy, Solomon Messing, and Lada A Adamic. 2015. Exposure to ideologically diverse news and opinion on Facebook. *Science* 348, 6239 (2015), 1130–1132.
12. Irene V Blair, John F Steiner, Diane L Fairclough, Rebecca Hanratty, David W Price, Holen K Hirsh, Leslie A Wright, Michael Bronsert, Elhum Karimkhani, David J Magid, and others. 2013. Clinicians' implicit ethnic/racial bias and perceptions of care among black and Latino patients. *The Annals of Family Medicine* 11, 1 (2013), 43–52.
13. Johan Bollen, Huina Mao, and Xiaojun Zeng. 2011. Twitter mood predicts the stock market. *Journal of computational science* 2, 1 (2011), 1–8.
14. Andrea Ceron, Luigi Curini, Stefano M Iacus, and Giuseppe Porro. 2014. Every tweet counts? How sentiment analysis of social media can improve our knowledge of citizens' political preferences with an application to Italy and France. *New Media & Society* 16, 2 (2014), 340–358.
15. Dan Cosley, Shyong K Lam, Istvan Albert, Joseph A Konstan, and John Riedl. 2003. Is seeing believing?: how recommender system interfaces affect users' opinions. In *Proceedings of the SIGCHI conference on Human factors in computing systems*. ACM, 585–592.
16. Robyn M Dawes. 1989. Statistical criteria for establishing a truly false consensus effect. *Journal of Experimental Social Psychology* 25, 1 (1989), 1–17.
17. Robyn M Dawes and Matthew Mulford. 1996. The false consensus effect and overconfidence: Flaws in judgment or flaws in how we study judgment? *Organizational Behavior and Human Decision Processes* 65, 3 (1996), 201–211.
18. Hyo Jin Do and Ho-Jin Choi. 2015. Korean Twitter Emotion Classification Using Automatically Built Emotion Lexicons and Fine-Grained Features.. In *PACLIC*.
19. Hyo Jin Do, Chae-Gyun Lim, You Jin Kim, and Ho-Jin Choi. 2016. Analyzing emotions in twitter during a crisis: A case study of the 2015 middle east respiratory syndrome outbreak in Korea. In *Big Data and Smart Computing (BigComp), 2016 International Conference on*. IEEE, 415–418.
20. Siamak Faridani, Ephrat Bitton, Kimiko Ryokai, and Ken Goldberg. 2010. Opinion space: a scalable tool for browsing online comments. In *Proceedings of the SIGCHI Conference on Human Factors in Computing Systems*. ACM, 1175–1184.
21. Leon Festinger. 1962. *A theory of cognitive dissonance*. Vol. 2. Stanford university press.
22. Peter Fischer, Andreas Kastenmüller, Tobias Greitemeyer, Julia Fischer, Dieter Frey, and David Crelley. 2011. Threat and selective exposure: the moderating role of threat and decision context on confirmatory information search after decisions. *Journal of Experimental Psychology: General* 140, 1 (2011), 51.
23. Dieter Frey. 1986. Recent research on selective exposure to information. *Advances in experimental social psychology* 19 (1986), 41–80.
24. Michel Galley, Kathleen McKeown, Eric Fosler-Lussier, and Hongyan Jing. 2003. Discourse segmentation of multi-party conversation. In *Proceedings of the 41st Annual Meeting on Association for Computational Linguistics-Volume 1*. Association for Computational Linguistics, 562–569.
25. Mingkun Gao, Hyo Jin Do, and Wai-Tat Fu. 2017. An Intelligent Interface for Organizing Online Opinions on Controversial Topics. In *Proceedings of the 22nd International Conference on Intelligent User Interfaces*. ACM, 119–123.
26. Kiran Garimella, Gianmarco De Francisci Morales, Aristides Gionis, and Michael Mathioudakis. 2016. Quantifying Controversy in Social Media. In *Proceedings of the Ninth ACM International Conference on Web Search and Data Mining (WSDM '16)*. ACM, New York, NY, USA, 33–42. DOI: http://dx.doi.org/10.1145/2835776.2835792
27. Kiran Garimella, Gianmarco De Francisci Morales, Aristides Gionis, and Michael Mathioudakis. 2017. Reducing Controversy by Connecting Opposing Views. In *Proceedings of the Tenth ACM International Conference on Web Search and Data Mining (WSDM '17)*. ACM, New York, NY, USA, 81–90. DOI: http://dx.doi.org/10.1145/3018661.3018703
28. Jeffrey Gottfried and Elisa Shearer. 2016. News Use Across Social Media Platforms 2016. (26 May 2016).
29. Dietmar Gräbner, Markus Zanker, Günther Fliedl, and Matthias Fuchs. 2012. *Classification of Customer Reviews based on Sentiment Analysis*. Springer Vienna, Vienna, 460–470. DOI: http://dx.doi.org/10.1007/978-3-7091-1142-0_40

30. Anthony G Greenwald and Mahzarin R Banaji. 1995. Implicit social cognition: attitudes, self-esteem, and stereotypes. *Psychological review* 102, 1 (1995), 4.

31. Catherine Grevet, Loren G Terveen, and Eric Gilbert. 2014. Managing political differences in social media. In *Proceedings of the 17th ACM conference on Computer supported cooperative work & social computing*. ACM, 1400–1408.

32. Kazi Saidul Hasan and Vincent Ng. 2014. Why are You Taking this Stance? Identifying and Classifying Reasons in Ideological Debates.. In *EMNLP*, Vol. 14. 751–762.

33. Tin Kam Ho. 1995. Random decision forests. In *Document Analysis and Recognition, 1995., Proceedings of the Third International Conference on*, Vol. 1. IEEE, 278–282.

34. Tin Kam Ho. 1998. The random subspace method for constructing decision forests. *IEEE transactions on pattern analysis and machine intelligence* 20, 8 (1998), 832–844.

35. Enamul Hoque and Giuseppe Carenini. 2014. Convis: A visual text analytic system for exploring blog conversations. In *Computer Graphics Forum*, Vol. 33. Wiley Online Library, 221–230.

36. Enamul Hoque and Giuseppe Carenini. 2015. Convisit: Interactive topic modeling for exploring asynchronous online conversations. In *Proceedings of the 20th International Conference on Intelligent User Interfaces*. ACM, 169–180.

37. Enamul Hoque and Giuseppe Carenini. 2016. Multiconvis: A visual text analytics system for exploring a collection of online conversations. In *Proceedings of the 21st International Conference on Intelligent User Interfaces*. ACM, 96–107.

38. Shih-Wen Huang, Pei-Fen Tu, Wai-Tat Fu, and Mohammad Amanzadeh. 2013. Leveraging the crowd to improve feature-sentiment analysis of user reviews. In *Proceedings of the 2013 international conference on Intelligent user interfaces*. ACM, 3–14.

39. Shafiq Joty, Giuseppe Carenini, and Raymond T Ng. 2013. Topic segmentation and labeling in asynchronous conversations. *Journal of Artificial Intelligence Research* 47 (2013), 521–573.

40. Joachim Krueger and Russell W Clement. 1994. The truly false consensus effect: an ineradicable and egocentric bias in social perception. *Journal of personality and social psychology* 67, 4 (1994), 596.

41. Audrey J Lee. 2005. Unconscious bias theory in employment discrimination litigation. *Harv. CR-CLL Rev.* 40 (2005), 481.

42. Weiyuan Li and Hua Xu. 2014. Text-based emotion classification using emotion cause extraction. *Expert Systems with Applications* 41, 4 (2014), 1742–1749.

43. Q Vera Liao and Wai-Tat Fu. 2014. Expert voices in echo chambers: effects of source expertise indicators on exposure to diverse opinions. In *Proceedings of the 32nd annual ACM conference on human factors in computing systems*. ACM, 2745–2754.

44. Q Vera Liao, Wai-Tat Fu, and Sri Shilpa Mamidi. 2015. It is all about perspective: An exploration of mitigating selective exposure with aspect indicators. In *Proceedings of the 33rd annual ACM conference on Human factors in computing systems*. ACM, 1439–1448.

45. Charles G Lord, Lee Ross, and Mark R Lepper. 1979. Biased assimilation and attitude polarization: The effects of prior theories on subsequently considered evidence. *Journal of personality and social psychology* 37, 11 (1979), 2098.

46. John D Marvel. 2015. Unconscious bias in citizens' evaluations of public sector performance. *Journal of Public Administration Research and Theory* 26, 1 (2015), 143–158.

47. Horace McCormick. 2015. The real effects of unconscious bias in the workplace. *UNC Executive Development, Kenan-Flagler Business School. DIRECCIÓN* (2015).

48. Sean A Munson, Stephanie Y Lee, and Paul Resnick. 2013. Encouraging Reading of Diverse Political Viewpoints with a Browser Widget.. In *ICWSM*.

49. Sean A Munson and Paul Resnick. 2010. Presenting diverse political opinions: how and how much. In *Proceedings of the SIGCHI conference on human factors in computing systems*. ACM, 1457–1466.

50. Eli Pariser. 2011. *The filter bubble: What the Internet is hiding from you*. Penguin UK.

51. Souneil Park, Seungwoo Kang, Sangyoung Chung, and Junehwa Song. 2009. NewsCube: delivering multiple aspects of news to mitigate media bias. In *Proceedings of the SIGCHI Conference on Human Factors in Computing Systems*. ACM, 443–452.

52. Lee Ross, David Greene, and Pamela House. 1977. The "false consensus effect": An egocentric bias in social perception and attribution processes. *Journal of experimental social psychology* 13, 3 (1977), 279–301.

53. Cass R Sunstein. 2009. *Republic. com 2.0*. Princeton University Press.

54. Songbo Tan and Jin Zhang. 2008. An empirical study of sentiment analysis for chinese documents. *Expert Systems with applications* 34, 4 (2008), 2622–2629.

55. Ryoko Tokuhisa, Kentaro Inui, and Yuji Matsumoto. 2008. Emotion classification using massive examples extracted from the web. In *Proceedings of the 22nd International Conference on Computational Linguistics-Volume 1*. Association for Computational Linguistics, 881–888.

56. Yiming Yang and Jan O Pedersen. 1997. A comparative study on feature selection in text categorization. In *Icml*, Vol. 97. 412–420.

57. John Zaller. 1992. *The nature and origins of mass opinion*. Cambridge university press.

58. Amy X Zhang, Lea Verou, and David R Karger. 2017. Wikum: Bridging Discussion Forums and Wikis Using Recursive Summarization.. In *CSCW*. 2082–2096.

59. Ding Zhou, Sergey A Orshanskiy, Hongyuan Zha, and C Lee Giles. 2007. Co-ranking authors and documents in a heterogeneous network. In *Data Mining, 2007. ICDM 2007. Seventh IEEE International Conference on*. IEEE, 739–744.

Visible Hearts, Visible Hands: A Smart Crowd Donation Platform

Chi-Hsien Yen*
Computer Science
University of Illinois at Urbana-Champaign
cyen4@illinois.edu

Yi-Chieh Lee*
Computer Science
University of Illinois at Urbana-Champaign
be341341@gmail.com

Wai-Tat Fu
Computer Science
University of Illinois at Urbana-Champaign
wfu@illinois.edu

ABSTRACT
On existing crowdfunding platforms, the allocation of money is often not regulated, which leads to less-than-ideal distribution of resources. For example, recent donations to hurricane victims through their crowdfunding campaigns often lead to overfunding of certain victims while underfunding others. Inspired by algorithms from economic theories, we proposed a Smart Crowd Donate system encourages donors to express preferences to multiple projects and reallocates funds dynamically across these preferences over time. We conducted a user study in which recruited 452 participants to simulate a small scale of crowdfunding. The findings of our user study supported the idea that the Smart Crowd Donate system has potential to efficiently distribute funds to projects and allows more projects to receive the amount of money they need.

Author Keywords
Crowdfunding; fundraising; donate; resource allocation;

INTRODUCTION
Crowdfunding sites such as Kickstarter, DonorsChoose, and GiveForward have received considerable attention, as exemplified by the growing numbers of projects and donations on such platforms. The key characteristic of crowdfunding is that anyone can raise money directly from the global "crowd" to help accomplish his or her design projects or various other purposes, bypassing traditional funding sources such as venture capitalists and financial institutions. In addition to raising funds for commercial purposes, crowdfunding websites have also been adopted by philanthropic organizations to attract potential donors and promote specific campaigns [20].

Typically, a crowdfunding project aggregates capital from many donors' small donations. Each donor may have a different perspective on the value of the project, but most intend to maximize the benefit of their donations with limited funds, leading them to give preference to lower-risk projects or donate less than their judged value [23]. This may result in some high-quality projects being unable to reach their donation goals, while a few superstar projects receive several times the amount of donations they were initially seeking [19]. For example, in September 2017, Hurricane Maria hit Puerto Rico and several other countries and caused tremendous damage and financial loss. To recover from the disaster, some organizations and individuals were raising fund through crowdfunding platforms. On current crowdfunding websites [9], we can find there were many on-going related campaigns; however, the funding distribution is inefficient - few campaign were highly overfunded, but many others were still far from their raising goals.

Previous studies [14, 24] have shown that success rates of the projects on crowdfunding websites are often low. While the majority of successful projects receive donations at or slightly above their target amounts, a significant proportion of projects attract funds totaling 200% of their target amount or more [14]. In addition, many projects receive donations only in the first few days after they are launched and thereafter slowly lose the attention of potential funders before eventually failing. These observations led us to speculate that the current "invisible hand" approach of matching massive numbers of small donations to crowdfunding projects is suboptimal, in the sense that the distribution of donations could be improved such that more high-quality projects would succeed.

Solomon et al. [19] demonstrated that superstar projects on crowdfunding websites affect the opportunity for mediocre projects to be funded because the former may set unrealistically high standards for fundable projects in donors' minds. Other studies have shown that social information systems reliant on user dynamics to distribute resources often lead to higher inequality and unpredictability [17], and this may help explain why the distribution of donations to crowdfunding projects is suboptimal. Previous studies [18] have also indicated that crowdfunding will require improved coordination methods, if scarce resources are to be effectively distributed.

In this paper, we present a new system for crowdfunding that renders donations more effective by spreading the benefit across more crowdfunding projects, along with the results of an experiment designed to test how the proposed method may impact crowdfundings complex dynamics. Specifically, the proposed method is inspired by economic theory's deferred acceptance algorithm [16] (Matching algorithm), which was originally used to help optimally allocate students to their

*The two first authors contributed equally to this work

*IUI'*18, March 711, 2018, Tokyo, Japan © 2018 Association for Computing Machinery. ACM ISBN 978-1-4503-4945-1/18/03 ...$15.00.
https://doi.org/10.1145/3172944.3172971

preferred high schools, by iteratively matching the students who were rejected in the previous round until most students match a school. This algorithm were also applied to various facets, such as wireless communications [4], social network for the exchange of resources [11], and assigning refugees to landlords [2]. These applications demonstrated the prospect of adopting matching algorithm to solve preference-based resource allocation problems. Therefore, we designed a new algorithm to fit the requirements of the crowdfunding environment, and then conducted an experimental simulation of crowdfunding to address the problems of how to distribute donations effectively.

Crowdfunding websites' current method of matching donors to projects is simply allowing each donor to choose a single project to donate to at a time. However, when donors are interested in multiple crowdfunding projects, it is not immediately clear how best to allocate these individuals limited capital into multiple projects in a way that effectively supports all of them. Our system therefore allows donors to select multiple projects simultaneously and decide the total amount of their donations. Our system then automatically spreads out their funds among their chosen set of projects based on the dynamics of ongoing crowdfunding activities.

In summary, the main contributions of this work are as follows. We propose a new donation system that allows donors to simultaneously support multiple projects in a more monetarily efficient way; and we also show how allocation of funding can be more desirable collectively when donors can express and rank their preferences to multiple projects and the system distributes their donations to multiple projects preferred by multiple donors.

RELATED WORK

Generosity is a long-standing tradition in modern societies. In the U.S.A., total giving to charities in 2015 was $373.25 billion, of which 71% came from individuals [21]. While donors are plentiful, prior research [6] has suggested that more than 15% of charitable giving was directed to poorly run organizations. Donors often have trouble assessing the effectiveness of charities, and sometimes rely on word-of-mouth or other social cues to help them make decisions. Andreoni [3] argued that because the impact of charitable giving cannot be quantified as easily as consumer products can, it is hard to predict behavior of individual donors. A few studies [15, 10] have shown that individual donors are concerned about the impact of their contributions, but in general, the effects of the perceived quality of charitable organizations on donating behavior has received relatively little scholarly attention [3].

Recently, people are choosing to donate to charities through many crowdfunding platforms. For example, GoFundMe aims to help nonprofit projects obtain capital; GiveForward provides a platform for patients to raise money for medical treatment; and DonorsChoose allows schoolteachers to seek funding for improvements in educational quality. These platforms strategies for encouraging potential donors to sponsor crowdfunding projects include donation matching and conditional donation [5], resulting in a wide array of cues that affect donors decision-making. For instance, information on past donors behavior may influence the decisions of future donors.

Research on Crowdfunding

Prior studies [12, 18, 23] have shown that policies regarding how donations can be made, how they are allocated, and how donors are rewarded will have significant impacts on the general process of matching donations with projects [12]. In general, these studies found that donors strive to maximize the impact of their donations, either to magnify the potential rewards to themselves (e.g., products they receive), or to promote greater community benefits (e.g., by helping more charitable projects succeed). However, relatively few researchers have studied the effects of new crowdfunding mechanisms [5]. Some of these mechanisms allow backers to provide more information about their project preferences. For example, Beltran et al. [5] proposed a mechanism called conditional donation, in which donors can specify conditions for their donations, and found that this encouraged more donations. Taken as a whole, results from such studies imply that giving potential donors more freedom to express their project preferences is desirable.

A number of studies have identified predictors of success for crowdfunding [24]. While many of these factors favor high-quality projects, others [12, 18] have shown that donation dynamics also greatly impact on the efficacy of crowdfunding campaigns. These dynamics are often not directly related to campaign quality. For example, rapid increases in donations often lead to a snowball effect, leading in turn to a rich-gets-richer effect similar to information cascades [1]. The rate of new donations also tends to increase when project deadlines are close, and when a project nears its target funding goal [1], suggesting that, all else being equal, donors prefer projects that are more likely to succeed. For example, by analyzing data from DonorsChoose, Wash [22] found that the size of the donation made by the last donor to a successful project tended to be much larger than the average donation to the same campaign, presumably because the donor knew his/her money was sufficient to help the project reach its goal. This suggests that donation dynamics and timings may play a significant role in influencing the allocation of donations. Indeed, when unregulated, they may lead to higher inequality and unpredictability of outcomes [17], which may undermine crowdfunding platforms ability to allocate funding to collectively preferred projects.

Charitable crowdfunding websites current method of matching donors to projects is simply to allow each donor to choose a single project to donate to at a time. Previous work [8] indicated that donors are motivated to support crowdfunding projects because of personal beliefs and philanthropic impulses, but worry that their donations will not be used effectively. Hence, how to optimize donors limited budgets in pursuit of more meaningful impacts is emerging as an important issue. When donors are interested in multiple projects, however, it is not immediately clear how best to allocate these individuals limited funds in a way that effectively supports all of them.

Algorithm 1 Donation Distribution Algorithm

```
procedure ALLOCATE
    donations_queue ← donations that need to be allocated. (new donation, or donations released from a failed project)

    while donation_queue is not empty do
        donation ← pop the first donation in donations

        // donate to projects that still need funding
        project_list ← prioritized projects specified in donation (based on (1) preference (2) deadline (3) money needed)
        while donation is not completely allocated do
            project ← the next project that is not successful yet from project_list
            allocate money to project without overfunding it

        // donate to the highest preferred project
        if donation is not completely allocated then
            project ← the highest preferred project in donation
            allocate remaining money to project
            released_donations ← same or less amount of donations previously allocated to project that could be reallocated
            push released_donations into donations_queue

        if donation is not completely allocated then
            donation could not be allocated (in this case, all the selected projects in donation are expired)
```

In mathematics and economics science, matching algorithms has been studied to pair agents from two sides of a market based on their preferences. For example, Gale and Shapley (1962) proposed deferred acceptance algorithm (DA) [7], which tentatively matches agents with their highest preferred choices, and iteratively matches the unpaired agents based on their next choices, while allowing already-matched pairs be changed if more preferable pair is found. The algorithm was originally used in school choice systems and stable marriage problems, but recent researchers have adopted it in different fields, such as wireless communications, where channel resources are allocated to multiple users with preferences [4], social cloud, where data storage or computational resources could be exchanged in a social network [11], and immigration issues, like assigning refugees to landlords in Swedan [2].

Although the algorithm could not be directly applied to crowdfunding because the market characteristics are essentially different from economics markets, the ideas of DA inspired us to design a donation allocation algorithm, which allows users to specify preferences over multiple campaigns and distributes donation based on preferences. Our algorithm tentatively allocates money to the user's highest preferred campaign, but defers the final allocation until the campaign is due, thus has the opportunity to reallocate money when better distribution is found. The algorithm is not proved to be stable or has other properties that DA has (which is not our intention in this paper); however, computer simulations were used to show that the algorithm improves overall campaign success rate in various settings [13, 25]. Lee et al. [13] used an agent-based simulation to explore the potential benefits of allowing donors to select multiple projects and distributing their donations by deferring final funding allocation. Yen et al. [25] further investigated this issue by simulating donors' different strategies of selecting crowdfunding projects in order to understand how the donors' behaviors may influence crowdfunding success rate. These works have shown pros and cons of deploying this algorithm by using agent-based simulation; however, it is still unclear how real users may use this new algorithm and how to map this algorithm to a proper interface design. Therefore, we designed an interface that integrates the proposed algorithm and conducted an usability test to evaluate the efficiency and effectiveness of the system through a crowdfunding experiment. In the following, we briefly describe how the algorithm works and how we designed a functioning crowdfunding platform that incorporates this preferential allocating algorithm.

SMART CROWD DONATE (SCD)

We named our algorithm Smart Crowd Donate (SCD). There are two major differences between SCD and current crowdfunding systems.

First, on existing crowdfunding platforms, donors must decide which project and how much money they want to donate without any systematic means of knowing what amount of money would be the most appropriate or helpful in each case. If donors spread their donations too thinly, many or all of the projects may fail because each receives too little money. On the other hand, if donors contribute to just a few projects, those projects may receive more money than they need, while others are starved of funding that they might otherwise have obtained. SCD, in contrast, enables donors to select multiple projects they want to donate to and specify a grand total amount of money that they want to donate to all of them. The system then automatically finds the optimal way to allocate money across the selected projects.

Second, after making a donation to a project on current platforms, a donor cannot reallocate it to one or more other projects if the first project fails to reach its donation goal, or if it attracts more money than it required. SCD allows all donations to be reallocated to other projects within a certain time period. We expect that by reallocating the money based on the preferences of the donors, our system could help more projects succeed.

In the following, we first describe the most unique feature of the proposed system, the donation distribution algorithm and conducted a user study to investigate how real users interact with our system.

Donation Distribution Algorithm

To realize the above two features, we developed the donation distribution algorithm. Every time a new donation is made or a project fails, the donations previously allocated to that project can be reallocated, and the procedure Allocate (Algorithm 1) is executed to redistribute the pledged money.

For each donation, the algorithm will first consider allocating the money to those projects that are ongoing but not successful yet. When a donor chooses multiple projects for a donation, they are prioritized based on three comparisons, in the order (1) projects with higher preference rankings, (2) projects that are closer to their deadlines, and (3) projects that need the least money. This priority is regard to the following three principles of our system attempt.

1. First, we tend to make the donors be satisfied with the donation distribution, thus, matching the funding to his/her higher preferred projects is essential.

2. Second, increasing the number of successful projects can make more overfunded money could be reallocated to other project. Therefore, if our system helps a project reach donation goal before their project deadline, the higher chance of its spare funding could be redistribute.

3. Finally, the donation continues to be allocated to fill those prioritized projects sequentially until there is no money left. The algorithm will not be overfunded any projects in this step.

Given these prioritization rules, money will be allocated to the lower-ranked projects only when the higher-ranked projects have either succeeded or expired. Otherwise, donors may feel dissatisfied on the grounds that the allocation has not followed their preferences. Also, projects closer to their deadlines are considered higher priority because even if they fail, our system can reallocate the money they were pledged to other projects. Where multiple projects are equally preferred and have the same deadline, the money is distributed to the project that needs less money, because it has a higher chance of succeeding.

If there is still money left after these allocation steps, the algorithm will assign the remaining money to the project with the highest preference ranking even if it is already successful. Then, the algorithm will attempt to move some money other than the donation from that project to other projects (the amount is equal to or less than the donation), because some previous donations may be reallocated. Therefore, more projects can benefit from the reallocated money, while the highest preferred project still succeeds.

In other words, in contrast to current systems, SCD requires that donations be able to move out of projects, as well as into them, in order to optimize overall resource utilization. We therefore set a fixed time period during which each donation may be removed and reallocated to other projects; among other things, this prevents a situation in which the donor never knows conclusively which projects their money has been allocated to.

Donation Methods

In our proposed system, each donor can select multiple projects at the same time, which is called a Multiple Selection (MS) donation. There are three possible different methods to give preferences towards multiple projects, as follows:

1. **MS with multiple Projects (Single-Lv):** In this method, a donor may select up to p projects and decide how much money they would like to donate in total (p is an adjustable parameter in our simulation). The donors do not have to rank their projects, which are all treated by the system as having same preference level.

2. **MS with multiple preference Levels (Sequence):** Here, the donor can select up to p projects and determine the amount of his/her total donation, but is required to rank all of their selected projects in a sequence. The system will allocate the money to projects with higher preferences first.

3. **MS with multiple Projects and Levels (Multi-Lv):** This method, we mix the first and second approaches described above. After choosing up to p projects, donors can group their selected projects into different preference levels, within which levels all projects are treated as equally preferred.

We select these three methods because they reflect the most common types of preferences a person may have towards many choices. When people like many projects but do not prefer any particular one, the preference follows Single-Lv method. When they rank all the projects as how students choose schools, they use Sequence method. Combined Single-Lv and Sequence is the Multi-Lv method. We are interested in understanding how the success rate will change by using different methods, and how people will react when the interface of each is given.

INTERFACE DESIGN

In addition to its novel fund-allocation methods, our system provides a new type of donation interface. Figure 1(a) shows the front page of this interface, which displays current projects on our crowdfunding site, and allows donors to click the heart-shaped icon to select the projects they might want to donate to. The main difference between our interface and those of previous crowdfunding sites is the donation page (Figure 1(b)), the design of which closely reflects the algorithm and three ranking systems described in the previous sections. However, if a donor prefers to donate to just one project, our system allows this. Donors can drag-and-drop

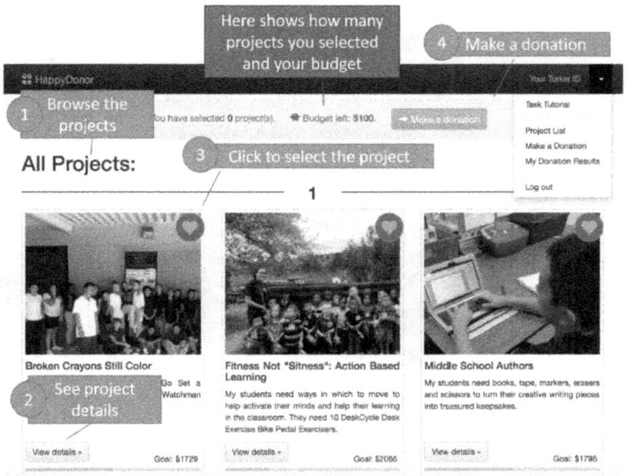

(a) The first page shows ongoing projects on our crowdfunding site

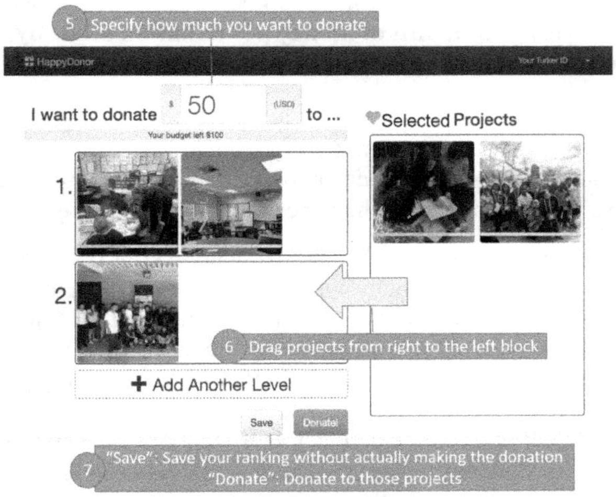

(b) User interface of our donation page on which donors can make a donation for the crowdfunding projects

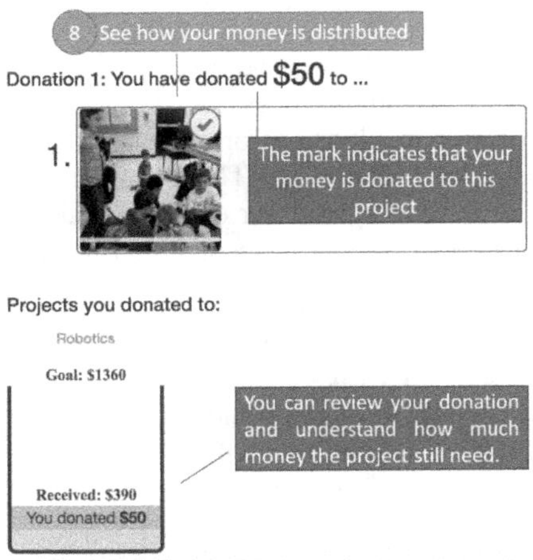

(c) User interface of our donation page on which donors can make a donation for the crowdfunding projects

Figure 1: This figure presents the interfaces we designed for our donation system. (a)Project list page (b)Donation page (c)Result page

project icons from "Selected Projects (right side)" to "Donation (left side)" and fill in the amount of money they want to donate via the "I want to donate" text box. Depends on the experiment condition a subject was assigned to, he or she can drag multiple projects into the same level (Single-Lv), or add multiple levels (Sequence), or do both (Multi-Lv).

Displaying Donation Results

One of the distinctive characteristics of our donation system is that it defers the final result of donation allocation. Because no other crowdfunding platforms do this, helping donors understand how our system distributes their money is therefore an important issue that may have a major effect on their reliance on our algorithm. Figure 1(c) presents our Donation Results interface. The top of the page shows the list of projects that the donor specified on the Donate page. The use of colorful vs. monochromatic images represents whether a given crowdfunding project is ongoing or failed, and the presence of a mark symbol at upper right indicates whether a donors funds have been distributed to that project.

At the bottom of the Donation Result page (Figure 1(c)), our interface shows the history of the pledged funds movements between a donors selected projects. We use a "cup" visualization to present the funding status of each project. The capacity of the cup denotes the raising goal of a given crowdfunding project; thus, when a new donation is assigned to a project, the liquid level (green part) increases proportionally based on the ratio of the new donation to the raising goal. However, a minimum height for the level of the liquid is assigned for purposes of visual clarity. When the cup has filled up completely, it indicates that the project has received enough money and succeeded.

EVALUATION

To explore the performance of our donation system, we conducted an online user study that simulated a crowdfunding site for educational fundraising campaigns. The study investigated the following questions: (1) How do the donors behave when using different donation methods on our crowdfunding site? (2) Whether does our algorithm distribute the donations to make more projects successful? (3) How satisfied are the donors with our donation system? and (4) How long is a donor willing to wait before learning the final distribution of their donation?

Method

Participants

We conducted this experiment on Amazon Mechanical Turk, with 452 participants (221 females). Their average age was 33 (SD = 10.03), and 49% of them had prior experience of using crowdfunding sites. After completing the experiment, which took between 10 and 20 minutes, each participant was paid US$.6 for their efforts.

Tasks

Project selection. In this study, we focused only on charitable (non-reward) crowdfunding campaigns in order to avoid any bias arising from the nature of the rewards offered a factor that the current version of our donation-distribution algorithm does not yet take into consideration. Therefore, we selected 32 real crowdfunding projects from DonorsChoose, which helps teachers raise funds for improving educational quality and students learning experience in the classroom. We chose equal numbers of these educational projects from two subject categories, Math & Science and Literacy & Language, to increase the likelihood that a given participant would be genuinely interested in at least some of them. In addition, we chose only projects with donation goals of between US$1,500 and US$2,300, so that the effect of donation goal on selecting projects is reduced when they make donation decisions. We intentionally included a much smaller number of projects in our study than appear on real crowdfunding platforms, because we wanted to encourage the participants to browse most or all of the projects on offer. Most of crowdfunding websites have functions to help sort tons of projects; however, the sorting function may influence donors' donating behaviors, for example, if a donor sorted projects by using deadline, they might tend to donate to the project which is close to the deadline. To ensure that all of the projects had an equal opportunity of being seen and read about, the order in which they appeared on the front page was randomized for each participant.

Project attributes setting. In order to render our crowdfunding site more similar to real-world situations, we controlled the status of each project. First, we divided each of the two thematic categories into four equal groups of four projects each. The first quarter of the projects were initially set as having received 0% of their donation goals; the second quarter, 25%; the third quarter, 50%; and the fourth, 75%.

We set the duration of each project at four weeks, but assigned them different start dates so that some would expire earlier than others. When the study began, a quarter of projects had their full four weeks left to run; a second quarter had three weeks remaining; another quarter, two weeks; and a fourth quarter, only one week to go.

The combination of four initial funding levels and four deadline settings yielded 16 subgroups among the projects, each containing two projects, one from each subject area.

Procedure

Based on the algorithm introduced above, our experiment probed four conditions. Each condition separately includes the same set of crowdfunding projects as described above, but the fundraising progress of the projects in each condition was independent of the other conditions.

Control Condition: This condition was a control group mimicking current crowdfunding sites on which donors only choose one project at a time and decide how much to donate to that project alone.

Single-Lv Condition: The participants assigned to this condition used **Single-Lv** donation method.

Sequence Condition: The participants assigned to this condition used **Sequence** donation method.

Multi-Lv Condition: The participants assigned to this condition used **Multi-Lv** donation method.

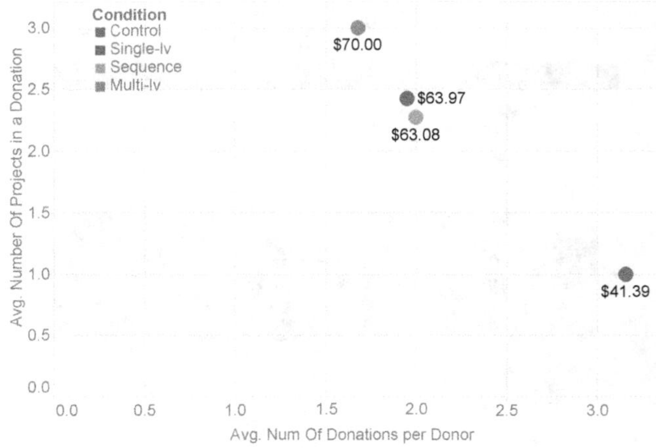

Figure 2: The scatter plot shows the relationship between average number of projects for each donation and average number of donations made by each donor. The labels are the average amounts of money per donation made by each donor.

Each participant was randomly assigned to one of these four conditions, resulting in each condition having approximately 113 participants in it. The experiment ran for 10 days.

Before the participants began to donate via our donation system, we presented them with a tutorial explaining the functions of our crowdfunding site and encouraging them to use it as they would use a crowdfunding site in the real world. Additionally, we informed them that if any crowdfunding project in the experiment successfully achieved its donation goal, we would donate a sum equal to 1% of what the participants had fictively donated to the real campaign [1]. It was hoped that this would encourage the participants to think more carefully about which crowdfunding projects they elected to support.

Each participant in each experimental condition was assigned the same donation budget, of US $100, and was allowed to decide whether to fully expend this budget or not. After they completed the donation process, our system showed them the initial allocation result and informed them that the final result will be revealed in 15 days. Then, we administered an online survey to investigate their decision-making process and preferences regarding our proposed interface and system.

After finishing the donation task, the participants were required to fill in a survey. The survey contained eight items scored using 5-point Likert scales (with 1 = strongly disagree and 5 = strongly agree) and an additional three items consisting of open-ended questions. All 11 items measured users experience with our donation system and their decision-making processes as donors.

RESULTS AND DISCUSSION

Behavior

Figure 2 displays the average number of projects in the four experimental conditions for each donation. Although donors

[1]We did donate money to the original campaigns that succeeded in our study as promised.

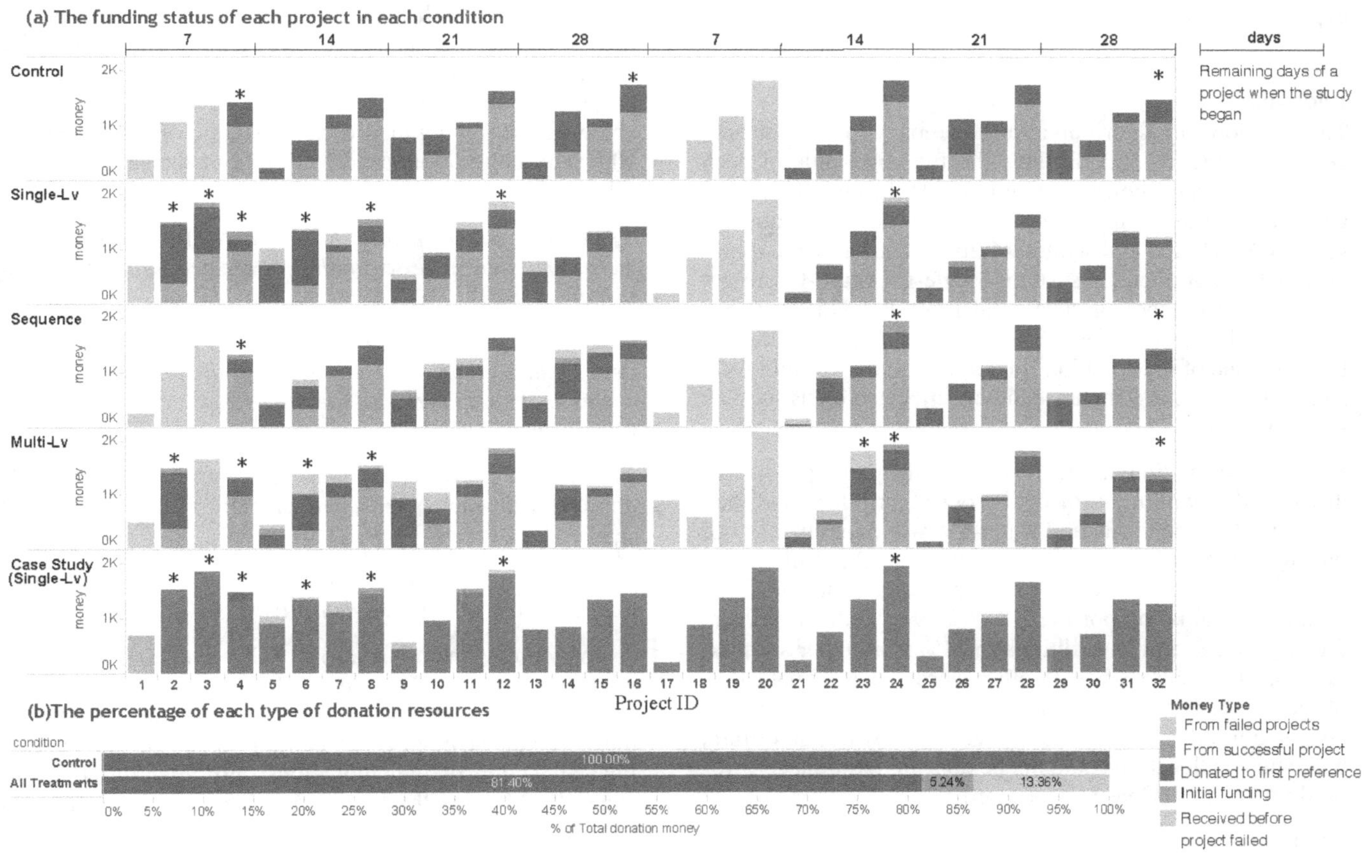

Figure 3: Money allocation among projects. Light blue: initial funding each project had when the study began. Dark blue: money allocated to the highest preferred project. Orange: money moved from successful projects. Pink: money moved from failed projects. Gray: money received by a project before it expired. '*' indicates the project succeeded at the end of the study.

could opt to fund just one project in Single-Lv, Sequence, and Multi-Lv, donors did chose to fund more than one projects in average (1 in Control condition, 2.42 in Single-Lv, 2.27 in Sequence, and 3.00 in Multi-Lv). In addition, as shown in Figure 2, the average number of donations made by each donor in Control condition was 3.16, as compared to 1.95 in Single-Lv, 2.00 in Sequence and 1.68 in Multi-Lv. On the contrary, the average amounts of money per donation made by each donor increase in Single-Lv, Sequence, and Multi-Lv ($41 in Control condition, $64 in Single-Lv, $63 in Sequence, and $70 in Multi-Lv). These findings imply that the donors did show different donation strategies when they utilized our system.

Within the non-control groups, as Figure 2 shows, Multi-Lv had a larger average donation amount than Single-Lv or Sequence, which also caused Multi-Lv's donation times to decrease. In other words, Multi-Lv donors placed multiple projects in the same donation and assigned more money to it. This may have been because donors in Multi-Lv had the most flexibility in arranging the crowdfunding projects they wanted to donate to.

The average number of projects contributed to per donor varied across the four experimental conditions, from as few as 3 (Control condition) to as many as 4.5 (Multi-Lv). This appears to suggest that our donation method encouraged donors to choose more crowdfunding projects. Though the variation was not high (no significant effect), it may have been restricted by the small size of the budgets assigned to the participants. Further research should seek to clarify this result via a larger range of donor budgets.

The more projects the donors chose to donate to, the more flexibility of our system could reallocate the donation. Our empirical user study showed that users generally placed two to three projects in a donation set, even though the interface allowed them to choose more than three. Again, a possible explanation for this may be linked to the small size of the budgets they were given, which may have led them to worry about spreading their limited funds too thinly to have a noticeable positive impact on the projects. Nor did we reveal our hypothesis to the participants that if donors chose more projects, the success rate of the experimental crowdfunding site as a whole would increase. In future research, it might be useful to study the effects on donors behaviors if we were to explain the potential benefits of our donation algorithm to the users.

Allocation

To show how our algorithm allocated money to increase success rates, Figure 3(a) displays the funding status of each project in each of the four conditions. At the end of our user study, three projects in Control condition, three in Sequence, seven in Single-Lv, and eight in Multi-Lv had succeeded, suggesting that our donation system (Single-Lv, Multi-Lv) might increase the number of successful projects. However, Sequence did not outperform SS. One possible explanation is that the scale of the donations in our user study was relatively small; therefore, less money can be reallocated by using such strict method.

Further investigation of how funds from the participants were distributed among the projects by our algorithm found that, in Single-Lv, Sequence, and Multi-Lv, while the majority of the money (81.4%) was allocated because the project was one of the highest preferred projects in a participants donation, a substantial proportion (13.36%) was reallocated from failed projects, and an additional 5.24% from other successful projects (Figure 3(b)). In other words, approximate 18% of the money in Single-Lv, Sequence, and Multi-Lv were reallocated to other projects for better usage by our algorithm, while this reallocation could not be done in traditional crowdfunding systems (Control condition).

The bottom row in Figure 3(a) provides an example of how our algorithm moved money to help more projects succeed. In condition Single-Lv, project 4 succeeded before its deadline, but kept receiving more money from the donors (shown as a red bar). Because the project had received sufficient support, the algorithm moved the additional funding to other projects that were also preferred by the donors (orange bars). Project 1, meanwhile, failed when its time limit expired. Our algorithm released the money it had received up to that point (purple bar) and moved it to other projects based on the donors preferences (pink). In all, its funds were moved to eight other projects, including projects 6, 8, and 12, which also succeeded in the end.

User Experience with SCD

Overall, the participants reported high levels of satisfaction with our donation system: They found it easy to use the ranking interface (Single-Lv=4.1, Sequence=3.8, and Multi-Lv=3.7). A one-way ANOVA with condition as the independent variable shows significance ($F(2, 340) = 3.3$, $p < .05$), and the post-hoc Tukey HSD test shows that the score of Single-Lv is significantly higher than that of Multi-Lv ($p < .05$). Most also reported that the results page was easy to understand (Control condition=4.34 Single-Lv=4.40, Sequence=4.13, and Multi-Lv=4.2).

We asked the participants who had placed more than one project in a donation (67.35% donors in Single-Lv, Sequence, and Multi-Lv) to explain why they had wanted to selected multiple projects. Most who had done so reported that it was difficult for them to choose between similar projects they wanted to donate to, and that they had therefore selected all of them and allowed the system to help them find the best way to distribute their donations among them. Because the budget was limited, some of the donors who had selected multiple projects reported that it was difficult to decide on a reasonable way of splitting their donations. Two of the participants who selected multiple projects described their experience as follows:

"There was not one project I only wanted to donate to. There were some that were so similar; it seemed wrong to choose just one." (S13)

"I wanted to help all of the choices that I made. The one hundred dollars made me feel limited on the choices I made. I wish I could help them all, there were some excellent creativity and needs." (S101)

The participants who only donated to one project held similar opinions with each other. For example:

"I selected one donation because I really wanted to go all-in on this project. I believe it has the potential to be extremely impactful this teachers students lives." (S43)

As previously mentioned, our SCD donation system announced that it would probably finish redistributing donors funds across the selected projects within 15 days. We asked the participants if they felt comfortable with knowing the final allocation of their donations only after this time had elapsed. Most of the participants reported a positive attitude toward this policy (Single-Lv=3.93, Sequence=3.96, and Multi-Lv=3.81). However, we also asked them how long they would ideally like to wait to know the final allocation results, if they were allowed to decide this.

Half the participants (n=224) reported that ideally, they would like to know the final results of their donation allocation within five days, while the other half (n=228) expressed that they were comfortable with waiting more than five days. It is reasonably clear that if the donation system adopts a longer deferral period, the overall success rate of crowdfunding will increase, and that a deferral period of greater than five days is sufficiently beneficial. The general acceptability to users of a six-day-plus deferral period (i.e., even those who preferred a shorter period did not appear to strongly prefer it) suggests that real-world use of our algorithm is feasible.

In summary, from the results of the user study, we demonstrated that (1) compared to the traditional method (SS), donors did show different donation strategies when they used our system (Single-Lv, Sequence, Multi-Lv), i.e., they chose more projects and assigned more money in a donation. (2) Our algorithm reallocated 18.4% of the money for better usage, and the number of successful projects in Single-Lv and Multi-Lv is higher than the other methods in our study. (3) donors showed positive attitudes toward our donation interfaces and system policies, reflecting the feasibility and practicability of our donation system.

DISCUSSION

Although large amounts of money are donated through crowdfunding platforms every year, success rates of projects on most such platforms are lower than 60%. Many factors may affect donors motivation to make donations, but we believe one of the main problems is the inefficiency of the current crowdfunding donation method. Because it is difficult for individual donors to assess how much money a project needs at any given time, a better approach is to encourage them to provide their private preferences, and allow the crowdfunding system to adaptively reallocate their donations to those projects that need funding the most. Moreover, from the perspective of project creators, this would allow more attention to be focused on the quality of their projects, and give less weight to funding goals and deadlines than has been the case with traditional crowdfunding platforms [17, 18]. Our study is an initial step in this direction.

Based on our experimental results, in general, donors are willing to trust a donation system to help them coordinate their donations to multiple projects. Although our donation methods allowed donors to put just one project in each donation if they wished, we found that most of them put multiple projects into a donation, which implies (1) that they trusted our donation system to coordinate and optimize their donations, and (2) that it was easy for them to use the system. In the post-study survey, some participants indicated that it was difficult to choose a specific project to donate to, and that they welcomed a way of distributing their donations more widely. This is perhaps especially true of charitable crowdfunding platforms, on which many projects may request comparable materials and/or have similar donation goals.

Moreover, donation methods should aim to provide high levels of freedom for algorithms to reallocate funding, but also high levels of user control, in terms of allowing users to express their preferences. Our results show that different designs of donation interface led to different donation behaviors. The donors made fewer donations, but put more projects and higher amounts of money into each donation, especially as compared to the SS method (Control condition). Multi-Lv provides the highest level of user control, in that they allow the placement of multiple projects in the same level as well as the addition of multiple levels. For these reasons, donors may be able to express their preferences more flexibly. Meanwhile, the more projects are selected in each donation, the more opportunity our system has to reallocate money, which results in more efficient overall distribution.

This method also causes delay of donation distribution. Although our survey result indicated that the participants felt comfortable with waiting 15 days to acquire final donation distribution, we conservatively regard this result. Although a longer delay period helps increase overall success rate as more opportunities of donation reallocation can be exploited, such a long delay time may cause frustration or dissatisfaction among users. Further studies are necessary to understand the delay issue when deploying this system in a real crowdfunding website.

Taken as a whole, the results of the user study indicate the usefulness of our new donation interface, especially for donors who want to make contributions to many projects at a time. This study shows potential pros and cons of deploying the donation distribution algorithm. Compared to the current donation method, SCD encourages donors to select multiple projects in a donation and express their preferences when donating. In addition, the experiment demonstrated how this system could effectively distribute funding to the projects based on donors' preferences. However, few disadvantages of using this method should be considered. For example, donors may take more time to pick up multiple projects and rank them while donating. Also, donors need to wait a certain amount of time to know the final funding allocation. These characteristics of the system might decrease their willingness to donate, preventing impulsive donations. Perhaps in the future crowdfunding site design, donors can choose to use either method in the interface, depending on how they like the way donations are allocated. In any cases, the developers of crowdfunding platforms should seek to strike a careful balance between the flexibility allowed to a donor when expressing preferences, and algorithms' freedom to allocate money.

LIMITATIONS AND FUTURE RESEARCH

This study has some limitations. First, we simulated a crowdfunding site in our experiment rather than applying our system to a genuine site, and only included non-reward, charitable crowdfunding campaigns. Deploying this system to other types of crowdfunding is one of the future research directions.

This kind of fund-reallocation enabled system may not fit reward-based crowdfunding (e.g., Kickstarter) well because donors on those platforms may only be interested in specific rewards. The algorithm should take value of rewards into account when reallocating donations in such scenarios.

Second, we recruited participants from Amazon Mechanical Turk to act as donors. Although this method can attract a variety of participants, it is not capable of simulating the enormous scale of the global audience for real crowdfunding sites. In our study, we assigned a fixed amount of budget to the participants; real donors, making donations with their own money, might have different considerations and reactions/behaviors, which limits the external validity of our study. It would therefore be useful to conduct a study using our system on actual donors. How many projects would a real user select? How would they structure their preferences? Would the reallocating feature affect their motivation to donate, and if so, in what way? In addition, our experiment only included 32 projects so the participants might have chance to review all projects before making decision. However, there are always thousands of projects in a real crowdfunding website, and the donors tend to use ranking and filter functions to help them find preferred projects, which may influence their donation behavior. In other words, it would be worth deploying our donation system on one or more real crowdfunding platforms to verify its benefits in the future.

Lastly, previous studies have indicated that many donors on crowdfunding sites may wait and see how many other donors support certain projects, because they want to choose projects without a high risk of failure [18]. Logically, this could result in a state of mutual hesitation that would harm the success rate of crowdfunding as a whole. It is possible to mitigate this deadline-driven strategies by our system, e.g., showing how many donors select a project in their donations (not necessarily donate to) to signal the social preference. Future studies should examine this question.

CONCLUSION

Existing crowdfunding platforms generally lack mechanisms for the effective coordination of donations. Our Smart Crowd Donation system allows donors to specify the total amount of money in a donation to multiple crowdfunding projects, which are then allocated the money in an optimal manner. The user study we conducted to evaluate this system found that (1) users could understand the interface well and use it in the intended way; (2) our algorithm could reallocate users money in a manner that caused more projects to succeed; and (3) users had positive attitudes to the overall donation experience, and no strongly negative ones toward the waiting time the system required. This SCD system can be seen as having potential for future use in crowdfunding research and practice to improve resource allocation.

ACKNOWLEDGMENTS

We thank the anonymous reviewers for their insightful comments. This research was supported by grants NSF SES-1419297 and NSF IIS-1441563.

REFERENCES

1. Agrawal, A. K., Catalini, C., and Goldfarb, A. Some simple economics of crowdfunding. Tech. rep., National Bureau of Economic Research, 2013.
2. Andersson, T., and Ehlers, L. Assigning refugees to landlords in sweden: Stable maximum matchings.
3. Andreoni, J. Philanthropy. *Handbook of the economics of giving, altruism and reciprocity 2* (2006), 1201–1269.
4. Bayat, S., Li, Y., Song, L., and Han, Z. Matching theory: Applications in wireless communications. *IEEE Signal Processing Magazine 33*, 6 (2016), 103–122.
5. Beltran, J. F., Siddique, A., Abouzied, A., and Chen, J. Codo: Fundraising with conditional donations. In *Proceedings of the 28th Annual ACM Symposium on User Interface Software & Technology (UIST)*, ACM (2015), 213–222.
6. Budak, C., and Rao, J. M. Measuring the efficiency of charitable giving with content analysis and crowdsourcing. In *Tenth International AAAI Conference on Web and Social Media* (2016).
7. Gale, D., and Shapley, L. S. College admissions and the stability of marriage. *The American Mathematical Monthly 69*, 1 (1962), 9–15.
8. Gerber, E. M., and Hui, J. Crowdfunding: Motivations and deterrents for participation. *ACM Transactions on Computer-Human Interaction (TOCHI) 20*, 6 (2013), 34.
9. GoFundMe, and project, H. www.gofundme.com/mvc.php?route=category&term=hurricane.
10. Gordon, T. P., Knock, C. L., and Neely, D. G. The role of rating agencies in the market for charitable contributions: An empirical test. *Journal of accounting and public policy 28*, 6 (2009), 469–484.
11. Haas, C. *Incentives and two-sided matching-engineering coordination mechanisms for social clouds*, vol. 12. KIT Scientific Publishing, 2014.
12. Kuppuswamy, V., and Bayus, B. L. Crowdfunding creative ideas: The dynamics of project backers in kickstarter. *UNC Kenan-Flagler Research Paper*, 2013-15 (2015).
13. Lee, Y.-C., Yen, C.-H., and Fu, W.-T. Improving donation distribution for crowdfunding: An agent-based model. In *Social, Cultural, and Behavioral Modeling: 9th International Conference, SBP-BRiMS 2016, Washington, DC, USA, June 28-July 1, 2016, Proceedings 9*, Springer (2016), 3–12.
14. Mollick, E. The dynamics of crowdfunding: An exploratory study. *Journal of business venturing 29*, 1 (2014), 1–16.
15. Parsons, L. M. The impact of financial information and voluntary disclosures on contributions to not-for-profit organizations. *Behavioral research in accounting 19*, 1 (2007), 179–196.
16. Roth, A. E. Deferred acceptance algorithms: History, theory, practice, and open questions. *international Journal of game Theory 36*, 3-4 (2008), 537–569.
17. Salganik, M. J., Dodds, P. S., and Watts, D. J. Experimental study of inequality and unpredictability in an artificial cultural market. *science 311*, 5762 (2006), 854–856.
18. Solomon, J., Ma, W., and Wash, R. Don't wait!: How timing affects coordination of crowdfunding donations. In *Proceedings of the 18th ACM Conference on Computer Supported Cooperative Work & Social Computing (CSCW)*, ACM (2015), 547–556.
19. Solomon, J., Ma, W., and Wash, R. Highly successful projects inhibit coordination on crowdfunding sites. In *Proceedings of the SIGCHI Conference on Human Factors in Computing Systems*, ACM (2016).
20. Tanaka, K. G., and Voida, A. Legitimacy work: Invisible work in philanthropic crowdfunding. In *Proceedings of the SIGCHI Conference on Human Factors in Computing Systems*, ACM (2016).
21. USA, G. Giving usa annual report 2015, 2015.
22. Wash, R. The value of completing crowdfunding projects. In *Proceedings of the International Conference on Weblogs and Social Media (ICWSM)*, AAAI (2013).
23. Wash, R., and Solomon, J. Coordinating donors on crowdfunding websites. In *Proceedings of the 17th ACM conference on Computer supported cooperative work & social computing (CSCW)*, ACM (2014), 38–48.

24. Xu, A., Yang, X., Rao, H., Fu, W.-T., Huang, S.-W., and Bailey, B. P. Show me the money!: An analysis of project updates during crowdfunding campaigns. In *Proceedings of the SIGCHI Conference on Human Factors in Computing Systems*, ACM (2014), 591–600.

25. Yen, C.-H., Lee, Y.-C., and Fu, W.-T. Improving the efficiency of allocating crowd donations with agent-based simulation model. In *International Conference on Social Computing, Behavioral-Cultural Modeling and Prediction and Behavior Representation in Modeling and Simulation*, Springer (2017), 248–253.

Ev'ry Little Movement Has a Meaning of Its Own:

Using Past Mouse Movements to Predict the Next Interaction

Tiffany C.K. Kwok[1], Eugene Yujun Fu[1], Erin You Wu[1], Michael Xuelin Huang[2], Grace Ngai[1], Hong-Va Leong[1]
[1]Department of Computing, Hong Kong Polytechnic University, Hong Kong, China
[2]Max Planck Institute for Informatics, Saarland Informatics Campus, Germany
[1]{csckkwok,csyfu,csywu,csgngai,cshleong}@comp.polyu.edu.hk
[2]mhuang@mpi-inf.mpg.de

ABSTRACT
User experience could be enhanced if the computer could understand human interaction intention. For instance, it could react to intercept and prevent interaction errors. This paper presents an approach to predicting users' intention in interaction tasks based on past mouse movements. We adopt a long short-term memory (LSTM) model to predict the users' intention via their next mouse click interaction, upon being trained with past mouse interaction behaviors. To evaluate, we consider two scenarios in daily computer usage: a more structured crowdsourcing annotation task and a more free-form, open-ended web search task. Our results indicate that we could predict the next interaction event with reasonable accuracy. We also conducted a pilot study to investigate the possibility of applying our model for non-intentional mouse click detection. We believe that our findings would be beneficial towards the development of better intelligent agents.

Author Keywords
User Intention; Mouse Interaction; Human-Computer Interaction; Non-intentional Mouse Click Detection;

INTRODUCTION

Understanding users' affect, intentions and behaviors has long been one of the goals of human-computer interaction research. A computer that knows users' intentions and understands users' behaviors could make intelligent decisions to enhance users' experience. Applications include estimating users' skill acquisition and learning progress [13], estimating task performance [1], predicting users' next action or interaction [19] or even distinguishing users' potential mistakes or errors [18].

IUI'18, March 7–11, 2018, Tokyo, Japan

ACM ISBN 978-1-4503-4945-1/18/03...$15.00
https://doi.org/10.1145/3172944.3173002

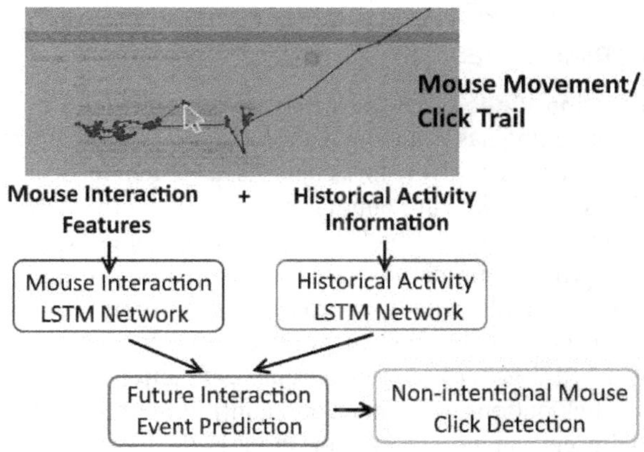

Figure 1. Model overview: A dual-stream LSTM

Almost all complex tasks on the computer require users to perform a series of actions. To enhance users' experience, it would be useful if an intelligent interface could anticipate what the user is going to do next and to prepare in advance, so as to deliver the right information at the right time.

A large body of work has explored user intention prediction during browsing activities. For example, browsing history and search queries were exploited to enhance online service recommendation [4]. Searching behaviors were studied to predict the next URL classes that a user intends to visit [14]. However, these methods relied on browsing context, and is thus hard to generalize to other tasks and activities.

Despite the importance of the mouse in daily computer usage [2], little attention has been paid to analyzing mouse interaction data to extract user information, such as identity [17] and mental state [12]. Far less has been studied for user intention prediction. Guo et al. used mouse movement and eye gaze features to predict ad clicking [10]. Diaz et al. investigated mouse movement behavior to predict searching results [3]. Some work has also proposed a task-agnostic prediction model. For example, Pasqual et al. predicted the mouse endpoint using movement template matching [16]. Ziebart et al. studied a probabilistic model to predict movement points from previous clicks [20].

Despite effort in previous work, most studies focus on either specific tasks, or predefined interfaces. A task- and interface-agnostic intention prediction is very challenging, as 1) it is uncertain when the user intends to click; 2) the travel distance of mouse movements may vary, and 3) it is highly affected by the nature of a task. To the best of our knowledge, we are the first to address these questions jointly. In this paper, we propose a dual-stream Long Short-Term Memory (LSTM) network [7,11] (Figure 1) to predict the *next interaction activity* based on mouse movement features only, and across two common and diverse tasks: crowdsourcing annotation and web search.

The contribution of this paper includes: We 1) predict the next mouse interaction event given past mouse behaviors; 2) evaluate our prediction models via two different tasks with reasonable accuracy; 3) apply our model to non-intentional mouse click detection.

EXPERIMENT DESIGN

Annotating Videos in a Crowdsourcing Interface

Crowdsourcing has been much used as a method of gathering massive training data for supervised machine learning methods. To make sure annotators can efficiently complete an annotation task, an intelligent assistant should be able to sense when annotators are distracted, confused or interrupted, and provide appropriate information. To this end, we need to be able to predict users' true intent. We considered a general crowdsourcing annotation task where users click buttons to annotate and confirm their answer, and model users' intentions via their mouse click events.

Subjects were asked to watch videos of people who are viewing emotion elicitation videos from the DISFA dataset [15] and annotate the video with the emotion(s) that the viewer is exhibiting based on the facial expressions. To ensure the annotation quality [6], we asked the annotators to self-report their confidence level for each annotation label(s) before submitting their labels and moving on.

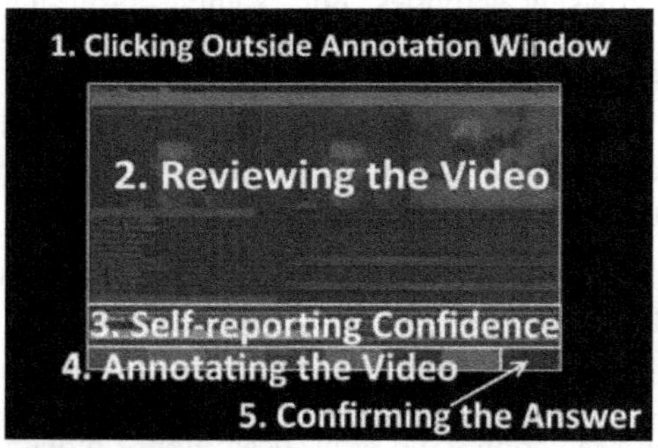

Figure 2. Interface of video annotation and its components

The interface for video annotation contains four basic components (Figure 2), which correspond to different user activities: 1) reviewing the video, 2) self-reporting, 3) annotating, and 4) confirming the annotation. Users sometimes click outside the window, generating a fifth kind of activity.

This experiment involved 15 subjects (seven females), all comfortable with computer usage. Each subject was asked to annotate 243 video clips. After viewing each clip, they were asked to report their confidence level before progressing to the next clip. In total, 18,059 clicks were collected.

Information Search

The crowdsourcing annotation task was performed on a relatively fixed and simple interface. For a more realistic scenario, we studied a web search task, which involved more complicated interactions: users could be choosing from returned links, looking for key information, opening a new tab or clicking the submit button.

Our web search experiment asked subjects to play a game similar to the search game "A Google a Day" [8]. Users were asked to find the answer to a given question by searching on the web. The question was formulated such that the answer cannot be found via a simple web search. We restricted the browser and search engine to Chrome and Google.

Since the web search may return *any* page, the interface of web search task is not fixed and we cannot classify a user's activity by the mouse click location as we did for the crowdsourcing task. Instead, we defined an event as a change in the currently-viewed page in the browser and did a rough classification of the content on the page, which serves as an indication of the users' intent. For instance, a "New Tab" probably means the user wants to start a new search, and users visiting a page linked to from the search results are probably in the state of finding information. We thus classified five types of activities: 1) reading the question, 2) starting new search, 3) deciding between the returned search results, 4) parsing information, and 5) clicking the submit button.

This experiment involved 15 subjects (seven females), all comfortable with computer usage. A user interface, only used for displaying questions and submitting answers, was designed for the purposes of repeatability and controllability. Each subject was asked to answer six questions. In total, 7,877 clicks were collected.

METHODOLOGY

We are interested in whether we can predict the next activity, i.e. the type of next mouse click event, given ***T*** seconds of mouse movement. We believe that since the activities are sequential and each activity is dependent on past ones, therefore, hidden information of users' intentions can be deduced from the activity history.

Long Short-Term Memory (LSTM) Model

We propose a two-stream LSTM framework to predict users' intentions (Figure 1). Our proposed network framework utilizes the historical activity information as well as the mouse interaction information to predict user's intentions. Instead of modeling the two types of features in one LSTM network, we model them via two separate LSTM networks and adopt a weighted average approach to fuse the mouse interaction and historical activity networks.

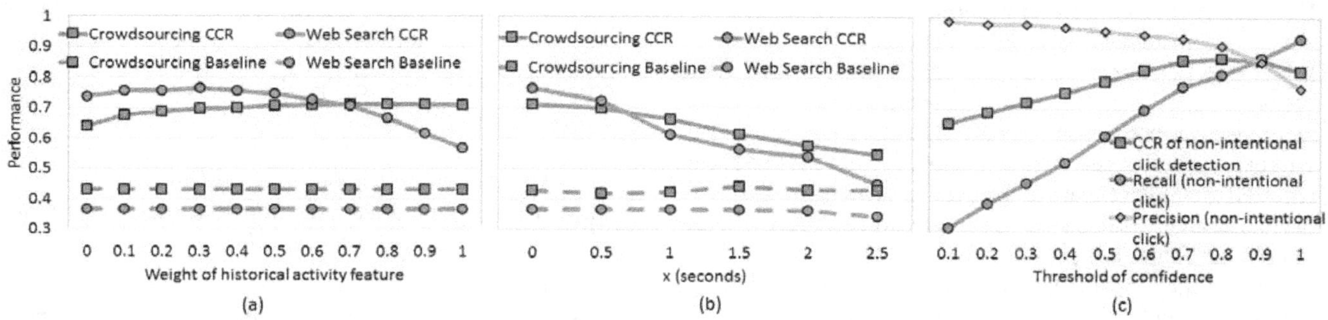

Figure 3. (a) Results of fusing the LSTM networks with different weights. (b) Results of predicting user's intention x seconds ahead. (c) Results of non-intentional mouse click detection.

Both networks are modelled as an LSTM with two layers and 64 neurons on each layer. We use the mini-batch stochastic gradient descent algorithm to learn the network parameters, where the batch size is set to 128 and momentum set to 0.8. The learning rate is initialized as 0.001 and decays by 10 times every 10,000 iterations. The whole training procedure stops after 30,000 iterations.

Mouse Interaction Features

We hypothesize that users' intention may be concealed behind mouse behaviors, especially in crowdsourcing and in web search tasks, where the mouse serves as a key input method. The mouse movements may vary depending on whether the user is reading text, watching videos, clicking links or making decisions. Our mouse interaction LSTM network uses features from mouse movements as input.

Table 1 shows our mouse movement features. The features are extracted from mouse interactions that happen within a time window before the current moment. Given a time window of T seconds, where T is the number of steps in our mouse interaction LSTM network, and a sampling rate of fs Hz gives us $T \times fs$ mouse feature vectors. Each mouse feature vector represents the mouse interaction information at that moment.

Descriptions	Features
Mouse coordinate	*x*, *y*
Mouse move speed	*x* speed, *y* speed, total speed
Mouse move acceleration	*x* acceleration, *y* acceleration, total acceleration
Mouse move angle	movement angle, angle difference
Mouse area of interest (AOI)	current AOI, previous AOI
Activity state	current activity state

Table 1. Mouse interaction features.

We also hypothesize that historical activity information may indicate what a user is going to do next. Thus, we provide the historical activity features as input to our historical activity LSTM network. Our historical activity features include the K most recent activities, where K is the number of steps in our historical activity LSTM network, and their durations. The input for a step S is the activity state and duration of the $(K\text{-}S)^{th}$ recent activity.

RESULTS AND DISCUSSION

We evaluate our model in three ways. First, we evaluate its performance in predicting the next activity – i.e. the interaction event that will happen immediately after the current moment. Then, we evaluate its performance on a the more challenging task of predicting a future event that *will happen* within the next 0s~2.5s. Finally, we evaluate our method on detecting non-intentional clicks.

Predicting the Next Activity / Interaction Event

We first evaluate our model for the scenarios in which it is known that an activity is about to occur. Our mouse interaction network considers mouse movements within the last $T = 1$ seconds, and our historical activity network considers the previous $K = 5$ activities. These parameters are chosen as it is known that information which is too far away from the prediction point is not too useful for understanding users' intention [5]. We randomly split the set 90%/10% for training/testing. Using ZeroR, which classifies all instances as the majority class in the training set, gives a baseline of 42.9% correctly classified rate (CCR) for the crowdsourcing task and 36.5% for the web searching task.

Figure 3(a) shows the results of fusing the LSTM networks with different weights. A higher weight W means that the historical activity information network has a greater influence on the prediction (and hence less influence for mouse activity). The figure shows that the crowdsourcing task, which has a fixed interface and a relatively fixed order of interaction, benefits more from the historical activity information, but, the web search task, which is relatively more free-form and unpredictable, benefits more from mouse interaction information. We achieve the best performance for crowdsourcing task when the weight of historical activity network W=0.8, and for web search when W=0.3.

Task	Baseline	Mouse interaction	Historical activity	Fusion
Crowdsourcing	42.9%	63.9%	70.9%	71.2%
Web Searching	36.5%	73.7%	56.8%	76.5%

Table 2. Performance of models using different features.

Table 2 presents the results of using only mouse interaction, historical activity, and the fusion of the two networks on the crowdsourcing and web search tasks respectively.

The results show that all models beat the baseline by more than 20%. Specifically, for the crowdsourcing task, the fused model outperforms baseline by more than 28%, and on the web search task, by 40%. The results are encouraging, implying that historical information and mouse behavior are indicative of users' next activity and thus their intention.

Predicting an Activity in the Future

We have evaluated our intention prediction model in predicting the next activity in two tasks with promising results. However, at this point, we have only investigated one aspect of user prediction – predicting what a user's intention will be, just before the activity occurs. If we want to develop an intelligent agent that can prepare in advance to assist the user in real situations – for example, to enlarge the target button just before it is pressed – we need to be able to predict the user's intention a few seconds ahead of the event. This is a more difficult task as we have less of the indicative historical data to work with.

We conduct a pilot experiment to investigate how well our prediction models could do in predicting a user's next activity x seconds ahead before it actually occurs. It aims to obtain some useful findings for developing an intelligent agent that can anticipate a user's next interaction. We believe that 2.5 seconds should be adequate for such purposes. In this experiment, we evaluated our prediction model with x varying from 0.5 to 2.5 seconds, with the same features and tasks as in previous experiments, with the only difference being that we are now predicting the activity that will occur x seconds after the current moment. This affects the mouse interaction features, since our statistics will not be able to cover entire mouse behavior.

Figure 3(b) shows the results. As we move further away from the interaction event, obviously, the performance drops, as it is difficult to predict too far into the future. However, we can see that it is possible to predict slightly ahead into the future with reasonable accuracy. For crowdsourcing, the performance of predicting 0.5 seconds ahead is very close to predicting just before the event (i.e. 0 seconds ahead). Both models achieve over 70% accuracy. For web search, the model achieves around 72% accuracy when predicting 0.5 seconds ahead, which is 4% lower than just before the event.

Non-intentional Mouse Click Detection

The ability to be able to predict users' intention could be used to enhance an intelligent system in multiple ways. One potential application is to detect non-intentional clicks. If the users' mouse click event is different from the predicted intention, that event may be an error and the system may need to take some corrective actions. We therefore investigate the feasibility of using our model to detecting non-intentional clicks from the user.

To produce non-intentional mouse click instances, 50% of the test set instances were randomly selected and randomly assigned to a different activity class. This gives an unintentional click detection baseline of 50%.

To classify the activities as correct or erroneous, we use the confidence values for each potential classification result returned by the LSTM. A min-max normalization is performed over the returned confidence values. We then compare the normalized confidence value of the labeled user activity class with a pre-selected threshold. If it is larger than the threshold, the mouse activity is classified as correct; otherwise it will be classified as an erroneous mouse click.

Figure 3(c) shows the results of non-intentional mouse click detection with different confidence thresholds. We observe that using 0.8 as the confidence threshold achieves the best balance between precision and recall. Our model thus reaches a non-intentional mouse click detection performance of 86.5%, with a precision of 90.7%.

DISCUSSION

This work uses LSTM to predict the next mouse interaction and to detect non-intentional clicks based on the mouse movement behaviors. Our results are promising, achieving a considerably higher performance than the baseline.

Our study is useful in numerous daily scenarios, including detection of non-intentional operations. Consider, for instance, a user unintentionally clicks on the interface. An intelligent interface, instead of allowing the error, should be able to filter out unintended actions, or at least ask for a confirmation. Furthermore, our studies can be used in conjunction with mouse-gaze coordination and incorporate the user mental states [12]. This can further conduce to spot and intercept important data-entry tasks [9]. Taken together, our study opens up new possibilities for advanced HCI applications, in particular, intelligent user interfaces.

CONCLUSION

In this paper, we investigated predicting users' mouse interaction activity. Our evaluation covers two contexts: a rigid, well-defined crowdsourcing annotation task, and a free-form, open-ended web searching task. We propose a way to train a popular neural network, the long short-term memory network, to predict mouse interaction activity with historical user mouse interaction data. We evaluated and discussed the performance of the model and investigated its potential for non-intentional click detection in a pilot study.

The results of our models on the task- and interface- agnostic intention prediction are quite promising. When provided with a sequence of users' behaviors, the LSTM network can predict the next interaction activity, achieving over 20% improvement over baseline. We can beat the baseline by more than 28% for crowdsourcing task and 40% for web search task by fusing the historical activity and mouse activity networks. When applying the prediction model into non-intentional mouse click detection problem, we observed that using 0.8 as the confidence threshold could best balance the precision and recall in our tasks. In non-intentional mouse click detection, a confidence threshold of 0.8 could yield an accuracy of 86% and a precision of 90%. This suggests that users' intention prediction models has potential as a means of providing information to the intelligent system, and corrective action could be taken in order to improve users experience. In future work, we will experiment with more sophisticated models that also take mouse-gaze coordination into consideration.

REFERENCES

[1] Brown, E.T., Ottley, A., Zhao, H., et al.Finding Waldo: Learning about Users from their Interactions. *IEEE Transactions on Visualization and Computer Graphics 20*, 12 (2014), 1663–1672.

[2] Chang, C., Amick, B.C., Menendez, C.C., et al.Daily Computer Usage Correlated with Undergraduate Students' Musculoskeletal Symptoms. *American Journal of Industrial Medicine 50*, 6 (2007), 481–488.

[3] Diaz, F., Guo, Q., and White, R.W.Search Result Prefetching Using Cursor Movement. *Proceedings of the 39th International ACM SIGIR conference on Research and Development in Information Retrieval - SIGIR '16*, (2016), 609–618.

[4] Elkahky, A.M., Song, Y., and He, X.A Multi-View Deep Learning Approach for Cross Domain User Modeling in Recommendation Systems. *WWW '15 Proceedings of the 24th International Conference on World Wide Web*, (2015), 278–288.

[5] Fu, Y., Kwok, T.C.K., Wu, Y.E., Leong, H.V., and Ngai, G.Your Mouse Revals Your Next Activity : Towards Predicting User Intention from Mouse Interaction. *COMPSAC '17 IEEE Computer Software and Applications Conference.*

[6] Georgescu, M. and Zhu, X.Aggregation of Crowdsourced Labels Based on Worker History. *WIMS '14 Proceedings of the 4th International Conference on Web Intelligence, Mining and Semantics (WIMS14)*, (2014).

[7] Gers, F.A., Schmidhuber, J.A., and Cummins, F.A.Learning to Forget: Continual Prediction with LSTM. *Neural Computation 12*, 10 (2000), 2451–2471.

[8] Google.A google a day. http://www.agoogleaday.com/.

[9] Gould, S.J.J., Cox, A.L., Brumby, D.P., and Wickersham, A.Now Check Your Input: Brief Task Lockouts Encourage Checking, Longer Lockouts Encourage Task Switching. *CHI '16 Proceedings of the 2016 CHI Conference on Human Factors in Computing Systems*, (2016), 3311–3323.

[10] Guo, Q. and Agichtein, E.Ready to Buy or Just Browsing?: Detecting Web Searcher Goals from Interaction Data. *SIGIR '10 Proceedings of the 33rd international ACM SIGIR conference on Research and development in information retrieval*, (2010), 130–137.

[11] Hochreiter, S. and Schmidhuber, J.Long Short-Term Memory. *Neural Computation 9*, 8 (1997), 1735–1780.

[12] Huang, M.X., Li, J., Ngai, G., and Leong, H.V.StressClick. *Proceedings of the 2016 ACM on Multimedia Conference - MM '16*, (2016), 1395–1404.

[13] Lalle, S., Toker, D., Conati, C., and Carenini, G.Prediction of Users' Learning Curves for Adaptation while Using an Information Visualization. *IUI '15 Proceedings of the 20th International Conference on Intelligent User Interfaces*, ACM (2015), 357–368.

[14] Maniu, S., O'Hare, N., Aiello, L.M., Chiarandini, L., and Jaimes, A.Search Behaviour on Photo Sharing Platforms. *Proceedings of IEEE International Conference on Multimedia and Expo (ICME)*, (2013), 1–6.

[15] Mavadati, S.M., Mahoor, M.H., Bartlett, K., Trinh, P., and Cohn, J.F.DISFA: A Spontaneous Facial Action Intensity Database. *IEEE Transactions On Affective Computing 4*, 2 (2013).

[16] Pasqual, P.T. and Wobbrock, J.O.Mouse Pointing Endpoint Prediction Using Kinematic Template Matching. *CHI '14 Proceedings of the SIGCHI Conference on Human Factors in Computing Systems*, (2014), 743–752.

[17] Pilankar, P.S. and Padiya, P.Multi-Phase Mouse Dynamics Authentication System using Behavioural Biometrics. *International Conference on Signal Processing, Communication, Power and Embedded System (SCOPES), 2016*, (2016), 1947–1950.

[18] Ratwani, R.M., McCurry, J.M., and Trafton, J.G.Predicting Postcompletion Errors Using Eye Movements. *Proceedings of the SIGCHI Conference on Human Factors in Computing Systems*, (2008), 539–542.

[19] Schwarz, J., Marais, C.C., Leyvand, T., Hudson, S.E., and Mankoff, J.Combining Body Pose, Gaze, and Gesture to Determine Intention to Interact in Vision-Based Interfaces. *CHI '14 Proceedings of the SIGCHI Conference on Human Factors in Computing Systems*, (2014), 3443–3452.

[20] Ziebart, B., Dey, A., and Bagnell, J.A.Probabilistic Pointing Target Prediction via Inverse Optimal Control. *IUI '12 Proceedings of the 2012 ACM international conference on Intelligent User Interfaces*, (2012), 1–10.

Modeling Expertise in Assistive Navigation Interfaces for Blind People

Eshed Ohn-Bar[1], João Guerreiro[1], Dragan Ahmetovic[1], Kris M. Kitani[1], Chieko Asakawa[1,2]
[1]Carnegie Mellon University, [2]IBM Research - Tokyo
{eshed1, jpvguerreiro, dragan1}@cmu.edu, {kkitani, chiekoa}@cs.cmu.edu

ABSTRACT
Evaluating the impact of expertise and route knowledge on task performance can guide the design of intelligent and adaptive navigation interfaces. Expertise has been relatively unexplored in the context of assistive indoor navigation interfaces for blind people. To quantify the complex relationship between the user's walking patterns, route learning, and adaptation to the interface, we conducted a study with 8 blind participants. The participants repeated a set of navigation tasks while using a smartphone-based turn-by-turn navigation guidance app. The results demonstrate the gradual evolution of user skill and knowledge throughout the route repetitions, significantly impacting the task completion time. In addition to the exploratory analysis, we take a step towards tailoring the navigation interface to the user's needs by proposing a personalized recurrent neural network-based behavior model for expertise level classification.

Author Keywords
blind navigation; knowledge; experience; interface adaptation; user modeling; personalization; recurrent neural networks.

INTRODUCTION
Navigation assistive technologies play an important role in increasing the independence of blind people. Current solutions for indoor navigation are now able to provide practical localization accuracy and guidance [2, 6, 7]. Although such interfaces are often static in the instructions they convey, the user's information needs depend on the user's knowledge of the environment and navigation techniques [3]. In order to accommodate these dynamic needs, we envision interfaces that are able to automatically identify the user's behavioral states and expertise level. By focusing on the evolution of user behavior as they gain task expertise, we aim to provide insights into this relatively unexplored dimension of user-system interactivity for navigation assistance for blind people.

Even considering accurate navigation assistance, mistakes are common when traveling unfamiliar routes [1]. The lack of knowledge and confidence may lead users to hesitate in

IUI'18, March 7–11, 2018, Tokyo, Japan
© 2018 ACM. ISBN 978-1-4503-4945-1/18/03...$15.00
DOI: https://doi.org/10.1145/3172944.3173008

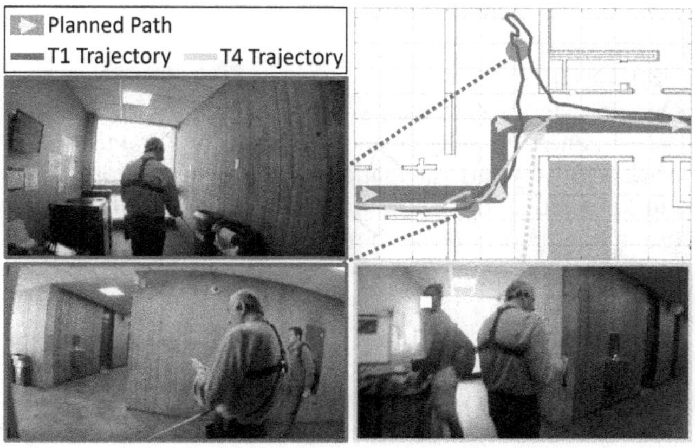

Figure 1. We model the evolution of user expertise throughout repetitions of a navigation task with a smartphone-based turn-by-turn navigation guidance interface. Given motion of blind users along a planned path (shown for one participant for trial 1, T1, and trial 4, T4), the model learns to categorize expert behavior. In the example, the left and immediate right turn in a portion of the portion is often missed in T1, but not in T4, due to better knowledge of the interface and route.

complex areas, walk slowly, miss a turn due to a late reaction or have longer error-recovery times (Fig. 1). Previous research has shown that route knowledge can also be acquired through maps or virtual navigation [5, 10, 20], but its utility is better assessed with real-world navigation tasks [14]. However, route learning and familiarization is a process that takes time and it is difficult to conduct long-term, longitudinal user studies to assess its evolution.

In general, as a user interacts with an interface repeatedly, we expect gradual adaptation and improvement to occur. Nonetheless, the extent of this phenomenon is not trivial, in particular for navigation tasks. For instance, guided navigation is known to negate route learning as people become reliant on the system [8], but indoor navigation systems for blind people face significant localization and safety challenges. An intelligent navigation interface for blind people must facilitate a certain level of situational awareness in order to avoid missing a turn, bumping into obstacles and pedestrians, or getting lost.

By employing an assistive navigation interface, our study emphasizes expertise in Human-Machine Interactivity settings, as opposed to general mobility. The analysis is relevant to scenarios where the cognitive load of the task is shared between the user and the system, and this is reflected in the way expertise evolves. For instance, users do not need to remember certain information, such as the direction of instructed turns, but instead they can attend to learning challenging route areas.

As a step towards assistive navigation interfaces that can accommodate each user's unique walking and learning style, this paper presents: (1) expertise evolution assessment - the results of a real-world repetition study with 8 blind participants aimed to quantify the gradual increase of task knowledge, and (2) expertise model - a deep learning-based system for modeling user expertise that can be used in adaptive user interfaces for identifying expert behavior and contextually assisting the user in real-time. We find that model personalization is essential as expertise manifests differently among users. Specifically, appropriately modeling personal expertise leads to an improvement in classification accuracy of up to 17%.

USER STUDY

Our first step was to assess how route exposure affects the performance, knowledge and behaviour of blind users while using a turn-by-turn navigation guidance smartphone app. To our knowledge, this is the first study that quantifies the evolution of expertise through real-world assisted navigation of blind people.

Participants

We recruited 8 blind participants (4m/4f), who use a white-cane as the primary navigation aid. Their ages range from 43 to 76 (M=65.63, SD=10.61) years old. Two participants do not own a smartphone and five had experience with navigation apps. The study took approximately two hours per participant, who were compensated for their time ($25 per hour).

Real-World Navigation and Apparatus

We used NavCog3 [21], an open-source[1] indoor navigation system that provides turn-by-turn instructions to guide a user to a destination. When the user reaches a turning point, the system provides a verbal instruction (*e.g.*, "*turn left*") and a short vibration and sound effect. When the user completes the turn, achieving the correct orientation, the vibration and sound are provided again together with the next instruction (*e.g.*, "*proceed 50 feet and turn right*"). While navigating that segment, the system provides periodic information about the remaining distance (*e.g.*, "*30 feet*"), and an "*approaching*" message right before the turn. Additionally, the system provides information about relevant landmarks and Points of Interest (POIs) when the user is within close proximity (*e.g.*, "*a restroom is on your right*").

We instrumented three buildings in our university campus ($58,800m^2$) with *iBeacons* and used an *iPhone 7* with the navigation app, which logged all events during the navigation tasks. Participants used their free hand to hold the smartphone and used *AfterShokz* bone-conductive headphones. Video was recorded for visualization and analysis purposes from a first-(participant) and third-person (researcher) perspective, using two *GoPRO* cameras.

Method and Procedure

The user study consisted of the repetition of two routes with similar complexities (number of turns and POIs), which order was counter-balanced among users. *Route A* has a total length of 500 feet, 8 turns and 13 landmarks/POIs, while *Route B* has a length of 250 feet, 7 turns and 10 landmarks/POIs. For their first route, participants walked the same route six times. It included three consecutive trials with the navigation app, a trial from memory (using only the white cane), another trial with the app, and a second trial from memory. The unassisted trials intended to make participants reason about the route and to gain insights on their ability to leverage the knowledge previously acquired. For their second route, participants walked the same route four consecutive times with the app. We avoided the walk from memory due to fatigue constraints. Immediately after each trial, participants were asked to describe the route (as in [4, 15]) by referring its turns, POIs and landmarks. Then, they walked with the researcher to the starting point through a different path. Participants took a longer break after finishing all trials of the first route, but only minor breaks (up to 1 minute) between same-route trials.

[1]HULOP: http://github.com/hulop

Design and Analysis

The analysis focuses on the comparison of the two extremes of route expertise, the first (T1) and last (T4) trials with the navigation app. To assess user performance we rely on task **Completion Time**. We did not focus on navigation errors as those depend mainly on the system accuracy. In contrast, completion time reflects the fast/slow recovery from errors. In order to assess participants' route knowledge with their verbal descriptions, we used and adapted metrics from prior research [10, 18, 24]: (1) **FormElementsError** reflects the number of wrong, missing or extra turns and is analyzed using the Levenshtein distance [16] between the correct and participant's description; (2) **POIsMentioned** refers to the number of POIs and landmarks referred by the participant; (3) **POIsCorrectLocation** refers to the POIsMentioned in the correct segment and side of the route. We ran *Shapiro-Wilkinson tests* to all dependent variables to check for normality, and used a *Paired-Samples t-test* when the variables have a normal distribution and a *Wilcoxon Signed Rank test* otherwise.

EXPLORATORY ANALYSIS

Performance and Route Knowledge

Fig. 2 shows a gradual increase in performance, depicted by a decrease in *Completion Time* over the four trials. Results show significant differences between the first and last trial for both routes, with an average decrease of 45.2 seconds in *Route A* and 56.5 in *Route B* ($p < 0.05$ in both routes).

Route description metrics show that participants were able to significantly improve their knowledge about the route structure (FormElementError) from the first to the last trial, in both routes ($p < 0.005$). Although participants were never able to report the full route structure, they were only able to report an average of 26% of the route after one trial, against 69% after the last trial. This can be explained by participants being "*focused on the instructions to guarantee I [they] reach the destination*". As they got more familiar with the route, they were able to retain more of its information.

The rate of *POIsMentioned* by the participants was very similar among trials ($p > 0.05$ in both routes). Participants ended up referring mostly to landmarks that had a direct impact on

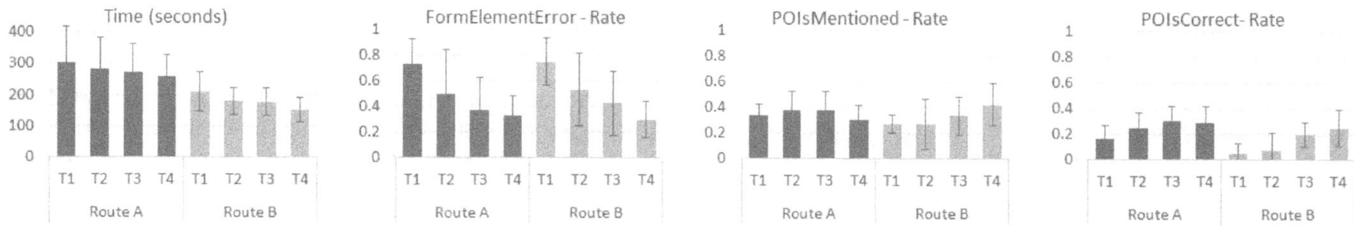

Figure 2. User performance metrics of completion time and route knowledge. Analysis is shown for each of the four trials and two routes in the study.

their navigation or landmarks/POIs close to the start or end of the route. For instance, the doors that users opened were mentioned in almost all trials, as well as floor changes next to a turning point. The rate of *POIsCorrect* increased slightly over time in *Route A* (n.s. $Z = -1.300$, $p = 0.194$), but significantly ($Z = -2.379$, $p < 0.05$) in *Route B*, showing a greater ability to incorporate the landmarks/POIs in the rest of the route.

The experimental procedure included walking the route from memory twice throughout the repetitions in order to further evaluate the evolving expertise. Although we found that most participants were not able to fully recall the routes, some participants were still able to complete the route when navigating from memory. One participant (out of four) completed *Route A* in their first unassisted trial, while three completed it on their second trial. All but one participant in *Route A* (and all in *Route B*) reached the last or second to last turn. In *Route B*, one and two participants completed the first and second unassisted trials, respectively.

Speed Analysis

The continuous location and orientation tracking provided by the phone and beacon signals enables us to analyze the impact of task knowledge on user walking style throughout the route. For instance, we can identify the frequency of user stopping or slowing down. Fig. 3 shows the walking speed distribution over all participants for each route and trial. Overall, average walking speeds increase over trials ($p < 0.001$), but more significantly on *Route A*, increasing from 0.54 meters per second (m/s) in T1 up to 0.64 m/s in T4. Since these speed values are computed over all time steps (including events of turning and stopping, resulting in low average speeds) and all participants, even small changes are significant. *Route B* has shorter segments and high density of turns and POIs, so users tend to walk slower. At times, we observed users walking more cautiously in this dense route in order to validate their route knowledge before continuing to move forward.

Throughout the repetitions, users were able to generally complete tasks faster by avoiding getting lost, not missing turns, and leveraging information about POIs and landmarks. Specifically, the number of hesitation events reported by the users decreased. Fig. 3(right) validates the reports, showing a reduction in the percentage of time users spent stopping or walking slowly (defined as any speed under 0.2 m/s). The observation that walking speed evolves in certain situations as users gain route navigation expertise motivated us to consider whether a sequence classification model can capture this subtle phenomenon. The model would have to account for our diverse group of participants, including their unique walking styles and mobility and orientation strategies.

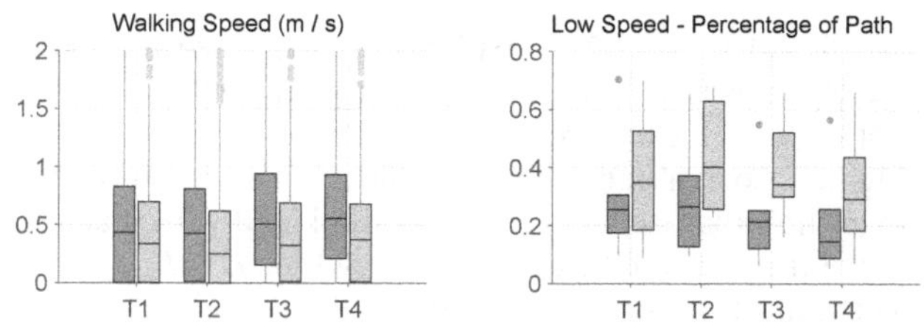

Figure 3. Box plots of walking speed (left) and percent of the path spent at low speed (right) over the four trials (color coding follows Fig. 2).

EXPERTISE CLASSIFICATION MODEL

With the overarching aim of developing navigation interfaces which can interpret the state of the user continuously, we propose a personalized behavior model for classifying route expertise.

Recurrent Neural Network Model

Given a sequence of observations of user walking and reaction patterns, we learn a model for user's behavioral states and expertise level. Following state-of-the-art approaches for sequential behavior modeling [9, 17, 19, 22], a Recurrent Neural Network (RNN) with Long Short-Term Memory (LSTM) hidden units [11] is trained. The model is trained for 100 epochs using Stochastic Gradient Descent (SGD) with momentum. In training, we use Dropout [23] and two 128-cell hidden layers.

Model Observations and Training

Our set of features is kept as general as possible to avoid overfitting to our specific settings, while reflecting our observations that user velocity changes throughout the trials. At each time step, the model observes sensor signals and events generated by the interface. The state of the user is parameterized by the tracked real-world position and orientation, $\mathbf{P} = [x, y, \theta]$. User movement is characterized by the linear velocity $\mathbf{S}$ in m/s and the angular velocity $\mathbf{A}$ in radians per second (r/s) components, derived from P. The model also has access to the current instruction $\mathbf{I}$ provided by the interface, encoded as a one-hot vector where each element in the vector corresponds to an instruction type. In the experiments, the instructions are clustered into four categories: approaching a turn, turn, proceed forward, and POIs/landmarks.

Modeling route expertise is formulated as classification between user behavior during T1, the initial navigation task, and T4, the last navigation task, for each route. The model generates route expert/novice labels, and these are compared with their trial number. To ensure the model generalizes well to different settings, each route is split into spatially disjoint sets used for cross validation. Over the entire collected dataset, sampling at 1 second intervals leads to a total of 5,147 samples.

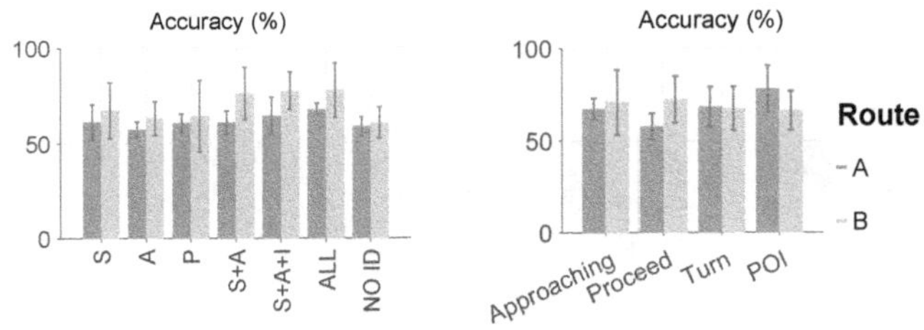

Figure 4. Behavior model performance for different feature combinations (left) and during different instruction events (right).

We found it crucial to explicitly personalize the expertise model. This is achieved by (1) adding the **person ID** as a one-hot vector to the feature space, and (2) modification of the training loss, so that in training time the 2-class log loss computed over the expertise label L_{expert} is combined with scalar multiple of the person ID classification log loss, $L = L_{expert} + \lambda L_{ID}$. The multi-task formulation can regularize training by encouraging the model to leverage person-specific cues [17, 12]. Adding the auxiliary training task will be shown useful for learning representations that can robustly generalize to unseen test cases.

Results and Analysis

Results for the behavior model in terms of normalized classification accuracy, computed as the average percentage of correctly classified instances for each class, are shown in Fig. 4. On the left, it studies expertise classification for different combinations of inputs to the model with the goal of analyzing the contribution of different cues for our modeling task.

A combination of all the proposed cues (**ALL**) is shown to produce the best classification results of 67.60% and 77.69% for *Route A* and *Route B*, respectively. We can observe how the velocity components $S+A$ alone account for a significant portion of the predictive power of the model. The model further benefits from incorporation of the instructional feature I, as it includes additional context regarding the evolution of expert behavior during specific navigation events. Interestingly, *Route B*, which contains a higher concentration of instructional and POI events, also provides more opportunities for the model to capture expert behavior (reflected by a higher classification accuracy). The position features provide a useful baseline, but result in only a small improvement when combined with the other features.

The person ID cue is shown to be essential for a flexible expertise model which can accommodate the large variations between T1 and T4 *among participants*. As shown in Fig. 4, without the explicit personalization in training (**NO ID**), the LSTM model performance deteriorates significantly, to 59.36% and 61.28% for *Route A* and *Route B*, respectively. This large drop in performance occurs with a model learned over the complete set of features (ALL). The need for personalization, in particular for our classification task, became clear during the user study. The large variability in mobility skills and learning styles makes expertise classification a challenging task; although the level of user task performance improved significantly between the initial and subsequent trials, the improvement and its rate was found to be highly personal. Therefore, it is not surprising that a non-personalized model is struggling at the task of identifying how each user's behavior changes along their own expertise spectrum.

A breakdown of the expertise classification results by different navigational instruction events is shown in Fig. 4. The figure analyzes user behavior changes in response to navigation instructions over the trials, as well as differences between the two routes. For instance, on *Route A*, the model is shown to perform best at POI/landmark-based instructions, such as doors or floor changes. Our data-driven model reveals how POI-related behavioral changes are a strong indicator for expert behavior, in particular on *Route A*. We can draw a similar conclusion for instructions of "*approaching*" a turn and "*proceed*" during navigation on the *Route B*. These results are in alignment with the findings in Fig. 2 and the unique properties of each route. On *Route A*, the common "*proceed*" instructions result in a more subtle difference between reactions of novice and experienced users. This is due to the several long forward segments throughout the route. Expertise classification of behavior during "*turn*" instructions is most consistent among the two routes when compared to other instructions. User behavior during turns is indeed more consistent with respect to the route properties, yet the model is still able to capture expertise-dependent behavior during turn events. This analysis demonstrates that our classification model is able to leverage several types of expertise-related cues specific to the route, the user, and the instructions provided.

CONCLUSIONS AND FUTURE WORK

This paper discussed challenges in deploying intelligent and adaptive assistive navigation interfaces for blind people. A real-world study with 8 blind participants explored how route expertise evolves with task repetition. Results show that both route knowledge and route completion time gradually improve. The results on timing and knowledge acquisition can be used to address some of the significant challenges faced by indoor navigation interfaces for blind people, including reduction in cognitive load and supporting the dynamic and personal needs of the user. The evolution of route expertise resulted in rich behavior characteristics which were captured with a personalized RNN model. The model was also used to gain insights into how user behavior changes with increased knowledge.

As future work, the exploratory analysis in this study can be complemented by the results of a real-world longitudinal study. The user performance findings can be used to compare with approaches that focus on other forms of route learning [10]. Although we kept our features as general as possible, additional cues, such as environmental context [13], may provide further classification performance improvements. The goal of our analysis was to compare two extremes of route expertise, yet we hope this study motivates future researchers to pursue additional general measures and models for user expertise level. Another next step would be to study how the interface should be modified to support each user and their identified expertise level.

ACKNOWLEDGMENTS

We thank the participants and the support of Shimizu Corporation, JST CREST (JPMJCR14E1) and NSF (1637927).

REFERENCES

1. Dragan Ahmetovic, Cole Gleason, Chengxiong Ruan, Kris Kitani, Hironobu Takagi, and Chieko Asakawa. 2016. NavCog: a navigational cognitive assistant for the blind. In *International Conference on Human-Computer Interaction with Mobile Devices and Services*.
2. Dragan Ahmetovic, Masayuki Murata, Cole Gleason, Erin Brady, Hironobu Takagi, Kris M. Kitani, and Chieko Asakawa. 2017. Achieving Practical and Accurate Indoor Navigation for People with Visual Impairments. In *Web for All*.
3. Nikola Banovic, Rachel L Franz, Khai N Truong, Jennifer Mankoff, and Anind K Dey. 2013. Uncovering information needs for independent spatial learning for users who are visually impaired. In *International ACM SIGACCESS Conference on Computers and Accessibility*.
4. Mark Blades, Reginald Golledge, R Jacobson, Robert Kitchin, and Yvonne Lippa. 2002. The effect of spatial tasks on visually impaired peoples' wayfinding abilities. *Journal of Visual Impairment & Blindness* 96, 06 (2002).
5. Julie Ducasse, Anke M Brock, and Christophe Jouffrais. 2018. Accessible interactive maps for visually impaired users. In *Mobility of Visually Impaired People*. Springer, 537–584.
6. Navid Fallah, Ilias Apostolopoulos, Kostas Bekris, and Eelke Folmer. 2012. The user as a sensor: navigating users with visual impairments in indoor spaces using tactile landmarks. In *SIGCHI Conference on Human Factors in Computing Systems*.
7. Navid Fallah, Ilias Apostolopoulos, Kostas Bekris, and Eelke Folmer. 2013. Indoor Human Navigation Systems: A Survey. *Interacting with Computers* 25, 1 (2013), 21.
8. Elliot Fenech, Frank Drews, and Jonathan Z Bakdash. 2010. The Effects of Acoustic Turn-by-turn Navigation on Wayfinding. 54 (2010).
9. Srujana Gattupalli, Dylan Ebert, Michalis Papakostas, Fillia Makedon, and Vassilis Athitsos. 2017. CogniLearn: A Deep Learning-based Interface for Cognitive Behavior Assessment. In *International Conference on Intelligent User Interfaces*.
10. João Guerreiro, Dragan Ahmetovic, Kris M. Kitani, and Chieko Asakawa. 2017. Virtual Navigation for Blind People: Building Sequential Representations of the real-world. In *International ACM SIGACCESS Conference on Computers and Accessibility*.
11. Sepp Hochreiter and Jürgen Schmidhuber. 1997. Long Short-Term Memory. *Neural Computation* 9, 8 (1997).
12. Hernisa Kacorri, Kris M. Kitani, Jeffrey P. Bigham, and Chieko Asakawa. 2017. People with Visual Impairment Training Personal Object Recognizers: Feasibility and Challenges. In *SIGCHI Conference on Human Factors in Computing Systems*.
13. Hernisa Kacorri, Eshed Ohn-Bar, Kris M. Kitani, and Chieko Asakawa. 2018. Environmental Factors in Indoor Navigation Based on Real-World Trajectories of Blind Users. In *SIGCHI Conference on Human Factors in Computing Systems*.
14. Rob Kitchin and RD Jacobson. 1997. Techniques to collect and analyze the cognitive map knowledge of persons with visual impairment or blindness: issues of validity. *Journal of Visual Impairment and Blindness* 91, 4 (1997), 360–376.
15. Orly Lahav and David Mioduser. 2008. Haptic-feedback support for cognitive mapping of unknown spaces by people who are blind. *International Journal of Human-Computer Studies* 66, 1 (2008), 23–35.
16. Vladimir I Levenshtein. 1966. Binary codes capable of correcting deletions, insertions, and reversals. In *Soviet Physics Doklady*, Vol. 10. 707–710.
17. Zachary C Lipton, David C Kale, Charles Elkan, and Randall Wetzell. 2016. Learning to diagnose with LSTM recurrent neural networks. In *International Conference on Learning Representations*.
18. Romedi Passini, Guylene Proulx, and Constant Rainville. 1990. The spatio-cognitive abilities of the visually impaired population. *Environment and Behavior* 22, 1 (1990), 91–118.
19. Haşim Sak, Andrew Senior, and Françoise Beaufays. 2014. Long short-term memory recurrent neural network architectures for large scale acoustic modeling. In *Annual Conference of the International Speech Communication Association*.
20. Jaime Sánchez, Marcia de Borba Campos, Matías Espinoza, and Lotfi B Merabet. 2014. Audio haptic videogaming for developing wayfinding skills in learners who are blind. In *International Conference on Intelligent User Interfaces*.
21. Daisuke Sato, Uran Oh, Kakuya Naito, Hironobu Takagi, Kris M. Kitani, and Chieko Asakawa. 2017. NavCog3: An Evaluation of a Smartphone-Based Blind Indoor Navigation Assistant with Semantic Features in a Large-Scale Environment. In *International ACM SIGACCESS Conference on Computers and Accessibility*.
22. Harold Soh, Scott Sanner, Madeleine White, and Greg Jamieson. 2017. Deep Sequential Recommendation for Personalized Adaptive User Interfaces. In *International Conference on Intelligent User Interfaces*.
23. Nitish Srivastava, Geoffrey E Hinton, Alex Krizhevsky, Ilya Sutskever, and Ruslan Salakhutdinov. 2014. Dropout: a simple way to prevent neural networks from overfitting. *JMLR* 15, 1 (2014), 1929–1958.
24. Koji Yatani, Nikola Banovic, and Khai Truong. 2012. SpaceSense: representing geographical information to visually impaired people using spatial tactile feedback. In *SIGCHI Conference on Human Factors in Computing Systems*.

AVEID: Automatic Video System for Measuring Engagement In Dementia

Viral Parekh*[1], Pin Sym Foong*[2], Shendong Zhao[2] and Ramanathan Subramanian[3]

[1]CVIT Lab
Int'l Institute of Information Technology, Hyderabad
viral@live.in

[2]NUS-HCI Lab
National University of Singapore, Singapore
pinsym@u.nus.edu,
zhaosd@comp.nus.edu.sg

[3]University of Glasgow, Singapore
Ramanathan.Subramanian@glasgow.ac.uk

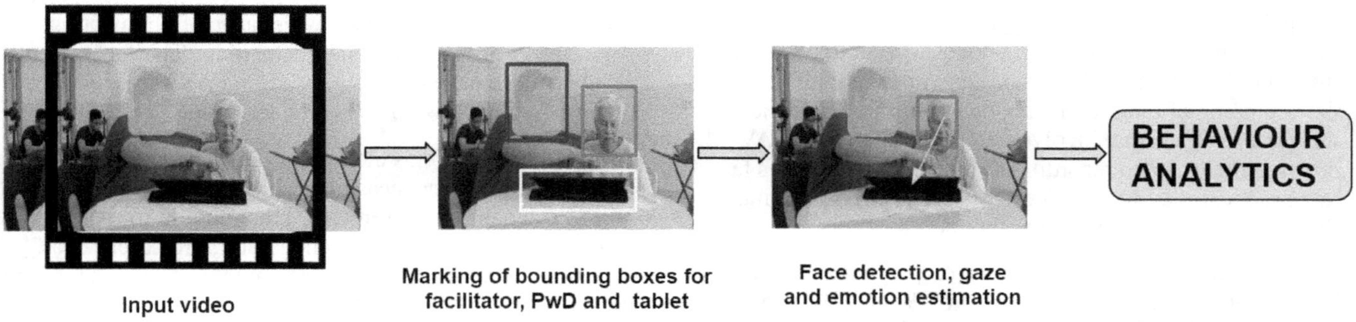

Figure 1. AVEID overview - The AVEID system enables non-intrusive and automated behavioral analytics of persons with dementia (PwD) by capturing their attention (gazing behavior) and attitude (emotion) characteristics.

ABSTRACT

Engagement in dementia is typically measured using behavior observational scales (BOS) that are tedious and involve intensive manual labor to annotate, and are therefore not easily scalable. We propose AVEID, a low cost and easy-to-use video-based engagement measurement tool to determine the engagement level of a person with dementia (PwD) during digital interaction. We show that the objective behavioral measures computed via AVEID correlate well with subjective expert impressions for the popular MPES and OME BOS, confirming its viability and effectiveness. Moreover, AVEID measures can be obtained for a variety of engagement designs, thereby facilitating large-scale studies with PwD populations.

Author Keywords

Engagement; Video-based analytics; Dementia

INTRODUCTION

Engagement activities for people with dementia (PwD) are an important, non-pharmacological method to promote quality of life and reduce undesirable outcomes such as apathy, depression and aggressive behaviors [2]. Hence, HCI researchers have been developing various systems to supply more interactive and interesting engagement activities for PwD. Examples of these are conversation support systems [1], art therapy [11] and music therapy [4]. Equally important are engagement measurement tools as they provide feedback to facilitators on the effectiveness of engagement systems, while also providing a basis for forming and adjusting interventions. As memory impairments in PwD preclude the use of self-reports as a measurement tool, researchers primarily use some form of observation to code outcome behavior. Behavioral coding requires the use of behavioral observational scales (BOS), and the training of coders who can accurately encode observed behaviors for robust inference. Due to these requirements, behavioral coding as a measurement tool presents the following challenges: 1) It is human-effort intensive; 2) Training coders is time-consuming; 3) Large-scale data annotation becomes tedious, and 4) It supports only coarse-grained behavior analytics due to limitations in human annotation capability.

Hence, automated measures of engagement might be useful for researchers. Despite the availability of such tools for neurotypical target groups, they are not appropriate for use with PwD. For example, PwD tend to resist any type of on-body physical instrumentation [10] so the use of wearable devices or bio-signal systems for measuring engagement is typically not viable. Patel et. al. [14] suggest that PwD require monitoring systems that are "unobtrusive, and preferably collected in a transparent way without patient intervention due to their cognitive impairment."

*indicates equal contribution

IUI'18, March 7–11, 2018, Tokyo, Japan

ISBN 978-1-4503-4945-1/18/03. . . $15.00

DOI: https://doi.org/10.1145/3172944.3173010

In this regard, we present AVEID, a low-cost and easy to use video-based system for measuring engagement in PwD. AVEID employs deep learning-based computer vision algorithms to continuously capture a dementia patient's engagement behavior during an interaction session, thereby enabling fine-grained behavior analytics. Consistent with BOS that quantify the patient's attention and attitude towards an engagement system, AVEID estimates the patient's attentional behavior based on gazing direction, and attitude based on facial emotions (Figs. 1,6). Gazing mannerisms have been extensively studied as cues indicative of attention/engagement during interactions [16, 18], while facial emotions are inherently reflective of a user's attitude towards the environment. Also, since deep learning systems are 'end-to-end' requiring no manual intervention for model synthesis, AVEID only requires manual annotation of bounding boxes to denote positions of the patient, facilitator (if present) and engagement device at the beginning of the examined video. Unlike gaze-tracking or wearable systems that involve specialized hardware, AVEID only requires a video recording as input. These features facilitate practical, day-to-day usage of AVEID in care homes by therapists or researchers from other domains.

We validated AVEID against human (expert behavioral coder) impressions corresponding to two well-known BOS, namely, the Menorah Park Engagement Scale (MPES) [8] and the Observational Measure of Engagement (OME) [2]. Experiments confirm that measures derived from AVEID agree well with human opinion. Furthermore, AVEID can save the time and effort expended by the behavioral coder, allow for personalized treatment and enable timely analytics on large sample sizes. AVEID measures would also be applicable across small-space engagement activities, facilitating replicability and ecological validity of engagement evaluation studies; we ultimately envision AVEID to provide a strong basis for effective non-pharmacological intervention in dementia care environments.

AVEID IMPLEMENTATION

Consistent with popular BOS used for measuring engagement with PwD, AVEID is designed to quantify the attention and attitude of the patient towards the engagement system over the observed period (Table 1). AVEID employs the patient's gaze focus as a cue towards inferring attention, while utilizing facial affect to infer attitude. We use the following terms to describe the system:

User: who operates AVEID to measure engagement.

Target subject: PwD undertaking an engagement activity.

Target activity space: the 2D area where we expect the PwD's gaze to be directed in order to engage with the designed activity. In the AVEID context, the engagement activity involves interaction with a tablet as in [6]. The applications used in tablets are categorized based on the interests and abilities of the PwD. As interest areas, these five are selected categories include reminiscence, household activities, games, arts and crafts and chatting.

Facilitator: a second person in the frame whose role is to support and promote engagement of the PwD.

AVEID MODULES

The AVEID system comprises four modules, namely, *User input, Face detection, Gaze and emotion detection* and *Behavior analytics* (Fig. 1).

The **User Input** module allows users to select the video for analysis, and enables them to mark bounding boxes corresponding to the target subject, target activity space and facilitator. This initialization needs to be performed at the beginning of each video for accurate face detection (under varied video acquisition conditions), and estimation of attentional measures.

The **Face Detection** module implements the *Tiny face* [7] state-of-the-art face detection method. Tiny face performs robust face detection across a wide range of illuminations, face sizes, head poses and facial occlusions. The face detection module detects patient's and facilitator's faces (within the input bounding boxes) in each video frame.

Gaze Detection forms the core of AVEID, as its output is used to compute *attention* measures, which are of prime importance in engagement measurement. This module implements the *GazeFollow* deep network architecture of Recasens et al. [15], and utilizes head orientation as a cue to determine where a target is gazing at [13, 17].

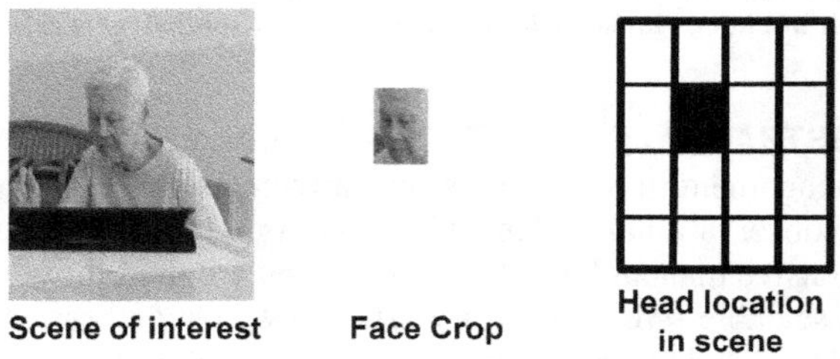

Figure 2. The three inputs utilized for gaze detection.

The target's gaze focus is determined based on three inputs (Fig.2): 1) An image (video frame) capturing the scene of interest, 2) Cropped head of the target (output of *Tiny face*), and 3) Location of the head in the scene (denoted by the highlighted grid square). The model comprises two computational pathways. The *gaze pathway* uses the target head appearance and location to produce a *gaze map* that estimates the general direction of the target's gaze. The *saliency pathway* examines scene content to output the *saliency map* that detects interesting objects capable of capturing the target's attention. The two maps are then combined to infer the target's gaze focus. As the target activity space and facilitator are the two entities of interest in AVEID, the gaze detection module outputs for each video frame, a label signifying whether the target is gazing at the *target activity space, facilitator or elsewhere*.

The **Emotion Detection** module implements the deep network for emotion recognition described in [12]. Given that recognizing emotions of elderly people is challenging even for trained human experts, the deep network described in [12] is fine-tuned with 950 elderly face examples from the FACES dataset [3]. The emotion detection module outputs per video frame a label corresponding to one of the six Ekman emotions plus neutral as illustrated in Fig. 6.

	MPES BOS	OME BOS	AVEID
Unit of Assessment	5-minute observed periods, coded with 0,1 or 2	Identified period of engagement, rated on a 7-point scale	User-specified observed periods of time (flexible granularity)
Attention	Active engagement (Did target activity), Passive engagement (Watched target activity), Other engagement.	Attention intensity (1 denoting no attention)	3 raw + 18 derived gaze-based statistics over observed period.
Attitude	Pleasure and anxiety as proportion over observed period.	Attitude valence with (1 denoting strongly negative, 3 denoting neutral, and 7 denoting strongly positive affect).	Proportion of negative and neutral-or-positive affect over observed period.

Table 1. Measuring attention and attitude via the MPES and OME scales, and the matching measures used with AVEID

The **Behavior Analytics** module processes the outputs of the gaze and emotion detection modules to compute measures reflecting the patient's *attention* and *attitude*. For characterizing attention, the per-frame gaze labels are combined to compute three raw (or basic) statistics, namely, gaze proportion on tablet, facilitator and elsewhere over the period of observation. In addition to these coarse-grained features, we also derived 18 fine-grained statistics from the gaze labels for analysis, described as follows.

Upon determining *episodes of focus* on the tablet, facilitator and other *entities* within the observation period, we computed the means and standard deviations (std) of these episode durations (**6 features** in total); likelihood of transitioning from one entity to another- e.g., transition from focusing on tablet to focusing elsewhere; this gives rise to **six transition probability features** corresponding to 3 permute 2 entity transitions. An additional *six gaze flux features* denoting gaze flux into and out of the three entities were obtained from marginal likelihoods– e.g., P(gaze flux into tab) = P(fac $\rightarrow$ tab) + P(others $\rightarrow$ tab), where $\rightarrow$ denotes a gaze transition.

To quantify attitude, we computed the proportions of positive (neutral or happy emotion) and negative (angry, sad or disgusted) affect over the observation period from the per-frame facial emotion labels.

In terms of computational hardware, AVEID requires a Graphics Processing Unit (GPU) for video processing. The current system is implemented on a Xeon processor with 64GB RAM, and 12 GB NVIDIA GeForce GTX 1080 Ti GPU memory.

BOS FOR VALIDATION

We validated AVEID by comparing the obtained attention and attitude measures against expert annotations acquired for the OME and MPES scales, whose descriptions follow.

The **Observational Measure of Engagement** (OME) [2] is an observational scale to directly assess engagement in PwD. For this BOS, observers are first required to detect *time periods denoting PwD engagement*, and score the attention and attitude levels of the patient within these engagement periods. OME represents a very coarse-grained assessment of PwD engagement, and can best facilitate examination of engagement periods, as no codings are made when the dementia patient is disengaged from the target activity. The **Menorah Park Engagement Scale** (MPES) [8] is a more fine-grained BOS, as PwD engagement is assessed over 5-minute time periods. Three types of engagement, namely, active engagement with the target device/activity, passive engagement and engagement with others, are measured in this BOS (Table 1).

EXPERT SCORE ACQUISITION

All annotated videos were as shown in Fig.1, where a PwD engages with an interactive tablet aided by a facilitator [6]. For OME scoring, a dementia care therapist with 10 years experience indicated periods of patient engagement in seven 15-minute video segments according to the following OME definition: "amount of attention the person was visibly paying to the stimulus (tablet) via eye movements; manipulating/holding and talking about it." [2]. MPES scores were provided by researchers trained to attain 0.8 (Kappa) inter-rater reliability. They scored 5-minute segments from 20 videos (30 minutes each), for active engagement (*Did target activity*), passive engagement (*Watched target activity*) and engagement with other stimuli (*Attention on activity other than target*) on an ordinal scale (Table 1). Table 2 summarizes the annotation statistics.

Bos	No. Videos	No. of Video Segments	Annotated by
OME	7	-	Therapist
MPES	20	130	Trained researchers

Table 2. Scores were obtained from experienced therapists or trained researchers.

VALIDATION STUDY RESULTS AND DISCUSSION

Measures of Attention

In the OME BOS, engagement periods are identified and then annotated for attention level and attitude. So, we computed the proportion of patient's gaze focus on the target activity space for a) those segments where the therapist indicated engagement, and b) the remaining video segments where the therapist inferred disengagement. Fig.3 presents the computed gaze proportions for seven videos. Higher distribution of gaze focus on tablet was clearly noted during engagement periods, as confirmed by a two-sample Kolmogorov-Smirnov test at $p<0.001$. Therefore, gaze focus on the target was sufficient to convey the notion of attention as with the OME.

The MPES BOS quantifies attention over 5-minute intervals. Fig. 4 presents Pearson correlations computed between active, passive and other engagement MPES scores, and the 21 AVEID attention features in the form of a 3×21 grayscale image. Negative and positive correlations are respectively denoted by darker and lighter shades. Red and cyan symbols respectively denote significant ($p<0.05$) and marginally significant ($p<0.1$) correlations.

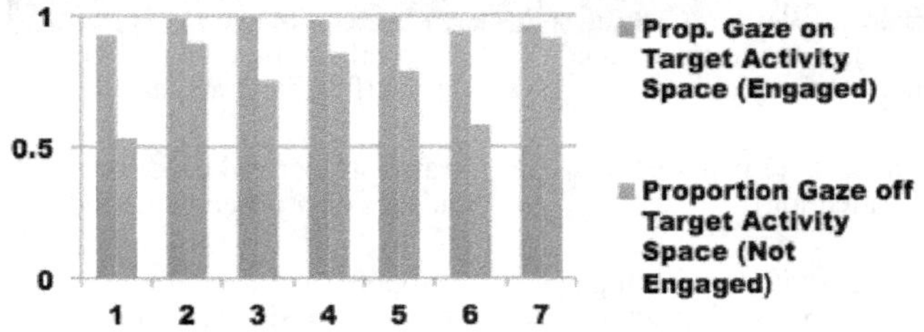

Figure 3. Gaze proportions on tablet (engagement device) during *engaged* and *not-engaged* periods as per OME BOS.

Active engagement is significantly and positively correlated with the extent of gaze focused on tablet, mean duration of tablet gazing episodes and std of these episodic durations, while being negatively correlated with the extent of gaze focus on the caregiver and other areas. Active engagement is also marginally and positively correlated with the gaze flux in and out of the target activity area, suggesting that focus on target activity area as well as periodic gaze switching when communicating with the facilitator are linked with higher active engagement scores as assessed by the expert.

On the other hand, passive engagement marginally and negatively correlates with the gazing durations on the facilitator. This pattern is concurrent with the MPES description of passive activity where the PwD behaves with less enthusiasm and is not having social interactions with the facilitator. The final MPES item, engagement with other, positively correlates with gazing on facilitator, and negatively with the mean and standard deviation of gazing episode durations on the target activity area. This suggests that engagement with other activities, as coded by the experts, is associated with behaviors where the PwD directs attention more toward the facilitator rather than toward the presented activity.

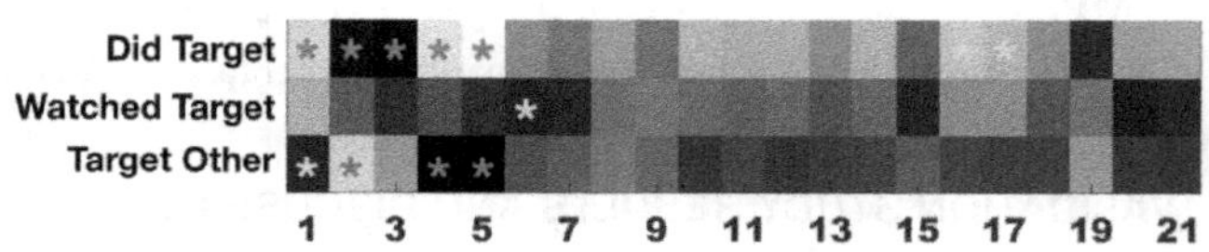

Figure 4. Correlations between gaze-based AVEID features and MPES scores for active (Did Tgt), passive (Watched Tgt) and other engagement (Tgt Other). Red and cyan marks denote correlations significant at (p<0.05) and (p<0.1).

To summarize, gaze on target as a correlate of engagement is validated by both the OME and MPES coding methods. Furthermore, attention measures computed via AVEID are able to capture a number of aspects concerning these BOS.

Measures of Attitude

Inferring facial emotions of PwD is a known challenge due to older adults exhibiting facial emotions in a controlled manner, ageing skin and muscles significantly modulating facial appearance, and indicating a prominently negative affect [5]. Additionally, PwD often display flattened affect [9]. However, greater engagement from the PwD should also elicit a positive reaction from the facilitator whose role is to promote such behavior. As facilitators are neurotypical adults whose facial emotions can be better recognized with available computer vision tools, we therefore examined if higher MPES attitude scores correlate better with the facilitator's facial emotions (Fig.6). This hypothesis turned out to be true, with pleasure scores correlating significantly and positively with the proportion of positive facial affect exhibited by the facilitator (r=0.24, p<0.01). Therefore, examining facilitator behavior (where possible) could provide crucial cues for measuring engagement in PwD.

Overall, results reveal that AVEID can effectively capture patient (and facilitator) behavior indicative of attention and attitude. Also, since AVEID measures are based on per-frame gaze and emotion labels, it is possible to go beyond coarse engagement measures that BOS provide. E.g., even though the patient's verbal behavior was not captured in the videos, the frequency with which the patient directs gaze towards the facilitator may serve as an effective cue to this end. Finally, gazing and attitude estimation can be reliably accomplished for small-space activities (where the patient's face is clearly visible), facilitating evaluation of multiple engagement designs.

CHALLENGES AND LIMITATIONS

Figures 5 and 6 illustrate the challenges involved in video-based engagement measurement for PwD, where the observation videos are captured under unconstrained settings. Fig.5 presents two examples of incorrect gaze focus estimation due to the closeness of the facilitator to the tablet, and due to the 2D video information being insufficient to model the 3D world. Likewise, in Fig. 6 (right), the patient's facial appearance is mistaken by the algorithm as an exhibition of sadness. It needs to be acknowledged that gazing behavior can only indicate passive engagement; the use of wearable physiological sensors [19] may be necessary for inferring cognitive engagement.

Figure 5. Incorrect gaze estimation examples (zoom to view).

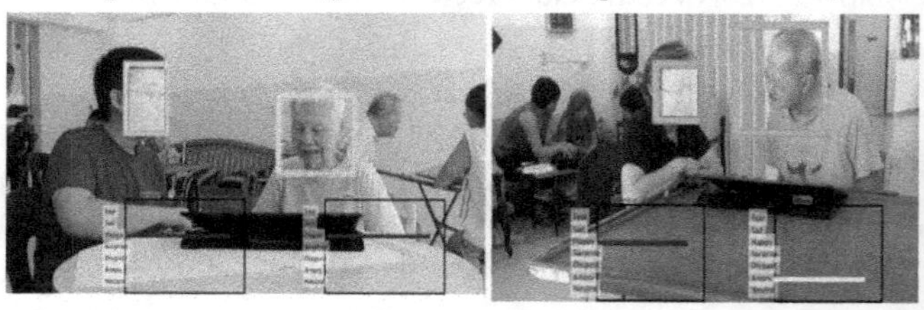

Figure 6. Exemplar emotion estimation results. Facial emotions of the PwD and facilitator are correctly identified (left). PwD's emotion is incorrect, but facilitator's emotion is correct (right) (zoom to view).

CONCLUSION

We present AVEID, a video-based analytics system that effectively capture various aspects of BOS employed for measuring engagement in PwD. AVEID currently measures only passive engagement (via gaze behavior), and inferring attitude from PwDs' facial emotions is highly challenging. Future work will address these limitations, and explore additional modalities (such as verbal behavior) for measuring engagement among PwD.

REFERENCES

1. Arlene J Astell, Maggie P Ellis, Lauren Bernardi, Norman Alm, Richard Dye, Gary Gowans, and Jim Campbell. 2010. Using a touch screen computer to support relationships between people with dementia and caregivers. *Interacting with Computers* 22, 4 (2010), 267–275.
2. Jiska Cohen-Mansfield, Maha Dakheel-Ali, and Marcia S Marx. 2009. Engagement in persons with dementia: the concept and its measurement. *The American journal of geriatric psychiatry* 17, 4 (2009), 299–307.
3. Natalie C Ebner, Michaela Riediger, and Ulman Lindenberger. 2010. FACES-A database of facial expressions in young, middle-aged, and older women and men: Development and validation. *Behavior research methods* 42, 1 (2010), 351–362.
4. Stu Favilla and Sonja Pedell. 2013. Touch screen ensemble music: collaborative interaction for older people with dementia. In *Proceedings of the 25th Australian Computer-Human Interaction Conference: Augmentation, Application, Innovation, Collaboration.* ACM, 481–484.
5. Mara Fölster, Ursula Hess, and Katja Werheid. 2014. Facial age affects emotional expression decoding. *Frontiers in Psychology* 5 (2014), 30. DOI: http://dx.doi.org/10.3389/fpsyg.2014.00030
6. Pin Sym Foong, Shengdong Zhao, Kelsey Carlson, and Zhe Liu. 2017. VITA: Towards Supporting Volunteer Interactions with Long-Term Care Residents with Dementia. In *Proceedings of the 2017 CHI Conference on Human Factors in Computing Systems (CHI '17).* ACM, New York, NY, USA, 6195–6207. DOI: http://dx.doi.org/10.1145/3025453.3025776
7. Peiyun Hu and Deva Ramanan. 2017. Finding tiny faces. In *2017 IEEE Conference on Computer Vision and Pattern Recognition (CVPR).* IEEE, 1522–1530.
8. Cameron J.Camp, Michael J. Skrajner, and Greg J. Gorzelle. *Engagement in Dementia. In Assessment Scales for Advanced Dementia.* HPP, Baltimore. 65–69 pages.
9. M Powell Lawton, Kimberly Van Haitsma, Margaret Perkinson, and Katy Ruckdeschel. 1999. Observed affect and quality of life in dementia: Further affirmations and problems. *Journal of mental Health and Aging* (1999).
10. Edward L Mahoney and Diane F Mahoney. 2010. Acceptance of wearable technology by people with AlzheimerâĂŹs disease: Issues and accommodations. *American Journal of Alzheimer's Disease & Other Dementias®* 25, 6 (2010), 527–531.
11. Alex Mihailidis, Scott Blunsden, Jennifer Boger, Brandi Richards, Krists Zutis, Laurel Young, and Jesse Hoey. 2010. Towards the development of a technology for art therapy and dementia: Definition of needs and design constraints. *The Arts in Psychotherapy* 37, 4 (2010), 293–300.
12. Hong-Wei Ng, Viet Dung Nguyen, Vassilios Vonikakis, and Stefan Winkler. 2015. Deep Learning for Emotion Recognition on Small Datasets Using Transfer Learning. In *Proceedings of the 2015 ACM International Conference on Multimodal Interaction (ICMI '15).* ACM, New York, NY, USA, 443–449. DOI: http://dx.doi.org/10.1145/2818346.2830593
13. Viral Parekh, Ramanathan Subramanian, and C. V. Jawahar. 2017. *Eye Contact Detection via Deep Neural Networks.* Springer International Publishing, Cham, 366–374. DOI: http://dx.doi.org/10.1007/978-3-319-58750-9_51
14. Shyamal Patel, Hyung Park, Paolo Bonato, Leighton Chan, and Mary Rodgers. 2012. A review of wearable sensors and systems with application in rehabilitation. *Journal of NeuroEngineering and Rehabilitation* 9, 1 (20 Apr 2012), 21. DOI: http://dx.doi.org/10.1186/1743-0003-9-21
15. Adria Recasens*, Aditya Khosla*, Carl Vondrick, and Antonio Torralba. 2015. Where are they looking?. In *Advances in Neural Information Processing Systems (NIPS).* * indicates equal contribution.
16. Elisa Ricci, Jagannadan Varadarajan, Ramanathan Subramanian, Samuel Rota Bulo, Narendra Ahuja, and Oswald Lanz. 2015. Uncovering Interactions and Interactors: Joint Estimation of Head, Body Orientation and F-Formations From Surveillance Videos. In *International Conference on Computer Vision (ICCV).*
17. Brian A. Smith, Qi Yin, Steven K. Feiner, and Shree K. Nayar. 2013. Gaze Locking: Passive Eye Contact Detection for Human-object Interaction. In *Proceedings of the 26th Annual ACM Symposium on User Interface Software and Technology (UIST '13).* ACM, New York, NY, USA, 271–280. DOI: http://dx.doi.org/10.1145/2501988.2501994
18. Ramanathan Subramanian, Jacopo Staiano, Kyriaki Kalimeri, Nicu Sebe, and Fabio Pianesi. 2010. Putting the Pieces Together: Multimodal Analysis of Social Attention in Meetings. In *ACM Multimedia.* 659–662.
19. R. Subramanian, J. Wache, M. Abadi, R. Vieriu, S. Winkler, and N. Sebe. 2017. ASCERTAIN: Emotion and Personality Recognition using Commercial Sensors. *IEEE Transactions on Affective Computing* (2017).

Voice Input Tutoring System for Older Adults using Input Stumble Detection

Toshiyuki Hagiya
KDDI Research, Inc. &
Kyoto University
to-hagiya@kddi-research.jp

Keiichiro Hoashi
KDDI Research, Inc.
hoashi@kddi-research.jp

Tatsuya Kawahara
Kyoto University
kawahara@i.kyoto-u.ac.jp

ABSTRACT
Many older adults are interested in smartphones but encounter difficulties in self-instruction and need support, especially text input. Voice input is a useful option for text input, but also presents some difficulties for older adults. In this paper, we propose a tutoring system for voice input that detects input stumbles using a statistical approach and provides instructions to overcome them. We construct the tutoring system based on the data from a user study with novice older adults. In an evaluation experiment, the number of input stumble and the sentence completion time of the participants using the tutoring system were significantly smaller than those without it. The results showed that the tutoring system resulted in the improvement of the efficiency of voice input for novice older adults.

Author Keywords
Voice input; older adults; tutoring system;

INTRODUCTION
Smartphones offer new opportunities to improve the lives of older adults [8]. Although these individuals would like to learn how to use smartphones [1], those who have never used one may face difficulties and some of them may give up on using a smartphone and go back to using their old feature phone, Therefore, providing support in the initial stages is very important. To make full use of the functions of a smartphone, it is essential to master text input, which is one of the operations that novice older adults find most difficult. Automatic speech recognition (ASR), which is an option of the text input, are easier to those who were unfamiliar with touch input [12]. However, users need to get accustomed to ASR, in order to input as intended. In addition, ASR needs to be used along with software keyboards when precisely input sentences are required, e.g., when dealing with documents. In this study, we developed a tutoring system for voice input that detects input stumbles using a statistical approach, and then provides instructions that help users resolve input stumbles independently. We outline our development of the tutoring system in three steps. First, we describe a user study that clarified the problems that older adults encounter with voice input. Second, we explain designing the structure of the tutoring system on the basis of the user study. Finally, we evaluate the performance of the resulting tutoring system.

IUI 2018, March 7–11, 2018, Tokyo, Japan.

https://doi.org/10.1145/3172944.3172995

RELATED WORK

Interface Design for Voice Input
At present, automatic speech recognition (ASR) is still imperfect, although many researchers have worked to improve its performance. Therefore, some research has been proposed for voice input interfaces to include the assumption that misrecognition occurs. Goto *et al.* [4] proposed a system to alter a sentence when users hesitate by lengthening a vowel during a phrase. Ogata *et al.* [11] proposed a system to display the result of ASR as a sentence that includes alternative word candidates. In a similar way, Liang *et al.* [9] proposed a simple gesture-based error correction interface where a user marks the error region once, and then the error region is replaced by the top candidate. Speech Recognizer for Android [2] gives feedback on the results of errors, such as audio recording errors and network-related errors. This function mainly gives feedback on the cause of equipment-side rather than user-side problems.

Tutoring System for Older Adults
A wealth of research has focused on designing better instructional resources to assist older adults. For example, Morrell *et al* [10] have studied what the optimal amount of guidance is. Rogers *et al.* [13] investigated the kind of resources most useful in the learning process, and found that step-by-step interactive tutorials were the most effective approach to the learning process for older adults. With respect to using smartphones, Leung *et al.* [8] surveyed and investigated how older adults learned. According to their report, older adults tend to prefer an instruction manual to trial-and-error. Kelleher *et al.* [6] proposed stencil-based tutorials that overlay step-by-step instructions on the screen. Hagiya *et al.* [5] proposed a tutoring system for text entry on smartphones that provided instruction about the next operation. However, tutoring systems for voice input have not been studied.

TUTORING SYSTEM FOR VOICE INPUT
As described in the previous section, although many studies deal with ASR and others with tutoring systems, tutoring systems for voice input have not been studied. Therefore, we propose a tutoring system for voice input that detects input

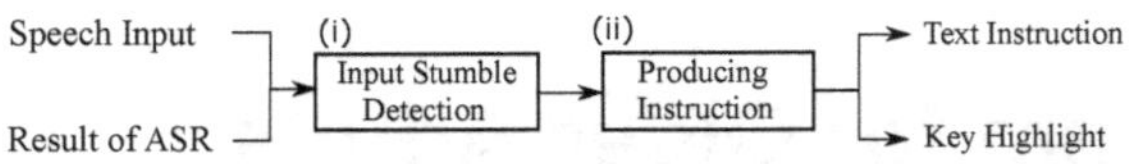

Figure 1. Block diagram of the voice input tutoring system

stumbles using a statistical approach and provides instructions that help users resolve input stumbles. As shown in Figure 1, the tutoring system is composed of two functions, (i) input stumble detection and (ii) producing instruction. The function of input stumble detection is to detect voice input stumble based on a model trained by features from such as acoustics and results of ASR. The function that produces instruction displays the instructions for the next operation, using text and key highlighting.

USER STUDY TO CLARIFY HOW NOVICE OLDER ADULTS MAKE INPUT STUMBLES

This study has two purposes: One is to clarify how novice older adults make input stumbles in smartphone voice input. Second is to collect the input data to construct a tutoring system. In this study, participants first input a statement by voice, and then are permitted to modify what was recognized, using a combination of voice and touch.

Participants

Ten older adults were recruited from a local social institution to take part in this experiment. There were five males and five females, ranging in age from 65 to 72 years, with a mean age of 69.8 (sd = 3.8). None of them owned a smartphone but all had owned a featurephone and had used their own PC routinely. None of them had tremor disorders, eye problems, or other relevant health problems.

Apparatus

Google Cloud Speech API [3] was used for ASR. As shown in Figure 2, a key for ASR was implemented on a software keyboard. After the key is pushed, a tone acknowledges the push, and the end of the tone announces the start of ASR. ASR terminates when the API detects the end of a speech or when five seconds have passed without input. Then Google Cloud Speech API outputs the N best candidates of recognition results and the highest confidence score between 0 and 1. The smartphone records the user's voice and the keys touched. All operations were also recorded by an overhead video camera. Participants used a Nexus 6 running Android 7.0.

Procedure

First, an overview of the experiment was explained and the informed written consent was obtained from the participants. Next, the participants were given explanations on how to operate a smartphone, including touch and swipe operations, and instructed on how to use the voice input and the software keyboard by a human tutor. Then, they input sentences to match a sentence presented in Japanese, using an application as shown in Figure 2. The sentences were selected from an email corpus collected originally from personal conversations via email. The corpus contained roughly 30,000 sentences (average character length = 23.6). Participants were asked to input twenty sentences within 60 minutes, with a ten-minute break after completing ten sentences. They operated the smartphone while holding it in their hand and sitting on a chair. They were instructed to type by themselves if possible. However, they were permitted to ask the human tutor when they lacked the confidence to perform the next action. After the experiment, they took part in an interview.

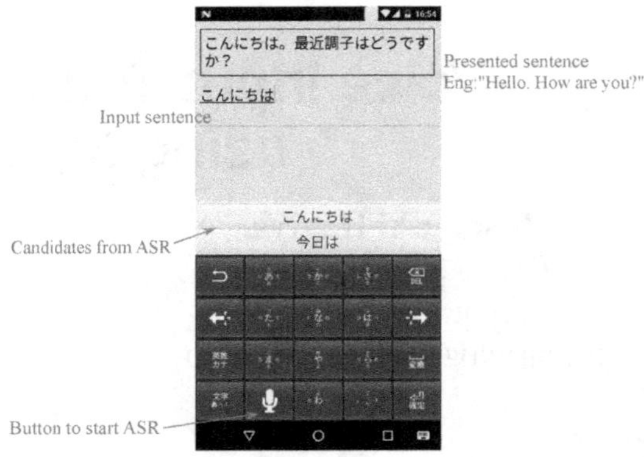

Figure 2. A screen of an input application and a software keyboard

Table 1. Input stumble of voice input

	Input stumble
(1)	Volume was too high for voice recognition
(2)	Volume was too low for voice recognition
(3)	Utterance started before ASR began working
(4)	Filler was inserted
(5)	Utterance paused due to long phrase
(6)	Intended homonyms were not displayed due to short utterance
(7)	Not knowing how to insert punctuation mark
(8)	Not knowing how to insert question mark
(9)	Not knowing how to select candidates
(10)	Not knowing how to delete a word
(11)	Forgetting to move cursor to end of sentence

Upon completion of this stage, three annotators independently extracted the patterns of input stumbles from the logs and the recorded videos, and defined categories of the stumbles based on discussion. Next, the annotators associated labeled input stumbles of each input sentence, and the labels given by at least two annotators were used in the next stage.

Results of the User Study

All participants completed the task, taking an average time of 27.3 minutes (sd = 7.4). Voice input stumbles fell into 11 categories, as shown in Table 1. The concordance rate of the annotation of the input stumble by Fleiss' kappa was 0.79. In the interview, many comments similar to these were made:

"It was easier to input by voice than touch, but it was difficult to correct it when I made mistakes. So I wanted to know how I should correct and why I failed."

This study showed that older adults have some difficulties for voice input and need instructions.

CONSTRUCTION OF TUTORING SYSTEM

In this section, we describe the construction of the two functions of the tutoring system for voice input.

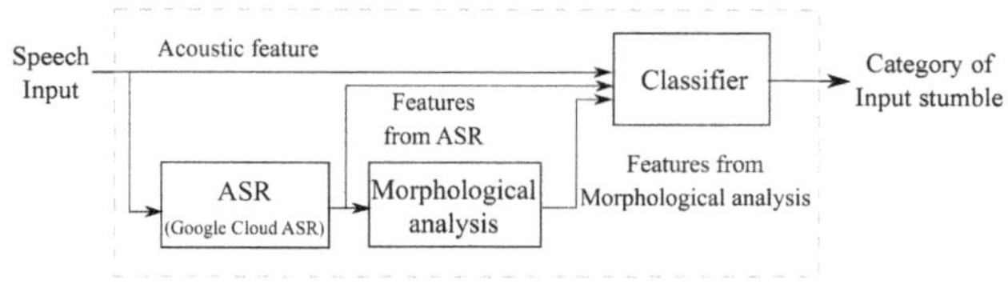

Figure 3. A block diagram of input stumble detection

Input Stumble Detection

Input stumble detection was constructed by machine learning based on data from the previous user study. The block diagram of input stumble detection is shown in Figure 3. First, acoustic features were extracted from speech input. Simultaneously, features from ASR including the confidence score and the candidates were the output from Google Cloud ASR. Next, the features from the morphological analysis of the results of ASR were extracted using Lucene-gosen [7]. Finally, the classifier of input stumbles was trained using the features and the labels.

To select the best machine learning algorithm, we compared the performance of four models, a linear regression, a C4.5, a support vector machine (SVM) using an RBF kernel, and a deep neural network (DNN) [14]. A DNN with five layers was trained by minimizing loss function with backpropagation and the stochastic gradient descent method with a dropout ratio of 50%.

A total of 28 features was used, 17 of which were acoustic features: the number of amplitude overflows, the duration of voice activity, five kinds of amplitude averages, namely time gaps between voice activity, 0.5 sec before and after the start and the end of voice activity, and the differences in the five kinds of averages. The remaining 11 features were textual features related to the ASR and morphological analysis results: the number of candidates, the confidence score, the length of the sentences, the number of morphemes, the ID of morphemes of sentence terminations, the number of conjunctions, the number of end-forms, the number of fillers, the number of homonyms of the shortest words (except particles), the time to the next operation, and the position of the cursor.

Features used for SVM and logistic regression were selected by L1 regularization. Those for a C4.5 were selected by stepwise backward selection of each participant with 10-fold cross-validation (CV). The F-measure from the 10-fold CV was 0.70 with a linear regression, 0.73 with C4.5, 0.72 with SVM and 0.73 with DNN. Anova $(\alpha = 0.05)$ showed no significant differences among these models, so we adopted C4.5 for use here as it had the highest rate of accuracy.

Producing Instructions

The definition of instructions to be presented to users was done manually, based on the observation of effective instructions given by human tutors. The instruction was provided by text and with overlaid key highlighting. The instruction provided for the input stumble of "Not knowing how to insert a punctuation mark" is exemplified in Figure 4. The instruction was displayed when there was no operation for 5 seconds after a detected input stumble, and remained on the screen for

Figure 4. Screen shot showing instructions after input stumble (7)

7 seconds or until the screen was touched. The time and the text of instructions were modified after discussions with three older adults (60s) who did not participate in this study. The texts were accordingly modified to show not only the method of operation but also the reason for the correction, as well as tips for voice input.

EVALUATION EXPERIMENT WITH TUTORING SYSTEM

Participants

Twenty older adults took part in this experiment. They were recruited from a local social institution and did not participate in the previous user study. There were ten males and ten females, ranging in age from 65 to 71 years, with a mean age of 68.6 (sd = 1.9). Ten participants did not use the tutoring system (group A), and the other ten used it (group B). None of these older adults owned a smartphone or had any previous experience of using a voice input, but all had owned a featurephone and all had routinely used their own PC. None of them had tremor disorders or other relevant health problems.

Procedure and Apparatus

The experiment was conducted in a similar way to the previous user study. In brief, an overview of the experiment was explained and the informed written consent was obtained from the participants. Next, the participants were given explanations on how to operate a smartphone and how to use the voice input and the software keyboard. While seated in a chair, they input 40 sentences to match the presented sentences. Participants first used voice input, then were permitted to modify the result with a combination of voice and touch. They had a ten-minute break after completing twenty sentences. After the experiment, they filled out a 5-point Likert-scale questionnaire, and took part in an interview. After all the participants had completed the experiment, three annotators labeled input stumbles in the logs. We adopted the labels given by more than two annotators.

Experimental Results

All participants completed the task. The concordance rate of annotation of input stumble using Fleiss' kappa was 0.85.

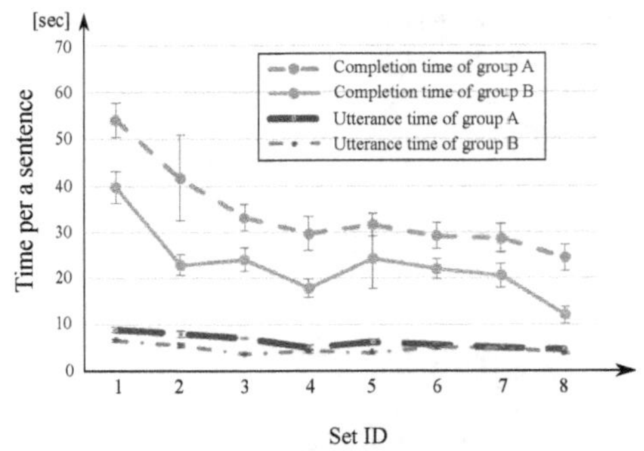

Figure 5. The average completion time and the utterance time for a sentence in each set

The detection performance of input stumble for group B using F-measure was 0.74. The word recognition rate of ASR was 91.1% for group A and 92.6% for group B, respectively. Welch's t-test ($\alpha = 0.05$) showed no significant difference between groups A and B. To evaluate the effect of the tutoring system, we adopted three metrics: the task completion time, number of input stumble, and the questionnaire.

Completion Time

To analyze the learning effect of our system, we conducted a chronological analysis of the performance of the subjects, by dividing all 40 sentences into 5 sets (8 sentences per set), and measuring the average completion time and utterance time for each set during the experiment. The results of the analysis are shown in Figure 5. The completion time of both groups decreased gradually. The completion times of group B were shorter than those of group A in all sets. Welch's t-test showed a significant difference between the completion time of both groups for the first set ($t(12) = 2.79, p < .05$) and the final set ($t(15) = 2.89, p < .05$). On the other hand, the utterance time of both groups decreased gradually, and there was no significant difference between the two groups.

Number of input stumbles

Figure 6 shows the number of input stumbles per sentence. As shown in the figure, the number of input stumbles of both groups decreased gradually, as did the completion time. The number of input stumbles in group B was less than in group A in all sets. Welch's t-test showed a significant difference between the number of stumbles of both groups for the first set ($t(16) = 3.05, p < .01$) and final set ($t(9) = 8.65, p < .01$).

Questionnaire results

The results of questionnaires are shown in Table 2. The scale is 1-5, where 5 indicates the highest level of agreement. The score of the items *"The voice input was useful"* were 3.7 in group A and 3.6 in group B, showing no significant difference. On the other hand, there was a 0.5 point inter-group score difference for *"The correction was easy"* and *"I can learn the voice input method by myself"*. A Wilcoxon signed-rank sum test ($\alpha = 0.05$) showed a significant difference between the groups for the only latter item.

DISCUSSION

In summarizing the results of the evaluation, the completion time and the number of input stumbles of group B were significantly smaller than those of group A. These results indicate that the tutoring system works effectively for novice older adults. Focusing on the time, the time taken to find out how to modify and the time to needed to modify sentences decreased as a result of using the system because the ratio of the utterance time to the completion time was small. In addition, there is a possibility that the amount of modification decreased because instructions influenced the input efficiency. Some participants of group B made a comment:

"I realized that ASR worked well when I want to input a long sentence or several sentences if I input each short sentence."

These comments imply that the instruction provided by the tutoring system worked effectively.

On the other hand, some participants made multiple input stumbles simultaneously in one voice input. However, the tutoring system provides an instruction only for the most probable input stumble. Therefore, in this case, they often did not know how to perform the next operation after resolving an input stumble. To detect multiple stumbles and provide step-by-step instruction is a topic for our future works.

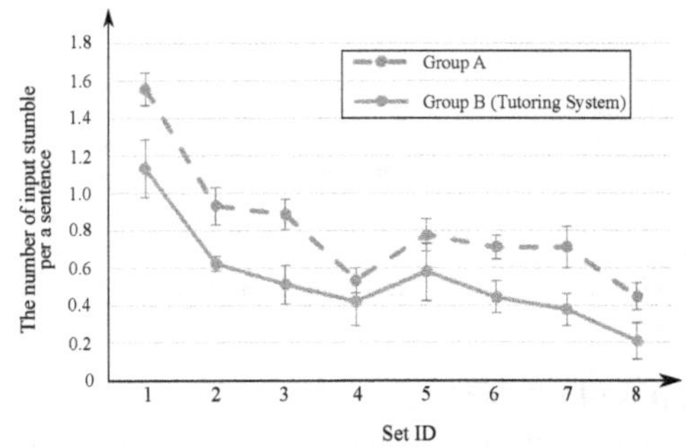

Figure 6. The number of input stumbles in a sentence in each set

Table 2. Questionnaire responses. The scales are 1-5, where 5 is higher agreement; the standard deviations are given in parentheses)

Question	group A	group B
The voice input was useful	3.7 (0.64)	3.6 (0.66)
The correction was easy	2.6 (0.66)	3.1 (0.70)
I can learn the way of the voice input by myself	3.7 (0.45)	4.2 (0.40)

CONCLUSION

We developed a tutoring system for voice input that detected input stumbles, and provided instructions. First, we conducted a user study to clarify the problems older adults encountered in voice input. Second, we constructed the tutoring system. Finally, we evaluated the performance of the tutoring system. In the evaluation experiment, the number of input stumble and the sentence completion time of the participants using the tutoring system were significantly smaller than those without it. The results showed that the tutoring system resulted in improvement in the efficiency of voice input for novice older adults. In future research, we are going to develop a system to detect multiple stumbles and provide step-by-step instructions to improve usability.

REFERENCES

1. Beverly Beisge and Marilyn Kraitchman. 2003. Senior Centers: Opportunities For Successful Aging. *Springer Publishing Company* (2003).
2. Google. 2017a. Android Developers. (2017). https://developer.android.com/index.html.
3. Google. 2017b. Cloud Speech API. (2017). https://cloud.google.com/speech.
4. Masataka Goto, Katunobu Itou, and Satoru Hayamizu. 2002. Speech Completion: On-demand Completion Assistance Using Filled Pauses for Speech Input Interfaces. In *Proceedings of the 7th International Conference on Spoken Language Processing (ICSLP '02)*. World Academy of Science, Engineering and Technology (WASET), 1489–1492.
5. Toshiyuki Hagiya, Toshiharu Horiuchi, and Tomonori Yazaki. 2016. Typing Tutor: Individualized Tutoring in Text Entry for Older Adults Based on Input Stumble Detection. In *Proceedings of the SIGCHI Conference on Human Factors in Computing Systems (CHI '16)*. ACM, 733–744.
6. Caitlin Kelleher and Randy Pausch. 2005. Stencils-based tutorials: Design and evaluation. In *Proceedings of the SIGCHI Conference on Human Factors in Computing Systems (CHI '05)*. ACM, 541–550.
7. Taku Kudoh, Tsuyoshi Fukui, Takashi Okamoto, and Matt Francis. 2017. lucene-gosen. (2017). https://github.com/lucene-gosen.
8. Rock Leung, Charlotte Tang, Shathel Haddad, Joanna Mcgrenere, Peter Graf, and Vilia Ingriany. 2012. How older adults learn to use mobile devices: Survey and field investigations. *ACM Transactions on Accessible Computing* 4, 3 (2012), 11:1–11:33.
9. Yuan Liang, Koji Iwano, and Koichi Shinoda. 2014. Simple Gesture-based Error Correction Interface for Smartphone Speech Recognition. In *Proceedings of the 15th Annual Conference of the International Speech Communication Association International Conference on Science and Technology for Humanity (INTERSPEECH '14)*. International Speech Communication Association (ISCA), 1194–1198.
10. Roger W. Morrell, Denise C. Park, Christopher B. Mayhorn, and Catherine L. Kelley. 2000. Effects of age and instructions on teaching older adults to use eldercomm, an electronic bulletin board system. *Educational Gerontology* 26, 3 (2000), 221–235.
11. Jun Ogata and Masataka Goto. 2005. Speech Repair: Quick Error Correction Just by Using Selection Operation for Speech Input Interfaces. In *Proceedings of the 9th European Conference on Speech Communication and Technology (Eurospeech '05)*. International Speech Communication Association (ISCA), 133–136.
12. Pei-Luen Patrick Rau and Jia-Wen Hsu. 2005. Interaction Devices and Web Design for Novice Older Users. *Educational Gerontology* 31, 1 (2005), 19–40.
13. Wendy A. Rogers, Elizabeth F. Cabrera, Neff Walker, D. Kristen Gilbert, and Arthur D. Fisk. 1996. A survey of automatic teller machine usage across the adult lifespan. *Human Factors* (1996), 38,1; 156–166.
14. Yuan Tang. 2016. TF.Learn: TensorFlow's High-level Module for Distributed Machine Learning. In *arXiv*. 1612.04251.

The I in Team: Mining Personal Social Interaction Routine with Topic Models from Long-Term Team Data

Yanxia Zhang
Delft University of Technology
Delft, Netherlands
Yanxia.Zhang@tudelft.nl

Jeffrey Olenick
Michigan State University
East Lansing, United States
olenickj@msu.edu

Chu-Hsiang Chang
Michigan State University
East Lansing, United States
cchang@msu.edu

Steve W. J. Kozlowski
Michigan State University
East Lansing, United States
stevekoz@msu.edu

Hayley Hung
Delft University of Technology
Delft, Netherlands
h.hung@tudelft.nl

ABSTRACT
Social interaction plays a key role in assessing teamwork and collaboration. It becomes particularly critical in team performance when coupled with isolated, confined, and extreme conditions such as undersea missions. This work investigates how social interactions of individual members in a small team evolve during the course of a long duration mission. We propose to use a topic model to mine individual social interaction patterns and examine how the dynamics of these patterns have an effect on self-assessment of mood and team cohesion. Specifically, we analyzed data from a 6-person crew wearing Sociometric badges over a 4-month mission. Our results show that our method can extract the latent structure of social contexts without supervision. We demonstrate how the extracted patterns based on probabilistic models can provide insights on common behaviors at various temporal resolutions and exhibit links with self-report affective states and team cohesion.

Author Keywords
Wearable; team dynamics; machine learning

INTRODUCTION
Understanding team process dynamics such as the relation between affect, cohesion and performance, plays an important role in a variety of HCI applications that support group collaborations. One open question is that how to support team work unobtrusively without disrupting their ongoing tasks, for example providing timely interventions to assist individual members or an entire team to overcome crucial situations [13]. Assessing an individual's affect and their perception of team cohesion is a crucial first step in mitigating negative feelings and preventing team failure. This becomes particularly challenging for long duration missions that can last for months or even years under persistent stress in confined spaces (e.g., in space or under water) as a team must live and work together during the entire period [12].

Social interactions are an essential part in our daily life. In particular, much information about social relationships are transmitted thorough face-to-face interactions [2, 3]. Previous works found that face-to-face interaction patterns of group members are linked to their productivity, performance and interaction efficacy [4, 18]. However, it is challenging to capture dynamic social interaction patterns in real environments manually when social networks are often constructed using questionnaires [2, 8]. Recent advances in wearable devices allow real-time detection of social interactions, for example using the Sociometric badges [18]. This type of wearable device augments an ID badge with sensors that can detect an individual's communication activities at the minute or second level including who they interact with, when it happens, and how long it lasts. These wearable sensors provide an attractive opportunity to study long term team process dynamics with unobtrusive continuous recording [12, 13].

This paper investigates how an individual's social interaction patterns evolve dynamically during the course of a team mission and whether they are linked to self-report mood and perceived cohesion. We hypothesize that there exist low dimensional structures to represent more frequent or normal behaviors of someone's daily social interaction patterns. We apply latent Dirichlet allocation (LDA) to discover the hidden structures and examine how observed events fit to the learned model. This allows us to model how social interaction behaviors unfold during the mission. In addition, we identify common behavioral patterns and track changes on both a short-term daily and long-term bi-weekly basis. Finally, we illustrate how the temporal dynamics of social interactions are related to affective state and perceived team cohesion.

IUI 2018, March 7–11, 2018, Tokyo, Japan.

http://dx.doi.org/10.1145/3172944.3172997

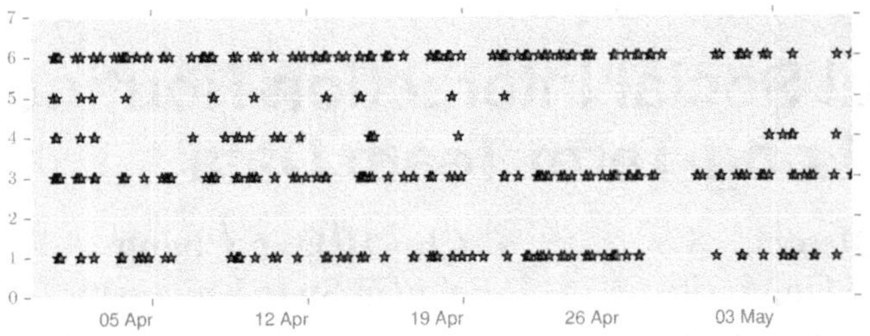

Figure 1. One month of face-to-face interactions detected for subject 2 from the badge. The y axis indicates the badge ID (1-6).

RELATED WORK

Social interaction patterns among groups can reveal rich information about individual and group states [4, 18, 3]. Existing research adopted social network analysis (SNA) to understand community behaviors in large organizations [4, 18, 8]. These works construct a graph via linking nodes based on communication levels between pairwise subjects and measure the state of communications within the network by graph's centrality, density and etc [8, 4]. Increasing amounts of research started to explore unsupervised machine learning methods to mine human behavior patterns [5, 3]. Eagle and Pentland applied principle component analysis (PCA) to model community behaviors from the bluetooth and location data in the reality mining dataset [5]. Their method extracted eigenbehaviors to represent the underlying structure in users' daily patterns. Huynh *et al.* applied LDA to discover activity routines (e.g., having lunch, driving car or sitting at desk) using wearable sensor data collected from one subject over 16 days [10]. Farrahi and Gatica-Perez applied several probabilistic topic models including LDA, the Author-Topic and N-gram Topic model to the daily location sequences of 97 mobile phone users over 16 months to mine individual and group mobility patterns [6, 7]. They used labeled cell tower data to extract human mobility routines such as "going home from work". The selection of number of latent topics and other parameters in these models is usually time-consuming and difficult for personalized applications. Nonparametric models have been introduced to overcome these challenges [15, 17].

In sum, previous works adopted LDA for identifying activity and mobility routines. There is little work that mines social interaction routines and investigates how their dynamics link to individual's affective states and perceived cohesion during a long mission. Moreover, compared to using SNA in complex organizations, this work focused on small teams which have inherently different dynamics than large communities [9].

THE DATASET

Team cohesion is considered to be a dynamic phenomenon rather than a stable construct. Existing research focused on team cohesion during short periods such as meetings [14]. However, team cohesion has rarely been investigated for long durations (e.g., months, years) [16, 12, 11]. To understand the dynamics of team cohesion, the dataset is collected from a team of 6 members over a 4-month mission. Participants wore badges from Sociometric Solutions during waking hours and whenever potentially engaged in social activities (thus not while exercising, or showering). Twice a day (in the morning just before lunch and just before dinner), participants completed an online survey. They were asked to rate their affective state for the day and perceived cohesion with the team in the previous hour. Informed consent was obtained from all subjects before starting the study. One participant withdrew from the experiment early for personal reasons.

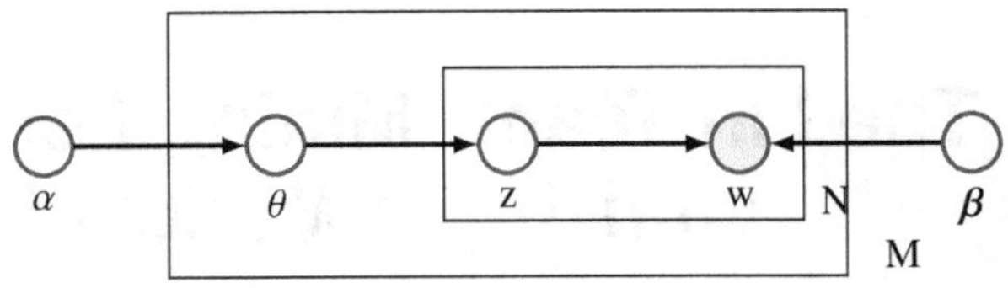

Figure 2. Graphical model representation of LDA model

The badge has an infrared sensor facing outwards with a unique identifier [18]. Figure 1 illustrates a month of infrared detection recording. The badge logs the identifier and the associated timestamp at second level when another badge is detected. The number of infrared detections of an id corresponds to the duration that one subject is within the face-to-face interaction range. The infrared detections are shown to be effective proxies for social interactions [2, 18]. For each subject, we extracted the infrared detections that consist of another's badge ID being detected $u \in \{1, 2, .., 6\}$ and its associated timestamp.

LDA FOR IDENTIFYING SOCIAL INTERACTION ROUTINE

Topic models (i.e., LDA [1]) have been successfully applied in text mining community to extract summaries of large and unstructured collection of documents. LDA treats words in documents as a generative probabilistic process, in which hidden variables describe the structure of how topics are composed of mixture of words and how documents are composed of mixture of topics (see Figure 2). Assuming we have a corpus D consisting of M documents and N words per document, LDA learns the topic proportions of these documents by representing each topic as a mixture of word distribution and each document as a mixture of topic-document distribution. The probability of each topic $\boldsymbol{\theta}$ is initialized with a Dirichlet prior distribution with hyperparameter α. The word probability over each topic is denoted as $p(w|z_n, \beta)$ with parameter β. For one document, we denote the full joint probability as:

$$p(\boldsymbol{\theta}, \mathbf{z}, \mathbf{w}|\alpha, \beta) = p(\boldsymbol{\theta}|\alpha) \prod_N p(z_n|\boldsymbol{\theta}) p(w|z_n, \beta) \quad (1)$$

After we marginalize out the hidden parameters:

$$p(\mathbf{w}|\alpha, \beta) = \int p(\boldsymbol{\theta}|\alpha) \prod_N \sum_z p(z_n|\boldsymbol{\theta}) p(w|z_n, \beta) \quad (2)$$

During the optimization process, LDA learns the parameters for documents generated by distributions over topics and words that maximize the posterior likelihood:

$$\mathbf{arg}\max_{\alpha,\beta} \, log p(\mathbf{w}|\alpha, \beta) \quad (3)$$

The idea of using topic models to discover latent structures is that we consider daily interactions of team members to be composed of a mixture of interactions related to the mission itself or just socializing. If we consider a social interaction routine as one topic that consists of commonly co-occurring interaction observations, we can consider each day to be a mixture of social interaction routines in the same way that a document is formed by a mixture of topics. Typically for data clustering, popular methods include KMeans which would hard assign a data sample to one particular cluster, or Gaussian mixture models (GMM) which would assign a soft membership score for each cluster assuming a Gaussian density. The benefit of LDA is that it provides a richer representation for topics that are composed of probabilistic description of words, in our case, the interaction events that we are interested in. LDA assumes the data follows multinomial distributions which is suitable for our application that the interaction instances detected from the badge are discrete counts for each interactant.

Identifying the common interaction patterns and the changes over time can reveal the social context of each individual in the team. We are interested in both the temporal context (e.g. morning, lunch time) of when interactions happen and social context of who why interact with. Examining how time and durations of interaction routines vary during different stages of the mission can provide insights on changes of individual's affect states and team cohesion [13]. For instance, an increase and decrease of interaction frequencies with more people can signify a change in roles or motivation in collaboration. A significant deviation from normal interaction routines might indicate a critical event (i.e., a huge argument) that requires timely intervention.

METHOD

Our first step is to convert raw infrared log data to word tokens and build a vocabulary. We consider one day recording as a document and each interaction observation as a word. Then, we form the document collections as features represented with word distributions over the built vocabulary. Finally, we use LDA to identify topics in the documents.

Feature extraction and word representation

We constructed a corpus consisting of documents $D = \{\mathbf{w}^1, ..., \mathbf{w}^M\}$ to represent the interaction data during M days, where one day $\mathbf{w}$ is a document in the corpus. Each document $\mathbf{w}$ consists of N words $\mathbf{w} = \{w_1, ..., w_N\}$ that represent interaction events within that day. The number of words N can vary daily depending on amounts of interactions during that day. One way is to encode words with semantic meanings that capture interaction status during the entire day continuously, for example, denote interactions as non-zeros and no interactions as zeros. However, this representation introduced data sparsity issues as social interaction events happened rarely compared to no interactions. To alleviate this issue, we encoded the word tokens with both the temporal and interactant information only when observations were available.

We used a non-overlapping windows of $\Delta_t = 60$ mins to extract observations and construct words w. We extracted word representations from pairwise (dyadic) interaction observations detected from the infrared sensor. The interaction word w for subject u_i is represented as:

$$w = [u_i, u_j, t] \tag{4}$$

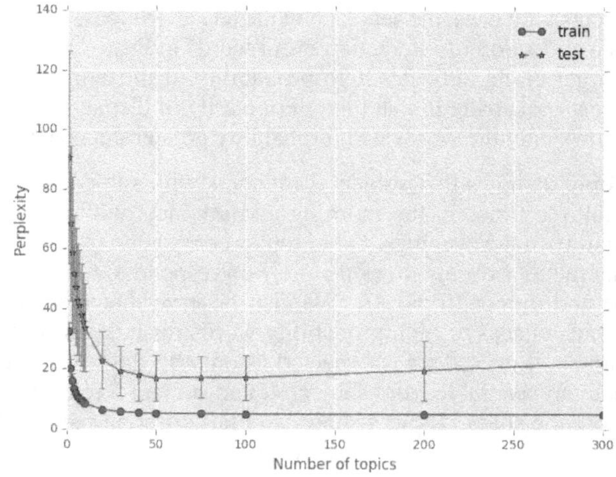

Figure 3. Five-fold cross validation to select number of topics

where u_i is the current subject, u_j is the other subject being detected, t is the temporal context that describes the hour of the day in a 24 hour format. In this way, we implicitly encode the interaction duration as more words will be generated when more interactions observed within a period of Δ_t.

Training and discovering topics

We performed LDA on each day that is considered as one document with a bag of interaction words. In doing so, we lose the inherent temporal ordering of the day but this can be reconstructed from the time index in w. During the training process, we weighted the informativeness of the words in the vocabulary using the term frequency and inverse document frequency (TF-IDF) score. We initialized the topic prior $\alpha = 1/T$ and word prior distribution $\beta = 0.01$ where T denotes the number of topics. The parameters were optimized via the variational Bayes method. The number of topics were selected via a five-fold cross validation, where each fold was populated without replacement by randomly selecting M/5 days (see Figure 3). We performed the cross validation experiments for five times. Perplexity is the commonly used measure to evaluate topic models, defined as $exp\{-\sum_d logp(\mathbf{w^d})/\sum_d N^d\}$, where $\mathbf{w^d}$ denotes words and N^d denotes number of words in document d. It is a decreasing function of log-likelihood where lower perplexity implies a better model. For LDA, we used part of the documents to learn the topic-word distributions in the training set. Then we compute the perplexity on the held-out test set. We found a number between 10 to 20 topics to be the optimal number of topics as the cross validated perplexity starts flattening out after 10 topics.

RESULTS

Extracting latent patterns

Following the word representation and topic extraction procedure results in a total of 103 documents and a vocabulary of 77 unique word tokens for subject 2. To illustrate the identified patterns, we plot the extracted 10 topics in Figure 4. Each topic is a distribution over words and corresponds to social interaction routines, in other words, a mixture of daily interaction events. For instance, topic 8 consists of two major interaction events with the same subject 6 in the late afternoons. Each row is a collection of interaction event words indicated as circles. Larger circle indicates high probability of those interaction events occurring in that topic. For clarity of display, Figure 4 shows only the words with probability greater than 0.01.

Topic 0 shows that subject 2 interacts with subject 1 and 3 multiple times in the morning and interacts with subject 1 mainly in the evenings. Other topics correspond to high level interactions during times that may correspond to lunch (topic 5) and dinner (topic 8). We also observe that there is no topic consists of high probability words for interaction with subject 4 or 5. This is expected as only 45 days of infrared data are available from subject 4, and subject 5 retired early from the study. Topic 4 shows a rather different pattern that represents group events involving 5 people and these group interactions only happened in the late evening. A similar topic to topic 4 has also been identified from the other team member's interaction data.

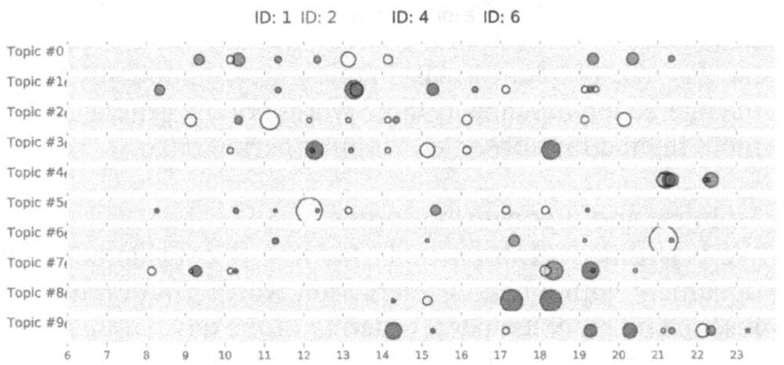

Figure 4. Ten most probable topics for subject 2. Each row is one topic and its associated word events. The circle color indicates the interactant and the size corresponds to the probability of that interaction event. The x axis shows hours of the day.

Analysis of topic dynamics

Short-term daily analysis: Each daily interaction can be represented as a mixture of the learned topics z from Figure 4 with proportions $\boldsymbol{\theta}$, where the topic activation $\theta^d_{z_i}$ (i = 0, ..., 9) represents the probability of topic z_i in a document d. As shown in Figure 5, the green area under the curve represents the probability of each topic occurring at a particular day which shows that topic activations vary daily. Topic 5 represents active interactions with subject 3 occurred regularly during 12-1pm during the first phase of the mission. During the second phase of the mission, topic 3 is more prevalent; subject 2 interacted more frequently with subject 6 during 12-1pm instead. They also interacted with subject 3 more often in the evenings (9-10pm, topic 6) compared to the first phase. Topic 4, which represents the late evening group events, occurred as one of the major topic on just one day in the third month.

Long-term bi-weekly analysis: We computed the marginal likelihood of topics for all events observed every two weeks to analyze more long term variations in routine. Figure 6 shows an increasing trend of topic 3 for the first three months with the highest peak at the end of the third month. By combing with the daily activations shown in Figure 5, we can infer that the peak period of topic 3 happened regularly for 3 weeks. In

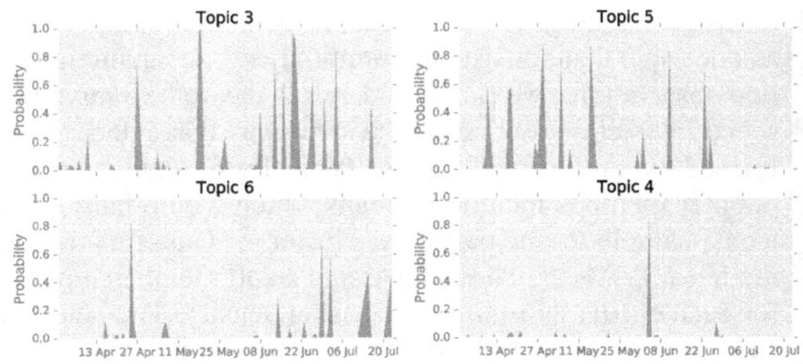

Figure 5. Daily activations of four topics for subject 2

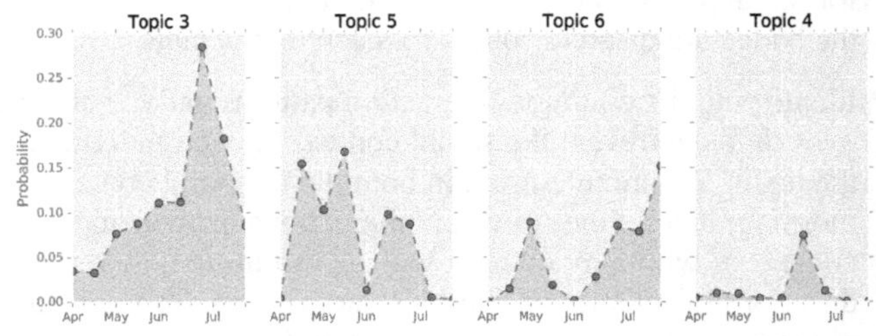

Figure 6. Topic activations aggregated every two weeks.

contrast, topic 4, that represents the entire group event has a peak period between June to July because the group events happened as the only topic ($\theta = 0.99$) on one day.

Correlating topics with self-report ratings

This final analysis aims to identify interaction patterns that are linked to an individual's affective state and their perception of the team's cohesion. The goal is to find out crucial events (words) in the topics that are related to changes in individual states and team process. This is achieved by using topic activations as features and computing correlations between topics and self-report ratings. During the entire mission, the team members filled in surveys about their mood (three variables) and team cohesion (two variables) twice a day.

We use the average of survey responses submitted within a day to represent daily ratings. In total, 94 days of infrared data and self-report surveys are available for subject 2. Three topics are found to be significantly correlated to the self-report ratings. Topic 4 is found to be negatively correlated to perceptions of task cohesion ($r = -0.41, p < 0.001$). This indicates that the late evening group events in topic 4 significantly influenced team cohesion which may require a group intervention. Social cohesion is found to be negatively correlated to topic 8 ($r = -0.35, p < 0.001$). This could be unpleasant interpersonal relationship caused by conflicts between subject 2 and subject 6 occurred during the mission. There is a medium negative correlation between topic 7 and feelings of being sad to pleased ($r = -0.23, p = 0.025$). These results suggest that different interaction routines have different effects on the affective states and perceived cohesion of subject 2. Especially, we found different topics between social and team cohesion which is consistent with previous findings that consider these two components separately in team cohesion [14].

CONCLUSION

We proposed to use LDA to mine an individual's social interaction patterns in a small team from longitudinal face-to-face interactions data collected from wearable sensors. We showed that the social interaction routines can be represented by low dimensional latent structures. Our method can identify common behaviors at different temporal resolutions which allows us to examine the dynamics of social interactions over the course of the mission. We envision our technique can be used to design intelligent user interfaces that support team management for long duration missions. Through continuous learning the normal behaviors from team interaction sensors, we can predict and assess how newly observed behaviors fit to the existing team work patterns. When anomalies or new patterns are detected, feedback intervention can be provided in real-time at either individual or group levels to maintain team effectiveness. In the future, we will extend the model from analyzing individual to group behavior. We will also investigate new method that can model events consisting of both discrete identity and continuous temporal variables.

ACKNOWLEDGEMENT

This research was supported by the project 'Resourceful Ageing' funded by NWO/STW under the Research through Design program (2015/16734/STW). Data used in the preparation of this manuscript were provided by S. W. J. Kozlowski, S. Biswas, & C.- H. Chang. Their research, which generated the data, was supported by the National Aeronautics and Space Administration (NASA; NNX13AM77G, S.W.J. Kozlowski, Principal Investigator). Any opinions, findings, conclusions and recommendations expressed are those of the authors and do not necessarily reflect the views of NASA.

REFERENCES

1. David M. Blei, Andrew Y. Ng, and Michael I. Jordan. 2003. Latent Dirichlet Allocation. *J. Mach. Learn. Res.* 3 (March 2003), 993–1022. http://dl.acm.org/citation.cfm?id=944919.944937
2. Tanzeem Choudhury and Alex Pentland. 2003. Sensing and Modeling Human Networks Using the Sociometer. In *Proceedings of the 7th IEEE International Symposium on Wearable Computers (ISWC '03)*. IEEE Computer Society, Washington, DC, USA, 216–. http://dl.acm.org/citation.cfm?id=946249.946901
3. T. M. T. Do and D. Gatica-Perez. 2011. GroupUs: Smartphone Proximity Data and Human Interaction Type Mining. In *2011 15th Annual International Symposium on Wearable Computers*. 21–28. DOI: http://dx.doi.org/10.1109/ISWC.2011.28
4. Nathan Eagle and Alex Pentland. 2005. Social Serendipity: Mobilizing Social Software. *IEEE Pervasive Computing* 4, 2 (April 2005), 28–34. DOI: http://dx.doi.org/10.1109/MPRV.2005.37
5. Nathan Eagle and Alex Sandy Pentland. 2009. Eigenbehaviors: Identifying structure in routine. *Behavioral Ecology and Sociobiology* 63, 7 (2009), 1057–1066.
6. Katayoun Farrahi and Daniel Gatica-Perez. 2011. Discovering Routines from Large-scale Human Locations Using Probabilistic Topic Models. *ACM Trans. Intell. Syst. Technol.* 2, 1, Article 3 (Jan. 2011), 27 pages. DOI: http://dx.doi.org/10.1145/1889681.1889684
7. K. Farrahi and D. Gatica-Perez. 2012. Extracting Mobile Behavioral Patterns with the Distant N-Gram Topic Model. In *2012 16th International Symposium on Wearable Computers*. 1–8. DOI: http://dx.doi.org/10.1109/ISWC.2012.20
8. James H Fowler and Nicholas A Christakis. 2008. Dynamic spread of happiness in a large social network: longitudinal analysis over 20 years in the Framingham Heart Study. *Bmj* 337 (2008), a2338.
9. Daniel Gatica-Perez. 2009. Automatic nonverbal analysis of social interaction in small groups: A review. *Image and vision computing* 27, 12 (2009), 1775–1787.
10. Tâm Huynh, Mario Fritz, and Bernt Schiele. 2008. Discovery of Activity Patterns Using Topic Models. In *Proceedings of the 10th International Conference on Ubiquitous Computing (UbiComp '08)*. ACM, New York, NY, USA, 10–19. DOI: http://dx.doi.org/10.1145/1409635.1409638
11. Steve WJ Kozlowski, S. Biswas, and CH Chang. August 2013 to December 2017a. *Measuring, monitoring, and regulating teamwork for long duration missions. National Aeronautics and Space Administration (NNX13AM77G).* Technical Report.
12. Steve WJ Kozlowski, CH Chang, and S. Biswas. January 2017b. Measuring team functioning via multiple methods. *NASA Human Research Program Investigators' Workshop* (January 2017).
13. Steve W.J. Kozlowski and Georgia T. Chao (in press). 2018. Unpacking Team Process Dynamics and Emergent Phenomena: Challenges, Conceptual Advances, and Innovative Methods. *American Psychologist* (2018).
14. Marjolein C. Nanninga, Yanxia Zhang, Nale Lehmann-Willenbrock, Zoltán Szlávik, and Hayley Hung. 2017. Estimating Verbal Expressions of Task and Social Cohesion in Meetings by Quantifying Paralinguistic Mimicry. In *Proceedings of the 19th ACM International Conference on Multimodal Interaction (ICMI 2017)*. ACM, New York, NY, USA, 206–215. DOI: http://dx.doi.org/10.1145/3136755.3136811
15. T. Nguyen, D. Phung, S. Gupta, and S. Venkatesh. 2013. Extraction of latent patterns and contexts from social honest signals using hierarchical Dirichlet processes. In *2013 IEEE International Conference on Pervasive Computing and Communications (PerCom)*. 47–55. DOI: http://dx.doi.org/10.1109/PerCom.2013.6526713
16. Eduardo Salas, Scott I Tannenbaum, Steve WJ Kozlowski, Christopher A Miller, John E Mathieu, and William B Vessey. 2015. Teams in space exploration: A new frontier for the science of team effectiveness. *Current Directions in Psychological Science* 24, 3 (2015), 200–207.

17. F. T. Sun, Yi-Ting Yeh, H. T. Cheng, C. Kuo, and M. Griss. 2014. Nonparametric discovery of human routines from sensor data. In *2014 IEEE International Conference on Pervasive Computing and Communications (PerCom)*. 11–19. DOI: http://dx.doi.org/10.1109/PerCom.2014.6813938

18. Benjamin N Waber, Daniel Olguin Olguin, Taemie Kim, Akshay Mohan, Koji Ara, and Alex Pentland. 2007. Organizational engineering using sociometric badges. *Available at SSRN 1073342* (2007).

Write-it-Yourself with the Aid of Smartwatches: A Wizard-of-Oz Experiment with Blind People

Syed Masum Billah **Vikas Ashok** **IV Ramakrishnan**
Department of Computer Science, Stony Brook University, NY, USA
{sbillah, vganjiguntea, ram}@cs.stonybrook.edu

ABSTRACT
Working with non-digital, standard printed materials has always been a challenge for blind people, especially writing. Blind people very often depend on others to fill out printed forms, write checks, sign receipts and documents. Extant assistive technologies for working with printed material have exclusively focused on reading, with little to no support for writing. Also, these technologies employ special-purpose hardware that are usually worn on fingers, making them unsuitable for writing. In this paper, we explore the idea of using off-the-shelf smartwatches (paired with smartphones) to assist blind people in both reading and writing paper forms including checks and receipts. Towards this, we performed a Wizard-of-Oz evaluation of different smartwatch-based interfaces that provide user-customized audio-haptic feedback in real-time, to guide blind users to different form fields, narrate the field labels, and help them write straight while filling out these fields. Finally, we report the findings of this study including the technical challenges and user expectations that can potentially inform the design of *Write-it-Yourself* aids based on smartwatches.

Author Keywords
Accessibility; visual impairments; blind; writing aid; wearables; directional guidance; audio-haptic; smartwatch.

INTRODUCTION
Although the Web has become the dominant medium for doing many transactional tasks such as online banking, online form-based registrations, and online shopping, printed materials such as paper forms, postal mails, checks, contracts and shopping credit-card receipts still abound in our daily lives. While paper-based transactions, especially filling out paper forms and affixing signatures on printed materials is straightforward for sighted people, they present significant barriers to blind people, notably writing. People with vision impairments form a sizeable population—over 21 million people with significant vision loss in the US alone and over 39 million blind people worldwide [29].

IUI'18, March 7–11, 2018, Tokyo, Japan

ACM ISBN 978-1-4503-4945-1/18/03…$15.00
https://doi.org/10.1145/3172944.3173005

To assist blind people with printed materials, existing assistive-technology (AT) solutions primarily employ OCR via cameras embedded in smartphones (KNFB Reader [3], Seeing AI [19]), Head-Mounted Displays [21] and custom-designed hardware (FingerReader [25]). All these ATs focus exclusively on reading printed content, and provide little-to-no support for writing (e.g. writing checks and signing credit-card receipts). Besides, a bigger problem is that in some cases an AT solution, especially ones based on special-purpose hardware designed to be worn on fingers [25], interfere with writing.

In this paper, we report on the feasibility of using off-the-shelf smartwatches with built-in audio-haptic feedback, as a *write-it-yourself (WiY)* AT to aid blind users to work with paper forms and paper receipts *independently*. To this end, we conducted a Wizard-of-Oz (WoZ) study with 12 blind participants to capture and understand the technical challenges, and user requirements and expectations that can potentially inform the design of smartwatch-based WiY aids. Our choice of smartwatches for the study was dictated by its growing popularity as the preferred wearable [23].

RELATED WORK
The use of braille, one of the oldest tactile-based read/write systems for the blind, has been steadily declining [20], hastened by advances in digital technologies, particularly speech, computer vision and OCR. A number of stand-alone reading applications, leveraging these advances, have emerged—examples include the pioneering Kurzweil Scanner [4] for desktops; KNFB Reader [3], Seeing AI [19] and Text Detective [5] for mobile phones; and FingerReader [25], OrCam [21], HandSight [26] for wearables devices. OCR, that underpin all of these stand-alone reading applications have several limitations—they are unusable in poor lighting conditions; they require careful camera framing so that a target object is completely visible and centered within the camera's field of view [15, 18]; they do not support complex documents and spatial data [16], and cannot determine which blocks of text to read, and in what order [9]. Reading apps on wearables such as [21, 25, 26] address some of these limitations. But they have other problems—they require specialized hardware and cameras and the ones designed to be worn on fingers interfere with writing. These reasons have prevented them from gaining mainstream acceptance.

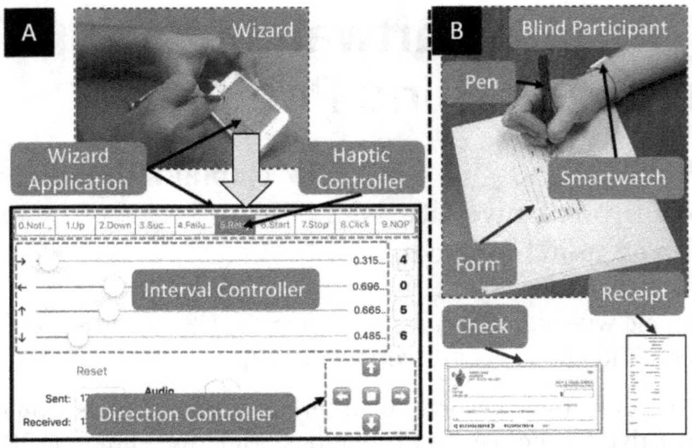

Figure 1. (A) The Wizard interface with customization option; (B) A blind participant writing on printed materials (e.g., a form, check) with a regular pen while wearing a smartwatch.

Crowd-sourcing of object recognition in images, using, say Mechanical Turk, has also been explored as an alternative to OCR, notable examples being VizWiz [8] and BeMyEyes [1]. Crowd-sourced solutions can conceivably be used as a WiY aid. But two major problems with these solutions are that the blind users lose privacy and have to depend on others to help with writing.

Audio-haptic cues for way-finding and for exploration of maps have been used in numerous projects [6, 11, 17, 18, 22, 24, 27]. These works use some combination of synthesized speech and sonification and haptic patterns for effective discrimination [10, 12, 14]. The drawback with these audio-haptic approaches is that they require extraneous hardware including several specialized haptic motors, ranging from 4 to 8, and mounted camera sensors. Pairing a smartphone with an off-the-shelf smartwatch that comes with built-in audio-haptic feedback is an attractive approach to solving the WiY problem without the need for such extraneous hardware, and thus has the potential to become an unobtrusive viable mainstream writing aid for blind individuals. The feasibility of such an approach is reported in the sequel.

METHOD

The experimenter in our WoZ study (i.e., the wizard) controlled the direction of participants' hand movements with audio-haptic feedback provided by a smartwatch worn by the participants (see Figure 1). The choice of the audio-haptic cues for different directions however, was self-customized by the participants themselves.

Participants

We recruited 12 blind participants (labeled as P1 to P12) through local mailing lists and word-of-mouth. No participant had any hearing or speech impairment. They varied in age from 30 to 60 (mean=40.5, median=35, SD=11.1), and gender (7 males, 5 females). All participants reported prior experience with audio-haptic feedback, which they had gained from using smartphones, game controllers, gloves and other devices. All participants except P5, P10 and P11, stated that writing was very much a part of their daily routine, e.g., paying bills, teaching their children, shopping, or at work. Those 3 participants only knew how to write their name and signature—2 of them (P5 and P11) were born blind, and P10 who lost his vision 20 years back had mostly forgotten how to write. All participants said that they sought help from others when writing on paper.

Apparatus

The smartwatch interface was designed as an Apple Watch App running in tandem with a *companion* Wizard App on an iPhone (see Figure 1); the latter let the experimenter transmit audio-haptic feedback instructions in real-time to the Watch App to control the hand movements of the participants during the writing process. In other words, the Wizard App was set up to help the wizard guide blind participants to different *fields* (e.g., name, signature, tip) on the printed forms by continuously transmitting these audio-haptic feedback instructions. The printed materials used in the study were sample templates of a bank check, restaurant receipt, and a personal-information form as shown in Figure 1.B.

Wizard App

The Wizard App (see Figure 1.A) has arrow keys (indicated by "Direction Controller" in the Figure 1A) that allows the experimenter to send different audio-haptic signals for different directions of hand movement. The exact audio-haptic pattern for each direction can be configured using the "Haptic Controller". Further, the time-intervals for the selected patterns can also be adjusted by moving the 4 sliders shown in the "Interval Controller".

Audio-Haptic Feedback

We used the 9 default audio-haptic patterns in Apple watch [2]. Figure 2 shows these patterns (labeled as AH0 to AH8). Each pattern consists of one or more individual haptic and audio signals. The amplitude and the duration of the haptic signals are shown in pink, while the audio signals are depicted in blue. For any hand-movement direction, one single pattern was relayed continuously, with the interval between two such patterns were set based on preference.

Procedure

The experimenter started the study with a brief background survey, and then introduced the participants to the Watch App. Prior to the study, participants were first exposed to the different audio-haptic signals, and then allowed to select the ones they preferred (including tuning of the associated vibration-stimulus intervals) for distinguishing between different directional hand movements. The participants were then asked to complete the following three tasks (ordering was counterbalanced): (A) Fill out the details in a sample check; (B) Write the tip amount, total amount and sign a sample restaurant receipt; and (C) Fill out the name, email, and country fields in a sample paper form. Participants unfamiliar with writing could sign the form fields instead of writing-in actual data.

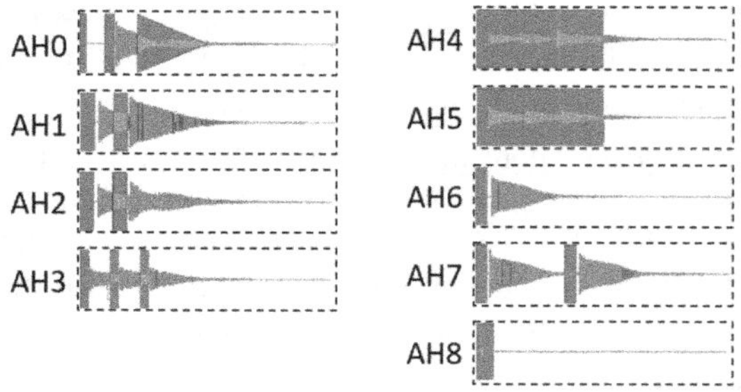

Figure 2. Nine audio-haptic feedback patterns (AH0 to AH8), pink for haptic and blue for audio signals.

For each task, the participants began by first taking a picture of the printed material with an iPhone provided by the experimenter. To take a picture, the participants were instructed to hold the iPhone directly above and parallel to the sample paper on the table, and continuously reposition the camera according to synthesized audio instructions, until the camera could capture the entire form within the picture frame. This was done to create an illusion that the participants were interacting with a fully-functional WiY application, rather than a wizard. To further strengthen this illusion, the participants were explicitly told that a background application sent this picture to the WiY application on the Watch via Bluetooth for processing and automatically generating audio-haptic guidance instructions.

After taking the picture of the paper form, the participants proceeded with the task by first placing their pen-tip at its top-left corner. They then moved their hand in the direction indicated by the received audio-haptic signal. The wizard ensured that the participants were guided to different fields one-by-one via their preferred audio and haptic cues. Feedback was also provided to ensure that the participants maintained a straight line while writing out the required information in the various printed fields.

At the end, the experimenter conducted a semi-constructed interview with preselected topics such as participant's writing proficiency, strategies, and usability of WiY. The interview culminated with participants making suggestions and recommendations. The entire session lasted for 2 hours.

Measures

All tasks were video-recorded. Audio-haptic preferences of users, including vibration-stimulus intervals were logged. Other collected data included task-completion times, user accuracy in correctly interpreting haptic cues, and task success rate. A task was considered a *success* if the required information was written reasonably straight and acceptably close to the intended fields; the judgement was left to the discretion of the experimenter. In total, the participants wrote into 108 fields (12 * 3 tasks/participant * 3 fields/task).

RESULTS

Participants' preferences: The participants' preferences of audio-haptic patterns for the four directions of hand movement, as well as the interval specification for each of these preferred patterns are shown in Figure 3. The order of

	AH0	AH1	AH2	AH3	AH4	AH5	AH6	AH7	AH8
P1	R	U				L		D	
P2	R					U	D		L
P3	L				R	U	D		
P4		R	L			U	D		
P5	R		L		U				D
P6		R		L	U				D
P7	R			D	U	L			
P8					R L			U D	
P9	L				R			U D	
P10		L		U	D		R		
P11	R				L		D	U	
P12	R	L		U			D		

Range (sec.)	Color
[0.3, 0.5)	
[0.5, 0.8)	
[0.8, 1.0)	
[1.0, 1.3)	
[1.3, 1.5]	

Figure 3. Participants' preferences (rows) for audio-haptic patterns (columns) for right (R), left (L), up (U), and down (D) directions. Color shades denote interval ranges for patterns.

preference was as follows: AH5 (18%), AH0 (16%), AH6, AH7 (both 12%), AH5, AH1 (both 10%); AH3 (8%), AH8 (6%) and AH2 (4%). Again, see Figure 2 for each pattern.

The participants stated that they could easily recognize the long persistent haptic pattern in AH5, as well as the long but gradually decaying haptic pattern in AH0. The gradually decaying nature of AH0 prompted them to set short intervals (0.3s to 0.8s), whereas, the persistent nature of AH5 made them to select a relatively longer interval (0.5s to 1.3s).

Since AH4 and AH5 are almost similar with the only difference being the underlying audio tone, majority (10) of the participants selected only one of these patterns during customization. Only participants P3 and P7 indicated that they were comfortable distinguishing AH4 from AH5 using audio cues, and so they picked both these patterns.

Interestingly, as seen in Figure 3, a couple of participants (P8 and P9) used a single pattern (AH7) to represent multiple directional movements (Up and Down), by selecting different intervals for the same pattern. P8 also used a single pattern (AH4) with different intervals for representing Right and Left directional movements. When inquired, these participants stated that they did not want to memorize too many patterns. Some participants selected certain patterns because these patterns reminded them of certain events in their daily lives. For example, P2, P3, P4 choose AH5 for Up because they felt that the tone of AH5 sounded like their morning wakeup alarm. Similarly, P10 stated that AH1 and AH6 resembled the indicator sounds of a car, and P12 said that AH1 sounded like heartbeat to her. We also noticed a trend in selecting patterns and intervals for the opposite direction movements. For example, if a strong pulse with a short interval was chosen for a direction, then a weaker pulse with a long interval was chosen for the opposite direction.

Task completion time: The average completion times for the 3 tasks (A, B, and C) were 185s (SD: 15.5s), 163s. (SD: 10.3s), and 240s (SD: 19.6s) respectively. To compare these completion times with that of sighed people, one author and 6 MS students (sighted) performed the same tasks. On an average, they took 33.2s (SD: 6.1s), 12.5s (SD: 5.7s) and 25.9s (SD: 8.3s) for tasks A, B, and C respectively.

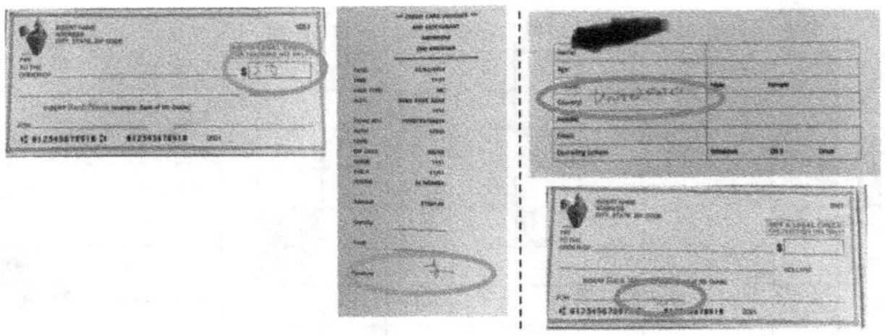

Figure 4. Ovals are target fields on the papers. Successful (left of dotted line) and unsuccessful (to the right) writing samples.

Interpretation accuracy: The participants interpreted the received audio-haptic patterns with an average accuracy of 97%. Participants themselves stated that since they handpicked their own patterns, it was easy for them to interpret the directional instructions.

Task success rate: The success rates as defined earlier, were 84%, 68%, and 45% for tasks A, B, and C respectively. Figure 4 presents examples of successful and unsuccessful tasks. The primary reason for failures was lack of prior calibration to accommodate hand-to-pen distance. Also, different participants had different pen-holding styles, which made it a little difficult for the wizard to predict where exactly on paper they would end up writing. For example, in Figure 4 (right), even if the participant P4 was properly guided to a field on the check, the written entry ended up overlapping with the line, thereby resulting in a failure. Another reason for failures was the limited space allotted to certain fields, especially in Tasks B and C. This was further exacerbated by the communication overhead between the Wizard app and the Watch app; in some cases, the participants accidently navigated past the target location before receiving a 'stop' haptic feedback.

User Requirements and Expectations

Feedback from participants shaped the formulation of these user expectations and interface design requirements:

U1. Goal notification: A distinct audio-haptic pattern to notify users that they have reached the destination field.

U2. Dimension notification: Audio feedback indicating the dimensions of a selected field in a relatable manner, such as "*this field has the width of a pencil*", or "*length is less than a credit card*".

U3. Discrete intervals: The selection of vibration intervals on a nominal scale with categories like "slow", "medium", "fast", and "very fast", instead of a continuous scale.

U4. Intelligent companion smartphone app: Narrate the text under fingertips like VoiceOver while navigating the picture of the printed material taken by the smartphone app. Also, double tapping on any form label in the picture should trigger their smartwatch to guide them to the corresponding field on the actual printed material.

U5. Picture taking with the smartwatch: Allow taking pictures of the printed materials with a smartwatch as an alternative for blind people who are not adept at taking pictures with smartphone apps such as KNFB Reader.

U6. Augmenting with a ruler or a credit card: Allow using a ruler or a credit card to assist with writing along a straight line, in addition to audio-haptic feedback.

U7. Wrist-Pace control: Control the speed of wrist movements with audio cues such as "slow down" and "speed up". Towards this, increasing or decreasing the haptic-pattern interval was not recommended since it was hard to distinguish different patterns with short intervals.

Discussion

The study revealed the following technical challenges:

C1. High precision motion tracking: Tracking algorithm should have millimeter range precision since users move their hands over a Letter size page.

C2. Detecting when the user starts writing: Tracking algorithm needs to know when the pen-tip touches the paper to provide audio-haptic guidance to help users maintain a straight line while writing.

C3. Calibration: Differences in the size of hands and pen-holding styles require sophisticated wrist-to-pen calibration to accurately track pen-tip location.

C4. Communication-overhead related issues: Proactively prevent the user from accidentally navigating past the target location on the form due to the unavoidable communication overhead between the smartphone and smartwatch.

C5. Mapping between picture and print material: Techniques are needed to estimate dimensional details of the printed material by analyzing the corresponding picture.

While most of these challenges are open problems, related research works in robotics can potentially be applied to our WiY system to address some of them. For example, for C1, user can initially register the top-left corner as the origin by pressing the crown of the watch when the pen tip is at that corner and further tracking can be made relative to the origin, by measuring short-range displacements using motion sensor data [13]. For C2 and C3, ideas proposed in [7, 28] where information (e.g., typed word) is inferred from smartwatch sensor data, can be used. For C4, the ideas underlying Proportion Integral and Derivative (PID) Controllers can be utilized. Finally, for C5, recent developments in the fields of computer vision and augmented reality can be explored.

CONCLUSION

Write-it-Yourself aids using smartwatches have the potential to become a transformative assistive technology that can empower blind people to work with printed materials independently without having to depend upon others; hence can make them more employable. Our WoZ study with blind participants gathered critical requirements and identified technical challenges that need to be addressed for realizing WiY aids in practice. This is a topic for future research.

ACKNOWLEDGMENTS

We thank the anonymous reviewers for their insightful feedback. This research is supported by NSF: IIS-1447549, NEI/NIH: R01EY02662, NIDILRR: 90IF0117-01-00.

REFERENCES

1. Be My Eyes. Retrieved from http://bemyeyes.com/.
2. 2017. Haptic Feedback. Retrieved from https://developer.apple.com/watchos/human-interface-guidelines/user-interaction/haptic-feedback/.
3. Knfb Reader. Retrieved from http://www.knfbreader.com/.
4. 1996. Kurtzweil 1000 for Windows. Retrieved from https://www.kurzweiledu.com/products/kurzweil-1000-v14-windows.html.
5. Text Detective. Retrieved from https://itunes.apple.com/us/app/text-detective/id541494875?mt=8.
6. Bardot, S., Brock, A., Serrano, M., and Jouffrais, C., 2014. Quick-Glance and in-Depth Exploration of a Tabletop Map for Visually Impaired People. In *Proceedings of the 26th Conference on l'Interaction Homme-Machine*. ACM, 165-170.
7. Beltramelli, T. and Risi, S., Deep-Spying: Spying Using Smartwatch and Deep Learning. Retrieved from https://arxiv.org/abs/1512.05616.
8. Bigham, J. P., Jayant, C., Ji, H., Little, G., Miller, A., Miller, R. C., Tatarowicz, A., White, B., White, S., and Yeh, T., 2010. Vizwiz: Nearly Real-Time Answers to Visual Questions. In *Proceedings of the 2010 International Cross Disciplinary Conference on Web Accessibility (W4A)*. ACM, 1-2.
9. Borodin, Y., Bigham, J. P., Dausch, G., and Ramakrishnan, I. V., 2010. More Than Meets the Eye: A Survey of Screen-Reader Browsing Strategies. In *Proceedings of the 2010 International Cross Disciplinary Conference on Web Accessibility (W4A)*. ACM, 1-10.
10. Brewster, S. and Brown, L. M., 2004. Tactons: Structured Tactile Messages for Non-Visual Information Display. In *Proceedings of the Fifth Australasian User Interface Conference (AUIC2004)*. ACS, 15-23.
11. Brock, A., Kammoun, S., Macé, M., and Jouffrais, C., 2014. Using Wrist Vibrations to Guide Hand Movement and Whole Body Navigation. *i-com 13*, 3, 19-28.
12. Choi, S. and Kuchenbecker, K. J., 2013. Vibrotactile Display: Perception, Technology, and Applications. *Proceedings of the IEEE 101*, 9, 2093-2104.
13. ChRobotics, Using Accelerometers to Estimate Position and Velocity. Retrieved from http://www.chrobotics.com/library/accel-position-velocity.
14. Hong, J., Stearns, L., Froehlich, J., Ross, D., and Findlater, L., 2016. Evaluating Angular Accuracy of Wrist-Based Haptic Directional Guidance for Hand Movement. In *Proceedings of the 42nd Graphics Interface Conference*. Canadian Human-Computer Communications Society, 195-200.
15. Jayant, C., Ji, H., White, S., and Bigham, J. P., 2011. Supporting Blind Photography. In *The proceedings of the 13th international ACM SIGACCESS conference on Computers and accessibility*. ACM, 203-210.
16. Kane, S. K., Frey, B., and Wobbrock, J. O., 2013. Access Lens: A Gesture-Based Screen Reader for Real-World Documents. In *Proceedings of the SIGCHI Conference on Human Factors in Computing Systems*. ACM, 347-350.
17. Lawrence, M. M., Martinelli, N., and Nehmer, R., 2009. A Haptic Soundscape Map of the University of Oregon. *Journal of Maps 5*, 1, 19-29.
18. Manduchi, R. and Coughlan, J. M., 2014. The Last Meter: Blind Visual Guidance to a Target. In *Proceedings of the 32nd annual ACM conference on Human factors in computing systems*. ACM, 3113-3122.
19. Microsoft, 2017. Seeing Ai. Retrieved from https://www.microsoft.com/en-us/seeing-ai/.
20. NFB, 2016. Statistical Facts About Blindness in the United States.
21. OrCam, 2017. Orcam: See for Yourself. Retrieved from https://www.orcam.com/myeye/.
22. Pielot, M., Poppinga, B., Heuten, W., and Boll, S., 2011. A Tactile Compass for Eyes-Free Pedestrian Navigation. In *Proceedings of the 13th IFIP TC 13 international conference on Human-computer interaction - Volume Part II*. Springer-Verlag, 640-656.
23. Piwek, L., Ellis, D. A., Andrews, S., and Joinson, A., 2016. The Rise of Consumer Health Wearables: Promises and Barriers. *PLoS Medicine 13*, 2 (02/02), e1001953.
24. Rümelin, S., Rukzio, E., and Hardy, R., 2011. Naviradar: A Novel Tactile Information Display for Pedestrian Navigation. In *Proceedings of the 24th annual ACM symposium on User interface software and technology*. ACM, 293-302.
25. Shilkrot, R., Huber, J., Ee, W. M., Maes, P., and Nanayakkara, S. C., 2015. Fingerreader: A Wearable Device to Explore Printed Text on the Go. In *Proceedings of the 33rd Annual ACM Conference on Human Factors in Computing Systems*. ACM, 2363-2372.
26. Stearns, L., Du, R., Oh, U., Jou, C., Findlater, L., Ross, D. A., and Froehlich, J. E., 2016. Evaluating Haptic and Auditory Directional Guidance to Assist Blind People in Reading Printed Text Using Finger-Mounted Cameras. *ACM Trans. Access. Comput. 9*, 1, 1-38.
27. Tsukada, K. and Yasumura, M., 2004. Activebelt: Belt-Type Wearable Tactile Display for Directional Navigation. In *Ubicomp 2004: Ubiquitous Computing: 6th International Conference, Nottingham, Uk, September 7-10, 2004. Proceedings*, N. DAVIES, E.D. MYNATT and I. SIIO Eds. Springer Berlin Heidelberg, Berlin, Heidelberg, 384-399.
28. Wang, H., Lai, T. T.-T., and Choudhury, R. R., 2015. Mole: Motion Leaks through Smartwatch Sensors. In *Proceedings of the 21st Annual International Conference on Mobile Computing and Networking*. ACM, 155-166.
29. WHO, 2014. World Health Organization. Visual Impairment and Blindness. Retrieved from http://www.who.int/mediacentre/factsheets/fs282/en/.

Responsive News Summarization for Ubiquitous Consumption on Multiple Mobile Devices

Rocio Chongtay
Institute for Design and Communication
University of Southern Denmark Kolding, Denmark
rocio@sdu.dk

Mark Last
Department of Software and Information Systems Engineering
Ben-Gurion University of the Negev
Beer-Sheva, Israel
mlast@bgu.ac.il

Bettina Berendt
Department of Computer Science
KU Leuven
Leuven, Belgium
bettina.berendt@cs.kuleuven.be

ABSTRACT
With the proliferation of online news read on devices ranging from desktops to smart watches, the need for meaningful summaries of long texts is growing. Manual summaries are labour-intensive and cannot be offered for all display sizes, whereas today's abstracts of most news texts are teasers designed to attract the reader's interest more than to provide an overview of an article's content suited to the reader's information needs. We propose responsive news summarization as a technological approach for filling this gap. Responsive news summarization provides an automatically generated content summary that has the right length for the device requesting the article, plus access to the full text. We describe the system prototype available at multisizenews.com along with the initial user study results and give an outlook on future work.

Author Keywords
Automatic Text Summarization; Responsive Web Design; Adaptive Text; Responsive News.

INTRODUCTION
News are increasingly read online and consumed continuously on the go. However, given the current plethora of devices ranging from desktop screens to smart watches, readers attracted by the teasers and interested in learning the contents of an article face an often unsatisfactory choice: They can either read (a) only the teaser or (b) the whole article or (c) a manually created summary (if one exists). The teaser is often automatically generated, but only repeats the first sentence or the first n characters of an article, and therefore does not provide an informative overview of its content. The full article is often too long to read, especially on small-screen devices and under the user's timing constraints, while fixed-size manual summaries may not be informative enough and still too long for smartphone and smartwatch screens. In addition, interfaces often require the reader to scroll down to the summary. It is obviously unrealistic to expect journalists to write, in addition to their full articles, summaries for each screen size available on the market. We therefore propose responsive news summarization as an automated approach for addressing this dilemma. Responsive news summarization offers a summary – rather than a teaser – that has the length optimized for the device requesting the article, plus access to the whole text. The summary is automatically generated on-demand. A prototype is demonstrated at the non-commercial site multisizenews.com. The current prototype hosts a set of sample articles obtained from the Open Platform API of The Guardian, and it offers a summary that fits the screen size of a device currently used by the reader together with the option to see summaries of alternative lengths. The current prototype offers four different summary lengths that roughly fit a desk-/laptop, tablet, smartphone, and smartwatch displays.

In Section 2, we give a brief background and overview of related work. In Section 3, we describe the proposed system and show examples. Section 4 presents the results of an initial user study. Section 5 concludes with an outlook on future research.

ACM IUI 2018, March 7 – 11, Tokyo, Japan.

ACM ISBN 978-1-4503-4945-1/18/03…$15.00
https://doi.org/10.1145/3172944.3172992

BACKGROUND AND RELATED WORK
The contribution of this paper is to propose the approach of responsive news summarization as well as to present a prototype. To the best of our knowledge, this is a novel approach and no directly comparable systems exist. On the other hand, we build on related work from automatic text summarization and its uses by news websites, as well as from Responsive Web Design.

High-quality summaries of news articles can significantly reduce the information overload of news consumers around the world. There is a distinction between extractive summarization, which is aimed at the selection of the most relevant sentences from a source text, and abstractive summarization, which generates a summary as a reformulated synopsis expressing the main idea of the input article. Unlike abstractive summarization methods, which require natural language processing operations, statistical summarizers work in an extractive manner, usually via ranking the fragments of a summarized text by a relevance score and selecting the top-ranked fragments (e.g., sentences) into a summary.

We have chosen MUltilingual Sentence Extractor (MUSE) [4-6] as our summarization engine. MUSE is a language-independent extractive summarization algorithm that ranks each sentence in an article by a score calculated as a weighted linear combination of multiple sentence features. By default, MUSE uses 31 language-independent sentence metrics, which are divided into three main categories: structure-, vector-, and graph-based, according to their text representation model. MUSE implements a supervised learning approach to extractive summarization, where the best set of weights for the sentence scoring metrics is found by a Genetic Algorithm trained on a collection of articles and their gold standard summaries. The resulting vector of weights is used for sentence scoring in summarizations of future articles. In multi-lingual summarization experiments presented in [4-6], MUSE has outperformed other single-document summarization systems, including TextRank [10], on benchmark document collections in three languages (English, Arabic, and Hebrew) MUSE was also chosen because it offers a configuration option not provided by most other summarization systems, but central to our approach: The length of the actual summary, containing the top-ranking sentences, can be limited in terms of the maximum number of characters, words or sentences, depending on the user needs and/or the size of the screen used to read the news. In any case, the extracted key sentences are shown in the order of their appearance in the original text.

The market for news summarization is evolving at a rapid pace. For example, Awesummly (Google Play Store) summarizes news in English and Hindi; Newser displays summaries of their curated news (http://www.newser.com); Gist - News Summaries (Apple App Store) provides 5-sentence summaries of news articles, and Wibbitz (http://www.wibbitz.com/) automatically creates short videos from text content. For other examples, see [3]. Summarization has also been deployed successfully on texts similar to news, including from Reddit and Medium (https://www.reddit.com/user/tldrrr?sort=top, https://medium.com/@mojojolo/automatic-summarization-in-medium-59b1747c1d36). However, all these applications provide either manual or automated summaries of fixed size, completely ignoring the constantly changing needs of mobile users.

Responsive Web Design (RWD) as defined in [8] is a web development approach where the representation of layout and content of a web page responds dynamically to the screen size and orientation of the device used to view it. One of the main goals of RWD is to deliver an optimal user experience with a design that eases reading and navigation across a wide range of devices with a minimum amount of resizing, panning, and scrolling. The basic elements of RWD are: (a) a flexible grid-based layout, (b) flexible images and media, (c) media queries, a module from the W3C specification (https://www.w3.org/TR/css3-mediaqueries/) and (d) the viewport meta tag's attribute *initial-scale=1* which sets the width of the content to the width of the viewport itself. Our main focus is on media queries, which given their context-aware nature play a crucial role for the web application proposed in this work. Media queries work like filters that can be applied to CSS styles. They use the so called "breakpoints" which are commonly based on the width of the visible area of a web page on the browser, by specifying the minimum and/or maximum width in pixels, but they can also use display type, height and orientation [9]. Basically, we use media queries to dynamically change the content and the style of the displayed information based on the characteristics of the device rendering the content.

The benefits of using RWD have been recognized by many, including news agencies, which have joined the trend of developing responsive websites, one of the many examples being the BBC which, in 2015, announced its RWD based website (http://www.bbc.com/news/technology-31966686).

In a new article, Leiva (2018) presents the responsive text summarization (RTS) approach aimed at allowing desktop web pages to be read in response to the size of the user's device. However, their proposed RTS tool, based on the TextRank algorithm, allows the designers to set the summary size only as a ratio of the original text length or the number of desired sentences (rather than the number of characters or words), which, of course, does not ensure that each summary will be readable on a small screen with at most one swipe.

SYSTEM ARCHITECTURE AND EXAMPLES

The Multisizenews digest application was designed as a website using RWD principles. The RWD approach was chosen to provide an application suitable for ubiquitous consumption by optimizing the amount of the shown content for any screen size.

The application is built on a multi-tier framework, see Figure 1: At the logic tier, when the multisizenews.com is opened (A), a request for news content is sent to a news portal API (B). For the current prototype, we used the Guardian Open Platform Content API (data tier). The news portal API processes the request and sends back the response with the news data, in this case in JSON format (C). The response contains some metadata as well as an array of news articles information (see a response example at https://content.guardianapis.com/search?q=all&api-key=test). The articles' title and text are extracted from the response returned by the request to the news API (D). MUSE automated text-summarization technique is then applied to these texts to generate news summaries of several sizes (E).

At the presentation tier, news articles are displayed on a grid of cards. Each news card contains information from the results, obtained from the news portal API specifically: headline, a thumbnail image (if available), category and date of publication. When the user selects a news article to read, a page with the news article is displayed combining the information shown in the card with the article's text in either full size or using the summary size (e.g., "medium", "small" or "tiny") optimized for the device being used to view it (F). Here, the media queries' breakpoints are matched with the browser's visible area on the device and the appropriate size for the article is displayed. The user interface also provides the users with the possibility to choose a different size of text to read independently of their device size.

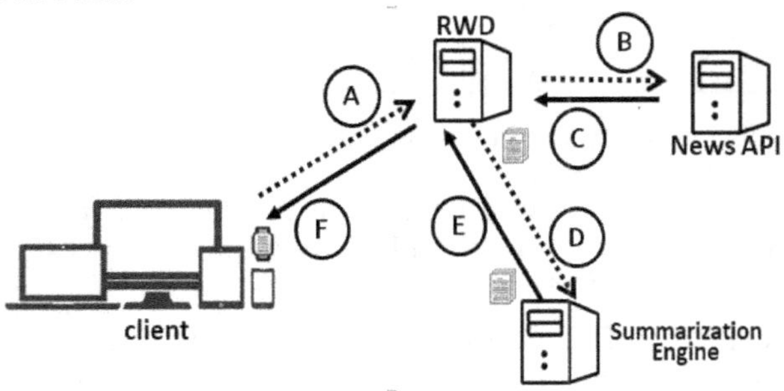

Figure 1: Multisizenews Framework

Examples of different display sizes are shown in Figure 2, and the functionality can be tested at http://multisizenews.com.

Figure 2: Multi-size news summaries, view examples on different device sizes.

It is important to note that the size "Tiny" (for smartwatches) has been chosen to fit two smartwatch screens (scrolling is required). This design decision is based on what other news apps for smartwatches offer, e.g. the New York Times. To illustrate the difference between a news teaser and one of MUSE-generated summaries, we show for the news article with the title: "High blood platelet count 'as good a cancer predictor as a lump in the breast'", the following teaser provided by the news API:

> "Common blood tests could help diagnose cancer early even in patients that show no other symptoms, study finds"

In contrast, the MUSE-generated summary in a size that fits on a smartphone screen ("small") provides the following overview of the news article:

> "This is a clue which can be used in practice by GPs to help them select patients for further investigation … most excitingly in some patients who may not already have other symptoms of cancer to achieve earlier diagnosis," said Sarah Bailey, co-author of the research from the University of Exeter. Within a year of the blood test, the team found that cancer was more common among those who had thrombocytosis: 11.6% of men and 6.2% of women were found to have cancer compared to 4.1% of men and 2.2% of women without a raised platelet count. In the general population about 1% of individuals over the age of 40 develop cancer each year. "We found cancer was more commonly diagnosed in men with raised platelet counts than it was in women with raised platelet counts and we believe that is because there are more causes of raised platelet counts in women that are not cancer," said Bailey"

The example shows that the automatically generated summaries give a better idea of what the news are about than the teasers provided by the API. This framework is designed in a modular fashion, which allows the integration of additional APIs/endpoints to retrieve news articles from other sources. In any case, the amount of displayed content, and performance have to be carefully balanced for a good user experience.

USER STUDY

An initial user study was implemented in order to evaluate the summaries with regard to six different aspects: Readability, Coherence, Relevance, Redundancy, Information Coverage, and Length. Design choices for the study, including the number of participants and the measures, reflected the focus on formative evaluation (Francik, 2015) as well as conventions in manual evaluation of textual summaries [11]. Eight users, four female and four male (age range 24-43), evaluated the summaries of five articles in three different sizes: Medium (620 words), Small

(135 words) and Tiny (350 characters). Table 1 shows the results of this study.

The main findings of this user study are as follows. The users are satisfied with the readability of most summaries though it slightly decreases for the summaries of shorter length. Also, the summaries' coherence is perceived as good in most cases.

The relevance of the shown content appears to be negatively affected by the summary size. In nearly all cases, the MUSE algorithm avoids presenting redundant information to the user. As expected, shorter summaries cover a smaller amount of the original content. For all three summary sizes, the users differed with respect to the evaluation of the summary length.

Summary Size	Article	Readability					Coeherence					Relevance					Redundancy			Inf. Coverage			Length		
		VG	G	A	DR	NR	VG	G	A	LC	NC	VG	G	A	LR	NR	N	S	MA	MO	AH	MLH	RL	TL	TS
Medium	A1	25.0	**50.0**	25.0			**50.0**	37.5	12.5			**50.0**	25.0	25.0			**50.0**	37.5	12.5	**100.0**			37.5	**62.5**	
	A2	25.0	**50.0**	25.0			**37.5**	**37.5**	25.0			25.0	**62.5**	25.0			**62.5**	25.0	12.5	**100.0**			37.5	**62.5**	
	A3	25.0	**37.5**	25.0	12.5		25.0	**37.5**	**37.5**				**50.0**	**50.0**			**62.5**	37.5		**100.0**			25.0	**75.0**	
	A4	25.0	**37.5**	25.0	12.5		25.0	**50.0**	25.0			25.0	**50.0**	25.0			**62.5**	37.5		**100.0**			**62.5**	37.5	
	A5	37.5	**50.0**	12.5			25.0	**50.0**	12.5	12.5		**37.5**	25.0	25.0	12.5		**62.5**	37.5		**87.5**	12.5		**62.5**	37.5	
Small	A1	37.5	**50.0**	12.5			12.5	**50.0**	37.5			12.5	**50.0**	37.5			**100.0**				**75.0**	25.0	37.5		**62.5**
	A2	12.5	**50.0**	37.5				**50.0**	37.5	12.5		12.5	**50.0**	25.0	25.0		**75.0**	25.0			**50.0**	**50.0**	**62.5**		37.5
	A3		**62.5**	37.5				37.5	**62.5**				**37.5**	**37.5**	25.0		**62.5**	37.5			25.0	**75.0**	25.0		**75.0**
	A4	37.5	**50.0**	12.5			12.5	**50.0**	25.0	12.5		12.5	**50.0**	25.0	12.5		**75.0**	25.0		25.0	**62.5**	12.5	**62.5**		37.5
	A5	25.0	**37.5**	25.0	12.5			**50.0**	37.5		12.5		**37.5**	**37.5**	12.5	12.5	**50.0**	**50.0**		12.5	**50.0**	37.5	**62.5**		37.5
Tiny	A1	25.0	**50.0**	25.0			25.0	**37.5**	**37.5**				37.5	**50.0**	12.5		**62.5**	37.5			12.5	**87.5**	37.5		**62.5**
	A2	25.0	**50.0**	25.0				**50.0**	37.5	12.5			37.5	**50.0**		12.5	**87.5**	12.5			**50.0**	**50.0**	**50.0**		**50.0**
	A3	25.0	**50.0**	25.0			12.5	**62.5**	25.0				**50.0**	**50.0**			**100.0**				12.5	**87.5**	**62.5**		37.5
	A4	12.5	**37.5**	**37.5**	12.5			**37.5**	**37.5**	25.0			**37.5**	**37.5**	12.5	12.5	**87.5**	12.5			12.5	**87.5**	**62.5**		37.5
	A5	12.5	**37.5**	**37.5**	12.5		12.5	**37.5**	**37.5**		12.5		37.5	**50.0**	12.5		**62.5**	37.5			12.5	**87.5**	**50.0**		**50.0**

Table 1 User study: five articles' summaries (Medium=620 words, Small=135 words and Tiny=350 characters) evaluation results (percentage) on Readability, Coherence, Relevance, Redundancy, Information Coverage and Length. The evaluation parameters are VG=very good, G=good, A=acceptable, DR=difficult to read, NR=not readable, LC=Little coherence, NC=no coherence, LR=Little relevance, NR=no relevance, N=none, S=some, MA=many, MO=Most, AH=about half, MLH=much less than half, RL=Right Length, TL=Too Long, TS=too Short.

CONCLUSIONS AND FUTURE WORK

We have presented a prototype of a responsive news summarization system, which is built with the following features: (a) real time access to top news articles from the news source and (b) real time summarization via MUSE summarization API. In future work, it will be augmented by (c) the option to customize the summary length to any number of words, thus allowing for a seamless adaptation to further screen and browser-window sizes. Additionally, the user experience will be enhanced by applying text segmentation into paragraphs for readability.

In a longer term, we plan to enhance the framework by integrating a semantic module based on Linked Data and entity expansion [2] that will retrieve additional related information to enrich the news content. The named entity tagging, available with MUSE API, can be used for this purpose.

Other possible improvements include adding a search option with functionalities for disambiguation, such as autocomplete, query expansion, and similarity search. Furthermore methods for multi-document summarization and for update summarization (see [1], for an overview of news summarization methods), could be used for additional news summarization applications.

We intend to evaluate the system with a larger group of users and tasks, to complement the NLP-centric measures now used by HCI-centric ones, and to relate user opinions to automated readability indexes such as Coleman-Liau or Flesch-Kincaid and similar criteria.

Together, these methods can help both news consumers by providing richer search interfaces and better summaries, and news producers by providing them with automated summarization tools and thereby simplifying the work of manually annotating textual content.

CREDITS

The prototype produced for this paper uses the Guardian Open Platform API (http://open-platform.theguardian.com/) and the Multilingual Sentence Extractor (MUSE) API (http://museec.ise.bgu.ac.il).

REFERENCES

1. B. Berendt, M. Last, I. Subašić, and M. Verbeke. 2014. New Formats and Interfaces for Multi-Document News Summarization and its Evaluation. In A. Fiori (Ed.), Innovative Document. Summarization. Techniques: Revolutionizing Knowledge Understanding, pp. 231–257.Hershey, PA: IGI Global.
2. E. Francik, E., 2015. Five, ten, or twenty-five – How many test participants? *Human Factors International.* www.humanfactors.com/newsletters/how_many_test_participants.asp
3. J. L. R. García, G. Rizzo, L. P. Romero, M. Hildebrand, and R. Troncy. 2015. Generating

semantic snapshots of newscasts using entity expansion. In: Cimiano P., Frasincar F., Houben GJ., Schwabe D. (eds) Engineering the Web in the Big Data Era. ICWE 2015. Lecture Notes in Computer Science, vol 9114. Springer, Cham, pp. 410–419.

4. Y.J. Kumar, O.S. Goh, H. Basiron, N.H, Choon, and P.C. Suppiah. 2016. A Review on Automatic Text Summarization Approaches. Journal of Computer Science., 12(4), 178–190.
5. M. Litvak and M. Last. 2013. Cross-lingual training of summarization systems using annotated corpora in a foreign language. Inf Retr., 16 (16):629–656.
6. M. Litvak, M. Last, and M. Friedman. 2010. A new approach to improving multilingual summarization using a genetic algorithm. In Proceedings of the 48th Annual Meeting of the Association for Computational Linguistics (ACL '10). Association for Computational Linguistics, Stroudsburg, PA, USA, pp. 927-936.
7. L. A. Leiva. 2018. Responsive text summarization. Information Processing Letters, 130, 52–57.
8. E. Marcotte. 2014. Responsive Web Design (2nd ed.). New York: A Book Apart.
9. C. Matthew. 2014. The Responsive Web. Manning Pub.
10. R. Mihalcea and P. Tarau. 2004. TextRank - bringing order into texts. In Proceedings of the Conference on Empirical Methods in Natural Language Processing (EMNLP 2004), (pp. 404-411). Barcelona, Spain.
11. H. Saggion and T. Poibeau. 2013. Automatic text summarization: Past, present and future. In *Multi-source, multilingual information extraction and summarization* (pp. 3-21). Springer Berlin Heidelberg.

Below the Surface: Unobtrusive Activity Recognition for Work Surfaces using RF-radar sensing

Daniel Avrahami
FXPAL
Palo Alto, USA
daniel@fxpal.com

Mitesh Patel
FXPAL
Palo Alto, USA
mitesh@fxpal.com

Yusuke Yamaura
FUJI XEROX
Yokohama, Japan
yamaura.yusuke@fujixerox.co.jp

Sven Kratz*
Harman International
Mountain View, USA
sven.kratz@harman.com

ABSTRACT
Activity recognition is a core component of many intelligent and context-aware systems. In this paper, we present a solution for discreetly and unobtrusively recognizing common work activities above a work surface *without* using cameras. We demonstrate our approach, which utilizes an RF-radar sensor mounted under the work surface, in two work domains; recognizing work activities at a convenience-store counter (useful for post-hoc analytics) and recognizing common office deskwork activities (useful for real-time applications). We classify seven clerk activities with 94.9% accuracy using data collected in a lab environment, and recognize six common deskwork activities collected in real offices with 95.3% accuracy. We show that using multiple projections of RF signal leads to improved recognition accuracy. Finally, we show how smartwatches worn by users can be used to attribute an activity, recognized with the RF sensor, to a particular user in multi-user scenarios. We believe our solution can mitigate some of users' privacy concerns associated with cameras and is useful for a wide range of intelligent systems.

Author Keywords
Activity recognition; Retail; Deskwork; Sensing; Radio Frequency Radar Sensor; IMU.

ACM Classification Keywords
Human-centered computing → Ubiquitous and mobile computing systems and tools

INTRODUCTION
Recognizing user activity is a core component of many intelligent and context-aware systems. Over the last several decades, activity recognition has been demonstrated in a wide range of domains, including physical activity, manufacturing, cooking, activities of daily living, and many more. In the physical world, systems rely on sensors to recognize activities. This includes sensors attached to objects (such as RFID tags, shake sensors etc. *c.f.* [5, 23]), sensors carried or worn on the user's body (such as accelerometers or IMUs, *c.f.* [3, 6, 10, 17, 25]), or instrumented in the environment (such as cameras, *c.f.* [11, 15, 24, 34, 39]). Indeed, cameras have many advantages for activity recognition, including a wide view of the space in which an activity takes place, not requiring instrumenting users, and, importantly, are low cost. However, intelligent systems that rely on cameras for activity recognition face a number of challenges. From a technical standpoint, cameras often require an unobstructed view of the activity and can be susceptible to changes in illumination (although a combination with non-visible light can mitigate this challenge). Furthermore, using cameras, particularly in private and semi-private spaces (such as offices and other businesses) poses potential violations (both real and perceived) of users' privacy. Indeed, a video or even a still frame captured by a camera can often be easily interpretable by a human observer. Thus, other methods must be explored to deliver activity-recognition solutions that can overcome some of users' privacy concerns associated with cameras.

Background
The work described in this paper originated from an engagement with a local convenience store chain interested in analytics of activities performed in the day-to-day operation of stores with the goals of process optimization and improved space utilization. Based on discussions, however, the use of cameras for capturing activities in the environment was to be avoided (other instruments, such as beacons and worn sensors were acceptable). To address this constraint, we explored solutions for recognizing activities performed above a work surface (Figure 1). Indeed, the use of cameras can be problematic in many other work environments, such as office spaces and medical facilities that could benefit from accurate activity recognition for both post-hoc and real time applications.

In this paper, we present our exploration of a solution for recognizing common activities performed above a work surface, focusing first on activities performed at a convenience-store's checkout counter and later on common office deskwork activities. Our proposed solution makes use of an RF-radar sensor, mounted under the work surface

IUI'18, March 7–11, 2018, Tokyo, Japan

ACM ISBN 978-1-4503-4945-1/18/03...$15.00
https://doi.org/10.1145/3172944.3172962

* - The work was performed while the author was at FXPAL

to perform activity recognition in a discreet and unobtrusive way. We show how smartwatches, worn by the users, can be used to attribute a performed activity to the correct user in multi-user scenarios. Our proposed solution is able to recognize a set of seven common activities performed at the counter with 94.9% accuracy and six common deskwork activities with 95.3% accuracy. Since our setup does not require the use of a camera, we believe it can benefit many intelligent systems by alleviating some of the privacy concerns associated with cameras.

This work makes the following contributions:

1. We present a solution for recognizing activities performed above a work surface using an RF-radar sensor and show that using multiple projections of RF signal leads to improved recognition accuracy.
2. Demonstrate our solution in two work domains: activities performed at a convenience-store's checkout counter, and common deskwork activities in an office environment.
3. Present a method for attributing a performed activity to the correct user in multi-user scenarios using a combination of RF-radar and IMU sensor data.

The remainder of the paper is organized as follows: we first review related work from the field of activity recognition. We then describe our solution, and present results for activity recognition in two domains. We then present a method for identifying the user performing an activity using a combination of RF and IMU data. We conclude with a discussion and areas for future work.

RELATED WORK

Activity recognition for intelligent and context-aware systems is a broad field of research and a large body of previous work exists. Activity recognition systems have been built that make use of sensors attached to objects, sensors carried or worn on the user's body, instrumented in the environment, or some combination.

Computer vision-based systems that take advantage of RGB images and/or depth images have been successfully used for a wide range of activity recognition tasks. Poppe *et al.* [24], Weinland *et al.* [34], and Ke *et al.* [15] provide surveys of image-based activity recognition systems and applications.

Damen *et al.* [11] used a body-mounted RGB-D camera to monitor workspace activity. They were able to track individual objects in the workspace and classify a set of basic work steps, e.g., packaging goods in a box. Zhang *et al.* [39] describe a system for the recognition of daily life activities of seniors, using an RGB-D camera. Lavania *et al.* [18] use computer vision and deep neural networks to perform activity recognition for a biology laboratory. Cameras have also been used for detecting affective state (*c.f.* [29]). Beyond several technical challenges associated with the use of cameras, they are considered particularly invasive and privacy compromising. In the papers discussed next, as well as in our proposed solution, the use of cameras was avoided.

Figure 1. Our two focus domains for recognizing activities performed above a work surface: a convenience-store checkout counter (top, ©Melissa Y.) and an office desk (bottom).

In addition to cameras, other sensors have been used for activity recognition. Several systems (*c.f.,* [2, 3, 6, 8, 10, 17, 25, 27]) demonstrated recognizing physical human activities (walking, running, cycling, etc.) using a worn IMU, now a common feature of smartphones and smartwatches (for a survey on activity recognition using acceleration sensors see [17]). Ward *et al.* [33] use a combination of accelerometers and microphones for activity recognition of assembly tasks in a workshop setting. Indeed, microphones from smartphones and smartwatches can also been used for recognizing other daily activities [30].

Another important approach for human activity recognition is to recognize the activity through the objects that are used. For example, Philipose *et al.* developed a system for recognizing Activities of Daily Living (ADLs) by attaching RFID tags to household objects [23]. In [5], activity recognition from objects was expanded to include accelerometers in the tagged objects to observe not only a user's proximity to the object but the interaction itself. Marquardt *et al.* [21] developed a vision-based tool for creating interaction that utilizes the physical relationship between people, devices, and (visually tagged) non-digital objects. Recently, Laput *et al.* [16] have explored the use of a multi-sensor unit to detect user interaction with everyday household devices, intentionally avoiding using cameras. They utilized different levels of sensor hierarchy to classify higher level human behaviors.

Activity Recognition for Work- and Retail Spaces

Some research exists that looked at recognizing activities within retail spaces, with much of the focus on understanding the behavior of shoppers (as opposed to store employees). Zeng *et al.* [38], for example, used changes in WiFi signals in the store to classify whether a shopper was walking or standing (and where).

Radhakrishnan *et al.* [25] use a combination of a smart band and mobile phone IMU-sensing to classify customer activities in a retail scenario. In our work, we compare the performance of activity recognition using RF-radar and IMU data (and also the combination of the two) showing significantly higher accuracy using RF sensing. It must be noted that our focus is on activities of store employees, and that unlike in [25] recognition is limited to activities performed above or just around the work surface.

Wimmer *et al.* [36] developed smart furniture that used networked capacitive sensors to perform activity sensing. Their CapTable is a wooden table equipped with capacitive sensors. These sensors allow tracking user hand locations and simple object manipulation tasks. Wimmer *et al.* share our goal of building a solution that is privacy-sensitive, unobtrusive and allows for implicit human-computer interaction. CapTable requires a rather complex instrumentation to cover the area of an entire work surface. In contrast, our proposed solution requires a minimal installation under an existing work surface such as a counter or a desk.

Prior work discussed applications for sensing and understanding activities and states in an office workplace environment. Understanding a knowledge-worker's state can be useful for determining whether and when they can be disrupted (*c.f.,* [4, 13, 14, 40]). Similarly, prior work looked at a worker's activities to promote physical breaks in the workplace to combat sedentary behavior (e.g., [7, 26]). However, understanding non-digital work activities performed by a worker is important for intelligent systems to make appropriate recommendations. For example, in Züger *et al.*'s system deployment, participants complained that the system incorrectly considered them available when, in fact, they were performing an activity with a high cognitive load, just not on the computer [40]. As we show later, our solution is able to recognize activities such as writing and reading paper documents, which would alleviate some of the challenges these participants experienced.

Prior Uses of RF Radar Sensors

Adib *et al.* [1] describe a system that uses an array of RF antennas placed behind a wall to detect humans through light materials, such as drywall. Using the sensor data, they implement 3D skeleton estimation, gestures (in-air drawing), and user identification. We were inspired by Adib *et al.*'s work, and our work similarly uses RF from behind a solid material (in our case, under a work surface, for activity recognition).

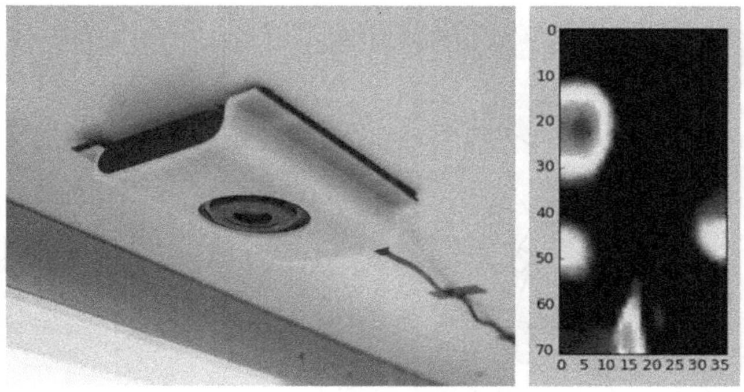

Figure 2. A Walabot Pro RF-radar sensor mounted under a work surface using a custom 3D-printed mount (left) and sample output image from the sensor (right).

Ding *et al.* [12] demonstrated using changes in backscatter communication between an active RF reader and an RFID tag to classify basic approaching and departure behavior.

For very short-range applications, RF sensing has been used to detect gestures and materials. Lien *et al.* [19] and Wang *et al.* [32] used a Google Soli to detect small finger gestures via a deep learning models. The RadarCat [37] project used a Soli sensor to detect different materials and user body locations. In contrast to the Walabot sensor used in our work, the Soli sensor has an operating frequency of 60 GHz, which gives it a high precision for fine details at short ranges. In long-range applications, Doppler radar range sensors with Support Vector Machine (SVM) and K-nearest neighbor (KNN) models were used by Liu *et al.* [20] to detect fall events of patients in long-term care facilities. Finally, a beam-scanning radar system was proposed by Wang *et al.* [31] for human location detection and detecting whether a person is sitting or standing. Our system, which we present next, extends this previous work with recognition of more detailed activities relevant for retail and workplace applications.

AN UNOBTRUSIVE ACTIVITY-SENSING SOLUTION

In this section, we introduce an unobtrusive, RF-sensor-based activity-recognition solution that can be easily deployed under a work surface. As discussed in the introduction, at this project's onset, our focus was on activity recognition for a convenience-store checkout counter, expanded later to include the applicability of the solution to an office environment. We contrast our solution to IMU-based activity recognition and investigate the potential value of combining RF sensing and a worn IMU, since in our target store environment, employees wear a smartwatch as part of a different pilot deployment.

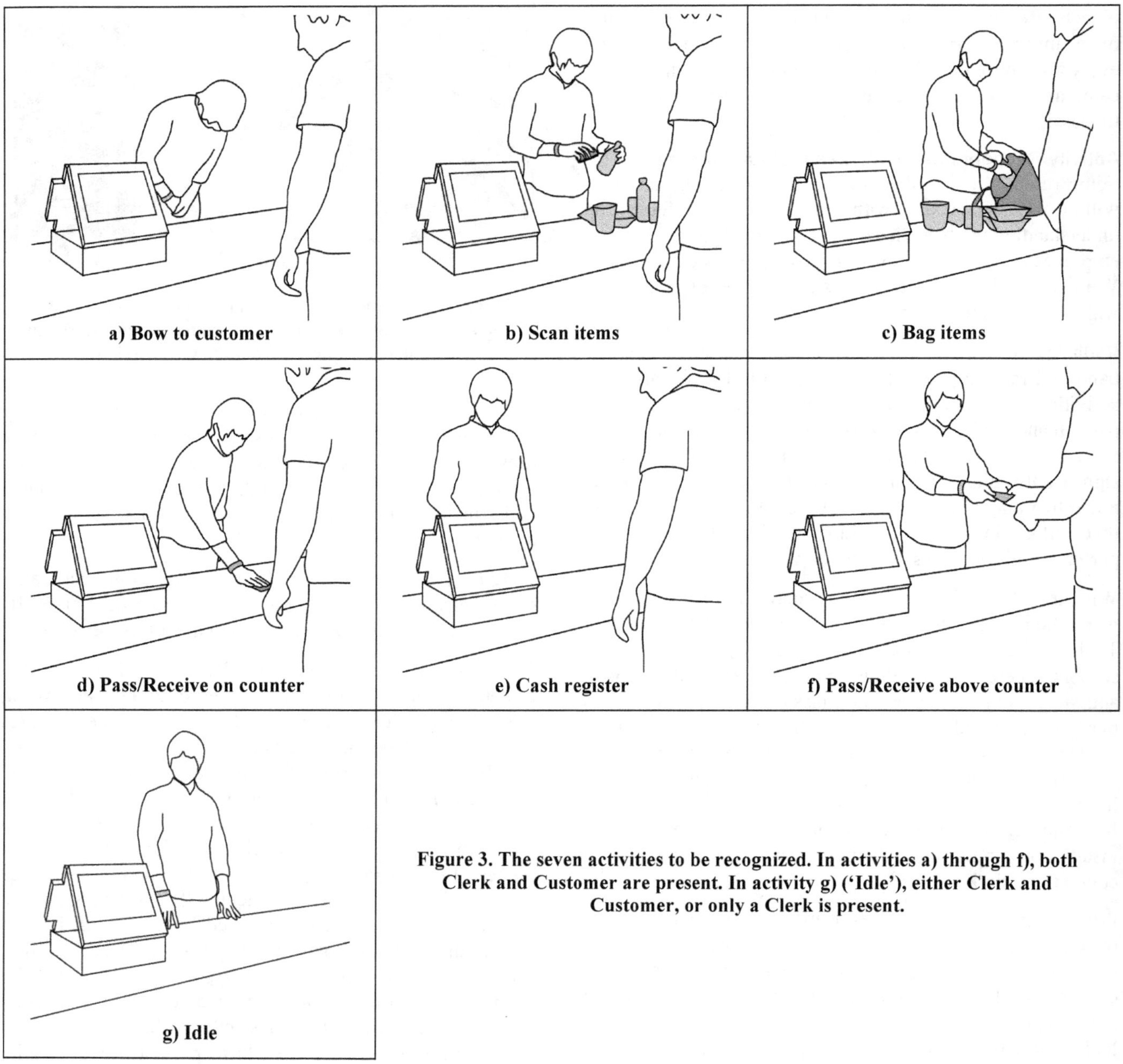

Figure 3. The seven activities to be recognized. In activities a) through f), both Clerk and Customer are present. In activity g) ('Idle'), either Clerk and Customer, or only a Clerk is present.

The section is organized as follows: We first describe the system components and setup used in our experiments. We next describe the construction of activity-recognition classifiers and provide analysis of how the use of multiple projections of RF-signal can improve recognition accuracy. Finally, we demonstrate the use of IMU and RF-sensor data for attributing action to a particular user in multi-user scenarios.

Implementation

For capturing RF data above and around a work surface, we use a Walabot Pro RF sensor[1]. The sensor operates in the frequency range of 3.3 – 10.3 GHz, which allows the sensor to "see" through different light dielectric materials such as wood, drywall, glass, etc. We mount the Walabot sensor under the work surface using a custom 3D-printed mount (see Figure 2, left).

The Walabot Pro sensor uses a 72mm x 140mm array of 18 antennas to generate a 3D representation by measuring the strength of the reflected signal from the area above the antenna array. The point cloud is projected into a 75 x 37 pixel image. The intensity of each pixel denotes the reflected energy received at that point, represented in *angle* and *distance* (see Figure 2, right). The average transmission power of RF signal is -16 dbm. We note that based on the

[1] https://walabot.com/

manufacturer's reports, no known health risks are associated with the device[2].

While the Walabot Pro sensor can capture data at 30fps, we presently capture RF sensor data at a sampling rate of 2fps. As shown later, this rate provides sufficient recognition accuracy and allows keeping the size of collected data small. For comparing to activity recognition using IMU data, we use the Microsoft Band 2[3]. We log IMU sensor data from the wearable sensor which consists of accelerometer and gyroscope data. The sampling rate of both these sensors is 62 Hz. Data are streamed from the Microsoft Band 2 over Bluetooth to a smartphone running Android OS and then transferred to a server for further processing. Lastly, we utilize the scikit-learn machine learning library [22] to train and test the different models presented next.

Activity Recognition: Checkout Counter

We first focus on recognizing activities performed at the convenience-store's checkout counter. For this purpose, we selected six common activities performed by the clerk in the checkout process (illustrated in Figure 3). The activities are: *Bowing to customer* (customary in Japan, where our project originated), *Scanning item barcodes with barcode scanner*, *Placing items into a bag*, *Passing or receiving an object on the counter* (this can be an item or payment), *Interacting with the cash register*, and *Passing or receiving an object above the counter* (this can be an item or payment). For these six activities, both clerk and one or more customers are typically present. Finally, we also included a seventh, '*Idle*' activity in which the clerk and customer are not performing any of the above activities, or the clerk is standing by herself or himself at the counter. It should be noted that our proposed system is generalizable and not constrained to the activities selected in this experiment.

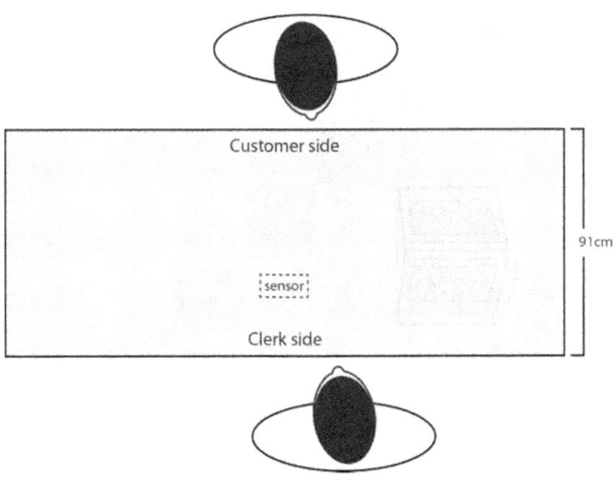

Figure. 4. The check-out counter environment simulated in our lab.

10-fold	Baseline (IMU only)	RF	RF + IMU
Logistic Regression	0.384	0.880	0.893
Naïve Bayes	0.307	0.562	0.564
KNN	0.585	0.880	0.884
SVM	0.507	**0.905**	**0.917**
Random Forest	**0.593**	0.818	0.832

Table 1. Activity recognition accuracy of different classifiers using different sensors combination based on a 10-fold cross validation.

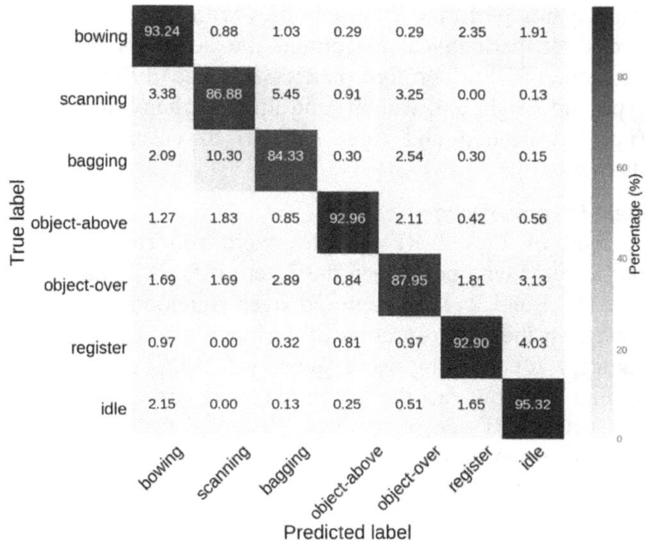

Figure. 5. Confusion matrix of activity recognition based on RF data only produced by the SVM classifier using 10-fold cross validation.

Setup

Unfortunately, to date, collecting data in the real store was not possible. Thus, a convenience-store counter was simulated in our lab using a 182cm x 91cm work-surface, as shown in Figure 4 (as described later, data for deskwork activity recognition, however, was collected in real offices). The Point-of-Sale (POS) was simulated using a large metal enclosure with a propped-up tablet. When the system is initialized, the first five seconds are used for calibration, and any objects present during those five seconds are considered background (thus, the POS is "invisible" to the system). Because in our use-case environment customers are expected or allowed only on one side of the counter, we designate one side of the counter the "Clerk" side (Figure 4, bottom), and the other side the "Customer" side (Figure 4, top).

Since people stand on both sides of the counter (a clerk on one side, and customer(s) on the other), the field of view of the Walabot's sensor was set to its maximum 180 degrees.

[2] https://walabot.com/walabot-tech-brief-416.pdf

[3] https://www.microsoft.com/microsoft-band/en-us

Data

10 participants from our lab volunteered to play the roles of Clerk and Customer, taking turns playing each role. When playing the role of a Clerk, participants wore a Microsoft Band 2 on the wrist of his or her dominant hand and stood on the appropriate side of the work surface. Participants then performed each of the 7 activities repeatedly for one minute (e.g., passing a grocery item back and forth). Participants were allowed to move left and right, but not move to the other side of the work surface. Each activity instance (e.g., a single bow, scanning a single item, etc.) took approximately one to three seconds (i.e., participants performed ~30 bows and scanned an item ~35 times).

To collect data for different scenarios, seven of the participants performed the activities with one "customer", and three participants performed the activities with two "customers". Furthermore, participants had different body types (in height and weight) and different hand dominance (i.e. left handed and right handed) to ensure a varied dataset.

Data Preprocessing

A total of 17,862 RF samples were collected from 10 participants who performed the 7 activities. IMU data from the MS Band 2 were captured over Bluetooth at 62 Hz. Based on the short duration of each activity instance, data samples for learning were generated using a 1500msec sliding window, as the mean intensity from each of 3 consecutive RF-sensor samples. Statistical features such as median, standard deviation, min, max, difference between max and min value, slope of the time series samples and a movement feature (which is extracted by taking the difference between the data sample and the mean value) were computed from the raw IMU data. These features were generated for each dimension of the IMU's accelerometer and gyroscope data.

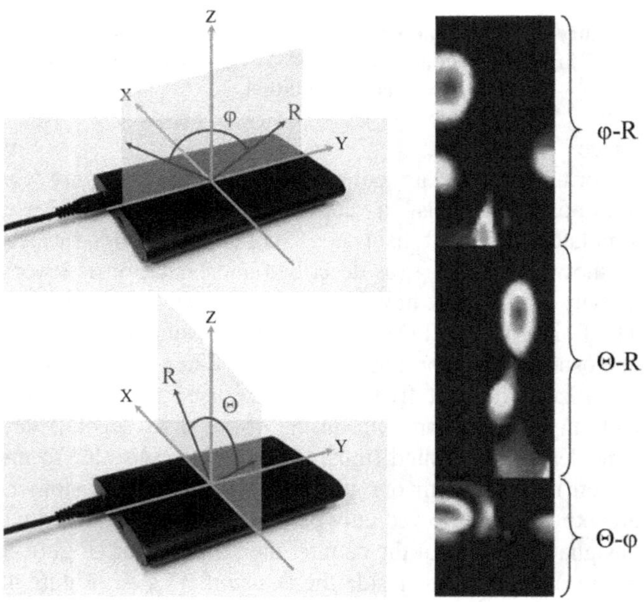

Figure 6. The Walabot sensor coordinate system (left), representing a half hemisphere area in which RF signal is transmitted and sensed. On right, the default projection (*top*), with two additional extracted projections (*center and bottom*) concatenated.

Results

We compare activity recognition performance when using the RF-sensor data only, the IMU data only, and when using a combination of the two. We report results from 10-fold cross validation evaluation; given the use of a sliding window in generating the data, we split the data into training and testing sets in a way that guaranteed to not have any overlapping samples in the sets.

The activity recognition performance was tested using five different classification techniques listed in Table 1. Our results show that classification accuracy using the RF sensor alone is high, much higher than that of baseline classification using the IMU data. This suggests the viability of this solution for unobtrusive activity

10-fold	RF (1 projection)	RF (3 projections)	RF (3 projections) + IMU
Logistic Regression	0.880	0.938	0.944
Naïve Bayes	0.562	0.604	0.604
KNN	0.880	0.915	0.921
SVM	**0.905**	**0.945**	**0.949**
Random Forest	0.818	0.881	0.886

Table 2. Comparing retail-activity recognition accuracy using 1 or 3 slices of RF signal, based on a 10-fold cross validation. Additional slices lead to accuracy gains.

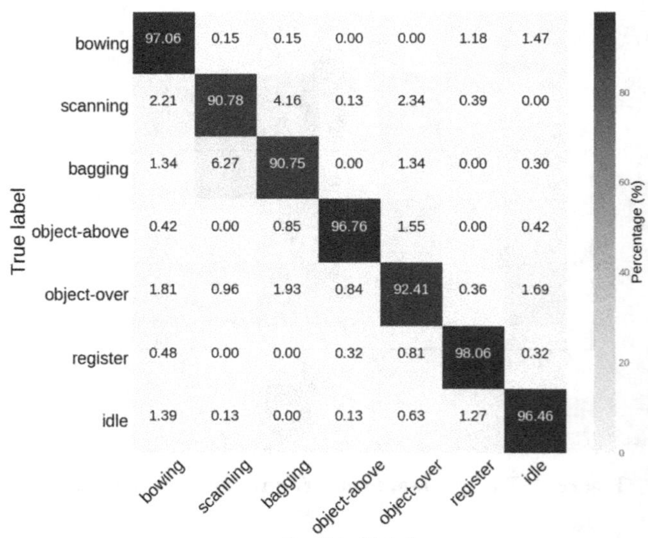

Figure 7. Confusion matrix of activity recognition based on RF data only produced by the SVM classifier using 10-fold cross validation.

recognition. Interestingly, we find that combining IMU and RF-sensor data does not provide meaningful accuracy gains. Figure 5 shows a confusion matrix for the seven clerk activities produced by the SVM classifier.

Multiple Projections of RF-signal for Improved Accuracy

One interesting area for investigation is whether extracting additional projections of RF data from 3D to 2D space would improve recognition accuracy further. Figure 6 illustrates the Walabot sensor's coordinate system. By default, the Walabot sensor outputs a single projection from 3D into 2D space, represented in angle φ and distance R (Figure 6, top). It is, however, possible to generate additional projections into 2D space using angle Θ (see Figure 6, bottom). For this test we generate 2 additional RF signal projections: A projection (Θ-R) that is perpendicular to the default slice (φ-R), and a projection (Θ-φ) that is a cross-section of (Θ-R) and (φ-R). The 3 projections are concatenated into a single image with a resolution of 187 x 37 pixels (see Figure 6, right). We evaluated this approach by performing a 10-fold cross validation on the same set of models as before.

Results

Even with recognition rates already high with a single projection, using the 3 projections resulted in overall improved accuracy, as can be seen in Table 2. For the best classifier (SVM), using 3 projections instead of the default projection reduced the error by 45%. Adding IMU data yielded only minor gains over the 3 projections of RF signal.

Leave-one-out	RF + IMU
Logistic Regression	**0.984**
Naïve Bayes	0.711
KNN	0.956
SVM	0.974
Random Forest	0.918

Table 3: Retail-activity classification accuracy using a leave-one-user-out validation.

Figure 7 shows a confusion matrix for the seven activities produced by the SVM classifier. Looking more closely at performance on the different activities, we see that, of all the activities, scanning and bagging were the most likely to be confused. Still, each of these activities is recognized correctly in more than 91% of the samples.

The improvement in overall accuracy suggests that the additional 2 projections capture important information present in different directions that isn't captured using a single projection.

To summarize, we are able to reach very high activity recognition rates for our seven activities using the RF sensor alone. As we show later, while IMU data did not generate a significant improvement in activity recognition accuracy, it can still play a role in an overall system for associating an activity with the user who performed it.

Figure 8. The six office deskwork activities to be recognized.

User Independence Test

Finally, to test how well the solution performs on new users, a leave-one-user-out evaluation was conducted on the retail activity dataset. This is important, for example, in the case of a new worker at the store. For each of the 10 users, the models are trained using data from 9 users and tested on the left-out user. We used the data generated with 3 projection RF signal for this evaluation. Table 3 shows the accuracy achieved using different classification models. Highest accuracy was achieved by the Logistic Regression classifier over all 10 users, at 98.4%. This result is very positive as it suggests that a system may be able to be bootstrapped with training data and yield reasonably high recognition accuracy for new users.

Activity Recognition: Office Deskwork

As discussed earlier, the ability to discreetly and unobtrusively recognize activities performed above a work surface could be valuable in other domains such as office environments, to allow intelligent systems to make better estimation of workers' state and availability. To investigate the applicability of the solution to office deskwork, we conducted a pilot exploration using our solution under office desks. We focused on six common deskwork activities, illustrated in Figure 8: *Writing (on paper), Reading (from paper), Eating, Drinking, Computer Work,* and *Idle* (e.g., reading off the screen). Finally, we also included a condition with the user not at their desk (either in the office, or away) that we call *Not at Desk*, as a seventh activity.

Setup

This dataset was collected in participants' personal offices. As such, the dataset represents naturalistic environments, including desk clutter present in different people's offices. Furthermore, by capturing data over time, we account for how such environments change.

Following lessons from the previous section, three projections were generated for each RF sample. Since, unlike the counter scenario, in this environment most activities are performed on one side of the work surface by one person, the field of view angles (Θ and φ) of the Walabot's sensor were set to 90 degrees (Refer to Figure 6 for details related to field of view).

Data

We collected data from 6 participants, all members of our lab. Data were collected in each participant's office, with the Walabot sensor mounted to the underside of the desk, coarsely under the location of the participant's keyboard. To accommodate the natural changes in people's offices and desk environments, such as bringing or removing papers, personal electronics, different food and drinks, etc., we collected the full set of activities from each participant on 5 different occurrences throughout the workweek. In each data-collection session, participants performed each of the activities at a time for two minutes. Participant chose in which order they wanted to perform the activities.

10-fold	Accuracy
Logistic Regression	0.831
Naïve Bayes	0.393
KNN	**0.953**
SVM	0.932
Random Forest	0.949

Table 4. Classification accuracy for deskwork activities in participants' offices.

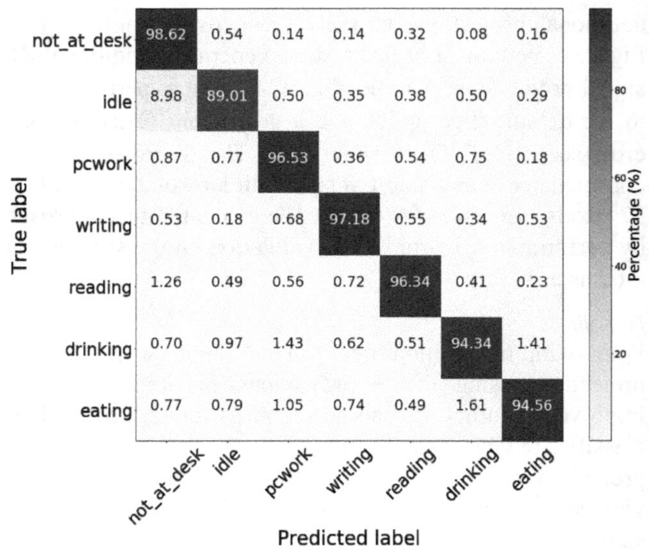

Figure 9. Confusion matrix for office deskwork activity recognition predicted by KNN using 10-fold cross validation.

The full dataset contained a total of 7 hours of RF sensor data (6 participants x 5 sessions x 2 minutes/activity x 7 activities), with *one full hour* of RF data for each activity. We note that even with this small number of participants, the data include rather diverse working styles: One of the participants uses an L-shaped desk with their computer at the intersection of the L. Another participant uses a sit-stand desk. Yet another participant uses an ergonomic pullout keyboard tray. (For this participant, the Walabot was mounted further back under the desk.)

Data Preprocessing

As before, a data sample is generated for every 1,500msec window as the mean intensity for each pixel using a sliding window. From each session and each activity, we trim the first and last 1 seconds. The dataset contained a total of 23,687 samples.

Results

Table 4 demonstrates the performance of five classification approaches based on 10-fold cross validation. With the exception of Naïve Bayes, most of the models were able to correctly classify the 7 activities with accuracy in the range of 83–95%. K-nearest neighbor (KNN) and Random Forest models gave the highest accuracy. The confusion matrix for the KNN classifier is shown in Figure 9. As can be seen, in about 8-9% of the cases when a participant was idle, the models incorrectly classified them as not at their desk. It is worth noting that while detecting Computer Work can be easily done by installing a tool on the user's computer, correctly detecting that a user is reading or writing (not on their computer) can be greatly beneficial to tools that detect presence and availability, such as [4, 40].

ATTRIBUTING ACTION IN MULTI-USER SCENARIOS

One challenge with using RF sensing for activity recognition is that when more than one user occupies the work space (for example, more than one clerk is working at the store), the system cannot tell which user is the one performing the activity that was recognized. In this section, we present our experiments for identifying the user performing an activity above the work space.

One approach to attempting to identify the user performing an activity in a multi-user scenario would be to train a "person classifier" using the RF sensor, similar to [1]. In [1], an antenna mounted behind a wall is used to identify human body parts from RF snapshots across time to distinguish between users. In our setup, however, the sensor is mounted under the work surface, getting only limited view of the users' body. Another approach is to use additional sensors to identify users, such as IMU data from smartwatches worn by users. As such, the system tries to identify which smartwatch was worn by the user performing the activity. This is analogous to work by Cho *et al.* [9] and Wilson and Benko [35] that correlated images from cameras and IMU data.

Data

To simulate a multi-user scenario in which two users each wear a smartwatch, we used the RF-sensor and IMU dataset collected earlier to generate the following: Each RF-data sample (representing a 1,500msec window) in the dataset was paired both with IMU data captured at the same time (i.e. "*Matching*"), but also with IMU data from a different activity and user (i.e. "*Mismatching*"), simulating the activity of a different user. By way of illustration, consider RF data sample captured while a user was scanning an item, paired with its corresponding IMU data as well as with mismatching IMU data recorded during a "Bowing" activity. The system's goal is to correctly link the RF data and its matching IMU data.

Process

We implemented the following 4-step process for matching RF and IMU data:

In step 1, the system performs activity recognition on the RF data alone, using an SVM classifier (this classifier was used as it provided the highest recognition accuracy). The activity classified with the highest likelihood is recorded, as denoted in equation 1.

1) $$Activity = argmax(\ p(activity|RF)\ )$$

In step 2, the system uses a Random Forest model to perform activity recognition on both matching and mismatching IMU data samples (the Random Forest classifier was chosen as it had the highest accuracy for IMU-only data). Recall that the system does not know which IMU sample is the matching one. For each IMU sample, the likelihood score for the *Activity* classified on the RF data is recorded, as denoted in equation 2 (continuing with our illustration, the likelihood of "Scanning", returned by each IMU data).

2) $$M_1 = p(Activity|IMU_1) \qquad M_2 = p(Activity|IMU_2)$$

In step 3, the system returns the IMU sample that produced a higher likelihood score as "Matching", as denoted in equation 3. In case the likelihood produced for both IMU samples is identical, the system returns *"Matching IMU Unknown"*.

3) $$Matching = argmax(M1,M2)$$

In the final step, the system returns a confidence score, denoted in equation 4, calculated as the absolute difference between the likelihoods returned for each IMU data sample. As we show later, this score is a good measure for the confidence in the system's choice between the two IMU samples.

4) $$Confidence = |M_1\text{-}M_2|$$

Results

We report the results of a 10-fold cross-validation evaluation. Our system correctly selected the matching IMU data in 64% of cases. Figure 10 shows the classification accuracy at different classification-confidence bands. It is apparent that classification returned by the system with a high confidence value likely corresponds to correct classification. Specifically, for all samples with a confidence greater than 0.2 (true for 66% of the data), classification accuracy is 88%. This result shows our

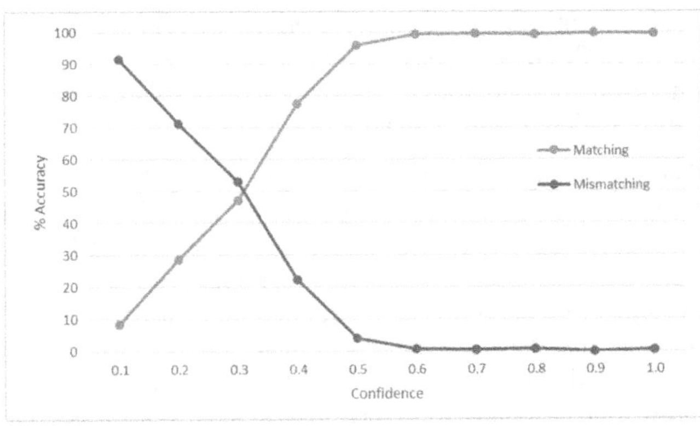

Figure 10. Distribution of prediction *accuracy* by prediction *confidence*, calculated as the absolute difference in likelihood score between both IMU samples.

approach performs well on a large segment of the data, and that the confidence metric provided by the system is a good indicator for the reliability of the classification. However, the large number of samples with a low confidence score suggests that further investigation is needed.

LIMITATIONS

A limitation of our dataset for convenience-store activities is that data were collected in a simulated checkout environment. Still, our data includes conditions of more than one customer, and included participants of different height and weight. In the future, we hope to deploy our system in a real store. Our deskwork dataset included activities performed in participants' real offices and accounted for daily variations in objects, clothing, and postures. However, in this pilot dataset of deskwork activities, activities were performed separately from one another. Whereas activities at the convenience store counter are rarely interleaved, at an office desk, multiple activities often occur at the same time (for example, working on the computer and drinking). Our work has also focused on a set of common activities, but more activities could be recognized. As such, a larger set, with more and interleaved activities needs to be collected, and an approach for recognition, such as in [28], can be attempted. Nonetheless, we believe our pilot office-desk activity dataset serves to demonstrate the potential applicability of our solution to this work domain.

DISCUSSION & FUTURE WORK

The results, presented in the previous section, illustrate how activities performed above a work surface can be recognized discreetly and unobtrusively, without requiring a camera. We further show that additional projection of RF signal greatly improves recognition accuracy. Finally, we also demonstrate the use of IMU data from a worn sensor for identifying the person performing the recognized activity in multi-user scenarios.

In our current work, samples were created as snapshots from the IMU and RF sensor. However, many of the activities we are interested in do have a temporal component, especially in the convenience-store counter environment (e.g., a scanning motion, a bagging motion). Thus, while the accuracy of our classifiers was very high, future similar solutions may need to explore features contained in the time domain.

One interesting question that came up during this work but is not currently addressed is that of activities that are performed above the work surface then transition off it (or start off the work surface and continue above it). For example, moving a box or a bag on and off a counter. It is possible that for such activities, data from the worn IMU sensor could provide a significant contribution. This would allow the system to more accurately determine the beginnings and completions of activities.

A potential extension for the work could involve attempting to include knowledge of the materials used or placed on the work surface. This could be done, for example, in a method similar to that used by [37]. Furthermore, the physical relationship between people and objects could be used to enhance both recognition and interaction, as in [21]. This information could then be supplied to the activity-recognition model as additional information.

Beyond the office desk and check-out counter use-cases, we expect that this solution could prove useful for other intelligent systems that rely on activity recognition but where the use of cameras may be prohibited. For meeting rooms, for example, detecting position and movement of meeting attendees could be used for augmenting meetings. It could also assist remote meeting participants to direct their attention appropriately. Also in work environments, this system could be used to monitor hot-desking utilization. In retail environments, our solution could be used to monitor customer position and interaction with products in a showroom. For such use-cases, the RF sensor could be used to detect the position of movement around a product display and would allow businesses to observe correlations between physical placement of products and sales.

Finally, as described in the Introduction, we chose to investigate the use of RF radar sensing as a potential replacement for the use of cameras for activity recognition. This was particularly important for environments where installing a camera may be prohibitive. Yet, it is an open question whether users would be more comfortable with the RF sensor mounted under the work surface compared to being observed by a camera. We speculate that it would be important to show users the output of the RF sensor as a way of highlighting the lack of humanly interpretable information in that data.

CONCLUSIONS

We present a solution for accurate, yet discreet and unobtrusive activity recognition solution that utilizes an RF-radar sensor mounted under a work surface. We further show how the use of the RF sensor in combination with a wrist-worn IMU can be used for attributing a recognized action to the correct user in multi-user scenarios. We demonstrated our solution in both specialized and general domains: a convenience-store counter and an office environment, and believe that this work has potential application in many other domains. We believe this paper places a useful tool in the toolbox of developers and designers of intelligent context-aware systems.

ACKNOWLEDGMENTS

We thank Matt Cooper for his comments and suggestions. We thank Jenn Marlow and Thi Avrahami for their help with the paper. Finally, we thank our participants for volunteering their time.

REFERENCES

1. Fadel Adib, Chen-Yu Hsu, Hongzi Mao, Dina Katabi, and Frédo Durand. 2015. Capturing the Human Figure Through a Wall. *ACM Trans. Graph.* 34, 6: 219:1–219:13. https://doi.org/10.1145/2816795.2818072
2. Oresti Baños, Miguel Damas, Héctor Pomares, Ignacio Rojas, Máté Attila Tóth, and Oliver Amft. 2012. A Benchmark Dataset to Evaluate Sensor Displacement in Activity Recognition. In *Proceedings of the 2012 ACM Conference on Ubiquitous Computing* (UbiComp '12), 1026–1035. https://doi.org/10.1145/2370216.2370437
3. Ling Bao and Stephen S. Intille. 2004. Activity Recognition from User-Annotated Acceleration Data. In *Pervasive Computing*, 1–17. https://doi.org/10.1007/978-3-540-24646-6_1
4. James "Bo" Begole, Nicholas E. Matsakis, and John C. Tang. 2004. Lilsys: Sensing Unavailability. In *Proceedings of the 2004 ACM Conference on Computer Supported Cooperative Work* (CSCW'04), 511–514. https://doi.org/10.1145/1031607.1031691
5. Michael Buettner, Richa Prasad, Matthai Philipose, and David Wetherall. 2009. Recognizing Daily Activities with RFID-based Sensors. In *Proceedings of the 11th International Conference on Ubiquitous Computing* (UbiComp'09), 51–60. https://doi.org/10.1145/1620545.1620553
6. Andreas Bulling, Ulf Blanke, and Bernt Schiele. 2014. A Tutorial on Human Activity Recognition Using Body-worn Inertial Sensors. *ACM Comput. Surv.* 46, 3: 33:1–33:33. https://doi.org/10.1145/2499621
7. Scott A. Cambo, Daniel Avrahami, and Matthew L. Lee. 2017. BreakSense: Combining Physiological and Location Sensing to Promote Mobility During Work-Breaks. In *Proceedings of the 2017 CHI Conference on Human Factors in Computing Systems* (CHI'17), 3595–3607. https://doi.org/10.1145/3025453.3026021
8. Ricardo Chavarriaga, Hesam Sagha, Alberto Calatroni, Sundara Tejaswi Digumarti, Gerhard Tröster, José Del R. Millán, and Daniel Roggen. 2013. The Opportunity Challenge: A Benchmark Database for On-body Sensor-based Activity Recognition. *Pattern Recogn. Lett.* 34, 15: 2033–2042. https://doi.org/10.1016/j.patrec.2012.12.014
9. Yongwon Cho, Yunyoung Nam, Yoo-Joo Choi, and We-Duke Cho. 2008. SmartBuckle: Human Activity Recognition Using a 3-axis Accelerometer and a Wearable Camera. In *Proceedings of the 2nd International Workshop on Systems and Networking Support for Health Care and Assisted Living Environments* (HealthNet'08), 7:1–7:3. https://doi.org/10.1145/1515747.1515757
10. Tanzeem Choudhury, Gaetano Borriello, Sunny Consolvo, Dirk Haehnel, Beverly Harrison, Bruce Hemingway, Jeffrey Hightower, Predrag "Pedja" Klasnja, Karl Koscher, Anthony LaMarca, James A. Landay, Louis LeGrand, Jonathan Lester, Ali Rahimi, Adam Rea, and Danny Wyatt. 2008. The Mobile Sensing Platform: An Embedded Activity Recognition System. *IEEE Pervasive Computing* 7, 2: 32–41. https://doi.org/10.1109/MPRV.2008.39
11. Dima Damen, Andrew Gee, Walterio Mayol-Cuevas, and Andrew Calway. 2012. Egocentric real-time workspace monitoring using an rgb-d camera. In *2012 IEEE/RSJ International Conference on Intelligent Robots and Systems (IROS)*, 1029–1036. https://doi.org/https://doi.org/10.1109/IROS.2012.6385829
12. Han Ding, Chen Qian, Jinsong Han, Ge Wang, Zhiping Jiang, Jizhong Zhao, and Wei Xi. 2016. Device-free Detection of Approach and Departure Behaviors Using Backscatter Communication. In *Proceedings of the 2016 ACM International Joint Conference on Pervasive and Ubiquitous Computing* (UbiComp'16), 167–177. https://doi.org/10.1145/2971648.2971699
13. James Fogarty, Scott E. Hudson, Christopher G. Atkeson, Daniel Avrahami, Jodi Forlizzi, Sara Kiesler, Johnny C. Lee, and Jie Yang. 2005. Predicting Human Interruptibility with Sensors. *ACM Trans. Comput.-Hum. Interact.* 12, 1: 119–146. https://doi.org/10.1145/1057237.1057243
14. Eric Horvitz, Paul Koch, and Johnson Apacible. 2004. BusyBody: Creating and Fielding Personalized Models of the Cost of Interruption. In *Proceedings of the 2004 ACM Conference on Computer Supported Cooperative Work* (CSCW'04), 507–510. https://doi.org/10.1145/1031607.1031690
15. Shian-Ru Ke, Hoang Le Uyen Thuc, Yong-Jin Lee, Jenq-Neng Hwang, Jang-Hee Yoo, and Kyoung-Ho Choi. 2013. A Review on Video-Based Human Activity Recognition. *Computers* 2, 2: 88–131. https://doi.org/10.3390/computers2020088
16. Gierad Laput, Yang Zhang, and Chris Harrison. 2017. Synthetic Sensors: Towards General-Purpose Sensing. In *Proceedings of the 2017 CHI Conference on Human Factors in Computing Systems* (CHI '17), 3986–3999. https://doi.org/https://doi.org/10.1145/3025453.3025773
17. Oscar D. Lara and Miguel A. Labrador. 2013. A survey on human activity recognition using wearable sensors. *IEEE Communications Surveys and Tutorials* 15, 3: 1192–1209. https://doi.org/https://doi.org/10.1109/SURV.2012.110112.00192
18. Chandrashekhar Lavania, Sunil Thulasidasan, Anthony LaMarca, Jeffrey Scofield, and Jeff Bilmes. 2016. A Weakly Supervised Activity Recognition Framework for Real-time Synthetic Biology Laboratory Assistance. In *Proceedings of the 2016 ACM International Joint Conference on Pervasive and Ubiquitous Computing* (UbiComp '16), 37–48. https://doi.org/10.1145/2971648.2971716
19. Jaime Lien, Nicholas Gillian, M. Emre Karagozler, Patrick Amihood, Carsten Schwesig, Erik Olson,

Hakim Raja, and Ivan Poupyrev. 2016. Soli: Ubiquitous gesture sensing with millimeter wave radar. *ACM Transactions on Graphics (TOG)* 35, 4: 142.

20. Liang Liu, Mihail Popescu, Marjorie Skubic, Marilyn Rantz, Tarik Yardibi, and Paul Cuddihy. 2011. Automatic fall detection based on Doppler radar motion signature. In *2011 5th International Conference on Pervasive Computing Technologies for Healthcare (PervasiveHealth) and Workshops*, 222–225. https://doi.org/https://doi.org/10.4108/icst.pervasivehealth.2011.245993
21. Nicolai Marquardt, Robert Diaz-Marino, Sebastian Boring, and Saul Greenberg. 2011. The Proximity Toolkit: Prototyping Proxemic Interactions in Ubiquitous Computing Ecologies. In *Proceedings of the 24th Annual ACM Symposium on User Interface Software and Technology* (UIST '11), 315–326. https://doi.org/10.1145/2047196.2047238
22. Fabian Pedregosa, Gaël Varoquaux, Alexandre Gramfort, Vincent Michel, Bertrand Thirion, Olivier Grisel, Mathieu Blondel, Peter Prettenhofer, Ron Weiss, Vincent Dubourg, Jake Vanderplas, Alexandre Passos, David Cournapeau, Matthieu Brucher, Matthieu Perrot, and Édouard Duchesnay. 2011. Scikit-learn: Machine Learning in Python. *Journal of Machine Learning Research* 12: 2825–2830.
23. M. Philipose, K. P. Fishkin, M. Perkowitz, D. J. Patterson, D. Fox, H. Kautz, and D. Hahnel. 2004. Inferring activities from interactions with objects. *IEEE Pervasive Computing* 3, 4: 50–57. https://doi.org/10.1109/MPRV.2004.7
24. Ronald Poppe. 2010. A survey on vision-based human action recognition. *Image and vision computing* 28, 6: 976–990.
25. Meera Radhakrishnan, Sharanya Eswaran, Archan Misra, Deepthi Chander, and Koustuv Dasgupta. 2016. Iris: Tapping wearable sensing to capture in-store retail insights on shoppers. In *Pervasive Computing and Communications (PerCom), 2016 IEEE International Conference on*, 1–8. https://doi.org/https://doi.org/10.1109/PERCOM.2016.7456526
26. Derek Reilly, Emma Westecott, David Parker, Samuel Perreault, Derek Neil, Nathan Lapierre, Kate Hartman, and Harjot Bal. 2013. Design-driven Research for Workplace Exergames: The Limber Case Study. In *Proceedings of the First International Conference on Gameful Design, Research, and Applications* (Gamification '13), 123–126. https://doi.org/10.1145/2583008.2583030
27. Attila Reiss and Didier Stricker. 2012. Creating and Benchmarking a New Dataset for Physical Activity Monitoring. In *Proceedings of the 5th International Conference on PErvasive Technologies Related to Assistive Environments* (PETRA '12), 40:1–40:8. https://doi.org/10.1145/2413097.2413148
28. Daniele Riboni, Timo Sztyler, Gabriele Civitarese, and Heiner Stuckenschmidt. 2016. Unsupervised Recognition of Interleaved Activities of Daily Living Through Ontological and Probabilistic Reasoning. In *Proceedings of the 2016 ACM International Joint Conference on Pervasive and Ubiquitous Computing* (UbiComp '16), 1–12. https://doi.org/10.1145/2971648.2971691
29. Chiew Seng Sean Tan, Johannes Schöning, Kris Luyten, and Karin Coninx. 2013. Informing Intelligent User Interfaces by Inferring Affective States from Body Postures in Ubiquitous Computing Environments. In *Proceedings of the 2013 International Conference on Intelligent User Interfaces* (IUI '13), 235–246. https://doi.org/10.1145/2449396.2449427
30. Edison Thomaz, Cheng Zhang, Irfan Essa, and Gregory D. Abowd. 2015. Inferring Meal Eating Activities in Real World Settings from Ambient Sounds: A Feasibility Study. In *Proceedings of the 20th International Conference on Intelligent User Interfaces* (IUI '15), 427–431. https://doi.org/10.1145/2678025.2701405
31. Guochao Wang, Changzhan Gu, Takao Inoue, and Changzhi Li. 2014. A hybrid FMCW-interferometry radar for indoor precise positioning and versatile life activity monitoring. *IEEE Transactions on Microwave Theory and Techniques* 62, 11: 2812–2822. https://doi.org/https://doi.org/10.1109/TMTT.2014.2358572
32. Saiwen Wang, Jie Song, Jaime Lien, Ivan Poupyrev, and Otmar Hilliges. 2016. Interacting with Soli: Exploring Fine-Grained Dynamic Gesture Recognition in the Radio-Frequency Spectrum. In *Proceedings of the 29th Annual Symposium on User Interface Software and Technology* (UIST '16), 851–860. https://doi.org/10.1145/2984511.2984565
33. Jamie A. Ward, Paul Lukowicz, Gerhard Troster, and Thad E. Starner. 2006. Activity recognition of assembly tasks using body-worn microphones and accelerometers. *IEEE transactions on pattern analysis and machine intelligence* 28, 10: 1553–1567. https://doi.org/https://doi.org/10.1109/TPAMI.2006.197
34. Daniel Weinland, Remi Ronfard, and Edmond Boyer. 2011. A survey of vision-based methods for action representation, segmentation and recognition. *Computer vision and image understanding* 115, 2: 224–241.
35. Andrew D. Wilson and Hrvoje Benko. 2014. CrossMotion: Fusing Device and Image Motion for User Identification, Tracking and Device Association. In *Proceedings of the 16th International Conference on Multimodal Interaction* (ICMI '14), 216–223. https://doi.org/10.1145/2663204.2663270
36. Raphael Wimmer, Matthias Kranz, Sebastian Boring, and Albrecht Schmidt. 2007. CapTable and CapShelf:

unobtrusive activity recognition using networked capacitive sensors. In *Networked Sensing Systems, 2007. INSS'07. Fourth International Conference on*, 85–88. https://doi.org/https://doi.org/10.1109/INSS.2007.4297395

37. Hui-Shyong Yeo, Gergely Flamich, Patrick Schrempf, David Harris-Birtill, and Aaron Quigley. 2016. RadarCat: Radar Categorization for Input & Interaction. In *Proceedings of the 29th Annual Symposium on User Interface Software and Technology* (UIST '16), 833–841. https://doi.org/10.1145/2984511.2984515
38. Yunze Zeng, Parth H. Pathak, and Prasant Mohapatra. 2015. Analyzing Shopper's Behavior Through WiFi Signals. In *Proceedings of the 2Nd Workshop on Workshop on Physical Analytics* (WPA '15), 13–18. https://doi.org/10.1145/2753497.2753508
39. Chenyang Zhang and Yingli Tian. 2012. RGB-D camera-based daily living activity recognition. *Journal of Computer Vision and Image Processing* 2, 4: 12.
40. Manuela Züger, Christopher Corley, André N. Meyer, Boyang Li, Thomas Fritz, David Shepherd, Vinay Augustine, Patrick Francis, Nicholas Kraft, and Will Snipes. 2017. Reducing Interruptions at Work: A Large-Scale Field Study of FlowLight. In *Proceedings of the 2017 CHI Conference on Human Factors in Computing Systems* (CHI '17), 61–72. https://doi.org/10.1145/3025453.3025662

Investigating Interactions for Text Recognition using a Vibrotactile Wearable Display

Granit Luzhnica
Know-Center
Graz, Austria
gluzhnica@know-center.at

Eduardo Veas
Know-Center
Graz, Austria
eveas@know-center.at

ABSTRACT
Vibrotactile skin-reading uses wearable vibrotactile displays to convey dynamically generated textual information. Such wearable displays have potential to be used in a broad range of applications. Nevertheless, the reading process is passive, and users have no control over the reading flow. To compensate for such drawback, this paper investigates what kind of interactions are necessary for vibrotactile skin reading and the modalities of such interactions. An interaction concept for skin reading was designed by taking into account the reading as a process. We performed a formative study with 22 participants to assess reading behaviour in word and sentence reading using a six-channel wearable vibrotactile display. Our study shows that word based interactions in sentence reading are more often used and preferred by users compared to character-based interactions and that users prefer gesture-based interaction for skin reading. Finally, we discuss how such wearable vibrotactile displays could be extended with sensors that would enable recognition of such gesture-based interaction. This paper contributes a set of guidelines for the design of wearable haptic displays for text communication.

Author Keywords
vibrotactile feedback; skin reading; stimulation; haptic display; wearable; user study; interaction, interaction design; gesture interaction; gesture recognition; HCI

INTRODUCTION
Reading is a fundamental skill in human development, as a way to acquire knowledge from written text, and also a major component in communication (e.g., letters, telegram, chat, email). To most people, reading is a visual task that recruits the most developed sense of vision to decode messages encoded in graphical symbols. People with visual impairments resort to the tactile sense for reading by using Braille. Besides them, non-impaired individuals can benefit from a means to perceive messages that do not recruit the visual or auditory senses. The primary feedback modalities of mobiles and wearables are visual and auditory. As such, they compete for visual and auditory attention and distract the user from important tasks.

IUI'18, March 7–11, 2018, Tokyo, Japan

ISBN 978-1-4503-4945-1/18/03...$15.00

DOI: https://doi.org/10.1145/3172944.3172951

Alternative display modalities, such as tactile displays, can reduce demands on the predominant visual display, but are largely under-utilised [4].

With the proliferation of wearable devices, devices with vibrotactile capabilities are accessible to a substantial number of end users. With them, it becomes possible to transmit generic symbols with abstract meanings [14, 29, 24] that can be combined in arbitrary messages (words, sentences) [14, 29]. Luzhnica et al. refer to this as vibrotactile *skin-reading*. While encoding alphanumeric symbols in tactile patterns to transmit words is not new [14], recent developments in vibrotactile technology and stimulation methods overcome issues in effective training, throughput, accuracy as well as portability [28]. Vibrotactile skin reading uses a vibrotactile display to convey dynamically generated textual information similar to refreshable Braille displays [43, 41]. However, it is much more portable, and mobile as the entire vibrotactile display is packed within a wearable glove or sleeve [29]. Moreover, it requires substantially less effort to learn. Recent research has demonstrated that sighted individuals are able to learn the entire English Alphabet (26 letters) within three hours of training [29] as opposed to six months of training required for learning Polish Alphabet (32 letters) using Braille [3]. While being able to efficiently transmit an alphabet is a necessary step, reading is inherently a much more complex task [38]. Learning to read is learning how to use the conventional forms of printed language to obtain meaning. For skin-reading, the print is transformed into vibrotactile patterns, so that reading entails obtaining meaning from them.

A common belief that reading is a sequential task, where *glide smoothly across the page*, is merely an illusion [37]. At the word level, well-established research postulated that words are recognized as units [22, 11, 40, 5] and they are even recognized before individual letters [5]. Reading depends on the mechanics of the visual system to stop at fixed spots in the text (fixations) and jump quickly to other spots (saccades, covering about 8 letter spaces) [37]. Skilled readers fixate on about $2/3$ of the words in a text. Beside forward movements to advance in reading, they reread nearby material backwards in the text about 10 to 15% of the time, occasionally driven by breakdowns on comprehension. Conversely, beginning readers fixate every word (often more than once), perform shorter saccades, and up to 50% of their eye movements are regressions, as they rely more on context to identify words [37]. Obtaining meaning from printed words is not sequential; it depends on processing words as units and uses backward jumps at word level to aid understanding.

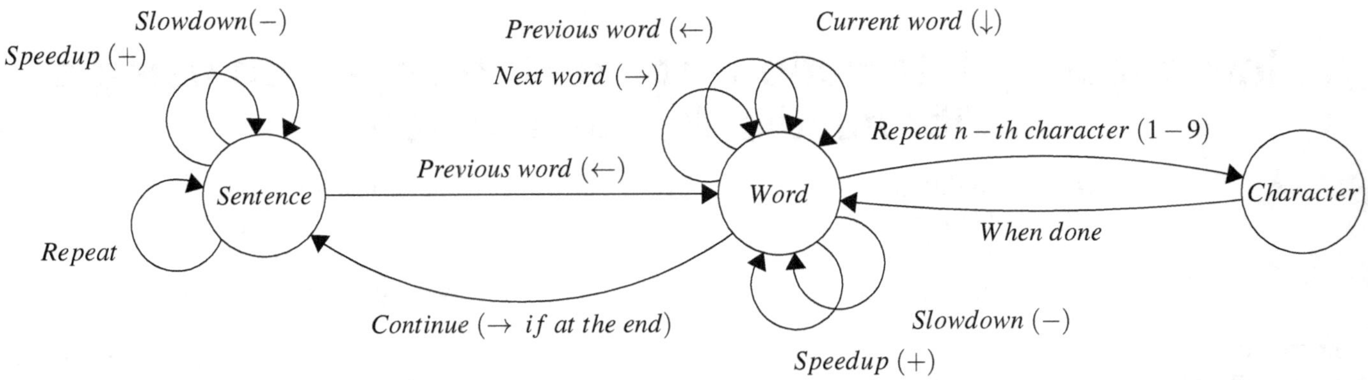

Figure 1. Interaction concept during sentence transmission. States (Sentence, Word and Characters) represent what the system is transmitting to user.

In Braille, it is not possible to form a global shape recognition of the entire word, so the text has to be processed character by character [7, 31, 30]. The perception and flow of information in Braille are controlled by moving the hand forward and occasionally backwards to revisit information [30, 20]. Thereby, Braille readers control reading speed, focus on particular letters or re-scan entire words. On the other hand, vibrotactile skin reading is passive: a pattern of vibrations is stimulated by the device from start to end while users have no control over the transmission. Yet, vibrotactile displays can evoke the perception of words as units, by means of tactile animations [21, 48]. The question that drives this research is what interactions are needed for efficient skin-reading? Users may not understand parts of the text due to lack of concentration or training. They need ways to pause, resume and jump to previous units of meaning or change the speed of transmission to account for progress in their reading skills.

In this paper, we propose using navigation interactions for skin reading to equip users with means of controlling the reading process. An interaction concept was created to enable reading interactions for vibrotactile displays. A formative study trained novice users to recognise letters and words, and tested their behaviour while skin-reading sentences. We analyse participants' interaction behaviours and a questionnaire to determine what interactions are useful and what are the preferred means of interactions. Finally, we map our interactions to gestures and discuss the wearable design choices that could allow the used wearable vibrotactile display to be extended for supporting such gesture-based interaction concept.

RELATED WORK

Starting with Braille's invention of the Braille coding in 1824, haptic displays have long been widely used by people with visual impairments. Research on tactile displays equipped with actuators has been ongoing since at least 1924 [13], where Gault [13] used a piezoelectric unit to convert entire recorded speech to touch. Similarly, Kirman [21] used a 15×15 vibrator matrix on the palm to teach six participants to differentiate between the patterns of 15 different words. Other researchers attempted to utilise a visually oriented approach, where a low-resolution image of the object is projected to an array of stimulators. For instance, White [52] transformed images captured from a video feed to a 20×20 vibrotactile display placed on the back. After training, participants were able to distinguish simple shapes like circle, square and triangle. Bliss [2] developed the first commercial device capable of capturing text from the video feed and then imprinting each letter on the finger with a 6×24 matrix of vibrators.

A more successful approach of transmitting information through haptics was provided by Geldard [14]. The device was named Vibratese and used five vibromotors on the chest to encode 45 symbols (letters, numbers and most frequent short words). The author reported that after 65 hours of training one participant was able to understand 38 wpm (words per minute). More recently, Luzhnica et al. followed a different encoding scheme using only the location of vibromotors to encode 26 letters of English alphabet [29]. The authors used six vibromotors on the back of the hand and were able to train users to perceive letters, words and phrases through skin within only five hours, although they needed repetition of stimuli.

A crucial aspect of tactile displays is how they encode information. It requires providing patterns that are discriminative while delivering them as fast as possible. Typically a combination of variations in amplitude [47, 49, 54], frequency [47, 49, 54], duration [16, 14] and body locations [14, 54, 34, 44] have been used. For instance, Geldard [14] in his Vibratese used five locations, a variation of three durations and three intensities to encode the desired symbols. Recently, Novich [35] showed that spatiotemporal encoding, where vibromotors in a pattern are turned on and off sequentially one after the other, results in significantly better discrimination than the spatially encoded patterns where all vibromotors in a pattern onset simultaneously. Liao [24] utilised such a spatiotemporal encoding to encode symbols on the wrist. Although such encoding works well [24, 35] in terms of being identified by participants, it is many times slower than the spatial encoding. Luzhnica [29] used a prioritised overlapping spatiotemporal encoding where vibromotors are activated in sequence after a gap, and they stay on until the pattern is finished. This method resulted in better recognition accuracy than spatial encoding, and it is faster than spatiotemporal encoding, as vibromotors share most of the activated time. Recent research leverages spatial acuity (sensitivity of locations of actuators) for achieving a better perception of encoded information [28, 27]. We employ the same method as Luzhnica [29] for encoding char-

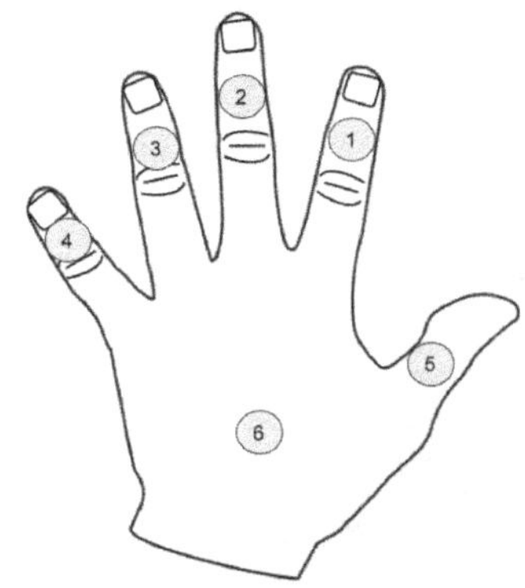

Figure 2. The vibrotactile display investigated in this paper containing six vibromotors. The design has been borrowed from [29]. The number of the vibromotor indicates the priority of activation.

acters, words and sentences namely for skin reading. Our contribution and novel aspect of this paper lie on proposing to equip users with interactions for skin reading.

INTERACTION CONCEPT

We design an interaction concept for textual vibrotactile skin reading, illustrated in Figure 1. The concept is based on a virtual fixation point metaphor. The fixation point represents the word that is currently being transmitted to the user. We will refer to it as the current word. While perceiving text/sentences, at whatever point in time, users have the possibility to request re-transmission of the current word. In this case, the system transmits the current word and transfers itself into the pausing state (corresponds to Word state in Figure 1) where no further text is transmitted until resumed. Let us assume that the user paused on the n-th word of a text. While on the pausing state, the user can repeat the current (n) word or navigate to the previous ($n-1$) word in the text. In this case, the fixation point shifts to the left in the text and the ($n-1$) word is transmitted and becomes the current word. At this point, the user can repeat the current word ($n-1$), regress to the previous one ($n-2$), or go to the next one (n). Hereby, the user navigates back an forth and scans the text. If the fixation point is at position n and the user navigates to the next word (beyond the point where it was paused), the system resumes and starts transmitting the rest of the words. Additionally, when the system is in the pause mode, the user can repeat particular characters of the fixated word. Furthermore, users can also change the speed of transmission which would proportionally change gaps between characters and words; and the activation time of each vibration motor (see Figure 4).

USER STUDY

To investigate our interaction concept and determine which of the interactions are useful for the user, we conducted a user study that combines participant training and testing of characters, words and sentences. An additional goal of the study was to investigate the word recognition process. However, the topic is out of the scope of this paper, and thus we will not discuss the results and findings concerning this investigation.

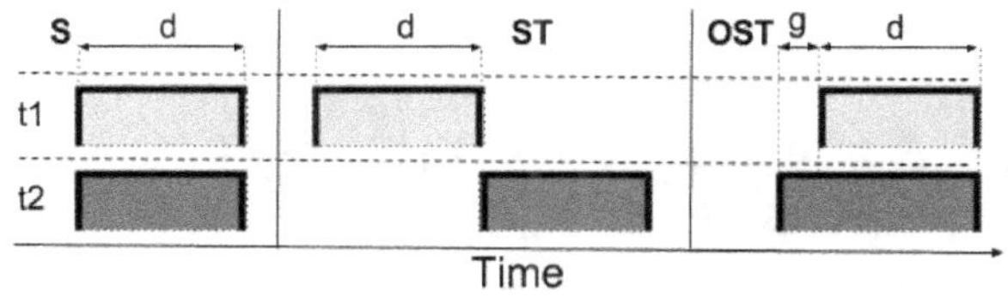

Figure 3. Pattern types composed of two vibromotors/locations: spatiotemporal (ST), overlapping spatiotemporal (OST), spatial (S). Base duration (d) represents the activation time of a vibromotor (t1 and t2). The gap between the activation of vibromotors is denoted by g.

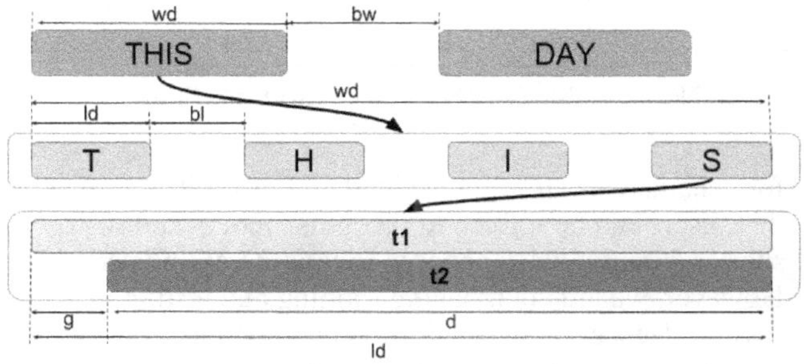

Figure 4. Stimulation process of characters, words and sentences. Base duration (d) represents the activation time of a vibromotor. Words in a sentence are transmitted in series separated by a gap (bw = 600 ms). Within words, characters are transmitted in series with a gap in between (bl = 200 ms). The characters are encoded using OST patterns where vibromotors are activated in sequence with a gap in between (g = 10ms).

Wearable Haptic Display Design

We use the glove-based design of Luzhnica et al [29] for the vibrotactile display. It contains six vibromotors placed on the back of the hand (see Figure 2). The vibromotors can be fitted in a fingerless glove, leaving the fingers free for interaction.

Vibrotactile Patterns and Encoding

Each character is encoded with one or two vibromotors using an OST (overlapped spatiotemporal) stimulation as introduced by Luzhnica and Veas. [28]. Figure 3 illustrates the details of OST and the differences with other stimulation forms. The activation of vibromotors is done in sequence, but they share most of the activation time. Moreover, the activation is prioritised based on the sensitivity of the finger as such prioritisation yields a higher accuracy of identification of locus [28]. Sensitivity order is assumed as reported on studies on the subject [9, 51, 19], suggesting that sensitivity decreases from the index finger towards the little finger: the index finger is more sensitive than the middle, ring, and pinky finger. The thumb has the lowest sensitivity [46]. For example, for a character encoded in index and pinky finger, the vibromotor on index finger would be activated first, and then after a gap, the vibromotor placed on the pinky finger. Figure 5 illustrates which vibromotors are used to encode each of the characters used in the study.

Figure 4 illustrates the technical details of the stimulation process of characters, words and sentences. Character encoding uses a base duration (d) of 200 ms and a 10 ms gap (g) between the activation of vibromotors. This means that the duration of a character (ld) is 200 ms for one vibromotor and 210 ms for two-vibromotor letters. When constructing words, a between letter gap (bl) of 200 ms is used to separate sequential letters. With such encoding, a word containing

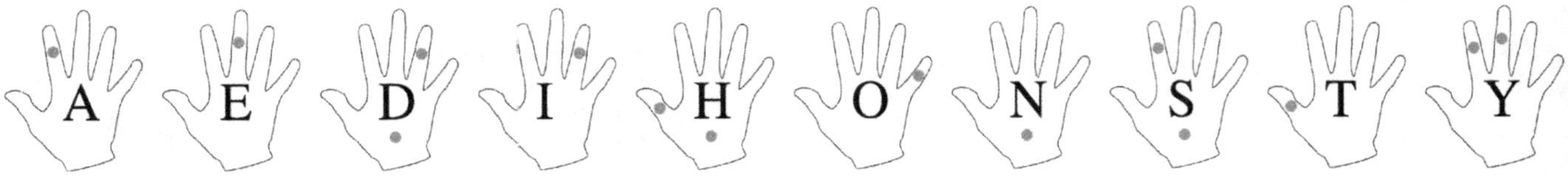

Figure 5. The encoding scheme of each character used during the study.

2-char	3-char	4-char	5-char
is	tea	easy	shiny
he	say	does	stand
it	hot	this	notes

Table 1. The list of words that are used during the experiment

four characters can be transmitted within 1400-1440 ms. Note that, users can be trained to recognise letters and words with shorter duration when exposed to longer training periods [29]. However, we aimed at having training and testing in a single session. Hence, we decided for longer durations. Additionally, sentence encoding uses a between word gap of 600 ms.

Characters

Similar patterns have been used to train users to recognise the entire English alphabet [29], and a wearable glove based layout capable of encoding 36 characters with only one or two vibromotors have been proposed [28], which demonstrate the capabilities of such wearable device for text reading. Nevertheless, in this study, we use only ten characters: A, E, I, O, T, N, S, H, D and Y. A small alphabet ensures a shorter period of training for characters and still enables us to create words and sentences for investigating interactions.

Words

With the chosen characters, we composed a list of 12 words, containing two to five characters. The words have been selected from the list of basic English words[1] and they will be used to train the user with words.

Sentences

We created a list of 29 sentences (see Table 2). But only 15 of them were stimulated during testing, whereas the rest are there just to create more choices. The goal of the sentences testing was to observe how participants interact with the system while reading a sentence and how well they perform.

He is the one, **She is the one**, **The tea is hot**, The sea is hot, **It is hot**, **He is hot**, She is hot, **Today is hot**, He says no, **She says no**, I say yes, **I say no**, **He says yes**, She says yes, I say yes, **This is easy**, It was easy, It is easy, **I hate this**, He hates this, **Hide this idea**, **It does stand**, This does stand, **It is done**, This is done, **This is shiny**, It is shiny, **It is noisy**, This is noisy.

Table 2. Sentences used during the experiment. All sentences (29) were presented to the user in a list to select from. Only the bold marked ones (15) are used to test the user. The rest of the sentences (14) are used as decoys to make the process more challenging.

Procedure

The entire study was organised in several blocks which we will refer to as rounds, each serving different purposes:

[1] `https://simple.wikipedia.org/wiki/Wikipedia:List_of_1000_basic_words`

Figure 6. A participant performing a round of sentence reinforcement

Character Training trained users to associate a symbol with a vibrotactile pattern. During this process, participants were stimulated with patterns representing a character, the character was displayed on the screen, and an audio spelling of the character is simultaneously played as shown in Figure 7. Such a simultaneous technique of tactile, auditory and visual stimulation has been demonstrated to be efficient [29].

Character Reinforcement. Participants were stimulated with a pattern and asked to input the character associated with it. After entering the answer, they were notified whether their input was correct and saw the correct answer (see Figure 7). This way they would learn from their mistakes. Participants were allowed to repeat the stimuli before answering.

Word Training exposed users to simultaneous stimulation of vibrotactile, auditory and visual stimuli all representing a word. The process was similar to character training, but instead of characters words were used. Words were transmitted as a series of characters (see Figure 4).

Word Reinforcement. This is similar to character reinforcement, but words are used instead. Participants are allowed repeat the stimuli. After stimulation, they were asked to select the answer from a list constructed with all the words shown in Table 1, plus 21 other words words including "No idea!". Participants were instructed to choose "No idea!" if they do not know what is stimulated. We also pointed out that for every stimulated word there are other similar words in the list and thus they should avoid guessing based on few characters. Upon entering the answer, participants were informed on the display what would have been the correct answer.

Words Testing: was similar to word reinforcement, but participants were not allowed to repeat the stimuli, and they were not notified the correct answer.

Sentence Reinforcement. The process was similar to the word reinforcement but used sentences instead of words. Participants were stimulated with a sentence and asked to select an answer from a list of sentences. As shown in Table 2, the list of choices contained 29 sentences plus the "No idea" op-

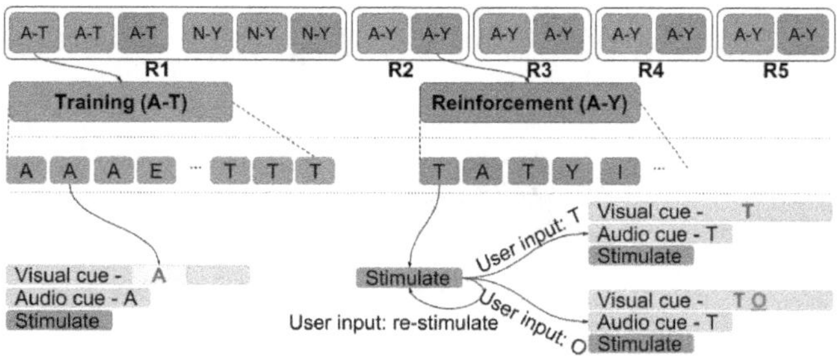

Figure 7. Character training and reinforcement process. Initially only five characters were introduced (A-T) then the next five letters (N-Y). For the the rest of letter training, all ten characters were used (A-Y). Colour coding: ● - train round, ● - reinforcement round.

tion. However, users were tested only in 15 sentences and the rest of them were used to make the process more challenging. Each sentence was composed of three to four words (see Table 2). The main purpose of sentence reinforcement was to study interactions during skin reading.

Participants went through five rounds of character training and reinforcement as shown in Figure 7. The first round was split into two short rounds, where only half of the characters are used in each (A-T and N-Y). This way participants were introduced first to five characters and then to the next five. The following four rounds used all ten characters. In every training round, a character was displayed three times whereas in the reinforcement rounds each character was tested twice.

Thereafter, participants went through a round of word testing followed by a round of reinforcement using words from Table 1. Then, users went through four rounds of word training each followed by a round of word reinforcement. Finally, users were subject to one round of word testing followed by one round of word reinforcement where they were exposed to a combination of words they trained on (from Table 1) and an equal number (balanced by word length) of words they did not trained on. To finish the study, participants were subject of one round of sentence reinforcement where each of 15 sentences (see Table 2) was tested once.

Interaction

During the sentence reinforcement rounds, participants could use the interaction concept presented in Figure 1. They, could repeat the current word by using the keyboard space key, navigate words using left and right arrow keys, change transmission speed by using up and down arrow keys. They could choose to re-stimulate only a particular letter by pressing a number from 1-9, which would re-stimulate the n-th letter of the current word. Additionally, participants were able to repeat the entire sentence by pressing S. During word reinforcement rounds, participants were also able to repeat the entire word or particular characters of it. Similarly, during the character reinforcement, participants could repeat the character.

Data Collection

First, all user responses and interactions during testing and reinforcement rounds were logged. Additionally, at the end of the session, users filled a questionnaire asking questions about how they would use such a wearable device on a daily basis. Initially, they were asked to rate whether they find the interactions for skin reading as: (i) Necessary, (ii) Optional or (iii) Not useful. Also, for each available interaction, users were asked to rate how often they think they would use it by selecting one of the available choices:

1. Continuously - every couple of seconds or minutes
2. Often - every couple of hours
3. Not very often - every couple of days or weeks
4. Rarely - few times only, and
5. Never.

Furthermore, we proposed three possible modes of interaction:

1. Gesture-based: the user uses hand gestures to interact,
2. Smartphone-based: an application in the user's smartphone is used to interact, and
3. Physical buttons based: physical buttons would be added to the vibrotactile glove for interaction.

Participants were asked to rate (0-10) how suitable each of the proposed modality would be for interactions with the wearable display. Furthermore, they were asked to choose one modality they would use for interactions/commands that they would use more often and one for the interactions they would use rarely.

Apparatus

Our device consisted of an Arduino Due board which controls $3.4mm$ vibrotactile motors of type ROB-08449 (Voltage range: $2.3V \sim 3.6V$; Amplitude vibration: $0.8G$).

Participants

Twenty-two (22) individuals (12 male and 10 female) aged between 17 and 38 (M=26.7, STD=5.5) years old participated in this study. The overall study took approximately 90 minutes. Only one of them was left-handed. All of them used the left hand for stimulation and the right to interact with the computer as depicted in Figure 6. One participant, for personal time constraint reasons, completed the character and word rounds but did not continue with sentence reinforcement round.

Results

Let us define four common variables: accuracy, repetition, total duration. Accuracy will be defined as a binary variable set to be one if the user's answer is correct. Repetition describes how many times a user repeated the stimulation (character, word or sentence) within a reinforcement round. The total duration represents the entire duration from the time stimulation was first initiated by the system until the user responded, including repetitions. Additionally, we define an interaction to be a repetition of any kind. E.g. during sentence reinforcement round, each repetition such as: current word, previous word, next word, a particular letter of the current word or the entire sentence is considered to be an interaction. Although, we will provide a brief overview of performance to give an impression of users training level prior to sentence reading, we will mostly focus on interactions during sentence reinforcement round as the reading performance is out of the scope of this paper.

Performance

Each character reinforcement round collected 20 probes (2 × 10 characters) for each user. Table 3 presents the results

Round	Accuracy	Total Duration (s)	Repetitions
1a	0.98 (0.15)	3.29 (4.03)	0.22 (0.60)
1b	0.82 (0.38)	5.06 (8.41)	0.57 (1.28)
2	0.86 (0.25)	5.57 (9.58)	0.72 (1.52)
3	0.95 (0.23)	5.58 (23.8)	0.72 (1.81)
4	0.95 (0.22)	4.39 (6.56)	0.63 (1.37)
5	0.95 (0.22)	3.33 (5.58)	0.39 (0.90)

Table 3. Results of character reinforcement rounds. Note that we consider the first two rounds (1a and 1b) as two parts of round one as each of them contained only half the characters. This table shows the correct recognition rate (accuracy), average total duration, average duration and average repetition rate.

Round Type	Accuracy	Total Duration (s)	Repetitions
With Repetition	0.81 (0.39)	12.41 (12.27)	2.32 (4.28)
No Repetition	0.55 (0.50)	9.34 (8.45)	0.0 (0.0)

Table 4. Results of word recognition in the last reinforcement (with repetitions) and testing (no repetitions) rounds.

of character recognition, including the average accuracy, repetition, duration and total duration. By the third round, participants could already recall characters with a high accuracy (M=95%). While on the next two rounds the accuracy does not improve, there is an improvement in repetition and duration which could be interpreted as them being more confident.

For the word recognition, we focus on the last round of reinforcement and testing as we consider them to be the end result of the word training process. Note that, in the reinforcement round users are allowed to repeat word or letters whereas in the testing repetitions are not allowed. In each of the two rounds, 24 probes were collected for each user. The recognition accuracy, total duration and repetition rate are presented in Table 4. Additionally, the user recognition accuracy (averaged per user) is shown in the Figure 8. Both Table 4 and Figure 8 reveal that when repetitions are allowed, participants achieve a higher accuracy. Furthermore, a chi squared test reveals that participants achieve a significant higher accuracy ($M = 0.81, STD = 0.39$) in the round where they can perform repetitions compared to the round where they are not allowed to repeat ($M = 0.55, STD = 0.5$); $\chi^2(2, 1056) = 81.67, p = 0.0$.

The sentence recognition round collected 15 probes for each user. The average accuracy, number of interactions, duration and total duration for sentence recognition are presented in Table 5. On average, users needed 37.29 seconds to recognise sentences with an accuracy of 82%.

Interactions

First, we analyse the interactions in the last round of word reinforcement. On average participants performed 2.32 (SD=4.28) interactions for each word. From the interactions, participants repeated 67% of words completely (at least once) whereas they repeated one or more single characters only in 6.8% of the words. Table 5 shows that participants needed on average needed 7.14 interactions to recognise sentences. Moreover, the histogram in Figure 11 shows that the vast majority of users needed a relatively low number of interactions. Eleven users needed on average five or fewer interactions per sentence but some users performed even over 20 interactions per sentence.

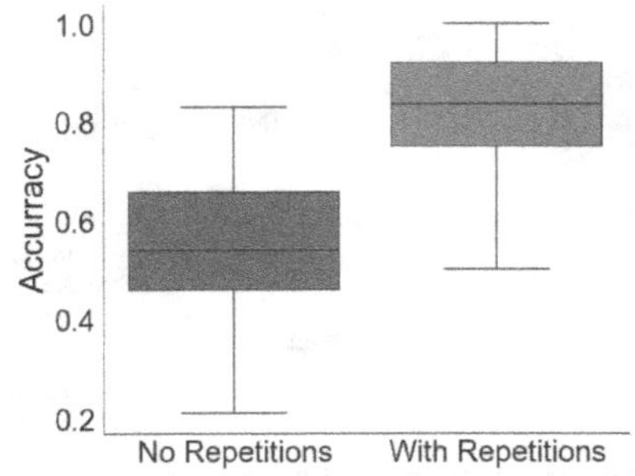

Figure 8. Averaged user accuracy for the last reinforcement (with repetitions) and testing rounds (without repetitions).

Generally, word repetition was used (at least once) in 82.8% of the sentences, character repetition in 6.3% of them and sentences were repeated entirely in 21.2% cases. Within word interactions, 62.8% of them were repetition of current word, 25.6% of them were repetition of the previous word and only 11.6% were a repetition of next word in the sentence.

Figure 9 shows the overall state transitions probabilities between interactions during sentence reading. The chart is constructed from the interaction data of the sentence reinforcement rounds. The transition plot in Figure 10 shows the state transitions probabilities for the first ten iterations of interactions. The start state represents the time point when the sentence is fully transmitted the first time. The finish state represents the user providing the answer for sentence recognition.

The most likely interaction at the start is repeating the current word (probability = 0.57). Participants were also likely to start with previous word interaction (0.23) which could be interpreted as they already understood the current word. Precipitants were also likely to start with repeating the entire sentence (0.17). After a current word repetition, participants were most likely to continue with another current word repetition (0.6), meaning that they did not understand the word from the last repetition. They were also fairly likely to continue with previous word (0.16) or next word repetitions (0.1). They were quite likely to provide the answer (0.10). After a previous word repetition, participants were most likely to continue with another previous word repetition (0.38), meaning that they understood the word that was repeated and they were scanning the sentence backwards. They were also highly likely to continue with current word repetition (0.36), in cases where they did not understand the repeated word. On the other hand, they were relatively less likely to continue with a next word interaction (0.1). They were quite likely to provide the answer (0.16), meaning that they finished backwards scanning. After the next word repetition, participants were most likely to use a current word repetition (0.48) in the case where the did not understand the repeated word. They were also likely to use the next word interaction (0.18) again; scanning forward the sentence, or use the previous word interaction (0.1). They were quite likely to provide the answer (0.22), meaning that they finished forward scanning.

After the entire sentence repetition, users were most likely to continue with another sentence repetition (0.47), which could be interpreted as some users were simply repeating the

Accuracy	Interactions	Total Duration (s)
0.82 (0.38)	7.14 (7.59)	37.29 (27.04)

Table 5. Averaged sentence recognition results (M, STD).

sentence over and over until they were able to understand it completely. Such an interaction was relatively less but still likely followed by current word repetition (0.13) or previous word repetition (0.09). Users also were likely (0.3) to provide an answer. A similar behaviour pattern occurs after character repetition. Users were most likely (0.9) to repeat character again as users who used this interaction were repeating different letters of the current word.

Only five users adjusted the transmission speed during sentence recognition. Two of them set it to a higher than the default speed whereas three of them did slow it down.

Additionally, we explored the relationship between sentence recognition accuracy and the number of interactions. Figure 11 shows that there is a positive Pearson correlation between the average recognition accuracy and the average number of interactions, meaning that users that interacted more, also recognised sentences more accurately; $r = 0.47, p = 0.03$.

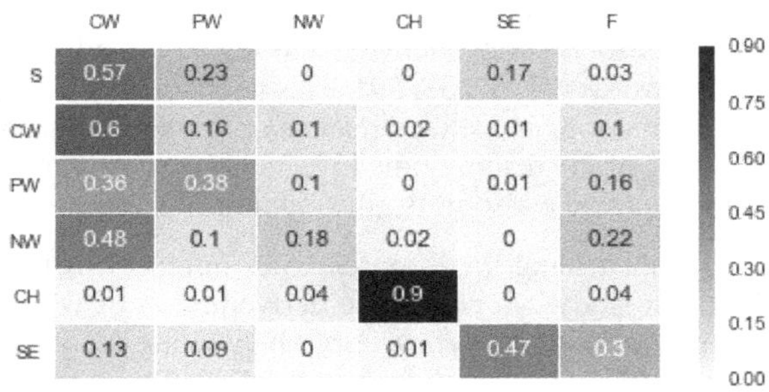

Figure 9. State transitions probabilities between interactions for sentence reading constructed from the sentence reinforcement round. Interaction states: S -start, CW - current word, PW -previous word, NW - next word, C - character, SE - sentence, F- finish.

Questionnaire

On the question of how useful they found the interaction concept when performing sentence reading, 76% (16) of users rated it as "Necessary", 24% (5) of them rated it as "Optional" and no user rated it as "Not useful". When asked why users thought such an interaction was optional, they all argued that with a proper amount of training they would get proficient and there would not be a need for such interaction.

User ratings on how frequent they think each of the commands/interactions they would use are presented in Figure 12. For all word repetition interactions: repeat the current word, previous word, and next word, the vast majority of participants thought that they would use them continuously (every couple of seconds or minutes). Quite contrary, for adjusting the speed the majority if users think that they would rarely use. For repeating the n-th character of the current word, there is some divergence. While most of the users think that they would never use it, two users think they would use it continuously, and another four think they would use it often.

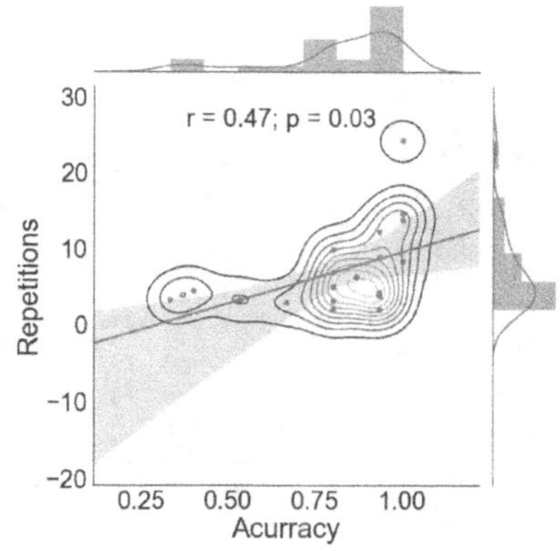

Figure 11. The relation between average sentence recognition accuracy and the average number of interaction. The bar plots on the top and on the side represent histograms and calculated the univariate distribution of the variable in the given axis. The contours represent the multivariate distribution of both variables. The straight line and the shades around it represent the fitted regression and its confidence. The Pearson correlation index and the confidence value are annotated as r and p.

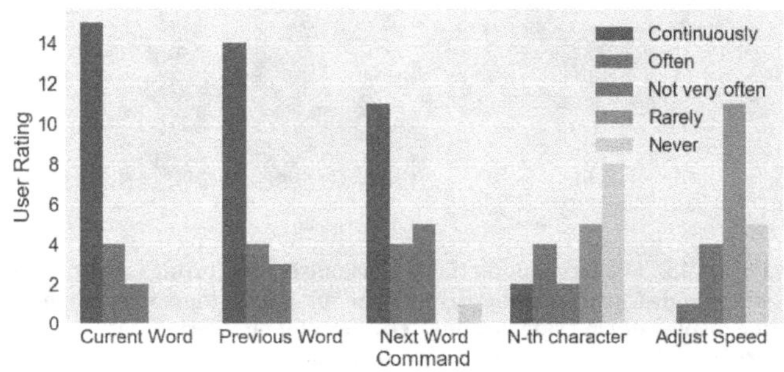

Figure 12. User ratings on how frequent they think they would use each of the interactions for text reading through a vibrotactile display.

User ratings on how suitable the proposed modalities of interaction would be for skin reading application are presented in Figure 13. Gesture interaction received the highest rating ($M = 7.9, STD = 1.7$). But, a paired t-test reveals that the difference with physical buttons interaction ($M = 6.57, STD = 2.99$) is not significant ; $t(42) = 1.72, p = 0.101$. On the other hand users rated gesture interaction ($M = 7.9, STD = 1.7$) significantly higher than interaction using a smart phone ($M = 4.76, STD = 2.64$); $t(42) = 4.1, p = 0.001$[2]. Additionally, when users were asked to choose one preferred modality of interaction for commands they would regularly and for ones they would rarely use, users mainly prefer gesture-based interaction for regular interactions and smartphone-based interaction for rarely used interactions (see Figure 13).

Discussion

Our study was designed to investigate and identify useful interactions for skin reading with a wearable vibrotactile display. The evidence from all sources such as user performance, interaction behaviour and questionnaire point out that when performing skin reading, users benefit from means of interactions with the vibrotactile display. First, the majority (76%) of the users explicitly expressed in the questionnaire that they

[2]The significance level is considered $\alpha = 0.025$ according to Bonferroni correction for two comparisons

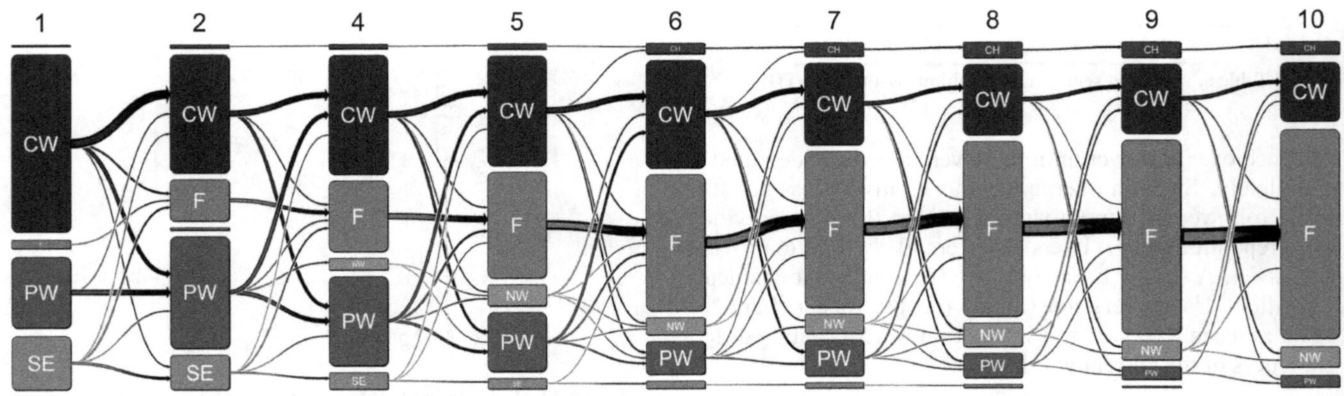

Figure 10. State transitions diagram between interactions for the first ten interaction during the sentence reading. Interaction states: S -start, CW - current word, PW -previous word, NW - next word, C - character, SE - sentence, F- finish. The size of the bar represents the probability of being in that state for the given interaction whereas the width of the arrow represents the probability of the state transition.

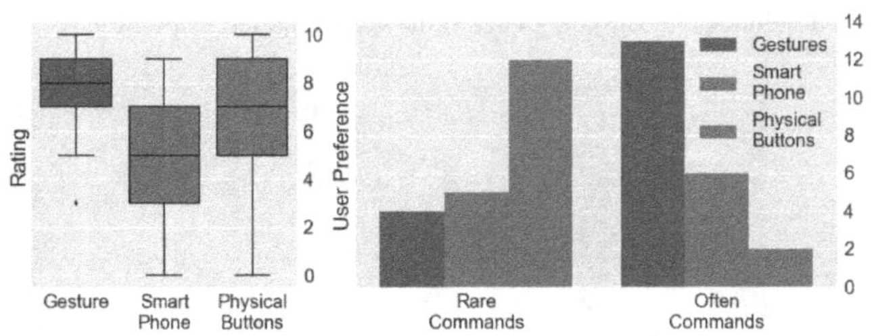

Figure 13. The box plot on the left visualises user ratings (0-10) on how suitable different modalities would be for interactions with a vibrotactile display during skin reading. The bar plot on the right visualises user preferences choices on which modality would be more useful for interactions/commands that they would use very often (at least every couple of hours) versus the interactions they would use rarely.

think having interactions similar to our experiment is necessary for skin reading. While some users (24%) expressed that when proficient, they would not need interactions, none of the believed that such interactions were not useful at all.

The necessity for interactions is also expressed in users' performance during sentence and words recognition. Interactions had a positive effect on the recognition accuracy. Participants performed significantly better (see Figure 8) in the word recognition rounds where repetition is allowed. Additionally, participants who on average performed more interactions in sentence recognition, achieved a better accuracy (see Figure 11).

Interaction usage also demonstrates that the interactions were necessary. Participants, on the last round of word recognition with repetition, on average needed 2.32 (SD=4.28) interactions for each word. Furthermore, they used on average 7.14 interactions for each sentence during sentence recognition.

As participants had no prior experience in skin reading, our study shows that at least for novice users, interactions are crucial. Users with minimal training can start perceiving words and phrases and would be able to understand them if the navigation interactions are at their disposal. Thereby, users do not need to become proficient before they can start using such a wearable device. On the other hand, as users' skin reading skills increase, they would presumably need fewer interactions. They might learn to recognise entire words as units similar to visual reading [53, 45, 11, 40, 5]. Nevertheless, that does not invalidate the need for interactions. First, users might need to repeat certain words from time to time as result of attention breaks or simply due to misperception. In both visual and Braille reading such interactions occur very often even if readers are not aware of it as it occurs unconsciously and naturally. Readers jump backwards to revisit already visited letters and words [22, 37, 38, 39]. This phenomenon is known as back regression, and skilled readers make regressions back in $10 - 15\%$ of the reading time [37, 38, 39]. Such regression is common practice also in Braille reading [30, 20].

Besides emphasising the importance of interactions in skin reading, our study can be used to derive details of which interactions are most important. Both behaviour analysis and questionnaire analysis confirm that word repetition, and navigation interactions are critical. Participants used word interaction in 82% of sentences and the vast majority of users were convinced that such interactions would constantly be used. Repeating the n-th character of a word was rated as unnecessary by users and was mostly irrelevant to sentence recognition. A closer look at the usage of this interaction reveals that it was only used by seven participants. One participant used it in every sentence; one user used it only in two sentences whereas five users used it only in one sentence. Thus, only one user used character repetitions regularly in sentence recognition, whereas the rest did try to use them in one or two sentences to explore how well that would work but did not continue afterwards with the rest of the sentences. Adjusting the speed seems not to be frequently used. It was used only by five participants. Participants set the speed they were comfortable with and used it for the rest of the sentence recognition. This was also mirrored in the questionnaire where most of the participants expressed that they would only use it a few times during the lifetime of such device. Most of the participants pointed out that they would use it in accordance with the progress of their skin reading skill.

Interestingly and contrary to expectations, the repetition of the entire sentence was used by some users. Although, they were a small number, yet we did not expect any user to rely on it.

Our prior expectation was that at first, users might be tempted to try it, but they would realise that it is challenging with their level of training to perceive the entire sentence at once. Such a scenario did occur with five users, where they used it only in four sentences or less. As shown in the Figure 10, at the first, second or third interactions some users switch to word-based interactions. Initially, they were curious and tried it for one or two iterations (see Figure 10), but then realised it was difficult and switched to other interactions. However, there were users who persisted using sentence repeats. Three users relied on this interaction almost entirely (used in more than 12 sentences), and two others used it moderately (in 7-9 sentences). Figure 10 shows that some participants repeatedly used this interaction until they provided an answer. Although it was interesting to provide such interaction in our study and explore user behaviour, only a small number of users used them. Moreover, in a real-world scenario, where text contains multiple sentences, and they are much longer, repeating the entire text might not very be useful as it does not scale.

The questionnaire reveals that the preferred modality for constantly used interaction would be gesture-based, whereas participants would prefer a settings smartphone application for rarely used interactions (adjusting the speed). For the constantly used interaction, one would need to provide a gesture-based system that would support the basic interactions: repeat the current word, go to previous word (and transmit it) and go to next word. Such a system would be a simplified version of the interaction system we initially designed (see Figure 1). Stopping and resuming to transmit the rest of the text could be automatically achieved using the current word and next word interaction as explained in Section Interaction Concept.

GESTURE BASED INTERACTION

Besides user preferences, from the engineering, designing and manufacturing perspective, a gesture-based interaction would be a perfect fit for a glove-based vibrotactile wearable display as the same glove could be equipped with sensing capabilities to enable gesture recognition. In this section, we map our interactions to hand gesture interactions and explore what sensors would we need to recognise them.

Gesture Mapping

Our study concluded that only the interactions related to word navigation are essential for skin reading. Here we map each of them to a hand-based gesture. The used gestures should be easy to remember, fast to perform, and contain simple movements so that they can be recognised with a minimal set of sensors. Thus, we map the previous word interaction to swiping left gesture and next word interaction to swiping right. The mapping is natural, as it corresponds to movement of focus point within the sentence. Additionally, the interactions are easy to perform and considered in the research community as natural hand gestures [42, 15, 26] meaning that most users would be familiar with them. As for current word interaction, we map it to swipe up gesture as it shares the simplicity and popularity with the other selected gestures.

Gesture Recognition

Gesture recognition has been a subject of many researchers. At a core abstract level, the main approaches for gesture recognition has been based on either environmental sensors such as: camera [8, 6, 12, 8, 1, 18], radar signals [10, 25] wifi [23, 36], etc... or hand/body-worn sensors such as : motion sensors, flexion and pressure sensors [26, 32, 56, 33, 57]. Even though each of them has its advantages and disadvantages, for our specific use case, wearable based sensors approach is a more suitable solution. First, it is not bound to the location (where sensors are placed) and second, adding the sensors to the same wearable glove, makes the setup much more convenient.

Many gesture recognition systems using wearable sensor have been proposed over the years, most of them rely on either hand worn sensors [26, 32, 56, 33, 57] or wrist-based sensors [17, 50, 55, 58]. For recognizing gestures, typically statistical and machine learning approaches such as neural networks [32, 56], support vector machines [26], linear discriminant analysis (LDA) [26, 15], logistic regression [26, 58], decision trees [58], etc.. have been employed.

Our gesture recognition system uses an existing framework and dataset of Luzhnica et al. [26]. The authors, collected data from 18 participants performing 31 gestures using a custom made data glove, where each participant performed each gesture 5-10 times. The data were annotated manually. Their data glove was equipped with seven inertial measurement units (IMU), one on each finger, one on the back of the palm and one on the wrist. Additionally, the glove was equipped with 13 bend sensors to cover main finger joint and wrist movement; and also five pressure sensors on each fingertip. The recording frequency of data glove was 85Hz (85 frames per second). For their recognition system, the authors used a sliding window approach upon which they extracted time domain features such as minimum, maximum, range, average, standard deviation and signal energy and time domain features such as Fast Fourier Transform for every sliding window. The authors evaluated different parameters for sliding window and different machine learning algorithms. They concluded that using LDA for dimensional reduction and then logistic regression for classification yielded the best results, where they achieved a f_1 score accuracy of 98.5%.

For our use case, we will use the same approach in data processing, algorithm, training and evaluation procedure and thus we will skip some of the extensive details (c.f., [26]). From the dataset provided by the authors [26], we use only three (swipe left, right and up) gestures and thus also explore what sensors we would need to correctly identify the given gestures. More precisely, we explore two particular sensors from their set: IMU on the back of the and the IMU on the wrist. Such motion sensors should be sufficient to capture motion characteristics of our gestures.

Considering that we reduce the number of gesture classes to three, the number of windows with rest class is very imbalanced. The rest class represents the data where the user is not performing any gesture such as: not moving or performing arbitrary movements. Thus we reduce the number of windows with rest class by randomly sampling a portion (5%) of them.

	Wrist				Palm			
	I	L	R	U	I	L	R	U
I	**385**	4	2	2	**386**	3	1	2
L	5	**61**	2	0	1	**68**	0	0
R	2	3	**54**	0	2	0	**57**	0
U	0	0	0	**60**	0	0	0	**60**

Table 6. Confusion matrix for classification in the test set using IMU on the wrist (left) and IMU on back of the hand (right). Classes: I - rest, L - swipe left, R - swipe right, U - swipe up.

In total, the entire resulting dataset (both training and test) contains 2959 windows. We use LDA for dimensional reduction and logistic regression for classification trained on the training set which represents the 80% the data. The test set (the rest 20% the data) will be used to report on performance.

With only the IMU on back of the hand, our classifier achieves a f_1 score accuracy of 98.4% on the test set. Using only the IMU on the wrist results in an accuracy of 96.5%.

Lessons Learnt

Overall using a single motion sensor (IMU) one would be able to recognise the necessary gesture-based interactions with a very high accuracy. The gestures can be better recognised by placing the sensor on the back of the hand (98.4%) as opposed to placing on the wrist (96.5%). The confusion matrix presented on Table 6 reveals that when using only the IMU on the wrist, there are some more misclassifications for classes left, right and the rest. Such misclassifications are less evident when using the IMU on the back of the hand. This could be explained by the fact that such gestures involve physical flexion and extension of the wrist which can easily be captured by the sensor on the hand but not on the wrist.

However, besides the accuracy, there are design and practical implications that might influence the decision of sensor location. First, there is a vibromotor located on the back of the hand of our vibrotactile wearable glove (see Table 2), which is approximately located nearby the IMU on the data glove used to record the data [26]. Having both IMU and a vibromotor nearby might introduce noise in measurements when the vibromotor is active. A possible overcome could be achieved by shifting in opposite direction (left and right) to maximise the space in between. Alternatively, one could move the IMU on the palm side of the hand. On the other hand, a wrist-worn device makes it impossible to wear it along watches or wristbands. However, considering that a lot of users might already possess smart watches or wristbands equipped with a motion sensor, the motion data from their existing watch or wristband could be used to classify the required hand gestures. This would reduce both costs and power consumption of the wearable vibrotactile display.

LIMITATIONS AND FUTURE WORK

One limitation of our interaction system is that it deals only with text reading and not text comprehension, and thus it does not offer means of navigation beyond neighbouring words. For instance, while reading, users might want to revisit text 3-4 sentences backwards to better comprehend the text. Although, jumping larger portions of the text such as sentences could be provided analogously to our current interactions. Such interaction could be mapped to rotation-based gestures like hand pronation and supination which could be easily be recognised using the motion sensors we proposed. For that, we would need to train users for longer periods so that they would be able to perceive and understand larger messages in the first place. Furthermore, we do not evaluate whether hand motion while performing the gesture could affect the ability of the user to perceive information during skin reading. Such effects need to be studied. If that were the case, a less convenient solution would be to use one hand for skin reading and the other one for interaction. We will consider both limitations mentioned above for conducting additional studies in the future.

CONCLUSION

This paper investigates interactions for skin reading using a wearable vibrotactile display. Initially, we designed an interaction concept for skin reading. We conducted a formative study with 22 users to evaluate our concept during word and sentence reading with a six-channel wearable vibrotactile display. Participants were trained to recognise ten characters, trained on words and then tested on word and sentence recognition, during which they were able to use the designed interactions. Furthermore, participants filled a questionnaire expressing their opinion about the interaction concept in general, different interactions within it and preferred modality of interaction.

The results of our study and analysis of questionnaire indicated that interactions are beneficial for skin reading. Furthermore, this study shaped our interaction concept by characterising interactions like character repetition as not necessary and transmission speed adjustment as less important. As a result, our end concept contains three main interactions all of them providing word repetition and navigation within the sentence. For such interactions, users preferred gesture-based interaction as an interaction modality. Following such a preference, we mapped our interactions to swipe-based hand gestures. Furthermore, we used motion sensors on the back of the hand and wrist to examine how well such gesture-based interactions would be recognisable using machine learning algorithms. Our results showed that a single motion sensor either on the wrist or hand is sufficient to recognise our gesture-based interactions the with a high accuracy. Also, hand (98.4%) is a better choice for locating the sensor compared to wrist (96.5%) in terms of gesture recognition accuracy. Such a sensor could be incorporated into the same wearable glove providing one single solution for both skin reading and interaction. Thus, our contribution could serve as a guideline for designers and manufactures of such wearable vibrotactile displays.

ACKNOWLEDGMENTS

This work was funded by MoreGrasp (H2020-ICT-2014-1 643955). The Know-Center is funded within the Austrian COMET Program - Competence Centers for Excellent Technologies - under the auspices of the Austrian Federal Ministry of Transport, Innovation and Technology, the Austrian Federal Ministry of Economy, Family and Youth and by the State of Styria. COMET is managed by the Austrian Research Promotion Agency FFG.

REFERENCES

1. Henrik Birk, Thomas B. Moeslund, and Claus B. Madsen. 1997. Real-Time Recognition of Hand Alphabet Gestures Using Principal Component Analysis. In *In 10th Scandinavian Conference on Image Analysis*.
2. J. C. Bliss, M. H. Katcher, C. H. Rogers, and R. P. Shepard. 1970. Optical-to-Tactile Image Conversion for the Blind. *IEEE Transactions on Man-Machine Systems* 11, 1 (March 1970), 58–65. DOI: http://dx.doi.org/10.1109/TMMS.1970.299963
3. Łukasz Bola, Katarzyna Siuda-Krzywicka, Małgorzata Paplińska, Ewa Sumera, Paweł Hańczur, and Marcin Szwed Szwed. 2016. Braille in the sighted: Teaching tactile reading to sighted adults. *PLoS ONE* (2016). DOI: http://dx.doi.org/10.1371/journal.pone.0155394
4. Stephen Brewster and Lorna M. Brown. 2004. Tactons: Structured Tactile Messages for Non-visual Information Display. In *Proceedings of the Fifth Conference on Australasian User Interface (AUIC)*. Australian Computer Society, Inc., Darlinghurst, Australia, Australia, 15–23. http://dl.acm.org/citation.cfm?id=976310.976313
5. James McKeen Cattel. 1886. The Time Taken up by Cerebral Operations. *Mind* os-XI, 42 (1886), 220–242. DOI:http://dx.doi.org/10.1093/mind/os-XI.42.220
6. Qing Chen, Nicolas D. Georganas, and E.M. Petriu. 2007. Real-time Vision-based Hand Gesture Recognition Using Haar-like Features. In *Instrumentation and Measurement Technology Conference Proceedings, 2007. IMTC 2007. IEEE*. 1–6. DOI: http://dx.doi.org/10.1109/IMTC.2007.379068
7. Meredyth Daneman. 1988. How reading braille is both like and unlike reading print. *Memory & Cognition* 16, 6 (01 Nov 1988), 497–504. DOI: http://dx.doi.org/10.3758/BF03197051
8. N.H. Dardas and Nicolas D. Georganas. 2011. Real-Time Hand Gesture Detection and Recognition Using Bag-of-Features and Support Vector Machine Techniques. *Instrumentation and Measurement, IEEE Transactions on* 60, 11 (Nov 2011), 3592–3607. DOI: http://dx.doi.org/10.1109/TIM.2011.2161140
9. Robert O. Duncan and Geoffrey M. Boynton. 2007. Tactile Hyperacuity Thresholds Correlate with Finger Maps in Primary Somatosensory Cortex (S1). *Cerebral Cortex* 17, 12 (2007), 2878. DOI: http://dx.doi.org/10.1093/cercor/bhm015
10. T. Fan, C. Ma, Z. Gu, Q. Lv, J. Chen, D. Ye, J. Huangfu, Y. Sun, C. Li, and L. Ran. 2016. Wireless Hand Gesture Recognition Based on Continuous-Wave Doppler Radar Sensors. *IEEE Transactions on Microwave Theory and Techniques* 64, 11 (Nov 2016), 4012–4020. DOI: http://dx.doi.org/10.1109/TMTT.2016.2610427
11. Dennis F. Fisher. 1975. Reading and visual search. *Memory & Cognition* 3, 2 (01 Mar 1975), 188–196. DOI: http://dx.doi.org/10.3758/BF03212897
12. Pragati Garg, Naveen Aggarwal, and Sanjeev Sofat. 2009. Vision based hand gesture recognition. *World Academy of Science, Engineering and Technology* 49, 1 (2009), 972–977.
13. Robert H Gault. 1924. Progress in experiments on tactual interpretation of oral speech. *The Journal of Abnormal Psychology and Social Psychology* 19, 2 (1924), 155.
14. Frank A. Geldard. 1957. Adventures in tactile literacy. *American Psychologist* 12, 3 (1957), 115–124.
15. Przemys Glomb, Michal Romaszewski, Sebastian Opozda, and Arkadiusz Sochan. 2012. Choosing and Modeling the Hand Gesture Database for a Natural User Interface. In *Proceedings of the 9th International Conference on Gesture and Sign Language in Human-Computer Interaction and Embodied Communication (GW'11)*. Springer-Verlag, Berlin, Heidelberg, 24–35. DOI: http://dx.doi.org/10.1007/978-3-642-34182-3_3
16. Eric Gunther. 2001. *Skinscape: A tool for composition in the tactile modality*. Ph.D. Dissertation. Massachusetts Institute of Technology.
17. Jaehyun Han, Sunggeun Ahn, and Geehyuk Lee. 2015. Transture: Continuing a Touch Gesture on a Small Screen into the Air. In *Proceedings of the 33rd Annual ACM Conference Extended Abstracts on Human Factors in Computing Systems (CHI EA '15)*. ACM, New York, NY, USA, 1295–1300. DOI: http://dx.doi.org/10.1145/2702613.2732849
18. Mokhtar M Hasan and Pramod K Mishra. 2012. Hand gesture modeling and recognition using geometric features: a review. *Canadian Journal on Image Processing and Computer Vision* 3, 1 (2012), 12–26.
19. Eve E. Hoggan, Sohail Anwar, and Stephen A. Brewster. 2007. *Mobile Multi-actuator Tactile Displays*. 22–33 pages. DOI: http://dx.doi.org/10.1007/978-3-540-76702-2_4
20. Barry Hughes, Arend W.A. Van Gemmert, and George E. Stelmach. 2011. Linguistic and perceptual-motor contributions to the kinematic properties of the braille reading finger. *Human Movement Science* 30, 4 (2011), 711 – 730. DOI:http://dx.doi.org/https://doi.org/10.1016/j.humov.2010.05.005 Special Issue: Progress in Graphonomics: A Perceptual Motor Skill Perspective.
21. Jacob H. Kirman. 1974. Tactile perception of computer-derived formant patterns from voiced speech. *The Journal of the Acoustical Society of America* 55, 1 (1974).
22. Kevin Larson. 2004. The Science of Word Recognition. *Advanced Reading Technology, Microsoft Corporation* (July 2004). https://www.microsoft.com/typography/ctfonts/WordRecognition.aspx

23. Hong Li, Wei Yang, Jianxin Wang, Yang Xu, and Liusheng Huang. 2016. WiFinger: Talk to Your Smart Devices with Finger-grained Gesture. In *Proceedings of the 2016 ACM International Joint Conference on Pervasive and Ubiquitous Computing (UbiComp '16)*. ACM, New York, NY, USA, 250–261. DOI: http://dx.doi.org/10.1145/2971648.2971738

24. Yi-Chi Liao, Yi-Ling Chen, Jo-Yu Lo, Rong-Hao Liang, Liwei Chan, and Bing-Yu Chen. 2016. EdgeVib: Effective Alphanumeric Character Output Using a Wrist-Worn Tactile Display. In *Proceedings of the 29th Annual Symposium on User Interface Software and Technology (UIST '16)*. ACM, New York, NY, USA, 595–601. DOI: http://dx.doi.org/10.1145/2984511.2984522

25. Jaime Lien, Nicholas Gillian, M. Emre Karagozler, Patrick Amihood, Carsten Schwesig, Erik Olson, Hakim Raja, and Ivan Poupyrev. 2016. Soli: Ubiquitous Gesture Sensing with Millimeter Wave Radar. *ACM Trans. Graph.* 35, 4, Article 142 (July 2016), 19 pages. DOI: http://dx.doi.org/10.1145/2897824.2925953

26. G. Luzhnica, J. Simon, E. Lex, and V. Pammer. 2016. A sliding window approach to natural hand gesture recognition using a custom data glove. In *2016 IEEE Symposium on 3D User Interfaces (3DUI)*. 81–90. DOI: http://dx.doi.org/10.1109/3DUI.2016.7460035

27. Granit Luzhnica, Sebastian Stein, Eduardo Veas, Viktoria Pammer, John Williamson, and Roderick Murray Smith. 2017. Personalising Vibrotactile Displays Through Perceptual Sensitivity Adjustment. In *Proceedings of the 2017 ACM International Symposium on Wearable Computers (ISWC '17)*. ACM, New York, NY, USA, 66–73. DOI:http://dx.doi.org/10.1145/3123021.3123029

28. Granit Luzhnica and Eduardo Veas. 2017. Vibrotactile Patterns using Sensitivity Prioritisation. In *Proceedings of the 2017 ACM International Symposium on Wearable Computers (ISWC '17)*. ACM, New York, NY, USA, 148–155. DOI: http://dx.doi.org/10.1145/3123021.3123032

29. Granit Luzhnica, Eduardo Veas, and Viktoria Pammer. 2016. Skin Reading: Encoding Text in a 6-channel Haptic Display. In *Proceedings of the 2016 ACM International Symposium on Wearable Computers (ISWC '16)*. ACM, New York, NY, USA, 148–155. DOI: http://dx.doi.org/10.1145/2971763.2971769

30. Susanna Millar. 2003. *Reading by touch*. Routledge.

31. Susanna Millar. 2004. *Reading by Touch in Blind Children and Adults*. Springer Netherlands, Dordrecht, 437–457. DOI: http://dx.doi.org/10.1007/978-94-017-1731-1_23

32. Kouichi Murakami and Hitomi Taguchi. 1991. Gesture Recognition Using Recurrent Neural Networks. In *Proceedings of the SIGCHI Conference on Human Factors in Computing Systems (CHI '91)*. ACM, New York, NY, USA, 237–242. DOI: http://dx.doi.org/10.1145/108844.108900

33. P. Neto, D. Pereira, J. Norberto Pires, and A.P. Moreira. 2013. Real-time and continuous hand gesture spotting: An approach based on artificial neural networks. In *Robotics and Automation (ICRA), 2013 IEEE International Conference on*. 178–183. DOI: http://dx.doi.org/10.1109/ICRA.2013.6630573

34. Hugo Nicolau, João Guerreiro, Tiago Guerreiro, and Luís Carriço. 2013. UbiBraille: Designing and Evaluating a Vibrotactile Braille-reading Device. In *Proceedings of the 15th International ACM SIGACCESS Conference on Computers and Accessibility (ASSETS '13)*. ACM, New York, NY, USA, Article 23, 8 pages. DOI: http://dx.doi.org/10.1145/2513383.2513437

35. Scott D. Novich and David M. Eagleman. 2015. Using space and time to encode vibrotactile information: toward an estimate of the skin's achievable throughput. *Experimental Brain Research* 10 (2015). DOI: http://dx.doi.org/10.1007/s00221-015-4346-1

36. Qifan Pu, Sidhant Gupta, Shyamnath Gollakota, and Shwetak Patel. 2013. Whole-home Gesture Recognition Using Wireless Signals. In *Proceedings of the 19th Annual International Conference on Mobile Computing & Networking (MobiCom '13)*. ACM, New York, NY, USA, 27–38. DOI: http://dx.doi.org/10.1145/2500423.2500436

37. Keith Rayner. 1998. Eye movements in reading and information processing: 20 years of research. *Psychological bulletin* 124 (1998), 372–422. http://scholar.google.com/scholar.bib?q=info:kPKV2_0qLzcJ:scholar.google.com/&output=citation&hl=en&as_sdt=2000&as_ylo=1998&as_yhi=1998&ct=citation&cd=0

38. Keith Rayner, Barbara R. Foorman, Charles A. Perfetti, David Pesetsky, and Mark S. Seidenberg. 2001. How Psychological Science Informs the Teaching of Reading. *Psychological Science in the Public Interest* 2, 2 (2001), 31–74. DOI:http://dx.doi.org/10.1111/1529-1006.00004 PMID: 26151366.

39. Keith Rayner, Timothy J. Slattery, and Nathalie N. Bélanger. 2010. Eye movements, the perceptual span, and reading speed. *Psychonomic Bulletin & Review* 17, 6 (01 Dec 2010), 834–839. DOI: http://dx.doi.org/10.3758/PBR.17.6.834

40. Gerald M. Reicher. 1969. Perceptual Recognition as a Function of Meaningfulness of Stimulus Material. *Journal of Experimental Psychology* 81, 2 (1969), 275.

41. Kailiang Ren, Sheng Liu, Minren Lin, Yong Wang, and Q.M. Zhang. 2008. A compact electroactive polymer actuator suitable for refreshable Braille display. *Sensors and Actuators A: Physical* 143, 2 (2008), 335 – 342. DOI: http://dx.doi.org/https://doi.org/10.1016/j.sna.2007.10.083

42. M. Romaszewski, P. Glomb, and P. Gawron. 2014. Natural hand gestures for human identification in a Human-Computer Interface. In *Image Processing Theory, Tools and Applications (IPTA), 2014 4th International Conference on*. 1–6. DOI: http://dx.doi.org/10.1109/IPTA.2014.7001997

43. A. Russomanno, S. OâĂŹModhrain, R. B. Gillespie, and M. W. M. Rodger. 2015. Refreshing Refreshable Braille Displays. *IEEE Transactions on Haptics* 8, 3 (July 2015), 287–297. DOI: http://dx.doi.org/10.1109/TOH.2015.2423492

44. Caitlyn E. Seim, David Quigley, and Thad E. Starner. 2014. Passive Haptic Learning of Typing Skills Facilitated by Wearable Computers. In *CHI '14 Extended Abstracts on Human Factors in Computing Systems (CHI EA '14)*. ACM, New York, NY, USA, 2203–2208. DOI: http://dx.doi.org/10.1145/2559206.2581329

45. Frank Smith. 1969. Familiarity of configuration vs discriminability of features in the visual identification of words. *Psychonomic Science* 14, 6 (01 Jun 1969), 261–262. DOI: http://dx.doi.org/10.3758/BF03329112

46. Annette Sterr, Lisa Green, and Thomas Elbert. 2003. Blind Braille readers mislocate tactile stimuli. *Biological Psychology* 63, 2 (2003), 117 – 127. DOI: http://dx.doi.org/10.1016/S0301-0511(03)00051-6

47. Ian R Summers, Jon J Whybrow, Denise A Gratton, Peter Milnes, Brian H Brown, and John C Stevens. 2005. Tactile information transfer: A comparison of two stimulation sites. *The Journal of the Acoustical Society of America* 118, 4 (2005), 2527–2534.

48. Hong Z. Tan, Nathaniel I. Durlach, William M. Rabinowitz, Charlotte M. Reed, and Jonathan R. Santos. 1997. Reception of Morse code through motional, vibrotactile, and auditory stimulation. *Perception & Psychophysics* 59, 7 (01 Jan 1997), 1004–1017. DOI: http://dx.doi.org/10.3758/BF03205516

49. David Ternes and K E MacLean. 2008. Designing Large Sets of Haptic Icons with Rhythm. In *EuroHaptics*, M. Ferre (Ed.). Springer, Madrid, Spain, 199–208. http://www.cs.ubc.ca/labs/spin/publications/spin/ternes2008eh.pdf

50. Wouter Van Vlaenderen, Jens Brulmans, Jo Vermeulen, and Johannes Schöning. 2015. WatchMe: A Novel Input Method Combining a Smartwatch and Bimanual Interaction. In *Proceedings of the 33rd Annual ACM Conference Extended Abstracts on Human Factors in Computing Systems (CHI EA '15)*. ACM, New York, NY, USA, 2091–2095. DOI: http://dx.doi.org/10.1145/2702613.2732789

51. Francisco Vega-Bermudez and Kenneth O Johnson. 2001. Differences in spatial acuity between digits. *Neurology* 56, 10 (2001), 1389–1391.

52. Benjamin W. White, Frank A. Saunders, Lawrence Scadden, Paul Bach-Y-Rita, and Carter C. Collins. 1970. Seeing with the skin. *Perception & Psychophysics* 7, 1 (1970), 23–27. DOI: http://dx.doi.org/10.3758/BF03210126

53. RS Woodworth. 1937. Experimental Psychology. New York: Holt, 1938. *Department of Psychology Dartmouth College Hanover, New Hampshire* (1937).

54. Cheng Xu, Ali Israr, Ivan Poupyrev, Olivier Bau, and Chris Harrison. 2011. Tactile Display for the Visually Impaired Using TeslaTouch. In *CHI '11 Extended Abstracts on Human Factors in Computing Systems (CHI EA '11)*. ACM, New York, NY, USA, 317–322. DOI: http://dx.doi.org/10.1145/1979742.1979705

55. Chao Xu, Parth H. Pathak, and Prasant Mohapatra. 2015. Finger-writing with Smartwatch: A Case for Finger and Hand Gesture Recognition Using Smartwatch. In *Proceedings of the 16th International Workshop on Mobile Computing Systems and Applications (HotMobile '15)*. ACM, New York, NY, USA, 9–14. DOI: http://dx.doi.org/10.1145/2699343.2699350

56. Deyou Xu. 2006. A Neural Network Approach for Hand Gesture Recognition in Virtual Reality Driving Training System of SPG. In *Pattern Recognition, 2006. ICPR 2006. 18th International Conference on*, Vol. 3. 519–522.

57. Xu Zhang, Xiang Chen, Wen-hui Wang, Ji-hai Yang, Vuokko Lantz, and Kong-qiao Wang. 2009. Hand Gesture Recognition and Virtual Game Control Based on 3D Accelerometer and EMG Sensors. In *Proceedings of the 14th International Conference on Intelligent User Interfaces (IUI '09)*. ACM, New York, NY, USA, 401–406. DOI: http://dx.doi.org/10.1145/1502650.1502708

58. Yixin Zhao, Parth H. Pathak, Chao Xu, and Prasant Mohapatra. 2015. Demo: Finger and Hand Gesture Recognition Using Smartwatch. In *Proceedings of the 13th Annual International Conference on Mobile Systems, Applications, and Services (MobiSys '15)*. ACM, New York, NY, USA, 471–471. DOI: http://dx.doi.org/10.1145/2742647.2745922

Can a Helmet-mounted Display Make Motorcycling Safer?

Renate Häuslschmid
LMU Munich
Munich, Germany
renate.haeuslschmid@ifi.lmu.de

Benjamin Fritzsche
IAV GmbH
Munich, Germany
max.vonbuelow@online.de

Andreas Butz
LMU Munich
Munich, Germany
butz@ifi.lmu.de

ABSTRACT

In this paper we investigate whether a helmet-mounted display for motorcyclists can provide similar benefits as the established head-up display (HUD) in cars. HUDs can increase driving safety by efficiently informing the driver. Given their high safety risks, such a technology seems overdue for motorcyclists. Only recently, several crowdfunding projects have raised substantial funding for helmet-mounted displays, however, none of them has released a commercial product yet.

In order to investigate display concepts, we developed an easy-to-reproduce and low-cost helmet-mounted display prototype and compared it to a conventional display setup. The helmet-mounted display was rated more attractive and induced a lower workload. Those motorcyclists who generally exceeded the speed limit before also rode significantly slower when using the head-mounted display. We argue that an intelligent HUD application that adapts to the rider's behavior and preferences could further enhance safety and improve user experience for motorcyclists. We encourage other researchers to replicate our setup and to investigate the impact of HUDs on motorcyclists' behavior and road safety.

Author Keywords

motorcycling, prototyping, rider-assistance system, head-up display, head-mounted displays, head-down display

INTRODUCTION

Motorcyclists are the road users who are exposed to the highest risks. The risk of death is 26 times higher for motorcyclists involved in a crash compared to a car passenger. This risk is twofold: Car drivers often overlook and crash into riders, but riders also often underestimate the road conditions, especially by simply misjudging curves and their own speed [1].

One reason for this misjudgment is the helmet's limitation of the rider's peripheral vision, which is crucial for realistic speed perception [17]. The helmet forces riders to move their head and eyes away from the road scene, e.g., to monitor blind spots or read dashboard information such as the speedometer. Those shifts of gaze and attention are dangerous since road events are time-critical and easily missed. Car drivers experience the same problem to a lower extent, as their vision is less limited and often extended by supportive displays. Head-up displays (HUDs) present information within the drivers' field of view (FOV) and support the dual task of road monitoring and information uptake simply by their position. Motorcyclists also desire those benefits, as several substantially supported fundraising campaigns show, e.g., of the Skully AR-1 (almost \$2.5 million) [8] and the Nuviz Ride (\$200.000) [4].

Figure 1. Our helmet-mounted display prototype uses a conventional smartphone, three optical lenses, a mirror and a transparent mirror (combiner). The see-through image is presented to the rider's right eye.

In this paper, we investigate whether a HUD for riders may indeed provide similar benefits as existing in-car HUDs or whether they rather disturb and distract the rider whose vision is already limited. Since there are no suitable commercial products on the market yet, we built a low-cost open hardware platform that implements a HUD for motorcyclists – called a helmet-mounted display (HMD) for the rest of this paper.

We compare this HMD with a standard motorcycle head-down display (HDD) setup in a riding simulator. We therefore developed an intelligent application with a variety of content. Riders are informed about the current speed, speed limits, and curve properties in order to improve their limited judgment described above. We present results both about the rider's behavior and workload and the systems' attractiveness.

IUI'18 March 7-11, Tokyo, Japan

ISBN 123-4567-24-567/08/06...\$15.00

DOI: http://dx.doi.org/10.1145/3172944.3172963

BACKGROUND & RESEARCH APPROACH

In order to fully understand the causes of motorcycle accidents and how to counteract them we first analyzed the road accident data from the GENESIS database of the German federal agency for statistics [9]: In 2014, 587 motorcyclists died on German roads. 73% of the deadly and 52% of the severe accidents happened on rural roads. In 53.5% of the cases the motorcyclists were involved in crashes with other road users and in 36.3% they swung off the road – e.g. in curves (46.3%). 35% of all accidents with injury to persons are caused by excessive speed. This percentage is 2.5 times higher compared to car drivers. NHTSA reports very similar accident statistics for the United States [1].

These statistics underline that motorcyclists are exposed to high risks of accident and death. However, a considerable factor of that danger is impaired judgment. Motorcyclists underestimate speed – particularly in curves. We hypothesize that informing the rider about speed, curves and the associated dangers may enhance safety for motorcyclists. Furthermore, we think that a display that presents such information within the riders' field of view will reduce the risk and effort of information uptake compared to the standard head-down display. Speed and road conditions are also shown in available and future helmet-mounted displays, as explained below.

RELATED WORK

Visual Aspects of Head-Up and Head-Mounted Displays

HUDs are reflected in the windshield (car-stabilized) and remain at a fixed position when the driver moves the head. For motorcyclists we used the visor to reflect the image into the visual field. The motorcycle HMD hence displays content at a fixed field of view position but moves along with the head, i.e., head-stabilized. This is a substantial difference between these two displays in terms of the relation between display content and the world outside. Truly world-stabilized content is technically hard to achieve in both displays.

The humans' visual field can be divided into the foveal (<2°), central (<10°), and peripheral (>10°) field of view [10, 27]. When looking straight on the road, the foveal and central visual fields perceive the road scene. This area needs to remain uncluttered to ensure clear visibility of the road scene [18]. Peripheral vision is important for, e.g., speed perception [17], but has generally less visual resources [38]. We think that the coverage of a small area within the near peripheral field through a transparent display (that also shows speed information) is the safest location for a HMD.

Chua et al. [18] investigated the response times and user preferences on see-through head-mounted displays in a divided attention scenario (like riding plus information uptake) and confirmed prior research for other display types, e.g., HUDs [24, 25]: The central location promoted the fastest response times but peripheral positions are more "comfortable, unobtrusive, and preferred". The location in the middle-right showed the best balance between performance and comfort. Furthermore, the response time increases with the complexity of the content.

As follows, the placement of the image is highly important: A central placement with the risk of occluding the road scene has to be well weighed up with a peripheral placement and its increased reaction times. As for the image distance, in-car HUDs and also AR and VR glasses often present the image in approximately 2 to 3 m [26] – which corresponds to the eyes' resting distance [23]. Furthermore, it is often preferred by the users and promotes the best performance [24]. A large image distance generally reduces the time and effort to switch back and forth between road scene and display but are often disliked by the users. Virtual images such as on a HMD often create a mismatch of accommodation and vergence. Furthermore, the images perceived by the two eyes differ considerably when using a monocular HMD. This causes a blending of those two images on long-term and is one of the major issues of monocular HMDs ('binocular rivalry') [11, 33, 39]. Those mismatches are exhausting for the eyes and need to be considered especially when designing a HMD for real-world use, e.g., by presenting the image to the dominant or both eyes [19].

When designing content for a helmet-mounted display, special attention to the dynamics of distraction is needed. Car HUDs produce specific types of distraction, such as visual tunneling and cognitive capture, in which a driver is distracted without being aware of it and the associated risk. This problem may be further increased by interactions the driver performs to reach a certain goal, or which are of long duration [22]. As drivers cannot process display content and road scene simultaneously, they can miss or react delayed to events in the road scene, although they are actually looking at it [34, 42]. Salient HUD content can also let drivers immediately withdraw their visual focus and attention from the road scene [40]. Similar problems have to be expected for motorcyclists.

Head-Up Displays for Car Drivers

A head-up display appears to the driver as a transparent overlay that is placed slightly (5°) below the line of sight. It overlays primarily asphalt and informs the driver about speed, speed limits and other traffic restrictions, vehicle status such as remaining gas, and route guidance [12, 16]. Most HUDs are reflected on the windshield to reach an increased virtual image distance of approximately 2 m. The prominent position and the increased distance allows the driver to glance faster back and forth between the road scene and the display. The driver can safely monitor the road scene while reading the HUD. Although there still is a risk of distraction, HUDs provide an overall safety benefit compared to other in-car displays [30, 32, 35, 43].

Head-Up Displays for Motorcyclists

One of the first attempts to increase motorcyclists' safety and comfort by providing information to them started in 2009 as the *Saferider project* [13, 14, 37]. In this project, several advanced riding assistance systems and in-vehicle information systems were developed and studied. Most approaches used a head-down display, however, one also focused on the helmet: The *smart helmet* provided audio output, haptic feedback through vibration and also a red, uni-color head-up display which overlaid the 'global visual field' [37] with gear, speed and distance to the next hazard. However, we did not find any further information about the HUD and the user studies on safety and comfort.

Similarly, Jenkins et al. [29] proposed a system for real-time rider alert and cueing for upcoming dangers. Information about the current speed, gear and hazards is displayed on a small screen below the left eye. The authors focused on the content and design of the display and did not describe the realization of the hardware or a user study in detail.

Mendes [36] displayed navigation and weather information on a self-made HMD which was based on a Recon Snow 2 display unit integrated into skiing glasses and a helmet. A user study with 7 participants showed that the helmet-mounted display was found to be overall useful. The participants did not like that the display was non-see-through and that they had to glance away from the road.

In contrast to the helmet-mounted approaches, Ito et al. [28] reflected a car-like HUD in the motorcycle's windshield. This leads to a bike-stabilized instead of a head-stabilized placement. Based on the assumption that the time to understand the display's content should not exceed 2 s, they suggested to display up to 5 Hiragana characters in the lower right or left corner of their windshield setup.

Realization of Helmet-Mounted-Displays

There are several approaches with varying fidelity to the realization of a road-ready helmet-mounted display. Below, we briefly introduce the most relevant ones.

The *BikeHUD* [2, 7] utilizes a non-see-through display which displays the image below the left eye and at an optically infinite distance. The display unit blocks the riders' view and requires a direct glance downwards for reading the content. The BikeHUD requires a wired connection to the bike.

Also the *SportVue MC2 HUD* [6] is wired to the motorcycle. The display is attached to the outside of the helmet at the upper part of the visor. As the helmet is available since 2005 and basically unchanged, the setup is rather basic and provides a simple monochromatic (red) image.

The *Reevu MSX1* [5] is also a rather simple version of a helmet-mounted display and presents a digital rear view mirror at the top edge of the helmet. As the distance to the eyes is very low, it is difficult to visually focus on the display.

The *Skully AR-1* [8] is a fundraising project that recently failed. The optical concept was similar to the Google Glass and the peripherally placed image was planned to display, e.g., a rear view camera and navigation information.

The *Nuviz Ride* [4] is also a fundraising project. The display unit is attached to the outside of the helmet and presents its image below the right eye. The helmet can be connected via Bluetooth to the smartphone and controlled via a customized control unit for the handlebar.

The *DigiLens MonoHUD* [20] is based on a micro display and a combiner. It presents the image – showing, e.g., speed, gear and warnings – between the center and the periphery of the right eye at a distance of 1.5 m.

Wagner et al. [41] developed a binocular HMD based on a laser, a mirror, and retinal scanning. The setup is rather complex and partially 3D-printed, but adaptable to the user.

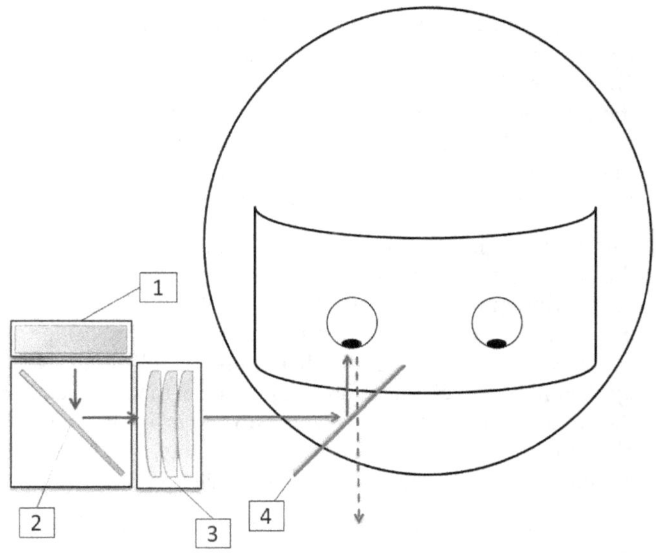

Figure 2. Our HMD prototype uses reflection as do in-car HUDs. The image of a smartphone (1) is first reflected on a mirror (2) and then fed through three optical lenses (3). The light rays are then reflected on a transparent mirror or combiner (4). The dotted line indicates where the rider perceives the image.

In contrast to these helmets, the *LiveMap* [3] helmet displays a binocular image at a distance of about 4 m and within the central field of view. The company justifies this placement by promising that they will limit the central display of complex content to very low speeds. The system is based on a projector, integrates sensors such as a Gyroscope and can be connected to the smartphone. The helmet is still under development.

The quality and number of see-through glasses and AR devices increases rapidly. Since only recently, toolkits such as the *Holokit* [1] and the *Aryzon DIY kit* [2] provide the possibility of experiencing and prototyping AR applications based on the own smartphone. As these setups are binocular, the image area is placed in the central visual field – overlaying the road scene but potentially providing interesting, advanced applications.

Since we aimed to investigate the actual benefits of helmet-mounted displays, we decided to aim for a helmet that is comparable to the recent developments. Accordingly, we decided for a monocular HMD with the image presented in the close periphery of the right eye. Just like the AR toolkits mentioned above, we used a smartphone as display and computing unit. We aimed for a prototype that is simple, low-cost, and easy to reproduce in order to make it available to other researchers and encourage further investigations in this field.

HELMET-MOUNTED-DISPLAY SETUP

We used a standard motorcycle helmet as the basis and extended it with a retainer and an attachable optical setup which consists of a smartphone, three lenses, a mirror and a combiner (transparent mirror). The optical setup follows the principle used for automotive head-up displays (depicted in fig. 2) and

[1] https://holokit.io

[2] https://www.kickstarter.com/projects/aryzon/aryzon-3d-augmented-reality-for-every-smartphone

also the DigiLens MonoHUD helmet [15, 20]: The light (image) is reflected in a combiner and directed into the user's eye. One or multiple mirrors can be placed in between to increase the light path length and so the distance between the virtual image and the user's eye. Also, one or several lenses can be integrated into the setup to adjust the light rays' angle and to further increase the virtual image distance.

Similar to augmented reality (AR) toolkits such as Holokit or the Aryzon, we decided to use a smartphone. It provides a fast computing unit, a bright and sharp display, sufficient power and a wireless WiFi or Bluetooth connection in one device and is hence highly suitable for such a do-it-yourself setup. Native applications or web pages are easy to implement and can use the smartphone's integrated sensors. For our setup we used a HTC One M8s smartphone with a 5" display, 1920×1080 px resolution and a luminance of approximately 450 cd/m^2.

For the mirror we selected a surface mirror made from premium steel which provides a clear image. In contrast, glass mirrors reflect the image twice and thereby produce a disturbing double image. We placed the mirror at an angle of 45° to the eye line which allowed us to attach the smartphone to the side of the helmet and achieve a smaller setup size.

As the same double image problem applies to the combiner, we selected a 0.75 mm thick acrylic glass. We cut the material into a large rectangle with rounded corners so that its edges are rarely visible to the user when placed between the eye and the nose. The combiner is attached to the helmet by means of a lego joint which allows the user to reposition the image.

To increase the virtual image distance we integrated three plano-convex acrylic glass lenses into the setup. Each lens has a diameter of 6.2 cm (usable area of approximately 5 cm) and a focal length of 27.5 cm. By placing the lenses directly next to each other, the overall focal length is reduced to 9.17 cm. When the distance between lens and light source corresponds exactly to the focal length, the light rays exit the lens in parallel, which places the image at optical infinity [21]. However, the experimenters perceive it to be at a distance of 1 to 2 m.

As most helmet-mounted displays, our setup presents the image to the right eye as it is regularly the lead eye [19]. Furthermore, we positioned the center of the lenses at eye level so that the image can be positioned and perceived as good as possible. When the combiner is positioned at 45° the setup covers a field of view of 37°×37° and is directly in front of the right eye. For the presented user study, we requested the participants to adjust the image position to their own preferences but within the range of 5° to 10° horizontally and 0° to -10° vertically.

The retainer and all containers for the optical setup are laser-cut from balsa wood panels to be lightweight yet stable. Including the smartphone, the setup weighs approximately 450 g. We attached an equivalent weight to the left side of the helmet which leads to a higher but balanced weight of 2500 g. The prices for all materials, excluding the smartphone, sum up to approximately 20€. All materials, laser cutter templates and a construction manual are available for download[3].

[3]https://doi.org/10.5282/ubm/data.117

USER STUDY

Study Design

The risk of accidents is highest on rural roads [9]. It is often caused by underestimating the current speed and the radius of bends. One approach to counteract this risk is to provide speed and road information to the rider on an additional display. In our study we compare two *display variants* – the standard head-down display placed close to the handlebar and a helmet-mounted display placed close to the riders' line of sight.

Information which is displayed permanently within the already limited field of view can cause distraction, increased workload, or rejection of the system. Consequently, it is crucial to identify the HUD content which is most effective, i.e., which riders experience as helpful but not too distractive. Based on related work and preceding interviews with experienced motorcyclists, we chose to test three gradations of the *display content*: (1) speed, (2) speed & speed limit, (3) speed & speed limit & curve information.

The user study follows a 2×3 within-subjects design with the independent variables *display variant* and *display content*. This corresponds to six conditions which are tested in a lab study due to legal restrictions and safety concerns. The content variations for each display variant are scheduled after each other to reduce switches between the display variants and confusion of the participant. The display variants as well as the display content variations are presented in a counterbalanced order to the participants.

HMD software for the study

We chose to test the same three gradations of the display content with both display variants: (a) speed, (b) speed & speed limit, (c) speed & speed limit & curve information. The content for our HMD is shown in fig. 4. The *speed* information aims to prevent misjudgment of the current speed and to induce a more appropriate speed (within the limits). A real HMD application may obtain the speed information from a (wireless) connection to the motorcycle or use GPS tracking. The speed is displayed as a digital speedometer in kilometers per hour (km/h). It is permanently displayed and continuously updated. As this content is assumed to be accessed the most often, it is displayed at a medium large size and closest to the riders line of sight.

The *speed limit* aims to support the driver in keeping track of the allowed speed and in understanding wether the current speed is appropriate and considered safe. This information is location-dependent and a road ready application may retrieve it from a map or navigation service provider, e.g., Google Maps. The speed limit icon is displayed next to the speedometer. It corresponds to the respective traffic sign and shows a number within a red circle. The speed limit is displayed to the right of the speedometer. During the study, it switches five times between 70 km/h and 110 km/h.

The *curve information* includes the direction of and the distance to the upcoming curve as well as a warning if it is sharp. The *direction of the curve* is presented as an arrow pointing to the left or right. It allows the rider to prepare for curves specifically in hilly terrain, where curves may not be visible in

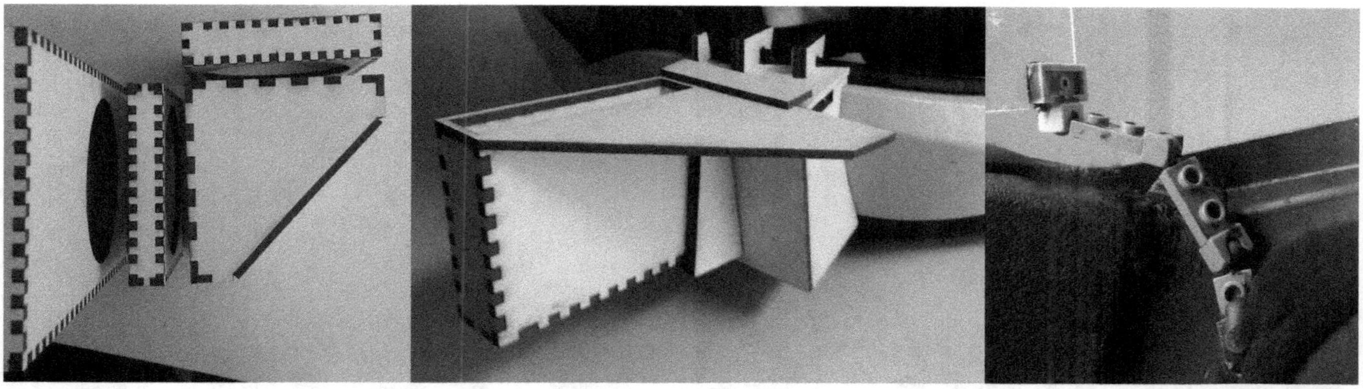

Figure 3. The retainers of all optical elements are laser cut, glued together and coated with an adhesive foil. The combiner is attached to the inside of the helmet by means of a lego joint which allows the user to adjust the image position.

time. Accordingly, we also display the *distance to the curve* as a countdown in 100 m steps. Since braking inside the curve may lead to a swinging off the road it is important to adjust the speed before the curve. The *curve warning* is displayed as a triangle surrounding the arrow if the upcoming curve is very sharp, to raise awareness for the danger. This part of the application is complex and needs to be intelligent in order to be helpful and safe but not disturbing: At first, it has to interpret the map data to detect upcoming curves and gather knowledge about their characteristics (e.g., their direction, sharpness, center and distance). The application also needs to retrieve data about the motorcycle in relation to its environment such as the current speed, lateral position on the lane (normally varies within the lane boundaries in curves to lower its sharpness) and the distance to the curve center (whether deceleration is needed and possible). Also contextual data such as weather (e.g. rain) and asphalt should be considered if possible. Furthermore, the application should learn from the users' riding abilities and behavior and potentially also consider data from other motorcyclists or similar curves. The application has to interpret all this data and to decide whether the riding behavior is appropriate and safe in the momentary situation and what information should be presented on the HMD. Our application considers the curve properties, and the speed and location of the motorcyclists but does not yet learn from the riders' behavior. The curve information is displayed only when approaching a curve. We decided for a prominent position above the speed information and a large size in order to emphasize its importance.

Riding Simulator

We used the driving simulator *Racer* [4] which provides settings specifically for motorcycle simulation. We implemented six riding tracks as two-lane roads in a hilly nature of grass fields and trees to obtain situations in which the road is not fully visible. We designed three homogenous tracks and particularly the curves based on the German Guidelines for Road Design [9]. According to those guidelines, curves should have a radius of 200 to 400 m for roads with a speed limit of 70 km/h and 400 to 900 m for roads with 110 km/h, respectively. In our study, the speed limit changes five times on each track and is either set to 70 km/h or to 110 km/h (90 km/h on average per track). We randomly scheduled eight curves to the left and eight to the right with an average radius of 400 m and followed by straight segments of 100 to 400 m. For a natural riding feeling, the road tilts in curves between 1° and 7° and for a distance of 100 to 1000 m. The rider has to constantly control the throttle and brake as the speed of the simulated motorcycle adapts naturally to the road.

The speed limit was communicated to the rider at the beginning of a straight road segment (after curves) by means of standard traffic signs next to the road. We did not present any other road signs. We inverted the three tracks in order to obtain the six homogeneous tracks required by the study design.

Procedure

At first, the experimenter introduced the participants to the topic and the procedure of the study. The participants were asked whether they consent to participate and if so to fill out a demographic questionnaire. Next, they received introductions to the motorcycle simulator and the two display variants. In this process, participants put on the helmet and calibrated the combiner. Before the test started, the experimenter advised participants to ride as they used to and sent them on a 3 min test drive to familiarize themselves with the simulator setup.

The test started with one of the two display variants. The participants rode three tracks with the same display variant but varying content and completed an intermediate questionnaire after each track. Then, the experimenter installed the other display variant and asked the participant to complete three more tracks and questionnaires. The study was closed with a final questionnaire and a discussion with the experimenter in which the participants reported their personal feedback. Participants needed approximately 9 to 10 min per track; the test duration hence summed up to an average of about 80 min.

Apparatus

Our apparatus consisted of the two display variants showing the HMD software – either on the head-down or the helmet-mounted display – as well as the riding simulator which was projected on a wall and controlled by means of a mock-up motorcycle setup.

[4] http://www.racer.nl

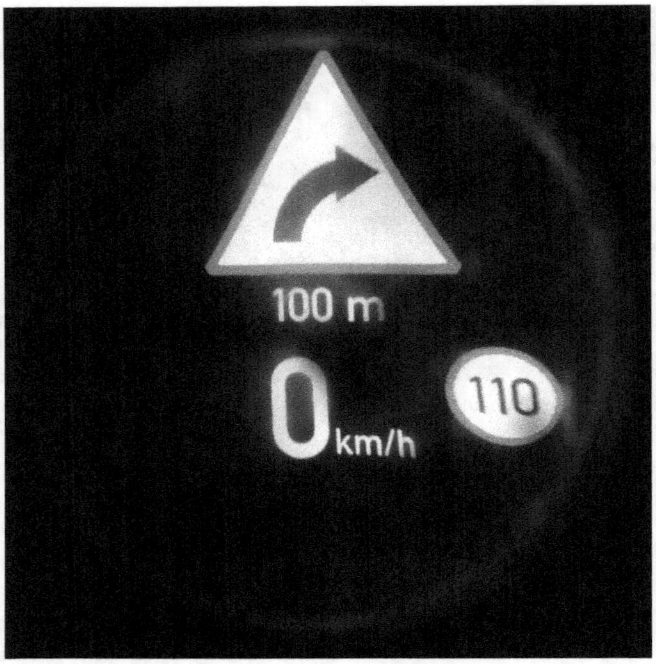

Figure 4. This photograph shows the virtual image created by our prototype. It presents the speedometer, speed limit and curve warning (content variant c)

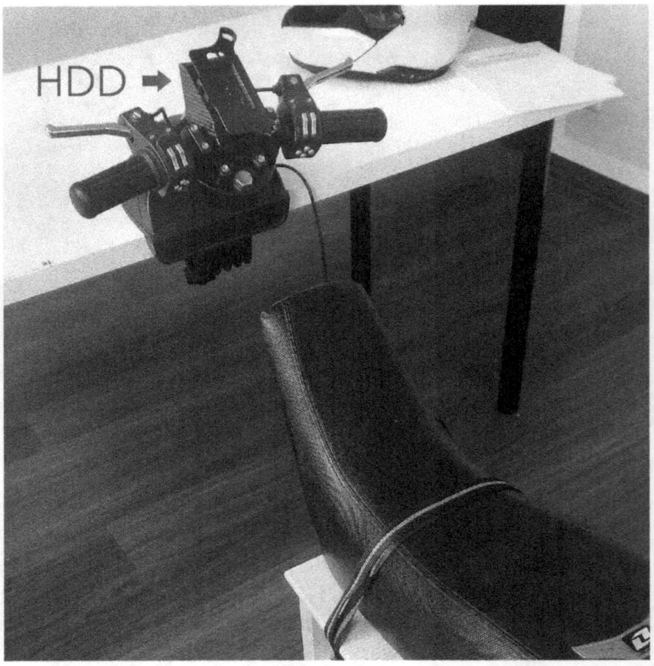

Figure 5. We used a gaming handlebar for the control of the riding simulator and a real motorcycle seat to create a realistic riding posture and feeling.

The two display variants were realized by the same smartphone which was either attached to the handlebar or, along with an additional weight for a balanced weight distribution, attached to the helmet. We used a HTC One M8s smartphone with a resolution of 1920×1080 px and a luminance of approximately 450 cd/m. The participants were asked to adjust the combiner so that the image was placed according to their own preferences but within an area of 5° to 10° horizontally and 0° to -10° vertically.

The HMD software was implemented in Processing and translated directly into an Android App. For wireless use, the application was connected to the riding simulator via WiFi. The interface measured 400 × 430 px which corresponds to 2.2 × 2.4 cm on the display as this was found to be sufficient in the pre-study interviews with motorcyclists.

The Racer riding simulator was projected on a wall at a distance of 2 m to the motorcycle setup and the horizon was set to be approximately at eye level. The handlebar contained a brake lever and a throttle controller and was controlled just like a real motorcycle handlebar at low speeds (i.e., turning the handlebar to the right made the simulated bike go right). We are aware that actual motorcycle physics differ at higher speeds, but were limited by the available simulator software. To obtain a realistic riding posture and feeling, we attached a real motorcycle seat to a stool. The simulator sound was also played back to the participants to further increase realism.

Participants

We recruited 24 participants (1 female) with a mean age of 30.8 years (SD=6.5) and an average motorcycling experience of 12 years. Our participants estimated to ride their motorcycles for on average of approximately 6000 km/year and to spend on average 57% on rural roads, 35.4% on urban roads and 7.6% on highways. Our participants described their riding style as anticipative (n=11), sportive (n=8), fast, defensive, careful, relaxed, and confident (n=3 each).

Results

Riding Behavior

To judge the riding behavior, we analyzed the speed of the logged telemetric data by means of repeated measures ANOVAs. Our participants rode marginally slower using the HMD (mean=95.7 km/h, SD=8.4) than using the HDD (mean=97.5 km/h, SD=9.3), but this difference is not statistically different. The mean speed limit can be calculated to 90 km/h for each track – 18 of our participants exceded the speed limit despite the display support. Excluding the participants who obey to the speed limits anyway, we find a significantly ($F_{1,17}$=4.77, p=0.043, r=0.22) reduced speed for the HMD (mean=98.44, SD=7.30) compared to the HDD (mean=101.05, SD=7.59).

The content variant in turn did not influence the riding behavior: Variant a presented a speedometer only and led to an average speed of 97.2 km/h (SD=9.1). Variant b presented the speed limit in addition and induced an average speed of 96.7 km/h (SD=8.6). Variant c also showed information about upcoming curves and led to an average speed of 96.0 km/h (SD=9.2). The order of variants a, b and c was counterbalanced in the study.

Workload

We measured the workload of each display and content variant by means of the standardized *Driver Activity Load Index* (DALI) questionnaire. The DALI questionnaire measures seven types of workload and uses a 6-point Likert scale. The results for all workload types are analyzed by means of Friedman and Wilcoxon tests and shown in fig. 6.

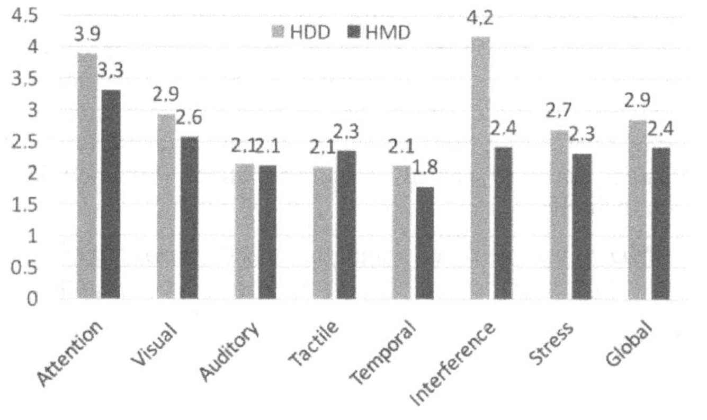

Figure 6. The head-mounted display (blue) induced a lower workload than the head-down display (orange). The HMD reduced the interference with the riding task and the visual workload significantly.

The two display variants induced a significantly different global workload (p=.001, Z=-3.21): We measured a mean value of 2.4 (SD=0.6) for the helmet-mounted display and 2.9 (SD=0.8) for the head-down display. The HMD received slightly lower values for all workload types – namely attention, interference, stress as well as visual and temporal workload – except for the auditory and tactile workload. The auditory workload values are irrelevant for the helmet since there was no auditory feedback other than the riding sound. The slightly higher tactile workload can be attributed to the higher weight of the helmet. However, the auditory, tactile, temporal and stress workload are not statistically different for the two variants. The visual workload of the HMD is significantly lower compared to the HDD (p=.04, Z=-2.06). Also, the HMD *interferes* significantly less with the primary task (p<.001, Z=-4.02) which means that the rider can focus more on the road scene.

Furthermore, we analyzed the workload for the three content variations: For variants a and b (see before), we calculated a global workload of mean=2.6 (SD=0.7 and SD=0.6). Variant c showed additional information about upcoming curves and led to a mean workload of 2.7 (SD=0.7). The results of the six workload types are highly consistent for all content variants. We did not find any significant differences.

System Attractiveness & Qualitative Feedback

We used the AttrakDiff [5] in combination with a self-designed questionnaire and open interviews to gather insights into the attractiveness and likability of the display and content variants.

The AttrakDiff questionnaire consists of 28 items with a 7-point Likert scale and provides insights into the pragmatic quality, the hedonic quality and the attractiveness. The results are shown in fig. 7. We measured a mean pragmatic quality (PQ) of 1.47 for the helmet and 0.44 for the HDD. The hedonic quality can be subdivided into stimulation and identity: We measured a mean stimulation (HQ-S) of 1.18 for the helmet and -0.97 for the HDD. For the identity (HQ-I), we calculated a mean of 1.2 for the helmet and 0.04 for the HDD. The attractiveness (ATT) of the helmet-mounted display reached a mean of 1.31 while the HDD was evaluated with a mean of

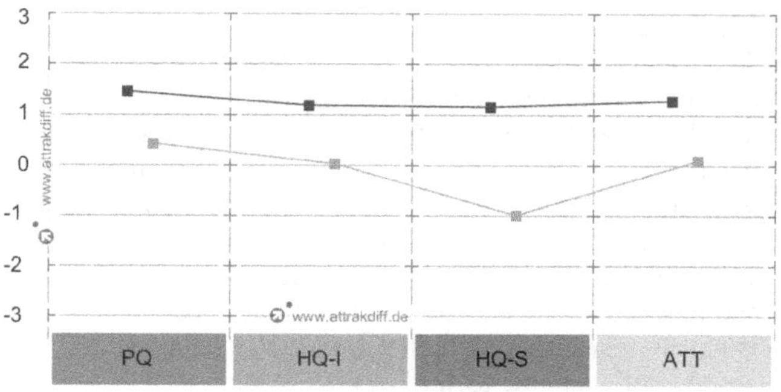

Figure 7. The head-mounted display (blue) was rated more attractive than the head-down display (orange). The AttrakDiff results are further supported by the feedback of our participants.

0.11. Overall, we measured a considerably different system attractiveness for the two display variants: The helmet was rated with a mean of 1.29 and the HDD with -0.38. Furthermore, we asked the participants to rate the weight of the helmet on a scale from 0 (light) to 7 (heavy). The helmet itself with the retainer only was rated with 3.83 and said to be somewhat heavier than normal. The helmet with the smartphone setup and the balance weight was rated with 5.58 and said to be notably heavier. In open interviews, we asked participants to report about their experience using the different display and content variants. Below, we summarize the participants' feedback for the two display variants.

Using the *helmet-mounted display*, participants liked the content variant with speed and speed limits best. The speed information was highly valued by most participants and commented as helpful, admonishing, and relaxing. Few participants said it was unnecessary and useful only in speed controls. We received opposing comments also about the curve information: While some participants regarded it as superfulous and disturbing and thought it would be ignored once one is used to the helmet. Others said the curve information was a good and trustworthy preparation and motivated them to adapt their riding behavior. Overall, many participants explicitly valued the image and its quality and position with attributes like *comfortable* and *beneficial*, however, some felt stressed and unconfident using this HMD and desired a brighter image. Participants also said that it was easy and fast to get accustomed to the HMD and to visually focus on the image. Many participants desired a navigation application and warnings.

Although we evaluated the *head-down display* position in a pre-study and verified it as realistic, some participants said it should be placed higher – others said it was as the usual location. We attribute this difference to varying placements in their own motorbikes. We observed, that participants who experienced the HMD before the HDD had a more critical and negative attitude towards the HDD and its position. Also for HDD use, participants preferred the content variant comprising speed and speed limit. The curve information was said to be not usable on the HDD. They explicitly mentioned the problem of upcoming curves and other critical situations: In such situations a glance away from the road situation is impractical and dangerous even if the additional information might be supportive – a (timely) presentation of critical information on the HMD was valued as highly beneficial.

[5] www.attrakdiff.de

DISCUSSION

As shown by accident statistics and fundraising projects and confirmed by the motorcyclists that we consulted for the system design and recruited for the study, motorcyclists need and desire technological support. Commercially available display helmets are rare and so far rather basic. Substantial research and development is currently undertaken to provide a more advanced support – based on the assumption that it will have the same benefits as car HUDs. Yet, the impact on motorcyclists is hardly researched, which can partially be attributed to the absence of available technology.

We approached this topic by designing a reproducible helmet-mounted display prototype based on a standard smartphone. It enables the fast and easy exploration, prototyping, and evaluation of HMD-based systems for motorcyclists. The HMD can be easily reproduced by means of a laser cutter, three optical lenses, a mirror, an acrylic glass panel for the combiner and a smartphone. The required materials and optical elements are low cost and sum up to approximately 20 €only. As our participants noted that a brighter image would be pleasant, we recommend to use an up-to-date smartphone with a display brightness of at least 500 cd/m^2. Furthermore, as the weight of the helmet was criticized by the participants, we recommend to use a phone with less than 150 g along with a lightweight helmet. Our participants explicitly remarked the high quality of the image and that it is easy to focus on it – which is generally problematic for monocular see-through displays.

With this setup, we ran a lab study about the benefits of such a helmet-mounted display in comparison to a standard motorcycle display setup. Before helmet-mounted displays can be tested and used on a real road, lab studies have to be performed in order to investigate the potential risks and benefits of such display without putting the rider or other road users at risk. As follows, we used a specific motorcycle simulator with realistic and homogenous riding tracks for the presented study.

As for the HMD application, we designed three variants with increasing amount of information and intelligence based on accident statistics and content provided on similar HMDs. We compared those display and content variants regarding attractiveness and workload as well as the impact on riding behavior. The HMD was valued as the more attractive system, however, this might be related to the novelty of the system. Many participants described the HMD image as comfortable and beneficial. Also, the helmet did receive better workload ratings – especially regarding visual load and interference of information uptake with the primary task. Both are highly relevant for safety and should be avoided especially in dangerous real-world situations. A helmet-mounted display seems to actually provide decreased workload and in turn a safety benefit; this is further supported by the riding behavior evaluation: Motorcyclists who normally generally exceeded the speed limits rode significantly slower when using the HMD. Kiefer [31] showed that drivers preferred the speedometer displayed on a HUD over the HDD version as it supported keeping the desired speed. Drivers adjust their speed only slightly – if at all – but seem to be more aware of it and more willingly to adhere to limits (as discussed by Gish et al. [24]).

Our results indicate that all three content variants induced a manageable workload. However, the individual feedback of our participants showed that the preferences vary considerably: Many participants found the content variant containing speed and speed limit the most attractive and useful. Some participants also wanted curve information or route guidance on their HMD.

HMD content is placed within the riders' already very limited visual field and can lead to clutter or occlusion. Consequently, the presentation of unnecessary or disliked information has to be avoided. As follows, an adaptable or personalizable HMD might be the best solution for all motorcyclists. We recommend to use the speedometer as a basis for future HMD applications and augment it according to the users' preferences or behavior: Riding behavior may change over time, e.g. depending on the weather, daytime, personal condition or mood. We think that a more advanced HMD application should also learn from the rider's behavior and abilities and display only the information that is momentary needed or helpful. For example, curve information may only be displayed before a dangerous instead of every curve which may further underline its importance and in turn motivate the rider to actually obey to it. A broad knowledge base that incorporates data from many motorcyclists and curves may also provide a good foundation for such application and allow for a more sophisticated calculation of a safe velocity.

CONCLUSIONS & FUTURE WORK

We investigated the question whether a HUD for motorcyclists will indeed provide similar and measurable benefits as existing HUDs in cars or whether they will disturb and distract the rider whose vision is already limited. Since there are no suitable commercial products on the market yet, we built a low-cost and easy-to-reproduce helmet-mounted display. In a user study, we presented the current speed, speed limits, and intelligent curve information to the riders on our HMD and compared it to a conventional motorcycle display setup. Our results indicate that the HMD induces a lower workload and interferes less with the riding task as the focus switches are easier; which is supported by the participants' feedback. The HMD was also rated more attractive than the head-down display. Furthermore, participants that exceeded the speed limit rode significantly slower with the HMD. As a consequence, we argue that a personalizable or adaptable system might be a good solution and should be researched in future.

By making all construction files publicly available, we encourage other researchers to replicate our HMD setup and to further investigate the impact on motorcyclists' behavior and road safety. As a next step, we are currently developing a binocular helmet-mounted display to enable research in the field of AR. Furthermore, we think that eye-tracking could provide deeper insights into the riders' glance behavior and more precisely quantify the HMD's risks and benefits.

REFERENCES

1. 2015. Traffic Safety Facts. 2013 Data. Motorcycles. (Report No. DOT HS 812 148). (2015).
2. 2016a. BikeHUD Adventure to Include Transparent Display and Front/rear HD Cameras. http://www.gizmag.com/bikehud-adventure-motorcycle-hud-heads-up-display/34894/?li_source=LI&li_medium=default-widget. (2016). last accessed on 2016-07-16.
3. 2016. LiveMap: Motorbike Helmet with Navigation | Unique Hi-tech Motorbike Helmet with Built-in Navigation System and Voice Controlled Interface. https://livemap.info/. (2016). last accessed on 2016-07-16.
4. 2016. NUVIZ - The Motorcycle Head-Up Display. http://www.ridenuviz.com/#intro. (2016). last accessed on 2016-07-14.
5. 2016. Reevu Motorbike Helmets. Reevu - The World's First Rear View Helmet. http://www.reevu.com/. (2016). last accessed on 2016-07-15.
6. 2016. Retro-fit Heads-up Display System for Motorcycle and Bicycle Helmets. http://www.gizmag.com/go/2430/. (2016). last accessed on 2016-07-16.
7. 2016b. Review: BikeHUD by BikeSystems, the First Motorcycle Heads-up Display. http://www.gizmag.com/bikehud-motorcycle-hud-heads-up-display-review/33884/. (2016). last accessed on 2016-07-16.
8. 2016. SKULLY AR-1 Augmented Reality Helmet. https://www.skully.com/. (2016). last accessed on 2016-07-15.
9. 2016. Statistisches Bundesamt Deutschland - GENESIS-Online. https://www-genesis.destatis.de/genesis/online. (2016). last accessed on 2016-07-12.
10. DIN 15996:2008. 2008. Bild- und Tonbearbeitung in Film-, Video- und Rundfunkbetrieben - Grundsätze und Festlegungen für den Arbeitsplatz. (2008).
11. David Alais and Randolph Blake. 1999. Grouping Visual Features During Binocular Rivalry. *Vision Research* 39, 26 (1999), 4341 – 4353. DOI: http://dx.doi.org/10.1016/S0042-6989(99)00146-7
12. Audi. 2017. Head-Up Display. (2017). https://www.audi-technology-portal.de/en/electrics-electronics/controls/head-up-display_en last accessed on 2017-08-21.
13. Evangelos Bekiaris, Stella Nikolaou, Roberto Montanari, Andrea Spadoni, Andrea Borin, Marco Pieve, Roberto Lot, Roberto Sartori, Veronique Huth, Frederik Diederichs, and others. 2010. SAFERIDER-Advanced Telematics for Enhancing the Safety and Comfort of Motorcycle Riders. In *17th ITS World Congress*.
14. Evangelos D. Bekiaris, A. Spadoni, and S. I. Nikolaou. 2009. SAFERIDER Project: New Safety and Comfort in Powered Two Wheelers. In *2009 2nd Conference on Human System Interactions*. 600–602. DOI: http://dx.doi.org/10.1109/HSI.2009.5091045
15. J. Alejandro Betancur. 2011. *Augmented Reality - Some Emerging Application Areas*. InTech, Chapter Physical Variable Analysis Involved in Head-Up Display Systems Applied to Automobiles. DOI: http://dx.doi.org/10.5772/25849
16. BMW. 2017. BMW Head-Up Display. (2017). https://secure.bmw.com/com/en/newvehicles/2series/active_tourer/2014/showroom/driving_assistance/bmw_head-up_display.html last accessed on 2017-08-21.
17. Mark W. Cannon. 1987. Recent Advances in Understanding Peripheral Vision. In *Proceedings of 30th Annual Meeting of the Human Factors Socitety*, Vol. 30. 601–60.
18. Soon Hau Chua, Simon T. Perrault, Denys J. C. Matthies, and Shengdong Zhao. 2016. Positioning Glass: Investigating Display Positions of Monocular Optical See-Through Head-Mounted Display. , Article 1 (2016), 6 pages. DOI:http://dx.doi.org/10.1145/2948708.2948713
19. James F. Collins and Loren K. Blackwell. 1974. Effects of Eye Dominance and Retinal Distance on Binocular Rivalry. *Perceptual and Motor Skills* 39, 2 (1974), 747–754. DOI:http://dx.doi.org/10.2466/pms.1974.39.2.747
20. Digilens. 2016-01-05T17:00:40+00:00. DigiLens Takes Motorcycle Head-Up Displays Miles Down the Road. http://www.digilens.com/digilens-takes-motorcycle-head-up-displays-miles-down-the-road/. (2016-01-05T17:00:40+00:00). last accessed on 2016-07-26.
21. G.R. Fowles. 1968. *Introduction to Modern Optics*. Holt, Rinehart and Winston.
22. Shaul Fox and Michael Hoffman. 2002. Escalation Behavior as a Specific Case of Goal-Directed Activity: A Persistence Paradigm. *Basic and Applied Social Psychology* 24, 4 (2002), 273–285. DOI: http://dx.doi.org/10.1207/s15324834basp2404_3
23. J. L. Gabbard, G. M. Fitch, and Hyungil Kim. 2014. Behind the Glass: Driver Challenges and Opportunities for AR Automotive Applications. *Proc. IEEE* 102, 2 (Feb 2014), 124–136.
24. Kenneth W. Gish and Loren Staplin. 1995. *Human factors aspects of using head up displays in automobiles: A review of the literature*. Technical Report.
25. Renate Haeuslschmid, Susanne Forster, Katharina Vierheilig, Daniel Buschek, and Andreas Butz. 2017. Recognition of Text and Shapes on a Large-Sized Head-Up Display. In *Proceedings of the 2017 Conference on Designing Interactive Systems (DIS '17)*. ACM, New York, NY, USA, 821–831. DOI: http://dx.doi.org/10.1145/3064663.3064736

26. Renate Haeuslschmid, Bastian Pfleging, and Florian Alt. 2016. A Design Space to Support the Development of Windshield Applications for the Car. In *Proceedings of the 2016 CHI Conference on Human Factors in Computing Systems (CHI '16)*. ACM, New York, NY, USA, 5076–5091.

27. Herbert Hagendorf, Joseph Krummenacher, Hermann-Josef Müller, and Torsten Schubert. 2011. *Wahrnehmung und Aufmerksamkeit: Allgemeine Psychologie für Bachelor*. Springer, Berlin Heidelberg, Germany. DOI: http://dx.doi.org/10.1007/978-3-642-12710-6

28. Kenichiro Ito, Hidekazu Nishimura, and Tetsuro Ogi. 2015. Head-up Display for Motorcycle Navigation. ACM Press, 1–3. DOI: http://dx.doi.org/10.1145/2818406.2818415

29. M. P. Jenkins and D. Young. 2016. BARRACUDA: An Augmented Reality Display for Increased Motorcyclist en Route Hazard Awareness. In *2016 IEEE International Multi-Disciplinary Conference on Cognitive Methods in Situation Awareness and Decision Support (CogSIMA)*. 68–72. DOI: http://dx.doi.org/10.1109/COGSIMA.2016.7497788

30. N. A. Kaptein. 1994. *Benefits of in-car head-up displays, TNO Report No.:TNO-TM 1994 B-20*. Technical Report. TNO Human Factors Research Institute.

31. Raymond J. Kiefer. 1991a. Effect of a Head-Up Versus Head-Down Digital Speedometer on Visual Sampling Behavior and Speed Control Performance During Daytime Automobile Driving, In SAE Technical Paper. (02 1991). DOI:http://dx.doi.org/10.4271/910111

32. R. J. Kiefer. 1991b. *Effect of a Head-up versus Head-down Digital Speedometer on Visual Sampling Behaviour and Speed Control Performance during Daytime Automobile Driving. Technical Report No. 910111*. Technical Report. SAE.

33. Robert S. Laramee and Ware Colin. 2002. Rivalry and Interference with a Head-mounted Display. *ACM Trans. Comput.-Hum. Interact.* 9, 3 (Sept. 2002), 238–251. DOI: http://dx.doi.org/10.1145/568513.568516

34. Yung-Ching Liu. 2003. Effects of Using Head-up Display in Automobile Context on Attention Demand and Driving Performance. *Displays* 24, 4?5 (2003), 157 – 165. DOI: http://dx.doi.org/10.1016/j.displa.2004.01.001

35. Yung-Ching Liu and Ming-Hui Wen. 2004. Comparison of Head-up Display (HUD) vs. Head-down Display (HDD): Driving Performance of Commercial Vehicle Operators in Taiwan. *International Journal of Human-Computer Studies* 61, 5 (2004), 679 – 697. DOI: http://dx.doi.org/10.1016/j.ijhcs.2004.06.002

36. Diogo Sanches Mendes. 2015. Motorcycle HUD for Navigation, Communication and Performance Monitoring. (2015).

37. Roberto Montanari, Andrea Borin, and Andrea Spadoni. 2011. SAFERIDER: Results from Yamaha Test Site on Advanced Rider Assistance System. In *Proceedings of the 9th ACM SIGCHI Italian Chapter International Conference on Computer-Human Interaction: Facing Complexity*. ACM, 132–138. http://dl.acm.org/citation.cfm?id=2037329.

38. Ronald R Mourant and Thomas H Rockwell. 1970. Mapping Eye-Movement Patterns to the Visual Scene in Driving: An Exploratory Study. *Human factors* 12, 1 (1970), 81–87. DOI: http://dx.doi.org/10.1177/001872087001200112

39. Eli Peli. 1999. Optometric and Perceptual Issues with Head-mounted Displays. *Visual instrumentation: Optical design and engineering principles* (1999), 205–276.

40. Tony Matthias Poitschke. 2011. Blickbasierte Mensch-Maschine Interaktion im Automobil. (2011).

41. Mathieu Wagner, Thibault North, Stéphane Bourquin, and Lucio Kilcher. 2016. Lightweight High-Brightness Helmet-mounted Head-up Display System, Vol. 9770. 97700F–97700F–8. DOI: http://dx.doi.org/10.1117/12.2203444

42. Christopher D. Wickens and William Horrey. 2008. Models of Attention, Distraction, and Highway Hazard Avoidance. In *Driver Distraction Theory, Effects, and Mitigation*, Michael A. Regan, John D. Lee, and Kristie L. Young (Eds.). CRC Press, Boca Raton, FL, USA, 57–69. DOI:http://dx.doi.org/10.1201/9781420007497.ch5

43. Christopher D. Wickens and J. J. Long. 1994. Conformal Symbology, Attention Shifts and the Head-up Display. In *Proceedings of the 38th Human Factor and Ergonomics Society Annual Meeting*. Human Factors Society, 6–10.

A Model for Detecting and Locating Behaviour Changes in Mobile Touch Targeting Sequences

Daniel Buschek
LMU Munich
Amalienstr. 17, 80333 Munich, Germany
daniel.buschek@ifi.lmu.de

ABSTRACT

Touch offset models capture users' targeting behaviour patterns across the screen. We present and evaluate the first extension of these models to explicitly address *behaviour changes*. We focus on user changes in particular: Given only a series of touch/target locations (x, y), our model detects 1) if the user has changed therein, and if so, 2) at which touch. We evaluate our model on smartphone targeting and typing data from the lab ($N = 28$) and field ($N = 30$). The results show that our model can exploit touch targeting sequences to reveal user changes. Our model outperforms existing non-sequence touch offset models and does not require training data. We discuss the model's limitations and ideas for further improvement. We conclude with recommendations for its integration into future touch biometric systems.

Author Keywords

Change point model; touch biometrics; regression; computational interaction

INTRODUCTION

A well-known aspect of mobile touch input is its inaccuracy: Users may not hit their target exactly, for example due to occlusion [4, 27], limited reach [5], finger orientation [17] and alignment [18], movement [15], and encumbrance [22].

Touch offset models [6, 16, 29] are a computational tool to address this problem: They use touch data to learn users' 2D targeting error patterns across the screen. The models can then shift future touches, improving touch accuracy. These models have also been used to recognise users based on their targeting patterns [10] and to infer hand posture [11] and finger [6].

However, none of these models considered touch *sequences*: 1) Touch corrections were applied per single touch [16, 29]. 2) Recognition of users and hand postures aggregated evidence over multiple touches [6, 10, 11]. Hence, it remains unexplored how to utilise structures within offset sequences, for example *changes* in the underlying behaviour patterns.

IUI'18, March 7–11, 2018, Tokyo, Japan

ACM ISBN 978-1-4503-4945-1/18/03...$15.00
https://doi.org/10.1145/3172944.3172952

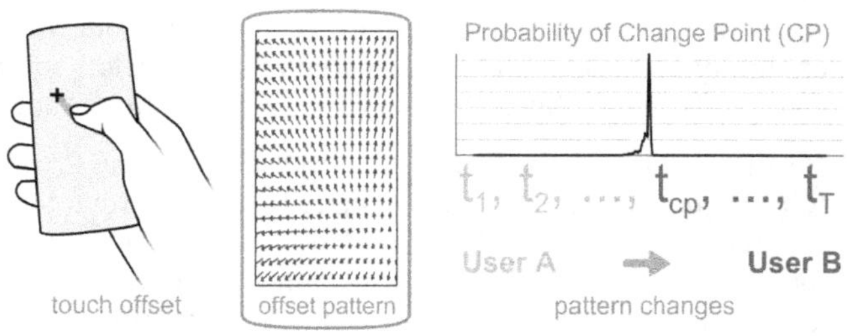

Figure 1. Left: Touch targeting errors (offsets) are measured between touch and target location. Centre: Offset models use regression on such touch targeting data to learn users' individual targeting behaviour patterns across the screen. Right: We extend this approach to touch sequences with behaviour changes, in particular changing users. In this example of a sequence of T touches $t_1, t_2, \ldots, t_T$, the user changes after cp touches. Our model exploits the resulting change in offset patterns (i.e. regression parameters) to 1) detect if a touch sequence contains a user change, and to 2) locate at which touch that change occurs.

Touch targeting is often sequential behaviour, for example when typing or navigating between or within apps. Hence, we argue that there is a gap between the actually sequential user behaviour and the existing offset models' non-sequential approach. This motivates our investigation of the first touch offset model that treats touches in sequences (Figure 1). Our model is thus able to address a new use case for utilising touch offsets: Exploiting behavioural (in)consistencies in targeting sequences to detect and locate changes in user behaviour over time. In particular, here we address the case of changing users.

Detecting user changes has great practical relevance, for example for informing interface adaptation and personalisation, and behavioural biometric systems that protect users' personal data and devices. Touch targeting is the most fundamental and common interaction on mobile devices today; yet it typically yields rather limited data (2D touch/target locations). Thus, detecting user changes purely based on targeting behaviour presents an important and challenging problem.

We contribute 1) a *novel touch offset model*, the first to extend existing offset models from single touches to touch sequences with change points; and 2) *detailed evaluations* of this model on touch targeting data in the lab ($N = 28$) and typing data in the wild ($N = 30$).

The results show that our model can exploit touch targeting sequences to reveal user changes. We discuss this as a building block for touch biometric systems, considering limitations and integration opportunities.

RELATED WORK

In mobile touch input, touch-to-target distances ("offsets") depend on the GUI target's location on the screen. Touch offset models aim to capture and utilise these patterns. Here, we relate our work to this line of research.

Henze et al. [16] collected touch targeting data with a smartphone game. They fitted fifth-order polynomial functions to correct offsets, reducing error rate by 7.79 %. These functions predicted *x*/*y* offsets based on touch *x*/*y*, respectively. Later, a user-specific "2D" offset model by Buschek et al. [11] used quadratic polynomials and considered both touch x and y to predict offsets for both dimensions. Our approach embeds such polynomials. In contrast to the related work, our model explicitly considers that the polynomial's parameters might change over time; this is the foundation for detecting changes.

Beyond linear models, Weir et al. [29] used Gaussian Process (GP) regression [23] for offset modelling to improve touch accuracy. Other work also included motion data into such models [20, 21]. Weir et al. [29] found that offset patterns are highly user-specific, and Musić and Murray-Smith [19] pointed out their speed-specific nature when tapping while walking. Thus, later work employed these GP offset models to personalise mobile messaging in context [9], and to identify and authenticate users [10]. This research motivates the use of touch offsets for touch biometrics in general, and in particular our investigation of an offset model that detects and locates user changes. The related work [10] also provides a baseline approach for comparison (see our evaluation).

All existing offset models needed recorded touch and target locations as training data. In particular, related work used 60 to 400 touches [6, 10, 11, 29]. Weir et al. [28] showed that this can be reduced, using a sparse model, namely a Relevance Vector Machine (RVM) [26]. Since our model looks for changes, not known behaviour, it does not require training data beyond the analysed sequence. Nevertheless, this related work motivates our investigation of detecting user changes in sequences of different lengths, showing that longer sequences (i.e. more touches) better reveal changes.

In summary, existing touch offset models employ regression to learn a mapping from sensed to intended location, using training data as a set, not a sequence. In contrast, our model considers touches as sequences of consistent targeting patterns (modelled with linear regression) with potential pattern changes (i.e. changing regression parameters). This novel approach to touch offset modelling enables our model to utilise touch targeting sequences to detect and locate behaviour changes.

APPLICATION CONTEXT

We highlight that our contribution in this paper is not a practical application, but a novel model and its detailed evaluation with a discussion of limitations and opportunities. Nevertheless, as a motivation for this line of research, here we provide examples of possible future applications for our model.

Automated guest mode: A smartphone could use our model as part of a system that detects user changes to automatically enter a "guest mode" for temporary device sharing. That mode could enable phone calls but block viewing private photos.

Detecting misuse: Consider that a user leaves behind an unlocked phone in a bar. A stranger might grab it to browse private data. The device could analyse the sequence of recent touches to detect if the user has changed. It could then lock itself or raise alarm, for example by sending an email with its GPS location to the legitimate owner or a trusted third party.

Personalisation on shared devices: Another use case is a shared device, for example a "family tablet". Different users might use it for online shoppping, without explicitly switching user accounts. It is thus not clear which user has seen which products and should be shown which recommendations in the future. To solve this problem, the device could detect user changes based on touch behaviour to automatically open a prompt asking for the new current user. It might also recognise the new user automatically upon detecting a change when combined with a user identification model. Moreover, detecting user changes in touch sequences also helps to assign parts of the browsing history to different users post hoc.

Note that we consider our model a *building block* among others – many practical applications benefit from combining it with other data and methods, as described in our discussion.

CHANGE POINT MODELLING FOR TOUCH SEQUENCES

Here, we first introduce the (linear) touch offset models that we then integrate into our change point model.

Overview: Touch Targeting Offset Models

We describe a touch $\mathbf{t}$ at screen location x, y as a vector $\mathbf{t} = (x, y)^T \in \mathbb{R}^2$. Abstractly, an offset model is a function $f(\mathbf{t})$ that maps a touch $\mathbf{t}$ to an offset $\mathbf{o} = (o_x, o_y)$. For training, this offset is typically measured between the touch location $\mathbf{t}$ and the target location (e.g. the target button's centre). In applications, adding the model's predicted offset to the touch yields a corrected touch location $\mathbf{t}' = (t_x + o_x, t_y + o_y)^T$. If the model works well, this correction shifts the touch towards the user's intended target, improving touch accuracy [6, 11, 29]. The model developed in this paper detects behaviour changes based on these offset patterns, instead of correcting touches.

Linear Touch Offset Models with Basis Functions

The linear touch offset models described in related work [6, 11] follow the general linear model, in matrix form defined as:

$$\mathbf{o} = \mathbf{X}\mathbf{w} + \varepsilon, \tag{1}$$

where $\mathbf{X}$ is the $T \times d$ design matrix with one row per touch (e.g. in an interaction sequence of T touches) and one column per basis function (explained below). Moreover, $\mathbf{w}$ contains the model's parameters, and $\mathbf{o}$ is a $T \times 2$ vector containing the observed offsets for both screen dimensions for all T touches. Finally, ε is Gaussian noise. See the related work for more details on parameters and how to estimate them from data [6].

The model uses basis functions Φ to transform the raw input touches. For example, the quadratic model described in related work [6, 11] uses $\Phi(\mathbf{t}) = (1, x, y, x^2, y^2)^T \in \mathbb{R}^5$. In general, basis functions allow the linear model to account for nonlinear relationships between touch locations and offsets.

Extending Offset Models to Sequences & Change Points

We adapt the change point model from Rasmussen [24], which uses Bayesian analysis and the general linear model. We decided to build upon this model, since it allows us to integrate the linear offset model described above with few adaptations. The result is the first touch offset model that analyses touches as sequences to detect behaviour changes.

Rationale

Intuitively, the model as described below "tries out" all possible splits of a touch targeting sequence into two parts, expecting each part to show different but consistent user behaviour. A change point then seems more likely for those splits of the observed data which match this expectation.

Formal Definition

We describe the parts relevant to our changes and use of the model. More background can be found in related work [24].

First, to be able to treat our two-dimensional output $\mathbf{o} \in \mathbb{R}^{T\times 2}$ with one-dimensional regression, we unroll it into a long vector $\hat{\mathbf{o}} = (o_{x1}, ..., i_{xT}, o_{y1}, ...o_{yT})^T \in \mathbb{R}^{2T\times 1}$ (as in [29]).

We define a matrix $\mathbf{G}_t \in \mathbb{R}^{T\times 2d}$ per timestep t (the "splits"):

$$\mathbf{G}_t = \begin{bmatrix} \mathbf{X}[1,...,t;1,..,d] & \mathbf{0}_{t,d} \\ \mathbf{0}_{T-t,d} & \mathbf{X}[t+1,...,T;1,..,d] \end{bmatrix} \quad (2)$$

Therein, $\mathbf{0}_{n,m}$ is a zero-filled matrix of dimension $n \times m$, and the $\mathbf{X}[...;...]$ denote submatrices of $\mathbf{X}$ which consist of rows and columns with the given lists of indices.

Next, we stack up these matrices $\mathbf{G}_t$ to $\hat{\mathbf{G}}_t \in \mathbb{R}^{2T\times 4d}$ to match the way we handle the 2D output with $\hat{\mathbf{o}}$:

$$\hat{\mathbf{G}}_t = \begin{bmatrix} \mathbf{G}_t & \mathbf{0}_{T,2d} \\ \mathbf{0}_{T,2d} & \mathbf{G}_t \end{bmatrix} \quad (3)$$

Using these matrices $\hat{\mathbf{G}}_t$, we define ρ_t as an intermediate step:

$$\rho_t = |\hat{\mathbf{G}}_t^T\hat{\mathbf{G}}_t|^{-1/2}[\hat{\mathbf{o}}^T\hat{\mathbf{o}} - \hat{\mathbf{o}}^T\hat{\mathbf{G}}_t(\hat{\mathbf{G}}_t^T\hat{\mathbf{G}}_t)^{-1}\hat{\mathbf{G}}_t^T\hat{\mathbf{o}}]^{-(T-d)/2} \quad (4)$$

Finally, normalisation of these ρ_t yields the probability $p(c_t|\hat{\mathbf{o}})$ of a change point c_t happening at time t:

$$p(c_t|\hat{\mathbf{o}}) = \rho_t \left(\sum_{s=1}^{T-1} \rho_s\right)^{-1} \quad (5)$$

Computing $p(c_t|\hat{\mathbf{o}})$ for all $t = 1, ..., T-1$ yields the posterior. For each timestep, we now have a probability describing how likely we think it is that the change happens there. The prior implied in the transformations leading to the equations above is uniform [24]: Before seeing the data, the model considers each time step to be equally (un)likely as a change point.

Model Limitations

The model in this specific form has two limitations: First, it only expects a single change point in a sequence. We focus on this case in our analyses to evaluate the fundamental model. However, as described in related work [24], the formal approach can be extended to multiple change points, in our case by modifying Equation 2 (e.g. to split into three parts). Even in its current form, the *detection* task (i.e. change in sequence or not?) works with multiple change points, as long as at least one of them is a clear enough change to our model.

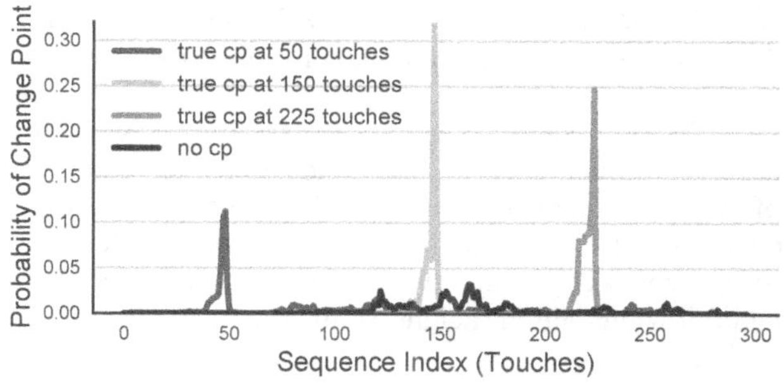

Figure 2. Posterior distributions for four example sequences, three with change points (at 50, 150, 225 touches), and one without a true change point. The plots show the probability of a change point at each touch in the sequence, as estimated by our model. Note how the probability mass concentrates around true change points and how the model remains "undecided" for the sequence with no true change point.

Second, the model formulation originally analyses sequences post hoc. For example, a touch biometric system could use it to detect user changes in touch data after a usage session. However, this approach can be turned into an online version by processing chunks of touches (e.g. the last N touches, updated at each touch). We return to these limitations in our discussion.

TOUCH SEQUENCE AND CHANGE POINT ANALYSES

Model Application I: Detecting Change Points

Intuitively, we decide that a change point is present in a touch sequence if our model's posterior $p(c_t|\hat{\mathbf{o}})$ shows a clear "peak" (i.e. low posterior entropy). In contrast, if the model cannot find a clear change point the posterior will be "flat" (i.e. high entropy). Figure 2 shows examples for each of these cases.

Implementing this approach, we decide if a change point is present or not based on the posterior entropy H:

$$H = -\sum_{t=1}^{T-1} p(c_t|\hat{\mathbf{o}}) \log p(c_t|\hat{\mathbf{o}}) \quad (6)$$

In practice, the actual decision can be made, for example, by comparing the entropy against a threshold.

Model Application II: Locating Change Points

A second task is to estimate *where* a change point is located within a sequence. Our model's posterior distribution also enables such estimates. For example, we can estimate the time step of the change point with the posterior mean location l_{mean}:

$$l_{\text{mean}} = \sum_{t=1}^{T-1} p(c_t|\hat{\mathbf{o}})t, \quad (7)$$

We could also use the maximum's location $l_{\max}$:

$$l_{\max} = \arg\max_t p(c_t|\hat{\mathbf{o}}) \quad (8)$$

We compare both approaches in our analyses. Our results show that l_{mean} yields more accurate estimates.

STUDY I - MOBILE TOUCH TARGETING IN THE LAB

We evaluate the described model on a published smartphone touch targeting dataset [6], collected in the lab. Per participant ($N = 28$), the dataset contains two sessions (a week apart), each with touches at 400 target locations per combination of the two independent variables: *hand posture* (right thumb, device in right hand; right index finger, device in left hand) and *target type* – crosshair, key (4×7 mm), app icon (9×9 mm), and full width button (height 9 mm).

Preprocessing

Following related work [6, 10], we removed outliers that result from participants hitting the screen by accident (e.g. accidental double tap). These touches are clearly too far away from the target to be intended targeting actions. We removed touches which are further away from their target than the task's mean offset length plus three standard deviations (1.4 % of the data).

Evaluation Procedure

The data contains touches from 28 users. Hence, to extensively test our model, we can create sequences with and without user changes as follows: For each pair of users u_i, u_j, we concatenate n_i touches from u_i with n_j touches from u_j to form one sequence (of length $n_i + n_j$) that has a user change (if $i \neq j$) or no such change (if $i = j$). Note that this concatenation introduces no artefacts (e.g. unusually long time gap) since the sequence is still just a list of touch and target locations.

We then analyse these concatenated sequences with our model. Ideally, the model would predict a change for all sequences with touches from two different users (i.e. $i \neq j$), and no change for all sequences with touches from a single user (i.e. $i = j$).

Moreover, by varying n_i and n_j, we can 1) shift the change point's location within the sequence, and 2) evaluate the model on sequences of different lengths overall.

Performance Measures

To measure model performance, we use the two standard measures receiver-operating-characteristic area-under-curve (ROC AUC) and equal error rate (EER) [14]: In our case, the ROC curve is obtained by varying the decision threshold applied to the model's "score" (i.e. entropy, Equation 6). The curve plots false positives (missing to detect a change) against true positives (rightfully detecting a change). A high area under this curve (AUC) means that cases with and without changes can be distinguished well. The maximum AUC score (1) indicates perfect distinction. Moreover, EER is the point on the ROC curve closest to the line "false positive rate equals false negative rate". An EER of $X\%$ means that in $X\%$ of cases the system would incorrectly detect a change, while in $X\%$ of actual changes it would fail to detect them.

Results – Detecting User Changes

Table 1 shows the results of detecting user changes with three different variations of our model (linear, quadratic, hyperbolic basis functions). The models analysed sequences of 300 touches with one hand posture and target type, with change points located at 150 touches (i.e. at 50 % of the sequence).

Target type	Hand posture	Change point detection accuracy									
		linear Φ		quadr. Φ		hyperb. Φ		rel. work		combined	
		AUC	EER	AUC	EER	AUC	EER	AUC	EER	AUC	EER
cross	thumb	0.96	12	0.97	8	0.96	10	0.85	23	0.97	8
	index	0.92	17	0.92	16	0.92	16	0.79	29	0.94	13
key	thumb	0.94	15	0.96	15	0.95	13	0.86	23	0.97	8
	index	0.92	15	0.91	17	0.92	16	0.83	23	0.93	15
app	thumb	0.88	19	0.88	17	0.88	15	0.80	29	0.91	13
	index	0.89	21	0.91	19	0.91	17	0.78	31	0.93	15
fill	thumb	0.72	33	0.70	35	0.68	33	0.49	48	0.64	40
	index	0.76	35	0.74	33	0.74	33	0.53	46	0.73	29

Table 1. Evaluation of change point detection for different targets, hand postures, and offset models (i.e. basis functions Φ), with sequences of 300 touches and a true change point at 150 touches. The second to last column shows the results using the approach from related work [10], the last column combines it with our approach.

Target type	Hand posture	Change point detection accuracy					
		true cp at 25%		true cp at 50%		true cp at 75%	
		AUC	EER	AUC	EER	AUC	EER
cross	thumb	0.91	16	0.96	10	0.91	17
	index	0.85	23	0.92	16	0.85	23
key	thumb	0.90	19	0.95	13	0.89	21
	index	0.86	20	0.92	16	0.85	21
app	thumb	0.82	24	0.88	15	0.83	24
	index	0.81	27	0.91	17	0.81	26
fill	thumb	0.61	40	0.68	33	0.64	37
	index	0.68	37	0.74	33	0.68	37

Table 2. Evaluation of change point detection for different locations of the change point within the analysed sequence (for sequences of length 300 and the hyperbolic offset model). The results show that the model performs better if a sufficient number of touches is observed for behaviour both *before* and *after* the change point.

Target Types and Hand Postures

Behaviour changes were clearer for interactions with smaller targets. The large *fill* targets in particular hide user-specific targeting behaviour, explained by their large area that allows for less consistent behaviour [10]. Changes were also clearer for thumb touches than index finger ones. Both findings are in line with related work [10], which analysed individuality of offsets touch by touch (not as sequences with change points).

Model Variations

Comparing variations of our model, the one with hyperbolic basis functions performs best overall. It beats the quadratic one only by a slight margin. This suggests that the complexity of offset patterns is sufficiently captured by quadratic/hyperbolic terms regarding the detection of changes.

Change Point Location in the Sequence

If a change occurs near the start or end of a sequence, either behaviour before or after the change is only observed for few touches. Hence, we are interested in evaluating how the model reacts to change points in different places.

Table 2 shows results for change points at 25 %, 50 %, and 75 % of the whole sequence. These results show that change points are easier to find with our model when a sufficient number of touches is observed for behaviour before and after them. This is to be expected: Behaviour changes are clearer if consistent behaviour can be observed around them, which only becomes evident with a certain number of touches. Nevertheless, visual inspection and high AUC values indicate that the model's posterior provides considerable evidence for change points even if they happen near the start/end of a sequence.

Sequence Length

We also analysed how evident change points appear to our model in sequences of different lengths. Figure 3 (left) shows the results: Changes are harder to spot in shorter sequences. In contrast, more data gives our model longer subsequences of consistent behaviour, making it easier to detect a change.

Comparison to Related Work / Non-Sequence Offset Models

Table 1 further shows results with the only previously published approach for distinguishing users purely based on touch offset patterns [10]. That approach uses non-sequence touch offset models [29] to evaluate and aggregate the likelihood of a specific user in contrast to others over all touches. Hence, it needs training data from the user that it seeks to distinguish from others; plus data from others.

Following the related work [10], for each evaluation case (see procedure above), we trained that model on data from u_i vs data from all others but u_j – using data from one study session, then testing on sequences concatenated from data of u_i and u_j from the other session. This is a recommended evaluation scheme from behavioural biometrics [8, 10]; further details on this model and approach can be found in said related work.

In contrast, our model does not require any data beyond the sequence at hand. Moreover, instead of aggregating single touches, it considers the sequence as such, that is, largely consistent behaviour over time, possibly changing at some point. Figure 3 shows that our sequence model is able to exploit more touches (EERs decrease per touch), while aggregation largely stagnates at higher EERs after a certain number of touches. The black regression lines in Figure 3 show this (EER in % falls -0.07 per touch with our model vs -0.02 with the non-sequence model).

Based on the results in Table 1, our model improves EERs by $\approx 40\,\%$ relative to the previously proposed approach for distinguishing users purely with touch offset patterns.

Model Combination

Finally, as the last column in Table 1 shows, it is possible to combine the "scores" obtained by both models (ours + related work [10]) to improve user change detection. We combined the models' outputs as a weighted sum, with weights informed by cross validation on one randomly chosen user's data. Intuitively, this combined model performs better since it utilises both indications of *known* behaviour and *change* of said behaviour: 1) The other model [10] trained as described above assesses if the behaviour matches to that of the expected user (u_i in our evaluation scheme, see above); and 2) our model assesses if the given sequence contains a behaviour change.

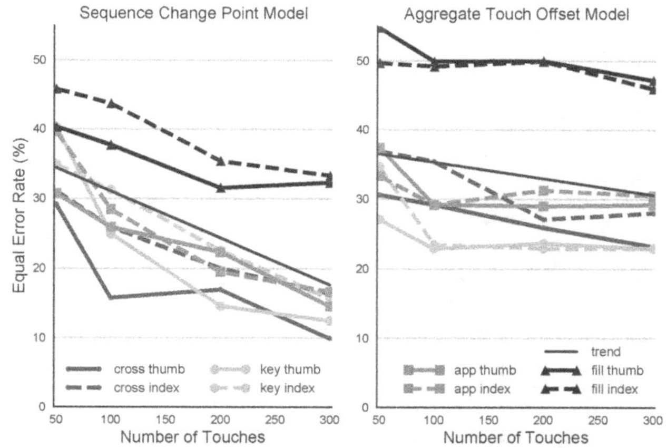

Figure 3. Change point detection for sequences of different lengths (true change point at 50 %). For our approach (left), more data leads to better accuracy (i.e. lower EER). In comparison, the previously proposed approach (right, [10]) remains at a higher error rate.

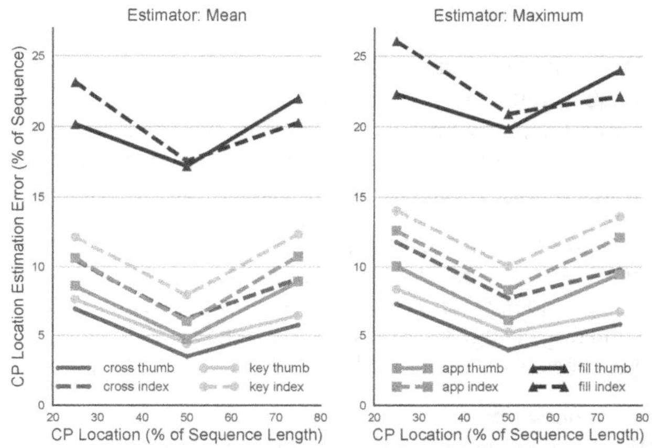

Figure 4. Change point location estimation (hyperbolic Φ, sequence with 300 touches). We measure the difference in percent of sequence length between predicted location and true location. We compare two estimators (left: mean, Equation 7; right: max, Equation 8) and three locations of the change point (x-axes: 25 %, 50 %, 75 % of sequence).

Results – Locating User Changes

We are also interested in detecting *where* a user change happens within a touch sequence. Our model inherently yields an estimate of this change point location (Equations 7 and 8). We again follow the described evaluation procedure, now only looking at cases with change points. We measure the distance between the estimated change point location and the true location, in % of the length of the whole sequence.

Target Types and Hand Postures

In line with results for detecting changes, estimating their locations is easier for thumb input than index finger touches (compare full vs dotted lines in Figure 4). Moreover, *fill* targets stand out with much higher estimation errors ($\approx$17.5 %), again explained by less consistent user behaviour for such large targets. In contrast, the model located changes for the smaller targets more accurately, with errors of 3.51 % to 8.00 %. For the tested sequence length, this means that changes are located within about 10 to 24 touches around the true point. To put this into context, in a typing sequence, for example, a user change might thus be located within up to 2 to 5 words.

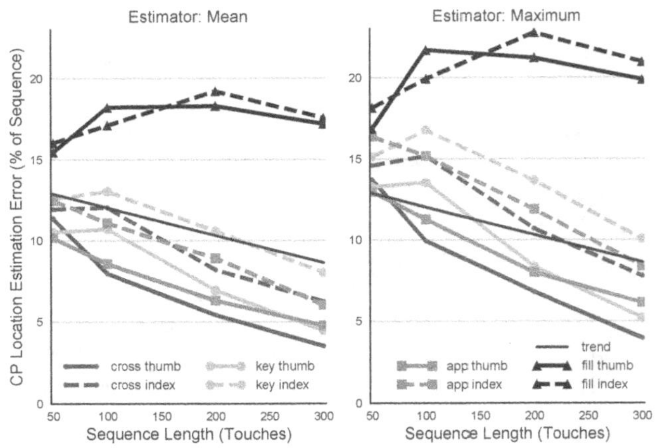

Figure 5. Change point location estimation for sequences of different lengths. The true change point is at 50 % of the sequence. The mean approach (Equation 7, left) is more accurate than the maximum approach (Equation 8, right). Overall, changes are more accurately located as more touches are observed.

Comparison of Change Point Location Estimators

Figure 4 (left vs right) shows two different approaches of estimating the change point location from our model's posterior: mean (Equation 7) and maximum (Equation 8). The mean estimator was more accurate for all targets and postures.

Change Point Location in the Sequence

Figure 4 shows results for changes at 25 %, 50 %, and 75 % of the sequence. In line with results for detecting changes, estimating change locations is easier when a sufficient number of touches is observed for behaviour before and after them.

Sequence Length

We also compared location estimation for sequences of different lengths. Figure 5 shows the results: Overall, change point estimation is more accurate relative to the length of the sequence as more touches are observed. An exception are the *fill* targets, again likely due to the highly inconsistent targeting behaviour evoked by their large area. Comparing both estimators, the mean approach is consistently better than the maximum approach for all tested sequence lengths. The trends are similar (error in % sequence length about -0.02 per touch).

STUDY II - MOBILE TOUCH TYPING IN THE WILD

We complement our lab analyses with evaluations on touch sequences collected from users' own everyday typing. This promises results of high ecological validity. In particular, an in-the-wild study allows us to observe targeting behaviour from a variety of everyday contexts for each user. This study is part of a larger research project (see [7] for further analyses); here we focus on targeting behaviour.

Apparatus

We modified Google's Android Open Source Project (AOSP) Keyboard[1] to record keyboard touch data. To protect users' privacy, the data was filtered on the device: In particular, we used a "trigram filter", which recorded touch locations only for three subsequent touches with a random chance of 10 %. After each recording, there was a minimum gap of at least one character. These parameters were tested in a pre-study to ensure that the recorded data would not reveal entered text. Typing in special text entry fields (e.g. name, address, password) was never recorded. Moreover, we added a "private mode" button to the keyboard with which participants could pause recording at any time.

We assessed hand posture via an experience sampling method (ESM): Our keyboard displayed a set of posture pictograms and asked participants to select their current hand posture. This posture selection overlay was shown when opening the keyboard, but no more than once every ten minutes.

Participants

We recruited 30 participants (15 female) via a newsletter and social media. Their mean age was 24 years (18-33); one was left-handed. Most were students and proficient touch keyboard users. They received a € 15 gift card as compensation.

Procedure

We deployed our app in a three-week field study on participants' own smartphones. App, study and examples of recorded data were explained in an initial meeting. In line with our university's regulations, people signed an informed consent form. Demographics were recorded with a questionnaire.

Participants then used their phone as usual. We did not instruct them, for example, to use certain hand postures (but we assessed postures via ESM, see apparatus).

After three weeks, we informed participants about the end of the study and asked them to uninstall the app. They also provided feedback in a post-study questionnaire. No data was recorded beyond the study.

Study Limitations

Samples in this study and the lab dataset are biased towards students and thus young people. Touch behaviour might be different for other user groups.

Moreover, our data might contain typing from non-participants (e.g. device sharing). However, all participants owned personal unshared devices. We also instructed them to use the "private mode" if they should need to share their device temporarily.

Since hand posture was assessed via ESM, it might not be perfectly accurate. A Likert question in the post-study questionnaire asked about this (*"I always selected the posture I was actually using"*). All but one person (strongly) agreed with this statement.

Finally, we only observed targeting behaviour while typing, not for tapping in general (e.g. app selection on home screen).

Preprocessing and Evaluation Procedure

In total, we recorded 204,685 touches with screen locations and the locations of their corresponding target keys. People used their own devices; related work [2, 13] pointed out that in this case touch locations need to be normalised for analyses across screen sizes. Hence, we normalised them using the recorded keyboard widths and heights.

[1] `https://android.googlesource.com/platform/packages/inputmethods/LatinIME/`, *accessed 7th October 2017.*

Hand posture	N	Change point detection accuracy									
		linear Φ		quadr. Φ		hyperb. Φ		rel. work		combined	
		AUC	EER	AUC	EER	AUC	EER	AUC	EER	AUC	EER
all	30	0.91	17	0.92	17	0.85	21	0.86	36	0.92	16
two thumbs	19	0.90	18	0.90	17	0.86	20	0.71	33	0.93	15
right thumb	12	0.88	16	0.88	20	0.84	23	0.64	38	0.87	19

Table 3. Change point detection on touch targeting sequences from typing in the wild (sequences of length 300 with true change point at 50 %).

Hand posture	N	Change point detection accuracy					
		true cp at 25%		true cp at 50%		true cp at 75%	
		AUC	EER	AUC	EER	AUC	EER
all	30	0.86	22	0.92	17	0.86	22
two thumbs	19	0.85	23	0.90	17	0.85	22
right thumb	12	0.81	26	0.88	20	0.81	26

Table 4. Evaluation of change point detection in the wild for different locations of the change point within the analysed sequence (for sequences of length 300 and the quadratic offset model).

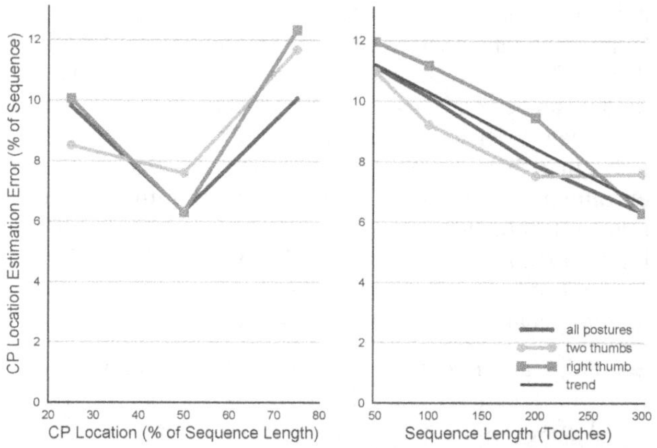

Figure 6. Change point location estimation on touch targeting sequences from typing in the wild. Left: Results for different locations of the change point within the sequence (of length 300 touches). Right: Results for sequences of different lengths (true change point at 50 %).

For the following analyses, we used the same evaluation procedure as in the first study. However, we have many more touches here than in the lab. To allow for comparisons to the first study, we subsample shorter sequences of the same lengths as in study one (up to 300 touches). To avoid introducing randomness by this procedure, we follow the common ten-fold cross-validation scheme, that is, repeating all analyses on different subsequences and reporting the averaged results.

Results

To avoid redundancy with our report of the lab study, here we focus on differences, comparisons and additional insights.

Model Variations

The model with quadratic basis functions performed best overall (Table 3). It outperformed the linear one only slightly. This suggests that the complexity of offset patterns for typing in the wild is sufficiently captured by linear/quadratic terms regarding the detection of user changes. In contrast to the lab, the hyperbolic model performed worse. One explanation is that this model overfits on noisy everyday data, whereas the simpler linear/quadratic models are more robust.

Hand Postures

Table 3 shows results for two postures, namely typing with both thumbs (i.e. two handed use) or with the right one only (i.e. one handed use). The number of participants per posture differs, since not everyone used every posture. Other postures (e.g. index finger) occurred as well, but were used too rarely and/or by too few people for a meaningful analysis here.

Direct comparisons are difficult due to the different numbers of participants. Nevertheless, the results suggest the tendency that typing with both thumbs revealed user changes better than typing with the right thumb. This is in line with related work on password typing biometrics [8], which found in a lab study that users are easier to distinguish by typing behaviour with both thumbs compared to one.

Change Point Location and Sequence Lengths

As in the first study, we evaluated different locations of the change point (Table 4) as well as different sequence lengths. The results confirmed the findings from the lab study: Behaviour changes are clearer 1) if consistent behaviour can be observed both before and after them for a sufficient number of touches, and 2) for longer sequences overall. The impact on AUCs and EERs was comparable to the first study.

Performance in the Lab vs in the Wild

Table 1 and Table 3 show overall comparable change point detection accuracy for key targets with our model. In contrast, the non-sequence touch offset model [10] performs a lot worse (EER 23 in the lab vs 36 in the wild). We explain this with varying contexts of typing in daily life (e.g. on the go vs at home). Relying on training data is challenging if that data was collected in a different context. In contrast, our model analyses the given sequence without training on previous recordings, rendering it more robust to changing everyday situations.

Model Combination

The combined model still overall performed best (Table 3), but the advantage was less distinct than in the lab; the linear version of our model performed better than the combined model for typing with the right thumb. This is explained by the overall worse performance of the non-sequence model.

Locating User Changes

For locating the change point (Figure 6), this study overall confirmed the findings from the lab. Changes are more accurately located by our model 1) when a sufficient number of touches is observed before and after them; and 2) as more touches are observed (error in % sequence length about -0.02 per touch).

DISCUSSION

Improving Offset Features for Touch Biometrics

Our analyses show that mobile touch targeting sequences reveal information about user changes. However, are the observed results "good enough" to consider the model useful for future research and (biometric) applications? We conclude that the answer is yes, as explained below.

First, our model presents several advances compared to prior work: 1) It outperforms the existing non-sequential method for exploiting touch offset patterns to detect changing users [10]. Comparing lab vs wild, it also better handles noisy real-world data. 2) Moreover, our model requires no training data. 3) Our model can be combined with the existing one [10] to improve user change detection accuracy overall. 4) Our EERs are also lower than those obtained for detecting user changes (between enrolment and authentication, i.e. using training data) with touch offset features on typing data in the lab [8] (our EER for typing 17-26 % vs 30 % in the related work). 5) Finally, to the best of our knowledge, we are the first to present a model for *locating* change points in sequences of touch offsets.

Second, regarding observed absolute EERs, we highlight our focus on touch offsets only: While this paper contributes a novel offset model, practical applications interested in detecting changing users can take into account more information. Related work showed that combining different behavioural biometrics improves accuracy [12]. This was also shown for the particular case of combining touch offsets with other touch features [8, 25]. Hence, related work demonstrates that improvements in utilising touch offsets, as achieved here, lead to overall better touch biometric systems.

We thus conclude that our model presents a useful novel building block for touch biometric systems that enables them to better exploit touch targeting (offset) sequences.

Modifying and Extending the Model

Online Change Point Detection

Some use cases require online change point detection. While our model analyses sequences post hoc, it can be integrated into an online version, for example, by processing the last N touches, updated per touch. We also plan to investigate dedicated online change point models (e.g. [1]) in future work.

Handling Multiple Change Points

Our model as described here assumes one change point. This is suitable for some applications, such as locking a phone or sending a warning email to its legitimate owner if a user change has been detected in the last touch sequence.

Other applications might involve (post hoc) analyses of interaction sequences that contain multiple user changes. The model formulation can be extended directly to multiple changes (see [24]). Even without modifications, *detecting* a change is possible if at least one change point is evident enough to our model. Thus, our model might be used in a "divide-and-conquer" scheme that (recursively) subdivides the sequence at a detected change to check the subsequences for further changes. We will investigate such extensions in future work.

Handling Short (Sub)Sequences

Our analyses revealed that user changes are harder to detect and locate if the model has little data to work with. This is the case for 1) short touch sequences and 2) short subsequences, that is, the user changes near the start/end of the sequence, such that only few touches are available for one of the users. To improve the model for such cases, it could be combined with an approach that uses recorded training data, as demonstrated with our combined model (also see next subsection).

Combining Change Detection and User Recognition

Our model detects user changes. Another task is to *recognise* users. For example, a touch biometric system might assign different parts of a finished browsing session on a shared device to specific users to inform future personal shopping recommendations based on who visited which website/product (see application context section). Such a task benefits from combining our model with a method to match the obtained subsequences (i.e. split at change points) to known users. One combination candidate is the model from prior work [10], which we already successfully combined with our model to improve the detection of changes itself (see Table 1 and 3).

Our model itself could also be used to help recognise a known user: Concatenate a previously recorded touch sequence with new touches. If our model detects no change point, this suggests that the new data comes from the same user as the old one. In contrast, if a change point is detected, this indicates that the new data comes from a different user. We plan to explore this idea further in future work, comparing it to other anomaly detection methods (see e.g. [3, 8]).

Causes of Changes in Mobile Touch Targeting Behaviour

We focussed on behaviour changes due to user changes, since 1) this extends related work on the user-specific nature of touch targeting behaviour [10, 29], and 2) promises to be useful as a building block for touch behaviour biometrics. Nevertheless, there are other reasons for changes in touch targeting behaviour, such as changing hand postures, starting to walk, and so on. Our model itself is flexible and could be applied for detecting other changes. An interesting challenge is to distinguish causes (e.g. new user or new hand posture?). To address this question our model could be combined with posture detectors [15, 30] and further information (e.g. application context, other sensor data).

Our model already reveals insights into the relative impact of context and user changes: Our typing data sequences contain touches from multiple postures ("all" postures row in Table 3) and likely from multiple contexts in the wild (e.g. at home vs on the go), yet the high AUCs indicate that our model still picked up user changes. This indicates that user changes are more pronounced in typing sequences than changing postures or situations – a promising result for touch biometrics.

Implementing and Integrating the Model in Applications

Our model has several favourable properties that facilitate easy implementation and integration: 1) It requires no training data. 2) It is lightweight (our implementation has about 30 lines of Python code). 3) The model runs fast and can utilise highly efficient matrix routines, since it can be written almost entirely in vectorised/matrix form.

CONCLUSION

Touch offset models capture 2D targeting behaviour patterns to improve touch accuracy or to recognise users and hand postures [6, 10, 16, 29]. We presented the first extension of these models to explicitly consider touches as *sequences*, enabling our model to assess *changes* in user behaviour. In particular, our model detects and locates user changes based on touch targeting offsets. This is useful, for example, to detect misuse, to manage multiple user accounts, or to inform user-specific personalisation and recommendation systems.

We evaluated our model on smartphone targeting and typing data from the lab ($N = 28$) and field ($N = 30$). Depending on hand posture, target, sequence length and change point location, it detects user changes with a best equal error rate of 8 %, and locates them with a best error of 3.5 % sequence length. Our model outperforms the existing non-sequence touch offset models for detecting user changes and does not require training data. We demonstrated that it can be combined with existing models to further improve accuracy. Our model also provides a posterior distribution, useful for locating user changes within sequences and for combining it with other probabilistic information (e.g. from other sensors).

Hence, our model allows researchers and applications interested in changes in users' mobile interaction behaviour to better exploit touch targeting (offset) sequences. By releasing our model and data, we thus hope to provide a useful novel building block for touch biometrics.

PROJECT RESOURCES

Our models and data are available on the project's website: http://www.medien.ifi.lmu.de/touch-change

ACKNOWLEDGEMENTS

We thank Benjamin Bisinger for his help with the field study. Work on this project was partially funded by the Bavarian State Ministry of Education, Science and the Arts in the framework of the Centre Digitisation.Bavaria (ZD.B). This research was supported by the Deutsche Forschungsgemeinschaft (DFG), Grant No. AL 1899/2-1.

REFERENCES

1. Ryan Prescott Adams and David J. C. Mackay. 2007. Bayesian Online Changepoint Detection. *arXiv.org* (2007), 7. DOI: http://dx.doi.org/arXiv:0710.3742v1
2. Naif Alotaibi, Emmanuel Pascal Bruno, Michael Coakley, Alexander Gazarov, Stephen Winard, Filip Witkowski, Alecia Copeland, Peter Nebauer, Christopher Keene, and Joshua Williams. 2014. Text Input Biometric System Design for Handheld Devices. In *Proceedings of Student-Faculty Research Day, Pace University*. 1–8. https://pdfs.semanticscholar.org/6bbf/41e3a8b1ceb7ec9cdd4bb2797dd5ebb7a1ff.pdf
3. M. Antal and L. Z. SzabÃş. 2015. An Evaluation of One-Class and Two-Class Classification Algorithms for Keystroke Dynamics Authentication on Mobile Devices. In *20th International Conference on Control Systems and Computer Science*. 343–350. DOI: http://dx.doi.org/10.1109/CSCS.2015.16
4. Patrick Baudisch and Gerry Chu. 2009. Back-of-device Interaction Allows Creating Very Small Touch Devices. In *Proceedings of the SIGCHI Conference on Human Factors in Computing Systems (CHI '09)*. ACM, New York, NY, USA, 1923–1932. DOI: http://dx.doi.org/10.1145/1518701.1518995
5. Joanna Bergstrom-Lehtovirta and Antti Oulasvirta. 2014. Modeling the Functional Area of the Thumb on Mobile Touchscreen Surfaces. In *Proceedings of the SIGCHI Conference on Human Factors in Computing Systems (CHI '14)*. ACM, New York, NY, USA, 1991–2000. DOI: http://dx.doi.org/10.1145/2556288.2557354
6. Daniel Buschek and Florian Alt. 2015. TouchML: A Machine Learning Toolkit for Modelling Spatial Touch Targeting Behaviour. In *Proceedings of the 20th International Conference on Intelligent User Interfaces (IUI '15)*. ACM, New York, NY, USA, 110–114. DOI: http://dx.doi.org/10.1145/2678025.2701381
7. Daniel Buschek, Benjamin Bisinger, and Florian Alt. 2018. ResearchIME: A Mobile Keyboard Application for Studying Free Typing Behaviour in the Wild. In *Proceedings of the 2018 CHI Conference on Human Factors in Computing Systems (CHI '18)*. ACM, New York, NY, USA. DOI: http://dx.doi.org/10.1145/3173574.317382
8. Daniel Buschek, Alexander De Luca, and Florian Alt. 2015a. Improving Accuracy, Applicability and Usability of Keystroke Biometrics on Mobile Touchscreen Devices. In *Proceedings of the 33rd Annual ACM Conference on Human Factors in Computing Systems (CHI '15)*. ACM, New York, NY, USA, 1393–1402. DOI: http://dx.doi.org/10.1145/2702123.2702252
9. Daniel Buschek, Alexander De Luca, and Florian Alt. 2015b. There is More to Typing Than Speed: Expressive Mobile Touch Keyboards via Dynamic Font Personalisation. In *Proceedings of the 17th International Conference on Human-Computer Interaction with Mobile Devices and Services (MobileHCI '15)*. ACM, New York, NY, USA, 125–130. DOI: http://dx.doi.org/10.1145/2785830.2785844
10. Daniel Buschek, Alexander De Luca, and Florian Alt. 2016. Evaluating the Influence of Targets and Hand Postures on Touch-based Behavioural Biometrics. In *Proceedings of the 2016 CHI Conference on Human Factors in Computing Systems (CHI '16)*. ACM, New York, NY, USA, 1349–1361. DOI: http://dx.doi.org/10.1145/2858036.2858165
11. Daniel Buschek, Simon Rogers, and Roderick Murray-Smith. 2013. User-specific Touch Models in a Cross-device Context. In *Proceedings of the 15th International Conference on Human-computer Interaction with Mobile Devices and Services (MobileHCI '13)*. ACM, New York, NY, USA, 382–391. DOI: http://dx.doi.org/10.1145/2493190.2493206
12. Heather Crawford, Karen Renaud, and Tim Storer. 2013. A framework for continuous, transparent mobile device authentication. *Computers & Security* 39, Part B (2013), 127 – 136.
13. Benjamin Draffin, Jiang Zhu, and Joy Zhang. 2014. *KeySens: Passive User Authentication through Micro-behavior Modeling of Soft Keyboard Interaction.*

Springer International Publishing, Cham, 184–201. DOI: http://dx.doi.org/10.1007/978-3-319-05452-0_14

14. Tom Fawcett. 2006. An introduction to ROC analysis. *Pattern Recognition Letters* 27, 8 (2006), 861 – 874. DOI: http://dx.doi.org/10.1016/j.patrec.2005.10.010

15. Mayank Goel, Jacob Wobbrock, and Shwetak Patel. 2012. GripSense: Using Built-in Sensors to Detect Hand Posture and Pressure on Commodity Mobile Phones. In *Proceedings of the 25th Annual ACM Symposium on User Interface Software and Technology (UIST '12)*. ACM, New York, NY, USA, 545–554. DOI: http://dx.doi.org/10.1145/2380116.2380184

16. Niels Henze, Enrico Rukzio, and Susanne Boll. 2011. 100,000,000 Taps: Analysis and Improvement of Touch Performance in the Large. In *Proceedings of the 13th International Conference on Human Computer Interaction with Mobile Devices and Services (MobileHCI '11)*. ACM, New York, NY, USA, 133–142. DOI: http://dx.doi.org/10.1145/2037373.2037395

17. Christian Holz and Patrick Baudisch. 2010. The Generalized Perceived Input Point Model and How to Double Touch Accuracy by Extracting Fingerprints. In *Proceedings of the SIGCHI Conference on Human Factors in Computing Systems (CHI '10)*. ACM, New York, NY, USA, 581–590. DOI: http://dx.doi.org/10.1145/1753326.1753413

18. Christian Holz and Patrick Baudisch. 2011. Understanding Touch. In *Proceedings of the SIGCHI Conference on Human Factors in Computing Systems (CHI '11)*. ACM, New York, NY, USA, 2501–2510. DOI: http://dx.doi.org/10.1145/1978942.1979308

19. Josip Musić and Roderick Murray-Smith. 2016. Nomadic Input on Mobile Devices: The Influence of Touch Input Technique and Walking Speed on Performance and Offset Modeling. *Human-Computer Interaction* 31, 5 (2016), 420–471. DOI: http://dx.doi.org/10.1080/07370024.2015.1071195

20. Josip Musić, Daryl Weir, Roderick Murray-Smith, and Simon Rogers. 2016. Modelling and correcting for the impact of the gait cycle on touch screen typing accuracy. *mUX: The Journal of Mobile User Experience* 5, 1 (19 Apr 2016), 1. DOI: http://dx.doi.org/10.1186/s13678-016-0002-3

21. Matei Negulescu and Joanna McGrenere. 2015. Grip Change As an Information Side Channel for Mobile Touch Interaction. In *Proceedings of the 33rd Annual ACM Conference on Human Factors in Computing Systems (CHI '15)*. ACM, New York, NY, USA, 1519–1522. DOI: http://dx.doi.org/10.1145/2702123.2702185

22. Albert Ng, Michelle Annett, Paul Dietz, Anoop Gupta, and Walter F. Bischof. 2014. In the Blink of an Eye: Investigating Latency Perception During Stylus Interaction. In *Proceedings of the SIGCHI Conference on Human Factors in Computing Systems (CHI '14)*. ACM, New York, NY, USA, 1103–1112. DOI: http://dx.doi.org/10.1145/2556288.2557037

23. Carl Edward Rasmussen and Christopher K. I. Williams. 2006. *Gaussian Processes for Machine Learning*. The MIT Press. http://www.ncbi.nlm.nih.gov/pubmed/15112367

24. Peter Rasmussen. 2001. Bayesian Estimation of change points using the general linear model. *Water Resources Research* 37, 11 (2001), 2723–2731. DOI: http://dx.doi.org/10.1029/2001WR000311

25. Pin Shen Teh, Ning Zhang, Andrew Beng Jin Teoh, and Ke Chen. 2016. A survey on touch dynamics authentication in mobile devices. *Computers and Security* 59 (2016), 210–235. DOI: http://dx.doi.org/10.1016/j.cose.2016.03.003

26. Michael E. Tipping. 2001. Sparse Bayesian Learning and the Relevance Vector Machine. *Journal of Machine Learning Research* 1 (2001), 211–244. http://www.ai.mit.edu/projects/jmlr/papers/volume1/tipping01a/abstract.html

27. Daniel Vogel and Patrick Baudisch. 2007. Shift: A Technique for Operating Pen-based Interfaces Using Touch. In *Proceedings of the SIGCHI Conference on Human Factors in Computing Systems (CHI '07)*. ACM, New York, NY, USA, 657–666. DOI: http://dx.doi.org/10.1145/1240624.1240727

28. Daryl Weir, Daniel Buschek, and Simon Rogers. 2013. Sparse Selection of Training Data for Touch Correction Systems. In *Proceedings of the 15th International Conference on Human-computer Interaction with Mobile Devices and Services (MobileHCI '13)*. ACM, New York, NY, USA, 404–407. DOI: http://dx.doi.org/10.1145/2493190.2493241

29. Daryl Weir, Simon Rogers, Roderick Murray-Smith, and Markus Löchtefeld. 2012. A User-specific Machine Learning Approach for Improving Touch Accuracy on Mobile Devices. In *Proceedings of the 25th Annual ACM Symposium on User Interface Software and Technology (UIST '12)*. ACM, New York, NY, USA, 465–476. DOI: http://dx.doi.org/10.1145/2380116.2380175

30. Ying Yin, Tom Yu Ouyang, Kurt Partridge, and Shumin Zhai. 2013. Making Touchscreen Keyboards Adaptive to Keys, Hand Postures, and Individuals: A Hierarchical Spatial Backoff Model Approach. In *Proceedings of the SIGCHI Conference on Human Factors in Computing Systems (CHI '13)*. ACM, New York, NY, USA, 2775–2784. DOI: http://dx.doi.org/10.1145/2470654.2481384

Ether-Toolbars: Evaluating Off-Screen Toolbars for Mobile Interaction

Hanae Rateau
ESTIA & University of Lille Sci. and Tech, CNRS, INRIA
hanae.rateau@inria.fr

Yosra Rekik
University of Lille Sci. and Tech, CNRS, INRIA
yosra.rekik@inria.fr

Edward Lank
University of Waterloo, INRIA
lank@uwaterloo.ca

Laurent Grisoni
University of Lille Sci. and Tech, CNRS, INRIA
laurent.grisoni@univ-lille.fr

ABSTRACT
In mobile touchscreebn interaction, an important challenge is to find solutions to balance the size of individual widgets against the number of widgets needed during interaction. In this work, to address display space limitations, we explore the design of invisible off-screen toolbars (ether-toolbars) that leverage computer vision to expand application features by placing widgets adjacent to the display screen. We show how simple computer vision algorithms can be combined with a natural human ability to estimate physical placing to support highly accurate targeting. Our ether-toolbar design promises targeting accuracy approximating on-screen widget accuracy while significantly expanding the interaction space of mobile devices. Through two experiments, we examine off-screen content placement metaphors and off-screen precision of participants accessing these toolbars. From the data of the second experiment, we provide a basic model that reflects how users perceive mobile surroundings for ether-widgets and validate it. We also demonstrate a prototype system consisting of an inexpensive 3D printed mount for a mirror that supports ether-toolbar implementations. Finally, we discuss the implications of our work and potential design extensions that can increase the usability and the utility of ether-toolbars.

Author Keywords
Around-device interaction; ether-widgets; ether-toolbar; deformation estimation; model; user study; mobile interaction

INTRODUCTION
Modern mobile computing devices have ever-increasing processing power and memory, thus allowing increasingly feature-rich applications. Unfortunately, feature rich interfaces often require access to these features through on-screen widgets. These widgets, while necessary, occupy screen pixels on a device for which screen size is heavily constrained. To address this issue of limited on-screen space, some previous works have proposed interaction techniques that allow the user to take advantage of a virtual or invisible space around the device either by considering the device as a window into a larger display space [15], or by arranging additional display content around the device [14], *around-device interaction*.

This paper explores the design of single-screen application interfaces using an interaction paradigm in which one part of the application interface – typically widgets – exists outside of the display screen but is invisible, thus reserving the on-screen display solely for application content. In this way we leverage both human memory and mobile device surroundings. We call such invisible off-screen widgets, *ether-widgets*, inspired from past research on representations for virtual space between displays [2].

We focus here specifically on ether-toolbars; arguably the toolbar is the widget that best exposes single-click access in a high-density container. In order to explore the design of ether-toolbars, we first examine three competing display metaphors that put ether-widgets off-screen: a ghost display similar to a Manhattan-style focus+context interface [5]; a zoom-based metaphor, which zooms the display such that widgets are scaled and translated off-screen; and a translation-based metaphor, where widgets are simply directly translated off-screen. The results of this study argue for the advantages of a translation-based metaphor. We then design a simple implementation of an ether-toolbar, leveraging the translation metaphor, and measure performance on the ether-toolbar in contrast to performance with on-screen toolbars. From the collected data, we leverage a model that estimates the ether-toolbar deformation as perceived by users and we validate it. Finally, we present a prototype drawing application that demonstrates ether-widgets, including a simple computer vision system that supports self-calibration of around-display input. We conclude by discussing potential enhancements to

IUI'18, March 7–11, 2018, Tokyo, Japan

DOI: https://doi.org/10.1145/3172944.3172978

ether-toolbars and implications for the design of additional ether-widgets in applications.

RELATED WORK

Researchers have frequently explored how non-display physical space around screens can be used to boost the efficiency, accuracy, or expressivity of input during direct input. Most relevant to our research, this section explores work in off-screen or around-device interactions.

Different ways have been explored to make the device's surroundings interactive. For example, in SideSight [3], Butler *et al.*augment the mobile device with infra-red proximity sensors along the sides of the device. These sensors can detect and track finger position near the device enabling multi-touch interaction around the device. Hoverflow [16] describes an augmented Apple Iphone with proximity sensors that recognizes *gestures above* the device. Medusa [1] also uses proximity sensors all around a tabletop in order to sense users arms. This enables to map a touch to an arm and a user. The Abracadabra input technique [11] from Harrison *et al.*uses magnetometers added to a smartwatch and a small magnet attached to the user's finger to sense the finger position in the space around the watch. Toffee [19] enables around-device interaction using acoustic time-of-arrival. A device is augmented with four piezo discs. Thanks to this setup, touches can be located when performed. Thus, it allows to place virtual buttons around the device. These works propose to modify the device in order to make it aware of its near surroundings. In this work, we present a 3D printed mount that just clips onto the tablet enabling finger tracking and contour detection around the tablet.

There have been numerous investigations into understanding and evaluating the performance of off-screen interaction. Research has focused on understanding off-screen midair pointing in static visualization conditions. For instance, Hasan et al. [13] examine the advantage of off-screen pointing in terms of navigation time when comparing off-screen pointing with Peephole and standard Flick & Pinch for map navigation – with or without the help of an overview. Gustafson et al. [9] measured the performance of "coordinate-based imaginary pointing" when using the non-dominant hand as a reference. Their findings showed that the performance deteriorated significantly when increasing distance between the target and the reference hand. Finally, Ens et al. [6] investigated off-screen pointing performance for Fitt's task with dynamic and continuous feedback. Two novel pointing techniques were proposed namely,*launch-adjust* and *glide*. In both of these techniques, a continuous feedback on the target position and the finger position is provided by using either the *wedge* technique [8] or an overview of the scene. Their findings indicated that further targets should be larger to minimize the error. Another interesting result is that the direction has a significant effect on the movement time. In particular, diagonal direction increases the movement time and that users tend to undershoot the target.

In the domain of pointing performance, Markussen et al. [18] investigated off-screen midair horizontal pointing performance on a distant display. They showed that the perceived space around the screen is modified depending on how far is the intended target position from the screen. Users tend to guess the intended position closer than it is from the screen. Hasan et al. [12] found that for midair target selection a *DownUp* gesture decreases the error rate but increases the trial time. In contrast, *LiftOff* gesture provides the best compromise between error rate and trial time. In their study of targeting around devices, they also indicated that the radial bins should be bigger than 4 cm wide and the input range should not extend beyond 40 cm around the device.

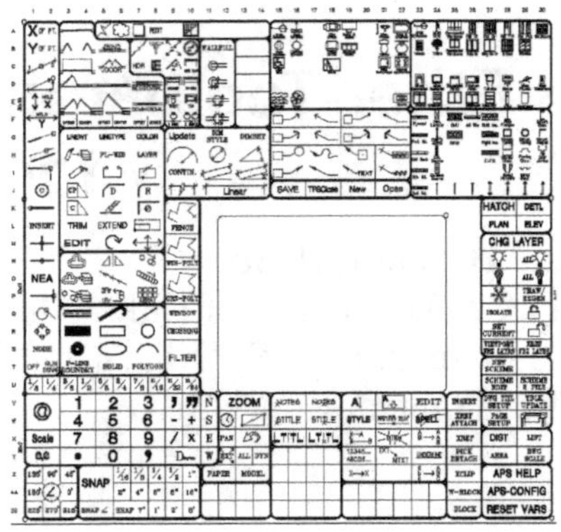

Figure 1: The AutoCAD tablet overlay.

In this paper, we are particularly interested in the placement of widgets around the device. The inclusion of around device widgets to support interaction has been leveraged in commercial systems in the past to support feature-rich applications. As one simple example of this, versions of AutoCAD included tablet overlays (Figure 1) that positioned widgets on a data tablet outside the screen area. The advantage of this interaction was that a widget-space could be created for feature-rich applications significantly larger than the display. The disadvantage of using around-device space is the need to either memorize widget placement or the need to provide some targeting aid such as the AutoCAD overlay.

EXPLORING ETHER-WIDGET METAPHORS

Our goal in this work is to explore around-device space as a placement for widgets within an application. While others have explored the placement of content around the device, we are not aware of any work exploring, specifically, the placement of widgets.

In typical feature rich personal computer applications, extensive command sets are often contained in a toolbar-like interface such as a ribbon [10]. While every interface widget has trade-offs associated with it, one advantage of the ribbon is its ability to allow users to prioritize recognition over recall. This particularly benefits novice users: it exposes functionality so the functionality can be discovered visually during interaction. However, the problem with the ribbon is that it consumes significant screen real-estate. For example, Word's ribbon contains up to three rows of widgets. If one images porting this to a multi-touch computer, and one adopts Android design guidelines, then a ribbon like toolbar will consume at least 7mm minimum target size plus 1mm minimum target spacing time three rows of target = 2.5cm of on-screen space.

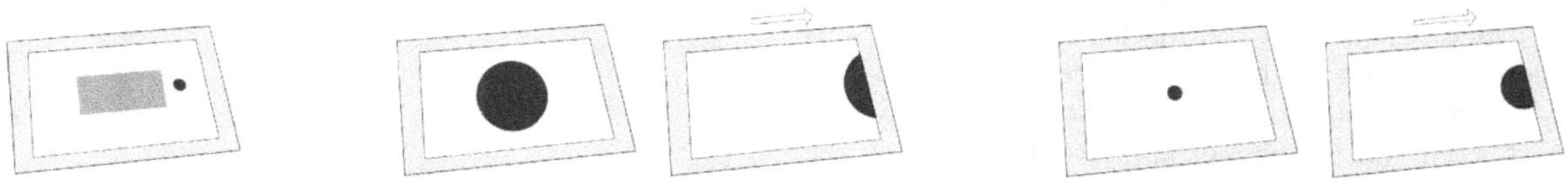

(a) Focus+Context (b) Translation: before translation (c) Translation: during translation (d) Zoomed: before zooming (e) Zoomed: during zooming

Figure 2: TThe three Ether-Widgets *metaphors* for target number 2. N.B: The arrow was not displayed to participants.

Our goal with off-screen target placement is to allow expert users to access features when they know the location of the features. However, to support the novice experience, it would also be good if widgets could be displayed on-screen, could migrate off during interaction, and could be recalled when needed so that users can find their desired command.

Given a user interface with many widgets and a content area, if the desire is to move the widgets off-screen we propose three primary metaphors for off-screen placement. First, the screen could be considered a porthole into a larger space or map area, and widgets could be located at a fixed location somewhere else in the ether; a peephole or focus+context widget arrangement. Second, the display could zoom into the content area, allowing the widgets to drift naturally off the edge of the display. Finally, the widgets could be contained in a panel that simply moves off-screen. In this section, we evaluate the three metaphors for around-device widget placement, *i.e.*, the placement of ether-widgets. Figure 2 presents each of these options.

Focus+Context Ether-Widgets

The first metaphor considers the display to be a type of focus+context viewport with a high resolution focus and an alpha-blended context that shows a scaled view of around-device widget space. Many researchers have explored the idea of embedded high-resolution displays within a lower resolution or larger surrounding environment [17, 4]. Our implementation is most similar to a *Manhattan* embedding as described by Carpendale *et al.* [4] where a high-resolution focus area overlaps the context. We use alpha-blending to represent the surrounding context during interaction. This focus+context metaphor has analogs to, for example, overview maps embedded in command-and-control games.

Zoomed Ether-Widgets

The second considers a zoomed version of the interface such that, as a result of zooming, the widgets move off-screen into the “ether” around the display. Zooming is a common technique used to allow detailed exploration of a region of interest while preserving the existence of context. In this implementation, during interaction the interface is enlarged such that content consumes the entire screen. This has the added benefit that ether-widgets are larger in size (and hence easier to target) than they would be if they existed on-screen.

Translation Ether-Widgets

In the third metaphor, we examine an approach where widgets are translated off the display. Translation, or linear movement, may be the easiest-to-track displacement of widgets because of the one-to-one mapping of perceived movement to actual movement (unlike, *e.g.*, zooming, where users must scale screen space to estimate distance). Translation is a common metaphor for toolbars and ribbons in standard graphical interfaces when these widgets are set to auto-hide. The animation depicts a translation of the widget into the windows titlebar. Given that the use translation is common for auto-hide in graphical interfaces, this metaphor may be the most familiar to users. As well, translation can be designed such that its perceived effect on content is minimized compared to zoom.

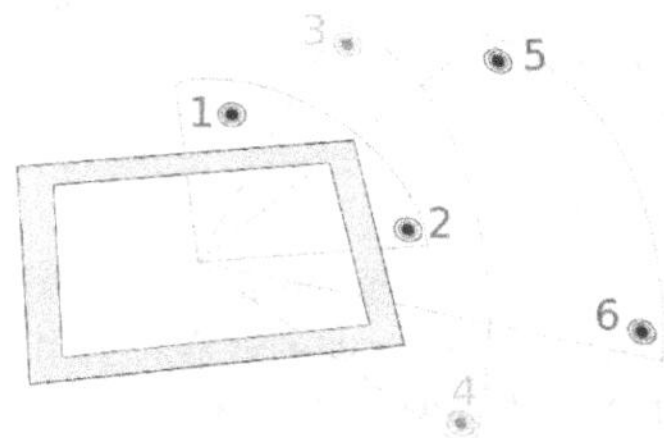

Figure 3: Targets positions where green targets are the near targets, the orange are the middle and the red ones are far ones.

EXPERIMENT 1: PILOT STUDY

We conducted a pilot study with eight participants to compare the impact of the three ether-widgets metaphors when selecting an off-screen target. The goal of this experiment was to contrast metaphors for off-screen target placement. The experiment ran on a 8.4-inch Samsung Galaxy Tab S is placed on a table. Participants sat at the table. To track the tablet, right hand and right index position, we used the OptiTrack system. One rigid body was attached to a glove we equipped the participants with. Another rigid body was attached to the tablet. For the index, we attached one marker to the fingertip. We implemented a simple tap recognizer that analyzed the Optitrack data. When a tap was performed, it was send to a NodeJS server with its coordinates in the reference frame of the tablet.

The task required participant to tap on an ether (off-screen) target as quickly and accurately as possible. Targets were displayed randomly one at a time within the off-screen space (see Figure 3). Each trial began after the previous target was selected and ended with the selection of the current target. In the *Focus+Context* condition, a gray rectangle representing the tablet surrounded by the off-screen space that contains the actual target are displayed on the screen (see Figure 2(a)). To start the trial, participant had to press the “start” button. In the *Translation* condition, first the target with its actual size (4 cm; 6 cm or 10 cm) and the background are displayed on the screen.

Then participant had to press the "start" button. Both the target and background are then moved until the target reaches its corresponding position in the ether-space (see Figure 2(b) and (c)). In the *Zoomed* condition, first the target with a diameter of 2 cm and the background are displayed on the screen. Then participant had to press the "start" button. The target is then simultaneously scaled and translated until it gets its corresponding size (4 cm; 6 cm or 10 cm) and position in the ether-space (see Figure 2(d) and (e)). We counterbalanced the ordering of ether-widget placement metaphors. We measured time, accuracy, and subjective responses from participants collected on a Likert scale.

RESULTS

We analyzed time, error, and subjective responses. All statistical analyses are multi-way ANOVA. Tukey tests are used post-hoc when significant effects are found. In the following, we report the results for each of the dependent variables.

We found mixed results for time and error dependent variables. For time, only *position* was significant ($F_{5,25} = 3.16$, $p = .023$), and the effect was not large. There were no other effects and no interactions.

Similarly, for accuracy, while significant effects were found for *metaphor* ($F_{2,10} = 10.27$, $p = .0038$), *size* ($F_{2,10} = 28.75$, $p < .0001$) and *position* ($F_{2,25} = 5.37$, $p = .0001$) with *metaphor* × *position* ($F_{10,59} = 2.35$, $p = .022$) and *size* × *position* ($F_{10,59} = 2.42$, $p = .019$) interactions on *accuracy*, post-hoc tests revealed that no one technique was consistently best. *Focus+context* is significantly more accurate than *zoomed* metaphor when selecting the targets 4 and 6 (far from the display), but *zoomed* has significant time × target effects. There are no significant advantages or disadvantages for the *translate* technique with report to other techniques.

In overall ranking, the *translation* metaphor was ranked 62.5% first, 25% second and 12.5% third. *Focus+context*, the next most preferred metaphor, was ranked 25% first, 37.5% second and 37.5% third. The *zoomed* technique was ranked 12.5% first, 37.5% second and 50% third.

ETHER-TOOLBAR DESIGN

In this section, we explore the design and efficacy of one potential ether-widget, an ether-toolbar. The overall goal of this follow-on study is to identify expected precision of ether-widgets for denser arrangements.

Results of the pilot study indicate that the translate metaphor is the most preferred and is statistically similar in speed and accuracy to other off-screen metaphors. As a result, we use the translate metaphor to place our ether-widget. One advantage to translate is that, conceptually, it is similar to widgets such as ribbons, where the animated auto-hide feature can be viewed as a translation of the widget to ether-space.

Ether-toolbars themselves may present both advantages and disadvantages as potential off-screen targets. First, their rectangular grid can be placed adjacent to the device, simplifying estimation of widget position; however, the density of their arrangement confounds accurate targeting, potentially nullifying any advantage of proximal placement. Second, toolbars have a natural migration pattern to drift off-screen via auto-hide options on standard toolbars, and this metaphor can be leveraged to support off-screen migration. Figure 4 shows a conceptual design for an Ether-Toolbar. During normal interaction, the toolbar is above the screen, and interacting in ether-space activates commands. Users can also choose to reveal the toolbar – for example, if they are novice users and do not know the location of controls. They do this using a bezel swipe, a standard mobile interaction technique that can be used to reveal above device controls.

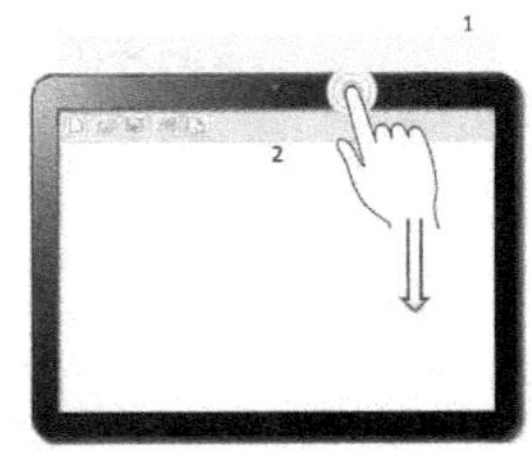

Figure 4: Conceptualization of Ether-Toolbar design. In typical interaction, the toolbar is positioned along the top of the tablet display, and, when a user interacts, they tap above the display on the toolbar in ether-space (1). By swiping down on the bezel, the toolbar can be revealed (2) and novice users can interact with it on the display. After interacting, it will be translated up and off the display again.

One advantage of this design is that it can co-exist naturally with standard mobile applications designed for tablets or smartphones (*e.g.*bezel swipe to reveal notifications). This technique, in novice mode, can be used identically. What ether-toolbar adds is an ability to directly access the above-device widgets without needing to reveal them, thus saving the bezel-swipe to reveal and the time-out to vanish, leaving the screen free for interaction.

EXPERIMENT 2 : ETHER-TOOLBAR ACCURACY

In this section, we evaluate the potential accuracy of ether-toolbars. We describe an experiment that varies the number of buttons and number of rows of buttons, we analyze precision, and we leverage this data to drive design recommendations for an overall implementation.

Participants

Ten new unpaid participants took part in our experiment. Participants' ages varied between 26 and 38 years. Nine participants were right handed.

Apparatus and Interface

The experiment ran on the same Samsung Galaxy Tab S. The tablet was placed on top of a 32" multi-touch screen which was inclined to horizontal. The 32" 3M multi-touch screen was used to detect tap locations around the tablet device. Participants sat in front of the tablet, which was placed in a fixed location at the bottom of the multi-touch screen as shown in Figure 5. An additional application was developed to log the touches on the multi-touch display – time and coordinates – in the reference frame of the tablet.

We implemented an Android applicationto simulate both an on-screen toolbar and an ether-toolbar in positions indicated

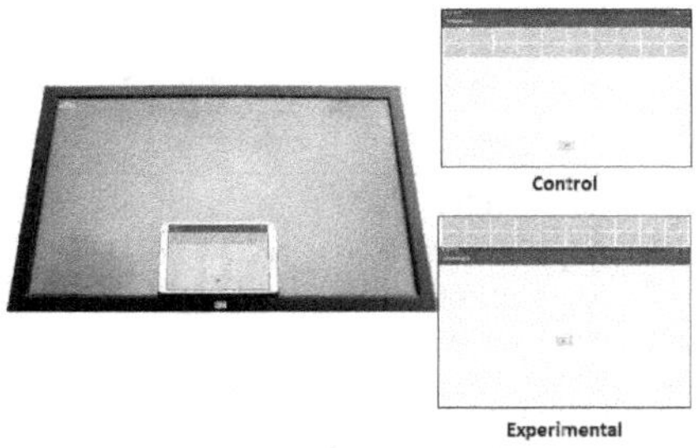

Figure 5: Screen-shot of the interface presented to participants. Here the grid is composed of two rows and ten buttons. The participant is asked to tap the 'B8' button.

in Figure 4. It included a control condition which pictured the toolbar on the screen and an experimental condition, with the ether-toolbar. The tablet displayed rectangles that represented the buttons at the top while a start button was 8cm under the first row of buttons. Each button had an identifier that gave the row (A-C, top to down - the letter "A" refers to the top row) and the column (1-number of buttons per row, right to left). For example, if we have a grid with two rows of eight buttons, B8 would identify the eighth button of the second row starting from the top-left corner of the grid (Figure 5). To perform a trial, a user would tap the start-button (pictured in Figure 5). The button label would change to reveal a target button to tap (row + column format), and the participant would then tap the button. The start button's position was changed for the control versus the experimental condition such that the distance made by the participant from start button to toolbar was fixed. This ensured that any timing differences were a result of the increase in task difficulty due to position estimation, and not due to increased distance to make.

Design

The experiment was a repeated measures design that included two conditions (on-screen vs ether-toolbar placement). We, also, examined 3 button densities within a row (5, 8, or 10 buttons per row) and we included 1, 2, or 3 rows of buttons. We limit our number of buttons per row to 10 because, in informal evaluation, it was deemed too difficult to accurately estimate the position of more than 10 buttons along the top of the display. Similarly, we use 3 rows of buttons because, in on-screen condition, users will interact with the widget on the display. Assuming minimum widget size of 1cm, 3 rows of buttons would cover 3cm on the display – approximately 25%.

Participants completed 15 trials within each configuration, where they clocked on five selected buttons three times each. We did not counterbalance condition (on-screen vs ether) between users. Instead, each user saw the on-screen condition first, to learn the toolbar placements and size, and then saw the ether condition second. This strategy was informed by our goal to evaluate the pointing precision on off-screen content that users habitually see on screen. For our other experimental factors, we began with one row of buttons, our simplest configuration, then allowed the complexity of the interface to gradually increase. We did this so we could easily determine at which point accuracy would begin to drop and to allow users to gradually learn button placement beginning with simple cases. Button density (5, 8, or 10) was counterbalanced.

Overall, our experiment was a $2 \times 3 \times 3$ repeated measures design clicking on five selected buttons three times each with 10 participants yield a total of 2700 individual button accesses.

Research Questions

We would expect ether-widget access to be both slower and more error prone than on-screen targeting. Given this assumption, the goal of this experiment is not to prove that fact – a failure for ether-widgets when compared to on-screen widgets – but instead to understand both the relative accuracy of users manipulating ether-widgets. With this in mind, we will examine overall speed and error rate, but then focus specifically on access patterns and how best to boost overall accuracy.

RESULTS

The dependent measures are *accuracy* (the proportion of correct button selection) and *trial time* (trial time is measured from the target apparition, to button successfully selected). All analyses are two-way ANOVA. Tukey tests are used post-hoc when significant effects are found.

Trial time and accuracy

Our primary interest is in how condition effects trial time and accuracy. RM-ANOVA did not reveal any condition effects for trial time, implying that there were no statistically significant differences between trial time when comparing ether or on-screen widget access. However, we did see significant main effects for accuracy.

Table 1 presents a snapshot of post-hoc accuracy analysis over our data set. These accuracies assume that button width and height were identical to on-screen button width and height, specifically button row height was 1cm and button width was 35mm per button for the 5 buttons configuration, 22mm per button for the 8 buttons configuration, and 17mm per button for the 10 buttons configurations, a result of the display width measuring 17.5cm.

Overall, we see that for 1-row, 5- and 8- button configurations, accuracy of off-screen targeting is quite high (85% for one row of five buttons and 87% for one row of eight buttons, respectively (not significant)). One interesting factor we observed was that, in multi-row configurations, buttons in the row farthest from the tablet had lower accuracy than buttons closer to the tablet, again unsurprising do the imprecision in distance estimation when moving away from the edge of the tablet. Interestingly, when examining Figure 6, we confirm that the farther the row is the larger it is perceived by participants. Additionally, Figure 6 shows that for the farthest row, participants consistently over-estimate its height.

Participants comments

All our participants felt that the task became more difficult and that they needed to concentrate to accomplish it from either R2B8 or R2B10 configurations. All our participants also preferred not to use 10 buttons per row for the ether-widgets condition. Some quotes are: "*10 buttons is really too much... I think I am unable to make the difference between*

	R1B5					R1B8					R1B10			
	On-screen		Ether-toolbar			On-screen		Ether-toolbar			On-screen		Ether-toolbar	
	Mean	s.d	Mean	s.d		Mean	s.d	Mean	s.d		Mean	s.d	Mean	s.d
A1	100	0	100	0	A1	100	0	90	9.97	**A1**★	100	0	70	29.93
A2	100	0	73.33	21.33	A2	100	0	76.66	23.95	**A2**★	100	0	60	23.45
A3	100	0	80	19.95	A4	100	0	86.66	17.42	**A8**★	96.66	6.53	50	22.31
A4	100	0	76.66	17	A7	100	0	83.33	14.60	**A9**★	96.66	6.53	66.66	21.77
A5	100	0	93.33	8.71	A8	100	0	96.66	6.53	**A10**★	100	0	86.66	17.42
	R2B5					R2B8					R2B10			
	On-screen		Ether-toolbar			On-screen		Ether-toolbar			On-screen		Ether-toolbar	
	Mean	s.d	Mean	s.d		Mean	s.d	Mean	s.d		Mean	s.d	Mean	s.d
A3★	93.33	8.71	18.33	20.9	**A2**★	100	0	16.66	22.3	**A2**★	96.66	6.53	10	9.97
A4★	96.66	6.53	23.33	19.59	**A3**★	100	0	23.33	23.95	**A5**★	90	13.94	18.33	15.74
A5★	100	0	20	17.42	**A8**★	96.66	6.53	13.33	14.44	**A8**★	93.33	8.71	10	13.94
B1	96.66	6.53	93.33	8.71	B1	96.66	6.53	90	19.59	B8	96.66	6.53	53.33	27.88
B2	86.66	17.42	73.33	25.39	B5	90	13.94	66.66	27.54	B9	100	0	68.33	26.87
	R3B5					R32B8					R3B10			
	On-screen		Ether-toolbar			On-screen		Ether-toolbar			On-screen		Ether-toolbar	
	Mean	s.d	Mean	s.d		Mean	s.d	Mean	s.d		Mean	s.d	Mean	s.d
A1★	100	0	13.33	19.95	**A7**★	96.66	6.53	16.66	10.88	**A1**★	100	0	6.66	8.71
A2★	100	0	3.33	6.53	**B2**★	86.66	10.66	41.66	25.41	**A6**★	96.66	6.53	3.33	6.53
B3★	86.66	10.66	46.66	22.20	**B6**★	93.33	13.06	43.33	30.87	**B7**★	96.66	6.53	15	12.36
B4★	96.66	6.53	23.33	17	C4	96.66	6.53	90	9.97	C4	96.66	6.53	56.66	21.88
C3	96.66	6.53	86.66	13	C8	90	9.97	100	0	C8	100	0	63.33	22.73

Table 1: Mean and s.d of accuracy.The significant difference between *on-screen* and *ether-toolbar* are **highlighted**★.

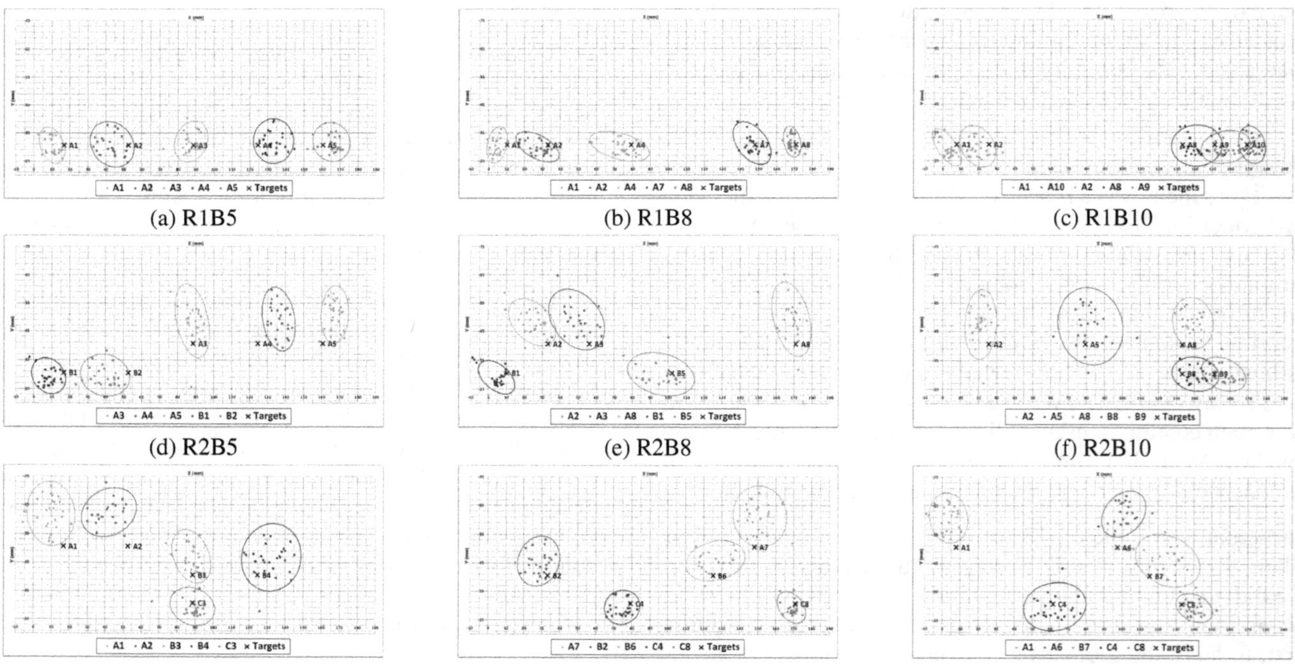

(a) R1B5 (b) R1B8 (c) R1B10

(d) R2B5 (e) R2B8 (f) R2B10

(g) R3B5 (h) R3B8 (i) R3B10

Figure 6: The taps of every participants for each configuration. The blue dots represent the taps in *expert mode.*

having 10 or 11 or 12 buttons (or even more)...", "*if I have the choice, I will stop at 8 buttons per row*" or "*I don't like selecting the off-screen buttons when there are 10, it is really very difficult*".

To better understand how participants performed, we report the different strategies described by participants in order to localize their ether-button target. This data was extracted from post-experiment interviews with participants.

- **Considering the two extremities of the tablet and its middle as references.** All participants used this strategy in order to estimate the target button's location. For instance, participants knew that the third button was exactly at the center of the screen in the 5 buttons configurations, whereas in the 8 buttons configurations the middle line of the screen was the line separating the fourth and the fifth button. Similarly with the extremities of the screen, participants knew the first and last buttons were at the extremities and then could estimate these buttons close neighbors.
- **Counting the number of buttons.** This strategy was mostly used at the very beginning of the experiment for five and eight buttons and was the primary strategy in the 10 button configurations: participants physically counted with their fingers the buttons while estimating the size of the buttons.

ETHER-TOOLBAR DEFORMATION MODEL

Results from Experiment 2 showed that the accuracy drops drastically for buttons in rows above the closest one from the tablet. Interestingly, when looking at the graphs in Figure 6 we can identify consistency in errors. Participants seem to estimate the buttons further and larger than they actually are but always in the same proportions for buttons of the same row. This observation means that a model that reflects how users perceive mobile surroundings for an ether-toolbar can be leveraged from the collected data with the ultimate goal of improving the accuracy. In addition, due to the deterioration of the performance for the configurations where there were 10 buttons and as also our participants felt that these configurations are difficult, we decide to limit the number of buttons per row to a maximum eight.

Deformation Model

Our goal here is to leverage a model that estimates the ether-toolbar deformation as perceived by users. Towards this ultimate goal, we, first, assume that we have 95% accuracy for the collected data for the different ether-configurations. Given this assumption, we then consider only the following 95% of the collected data: for each configuration, for each target button, we calculated the two barycenters x_{mean} and y_{mean} of respectively the x coordinate (*i.e.*, the position of the tap along the top side of the tablet) and y coordinate (*i.e.*, the position of the tap above the tablet) of the all collected taps for this button. For each barycenter (x_{mean} and y_{mean}), we then extract 95% of the data (X_{95} and Y_{95}) that are the nearest to it. In the following, we describe the deformation of the ether-button through the y axis and then through the x axis.

In order to determine the deformation of the ether-buttons through the y axis, we consider the data extracted in Y_{95} and ran a partitioning algorithm based on the Fisher-Jenks grouping algorithm [7]. The Fisher-Jenks algorithm classifies unidimensional values in a predefined number of groups (three in our case) by minimizing the intra-group variance. The output of the partitioning gives us the barycenters of the three groups (corresponding to the barycenters of the three rows) and the intervals representing the boundaries of the groups on the y axis (corresponding to the height of the each row). Table 2 summarized the results. We then consider participants comments and our findings for the farthest row to refine our model as follow: we multiply the height of the farthest row by two to make them as if they have an "unlimited height".

	Lower (mm)	Upper (mm)	Size (mm)
Closest row	14.67	28.57	13.89
Middle row	28.57	43.91	15.35
Farthest row	43.91	62.91	19.00

Table 2: Corrected boundaries of the ether-toolbar rows in mm. The Y axis origin is the tablet top side.

We then made the same analysis for the x axis though the accuracy rate is 89.73%. We found that the barycenters shift by 2.36mm on average. The major deformations (5mm) happen for the left-most and right-most buttons and their closest neighbors. This can be explain by the fact that participants took the screen extremities as reference points for the left-most and right-most target buttons. Using only the Fisher-Jenks classification algorithm, we found the groups sizes were always smaller than the actual buttons size. Due to these minor deformations along the x axis, we decided to only modify the ether-toolbar along the y axis.

Experiment 3: Validation

A third experiment, similar to the second, was used to validate our ether-widgets deformation estimation. The same apparatus, task, and design were used, but with only 2 buttons densities conditions (5 and 8) and 3 new participants: 3 participants x 2 toolbar placements x 3 row conditions x 2 buttons densities x 5 buttons x 3 repetitions = 540 individual button accesses.

RM-ANOVA did not reveal any condition effects for the accuracy, with an overall of accuracy of 94.23% (sd=2.83) for the ether-toolbar condition and 99.62% (sd=.73) for the on-screen toolbar condition. This findings indicate that our estimation of the deformation of ether-toolbar performed well with our validation data.

PROTOTYPE: DRAWING WITH ETHER-TOOLBAR

While much of our design work explored ether-toolbars, we designed a prototype application that explores the ether-widget space more fully. We implemented "Ether-Draw", a prototype application that supports ether-widgets and includes a low-cost mirror mount that supports self-calibration of around-display input.

When the user starts a new project with the Ether-Draw application, the ether-toolbar is not integrated into the application GUI. However, Ether-Draw provides the users the ability to create new personalized ether-widgets in real time and depending on their need. When creating a new ether-button, users have to memorize the position of the button and the associated command. To help them remember, and to make the presence of the button more explicit for demonstration purposes, users can draw a marker at the position of the ether-button. This physical representation of the button is depicted in our Figures for clarity, but is strictly optional.

Two main ether-button types can be created: (1) *ether-button export* and (2) *ether-button import*. In the *ether-button export* case, users can configure a particular command through the GUI (*e.g.*, red circle) and save it outside the screen. To save the command, users have to perform a long tap on the current tool widget to activate the export mode. When a tap is detected, an ether-button is created outside the screen where the tap was made. In the *ether-button import* case, users can draw a shape on the paper-sheet next to the tablet and import it in the application. Like the *ether-button export*, a button is created at the drawing location so that the shape can also be reused later in the application.

Hardware and implementation details

The prototype was implemented on a Samsung Galaxy Tab S of 8.4". We designed a 3D printed mount where a mirror was fixed above the front camera of the tablet. The mount allowed users to adjust the mirror so it shows the space at the right side of the tablet (See Figure 7).

The drawing application supports different shapes (rectangles, ellipses and lines) and different stroke styles, thicknesses and colors, as well as filling colors for closed shapes. A calibration button allows users to see the camera image so they can adjust the mirror position and orientation (Figure 8). The application runs on Android. The OpenCV library is used to process the camera image in order to track the finger and detect the drawing contours for *tool import*. Since we only need to map 2D coordinates of the virtual buttons in the camera image and the finger position, we do not need the finger position in space. We only use the image coordinate. The finger is tracked using an OpenCV background removal algorithm.

A tap sound recognizer that runs in the background has also been implemented to allow users to export and select tools. When a tap is detected, a virtual button that saves the current command is created where the finger was at the moment of the tap. If not, we search the nearest virtual button from the finger position that is not further than 100 pixels.

Figure 7: 3D printed mount that supports the mirror.

DISCUSSION AND IMPLICATIONS

Ether-toolbars leverage simple computer vision and spatial memory to support interaction. Thanks to the simple deformation model provided, ether-toolbars obtain an accuracy that is statistically equivalent to on-screen targets. We observe from the model that the further the row from the tablet, the larger it has to be. This confirms the results of the works of Gustafson *et al.*[8] and of Ens *et al.*in [6] discussed in the related work concerning target pointing with report to a reference point (hand or device). Whereas the study presented by Markussen *et al.*[18] found that for *midair* gestures around a distant TV screen, users tend to guess the target position closer than it actually is.

The added advantage is that relatively low-cost hardware additions to current commodity smartphones can support their implementation.

In the domain of intelligent user interfaces, one important area of inquiry is an understanding of how much intelligence is needed to support interaction. Whether complex algorithms must be implemented or significant external sensing must be used to support novel user interactions is often an open question. Some past research has explored this, including the use of time-of-arrival signals [19] to support around-device interaction. Our research falls within this domain, exploring specifically the question of whether simple computer vision algorithms can support around-device interaction.

Alongside the question of simplicity, another area of inquiry in around-device interaction involves precision. Specifically, our work provides evidence that high-density interaction surfaces can be supported in the space around portable devices, provided one understands how distance affects targeting precision. We do this via the high degree of consistency between our two user studies of toolbar targeting, where we show that targeting precision is statistically equivalent – even for up to 24 tiled buttons, 3 rows of 8 – located immediately adjacent to the display. This represents a significant enhancement over other recent work in around-device interaction, where fewer, larger, more separated spaces were used in around-device interaction [12].

CONCLUSIONS AND NEXT STEPS

We presented ether-widget design for mobile interaction. Ether-widgets leverages both users short term spatial memory and sensing technologies of mobile devices to expand the interaction space around the device. We first explored three ether-widget metaphors. Through a pilot study, we showed that the translation metaphor is the most preferred while providing the same accuracy and speed than Focus+context and zoomed metaphors. We then explored the design and efficiency of one particular type of ether-widgets, the ether-toolbar while using the translation metaphor. We designed an experiment to understand the relative accuracy of users when interacting with an ether-toolbar. Our findings indicate that 10 buttons per row is not adapted for ether-toolbar as it is both less preferred by participants and deteriorated significantly the performance. Importantly, our findings indicate that the farther the row is from the tablet the larger it is perceived by users. Through Fisher partitioning algorithm, we then proposed a model that estimate the ether-toolbar deformation as perceived by users. We validate our model with three new participants and we reach 94% of accuracy with no statistical difference with on-screen toolbars. This result supports the idea that off-screen interaction around the device is suitable for feature rich applications without deteriorating the performance compared to

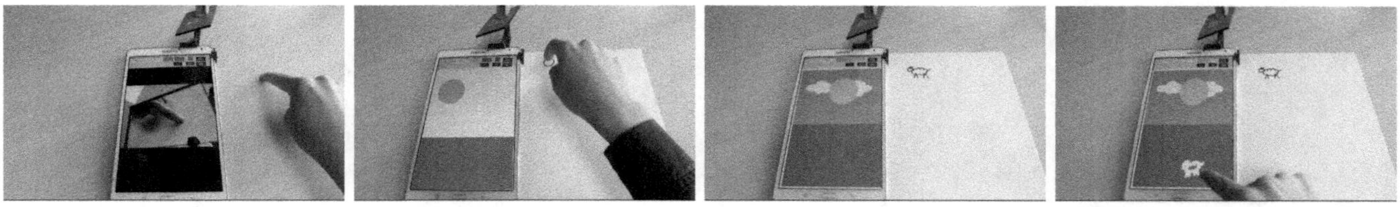

(a) Calibration (b) Exportation (c) Importation (d) Use of imported drawing

Figure 8: Application to support drawing using ether-widgets: (a) calibration step; (b) a user exporting a yellow circle command outside the screen; (c) a user creating/importing a new sheep command; (d) a user using the sheep command.

on-screen interaction. We finally presented "ether-draw", a prototype application that supports personalized ether-toolbar. We hope that our findings will contribute towards the adoption of ether-widget design and will enable the design of additional ether-widgets in applications.

Among possible future work, it would be interesting to study the effect of the different sides of the tablet on the performance of ether-toolbar as well as the effect of the device (*e.g.*, using a smartphone). Further work would, also, investigate new prototype applications that take advantage of the combination of the mobile device and its surrounding space. In the long term, it would also be interesting to evaluate user expertise development on non-visual targets, and how expertise influences accuracy and ether-widgets space perception.

REFERENCES

1. Michelle Annett, Tovi Grossman, Daniel Wigdor, and George Fitzmaurice. 2011. Medusa: A Proximity-aware Multi-touch Tabletop *(UIST '11)*.
2. Patrick Baudisch, Edward Cutrell, Ken Hinckley, and Robert Gruen. 2004. Mouse Ether: Accelerating the Acquisition of Targets Across Multi-monitor Displays *(CHI EA '04)*.
3. Alex Butler, Shahram Izadi, and Steve Hodges. 2008. SideSight: multi-"touch" interaction around small devices. In *(UIST '08)*.
4. Sheelagh Carpendale, John Ligh, and Eric Pattison. 2004. Achieving Higher Magnification in Context *(UIST '04)*.
5. Andy Cockburn, Amy Karlson, and Benjamin B. Bederson. 2009. A Review of Overview+Detail, Zooming, and Focus+Context Interfaces. *ACM Comput. Surv.* (2009).
6. Barrett Ens, David Ahlström, Andy Cockburn, and Pourang Irani. 2011. Characterizing User Performance with Assisted Direct Off-screen Pointing *(MobileHCI '11)*.
7. Walter D. Fisher. 1958. On Grouping for Maximum Homogeneity. *J. Amer. Statist. Assoc.* 53, 284 (1958), 789–798.
8. Sean Gustafson, Patrick Baudisch, Carl Gutwin, and Pourang Irani. 2008. Wedge: Clutter-free Visualization of Off-screen Locations *(CHI '08)*.
9. Sean Gustafson, Daniel Bierwirth, and Patrick Baudisch. 2010. Imaginary Interfaces: Spatial Interaction with Empty Hands and Without Visual Feedback *(UIST '10)*.
10. Jensen Harris. 2008. The Story of the Ribbon. *Presentation at MIX08* (2008).
11. Chris Harrison and Scott E. Hudson. 2009. Abracadabra: Wireless, High-precision, and Unpowered Finger Input for Very Small Mobile Devices *(UIST '09)*.
12. Khalad Hasan, David Ahlström, and Pourang Irani. 2013. Ad-binning: Leveraging Around Device Space for Storing, Browsing and Retrieving Mobile Device Content *(CHI '13)*.
13. Khalad Hasan, David Ahlström, and Pourang P. Irani. 2015. Comparing Direct Off-Screen Pointing, Peephole, and Flick & Pinch Interaction for Map Navigation *(SUI '15)*.
14. Khalad Hasan, David Ahlström, Junhyeok Kim, and Pourang Irani. 2017. AirPanes: Two-Handed Around-Device Interaction for Pane Switching on Smartphones *(CHI '17)*.
15. Bonifaz Kaufmann and Martin Hitz. 2012. X-large Virtual Workspaces for Projector Phones Through Peephole Interaction *(MM '12)*.
16. Sven Kratz and Michael Rohs. 2009. HoverFlow: Expanding the Design Space of Around-device Interaction *(MobileHCI '09)*.
17. Edward Lank and Son Phan. 2004. Focus+Context Sketching on a Pocket PC. In *CHI '04 Extended Abstracts on Human Factors in Computing Systems (CHI EA '04)*.
18. Anders Markussen, Sebastian Boring, Mikkel R. Jakobsen, and Kasper Hornbæk. 2016. Off-Limits: Interacting Beyond the Boundaries of Large Displays *(CHI '16)*.
19. Robert Xiao, Greg Lew, James Marsanico, Divya Hariharan, Scott Hudson, and Chris Harrison. 2014. Toffee: Enabling Ad Hoc, Around-device Interaction with Acoustic Time-of-arrival Correlation *(MobileHCI '14)*.

Organic Visualization of Document Evolution

Ignacio Perez-Messina
Computer Science Dept.
Universidad de Chile
Santiago, Chile
iperez@dcc.uchile.cl

Claudio Gutierrez
Computer Science Dept.
Universidad de Chile
Santiago, Chile
cgutierr@dcc.uchile.cl

Eduardo Graells-Garrido
Data Science Institute
Universidad del Desarrollo
Santiago, Chile
egraells@udd.cl

ABSTRACT
Recent availability of data about writing processes at keystroke-granularity has enabled research on the evolution of document writing. A natural task is to develop systems that can actually show this data, that is, user interfaces that transform the data of the process of writing –today a black box– into intelligible forms. On this line, we propose a data structure that captures a document's fine-grained history and an organic visualization that serves as an interface to it. We evaluate a proof-of-concept implementation of the system through a pilot study using documents written by students at a public university. Our results are promising and reveal facets such as general strategies adopted, local edition density and hierarchical structure of the final text.

Author Keywords
Text Production; Writing Process; Information Visualization.

INTRODUCTION
Writing is an old and relevant human skill whose standard product is text. Due to the widespread use of information technologies, most text available today is stored in digital platforms, such as the Web. Although static in their final form, documents –collaborative ones in particular– are works-in-progress, meaning they are still subject to their writing process, and thanks to versioning systems, they are being stored as such. Currently, we do not fully understand the importance of this data, even though the way we write is tied to how we learn and structure our knowledge [2]. This may be in part because, as stated by Grésillon and Perrin in the Handbook of Writing and Text Production, "The written (the product) aims at overcoming the writing (the process)" [6], which means that the better the quality of a text, the less we know about its development.

This lack of understanding, and of research on this topic, may be due to the fact that data was not easily available. But today, Web services such as Google Drive keep records of document changes at keystroke-level, so as data has become widely available, a new avenue of research has opened that could have a great impact on natural language processing and generation, namely the study of text in its temporal, mutable form.

IUI'18, March 7–11, 2018, Tokyo, Japan

ISBN 978-1-4503-4945-1/18/03. . . $15.00

DOI: https://doi.org/10.1145/3172944.3173004

A vast work on text visualization is available, mainly addressing text corpora exploration and classification while there is little research on individual documents and their production process (the most extensive survey on text visualization [11] does not consider versioned text as a specific data source). On the latter, most work focuses on collaboration at the coarse granularity of versioned text (*e.g.*, Wikipedia content) and is not suited for research on individual writing.

In this paper, we propose an interactive visualization method in the largely unexplored field of fine-grained text production data. With an organic design that mimics plant metabolism and behavior, the proposed visualization shows the whole fine-grained history of a document in one image (a plant) and displays its development in time with animation (its growth). It also provides access to its textual content interactively, through which a naturally occurring segmentation of the text (the plant's branches) can be produced. By allowing the complex behavior of producing text to visually emerge, it fosters exploration of its structure and evolution through time, which could reveal the information hidden in fine-grained versioning data.

We evaluated our interactive visualization through a pilot study, where we visualized and analyzed documents written by engineering students. The results show different characteristics of the writing process that emerged from the visualization: general strategies adopted, local edition density, and global text structure. These results evoke interesting applications for automated text analysis such as new text segmentation algorithms and document classifiers based on writing process rather than word choice. We conclude that the study and visualization of fine-grained text data enables a deeper understanding of documents, as it permits to augment the final product with the trace of the decisions performed during its production.

BACKGROUND
Currently most user interfaces for text visualization focus on finished text, *i.e.*, the final product of the writing process of an agent, or a corpus of such products (visual text summarization [7], topic modeling [15], mapping content structure [18], recommender systems [5], among others [16]).

There is little work on visualization of the process itself that generates a document, particularly in the case of the human *writing* process [6]. The challenge here is to understand the structure and evolution of text according to several updates, each of which may add new content and/or delete prior content.

Currently, there are two prominent sources for this kind of visual interaction: collaborative user-generated content and individual research-generated.

Regarding collaborative content, the most common data source is Wikipedia, with tools like History Flow [19], that visualizes the *revision history* of Wikipedia articles, and the Notabilia project [17], which visualizes collective deliberation. DocuViz [20] applied the History Flow approach to collaborative documents in Google Docs and Kim et al. [8] proposed using only document *deltas* in this same line of visualization.

There are studies that focus on individual writing process [12]. Perrin and Wildi developed a statistical method to infer writing phases using cursor movement data [14]. Caporossi and Leblay [1] showed a graph-based visualization of the writing of a paragraph with data from ScriptLog (a keystroke logging program), where nodes represent operations; and edges their topological and temporal relations.

Evolution of single documents has thus been researched either from a collaborative, large-scale perspective using coarse data or from an individual, fine-grained one but only at very small scale. To the best of our knowledge, there is no visualization in between that encompasses these dimensions as a whole, therefore uniting writing process research. The system we describe next aims at filling this gap.

SYSTEM DESIGN

Following Wise's ecological [21] and Fry's organic information design [4] approaches, we created a plant-like structure of interdependent units. With this design, a document is not shown as something linear and static, but rather as emergent and dynamic; it grows and dies as it is produced. We implemented our prototype using the Processing language [3] as it is commonly used for organic visualization systems and data from Google Docs.

Here we describe the different stages of the pipeline needed to arrive at such depiction: the definition and grouping of text operations, the data structure holding those operations, and the visual design that shows the data structure. We denote by *agent* the writing agent and leave the word *user* for the user of the system.

Operation Grouping and Locality Criteria

We define a document as a chain of atomic (distinguishable in time) operations (insertions and deletions) and group these operations according to a locality criteria. As the retrieved operations usually correspond to single keystrokes, we group adjacent ones into the largest locality-preserving chain (*i.e.*, in such a way that no voluntary change in cursor position takes place between any two of these operations), thus resulting in larger operations we call *bursts*. Bursts are more coherent and significant than single keystrokes because they allow undoing as long as the agent does not actively change cursor position, so correction of typographical errors and low-level information of the writing process [6] are filtered out. Bursts are then rearranged spatially according to their insertion position in the document (in the same way as in Kollberg's S-notation [10]).

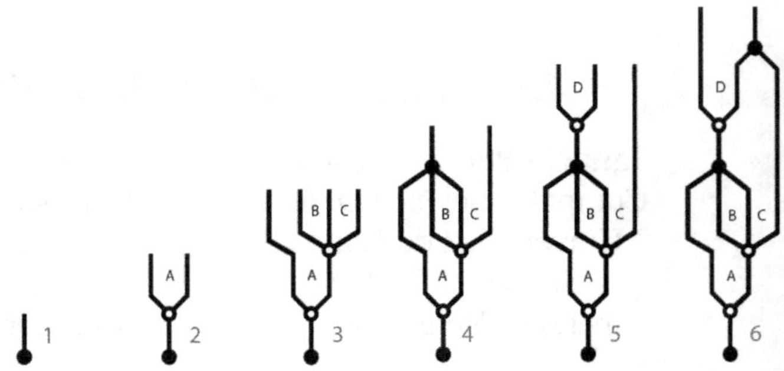

Figure 1. Progression of a document's data structure. Deletion nodes are black circles, insertion nodes are white circles and POIs are "null" nodes (leaves). Edge direction is "upward." From left to right: (1) Empty document. (2) Insertion of "A." (3) Insertion of "BC" at position 2, resulting in string "ABC." (4) Simultaneous deletion of "AB." (5) Insertion of "D" before "C," resulting in string "DC." (6) Deletion of "C." Final document contains only string "D."

Data Structure for Text Evolution

We store the operations and their spatial relations as a Planar Directed Acyclic Graph in which internal nodes represent operations, leaves represent *Places of Insertion* (POIs, which are the points between characters and elements where the blinking cursor can be), and edges are topological relations between them and direction follows the arrow of time (see Fig. 1). An empty document starts as a (root) node leading to a single leaf, at which point only an insertion can take place (as a deletion needs more than one POI to take place). When the agent types, an operation node containing the inserted string replaces the null node at the leaf, from which $n + 1$ edges emerge, where n is the number of characters inserted. Each of these edges contains a new POI and the POI where the insertion took place is no longer reachable since it becomes an internal node.

The aforementioned process goes on recursively, always maintaining a tree structure. This, however, does not hold when considering deletions. In the case of a deletion of m characters, the $m + 1$ corresponding adjacent edges are bundled together into a single operation node with one leaf. Note that this radically changes the original insertions-only tree structure since a deletion may encompass many levels of the hierarchy.

Visual Representation

We used a glyph-based approach to visualize the aforementioned data structure, in which glyphs (the visual unit that conveys meaning) act as interdependent units and build upon each other as stems of a plant. Intuitively, an insertion "opens up" space in the document, by splitting one leaf into many, while deletions "close" it, by joining many leaves back into one. The glyph designed to represent insertion nodes is, therefore, a stylized multiplexer. Deletion nodes, on the other hand, do not have their own glyph but retroactively affect insertion glyphs (changing the look of glyphs that were already placed). Figure 2 illustrates this.

Seeing the visualization as a mapping from the data structure to the visual space, the rules that define this mapping are:

1. For each insertion node, there is one glyph that represents it and its first-level out-edges.

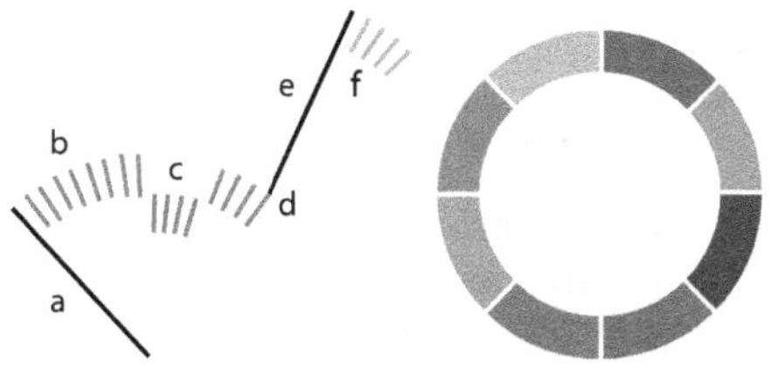

Figure 2. Glyph scheme of two related nodes (left) and cyclic color palette (right). A glyph is composed by an arc (b, f), which is composed by the node's out-edges (making its length proportional to the characters inserted), and a support line (a, e). When a string is deleted, the correspondent part of the arc loses opacity and falls toward the center (c). Children nodes are placed as coming out from the POI they originated from (d). In this example, an insertion of size 15 was followed by a deletion of size 3 at position 10, and then writing was resumed at the end of the document.

2. An edge leading from an insertion node to another means that the correspondent glyphs are related, precisely the latter is placed on top of the former, at the position corresponding to its relative POI within its parent.

3. And edge leading to a deletion node changes the glyph as shown in Figure 2.

Aesthetics. Preliminary prototypes showed the need for decreasing glyph overlap: to avoid, at the same time, straight and spiraling branches. Thus, a "phototropism factor" is applied to the growth of the tree, mimicking the plant behavior of growing towards a light source. Time is represented using a cyclical eight-color categorical palette (see Figure 2, right): nodes are colored according to the session (considered here as a day of writing) in which they were added. The radius of the arc doubles in case its center angle was to surpass π.

Interaction. "Phototropism" and arc length-node size ratio can be dynamically manipulated to globally change the shape of the tree and improve visibility. When a glyph is selected, the textual contents of its branch (deleted and active children) are displayed on the screen in a notation similar to S-notation [13]. Left-clicking hides/shows the branch.

PILOT STUDY

We performed a pilot study, where computer science students from a public university were asked to share their documents written in Google Drive. In total, we obtained 60 documents of different lengths (from a few paragraphs to full-length articles) and purposes (though they were all course assignments). Most of them were ruled out before visual analysis due to being incomplete or too complex. The five documents shown here were selected due to their complementariness (see Table 1). For each one, we identified the visualization's branching structure, which leads to a hierarchic segmentation of the tree. Then, we inspected each branch's content and identified which part of the document corresponded to the branch. We also took note of branch length and breadth, and important deletions, which we interpreted in the context of each document.

There are three dimensions of document evolution that, according to the analysis, are well captured by our system:

- *The internal organization of the text and its hierarchic structure* (Fig. 3). We observed that branches of a tree mostly correspond to the global text structure, which is a direct consequence of the proposed data structure. In Cases A and C, branches match paragraph divisions, as they have no other hierarchical level. Cases B and E have a typical hierarchical organization (cover information, sections, and bibliography) which is perfectly matched by the relations of the correspondent branches. Case D has also no more structure than paragraph-level as can be intuited by its "one big branch" appearance.

Table 1. Description of document case studies.

Doc	Description	Words	Operations
A	Two-item summary	312	1307
B	Three-question assignment	1567	7136
C	One-question assignment	657	3015
D	Unstructured essay	5242	15411
E	Structured assignment	1135	4350

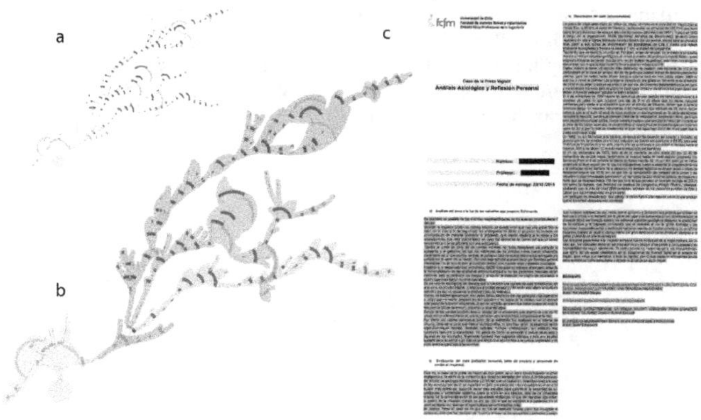

Figure 3. Analysis of document B. From the raw visualization (a) we identified its branching structure (b. The colors were manually added). Inspecting each branch's content produces a correspondent segmentation of the text (c. Highlights were manually added to match correspondent colors in b). This shows that the branching structure of the tree is the same as the hierarchic structure of the document: the cover title splits into two, the bibliography and the body, which splits also into three sections.

- *Some patterns and strategies adopted by agents* (Fig. 4). Thanks to the particular data structure and the visual representation of deletions, the strategies used to write the document can be observed. Cases B and E, show a well-defined hierarchical structure, meaning their writing bore the final structure in mind from the beginning, something that can be expected in a course assignment. Case C shows a draft that was rewritten and erased (similarly, D shows the rewriting of pasted text), while A was written almost linearly, without important deletions.

- *The amount of work put into the document and its different parts* (Fig. 5). This dimension emerges from the color scheme and the grouping of operations into bursts. Case studies A, B, C and E have branches of only one color, meaning they were introduced during one session with no later rewriting, whereas D has branches showing many appendices of different colors, meaning they were reread and edited in posterior sessions. Moreover, the highest edition

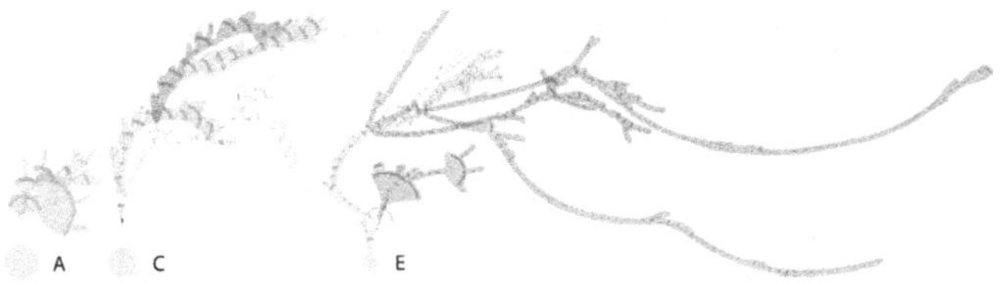

Figure 4. Visualization of documents A, C and E. Note that the branching structure in each case was manually highlighted. A Shows two branches, corresponding to its two paragraphs. C features four main branches, one of which (the faint-looking one) was completely deleted and from which the other branches arise. E is more complex, each branch mapping to a section of the text (same as case B). These cases show different writing strategies: almost linear (A), draft and rewrite (C), and hierarchically structured (E).

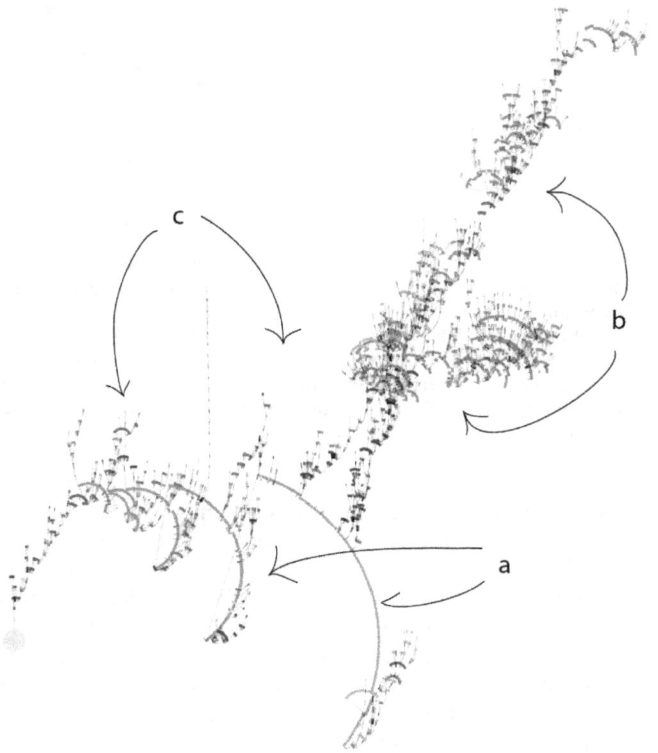

Figure 5. Analysis of D. Very long arcs (a) denote copy/pastes. Branches extending from these arcs (b) are their rewriting (note that the largest arc was almost completely deleted) and have the highest density of changes. Little branches of different colors (c) are later additions.

density is concentrated around the deletion of a large piece of text that was pasted from another document.

In summary, we observed that the system captures important components of the writing process, mainly through its underlying data structure and its decentralized depiction of operations rather than whole versions.

DISCUSSION AND CONCLUSIONS

Our results shed light on the dynamic origins of text and the structures underlying the process of writing. These findings could be useful in natural language processing, *e.g.*, by including human-writing processes into automated text generation, topic segmentation or document summarization. A direct application of our system is a real-time writing-aid in document writing tools, which returned to the document its heterogeneity, for example, showing the relative age of parts of a text, their need for updating and the thread they belong to.

Scope and Future Work. A rightful critique is that, owing to its lack of a different glyph for deletion nodes, the visualization captures only a subset of the data structure, *i.e.*, it is only a spanning tree of the whole graph, which leads to the non-uniqueness of a document's representation: a design fault because it forces a degree of freedom not present in the data [9]. Future work, then, should include the design of deletion nodes so that they play a structural role. Also, having a way to differentiate agents would capture on-line collaborative behavior, which is a very appealing line of study. Displacing text (cut and paste actions inside the document) is not yet captured by the system due to that cutting/pasting is not a specific type of operation in the data, so further preprocessing is required to recognize this behavior. Finally, the pilot study showed that coloring a tree by its branching structure is important for analysis, so a useful feature would be the automatic segmentation of text by branching structure and the consequent visual mapping from the tree to the document.

Conclusions. We have presented a novel visualization design for document evolution, which combines an operational view of the document with an organic visual scheme, and shown that it renders visible some facets of the complex behavior in the process of writing. It can be used, for example, to get an overview of the whole of a document's history in a single image, which is enough to give an idea of the amount of work put into it and the general strategy adopted, and as an interface to its content. Examples of such strategies are rewriting from a draft, writing with a structure in mind, one- *vs.* many-session writing, etc. These features are something that, for a single session or single agent document and at this level of granularity, to the best of our knowledge, available systems cannot provide. Also, with its interactive functions, the system can be used to produce a segmentation of a document, which in some cases coincides with its hierarchical structure, but in any case is a naturally occurring segmentation which follows the thread of thought of the agent. We present this approach and system to provide an integration of computer-aided writing research by proposing a clear focus on the document as a well-defined temporal object. Text analysis should not be abstracted from a document's history when possible, and this approach proves a fair candidate for a first step towards, what we'd like to call, diachronic text analysis.

ACKNOWLEDGEMENTS

The authors would like to thank Tobias Schreck for a fruitful discussion about the visual representation, and James Somers for the knowledge on how to download data from Google Docs. Claudio Gutierrez also thanks CIWS.

REFERENCES

1. Gilles Caporossi and Christophe Leblay. 2011. Online writing data representation: a graph theory approach. In *International Symposium on Intelligent Data Analysis*. Springer, 80–89.
2. Janet Emig. 1977. Writing as a mode of learning. *College composition and communication* 28, 2 (1977), 122–128.
3. Ben Fry. 2007. *A Processing: Programming Handbook for Visual Designers and Artists*. MIT Press.
4. Benjamin Jotham Fry. 2000. *Organic information design*. Ph.D. Dissertation. Massachusetts Institute of Technology.
5. Eduardo Graells-Garrido, Mounia Lalmas, and Ricardo Baeza-Yates. 2016. Data portraits and intermediary topics: Encouraging exploration of politically diverse profiles. In *Proceedings of the 21st International Conference on Intelligent User Interfaces*. ACM, 228–240.
6. Almuth Grésillon and Daniel Perrin. 2014. Methodology: From speaking about writing to tracking text production. *Handbook of writing and text production* 10 (2014), 79–111.
7. Enamul Hoque and Giuseppe Carenini. 2015. Convisit: Interactive topic modeling for exploring asynchronous online conversations. In *Proceedings of the 20th International Conference on Intelligent User Interfaces*. ACM, 169–180.
8. Seungyeon Kim, Joshua V Dillon, and Guy Lebanon. 2012. Cumulative Revision Map. *arXiv preprint arXiv:1205.3205* (2012).
9. Gordon Kindlmann and Carlos Scheidegger. 2014. An algebraic process for visualization design. *IEEE transactions on visualization and computer graphics* 20, 12 (2014), 2181–2190.
10. Py Kollberg and Kerstin Severinson Eklundh. 2002. STUDYING WRITERS'REVISING PATTERNS WITH S-NOTATION ANALYSIS. *Studies in Writing* 10 (2002), 89–104.
11. Kostiantyn Kucher and Andreas Kerren. 2015. Text visualization techniques: Taxonomy, visual survey, and community insights. In *Visualization Symposium (PacificVis), 2015 IEEE Pacific*. IEEE, 117–121.
12. Muhammad M Abdel Latif. 2008. A state-of-the-art review of the real-time computer-aided study of the writing process. *International Journal of English Studies* 8, 1 (2008), 29–50.
13. Daniel Perrin. 2003. Progression analysis (PA): Investigating writing strategies at the workplace. *Journal of Pragmatics* 35, 6 (2003), 907–921.
14. Daniel Perrin and Marc Wildi. 2009. 28 Statistical modeling of writing processes. *Traditions of writing research* (2009), 378.
15. Carson Sievert and Kenneth E Shirley. 2014. LDAvis: A method for visualizing and interpreting topics. In *Proceedings of the workshop on interactive language learning, visualization, and interfaces*. 63–70.
16. Artur Šilić and Bojana Dalbelo Bašić. 2010. Visualization of text streams: A survey. In *International Conference on Knowledge-Based and Intelligent Information and Engineering Systems*. Springer, 31–43.
17. Dario Taraborelli and Giovanni Luca Ciampaglia. 2010. Beyond notability. Collective deliberation on content inclusion in Wikipedia. In *Self-Adaptive and Self-Organizing Systems Workshop (SASOW), 2010 Fourth IEEE International Conference on*. IEEE, 122–125.
18. Frank Van Ham, Martin Wattenberg, and Fernanda B Viégas. 2009. Mapping text with phrase nets. *IEEE transactions on visualization and computer graphics* 15, 6 (2009).
19. Fernanda B Viégas, Martin Wattenberg, and Kushal Dave. 2004. Studying cooperation and conflict between authors with history flow visualizations. In *Proceedings of the SIGCHI conference on Human factors in computing systems*. ACM, 575–582.
20. Dakuo Wang, Judith S Olson, Jingwen Zhang, Trung Nguyen, and Gary M Olson. 2015. DocuViz: visualizing collaborative writing. In *Proceedings of the 33rd Annual ACM Conference on Human Factors in Computing Systems*. ACM, 1865–1874.
21. James A Wise. 1999. The ecological approach to text visualization. *Journal of the Association for Information Science and Technology* 50, 13 (1999), 1224.

Coupling Story to Visualization: Using Textual Analysis as a Bridge Between Data and Interpretation

Ronald Metoyer, Qiyu Zhi, Bart Janczuk, Walter Scheirer
University of Notre Dame
Notre Dame, USA
{rmetoyer, qzhi, bjanczuk, walter.scheirer}@nd.edu

ABSTRACT
Online writers and journalism media are increasingly combining visualization (and other multimedia content) with narrative text to create narrative visualizations. Often, however, the two elements are presented independently of one another. We propose an approach to automatically integrate text and visualization elements. We begin with a writer's narrative that presumably can be supported with visual data evidence. We leverage natural language processing, quantitative narrative analysis, and information visualization to (1) automatically extract narrative components (who, what, when, where) from data-rich stories, and (2) integrate the supporting data evidence with the text to develop a narrative visualization. We also employ bidirectional interaction from text to visualization and visualization to text to support reader exploration in both directions. We demonstrate the approach with a case study in the data-rich field of sports journalism.

ACM Classification Keywords
Human-centered computing: Information visualization; Computing methodologies: Information extraction

Author Keywords
narrative visualization; text analysis; text visualization interaction; deep coupling.

INTRODUCTION
Integrating narrative text with visual evidence is a fundamental aspect of various investigative reporting fields such as sports journalism and intelligence analysis. Sports journalists generate stories about sporting events that typically generate tremendous amounts of data. These stories summarize the event and build support for their particular narrative (e.g. why a particular team won or lost) using the data as evidence. Intelligence analysts carry out similar tasks, collecting data as evidence in support of the narrative that they construct to inform decision makers [1]. Such a process would also be familiar to digital humanities scholars who routinely distill meta-narratives by automatic means from large corpora consisting of literary texts [12, 8]. Support for linking visualizations of this information to the text is an underexplored area that could benefit each of these users.

When visual evidence is provided, it is often presented completely independently of the narrative text. ESPN[1], for example, routinely presents journalistic articles on web pages that are separate from relevant videos, interactive visualizations, and box score tables that all present information about the same game event (See Figure 1). This approach may limit the reader's ability to interpret the writer's narrative in context. For example, a reader might be interested in more detail surrounding a specific element described in the narrative text because she may not agree with the statement. Alternatively, the reader might also be interested in finding the writer's particular take on a specific player of interest or time in the game that she came across while exploring the data visualization. This bidirectional support for interpretation is currently lacking. We leverage the existing skill set of the writer and combine it with computational methods to automatically link the writer's narrative text to visualization elements in order to provide that context in both directions.

RELATED WORK
Narrative visualizations are data visualizations with embedded "stories" presenting particular perspectives using various embedding mechanisms[14]. Segel et al. [14] discuss the utility of textual "messaging"and how author-driven approaches typically include heavy messaging while reader-driven approaches involve more interaction. Kosara and Mackinlay [9] and Lee et al. [11], on the other hand, adopt a view of storytelling in visualization as primarily consisting of communication separate from exploratory analysis. This view matches the way journalists use various data sources including videos and notes to create compelling stories [9].

We attempt to provide equal flexibility to the reader and author. Our proposed method for coupling textual stories to data visualizations can not only assist writers in constructing their message and framing the data [5, 9] but also create exploratory interaction mechanisms for readers. The linking of subjective narrative with objective data evidence can serve to reinforce

[1] espn.go.com

IUI'18, March 7–11, 2018, Tokyo, Japan
ACM ISBN 978-1-4503-4945-1/18/03...$15.00
DOI: https://doi.org/10.1145/3172944.3173007

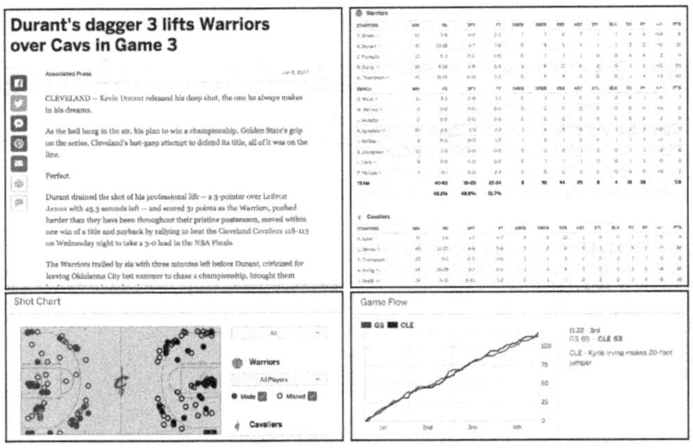

Figure 1. Sites such as www.espn.com provide the reader with several forms of content, but they are often presented independent of one another. Here we see typical narrative text on the upper left, box score in the upper right, and visualizations (shot chart and game flow time series) along the bottom. Each of these elements is shown on a separate web page on the ESPN site. All content from www.espn.com

author communication and give readers the ability to explore their own interpretations of the story and the event. This approach can be viewed as providing a "close reading" of the narrative, using the visualization as a means for providing the semantic context [7] as opposed to a distant reading where the actual text is replaced by abstract visual views [12].

We are not the first to investigate the coupling of text to visualization. Chul Kwon et al. [10] directly, but manually, tie specific text elements to visualization views to support interpretation of the author's content. Others analyze text to automatically generate elements of narrative visualization such as annotations [6, 2]. Likewise, Dou et al. [3] also analyze text, but from large scale text corpora, to identify key "event" elements of who, what, when and where and use that information to construct a visual summary of the corpora and support exploration of it. We build on these approaches, automatically linking text to visualization elements, but focus on a single data-rich text document. In addition, we explore the use of links from the visualization back to the text.

SPORTS STORIES: BASKETBALL

To ground the discussion, we focus on the data-rich domain of sports, specifically basketball, for which we have a significant set of narratives and data published regularly online. Sports events produce tremendous amounts of data and are the subject of sports journalists and general public fans. Basketball is no exception. Data regarding player position and typical basketball "statistics" are collected for every game in the National Basketball Association (NBA)[2]. These data typically include field goals (2pt and 3pt), assists, rebounds, steals, blocked shots, turnovers, fouls, and minutes played. The NBA has recently begun to track the individual positions of players throughout the entire game, leading to spatial data as well as various derived data such as the total number of times a player touches the ball (i.e., touches). The data is rich in space, time, and discrete nominal and quantitative attributes.

[2]http://stats.nba.com/

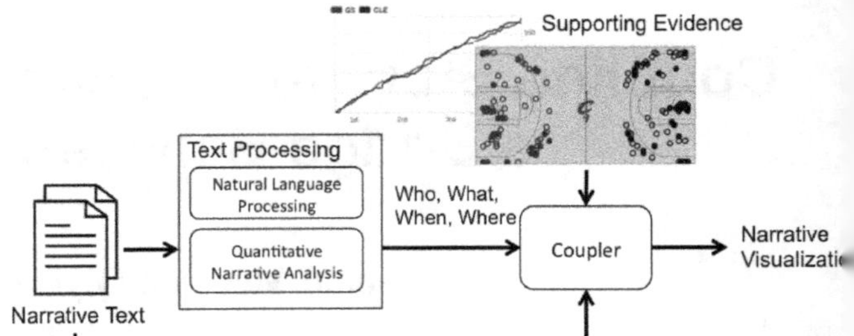

Figure 2. Software architecture for deep coupling of narrative text and visualization components.

OVERVIEW

Our approach is based on a detailed analysis of narrative text to identify key elements of the story that can directly index into the visualizations (and vice versa) to create a *deep coupling*. The system architecture is shown in Figure 2. Raw text is provided as input to the text processing module. This module analyzes the text to extract the four key narrative elements - who, what, when, and where (4 Ws). The coupler then indexes into the multimedia and vice versa with these Ws. We focus solely on data visualization multimedia elements (charts, tables, etc.) as the supporting evidence, however, evidence such as video, images, and audio could be treated similarly.

IDENTIFYING STORY ELEMENTS

A story is defined by characters, plot, setting, theme, and goal which are also sometimes referred to as the five Ws: who, what, when, where and why. These are the elements considered necessary to tell and/or uncover, in the case of intelligence investigation, a complete story [1].

In sports, there are clear mappings for these essential elements. In basketball, for example, there are players, coaches, referees, and teams (who), locations/spaces on the basketball court such as the 3-point line or inside the key (where), distinct times or time periods such as the 4th quarter, or 3-minutes left (when), and particular game "stats" such as shots, fouls, timeouts, touches, etc. (what). Our first step is to extract these elements.

We first segment the text into sentences and for each sentence, we seek to determine if it contains a reference to who, what, when, or where. Consider the following sentence from an Associated Press story from Game 3 of the 2017 NBA Finals between the Cleveland Cavaliers and the Golden State Warriors [3]: *The Warriors trailed by six with three minutes left before Durant, criticized for leaving Oklahoma City last summer to chase a championship, brought them back, scoring 14 in the fourth.* From the second clause in this sentence, we would expect to extract a Who (Durant), a What (14 points), a When (the fourth), and no Where elements.

Who: Extracting the story characters is straightforward, especially for a particular domain. In the NBA case, we can obtain a complete list of all teams, players, coaches, and referees in the league. A more general solution, however, could utilize a

[3]http://www.espn.com/nba/recap?gameId=400954512

named-entity identifier such as the Stanford Core NLP Named Entity Recognizer [4].

What: The "What" of a basketball story, or any sports story in general, refers to the game statistics of interest. While it would seem straightforward to look for mentions of numbers and/or specific stat names since numbers and names are generally used to describe these stats (e.g. 25 points, 10 rebounds, five 3-pointers), this is not always the case. Consider the many ways to refer to the points scored stat: Durant scored 25 points, Durant added 15, or even, Durant outscored the entire Cavalier team in the second quarter.

To identify stats, we take inspiration from the digital humanities [4] and build a "story grammar" to parse the narrative. The stats story grammar is a set of manually designed production rules for creating and/or matching variations of mentions of stats. While the grammar-based approach is appropriate for identifying most mentions of stats, it is only as effective as the grammar specification and a new variation of a stat mention will not be recognized. We therefore use the grammar to generate training data for an SVM classifier for stats.

We run the sentences of 13 stories/blog posts through the stats story grammar to label the sentences as STAT or NO STAT. We then use these positive (STAT) sentence-classification pairs as training data for the SVM classifier. Specifically, for each sentence that contains a statistic, we create a 10-word window around the statistic to use as a feature vector. All such windows are provided as training examples in order to learn the general textual context that surrounds mentions of stats. After training on approximately 600 such windows, the classifier achieves 98% accuracy on a test data set of approximately 150 sentences and it finds additional statistic mentions that were not classified correctly by the grammar.

When and Where: We currently extract both times and locations using only a grammar with acceptable results because there are a limited number of ways to specify times and places in basketball. A classifier similar to that developed for stats could also be generated for both times and places to boost performance if necessary.

Narrative Text to Visualization Coupling

The text analysis stage results in a list of Ws for each sentence in the narrative, stored as a .json object with W-value pairs. This information is then provided to the "coupling" component. The coupler associates each sentence with the appropriate visualization(s) (i.e., those that support the specific Ws in the sentence) and initializes the visualization to show the data for the particular person (who), stat (what), time (when), and location (where) mentioned in the sentence.

In Figure 3, the user has hovered over the sentence highlighted on the left side. The mentioned player is highlighted in the box score on the right (Kevin Durant) and his player profile is shown at the bottom left. The specific mentioned time in the game is marked in the time series visualization (3 minutes left), the specific quarter that is mentioned is selected in the time series visualization (fourth quarter), and the shot chart in the upper left of the visualization shows the shots attempted (both made and missed) by Kevin Durant in the 4th quarter. This visualization initialization provides the context for the writer's interpretation of what was important, and allows the reader to ask their own questions, such as: How many shots did Durant have to take in the 4th quarter to score 14 points?

Interaction Design

No guidelines or principles currently exist for the design of tightly coupled reader interaction with narrative text and visualization concurrently. We chose a multi-view or "partitioned poster" layout [14] to allow for all visualizations to be accessible in a single view along with the narrative text. Interaction is guided by basic multi-view coordination principles [13]. We assume each data table consists of items described by attributes - both of which can correspond directly to one of the four Ws of a story. Thus a visualization can be directly parameterized by one or more of the 4Ws from a sentence.

We coordinate text views with visualization views and vice versa. User interaction (e.g., mouse over, selection) with specific sentences results in the corresponding Ws being brushed in the linked visualizations. Likewise, user interaction with the visualization components results in the corresponding Ws being highlighted in the narrative text. For example, in Figure 3, users can select a row (i.e. a player) in the box score tables and that player's data is then highlighted (brushing and linking) in all other views (e.g. shots in the short chart and mentions in the time series). That player's profile is also displayed in detail at the bottom left (details on demand). All visualizations support tooltip details where appropriate.

Navigation Between Text and Visualization

The reader must be able to navigate from the narrative text to the visual representations and vice versa. As the reader browses the text, sentences are highlighted to show the current sentence of interest and the visualizations update to reflect the corresponding Ws from the highlighted text. The user can click on a sentence to indicate that he is interested in exploring the data context around that aspect of the narrative, thus, we freeze the state of the visualizations. The user can then interact with the visualizations, using mouse-overs to get further details. Any direct interaction, such as a click on an element or brush to select a time series range, results in updating all visualizations and the highlighted narrative text given the new selected Ws. The user can now continue to explore the visualizations or can navigate back to the narrative text at any time to examine the writer's commentary with regards to the selected Ws.

CASE STUDY: SPORTS NARRATIVES

To gain an initial understanding of the potential opportunities and pitfalls that this approach presents, we conducted an informal case study with a domain expert user with 4.5 years of experience as a media producer for Bleacher Report[5] and multiple collegiate sports media outlets. We gave the user a brief introduction to the interface and asked him to explore a game recap of Game 3 of the 2017 NBA finals and provide feedback using a "Think Aloud" protocol.

[4]https://nlp.stanford.edu/software/CRF-NER.shtml

[5]www.bleacherreport.com

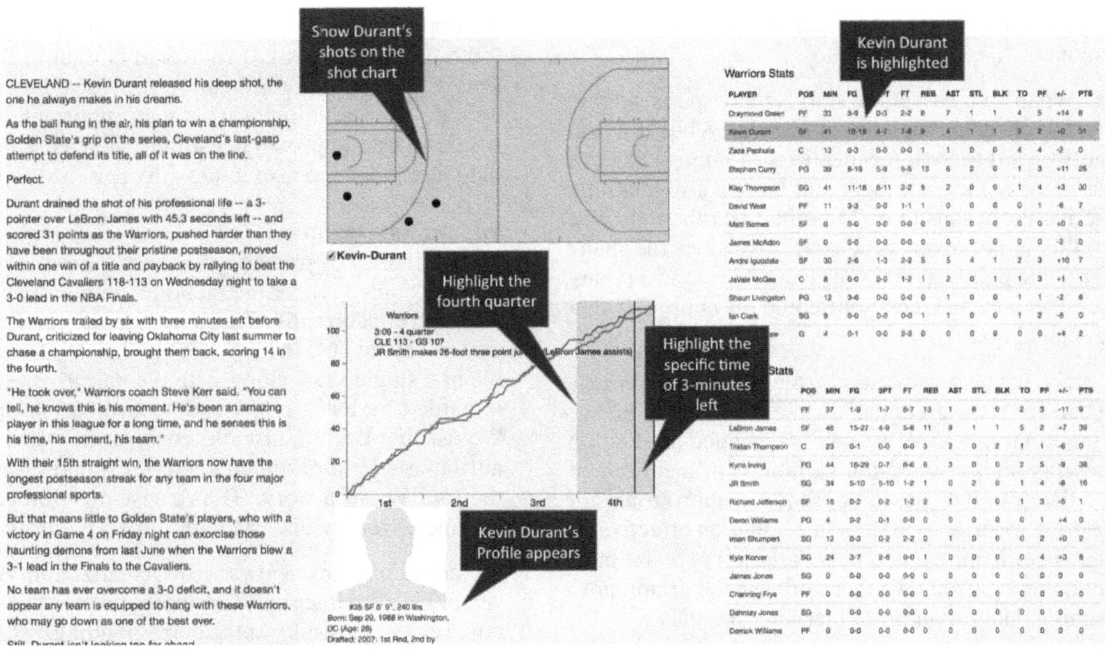

Figure 3. Coupling from text to visualization. The user has selected a passage that reads: The Warriors trailed by six with three minutes left before Durant, criticized for leaving Oklahoma City last summer to chase a championship, brought them back, scoring 14 in the fourth. Story excerpt from the Associated Press.

Our user immediately grasped the navigation concept and was easily able to move from reading/scanning the narrative text to the visualization and back to the narrative text. His general impression was that there was great value in being able to more deeply explore the specific narrative presented by the author: *I love the idea of being able to experience the article, but really dial-in on a specific part of it myself.* He was also intrigued by the potential to more deeply tie the text phrasing to the visuals. *If the writer emphasized the number of points Curry had from the paint, I'd be interested in seeing that visually, and also exploring for myself where else he may have scored from. I'd like to select areas like the paint, midrange, and 3-pointers and beyond to see the shots he took in those areas.*

Our user also articulated several areas for improvement. For example, he found the box score filtering by selecting a player row to be extremely useful, but wanted even more control. *I'd like to select both a player row and a stat column so I could more specifically look for a specific stat for that player in the other charts like the time series view.* He also recommended a more subtle tie from the visualization to the narrative text might be more effective. Currently, data items selected through direct interaction with the visualization causes the sentences that mentioned those items to be highlighted in the narrative. This was sometimes overwhelming because some sentences may have directly mentioned specific players and their stats while others may have simply provided commentary or mentioned the player in a secondary role. A deeper analysis of the text to understand the saliency of the sentence with regards to the selected data should be explored. Finally, our user desired a more granular link to the text. *It would be useful if the text highlighted the types of elements - player, stats, times, etc., with different colors* . Future versions could employ color encodings to distinguish the 4Ws in the text.

CONCLUSION AND FUTURE WORK

We have presented a novel approach to automatically couple narrative text to visualizations for data-rich stories and demonstrated the approach in the basketball story domain. This serves only as an introductory step for using text analysis to tightly integrate visualization with narrative text. There are several exciting avenues of research that remain to be explored.

First, Where is the 5th W? We have not attempted to analyze the text to understand the "Why" of the narrative. A more nuanced narrative analysis is necessary to take semantics and topics into account when coupling to the visualization.

Our approach is carried out completely offline. One can imagine, however, a real-time version that operated online as the journalist writes the story - suggesting a set of initialized candidate visualizations to support the most recently completed sentence. Our case study user was intrigued by the possibility that the tool could influence how journalists write. *I wonder if a writer might use specific phrasing as a tool for leading the reader to particular elements of the game?* It would be interesting to study how real-time interactive visualization coupling might influence the writing style of journalists.

This approach should transfer well to any sport where stories typically consist of discussions of players, teams, the field (or pitch, court, etc.), times, and game stats. We suspect it can also be extended to data-rich news stories as well, however, these will require more sophisticated algorithms for extracting the Ws given the more general language and context. Finally, a thorough evaluation of the approach is needed. We are in the process of conducting a crowdsourced study to examine the effects of this type of coupling on the reading experience.

REFERENCES

1. Ruben Arcos and Randolph Pherson. 2015. *Intelligence Communication in the Digital Era: Transforming Security, Defence and Business*. Springer.
2. Chris Bryan, Kwan-Liu Ma, and Jonathan Woodring. 2017. Temporal summary images: An approach to narrative visualization via interactive annotation generation and placement. *IEEE transactions on visualization and computer graphics* 23, 1 (2017), 511–520.
3. Wenwen Dou, Xiaoyu Wang, Drew Skau, William Ribarsky, and Michelle X Zhou. 2012. Leadline: Interactive visual analysis of text data through event identification and exploration. In *Visual Analytics Science and Technology (VAST), 2012 IEEE Conference on*. IEEE, 93–102.
4. Roberto Franzosi. 2010. *Quantitative narrative analysis*. Number 162. Sage.
5. Jessica Hullman and Nick Diakopoulos. 2011. Visualization rhetoric: Framing effects in narrative visualization. *IEEE transactions on visualization and computer graphics* 17, 12 (2011), 2231–2240.
6. Jessica Hullman, Nicholas Diakopoulos, and Eytan Adar. 2013. Contextifier: automatic generation of annotated stock visualizations. In *Proceedings of the SIGCHI Conference on Human Factors in Computing Systems*. ACM, 2707–2716.
7. Stefan Jänicke, Greta Franzini, Muhammad Faisal Cheema, and Gerik Scheuermann. 2015. On close and distant reading in digital humanities: A survey and future challenges. *Proc. EuroVis, Cagliari, Italy* (2015).
8. Matthew L. Jockers. 2013. *Macroanalysis: Digital Methods and Literary history*. University of Illinois Press.
9. Robert Kosara and Jock Mackinlay. 2013. Storytelling: The next step for visualization. *Computer* 46, 5 (2013), 44–50.
10. Bum Chul Kwon, Florian Stoffel, Dominik Jäckle, Bongshin Lee, and Daniel Keim. 2014. VisJockey: Enriching Data Stories through Orchestrated Interactive Visualization. In *Poster Compendium of the Computation+ Journalism Symposium*, Vol. 3.
11. Bongshin Lee, Nathalie Henry Riche, Petra Isenberg, and Sheelagh Carpendale. 2015. More than telling a story: Transforming data into visually shared stories. *IEEE computer graphics and applications* 35, 5 (2015), 84–90.
12. Franco Moretti. 2013. *Distant Reading*. Verso Books.
13. Chris North and Ben Shneiderman. 2000. Snap-together visualization: a user interface for coordinating visualizations via relational schemata. In *Proceedings of the working conference on Advanced visual interfaces*. ACM, 128–135.
14. Edward Segel and Jeffrey Heer. 2010. Narrative visualization: Telling stories with data. *IEEE transactions on visualization and computer graphics* 16, 6 (2010), 1139–1148.

CARDINAL

Computer-Assisted Authoring of Movie Scripts

Marcel Marti
ETH & Disney Research
Zürich, Switzerland
marmarti@student.ethz.ch

Jodok Vieli
ETH & Disney Research
Zürich, Switzerland
jvieli@student.ethz.ch

Wojciech Witoń
ETH & Disney Research
Zürich, Switzerland
witon.wojciech@gmail.com

Rushit Sanghrajka
Disney Research Los Angeles
Burbank, CA, USA
rush.sanghrajka@utah.edu

Daniel Inversini
Disney Research Zürich
Zürich, Switzerland
daniel.inversini
@disneyresearch.com

Diana Wotruba
Disney Research Zürich
Zürich, Switzerland
dwotruba@operamail.com

Isabel Simo
Disney Research Zürich
Zürich, Switzerland
isabel.simo@disneyresearch.com

Sasha Schriber
Disney Research Zürich
Zürich, Switzerland
sasha.schriber
@disneyresearch.com

Mubbasir Kapadia
Rutgers University
New Brunswick, NJ, USA
mubbasir.kapadia@rutgers.edu

Markus Gross
ETH & Disney Research
Zürich, Switzerland
grossm@inf.ethz.ch

ABSTRACT

We present CARDINAL, a tool for computer-assisted authoring of movie scripts. CARDINAL provides a means of viewing a script through a variety of perspectives, for interpretation as well as editing. This is made possible by virtue of intelligent automated analysis of natural language scripts and generating different intermediate representations. CARDINAL generates 2-D and 3-D visualizations of the scripted narrative and also presents interactions in a timeline-based view. The visualizations empower the scriptwriter to understand their story from a spatial perspective, and the timeline view provides an overview of the interactions in the story. The user study reveals that users of the system demonstrated confidence and comfort using the system.

IUI'18, March 7–11, 2018, Tokyo, Japan

ISBN 978-1-4503-4945-1/18/03...15.00

DOI: https://doi.org/10.1145/3172944.3172972

Author Keywords

computer-assisted authoring; natural language processing; previz; scriptwriting.

INTRODUCTION

Movies tell complex and detailed stories to viewers through an intricately planned narrative structure. These stories are traditionally authored in text editors. Existing applications allow for organization of material, but lack support for visualizations that highlight different aspects of a script.

Information extraction and visualization of the various elements of the story can help scriptwriters analyze when and where actions and interactions between actors in the scenes of the script unfold. The lack of specialized visualizations hinders story writers from discerning if their description of the story matches their creative intent. Characters movements and interactions in the script may be complex and difficult to follow solely through the text.

Extracting information from scripts to visualize it in novel and helpful ways is challenging due to the lack of meta information about different parts of a script. Scriptwriters, just like any other people, develop their own habits over time. While there is an industry standard format, scripts differ a lot in the implementation of this standard. New visualizations should not need manual input from scriptwriters. These tools should not interrupt or change the work-flow of scriptwriters, making this problem difficult to approach and solve. All data must be extracted from text alone, requiring sophisticated parsing capabilities.

Existing solutions like Final Draft [6] or Adobe Story [1] provide some tools that allow scriptwriters to plan certain aspects of their script, but the main focus is on organizing scenes, locations and actors without visualizations of interactions and movement. These features require the application to be aware of details of the written script, which traditional scriptwriting applications do not do in a sufficient capacity.

We propose CARDINAL, a script authoring application taking a natural language processing based approach to provide new visualizations for scriptwriters. CARDINAL provides line visualizations that allow users to properly plan parallelism in actions and clearly visualizes which actors are interacting with whom at which point in time in the script. Furthermore, CARDINAL also provides an automatically generated three-dimensional preview of the written script that allows scriptwriters to not only detect logical errors in their script but also provides an easy way to keep in mind what the authored story currently could look like in a production setting. These different views in CARDINAL are possible by virtue of intelligent automated analysis of these natural language scripts and generate intermediate representations of scripts, that allow us to view the scripts in different types of ways.To extract the information needed to automatically generate these visualizations from a text, CARDINAL employs a natural language processing solution that translates text in the script into actions that are used by the application. While the application stays true to its roots and sticks close to the industry standard format of scripts, the functionally is extended in reasonable and automated ways. Other than in traditional scriptwriting tools, scriptwriters can now follow the action in a script much more easily by simply looking at the interaction view or the generated preview.

We show how these new visualizations work and look and how they are implemented in a proof-of-concept prototype. We also mention the challenges that come with each feature. Our expectation of the usefulness and efficiency of our novel visualizations for extracting data from scripts is corroborated with a user study, which confirms that subjects take less time to extract information while also reducing the fraction of wrong answers when using our visualizations.

RELATED WORK

CARDINAL uses sophisticated natural language processing frameworks based on Stanford's Core NLP framework [14]. To get the best results for our interface, we also use dependency resolution [4] and coreference resolution [13]. Natural language is also used by other systems such as LyriSys, which uses it towards generating lyrics [24]. LISA [19] uses a similar natural language-based approach to extract information about stories and automatically flags logical problems within the story.There are various other attempts that focus on extracting narrative information, and some require further user input [5, 7], others focus on other aspects of the narratives such as affect [8]. Sanghrajka et al. propose a framework for narrative extraction in screenplays in [20].

Pavel et al. [17] propose a new way to visualize, search and browse in movie plots based on synchronized captions, scripts and plot summaries. Won et al. [25] have also worked in the domain of creating previsualizations from text-based directives. Newer visualization tools are being introduced in other domains as well, which make use of combined models, neural networks and other newer technologies [21, 2].

Randall Munroe's narrative charts are a notable example of timelines created for stories [16]. Munroe's charts, though hand-crafted, are a descriptive summarization of character interactions and can serve as an effective reference tool. Ruben et al. even propose tools to work with audio based stories [18]. In [23] Tapaswi et al. present a new way to automatically summarize the storyline of movies and TV episodes by visualizing character interactions as a chart. In this work, the authors also present a timeline-based chart where each character of a story is represented by a horizontal line. These lines join, split and fade in or out based on whether a character is part of the scene. In CARDINAL, we try to take the timeline one step further and do not only represent character interactions on a per-scene level but instead go deeper to a per-action level. We visualize dialogues and actions and join or split lines within each scene based on those interactions.

CARDINAL uses affordances as atomic actions executable by smart objects. CANVAS [10] is an authoring system that is built on top of a smart object and affordance system as well. (Kapadia et al.) describe a computer-assisted visual authoring tool for synthesizing multi-character animations from sparsely-specified narrative events. Other than CARDINAL, CANVAS uses a storyboarding approach to specifying a narrative that is then completed automatically by the system.

Storyboarding is also used by StoryCrate [3], where Bartindale et al. present a tangible tabletop prototype for live storyboarding in film production. In their work on behavior trees, Kapadia et al. [11] describe a new approach to modeling multi-character behavior using behavior trees. This work is continued in [12] and [9] where a new approach to integrating interactivity into behavior trees is presented.

From the related work discussed in this section, CARDINAL sets itself apart as a unique application which uses natural language understanding to extract affordance-based information from the script and simultaneously performs previsualization to provide the author with multiple representations of the narrative they are creating with the application.

OVERVIEW

CARDINAL distinguishes itself from traditional scriptwriting tools by focusing on assisting scriptwriters during the process of authoring stories. Figure 1 depicts an overview of the structure of components and features of CARDINAL. This section gives important terms and then briefly describes the various views shown in the framework.

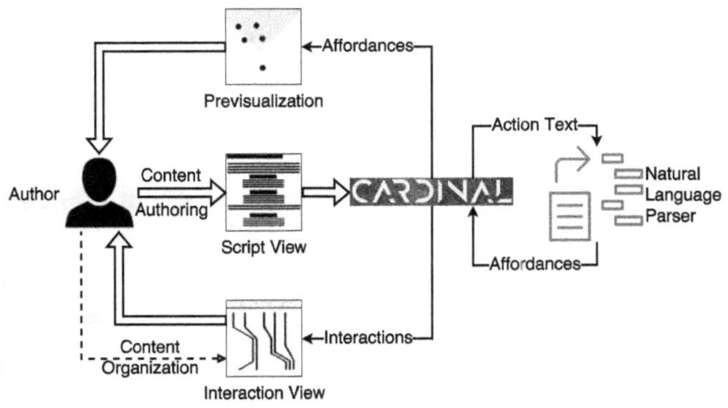

Figure 1: Conceptual framework of CARDINAL. The user authors a movie script mostly in a textual script view. The system takes the text and stores it in an internal meta-annotated representation format. Text of actions is further passed to a natural language processing server and transformed into affordances, which are then used in other visualizations.

Terminology

Special Sets

CARDINAL stores sets of smart objects, affordances and affordance instances in different places, each representing different structures in the application. These special sets are defined in the system and are constructed from the current script. The various special sets are described below.

Smart Objects

Smart object $\mathbf{S} =< \mathbf{A}, \mathbf{s_s}, \mathbf{s_d} >$ is an object that has a list of affordances $\mathbf{A} \subseteq \mathbf{A_{all}}$, which represent the actions and interactions offered by that smart object. Each smart object, at any time, has a position and an orientation (which are represented using position-, forward- and up-vectors), and has a static significance value $\mathbf{s_s}$ and a dynamic significance value $\mathbf{s_d}$ that are both used to compute how much that object adds to the significance of a position in a scene. An actor is an example of a smart object.

Affordances

Affordance is a definition of a possible action such as walking, cheering and waving, and is represented as a three-value tuple: $\mathbf{A} =< \mathbf{O}, \mathbf{U}, \mathbf{v} >$ – $\mathbf{O}$ denotes the owner, $\mathbf{U}$ denotes the set of users for the affordance. The direction of initiation for affordances is usually reversed – the user of an affordance initiates the affordance, while the owner of the affordance controls the affordance. Every affordance also has a vector $\mathbf{v}$ associated with it. This vector is used to map the verbs from the script text to the closest affordance, which is described in Section 4. An "action" is an individual instance of an affordance.

One example that showcases the reversed flow of control particularly well is a ball. A ball offers an affordance to be picked up – it is initiated by an actor (user) which uses the hands of an actor. The ball knows how it is supposed to be picked up and controls the actor trying to pick up the ball. For simple affordances, this reversed flow of control is not easily seen.

Interactions

Interactions $\mathbf{I} \subseteq \mathbf{A_S}$ are sets of affordances that describe how a set of actors interacts with each other and with objects in the scene. Interactions can span a long time and can contain affordances that happen in sequence. Interactions cannot span across scene boundaries.

Views

In CARDINAL, we introduce a variety of views that focus on different aspects of the script: the text-based script view, the interaction view highlighting exact timings and parallelism in actions, and the preview that comes with different filters and focuses on planning spatial properties of a story. These views are shown in Figure 2.

Script View

The script view is the text-based view of CARDINAL. Just like in traditional scripts, it allows scriptwriters to create, edit and remove parts of the script. It sticks to the industry standard for scripts.

Interaction View

The interaction view shows the evolution of each actor in a scene as a graphical 2D representation of the script. In order to be fully distinguishable, every actor has its own color and line. The interaction view is created automatically from the parsed script.

2D/3D Preview

Keeping track of movement and locations in 360-degree movies purely based on a textual representation of a story is difficult. CARDINAL provides a solution to these problems by automatically generating a 2D as well as a 3D preview of the authored story. Text entered as actions is passed to a natural language processing subsystem, which in turn maps the action text to an action vocabulary and produces animations for the actors in the preview scene. This automatically generated preview comes with a set of predefined filters that each highlight different features of the story.

The different views allow the user to interact and view the script in multiple ways, which current scripting tools lack. The views are not only for viewing but also allow for editing. The interaction view allows the user to make edits in terms of interactions as opposed to the raw text in script view. This novel approach is the core of CARDINAL and its focus on the assisted authoring of scripts.

SCRIPT VIEW

The main tool of every scriptwriter is a script view. Just like in traditional scriptwriting applications, CARDINAL allows authors to write their scripts in a well-known format. Unlike traditional scripts, however, CARDINAL improves upon existing tools by further highlighting actors. Each actor is assigned a unique color upon creation that identifies him throughout the application in actions, the automatically generated preview and the interaction view.

The four different elements commonly found in movie scripts, are represented in CARDINAL by modules that an author can drag and drop into the script view: **Dialogs** have

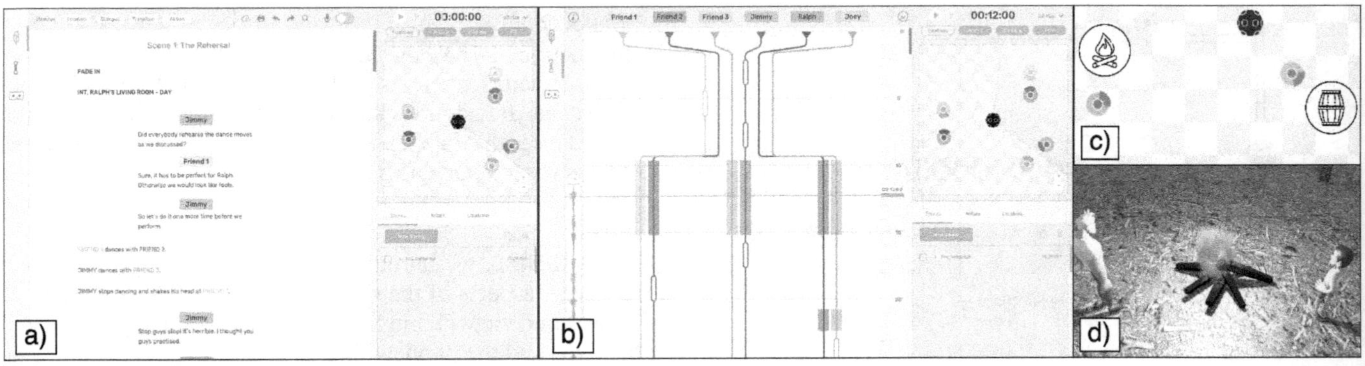

Figure 2: The various views of the CARDINAL system: a) Script View, b) Interaction View, c) 2D-Preview, d) 3D-Preview.

a heading with an actor name, followed by the dialog text, **Actions** describe things happening that aren't dialog, and include movement, interactions and circumstantial descriptions, **Locations** start with a shortcut for exterior (EXT.) or interior (INT.) scenes, **Transitions** describe changes from one scene to another. Each module has a start- and an end-time that is automatically computed based on its relative position in the existing script view. Since the script view has no way of showing parallelism in actions, modules are inserted in the script view in a way that all modules following the new module are shifted forward in time by the duration of the new module.

Affordances extraction

In the script view, all information used by other visualizations is extracted. Text in action modules is sent to a remote natural language processing (NLP) service, responsible for parsing the text and sending it back in a form of subject-verb-object triples. These triples are then interpreted and checked for correctness. The parsed subjects and objects are searched for by name in the list of all available objects in the current project. If the subject is found, the list of affordances offered by it is searched for an affordance that represents the relation in the parsed action.

If neither the subject nor the object is found, the script view shows a warning, explaining that no object with the specified parsed name could be found. If the relation is not found, then a warning is displayed that the subject does not have an affordance of the specified name. This functionality allows for an efficient work-flow where actions are automatically parsed and translated into affordances that can be then used by the preview and the interaction view to reflect a current content of the script.

Natural Language Processing

Scriptwriters are able to provide an input in natural language in the form of the main story plot, i.e., interactions between characters, and dialogs (locations and transitions are chosen from predefined options). With the help of a Stanford CoreNLP framework [14] a semantic analysis of the action text is performed, automatizing a process of creating affordances.

A story is assumed to be divided into separate modules (paragraphs), consisting of logically connected sentences. A first step involves applying co-reference resolution to the whole text in one paragraph – pronouns, such as 'he', 'they', 'it', are assigned the real names of actors, objects and places based on previously analyzed sentences. Then, single sentences and words (tokens) are extracted. Relations between tokens are analyzed using dependency graphs [4].

The main parsing task involves extracting subjects (nouns), relations (verbs) and objects (often nouns), i.e., `relation triples`, as well as relation modifiers (mostly adverbs), which describe a way affordances are performed (walking could be either fast or slow). Also, more complicated structures of sentences are handled, containing, e.g., auxiliary verbs and continuous forms of verbs, i.e., a sentence "Adam is gone" would be recognized as a state of the person, in contrast to sentence "Adam is going to Isa", being a proper action.

Nominal modifiers ("talk **with** someone"), and relational objects ("talk with **someone**") are extracted as well, but they are analyzed in the way that the final output of the parser consists of only triples and modifiers, i.e., a relation would be "talk with" and an object would be "someone". If more than one object is specified in the sentence, then for each of them an independent triple is created. Each module and each sentence in the module are indexed which is used to provide proper timings — as a result, all triples generated from one sentence are assigned the same time and resulting actions are executed simultaneously. An exception from this rule occurs when timing words are used, i.e., in a sentence "Before Isa shakes Marcel's hand, she cries." the second action is performed first.

Creating new affordances requires defining at least possible owners O and users U, associated relations (verbs) and relevant animations. As a result, a set of affordances set up in CARDINAL is finite, requires much time to be extended, and thus it is intractable to create a complete library of affordances corresponding to every word possibly used by a scriptwriter. We resolve this problem by assigning to every created affordance a vector $\mathbf{v}$, which is an embedding of an associated relation (verb) extracted using Word2vec [15]. Each extracted relation triple is mapped to one of the previously defined affordances by looking for a most similar verb to an extracted relation in a set of relations associated with previously defined affordances based on a cosine similarity of vectors. In cases when the system fails to understand the action, it does not perform a visualization and displays a message to the user.

INTERACTION VIEW

The interaction view visualizes a movie script as a set of lines, one for each actor. This visualization shows the interactions between actors and groups them accordingly. A user is able to immediately extract information crucial for each scene, such as participating actors, their interactions over time, and the timing relative to other affordances in the scene. Professional production of movies involves a lot of people not equally familiar with the script – the interaction view will offer a lead-in in any stage of the production.

A system that helps to create a video content should not only help understand the script and detect flaws and inconsistencies but once the problems are apparent one should be able to change and correct the script. The interaction view meets this requirement as it is fully interactive – a user is able to add and remove actors and affordances, as well as change the timing of each affordance separately by dragging and scaling a graphical element to the desired form. Changes made here are consistent with all other views.

The visualization is built dynamically based on the intermediate representation produced by the script view. Every **actor** has its dedicated column, serving as a beginning of a character's line. The line always starts at the same place at the top, but moving down it can move horizontally dependent on other actors the character interacts with. The lines move back to their dedicated columns as soon as the interaction finishes. Each **affordance** is represented as a graphical element drawn on the line of its owner. In order to provide a clear overview we distinguish dialogs and other interactions by using different graphical elements. The relative position on the vertical axis gives information about the order, while the length gives insight into a relative duration of the affordance. A more detailed description of the affordance appears while hovering the mouse over the graphical element. The dialog elements then show the name of the affordance, all involved users and (if applicable) a content of the actual dialog.

Figure 3 shows an example way a user can interact with `CARDINAL`, by providing a text in the script view, which is later automatically split into submodules and translated into affordances. The interaction view then visualizes these affordances and allows a user to change their order or duration, what is reflected back in the script view.

Interactions

In order to visualize a context of the individual affordance we designed **interactions**. An interaction i groups related affordances (e.g., a dialog interaction consists of multiple talk affordances) and is visualized by joining corresponding lines for the time of interaction. The main difficulty in creating the interaction view is to identify related affordances. We came up with several definitions for a relation between affordances and different approaches to group them. We introduce following nomenclature: $a_1 \backsim a_2$ means that affordances a_1 and a_2 are related to each other, $c_1 \vdash c_2$ means that characters c_1 and c_2 are close to each other. Both aforementioned relations are reflexive and symmetric, but not transitive.

We define $\mathbf{A_S}$ as a set of all affordances, $\mathbf{I_S}$ – a set of all interactions in the current scene, and a function $\mathbf{F_P}$ returning a set of all owners $\mathbf{O}$ and users $\mathbf{U}$ of one or more affordances or interactions. Between affordances there can be:

1. **No relation** Affordances are not related to each other.
$$a_1 \not\backsim a_2$$
2. **Relation by locality** Affordances are related based on the location of their owner. Affordances with proximate actors are related to each other.
$$O_1 \vdash O_2 \implies a_1 \backsim a_2$$
3. **Relation by participation** Affordances are related based on common actors.
$$\mathbf{F_P}(a_1) \cap \mathbf{F_P}(a_2) \neq \emptyset \implies a_1 \backsim a_2$$

Grouping

An interaction consists of a group of pairwise related affordances. The need for recognizing these groupings is to understand when affordances require characters to be together, which will then be used in creating the grouped lines for the interaction view. These groups can be:

1. **Exclusive** Actors can only be in one interaction at a time.
$$\forall i_1, i_2 \in \mathbf{I_S}, i_1 \neq i_2 \implies \mathbf{F_P}(i_1) \cap \mathbf{F_P}(i_2) = \emptyset$$
2. **Inclusive** No restriction on the actors of an interaction, they can be part of one or more interactions.

Spatial interactions

Scripts use location relative to other actors or objects in the scene rather than absolute location. This allows us to determine each actor's location at any time based on the initial location of the actor and spatial affordances like *go to someone* and *go to some object*. Therefore, groups created by locality are always exclusive. The main benefit of this approach is it's simplicity while reflecting our intuitive understanding of interactions in most scenarios: people interact with their immediate surroundings. However, there are scenarios where interactions created by locality ignore certain affordances. *Point at someone* or *greet someone* don't require their users to be proximate to the owner. Nevertheless, one could visualize these affordances by connecting the actors with dotted lines.

Exclusive interactions by participation

The *related* relation is not transitive. Therefore, actors might very well be in two different groups of related affordances. For exclusive interactions, we don't allow this behavior. We have to select affordances which we won't take into account for creating the interactions. We propose the following selection criteria:

1. **Occurrence count:** We count the number of occurrences of actors in each group of related affordances. For every

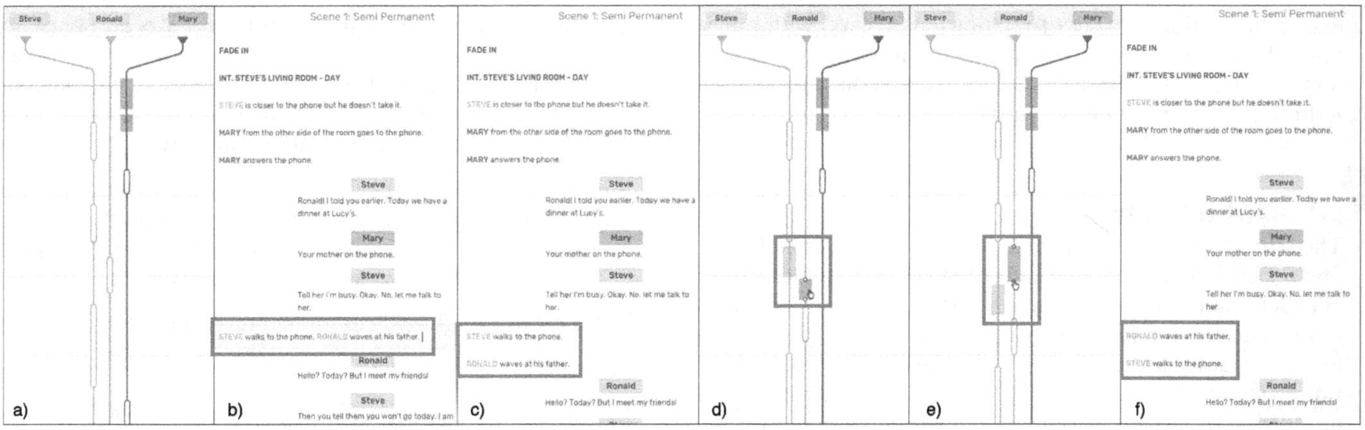

Figure 3: Figures a) to c) – `CARDINAL` automatically parses action modules into affordances that are animated in the preview and shown in the interaction view, and splits the text into two separate modules. Figures d) to f) – the interaction view allows users to arrange affordances happening in parallel by providing tools necessary to modify their start times and duration (here a user increases a length of the movement affordance to make Ronald move a bit slower and before Steve).

affordance, we go through its actors and look for the group having the highest occurrence count. That's the group that "wins" this affordance, in every other group this affordance is discarded. To prevent equal counts we weight the occurrences by the importance of each affordance.

2. **Affordance importance:** Affordances are assigned a weight between 0 and 1. We propose the following ordering from highest to lowest importance: dialogs, affordances with small range (*touch* or *hold*), affordances with hight range (*point at* or *wave at*), affordances without specified targets (*cheer* or *clap*).

Inclusive interactions by participation

Inclusive interactions are created from the related affordances without further selection necessary because we allow actors to be part of multiple interactions. This approach is the most correct in the sense that we do not ignore any affordances. However, there is a significant increase in visual complexity. Multiple parallel lines are needed to visualize an actor being part of multiple interactions.

Figure 4 presents adding a new affordance in the interaction view and an automatic grouping of existing affordances. Figure 5 visualizes different grouping approaches described above: exclusive and inclusive interactions by participation as well as exclusive interactions by location.

PREVISUALIZATION OF MOVIE SCRIPTS

`CARDINAL` uses the natural language text in the script view and translates it into an intermediate representation (IR). This intermediate representation is made of modules, which describe affordances and their respective timings in the scene, as described in the script view section. The IR is used throughout the system to automatically generate visualizations. For previsualizations, we generate a behavior tree based on these affordances which plays animations and handles movements. Our system uses the ADAPT [22] framework to generate the behavior trees.

Behavior Trees for Script Visualization

Behavior trees have been used before in ADAPT to display animations and sequences of animations. For `CARDINAL`, behavior trees have the additional benefit of providing an easy structure to encode dependencies among different affordances. Our implementation is based on the same framework as ADAPT and comes with the basic building blocks of behavior trees, such as the action nodes, sequence nodes, selector nodes, loop nodes and wait nodes. A simple example of a behavior tree that is automatically generated by our system is provided in the supplementary document. `CARDINAL` uses these node types to encode the movie script in a behavior tree by forming blocks of overlapping affordances, effectively handling dependencies in a way that keeps all potential errors local to each block. The behavior tree in `CARDINAL` is constructed by a dispatcher that maps affordance descriptions to their corresponding instances:

$$d(a) : \mathbf{A}_S \rightarrow \mathbf{N}_S \cup \varnothing \tag{1}$$

The function d maps each affordance instance of a scene to either a node in that scene or to nothing, $\varnothing$. If an affordance instance is mapped to nothing, there is no behavior tree node implementation available for that affordance, which makes it a virtual affordance. Each behavior tree node in `CARDINAL` is annotated with the start and end time of the corresponding affordance. Additionally, each node has access to its affordance instance, and therefore to its owners and users, allowing nodes to affect the participants of their coupled affordance instance in terms of a predefined, shared behavior. The nodes are represented in the equation below, where t_s and t_e are start time and end time.

$$\begin{gathered} \mathbf{N}_S = \{d(a) \mid a \in \mathbf{A}_S\} \\ n \in \mathbf{N}_S = < a, t_s, t_e >, t_s \leq t_e \\ a \in \mathbf{A}_s = \text{Source affordance instance.} \end{gathered} \tag{2}$$

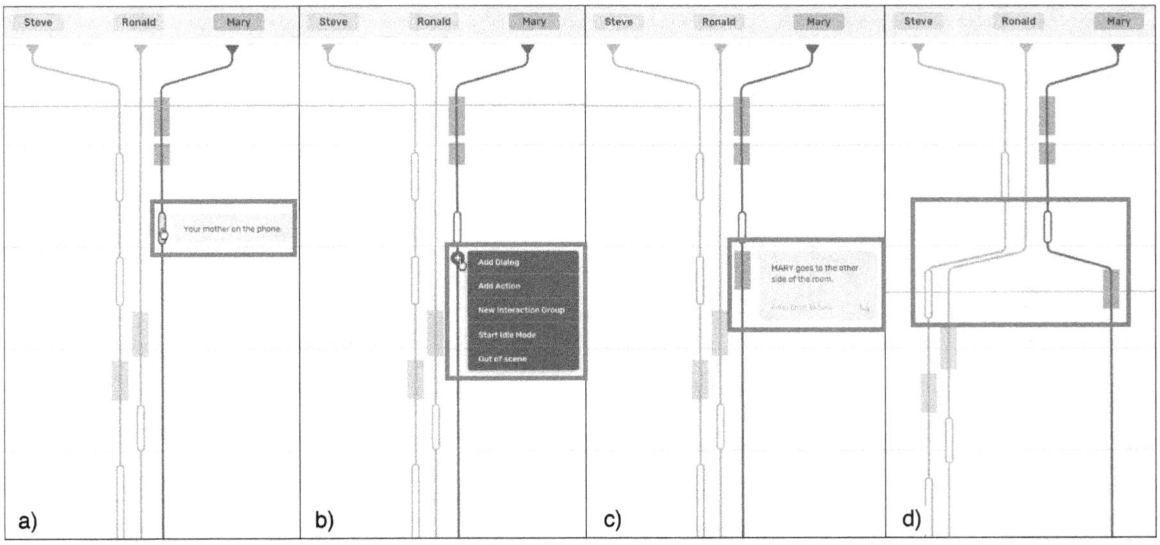

Figure 4: The interaction view can also be used to author affordances for actors. This gives scriptwriters the flexibility needed to fine-tune their story. CARDINAL automatically splits actors into interaction groups: a) the user looks at a dialog in the interaction view and realizes that the actor should be moving away from its current interaction group, b) the user adds a movement affordance directly in the interaction view, c) the movement affordance appears in the interaction view and all other visualizations, d) the movement of the actor away from its current group causes the interaction view to split the actors into two interaction groups.

Tree Construction

CARDINAL groups overlapping affordance instance nodes $n \in \mathbf{N}$ into parallel sequences and prepends them with a wait node with access to a shared watch. If a new node overlaps multiple existing nodes, the existing nodes are first grouped into a single sequence node and that node is then grouped in parallel with the new node. This approach keeps errors in check by making sure they stay block-local.

For example, A block b_2 will only start executing once its predecessor block b_1 has finished executing because the behavior tree effectively encodes a dependency between block b_2 and block b_1: $b_1 \leq b_2$. If an affordance in block b_1 is out of control and takes longer than planned, the behavior tree ensures that the story will be correctly displayed again as soon as it enters block b_2, effectively keeping an error block-local. This approach has the downside that there is a degenerate case where each inserted affordance overlaps with the previous one, resulting in one giant block without encoded dependencies. In the end, the result of this dispatching process is a behavior tree that encodes the written story.

CARDINAL uses two subtrees that are looped. The first subtree, the reset-tree, resets all actor positions and orientations to their original values. The second subtree, the story-subtree, contains the affordance- and compound-nodes.

Affordance Nodes

Affordance nodes are behavior tree nodes that are instantiated by the dispatcher, which turns an affordance instance into an affordance node that has access to its source instance. These affordance nodes are then inserted into the behavior tree as described in the previous section. Something that is not obvious is that these affordance nodes themselves have children. Affordance nodes are therefore compound nodes: $n \in \mathbf{N}_S = < a, t_s, t_e, C >$, where $\mathbf{N}_S$ is the set of all BT nodes, and $\mathbf{C}$ is the set of the BT nodes that are child nodes.

To provide the functionality needed to generate character visualizations by animating 3D models, CARDINAL uses a similar approach to ADAPT [22], where each character is controlled by an animation controller that is split into three layers: Head, Hands, and Body. Animations for these layers are cleverly blended together, but only one animation per layer is allowed at any time. If a new animation is played for the same layer, the old animation will stop and the controller blends into the new animation. These animation changes are available as behavior tree nodes and are the building blocks of affordances. All of this processing done to produce behavior trees can then be used for 2D or 3D preview.

Previews

2D-Preview

The 2D-preview is a top view of the scene. This preview excludes all detail apart from locations of actors and important objects and hence is perfect for planning movement and spatial relationships between actors. The 2D preview is based on the state managed and modified by the behavior tree. Each actor is assigned a symbol in the color of that actor, that shows the location and the direction they are looking. Another feature for which the 2D-preview provides functionality is the camera. The camera is a smart object type with its own set of affordances that deal with camera movement and focus. The 2D-preview helps you visualize the field of view of the camera and allows users to verify whether all desired actors are in view. This preview is shown in Figure 6.

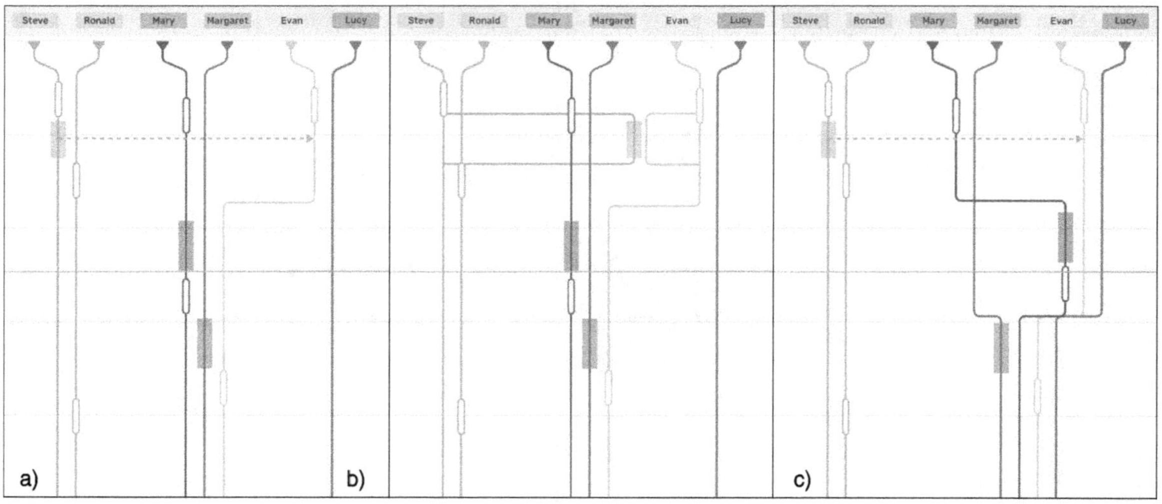

Figure 5: The different definitions for relations between affordances and different approaches for grouping them together result in different looking interactions views for the same story: a) exclusive interactions as grouped affordances related by participation, b) inclusive interactions as grouped affordances related by participation, c) exclusive interactions as grouped affordances related by location.

Figure 6: The 2D-Preview is mainly used to resolve conflicts and issues regarding positioning and movement of characters. Authors can resolve conflicts by making actors move to different positions: a) the user sees that three characters that are not supposed to like each other are standing around a campfire, b) the user adds another object, a barrel, c) the user makes one of the three characters walk to the barrel instead of the campfire to resolve the situation.

3D-Preview

The 3D-Preview allows authors to watch their stories as they are authored. Affordances that are added to a scene are immediately translated into animations represented by behavior tree nodes and can then be viewed in this preview. This view allows users to visualize the locations of actors as well as how they interact with each other. It shows all parts of an interaction: When, Where and How. This makes the preview less focused than other, more specialized visualizations but provides an animated version of the story. The 3D-Preview uses the ADAPT framework [22] and an example is presented in Figure 7.

DEMONSTRATION AND USER STUDY

We demonstrated `CARDINAL` and its efficacy of authoring scripts, which is shown in this paper. Figure 2 demonstrates the various views of `CARDINAL` used to author a script. Figures 3, 4 and 5 show the usage of the interaction view of `CARDINAL` for editing the script. Finally, Figures 6 and 7 demonstrate the visualization features of the `CARDINAL` system. Please look at the supplementary video for a more detailed demonstration.

We also conducted a user study to assess whether the visualization possibilities of the `CARDINAL` system help the user to understand stories better. Each subject was asked to answer comprehension questions about a given script using either the `CARDINAL` system or a control system. As a control system, we used Trelby, an open source scriptwriting system similar to Final Draft. Extended user study results and all the user study data can be found in the supplementary document.

Method

Each subject was provided with a short introduction. The introduction included a tutorial for every system we used in the study. All the subjects carried out the experiment on a similar PC with two monitors. One monitor showed the script the other one showed the questions. To prevent any learning effect we prepared two different stories (A and B). The stories had the same structure e. g. the same number of actors, interactions, and objects. We prepared questions which we adapted to the respective story, not differentiating on the logic. Every subject answered the questions about one story using the traditional scripting tool and then answered the questions about the other story using the `CARDINAL` system. We used the number of concurrent interactions in the script to control the difficulty of the task. Before every set of questions we asked a control question to ensure that the adjustment to the new system does not influence our results. We

Figure 7: An example sequence of images from the 3D-Preview

assigned story A and story B evenly to the two systems in order to decrease the systematic error. The answers to the questions were typed into an editor window where a script was running that enabled us to measure the time used to answer each question precisely. After the experiment, the subjects were asked standard usability questions about the CARDINAL system. The subjects were all Disney Research associates or their friends. We rewarded each of them with a cinema ticket at the end of the experiment. It is important to note that this is simply a preliminary user study: the participants used were not expert scriptwriters. The purpose of this user study hence was not to author scripts but to evaluate how comfortable participants felt using the system with an existing script.

Metrics

Factors

The system used to answer the questions and the story A and B were treated as factors in our experiment.

Dependent variables

We logged two main metrics to capture the performance of each subject. The first measure is the time needed to answer the questions. We measured it in seconds. The second measure was correctness of the answers. We handled correctness strictly and marked the questions either correct or incorrect. These metrics are treated as dependent variables (DV).

Results

We recorded 16 subjects from the age of 22 up to 39, 37.5% females. The subjects didn't have any prior experience in scriptwriting. All subjects used both scripting systems with two different stories. The results showed a decrease in the time used to answer question when the CARDINAL system was used.

The statistical analysis was conducted as follows: first, we verified with a paired t-test that the system used had no influence the correctness of the answers. Then we conducted a 2-way mixed model ANOVA to confirm that users are significantly faster to find content in a story when using the CARDINAL system compared to a traditional system.

Paired t-test

A paired-samples t-test was used to determine whether there was a statistically significant mean difference between the sum of all correctly answered questions using the CARDINAL authoring tool compared to traditional scripting. Data are mean $\pm$ standard deviation unless stated otherwise. No outliers were detected that were more than 1.5 box-lengths from the edge of the box in a boxplot. The assumption of normality was not violated, as assessed by Shapiro-Wilk's test (p >.5). Participants did not differ significantly in the amount correct of answers, whether they were shown the CARDINAL scripting tool (3.75 $\pm$ 1.3) or the traditional scriptwriting tool (3.94 $\pm$ 1.2), t(15) =3.6, p = .72, d=0.009.

Thus, we ensured that the difference was not due to the quality of the answer but rather due to efficiency. Accordingly, all the following analysis were on time the task required.

2-way mixed model ANOVA

We treated the system as within-subject and the two stories as between-subject. There were no outliers, as assessed by examination of studentized residuals for values greater than ± 3. The data were normally distributed, as assessed by Shapiro-Wilk's test of normality ($p > .05$), but only trending for CARDINAL story for those who started with story b ($p = .04$). As the normal Q-Q plot showed approximate normality, and ANOVA can tolerate data that is non-normal (skewed or kurtotic distributions) with only a small effect on the Type I error rate, we proceeded without any transformation of data. There was homogeneity of variances ($p > .05$) and covariances ($p > .05$), as assessed by Levene's test of homogeneity of variances and Box's M test, respectively. There was no statistically significant interaction between the authoring tool and the plot of the story, $F(1,14) = .567$, $p < .46$, partial $\eta 2 = .04$), and also no main effect of story plot was significant ($RT, F(1,14) = .23$, $p < .64$, partial $\eta 2 = .16$. Thus any systematic effect of story content on extracting relevant information from scriptwritings can be discarded.

The main effect of tool, however, showed a statistically significant difference in mean RT for different scriptwriting tools ($F(1,14) = 29.5$ $p < .0005$, partial $\eta 2 = .68$). We did find similar results when further tested whether main effect for scriptwriting tool was different for the interaction view ($F(1,14) = 9.48$, $p < .008$, partial $\eta 2 = .4$), or the preview ($F(1,14) = 25.37$, $p < .005$, partial $\eta 2 = .64$), and neither a main effect for nor interaction with story plot ($p > .05$).

Usability

The usability user study revealed that users feel both more comfortable as well as more confident using our provided visualizations. Some users noted that having a summary of actions and interactions for each actor in the scene would help tremendously to identify dominating figures in the story. Furthermore, being able to smoothly move through time increases the value of the three-dimensional preview immensely. Some users notified us about more subtle animations being really hard to see, raising the need for much more intricate camera controls for the visualizations. Fortunately, all features apart from the actor summary are already planned for the final product.

CONCLUSION

In this paper, we demonstrate the benefits of using CARDINAL as an authoring system for movie scripts. Almost all the subjects in the user study mentioned that it was laborious to work with the traditional system. The user study confirms the premise that users spend less time and effort and rate it subjectively easier to find specific information in a story using the CARDINAL system compared to a traditional one. In terms of correctness of the answers, the study showed no significant difference between the two systems.

In order to make the two authoring tools comparable (which is difficult as they have different features), we tried to focus on efficiency and response time while keeping the difficulty of finding the correct answer constant, which was successful (t-test). However, future studies using different story plots especially in terms of complexity can confirm whether CARDINAL also helps in increasing the success rate of finding correctness and quality of answers.

CARDINAL also has certain limitations in the accuracy of visualizations based on the description provided. It fails to understand adverbs or adjectives such as "suddenly" or temporal constraints in the current prototype version, which need to be addressed in the final version of the system.

Additionally, future work can also focus on extending visualization of movie scripts to visualization of other textual narratives. Scripts provide the system with a structure of text and dialog that stories in other forms do not; however, other work has been done to understand information from stories [8]. The ability of visualization quality depends upon the ability of the natural language parser, which acts as a limitation for CARDINAL. However, as seen in the demonstration video, CARDINAL clearly still can be used as a state of the art tool that can be used for authoring of movie scripts.

REFERENCES

1. Adobe Story 2012. Adobe Story. (2012). https://story.adobe.com.
2. Jordan Barria-Pineda, Julio Guerra, Yun Huang, and Peter Brusilovsky. 2017. Concept-Level Knowledge Visualization For Supporting Self-Regulated Learning. In *Proceedings of the 22Nd International Conference on Intelligent User Interfaces Companion (IUI '17 Companion)*. ACM, New York, NY, USA, 141–144. DOI: http://dx.doi.org/10.1145/3030024.3038262
3. Tom Bartindale, Alia Sheikh, Nick Taylor, Peter Wright, and Patrick Olivier. 2012. StoryCrate: Tabletop Storyboarding for Live Film Production. In *Proceedings of the SIGCHI Conference on Human Factors in Computing Systems (CHI '12)*. ACM, New York, NY, USA, 169–178. DOI: http://dx.doi.org/10.1145/2207676.2207700
4. Danqi Chen and Christopher D Manning. 2014. A Fast and Accurate Dependency Parser using Neural Networks. In *Empirical Methods in Natural Language Processing (EMNLP)*.
5. David Elson. 2012. *Modelling Narrative Discourse*. Ph.D. Dissertation. Columbia University.
6. Final Draft 1990. Final Draft. (1990). http://www.http://finaldraft.com.
7. Mark Mark Alan Finlayson. 2012. *Learning narrative structure from annotated folktales*. Ph.D. Dissertation. Massachusetts Institute of Technology.
8. Amit Goyal, Ellen Riloff, and Hal Daumé III. 2010. Automatically producing plot unit representations for narrative text. In *Proceedings of the 2010 Conference on Empirical Methods in Natural Language Processing*. Association for Computational Linguistics, 77–86.
9. Mubbasir Kapadia, Jessica Falk, Fabio Zünd, Marcel Marti, Robert W. Sumner, and Markus Gross. 2015. Computer-assisted Authoring of Interactive Narratives. In *Proceedings of the 19th Symposium on Interactive 3D Graphics and Games (i3D '15)*. ACM, New York, NY, USA, 85–92. DOI: http://dx.doi.org/10.1145/2699276.2699279
10. Mubbasir Kapadia, Seth Frey, Alexander Shoulson, Robert W. Sumner, and Markus Gross. 2016. CANVAS: Computer-assisted Narrative Animation Synthesis. In *Proceedings of the ACM SIGGRAPH/Eurographics Symposium on Computer Animation (SCA '16)*. Eurographics Association, Aire-la-Ville, Switzerland, Switzerland, 199–209. http://dl.acm.org/citation.cfm?id=2982818.2982846
11. Mubbasir Kapadia, Nathan Marshak, and Norman I. Badler. 2014. ADAPT: The Agent Development and Prototyping Testbed. *IEEE Transactions on Visualization and Computer Graphics* 99, PrePrints (2014), 1. DOI: http://dx.doi.org/10.1109/TVCG.2014.251
12. Mubbasir Kapadia, Fabio Zund, Jessica Falk, Marcel Marti, Robert W. Sumner, and Markus Gross. 2015. Evaluating the Authoring Complexity of Interactive Narratives with Interactive Behaviour Trees. In *Foundations of Digital Games (FDG'15)*. 9.
13. Heeyoung Lee, Angel Chang, Yves Peirsman, Nathanael Chambers, Mihai Surdeanu, and Dan Jurafsky. 2013. Deterministic Coreference Resolution Based on Entity-Centric, Precision-Ranked Rules. *Computational Linguistics* 39, 4 (2013), 885–916. DOI: http://dx.doi.org/10.1162/COLI_a_00152
14. Christopher D. Manning, Mihai Surdeanu, John Bauer, Jenny Finkel, Steven J. Bethard, and David McClosky. 2014. The Stanford CoreNLP Natural Language Processing Toolkit. In *Association for Computational Linguistics (ACL) System Demonstrations*. 55–60. http://www.aclweb.org/anthology/P/P14/P14-5010

15. Tomas Mikolov, Kai Chen, Greg Corrado, and Jeffrey Dean. 2013. Efficient Estimation of Word Representations in Vector Space. *CoRR* abs/1301.3781 (2013). http://arxiv.org/abs/1301.3781

16. Randall Munroe. 2009. Movie narrative charts. *Xkcd. com. http://xkcd. com/657* (2009).

17. Amy Pavel, Dan B. Goldman, Björn Hartmann, and Maneesh Agrawala. 2015. SceneSkim: Searching and Browsing Movies Using Synchronized Captions, Scripts and Plot Summaries. In *Proceedings of the 28th Annual ACM Symposium on User Interface Software & Technology (UIST '15)*. ACM, New York, NY, USA, 181–190. DOI: http://dx.doi.org/10.1145/2807442.2807502

18. Steve Rubin, Floraine Berthouzoz, Gautham J Mysore, Wilmot Li, and Maneesh Agrawala. 2013. Content-based tools for editing audio stories. In *Proceedings of the 26th annual ACM symposium on User interface software and technology*. ACM, 113–122.

19. Rushit Sanghrajka, Daniel Hidalgo, Patrick P. Chen, and Mubbasir Kapadia. 2017. LISA: Lexically Intelligent Story Assistant. *Proceedings of the 13th Artificial Intelligence and Interactive Digital Entertainment Conference* (2017).

20. Rushit Sanghrajka, Wojciech Witoń, Sasha Schriber, Markus Gross, and Mubbasir Kapadia. 2018. Computer-assisted Authoring for Natural Language Story Scripts. *30th Conference on Innovative Applications of Artificial Intelligence (IAAI-18)* (2018).

21. Shilad Sen, Anja Beth Swoap, Qisheng Li, Brooke Boatman, Ilse Dippenaar, Rebecca Gold, Monica Ngo, Sarah Pujol, Bret Jackson, and Brent Hecht. 2017. Cartograph: Unlocking Spatial Visualization Through Semantic Enhancement. In *Proceedings of the 22Nd International Conference on Intelligent User Interfaces (IUI '17)*. ACM, New York, NY, USA, 179–190. DOI: http://dx.doi.org/10.1145/3025171.3025233

22. Alexander Shoulson, Nathan Marshak, Mubbasir Kapadia, and Norman I Badler. 2014. Adapt: the agent developmentand prototyping testbed. *IEEE Transactions on Visualization and Computer Graphics* 20, 7 (2014), 1035–1047.

23. Makarand Tapaswi, Martin Bäuml, and Rainer Stiefelhagen. 2014. StoryGraphs: Visualizing Character Interactions as a Timeline. *2014 IEEE Conference on Computer Vision and Pattern Recognition* (2014), 827–834.

24. Kento Watanabe, Yuichiroh Matsubayashi, Kentaro Inui, Tomoyasu Nakano, Satoru Fukayama, and Masataka Goto. 2017. LyriSys: An Interactive Support System for Writing Lyrics Based on Topic Transition. In *Proceedings of the 22Nd International Conference on Intelligent User Interfaces (IUI '17)*. ACM, New York, NY, USA, 559–563. DOI: http://dx.doi.org/10.1145/3025171.3025194

25. Jungdam Won, Kyungho Lee, Carol O'Sullivan, Jessica K. Hodgins, and Jehee Lee. 2014. Generating and Ranking Diverse Multi-character Interactions. *ACM Trans. Graph.* 33, 6, Article 219 (Nov. 2014), 12 pages. DOI: http://dx.doi.org/10.1145/2661229.2661271

Interactive Storytelling for Movie Recommendation through Latent Semantic Analysis

Kodzo Wegba, Aidong Lu[1], Yuemeng Li
University of North Carolina at Charlotte
Charlotte, USA
{kwegba1, aidong.lu, yli60}@uncc.edu

Wencheng Wang
State Key Laboratory of Computer Science
ISCAS, Beijing, China
whn@ios.ac.cn

ABSTRACT
Recommendation is essential to many online services; however current systems often provide limited interaction and visualization mechanisms, affecting the user satisfaction of recommendation. This paper presents an interactive recommendation approach for the general public without any knowledge of recommendation or visualization algorithms. Our approach emphasizes interactivity, explicit user input, and semantic information convey with the following two components. First, we propose a Latent Semantic Model that captures the statistical features of semantic concepts on 2D domains and abstracts user preferences for personal recommendation, so that high-dimensional spectral space from the rating records can be understood and interacted with directly. Second, we propose an interactive recommendation approach through a storytelling mechanism for promoting the communication between the user and the recommendation system. We demonstrate and evaluate our approach with a real dataset. Our approach can also be extended to other applications including various online recommendation systems.

Author Keywords
Recommender systems; interactive storytelling; latent semantic analysis.

INTRODUCTION
Online retailers and content providers nowadays offer a huge amount of products or services, which are often overwhelming for consumers. While many recommendation algorithms have been developed, including the prevailing top-N recommendation approaches [12], interaction mechanisms for consumers to adjust search preferences or recommendation results can still be improved [33].

The challenges for improving user satisfaction of interactive recommendation systems come from several aspects. First, the satisfaction of consumers vary with factors that often require explicit input from users. Second, useful information for assisting users to find the right movies, such as the similarities between recommended and rated movies, is often completely hidden from users. Third, complex recommendation algorithms and visualization systems are often too complicated for general consumers to use.

This work attempts to solve the problems with an interactive storytelling approach, which simulates the scenario of an expert recommending movies to a user – an expert generally selects movies for a user based on his or her watch history, makes recommendations, listens to the feedback, and continues to recommend more movies until the user finds a movie to watch. Similarly, our approach adopts such a continuous and interactive recommendation process that allows the user to orientate search results actively and explicitly. This requires us to study the personal movie features from rating statistics and convey useful information effectively.

Our work consists of two components, a model of latent semantic analysis and an approach of interactive recommendation. We first present a latent semantic model (LSM) built upon the high-dimensional latent space factorized from the movie rating records, as they are the most commonly used data for online recommendation. Our model collects a set of semantic concepts, including like, dislike, familiarity, diversity, typicality, and un-typicality, that can be used for two purposes: one is to help a user to correlate new recommended movies to the movies the user has watched, the other is to allow the user to specify the preferences of recommendation explicitly. We abstract the statistical features of semantic concepts among the high-dimensional latent space and automatically identify suitable 2D domains for recommendation.

We then present an interactive storytelling system that recommend movies in an animated comic strip style to promote the communication between the user and recommendation system. We employ the LSM to generate recommendation stories by assigning movies with suitable characters, roles, and narrative structures for describing a group of recommended movies. The recommendation stories are constructed automatically to attract user attention and can be adjusted flexibly during the interactive recommendation process. Different from previous online recommendation systems, our approach reveals information that is generally hidden from users and allows interactive exploration of movie similarities. We have also performed a controlled user study and a questionnaire to evaluate our approach. The results demonstrate that interac-

[1]Corresponding author

IUI 2018, March 7–11, 2018, Tokyo, Japan.

http://dx.doi.org/10.1145/3172944.3172979

tive recommendation is very promising for engaging user participation and providing better recommendation experiences.

RELATED WORK

Storytelling and Narrative Visualization

"Storytelling" has a long history in communication [18, 42, 35, 27, 30, 52]. Similarly, narrative visualization also refers to using data stories to improve visual communication [21, 23, 43, 47]. Specifically, it refers to "a series of events, facts, etc., given in order and with the establishing of connections between them" from the Oxford English Dictionary and it is often simplified to structures like beginning, middle, and end in visualization systems [44].

Several interactive or automatic storytelling approaches have been developed for applications ranging from general visualization process [11, 17] to specific problems, such as medical vis [51], geo vis [14], scientific vis [53], sequence vis [23], communication [29], and multi-dimensional vis [6]. Storytelling has been shown to be effective on conveying data in a number of applications [13, 45]. For visualization tasks, while storytelling did not seem to increase user-engagement in exploration [5], annotated visualizations were proven to be better in balancing graphical salience and relevance [22] and graph comics were useful to help a general audience understand complex temporal changes [2]. Nonetheless, it is clear that a flexible creation process should be provided and adjusted according to application requirements [36, 16, 1].

Different from other storytelling techniques, we present a highly interactive storytelling approach that simulates human communication with two features - continuous updating stories with or without user inputs and allowing interaction in all stages of interactive recommendation.

Visualization and Interactivity for Recommendation

For recommender systems, graph visualizations are often adopted [10, 50, 48]. For example, PeerChooser [37] provided an interactive graphical explanation interface for users to adjust their search requirements through varying levels of granularity of the graph neighborhood. Except graph, styles of 2D layouts [24], 3D map-based visualization [28], Venn diagrams [38], hyperbolic and multi-modal view [34], and radial displays [3] have also been explored.

Interactive recommendation approaches have also been developed [4, 49, 54]. For example, Gretarsson et al. [19] visualized recommended users in social networks with node-link diagram and grouped relevant nodes on the recommendation list in parallel layers. Loepp et al. presented an interactive recommendation approach by having users to choose between two sets of sample items iteratively and extracting latent factors [33]. Recently, Loepp et al. [32] presented MyMovieMixer for interactively expressing user preferences over the hybrid recommendation process. They often show that user engagement and overall satisfaction are improved. In addition, explanation interfaces can provide system transparency and thus increase user acceptance [46, 8].

Also related to this work is conversational recommender systems [7, 9], which intelligently select what information to elicit from the user in different situations. Our storytelling approach is similar to conversational recommender systems on the aspect of the interactive process, however our approach does not require the input of a user and it continuously presents new recommendations in a storytelling fashion with/without user inputs.

LATENT SEMANTIC MODEL FOR INTERACTIVE RECOMMENDATION AND MOVIE EXPLORATION

Our interactive recommendation approach for general users is consisted of two components: LSM for abstracting personal movie preferences (this section) and interactive recommendation with story generation (the next section). During this work, the designs of LSM and interactive recommendation system are simultaneously proceeded to ensure that the same set of semantic concepts can be used for both interactive recommendation and exploration of movies.

Latent Space from Collaborative Filtering

The latent factor models are the primary approaches of Collaborative Filtering (CF) techniques, which have been successfully adopted by a number of commercial systems [26]. The latent factor models based on Singular Value Decomposition (SVD) establish recommendations by transforming both movies and users to the same latent factor space, thus making them directly comparable. We choose this latent space as it can be used to explore not only recommended movies, but also the distribution patterns of movies and users for semantic analysis.

The latent space can be used to interpret a number of preference / relevance features. For example, a dimension from comedy to drama can be used to represent the taste of a user favoring these two movie genres. In majority of cases, the latent space captures statistical distribution of rating records that combine features from all users, which are often hard to describe or understand directly. To distinguish users from movies, we reserve special indexing letters of u and v for users and i and j for movies. A rating r_{ui} indicates the preference of a user u on a movie i, where rating values are in the set of $\{1,2,...,5\}$ with 1 for no interests.

We generate the latent space with the factorization of user-movie rating matrix using SVD. For a user-movie matrix M with m users and n movies, the SVD algorithm factorizes M into three matrices such that $M = USV^T$. It is common to truncate these matrices to yield U_k, S_k, and V_k, in order to decrease the dimensionality of the vector space, and only leave the strongest effects in the model by dropping dimensions with small singular values [15].

Recommendable Movies and Degrees

In a recommendation approach, we are interested in two things the most: recommendable movies and recommendation degrees for interpreting how likely we would recommend a movie. We follow a typical recommendation algorithm by adjusting rating history with the normalization of global effects. This step balances the tendencies that some users like to give higher ratings than others and some movies receive higher ratings than others, therefore the adjusted ratings

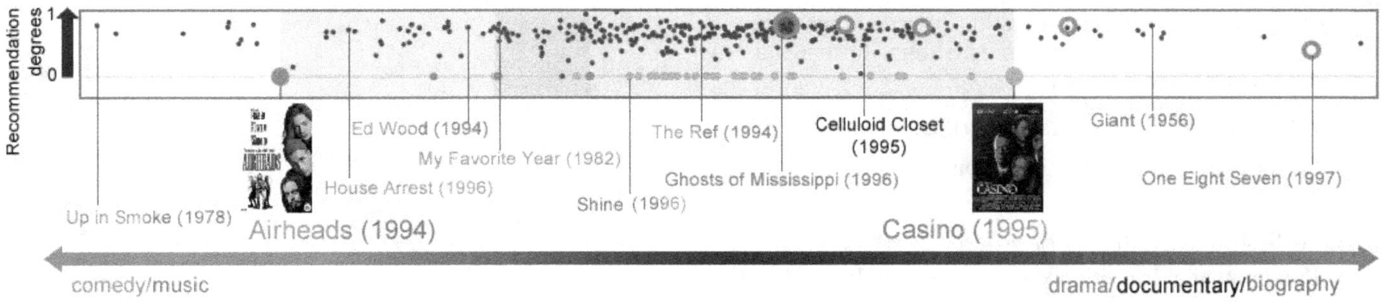

Figure 1. An example from our latent semantic model for interactive recommendation and abstraction of user preferences. It demonstrates the preference of a user on drama/documentary/biography movies (green zone toward the right) over comedy/music genres (orange zone toward the left). Our approach identifies a 2D visualization domain, where the horizontal axis layouts movies based on features from the user's watch history, and the vertical axis highlights the most recommendable movies on the top. Two example movie posters, one liked movie "Casino" and one disliked movie "Airheads", are also provided to demonstrate the latent dimension. For illustration purpose, we also add the arrowed line at the bottom and several movie titles to demonstrate the movie distributions. The movies selected to recommend are enlarged as blue circles, recommendable movies are shown as purple nodes, watched and liked movies as green nodes, and disliked movies as orange nodes.

$\hat{r_{ui}}$ are more accurate to compare different users or different movies. Denote a_u as the average rating given by user u, a_i as the average rating of movie i, and A and B as the averages of all users and all movies respectively.

$$\hat{r_{ui}} = r_{ui} - (a_u - A) - (a_i - B) \tag{1}$$

Our recommendation algorithm starts by mapping each user into the latent space by multiplying the adjacency matrix M and the V_k component of SVD. We denote this product as $C = M \times V_k$, where C_u represents a row vector for user u from the matrix C. We then compute the cosine similarity s_{uv} between users u and v with the C_u and C_v coordinates [31].

$$s_{uv} = \frac{\sum_{l=1}^{k} C_{ul} \times C_{vl}}{\sqrt{\sum_{l=1}^{k} (C_{ul})^2} \times \sqrt{\sum_{l=1}^{k} (C_{vl})^2}} \tag{2}$$

Next, we select a list of similar users with positive similarity coefficients, as recommendable movies are generally selected based on ratings from similar users. We denote this set as $S_u = \{v | s_{uv} \geq 0\}$ for user u. For a new user with no rating record, all the similarity coefficients s_{uv} are zero and the set S_u contains all the users.

We further select the list of recommendable movies L_u for the user u by choosing movies that have not been watched by u, but received positive ratings from similar users as follows, where the positive rating threshold w_c is initialized as 3 and can be adjusted for different numbers of recommendable movies.

$$L_u = \{i | v \in S_u, \hat{r_{vi}} \geq w_c \; and \; r_{ui} = 0\}. \tag{3}$$

In addition, we measure the recommendation degree of a movie i for user u by b_{ui}. The movies with high b_{ui} degrees are more likely to be recommended during the interactive recommendation process. It is calculated as the average rating from similar users with positive cosine similarities. For any $i \in L_u$,

$$b_{ui} = \sum_{v \in S_u \; and \; r_{vi} \neq 0} \{r_{vi} \times s_{uv}\} / \sum_{v \in S_u \; and \; r_{vi} \neq 0} \{r_{vi}\} \tag{4}$$

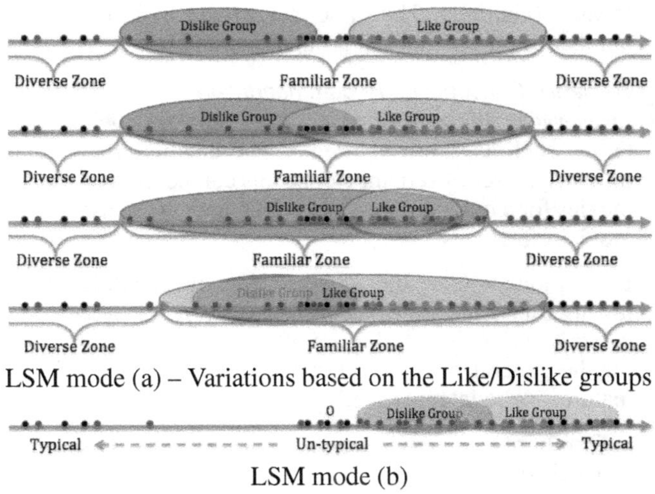

Figure 2. The LSM maps the distribution of a set of semantic concepts in the latent space. We separate the two modes of LSM for clarity – (a) includes concepts of like, dislike, familiarity and diversity and (b) includes concepts of typicality and un-typicality. The movie nodes are colored based on the groups – liked in green, disliked in orange, recommendable in blue, and not recommendable in black.

We normalize the s_{uv} and b_{ui} values to range of $[-1, 1]$ and $[0, 1]$ respectively to balance the differences among users.

Latent Semantic Model

While the latent space has been widely used in recommendation algorithms, it is a high-dimensional space and not directly suitable for visualization or interaction. Our goal of the LSM is to identify semantic concepts and visualization domains that can be used in interactive recommendation and exploration of movie similarities. Our approach is consisted of the following three steps.

Separating Movie Groups

To identify recommendable movies, we separate all the movies in the database to five groups based on the rating history of the user and our estimation of recommendation degrees. For any user u, each movie belongs to one and only one of the following groups.

- Like (with positive ratings from u): $G_+ = \{i|r_{ui} \geq \tau_+\}$
- Dislike (with negative ratings from u): $G_- = \{i|0 < r_{ui} < \tau_-\}$
- Neutral: $G_{neu} = \{i|\tau_- \leq r_{ui} < \tau_+\}$
- Recommendable (with positive recommendation degrees): $G_r = \{i|b_{ui} \geq \tau_r\}$ and not specified as "thumb-down" by the user during interaction recommendation process
- Not recommendable (with negative recommendation degrees): $G_n = \{i|b_{ui} < \tau_r\}$ or specified as "thumb-down" by the user during interaction recommendation process

The thresholds of positive rating τ_+ and negative rating τ_- are set to value 3, and the threshold of recommendation degree τ_r to value 0 initially. The values can be adjusted to control the number of movies in each group.

Semantic Concepts for Recommendation

In everyday life, we often describe an object with several terms, such as families, friends, and enemies for a person. Similarly, a set of semantic concepts can be used to describe movies for a quick impression, which may assist users to find movies effectively.

In addition to "like" and "dislike", we have identified the following four semantic concepts for recommendation based on two criteria – concepts that are often used in recommendation for the general public; and concepts with clear distribution features in the latent space.

- Familiarity – movie styles that the user has already watched;
- Diversity (Un-familiarity) – a broad range of movie styles that the user is not familiar with;
- Typicality – movie styles that can be well defined based on combined movie features;
- Un-typicality – movie styles that are unclear to a feature.

Next, we describe the distribution features of semantic concepts in the latent space. As illustrated in Figure 2, we can identify the familiar zone by including both the like and dislike groups – all the movies that have been watched by the user u. The diverse zones are regions outside the familiar zone and there are generally two diverse zones on each side of a latent dimension. Figure 3 uses examples from real scenarios to show the variations of the LSM mode (a).

The LSM mode (b) between typicality and un-typicality utilizes the distance of a movie to the Origin of the latent space. Since both the U_k and V_k from the latent space demonstrate clustering features of similar users and movies [39], the distances in the latent space can interpret the similarity degrees. For example, on a latent dimension which contains comedy movies on one side and drama movies on the other, the movies with combined comedy/drama or other genres are distributed near the Origin. This feature is similar to spectral spaces that nodes with few connections are often located

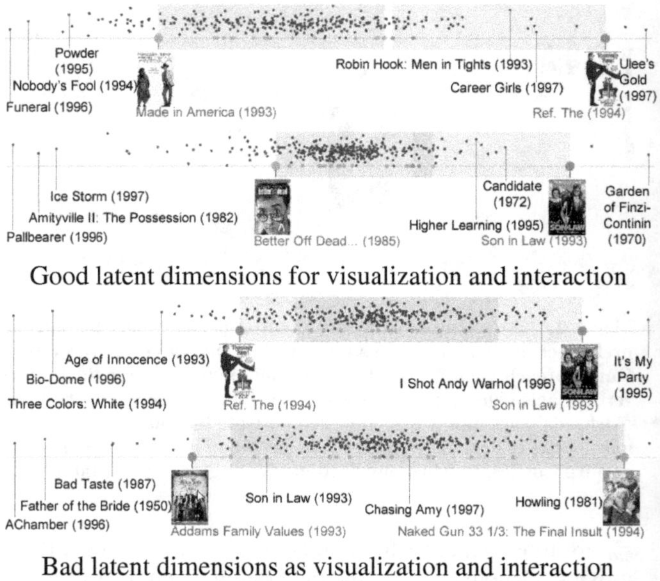

Figure 3. Good and bad example latent dimensions that are selected based on criteria described in Section 3.3.3. The liked and disliked zones are highlighted with shaded rectangles in green and orange respectively. The recommendable movies are colored in purple, "liked" movies in green, and "disliked" movies in orange.

close to the Origin [20]. What's important is that this feature preserves for general latent dimensions describing combined movie features or styles, with only un-typical movies corresponding to the latent dimension located close to the Origin. As shown in Figure 2 mode (b), any latent dimension can be modeled as typical to untypical to typical zones. The two typical zones correspond to two opposite features represented by the latent dimension.

While the distribution features of semantic concepts on the latent dimensions are clear, the relative locations among the semantic zones vary depending on the Origin and the familiar zone. For example, the Like and Dislike zones can appear on either side of the Origin or Overlap with the Origin. Nonetheless, they all provide valuable semantic information for interactive recommendation. We generally adjust thresholds of τ_+, τ_-, and τ_r to make sure that all the semantic zones contain recommendable movies.

Selecting Dimensions for Visualization and Interaction

In the latent space, each dimension describes certain joint statistical features of movies and users. We are interested in searching for dimensions that can help users understand movie relationships and are suitable for visualization and interaction. We need to select not only one, but also a set of suitable dimensions, so that multiple aspects of recommendable movies can be covered. However, not all the dimensions in the k-dimensional latent space are suitable for recommendation, as they may represent features of irrelevant movies or users, repeated features from other dimensions, or features that are hard to understand. Therefore, we go through the following process of selection based upon the distribution of the semantic concepts.

The selection is based on the combined information of user history, recommendation degrees, and explicit information from user interaction – thumb up/down for specific movies, which is described in the section 4. We prefer to choose the dimensions that separate the semantic zones with the following three factors: **Group sizes.** For each dimension, we measure the region of the like group as R_+, the dislike group as R_-, the overlapped region as R_o, and the combined range as R. It is ideal that R_+ occupies a large portion of R, as majority recommendable movies are selected within or close to this region. This factor is simplified as R_+/R. **The overlapping region.** We try to avoid the third and fourth cases of LSM mode (a) in Figure 2, which happens when one group is located inside another. They are less desirable as the meanings of such dimensions are hard to describe and understand. We set large penalty to avoid large overlapping ratios for R_o/R_+ and R_o/R_-. **The distribution of recommendable movies.** Inside R_+, it is ideal that the recommendable movies are evenly distributed. This factor helps to remove the dimensions with many movies mapping to a small range, which indicates that these movie features and differences are not well represented on the dimensions. We measure this factor with standard deviation θ_+ of recommendable movies in R_+.

Specifically, we use the following D_v equation to measure if a latent dimension v is suitable as a visualization domain, where w_+, w_o and w_θ are the weights for the three factors described above.

$$D_v = (\frac{R_+}{R})^{w_+} \times (1 - \frac{R_o}{R_+})^{w_o} \times (1 - \frac{R_o}{R_-})^{w_o} \times (\frac{R_+}{\theta_+})^{w_\theta} \quad (5)$$

Next, we filter the set $S_d = \{v | D_v > \tau_v\}$, composed of latent dimensions with high D_v values, by removing similar dimensions. This is achieved by comparing the locations of movies to the groups on the two dimensions. Among the similar dimensions with high D_s values, only the dimension with the highest D_v value is kept in S_d.

$$D_s(p,q) = \sum_{i \in L_u} w_i \cdot [(i \in R_{+p}) \oplus (i \in R_{+q}) + (i \in R_{-p}) \oplus (i \in R_{-q})] \quad (6)$$

where, $p \in S_d$ and $q \in S_d$ are latent dimensions, w_i is the weight for each movie to incorporate user preference, R_{+p} and R_{-p} are the ranges of like and dislike groups on p. We set $w_i = 1$ for all movies initially and double the value when the user clicks the thumb-up/down buttons.

INTERACTIVE STORYTELLING

We use storytelling as a metaphor for the process of interactive recommendation. This section presents our strategies to construct recommendation stories automatically through the LSM from the aspects of characters, roles, user interaction and narrative structures respectively.

Connecting Recommendation to Storytelling

To simulate this communication process, we present an interactive recommendation mechanism that treats the procedure of recommending movies as storytelling. As described in the introduction, interactive recommendation simulates the scenario of an expert recommending movies to a user. During recommendation, the expert generally presents one or several movies and provides reasons of recommendation, such as high popularity, high similarity to a movie the user likes, or special features. The user may respond by indicating his or her preferences on the recommended movies, such as "recommend more movies like this" or "no more movies like that". This process continues until the user finds an interesting movie to watch. Therefore, we design a **recommendation story** as a set of recommendable movies and brief reasons of recommendation and an **interactive recommendation** approach as a continuous storytelling process, which can be adjusted promptly with user interaction.

The interactive storytelling pipeline starts with exploring movie database for a user, selecting recommendable movies, and collecting necessary information. The interactive storytelling pipeline contains a loop indicating a continuous and interactive process of recommendation until a desirable movie is identified. Among which, the user can provide feedback to request new recommendation stories that reflect user inputs. The user can also adjust the visualization interactively, such as replaying a recommended movie or finishing the story immediately. If the user does not provide an input, the loop continues to different recommendation stories to achieve the effect of "how about some other types of movies you may like?" The automatic switch between different recommendation stories can avoid users getting bored from similar movies. During the process, the user can also use our interaction tools to explore additional information of movies.

Character. The character in an ordinary story is generally a person. In our recommendation stories, the characters are movies. Similar to the human characters, each movie character maintains a different relationship with the user, such as a rated movie, a favorite movie, or a recommendable movie. The movie characters are also related to each other, such as being rated by the same users or have similar rating averages. Since our focus is recommendation, the leading characters are recommendable movies, whose relationships with the user can be represented with LSM and recommendation degrees.

Role A role describes what function each character serves in the story. The roles of recommendable movies provide a mechanism for users to explore the movie database. Before going through the movie details, the roles of a movie provide a quick catch of the movie features, such as a typical drama movie which is very similar to one of the user's favorite movies. This provides the user a quick way to find several interested movies to explore.

In recommendation stories, we use the semantic concepts from LSM to describe the roles, such as a "liked" movie that the user rated high or a "typical" movie that has strong features of certain movie genres. Each movie character can play multiple roles, such as familiarity and un-typicality, just like a human character can be both a colleague and a friend. The actual roles of a movie character are determined by the locations among the semantic zones on selected latent dimensions, as shown in Figure 2.

User Interaction During Recommendation

For interactive recommendation, the user interaction becomes an important component of the storytelling pipeline. To allow active user interaction with the storytelling pipeline, we provide three groups of explicit interaction functions as follows:

The first group of interaction functions is for users to specify the preferred movie types between options of familiar (f) / diverse and typical (t) / untypical movies. The parameter values become effective immediately on generating the new recommendation stories. For a specific movie, the user can click thumbs-up (like) and thumbs-down (dislike) buttons, so that the specified movie is moved to the like or dislike groups (the group of not recommendable is removed from the recommendation process). We also increase the w_i value (a parameter to control the effects of user selection) of the movie in equations 5 and 6 for choosing latent dimensions for new stories. For each dimension v, the new measurement D'_v contains components from both data distribution by D_v and user interaction. We detect if the user preference is aligned with LSM, especially if a liked movie is in the like range and if a disliked movie is in the disliked range.

$$D'_v = D_v + w_i \times \left(\sum_{i \in (U_+ \cap R_+) \cup (U_- \cap R_-)} b_{ui} - \sum_{i \in (U_+ \cap R_-) \cup (U_- \cap R_+)} b_{ui} \right) \quad (7)$$

where U_+ and U_- are the sets containing all liked or disliked movies specified by the user.

The second group of interaction functions is to control the recommendation process. The users can replay, pause, and stop the current recommendation story, or play more stories (the default is continuing to recommend additional movies).

The third group is to explore movie details. If finding an interesting movie, the user can click the movie poster or movie node on the interface to view details. The users can also mouse over a movie node anytime to reveal a set of basic information, including user rating, average rating, popularity, title and genres.

Automatic Generation of Narrative Structures

A narrative structure refers to the sequence of events in a story. In recommendation stories, each event is a recommendable movie and brief reasons of recommendation. The sequence of a set of recommendable movies in a narrative structure is crucial to improve users' understanding of the movies effectively.

Considering the short attention of users in online recommendation, we prefer simple stories that can finish in a very short duration. Therefore, we generate each recommendation story only with one latent dimension selected with LSM. As each latent dimension reflects one combined movie / user feature, such recommendation stories simulate the effect that we recommend movies from one combined movie feature to another, such as popular drama/comedy movies to unpopular documentary movies. Other designs of recommendation stories using our LSM are also feasible. For example, long stories can be generated by connecting different latent dimensions. Due to the focus of our interactive recommendation approach, we only use short stories in this work.

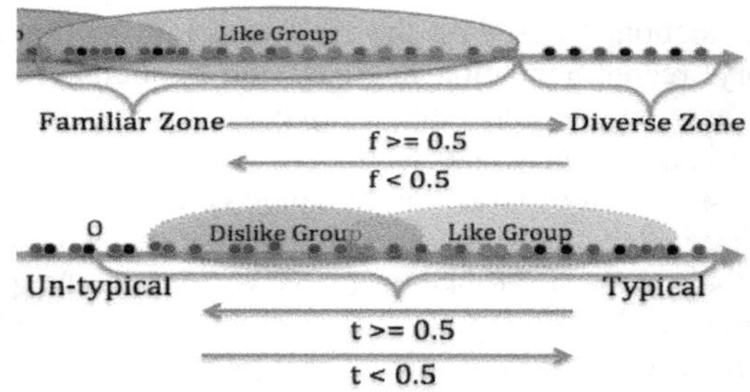

Figure 4. The four linear narrative structures based on the user preferences of t – typical, u=1-t – un-typical, f – familiar, and d=1-f – diverse.

Based on a latent dimension, we try to maintain smooth story transitions by generating linear narrative structures among the four semantic concepts: familiarity, diversity, typicality, and un-typicality. This is achieved by identifying a starting point, choosing narrative structures based on user preferences, and selecting recommendable movies.

The **starting point** of a story is determined according to user preferences of f and t, shown in Figure 4. The default values are 0.5 for both f and t, although we favor typical over untypical and familiar over diverse movies, which is consistent with the preferences of majority users. The following list is the order we set as default.

High familiarity: starting from the like group

High diversity: starting from the diverse zone closer to like group

High typicality: starting from the typical zone closer to like group

High un-typicality: starting from the un-typical zone

The **order** of recommended movies also considers user preferences. As shown in Figure 4, we use the four narrative structures to cover all combinations of the two user preferences of f and t. The narrative structures are designed to be linear sequences, so that users can expect very similar narrative visualization during the interactive recommendation process. Since the narrative structure is on one latent dimension each time, two zones from the LSM are involved. The ranges of the latent dimension to select recommended movies are also shown in Figure 4. During the interactive storytelling process, we switch narrative structures between the two options randomly to avoid simply repeated stories.

The **selection of recommended movies** is based on the sample rates computed according to user preferences of f and t. Assume a set G_T of T recommended movies is selected for each narrative structure. When the structure is between typicality and un-typicality, we determine the number of recommended movies from the typical zone as s_t and un-typical zone as s_u:

$$s_t = \lceil t * T \rceil; \quad s_u = T - s_t \quad (8)$$

Similarly, when the structure is between familiarity and diversity, the sampling numbers for familiar zone s_f and diverse zone s_d are:

$$s_f = \lceil f * T \rceil; \quad s_d = T - s_f \tag{9}$$

Inside each zone, we select recommended movies with the following procedure that is composed of a local sampling and a random test procedure. We first randomly pick a location l and choose the best candidate within a local window by combining all three factors: the recommendation degree b_{ui} of a candidate movie i, the distance of movie i to location l, and the similarity of movie i to the set of q movies that are specified by the user. On the latent dimension V_p, assume the location of movie i is $V_p(i)$. The effect of a user specified movie is set to be within a location window δ with a truncated Gaussian function $G_q()$, with high weights for thumb-up movies and low weights for thumb-down movies. The movie i with the highest value from the following combined measurement is selected as the best candidate.

$$b_{ui} \cdot \overbrace{G_1(|V_p(u_1) - V_p(i)|) \cdot \ldots \cdot G_q(|V_p(u_q) - V_p(i)|)}^{q=|U_+ \cup U_-|} / |V_p(i) - l| \tag{10}$$

The purpose of an additional random test is to ensure that our selections of recommendable movies are consistent with both user preferences of f and t, although only one factor is used to determine the narrative order. If the selected movie i passes the random test, we add it to the selected set G_T; otherwise we pick another random location and perform the local sampling again. For example, for the narrative structure between familiarity and diversity, we try to maintain an average typicality value close to the user preference t. We measure the typicality value of a movie i as $t(i) = |V_p(i)|$. The test is determined by if the movie i can make the average typicality value closer to t.

$$\left|\frac{(\sum_{i \in G_T} t(i)) + t(i)}{|G_T| + 1} - t\right| < \left|\frac{\sum_{i \in G_T} t(i)}{|G_T|} - t\right| \tag{11}$$

Similarly, for the narrative structure between typicality and un-typicality, we measure the familiarity value of a movie i given the center location of the like group c_+ as $f(i) = |V_p(i) - c_+|$. The random test is performed by replacing the $t(i)$ with $f(i)$ in the above equation.

Since the movie database is generally large, we can assume that there are always enough movies to recommend. In the cases that the recommendable movies run out, we can adjust the parameters τ_+ and τ_- to include additional movies.

INTERACTIVE RECOMMENDATION SYSTEM

The interface of our system is designed to be consistent with popular commercial recommendation systems, as shown in Figure 5. Our system also supports the following features of interactive recommendation.

Example-based Narrative Structure

The visualization of the latent dimension plays an important role in illustrating the recommendable movies and the movie distributions. To describe the narrative structure visually, we design an example-based approach shown in Figures 1, 3, 5, which uses two movies that have been watched by the user,

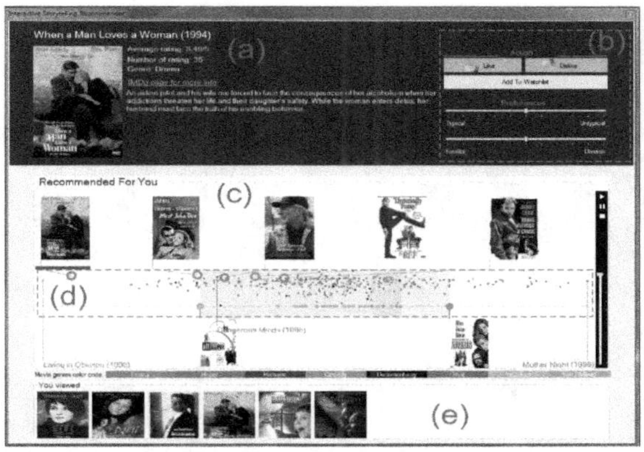

Figure 5. The interface of our recommendation system. Similar to online movie recommendation systems, our interface includes (a) basic information of a selected movie, (c) a list of recommendable movies, and (e) watch history. We also add (b) for explicit input of user preferences and (d) visualization for exploring recommendable movies.

one on each side of the familiar zone, to describe the combined features of that latent dimension. Since the combined features are generated simply from data statistics, they generally cannot be described with languages or equations. The example movies help the users to understand the overall trend of the latent dimension and provide a quick impression of a new movie by the distances to the two examples. All the recommendable movies are located on the 2D domain of latent dimension and recommendation degree, providing additional visual cues for recommendation reasons.

Animation Effects

Our system provides fully automatic animations to "tell" a recommendation story with the following three sets of animation effects.

The first animation set is to introduce the system components. Step by step, each component is highlighted with a brief description as shown in images (a-d) in Figure 6. The user can replay or skip to the next animation set anytime.

The second animation set is to present the narrative structure of a recommendation story. We use our example-based approach to animate the recommended movies for user attention and the two example movies from left to right for providing the impression of dimension meanings. Specifically, each example movie poster is animated by changing its size and the movie node is also animated simultaneously, as shown in Figure 6 (e-h).

The third animation set is to present a recommendation story, as shown in images (i-l) in Figure 6. We start to highlight the selected movie by flashing the movie node in the visualization panel when its poster in the recommendation list is animated. A green line under the movie poster also indicates the focused movie. Then, we switch the visualization gradually to provide detailed information of a selected movie. Specifically, the movie nodes in the visualization panel are progressively scaled to their maximum recommendation degree. We use the same animation procedure for all the selected movies in the

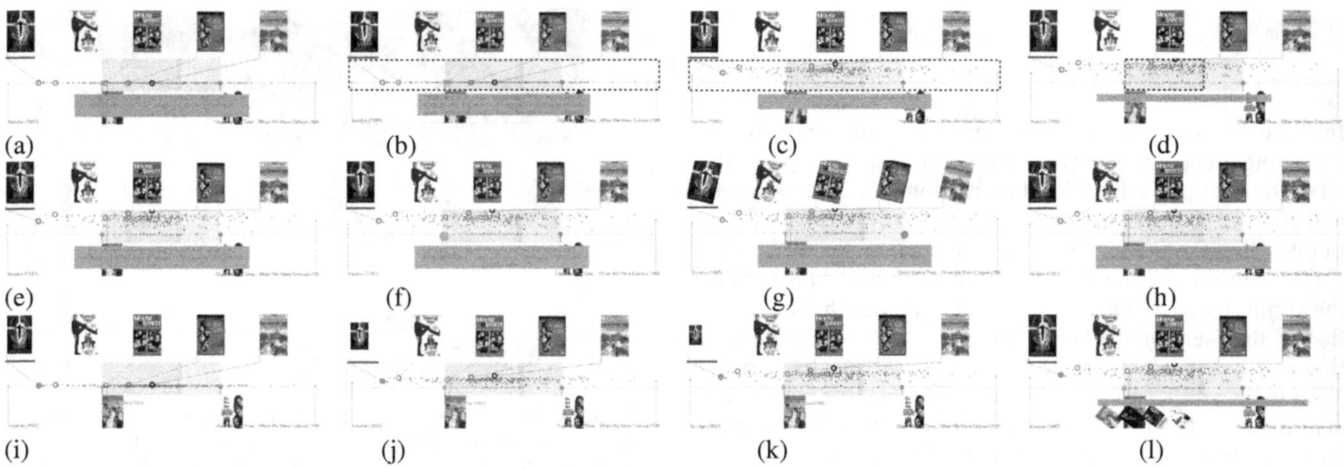

Figure 6. Example snapshots of the interactive recommendation process. We start by introducing the system interface to a new user, such as the use of rating history (a), color code (b), recommendation degree (c) and the liked zone (d). We also use example movies to illustrate the latent dimension and attract user attention with poster transitions (e-h). Next, we introduce the first recommended movie by animating the movie node and showing a green line under its poster (i). The visualization domain is animated gradually with more details (i-l). The same procedure (i-l) is used to animate additional recommended movies respectively.

story to avoid confusion. The user can observe all the information or switch anytime to the next recommended movie.

When the animation of a recommendation story ends or the user selects a movie for further exploration, a new story is generated automatically. The system re-introduces the new narrative structure and repeats the animation sequences to convey the story behind the new selected movies.

System Performance

The preprocess of our system includes the computation described in Section 3, including process of rating records, construction of SVD space, selection of recommendable movies and latent dimensions for the user. The performance of this stage is depended on the sizes of movie database and rating records. The preprocess takes 3-10 seconds for 30,000 ratings from 940 users for 370 movies and several minutes for the Movie100K dataset on a desktop computer with Intel Core i7 2.93 GHz processor.

During interactive recommendation stage, all the visualization and interaction processes described in Section 4 and 5 are interactive. This is essential for providing smooth user interaction in an online system. It is achieved by only keeping the relevant data to the user during run time. The performance is the main reason that rating records are used in our approach and many other popular online systems.

CASE STUDIES

This section describes three case studies using the MovieLens100K dataset [41]. The dataset has 100K ratings from 1 to 5 and 1682 movies from different categories rated by 943 users. We have select users with different backgrounds and rating histories to demonstrate our approach.

The first user is a 21 year old male working in entertainment. As shown in Figure 5, a latent dimension is identified between comedy movies toward the right and drama/romance/biography genres toward the left. As the default preference settings of 0.5/0.5 for typicality/un-typicality and familiarity/diversity, our recommendation system starts with movies of drama genre in the familiar zone and continues to drama and romance types for diversity. The recommended movies are: When a Man Loves a Woman (1994, Drama and Romance), Meet John Doe (1941, Drama, Romance and Comedy), Nobody's Fool (1994, Drama and Comedy), Ref The (1994, Comedy and Drama), and Rebel Without a Cause (1995, Drama).

We compare the recommendation results with the user's watch history. The user has rated 44 movies. Among which, about 68% of the movies are drama or a combination of drama and romance genres. Their average rating is high (4.30). The movies of other genres received lower ratings, especially comedy movies. Therefore, our result captures the user's preference of drama movies over comedy types.

The second user is a 28 year old male student. Figure 7 shows the first recommendation results for the user. The latent dimension spreads out movies in drama, documentary and comedy genres, with the combined features of positive influence (such as love and drama) toward the left direction and negative influence (such as horror) toward the right. Five movies are recommended from diverse to familiar zones: Wonderland (1997, Documentary), Fearless (1993, Drama), Man Without a Face (The 1993, Drama), Everest (1998, Documentary), and Miracle on 34th Street (1994, Drama).

Without user input, our system continues to additional recommendations with a new set of movies as shown in the first row of Figure 8. The user can also adjust the recommendation preferences and select their interested movies, shown on the second and third rows of Figure 8.

We compare the recommendation results with the user's watch history. He has an average rating of 3.64 for 34 movies from comedy, drama, horror, and romance genres. The rating records suggest that he likes drama and romance movies. Our recommendation results recommend majority movies in the familiar zone of the user and also introduce mixed adventure/documentary/drama movies for diversity.

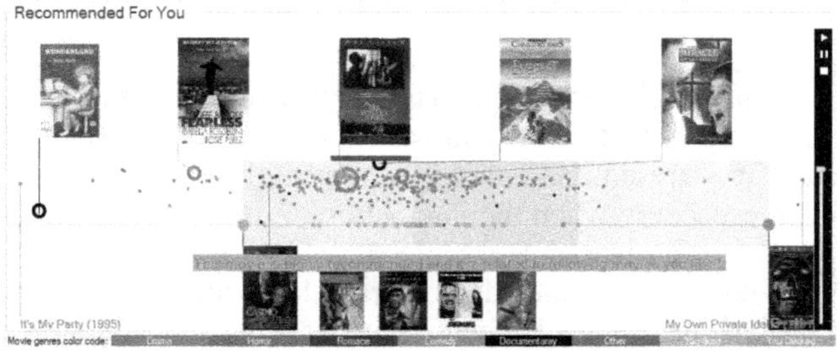

Figure 7. The result of the second user describes the user preference of love/drama movies he liked toward the left to horror/comedy movies he disliked toward the right.

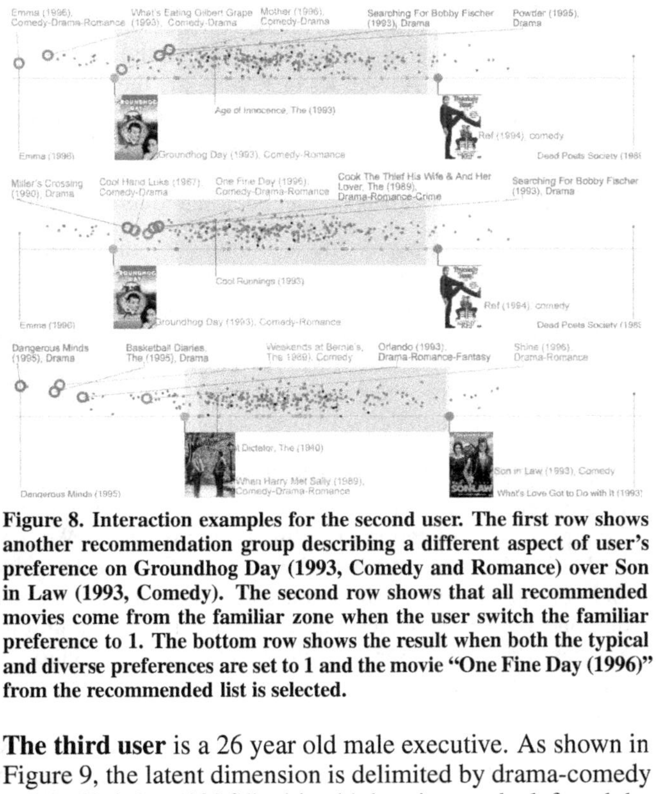

Figure 8. Interaction examples for the second user. The first row shows another recommendation group describing a different aspect of user's preference on Groundhog Day (1993, Comedy and Romance) over Son in Law (1993, Comedy). The second row shows that all recommended movies come from the familiar zone when the user switch the familiar preference to 1. The bottom row shows the result when both the typical and diverse preferences are set to 1 and the movie "One Fine Day (1996)" from the recommended list is selected.

The third user is a 26 year old male executive. As shown in Figure 9, the latent dimension is delimited by drama-comedy movie "Sabrina (1996)" with a high rating on the left and the comedy movie "Down Periscope (1996)" with a low rating on the right. Our system recommends five movies from drama movies combined with other genres in the familiar zone, such as Cool Hand Luke (1967, Comedy and Drama), Philadelphia Story (1940, comedy romance), Private Part (1997, Comedy and Drama), Sophie's Choice (1982, Drama and Romance) and Friday (1995, Comedy and Drama).

We compare the recommendation results with the user's watch history. He has rated 120 movies of several genres, such as comedy, drama, and horror. Most of his ratings were 1 or 2 stars and he only rated six movies with 4 or 5 stars. Our result reflects his low rating records with a large dislike region and a small like region. The latent dimension describes movie types from drama-comedy movies toward the left, to various other movie genres that the user has rated low toward the right. Such users are generally picky on movie selections, but our model still captures his favorite movie types and creates a matching recommendation group.

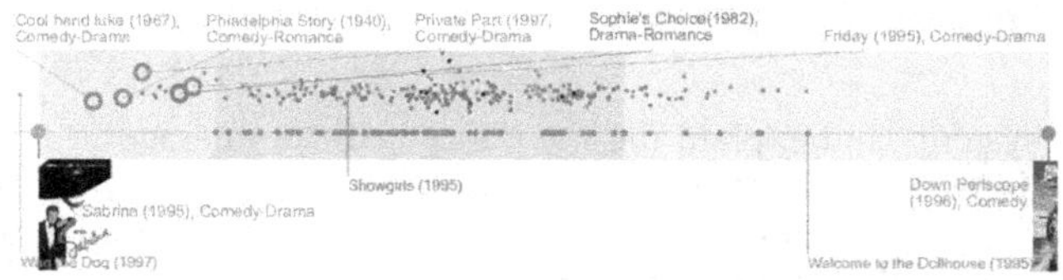

Figure 9. The result of the third user demonstrates a picky user who has rated many movies low. Our approach identifies the user's preference on comedy-drama movies (toward the left) over the other genres (toward the right).

EVALUATION OF INTERACTIVE RECOMMENDATION

To evaluate the effectiveness of our approach, we have conducted a controlled user study and a questionnaire. Our goal is to identify promising aspects of interactive recommendation from the perspectives of general users, especially on the search experience and user satisfaction.

As we focus on if and how an interactive mechanism can improve the recommendation experience, our hypotheses are as follows: **H1**: Interactive recommendation engages longer user attention by providing connections between recommended and user-rated movies. **H2**: Interactive recommendation provides a better search experience for users. **H3**: Interactive recommendation improves the user satisfaction of recommendation results.

User Study

For a controlled user study, we have developed two similar systems with the same recommendation algorithm. One system uses interactive recommendation, and the other uses the conventional top-K recommendation list. All the other factors, including movie posters and descriptions, are exactly the same for the two systems.

Data and Stimuli: Two independent movie groups of the same sizes are selected from the Movie100K dataset. Both groups contain movies of different types, as movie recommendation systems always handle a variety of movies. Specifically, one group contains the categories of drama and documentary, and the other group contains comedy and horror. For each group, 100 movies with more than 10 ratings are randomly selected.

For fairness, we use the same recommendation algorithm for both systems. The only difference is that the top-K list system uses the largest recommendation degrees, while the interactive version uses the narrative structures to select movies. The actual recommendation results are also affected by the user history and interaction during the study.

Subjects: Twenty one subjects (S1-S21) with normal or corrected vision participated in the experiment.

Procedures: Before the user study, we perform a training session to introduce the two systems. We demonstrate the

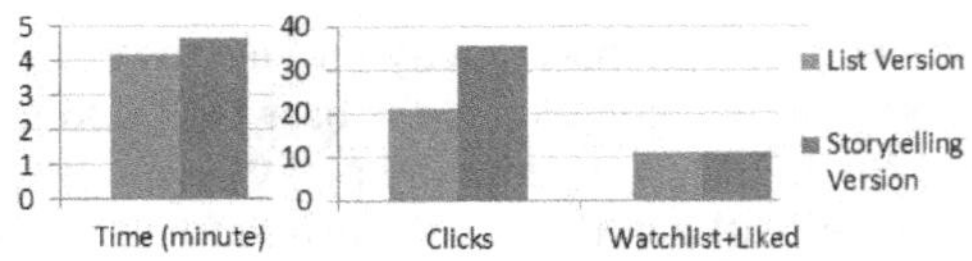

Figure 10. The averages of duration, movie clicked, and watchlist and liked clicked. The first two are statistically different, confirming our hypothesis of H1 on engaging users.

systems and explain the interfaces and the interaction functions. We also set up a user profile by asking the subject to rate 10 randomly selected movies from each group (randomness avoids all pre-selected movies are similar). We also encourage any questions from the subjects and try to address all during the training.

During the user study, each subject is asked to use both systems to perform the same task – searching for movies, which is very similar to the real-life scenarios. We alternate the two data groups for the two systems randomly among all the subjects. For each pair of system and data group, the subject needs to find three movies to add to the watchlist and "thumb-up" at least ten movies to watch later. Since our data groups are much smaller than the movie collections available in online stores, we set a time limit of 5 minutes for each system.

Questionnaire

We have also performed a questionnaire on user opinions of interactive recommendation at the end of the user study. The questions include basic information of subjects. Example questions are listed as follows: All the rating questions are scaled from 1 – Very dissatisfied to 5 - Very Satisfied.

1. Rate the two systems for recommendation experience?
2. Rate the two systems for recommendation results?
3. Rate how useful the listed information for recommendation: storyline, interaction, and animation?
4. Any suggestions to improve the systems.

Results and Discussions

Both systems automatically record several types of user interaction during the study, including the duration of each session, the numbers of movies clicked as "thumb-up", "thumb-down", added to watchlist, and number of mouse over function. In general, the averages of user interaction for the interactive system are larger than the top-K list system, indicating that the interactive system is more likely to engage users and encourage interaction and exploration.

To evaluate our hypothesis of H1 on engaging users, we compare the paired records of duration, movie clicked, and added to watchlist+like clicked. Figure 10 shows the averages from both systems. The one-tail p-value of time durations is 0.04, which is statistically significant between the two systems. This result is consistent with our hypothesis of H1 that the interactive system attracts longer user attention. In fact, the majority of subjects used the entire 5 minutes on the interactive system and the significance between the two systems can be larger if without the time limit.

The one-tail p-value for comparing the number of movie clicked is 0.0004, showing that subjects find significantly more movies they are interested in with the interactive system

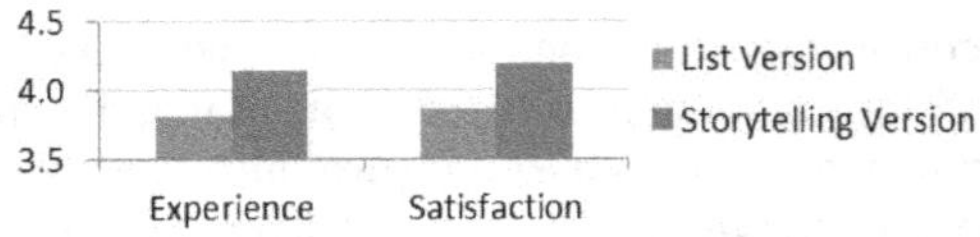

Figure 11. The averages of recommendation experience and user satisfaction for interactive system are higher than the top-K list system.

than the top-K list system. The numbers of the like+watchlist clicks represent favorite movies found by subjects and their averages are similar. During the user study, we have observed that especially when the interaction of data analysis leads to useful information, the subjects tend to explore additional movies. These results demonstrate that while the interactive system does not lead to better search results, it encourages significantly more interaction than the top-K list system. This is consistent with the design of our interactive recommendation approach, which simulates the communication between a user and an expert for engaging users.

To evaluate our hypothesis H2 and H3 on recommendation experience and user satisfaction, we compared the ratings from the questionnaire. As shown in Figure 11, the averages of the interactive system are both higher than the top-K list system, although not statistically significant. Also, during the user study, the subjects seldom pause or stop the animation, indicating strong interests on the recommendation stories.

The results of this user study are limited by the number of participants. It will be interesting to study the latent parameter selections with carefully controlled longer sessions and improve our questionnaire with user-centric evaluation frameworks [25, 40]. As it takes times for the general users to learn and accept such new technologies, we also need additional studies to evaluate the effectiveness of storytelling.

CONCLUSIONS AND FUTURE WORK

This paper presents an interactive recommendation approach for a popular application of online movie services. We have studied a latent semantic model which translates abstract data and complex recommendation algorithms to a set of semantic concepts and provides explicit interaction of search preferences. Based on LSM, our interactive recommendation approach automatically selects movies for recommendation and visualizes them in an animated comic strip fashion. Different from traditional recommendation algorithms, the interactive recommendation approach emphasizes the visual communication between users and recommendation systems for engaging users and improving search experiences.

As future work, we plan to perform formal evaluations on the effectiveness of interactive recommendation. We are interested in developing different versions of narrative visualization for different needs. We are also interested in integrating other techniques for movie recommendation, such as text analysis for mining useful information from reviews.

ACKNOWLEDGMENTS

We thank for reviewers for the helpful comments. This work was partially supported by the National Science Foundation under Grant Nos. 1564039 and 1629913, and National Natural Science Foundation of China (Project No.: 61661146002).

REFERENCES

1. Fereshteh Amini, Nathalie Henry Riche, Bongshin Lee, Christophe Hurter, and Pourang Irani. 2015. Understanding data videos: Looking at narrative visualization through the cinematography lens. In *Proceedings of the 33rd Annual ACM Conference on Human Factors in Computing Systems*. ACM, 1459–1468.
2. Benjamin Bach, Natalie Kerracher, Kyle Wm Hall, Sheelagh Carpendale, Jessie Kennedy, and Nathalie Henry Riche. 2016. Telling Stories about Dynamic Networks with Graph Comics. In *Proceedings of the Conference on Human Factors in Information Systems (CHI)*. ACM, New York, United States.
3. Fedor Bakalov, Marie-Jean Meurs, Birgitta König-Ries, Bahar Sateli, René Witte, Greg Butler, and Adrian Tsang. 2013. An Approach to Controlling User Models and Personalization Effects in Recommender Systems. In *Proceedings of the 2013 International Conference on Intelligent User Interfaces (IUI '13)*. 49–56.
4. Svetlin Bostandjiev, John O'Donovan, and Tobias Höllerer. 2012. TasteWeights: A Visual Interactive Hybrid Recommender System. In *Proceedings of the Sixth ACM Conference on Recommender Systems (RecSys '12)*. 35–42.
5. Jeremy Boy, Françoise Detienne, and Jean-Daniel Fekete. 2015. Storytelling in Information Visualizations: Does It Engage Users to Explore Data?. In *Proceedings of the ACM Conference on Human Factors in Computing Systems (CHI '15)*. 1449–1458.
6. C. Bryan, K. L. Ma, and J. Woodring. 2016. Temporal Summary Images: An Approach to Narrative Visualization via Interactive Annotation Generation and Placement. *IEEE Transactions on Visualization and Computer Graphics* (2016).
7. Giuseppe Carenini, Jocelyin Smith, and David Poole. 2003. Towards More Conversational and Collaborative Recommender Systems. In *Proceedings of the 8th International Conference on Intelligent User Interfaces (IUI '03)*. 12–18.
8. Li Chen and Feng Wang. 2017. Explaining Recommendations Based on Feature Sentiments in Product Reviews. In *Proceedings of the 22Nd International Conference on Intelligent User Interfaces (IUI '17)*. 17–28.
9. Konstantina Christakopoulou, Filip Radlinski, and Katja Hofmann. 2016. Towards Conversational Recommender Systems. In *Proceedings of the 22Nd ACM SIGKDD International Conference on Knowledge Discovery and Data Mining (KDD '16)*. 815–824.
10. Tarik Crnovrsanin, Isaac Liao, Yingcai Wuy, and Kwan-Liu Ma. 2011. Visual Recommendations for Network Navigation. In *Proceedings of the 13th Eurographics / IEEE - VGTC Conference on Visualization (EuroVis'11)*. 1081–1090.
11. Pedro Cruz and Penousal Machado. 2011. Generative storytelling for information visualization. *IEEE computer graphics and applications* 31, 2 (2011), 80–85.
12. Mukund Deshpande and George Karypis. 2004. Item-based top-N Recommendation Algorithms. *ACM Trans. Inf. Syst.* 22, 1 (Jan. 2004), 143–177.
13. Pierre Dragicevic, Anastasia Bezerianos, Waqas Javed, Niklas Elmqvist, and Jean-Daniel Fekete. 2011. Temporal distortion for animated transitions. In *Proceedings of the SIGCHI Conference on Human Factors in Computing Systems*. ACM, 2009–2018.
14. R. Eccles, T. Kapler, R. Harper, and W. Wright. 2007. Stories in GeoTime. In *Visual Analytics Science and Technology, 2007. VAST 2007. IEEE Symposium on*. 19–26.
15. Michael D. Ekstrand, John T. Riedl, and Joseph A. Konstan. 2011. Collaborative Filtering Recommender Systems. *Found. Trends Hum.-Comput. Interact.* 4, 2 (Feb. 2011), 81–173.
16. A. Figueiras. 2014. How to Tell Stories Using Visualization. In *Information Visualisation (IV), 2014 18th International Conference on*. 18–26.
17. D. Fisher, A. Hoff, G. Robertson, and M. Hurst. 2008. Narratives: A visualization to track narrative events as they develop. In *IEEE Symposium on Visual Analytics Science and Technology*. 115–122.
18. Nahum Gershon and Ward Page. 2001. What Storytelling Can Do for Information Visualization. *Commun. ACM* 44, 8 (Aug. 2001), 31–37.
19. Brynjar Gretarsson, John O'Donovan, Svetlin Bostandjiev, Christopher Hall, and Tobias Höllerer. 2010. Smallworlds: Visualizing social recommendations. *Computer Graphics Forum* 29, 3 (2010), 833–842.
20. Xianlin Hu, Aidong Lu, and Xintao Wu. 2013. Spectrum-Based Network Visualization for Topology Analysis. *Computer Graphics and Applications, IEEE* 33, 1 (Jan 2013), 58–68.
21. Jessica Hullman and Nicholas Diakopoulos. 2011. Visualization rhetoric: Framing effects in narrative visualization. *Visualization and Computer Graphics, IEEE Transactions on* 17, 12 (2011), 2231–2240.
22. Jessica Hullman, Nicholas Diakopoulos, and Eytan Adar. 2013a. Contextifier: Automatic Generation of Annotated Stock Visualizations. In *Proceedings of the SIGCHI Conference on Human Factors in Computing Systems (CHI '13)*. 2707–2716.
23. Jessica Hullman, Steven Drucker, Nathalie Henry Riche, Bongshin Lee, Danyel Fisher, and Eytan Adar. 2013b. A Deeper Understanding of Sequence in Narrative Visualization. *IEEE Transactions on Visualization and Computer Graphics* 19, 12 (2013), 2406–2415.

24. Anne-Marie Kermarrec and Afshin Moin. 2012. *Data Visualization Via Collaborative Filtering*. Research report. Inria. 23 pages. https://hal.inria.fr/hal-00673330

25. Bart P. Knijnenburg, Martijn C. Willemsen, Zeno Gantner, Hakan Soncu, and Chris Newell. 2012. Explaining the user experience of recommender systems. *User Modeling and User-Adapted Interaction* 22, 4 (01 Oct 2012), 441–504.

26. Yehuda Koren. 2008. Factorization Meets the Neighborhood: A Multifaceted Collaborative Filtering Model. In *Proceedings of the 14th ACM SIGKDD International Conference on Knowledge Discovery and Data Mining (KDD '08)*. 426–434.

27. R. Kosara and J. Mackinlay. 2013. Storytelling: The Next Step for Visualization. *Computer* 46, 5 (2013), 44–50.

28. Johannes Kunkel, Benedikt Loepp, and Jürgen Ziegler. 2017. A 3D Item Space Visualization for Presenting and Manipulating User Preferences in Collaborative Filtering. In *Proceedings of the International Conference on Intelligent User Interfaces (IUI)*. 3–15.

29. Bongshin Lee, Rubaiat Habib Kazi, and Greg Smith. 2013. SketchStory: Telling More Engaging Stories with Data Through Freeform Sketching. *IEEE Transactions on Visualization and Computer Graphics* 19, 12 (Dec. 2013), 2416–2425.

30. Bongshin Lee, N.H. Riche, P. Isenberg, and S. Carpendale. 2015. More Than Telling a Story: Transforming Data into Visually Shared Stories. *Computer Graphics and Applications, IEEE* 35, 5 (2015), 84–90.

31. Jure Leskovec, Anand Rajaraman, and Jeffrey David Ullman. 2014. *Mining of massive datasets*. Cambridge University Press.

32. Benedikt Loepp, Katja Herrmanny, and Jürgen Ziegler. 2015. Blended Recommending: Integrating Interactive Information Filtering and Algorithmic Recommender Techniques. In *Proceedings of ACM Conference on Human Factors in Computing Systems*. ACM, 975–984.

33. Benedikt Loepp, Tim Hussein, and Jüergen Ziegler. 2014. Choice-based preference elicitation for collaborative filtering recommender systems. In *Proceedings of the SIGCHI Conference on Human Factors in Computing Systems*. ACM, 3085–3094.

34. Hangzai Luo, Jianping Fan, Daniel A Keim, and Shin'ichi Satoh. 2009. Personalized news video recommendation. In *Advances in Multimedia Modeling*. Springer, 459–471.

35. Kwan-Liu Ma, I. Liao, J. Frazier, H. Hauser, and H.-N. Kostis. 2012. Scientific Storytelling Using Visualization. *Computer Graphics and Applications, IEEE* 32, 1 (2012), 12–19.

36. Alex Mitchell and Kevin McGee. 2011. Limits of rereadability in procedural interactive stories. In *Proceedings of the SIGCHI Conference on Human Factors in Computing Systems*. ACM, 1939–1948.

37. John O'Donovan, Barry Smyth, Brynjar Gretarsson, Svetlin Bostandjiev, and Tobias Höllerer. 2008. PeerChooser: Visual Interactive Recommendation. In *Proceedings of the SIGCHI Conference on Human Factors in Computing Systems (CHI '08)*. 1085–1088.

38. Denis Parra, Peter Brusilovsky, and Christoph Trattner. 2014. See What You Want to See: Visual User-driven Approach for Hybrid Recommendation. In *Proceedings of the 19th International Conference on Intelligent User Interfaces (IUI '14)*. 235–240.

39. Li Pu and Boi Faltings. 2013. Understanding and Improving Relational Matrix Factorization in Recommender Systems. In *Proceedings of the 7th ACM Conference on Recommender Systems (RecSys '13)*. 41–48.

40. Pearl Pu, Li Chen, and Rong Hu. 2012. Evaluating recommender systems from the user's perspective: survey of the state of the art. *User Modeling and User-Adapted Interaction* 22, 4 (01 Oct 2012), 317–355.

41. GroupLens Research. 2015. MovieLens100k: Movie rating Dataset. (2015). http://grouplens.org/datasets/movielens/

42. M.O. Riedl and R.M. Young. 2006. From linear story generation to branching story graphs. *Computer Graphics and Applications, IEEE* 26, 3 (2006), 23–31.

43. Arvind Satyanarayan and Jeffrey Heer. 2014. Authoring Narrative Visualizations with Ellipsis. *Comput. Graph. Forum* 33, 3 (2014), 361–370.

44. Edward Segel and Jeffrey Heer. 2010. Narrative visualization: Telling stories with data. *Visualization and Computer Graphics, IEEE Transactions on* 16, 6 (2010), 1139–1148.

45. Eric Spaulding and Haakon Faste. 2013. Design-driven narrative: using stories to prototype and build immersive design worlds. In *Proceedings of the SIGCHI Conference on Human Factors in Computing Systems*. ACM, 2843–2852.

46. Nava Tintarev and Judith Masthoff. 2015. *Explaining Recommendations: Design and Evaluation*. Springer US, Boston, MA, 353–382.

47. Chao Tong, Richard Roberts, Rita Borgo, Robert S Laramee, Kodzo Wegba, Aidong Lu, Yun Wang, Huamin Qu, Qiong Luo, and Xiaojuan Ma. 2018. Storytelling and Visualization: A Survey. In *Proceedings of the 9th International Conference on Information Visualization Theory and Applications (IVAPP)*.

48. Katrien Verbert, Denis Parra, Peter Brusilovsky, and Erik Duval. 2013. Visualizing Recommendations to Support Exploration, Transparency and Controllability. In *Proceedings of the 2013 International Conference on Intelligent User Interfaces (IUI '13)*. 351–362.

49. Jesse Vig, Shilad Sen, and John Riedl. 2009. Tagsplanations: Explaining Recommendations Using Tags. In *Proceedings of the 14th International Conference on Intelligent User Interfaces (IUI '09)*. 47–56.

50. Michail Vlachos and Daniel Svonava. 2012. Recommendation and visualization of similar movies using minimum spanning dendrograms. *Information Visualization* (2012).

51. Michael Wohlfart and Helwig Hauser. 2007. Story Telling for Presentation in Volume Visualization. In *Proceedings of the 9th Joint Eurographics / IEEE VGTC Conference on Visualization (EUROVIS'07)*. 91–98.

52. Wita Wojtkowski and W Gregory Wojtkowski. 2002. Storytelling: its role in information visualization. In *European Systems Science Congress*.

53. Li Yu, Aidong Lu, William Ribarsky, and Wei Chen. 2010. Automatic Animation for Time-Varying Data Visualization. *Computer Graphics Forum* 29, 7 (2010), 2271–2280.

54. Fajie Yuan, Guibing Guo, Joemon M. Jose, Long Chen, Haitao Yu, and Weinan Zhang. 2017. BoostFM: Boosted Factorization Machines for Top-N Feature-based Recommendation. In *Proceedings of the 22Nd International Conference on Intelligent User Interfaces (IUI '17)*. 45–54.

An Active Tangible User Interface Framework for Teaching and Learning Artificial Intelligence

Clifford De Raffaele
Middlesex University
Pembroke, PBK 1776, Malta
cderaffaele@ieee.org

Serengul Smith
Middlesex University
London, NW4 4BT, UK
s.smith@mdx.ac.uk

Orhan Gemikonakli
Middlesex University
London, NW4 4BT, UK
o.gemikonakli@mdx.ac.uk

ABSTRACT

Interactive and tangible computing platforms have garnered increased interest in the pursuit of embedding active learning pedagogies within curricula through educational technologies. Whilst Tangible User Interface (TUI) systems have successfully been developed to edutain children in various research, TUI architectures have seen limited deployment in more complex and abstract domains. In light of these limitations, this paper proposes an active TUI framework that addresses the challenges experienced in teaching and learning artificial intelligence (AI) within higher educational institutions. The proposal extends an aptly designed tabletop TUI architecture with the novel interactive paradigm of active tangible manipulatives to provide a more engaging and effective user interaction. The paper describes the deployment of the proposed TUI framework within an undergraduate laboratory session to aid in the teaching and learning of artificial neural networks. The experiment is assessed against currently adopted educational computer software and the obtained results highlight the potential of the proposed TUI framework to augment students' gain in knowledge and understanding of abstracted threshold concepts in higher education.

Author Keywords

Tangible User Interface; Computer-aided instruction; Higher Education; Artificial Neural Networks.

ACM Classification Keywords

• **Human-centered computing~Mixed / augmented reality** • Human-centered computing~Interactive systems and tools • **Social and professional topics~Computational science and engineering education** • **Social and professional topics~Adult education** • **Applied computing~Interactive learning environments** • Hardware~Emerging interfaces

IUI'18, March 7–11, 2018, Tokyo, Japan

ACM ISBN 978-1-4503-4945-1/18/03...$15.00
https://doi.org/10.1145/3172944.3172976.

INTRODUCTION

Through the rapid evolution of technology, emerging interaction techniques have provided the educational domain with new and smarter possibilities to support cognitive learning processes [28]. This evolution has brought with it a higher standard of intuition which necessitates users to exert less effort to make use of computer systems [34]. Thus led technology to new interaction paradigms of touchscreens, gesture recognition devices and tangible interfaces which are slowly replacing the conventional computing peripherals such as mice, keyboards and controllers [23].

As educators seek to engage evermore in active learning concepts and constructive-based solutions instead of the traditional exposition-based teaching methods that follow a "teaching-by-telling" methodologies [38], interest in educational technology has augmented as a promising means to enable modes of autonomous learning [39]. The introduction of such novel and smarter interaction technologies within the educational industry has been supported by multiple academic researchers so to provide an enhanced and enriched teaching and learning experience [3,42].

In particular, TUI systems provide an uniquly intuitaive user paradigm for students which operate through physical manipulation natively interlaced digital data representations [19]. This concept improves the interaction domain between human and computing machines by enabling users of TUI systems to take advantage of innate spatial and environmental skills [29], whilst interacting with and configuring physical objects [33]. Moreover, substituting real-life familiar objects instead of digital controlling options enables TUI systems to increase an application's intuitiveness which eases out the understanding of the concepts explained.

The introduction of Tangible User Interfaces (TUIs) as an educational technology quickly received interest in such a context especially for its effectiveness towards augmenting student motivation [6]. Following a comparative study with Graphical User Interfaces (GUIs) on creative design processes, the interaction techniques provided by TUI architectures outlined a substantial enhancement in student's design abilities as well a reduction of the cognitive load needed to interact with the technology [12].

Alternate studies further concluded that graspable/tangible user interfaces provide better retention of knowledge amongst students in educational applications [3] and are remarked as instruments that help learners in areas of; "development, sensory engagement, accessibility, collaborative activities and understanding of the world around them" [45].

The usefulness of TUIs for augmenting user's ability in problem-solving environments was also outlined by [32], which proposes a generic intelligent TUI system, 'Combinatorix', which allows students to explore and learn problem-solving techniques by manipulating physical objects and exposing potential solutions. The evaluation of this study showed that by aiding to picture all possible options to a given problem, the TUI system resulted in reduced cognitive stress amongst the evaluated students [32]. Similarly, 'AstroGrasp' was created to facilitate learning on astronomy concepts which allows students to interact with physical representations of the Earth and Moon, whilst observing representation of rays and shadows [1].

'Augmented Chemistry' embedded the TUI concept with augmented reality to allow students to inspect and interact and visualize imported molecular compounds from an extensive scientific database [4]. These enhancements in tangible manipulation and visualization were also corroborated in the study by [15] which developed a TUI which to aid explaining thermal transfer between objects. This was achieved by heating up an experimental material, whilst thermocouples monitored the heat transfer, which was subsequently displayed on the explainable tangible user interface provided.

Apart from these bespoke implementations in advanced education, the potential of this technology was mainly investigated in the primary educational domain. Examples like 'BrainExplorer' provide an insight into the effectiveness of engaging users is more creative ways via "interactive storytelling systems" [40], that seek to eliminate the use of textbooks whilst providing a hands-on experience. Authors in [31] further attest that such the smarter paradigms provided via TUI systems help students more effectively in tasks such as "memorizing scientific terminology, understanding a dynamic system, and transferring knowledge to a new situation".

Yet, whilst integration of these learning benefits together with the inherent attractive and eye-catching aspects of TUI systems [14] led to positive results when integrated within younger learning environments, the technology has so far lacked equal successful application within higher educational institutions (HEIs). This peculiar domain provides a number of unique challenges with respect to the adoption of effective and intelligent educational systems to help students overcome their "concrete operational phase" when learning new concepts [43]. Thus, this requirement necessitates TUI technology to aptly mitigate the challenges faced in engaging a mature audience with concepts of higher orders of complexity and abstraction from concrete experiences [27].

In contrast to the implementations in literature, this paper introduces a novel interaction concept within TUI frameworks by augmenting interactive surface architectures with active tangible manipulatives. This unique interactive paradigm presents TUI architectures with a smarter way to engage users and intelligently influence their scope of interaction. To further the limited successes identified in the literature on the of the efficacy of tangible systems in higher education, the proposed TUI architecture will be investigated for its ability to aid in the teaching and learning of abstracted Artificial Intelligence (AI) concepts such as Artificial Neural Networks (ANNs). The paper is organized so that a review of computer-aided techniques used to educate ANNs is presented in Section II. Section III outlines the proposed smart interactions within an adapted TUI architecture from both a tangible and digital perspective. The obtained results from deploying the system within a university programme are presented and discussed in Section IV. Finally, the last section outlines a brief conclusion of the presented work and the suitability aspects to this smart tangible computing in education.

ARTIFICIAL NEURAL NETWORKS

Within the domain of computer science, ANNs have quickly gained popularity as highly versatile machine learning algorithms with applicability in a myriad of applications ranging from image processing to autonomous control [18]. Defined by [11] as; "a computing system made up of a number of simple, highly interconnected processing elements, which process information by their dynamic state response to external inputs", this AI algorithm is further strengthened by feedback techniques such as back-propagation that provide a semi-supervised learning approach to optimize an output function convergence [7].

The ability of ANNs to address problems in classification, regression, time-series forecasting and complex system modeling [2] has consequently made the tuition of this machine learning (MLA) algorithm a stable within computer science and engineering degree programmes [13]. Yet, despite its widespread adoption, the complex nature of the ANN algorithmic processes poses a common difficulty to teaching within HEI contexts, thus leading academics to often rely on application software packages to aid in their educational delivery [30].

Amongst the most popular environments in use for this purpose are the Waikato Environment for Knowledge Analysis (WEKA) and MATLAB^{TM}, which allow students to process real datasets whilst making use of prebuilt libraries and toolboxes [13,16]. Both platforms provide user's the ability to preprocess, classify, cluster, associate, visualize and select attributes for given data. However, albeit these tools allow students to analyze the results of

ANNs, their use is often overwhelming for inexperienced users and often hinders the student's abilities deeply learn the algorithmic processes.

Addressing the visualization limitations above is commonly achieved through using bespoke educational software for ANNs. Applications such as TensorFlow allow students to interact with simulators online to allow customization of neural network architectures and visualize the obtained results [37]. Similarly, the Sharky Neural Network application adopts animation aspects to introduce students to simulated process and adaptably visualize the obtained results [35]. Whilst contributing to the visualization aspects of teaching and learning ANNs, these packages however often lack technical flexibility . This limits the ability for students to experiment with operational parameters in order to conceptualize their understanding [26].

More adaptable platforms such as Scikit-Learning [8] and Theano [41] allow students to easily set up and customize neural networks by making use of implementation libraries. Packages such as Pylearn2 [17] and Pyevolve [9] further extend ANNs with other MLAs, such as genetic algorithms, to extract further analysis from the obtained data. Comparably, the Caffe package facilitates the adoption of ANNs in image datasets and allows for the development of neural network architectures for detecting and classifying objects within images [20]. The technical capabilities of these applications however often technically overburden students with significant coding requirements and thus limits their ability to properly comprehend the underlying concepts of the ANN algorithmic process.

To this end, learns often resort to audiovisual media for studying the complex operational details of such algorithms, seeking educational channels on YouTube and virtual learning platforms to provide explanations and video-led examples [24]. Nevertheless, the sole use of diagrammatic representations and narration to explain the ANNs concepts, is functionally tantamount to the traditional lecturing approaches adopted within HEIs, which active learning pedagogies aimed to explicitly replace and augment using more engaging approaches.

PROPOSED ACTIVE TUI FRAMEWORK

In light of the above limitations to adopt educational technologies in this fundamental AI technique, this paper provides a contribution to enhance the teaching and learning of abstract concepts, such as those present in ANNs, using a real-time interactive educational tangible platform. Furthermore, in distinction from the current literature on TUI systems, this research proposes a novel interaction paradigm achieved by adopting active tangible manipulatives on an interactive surface architecture. This smarter technology is developed to aid mitigate the peculiar and augmented conceptual complexity experienced within HEI environments.

Physical Overview

The architectural system model proposed by this active TUI framework is that of an interactive tabletop design augmented with tangible computing. Based loosely on the MCRpd model proposed by [19], the proposal extends the interaction and feedback methodologies of TUI systems by integrating active microprocessor-controlled objects with a tabletop configuration. This design was conceived to enable the provision of additional manipulation capabilities which aid in the representation of abstracted educational concepts such as ANNs to HEI students.

Considerations in hardware design were also undertaken to account for the peculiar nature of HEI which intrinsically caters for different student demographics. The advanced complexity levels of ANN process necessitated the need to various simultaneous visualizations and interactions to be undertaken hence needing larger interactive surface area than conventional tabletop systems. This was mitigated by designing a 1.3m^2 interactive surface area tabletop whilst constraining the overall height dimensions to 90cm so as to retain comfortable reach and interaction by adult HEI students as detailed in [25]. These scaled architectural dimensions aided to engage larger numbers of students in collaborative interaction whilst accommodating for the comfortable visual and interaction dimensions of average-height HEI students.

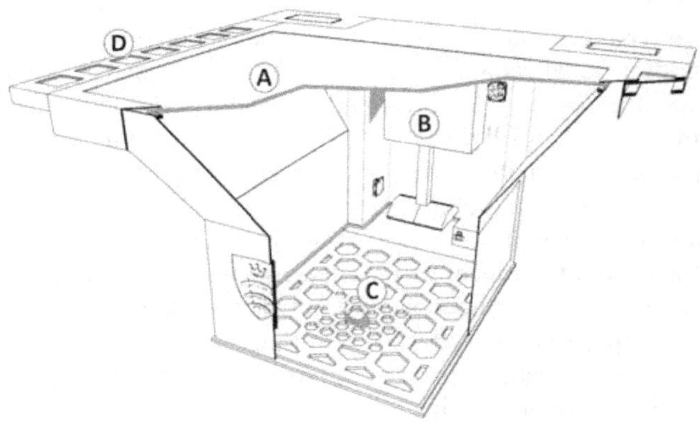

Figure 1. Construction cross-section of the proposed TUI: a) Tabletop interactive surface, b) Short-throw projector, c) Wide-angle CCD camera with IR band-filter, d) Side trays with illuminated TUI placeholders

As depicted in Figure 1, these design constrictions were addressed by making use of a short-throw projector mounted underneath a semi-transparent surface. The latter, made from an acrylic panel, was chosen due to its ability to clearly capture the projected image whilst allowing tangible objects to be seen from underneath. A wide-angle camera was employed to capture the surface area and provide visual feedback to the system. In tandem with the reacTIVision framework [21], the setup allows the conversion of tangible manipulation into digital control of the TUI software.

The active aspects of the proposed TUI system were designed using a distributed embedded microprocessor architecture. Adjacent to the table two tangible placeholder shelves were designed, as shown in Figure 1d, with integrated individually-controlled RGB lighting for each unique placeholder. This further enabled the system to direct students on appropriate use of TUI elements in a non-coercive approach.

Active Tangible Interaction

The proposed TUI framework presents an innovative interactive engagement paradigm to students by yielding an additional domain of user interaction through a set of active 3D physical objects. These objects were adapted by the TUI framework to allow the real-time design and configuration of neural network topologies as well as their operational parameters. The altering of these digital parameters using physical manipulatives is a central concept to TUI systems and hence a fundamental objective was to provide students with a heightened sense of intuitiveness and familiarity with tangible objects, thus reducing the barriers of interactivity commonly experienced by mature HEI students.

The active tangible concept was developed by embedding tangibles with autonomous computational architectural units that communicate wirelessly with a central processing server. To this end, within the base of each tangible object, an Arduino Nano™ was integrated, together with a small LiPo battery and a Bluetooth® communication module. This bi-directional communication architecture enabled each tangible object to independently transmit and receive data from the server processor via a serial communication protocol. To enable the optical recognition of objects by the computer-vision toolkit, a unique 'amoeba' marker [5] was attached underneath each object. This provided the framework the capability to passively track and intelligently control active components within tangibles. Furthermore, this approach introduced real-time multichannel user feedback through passive computer-vision and active tactile/analog interaction.

To aid in the teaching and learning process of ANN concepts, a 'horse-racing analysis' contextual example was adopted to explain the artificial intelligence algorithm. This context simulated the relational model of horse race time based on parametrical data of speed and health. The selection of this domain exploited the inherent familiarization and prior exposure of HEI students with the typical data of this application domain, hence perceptively reducing the cognitive load experienced by students whilst interacting with the novel framework. The aesthetic design and functionality of tangible objects were subsequently further adopted to symbolize and represent different ANN parameters ranging from input, hidden and output nodes as well as network parameters and configuration adapters. As pictured in Figure 2, these neural network concepts are innately expressed by the tangible objects within the 'horse-racing' context in an instinctively recognizable manner.

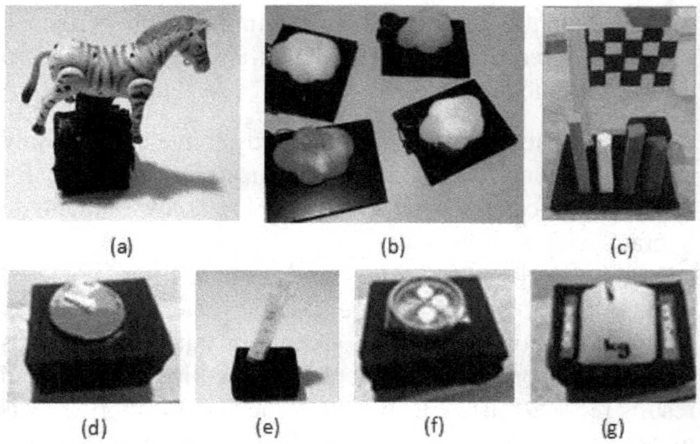

Figure 2. Active tangible objects contextualized for ANN operations including;
a) Horse - Context Simulator Controller,
b) Clouds – Hidden Layer nodes,
c) Finish Podium – Output Visualization,
d) Speedometer – Input Speed Value,
e) Syringe – Input Health Value,
f) Chronograph – Output Time Value,
g) Weight – Synapse Weight Adjustment.

Through embedded interaction with digital and physical feedback, these devices provided the TUI framework with the ability to computationally couple physical manipulations with ANN operands. These interactions are further elucidated in the following systematical descriptions:

- Horse Simulator Controller (Figure 2a) – The horse tangible represents the contextual data scenario and consequently triggers the loading of the appropriate dataset on the neural network AI algorithm. Students dynamically use this tangible to alter between setup and configuration modes of the designed ANN using positional shifting of the manipulative. Rotating the tangible at any stage in execution mode further controls and alters the training rate of the algorithm. This configuration interaction hence allows students to visualize and understand the training and convergence process in different modes of speed. The dynamic interaction is further communicated to the user via actively controlled feedback which via embedded actuators animates the figurines legs to simulate a functional galloping action whose pace is directly mapped with the ANN training rate.
- Cloud Nodes (Figure 2b) – A set of active cloud nodes were used to represent the abstruse nature of hidden layer nodes in ANN. Hence, by dynamically adding or removing these abstracted nodes, students were enabled to design and visualize the behavioural effects of differently configured topologies. The active tangibles were composed of translucent polylactide (PLA) material into which an actively controlled Light-Emitting-Diode (LED) was embedded. This intelligent interface aided student engagement by providing a color-coded relational

representation of output synapses. In addition, pervasive feedback interaction is used during the convergence process to intelligently engage student attention towards computational executions by timely triggered light strobes from the tangible.

- Result Podium (Figure 2c) – This finish line tangible embedded the representation of output results computed after each ANN iteration. By rotating the tangible, students can alter the result visualization of either the tabulated output values or a graphical representation of the estimated percentage error fed back though each back-propagation epoch.
- Speedometer (Figure 2d) – This active input tangible was designed to represent the variable speed of the simulated racing-horse input data. Via rotational interactions, students could alter the nodes input value which would be interactively reflected visually in both a displayed digital value as well as through proportionate dynamic analogue servo movement of the physical speedometer's hand.
- Syringe (Figure 2e) – The second input parameter was altered by users through the physical use of a syringe. This active tangible allowed students to alter the horse health data value which was exemplified as an input parameter to the ANN topology.
- Chronograph (Figure 2f) – This tangible output representation provided students the ability to toggle through testing or training simulation modes on the network. By actively engaging with the tangible through positional and rotational interactions, students can provide the ANN with an expected output data value, which would allow students to visualize the convergence process of the neural network to the newly trained outcome. Alternatively, the removal of this object indicated algorithmic testing conditions where the ANN needed to derive the output data.
- Weight Adjustment (Figure 2g) – This active TUI tangible was designed to allow students to experimentally learn and interact with the ANN operations. The translucent weight symbol, allowed students to select and configure internal ANN synapses by tangibly engaging with their parameters. By dynamically altering the RGB light from an embedded LED, the TUI framework provided intelligent feedback to users by changing its internal color to match that of the linked synapse. This mitigated the potential graphical clutter of complex topologies by allowing the TUI framework to provide positional assurance to students on the intended selection. Rotational interaction during setup stage also allowed students to configure the synaptic activation function whilst during configuration mode, the interaction would override the synaptic weight value with users input. This data value was further actively related back to students through a relational variation of lighting intensity of the physical tangible's LED.

Digital User Interaction

The proposed TUI framework embedded digital information through an interweaved GUI that provided an intuitive physical interactive experience. In stark contrast to the limitations imposed by Windows, Icons, Menus, Pointers (WIMP) systems, the proposed TUI architecture endowed additional flexibility options that were exploited to augment user immersion and learning processes.

The graphical interface was produced and implemented using Adobe Illustrator and the Unity™ game development environment. The framework behavioural interaction was programmed using C# which allowed the integration of animations based on the tangible information obtained through the TUIO communication protocol [22]. Furthermore, the framework integrated with a developed Python neural network simulator which whilst providing authentic representation of real-time data through functional AI computation also unbounded students in their flexibility to customize and configurate ANNs.

The GUI interface pervasively aids student interaction by providing subtle visual cues which are designed to aid in the experimental learning process and digitally interlink with physical manipulation. The interweaved design elements between visual animations, TUI execution and user interaction of the proposed TUI framework are systematically detailed in this subsection through a review of the framework's operation sequence.

The startup interface, illustrated in Figure 3a, presents students with a sectional layout to aid in the stage design of the ANN. As shown within Figure 3, by suitably embedding visual iconic symbols, students are guided through the TUI interaction through projected cues. These help to instinctively stimulate tangible interaction using appropriate placeholder indication. Once objects are placed on the interactive surface, the TUI framework makes use of digital timers, animated via radial filling as shown in Figure 3c, to allow users to assert their decided actions through physical manipulations. Following the successful registration of user interactions, the framework progressively advances through execution/customization stages, providing students with the ability to personalize the pace at which they progress through their learning process.

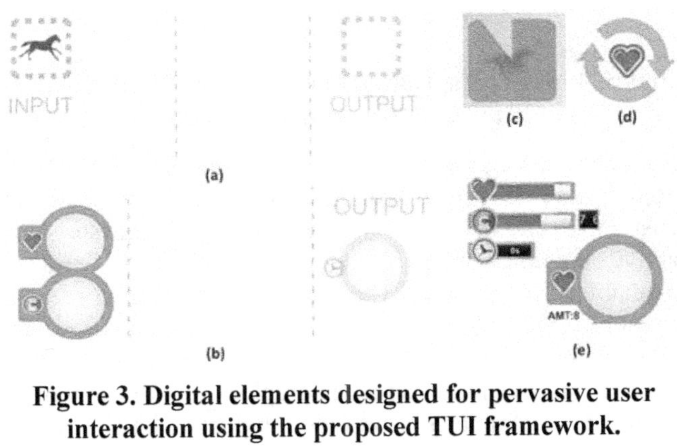

Figure 3. Digital elements designed for pervasive user interaction using the proposed TUI framework.

Subsequent to the loading of the 'horse-racing' dataset, via the 'horse' scenario controller, the TUI framework presents the contextual network's hyperparameters by visualizing the distinct input and output nodes of the ANN as illustrated in Figure 3b. Simultaneously, embedded LEDs actively flash on the respective input tangibles, pervasively diverting the student's attention towards the applicable interactive objects. Visual imagery further this smart interaction by helping students associate the digital/physical computational coupling by using indicative elements as pictured in Figure 3d. By manipulating the appropriate tangible, students are able to customize the input/output parameters for health, speed and time values, thus experimentally designing and configuring their custom simulation. Interactive feedback is provided during this stage by blending the use of pertinent icons, completion bars, and variable value scrolls, as shown in Figure 3e. This customization process is further reinforced within the TUI framework by the physical feedback provided using active actuators and input sensors on tangibles.

The use of proxemic interaction is also embedded within the tangible user interface by allowing students to dynamically configure synaptic links between nodes by placing the respective tangibles in physical proximity. This allows students to freely customize and experiment with ANN topologies augmenting the students' cognitive and learning process through user-centric progressive complex adaptions. To pervasively guide user's interaction, cloud tangibles which at setup stage represent the insertion of hidden nodes, are also interactively animated, by lighting up internally using the embedded LEDs as shown in Figure 4a. Once utilized and connected, color-coded internal synaptic links are projected on these tangible 'hidden' nodes, representing their connected topology as illustrated in Figure 4b.

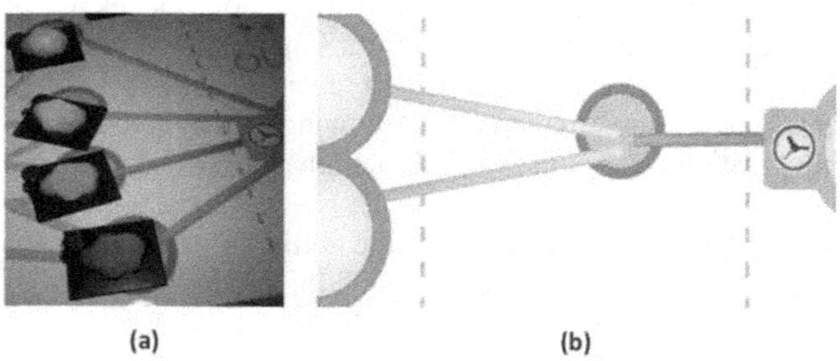

Figure 4. The configuration of hidden nodes and synapses using active cloud tangibles.

Following the connection of the ANN topology, the weight adjustment controller can optionally be utilized to customize the activation function on the synapse. This active tangible object is timely animated to indicate availability to the user. Thus, once placed near a created synaptic link, students can alter the selection of an algorithmic function. Making use of rotational interaction guided via pertinent circular graphics as illustrated in Figure 5, the framework provides students with the ability to experiment with different functional operands, which are visually explained to students using familiar mathematical graphs.

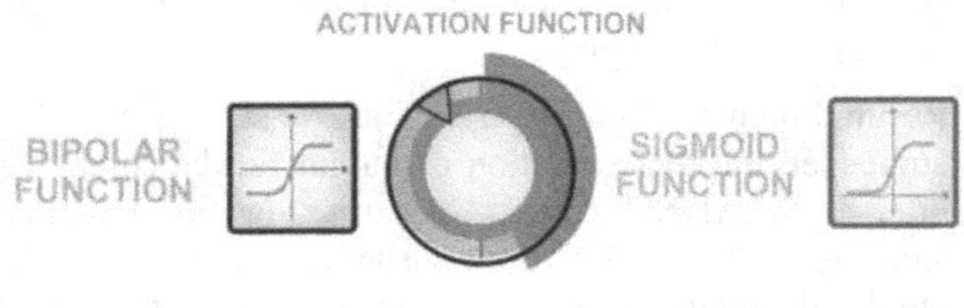

Figure 5. Selection of synapse activation function through rotational interaction and dynamic digital feedback.

Whilst the ANN is being constructed, students are provided with the option to switch between setup and configuration mode led through visual projection of graphics adjacent to the horse controller as shown in Figure 6a. Once the tangible is positionally dragged onto the 'start' placeholder, the input graphical information is summarized for users as shown in Figure 6b, whilst a new set of visual operands is projected near the tangible object. As shown in Figure 6b, these rotational cues provide the user to set the ANN training rate, hence idling or speeding up the simulation as desired. In tandem with this interaction, the TUI framework actively governs the tangible controller to provide real-time interactive feedback by altering the actuated galloping motion of the horse in relational speed to the rotational digital selection.

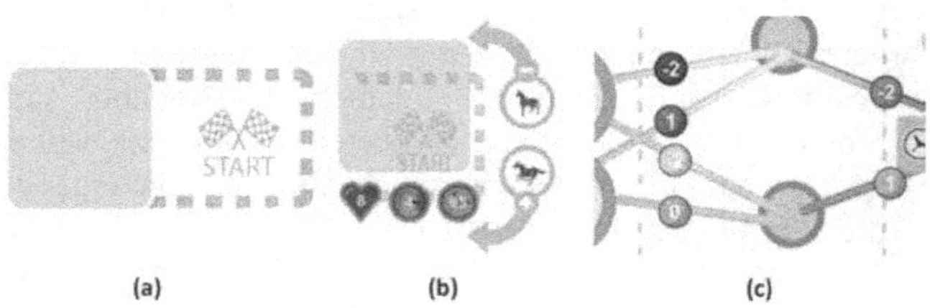

Figure 6. Visual digitization provided by the TUI framework in configuration mode.

At the start of the simulation in configuration mode, synapses are individually assigned random weights as common in most ANN implementations. This visual representation makes use of a suitably designed color-coding scheme, as shown in Figure 6c, to facilitate the student's association of data. To further the experimental learning capabilities imparted by the TUI framework, the proposed implementation multiplexed the use of the 'weight adjustment' object to enable customization of the initial data in configuration mode. The active tangible is therefore illuminated in varying light colors whilst the framework transitions to configuration mode, providing a persuasive indication to users via the physical domain on its potential use. Once placed on the interactive surface, the weight tangible is digitally augmented with a dynamic color wheel, illustrated in Figure 7a, which allows the user to accurately position and select individual synapses. Following the elapse of the interaction timer, the tangible object interactively changes light color to match the locked-in synoptic, indicating to the user the ability to configure specific data values on synapses via rotational interaction and digital visualizations as shown in Figure 7b.

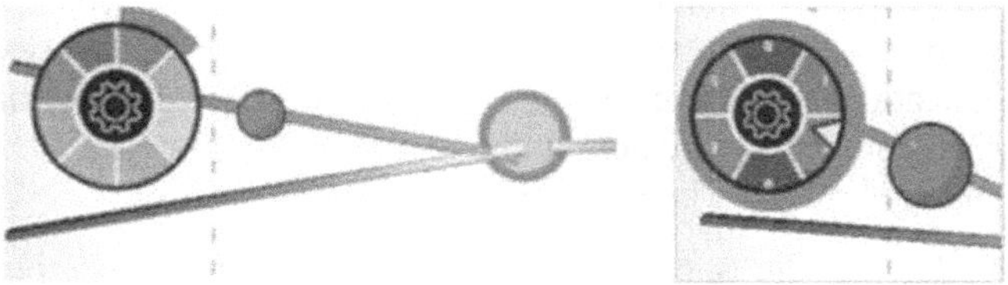

(a) (b)

Figure 7. Tangible interaction allowing students to experimentally configure synaptic weight values.

Consequent to the interactive customization of values, the framework aids students understanding the conceptual operation and convergence process of ANN through animated visuals. As shown in Figure 8a, data values are visualized traversing through nodes and synapses whilst appropriate animations are able to explain the mathematical value adjustments as signals propagate through the designed network. These dynamic visualizations provide a more intuitive understanding to the underlying concepts and procedural effects of the algorithm's iterations. Furthermore, at the end of each animated epoch, the underlying ANN scripts compute and display the resultant values of the last few iterations in a tabular graphic projected adjacent to the podium tangible. By physically altering this output tangible, students are further able to graphically interpret the convergence error computed through the last iterations, dynamically monitoring the effects of weight tuning on the algorithms backpropagation adjustments and accuracy.

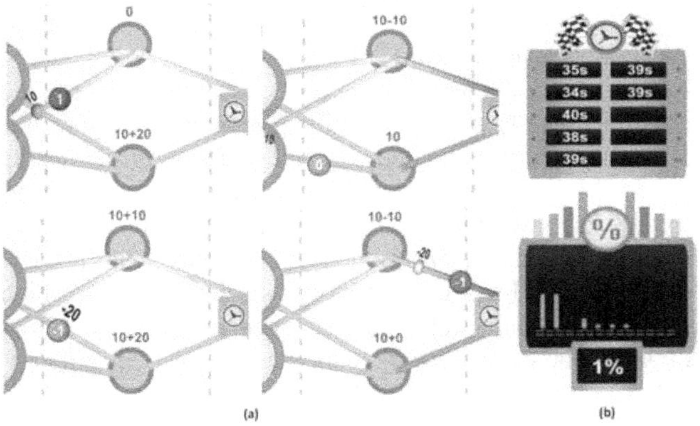

Figure 8. Digital visualizations highlighting internal computations:
a) Animated weight propagation and value calculation, b) Output result times per iteration together with backpropagated error percentage for convergence.

Once the AI algorithm is sufficiently converged, students are able to further engage with the TUI framework to utilize and understand the developed ANN in predictive AI testing mode. In this mode of execution, the interweaved and perceptually coupled digital and physical domains, as pictured in Figure 9, enable students to self-evaluate the suitability and accurateness of their designed ANN topology by testing its validity on new input datasets. This allows students to individually self-assess their progress and uniquely customize the pace of their learning experience so as to obtain a deeper understanding of the AI concept.

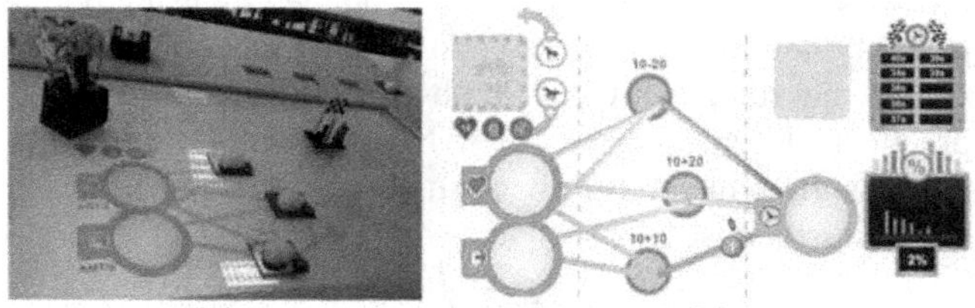

(a) (b)

Figure 9. Perceptually and computationally coupled ANN model within; a) the physical domain, and b) the digital domain.

EXPERIMENTAL EVALUATION

The developed TUI framework was deployed for evaluation at Middlesex University Malta within undergraduate degrees in Computer Science and Information Technology. Convenience sampling was undertaken to select 32 students studying the module of Artificial Intelligence who voluntarily offered to participate in the evaluation study. This population sample size was deemed adequate in line with the guidelines in [44]. The undergraduate participants were either in their second or third year of study and varied in age between 18 and 24.

To evaluate the effectiveness of the proposed TUI framework, a direct comparison was undertaken against currently employed PC-based educational technology using a GUI educational simulator. To ensure no additional experimental variables are introduced in the evaluation, a similar GUI software was developed to that created on the TUI framework. As visualized in Figure 10, the educational software was optimized for GUI interaction and usability whilst retaining identical functionality and educational capabilities.

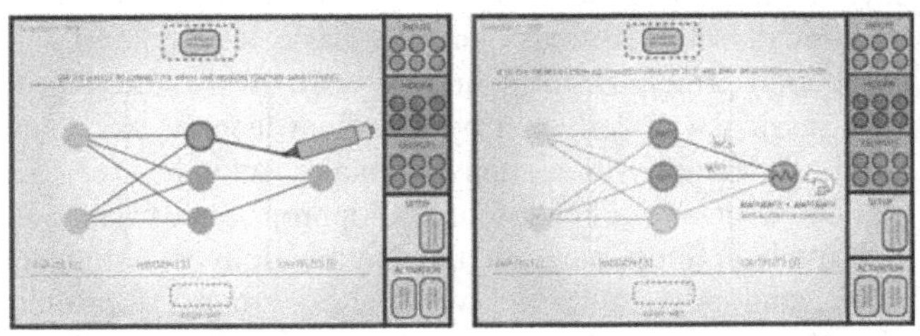

Figure 10. GUI software developed for comparative evaluation.

Artificial neural networks is a foundational topic within the selected course and commonly forms a threshold concept towards the student's progress and understanding of more complex algorithms. Hence, to maximize the evaluation potential of the proposed TUI framework, the experimental sessions were scheduled to coincide with the natural delivery of this topic within the curriculum.

Evaluation Methodology

An evaluation methodology was implemented which was designed to yield a quantitative analysis of the effectiveness and suitability of the proposed TUI framework in HEI contexts. This evaluation data was obtained by using both a usability questionnaire and an open-ended assessment where questions covered both theoretical as well as practical design aspects of ANN concepts. Figure 11 outlines the sequential flow of student evaluation, lecturing and assessment sessions;

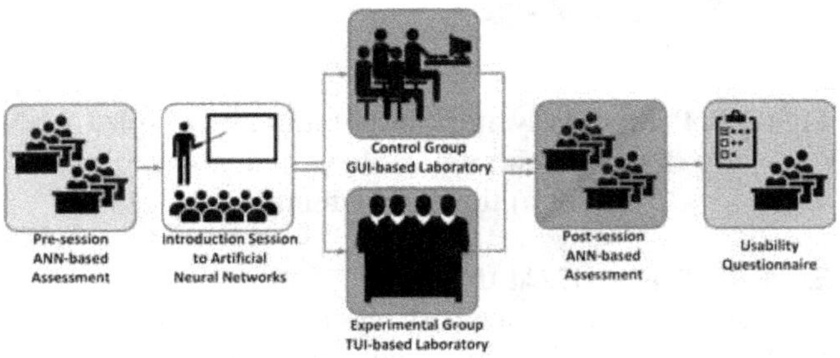

Figure 11. Evaluation stages designed for assessing the suitability of educational technologies for ANN concepts.

To mitigate the potential bias introduced by the students' apriori knowledge of ANN potentially acquired from their related work experience and varied demographics, a differential evaluation methodology was adopted to provide summative assessment on the level of knowledge gain obtained by students [10,36]. To this end, upon commencement all students were provided with a timed pre-session assessment on ANN knowledge. This examination was composed of 12 open-ended questions and covered various aspects of detail and conceptual understanding of the ANN concept. The results obtained from this assessment provided an individualistic knowledge baseline for each student prior to being provided formal tuition on ANN.

Following this initial assessment, students collectively attended a short introductory session. This was delivered in traditional lecture format, whereby basic terminology and foundation principles for neural networks were introduced. This session was delivered by the usual lecturer using the standard lecture slides conventionally adopted for the module to ensure a consistent and appropriate explanation is provided. Subsequent to the lecture delivery, students were randomly split in two equal groups for their laboratory/seminar session on the topic. These cohorts composed the experimental and control groups respectively for the evaluation methodology described. As illustrated in Figure 11 during the laboratory sessions, students sub-grouped in sets of four (4) to solve a number of given group work tasks. The latter were identical to both cohorts and involved the experimental design, construction and analysis of different ANNs topologies within a 'horse-racing' contextual example. The designed variable within the experiment was to enable students within different groups to utilize a different educational technology to undertake and solve the laboratory tasks. Thus, whilst the control group students adopted the traditional GUI-based educational software shown in Figure 10, the experimental group students were able to interact with the proposed TUI adaption pictured in Figure 9.

Following the successful completion of their respective tasks, all students were provided with a usability questionnaire for the respective educational technology utilized as well as a second assessment using similar open-ended questions on ANN concepts. The questions in this examination were designed to assess the various aspects of conceptual understanding including theoretical, detail-focused, procedural and problem-based knowledge as shown in the following questions extract:

- *Why is a Hidden Layer used in an ANN?*
- *How does adding more Hidden Layers affect data?*
- *What happens every time the data passes through Synapse?*
- *Why is the result difference of the Expected Output and Actual Output important?*

These quantitative assessments were designed to provide an evaluation on the knowledge gain obtained by each individual student during the respectively attended session. Equitable analysis on the assessment grades together with the quantified subjective evaluation provided by students in relation to the interactivity and usability of the designed educational technology were able to aid evaluate the respective aptness and efficacy of the proposed TUI framework in HEI contexts.

Results and Discussion

The grades obtained by students within each of the assessment sessions are visually presented in Figure 12. The figure provides a comparative evaluation of the results obtained by students in each distinct question during their pre-session assessment (green) as well as their subsequent post-session assessment following interaction with a GUI-based or TUI-based laboratory session (red or blue respectively). This data was evaluated for each individual student in both educational cohorts using a paired-sample t-test.

Results outlined that students undertaking the control laboratory improved their mark to 39.1% (σ: 15.6) from their initial pre-test score of 15.4% (σ: 3.1). On the other hand, students who engaged with the proposed TUI framework during the experimental setup achieved a post-test average grade of 71.2% (σ: 14.4). Thus, in contrast to the 23.7% (σ: 16.4) knowledge gain obtained during the GUI-based computer laboratory sessions, the proposed TUI framework provided students with a knowledge gain of 55.8% (σ: 13.7) at $p < 0.001$ as shown in the overall comparison in Figure 13.

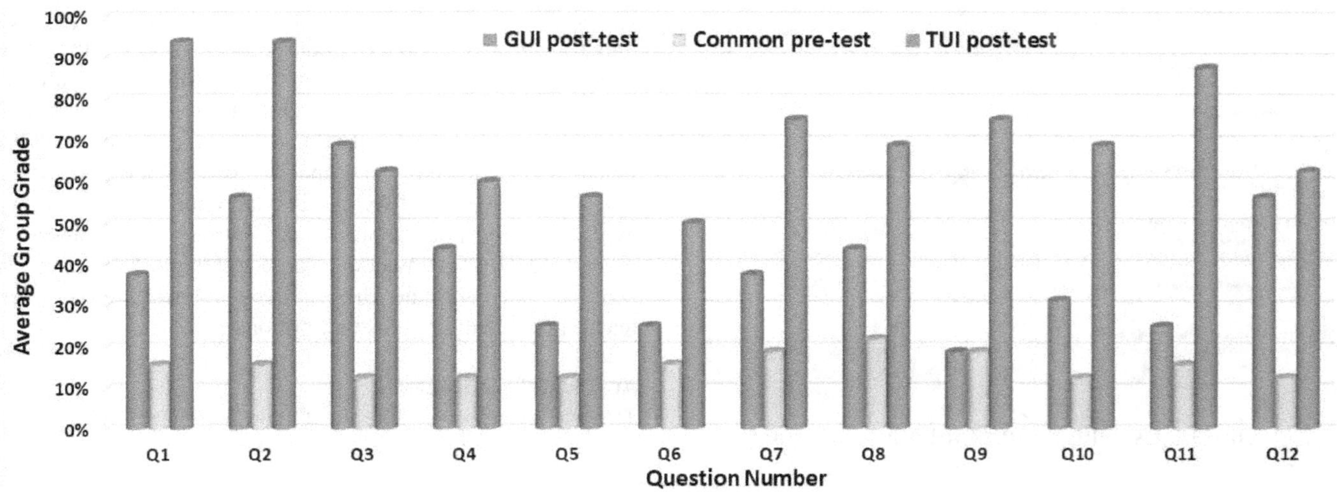

Figure 12: Average grade obtained for each assessed question during the: (left) Post-test of GUI control group, (center) Pre-test undertaken by all students prior to formal tuition on ANN, (right) experimental group after using the proposed TUI framework.

Analyzed under an independent samples t-test, the proposed TUI framework resulted in a knowledge acquiring difference of 32% (σ: 6.1) at $p < 0.001$ with respect to the control student cohort. This difference was directly attributed to the effectiveness of the proposed tangible interactive framework to engage students with abstracted ANN operational concepts. This was achieved in stark contrast to the experimental control group which by adopting a feature-identical GUI setup, illustrated the limited capabilities of the educational technologies adopted conventionally in HEIs.

he remarkable achievements obtained through the TUI interaction were further analyzed to obtain a deeper insight into the teaching and learning capabilities delivered by the framework. The nature of the open-ended questions delivered within assessments were thus segmented according to the different aspects of knowledge evaluated, as shown in Figure 13.

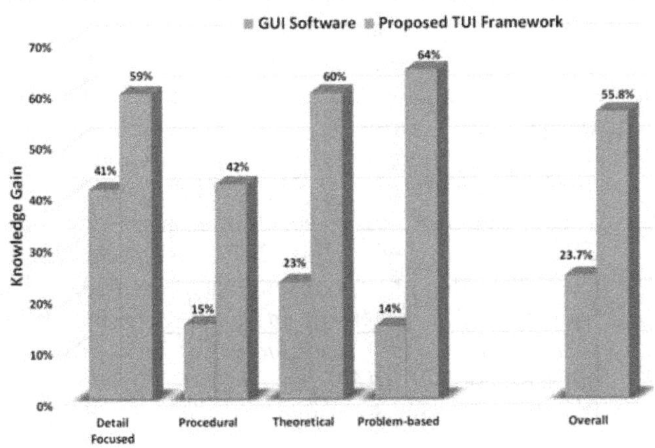

Figure 13. Knowledge gain analyses between educational technologies.

The aggregated results in Figure 13 show that both technologies performed with equitable effectives on 'detail oriented' aspects of knowledge with Q3 in Figure 12 showing a marginal increased ability by GUI software to aid in teaching and learning theoretical definitions. Conversely however, results in Figure 13 immediately highlight the ability of the proposed TUI framework to aid students understand the procedural and theoretical aspects of ANN concepts deeper than that provided by similar GUI software. This can be attributed to the students' ability to tangibly interact with the system's active functionality using instinctive manipulations and feedback channels that augment focus and understanding of the conceptual representations. Furthermore, as outlined by performance difference in answering problem-based questions, the intrinsic capability of the proposed TUI framework to contextualize ANN operation within a familiar environment by using adequately designed tangible representations aids students to assimilate knowledge, thus heightening their ability to apply and understand the underlying abstracted concepts in problem-oriented scenarios.

The aptness of the proposed TUI framework for adoption in HEI was also evaluated using a usability questionnaire that was provided to both groups of students after interacting with their respective educational technology. Using a bi-polar five-level Likert scale, students were asked to quantify their experience in various aspects of their educational pursuit. The subjective usability results presented in Figure 14 outline the effectiveness of the appropriately designed TUI framework to be interacted by users in an intuitive, productive, and ultimately enjoyable manner. Student's feedback demonstrated that albeit the GUI and TUI systems used projected the same information, the information in the TUI framework was perceived to be more effective in understanding and completing the intended ANN tasks.

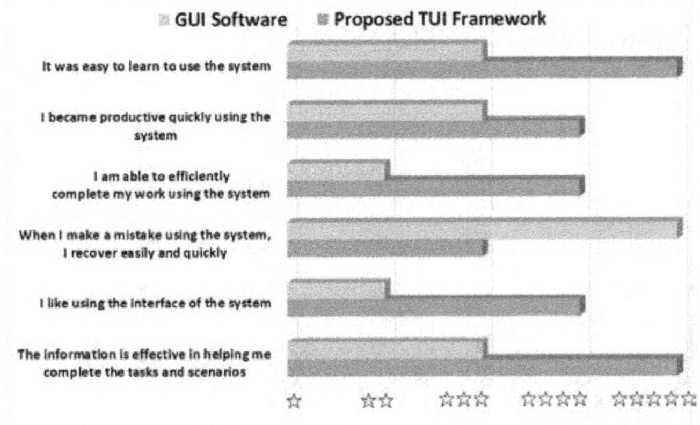

Figure 14. Usability results for both educational technologies.

As shown in Figure 14, a limiting usability factor was conversely noted in the easiness for users to recover the ANN to earlier versions, which when compared to 'back button' deployments in GUI software, the proposed TUI framework necessitated users to redefine parameters and connections by manipulating tangibles accordingly. Nevertheless, questions relating to efficiency in achieving the intended outcome illustrate that students still felt more productive when operating a TUI interface in developing and analyzing different ANN configurations. This statement was confirmed objectively by timing the duration that students took to collaboratively finish their assigned laboratory tasks successfully.

A combined interpretation of results corroborates on the effectiveness of the proposed TUI architecture to interlace the digital information within the tangible domain through a more immersive interface using the novel active tangible interaction paradigm. This reflected on the framework's heightened ability to engage multiple students together whilst facilitate the collaborative learning and engagement on contextual problem-solving scenarios. Whilst the paper described the TUI framework in context of a 'horse-racing' scenario for designing ANN topologies, the observed benefits from adoption of an active TUI framework can be equitably transferred to other AI contexts in light of the described TUI design considerations.

CONCLUSION

The contribution of this paper lies at the confluence of AI education and human-computer interaction. By addressing the limitations of educational technologies in higher educational contexts, this paper proposes an active TUI framework design which is able to cater for the peculiar teaching and learning requirements for abstracted concepts in HEI. Furthering the interactive paradigm of this technology, the described framework actively engages students by interweaving the physical and digital domains of interaction via the novel adoption of active tangible manipulatives on tabletop architectures. Contextualized for teaching and learning ANN algorithms, the proposed TUI framework was deployed in an evaluation process undertaken within an AI undergraduate programme. The experimental and collaborative learning paradigms provided by the tangible architecture led to engaged students achieving an increase in knowledge gain of 32% when experimentally compared to colleagues using traditional GUI software. In tandem with usability evaluation, the paper outlines the aptness and efficacy of embedded TUI frameworks as an educational technology in HEI to help mitigate the challenges encountered when teaching and learning abstract notions.

ACKNOWLEDGMENTS

The authors would like to thank Middlesex University Malta undergraduate students Mr. Maurice Sultana, Mr. Ian Farrugia, Mr. Mohamed Dekna and Mr. Ryan Tabone for their valued contribution in the development, implementation, and evaluation of this work.

REFERENCES

1. H Agrawal and K Sorathia. 2013. AstroGrasp: a tangible user interface for teaching basic astronomy concepts. *Proceedings of the 11th Asia Pacific Conf*: 123–128. https://doi.org/10.1145/2525194.2525207
2. A. S. Ahmad, M. Y. Hassan, M. P. Abdullah, H. A. Rahman, F. Hussin, H. Abdullah, and R. Saidur. 2014. A review on applications of ANN and SVM for building electrical energy consumption forecasting. *Renewable and Sustainable Energy Reviews* 33: 102–109. https://doi.org/10.1016/j.rser.2014.01.069
3. Xavier Alaman, Juan Mateu, and Maria J. Lasala. 2016. Designing virtual world educational applications. *2016 IEEE Global Engineering Education Conference (EDUCON)*, April: 1134–1137. https://doi.org/10.1109/EDUCON.2016.7474697
4. Joakim Almgren, Richard Carlsson, Henrik Erkkonen, Jonas Fredriksson, Sanne Moller, Henrik Rydgard, Mattias Osterberg, and Morten Fjeld. 2005. Tangible User Interface for Chemistry Education: Visualization, Portability, and Database. *Visualization, Portability, and Database. Proc. SIGRAD 2005*, 16: 19–24.
5. Ross Bencina and Martin Kaltenbrunner. 2005. The Design and Evolution of Fiducials for the reacTIVision System. In *Proc. 3rd International Conf on Generative Systems in the Electronic Arts.*
6. Lorena Blasco-Arcas, Isabel Buil, Blanca Hernández-Ortega, and F. Javier Sese. 2013. Using clickers in class. the role of interactivity, active collaborative learning and engagement in learning performance. *Computers and Education* 62: 102–110. https://doi.org/10.1016/j.compedu.2012.10.019
7. P.J. Braspenning, F. Thuijsman, and A. Weijters. 1995. *Artificial neural networks: an introduction to ANN theory and practice*. Springer Science & Business Media.
8. Lars Buitinck, Gilles Louppe, Mathieu Blondel, Fabian Pedregosa, Andreas Mueller, Olivier Grisel,

Vlad Niculae, Peter Prettenhofer, Alexandre Gramfort, Jaques Grobler, Robert Layton, Jake Vanderplas, Arnaud Joly, Brian Holt, and Gaël Varoquaux. 2013. API design for machine learning software: experiences from the scikit-learn project.

9. Andrew Butterfield, Vivek Vedagiri, Edward Lang, Cath Lawrence, Matthew J Wakefield, Alexander Isaev, and Gavin A Huttley. 2004. PyEvolve: a toolkit for statistical modelling of molecular evolution. *BMC Bioinformatics* 5, 1: 1. https://doi.org/10.1186/1471-2105-5-1
10. Alejandro Catala, Javier Jaen, Adria A. Martinez-Villaronga, and Jose A. Mocholi. 2011. AGORAS: Exploring creative learning on tangible user interfaces. In *Proceedings - International Computer Software and Applications Conference*, 326–335. https://doi.org/10.1109/COMPSAC.2011.50
11. Caudill and Maureen. 1986. Neural networks primer, part I. *AI Expert* 2, 12: 46–52.
12. Tilanka Chandrasekera and So-Yeon Yoon. 2015. The Effect of Tangible User Interfaces on Cognitive Load in the Creative Design Process. *Proceedings of the 2015 IEEE International Symposium on Mixed and Augmented Reality - Media, Art, Social Science, Humanities and Design*: 6–8. https://doi.org/10.1109/ISMAR-MASH'D.2015.18
13. P. Díaz-Moreno, J. J. Carrasco, E. Soria-Olivas, J. M. Martínez-Martínez, P. Escandell-Montero, and J. Gómez-Sanchis. 2016. Educational Software Based on Matlab GUIs for Neural Networks Courses. In *Handbook of Research on Computational Simulation and Modeling in Engineering*. 333–358. https://doi.org/10.4018/978-1-5225-0159-6.ch075
14. Darren Edge and Alan Blackwell. 2006. Correlates of the cognitive dimensions for tangible user interface. *Journal of Visual Languages and Computing* 17, 4: 366–394. https://doi.org/10.1016/j.jvlc.2006.04.005
15. Ruwan Fernando, Karine Dupre, and Henry Skates. 2016. Tangible user interfaces for teaching building physics: Towards continuous designing in education. In *CAADRIA 2016, 21st International Conference on Computer-Aided Architectural Design Research in Asia - Living Systems and Micro-Utopias: Towards Continuous Designing*, 693–702.
16. Eibe Frank, Mark A Hall, and Ian H Witten. 2016. The WEKA Workbench. *Morgan Kaufmann, Fourth Edition*: 553–571.
17. Ian J. Goodfellow, David Warde-Farley, Pascal Lamblin, Vincent Dumoulin, Mehdi Mirza, Razvan Pascanu, James Bergstra, Frédéric Bastien, and Yoshua Bengio. 2013. Pylearn2: a machine learning research library.
18. Satoshi Ishibushi, Akira Taniguchi, Toshiaki Takano, Yoshinobu Hagiwara, and Tadahiro Taniguchi. 2015. Statistical localization exploiting convolutional neural network for an autonomous vehicle. In *IECON 2015 - 41st Annual Conference of the IEEE Industrial Electronics Society*, 1369–1375. https://doi.org/10.1109/IECON.2015.7392291
19. Hiroshi Ishii. 2008. Tangible bits: beyond pixels. *Proceedings of the 2nd international conference on Tangible and Embedded Intreaction (TEI '08)*: xv–xxv. https://doi.org/10.1145/1347390.1347392
20. Yangqing Jia, Evan Shelhamer, Jeff Donahue, Sergey Karayev, Jonathan Long, Ross Girshick, Sergio Guadarrama, and Trevor Darrell. 2014. Caffe: Convolutional Architecture for Fast Feature Embedding. In *Proceedings of the ACM International Conference on Multimedia - MM '14*, 675–678. https://doi.org/10.1145/2647868.2654889
21. Martin Kaltenbrunner and Ross Bencina. 2007. reacTIVision: a computer-vision framework for table-based tangible interaction. *Proceedings of the 1st international conference on Tangible and embedded interaction*: 69–74. https://doi.org/10.1145/1226969.1226983
22. Martin Kaltenbrunner, Till Bovermann, Ross Bencina, and Enrico Costanza. 2005. TUIO: A protocol for table-top tangible user interfaces. *Neuroinformatics*: 1–5.
23. Andrew Manches, Pauline Duncan, Lydia Plowman, and Shari Sabeti. 2015. Three questions about the Internet of things and children. *TechTrends* 59, 1. https://doi.org/10.1007/s11528-014-0824-8
24. Barton Poulson. 2016. Artificial neural networks. Retrieved 26 September 2017 from https://www.lynda.com/Big-Data-tutorials/Artificial-neural-networks/420305/505154-4.html
25. Clifford De Raffaele, Geoffrey Buhagiar, Serengul Smith, and Orhan Gemikonakli. 2017. Designing a Table-Top Tangible User Interface System for Higher Education. In *IEEE International Conference on Smart Systems and Technologies (SST)*, 286–291. https://doi.org/10.1109/SST.2017.8188711
26. Clifford De Raffaele, Serengul Smith, and Orhan Gemikonakli. 2016. The aptness of Tangible User Interfaces for explaining abstract computer network principles. In *Proceedings - Frontiers in Education Conference, FIE*. 1–8. https://doi.org/10.1109/FIE.2016.7757573
27. Clifford De Raffaele, Serengul Smith, and Orhan Gemikonakli. 2016. Teaching and learning queueing theory concepts using Tangible User Interfaces. In *2016 IEEE Int Conference on Teaching, Assessment, and Learning for Engineering (TALE)*, 194–201. https://doi.org/10.1109/TALE.2016.7851794
28. Clifford De Raffaele, Serengul Smith, and Orhan Gemikonakli. 2017. The Application of Tangible User Interfaces for Teaching and Learning in Higher Education. In *Innovative Teaching and Learning in Higher Education* (illustrate), John Branch (ed.). Libri Publishing, 215–226.
29. Clifford De Raffaele, Serengul Smith, and Orhan Gemikonakli. 2017. Explaining multi-threaded task

scheduling using tangible user interfaces in higher educational contexts. In *2017 IEEE Global Engineering Education Conf (EDUCON)*, 1383–1390. https://doi.org/10.1109/EDUCON.2017.7943028

30. J.V. Ringwood and G. Galvin. 2002. Computer-aided learning in artificial neural networks. *IEEE Transactions on Education* 45, 4: 380–387. https://doi.org/10.1109/TE.2002.804401
31. B Schneider, J Wallace, P Blikstein, and R Pea. 2013. Preparing for Future Learning with a Tangible User Interface: The Case of Neuroscience. *IEEE Transactions on Learning Technologies* 6, 2: 117–129. https://doi.org/10.1109/TLT.2013.15
32. Bertrand Schneider, Paulo Blikstein, and Wendy Mackay. 2012. Combinatorix: Tangible user interface that supports collaborative learning of probabilities. *ITS '12 Proceedings of the 2012 ACM international conference on Interactive tabletops and surfaces*: 129–132. https://doi.org/10.1145/2396636.2396656
33. Bertrand Schneider, Patrick Jermann, Guillaume Zufferey, and Pierre Dillenbourg. 2011. Benefits of a tangible interface for collaborative learning and interaction. *IEEE Transactions on Learning Technologies* 4, 3: 222–232. https://doi.org/10.1109/TLT.2010.36
34. Orit Shaer, Consuelo Valdes, Sirui Liu, Kara Lu, Kimberly Chang, Wendy Xu, Traci L. Haddock, Swapnil Bhatia, Douglas Densmore, and Robert Kincaid. 2014. Designing reality-based interfaces for experiential bio-design. *Personal and Ubiquitous Computing* 18, 6: 1515–1532. https://doi.org/10.1007/s00779-013-0752-1
35. SharkTime Software. 2013. Sharky Neural Network - Classification neural network in action. Retrieved 26 September 2017 from http://sharktime.com/us_SharkyNeuralNetwork.html
36. Alexander Skulmowski and Günter Daniel Rey. 2017. Bodily effort enhances learning and metacognition: Investigating the relation between physical effort and cognition using dual-process models of embodiment. *Advances in Cognitive Psychology* 13, 1: 3–10. https://doi.org/10.5709/acp-0202-9
37. Daniel Smilkov and Shan Carter. 2017. A Neural Network Playground.
38. Julia E. Stephenson, Clifford Brown, and Darren K. Griffin. 2008. Electronic delivery of lectures in the university environment: An empirical comparison of three delivery styles. *Computers and Education* 50, 3: 640–651. https://doi.org/10.1016/j.compedu.2006.08.007
39. Akiko Takahashi, Yasuhiro Kashiwaba, Toshiaki Okumura, Toshihiko Ando, Kuniaki Yajima, Yoshihiro Hayakawa, Motomu Takeshige, and Tatsuo Uchida. 2016. Design of advanced active and autonomous learning system for computing education - A3 learning system. In *Proceedings of 2015 IEEE International Conference on Teaching, Assessment and Learning for Engineering, TALE 2015*, 77–82. https://doi.org/10.1109/TALE.2015.7386020
40. Joshua Tanenbaum and Angela Tomizu. 2008. Narrative Meaning Creation in Interactive Storytelling. *International Journal of Computational Science* 2, 1: 3–20.
41. Theano Development Team. 2016. Theano: A Python framework for fast computation of mathematical expressions. *arXiv e-prints* abs/1605.0.
42. Danli Wang, Lan Zhang, Chao Xu, Haichen Hu, and Yunfeng Qi. 2016. A Tangible Embedded Programming System to Convey Event-Handling Concept. *Proceedings of the TEI '16: Tenth International Conference on Tangible, Embedded, and Embodied Interaction - TEI '16*: 133–140. https://doi.org/10.1145/2839462.2839491
43. K.A. Williams and A.M.L. Cavallo. 1995. Reasoning Ability, Meaningful Learning, and Students' Understanding of Physics Concepts: Relating Students' Reasoning Ability and Learning Styles To Their Physics Misconceptions. *Journal of College Science Teaching* 24, 5: 311–314.
44. Carmen R. Wilson Van Voorhis and Betsy L Morgan. 2007. Understanding Power and Rules of Thumb for Determining Sample Sizes. *Tutorials in Quantitative Methods for Psychology* 3, 2: 43–50. https://doi.org/10.20982/tqmp.03.2.p043
45. Oren Zuckerman, Saeed Arida, and Mitchel Resnick. 2005. Extending Tangible Interfaces for Education: Digital Montessori-inspired Manipulatives. *CHI'05 Proceedings of the SIGCHI Conference on Human Factors in CS*: 859–868. https://doi.org/10.1145/1054972.1055093

Familiarisation: Restructuring Layouts with Visual Learning Models

Kashyap Todi[1,2] kashyap.todi@gmail.com
Jussi Jokinen[1] jussi.jokinen@aalto.fi
Kris Luyten[2] kris.luyten@uhasselt.be
Antti Oulasvirta[1] antti.oulasvirta@aalto.fi

[1]Department of Communications and Networking
Aalto University
Helsinki, Finland

[2]Hasselt University - tUL - Flanders Make
Diepenbeek, Belgium

ABSTRACT
In domains where users are exposed to large variations in visuo-spatial features among designs, they often spend excess time searching for common elements (*features*) in familiar locations. This paper contributes computational approaches to restructuring layouts such that features on a new, unvisited interface can be found quicker. We explore four concepts of *familiarisation*, inspired by the human visual system (HVS), to automatically generate a familiar design for each user. Given a history of previously visited interfaces, we restructure the spatial layout of the new (unseen) interface with the goal of making its elements more easily found. *Familiariser* is a browser-based implementation that automatically restructures webpage layouts based on the visual history of the user. Our evaluation with users provides first evidence favouring familiarisation.

Author Keywords
Visual search; Graphical layouts; Computational design; Adaptive user interfaces

INTRODUCTION
This paper addresses a common predicament in interaction with graphical user interfaces: from blogs to banking and mobile apps, users encounter a wide diversity of visual designs. Even when serving the same purpose, designs differ in terms of element positions, colouring, images, and widget types. While visual uniqueness provides for identity and brand recognition, it also implies that users are constantly confronted with learning, relearning, and accustoming to navigating new structures and different styles. For the visual system, this poses a challenge to constantly adapt the use of visual attention. By understanding how this happens, we could design and adapt interfaces automatically such that elements can be more easily found. This could make interface ecologies more usable and enjoyable for users who care less about brand identity.

Our work is motivated by the observation that the added effort experienced upon encountering unfamiliar or atypical designs depends on the cost related to visual search for new and unfamiliar visual layouts [8, 18, 35]. Consider taking a familiar design and moving an element to a different position. Users would first seek the element in its expected place and, upon failing, continue with some search strategy to locate the element that was moved, or simply give up. However, designs are likely to differ in more than one feature, requiring 'guessing' of element positions, and further frustration.

This paper investigates computational principles that restructure unfamiliar designs to designs the user considers to be familiar. More formally, our goal can be defined as follows: *Given a new design d, unfamiliar to the user, and a history of previously visited visual designs H ($d \notin H$), restructure d to minimize costs to visual search to the user.* By 'restructuring' we refer to manipulations to the visio-spatial layout, such as moving, resizing, and recolouring elements. In this paper, we call techniques that achieve this *familiarisation techniques*. These techniques exploit the capability of operating systems and browsers to change an interface design dynamically. Such computer-driven familiarisation complements efforts at design-time to ensure *consistency* and adherence to design standards and guidelines [26, 31]. At the user-end, familiarisation exploits the known processes of human visual system in visual search. This ensures that the familiarised layouts are more usable due to predictable element locations and layout structures. While consistency enforced at design time can only approximate what the user population has experienced, ensuring consistency through active familiarisation at runtime allows, in principle, 'perfect consistency' for an individual.

There are multiple competing principles on which familiarisation can be based, depending on how familiarity is defined. As these principles can lead to different techniques of familiarisation, it is important to explore their assumptions, implementations, and results. To this end, we define and formalise four principles of familiarisation, informed by theories of human visual system (HVS) and visual learning. These are implemented in *Familiariser*, a browser-based system that dynamically restructures interface layouts to make them easier to use. Results from our study indicate that familiarisation can reduce visual search times by over 10%, and also leads to over 23% lesser eye-gaze fixations.

IUI'18, March 7–11, 2018, Tokyo, Japan

DOI: https://doi.org/10.1145/3172944.3172949

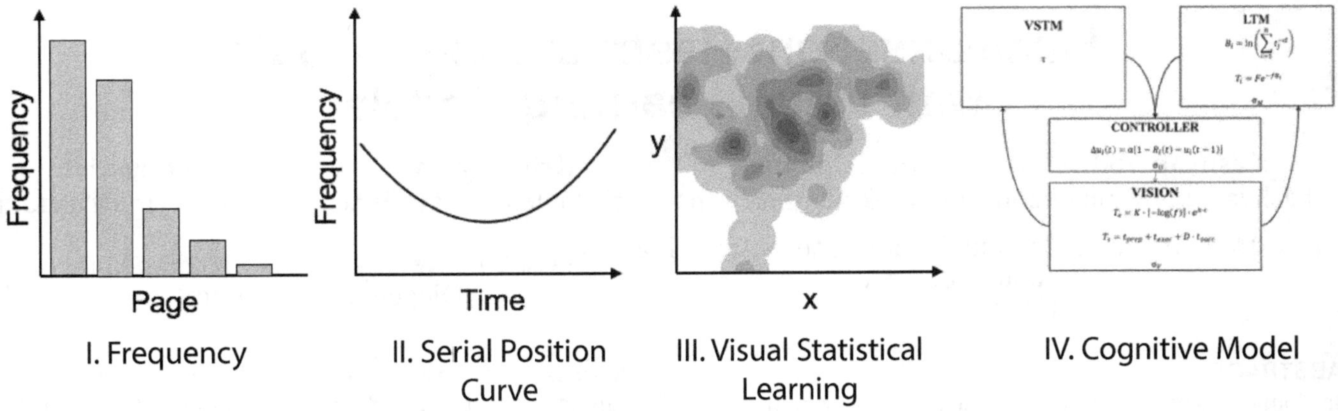

Figure 1. An illustration of the four principles for modelling familiarity. I selects the page with highest frequency; II considers frequency and time, selecting the page with the highest value on the curve; III considers positional (xy) information, and creates a probability distribution of features; IV uses a cognitive model of visual search to determine feature locations.

Overview: Four Familiarisation Principles

Familiarisation techniques can be generally defined as functions that take as input user history H and a new design d, and yield a restructured design d': $f(d,H) \rightarrow d'$. In this paper, we explore four principles with different theoretical underpinnings and consequences to how restructuring operates and how they influence results. Section *'Modelling Familiarity'* elaborates on each of these principles in greater detail.

I. Frequency: The most straightforward approach is to simply take the most *frequently used design* from H. Any new design within the same domain would be restructured such that elements appear in roughly the same places. While this design is likely to be recognizable, and simple to implement, the approach does not take into account the fact that most recent experiences are likely to dominate recall. Something that might have been frequently used in the past might be partially forgotten and overshadowed by the most recently encountered designs.

II. Serial Position Curve: The second principle implements the well-known serial position function of long-term recall [10]. Extensive empirical research on long-term and short-term memory has shown that the first and the most recently encountered objects are better recalled than ones in the middle. We implement a mathematical function that describes the relationship between order and recall probability. This is used to choose the most-likely-to-be-recalled design in H according to this function. A limitation of this and the first approach is that the visual features might not be adequately described by a single design.

III. Visual Statistical Learning: The third principle is visual statistical learning (VSL), according to which visual attention relies on a probabilistic internal model sensitive to the characteristics of the environments they have encountered before. We implement this hypothesis by building a statistical model of visual features in H. It is used to estimate the 'most probable' location of a given element. We then restructure a layout, element by element, considering this function, and finally align the elements so that they appear orderly.

IV. Cognitive Model: In our final technique, we train a cognitive model of layout learning with H and use its prediction on an empty canvas to predict the most likely positions of the elements of d. The model simulates learning of visual positions, and generates visual search patterns and times, given a layout and knowledge on that layout [18]. As an input it requires H and associated visitation durations, and optionally also considers element frequencies or relevance of elements. In this, it is similar to the previous approach. However, the model generates the actual eye movement patterns and visual search times, in addition to generating the memorability of location elements. It also simulates forgetting of layouts that have been visited only shortly and further back in time. This allows the model to be used for evaluating automatically how the familiarised layout will impact the user's behaviour, as well as how the user learns the new layout.

RELATED WORK

At its core, our work is situated within the domains of layout generation and restructuring, and user interface adaptation. We discuss prior literature that has dealt with these two themes, and draw comparisons to our work.

Layout Generation and Interface Restructuring

Automatic generation of layouts, and restructuring existing designs, have received significant attention by researchers and practitioners. One of the main rationales behind automatic generation is that it simplifies or eliminates the design task, making it possible for programmers or non-designers to create interfaces. Restructuring of designs allow for systematic improvement in usability and aesthetics of interfaces. Prior works have often used rules and heuristics to generate layouts that adhere to specific design guidelines [3, 6, 27, 28, 30], or example-based retargeting by mining existing designs [20, 21]. Our work situates itself in the area of model-based interface generation. Model-based techniques [5, 6, 30, 34] tackle the design problem by first abstracting the user interface as a set of models, which are then used to steer the generation or restructuring. There have been several prior systems, dating back to the 1980s, such as [4, 17, 24, 29, 36], that apply model-based approaches to interface (re-)design.

The above techniques and implementations have largely considered the user population as a whole, and not individuals or groups of users. There has also been some significant work done to address different groups of users. Ability-based design [38] focuses on creating interfaces that take into account different requirements or restrictions, and optimise them towards specific abilities (e.g. [14, 33]). Culture-based design [19] took into account differences among different cultures, and used this as a basis for creating multiple designs of the same interface, each suited to a specific group of users. While all these works have considered a subset of the population, or specific preferences and requirements of groups of users, they generally do not address design on the per-user level, and also do not take into account individual users' past experiences or usage history. In contrast, with SUPPLE, Gajos et al. [11, 13] defined user interface generation as an optimisation problem that took a set of user interactions as input, and used this to generate an optimal solution. By doing so, the system could take into account specific user requirements and abilities, and create individualised interfaces for each user. HIGHLIGHT [23] enabled re-authoring of existing websites based on tracing how the user interacts with the site, and created mobile versions customised to the user tasks and mobile devices. UNIFORM [25] bears a lot of resemblance to our work, as it takes into account a user's history to automatically generated remote control interfaces. UNIFORM differs from our work since it does not restructure existing interfaces, yet focuses on generating consistent user interfaces that provide access to existing functionalities on new platforms. Additionally, the user history is limited to one source design, and the work focuses on the engineering aspects of restructuring an interface to match the source, and not on the systematic selection or generation of source designs from an extended history. The general approach adopted by previous works on per-user model-based interface generation has been to model the user as a one-time activity, before generating an optimised interface. Familiarisation, on the other hand, captures the complete user history, and each time a new interface is encountered, it generates a just-in-time redesigned interface based on an updated familiarity model. Interfaces can thus evolve over time and usage, and (re-)design becomes a continuous activity.

Run-time Adaptation of Interfaces

As highlighted above, familiarisation presents an approach to adapt and restructure interfaces at runtime. Such an approach falls under the category of 'adaptive user interfaces'—interfaces that can adapt or modify themselves while being used. There have been several works on adaptive UIs previously. Past systems have used different criteria for adapting interfaces. For example, the Walking User Interface in [38] adapted based on whether the user is stationary or walking. In the [12], Gajos presents UIs that adapt to users' current tasks. In contrast to use scenario or current task, Familiariser adapts an interface layout based on users' history, and exposure to previous interfaces belonging to the same domain. A common criticism and shortcoming of adaptive UIs is that unpredictability and cost of adaptation can negate the benefits provided [15, 22]. Since we focus on adapting newly visited interfaces that the user has not previously used or learnt, it does not suffer from these drawbacks. Thus, by incorporating model-based design generation, and just-in-time interface adaptation, our work attempts to leverage recall and visual learning, and provide users access to interfaces tailored to their expectations and mental models.

MODELLING FAMILIARITY

What we call 'familiarity' is a complex cognitive phenomenon influenced by several factors related to how people learn visual search. We approach the problem by exploring progressively sophisticated principles inspired by theories of HVS and human memory.

At the highest level, these principles break down to two groups: (a) page-wise familiarity; (b) feature-wise familiarity. In *page-wise familiarity*, an entire layout (e.g., webpage) is recognised as one unit. It is assumed that users learn and recall entire pages and their visual layouts. On the other hand, feature-wise familiarity considers high-level features on webpages as individual units. For example, logos, navigation menus, and search-boxes, can be considered as features, and users learn and recall these recurring features across different pages. Based on these two cases, we explore four principles:

Principle I: Frequency

This is the most straightforward *page-wise* approach to defining familiarity. It is informed by the frequency effect: frequently encountered items are more likely to be recalled than less frequently encountered. More specifically, the number of encounters directly affects both retrieval time and retention probability: more frequently practised items are recalled faster and easier [2]. The interface (webpage) that has been encountered the most number of times (i.e., most frequently visited), and for the longest durations, is assumed to be the most familiar to the user, and is thus used as the base design to which new pages are familiarised:

$$f_{page} = n_{visits} * t_{average} \tag{1}$$

where f_{page} is the familiarity score of a page, n_{visits} is number of visits, and $t_{average}$ is average duration of visits (in seconds). This results in a one-to-one retargeting of one page to another.

Principle II: Serial Position Curve

While frequency of usage can be a reasonable method to predict the most familiar interface in simple scenarios, as user histories get larger over time, this is susceptible to failure. Usage-based aspects such as first exposure to a page, recency of visits, and intervals between visits, are not considered by the first model. Firstly, not only frequency of rehearsals, but also their recency, affects recall time and probability: recently encountered and practised items are recalled faster and more probably [2]. In addition to recency, there is also an effect of primacy, where items that have been encountered first are better remembered than later items [16]. Together, the primacy and recency effects create a U-shaped curve (a *serial position curve*). It maps items encountered in the past to probability of recall: the first and last items are more likely to be recalled better.

This leads to a *page-wise* approach that considers:

1. *Frequency (v):* The frequency of visits to a given page, denoting how often a page is visited.
2. *Recency (r):* The recency of visit to a page, denoting when the page was last visited.
3. *Primacy (p):* The order of visits to different pages, or the sequence in which unique pages are encountered.

For each of these, scores are calculated for every page in the history by ranking them. By aggregating scores for all factors, for each page, we can calculate a familiarity score for every page, and hence determine the most familiar interface. Thus, we compute the following scores:

1. *Frequency Score (S_v):* This is the ratio of the visit count for the given page to the total visit count of all pages in the history.
$$S_v = n_{page}/n_{total} \tag{2}$$
where S_v is the frequency score, n_{page} is number of visits to page, and n_{total} is total number of visits to all pages.
2. *Recency Score (S_r):* This takes into account the decaying aspect of memory. The number of other pages that are visited since the user last visited the given page negatively influences the familiarity. The score is normalised (most recently visited page has a score of 1), and this reduces as recency increases
$$S_r = 1 - r_{page}/n_{total} \tag{3}$$
where S_r is the recency score, r_{page} is recency of a page, and n_{total} is total number of visits to all pages.
3. *Primacy Score (S_p):* Pages that are encountered first tend to be better recalled than later pages. This effect is known as primacy, and the *primacy score* takes this into account, where earlier pages have a higher score. The score is normalised (first visited page has a score of 1), and subsequently reduces for following pages.
$$S_p = 1 - ((p_{page} - 1)/n_{pages}) \tag{4}$$
where S_p is the primacy score, p_{page} is visit order number for the page, and n_{pages} is number of unique pages visited.

By aggregating these scores, we derive the familiarity score for a page:

$$F_{page} = \alpha * S_v + \beta * S_r + \gamma * S_p \tag{5}$$

where F_{page} is the familiarity score for the page, α, β, γ are weights for the three factors, and $\alpha + \beta + \gamma = 1$.

In our implementation, we assign equal weights to frequency and recency, and suggest that order has a lower effect on familiarity, thus assigning it a lower weight. Thus, the values we use are: $\alpha = \beta = 0.4$, $\gamma = 0.2$.

The page with the highest familiarity score ($max\ F_{page}$) is considered to be the familiar page for a user, and is selected as the basis for familiarisation.

Figure 2 presents a sample scenario, where a user visits four unique pages multiple times. As the user visits different pages, Figure 2(a) illustrates evolution in recorded usage metrics and scores, along with page selection results as per principles I and II.

Principle III: Visual Statistical Learning

This definition takes into account the statistical frequency with which different design features occurred in history H. This hypothesis is based on theories of visual statistical learning [7], according to which visual search strategies are sensitive to the statistical structure of the visual environment.

A *feature* is defined as a high-level semantic element, and can be composed of multiple low-level elements. For example, a website's logo is a feature, and could be composed of an image and a link element. By aggregating the commonly found positions of each feature among the visited pages in a user's history, we can determine the most familiar characteristics for each feature, and use this as the familiar design. Unlike in the previous principles, the resultant familiar design here is not a single page from the history, but a *feature mesh* consisting of familiar features from multiple pages in the user's history.

To generate this feature mesh, or familiar design, we first generate spatial probability distribution maps for each encountered feature. In these maps, for pages in the history, every for every pixel occupied by a particular feature, the spatial probability is incremented. Features are weighed according to familiarity scores (F_{page}) of each page (from #2). Thus, a feature appearing on a more familiar page has a higher influence on the probability distribution. For each feature, the value (position) with the highest probability is selected to create the familiar design consisting of all detected features. Figure 2(b) illustrates the computed probability distribution maps and selected positions for different features, for the given scenario.

Principle IV: Visual Sampling Based on a Generative Cognitive Model

This definition uses a generative approach, where a model of visual search is used to generate gaze fixations as the simulated user is searching targets on a layout. The simulation integrates models of eye movements, visual short-term memory, and associative long-term memory, and proposes that visual search is the interaction of these three resources [18]. Given a user history with layouts, including locations of elements on the layouts, the model generates eye movement patterns as it simulates human-like visual search on the layouts. Using the model of eye movements [32], the simulation encodes elements on the layout until it has found the target. For each element, the encoding time is

$$T_e = K \cdot [-log(f)] \cdot e^{k \cdot \varepsilon}, \tag{6}$$

where f is the frequency of the object, either supplied externally to the model or assumed to be uniform, ε is the distance of the target from current eye fixation, and K and k are scaling constants, adapted from the literature [32]. T_e increases

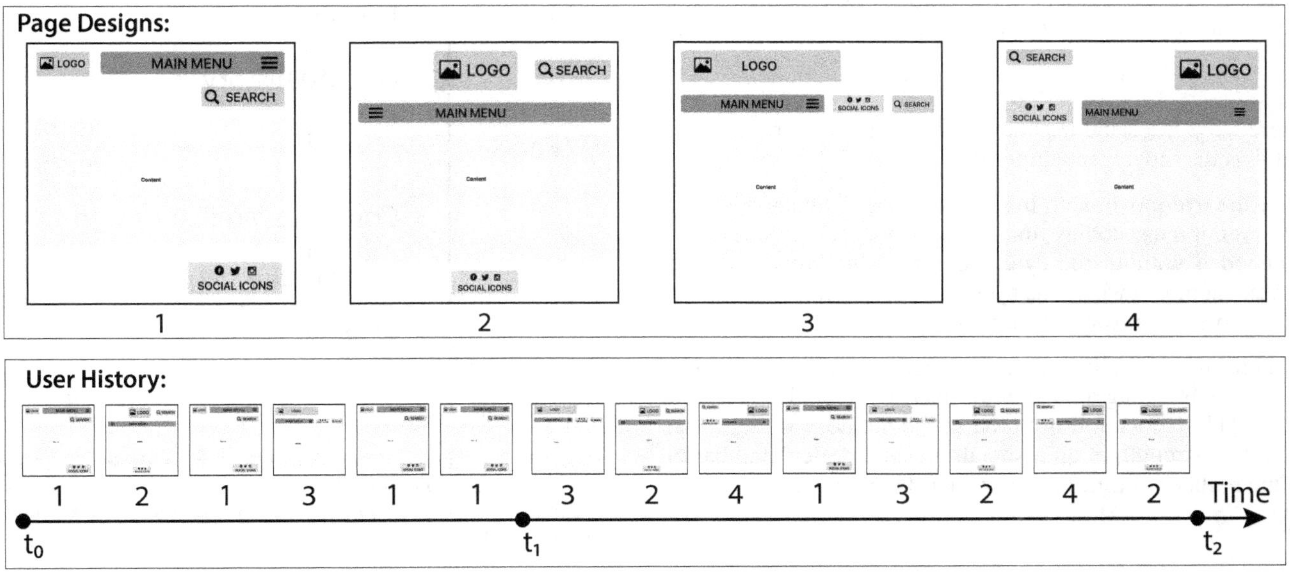

Timestamp	Page	Frequency (v)	Recency (r)	Primacy (p)	Frequency Score (S_v)	Recency Score (S_r)	Primacy Score (S_p)	Familiarity Score (F_{page})	
t_1	**1**	**3**	0	1	0.667	1.000	1.000	**0.867**	← Selected by I and II
	2	1	4	2	0.167	0.333	0.667	0.333	
	3	1	2	3	0.167	0.666	0.333	0.400	
	4	0	-	-	-	-	-	0	
t_2	**1**	**5**	4	1	0.357	0.714	1.000	**0.629**	← Selected by I
	2	4	0	2	0.286	1.000	0.750	**0.664**	← Selected by II
	3	3	3	3	0.214	0.786	0.500	0.500	
	4	2	2	4	0.143	0.857	0.250	0.479	

(a) Usage Metrics and Scores

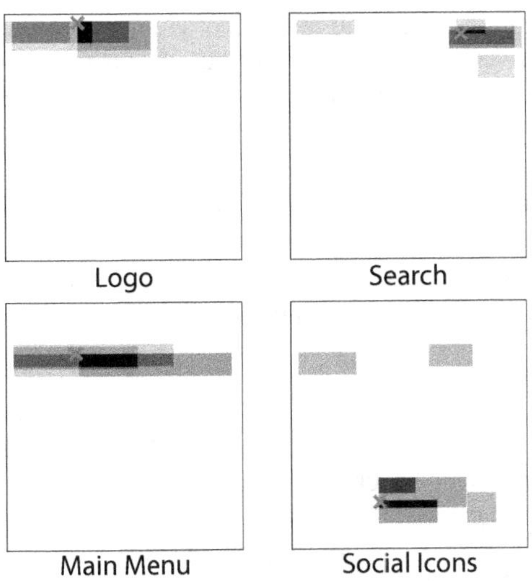

(b) Probability Distribution Maps (for III)

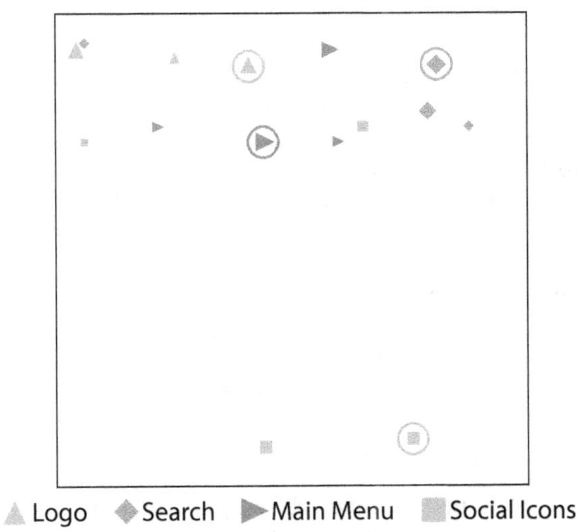

(c) Activations (for IV)

Figure 2. Scenario with 4 different page designs. The user history shows a timeline of page visits (for simplicity, uniform visit durations are assumed across pages). (a) Evolution of metrics and scores at two timestamps (t_1, t_2), and page selection outcomes. (b) Computed probability distribution maps for key features at t_2. Red $\times$ symbols indicate the selected position for each feature. (c) Activations for features at t_2. Circled activations indicate the predicted positions for each feature.

exponentially as the target is further from the fixation, but the visual system may compensate this by initiating a fast eye movement to gaze closer to the target, with movement time of

$$T_s = t_{prep} + t_{exec} + D \cdot t_{sacc}, \tag{7}$$

where t_{prep}, t_{exec}, and t_{sacc} are constants from literature [32] and D is the movement amplitude.

After the eye movement, the target needs to be encoded (6). However, if the encoding time is less than t_{prep}, then the target is encoded without the eyes moving. This creates an eye movement model where the eyes move only when the target is too far to encode from the current gaze point.

In addition to visual search, the model simulates learning of layouts by using an activation-based associative memory model [1], its location is stored in the memory storage. An activation strength of an association can be calculated based on the number of times the target has been found:

$$B_i = \ln(\sum_{j=1}^{n} t_j^{-d}), \tag{8}$$

where t_j is the time since the j:th time of finding the target i, and d is a decay parameter, set from literature [18]. As the model learns the layout, it can use the associative memory to recall the position of the target without having to visually search for it. The model is able to recall the position of the target, if $B_i > 0$, with noise added from normal distribution [18]. Recall time is:

$$T_i = Fe^{-fB_i}, \tag{9}$$

where F and f are scaling constants, set based on literature [18].

Longer history with a layout results in higher associative activations, and faster, more expert-like performance in finding targets. From the activations, the model can predict where the user will gaze, given a layout and user history. Figure 2(c) illustrates activations, and predicted positions, for the given scenario.

FAMILIARISER: SYSTEM OVERVIEW

We implemented the above principles of familiarity in *Familiariser*, a browser-styled application that allows users to visit webpages and enables access to familiarised versions, adapted towards each user. As illustrated in Figure 3, when a user visits a page, the following pipeline is executed:

1. **Parse page:** The page source (HTML) is parsed by the system. Key elements, representing high-level features, are detected and labelled.

2. **Update history:** If the visited page does not exist in the history, it is added; if it was previously visited, the corresponding entry in the history is updated for the page. Additionally, familiarity scores, described in the previous section, are updated for every page in the user history.

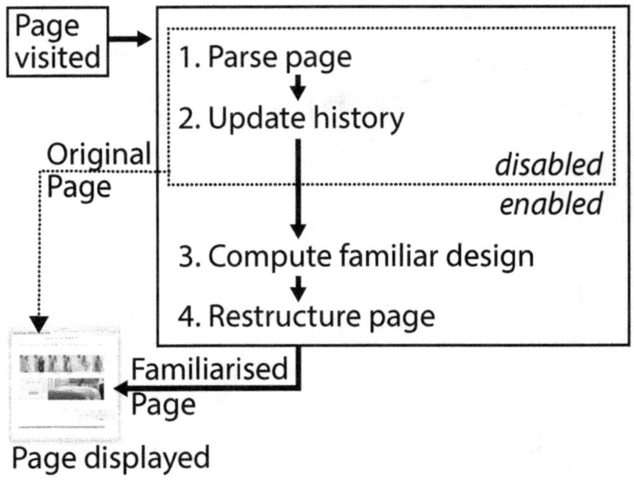

Figure 3. To compute a restructuring for a page, the history is updated for visited pages. Once familiarisation is enabled, the familiar design is computed using an HVS principle, and restructuring is instantiated via layout optimisation prior to rendering on a web browser.

While familiarisation is disabled, the pipeline ends at this point, and the original page is displayed as is. Once familiarisation is enabled, the following steps (3 and 4) are executed to familiarise the page.

3. **Compute familiar design:** Based on usage history, we compute the familiar page design, to be used as the basis for restructuring the new page.

4. **Restructure page:** The new page is restructured using positional values of matching features from the familiar design, and repositioning the corresponding elements on the visited page. Overlaps may occur in the restructured page. Familiariser resolves any such overlaps while attempting to best maintain relative alignments of elements on the page. This ensures a valid layout, without obscuring or omitting any contents. The familiarised page is finally displayed to the user.

Figure 4 illustrates two examples of results obtained by Familiariser, given a user history and original (unfamiliar) page, for each of the four principles of familiarity.

In the remainder of this section, we describe the various components of the system in greater detail.

Page Parsing

A *feature* can be defined as a task-level element [37]. They are actionable elements, with a well-defined purpose, such as the logo, search bar, buttons or icons to login and access a user account, or the shopping cart on e-commerce sites, etc. Features can be composed of several low-level HTML DOM elements. For familiarisation, it is necessary to first detect these features on a given page. Prior works have explored element detection when underlying sources were not available. Prefab [9] presented a pixel-based approach to reverse-engineering the GUI. Sikuli [39] allowed users to take screenshots of widgets and elements, and use these for search and automation of visual interfaces. For webpages, however, the underlying source files are openly accessible.

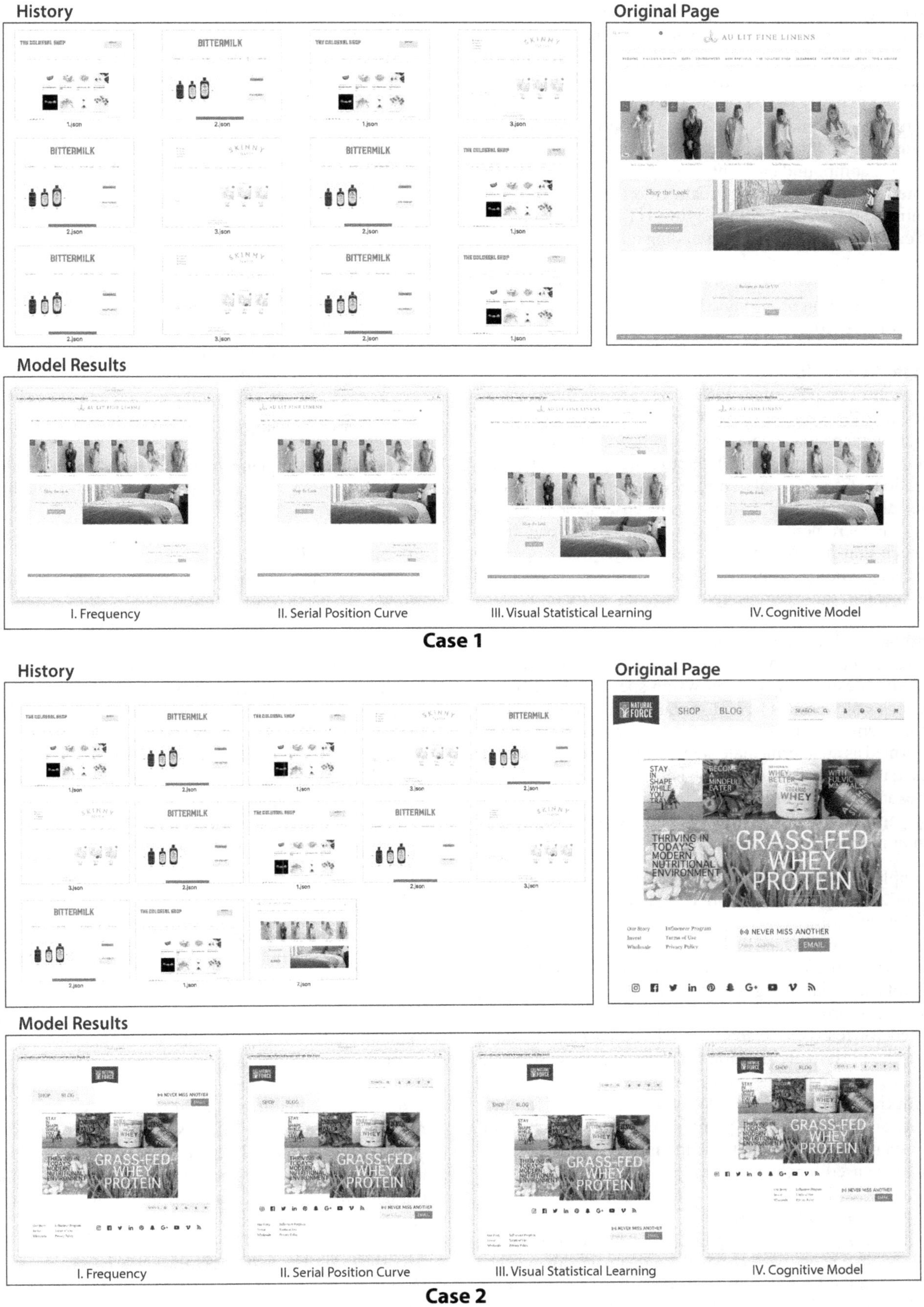

Figure 4. A visual comparison of the results for the four presented familiarity models, for two independent cases. For a given user history, when a new (unfamiliar) page is visited, each of the models may produce varying results.

Previously, Webzeitgeist [20] used CSS selectors to detect common features. Familiariser parses the underlying DOM tree of a page, and analyses DOM tags, identifiers, and linked CSS classes, of elements to automatically detect features on the page. We use partial string matching to detect commonly-used names, and map them to corresponding features. A feature can either be a leaf node in the DOM tree, or a compound element consisting of several smaller elements. The detection of features relies on appropriate naming and tagging of underlying HTML elements, and this can be a limiting factor in finding all matching features across different pages. Feature recognition could be improved by employing other computational methods, such as image recognition or machine learning, but this is out of the scope of this work.

Usage History Updates

For each user, page visit history is recorded, and usage-based metrics are updated each time new pages are visited. For each page, a unique entry in the history is maintained, and includes information related to time spent on the page (duration), frequency of visits, recency, and order of visits. When an existing page in history is re-visited, the frequency (f_{page}) is incremented, and the recency of that page is reset such that it is the "most recent" page (i.e. $r_{page} = 0$). For every other page in the history, the recency (r_{page}) is incremented, thus decreasing the recency score (S_r).

Familiar Design Computation

All pages in the history are considered to compute the familiar layout design. For web browsing specifically, different categories of websites have distinctly different features. To avoid mismatch in domain, website categorisation can be performed as an intermediate step, and only pages within the same category as the currently-visited page are considered. For example, if the user intends to visit a shopping website, only pages from the shopping domain are considered while computing the base layout design.

Principles I and II consider a single page as the 'familiar design'. Familiarity scores are calculated accordingly, and the highest-scoring page is selected. Matching features are extracted from the familiar design, and their xy positions are used for the base layout design. Principles III and 4 compute familiar designs based on all pages in the user history. For principle III, probability distribution maps are created for features detected on all visited pages. Using these, the most likely position for each feature is estimated, resulting in a base design where all feature are located appropriately. For principle IV, activation points for each feature are computed. The point with the highest activation, for a feature, is predicted to be the most familiar position, and hence used for the base design.

Target Page Restructuring

The base design that is computed is used to restructure the newly-visited page. Features on the target page are matched to those on the base design, and repositioned accordingly. In [21], retargeting occasionally resulted in truncated or cropped content due to size mismatch. In our approach, while repositioning, dimensions of the original elements are maintained so as to avoid truncation of contents. This can however result in some overlapping or occlusion of elements.

Overlap Resolution

Overlaps are resolved by setting up a series of overlap-redressal rules. Examples of rules used in Familiariser are as follows:

(a) Left-alignment or top-alignment of two (or more) elements should not be violated. If this is violated, a penalty is applied.

(b) Movement of any element from its preferred (horizontal) location entails a penalty.

(c) The vertical or horizontal sequence of any pair of elements should be honoured.

(d) The canvas width should not be changed. The height may be changed if needed.

The rules are implemented using any standard integer-linear programming solver, resulting in a valid layout without overlaps.

Enabling Familiarisation

During the initial stages of browsing, familiarisation is *disabled.* As users visit different pages, they gradually learn visual layouts of these, thus increasing chances of recall during future visits. Once a user is fluent with a small set of pages, familiarisation is *enabled*, and newly visited pages are be adapted to computed familiar designs. However, we need to determine the ideal moment to enable familiarisation, to make it effective. There is a trade-off between familiarising too early and too late. If enabled too early, users may not have learnt visited pages sufficiently, thus future pages would not benefit from adaptation. On the other hand, if familiarisation is delayed, then users might have already been exposed to a large number of diverse designs, thus making recall harder. For the purpose of our study, we determined (by trial-and-error) that enabling familiarisation after 25 page visits was favourable, given that the number of unique pages was less than or equal to 5. For future systems, familiarity scores can be used to empirically determine when to enable familiarisation, or this could be customisable per user.

With automatic (always-on) familiarisation, pages are automatically adapted once enabled. Familiariser also supports manual (on-demand) familiarisation, where users can request for a familiarised version of page. Here, the original page is displayed by default, and a familiarised version is rendered only when requested. This is similar to how web services such as translation and reader-friendly modes enable users to request for adapted versions of a page. Manual familiarisation obviates the need for a determining a fixed point at which adaptations are enabled.

ARCHITECTURE AND IMPLEMENTATION

Familiariser is implemented in Swift, on MacOS 10.13, as a standalone browser-styled application. In the back-end, the application contains a history model for each user, containing a dictionary of visited websites. Along with the website URL, and parsed contents, each website object also contains relevant usage information required for modelling familiarity (as described in section 'Modelling Familiarity'). Every time a new page is visited, custom JavaScript code parses the page source, and converts the page into a flattened JSON file, containing absolute (xy) positions of elements, as they appear on the browser, and other element properties, such as tags and CSS styles, required to recreate the page and to infer features. The JSON file is parsed, to construct a webpage object. The cognitive learning model (described in principle IV) is implemented using Common Lisp. Each time familiarisation is required, a CSV file containing relevant history information, including access timestamp, duration, and linked JSON file name, is generated. The CSV file and required JSON files for all webpages are passed as input to the learning model. As output, the model generates a CSV file containing activation points for all detected features, along with confidence values, and returns this to Familiariser. Familiariser uses this to select the desirable positions for features, to generate the familiar design. Overlaps in layout elements are resolved by passing a file containing element positions to a Java application. The application applies overlap-redressal rules to each element. We use an IBM CPLEX linear programming solver to optimally resolve any detected overlaps. The solver returns a corresponding file with resultant element positions. This is used by Familiariser to generate the final valid layout, which is then displayed to the user.

EVALUATION

The goal of our evaluation is to verify the concept of familiarisation, and the presented system. We seek to answer the question: *Does familiarisation improve performance in web browsing for end-users?* To this end, we conducted a comparative user study, and report on quantitative results. We compared original (unmodified) designs against familiarised designs in a study where users were asked to point-and-click on different features on the displayed page. We used the visual statistical learning principle (principle III) for familiarisation as these selection tasks were quite brief in duration. As dependent variables, we analysed visual search time, approximated by pointing time, and number of eye-gaze fixations per target feature. Comparing these two cases enables us to evaluate the potential effects of familiarisation during real-world usage. For the test case, we chose the domain of shopping websites, a frequently used category of webpages that are also plenty in number. These websites typically contain similar features yet vary vastly in their layouts and presentation of these features. This makes them a good test candidate for Familiariser, and provides a realistic use scenario for the study.

Study Tasks

For the study, participants were given the task of selecting (clicking on) a feature element on the displayed webpage, in a browser-based application. Webpages were selected randomly, from a dataset of 30 shopping sites. The target feature was also selected randomly from the page, and included commonly occurring elements, such as logos, navigation menus, search boxes, among others. Participants were requested to perform tasks quickly yet accurately as possible, and avoid unnecessary pauses. As tasks were performed, the software logged mouse movements, click events, and eye gaze information, including eye position (averaged) and fixations.

Apparatus

A 13" MacBook Pro with Retina Display (2560-by-1600 pixels), running MacOS 10.13, was used for the study. The browser-based Familiariser software was displayed as a full-screen application. We selected 30 shopping websites to create the dataset, excluding commonly-used shopping pages to avoid bias. Webpages used in the dataset were rendered offline to avoid delays. Tasks were completed using the in-built trackpad. All cursor motions and events were logged by the study software. For eye-tracking, an EyeTribe Tracker[1] was used, along with a custom Python program to log gaze positions and fixations.

Participants

We recruited 16 participants, aged 21 to 36 (mean 29), with no visual impairments. All participants reported frequent web usage (daily), and also reported exposure to shopping websites. Participants completed tasks with both original (unmodified) and test (familiarised) pages, in a within-subject study design.

Method

During the experiment, participants were exposed to a set of different websites. Before a website was displayed, they were presented with the task of selecting (clicking on) a particular feature element (e.g. logo, main menu, search box) on the page. The target feature element was selected at random from the page to be displayed. The timed trial started once the participant confirmed they were ready, by clicking on a confirmation button. This button was consistently placed at the centre of the screen, ensuring a constant starting point for the cursor during all trials.

The experiment was divided into two phases: *Learning Phase* and *Test Phase*.

1. Learning Phase

For each participant, the system selected 5 webpages, at random, from the dataset of 30 pages, for the learning phase. The learning dataset thus varied for each participant. During each trial, a page from this subset was selected at random, and the participant was asked to point and click at a randomly chosen feature on the page. A total of 25 trials were performed during this phase, and this was used to construct the 'usage history' for the participant.

2. Test Phase

Once the participant had experienced this subset of pages in the training phase, the experiment moved on to the test phase. The 5 pages used in the learning phase were stored in the user history, and excluded from the test dataset. Similar to the learning phase, participants again browsed to randomly selected pages, and were asked to select a target feature on the page. During the test trials, either the original (unmodified) page or a familiarised version was presented to the user, chosen

[1] www.theeyetribe.com

	Visual Search Time	Fixation Count
Original	2.8 seconds	3.4
Familiarised	2.5 seconds	2.6

Table 1. Summary of results for average visual search time and fixation count per target feature.

at random. Participants performed a total of 100 timed trials during the test phase.

The average duration of the study was approximately 30 minutes for each participant.

Results

We created a linear mixed model with search time as dependent variable, page type (Original vs. Familiarised) as fixed independent variable, and participant id and page URL as random variables. Grand mean search times were Original = 2.8 seconds and Familiarised = 2.5 seconds. The difference was statistically significant, $t(663) = 5.3, p < .001$, with model $F(1,663) = 28.5, p < .001$. In standardised units, the benefit of familiarised layout was $\beta = 0.35$.

We compared similarly the number of fixations per target. Grand mean fixation counts were Original = 3.4 and Familiarised = 2.6. The difference was statistically significant, $t(596) = 4.7, p < .001$, with model $F(1,596) = 22.3, p < .001$. In standardised units, the benefit of familiarised layout was $\beta = 0.35$.

The above results indicate that familiarisation improved user performance by reducing both visual search time and number of gaze fixations. Our study evaluates familiarisation using the visual statistical learning principle. A comparison of all four principles requires a more extensive study, and is left as subject of future work.

DISCUSSION

Our work on familiarisation of visual designs situates itself in the field of automatically generated user interfaces that adapt to individual users. It deals with concepts of recall and visual learning to make interfaces appear closer to each user's expectations. We explore four principles of familiarity, inspired by the human visual system, and grounded in literature. Familiariser implements these in an end-user system that captures users' history, and restructures newly visited pages based on automatically generated familiar layout designs. Results from the empirical study provide evidence for our approach. Familiarisation significantly improves visual search time by over 10%, and reduces the number of fixations by over 23%, while searching for features on a given design.

The cost of adaptation is often a concern for adaptive user interfaces. Our work circumvents this as familiarisation restructures only new and unfamiliar designs, instead of continuously adapting or modifying frequently-used layouts. One could criticise our approach for compromising brand identity, or undermining the designer, by modifying designs. However, we argue that usability of an interface supersedes these aspects for the end-user. Additionally, Familiariser addresses this by allowing users to optionally view either original or familiarised versions of designs. Commercial browsers have also used such techniques to improve usability of webpages. For instance, 'reader-friendly mode' on browsers allows users to switch between the original page and a version enhanced for reading.

There are certain limitations for applying familiarisation universally, as it requires (1) logging of a user's history of seen layouts, (2) detailed information and representation of layouts, (3) just-in-time computations of familiar design, and (4) instantiation of page restructuring in runtime, prior to rendering it on a display. By exploring a range of principles for familiarisation, we provide alternatives that enable systems to circumvent some of these limitations. The basic frequency-based approach (principle I) is straightforward to implement, and requires minimal user history information. Serial-position curve (II) requires some additional usage information, and requires calculations of various scores to select a page as the familiar design. The feature-based principles (III and IV) require detailed information about the interface layout, and are computationally more expensive, but offer more accurate representations for a user.

While this paper, and our implementation, focuses on repositioning of features, future familiarisation efforts can apply our work to address other interface aspects, such as colours, fonts, and other visuo-perceptual properties. Such properties are often position-agnostic, and thus for these page-wise familiarisation (I or II) is preferred. Apart from addressing additional interface properties, usability and experience with user interfaces can be further improved. Future systems can explore a dual-optimisation strategy, where the familiarity model can be combined with other predictive models of human perception. Additionally, more interfaces can be covered by applying the concept of familiarity to a variety of mediums (digital, physical, hybrid). For instance, it can be possible to familiarise physical interfaces, adapting them to resemble previously encountered digital or physical interfaces. Finally, by providing a formal model of familiarity, we can implicitly gain an understanding of "unfamiliarity". This opens up possibilities of other applications such as 'unfamiliarisation' or diversification of interfaces. This could encourage alternative design goals such as exploration, or be used to draw users' attention to certain elements.

More information and material related to this paper can be found at `http://www.kashyaptodi.com/familiarisation`.

ACKNOWLEDGEMENTS

The project has partially received funding from the Academy of Finland project COMPUTED and the European Research Council (ERC) under the European Union's Horizon 2020 research and innovation programme (grant agreement 637991).

Among others, we thank Niraj Damaya for code related to overlap resolution, Markku Laine for his useful comments, and study participants for their time and involvement.

REFERENCES

1. John R Anderson, D Bothell, C Lebiere, and M Matessa. 1998. An integrated theory of list memory. *Journal of Memory And Language* 38, 4 (1998), 341–380. DOI: http://dx.doi.org/10.1006/jmla.1997.2553
2. John R Anderson, Jon M Fincham, and Scott Douglass. 1999. Practice and retention: A unifying analysis. *Journal of Experimental Psychology-Learning Memory and Cognition* 25, 5 (1999), 1120–1136.
3. Yigal Arens, Lawrence Miller, Stuart C. Shapiro, and Norman K. Sondheimer. 1988. Automatic Construction of User-interface Displays. In *Proceedings of the Seventh AAAI National Conference on Artificial Intelligence (AAAI'88)*. AAAI Press, 808–813. http://dl.acm.org/citation.cfm?id=2887965.2888108
4. Gilles Bailly, Antti Oulasvirta, Timo Kötzing, and Sabrina Hoppe. 2013. MenuOptimizer: Interactive Optimization of Menu Systems. In *Proceedings of the 26th Annual ACM Symposium on User Interface Software and Technology (UIST '13)*. ACM, New York, NY, USA, 331–342. DOI: http://dx.doi.org/10.1145/2501988.2502024
5. C. M. Beshers and S. Feiner. 1989. Scope: Automated Generation of Graphical Interfaces. In *Proceedings of the 2Nd Annual ACM SIGGRAPH Symposium on User Interface Software and Technology (UIST '89)*. ACM, New York, NY, USA, 76–85. DOI: http://dx.doi.org/10.1145/73660.73670
6. François Bodart, Anne-Marie Hennebert, Jean-Marie Leheureux, and Jean Vanderdonckt. 1994. Towards a Dynamic Strategy for Computer-aided Visual Placement. In *Proceedings of the Workshop on Advanced Visual Interfaces (AVI '94)*. ACM, New York, NY, USA, 78–87. DOI:http://dx.doi.org/10.1145/192309.192328
7. Zoya Bylinskii, Nam Wook Kim, Peter O'Donovan, Sami Alsheikh, Spandan Madan, Hanspeter Pfister, Fredo Durand, Bryan Russell, and Aaron Hertzmann. 2017. Learning Visual Importance for Graphic Designs and Data Visualizations. *arXiv preprint arXiv:1708.02660* (2017).
8. Marvin M Chun and Yuhong Jiang. 1998. Contextual cueing: Implicit learning and memory of visual context guides spatial attention. *Cognitive psychology* 36, 1 (1998), 28–71.
9. Morgan Dixon and James Fogarty. 2010. Prefab: Implementing Advanced Behaviors Using Pixel-based Reverse Engineering of Interface Structure. In *Proceedings of the SIGCHI Conference on Human Factors in Computing Systems (CHI '10)*. ACM, New York, NY, USA, 1525–1534. DOI: http://dx.doi.org/10.1145/1753326.1753554
10. Peter A Frensch. 1994. Composition during serial learning: A serial position effect. *JOURNAL OF EXPERIMENTAL PSYCHOLOGY LEARNING MEMORY AND COGNITION* 20 (1994), 423–423.
11. Krzysztof Gajos and Daniel S. Weld. 2004. SUPPLE: Automatically Generating User Interfaces. In *Proceedings of the 9th International Conference on Intelligent User Interfaces (IUI '04)*. ACM, New York, NY, USA, 93–100. DOI:http://dx.doi.org/10.1145/964442.964461
12. Krzysztof Z. Gajos, Mary Czerwinski, Desney S. Tan, and Daniel S. Weld. 2006a. Exploring the Design Space for Adaptive Graphical User Interfaces *(AVI '06)*. ACM, New York, NY, USA, 201–208. DOI: http://dx.doi.org/10.1145/1133265.1133306
13. Krzysztof Z. Gajos, Jing Jing Long, and Daniel S. Weld. 2006b. Automatically Generating Custom User Interfaces for Users with Physical Disabilities. In *Proceedings of the 8th International ACM SIGACCESS Conference on Computers and Accessibility (Assets '06)*. ACM, New York, NY, USA, 243–244. DOI: http://dx.doi.org/10.1145/1168987.1169036
14. Krzysztof Z. Gajos, Jacob O. Wobbrock, and Daniel S. Weld. 2007. Automatically Generating User Interfaces Adapted to Users' Motor and Vision Capabilities. In *Proceedings of the 20th Annual ACM Symposium on User Interface Software and Technology (UIST '07)*. ACM, New York, NY, USA, 231–240. DOI: http://dx.doi.org/10.1145/1294211.1294253
15. Saul Greenberg and Ian H. Witten. 1985. Adaptive personalized interfaces–A question of viability. *Behaviour & Information Technology* 4, 1 (1985), 31–45. DOI:http://dx.doi.org/10.1080/01449298508901785
16. Richard NA Henson. 1996. Unchained memory: Error patterns rule out chaining models of immediate serial recall. *The Quarterly Journal of Experimental Psychology: Section A* 49, 1 (1996), 80–115.
17. Christian Janssen, Anette Weisbecker, and Jürgen Ziegler. 1993. Generating User Interfaces from Data Models and Dialogue Net Specifications. In *Proceedings of the INTERACT '93 and CHI '93 Conference on Human Factors in Computing Systems (CHI '93)*. ACM, New York, NY, USA, 418–423. DOI: http://dx.doi.org/10.1145/169059.169335
18. Jussi P. P. Jokinen, Sayan Sarcar, Antti Oulasvirta, Chaklam Silpasuwanchai, Zhenxin Wang, and Xiangshi Ren. 2017. Modelling Learning of New Keyboard Layouts. In *Proceedings of the 2017 CHI Conference on Human Factors in Computing Systems (CHI '17)*. ACM, New York, NY, USA, 4203–4215. DOI: http://dx.doi.org/10.1145/3025453.3025580
19. Andruid Kerne, William A. Hamilton, and Zachary O. Toups. 2012. Culturally Based Design: Embodying Trans-surface Interaction in Rummy. In *Proceedings of the ACM 2012 Conference on Computer Supported Cooperative Work (CSCW '12)*. ACM, New York, NY, USA, 509–518. DOI: http://dx.doi.org/10.1145/2145204.2145284

20. Ranjitha Kumar, Arvind Satyanarayan, Cesar Torres, Maxine Lim, Salman Ahmad, Scott R. Klemmer, and Jerry O. Talton. 2013. Webzeitgeist: Design Mining the Web. In *Proceedings of the SIGCHI Conference on Human Factors in Computing Systems (CHI '13)*. ACM, New York, NY, USA, 3083–3092. DOI: http://dx.doi.org/10.1145/2470654.2466420

21. Ranjitha Kumar, Jerry O. Talton, Salman Ahmad, and Scott R. Klemmer. 2011. Bricolage: Example-based Retargeting for Web Design. In *Proceedings of the SIGCHI Conference on Human Factors in Computing Systems (CHI '11)*. ACM, New York, NY, USA, 2197–2206. DOI: http://dx.doi.org/10.1145/1978942.1979262

22. Talia Lavie and Joachim Meyer. 2010. Benefits and Costs of Adaptive User Interfaces. *Int. J. Hum.-Comput. Stud.* 68, 8 (Aug. 2010), 508–524. DOI: http://dx.doi.org/10.1016/j.ijhcs.2010.01.004

23. Jeffrey Nichols and Tessa Lau. 2008. Mobilization by Demonstration: Using Traces to Re-author Existing Web Sites. In *Proceedings of the 13th International Conference on Intelligent User Interfaces (IUI '08)*. ACM, New York, NY, USA, 149–158. DOI: http://dx.doi.org/10.1145/1378773.1378793

24. Jeffrey Nichols, Brad A. Myers, Michael Higgins, Joseph Hughes, Thomas K. Harris, Roni Rosenfeld, and Mathilde Pignol. 2002. Generating Remote Control Interfaces for Complex Appliances. In *Proceedings of the 15th Annual ACM Symposium on User Interface Software and Technology (UIST '02)*. ACM, New York, NY, USA, 161–170. DOI:http://dx.doi.org/10.1145/571985.572008

25. Jeffrey Nichols, Brad A. Myers, and Brandon Rothrock. 2006. UNIFORM: Automatically Generating Consistent Remote Control User Interfaces. In *Proceedings of the SIGCHI Conference on Human Factors in Computing Systems (CHI '06)*. ACM, New York, NY, USA, 611–620. DOI:http://dx.doi.org/10.1145/1124772.1124865

26. Jakob Nielsen. 1993. *Usability Engineering*. Morgan Kaufmann Publishers Inc., San Francisco, CA, USA.

27. Peter ODonovan, Aseem Agarwala, and Aaron Hertzmann. 2014. Learning Layouts for Single-PageGraphic Designs. *IEEE Transactions on Visualization and Computer Graphics* 20, 8 (Aug. 2014), 1200–1213. DOI: http://dx.doi.org/10.1109/TVCG.2014.48

28. Peter O'Donovan, Aseem Agarwala, and Aaron Hertzmann. 2015. DesignScape: Design with Interactive Layout Suggestions. In *Proceedings of the 33rd Annual ACM Conference on Human Factors in Computing Systems (CHI '15)*. ACM, New York, NY, USA, 1221–1224. DOI: http://dx.doi.org/10.1145/2702123.2702149

29. D. R. Olsen, Jr. 1989. A Programming Language Basis for User Interface. In *Proceedings of the SIGCHI Conference on Human Factors in Computing Systems (CHI '89)*. ACM, New York, NY, USA, 171–176. DOI: http://dx.doi.org/10.1145/67449.67485

30. Angel R. Puerta, Henrik Eriksson, John H. Gennari, and Mark A. Musen. 1994. Model-based Automated Generation of User Interfaces. In *Proceedings of the Twelfth National Conference on Artificial Intelligence (Vol. 1) (AAAI '94)*. American Association for Artificial Intelligence, Menlo Park, CA, USA, 471–477. http://dl.acm.org/citation.cfm?id=199288.184583

31. John Rheinfrank and Shelley Evenson. 1996. Design languages. In *Bringing design to software*. ACM, 63–85.

32. Dario D Salvucci. 2001. An Integrated Model of Eye Movements and Visual Encoding. *Cogn. Syst. Res.* 1, 4 (Feb. 2001), 201–220. DOI: http://dx.doi.org/10.1016/S1389-0417(00)00015-2

33. Sayan Sarcar, Jussi Jokinen, Antti Oulasvirta, Xiangshi Ren, Chaklam Silpasuwanchai, and Zhenxin Wang. 2018. Ability-Based Optimization: Designing Smartphone Text Entry Interface for Older Adults. *IEEE Pervasive Computing* (2018).

34. A. Sears. 1993. Layout appropriateness: a metric for evaluating user interface widget layout. *IEEE Transactions on Software Engineering* 19, 7 (Jul 1993), 707–719. DOI:http://dx.doi.org/10.1109/32.238571

35. Andrew Sears, Julie A Jacko, Josey Chu, and Francisco Moro. 2001. The role of visual search in the design of effective soft keyboards. *Behaviour & Information Technology* 20, 3 (2001), 159–166.

36. Kashyap Todi, Daryl Weir, and Antti Oulasvirta. 2016. Sketchplore: Sketch and Explore with a Layout Optimiser. In *Proceedings of the 2016 ACM Conference on Designing Interactive Systems (DIS '16)*. ACM, New York, NY, USA, 543–555. DOI: http://dx.doi.org/10.1145/2901790.2901817

37. Martijn Van Welie and Gerrit C Van der Veer. 2003. Pattern languages in interaction design: Structure and organization. In *Proceedings of interact*, Vol. 3. 1–5.

38. Jacob O. Wobbrock, Shaun K. Kane, Krzysztof Z. Gajos, Susumu Harada, and Jon Froehlich. 2011. Ability-Based Design: Concept, Principles and Examples. *ACM Trans. Access. Comput.* 3, 3, Article 9 (April 2011), 27 pages. DOI:http://dx.doi.org/10.1145/1952383.1952384

39. Tom Yeh, Tsung-Hsiang Chang, and Robert C. Miller. 2009. Sikuli: Using GUI Screenshots for Search and Automation. In *Proceedings of the 22nd Annual ACM Symposium on User Interface Software and Technology (UIST '09)*. ACM, New York, NY, USA, 183–192. DOI: http://dx.doi.org/10.1145/1622176.1622213

Two Tools are Better Than One: Tool Diversity as a Means of Improving Aggregate Crowd Performance

Jean Y. Song, Raymond Fok, Alan Lundgard, Fan Yang, Juho Kim[†], Walter S. Lasecki

CROMA Lab | MISC Group
Electrical Engineering and Computer Science
University of Michigan – Ann Arbor
{jyskwon, rayfok, arlu, yangtony}@umich.edu
wlasecki@umich.edu

[†]KIXLAB
School of Computing
KAIST – Daejeon, Republic of Korea
juhokim@kaist.ac.kr

ABSTRACT

Crowdsourcing is a common means of collecting image segmentation training data for use in a variety of computer vision applications. However, designing accurate crowd-powered image segmentation systems is challenging because defining object boundaries in an image requires significant fine motor skills and hand-eye coordination, which makes these tasks error-prone. Typically, special segmentation tools are created and then answers from multiple workers are aggregated to generate more accurate results. However, individual tool designs can bias how and where people make mistakes, resulting in shared errors that remain even after aggregation. In this paper, we introduce a novel crowdsourcing workflow that leverages *multiple tools* for the same task to increase output accuracy by reducing systematic error biases introduced by the tools themselves. When a task can no longer be broken down into more-tractable subtasks (the conventional approach taken by microtask crowdsourcing), our multi-tool approach can be used to further improve accuracy by assigning different tools to different workers. We present a series of studies that evaluate our multi-tool approach and show that it can significantly improve aggregate accuracy in semantic image segmentation.

CCS Concepts

•Information systems → Crowdsourcing; •Human-centered computing → Human computer interaction (HCI); •Computing methodologies → *Computer vision;*

Author Keywords

Crowdsourcing; human computation; multi-tool aggregation; tool diversity; semantic image segmentation; computer vision

IUI'18, March 7–11, 2018, Tokyo, Japan

ISBN 978-1-4503-4945-1/18/03...$15.00

DOI: https://doi.org/10.1145/3172944.3172948

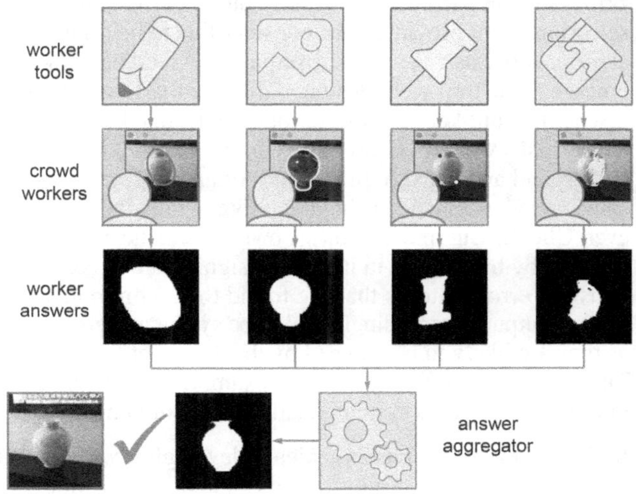

Figure 1: This paper introduces an approach to leveraging *tool diversity* that uses multiple different tools for the same task to improve aggregate crowd performance by reducing systematic error biases that might otherwise result from using any one tool type alone. Our findings on an image segmentation task demonstrate that tool diversity can provide output at least comparable to the best constituent tool and always yields significantly better results than the weakest constituent tool.

INTRODUCTION

The goal of *image segmentation* is to demarcate objects in a visual scene from the background, allowing computer vision (CV) systems to learn to recognize specific objects. These CV systems can, in turn, enable autonomous cars to identify pedestrians, surveillance drones to focus on potential threats, and in-home robots to help people with motor or mobility impairments live more comfortably and independently.

Perceiving the boundaries of physical objects comes naturally for people, but it remains a challenging open problem for CV systems due to the complexity of understanding the semantics of visual scenes [14, 26]. Crowd-powered object segmentation tools can bridge this gap by leveraging human understanding to produce large, manually-demarcated training data sets (e.g., [2, 12, 25]) for CV systems. However, designing crowd-powered tools that produce high-accuracy training data and scale efficiently (with respect to human-time cost) remains an open problem because the task of manually marking object boundaries requires significant hand-eye coordination and fine motor skills, resulting in a high error rate if these tasks are performed too quickly by workers.

Many web-based image segmentation tools (e.g., [1, 2, 5, 11, 24, 32]) have been designed to help workers reduce the effort needed to complete a task and to increase the accuracy of their output. However, different tool designs induce different error biases in worker performance, which can lead to systematic mistakes when only a single tool is used. For example, some tools [2, 32] provide polygon drawing functionality to help trace object boundaries, but [2] reported that workers often skip selecting part of the object if automatic scrolling during selection is not provided. We consider this to be a *systematic error bias* because the same error pattern would be unlikely to emerge if the tool were designed differently. In other words, it would be unlikely for worker outputs from Click'n'Cut [5] (which asks workers to use left/right mouse clicks to identify foreground and background regions of an image) to make the same mistakes as when using the polygon drawing tool. However, Click'n'Cut may exhibit its own systematic error pattern, induced by limitations in its own design. More generally, we consider error patterns that are found to be common among worker outputs from a single tool to be systematic error biases, as they are likely to be induced by the design of the tool itself. These errors are different from, for example, human perceptual biases that may also systematically affect outcomes.

In this paper, we propose the idea of leveraging *tool diversity* as a means of overcoming these systematic error biases by improving aggregate crowd performance. Tool diversity is the extent to which tools designed for the same task differ from one another in the systematic error biases that they induce. Unlike standard aggregation methods in crowdsourcing, which try to design and use the best single tool available with many workers in order to reach high accuracy, we show that using multiple effective tools can diversify the error patterns in worker responses, and help systems achieve higher *combined* accuracy (Figure 1). This insight is motivated by ensemble learning methods in machine learning that use multiple learning algorithms to obtain better prediction than can be obtained from any of the constituent algorithms alone [7].

To demonstrate our proposed workflow, we introduce a multi-tool crowd-powered image segmentation system, FourEyes, which leverages pairs of tools to generate better aggregate responses. Our evaluation shows the effectiveness of tool diversity through comparisons of aggregate crowd performance across different tool pairings with equally-sized groups of workers using the same tools. We show that the output accuracy of heterogeneous tool pairs are better than homogeneous sets. Moreover, we model the multi-tool aggregation problem as an optimization problem and use expectation maximization (EM) [6] to estimate consensus image segmentations. For certain tool pairs, EM-based multiple tool aggregation significantly improved output accuracy over majority voting. Finally, we characterize our problem and summarize the properties of crowdsourcing tasks that are amenable to our approach: those that are objective, are tractable enough for workers to produce nearly-correct responses, and increase in correctness as additional answers are provided, can benefit from our approach.

The key contributions of this research are:

- A novel crowdsourcing approach that combines input across different *types* of tools to improve aggregate quality.
- FourEyes, a crowd-powered image segmentation system that implements our approach, combining the output of four different tool types to improve the collective accuracy of a group of workers using a single segmentation tool.
- Experimental results from 51 objects across 12 indoor scenes segmented by 288 crowd workers using four different tools that validate our system's effectiveness and suggest the benefits of our multi-tool approach.

RELATED WORK

Conventional approaches to improving crowd worker output accuracy include microtask decomposition and consensus-based aggregation. These approaches are usually intended to reduce task complexity and correct for variance in individual worker responses, respectively. However, when it comes to systematic error biases induced by a tool's design, errors can persist even after decomposition or aggregation, since all workers use the same tool and the tool used in the workflow may still induce biases in worker responses. Our tool diversity strategy builds on prior work in crowdsourcing workflows and answer aggregation strategies to reduce these systematic error biases. In this section, we discuss related work in designing crowdsourcing workflows and improving output quality by answer aggregation.

Crowdsourcing Workflows

In crowdsourcing, breaking large tasks into smaller microtasks has been a popular strategy to increase the accuracy of crowd workers' answers. Microtasks are small, context-free units of work that are widely used in crowdsourcing workflows. Crowdsourcing platforms, such as Amazon Mechanical Turk, post these small units of work that (typically quasi-anonymous [22]) crowd workers can accept and complete. Soylent [3] showed that dividing a larger task into Find-Fix-Verify steps improves the accuracy of crowd workers' answers in document editing tasks. ToolScape [16] introduced a Find-Verify-Expand workflow to enhance the process of extracting different steps in how-to videos.

Other research has explored how to use crowd workflows to collectively accomplish what no single worker could alone. For instance, continuous [20, 18] or instantaneous [27] crowdsourcing workflows have made real-time crowdsourcing possible. These allow systems to get on-demand human responses when immediate judgments are needed. TimeWarp [19] introduced a workflow that invites a group of workers to perform a task that otherwise cannot be accomplished by a single worker.

In their speech captioning application, working in a group helps avoid a systematic bias of the captioning task without adding any delay. CrowdMask [15] uses a pyramid workflow to mask private content in images. While the system cannot hide sensitive content from a single worker, their method segments and distributes segments of user content so that workers can mark potentially private content without fully viewing it. Similarly, WearMail [34] introduced a workflow that allowed crowds to train a system on demand to accomplish an email search task without ever revealing email contents to workers.

Our work contributes to this line of research by introducing a novel crowdsourcing approach that aggregates multiple crowd-powered tools to offer better performance than from any of the constituent tools alone. To the best of our knowledge, we are the first to study methods for using tool diversity to increase aggregate accuracy in a crowdsourcing environment.

Improving Output Quality by Aggregating Answers

A common strategy to improve output quality in crowdsourcing systems is to aggregate independent workers' answers on the same task into a single response, typically via a consensus method like voting. Even simple majority voting has been shown to produce accurate results for crowdsourcing tasks, such as linguistic annotation tasks [33] and document editing tasks [3]. In terms of image segmentation tasks, ground truth segmentations of objects have been generated via majority pixel voting with manually-collected answers from multiple crowd workers or experts [12, 25]. More sophisticated approaches using unsupervised learning have been used to weight workers' answers by using models of their abilities [4, 23, 36, 37]. Deluge [4] models workers' sensitivity and specificity to detect noisy workers, and LazySusan [23] tracks workers by assigning different weights based on the accuracy of a worker's answer. In [36] and [37], the authors present probabilistic approaches to model not only the workers, but also the properties of the data being labeled.

One well-known weighted aggregation method is the EM algorithm [6], which predicts unknown (latent) correct answers by estimating weights for each crowd worker's answers. Dawid and Skene [6] showed that the EM algorithm significantly outperforms majority voting when a majority of workers' responses are correct and they are conditionally independent given the ground truth answer. The EM algorithm is suitable for utilizing tool diversity in image segmentation tasks because: i) the majority of the pixels selected by any tool are assumed to be correct and ii) the tools' performances are independent of each other. When designing tools, a tool's abilities are not known in advance because designers are typically unaware of the input images that the system will see. Because the performance of each tool can vary with images or object types, we can consider a tool's ability as the latent variable to be predicted. Therefore, we apply the EM algorithm across different tools with the goal of maximizing the performance of the aggregated output.

APPROACH

Prior work has used task decomposition—the process of breaking down larger tasks into more manageable, focused pieces of work—to make tasks more approachable for non-expert crowd workers. Once task decomposition has been used to break down a larger unit of work as much as possible within a corresponding workflow, most crowdsourcing systems then recruit multiple workers in parallel to further improve accuracy by aggregating their answers. We propose using multiple different tools across different workers to complete the same [sub]task, instead of having all workers complete the same task with the same interface or tool. Our proposed approach fills in the gap where traditional task decomposition leaves off.

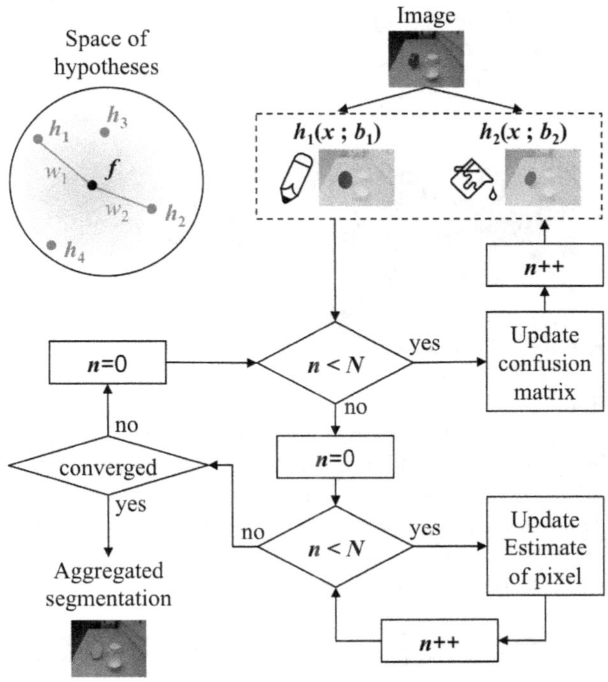

Figure 2: The top left diagram shows the hypothesis space of the possible segmentation tools, including the best performing tool (f) and other possible hypotheses ($h_1 \ldots h_4$). The flowchart on the right shows the EM algorithm we adopted for the optimization. Two different image segmentation tools, h_1 and h_2, each with different biases, b_1 and b_2 (respectively), pass segmented images to the system. We estimate the weights,w_1 and w_2 to approximate the performance of f.

Our work is conceptually motivated by ensemble learning in machine learning. Ensemble learning methods are machine learning algorithms that construct a set of learning algorithms and predict a new data point by taking a weighted vote of the predictions from each learning algorithm [7, 8]. It has been proven that ensembles can often perform better than any single member [7]. Algorithm accuracy (i.e., better than random guessing) and diversity are necessary and sufficient conditions for a combination of algorithms to be more accurate than any of its individual constituents [13]. The top left diagram in Figure 2 shows how ensemble methods work. In the diagram, a learning algorithm can be viewed as searching a space of hypotheses to identify the best performing hypothesis f, which

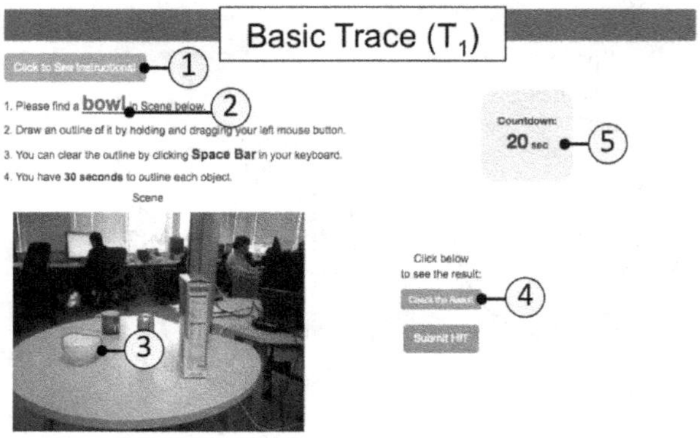

Figure 3: Overview of the Basic Trace image segmentation tool. (1) shows the full instruction when clicked. (2) describes the query object which is shown to the workers in random order. (3) shows an example of a trace line a worker provided. (4) shows the segmentation result when clicked. (5) is the task timer, which serves as an encouragement to workers to consider time in their work.

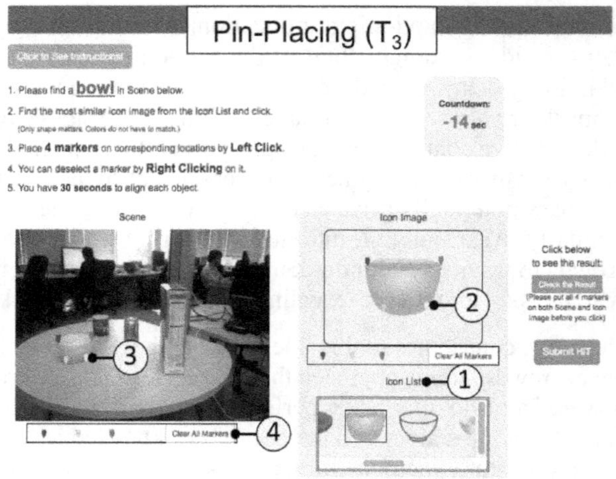

Figure 5: Overview of the Pin-Placing image segmentation tool. (1) shows template images list. (2) and (3) show examples of chosen points by a worker. (4) lets workers reset the points to start over.

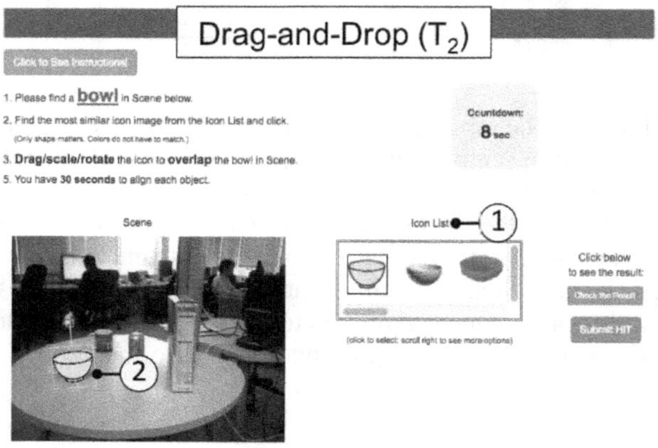

Figure 4: Overview of the Drag-and-Drop image segmentation tool. (1) shows the template images list. (2) shows an example of the chosen template image being aligned to the query object.

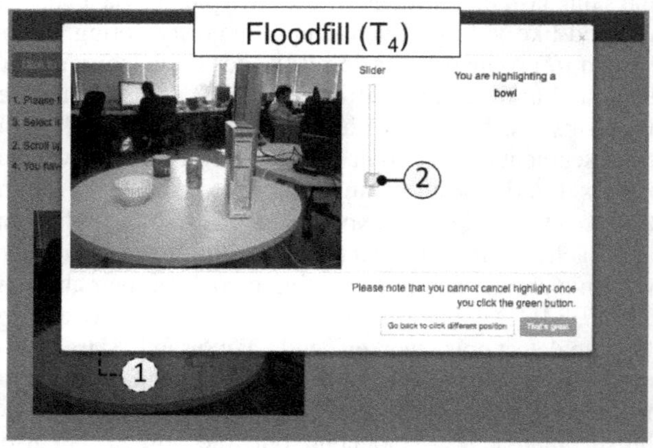

Figure 6: Overview of the Floodfill image segmentation tool. (1) shows that a worker can click on a query object in the given scene. (2) is a slider that allows workers to adjust a parameter to control the propagation of the selection area.

can be computationally difficult to find. Ensemble learning constructs a combination of two alternative hypotheses h_1 and h_2 with proper weights (w_1 and w_2), and approximates the best hypothesis f by averaging the two. Our tool diversity approach is analogous to ensemble learning methods in that two image segmentation tools are combined to produce a better segmentation result. In Figure 2, the bottom left shows two different realizations of web-based image segmentation tools, $h_1(x;b_1)$ and $h_2(x;b_2)$, with different error biases, b_1 and b_2, respectively. We propose using the EM method to optimize the weights w_1 and w_2 that maximize the combined accuracy of h_1 and h_2.

CHOOSING THE TOOLS

In this section, we introduce four web-based segmentation tools that we designed to instantiate and test the tool diversity concept. We considered one key question when designing the tools: "How can we diversify the errors produced by different tools?" Because it is hard to predict what errors will be induced by a given tool, we built tools specialized to work well with objects with different characteristics, such as small or transparent objects, objects with fuzzy materials, and reflective surfaces. These objects are current challenges to both automatic segmentation methods and human annotators. The way we built these tools increases the likelihood that each tool performs differently for different types of objects, resulting in greater error diversity. We categorized these object types into three groups and created tools that are designed to minimize errors in each particular object category. The spaces we explored and the tools we designed are summarized in Figure 7. We used the Question (Q), Option (O), and Criteria (C) representation [28] of the design space for deciding which tools to build. The Question indicates a key design issue, the

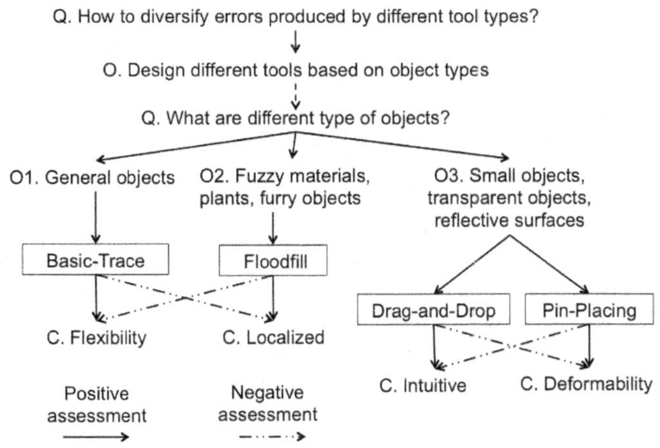

Figure 7: Design space we considered when choosing the tools for the study. We used the Question (Q), Option (O), and Criteria (C) representation of the design space.

Option node suggests possible answers to the Question, and the Criteria item represents the core properties expected from choosing an Option. For one of the Options (O3 in Figure 7), we differed the interface in two ways (Drag-and-Drop and Pin-Placing) so that the interaction of users can create different artifacts. We observed that different interactions lead to different error patterns, so we include both of the tools in the experiment section. In the rest of this section, we provide detailed descriptions of the four tools developed.

Basic Trace

The first tool is a free-form drawing tool shown in Figure 3. With Basic Trace, workers click and drag their mouse to trace the outline of the query object in a scene (Figure 3 ③). Once a worker submits the initial trace line, a simple image processing algorithm connects the gaps and fixes the irregularities in the traced line in order to form a smooth shape. It then highlights the pixels inside the traced shape, and returns the result as the final object segmentation. Of the four tools, the Basic Trace is the most manual, with the highest degree of freedom. The strength of this tool is that it is highly flexible and workers can segment any type of objects if sufficient time is given. However, the weakness of the tool is that if a worker is idle and not careful enough, the output can easily be very poor, e.g., a worker may draw a rough box around an object instead of carefully following the demarcation from the background.

Drag-and-Drop

The second tool lets workers select an object template from a list (Figure 4 ①), which is generated by searching images of a target object from an image search engine like Google or Bing. These images are then filtered for transparency and size, and the top N (in this paper we use $N = 12$) are downloaded to construct a template list for each query object. Workers are asked to select the template that most accurately matches that object in the scene based on its shape, proportion of dimensions, and perspective. In Drag-and-Drop, workers overlay their selected template onto the object identified in the scene (Figure 4 ②). Workers are able to scale, rotate, and drag the template to adjust the angle and dimensions of the template in an attempt to closely match the shape of the actual object. Based on a worker's transformation of the template, the system determines the final object segmentation by identifying and annotating the overlapping pixels between the template and the scene. The strength of this tool is that it is very intuitive to use. However, the weakness of the tool is that it is hard to map deformable objects, or even rigid objects if being viewed from different perspectives.

Pin-Placing

The third tool is also a template-based tool called Pin-Placing. A template list is generated in the same manner as in Drag-and-Drop (Figure 5 ①). With this tool, workers select four arbitrary points on their selected object template (Figure 5 ②), and pair them with four corresponding points on the object in the scene (Figure 5 ③). Workers can modify individual points, or clear all points at once (Figure 5 ④). After the four pairs of points are submitted, an automatic transformation algorithm is run to transform the template image to produce the final object segmentation. Note that four pairs of control points are the minimum necessary to perform a non-linear deformation between two images, given the perspective limitation inherent in a fixed-angle view in two dimension. Pin-Placing's working mechanism is similar to sophisticated techniques (e.g., that professional radiologists use for diagnosing lesions), but it is more intuitive to novice workers. One drawback of template-based approaches is that if an object in a scene has an atypical shape, none of the template images in the list may have a shape similar to the object. In this case, a possible solution may be to let workers ask to switch to a different tool that does not require choosing a template image.

We note that the two template-based tools, Drag-and-Drop and Pin-Placing, force workers to select occluded parts of a target object when there exist overlaps with other objects. This is a more useful functionality in domains like robotics, where ground truth object geometry includes hidden parts as well. However, in this study, we only consider the visible parts of a target object as the region of interest because it is a more general way of indicating objects in two-dimensional image segmentation. As a consequence, the tools necessarily select more false positive regions than the other tools.

Floodfill

Floodfill (AKA Bucket-fill) is a mostly autonomous tool, combining a simple region growing method [35] with minimal human input to initialize the seed point and tune a threshold parameter. Workers click on the object they want to segment (Figure 6 ①) and adjust a slider to tune one of the algorithm's threshold parameters (Figure 6 ②). This triggers the RGB Floodfill algorithm which highlights all neighboring pixels sharing an RGB value similar to the seed point that was clicked. If the segmentation is unsatisfactory, either failing to select the entire object or exceeding the object boundary, workers can adjust the slider to modify the highlighted area. The tool is strong if the shape of an object is complex with many curves, but only when the object is mostly monochromatic. If a query object consists of polychromatic or shaded regions, the selection area can be smaller than the actual object boundaries because the algorithm cannot propagate across these regions.

SYSTEM INTERFACES

To collect image segmentations from the crowd, we created a system named FourEyes that implements the tools above. FourEyes begins by receiving a scene image and the user's request in the form of a natural language query, e.g., "mark the bowl." The query is parsed to find nouns and then the nouns are displayed to workers (Figure 3 ②) in order to help identify objects that need to be segmented from the scene. For each tool, a short four to five steps of instruction including the target object name is displayed to workers while conducting the task. Also, workers can check the segmentation result before they submit their work ("Check the Result" button in Figure 3 ④). To discourage workers from idling, we embedded a task timer (Figure 3 ⑤) that counts down from t seconds and goes into negative when time runs out. In this paper, we used $t = 30$ in all experimental conditions. The timer does not impact workers other than to serve as an encouragement to consider time in their work.

EXPERIMENTS

To understand the effect of tool diversity on improving aggregate crowd performance, we recruited 288 crowd workers using LegionTools [10] and routed them from Amazon Mechanical Turk to FourEyes. Workers were given one of the four tools to perform a task of image segmentation. Note that we gave different tools to different workers because we consider the smallest unit of microtask as one worker segmenting one object using a single tool. We recruited six unique workers for each tool-scene pair (four tools and 12 scenes), resulting in a total of 1224 object segmentations.

Dataset

We chose a dataset that included various indoor objects. The dataset included 12 different visual scenes, each containing three to seven objects, for a total of 51 objects. The scenes were gathered from publicly-available datasets[1,2], and represent typical indoor scenarios with commonplace objects. They ranged from a living room to a tabletop, and contained everyday objects (e.g., a plant, laptop, soda can, cereal box, flashlight, etc.). In the experiment, each worker was shown one scene and a series of objects to segment depending on the number of objects in the scene. For each task, the order of objects in each list was randomized to avoid any ordering bias. Each worker was given one scene with one tool to perform a segmentation task.

Instructions and Payment

Before crowd workers could begin the task, they were shown a short instructional video demonstrating the goal of the task and how to use the tool they would be provided with. The two tools Drag-and-Drop and Pin-Placing have longer videos because they explain choosing the most similar template image. This additional step delayed workers' performance time in the actual experiment as well. Workers were also shown pictures exemplifying desired and undesired segmentations (same example images for all tools) so that they understand the aim of the task to create a detailed boundary of a target object in a scene. If the worker decided to proceed, they were directed to the FourEyes worker UI and their subsequent interactions with the UI were recorded. Task instructions were also accessible at any time if necessary (Figure 3 ①). Each worker was paid between \$0.35 and \$0.60 per task, proportional to the number of objects they had to segment and on the expected time of a given tool (a pay rate of ~\$10/hr). The expected time of each tool was determined by its average latency time from a dozen of preliminary experiments.

[1]https://rgbd-dataset.cs.washington.edu/dataset.html/

[2]https://www.doc.ic.ac.uk/ ahanda/VaFRIC/iclnuim.html/

Segmentation Quality Evaluation

To assess success on the image segmentation task, we measured the accuracy of each by comparing the similarity to the ground truth segmentation that was generated manually by the authors for the experiments. One author carefully completed the task and another author verified the quality of the resulting ground truth.

We used precision, recall, and F_1 score (the harmonic mean of precision and recall) to compute the pixel-level similarity (Equation 1). To do this, the number of true positive, false positive, and false negative pixels were counted for each crowdsourced segmentation.

$$\begin{aligned} \text{Precision} &= \frac{\text{true positive}}{(\text{true positive} + \text{false positive})} \\ \text{Recall} &= \frac{\text{true positive}}{(\text{true positive} + \text{false negative})} \\ \text{F1Score} &= \frac{2 \times \text{Precision} \times \text{Recall}}{(\text{Precision} + \text{Recall})} \end{aligned} \qquad \text{(Eq. 1)}$$

Results

The different tools had different error patterns (trade-offs) in terms of precision and recall. Figure 8 shows example worker segmentations from each tool, alongside the ground truth. Figure 9 shows precision-recall scatter plots of the segmentation result with each dot representing one object. We averaged the precision and recall of six workers who segmented the same object with the same tool, so one dot represents the average precision-recall of an object. As shown in Figure 9 (a) and (b), Basic Trace and Drag-and-Drop tended to show high recall but low precision. We observed that with these two tools, workers tended to select objects by putting large margins around the objects, resulting in high recall but low precision. Examples of segmentation using these two tools are shown in Figure 8 (a) and (b), respectively. Meanwhile, Pin-Placing resulted in the most scattered performance as shown in Figure 9 (c). This implies that the performance of the tool varies a lot depending on object types. An example of using Pin-Placing is shown in Figure 8 (c). In the example, a worker selected a template image that is very different from the query object, resulting in both low precision and low recall. Lastly, Figure 9 (d)

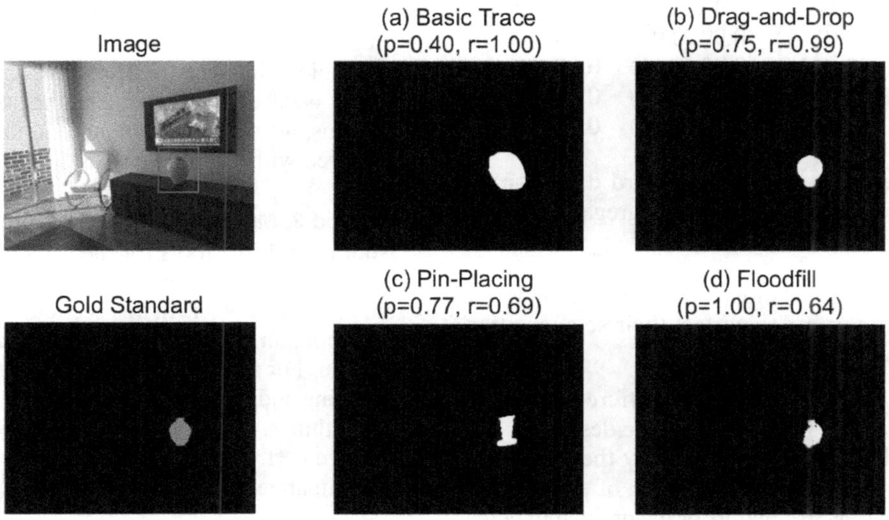

Figure 8: Original image (top left), ground truth image (bottom left), and exemplar segmentations using the four tools with their precision and recall values reported on top. (a) Basic Trace, (b) Drag-and-Drop, (c) Pin-Placing, and (d) Floodfill. In summary, the different tools have different precision-recall patterns. Therefore, we can expect that EM-based multiple tool aggregation would increase the overall accuracy of the segmentation task.

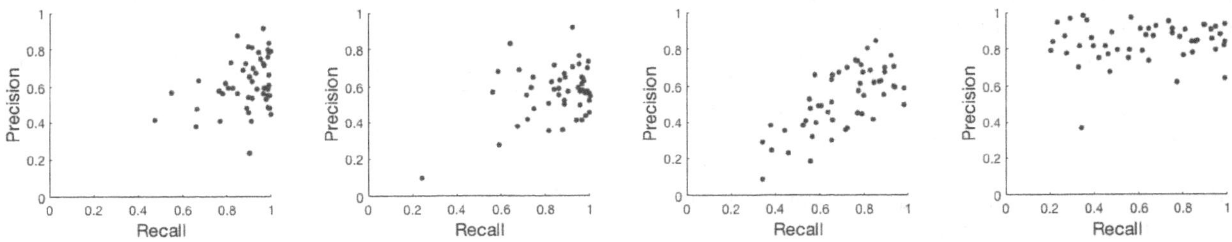

(a) Basic Trace (b) Drag-and-Drop (c) Pin-Placing (d) Floodfill

Figure 9: Precision-recall scatter plot of four different tools. We can see that the error patterns are diverse across different tools in terms of precision and recall. Basic Trace (a) and Drag-and-Drop (b) show high recall but low precision, Pin-Placing (c) shows the most scattered pattern, implying that the tool's performance highly depends on the query object, and Floodfill (d) shows high precision but low recall.

	Precision	Recall	F_1 score
Basic Trace	0.62 (0.14)	0.89 (0.12)	0.71 (0.13)
Drag-and-Drop	0.57 (0.14)	0.86 (0.15)	0.66 (0.13)
Pin-Placing	0.53 (0.17)	0.71 (0.17)	0.58 (0.17)
Floodfill	0.84 (0.11)	0.63 (0.25)	0.67 (0.20)

Table 1: Average performance (and standard deviation) of the four individual tools.

shows that Floodfill tended to give high precision but low recall performance. We observed that the selection area with Floodfill tended to be smaller than the actual object boundaries due to boundaries that were shaded or colored differently. An example segmentation of using Floodfill is shown in Figure 8 (d). Because one side of the vase was much brighter, a worker could not select the entire image with the seeded region growing algorithm.

Average accuracy metrics for each tool are summarized in Table 1. Since F_1 score is the harmonic mean of precision and recall, we use F_1 *score* as our measure of overall accuracy. In general, Floodfill gave the best performance in terms of precision and Basic Trace gave the best recall and F_1 score.

To calculate latency, we measured overall task time starting from when the worker began interacting with the task to when the worker clicked "submit" at the end of the task. After dropping outliers more than two standard deviations (2σ) from the mean latency, Basic Trace's average latency was 14.37 seconds ($\sigma = 8.08$), Drag-and-Drop's was 24.89 seconds ($\sigma = 11.25$), Pin-Placing's was 20.77 seconds ($\sigma = 7.90$), and Floodfill's was 12.62 seconds ($\sigma = 10.41$). The template-based tools had a higher segmentation latency than the other two tools. This was expected because the template-based tools are more involved and perhaps less intuitive to general-purpose crowd workers. Using Floodfill, some workers managed to

	Precision	Recall	F_1 score
Basic Trace	0.62 (0.17)	0.99 (0.04)	0.74 (0.14)
Drag-and-Drop	0.57 (0.16)	0.95 (0.11)	0.69 (0.14)
Pin-Placing	0.56 (0.17)	0.82 (0.16)	0.66 (0.16)
Floodfill	0.86 (0.12)	0.69 (0.23)	0.73 (0.17)

Table 2: Average performance (and standard deviation) of pixel-level majority voting on single-tool aggregation.

produce a satisfactory segmentation within three seconds, but others spent extra time trying to perfect their segmentation, with diminishing returns in accuracy.

From these primary results, we observed different error patterns (Figure 9) across the four tools that we designed. The result matches our design intent to diversify the errors produced by different tools. Now we can think of each tool as alternate hypotheses h_1, h_2, h_3, and h_4 of the optimal hypothesis f, with different error biases b_1, b_2, b_3, and b_4, respectively. As in ensemble learning, we expect that aggregating the different tool pairs will improve the output accuracy by reducing accumulated systematic error biases.

COMPARISON OF AGGREGATION METHODS

In order to evaluate the effectiveness of our tool diversity approach, we conducted a series of studies to examine the performance improvement achieved from an ensemble of two tools. As a baseline condition, we first investigate the segmentation quality of single tool aggregation based on majority voting of four different workers. We implement a pixel-level majority voting method, with each answer weighted equally. In the second study, we do the same majority voting, except on two tool pairs combining four workers' answers from two different tools. In the last study, we apply the EM method on multiple tool aggregation of two tools to optimize the tools' weights adaptively per object. Our studies show that the tool diversity approach is a safe design strategy that guarantees performance at least as good as the superior constituent tool.

Method 1. Single-Tool Aggregation (Baseline)

Single tool aggregation combines answers from the four workers who used the same tool to segment target objects. We ran 10 random sampling of all possible worker pairs from the collected data. This was performed to avoid any bias from accidentally choosing a good or bad pair of workers. For each query object in the scene, pixel-level majority voting was performed to annotate each pixel as either background or object. If more than two workers labeled a pixel as belonging to the query object, then the pixel was included. The accuracy of the final segmentation was computed as in the Segmentation Quality Evaluation section. The results of 10 random sampling were averaged per each query object. We summarized the average results in Table 2.

The change in precision was not significant with single tool aggregation compared to the average precision without aggregation. However, recall and F_1 scores improved. For example, recall of Basic Trace increased by 11% ($p < .01$) compared to its average performance without aggregation (see Table 1).

The increase in recall is a natural consequence of answer aggregation with low agreement thresholds. If the agreement threshold is higher, recall would decrease because more consensus is needed to annotate a pixel as an 'object'. In the next sections, we observe if and how further improvements can be achieved with multiple tool aggregation.

Method 2. Multiple Tool Aggregation (Uniform Voting)

Adding multiple tools for the same task can improve the aggregate accuracy when the tools compensate systematic error biases of each other. In this section, we focus on the results of two-tool pairs to provide a more in-depth evaluation and discussion. For all possible pairs of two tools, we ran 10 random sampling and chose two workers from each tool (combinations of six things, taken two at a time), a total of four workers. The average performance of all possible tool pairs as in Method 1 is summarized in Table 3.

	Precision	Recall	F_1 score
Basic Trace × Drag-and-Drop	0.61 (0.13)	0.99 (0.02)	0.74 (0.10)
Basic Trace × Pin-Placing	0.60 (0.13)	0.95 (0.07)	0.72 (0.11)
Basic Trace × Floodfill	0.74 (0.13)	0.93 (0.12)	0.81 (0.12)
Drag-and-Drop × Pin-Placing	0.57 (0.15)	0.92 (0.11)	0.69 (0.13)
Drag-and-Drop × Floodfill	0.70 (0.12)	0.92 (0.09)	0.78 (0.09)
Pin-Placing × Floodfill	0.70 (0.13)	0.86 (0.13)	0.76 (0.12)

Table 3: Average performance (and standard deviation) of pixel-level majority voting of all possible tool pairs.

Multiple tool aggregation improves F_1 scores compared to single tool aggregation. Every tool pair except Basic Trace × Pin-Placing (0.72) showed increased F_1 scores compared to the single constituent tools. The pair gave better F_1 scores than aggregating Pin-Placing alone (0.66), but gave a 2.7% lower F_1 score than aggregating Basic Trace alone (0.74). However, there was no statistically significant difference between single tool aggregation of Basic Trace versus multiple tool aggregation of Basic Trace × Pin-Placing pair. One notable finding about the result is that the highest F_1 score achievable from single tool aggregation is 0.74 (aggregating Basic Trace alone), whereas that from multiple tool aggregation is 0.81 (aggregating Basic Trace × Floodfill pair), which is a 9.5% ($p < .01$) performance improvement with mixing tools. To emphasize the performance improvement in terms of F_1 score, we compared the F_1 scores of multiple tool aggregations (blue bars) with their constituent tools (red and green bars) in Figure 10.

Method 3. Multiple Tool Aggregation (EM method)

For this study, we used the same 10 worker groupings from Method 2 to do a fair performance comparison. We used the EM method from Dawid and Skene [6] to estimate the labels

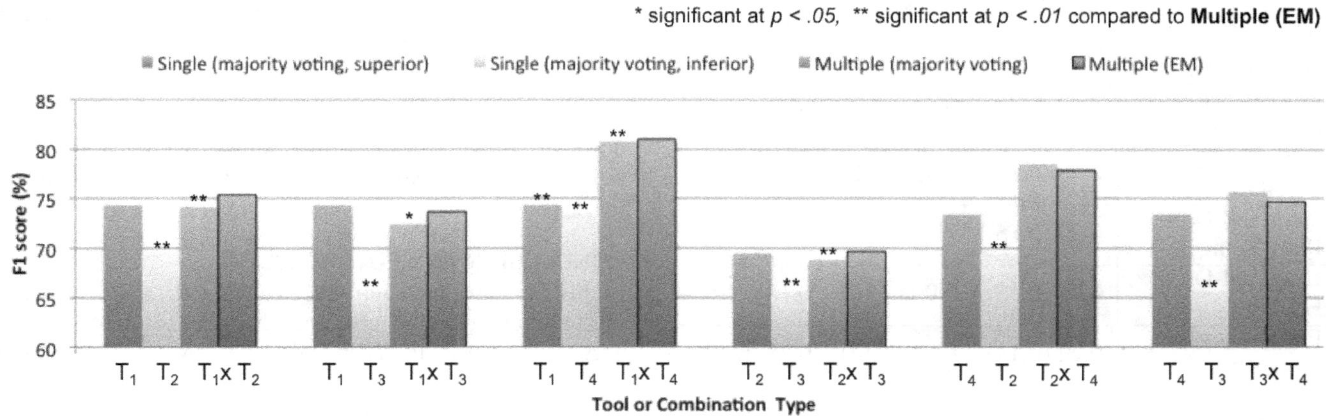

Figure 10: Accuracy (F_1 score) comparison of different aggregation methods based on four tools: Basic Trace (T_1), Drag-and-Drop (T_2), Pin-Placing (T_3), and Floodfill (T_4). Blue bars are multiple tool aggregation with majority voting and purple bars are multiple tool aggregation with the EM method. Red bars are single tool aggregation of the better performing tool and green bars are single tool aggregation of the less performing tool among the two constituent tools. * significant at $p < .05$; ** significant at $p < .01$ both compared to EM-based multiple tool aggregation (two tailed t-test). The tool diversity strategy always performed significantly better than the inferior constituent tool, and performed at least comparable to the superior tool.

of each pixel. We consider the ground truth labels as latent variables and estimate them jointly with the unknown parameters, the weight per tool, of our model. We model our problem of estimating the correct consensus image segmentations as follows:

Assume M crowd workers segment an object in an image A having N total pixels. Each pixel is labeled as either 1 (object) or 0 (background) by workers. The label a worker m assigns to each pixel is denoted as $z_{mn} \in \{0,1\}$. We denote all labels from worker m as a vector Z_m. The true label Y_n, where $n = 1,\ldots,N$, of each pixel is unknown. The true labels of A to be estimated are denoted as a vector Y. In the Dawid-Skene algorithm, it is assumed that the probability of worker m labeling a pixel is independent of choosing a pixel, i.e., it is a constant over n. In addition, we denote by θ the confusion matrices set to be estimated. We can estimate the true labels Y by maximizing the marginal log-likelihood of the observed worker labels.

$$l(\theta) := \log\Big(\sum_{Y\in\{0,1\}^n} L(\theta;Y,Z)\Big). \qquad \text{(Eq. 2)}$$

The EM algorithm works iteratively by applying two steps: the expectation step and the maximization step.

E Step: Calculate the expected value of the log-likelihood function, with respect to the conditional distribution of Y given Z under the current estimate of θ:

M Step: Find the estimate θ that maximizes the expectation of marginal log-likelihood.

The E and M steps are repeated until the estimations converge. The diagram on the right side of Figure 2 shows how the process is applied to our problem. The scene image is given as an input to two tools h_1 and h_2 that have different error models b_1 and b_2, respectively. Crowd workers use the tools to segment a query object, and the responses are transferred to the EM algorithm. Initial latent variables are set as the majority voting result, and the confusion matrix for each response is updated based on the initial assumption of the latent variables. Confusion matrices are updated by counting the number of false positive, false negative, true positive, and true negative pixels. Once the confusion matrices are updated for every pixel, the new estimations of latent variables are updated until convergence. The accuracy of multiple tool aggregation with the EM method is summarized in Table 3. The comparison of F_1 scores of the tool pairs with that of the constituent tools is summarized in Figure 10. The numbers for majority voting on single tool aggregation are obtained from Method 1, and the numbers for majority voting on multiple tool aggregation are obtained from Method 2. The p-values were computed using two tailed t-tests with Bonferroni correction applied after each t-test. The results show that the EM-based multiple tool aggregation always performed significantly better than the inferior constituent tool, and performed at least as well as the superior constituent tool.

The summarized result shows that the EM method significantly improves the performance of the tool pairs compared to uniform majority voting, except for the two tool pairs (Drag-and-Drop × Floodfill pair and Pin-Placing × Floodfill pair). From these exceptions, we observed that the trade-off between precision and recall was low because drop in recall was larger than the gain in precision, resulting in the overall F_1 scores not benefiting much from using the EM algorithm. Although there was a significant performance improvement, the gain using EM was small (under 3%).

DISCUSSION

We observed that the two highest aggregate-performance tool pairs were combinations of a high-precision (but low-recall)

	Precision	Recall	F_1 score
Basic Trace × Drag-and-Drop	0.63 (0.14)	0.98 (0.02)	0.75 (0.11)
Basic Trace × Pin-Placing	0.63 (0.14)	0.93 (0.09)	0.74 (0.12)
Basic Trace × Floodfill	0.75 (0.13)	0.93 (0.12)	0.81 (0.12)
Drag-and-Drop × Pin-Placing	0.59 (0.15)	0.90 (0.12)	0.70 (0.13)
Drag-and-Drop × Floodfill	0.71 (0.13)	0.90 (0.11)	0.78 (0.10)
Pin-Placing × Floodfill	0.72 (0.14)	0.81 (0.14)	0.75 (0.14)

Table 4: Average performance (and standard deviation) of all possible tool pairs using per-pixel EM algorithm-based weighted voting.

tool and a high-recall (but low-precision) tool, as shown in the third and fifth bar groups in Figure 10. Precision and recall often have an inverse relationship, where one can be increased at the cost of reducing the other. In the crowdsourcing literature, research has investigated different payment schemes to observe the trade-off between precision and recall on object annotation tasks [29]. Our work suggests that different tools can be built to target either high precision or high recall so that the harmonic means of both can be maximized by aggregating results from two methods. More generally, our results indicate that leveraging tool diversity in crowdsourcing tasks can improve aggregate crowd performance by compensating for various types of inherent individual systematic error biases.

Generalizability

While we demonstrate this new crowdsourcing paradigm using an image segmentation task, it could benefit any task where different approaches to solving the same problem can be devised. Specifically, tasks that have the following properties would be especially amenable to our approach:

- Expected correctness grows non-negatively with added worker input. In other words, on average, quality improves (collective answers converges to correct) as more worker responses are collected. Problems where majority voting works would belong to this class.
- The task is tractable enough to yield approximately-correct responses from workers, but responses can be expected to have imperfections. asks such as real-time captioning [18] or handwriting recognition [30] are examples of such tasks.
- The task has an objectively correct answer, but also tolerates imperfections from workers' responses. For example, creative writing tasks would *not* be a good fit because there is no single correct answer, and they do not tolerate imperfections well (e.g., incomplete sentences).
- The expected human error is distributed differently when using different tools. This way, a diverse tool set can complement a broad range of error types. If this were not the case (i.e., if the errors were all biased in the same direction), then we would not expect multiple tools to be significantly more effective than a single one alone.

Many common crowdsourcing problems (e.g., in computer vision, natural language processing, or robotic/UI manipulation) have these properties, suggesting that a range of domains beyond the one explored in this paper may also benefit from our approach.

CONCLUSION AND FUTURE WORK

In this paper, we have introduced a generalizable crowdsourcing approach of leveraging tool diversity to increase output accuracy of a system. When building a crowd-powered system, different tool designs can induce different worker performance, leading to systematic error biases when only a single tool is used for a task. We have shown that these systematic error biases can be reduced by using multiple tools to improve aggregate crowd performance on image segmentation tasks.

Overall, our findings open new opportunities and directions for pursuing a deeper understanding of how tool designs influence the aggregate performance on diverse crowdsourcing tasks. Future work may investigate ways to generalize methodologies for leveraging tool diversity in other domains, such as video coding [17], annotation of fine-grained categories [9], or activity recognition [21]. Tool diversity may also help seamlessly integrate computer and human input [31] to more efficiently train machine learning algorithms.

ACKNOWLEDGMENTS

The authors would like to thank Stephanie O'Keefe and Kyle Wang for their input on this work. This research was supported in part by the Denso Corporation, Toyota Research Institute, and MCity at the University of Michigan. This research was also supported in part by the Next-Generation Information Computing Development Program through the National Research Foundation of Korea (NRF) funded by the Ministry of Science and ICT (NRF-2017M3C4A7065960).

REFERENCES

1. Amy Bearman, Olga Russakovsky, Vittorio Ferrari, and Li Fei-Fei. 2016. What's the point: Semantic segmentation with point supervision. In *European Conference on Computer Vision*. Springer, 549–565.
2. Sean Bell, Paul Upchurch, Noah Snavely, and Kavita Bala. 2013. OpenSurfaces: A richly annotated catalog of surface appearance. *ACM Transactions on Graphics (TOG)* 32, 4 (2013), 111.
3. Michael S Bernstein, Greg Little, Robert C Miller, Björn Hartmann, Mark S Ackerman, David R Karger, David Crowell, and Katrina Panovich. 2015. Soylent: a word processor with a crowd inside. In *Communications of the ACM*, Vol. 58. ACM, 85–94.
4. Jonathan Bragg, Mausam, and Daniel S. Weld. 2013. Crowdsourcing multi-label classification for taxonomy creation. In *First AAAI conference on human computation and crowdsourcing*.
5. Axel Carlier, Vincent Charvillat, Amaia Salvador, Xavier Giro-i Nieto, and Oge Marques. 2014. Click'n'Cut:

Crowdsourced interactive segmentation with object candidates. In *Proceedings of the 2014 International ACM Workshop on Crowdsourcing for Multimedia*. ACM, 53–56.

6. Alexander Philip Dawid and Allan M Skene. 1979. Maximum likelihood estimation of observer error-rates using the EM algorithm. *Applied statistics* (1979), 20–28.

7. Thomas G Dietterich and others. 2000. Ensemble methods in machine learning. *Multiple classifier systems* 1857 (2000), 1–15.

8. Yoav Freund and Robert E Schapire. 1995. A desicion-theoretic generalization of on-line learning and an application to boosting. In *European conference on computational learning theory*. Springer, 23–37.

9. Timnit Gebru, Jonathan Krause, Jia Deng, and Li Fei-Fei. 2017. Scalable annotation of fine-grained categories without experts. In *Proceedings of the 2017 CHI Conference on Human Factors in Computing Systems*. ACM, 1877–1881.

10. Mitchell Gordon, Jeffrey P Bigham, and Walter S Lasecki. 2015. LegionTools: a toolkit+ UI for recruiting and routing crowds to synchronous real-time tasks. In *Adjunct Proceedings of the 28th Annual ACM Symposium on User Interface Software & Technology*. ACM, 81–82.

11. Sai Gouravajhala, Jean Y Song, Jinyeong Yim, Raymond Fok, Yanda Huang, Fan Yang, Kyle Wang, Yilei An, and Walter S Lasecki. 2017. Towards Hybrid Intelligence for Robotics. *Collective Intelligence Conference (CI)* (2017).

12. Danna Gurari, Mehrnoosh Sameki, and Margrit Betke. 2016. Investigating the Influence of Data Familiarity to Improve the Design of a Crowdsourcing Image Annotation System. *HCOMP* (2016).

13. Lars Kai Hansen and Peter Salamon. 1990. Neural network ensembles. *IEEE transactions on pattern analysis and machine intelligence* 12, 10 (1990), 993–1001.

14. Kaiming He, Georgia Gkioxari, Piotr Dollár, and Ross B. Girshick. 2017. Mask R-CNN. *CoRR* abs/1703.06870 (2017).

15. Harmanpreet Kaur, Mitchell Gordon, Yiwei Yang, Jeffrey P Bigham, Jaime Teevan, Ece Kamar, and Walter S Lasecki. 2017. Crowdmask: Using crowds to preserve privacy in crowd-powered systems via progressive filtering. In *Proceedings of the AAAI Conference on Human Computation (HCOMP 2017).*, *HCOMP*, Vol. 17.

16. Juho Kim, Phu Tran Nguyen, Sarah Weir, Philip J. Guo, Robert C. Miller, and Krzysztof Z. Gajos. 2014. Crowdsourcing Step-by-step Information Extraction to Enhance Existing How-to Videos. In *Proceedings of the 32Nd Annual ACM Conference on Human Factors in Computing Systems (CHI '14)*. ACM, New York, NY, USA, 4017–4026.

17. Walter S. Lasecki, Mitchell Gordon, Danai Koutra, Malte F. Jung, Steven P. Dow, and Jeffrey P. Bigham. 2014. Glance: Rapidly coding behavioral video with the crowd. In *Proceedings of the 27th annual ACM symposium on User interface software and technology*. ACM, 551–562.

18. Walter S. Lasecki, Christopher Miller, Adam Sadilek, Andrew Abumoussa, Donato Borrello, Raja Kushalnagar, and Jeffrey Bigham. 2012. Real-time captioning by groups of non-experts. In *Proceedings of the 25th annual ACM symposium on User interface software and technology*. ACM, 23–34.

19. Walter S. Lasecki, Christopher D. Miller, and Jeffrey P. Bigham. 2013. Warping Time for More Effective Real-time Crowdsourcing. In *Proceedings of the SIGCHI Conference on Human Factors in Computing Systems (CHI '13)*. ACM, New York, NY, USA, 2033–2036.

20. Walter S. Lasecki, Kyle I. Murray, Samuel White, Robert C. Miller, and Jeffrey P. Bigham. 2011. Real-time crowd control of existing interfaces. In *Proceedings of the 24th annual ACM symposium on User interface software and technology*. ACM, 23–32.

21. Walter S. Lasecki, Young Chol Song, Henry Kautz, and Jeffrey P. Bigham. 2013. Real-time crowd labeling for deployable activity recognition. In *Proceedings of the 2013 conference on Computer supported cooperative work*. ACM, 1203–1212.

22. Matthew Lease, Jessica Hullman, Jeffrey P Bigham, Michael S Bernstein, Juho Kim, Walter S. Lasecki, Saeideh Bakhshi, Tanushree Mitra, and Robert C Miller. 2013. Mechanical turk is not anonymous. *Social Science Research Network (SSRN)* (2013).

23. Christopher H. Lin, Mausam Daniel, and S. Weld. 2012. Crowdsourcing control: Moving beyond multiple choice. In *In: Proceedings of the 28th Conference on Uncertainty in Artificial Intelligence, UAI*.

24. Di Lin, Jifeng Dai, Jiaya Jia, Kaiming He, and Jian Sun. 2016. Scribblesup: Scribble-supervised convolutional networks for semantic segmentation. In *Proceedings of the IEEE Conference on Computer Vision and Pattern Recognition*. 3159–3167.

25. Tsung-Yi Lin, Michael Maire, Serge Belongie, James Hays, Pietro Perona, Deva Ramanan, Piotr Dollár, and C Lawrence Zitnick. 2014. Microsoft coco: Common objects in context. In *European conference on computer vision*. Springer, 740–755.

26. Jonathan Long, Evan Shelhamer, and Trevor Darrell. 2015. Fully Convolutional Networks for Semantic Segmentation. In *The IEEE Conference on Computer Vision and Pattern Recognition (CVPR)*.

27. Alan Lundgard, Yiwei Yang, Maya L. Foster, and Walter S. Lasecki. 2018. Bolt: Instantaneous Crowdsourcing via Just-in-Time Training. In *Proceedings of the 2018 CHI Conference on Human Factors in Computing Systems (CHI '18)*. ACM, New York, NY, USA.

28. Allan MacLean, Richard M Young, Victoria ME Bellotti, and Thomas P Moran. 1991. Questions, options, and criteria: Elements of design space analysis. *Human–computer interaction* 6, 3-4 (1991), 201–250.
29. Andrew Mao, Ece Kamar, Yiling Chen, Eric Horvitz, Megan E Schwamb, Chris J Lintott, and Arfon M Smith. 2013. Volunteering versus work for pay: Incentives and tradeoffs in crowdsourcing. In *First AAAI conference on human computation and crowdsourcing*.
30. Tom Ouyang and Yang Li. 2012. Bootstrapping Personal Gesture Shortcuts with the Wisdom of the Crowd and Handwriting Recognition. In *Proceedings of the SIGCHI Conference on Human Factors in Computing Systems (CHI '12)*. ACM, New York, NY, USA, 2895–2904.
31. Olga Russakovsky, Li-Jia Li, and Li Fei-Fei. 2015. Best of both worlds: human-machine collaboration for object annotation. In *Proceedings of the IEEE Conference on Computer Vision and Pattern Recognition*. 2121–2131.
32. Bryan C Russell, Antonio Torralba, Kevin P Murphy, and William T Freeman. 2008. LabelMe: a database and web-based tool for image annotation. *International journal of computer vision* 77, 1 (2008), 157–173.
33. Rion Snow, Brendan O'Connor, Daniel Jurafsky, and Andrew Y Ng. 2008. Cheap and fast—but is it good?: evaluating non-expert annotations for natural language tasks. In *Proceedings of the conference on empirical methods in natural language processing*. Association for Computational Linguistics, 254–263.
34. Saiganesh Swaminathan, Raymond Fok, Fanglin Chen, Ting-Hao Kenneth Huang, Irene Lin, Rohan Jadvani, Walter S. Lasecki, and Jeffrey P. Bigham. 2017. WearMail: On-the-Go Access to Information in Your Email with a Privacy-Preserving Human Computation Workflow. In *Proceedings of the 30th Annual ACM Symposium on User Interface Software and Technology*. ACM, 807–815.
35. Shane Torbert. 2016. *Applied computer science*. Springer. 158 pages.
36. Peter Welinder, Steve Branson, Pietro Perona, and Serge J. Belongie. 2010. The Multidimensional Wisdom of Crowds. In *Advances in Neural Information Processing Systems*. Curran Associates, Inc., 2424–2432.
37. Jacob Whitehill, Ting fan Wu, Jacob Bergsma, Javier R. Movellan, and Paul L. Ruvolo. 2009. Whose Vote Should Count More: Optimal Integration of Labels from Labelers of Unknown Expertise. In *Advances in Neural Information Processing Systems*. Curran Associates, Inc., 2035–2043.

Visualizing Gaze Direction to Support Video Coding of Social Attention for Children with Autism Spectrum Disorder

Keita Higuch[1] **Soichiro Matsuda**[2] **Rie Kamikubo**[1] **Takuya Enomoto**[3]
Yusuke Sugano[4] **Junichi Yamamoto**[3] **Yoichi Sato**[1]

[1]The University of Tokyo [2]Tsukuba University [3]Keio University [4]Osaka University

ABSTRACT

This paper presents a novel interface to support video coding of social attention in the assessment of children with autism spectrum disorder. Video-based evaluations of social attention during therapeutic activities allow observers to find target behaviors while handling the ambiguity of attention. Despite the recent advances in computer vision-based gaze estimation methods, fully automatic recognition of social attention under diverse environments is still challenging. The goal of this work is to investigate an approach that uses automatic video analysis in a supportive manner for guiding human judgment. The proposed interface displays visualization of gaze estimation results on videos and provides GUI support to allow users to facilitate agreement between observers by defining social attention labels on the video timeline. Through user studies and expert reviews, we show how the interface helps observers perform video coding of social attention and how human judgment compensates for technical limitations of the automatic gaze analysis.

Author Keywords

Video Coding Support, Children with ASD, Social Attention

INTRODUCTION

Autism spectrum disorder (ASD) is a neurodevelopmental disorder characterized by impairments in social communication and repetitive patterns of behaviors [3]. In 2016, Autism and Developmental Disabilities Monitoring (ADDM) Network reported that 1 in 68 children has been identified with ASD [13]. Children with ASD often face difficulties with daily functions.

Assessments of children with ASD are designed to measure and facilitate development of social communication skills such as imitation, pretend play, and joint attention. Therapeutic activities for developing these skills have been introduced into actual sites for ASD children's support. Recent studies revealed that the therapeutic activities can significantly affect their sociability in the long term [8, 33].

IUI'18, March 7–11, 2018, Tokyo, Japan

DOI: https://doi.org/10.1145/3172944.3172960

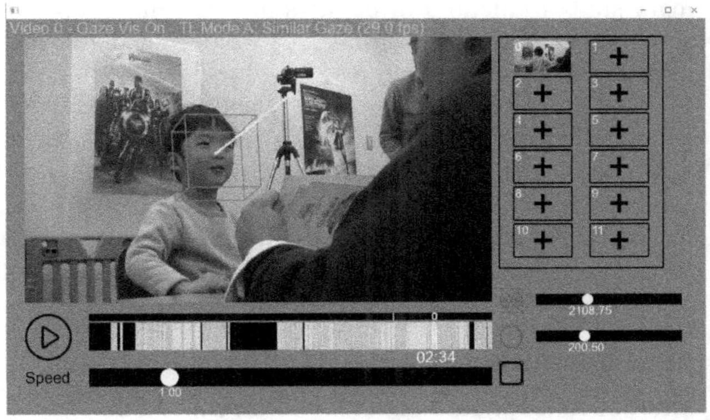

Figure 1. Proposed gaze visualization and video coding interface. The interface provides supportive features for video coding of social attention in assessments of children with autism spectrum disorder (ASD). Note that a child with typical development (TD) is shown in this picture.

Several structured therapeutic activities are supplemented with video recordings for evaluation. The evaluations are often performed as a post process of manual annotation of video recorded assessments [30, 6, 1, 2]. The video recordings are usually long and include many redundant scenes such as intervals of the session and breaks. Video coders (observers) have to locate scenes of assigned tasks in therapeutic sessions in lengthy videos and carefully extract attentive behaviors of children, such as eye contact and joint attention, for evaluating their social skills. Consequently, video coding of therapeutic activities requires a lot of effort from the observers. To make therapeutic activities more efficient, it is important to reduce the cost of video coding.

Partly because of such therapeutic demands, automatic analysis of attentive behaviors has been one of the central topics in the eye tracking community. However, despite recent advances in machine learning-based remote gaze estimation [48, 26, 49] and wearable camera-based eye contact detection [43, 12, 47], fully automatic detection of social attention under diverse environments is still challenging. Computer vision methods often suffer from various error factors, including diverse illumination conditions and occlusions, and we cannot fully rely on the automatic detection results. This issue becomes more critical in the case of therapeutic activities because incorrect evaluations must be avoided.

In this paper, we propose a supportive intelligent interface for video coding of therapeutic activities, as shown in Figure 1.

We take an approach where we use state-of-the-art computer vision-based automatic video analysis to help guide human evaluation and judgment of social attention behaviors. The proposed interface visualizes the results of gaze estimation of target video images. Moreover, we provide users with features to define social attention labels in the videos in relation to the estimated gaze positions. Using sample-based or image region-based extraction methods, users can view candidates that indicate the parts of the videos with potential target social-attention behaviors such as eye contact.

The contribution of this study is threefold: 1) we interviewed six professional therapists for children with ASD as a preliminary study to identify difficulties in evaluating therapeutic activities with video recordings, 2) we designed a novel interface to support evaluation of lengthy videos to find target social attention of children with ASD, and 3) through user studies, we confirmed that the interface helps observers perform video coding of social attention, and we determined how it can be improved for evaluating therapeutic activities. We also discussed the impact of automatic detection errors in video coding tasks, and concluded that the proposed interface is still useful even with imperfect automatic video analysis.

RELATED WORK

Interactive technologies for Children with ASD

Interactive technologies for children with ASD have been developed in the context of Human-Computer Interaction (HCI) to care for and aid impairments such as social communication and repeated patterns [8]. These technologies for the assessment of social skills are aimed at developing reception to and production of social signals [10]. Successful interactive technologies have introduced tablet computers [29, 31, 20], special electronic devices [28, 38, 39, 9], and virtual avatars [19, 25, 46] for enabling therapeutic activities with information and communications technology (ICT). These computer-supported systems allow therapists to automatically code low-level behaviors of children with ASD [40, 38, 28].

With that said, therapeutic activities in face-to-face settings with expert therapists are still important to assess and develop social skills of children with ASD. To accurately evaluate, therapists frequently perform video-based coding with recorded videos during therapeutic activity [30, 6, 1, 2]. However, video coding presents several difficulties in marking social attention in long video recordings. To address these difficulties, this work aims to support video coding of therapeutic activity for children with ASD by visualizing computer-estimated gaze direction.

Intelligent User Interfaces for Video Annotation and Browsing

Previous work developed interfaces to support video annotation (coding) of behaviors for manual annotation by observers [42, 17]. To reduce the effort of video coding, previous work introduced automatic behavior detection features such as sign language [15], transcription of speech [7], and facial expression [16]. Unlike these works, we introduce gaze analysis of videos of children with ASD to offer video coding support to experts. To this end, we performed interview studies with experts and designed supportive features to find target social attention from long video recordings of therapeutic activities. The novelties of the features are twofold: 1) introducing automatic gaze analysis to help users to detect attention behaviors, and 2) allowing users to define social attention labels for highlighting candidates of target social attention in video coding tasks.

Recent works also aimed at developing new tools for efficiently browsing diverse videos such as education [24], surveillance [36, 35], sports [27], and first-person videos [18]. These works used computer vision techniques and developed novel GUI supports for video browsing such as direct manipulation [32, 21, 22], content-aware fast-forwarding [18, 11, 34], and a colored video timeline [18, 14]. The colored timeline highlights part of a video in the timeline based on automatic detection results to indicate cues of important scenes to observers. Despite the benefits of the previous interface, it only used static data from preprocessing for the highlights. In this work, we developed a new interactive colored timeline feature of which highlighted parts change based on real-time user input.

Detecting and Analyzing Social Attention

With the progress in machine learning methodologies, automatic attention analysis has significantly improved. State-of-the-art face and facial landmark detection methods [4, 5, 41] are very robust even in challenging conditions, and calibration-free, appearance-based gaze estimation methods have advanced with large-scale datasets and deep learning techniques [48, 26, 49]. Although such learning-based methods have an advantage in that they require only a consumer RGB camera, they still suffer from various error factors, and the accuracy (average error: 5 degrees) is far less than commercial eye trackers. For this reason, we use a computer vision method with the GUI in video coding therapeutic activities.

Recent studies also aimed at automatically detecting events of social attention, such as joint attention [23, 45] and eye contact [43, 37, 44, 12], with wearable cameras or eye trackers. However, there are several fundamental difficulties in detecting attentive behaviors with wearable devices. First, it is difficult for children to wear cameras or eye trackers, and the approach is not always applicable in practical situations. Second, as discussed in [47], the definition of eye contact depends on the target object, and it is almost impossible to *pre-train* robust eye contact detectors without knowing the target object. Finally, social attention also highly depends on the context of interaction. Eye contact in social interaction has multiple meanings [30], and observers need to understand the meaning of social attention. These difficulties also motivated us to use automatic video analysis in a supportive manner for guiding human judgment.

DESIGN CONSIDERATION

Preliminary Study

To design a support interface for video coding, we first performed interviews of six experts (two female, four male) of children with ASD. The experts have over five years of experience with clinical assessments and academic studies. The semi-structured interview sessions took place in a private room at their facility, where we asked the following three questions: 1) In what situations do you use video recording for evaluations of assessments? 2) Are there any difficulties with the video coding–if so, what? 3) Do you want to use new technologies for video scoring–if so, what kind of support is crucial?

In addition to the interviews, we also observed how the experts performed the video coding. The experts showed us videos of assessments of the developing social skills of children with ASD according to the ethical code of our institute. They also showed their video coding tools [1] and described how they perform evaluations of therapeutic activities from the recorded videos.

Use of Video Recordings

According to the interviews, the experts frequently use video recordings for evaluations of assessments of children with ASD. Typically, target behaviors such as eye contact, joint attention, and imitations are clearly defined for each assessment session. Target behaviors can appear multiple times in each recording session, and the experts need to repeatedly review the recordings to code correctly.

There are two levels of video coding children's behaviors. The first level is identifying large actions and reactions of a child, such as pointing and imitations. These target behaviors are often clear in the recorded videos, and observers can easily confirm whether a child did the target actions/reactions. The second level is identifying more complex attentive behaviors, including eye contact (face looking) and joint attention with the therapist. Such attentive behaviors are important to measure the social skills of children.

The experts are generally welcome to use new tools to reduce their efforts and improve their productivity. However, it is not always possible to use hardware support (such as eye trackers) in face-to-face settings. This is one of the main reasons why the experts rely on video coding. Since software support tools for video coding are still quite limited, they sometimes recruit undergraduate students as assistants for video coding.

Difficulties of Video Coding

There is a fundamental ambiguity in finding attention in 2D video observations. Observers need to carefully examine the facing and gazing directions of children to predict their attention. This requires a huge effort for observers to identify target attentive behaviors particularly in the case of complex social attention.

In addition, video recordings are usually long (10 to over 60 minutes) because they continuously capture videos of entire therapeutic activities that include both on-task and off-task (*e.g.*, break) scenes. Therefore, observers spend a long time locating on-task scenes in long videos, and it is sometimes difficult to find all of the target behavior instances in the videos.

Our Approach

The main goal of this work is to address the above difficulties of video coding social attention in face-to-face settings (Figure 2). We take the approach of using recent advancements in computer vision technologies that allow us to detect attention behaviors (*e.g.*, gaze directions) from videos. However, robust, fully automatic recognition of social attention is still difficult due to limited accuracy and the ambiguity of attention (*i.e.*, attention dependent on contexts of social interaction) [49, 30]. This limitation motivated us to design a new approach using automatic video analysis to support guiding human judgment for facilitating agreement between observers.

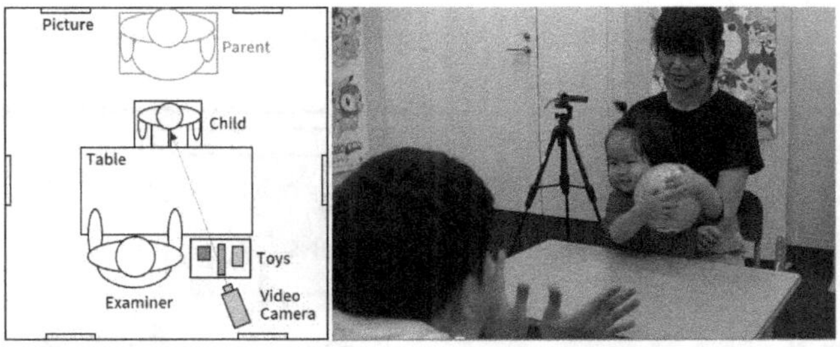

Figure 2. Example of target setting: assessments of children with ASD in a face-to-face setting (redrawn based on [30])

Considering the underlying difficulty and ambiguity of social attention judgment, we propose that gaze direction for video coding helps observers' judgments of social attention. We expect the visualization facilitates agreement between observers. In addition, to address the difficulty in finding multiple targets from a lengthy video, our interface provides supportive features that highlight candidates of targets based on user-defined social attention labels. Following prior work that reported the benefits of colored timelines (*i.e.*, [18, 14]), we also propose highlighting detection results in the video timeline of the interface. These features narrow down candidate frames of social attention in long video recordings and are expected to reduce observers' efforts.

PROPOSED INTERFACE

Based on the preliminary study, we propose a novel video coding interface that provides supportive features using computer vision techniques. Figure 3 shows the overview of the proposed framework. As a preprocessing step, the face and gaze direction of the target child is automatically detected in each frame of the input video. The proposed interface uses these detected data to visualize gaze directions.

Gaze Analysis

We use the OpenFace toolkit [5] to detect and track the target child's face. The toolkit provides 2D facial bounding boxes, facial landmark locations, and 3D head poses. Since the input video often contains many non-target faces, such as those of parents, our interface allows observers to define a target region of interest (ROI) in the input video frames. The ROI indicates the working area of children during therapeutic activities, and our interface ignores faces detected outside the ROI.

After face detection, the state-of-the-art appearance-based gaze estimation method [49] is then applied to estimate gaze directions of detected faces. 3D head poses are used to crop normalized face images and the face images are fed into a pre-trained full-face convolutional neural network for gaze

[1]Microsoft Media Player with Microsoft Excel, BECO2 and Noldus Observer

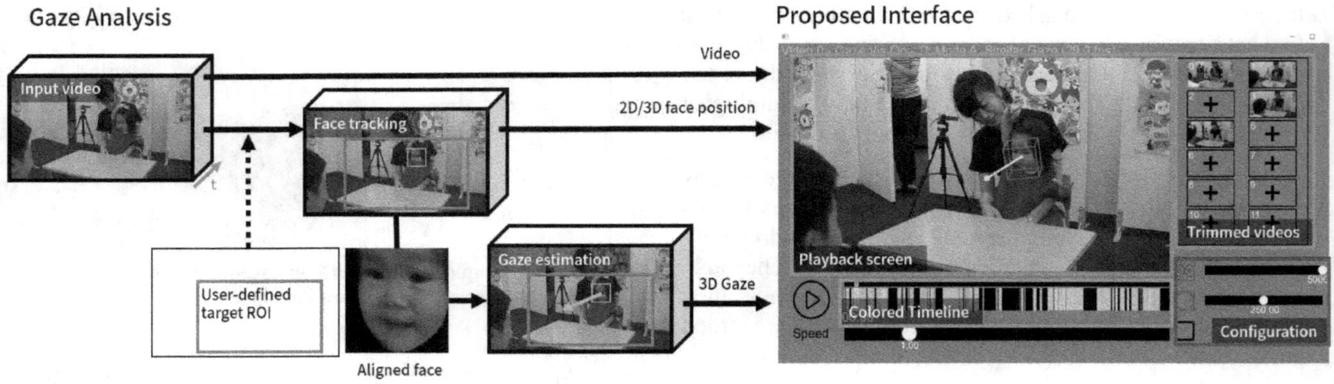

Figure 3. Overview of gaze analysis and the proposed interface: Gaze analysis takes face tracking and gaze estimation stages (Left). The proposed interface provides basic functions of video coding and supportive features for finding target social attention (Right).

estimation. Assuming that the camera's intrinsic parameters were obtained through camera calibration, this process provides the 3D gaze vectors of the target child defined in the camera coordinate system.

Interface Design

The right part of Figure 3 shows the proposed interface, which contains basic functions of video coding tools such as the playback screen, the video timeline, and the configuration panels. Parts of the video timeline can be highlighted based on detection results. The interface also has an annotation slider on the top of the timeline. Observers are allowed to mark on the slider by pressing a key to manually annotate when they find target social attention.

Visualizing Gaze Analysis Results

The interface also shows results of detected information on video images. We visualize both 3D face boxes and 3D gaze vectors projected onto video images. Proper lengths of gaze vectors differ by face positions and the context of the videos. The interface thus provides a slider to adjust the lengths of gaze vectors. The interface draws gaze vectors from the center of the face to the gaze position of the selected length.

The interface also shows face detection results on the video timeline. Previous studies revealed that highlighting analysis results in video timelines is beneficial for finding specific information from videos [14, 18]. We introduce this benefit into the video coding interface. As shown in Colored Timeline of Figure 3 (right), the interface visualizes face detection results in the video timeline. Gray regions indicate that a child's face appeared in a defined detection region. The black region shows that no face is detected in the region. This visualization was designed to help observers guess when a child was working on given tasks during video recordings.

Supportive GUI Features for Finding Target Social Attention

The interface also provides supportive features to interactively highlight candidates of target behaviors based on user-defined social attention labels. To define target labels, we propose two types of selection methods. The first is an sample-based method that allows observers to select samples of gaze direction as a target social attention label. Candidates of the target are then extracted and highlighted based on a distance-based search. The second is a region-based method that allows observers to draw a region on video frames. Candidates of the target are then highlighted if visualized gaze points appear inside of the target region. These methods work as GUI supports of the proposed interface. To address errors of gaze estimation results, the approach enables interactive adjustments of a detection threshold or region.

Sample-based highlight allows users to select 3D gaze positions as samples of their observational targets of social attention. Such user-defined labels are used to highlight frames detected based on the 3D distance between the center of sample gaze points and other gaze points in each frame. The gaze points are the tips of the gaze vectors whose lengths observers freely set from the face positions. The interface also allows the users to define a threshold of the distance for highlighting frames in the video timeline as the candidates.

Figure 4 (A) shows a process of using the sample-based highlight. In this mode, observers need to find the first sample of target social attention and mark it on the interface (A1). The interface then highlights detected candidates as green on the timeline (A2). The gaze vector is also highlighted as green if the seek bar of the timeline is set on detected frames. Observers can change the detection threshold of candidates (A3) and add further target labels (A4).

Region-based highlight allows users to set a rectangle on the video images as a target region of social attention. In the frames where the projected points of gaze vector tips on the playback screen are detected within the user-selected region, the interface highlights those frames on the timeline as the candidates. Unlike the sample-based highlights, the users can select the target regions multiple times and the highlighted candidates are updated according to the newly selected region.

Figure 4 (B) shows a process on using the region-selected highlight. Observers need to set a target region on the playback screen to highlight candidate frames by dragging the mouse (B1). In the selection process, green points on

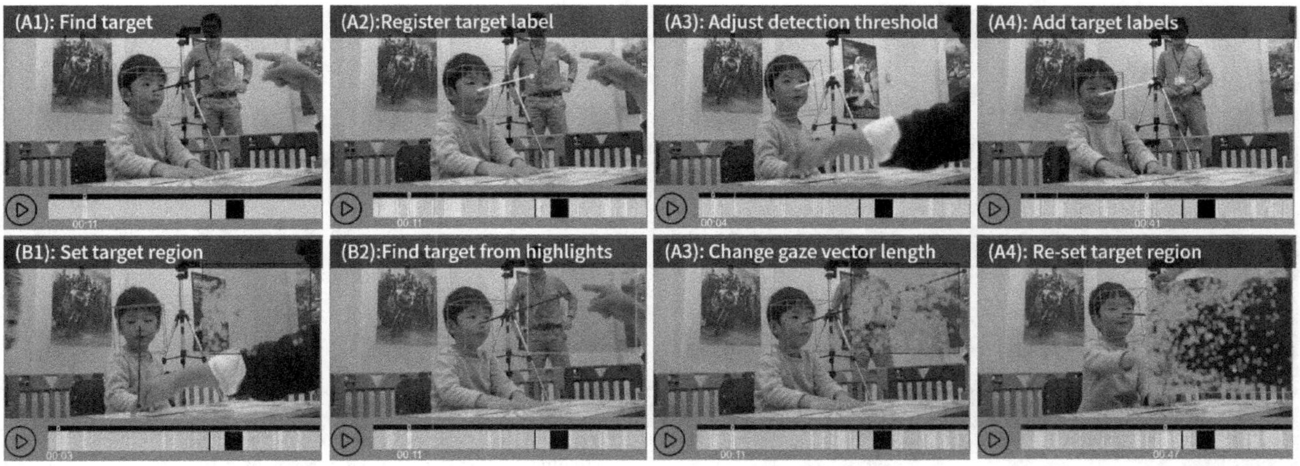

Figure 4. GUI supports for highlighting candidates of target social attention: (A1-4) Sample-based highlight, and (B1-4) Region-based highlight.

the screen indicate the detected gaze tips of each frame. The detected frames are also visualized on the video timeline. The rectangle of the selected region is highlighted if the seek bar of the timeline is set on detected frames (B2). Observers are allowed to change the length of the gaze vector (B3) and target regions (B4) based on their preference.

Video Trimming Function

The interface supports interactive video trimming for long videos. Video recordings of assessments are usually long and contain on-task scenes in limited parts. Observers spend a lot of effort finding and repeatedly checking the scenes in video coding. To reduce this effort, this feature aims to support observers in easily trimming important scenes from long videos. To trim the video, observers select a region in the timeline by dragging the right button of a mouse. Observers then click rectangles on the right side of the interface to make a new trimmed video. We expect the trimming function to reduce the effort of repeatedly finding and playing on-task scenes.

DATA COLLECTION FOR THREE EVALUATIONS

We created a novel video dataset of therapeutic activities for both children with typical development (TD) and ASD. We designed three evaluation studies for the visualization of gazes and the proposed interface. The first evaluation is confirming the effectiveness of visualizing gaze estimation results by a simple task. This task is designed to see whether the visualization helps observers with video coding of social attention, more specifically face looking of children, even without GUI supports. The second evaluation is revealing how the proposed features of the interface are used in a simple video coding task such as usability. We employed the baseline coding interface with two variations of the proposed features. We recruited both non-expert and expert therapists for the evaluation to understand the usability of the proposed interface with enough numbers of participants. Note that the usability for non-experts is also important because, in our interviews, experts mentioned that undergraduates are sometime recruited for video coding of assessments. We finally performed expert reviews in which experts use the proposed interface for video recordings of realistic therapeutic activities. We aimed to see how the proposed features can be used for our target of video coding.

Dataset

We recruited three expert therapists to perform professional therapeutic activities. We also recruited two children with TD (4-year-old boy and 2-year-old girl) and two children with ASD as targets of assessments. According to the ethical code of our institute, we used video recordings of children with ASD only for the evaluation of expert reviews.

We recorded scenes of therapeutic tasks assigned to children (Figure 5). More specifically, the experts performed imitation and naming tasks with the children. The imitation task is designed to see whether a target child is able to imitate several actions of the therapists. The naming task is used to see development of social interaction. In the task, a therapist shows or points to a picture card for the target child to look at and respond to by naming what is in the picture (e.g., animals). We captured video recordings for both children with TD and ASD during the social interaction tasks (the first row of Figure 5).

We also recorded a structured assessment program to evaluate the effectiveness of the proposed interface with actual therapeutic activities. We selected the early social communication scales (ESCS) [30], a video-recorded, structured observation measure to detect social disabilities in children. More specifically, ESCS was designed to provide measures of individual differences in nonverbal communication skills that typically emerge in children between 8 and 30 months of age. ESCS' settings (Figure 2) and nine tasks that are designed to detect specific social abilities such as joint attention, social interaction, and behavior requests are clearly defined. We simplified the use of ESCS to reduce the effort of children by choosing four typical tasks. We captured video recordings during the ESCS sessions with two children with TD (second and third rows of Figure 5).

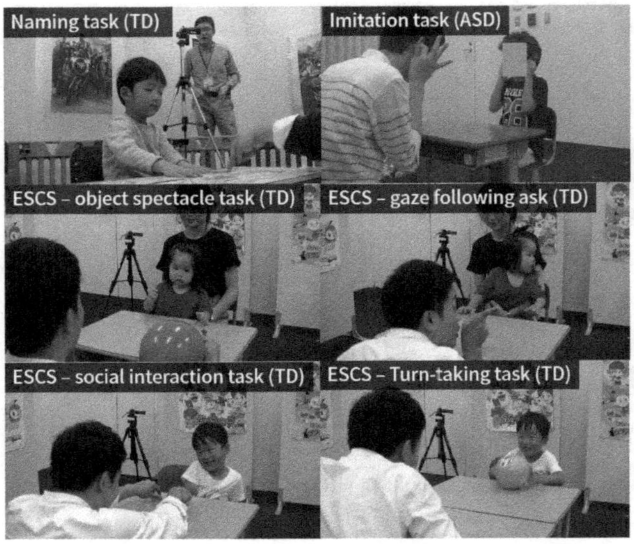

Figure 5. Our video dataset. The dataset contains general assessments (the first row) and a structured measurement program (the second and third rows) for both children with typical development (TD) and autism spectrum disorder (ASD). To follow the ethical code of our institute, the face of the child with ASD is hidden in the picture

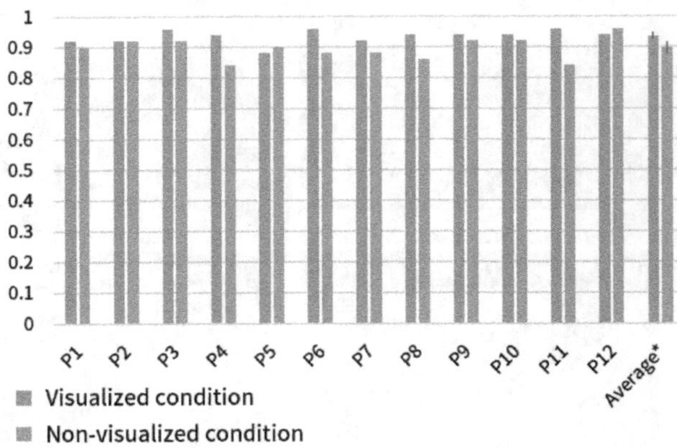

Figure 6. Result of agreement ratio. The Mann-Whitney U test revealed significance for the average agreement ratios ($p = 0.004$). Error bars indicate 95 % confidence interval.

EVALUATION 1: EFFECT OF VISUALIZING ESTIMATED GAZE

We first aimed to confirm our basic assumption that visualizing gaze direction helps to detect social attention activities. To this end, we used a single image to perform a simple study in which participants judged whether a child made face-looking behavior or not. We compared visualized and non-visualized conditions to see how visualized gaze direction changed observers' judgments. We recruited 12 participants who were non-experts of children with ASD but had enough experience with computers in their studies and works.

Task

Participants were asked to code whether a child on a given image looked at a therapist's face (face looking behavior). We requested that the participants quickly and accurately judge the face looking of a target child. The participants simply selected an answer from two keys (yes/no) for 100 images.

From our dataset of children with TD, we captured 50 images of scenes involving face looking behaviors performed by a target child and 50 images for non-face looking behaviors. The set of images had a variety of children, therapists, situations, and fixation targets in non-face looking behaviors. We shuffled the order of 100 images and randomly labeled half of the images with 0 and the other half with 1. Half of the participants saw images of 0 labels with visualized gaze and images of 1 labels without gaze visualization. The other half had reversed conditions.

Evaluation and Results

We compared answers for visualized images with answers for non-visualized images in terms of agreement ratio and response times. For the agreement ratio, we compared participants' selections with our selection for visualized and non-visualized conditions. We also calculated average response times for the conditions. As part of the participants' objective feedback, we also asked participants to identify in which conditions (*i.e.*, visualized and non-visualized conditions) was it easy to judge face looking after their tasks.

Figure 6 shows the results of agreement ratios for each participant. Average agreement ratios of visualized and non-visualized conditions are 0.93 (SD: 0.03) and 0.89 (SD: 0.04), respectively. The Mann-Whitney U test revealed the significance of the agreements ratio ($p = 0.004$). Average response times for visualized and non-visualized conditions were 2.00 seconds (SD: 0.34) and 2.00 seconds (SD: 0.38), respectively, so no significance was observed by the Mann-Whitney U test. In terms of objective feedback, all participants agreed that it was easy to judge face looking in the visualized condition. Despite there being no difference in the response times, we confirmed the assumption that the visualized gaze direction of a child helps observers facilitate agreements for coding social attention.

EVALUATION 2: INTERFACE USABILITY

We performed a study to evaluate the proposed features in addition to the overall functions of our system. We aimed to see how the experience of searching for target social-attention behaviors from therapeutic activity videos was affected by our system. We recruited two types of participant groups, non-experts (n = 12) and experts (n = 5), in video coding and observation of social attention. They were asked to complete three sets of tasks under different conditions in using the proposed interface features.

Conditions

The participants completed the tasks under the counterbalanced conditions, which were as follows:

Baseline (None)

Under this condition, they performed the assigned tasks without the visualization of gaze estimation, highlight features of face-detection results, or user-defined attention labels. The participants were given only the basic functions of video coding tools, including the playback screen, the video timeline, and the speed configuration. The interface had an annotation slider with which they could position a mark by pressing a key.

Proposed User-Defined Highlight: Sample-based (Sample)
While the basic functions described above were provided, under this condition the participants were expected to utilize the sample-based highlight features. They were instructed to sample out target social attention by marking it on the annotation slider to signify highlights of closely detected candidates on the timeline. The condition came with a slider handle to control the threshold of the distance of the 3D gaze positions at frames marked in relation to other frames.

While activating one of the user-defined highlight features, the visualization of gaze estimation and the face-detection highlights were always available. The participants could freely manipulate the length of the stick for gaze direction using the slider handle.

Proposed User-Defined Highlight: Region-based (Region)
Under this condition, the participants were expected to utilize the region-based highlight features. They were instructed to select a rectangular region on the video content, and the frames that included gaze positions detected within the region were highlighted.

Task and Procedure
The participants were given 3-minute-long video clips from the therapeutic activity recordings to search for scenes in which the child looked at the face of the therapist in the assessments. We assigned the participant to code the target behaviors within three-second intervals. The clips we used were from the data collected in the recordings of the 4-year-old boy with TD. The participants were asked to annotate a mark on the slider located on top of the timeline every time they found the target scenes. They performed these manual annotation tasks of finding target social attention behaviors under different usage of the interface features described above. Prior to each usage condition, a practice session was provided to allow the participants to get familiar with the interface.

After the experimental sessions, the participants were also given Likert scale survey questions to rate the ease of tasks under each condition and the effectiveness of features for *Sample* and *Region* conditions. The study then proceeded to interviews to understand the reasons for their ratings in the context of use and to receive their subjective feedback towards the proposed features of our system.

Quantitative Evaluation
We calculated the total averages of agreement ratios between all of the participants in each video clip. The results of *Sample*, *Region*, and *None* are 88%, 86%, and 86%, respectively. We also compared average completion times. The results of *Sample*, *Region*, and *None* are 346.98 (SD:123.94), 363.31 (SD:97.68), and 293.78 (SD:92.87). The Friedman test revealed no significant difference within the conditions. Note that these results are not surprising because the video recordings used in this evaluation are short in length (only 180 seconds), and the participants were requested to manipulate several GUI components relevant to the proposed features.

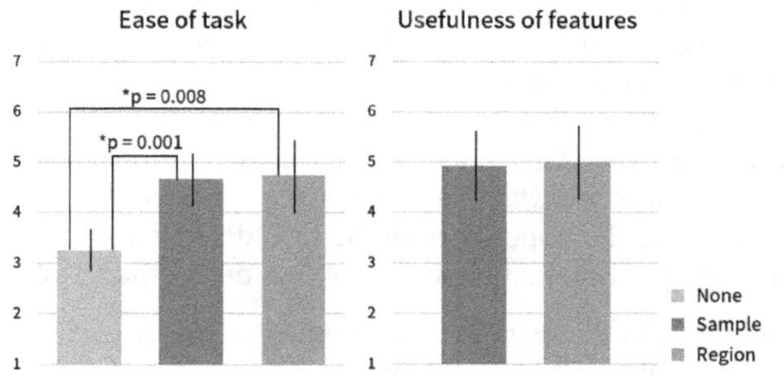

Figure 7. Results of objective feedback for the ease of tasks and usefulness of features from 12 non-experts. The Friedman and Mann-Whitney U tests revealed significance in the ease of tasks for *None-Sample* ($p = 0.001$) and *None-Region* ($p = 0.008$). No significance was observed in the usefulness of features from the non-experts. Error bars indicate 95 % confidence interval.

In the objective feedback from 12 non-experts, given that the averages regarding the ease of tasks in *Sample*, *Region*, and *None* were 4.67 (SD:1.07), 4.75 (SD:1.54), and 3.25 (SD:0.87), respectively, the Friedman test revealed significance within conditions (left of Figure 7). The Mann-Whitney U test revealed significance in *None-Sample* ($p = 0.001$) and *None-Region* ($p = 0.008$). Among five experts, the average answers for *Sample*, *Region*, and *None* were 5.2 (SD:1.10), 5.4 (SD:1.52), and 5 (SD:2.12), respectively. Given that the average answers from non-experts regarding the usefulness of features for *Sample* and *Region* were 4.92 (SD:1.51) and 5 (1.60), no significance was revealed by the Mann-Whitney U test (right of Figure 7). The answers from experts were 5.4 (SD:0.55) and 5.2 (SD:1.48). Overall, we observed positive objective feedback for two of the proposed features.

Subjective Feedback
We generally received positive feedback towards our system, as it was helpful in quickly estimating which portion of the timeline had information relevant to the completion of the task. They viewed the timeline highlights as an effective means of understanding the overall structure of the video content. The participants from both groups reported the highlighted candidates as: *"clues to determine the search portion in the videos."*[2]

Highlights on the timeline were found to be useful in estimating the sections participants needed to pay attention to. Many non-expert participants mentioned the fatigue level involved in not using the highlight features. One stated: *"The task itself becomes tiring. I had to constantly focus on the video."* In having no highlights, the experts mentioned how they were able to perform observational tasks at different attention levels. One expert participant who often performs video coding for counseling purposes reported: *"I became careful in observing*

[2]In this paper, italic fonts in double quotations denote translated speech from other languages.

the video when approaching the highlighted frames." We also observed that they often configured the speed slider to slow down the video or to move frame by frame to check around the estimated target frames. They added: *"I relaxed my attention while watching the content during dark-highlighted frames. That was not stressful."* Both groups of participants strongly emphasized the importance of the face-detection information in roughly estimating unnecessary sections of the content.

The majority of the participants preferred the use of sample-based highlights because they controlled system feedback by having visualized information (their markings on the video). Even though many reported cases of low accuracy of the system feedback, their acceptance of use was motivated by their flexibility in changing the thresholds to see the relationships between user-marked frames and others. Three non-expert participants articulated: *"I relied on my eyes to judge in the end"* in order to determine whether what they observed was valid. One expert explained: *"I can choose the relevancy of the candidates given on my own."*. On the other hand, few participants expressed a preference for the region-based highlights due to the lack of ease-of-use elements. They had to constantly change the parameters of the visualized gaze direction stick and re-select the region throughout the video content.

Among the participants, we observed a tendency to run through the whole video at least twice, and the highlights were then utilized to check the quality of their work annotating target behaviors. Without the highlights, non-expert participants observed: *"It took a lot of effort to look over the work without any guidance."* In comparing their work with the system-offered candidates, an expert participant said: *"Seeing how my annotated frames matched the highlights at the end increased my confidence level in my work."* In addition to minimizing coding errors, the participants also checked if they missed any relevant frames by going through the candidates. Without the highlight features, no clues were given on the timeline to effectively run through the frames all over again.

EVALUATION 3: EXPERT REVIEWS

This section explores the application of our system in the actual practice of video-based evaluations of social attention. We assigned five experts to review the interface under a given sets of tasks for video coding. In order to set practical conditions for using the interface for video coding, the study used a 3-minute-long clip from the therapeutic activity recording of the ASD child in the first session and proceeded with the whole 12-minute recording of the activities done by the two-year-old girl with TD. Rather than emphasizing multiple dataset scenarios with diverse children groups, we followed the ESCS coding tasks, which were generally performed on children with TD and ASD, and qualitative methods to gain thorough implementation aspects of the interface.

Task and Procedure

The task of the first session was to freely utilize the features (including sample- or region-based highlights, along with gaze-estimation and face-detection results visualized) to search for frames with target social attention as given in the interface usability study. It was followed by a session using our interface to perform simplified ESCS coding tasks for our expert-review purposes. In this scenario, the experts carefully observed and analyzed the long recordings for target attributes that fit behavioral categories structured by ESCS forms. We conducted unstructured interviews after each session to gain natural reviews of the features of our proposed interface and possible extension of the function provided in support of the complex and high-effort tasks of video coding.

The experts were instructed to trim video segments based on the ESCS coding tasks using our video-trimming function and to fill out our simplified version of ESCS forms. The example coding measures included a child's eye contact behaviors while playing with a given toy or when alternating their gaze between a moving toy and the examiner (in the category of initiating joint attention), requesting a toy (in the category of initiating behavioral requests), or interacting with the examiner in some way, such as singing (in the category of responding to social interaction).

Subjective Feedback

When analyzing the social-attention behaviors of children with ASD, all of the experts articulated how they made far less eye contact (face looking) and how this nature influenced the implementation reliability. Two experts mentioned that the sample-based timeline visualization for eye contact was particularly reliable in this task. One of them said: *I was amazed to see how the system was able to detect those few frames of limited social-attention behaviors."*

Since the clips from the ASD-child recordings involved content in which the child was mostly on the seat, one expert extended the use of the region-based highlights to select an area where there would not be any gaze direction or positions. This was found to be an effective way to visualize which portion of the video had unnecessary content.

The experts mentioned the use of timeline visualization features when trimming video clips. It was interesting to see how the system was implemented in the actual context of video coding. Face-detection was especially useful for long videos as a way to know which sections had unnecessary content such as a child being out of the frame. Moreover, the sample-based highlights gave hints as to which video segments most likely had experimental tasks. Since ESCS experiments usually come with strict procedures, the clipping feature was more useful in a video involving a child with ASD when it was difficult to estimate how the procedures would go. Knowing the overall structure of the video beforehand explicitly influenced the effectiveness of the highlights on the timeline.

FINDINGS

Benefits of Visualizing Gaze Estimation

Visualization of gaze estimation results on the video images helps video coding to facilitate agreements for assessing social attention. As shown in results in evaluation of visualizing gaze directions, this can be seen as minimizing the variability of judgment due to personal interpretation. The visualization can thus encourage the confirmation of target behaviors for the observers, whether they observed eye contact in the video frame.

Visualized gaze can be also used to define the labels necessary for highlighting candidates for target social-attention behaviors. For sample-based highlights, the observers search and select the representative line of sight from the visualized gaze directions. To make use of the region-based highlights, the observers perceive how the gaze directions are related to the defined areas of attention.

Benefits of Highlighting Detection Results over the Timeline

Using our detection methods to visualize candidates on the timeline supports observers in narrowing down parts of the videos to find target social attention. Face-detection highlights provide the initial support in understanding the general structure of the video content. The redundant parts of the video, such as when the child is off the seat or outside the camera's field of view, can be easily determined. In addition, the highlights related to gaze estimation come in handy when looking for parts that contain potentially relevant content. Using the sample-based features or region-selected features allows the observers to further narrow down the search with the ability to select the levels of candidate information they prefer to see on the timeline slider.

The benefit of reducing the search levels is that the cognitive load of complex observation is relieved because the observers know where to focus while the video is running. Without the highlight features, the majority of the participants mentioned how they had to remain attentive throughout the entire video. The video-coding experts reported ease in grabbing parts of the video that involved content that was outside the scope of the observational task. Expert feedback stated that the timeline highlights significantly minimized the effort in analyzing the video for potential frames with target social attention behaviors.

Considerations for Detection Error

It is important to discuss the impact of automatic detection errors. The accuracy of gaze estimation technology is still limited, and the analysis results of the datasets used in the evaluations revealed several types of errors. The face of the two-year-old child could not always be detected; the face detection results in the images of that child were not as stable as those from the four-year-old child's images (Left of Figure 8). Gaze estimation bias was also observed due to the occlusion of children's faces and the lack of relevant face images in the learning datasets (Right of Figure 8). In addition, the experts mentioned certain behaviors that could be uniquely found in ASD children, and the example case was of tilting the head downward while rolling eyes upward. Even though we did not observe those behaviors in the dataset we used, the experts reported the expected negative aspects considering various behavioral factors impacting the gaze estimation results.

Regarding the video coding performance from the ASD child experiments, the experts reported that they felt more confident in their own observational skills rather than relying on the system feedback. This was due to the fact that ASD children seldom make easy-to-define social attention behaviors. For instance, the expert observers were able to tell that the child

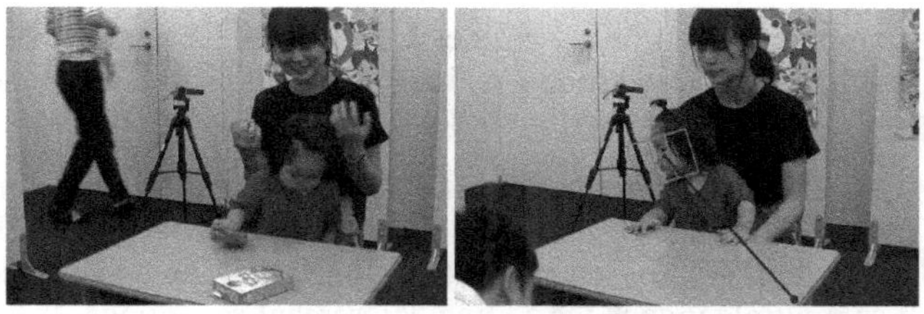

Figure 8. Failure cases of face detection (Left) and gaze estimation (Right)

looked at objects or somewhere else in the environment even though their eyes seemed to be directed towards the face of the examiner.

Despite several detection challenges, the proposed interface along with the special features was still useful in finding target social attention. Since the observers relied on their own observational skills in making final judgments of target behaviors, their feedback on the use of the interface was positive. Simply offering the possibilities of relevant parts gave them general directions of where to focus in the long videos. The functions where the observers could manipulate the levels of possibility feedback met their search needs as well. They could choose to see limited numbers of options with higher-level relevancy and then expand more options to browse for potentially relevant frames. In support of the complex observational tasks, rather than automating them completely, our interface encouraged the observers to effectively utilize their human skills by being able to see which parts needed to be browsed quickly or thoroughly.

LIMITATION

The main limitation of this work is that we evaluated the proposed interface with limited variations of videos in the user studies. Video recording of therapeutic activities are usually long, but we only used videos 180 seconds long in the interface usability study (Evaluation 2). Even though primary findings of the proposed features were revealed in the study, we plan to perform additional user studies with realistic video lengths. The evaluations also only used the videos of therapeutic activities recorded in a face-to-face setting. Therefore, we plan to collect a new dataset of other settings (e.g., floor setting), and evaluate the proposed interface to reveal further requirements for improving the supportive features.

CONCLUSION AND FUTURE WORK

This paper presents a novel interface to support video coding of social attention for the assessments of children with ASD. Based on interview study with professional therapists, we designed our interface to use computer vision-based automatic video analysis in a supportive manner for guiding human judgment.

We performed three evaluations to find the effectiveness of the proposed interface. We found benefits of gaze visualization and supportive features for finding target social attention. Through evaluations, we also found that, through our proposed interface, human judgment often compensates for the technical failure of the automatic gaze analysis. Although computer vision-based gaze estimation still has some technical limitations, the proposed interface could make assistance for complex video coding tasks.

One of our most important future works is extending the proposed interface for use with multiple video sources. In the interview sessions, an expert mentioned that they sometimes use multiple videos for coding assessment recordings. While multiple video sources can lead to more accurate and detailed analysis of social attention, it will open new challenges for efficient visualization. We also plan to explore supportive features with more advanced automatic attention analysis approaches and perform more deployment studies during actual therapeutic activities.

ACKNOWLEDGMENTS

This work was supported by JST CREST Grant Number JPMJCR14E1 and JPMJCR14E2, Japan. We thank all collaborators in our user studies and dataset for their support.

REFERENCES

1. Catherine Aldred, Jonathan Green, and Catherine Adams. 2004. A new social communication intervention for children with autism: pilot randomised controlled treatment study suggesting effectiveness. *Journal of Child Psychology and Psychiatry* 45, 8 (2004), 1420–1430. DOI: http://dx.doi.org/10.1111/j.1469-7610.2004.00338.x

2. Nadig AS, Ozonoff S, Young GS, Rozga A, Sigman M, and Rogers SJ. 2007. A prospective study of response to name in infants at risk for autism. *Archives of Pediatrics Adolescent Medicine* 161, 4 (2007), 378–383. DOI: http://dx.doi.org/10.1001/archpedi.161.4.378

3. American Psychiatric Association and others. 2013. *Diagnostic and statistical manual of mental disorders (DSM-5®).* American Psychiatric Pub.

4. T. Baltrusaitis, P. Robinson, and L. P. Morency. 2013. Constrained Local Neural Fields for Robust Facial Landmark Detection in the Wild. In *2013 IEEE International Conference on Computer Vision Workshops*. 354–361. DOI: http://dx.doi.org/10.1109/ICCVW.2013.54

5. T. Baltrusaitis, P. Robinson, and L. P. Morency. 2016. OpenFace: An open source facial behavior analysis toolkit. In *2016 IEEE Winter Conference on Applications of Computer Vision (WACV)*. 1–10. DOI: http://dx.doi.org/10.1109/WACV.2016.7477553

6. Grace T. Baranek. 1999. Autism During Infancy: A Retrospective Video Analysis of Sensory-Motor and Social Behaviors at 9–12 Months of Age. *Journal of Autism and Developmental Disorders* 29, 3 (01 Jun 1999), 213–224. DOI: http://dx.doi.org/10.1023/A:1023080005650

7. Ronald Böck, Ingo Siegert, Matthias Haase, Julia Lange, and Andreas Wendemuth. 2011. ikannotate–a tool for labelling, transcription, and annotation of emotionally coloured speech. *Affective Computing and Intelligent Interaction* (2011), 25–34.

8. Sofiane Boucenna, Antonio Narzisi, Elodie Tilmont, Filippo Muratori, Giovanni Pioggia, David Cohen, and Mohamed Chetouani. 2014. Interactive Technologies for Autistic Children: A Review. *Cognitive Computation* 6, 4 (01 Dec 2014), 722–740. DOI: http://dx.doi.org/10.1007/s12559-014-9276-x

9. LouAnne E. Boyd, Xinlong Jiang, and Gillian R. Hayes. 2017. ProCom: Designing and Evaluating a Mobile and Wearable System to Support Proximity Awareness for People with Autism. In *Proceedings of the 2017 CHI Conference on Human Factors in Computing Systems (CHI '17)*. 2865–2877. DOI: http://dx.doi.org/10.1145/3025453.3026014

10. Laurence Chaby, Mohamed Chetouani, Monique Plaza, and David Cohen. 2012. Exploring multimodal social-emotional behaviors in autism spectrum disorders: an interface between social signal processing and psychopathology. In *Privacy, Security, Risk and Trust (PASSAT), 2012 International Conference on and 2012 International Confernece on Social Computing (SocialCom)*. IEEE, 950–954.

11. Kai-Yin Cheng, Sheng-Jie Luo, Bing-Yu Chen, and Hao-Hua Chu. 2009. SmartPlayer: User-centric Video Fast-forwarding. In *Proceedings of the ACM CHI Conference on Human Factors in Computing Systems (CHI)*. ACM, New York, NY, USA, 789–798. DOI: http://dx.doi.org/10.1145/1518701.1518823

12. Eunji Chong, Katha Chanda, Zhefan Ye, Audrey Southerland, Nataniel Ruiz, Rebecca M. Jones, Agata Rozga, and James M. Rehg. 2017. Detecting Gaze Towards Eyes in Natural Social Interactions and Its Use in Child Assessment. *Proc. ACM Interact. Mob. Wearable Ubiquitous Technol.* 1, 3, Article 43 (Sept. 2017), 20 pages. DOI: http://dx.doi.org/10.1145/3131902

13. DL Christensen, J Baio, and K Van Naarden Braun. 2016. Prevalence and Characteristics of Autism Spectrum Disorder Among Children Aged 8 Years – Autism and Developmental Disabilities Monitoring Network. *MMWR Surveill Summ* 65, SS-3 (2016), 01–23. http://dx.doi.org/10.15585/mmwr.ss6503a1.

14. Manfred Del Fabro, Bernd Münzer, and Laszlo Böszörmenyi. 2013. *Smart Video Browsing with Augmented Navigation Bars.* Springer Berlin Heidelberg, Berlin, Heidelberg, 88–98. DOI: http://dx.doi.org/10.1007/978-3-642-35728-2_9

15. Philippe Dreuw and Hermann Ney. 2008. Towards automatic sign language annotation for the elan tool. In *Proceedings of LREC*.

16. Damien Dupre, Daniel Akpan, Elena Elias, Jean-Michel Adam, Brigitte Meillon, Nicolas Bonnefond, Michel Dubois, and Anna Tcherkassof. 2015. Oudjat: A configurable and usable annotation tool for the study of facial expressions of emotion. *International Journal of Human-Computer Studies* 83 (2015), 51 – 61. DOI: http://dx.doi.org/10.1016/j.ijhcs.2015.05.010

17. Laura Hänninen and Matti Pastell. 2009. CowLog: Open-source software for coding behaviors from digital video. *Behavior Research Methods* 41, 2 (2009), 472–476.

18. Keita Higuchi, Ryo Yonetani, and Yoichi Sato. 2017. EgoScanning: Quickly Scanning First-Person Videos with Egocentric Elastic Timelines. In *Proceedings of the 2017 CHI Conference on Human Factors in Computing Systems (CHI '17)*. 6536–6546. DOI: http://dx.doi.org/10.1145/3025453.3025821

19. Ingrid Maria Hopkins, Michael W. Gower, Trista A. Perez, Dana S. Smith, Franklin R. Amthor, F. Casey Wimsatt, and Fred J. Biasini. 2011. Avatar Assistant: Improving Social Skills in Students with an ASD Through a Computer-Based Intervention. *Journal of Autism and Developmental Disorders* 41, 11 (01 Nov 2011), 1543–1555. DOI: http://dx.doi.org/10.1007/s10803-011-1179-z

20. Debora M Kagohara, Larah van der Meer, Sathiyaprakash Ramdoss, Mark F OâĂŹReilly, Giulio E Lancioni, Tonya N Davis, Mandy Rispoli, Russell Lang, Peter B Marschik, Dean Sutherland, and others. 2013. Using iPods and iPads in teaching programs for individuals with developmental disabilities: A systematic review. *Research in developmental disabilities* 34, 1 (2013), 147–156.

21. Thorsten Karrer, Malte Weiss, Eric Lee, and Jan Borchers. 2008. DRAGON: A Direct Manipulation Interface for Frame-accurate In-scene Video Navigation. In *Proceedings of the ACM CHI Conference on Human Factors in Computing Systems (CHI)*. ACM, New York, NY, USA, 247–250. DOI: http://dx.doi.org/10.1145/1357054.1357097

22. Thorsten Karrer, Moritz Wittenhagen, and Jan Borchers. 2012. DragLocks: Handling Temporal Ambiguities in Direct Manipulation Video Navigation. In *Proceedings of the ACM CHI Conference on Human Factors in Computing Systems (CHI)*. ACM, New York, NY, USA, 623–626. DOI: http://dx.doi.org/10.1145/2207676.2207764

23. Hiroshi Kera, Ryo Yonetani, Keita Higuchi, and Yoichi Sato. 2016. Discovering Objects of Joint Attention via First-Person Sensing. In *The IEEE Conference on Computer Vision and Pattern Recognition (CVPR) Workshops*.

24. Juho Kim, Philip J. Guo, Carrie J. Cai, Shang-Wen (Daniel) Li, Krzysztof Z. Gajos, and Robert C. Miller. 2014. Data-driven Interaction Techniques for Improving Navigation of Educational Videos. In *Proceedings of the ACM Symposium on User Interface Software and Technology (UIST)*. ACM, New York, NY, USA, 563–572. DOI: http://dx.doi.org/10.1145/2642918.2647389

25. E. I. Konstantinidis, A. Luneski, C. A. Frantzidis, P. Costas, and P. D. Bamidis. 2009. A proposed framework of an interactive semi-virtual environment for enhanced education of children with autism spectrum disorders. In *2009 22nd IEEE International Symposium on Computer-Based Medical Systems*. 1–6. DOI: http://dx.doi.org/10.1109/CBMS.2009.5255414

26. Kyle Krafka, Aditya Khosla, Petr Kellnhofer, Harini Kannan, Suchendra Bhandarkar, Wojciech Matusik, and Antonio Torralba. 2016. Eye tracking for everyone. In *Proceedings of the IEEE Conference on Computer Vision and Pattern Recognition*. 2176–2184.

27. Justin Matejka, Tovi Grossman, and George Fitzmaurice. 2014. Video Lens: Rapid Playback and Exploration of Large Video Collections and Associated Metadata. In *Proceedings of the ACM Symposium on User Interface Software and Technology (UIST)*. ACM, New York, NY, USA, 541–550. DOI: http://dx.doi.org/10.1145/2642918.2647366

28. Soichiro Matsuda, Eleuda Nunez, Masakazu Hirokawa, Junichi Yamamoto, and Kenji Suzuki. 2017. Facilitating Social Play for Children with PDDs: Effects of Paired Robotic Devices. *Frontiers in Psychology* 8 (2017), 1029. DOI:http://dx.doi.org/10.3389/fpsyg.2017.01029

29. David McNaughton and Janice Light. 2013. The iPad and Mobile Technology Revolution: Benefits and Challenges for Individuals who require Augmentative and Alternative Communication. *Augmentative and Alternative Communication* 29, 2 (2013), 107–116. DOI: http://dx.doi.org/10.3109/07434618.2013.784930 PMID: 23705813.

30. Peter Mundy, Christine Delgado, Jessica Block, Meg Venezia, Anne Hogan, and Jeffrey Seibert. 2003. Early social communication scales (ESCS).

31. Leslie Neely, Mandy Rispoli, Siglia Camargo, Heather Davis, and Margot Boles. 2013. The effect of instructional use of an iPad on challenging behavior and academic engagement for two students with autism. *Research in Autism Spectrum Disorders* 7, 4 (2013), 509 – 516. DOI:http://dx.doi.org/10.1016/j.rasd.2012.12.004

32. Cuong Nguyen, Yuzhen Niu, and Feng Liu. 2013. Direct Manipulation Video Navigation in 3D. In *Proceedings of the ACM CHI Conference on Human Factors in Computing Systems (CHI)*. ACM, New York, NY, USA, 1169–1172. DOI: http://dx.doi.org/10.1145/2470654.2466150

33. Maria B Ospina, Jennifer Krebs Seida, Brenda Clark, Mohammad Karkhaneh, Lisa Hartling, Lisa Tjosvold, Ben Vandermeer, and Veronica Smith. 2008. Behavioural and developmental interventions for autism spectrum disorder: a clinical systematic review. *PloS one* 3, 11 (2008), e3755.

34. Suporn Pongnumkul, Jue Wang, Gonzalo Ramos, and Michael Cohen. 2010. Content-aware Dynamic Timeline for Video Browsing. In *Proceedings of the ACM Symposium on User Interface Software and Technology (UIST)*. ACM, New York, NY, USA, 139–142. DOI: http://dx.doi.org/10.1145/1866029.1866053

35. Yael Pritch, Alex Rav-Acha, Avital Gutman, and Shmuel Peleg. 2007. Webcam Synopsis: Peeking Around the World. In *Proceedings of the IEEE International Conference on Computer Vision (ICCV)*. IEEE, Washington, DC, USA, 1–8. DOI: http://dx.doi.org/10.1109/ICCV.2007.4408934

36. Alex Rav-Acha, Yael Pritch, and Shmuel Peleg. 2006. Making a Long Video Short: Dynamic Video Synopsis. In *Proceedings of the IEEE Conference on Computer Vision and Pattern Recognition (CVPR)*. IEEE, Washington, DC, USA, 435–441. DOI: http://dx.doi.org/10.1109/CVPR.2006.179

37. Brian A. Smith, Qi Yin, Steven K. Feiner, and Shree K. Nayar. 2013. Gaze Locking: Passive Eye Contact Detection for Human-object Interaction. In *Proceedings of the 26th Annual ACM Symposium on User Interface Software and Technology (UIST '13)*. 271–280. DOI: http://dx.doi.org/10.1145/2501988.2501994

38. Kenji Suzuki, Taku Hachisu, and Kazuki Iida. 2016. EnhancedTouch: A Smart Bracelet for Enhancing Human-Human Physical Touch. In *Proceedings of the 2016 CHI Conference on Human Factors in Computing Systems (CHI '16)*. 1282–1293. DOI: http://dx.doi.org/10.1145/2858036.2858439

39. B. Takacs. 2005. Special education and rehabilitation: teaching and healing with interactive graphics. *IEEE Computer Graphics and Applications* 25, 5 (Sept 2005), 40–48. DOI:http://dx.doi.org/10.1109/MCG.2005.113

40. Joshua Wade, Arpan Sarkar, Amy Swanson, Amy Weitlauf, Zachary Warren, and Nilanjan Sarkar. 2017. Process Measures of Dyadic Collaborative Interaction for Social Skills Intervention in Individuals with Autism Spectrum Disorders. *ACM Trans. Access. Comput.* 10, 4, Article 13 (Aug. 2017), 19 pages. DOI: http://dx.doi.org/10.1145/3107925

41. Yandong Wen, Kaipeng Zhang, Zhifeng Li, and Yu Qiao. 2016. *A Discriminative Feature Learning Approach for Deep Face Recognition*. Springer International Publishing, Cham, 499–515. DOI: http://dx.doi.org/10.1007/978-3-319-46478-7_31

42. Peter Wittenburg, Hennie Brugman, Albert Russel, Alex Klassmann, and Han Sloetjes. 2006. ELAN: a professional framework for multimodality research. In *Proceedings of LREC*, Vol. 2006. 5th.

43. Zhefan Ye, Yin Li, Alireza Fathi, Yi Han, Agata Rozga, Gregory D. Abowd, and James M. Rehg. 2012. Detecting Eye Contact Using Wearable Eye-tracking Glasses. In *Proceedings of the 2012 ACM Conference on Ubiquitous Computing (UbiComp '12)*. ACM, New York, NY, USA, 699–704. DOI: http://dx.doi.org/10.1145/2370216.2370368

44. Z. Ye, Y. Li, Y. Liu, C. Bridges, A. Rozga, and J. M. Rehg. 2015. Detecting bids for eye contact using a wearable camera. In *2015 11th IEEE International Conference and Workshops on Automatic Face and Gesture Recognition (FG)*, Vol. 1. 1–8. DOI: http://dx.doi.org/10.1109/FG.2015.7163095

45. Hiroshi Kera Ryo Yonetani Keita Higuchi Yifei Huang, Minjie Cai and Yoichi Sato. 2017. emporal Localization and Spatial Segmentation of Joint Attention in Multiple First-Person Video. In *The International Conference on Computer Vision (ICCV) Workshops*.

46. Hanan Makki Zakari, Minhua Ma, and David Simmons. 2014. *A Review of Serious Games for Children with Autism Spectrum Disorders (ASD)*. Springer International Publishing, Cham, 93–106. DOI: http://dx.doi.org/10.1007/978-3-319-11623-5_9

47. Xucong Zhang, Yusuke Sugano, and Andreas Bulling. 2017. Everyday Eye Contact Detection Using Unsupervised Gaze Target Discovery. DOI: http://dx.doi.org/10.1145/3126594.3126614

48. Xucong Zhang, Yusuke Sugano, Mario Fritz, and Andreas Bulling. 2015. Appearance-based gaze estimation in the wild. In *Proceedings of the IEEE Conference on Computer Vision and Pattern Recognition*. 4511–4520.

49. Xucong Zhang, Yusuke Sugano, Mario Fritz, and Andreas Bulling. 2017. It's Written All Over Your Face: Full-Face Appearance-Based Gaze Estimation. In *Proc. of the IEEE Conference on Computer Vision and Pattern Recognition Workshops (CVPRW)* (2017-05-18). https://perceptual.mpi-inf.mpg.de/files/2017/05/zhang_cvprw2017.pdf

Quester: A Speech-Based Question Answering Support System for Oral Presentations

Reza Asadi, Ha Trinh, Harriet J. Fell, Timothy W. Bickmore
Northeastern University
Boston, USA
asadi, hatrinh, fell, bickmore@ccs.neu.edu

ABSTRACT
Current slideware, such as PowerPoint, reinforces the delivery of linear oral presentations. In settings such as question answering sessions or review lectures, more extemporaneous and dynamic presentations are required. An intelligent system that can automatically identify and display the slides most related to the presenter's speech, allows for more speaker flexibility in sequencing their presentation. We present Quester, a system that enables fast access to relevant presentation content during a question answering session and supports nonlinear presentations led by the speaker. Given the slides' contents and notes, the system ranks presentation slides based on semantic closeness to spoken utterances, displays the most related slides, and highlights the corresponding content keywords in slide notes. The design of our system was informed by findings from interviews with expert presenters and analysis of recordings of lectures and conference presentations. In a within-subjects study comparing our dynamic support system with a static slide navigation system during a question answering session, presenters expressed a strong preference for our system and answered the questions more efficiently using our system.

Author Keywords
Presentation assistance; question answering support systems; natural language and speech processing.

INTRODUCTION
Conventional presentation tools, such as PowerPoint and Keynote, are designed to support presenters in doing what they do best, deliver standard, scripted, linear, and rehearsed presentations in a polished, but fixed and invariant manner. Unfortunately, these tools do not provide good support for speakers who want to deliver more extemporaneous talks in which they dynamically adapt their presentation to input or questions from the audience, evolving audience needs, or other contextual factors such as varying or indeterminate presentation time, real-time information, or more improvisational or experimental formats. At best, current slideware only provides simple indexing mechanisms to let speakers hunt through their slides for material to support their dynamically evolving speech, and speakers must perform this frantic search while the audience is watching and waiting.

IUI'18, March 7–11, 2018, Tokyo, Japan

ACM ISBN 978-1-4503-4945-1/18/03...$15.00
https://doi.org/10.1145/3172944.3172974

Perhaps the most common situations in which speakers must provide such dynamic presentations are in Question and Answer (QA) sessions at the end of their prepared presentations. Speakers' remarks are entirely driven by the questions from the audience, which arrive in an unscripted order, and the questions themselves are often entirely unanticipated. A significant portion of these QA sessions is often taken up by the speaker searching through their slides for material to support their responses.

Several solutions have been developed to support non-linear, dynamic presentations [6, 12, 17]. However, they require authoring of pre-planned paths and multiple branches in presentation scripts. An alternative approach is to dynamically offer branching options in real time based on tracking of the presenter's speech content, thereby eliminating the need for prior preparation. However, incorporating speech input is challenging as it depends on the accuracy of automatic speech recognition (ASR) and the speech during QA sessions is generally spontaneous.

In this effort, our aim is to develop slideware technology to support these dynamic speaker-led presentations, by having a system track the presenter's speech and automatically index supporting slides in real time. Our system, called *Quester*, matches a presenter's speech to slides based on slide contents and notes, and presents the top-ranked slides along with content keywords to the presenter so he or she only has to skim a handful of the most relevant slides and click on the one they want to show. We evaluated Quester in simulated post-presentation QA sessions, but it can be used to support any kind of speaker-led dynamically-structured presentation, such as a lecture on a subset of topics in a slide deck based on student or audience requests. Our contributions include:

1. Identification of current practices and requirements for dynamic presentations, through analysis of interviews with expert presenters and recordings of existing QA sessions;

2. Development of the Quester system to automatically suggest and display presentation content based on speech;
3. Validation of Quester in a comparative study that demonstrates its potential to improve the presenter's experience and performance during QA sessions, compared to standard slideware practice.

RELATED WORK

We review previous work regarding slideware support for non-linear and dynamic presentation, and current advances in QA support systems.

Non-Linear Presentations

Experts such as Tufte [18], criticize the linear structure of PowerPoint presentations and argue that although it helps the presenter, it is not "audience-oriented" and can reduce the overall quality of the presentations. The "sequentiality" of slides makes it difficult to display them in arbitrary orders, and thus may discourage presenters from navigating to related slides in order to respond to the audience questions during the presentation [22]. In contrast, free-form presentations can encourage discussions, creative thinking, and communication of new ideas [8].

QA sessions are a common setting for dynamic presentations. Anthony et al. [1] reported their observations of presenter performance during QA sessions in conference talks, which can inform the design of QA support systems. They observed the tendency of question askers to refer to something that was mentioned in the presentation before asking their question, and that presenters often repeat or rephrase questions before answering, as recommended in self-help presentation books.

Presentation Support Systems

Previous research has developed novel presentation systems to support a more dynamic approach to presenting. One of the challenges in designing these systems is to avoid distraction and excessive cognitive load that dynamic interfaces may cause [7]. Moskovich et al. [12] developed an interface for authoring and delivering customizable presentations using a hierarchical presentation structure and predefined paths. During delivery, the presenter can change the presentation path based on audience feedback or time constraints. The NextSlidePlease system [17] provides a graph-based authoring system and a presentation path suggestion algorithm to support interactive presentations. It helps users prioritize presentation content based on remaining time during presentation delivery. Using the HyperSlides system [6], presenters can author hierarchical hyperlinked non-linear presentation slides. Finally, the Palette [13] and PaperPoint [16] systems use paper-based slide cards to provide random access to single digital slides.

One of the main challenges in providing automated support for non-linear presentations is capturing speakers' dynamic and evolving communicative intent during delivery. Inferring intent from the presenters' speech content is an ideal approach, since it requires no additional effort by the speaker. There have been limited studies on taking advantage of the presenter's speech content to support presentations. Rogina et al. [15] matched speech transcripts with slide content to automatically advance slides and display additional related documents. IntelliPrompter [3] is a speech-based note display system that tracks a presenter's coverage of slide notes and cues them about their next speaking point.

Related Information Retrieval Methods

Studies in audio lecture indexing and retrieval have explored methods for matching voice data with text sources, which can be used in non-linear presentation support systems. Yamamoto et al. [20] compared the results of ASR with the textbook used in the lecture to segment lecture recordings into topics. They calculated the similarity between word vectors from the speech transcript and the textbook. Yang et al. [21] extracted keywords from video lectures using the ASR output and text information extracted from videos. Cao et al. [5] associated the text extracted from PowerPoint slides with lecture videos to support video-based QA on videotaped lectures.

Several related studies have used information retrieval techniques for automatic question answering. Yen et al. [23] evaluated a context-ranking model used for QA. The ranking was performed by predicting the relevancy of the input passage to a given question using features such as part of speech, named-entity class, and the degree of match between the passage words and question terms. Yih et al. [24] measured the semantic similarity of entities and relations extracted from questions with the content of the knowledge base to perform open domain QA. Semantic parsing was performed using a neural network-based semantic model.

To our knowledge, there have been no studies to date that investigate the application of speech-based content suggestions to support dynamic presentations in real time.

FORMATIVE STUDIES

To enrich our understanding of dynamic presentations, we conducted interviews exploring current practices of preparing and delivering extemporaneous talks. We supplemented our qualitative research with a quantitative analysis of post-presentation QA sessions from videotaped conference presentations and lectures.

Interviews of Expert Presenters

We recruited 8 university professors (4 female, 4 male, P1-8) from computer science and history departments. All participants had extensive experience giving presentations in various settings, from conference presentations to classroom lectures, seminars, workshops and panel discussions. We conducted semi-structured interviews with open-ended questions about general presentation preparation and delivery practices, potential issues of linear presentations, and strategies for dynamic presentation support. Each interview lasted between 30-45 minutes.

The interviews were recorded, transcribed and coded using thematic analysis techniques [4]. Our initial open coding process resulted in 96 active codes capturing actions in data. Using affinity diagraming, we categorized these codes into the following three themes.

Need for Dynamic Presentations

Participants identified a variety of situations that require a more dynamic approach to presenting. The most cited scenario is post-presentation QA sessions. In these sessions, it is a common practice for presenters to navigate back to previously presented slides, or spontaneously show additional backup slides to support their responses:

"We will definitely build in backups and we encourage students to incorporate backups... During the question period, you feel like a million bucks if someone is like, 'well what about this?', and then you say, 'well look at this!'" [P4]

Similar to QA sessions, unscripted presentations are also required for discussion-based settings such as *"flipped classrooms"* [P1] or *"review classes"* [P4]. In these scenarios, "*inevitably it involves a lot of shuffling. Someone just says, 'I have a question about TCP', and then OK, I have to go find that deck, and find that specific thing that you are talking about. So that's two hours of jumping around in random places"* [P4].

In flexible and interactive settings such as classrooms or seminars, presenters also dynamically tailor their delivery based on their real-time evaluation of the audience's level of understanding: *"I'll have a series of topics or modules that I want to cover in a class time, and some expand and some may contract depending on where the students are and their understanding and interest level"* [P1]. In some cases, presenters also spontaneously select a subset of topics to present based on audience interest: *"A lot of my presentations are play on adventure type things, where at some point I ask, 'hey what do you guys want to talk about?'"* [P8]. Most participants also mentioned the need for dynamically adapting their delivery due to time limit.

Preparing for Unscripted Interactions

Presenters often include backup slides at the end of their slide deck to prepare for QA sessions:

"If I am less familiar with a topic then I'm more likely to have some more backup slides... I think the act of creating the slide is very important... at least it will put you at ease" [P2]

These backups can be new slides containing supporting material for anticipated audience questions, or existing slides that are *"copied and pasted from other slide decks"* [P8]. They can also be results of a timed rehearsal process, in which some slides are moved from the main slide deck to the backup section due to time constraints.

Presenters often write speaking notes for new presentations or when highly visual slides are used. Short, bullet point-style notes are generally preferred, although more verbose notes and specific wordings may also be used for important points when presenters really want to *"get it across"* [P3]. In certain settings such as history conferences, it is also common to recite full scripts during presentations. Another approach is to make *"those slides your notes"* [P5], but this often results in text-heavy slides that are not desirable.

In addition to key speaking points, presenters also add *"supplemental material"* [P1] in their notes, such as more detailed explanations of a concept or additional information taken from an existing paper, which may be used when audiences ask related questions.

Nonlinear Slide Navigation

Most dynamic presentations require nonlinear access to relevant slides. The inability to quickly navigate to needed slides could cause significant disruption in the talk flow:

"It is disruptive if you can't get there quickly, and anytime you muck with the computer you are risking messing yourself up... The last thing you want to do is wasting your time trying to find your slide" [P2]

Presentation Venue	Num. of Pres. Analyzed	Avg. Length of Pres. (MM: SS)	Avg. Num. of Slides	Avg. Length of QA (MM: SS)	Avg. Num. of Questions	Percentage of Questions	
						Refer (%)	Extra (%)
CHI	10	14:24	33.1	3:30	3.2	9	3
NEAB-PD	5	20:36	28.2	5:37	4.4	0	9
FECE	5	19:24	15.4	7:57	5	8	0
Lectures	5	60:20	51.8	-	12.8	8	0

Table 1. Statistical analysis of conference presentations and lectures

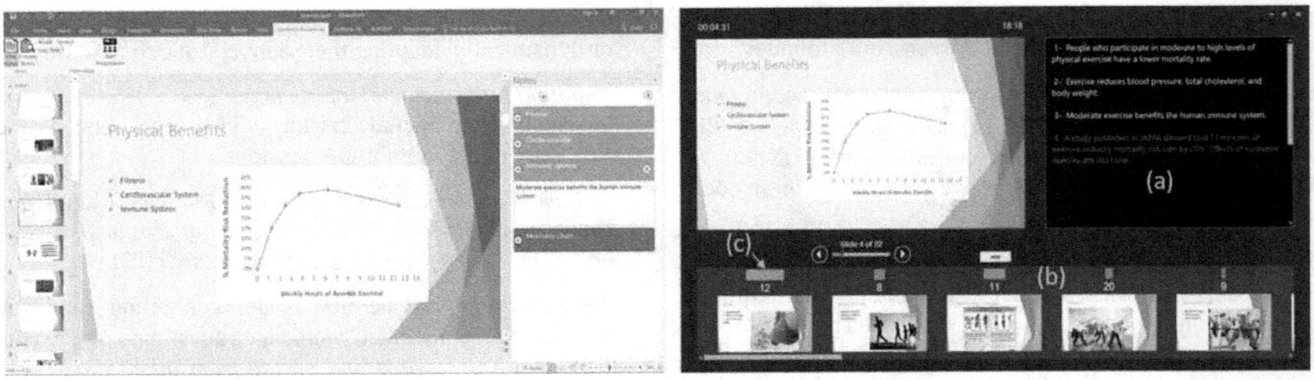

Figure 1. Note Authoring Environment (Left) and Presenter View (Right): (a) notes pane with an extra note topic in red, (b) slide navigation pane showing the most related slides, c) green bars showing the degree of slide relatedness to speech input

This disruption and delay time in searching for slides could lead to negative audience experience: *"I have seen people go through 30 slides and finally go, 'is this the slide you meant? or this slide?... it is a disaster"* [P1]. Instead of skipping through slides in sequence, a more recommended method is to exit the presenter view and then directly select a slide thumbnail from the slide navigation pane. However, this can still lead to a long delay time, especially for big slide decks. Another tactic is to add slide numbers on slides and use them for direct keyboard navigation. However, this can still be problematic if slide numbers are misremembered. Due to these difficulties, presenters may opt to not show supporting slides during QA sessions, even though they might have spent time preparing them, unless they are confident that they know *"where the slide is and it's very easy to quickly go to slide"* [P1].

To facilitate slide navigation, participants suggested having a dedicated *"question mode that you could have flags for particular slides that you anticipated you needed"* [P3], or indexing slides by key phrases, so that *"you know that a certain word would be phrase to a slide"* [P4]. One participant envisioned a speech-based technology that could automatically display relevant slides based on the presenter's speech:

"If there was a technology where the screen would go black and within 5 seconds the slide I wanted would come up that would be great... If I could speak into my clicker and say, you know, 'show me the slides that have this on it' and maybe a few slides would pop up and I would click on the one" [P6]

In summary, findings from our interview analysis highlights the need for more intelligent support for seamless nonlinear slide navigation during dynamic presentation delivery.

Analysis of Question Answering Sessions

To better understand the quantitative characteristics of QA sessions, we analyzed video recordings of 20 conference presentations and 5 lectures. Conference presentation samples were chosen from 3 different venues: CHI Conference, National Education Alliance for Borderline Personality Disorder (NEAB-PD), and Fostering Entrepreneurship in the Creative Economy (FECE). Lectures were chosen from the Simons Institute interactive learning series about different topics in computer science. We annotated the duration of presentations, number of slides, length of QA sessions, and the number of questions asked. For lectures, we examined all questions asked during and after the presentation.

Based on our analysis, a typical 20-minute conference presentation had 32 slides on average, while a typical 60-minute lecture had 51. Navigating through such a large slide deck to search for a specific slide would potentially be difficult and time consuming.

In total, 145 questions were asked. We categorized the presenters' strategies for responding to questions into two groups: 1) going back to a slide presented before (Refer); and 2) showing an extra slide (Extra) (Table 1).

On average, each QA interaction took 59 seconds, including the question, optionally repeating the question by speaker, optionally searching for and displaying a slide, and answering the question. For 10% of questions, presenters navigated to a slide (either previously presented or extra) to answer the questions. In 70% of these cases, the speakers moved though slides linearly. In the remaining 30%, they exited the presenter view to search for a slide. Navigating to a slide on average took 13.1 seconds, which comprises 22% of each QA interaction duration.

DESIGN OF QUESTER

Informed by our literature review and formative studies, we developed Quester, a question answering support system as an add-in for Microsoft PowerPoint.

Quester supports fast, nonlinear access to relevant presentation content by listening to speech input and dynamically suggesting the most related slides and note sections. Speech input can be received directly from the audience asking a question or from the presenter repeating or rephrasing the question. The system ranks presentation slides based on their textual content, slide notes, and metadata of slides' visual elements. To further assist presenters in identifying target content, it also highlights the section of the slide notes that is most related to the uttered question. Quester also provides an interface for presenters to privately preview and search for relevant content without exposing the search process to the audience.

Note Authoring Environment

Our system provides a note authoring interface integrated within PowerPoint 2016 (Figure 1). The presenters can divide the notes for each slide into sections called topics. This segmentation allows for highlighting specific sections of notes that are related to a question. This also makes it possible to separate extra notes from the main presentation notes. Extra notes may contain supplemental material that are not presented during the main delivery, but the presenter can refer to them during QA. They are distinguished from main notes with a different font color (Figure 1).

Presentation Mode

During the presentation, Quester displays the slide, notes, and timing information, similar to PowerPoint's Presenter View. It also provides a slide navigation pane (Figure 1).

Slide Navigation Pane

Located at the bottom of the Presenter View, the slide navigation pane displays 5 slide thumbnails at each moment, but the presenter can scroll to see the rest of slides. The number of visible slide thumbnails was chosen empirically based on trade-offs between quick accessibility and visual and cognitive load. Corresponding slide numbers are shown above each slide thumbnail. The slide navigation pane is hidden by default to avoid distraction during the presentation, but it is automatically shown when the presenter navigates to the last slide that he/she has planned to present (which can be set in the authoring environment). Users can also manually toggle the visibility of the navigation pane during the presentation.

The order of the slides displayed in the navigation pane is based on their semantic closeness to the speech input. It changes dynamically as new speech input is received and processed (with a 500 ms delay). To minimize potential distraction caused by rapid changes in the order of slide thumbnails, Quester does not change the slide orders once they appear in the visible portion of the Navigation pane. To indicate the degree of semantic match of each slide to recent speech, the system displays green bars with varying sizes above each slide thumbnail.

Presenters can hover over each slide thumbnail to privately see a preview of its content. This preview appears as a modal window over the presenter view and contains the slide and notes in smaller size (Figure 2). If the presenter wants to show a slide from the navigation pane to the audience, he/she can click on a thumbnail and the presentation will jump to that slide.

Note Highlighting

When the speaker displays a slide using the navigation pane, the note topic most related to the speech content is detected and the keywords in that topic are highlighted. Highlighting is done by changing the color of keywords and increasing the font size. Also, the notes pane is scrolled to display that topic at the top (Figure 2).

In the next section, we describe our technical approach to estimating the semantic closeness between the slide content and speech content.

Semantic Match Scoring

Before presentation, slide contents are automatically processed to extract their keywords, and weights are assigned to the keywords based on their importance in the slide. During the presentation, the system scans the presenter's speech content for these keywords, and based on the weights of detected keywords, slides and note topics are scored. The detailed description of the scoring system is available in [2]. In following subsections, we briefly explain the steps in this process.

Content Processing

The content used for semantic matching includes slide title and text content, slide notes, and metadata about the visual elements in each slide. The metadata is generated by extracting the type of each element in the slide and adding corresponding descriptive words for the element to slide content. For example, if a slide contains a chart, the system adds the words "plot", "graph", and "chart" to the slide content. This metadata allows the system to handle

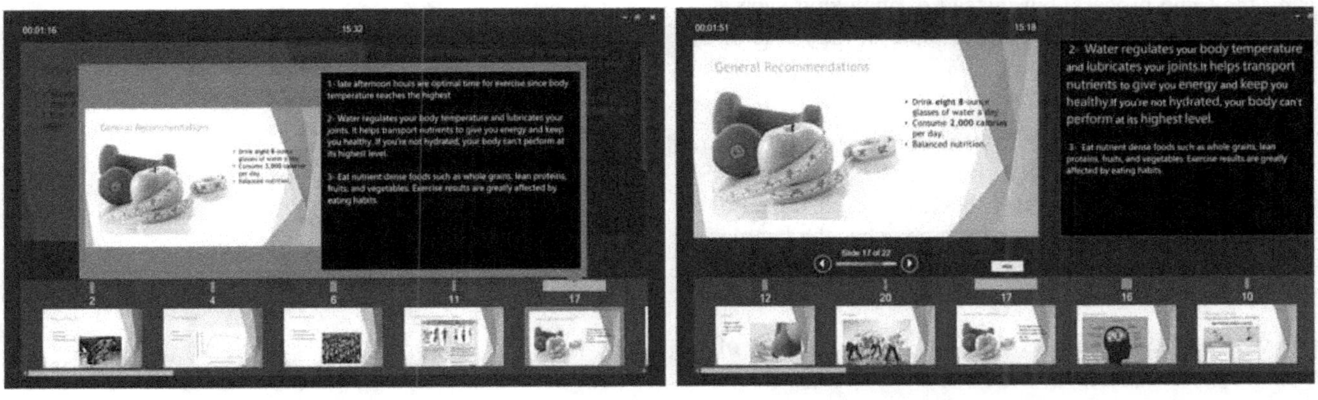

Figure 2. (Left) Slide Preview displayed when the presenter hovers the mouse over a slide thumbnail; (Right) Note pane is scrolled to display the most relevant note topic at the top with highlighted keywords

questions that refer to specific visual elements of a slide (e.g. *"Can you go back to the slide with the graph on it?"*).

The system segments the slide content into sentences, and performs part of speech tagging using the Stanford CoreNLP tools [9]. It removes stop words, adverbs, and symbols from the content and stores the remaining words as content keywords. It then lemmatizes the keywords and extracts their synonyms using WordNet [11].

Keyword Weighting

The system assigns slide-level and topic-level weights to each keyword based on its importance in the slide content and the note topic containing it, respectively.

Slide-level keyword weights are the result of a multiplication of values calculated using two methods:

Term frequency - inverse document frequency: This is a common measure in information retrieval, which is calculated by multiplying the frequency of keyword k in slide by its inverse document frequency:

$$idf_k = \log\left(\frac{|P|}{|\{\forall S \epsilon P | k \epsilon S\}|}\right) \quad (1)$$

P is the set of slides and the denominator is the number of slides containing keyword k.

Word similarity: This method assigns a higher weight to keywords that are semantically closer to other keywords in the same slide compared to the keywords in other slides. The similarity between keywords is calculated as follows:

$$sim(k_i, k_j) = \sqrt{\sum_{l=0}^{n} (v(k_i)_l - v(k_j)_l)^2} \quad (2)$$

$v(k)$ is the word vector representation of keyword k. We used a pre-trained GloVe [14] vector representation with 1.9 million uncased words and vectors with 300 elements, trained using 42 billion tokens of web data from Common Crawl.

We also assigned a topic-level weight for each keyword using the same process, but instead of analyzing each slide in the slide deck we analyze each topic in the notes of the slide containing that keyword.

Content Scoring

During a presentation, the system uses the IBM Watson cloud-based ASR[1] to transcribe the speech. This ASR system provides a list of hypotheses for each time frame, called word alternatives. Our system matches the lemmas of these word alternatives against each slide keyword lemma and its synonyms.

The score for each slide is the sum of the weights of its keywords that were spotted in speech. Similarly, the score for each topic will be the sum of the weights of its detected keywords.

Recency Model

The recency of keywords is important, so the keywords detected during a previous question do not affect the scores related to the current question being answered. To eliminate the effects of outdated keywords, the simplest solution is to require the presenter to manually reset slide scores before each new question. However, this imposes an extra burden on the presenters and they might forget to do so. Therefore, we developed and evaluated two models that take into account the recency effect.

Our system stores detected keywords in a stack and if a keyword that is already put in the stack is detected again, it is moved to the top. Therefore, the most recent keywords will always be at the top of the stack. We examined 2 recency models:

Window model: Similar to previous work in word completion [19], we calculated slide scores based on only the top n keywords in the stack. For example, if n=2 then the model only considers the last 2 detected keywords.

Decay model: The model calculates slide scores after modifying the keyword weights based on the keyword positions in the stack. Keyword weights are modified using the following equation:

$$w = w_0 b^t \qquad 0 < b \leq 1 \qquad 0 \leq t \quad (3)$$

in which, w_0 is the original weight of keyword, b is the decay base, and t is the distance of keyword from the top of the stack. For b=1 the weights are the same as the original weights (i.e., no recency model). As b gets smaller, the decaying effect will be stronger and keywords detected further in the past will have a smaller effect on slide scores.

We performed theoretical evaluations of these two models using a corpus of presentations and questions collected from a user study that we describe in the next section.

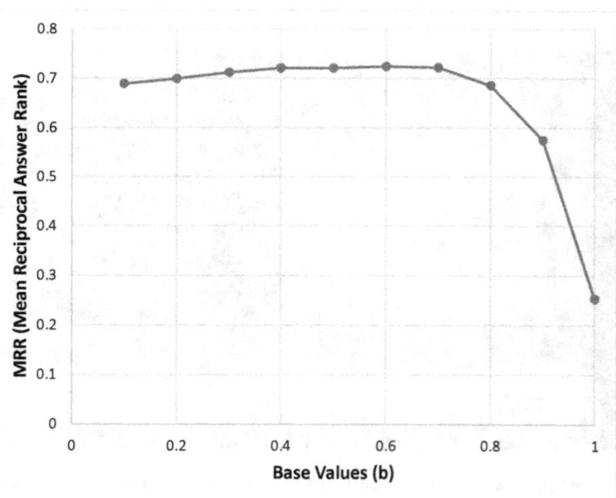

Figure 3. Performance of the decay recency model with different base values

[1] https://www.ibm.com/watson/services/speech-to-text/

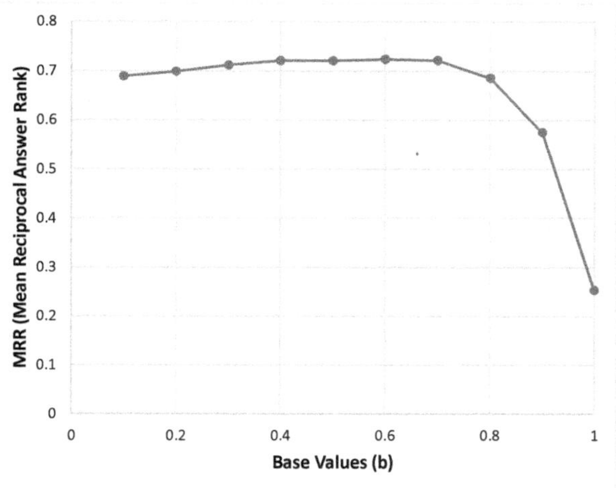

Figure 3. Performance of the decay recency model with different base values

Corpus of Evaluation Presentations and Questions

To support both theoretical and user evaluations of different aspects of Quester, we developed a standardized corpus consisting of two short (7-slide) presentations on the topics of Exercise and Nutrition, along with a set of audience questions and extra QA slides for each.

To generate a corpus of audience questions for each presentation, we recruited 8 participants (college educated with presentation experience) to view videotaped presentations of a researcher giving each of the short presentations, then generating 10 questions each, resulting in an initial set of 80 questions per presentation. After removing redundant, unclear, and rhetorical questions, we further curated the questions, resulting in 40 audience questions per presentation. 4 of these 40 questions required display of slides previously presented in the main presentation (e.g. *'Can you explain more about the graph on sleep?'*), and 2 required display of extra slides (e.g. *'Can you show me a sample weekly menu?'*) (reflecting the Refer and Extra percentages in Table 1). The remaining questions could be answered using additional content, with or without displaying supporting slides.

To generate the extra / backup slides to provide support for the audience questions, we categorized the 36 questions for each presentation into 15 topics per presentation, and had two writers create an additional 15 slides with accompanying speaker notes for each presentation. The writers also created additional notes for the original 7 slides to help answer the 4 Refer questions for each presentation.

The resulting slide notes for the Nutrition presentation contained 1562 words segmented into 55 topics. The slide notes for the Exercise presentation contained 1371 words in 58 topics. Our corpus roughly matched a corpus of presentation slides and notes gathered in a previous study [2] on several metrics: the notes for each slide contained 73.3 words and 2.82 topics on average.

Model Evaluation

We used our presentation corpus to evaluate the accuracy of the matching algorithm using both recency models with different parameter values.

To ensure that the system performance does not depend on specific order of questions, we evaluated the system with 10 different randomized permutations of questions and calculated the average performance for all permutations. For each permutation of questions, we passed each question to the system as input to assign scores to the slides using different models and parameter values. The system then ranked the slides based on their scores.

Measures

A common measure for evaluating the performance of QA systems is the mean reciprocal answer rank (MRR):

$$MRR_m = \frac{1}{|Q|}\sum_{q \in Q}\frac{1}{Rank_m(q)} \quad (4)$$

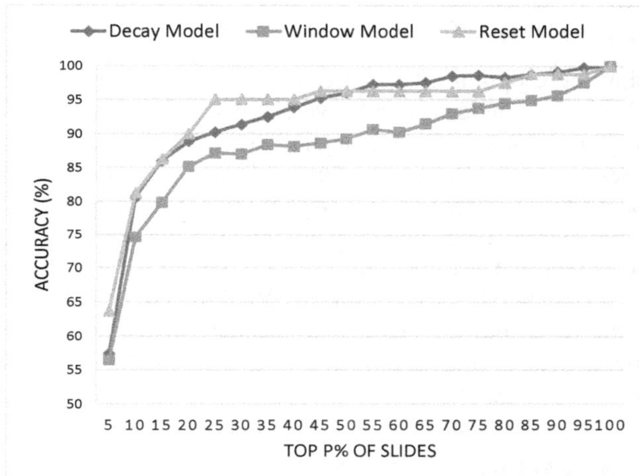

Figure 4. Comparison of different recency models

In which, $Rank_m(q)$ is the rank of the slide containing the answer to question q using model m, and Q is the set of all questions.

We also measured the performance of our system using an accuracy measure more tailored to our application. We calculated the proportion of questions for which the slide containing the answer was included in the top $p\%$ of slides with the highest match scores:

$$accuracy_{m,p} = \frac{|\{\forall q \in Q | Rank_m(q) < p\}|}{|Q|} \quad (5)$$

Results

Window Model: We evaluated this model for different values of n. We found that $n = 4$ resulted in the best MRR value of 0.70.

Decay Model: We evaluated this model for different values of b. Based on the evaluation, $b = 0.6$ resulted in the best

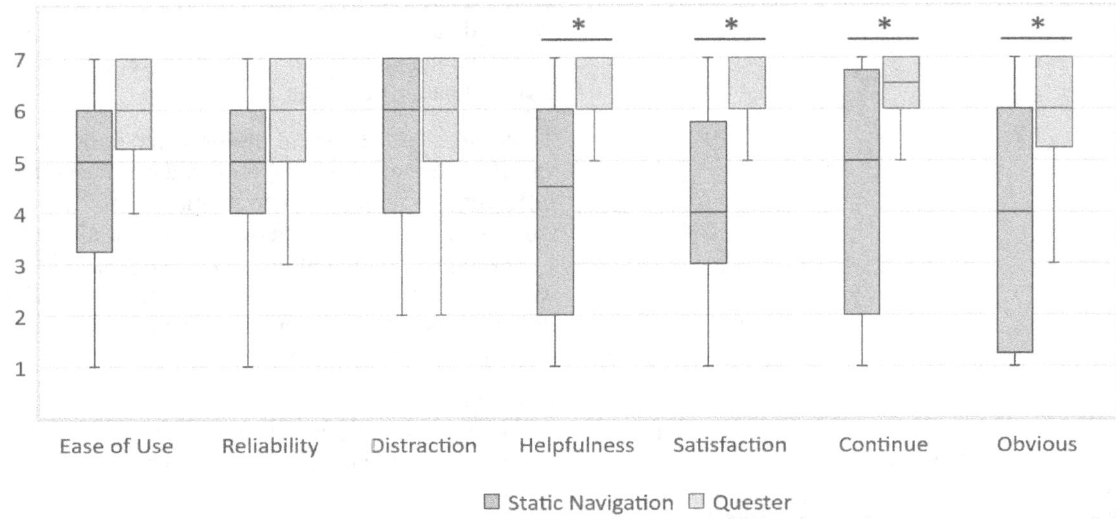

Figure 5. Presenters' absolute usability ratings of two QA support systems (* indicates statistical significances)

MRR value of 0.73. Figure 3 displays the MRR values of decay model for different base (*b*) values.

Using these optimized parameters (*b*=0.6 for decay model and *n*=4 for window model), we compared the accuracy of decay and window models against a system in which the scores are manually reset before each new question (Reset model). In our interface, we display the top 5 slides at any moment which corresponds to a *p* value of 22%. As shown in Figure 4, the accuracy of the Decay model for p=22% is 90.2% compared to 87.1% for the Window model and 95% for the Reset model. The actual accuracy of the system is expected to be lower than these values due to ASR errors. Based on these evaluations we decided to use the decay recency model with b=*0.6* in our system.

USER EVALUATION OF QUESTER

To examine the effectiveness of dynamic speech-based slide matching in Quester in improving presenters' experience and performance during a QA session, we conducted a user study comparing Quester against the static slide navigation supported in most conventional slideware.

For our Control condition (the Static Navigation), we extended PowerPoint with a Navigation pane similar to the one in Quester, but which always displays slides in the same linear order that they appear in the slide deck. As in Quester, the presenter can hover the mouse over each slide thumbnail to preview the slide and notes. Once the presenter clicks on a slide thumbnail to show the slide to the audience, the system displays the corresponding notes without highlighting the most related note topic.

Participants

We recruited 16 students and professionals (10 female, 6 male, ages 19-32, mean 23), with backgrounds in science, technology, business and arts. Of these participants, 2 were categorized as low competence public speakers, 5 were categorized as high competence public speakers, and 9 had moderate competence, according to the Self-Perceived Communication Competence Scale [10]. Participants were compensated for their participation.

Procedure

We asked each participant to rehearse and deliver two 3-minute presentations on the topics of Exercise and Nutrition, using the PowerPoint slide decks and notes prepared in our QA corpus. After each presentation, presenters engaged in a brief QA session during which they were asked to answer a set of 8 questions randomly selected from our 40-question corpus for each presentation, using a different QA support system. For each 3-minute talk, the participants were asked to only present the first 7 slides in the slide deck. The remaining 15 slides were extra material that could be used during the QA session.

During the delivery and QA session, the experimentation room was set up with a 42-inch display monitor for slide projection, a tripod-mounted microphone for recording the presenter's speech, and a secondary 15-inch computer screen displaying the Presenter View.

The study was a within-subject, single-session design in which each participant tested both conditions: *Quester vs. Static Navigation.* Each session lasted approximately 90 minutes. The ordering of the conditions and the slide decks were randomly assigned and counterbalanced.

At the beginning of the session, we introduced participants to the task of delivering two short presentations followed by QA sessions. For each condition, we gave participants 20 minutes to review the presentation content and rehearse their talk. We instructed them to review all 22 slides and notes, to prepare for both the presentation and the QA session. All participants confirmed that 20 minutes was sufficient for them to prepare.

Following each rehearsal, we gave participants brief instructions on how to use one of the two QA support systems and asked them to practice answering a sample question using the system. We asked participants to repeat the question aloud using their own words, before answering the question.

Following each practice round, we asked participants to give their final, videotaped presentation in front of the experimenter. After each presentation, the experimenter read aloud the randomly generated set of 8 questions, one at a time, for the presenter to answer. The presenter could ask the experimenter to repeat a question if they did not hear it clearly, and could skip any questions if they did not know the answer. Each QA session lasted approximately 5 minutes and was videotaped, with self-report measures gathered after each session. After the participant completed both conditions, we conducted a semi-structured interview, prompting for comparisons of the two QA support systems and suggestions for improvement. Self-report Measures of Presenter Experience

We assessed the presenters' experience with the QA support systems using the following self-report measures.

Absolute Usability Rating of QA Support System

We asked presenters to rate the usability of each QA support system after each QA session, using a 7-item, 7-point composite scale, as shown in Figure 5.

Figure 5 shows the results of the presenters' absolute usability ratings of the two QA support systems. Results of a repeated-measures ANOVA test on the composite usability rating (Cronbach's α=0.93) showed that Quester was rated significantly higher than the Static Navigation condition ($F_{1,15}$=10.337, p=.006, partial η^2=.408).

Results of Wilcoxon signed-rank tests on individual scale items showed that Quester was rated significantly better than the Static Navigation condition on *helpfulness* (Z=-2.55, p=.011), *satisfaction* (Z=-2.81, p=.005), *desire to continue using the system in future presentations* (Z=-2.50, p=.013), and *how obvious it was to see what the answer is* (Z=-2.97, p=.003). There were also trending effects of the condition on *ease of use* (Z=-1.95, p=.051) and *reliability* (Z=-1.80, p=.072), in favor of Quester. No significant difference was found between the two conditions in the rating of *distraction* (p=.258).

Relative Usability Rating of QA Support Systems

After presenters completed both conditions, we asked them to directly compare and indicate which of the two QA support systems performed better on the same 7 criteria included in the Absolute Usability Rating.

Results of Chi-square tests revealed significant preferences of presenters towards Quester on all 7 criteria. Compared to the Static Navigation condition, Quester was rated to be significantly better in terms of *ease of use* (χ2(1)=9.0, p=.003), *reliability* (χ2(1)=6.25, p=.012), *distraction* (χ2(1)=4.0, p=.046), *helpfulness* (χ2(1)=12.25, p<.001), *satisfaction* (χ2(1)=12.25, p<.001), *desire to continue using the system in future presentations* (χ2(1)=12.25, p<.001), and *how obvious it was to see what the answer is* (χ2(1)=12.25, p<.001).

In summary, results of both absolute and relative usability ratings demonstrated a strong preference of the presenters for Quester.

Rating on scale 1-7 *1 - not at all* *7 - very much*	**Static**	**Quester**	**p**
How ***nervous*** were you...?	3.44 (1.55)	2.94 (1.34)	.143
How ***competent*** were you...?	4.63 (1.46)	5.25 (1.24)	.249
How would you rate the ***overall quality***...?	5.06 (1.12)	5.31 (1.19)	.434

Table 2. Presenters' self-perceived ratings of their QA performances (Mean (SD) and p-value of Wilcoxon tests

Self-perceived Rating of QA Performance

After each QA session, we asked presenters to assess their own QA performance using a 3-item, 7-point scale, evaluating their self-perception of their *nervousness*, *competency*, and *overall quality* of their performance.

As shown in Table 2, results of the ratings showed improvements in all measures with Quester. However, results of Wilcoxon signed rank tests showed no significant differences between the two conditions in any measures.

Objective Measures of Presenter Performance

We analyzed video recordings of all QA sessions and calculated the following objective measures of the presenter's system usage and performance:

Utilization Rate: measured as the percentage of times that the presenter used the QA support system to answer a question, either by navigating through slides and notes to search for the correct answer and/or clicking on a slide to show to the audience. In both conditions, we asked participants to use the QA support systems in any way they wanted, and they could always choose to answer a question without using the systems.

Correctness of Answers: measured as the percentage of questions that were correctly answered, either with or without using the QA systems.

Efficiency: For each correct answer found, we measured the delay time (in seconds) taken from the moment the presenter finished repeating the question until the moment he/she started answering the question.

Number of Incorrect Slides Shown: measured as the number of incorrect slides shown to the audience before reaching a correct slide. This metric was calculated each time the presenter showed a correct slide to the audience. In 19% of cases, presenters did not show the correct slides.

A research assistant annotated the QA session recordings to check for the correctness of the presenter's answers and the delay time for each correct answer. For each question, the annotator compared the presenter's answer to the target answer included in the speaking notes. An answer was considered correct if it covered the main points in the target answer in sufficient details (but not necessarily word-for-word). 12.5% of the recordings (4 out of 32 recordings, 2 from each condition) were randomly chosen and annotated by another annotator to assess the reliability of our coding. The inter-rater reliability was adequate, with Cohen's Kappa of 0.73 for correctness, and intraclass-correlation of 0.96 for efficiency.

We performed Shapiro-Wilk tests to check the normality of our data. Our data for all measures were not normally distributed, thus we analyzed our data using non-parametric tests (Wilcoxon signed rank tests). Results of the objective measures are shown in Table 3. There was a significant difference in utilization rate between the two conditions (Z=-1.97, p=.048), in favor of Quester. There was also a significant difference in the answer response delay time (for correct answers) between the two conditions (Z=-2.04, p=.041), in favor of Quester. There were no significant differences between the conditions on the Correctness of Answers (Z=-0.77, p=.441), or the Number of Incorrect Slides Shown (Z=-1.35, p=.176).

Measures	Static	Quester	p
Utilization Rate (%)	59.37 (36.37)	74.22 (32.1)	**.048**
Correctness of Answers (%)	77.53 (23.0)	81.11 (16.35)	.441
Efficiency (seconds)	16.28 (11.15)	8.36 (6.43)	**.041**
Number of Incorrect Slides Shown	2.09 (3.25)	0.46 (0.69)	.176

Table 3. Objective measures of presenters' system usage and performance during QA sessions (Mean (SD) and p-value of Wilcoxon signed rank tests)

System Accuracy

To evaluate the performance of Quester, we analyzed system logs and calculated the system accuracy at both slide and note topic levels. *Slide-level accuracy* was measured as the percentage of times that the correct slide appears in the top 5 recommended slides for each question. *Topic-level accuracy* was measured as the percentage of times that the correct note topic was highlighted when the presenter clicked on the correct slide for a question. The average *slide-level accuracy* was 84.37% (SD=17.38), and the average *topic-level accuracy* was 74.05% (SD=32.31).

Qualitative Findings

We performed high-level coding of our semi-structured exit interview transcripts and derived three main themes.

Impact on User Experience

15 of 16 participants expressed strong preferences for Quester, citing its positive effects in time saving that encouraged them to actually use the system more: *"The first system [Static], I didn't use it much because you need to actually go in and search yourself. The other system [Quester] will do it for you and you will save time"* [P1]. This is the most important benefit of Quester, as long delay time could *"interrupt your train of thought"* [P12] and lead to negative impressions from the audience. Quester was also found to help reduce the memorization load required to *"remember where everything you put in the presentation is"* [P12]. In addition, two participants specifically reported that our system helped increase their confidence: *"When I had to look into the slides, there is a lot less lag time, and that lack of lag time made me feel more confident, because I wasn't keeping the audience stalling"* [P11]. One participant, however, preferred the Static Navigation system over Quester, because he felt that it was more *"organized"* [P2] and easy to simply skip through slides in order.

Level of Distraction

11 of 16 participants indicated that they experienced no distraction with Quester, as one participant explained: *"I wasn't looking at the computer until I had repeated the question, at which point it was already adjusted to include the right proportion of the slides and the likelihood. So it wasn't distracting to me"* [P11]. Several participants specifically reported that they felt the static navigation system was actually more distracting, because: *"While scrolling down I happened to see all the slides. And my mind started thinking about all the slides"* [P6].

However, 2 participants reported that the changing green bars that indicate slide likelihood was confusing and distracting. In addition, 3 participants mentioned that when the system failed to show correct slides, it was difficult and distracting for them to search for relevant slides themselves, as the slides *"were not in the orderly manner"* [P5]. One potential solution is to combine both dynamic and static navigation approaches, allowing the presenter to switch back to static navigation when the dynamic slide recommendations are not accurate.

Suggestions for Improvement

Some participants had suggestions for improving the appearance of slide recommendations. They proposed using color codes rather than varying sizes of the green bars to indicate different ranges of slide probability. 2 participants also suggested simply displaying the recommended slides in the descending order of probability. Participants also proposed novel ways to extend the system functionality. For example, the system could automatically display relevant information from external resources, such as webpages or existing documents.

CONCLUSION

We developed Quester, a system that provides dynamic speech-based slide ranking for speakers giving non-linear presentations, such as during post-presentation QA sessions. In our evaluation study, presenters rated Quester significantly higher, used it significantly more, and answered audience questions significantly faster, compared to a system that only provided linear slide navigation.

As future work, we aim to further evaluate the effectiveness of Quester in more realistic settings, ideally using slide decks that are authored by the participants themselves. Other future directions of research include novel forms of displays and prompts to help presenters give adaptive but coherent presentations, with supporting media (e.g. external resources or dynamically-updated data visualizations) automatically provided by the system.

ACKNOWLEDGMENTS

This work is supported in part by the National Science Foundation under award IIS-1514490. Any opinions, findings, and conclusions or recommendations expressed in this material are those of the authors and do not necessarily reflect the views of the National Science Foundation.

REFERENCES

1. Laurence Anthony, Deborah C Turk, Atsuko K Yamazaki and Thomas Orr. 2006. Q&A: Published advice vs. real-world difficulties. in *International Professional Communication Conference, 2006 IEEE*, IEEE, 11-21.
2. Reza Asadi, Harriet J Fell, Timothy W Bickmore and Ha Trinh. 2016. Real-Time Presentation Tracking Using Semantic Keyword Spotting. in *Interspeech*.
3. Reza Asadi, Ha Trinh, Harriet J. Fell and Timothy W. Bickmore. 2017. IntelliPrompter: speech-based dynamic note display interface for oral presentations *Proceedings of the 19th ACM International Conference on Multimodal Interaction*, ACM, Glasgow, UK, 172-180.
4. Virginia Braun and Victoria Clarke. 2006. Using thematic analysis in psychology. *Qualitative research in psychology*, 3 (2). 77-101.
5. Jinwei Cao and Jay F Nunamaker. 2004. Question answering on lecture videos: a multifaceted approach. in *Proceedings of the 4th ACM/IEEE-CS joint conference on Digital libraries*, ACM, 214-215.
6. Darren Edge, Joan Savage and Koji Yatani. 2013. HyperSlides: dynamic presentation prototyping. in *Proceedings of the SIGCHI Conference on Human Factors in Computing Systems*, ACM, 671-680.
7. Wilbert O Galitz. 2007. *The essential guide to user interface design: an introduction to GUI design principles and techniques*. John Wiley & Sons.
8. Rhema Linder, Nic Lupfer, Andruid Kerne, Andrew M Webb, Cameron Hill, Yin Qu, Kade Keith, Matthew Carrasco and Elizabeth Kellogg. 2015. Beyond slideware: How a free-form presentation medium stimulates free-form thinking in the classroom. in *Proceedings of the 2015 ACM SIGCHI Conference on Creativity and Cognition*, ACM, 285-294.
9. Christopher D Manning, Mihai Surdeanu, John Bauer, Jenny Rose Finkel, Steven Bethard and David McClosky. 2014. The stanford corenlp natural language processing toolkit. in *ACL (System Demonstrations)*.
10. James C. McCroskey and Linda L. McCroskey. 1988. Self-report as an approach to measuring communication competence. *Communication Research Reports*, 5. 108-113.
11. George A Miller. 1995. WordNet: a lexical database for English. *Communications of the ACM*, 38 (11). 39-41.
12. Tomer Moscovich, Karin Scholz, John F Hughes and D Salesin. 2004. Customizable presentations, Technical Report CS-04-16, Computer Science Department, Brown University.
13. Les Nelson, Satoshi Ichimura, Elin Rønby Pedersen and Lia Adams. 1999. Palette: a paper interface for giving presentations. in *Proceedings of the SIGCHI conference on Human Factors in Computing Systems*, ACM, 354-361.
14. Jeffrey Pennington, Richard Socher and Christopher Manning. 2014. Glove: Global vectors for word representation. in *Proceedings of the 2014 conference on empirical methods in natural language processing (EMNLP)*, 1532-1543.
15. Ivica Rogina. 2002. Lecture and presentation tracking in an intelligent meeting room. in *Proceedings of the 4th IEEE International Conference on Multimodal Interfaces*, IEEE Computer Society, 47.
16. Beat Signer and Moira C Norrie. 2007. PaperPoint: a paper-based presentation and interactive paper prototyping tool. in *Proceedings of the 1st international conference on Tangible and embedded interaction*, ACM, 57-64.
17. Ryan Spicer, Yu-Ru Lin, Aisling Kelliher and Hari Sundaram. 2012. NextSlidePlease: Authoring and delivering agile multimedia presentations. *ACM Transactions on Multimedia Computing, Communications, and Applications (TOMM)*, 8 (4). 53.
18. Edward R Tufte. 2003. *The cognitive style of PowerPoint*. Graphics Press Cheshire, CT.
19. APJ van den Bosch. 2011. Effects of context and recency in scaled word completion. *Computational Linguistics in The Netherlands journal*.
20. Natsuo Yamamoto, Jun Ogata and Yasuo Ariki. 2003. Topic segmentation and retrieval system for lecture videos based on spontaneous speech recognition. in *Interspeech*.
21. Haojin Yang and Christoph Meinel. 2014. Content based lecture video retrieval using speech and video text information. *IEEE Transactions on Learning Technologies*, 7 (2). 142-154.

22. Joann Yates and Wanda Orlikowski. The PowerPoint presentation and its corollaries: How genres shape communicative action in organizations. *Communicative practices in workplaces and the professions: Cultural perspectives on the regulation of discourse and organizations*. 67-91.
23. Show-Jane Yen, Yu-Chieh Wu, Jie-Chi Yang, Yue-Shi Lee, Chung-Jung Lee and Jui-Jung Liu. 2013. A support vector machine-based context-ranking model for question answering. *Information Sciences*, 224. 77-87.
24. Scott Wen-tau Yih, Xiaodong He and Chris Meek. 2014. Semantic parsing for single-relation question answering.

EASEL: Easy Automatic Segmentation Event Labeler

Isaac Wang[1], Pradyumna Narayana[2], Jesse Smith[1], Bruce Draper[2], Ross Beveridge[2], Jaime Ruiz[1]

[1]Department of CISE
Gainesville, Florida, USA
{wangi, jd.smith, jaime.ruiz}@ufl.edu

[2]Department of Computer Science
Fort Collins, Colorado, USA
{prady, draper, ross}@cs.colostate.edu

ABSTRACT

Video annotation is a vital part of research examining gestural and multimodal interaction as well as computer vision, machine learning, and interface design. However, annotation is a difficult, time-consuming task that requires high cognitive effort. Existing tools for labeling and annotation still require users to manually label most of the data, limiting the tools' helpfulness. In this paper, we present the Easy Automatic Segmentation Event Labeler (EASEL), a tool supporting gesture analysis. EASEL streamlines the annotation process by introducing assisted annotation, using automatic gesture segmentation and recognition to automatically annotate gestures. To evaluate the efficacy of assisted annotation, we conducted a user study with 24 participants and found that assisted annotation decreased the time needed to annotate videos with no difference in accuracy compared with manual annotation. The results of our study demonstrate the benefit of adding computational intelligence to video and audio annotation tasks.

Author Keywords

Data annotation tools; gesture segmentation; gesture analysis

INTRODUCTION

Gestural research—research focused on the use of gestures as input or channel of communication—has resulted in significant breakthroughs in user interaction (e.g., the Microsoft Kinect, mobile phones, surface gestures). Furthermore, gestural research has broad applications to research focused on multimodal communication, computer vision, machine learning, and interface design. Much of this research relies on video annotation, the process of identifying significant gestures and events in recorded video and then assigning them a shared label. For instance, this approach is used for studying multimodal interaction [10] and is also required for creating ground truth labels in large video datasets, such as the ChaLearn Gesture Dataset 2011 [6]. Often, annotation is done using simple media or text editors [12]. However, this is a difficult and time-consuming task; for example, a 5-minute video could take an hour for a single researcher to properly annotate.

IUI'18, March 7–11, 2018, Tokyo, Japan

ACM ISBN 978-1-4503-4945-1/18/03…$15.00
https://doi.org/10.1145/3172944.3173003

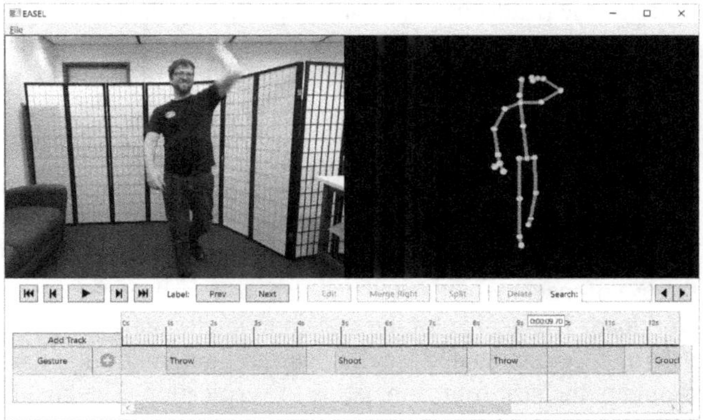

Figure 1. EASEL's user interface, showing the video player (top) and the annotation timeline (bottom).

Given the critical role of video annotation, researchers have developed several specialized tools for performing such analyses. These include programs designed to facilitate the annotation of audio and video for motion-tracking [9], multimodal discourse [8,12,16,18], and semantic description [2,4]. For instance, the ELAN annotation tool [18] uses a hierarchical system of annotations to transcribe and analyze speech components in video and audio files for multimodal studies. Similarly, ANVIL [8] and EXMARaLDA [16] are also used for annotation and transcription but go a step further by including the ability to define custom annotation schemes and built-in analysis functions to parse and visualize the annotated data. However, due to limited and varying feature sets (e.g., inability to handle common video formats, or insufficient support for a specific method of analysis), these annotation systems are often inappropriate for use in research areas for which they were not designed [12].

Additionally, although these tools provide interfaces that help facilitate annotation, they still require users to manually annotate most of the data, limiting their helpfulness. Few tools introduce methods to automate the process. For instance, Aydınlılar and Yazıcı [2] present a tool that helps automatically label semantic content in video. Likewise, the SorTable tool [15] helps automate continuous labeling, but by simplifying the process to better leverage both human and machine capabilities. In the same vein, we saw a potential for including assisted annotation for gesture labeling, as annotating videos can still be a tedious endeavor even when utilizing specially designed tools. Thus, we developed the Easy Automatic Segmentation Event Labeler (EASEL) from the ground up as a flexible but powerful annotation tool, supporting multiple video formats, requiring little configuration to get started, and featuring assisted annotation to aid in the gesture annotation process.

In this paper, we present EASEL, a tool supporting gesture analysis with Microsoft Kinect recordings that uses automatic gesture segmentation and recognition to streamline the annotation process, a feature we call *assisted annotation.* We describe the design of EASEL and how assisted annotation can benefit users when annotating videos. We also describe the results of a user study evaluating the efficacy of assisted annotation, showing how it can help reduce the time needed to annotate videos by offloading some of the work to the system.

SYSTEM OVERVIEW

EASEL is a tool designed for the annotation of multimodal communication and full-body motion gesture data. The main emphasis of EASEL is the inclusion of assisted annotation, or the use of machine-generated annotations to reduce the user's workload. The goal is for the system to intelligently assist the user by recognizing and labeling gestures automatically, thus changing the task from annotation to verification. The goal is not only to speed up annotation, but also reduce the amount of effort needed to complete the task.

EASEL's UI has two main components: the video player and the annotation timeline (Figure 1). These were designed to function similar to video editing software and other annotation tools [8,16,18], offering a level of familiarity for users. The video player was designed with the goal of allowing simultaneous playback of multiple videos. This allows for playback of videos from different angles or multiple parties, and can also display a video side-by-side with the corresponding Microsoft Kinect skeleton. Additionally, a requirement of the video player was supporting a variety of modern video formats; most existing annotation tools rely on the Java Media Framework [19], which lacks modern codec support (e.g., MPEG-4). EASEL uses the Microsoft Media Foundation framework [20] and supports modern video formats such as MPEG-4 and H.264.

The annotation timeline was designed to visually represent annotations using *musical score*, or *piano roll,* notation, which is particularly suited for depicting multimodal, multi-level, and multi-party communication [16] because it supports the combination of annotation and visualization [13]. The timeline displays annotations on individual tracks, allowing multiple attributes (e.g., gesture, intent, speech) to be labeled for the same video. The start/end times of each annotation can be dragged, and the annotation's label can be edited by double-clicking on the annotation and typing in a label. The timeline was also designed with the goal of not requiring any extensive setup before starting annotation; instead, EASEL allows users to define new tracks and labels as needed, adding a degree of simplicity and flexibility.

Annotating Videos with EASEL

We describe how a user would annotate a Kinect recording with EASEL. Although EASEL can open a variety of video formats for general use, EASEL currently supports XEF

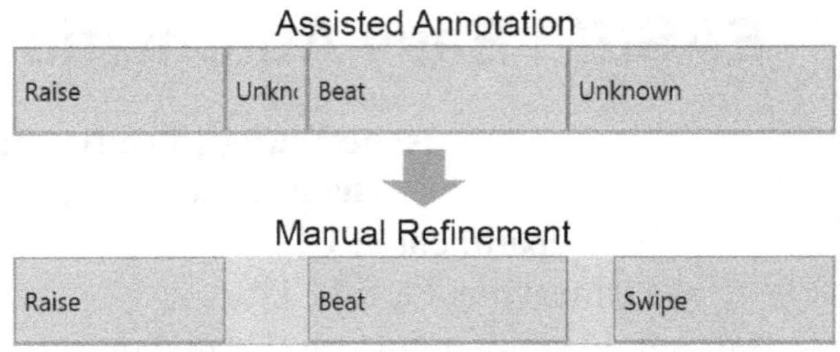

Figure 2. EASEL supports assisted annotation by segmenting and recognizing gestures to prepopulate the timeline. The user then manually refines annotations as needed.

recordings from Kinect Studio [21] for assisted annotation, but could conceivably handle similar formats as well. First, the Kinect XEF file is extracted into RGB video and skeleton data (describing body joint positions for each frame in the video). The video is directly loaded by EASEL for annotation and shows up in the video player. The skeleton data is loaded by the assisted annotation module, which segments and labels gestures in the skeleton data stream. This is shown in the annotation timeline, prepopulating the timeline with annotations (Figure 2). The first time the user loads a video (before any gestures are defined), EASEL will still auto-segment the data into annotations marking when it thinks a gesture occurred, labeling each annotation as "Unknown." The user then goes through the annotations, manually refining the start/end times or correcting the label if needed. These gesture annotations are saved to a database, and, the next time a video is loaded, EASEL will try to auto-label the data by recognizing the previously labeled gestures, effectively getting better as the user annotates more gestures.

IMPLEMENTATION

EASEL is written primarily in C#, with portions written in C++ to interface with Microsoft's native Media Foundation libraries. Other portions of EASEL, such as our implementation of Dynamic Time Warping (DTW) for gesture recognition, are also written in C++ for increased performance. EASEL uses Windows Presentation Foundation (WPF) as its GUI framework and supports systems running the .NET 4.5 runtime (Windows 7 or above). This operating system requirement was selected to take advantage of the Media Foundation library, which provides native video and audio playback for a large number of file formats and codecs and is the most up-to-date media playback framework currently supported by Microsoft.

Assisted Annotation

To streamline the annotation process, EASEL implements assisted annotation, reducing the need to manually identify gestures. Our approach consists of two parts: gesture segmentation, which first segments the video into potential gestures, and gesture recognition, which tries to label each potential gesture by recognizing previously labeled gestures.

Gesture Segmentation

Segmentation is one of the most time-consuming tasks when annotating video, audio, or motion capture data, and thus is an excellent candidate for improvement by automatic methods. EASEL can automatically segment a video into discrete gestures by estimating curvatures in high dimensional space using the ACE-PC technique by Arn et al. [1]. This method was chosen because of its ability to handle "open-world" gesture segmentation, i.e. identifying motions as potential gestures without any prior training. This method operates on a stream of multidimensional motion data over time and is not specific to the Kinect, making it possible to work with other types of input (e.g., accelerometer data for mobile interaction). After the motion data is loaded and segmented, these potential gestures appear as candidate annotations in the timeline.

Gesture Recognition

The output from gesture segmentation is further enhanced by attempting to automatically determine a label for each candidate annotation created. This is done by extracting the Kinect skeleton data for a given annotation and running a gesture matching or recognition technique on it. The annotation is then given a label based on a detected match.

As a simple baseline technique, we implemented a version of dynamic time warping (DTW) [14] for gesture recognition. As a template-based approach, DTW is particularly suited for EASEL, as it does not require training and can automatically recognize new gestures as they are added to the gesture database. For our implementation, the motion from the skeleton data is normalized by subtracting the spine base from every joint. Once a few instances of gestures have been labeled and stored in the database, EASEL will try to match new annotations against these gestures. A threshold is used to ensure that suggested labels are close enough matches (calibrated by finding an optimal threshold against the G3D [3] and EGGNOG [17] datasets, as they represent the typical use case for EASEL). If the similarity score of the closest matched gesture is below the threshold, then the annotation is pre-filled with the matched label. Otherwise, the annotation is classified as "Unknown," leaving the user to label it manually.

EVALUATION

We conducted a within-subject user study to evaluate the efficacy of assisted annotation in gesture annotation systems. We developed two versions of the system: *Assisted*, which included assisted annotation, and *Manual*, which did not. Our goal was to determine if:

(G1) Using *Assisted* results in decreased time to annotate videos than *Manual*.
(G2) The accuracy of annotations is higher when using *Assisted* as opposed to *Manual*.
(G3) *Assisted* decreases the task load involved with video annotation.

Participants

We recruited 24 participants (16 female, 8 male) from a local university through word-of-mouth and inter-departmental emails. Participants were between the ages of 19 and 29 (mean = 22.5, SD = 3.2). Seven participants had prior experience with similar video annotation software. Each participant was compensated with $20 in Amazon gift cards. Our study was approved by our Institutional Review Board.

Procedure

Participants were asked to complete two one-hour sessions on separate days (no more than three days apart). At the start of each session, participants were given a brief tutorial to the annotation task and given a reference sheet describing the gestures used in the videos. For each task, participants were asked to watch a video of a person performing gestures and use EASEL to annotate when and what gestures were performed, with an emphasis on ensuring that the entire gesture was annotated. Each session consisted of 10 trials: participants annotated a set of 10 videos by a single actor in the first session, and a set of 10 videos with a different actor in the second session. Participants used both versions of the system (*Assisted* and *Manual*), one for each session. The order of exposure to the two systems was counterbalanced.

We measured the time it took for participants to annotate each video. Annotations were also saved for later comparison against ground truth. At the end of each session, we asked participants to complete a short questionnaire to describe their experience with the system. The questionnaire included the questions from the NASA-TLX survey [7] for measuring task load, asking participants to rate their perceived workload across six continuous scales.

Videos Used in the Experiment

We created a small dataset of people performing gestures. The gestures in the dataset were based on the gaming gesture sets used in the MSRC-12 dataset by Fothergill et al. [5]. Each video contained a sequence of 10 gestures randomly selected from a gesture set containing six distinct gestures. There were two different sets of gestures: *Iconic* (crouch, shoot, throw, change, kick, goggles) and *Metaphoric* (raise, swipe, wind, bow, protest, beat). We recorded videos of four different actors, each performing gestures in 10 videos: five videos with *Iconic* gestures and five with *Metaphoric* gestures, resulting in 40 videos, each 30 seconds on average. The order of videos in each set was randomized, and the video sets used in the study sessions were counterbalanced.

To compare the accuracy of participants' annotations, we had three expert annotators independently create a set of annotations for all videos. Experts correctly labeled all gestures, giving us three sets of start/end times for each gesture. The start times and end times for each gesture were averaged to create a ground truth set of annotations.

Results

To compensate for learning effects, we treated the first half of the session as practice, using the latter five trials for analysis. The results from these trials were averaged to get the mean task time and annotation accuracy for each session.

Time Performance

We analyzed the time it took for participants to complete each task. Figure 3 shows boxplots comparing the distribution of task times for the two system conditions. The average task time was 166.9 seconds (SD = 50.5) when using

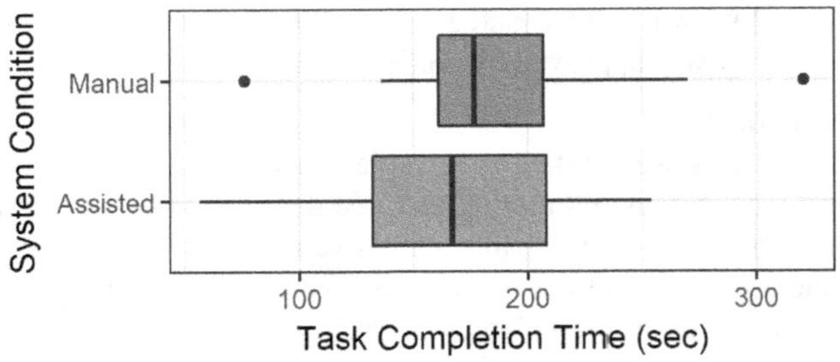

Figure 3. Boxplots comparing the average task completion time between the two system conditions. The *Assisted* system was faster (p < 0.05) than the *Manual* system.

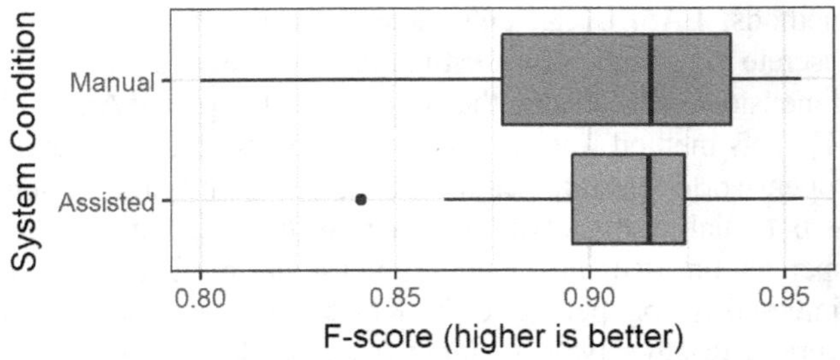

Figure 4. Boxplots comparing annotation accuracy (F-score) between the two system conditions. There was no significant difference in accuracy.

the *Assisted* system, compared with 188.2 seconds (SD = 50.7) for the *Manual* system. A within-subjects repeated measures ANOVA revealed a significant effect of system on task time ($F_{1,22} = 4.84$, $p < 0.05$), and no ordering effect of the system was observed ($p > 0.05$). Additionally, no interaction effects were observed ($p > 0.05$). We saw that, on average, participants using the *Assisted* version of EASEL completed tasks 11.3% faster than those using the *Manual* version. This indicates that assisted annotation is helping users accomplish tasks rather than being a hindrance.

Annotation Accuracy

We computed a frame-wise F-score [11] for each annotation, calculating precision and recall based on the number of frames matched against ground truth. F-scores were then averaged for each trial. The average F-score was 0.91 (SD = 0.03) for trials using the *Assisted* system and 0.90 (SD = 0.04) for trials using the *Manual* system (Figure 4). ANOVA revealed no significant difference in F-score between the two system conditions. The average F-scores for both conditions were similar to that of the expert annotators, who had an average F-score of 0.92. Thus, we found no difference in annotation accuracy, even when automatically labeled.

Task Load

We analyzed the results from the NASA-TLX survey to see if there was any reduction in task load when using the *Assisted* version of EASEL. We computed a raw TLX score averaging the values (between 0-100) from the six scales presented in the survey. The overall TLX score (lower is better) was 22.8 (SD = 16.5) for the *Assisted* condition and 27.9 (SD = 15.8) for the *Manual* condition. ANOVA revealed no significant difference in TLX scores between the two system conditions. When comparing scores individually across the six scales, we did not find any significant differences, although average scores for the *Assisted* condition were lower than *Manual* for each scale.

Discussion

Our evaluation study aimed to determine if including assisted annotation in gesture annotation tools improves task performance and decreases task load. From our results, we saw that task times in the *Assisted* condition were 11.3% faster on average (fulfilling goal G1), which quickly adds up when dealing with a large number of videos. One possible concern with the increase in speed is a decrease in quality; however, we found no significant difference in annotation accuracy between the two system conditions. Although we did not fulfill G2, we found that the accuracy of annotations for both conditions was comparable to that of experts. Thus, the inclusion of assisted annotation helped reduce annotation time while still retaining accuracy.

To determine how we could improve performance in future iterations, we took a closer look at the data to identify if there were any areas of EASEL that could be refined. Thus, we looked at how often users made changes to the machine-generated annotations. We found that gesture segmentation is not yet perfect, requiring adjustments to the start/end times for 72% of generated annotations. In contrast, only 32% of labels needed to be edited. Thus, improving automatic segmentation is a focus of future work, as it would decrease the need to manually edit annotations and further improve temporal performance.

CONCLUSION AND FUTURE WORK

In this paper, we presented EASEL, a video annotation tool that uses gesture segmentation and recognition to automatically label gestures in Kinect recordings. We showed how assisted annotation can improve temporal performance for gesture annotation with no difference in accuracy. The ability to have the system share the workload through assisted annotation has the potential to make video annotation tools more effective and intelligent. Our results not only affirm the benefits of assisted annotation for gesture annotation in EASEL, but also open up new possibilities for adapting the feature to work for other research domains. Future work will include incorporating automatic speech and affect recognition as well as expanding segmentation and recognition to easily support data formats other than Kinect recordings. The use of other segmentation and recognition techniques and ways to continually improve assisted annotation with live user feedback will also be explored.

ACKNOWLEDGEMENTS

This work was partially funded by the U.S. Defense Advanced Research Projects Agency and the U.S. Army Research Office under contract #W911NF-15-1-0459.

REFERENCES

1. Robert Arn, Pradyumna Narayana, Teegan Emerson, Bruce Draper, Michael Kirby, and Chris Peterson. Motion Segmentation via Generalized Curvatures. Under review in *IEEE Transactions on Pattern Analysis and Machine Intelligence*.

2. Merve Aydınlılar and Adnan Yazıcı. 2013. Semi-Automatic Semantic Video Annotation Tool. In *Computer and Information Sciences III*. Springer, London, 303–310. https://doi.org/10.1007/978-1-4471-4594-3_31
3. Victoria Bloom, Dimitrios Makris, and Vasileios Argyriou. 2012. G3D: A gaming action dataset and real time action recognition evaluation framework. In *IEEE Computer Society Conference on Computer Vision and Pattern Recognition Workshops*, 7–12. https://doi.org/10.1109/CVPRW.2012.6239175
4. Stamatia Dasiopoulou, Eirini Giannakidou, Georgios Litos, Polyxeni Malasioti, and Yiannis Kompatsiaris. 2011. A Survey of Semantic Image and Video Annotation Tools. In *Knowledge-Driven Multimedia Information Extraction and Ontology Evolution*. Springer, Berlin, Heidelberg, 196–239. https://doi.org/10.1007/978-3-642-20795-2_8
5. Simon Fothergill, Helena Mentis, Pushmeet Kohli, and Sebastian Nowozin. 2012. Instructing People for Training Gestural Interactive Systems. In *Proceedings of the SIGCHI Conference on Human Factors in Computing Systems* (CHI '12), 1737–1746. https://doi.org/10.1145/2207676.2208303
6. Isabelle Guyon, Vassilis Athitsos, Pat Jangyodsuk, and Hugo Jair Escalante. 2014. The ChaLearn gesture dataset (CGD 2011). *Machine Vision and Applications* 25, 8: 1929–1951. https://doi.org/10.1007/s00138-014-0596-3
7. Sandra G. Hart and Lowell E. Staveland. 1988. Development of NASA-TLX (Task Load Index): Results of Empirical and Theoretical Research. In *Advances in Psychology*, Peter A. Hancock and Najmedin Meshkati (eds.). North-Holland, 139–183. https://doi.org/10.1016/S0166-4115(08)62386-9
8. Michael Kipp. 2001. Anvil - A Generic Annotation Tool for Multimodal Dialogue. In *Proceedings of the 7th European Conference on Speech Communication and Technology (Eurospeech)*, 1367–1370.
9. Michael Nebeling, David Ott, and Moira C. Norrie. 2015. Kinect Analysis: A System for Recording, Analysing and Sharing Multimodal Interaction Elicitation Studies. In *Proceedings of the 7th ACM SIGCHI Symposium on Engineering Interactive Computing Systems* (EICS '15), 142–151. https://doi.org/10.1145/2774225.2774846
10. Francis Quek, David McNeill, Robert Bryll, Susan Duncan, Xin-Feng Ma, Cemil Kirbas, Karl E. McCullough, and Rashid Ansari. 2002. Multimodal Human Discourse: Gesture and Speech. *ACM Trans. Comput.-Hum. Interact.* 9, 3: 171–193. https://doi.org/10.1145/568513.568514
11. C. J. Van Rijsbergen. 1979. *Information Retrieval.* Butterworth-Heinemann, Newton, MA, USA.
12. Katharina Rohlfing, Daniel Loehr, Susan Duncan, Amanda Brown, Amy Franklin, Irene Kimbara, J-T Milde, Fey Parrill, Travis Rose, Thomas Schmidt, and others. 2006. Comparison of multimodal annotation tools: Workshop report. *Gesprächsforschung* 7.
13. R. Travis Rose, Francis Quek, and Yang Shi. 2004. MacVisSTA: a system for multimodal analysis. In *Proceedings of the 6th international conference on Multimodal interfaces*, 259–264.
14. Hiroaki Sakoe and Seibi Chiba. 1978. Dynamic programming algorithm optimization for spoken word recognition. *IEEE Transactions on Acoustics, Speech, and Signal Processing* 26, 1: 43–49. https://doi.org/10.1109/TASSP.1978.1163055
15. Advait Sarkar, Cecily Morrison, Jonas F. Dorn, Rishi Bedi, Saskia Steinheimer, Jacques Boisvert, Jessica Burggraaff, Marcus D'Souza, Peter Kontschieder, Samuel Rota Bulò, Lorcan Walsh, Christian P. Kamm, Yordan Zaykov, Abigail Sellen, and Siân Lindley. 2016. Setwise Comparison: Consistent, Scalable, Continuum Labels for Computer Vision. In *Proceedings of the 2016 CHI Conference on Human Factors in Computing Systems* (CHI '16), 261–271. https://doi.org/10.1145/2858036.2858199
16. Thomas Schmidt and Kai Wörner. 2009. EXMARaLDA—Creating, analyzing and sharing spoken language corpora for pragmatics research. *Pragmatics-Quarterly Publication of the International Pragmatics Association* 19, 4: 565.
17. Isaac Wang, Mohtadi Ben Fraj, Pradyumna Narayana, Dhruva Patil, Gururaj Mulay, Rahul Bangar, J. Ross Beveridge, Bruce A. Draper, and Jaime Ruiz. 2017. EGGNOG: A Continuous, Multi-modal Data Set of Naturally Occurring Gestures with Ground Truth Labels. In *2017 12th IEEE International Conference on Automatic Face Gesture Recognition (FG 2017)*, 414–421. https://doi.org/10.1109/FG.2017.145
18. Peter Wittenburg, Hennie Brugman, Albert Russel, Alex Klassmann, and Han Sloetjes. 2006. Elan: a professional framework for multimodality research. In *Proceedings of the 5th International Conference on Language Resources and Evaluation (LREC 2006)*, 1556–1559. Retrieved from http://tla.mpi.nl/tools/tla-tools/elan/
19. JMF 2.1.1 - Supported Formats. Retrieved October 3, 2017 from http://www.oracle.com/technetwork/java/javase/formats-138492.html
20. Supported Media Formats in Media Foundation (Windows). Retrieved January 10, 2017 from https://msdn.microsoft.com/en-us/library/windows/desktop/dd757927
21. Kinect Studio. Retrieved October 3, 2017 from https://msdn.microsoft.com/en-us/library/dn785306.aspx

An Evaluation of Inclusive Dialogue-Based Interfaces for the Takeover of Control in Autonomous Cars

Ioannis Politis
Patrick Langdon
Damilola Adebayo
Mike Bradley
P. John Clarkson
Engineering Design Centre
University of Cambridge
Cambridge, UK
{ip332, pml24, mdb54, dada2, pjc10}@cam.ac.uk

Lee Skrypchuk
Alexander Mouzakitis
Jaguar Land – Rover Research & Technology
Coventry, UK
{lskrypch, amouzak1}@jaguarlandrover.com

Alexander Eriksson
Swedish National Road and Transport Research Institute (VTI)
Göteborg, Sweden
alexander.eriksson@vti.se

James W. H. Brown
Kirsten Revell
Neville Stanton
Transportation Research Group
University of Southampton
Southampton, UK
{j.w.brown, k.m.revell, n.stanton}@soton.ac.uk

ABSTRACT
This paper presents formative research to inform the design of intelligent automotive user interfaces. It describes an evaluation of dialogue-based interfaces, mediating the driver to take back control from the autonomous mode of a car. Four concepts designed to increase driver Situation Awareness were evaluated in a driving simulator. They used dialogue-based interaction, where driving-related information was either asked from or repeated by the driver, with the alternative of a countdown-based interface with no additional information. An inclusive set of participants, with a wide age spectrum, tested the interfaces. The shorter and simpler interaction of the countdown timer was most accepted. The interface seeking answers to driving-related questions came next, and the interface requiring repetition of driving-related information, even when augmented by visual and tactile cues, was least accepted. Design guidelines on utilizing dialogue as a means of keeping the driver in the loop during a takeover were thus derived.

Author Keywords
Autonomous cars; dialogue system; evaluation; takeover of control; inclusive design.

INTRODUCTION
Autonomous cars are reaching the roads, and expected to become more widespread in the near future [15,32], although not without concerns from the public over their impact [36]. This has motivated a significant body of research in public opinion about these vehicles [21,36–40], anticipated behaviours when interacting with the technology within these cars [29], and user interface interventions to make this interaction more safe and usable [11,24,42,45]. As described in SAE J3016 [17], car autonomy is a spectrum rather than a binary state. This standard defines levels of autonomy, ranging from 0 (No Driving Automation) to 5 (Full Driving Automation), with decreasing expected driving engagement as levels increase. Both ends of this spectrum have relatively straight forward driver engagement expectations; level 0 expects full engagement, and level 5 expects no engagement. The problem arguably becomes harder in the intermediate levels, where *some* driving engagement is expected. This has triggered extensive research on how to design for *some* driving engagement, and better support this transition between car and driver control, the takeover. Available approaches have investigated amongst others new interfaces utilizing rich displays, expected to keep the driver alert [2,9,31,33,34], as well as made efforts in modelling the tasks that take place during takeovers, so as to better design for them [1,27,44].

The approach of this paper is one of Inclusive Design [5,18], considering a diverse user group in terms of capabilities in the design cycle. We are interested to investigate the opinions and difficulties of such a group regarding the problem of takeovers, and aim to design solutions that will satisfy users of varying demographics and degrees of functional capability. There are studies investigating opinions on such groups on the topic, *e.g.* [23,35]. An emerging requirement is simple, safe, and easy to use interfaces, enhancing the driver's capabilities. Voice control has explicitly been suggested as a means of achieving this [35]. Further, existing studies in automation have outlined the merits of using dialogue interaction as a means to reduce workload in other modalities, but also as a facilitator of Situation Awareness (SA) [12,26,30]. We therefore decided to take the approach of designing a set of dialogue systems as a start. We explored different types of potential dialogue interactions, in terms of how users perceive them, and how they behave when exposed to them. We designed an experiment evaluating the dialogue interfaces, and results confirmed that simplicity of the interfaces is paramount, even at the cost of available in-

IUI'18, March 7–11, 2018, Tokyo, Japan

ACM ISBN 978-1-4503-4945-1/18/03…$15.00
https://doi.org/10.1145/3172944.3172990

formation regarding the road. The rest of this paper will describe the experiment, and conclude with views on how to better design simple takeover interfaces, that facilitate SA.

DIALOGUE-BASED INTERFACES DESIGNED

A set of dialogue-based interfaces were designed, addressing the takeover process in a step-based approach, and aiming to be facilitators of varying degrees of SA [8]. Using input from prior studies [12,35], the goal was to achieve a natural verbal interaction with the vehicle, that is likely to put less strain on the driver's attentional resources when resuming control [16,46,47]. Although there are available takeover strategies involving speech output from the car *e.g.* [12,33], there are no approaches to the authors' knowledge utilising a natural dialogue for the takeover. This difference is important, as it involves a significant added effort from the driver in order to achieve the takeover. To reflect some fundamentally different dialogue structures, four systems were designed. They envisaged a case of an SAE Level 3 autonomous vehicle system, and a takeover due to sensor degradation. All systems were adaptations of emerging ideas from a design workshop with members of the automotive industry and the academia, which had taken place in the authors' home institution. All systems required an initial confirmation of readiness to assume control of the vehicle, which was a basic form of dialogue. After the confirmation was given, there were the following alternatives:

- A **Countdown-Based (CB)** system, where there was no further dialogue required, only a button press from the driver to assume control, and a countdown of 60 *sec* in blocks of 10 *sec*. This concept was simulating common available takeover concepts from the industry, *e.g.* [43], with the addition of an initial dialogue-based confirmation of readiness.
- A **Repetition-Based (RepB)** system, prompting the driver to repeat information, uttered by the system, about essential driving features when resuming control, including hazards, current lanes, current fuel level, current speed, intended exit, and immediate actions to be taken. This concept was based on aviation readbacks [4], a standard practice of pilots repeating important information to air traffic controllers. Although readbacks aim to reduce misunderstandings between air traffic controllers and pilots, the rationale of using such a technique in the automotive domain, was that it might benefit a similar interaction during a takeover, and possibly increase driver SA.
- A **Response-Based (ResB)** system, asking the driver to provide the same information as the RepB system by answering to related questions, posed by the system, instead of asking them to repeat it. This provided an analogous interaction to RepB, expecting higher engagement from the driver's side, as they would need to find and verbalise the required information rather than solely repeating it, similarly to answering SA-related questions in the Situation Awareness Global Assessment Technique (SAGAT) [7].
- A **Multimodality-Based (MB)** system, identical to the RepB system, with added multimodal information, *i.e.* LED strips in amber colour, animating on either side of the driver and simulating the position of surrounding traffic, as well as ambient vibrations, augmenting the utterances of the dialogue system. The rationale was that multimodal cues have repeatedly shown benefits informing the driver about events on the road [33,34], and multimodal information has emerged as requirement in qualitative studies in this domain [35].

An experiment evaluating the above dialogue systems was designed, aiming to evaluate users' performance and views when exposed to the dialogue-based takeover interfaces.

EXPERIMENT

The designed experiment used a within subjects design, with Type of Interface (ToI – CB, RepB, ResB, MB) as the single independent variable. The dependent variables were Perceived Workload (PW, using the National Aeronautics and Space Administration Task Load Index – NASA-TLX, Raw TLX adaptation [13,14]), Perceived Acceptance (PA, using the Acceptance Scale – AS [22]), Perceived Usability (PU, using the System Usability Scale – SUS [3]), Perceived Situation Awareness (PSA, using the Situation Awareness Rating Technique – SART [41]), Dialogue Performance (DiP – performance during the verbal interaction with the different dialogue systems), Time to Takeover (TT – the time from the start of the dialogue interaction until participants resumed control of the car), and Driving Performance (DrP – Speed, Longitudinal Acceleration, and Absolute Angle Input). It was hypothesized that ToI would influence these measures.

Participants

49 participants (24 female), aged between 17 and 86 years ($M = 45.51$, $SD = 17.36$) participated in the experiment. They all held a valid driving license, and had between 1 and 70 years of driving experience ($M = 25.68$, $SD = 17.58$). In order to adhere to the principles of Inclusive Design [20], effort was made to recruit representative population samples in terms of age and gender. Thus, there were 7 males and 5 females in the age band of 17 – 34, 11 males and 13 females in the age band of 35 – 56, and 7 males and 6 females in the age band of 57 – 86. The recruitment was opportunistic, however the resulting sample displayed a wide variety of ages, distributed between genders.

Equipment

A low fidelity driving simulator was used for the experiment[1]. It consisted of three computer screens, depicting the front and sides of the road scene, a gaming car seat, a gaming steering wheel, and a centre stack software, running on a separate computer, depicting current speed, state of automation,

[1] http://stisimdrive.com/

	CB	RepB	ResB	MB
PW (*M, SD, SE*)	22.38, 14.35, 2.05	22.91, 11.80, 1.69	29.72, 15.56, 2.22	26.32, 13.52, 1.95
PU (*M, SD, SE*)	85.15, 11.55, 1.65	77.35, 12.63, 1.80	75.26, 13.62, 1.97	75.89, 14.42, 2.08
PA (*M, SD, SE*)	1.05, 0.76, 0.11	0.14, 1.05, 0.15	0.37, 1.01, 0.14	0.20, 1.08, 0.16
Ranking (*Median*)	1	3	2	3
DiP (*% Correct*)	86.36	85.71	32.65	75.00
TT in ***sec*** (*M, SD, SE*)	19.79, 9.30, 1.37	48.61, 4.67, 0.67	47.79, 10.04, 1.43	49.65, 6.39, 0.93
AAI in ***deg*** (*M, SD, SE*)	0.36, 0.34, 0.05	1.12, 1.26, 0.17	1.45, 2.53, 0.36	1.21, 1.19, 0.17

Table 1: Results of Perceived Workload (PW – NASA-TLX), Perceived Usability (PU – SUS), Satisfaction score of Perceived Acceptance (PA – AS), Ranking of preferences, Dialogue Performance (DiP), Time to Takeover (TT), and Absolute Angle Input (AAI). Mean (*M*), Standard Deviation (*SD*), Standard Error (*SE*), Median, and Percentage values are reported as appropriate.

upcoming exits, desired lane to be in, and a pictorial representation of surrounding traffic. The simulator was depicting a circa ten-mile-long route, with straight rural roads, and a motorway with no major turns. When in autonomous mode, participants were using a 10-inch tablet to perform a secondary task. Their movements were filmed with a wide angle camera. Only used in MB interface, there were also two LED strips mounted on the wall on either side of the car seat, and a Tactile-Acoustic Device (TAD) [19], translating audio information into ambient vibrotactile stimuli.

Procedure

Participants were welcomed and had the purpose of the experiment explained to them. After answering to demographics questions, they were given a £20 web voucher for their time. They were then introduced to the driving simulator, completing a short drive. Other than a general description of the dialogue systems, provided by the experimenter, there was no prior training with the systems before the main part of the experiment. Their interaction with the different types of interfaces followed, counterbalanced through a Latin square. Participants were instructed to play a tablet memory game, used also in [33,34], and come back to driving whenever requested. In each interaction, there were three takeover requests, approximately when 10%, 40% and 70% of the route was completed. Requests were spoken by a female text-to-speech voice (Microsoft Anna [28]). Participants were expected to interact with the dialogue interfaces, and press a button on the steering wheel to take over control once the dialogues were completed. Recognition of their responses was based on Wizard-of-Oz, meaning that there was no actual dialogue system, but the experimenter was manipulating software on another computer, choosing the appropriate utterances based on the participants' responses, in line with studies like [6,25]. Any wrong or missed answers by participants regarding road-related information were counted as errors, affecting their DiP. The latter was scored as 0 if no mistakes were made, or 1 if any number of mistakes were made, including failing to acknowledge readiness to takeover. In the case of CB interface, failing to acknowledge readiness of takeover was the only possible mistake, as there was no further dialogue. TT was calculated from the time any dialogue interface required verbal confirmation of readiness, until participants had completed all steps of the verbal interaction and took over by pressing the button when ready (in the cases of RepB, ResB, and MB), or by the time participants pressed the button to take over control, as no further confirmation was required (in the case of CB). When participants assumed control in each of the three takeovers, they were asked to drive as normal for 60 *sec*, during which time their driving performance was logged, and they were then reminded to give control back to the car. After the interaction with each interface, lasting about 15 *min*, the NASA-TLX, AS, SUS, and SART questionnaires were administered, in this order. After all interfaces had been tested, a ranking of concepts was performed, concluding with a short interview (not to be discussed in detail in this paper). The experiment lasted in total about 90 *min*.

Results

Data for Perceived Workload, Perceived Acceptance, Perceived Usability, and Perceived Situation Awareness were analysed using a one-way ANOVA, with ToI as a factor, and planned contrasts between conditions. A significant effect of ToI on PW ($F(3,191) = 2.95$, $p < 0.05$, $\omega = 0.17$), revealed that ResB was perceived as inducing significantly higher workload than CB, and RepB. A significant effect of ToI on PA, in the Satisfaction score ($F(3,191) = 8.71$, $p < 0.001$, $\omega = 0.33$), revealed that CB had significantly higher perceived satisfaction than RepB, ResB, and MB. A significant effect of ToI on PU ($F(3,190) = 5.97$, $p < 0.01$, $\omega = 0.27$), revealed that CB had significantly higher PU than RepB, ResB, and MB. There were no significant effects observed in terms of PSA. Further, a Friedman test revealed that participants' rankings of the ToI were significantly different across interfaces ($\chi^2(3) = 47.12$, $p < 0.001$). Wilcoxon tests with Bonferroni correction, revealed that CB was significantly preferred to RepB, ResB, and MB, and ResB was significantly preferred to MB. Data for DiP were treated as dichotomous and analysed with Cochran's Q tests. These revealed that ResB induced more errors than CB ($Q(1) = 22.00$, $p < 0.001$), RepB ($Q(1) = 19.88$, $p < 0.001$), and MB ($Q(1) = 15.38$, $p < 0.001$). In terms of TT, a one-way ANOVA, with ToI as a factor, and planned contrasts between conditions found a significant effect of ToI on PW ($F(3,187) = 156.16$, $p < 0.001$, $\omega = 0.84$), revealing that TT in CB was significantly shorter than RepB, ResB, and MB. Concluding, a one-way ANOVA, analysing DrP, specifically Absolute Angle Input (AAI), with ToI as a factor, and planned contrasts between conditions found a significant effect of ToI on AAI ($F(3,190) = 4.62$, $p < 0.01$, $\omega = 0.23$), revealing that AAI in CB was significantly lower than RepB, ResB, and MB. No other driving metrics were found to elicit any significant effects. See Table 1 for all results. Finally, two-way mixed ANOVAs revealed no significant effect of age on the results.

DISCUSSION

The subjective results of the experiment favoured simplicity, regardless of age. The Countdown-Based interface, which required the shortest Time to Takeover, and allowed the participants to choose the moment of takeover, induced higher Perceived Usability and Acceptance, and was the highest ranked interface. This suggests that the desired interaction during takeover needs to be succinct and under participant's timing control. This is in line with [23,35], where a simplicity of interaction was found to be desirable. The longer interactions of the rest of the concepts, although arguably doing more to increase SA, were less preferred. Interview results (to be discussed in detail elsewhere), supported this argument, since participants acknowledged that CB was doing the least to support their knowledge of what was happening on the road, but appreciated its short duration and sense of control it elicited. We note, that the shorter interaction time and less errors of CB were a result of the design, and were not an indicator of higher performance or SA, since no driver information was provided in CB. Arguably, participants may have established SA to their satisfaction through the simulation. As a guideline, intelligent dialogue systems for takeovers should enable a straight forward interaction, providing only essential information. The only quantitative result in terms of driving performance that differed across types of interface, was a lower Absolute Angle Input for CB after the takeover, indicating a smoother steering behaviour. This finding could arguably be attributed to lower disruption to the driving task (as was observed in [33]).

The next concept in order of preference was Voice Autopilot Assistance, which interestingly was the concept inducing the highest perceived workload and resulting in the most dialogue mistakes. This is an expected result, as ResB required the longest interaction, and required answers rather than repetitions (like RepB and MB) or no action (like CB). This supports the argument that making the driver think about what is happening on the road before taking over was not disliked as an idea. Interview responses mentioned that if there were some shortcuts in the interaction of ResB, allowing participants to choose the moment of takeover, it would be preferable, as that ResB was less laborious than simply repeating information like in RepB and MB. This will be attempted in future studies, using the learnings of this experiment to design interfaces that will still facilitate SA without requiring long utterances. Finally, the use of multimodal displays in MB made little difference in subjective results, possibly because the cues were subtle, so as not to annoy, but as a result they were often not noticed. Future studies will evaluate more prominent cues during takeover interactions.

We argue that the observed results reflected the full embodiment of the tested techniques; CB simulated a short interaction with the least engagement, RepB and MB required repetition of all phrases, offering no shortcuts, and ResB required answers to all questions, with no shortcuts either. Future studies will attempt to amalgamate the tested approaches, offering an Augmented Countdown-Based interface, which will enable succinct interaction (see also [10]), but also inform the driver to facilitate SA. Increasing SA is imperative in a takeover interface [12,30], and a desirable quality recognised in user views. More objective measures of SA will be used in future studies, requiring specific responses to more critical road events, as opposed to an uneventful scenario simulated in this study, since richer road scenes may have an effect on observed driver behaviours.

CONCLUSIONS

This study evaluated a set of dialogue-based interfaces for the takeover of control in an autonomous car. The simplicity and personal choice about when to takeover of the countdown interface was appreciated the most, and the interface requiring response to questions about the road, thus engaging the driver the most, came next. The interfaces requiring repetition of phrases were the least preferred, even when multimodally augmented. In order to better facilitate Situation Awareness, an amalgamation of the best performing techniques is proposed.

ACKNOWLEDGMENTS

This work was funded by EPSRC and Jaguar-Land Rover, as part of the project Human Interaction: Designing Autonomy in Vehicles (HI:DAVe), Project Grant Number: EP/N011899/1.

REFERENCES

1. V. A. Banks, N. A. Stanton, and C. Harvey. 2014. Subsystems on the road to vehicle automation: Hands and feet free but not "mind" free driving. *Safety Science* 62: 505–514. http://doi.org/10.1016/j.ssci.2013.10.014
2. S. S. Borojeni, L. Chuang, W. Heuten, and S. Boll. 2016. Assisting Drivers with Ambient Take-Over Requests in Highly Automated Driving. In *AutomotiveUI 2016*, 237–244. http://doi.org/10.1145/3003715.3005409
3. J. Brooke. 1996. SUS-A quick and dirty usability scale. *Usability evaluation in industry* 189, 194: 4–7.
4. Civil Aviation Authority. 2015. *Radiotelephony Manual.*
5. Clarkson, J., Coleman, R., Keates, S., and C. Lebbon. 2013. *Inclusive design: Design for the whole population.* Springer.
6. B. Dhillon, R. Kocielnik, I. Politis, M. Swerts, and D. Szostak. 2011. Culture and Facial Expressions: A Case Study with a Speech Interface. In *INTERACT 2011*, 392–404.
7. M. R. Endsley. 1988. Situation awareness global

assessment technique (SAGAT). *Aerospace and Electronics Conference, 1988. NAECON 1988., Proceedings of the IEEE 1988 National*: 789–795. http://doi.org/10.1109/NAECON.1988.195097

8. M. R. Endsley. 1995. Toward a Theory of Situation Awareness in Dynamic Systems. *Human Factors: The Journal of the Human Factors and Ergonomics Society* 37, 1: 32–64. http://doi.org/10.1518/001872095779049543
9. A. Eriksson, S. M. Petermeijer, M. Zimmerman, J. C. F. De Winter, K. J. Bengler, and N. A. Stanton. 2017. Rolling out the red (and green) carpet: supporting driver decision making in automation-to-manual transitions. *IEEE Transactions on Human-Machine Systems*: In Press. http://doi.org/10.1002/elan.
10. A. Eriksson and N. A. Stanton. 2017. The chatty co-driver: A linguistics approach applying lessons learnt from aviation incidents. *Safety Science* 99: 94–101. http://doi.org/10.1016/j.ssci.2017.05.005
11. Y. Forster, F. Naujoks, and A. Neukum. 2016. Your Turn or My Turn ? Design of a Human- Machine Interface for Conditional Automation. In *AutomotiveUI 2016*, 253–260. http://doi.org/10.1145/3003715.3005463
12. Y. Forster, F. Naujoks, and A. Neukum. 2017. Increasing anthropomorphism and trust in automated driving functions by adding speech output. *IEEE Intelligent Vehicles Symposium, Proceedings* 2, Iv: 365–372. http://doi.org/10.1109/IVS.2017.7995746
13. S. G. Hart. 2006. Nasa-Task Load Index (NASA-TLX); 20 Years Later. *Proceedings of the Human Factors and Ergonomics Society Annual Meeting* 50, 9: 904–908. http://doi.org/10.1177/154193120605000909
14. S. G. Hart and L. E. Staveland. 1988. Development of NASA-TLX (Task Load Index): Results of Empirical and Theoretical Research. *Advances in Psychology* 52: 139–183. http://doi.org/10.1016/S0166-4115(08)62386-9
15. A. Hawkins. 2017. Ford and Lyft will work together to deploy autonomous cars. *The Verge*. Retrieved from https://www.theverge.com/2017/9/27/16373574/ford-lyft-self-driving-car-partnership-gm
16. W. J. Horrey and C. D. Wickens. 2004. Driving and Side Task Performance: The Effects of Display Clutter, Separation, and Modality. *Human Factors* 46, 4: 611–624. http://doi.org/10.1518/hfes.46.4.611.56805
17. SAE J3016. 2016. *Taxonomy and Definitions for Terms Related to Driving Automation Systems for On-Road Motor Vehicles*.
18. M. Jeon, I. Politis, S. E. Shaldover, C. Sutter, J. Terken, and B. Poppinga. 2016. Towards Life-Long Mobility: Accessible Transportation with Automation. In *AutomotiveUI 2016 EA*.
19. M. Karam, F. A. Russo, and D. I. Fels. 2009. Designing the model human cochlea: An ambient crossmodal audio-tactile display. *IEEE Transactions on Haptics* 2, 3: 160–169. http://doi.org/10.1109/TOH.2009.32
20. S. Keates and P. J. Clarkson. 2002. Countering design exclusion through inclusive design. *ACM SIGCAPH Computers and the Physically Handicapped* 44, 73–74: 69. http://doi.org/10.1145/960201.957218
21. M. Kyriakidis, R. Happee, and J. C. F. De Winter. 2015. Public opinion on automated driving: Results of an international questionnaire among 5000 respondents. *Transportation Research Part F: Traffic Psychology and Behaviour* 32: 127–140. http://doi.org/10.1016/j.trf.2015.04.014
22. J. D. Van Der Laan, A. Heino, and D. De Waard. 1997. A simple procedure for the assessment of acceptance of advanced transport telematics. *Transportation Research Part C: Emerging Technologies* 5, 1: 1–10. http://doi.org/10.1016/S0968-090X(96)00025-3
23. P. Langdon, I. Politis, M. Bradley, L. Skrypchuk, A. Mouzakitis, and P. J. Clarkson. 2017. Obtaining design requirements from the public understanding of driverless technology. In *International Conference on Applied Human Factors and Ergonomics*, 749–759. http://doi.org/10.1007/978-3-319-60441-1_72
24. D. R. Large, V. Banks, G. Burnett, and N. Margaritis. 2017. Putting the Joy in Driving : Investigating the Use of a Joystick as an Alternative to Traditional Controls within Future Autonomous Vehicles. In *AutomotiveUI 2017*, 31–39.
25. D. R. Large, G. Burnett, B. Anyasodo, and L. Skrypchuk. 2016. Assessing Cognitive Demand during Natural Language Interactions with a Digital Driving Assistant. In *AutomotiveUI 2016*, 67–74. http://doi.org/10.1145/3003715.3005408
26. K. J. Lee, Y. K. Joo, and C. Nass. 2014. Partially Intelligent Automobiles and Driving Experience at the Moment of System Transition. In *CHI 2014*, 3631–3634.
27. R. McCall, F. McGee, A. Meschtscherjakov, N. Louveton, and T. Engel. 2016. Towards A Taxonomy of Autonomous Vehicle Handover Situations. In *AutomotiveUI 2016*, 193–200. http://doi.org/10.1145/3003715.3005456
28. Microsoft. 2012. Microsoft Speech Platform. Retrieved from http://msdn.microsoft.com/en-us/library/hh361572.aspx
29. F. Naujoks, D. Befelein, K. Wiedemann, and A. Neukum. 2017. A Review of Non-driving-related Tasks Used in Studies on Automated Driving. In *International Conference on Applied Human Factors and Ergonomics*, 525–537. http://doi.org/10.1007/978-3-

319-60441-1

30. F. Naujoks, Y. Forster, K. Wiedemann, and A. Neukum. Speech improves human-automation cooperation in automated driving. *Mensch und Computer 2016 – Workshopband.* http://doi.org/10.18420/muc2016-ws08-0007
31. F. Naujoks, C. Mai, and A. Neukum. 2014. The effect of urgency of take-over requests during highly automated driving under distraction conditions. In *Proceedings of the 5th International Conference on Applied Human Factors and Ergonomics AHFE 2014*, 431–438.
32. Phys.org. 2017. GM unit says it has "mass producible" autonomous cars. *Phys.org.* Retrieved from https://phys.org/news/2017-09-gm-mass-autonomous-cars.html
33. I. Politis, S. Brewster, and F. Pollick. 2015. Language-Based Multimodal Displays for the Handover of Control in Autonomous Cars. In *Automotive UI 2015*, 3–10.
34. I. Politis, S. Brewster, and F. Pollick. 2017. Using Multimodal Displays to Signify Critical Handovers of Control to Distracted Autonomous Car Drivers. *International Journal of Mobile Human-Computer Interaction (IJMHCI)* 9, 3: 1–16.
35. I. Politis, P. Langdon, M. Bradley, L. Skrypchuk, A. Mouzakitis, and P. J. Clarkson. 2017. Designing autonomy in cars: A survey and two focus groups on driving habits of an inclusive user group, and group attitudes towards autonomous cars. In *International Conference on Applied Human Factors and Ergonomics*, 161–173. http://doi.org/10.1007/978-3-319-60597-5_15
36. C. Rödel, S. Stadler, A. Meschtscherjakov, and M. Tscheligi. 2014. Towards Autonomous Cars: The Effect of Autonomy Levels on Acceptance and User Experience. *Automotive UI 2014*: 1–8. Retrieved December 16, 2014 from http://dl.acm.org/citation.cfm?id=2667330
37. B. Schoettle and M. Sivak. 2014. *A survey of public opinion about autonomous and self-driving vehicles in the US, the UK, and Australia.*
38. B. Schoettle and M. Sivak. 2014. *Public Opinion About Self-Driving Vehicles in China, India, Japan, The U.S., The U.K. and Australia.* http://doi.org/UMTRI-2014-30
39. B. Schoettle and M. Sivak. 2015. *Motorists' Preferencesfor Different Levels of Vehicle Automation.*
40. B. Schoettle and M. Sivak. 2016. *Motorists' Preferences for Different Levels of Vehicle Automation: 2016.*
41. R. M. Taylor. 1989. Situational Awareness Rating Techniqu (SART): The development of a tool for aircrew systems design. *Situational Awareness in Aerospace Operations (AGARD-CP-478 pp. 3/1-3/17).*
42. T. Van Veen and J. Terken. 2017. Situation Awareness in Automated Vehicles through Proximal Peripheral Light Signals. In *AutomotiveUI 2017*, 287–292.
43. Volvo. Autopilot - Self-driving Volvos by 2017. Retrieved from https://www.volvocars.com/au/about/innovations/intellisafe/autopilot
44. M. Walch, K. Lange, M. Baumann, and M. Weber. 2015. Autonomous Driving: Investigating the Feasibility of Car-Driver Handover Assistance. In *AutomotiveUI '15*, 11–18. http://doi.org/10.1145/2799250.2799268
45. M. Walch, T. Sieber, P. Hock, M. Baumann, and M. Weber. 2016. Towards Cooperative Driving: Involving the Driver in an Autonomous Vehicle's Decision Making. In *AutomotiveUI 2016*, 261–268. http://doi.org/10.1145/3003715.3005458
46. C. D. Wickens. 1980. *The structure of attentional resources.*
47. C. D. Wickens. 2008. Multiple Resources and Mental Workload. *Human Factors: The Journal of the Human Factors and Ergonomics Society* 50, 3: 449–455. http://doi.org/10.1518/001872008X288394

Visualizing Reviews Summaries as a Tool for Restaurants Recommendation

Yaakov Danone
The University of Haifa
Haifa, Israel
dnkobi@gmail.com

Tsvi Kuflik
The University of Haifa
Haifa, Israel
tsvikak@is.haifa.ac.il

Osnat Mokryn
The University of Haifa
Haifa, Israel
ossimo@gmail.com

ABSTRACT

Online customers' opinions about products and services, in the form of reviews, are a major part of today's web culture. However, customers, when looking for a product or service, do not have the time or the desire to read even a small part of the available product reviews (which themselves may be lengthy and not easy to read). Moreover, they often would like to examine reviews of similar products, and get a comprehensive picture of how different aspects of these products compare. In this work, by introducing a generic framework for analyzing and presenting a visual summary based on comparative sentences extracted from customer reviews, we offer the user an easy and intuitive understanding of the differences between a set of products.

The contribution of this study is twofold: First, it focuses on reviews of intangible services (using the restaurant domain as a case study), unlike most of the related studies that consider physical products. Second, it combines state-of-the-art text analysis techniques with an intuitive visualization into an easy to use prototype to visualize summarized service comparisons to the users.

The system's usefulness and intuitiveness were confirmed in multiple user studies.

Author Keywords

Visualizing comparisons; Reviews summarization; Information visualization.

ACM Classification Keywords

• Human-centered computing~Social recommendation • Human-centered computing~Information visualization • Human-centered computing~Empirical studies in HCI

INTRODUCTION

Customer reviews are based on the experience of using the product "in the field" and thus provide more information than the technical evaluation of experts, and obviously, more than the product description provided by the seller [45]. Studies show that customer reviews have a major impact on consumer purchase decisions [29, 13, 28, 46]. In many cases, to better explain and illustrate the differences between products they are reviewing, consumers compare them with similar products, identifying their relative strengths and weaknesses [42]. Comparisons are different from opinions and sentimental evaluations. While opinions and sentimental evaluations are subjective, comparisons can be either subjective or objective [1]. For example, an opinion sentence about a car may be "Car X is very nice". A subjective comparative sentence may be "Car X is much better than Car Y". An objective comparative sentence may be "Car X is 2 feet longer than Car Y". Each statement has different language constructs, and therefore, they should be treated differently than general opinion statements [15].

IUI'18, March 7–11, 2018, Tokyo, Japan

ACM ISBN 978-1-4503-4945-1/18/03…$15.00
https://doi.org/10.1145/3172944.3172947

Today's information overload, where there are too many reviews and opinions available, make it hard to present a compact representation of a product's accumulated reviews to a customer [45]. Reviews can be lengthy, making it hard for the interested reader to understand and exploit them [12]. When focusing on the restaurants domain it is worth noting that differently from reviews of physical goods, in reviews of intangible services, customers tend to "tell stories" and report on their experiences using longer and more complex sentences [24].

One way of addressing this information overload is by generating a summary of reviews, which can be done in various ways. In our study, following past research, we used comparisons as a key factor in summarizing reviews, following [15, 42]. Comparative sentences have a similar structure and they appear in both physical goods and intangible services reviews, so it is reasonable to assume that the approach suggested by [42] may be applied also to restaurant services reviews. To present these summaries to end users, we apply information visualization techniques. Specifically, this work addresses the following research question: **How can visualization of comparison statements extracted from restaurant reviews help the customer in understanding the strengths and weaknesses of a restaurant, with respect to features in which she is interested?**

To answer the above question, the following challenges have been addressed, integrating state of the art research results with simple, intuitive visualizations:

- How to identify a comparison sentence in restaurant reviews?

- How to extract a comparison relation from a comparison sentence in restaurant reviews?

- How to find the direction of the comparison relation?

- How to summarize and visualize an integrated set of comparison sentences about features of interest extracted from reviews for the customer to use?

As a first step in the study, a prototype system that addresses the above challenges using simple common visualizations was developed and evaluated.

RELATED WORK

Consumer products and subsequently their reviews may be classified into one of two categories: physical goods and intangible services [22]. Generally, in physical product reviews, customers write about the features they liked/disliked, without adding much extraneous information. This contrasts with reviews of intangible services. In reviews of the latter type, customers tend to report on their experiences using complex and longer sentences [24]. For example, "*The food is just Ok. Their Happy Hour menu is pretty good. However, if it wasn't for Lynette, the bartender, I probably wouldn't frequent this place as much as I do. She is awesome, friendly, makes SPECTACULAR drinks . . . overall she makes what would be an A-OK experience, simply marvelous!!*" The example taken from a restaurant review talks about the restaurant's physical goods such as food and its intangible services such as the staff. Different from the physical goods, there are multiple mentions of the service that is being reviewed (the bartender) and opinions are given via different and complex expressions referring to the features or subcomponents of the reviewed service. Cruz et al. [4] confirmed the importance of the domain being examined in the field of Opinion Mining (OM) for building accurate opinion extraction systems, while indicating that people express their opinions on a given domain differently. Restaurants provide physical goods (the food) as well as services in the form of ambience or settings. To the best of our knowledge, most existing works, which utilized comparative sentences, focused mainly on pure physical product reviews, as demonstrated by [16, 42, 11, 17, 40]. Few studies did address services, including Gu and Yoo [10] that dealt with restaurants reviews in Korean. They identified comparison sentences as those containing one of the words {than, compared to, far, more} in Korean, and used semantic rule labeling on the resulted sentences. We assume that there may be a few more that we missed, but in general, the focus was on products reviews. In this study we analyze services provided by restaurants, as a case study, focusing on their intangible features as opposed to their physical aspects.

Previous work also tried to eliminate the need to read every review. One basic application, suggested by Turney [38], presented a simple unsupervised learning algorithm for classifying reviews as recommending (thumb up) or not recommending (thumb down), where the customer can promote the review by selecting it as useful or not. Another approach is to summarize the reviews. For example, Hu and Liu [12] identified the features of a particular product in the reviews and classified reviews as positive or negative with respect to these features, producing a summary about the products. Their work was a pioneering effort in OM and was followed by other studies like [44], which created a product ranking system derived from customer reviews. Their study aimed to develop a tool that selected the highest rated products based on their past reviews. It used a weight-directed graph that showed the quality of the products based on their reviews and presented the results as a ranked table for the top-rated products. Another attempt to summaries reviews and opinions was that of Ying and Jiang [43], which used text quality and subjectivity to decide which sentences are good summary sentences.

A comprehensive survey of reviews and text summarizing with the different approaches can be found in Liu and Zhang [21]. The works of Hu and Liu [12] and Zhang et al. [44], as well as most of the similar works in the field, focused on digital cameras, TVs and other electronic products and did not consider intangible services which is the focus of our study.

Comparative Sentence Mining

In a typical customer review, there are two kinds of judgmental sentences [44]:

1. Subjective sentences: Sentences with opinions, positive or negative, about an entity.

2. Comparative sentences: Sentences that compare objects.

The latter sentence type, comparative sentences, is one of the most important ways of evaluating an entity or event [14, 15] and a rich information source for identifying the relative strengths and weaknesses of products compared with their competitors [42]. We believe that this type of sentences can potentially be used as a key factor in summarizing customer reviews; therefore, our work focused on visualization of comparative sentences.

Jindal and Liu [14,15] were pioneers in analyzing comparisons using natural language processing (NLP) techniques and were the first to try to identify and extract comparative sentences from customer reviews. In their work, they had two main objectives:

1. Identify comparative sentences in the text.

2. Identify and extract comparative relations from comparative sentences.

They applied Class Sequential Rules (CSR, see [20]) to identify comparative sentences. To build a CSR training dataset, they treated each sentence as a sequence and manually defined it as belonging to either a comparative or non-comparative class. They identified the comparative keyword in a sentence (for example, adjectives with morphemes such as er/est, or general comparative keywords such as more, less, same, prefer, lead, beat etc.) and used a radius of words before and after the keyword to capture a sequence. Although their use of comparative keywords identified most of the corpus' comparative sentences, many sentences among these were not comparative (they achieved high recall 98% but with low precision 32%). Comparative keywords together with CSR and Naïve Bayes (NB) classifier gave an overall precision of 79% and an overall recall of 81% in distinguishing between comparative and non-comparative sentences. Originally, the actual words created too many patterns. To overcome this limitation, the authors changed each word (beside the comparative keyword) in the radius to its matched Part of Speech (POS) tag, and this way, the patterns emerged. In addition, Jindal and Liu [14] defined four types of comparative sentences: "non-equal gradable", "equative", "superlative" and "non-gradable". Their method, however, cannot identify the direction of the "non-equal gradable" (better/worse) sentence, which makes it inadequate to judge the sentiment polarities of customers, based on the comparative sentence. Xu et al. [42] improved Jindal and Liu's [14, 15] work by adding direction to the comparative relation and proposed a new form of the comparative relation:

<direction> (<product1>, <product2>, <attribute>, <sentiment>).

They recognized four possible directions: '>', which means P1 is better than P2, '<' worse, '=' equal and '~' no comparison. To extract a comparative relation, at first, Xu et al. [41] had to recognize the product names, the attribute and the sentiment phrase. Since the domain in their work was smartphones, the set of products and attributes is finite. They created a list that included most of the product names and attributes in the smartphone domain. For the sentiment phrases, the authors built a comparative keyword set from known lexical resources [27,6,7] (the same lexicon resources that was used by Jindal and Liu's [14,15] and also in this work). Next, they searched for the direction of a comparative relation. Finding the direction is not a trivial task; there are many comparative sentences that use the same comparative keyword but have opposite directions. For example, the following are restaurant reviews:

1. The Front Porch: "The food here is sooooo much better than Cha Cha Cha!"

2. Zazie: "I personally think the food is better at Citizen Cake".

The first comparative sentence in the example appears in a review about a restaurant, The Front Porch. The comparative keyword in the sentence is 'better' and the direction is in favor of the first restaurant over the second restaurant, Cha Cha Cha. The second comparative sentence contains the same comparative keyword 'better', even the attribute 'food' is the same, but the direction is opposite—in favor of the second restaurant.

To address this challenge, Xu et al. [42] found the connection between the words and the entities in the sentence as well as between the different comparative relations in the comparative sentence. For that purpose, they enhanced the one-level Conditional Random Field (CRF)[1], making it into a two-level CRF model. They used the different levels of the model and encoded the model to calculate the probability of finding the direction of each comparative relation. They used the word, entity and between-relations functions to consider the characteristics of the comparative sentence and decided the right direction of each comparative relation based on the characteristics. In this way, they managed to identify the directions for the relations with an overall accuracy of 66.17% and an average F-score result of 56.68 as shown in Table 2.

Table 2: Performance of the two-level CRF when identifying the direction of the relations ([Xu et al. 2011])

Direction	*Precision (%)*	*Recall (%)*	*F-score (%)*
>	76.63	81.90	78.56
<	59.72	48.39	51.77
=	61.11	23.33	31.19
~	54.29	83.33	65.20
Average	**62.94**	**59.24**	**56.68**

Xu et al. [42] visualized the results of the comparison of several items using a comparative relation map, which an undirected graph. The main node, in the center of the graph, represents the candidate product, to which other products are compared. It is connected to the other products via links, where each link represents comparisons based on one predefined feature. In the middle of each link, there is a red or a blue box. The red box grows in direct relation to the number of positive comparisons in favor of the main product and the blue box grows in direct relation to the number of positive comparisons in favor of competitors.

Still, the work of Xu et al. [42] was limited to the smartphone domain – a specific product with a well-defined set of features while we aim at services which has a wider set of features, not all of them are well defined. In addition, a consultation with a visualization expert confirmed that the comparative relation map visualization is not very intuitive, and necessitates the user getting instructions or training before using it.

Information Visualization

Information visualization is intended to provide an easily understandable interpretation of a huge and complex amount

[1] CRF is a framework for building probabilistic models to segment and label sequential data [19, 32].

of information, while creating visual representations of it that exploit the individual's perceptual and cognitive problem-solving capabilities [18,41]. Many studies in OM use visualization techniques to summarize customers' opinions of products from online reviews. Miao et al. [26] used a pie chart to present the proportion of positive and negative reviews of a product's specific feature. Gamon et al. [9] used a tree map to present common words used to describe features of vehicles. Shamim et al. [33] categorized visualization techniques used in OM into four categories:

1. Radial visualization: Opinion wheel and spider graph.

2. Graph visualization: Coordinated, comparative relation map, positioning map, line graph and pie chart.

3. Hierarchical visualization: Tree map and visual summary report.

4. Bar chart: Glowing bars, bars with different shapes and bar chart.

Usability, quality and expressiveness are important aspects of data usability and visualizations [8]. How can usability, however, be measured? Some approaches explain and define usability measurement aspects [25,34,2]. Bai et al. [2], for instance, defined seven visualization assessments: psychology of the observer, visual representation model, visual impact, overall performance, overall design style, information quality, and information presentation model. Another usability measurement is the System Usability Scale (SUS) [3], which is a standard questionnaire that is commonly used and contains 10 questions to measure the usability of a system.

TOOLS AND METODS

This study followed a "design study" approach [39]. Prototypes providing solutions for the individual research questions were developed, and then we developed research prototype that enabled us to demonstrate and evaluate these solutions using a publicly available dataset.

Dataset

For our experimentation, we used a dataset extracted from Yelp[2]. It contains approximately 270,000 Restaurant reviews taken from the San Francisco area (see [5] for details). In addition, for completion purposes, 50,000 more reviews were taken from the Yelp Dataset Challenge[3], 320,000 restaurant reviews overall. From this dataset, a set of 1,738 sentences that named another restaurant (hence they potentially contain comparisons) was extracted. They were manually analyzed by the first author and 1,380 of them were identified as comparative sentences.

Comparative Relations

Previous work [14,15] showed how to identify comparative sentences accurately. In the scope of this research, sentences appearing in a review of a restaurant that contained another restaurant's name together with a comparative keyword were considered to be comparative sentences. To find a second restaurant name, as a preliminary requirement, we needed a database of reviews where each review would be marked with the name of the restaurant the review was written about. We extracted all the names from the reviews and saved them into a list that used to identify a second restaurant name in a sentence. To extract comparison relations from comparison sentences, we needed to identify the entities in the sentence, namely the restaurants, the attributes and the comparative keywords. Following Xu et al. [42], for automatic identification of the attributes in comparative sentences, we manually collected the attributes from our dataset and saved them into a restaurants ontology that contained 242 attributes. In addition, we built a comparative keyword list, with comparative keywords collected from available lexical resources [27,6,7] that contained 143 comparative keywords and phrases. We do not claim that our lists are complete, but we do believe that we have a sizable number of indicative words and phrases.

To discover the direction of the comparative relations, we implemented the CRF technique used by Xu et al. [41]. It offers a natural formalism for exploiting the dependence structure among entities and directly model the conditional probability distribution of the output given the input, so they can exploit the rich and global features of the input without representing the dependencies in it [37]. Therefore, CRFs offer several advantages when modelling complicated and long-range dependencies in an intuitive way [42].

For POS tagging, we used the Stanford Parser [36, 23] that can automatically annotate with high accuracy.

The performance of the techniques we experimented with was evaluated using accuracy, precision, recall, and the F1 measure [35].

Visualization

To select the visualizations to be used in our framework, we examined a few known visualization techniques. We selected those that seemed to match our needs, consulted with a visualization expert about them and performed a user study where we used the SUS questionnaire with additional open and closed questions to gather information about user experience and preferences with respect to these visualization techniques. This enabled us to select one technique that was preferred by the users, for presenting the comparisons from the customer reviews.

There are many attributes in the restaurant domain and we need to visually present them to a customer while at the same time provide a comprehensive overview of the reviews. Hence, we reduced and indexed the attributes into categories. Saad and Conway [31] cataloged the factors involved in

[2] www.yelp.com

[3] http://www.yelp.com/dataset_challenge

customer satisfaction in the restaurant industry into the following five categories:

1. Responsiveness (In this research called Service): Are the employees attentive, helpful and professional in responding to the customer's needs?

2. Food quality/reliability: Is the food fresh, tasty and agrees with the customer, i.e., type of food (Italian, Indian, etc.), food properties (drinks, lunch, dessert, etc.)?

3. Design and appearance: This relates to the restaurant lighting, available parking, location, procedures, features, cleanliness, decoration and the general environment.

4. Price: How much has the customer paid for his food and items?

5. Satisfaction: What is the customer's overall satisfaction and experience?

We used the above categories to help our users focus on a limited number of attributes presented simultaneously.

VISUALIZING SUMMARISED COMPARISONS

We developed a framework for extracting, processing and integrating comparison sentences drawn from customer reviews and then presenting a summary of the comparisons in an intuitive, visual way.

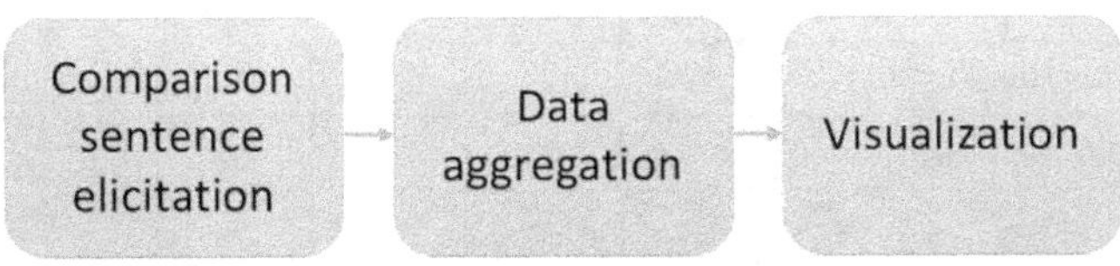

Figure 5: The main stages of the abstracted framework

As presented in Figure 5, the framework has three main components: Comparison sentence elicitation, data aggregation and visualization. The first step is to read the data and extract the comparative relations out of it, then aggregate and summarize the comparisons and reach a conclusion, and finally, present the results in an intuitive visualization. The following sections describe the implementation of a prototype that follows the suggested framework by:

- Compiling training datasets and extracting patterns and lexicons from the datasets to be used by the methods for identifying comparative relations from the reviews.

- Implementing extraction methods to extract comparative relations from incoming sentences.

- Selecting a visualization technique and developing an interactive visual user interface.

Extracting Comparative Relations

For automatic identification of comparative relations, we used the set of patterns extracted from our dataset, as described above. Following Xu et al. [42] method, the restaurants names, the attributes that are compared in the relations, and the comparative keyword in every sentence were extracted and represented in the standard form as:

<direction> {<restaurant1>, <srestaurant2>, <attribute>, <comparative keyword>}

Each comparative sentence was manually tagged with one of the four directions: >, <, = and ~, when > indicates that the first restaurant is better than the second restaurant, < worse, = equal and ~ has no gradable comparison. We used the standard forms of patterns identified using our training set and the pre-defined lists of entities (restaurants names, attributes, relations) to identify comparison sentences, comparison relations and relations directions in our test set.

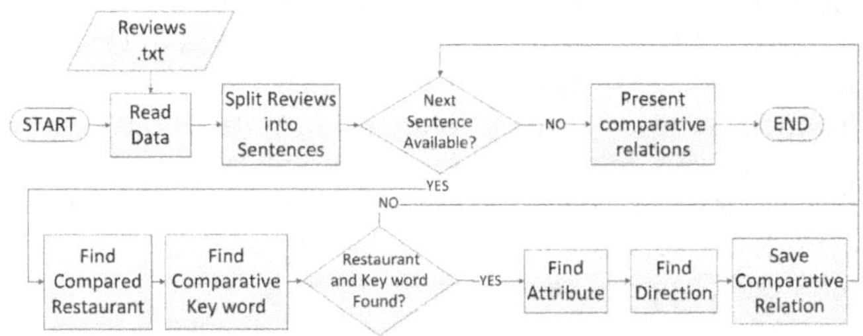

Figure 6: Workflow for implementing the framework

Figure 6 shows the workflow for the framework implementation. The analysis process starts by searching for the entities: the name of a second restaurant. Then finding a comparative keyword and the compared attribute from the predefined lists. In sentences that contain multiple entities, to verify which entity is right for the comparative relation we adopted the simple "closest first" approach, following Xu et al. [42]. The closest comparative keyword to the compared restaurant name in the sentence was selected, and following this, the closest attribute to the comparative keyword was selected. To find the direction of the comparative relation out of the four (>, <, =, ~) we first tried to use our own modified CSR method, hoping to receive better results than related works like the work of Xu et al. [42]. We used the POS tagging together with the comparative keywords to create CSR sequences: for every sentence from the dataset, we isolated the words around the comparative keywords by an optimal radius of words after evaluating the different options. As presented in Table 3 below, radius of three words for the new sentences combined with a radius of four words for the training patterns produced the best results in our experiment. To reduce the number of patterns, the POS tag of each word was used instead of the word itself (beside the keyword, which is left as is). Last, we matched a direction as a class to the generated sequence based on the direction manually defined earlier, we used four classes for the four directions (>, <, =, ~ as presented in [42]).

Unfortunately, in our experiment, the existing CRF method produced slightly better results than our modified CSR method (see table 4 for the CRF results). Accordingly, CRF as presented in [42], is the preferred method to identify the directions of comparative relations.

Table 3: The results using different radii to create patterns for the CSR method

		POS radii for the training patterns			
	F1	3	4	5	6
POS radii new **sentences**	2	60.21	59.17	59.55	58.77
	3	63.03	63.63	60.89	62.07

For selecting possible information visualization methods to present the comparative sentence to the customer, we consulted with a visualization expert on how to present the comparative relations that were extracted from the reviews as a preliminary stage in selecting the visualization techniques. As mentioned above, Shamim et al. [33] categorized the known visualization techniques in OM into four main categories: Radial visualization, graphs, hierarchical visualization and bar charts. From these categories, we selected six known visualization techniques that seemed to meet most of our needs. The six visualizations considered were: bar graph, spider graph, pie chart, tree map, table and comparative relation map.

The conclusions from the interview were to experiment with three visualization methods—bar graph, table and spider graph—and to compare only three restaurants in each visualization. In addition, for the table to be more precise and abundant, it was decided that each cell in the visualization table would be filled with the percentage and colors reflecting the restaurant ratings. In contrast to the expert's recommendation to consider testing time and performance measurements, we decided to focus only on usability since the visualizations were intuitive and the users were expected to be familiar with them. The visualizations were evaluated in a web-based user study, where we asked the participants a few informative questions about some information that was presented by the different visualizations (it was a simple comparative task) to allow them to reason about the visualizations. Then the participants used SUS to evaluate different visualizations. This process was repeated for all three visualizations. Last, the participants were asked which method he or she most preferred and why.

The experimental prototype

For experimental purposes, a Restaurant Comparison Presentation tool was developed, in order to enable us to assess the restaurant comparison visualization is a realistic setting. The tool contains three main sections: A Visualization window, a Data Grid (with the comparisons) and a Setup section that enables the user to choose how he or she wants to see the comparisons. The user can select attributes, restaurants for comparison, and a visualization method. Three visualization methods were used: bar graph, spider graph and table (see Figures 7, 8 and 9).

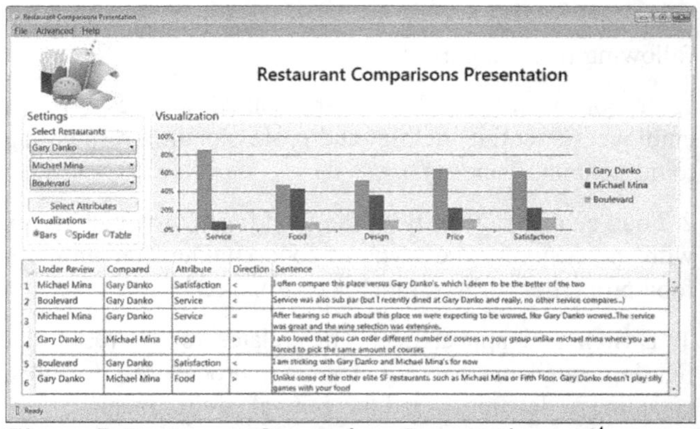

Figure 7: Restaurant Comparison Presentation tool[4]

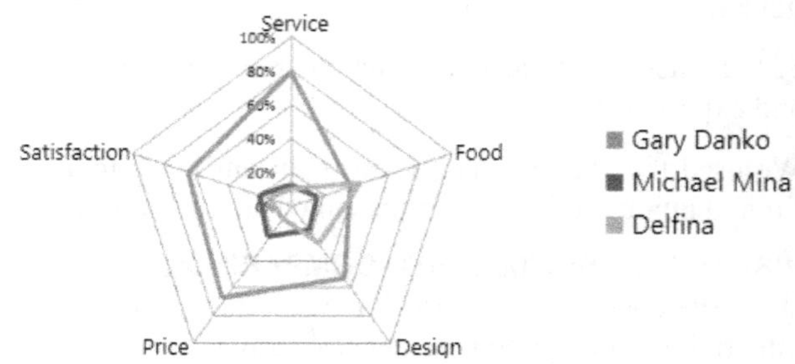

Figure 8: Spider graph visualization

	Service	Food	Design	Price	Satisfaction
Gary Danko	78%	39%	53%	67%	65%
Michael Mina	13%	17%	18%	24%	22%
Delfina	9%	44%	29%	9%	13%

Best / Middle / Worst

Figure 9: Table based visualization

EXPERIMENTAL SETUP AND EXPERIMENTAL RESULTS

To evaluate our framework, new comparative sentences were extracted from the dataset of reviews about restaurants in the San Francisco area. These were used as a test set and a gold standard. To build the test set, we randomly selected 10 restaurants and manually analyzed their reviews. The entities and the directions of the relations were manually extracted from each sentence. In this way, 456 comparative sentences were ready for the testing. Using the test set, we executed our implemented methods and compared the results achieved.

Table 4: The results of using CRF to find the direction of comparative sentences

Direction	Recall	Precision	% in Dataset	F1
>	40.00	40.51	17.58	40.25
<	75.57	73.88	57.58	74.72
=	68.57	72.73	23.08	70.59
~	50.00	44.44	1.76	47.06
Mean:	67.25	67.23	100.00	67.22

[4] available for downloading at: http://doi.org/10.5281/zenodo.1111755

Results of Comparative Relation Extraction

First, we evaluated the ability of CRF to identify comparative relations and the direction of the relations. It had an overall success of 67.22% (See table 4 for results). Next, given the fact that our list of attributes in comparative sentences is finite and most likely does not contain all the attributes available in the domain, we measured how well the attributes were found in the new dataset. We automatically extracted the attributes from the test set using our attributes list and compared it to the ones manually found it the new dataset. We used the accuracy parameter to evaluate the results. The right attribute was successfully found in the comparative sentences with an accuracy of 82%.

In addition, multiple attributes occasionally appear in the sentences while only one should match the comparative relation. By experimenting, we verified that it is better to use the attribute closest to the comparative keyword and not the one closest to the second restaurant name. We found that searching for the attributes closest to the comparative keyword in the sentence, correctly identified 82% of the attributes compared with 77% attributes that were closest to the second restaurant name.

Another experiment regarding the "inverted" comparative sentence (not, unlike, etc.) was also conducted. Such words invert the direction of the relation in the sentence. We tested all radii from zero (not searching) to six words before the comparative keyword to search for such inverted words. A distance of four words before the keywords while searching for "inverting" words worked best in our settings. Table 5 presents the final F-score results for finding comparative direction using the different distances while searching for "inverting" words:

Table 5: F-score results of finding the direction of the relation using the different radii to search for "inverted" comparisons (not, unlike, etc.)

Radius	0	1	2	3	4	5	6
F1	64.86	65.34	65.54	65.76	**67.22**	66.71	66.16

The Selected Visualization Technique

To evaluate and decide which visualization technique to use for presenting the comparisons of customer reviews, three visualization techniques were evaluated using an online questionnaire based on SUS. To date, 117 participants (recruited via social media) have responded to the questionnaire: 38% men and 62% women from different demographic layers. The final SUS results (from 0 to 100) of the questionnaire are presented in Table 6.

The bar graph is the most favored method, receiving a total SUS score of 82, followed by the table, a close second with 80, and then by the spider graph, which only received a score of 49.

Table 6: The results of the SUS questionnaire evaluating the visualization methods.

	Average SUS Score	Median	STD
Bar Graph	82	87	20
Table	80	87	19
Spider	49	47	24

Although the statistical ANOVA test between the table and the bar graph showed—with a confidence level of 95%--that there is no significant difference between the table and the bar graph, 65% of the volunteers declared that bar graph is their favorite visualization technique, 28% voted for the table and only 7% voted for the spider. Most volunteers declared the bar graph is the most "common", "clear", "simple", "eye pleasing", "intuitive", etc. technique.

Evaluating the Visualization of Restaurant Comparisons

To evaluate and examine the performance and usability of the implemented framework, we used the Restaurant Comparison Presentation prototype. 15 users tested the system functionality and answered the SUS questionnaire. The average SUS score was 86, the median was 90 and the standard deviation was 13, which show that overall, the users were highly satisfied with the system.

DISCUSSION

This study aimed to provide customers with a quick, visual overview of a large body of restaurant reviews. This goal was achieved by visualizing the results of uncovering and analyzing comparison sentences appearing in the reviews. As the suggested approach is generic, the same approach may be extended to additional domains besides the restaurant domain, which when applied, alleviates the information overload facing consumers today when looking at service and product reviews.

In this study, we followed Xu et al. [42] that, in their research, addressed sentences as either comparative or not comparative and assumed all comparative sentences have a clear direction, although they did not address "non-gradable" sentences such as "*It's different than Beretta*". In such sentences, though a comparison is being made, there is no clear direction. Therefore, in our research, we used the same directions as in Xu et al. [42] and considered the not comparative (~) direction as a non-gradable comparative. We found that 3.10% of the sentences in our data set were "non-gradable" sentences.

When comparing our results to the results obtained by Xu et al. [41], it can be noticed that by applying the same approach we achieved better results in general, but the results for the specific relations were quite different. This is an interesting issue for further analysis. In identifying the direction of the comparative relations, identifying "better" and "not equal" relations was less successful compared with "worse" and "equal" relations. We suspect that this is due to reviewers' tendencies to use "worse" and "equal" relations more in their reviews, leading these to be selected more often as the right direction for the relation, thereby causing the skew among the results.

All in all, we found that the users appreciated the idea of using simple, visualized summaries of comparisons of features of interest. Hence it seems that this is a direction for future research - better automation and experimentation in additional domains.

Regarding visualization, it is worth noting that there are several good approaches by commercial systems that do summarize restaurant reviews and provide them to consumers with some visualization aspects. For example, Yelp highlights excerpts with bold keywords. We go a step further and in addition to focusing on comparison sentences, we also provide visual representations of the opinions regarding the selected features, which is much more informative than highlighting keywords.

This study had a few limitations. We found out that 9% of the comparison sentences in our dataset do not contain comparative keywords, unlike previous studies [14,15,42], which asserted that almost all their comparison sentences contained comparative keywords (98% but with low precision). Hence, without comparative keywords, we were unable to predict the direction of the relation; comparative sentences without a comparative keyword were discarded. For example: "*Sorta wish I went to their sister restaurant, SPQR.*"; "*It's no Gary Danko's but they know their fish.*" and more. Another limitation relates to the restaurants' names, which can contain an attribute as well as mentioned in the sentence with a nickname. For example, Lime, Americano is also a restaurant and also a food or attribute. Sometimes, restaurants have nicknames; for example, Anchor and Core are sometimes called A&C, or Foreign Cinema is FC, etc. Nicknames that were not recognized by the restaurant lists were ignored as well. Another limitation was found vis-à-vis synonyms. For example, the comparative keyword 'like' in some cases is not a comparative keyword and has a different meaning. It can be used as a synonym for 'love' and not for 'same'. The same is true for 'even', which can be similar to 'equal' or can be a 'contrast' word. One solution for such issues is using the comparative keyword with POS tagging and learning how to distinguish between meanings, but doing so exceeds the scope of this research and should be considered as future work.

Then, a limitation exists regarding the assumption that each sentence contained only one comparison relation in it. In a long comparative sentence, there can be multiple relations separated by delimiters such as commas (",") and conjunctions such as "and" and "but". Multi-comparisons and complex sentences were treated as if they contained only one comparison. For example, the comparison from the Credo restaurant review, "*Sorry Barbacco...Credo has much better food and wine!*" In this example, the reviewer describes two comparative relations in one sentence. One relation claims that Credo has better food than Barbacco and the other claims that Credo also has better wine. Alternatively, there are comparative sentences that do not contain any comparative keyword or attribute.

Regarding visualization, we selected a few well-known visualizations for experimentation, following an expert recommendation. It is possible that a more thorough evaluation of possible visualizations that can be used would have resulted in better results and better users' satisfaction. Related to that is the simplicity of the evaluation – we used SUS to elicit users' opinion about the usability of the system, while defining a specific task may have resulted in better understanding. We see these aspects as ideas for future work.

Finally, the evaluation was done with 15 subjects, a very small number of participant that limits the significance of the evaluation. Again, this is an issue for future research that will extend the current study and address the limitations noted above.

CONCLUSIONS AND FUTURE WORK

In this study, we suggested, demonstrated and evaluated a generic framework for visualizing comparisons of restaurants with respect to the features the user is interested in, in order to allow the user to better assess the quality of a given restaurant. We hypothesized that visualized summaries will be perceived informative and easy to use and this hypothesis was confirmed in a user study. The suggested framework is not limited to restaurants review, but can be applied in any domain where comparisons of features are used in reviews.

There are a few directions that could be examined in future work. First, the various vocabularies used in this research were pre-compiled and dedicated to the restaurant domain. To make the framework more general, and to use different domains, new attribute lists need to be compiled for each domain. This requirement makes the system quite difficult to adapt. It may be worthwhile considering Liu's [20] Label Sequence Rules (LSR) method to find the entities in a sentence. The method might be adapted to create a more global framework that does not require entering fixed attributes and does not depend on the domain.

Another idea for future work is to explore the sentiments in the sentences [30] and enhance the methods for finding the direction using these sentiments as another indicator to support the decision about the correct comparative direction.

Finally, to improve the visualization method, instead of using an existing one, a new method, dedicated specifically to presenting comparative sentences, should be developed. The classic methods are excellent, and together with a data grid, present comparisons in an intuitive way, but maybe there is another method, as yet unknown in the field, which might be even better. A more thorough evaluation (like performing a search and evaluation task) may help understand better the pros and cons of the different visualizations. As part of this extension, a large-scale user study will be carried out.

REFERENCES

1. Arora, S., Joshi, M., & Rosé, C. P. (2009). Identifying types of claims in online customer reviews. In Proceedings of Human Language Technologies: The 2009 Annual Conference of the North American Chapter of the Association for Computational Linguistics, Companion Volume: Short Papers, 37-40. ACL.
2. Bai, X., White, D., & Sundaram, D. (2011). Purposeful visualization. In System Sciences (HICSS), 2011 44th Hawaii International Conference on (pp. 1-10). IEEE.
3. Brooke, J. (1996). SUS-A quick and dirty usability scale. Usability Evaluation in Industry, 189(194), 4-7.
4. Cruz, F. L., Troyano, J. A., Enríquez, F., Ortega, F. J., & Vallejo, C. G. (2013). 'Long autonomy or long delay?' The importance of domain in opinion mining. Expert Systems with Applications, 40(8), 3174-3184.
5. Removed for annoymization.
6. Esuli, A., & Sebastiani, F. (2006). Sentiwordnet: A publicly available lexical resource for opinion mining. In Proceedings of Language Resources and Evaluation Conference, Vol. 6, 417-422.
7. Fei, Z., Huang, X., & Wu, L. (2006). Mining the relation between sentiment expression and target using dependency of words. In Proceedings of the 20th Pacific Asia Conference on Language, Information and Computation (PACLIC20), Wuhan, China, 257-264.
8. Freitas, C. M., Luzzardi, P. R., Cava, R. A., Winckler, M., Pimenta, M. S., & Nedel, L. P. (2002). On evaluating information visualization techniques. In Proceedings of the Working Conference on Advanced Visual Interfaces, 373-374. ACM.
9. Gamon, M., Aue, A., Corston-Oliver, S., & Ringger, E. (2005). Pulse: Mining customer opinions from free text. In Advances in Intelligent Data Analysis VI, 121-132. Springer Berlin Heidelberg.
10. Gu, Y. H., & Yoo, S. J. (2010). Searching a best product based on mining comparison sentences. In SCIS & ISIS SCIS & ISIS 2010, 929-933. Japan Society for Fuzzy Theory and Intelligent Informatics.
11. He, S., Yuan, F., & Wang, Y. (2012, April). Extracting the comparative relations for mobile reviews. In Consumer Electronics, Communications and Networks (CECNet), 2012 2nd International Conference on, 3247-3250). IEEE.
12. Hu, M., & Liu, B. (2004, August). Mining and summarizing customer reviews. In Proceedings of the Tenth ACM SIGKDD International Conference on Knowledge Discovery and Data Mining (168-177). ACM.
13. Hu, N., Liu, L., & Zhang, J. J. (2008). Do online reviews affect product sales? The role of reviewer characteristics and temporal effects. Information Technology and Management, 9(3), 201-214.
14. Jindal, N., & Liu, B. (2006b). Identifying comparative sentences in text documents. In Proceedings of the 29th Annual International ACM SIGIR Conference on Research and Development in Information Retrieval (pp. 244-251). ACM.
15. Jindal, N., & Liu, B. (2006a). Mining comparative sentences and relations. In Association for the Advancement of Artificial Intelligence, Vol. 22, 1331-1336.
16. Kessler, J. S., Eckert, M., Clark, L., & Nicolov, N. (2010). The ICWSM 2010 JDPA sentiment corpus for the automotive domain. In 4th International AAAI Conf. on Weblogs and Social Media Data Workshop Challenge (ICWSM-DWC), Washington, DC.
17. Kessler, W., & Kuhn, J. (2013). Detection of product comparisons-how far does an out-of-the-box semantic role labeling system take you?. In EMNLP 1892-1897.
18. Khan, M., & Khan, S. S. (2011). Data and information visualization methods, and interactive mechanisms: A survey. International Journal of Computer Applications, 34(1), 1-14.
19. Lafferty, J., McCallum, A., & Pereira, F. C. (2001). Conditional random fields: Probabilistic models for segmenting and labeling sequence data. In Proceedings of the 18th International Conference on Machine Learning 2001 (ICML 2001) 31-36. ACM.
20. Liu, B. (2007). Web data mining: exploring hyperlinks, contents, and usage data. Springer Science & Business Media.
21. Liu, B., & Zhang, L. (2012). A survey of opinion mining and sentiment analysis. In Mining Text Data (pp. 415-463). Springer US.
22. Lovelock, C. H. (1983). Classifying services to gain strategic marketing insights. Journal of Marketing, 9-20.
23. Manning, C. D., Surdeanu, M., Bauer, J., Finkel, J. R., Bethard, S., & McClosky, D. (2014). The Stanford CoreNLP Natural Language Processing Toolkit. In ACL (System Demonstrations) 55-60.
24. Marrese-Taylor, E., Velásquez, J. D., & Bravo-Marquez, F. (2014). A novel deterministic approach for aspect-based opinion mining in tourism products reviews. Expert Systems with Applications, 41(17), 7764-7775.
25. Mayhew, D. J. (1991). Principles and guidelines in software user interface design. Prentice-Hall, Inc.

26. Miao, Q., Li, Q., & Dai, R. (2009). AMAZING: A sentiment mining and retrieval system. Expert Systems with Applications, 36(3), 7192-7198.

27. Miller, G. A. (1995). WordNet: A lexical database for English. Communications of the ACM, 38(11), 39-41.

28. Mudambi, S. M., & Schuff, D. (2010). What makes a helpful review? A study of customer reviews on Amazon.com. MIS Quarterly, 34(1), 185-200.

29. Pang, B., & Lee, L. (2008). Opinion mining and sentiment analysis. Foundations and Trends in Information Retrieval, 2(1-2), 1-135.

30. Ravi, K., & Ravi, V. (2015). A survey on opinion mining and sentiment analysis: Tasks, approaches and applications. Knowledge-Based Systems, 89, 14-46.

31. Saad Andaleeb, S., & Conway, C. (2006). Customer satisfaction in the restaurant industry: an examination of the transaction-specific model. Journal of Services Marketing, 20(1), 3-11.

32. Sha, F., & Pereira, F. (2003). Shallow parsing with conditional random fields. In Proceedings of the 2003 Conference of the North American Chapter of the Association for Computational Linguistics on Human Language Technology-Vol. 1, 134-141). ACL.

33. Shamim, A., Balakrishnan, V., & Tahir, M. (2014). Evaluation of opinion visualization techniques. Information Visualization, 147387/1614550537.

34. Smith, S. L., & Mosier, J. N. (1984). Design guidelines for user-system interface software (No. MTR-9420). MITRE CORP BEDFORD MA.

35. Sokolova, M., Japkowicz, N., & Szpakowicz, S. (2006). Beyond accuracy, F-score and ROC: A family of discriminant measures for performance evaluation. In Australasian Joint Conference on Artificial Intelligence, 1015-1021. Springer Berlin Heidelberg.

36. Stanford Natural Language Processing Group, (2009). The Stanford Parser: A statistical parser, http://nlp.stanford.edu/software/lex-parser.shtml.

37. Sutton, C., & McCallum, A. (2006). An introduction to conditional random fields for relational learning. Introduction to statistical relational learning, 93-128.

38. Turney, P. D. (2002). Thumbs up or thumbs down?: Semantic orientation applied to unsupervised classification of reviews. In Proceedings of the 40th Annual Meeting of the Association for Computational Linguistics, 417-424. ACL.

39. Von Alan, R. H., March, S. T., Park, J., & Ram, S. (2004) Design science in information systems research. MIS Quarterly, 28(1), 75-105.

40. Wang, W., Zhao, T., Xin, G., & Xu, Y. (2014). Recognizing Comparative Sentences from Chinese Review Texts. International Journal of Database Theory and Application, 7(5), 29-38.

41. Ware, C. (2012). Information visualization: Perception for design. Elsevier.

42. Xu, K., Liao, S. S., Li, J., & Song, Y. (2011). Mining comparative opinions from customer reviews for Competitive Intelligence. Decision support systems, 50(4), 743-754.

43. Ying, D., & Jiang, J. (2015). Towards opinion summarization from online forums. ACL.

44. Zhang, K., Narayanan, R., & Choudhary, A. (2009). Mining online customer reviews for ranking products. Technical Report, EECS Dept, Northwestern Univ.

45. Zhang, K., Narayanan, R., & Choudhary, A. (2010, June). Voice of the customers: Mining online customer reviews for product feature-based ranking. In Proceedings of the 3rd Conference on Online Social Networks, 11.

46. Zhang, L., & Liu, B. (2014). Aspect and entity extraction for opinion mining. In Data Mining and Knowledge Discovery for Big Data, 1-40. Springer Berlin Heidelberg.

Citicafe: An Interactive Interface for Citizen Engagement

Shubham Atreja
IBM Research
India
satreja1@in.ibm.com

Pooja Aggarwal
IBM Research
India
aggarwal.pooja@in.ibm.com

Prateeti Mohapatra
IBM Research
India
pramoh01@in.ibm.com

Amol Dumrewal
IIT Madras
India
proamold@cse.iitm.ac.in

Anwesh Basu
University of Texas
Austin, USA
anwesh@utexas.edu

Gargi B. Dasgupta
IBM Research
India
GaargiDasgupta@in.ibm.com

ABSTRACT

Community engagement is a new and emerging trend in urban cities driven by the mission of developing responsible citizenship. Technology is playing a vital role in helping this mission. For example, over the last couple of years, there have been a plethora of social media avenues to report civic issues and complaints. We present one such contribution of technology, in terms of an intelligent platform, "Citicafe". The platform has a conversation based interface that enhances citizen engagement by enabling a direct communication with them. The platform ingests data from different sources, which is exploited by a virtual agent to enable informed interactions. It can help citizens to (a) report problems and (b) gather information related to civic issues for different locations and their neighborhoods. We report the results of a user study carried out to establish the effectiveness of our interface and draw a comparison with an existing platform. A detailed qualitative and quantitative analysis of the survey results shows a definite and statistically significant ($p < 0.05$) preference for our interface over the existing platform.

Author Keywords

clustering; topic modeling; natural language; conversational agent; CRF; social good; citizen engagement; knowledge mining

INTRODUCTION

Recent years have seen the emergence of the theme of responsible citizenship. The belief therein is that citizens have the inherent capacity to solve their own problems and that social transformation is within the reach of all communities. Social media provides citizens a viable platform to come together on civic issues. Social media sites like Twitter, Facebook, and other online complaint boards have become important avenues to log civic-related issues and complaints. Citizens can use mobile applications to take a picture, add a description and report their issues along with their locations. Several studies have shown the importance of these sites in enhancing civic awareness among citizens [1, 2, 3]. These sites help the concerned authorities to gain high-level understanding of affected situations, severity of problems and the number of affected citizens, and take actions accordingly. With the advent of smart city technologies, a lot of initiatives are being carried out to improve social, economic and governance systems [4]. It will be ideal if these initiatives also take into account the needs and the ease of use of these sites by the citizens.

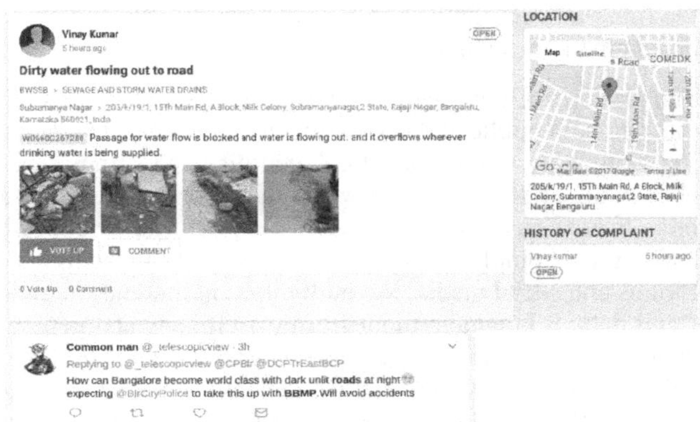

Figure 1: Snapshot of complaints

Figure 1 shows a snapshot of complaints from two online sources on road issues in Bangalore. As can be seen in the figure, they do not represent a standardized way of reporting complaints. Complaints can be descriptive, containing images or they can be short (as shown in the Twitter example). Further, there is also a need to process these complaints in real-time, so that the processed information is readily available to the authorities and to the citizens.

A different challenge is to get the citizens involved and motivated in improving their neighborhood and presenting them with relevant information as and when required. Often times, once the complaint is registered, there is no formal or infor-

IUI'18, March 7–11, 2018, Tokyo, Japan

ISBN 978-1-4503-4945-1/18/03...$15.00

DOI: https://doi.org/10.1145/3172944.3172955

mal feedback given back to the citizen. Also, there are not many avenues that allow citizens to be more engaged or better informed, avenues from where a citizen can request civic or public services information.

In consideration of the above-mentioned points, we designed and built a conversation-based intelligent platform, "CitiCafe". In this paper, we present a prototype of the platform for the city of Bangalore in India. The platform consists of a virtual agent with a natural language interface that can present citizens with relevant information and help them register complaints by asking specific questions. The citizens can interact with the agent using some of the popular social media platforms like Twitter, Facebook Messenger, Slack. Virtual agent has assumed great importance today having found wide applications in different domains [5, 6]. However, the use of virtual agents is not visible for social good. To the best of our knowledge, ours is the first platform that uses a virtual agent to enhance citizen engagement through a direct correspondence.

The platform also consists of a visual dashboard, Kibana [30], that can help public authorities and civic agencies by presenting them with various statistical analytics and summaries to get a better understanding of where the pressing issues are. In order to create a knowledge base for our platform, we collected and curated complaints from different sources like complaint forums and social media. We built different modules to understand natural language input from the citizens and generate appropriate responses. We conclude our paper by carrying out a detailed user study to establish the ease of use and ease of learning of our platform and draw comparisons with another existing platform.

RELATED WORK

Wide varieties of civic issues exist in an urban landscape, ranging from road condition, garbage dumps, pollution levels etc. Addressing such issues is important for the holistic development of the society and the first step towards that is citizen participation. Social media can provide a convenient interface for citizens to raise their concerns and get involved with the concerned authorities [1, 2, 3]. Although Twitter and Facebook are widely popular, there exist specific platforms [7, 8, 9, 10, 11] where citizens can report civic issues and raise complaints. In the city of Bangalore, ichangemycity.com [7] is one such platform that is very popular. Such platforms that allow citizens to register complaints often require extra effort on their part in terms of installing an application and one-time registration. Registering a complaint also requires additional information in terms of location of the complaint, the category it belongs to, etc. On top of this, there is no formal or informal feedback given back to the citizens regarding the time it will take to resolve updating them about the status. Sometimes, duplicate complaints catering to the same issue are registered, as they are raised by different citizens. These difficulties discourage the citizens to register their complaints. Some people may often choose not to go through this hassle but still talk about their issues on social media. Some works try to analyze social media (Twitter) to mine opinions and issues that people talk about [12, 13]. "Twitter Seva" [14] is another initiative launched by Twitter in partnership with government authorities. The initiative aims to improve public service engagement by allowing real time monitoring of complaints via Twitter. However, this platform doesn't provide a chat interface for citizen interaction. Our platform is embedded with a virtual agent that can interactively help the citizens in registering their complaints. The citizens can interact with the agent via existing social media channels. To make it further convenient, the agent is equipped with modules to automatically identify the location and category of the civic issue from the user input. Once the complaint is registered, the agent can provide feedback based on other complaints that are already present. The agent also regularly updates the citizens on the status of their complaints.

Another dimension of work uses the complaints registered on different platforms to facilitate further analysis. Bansal et al analyze such complaints to allow proactive maintenance [15]. Most other works use various text mining approaches to analyze complaints, gain insights and identify prominent issues [16, 17, 18]. However, the output of such analysis is not available to the citizens on a real time basis, that too in a chat based interface. Our platform's virtual agent can answer various informative queries, providing details about neighborhoods, status of civic amenities etc. All this is enabled by aggregating and analyzing information from different sources.

Some civic agencies also have their own platforms to streamline the complaint management process [19, 20, 21]. It enables the civic agencies to improve their operations and generate actionable insights by taking into account input from different sources. Such platforms often have a static interface that present varied analytics on top of the complaints that have been received. Using our platform, the civic agencies can generate these insights dynamically by interacting with the platform.

SYSTEM OVERVIEW

This section describes the working principles of Citicafe that is broken into various components: i. User Interface ii. Understanding Input iii. Response Generation iv. Knowledge Mining and v. Continuous Learning as shown in Figure 2. All the interactions with Citicafe are stored in a Cloudant database. The stored information includes the input from the user, the response generated and the feedback received, which can be exploited for continuous learning of the agent and to identify users for crowd sourcing validation of the complaints (sub-section: Continuous Learning and Proactive Interaction).

User Interface

Citicafe can be accessed via existing social media channels and supports multiple interfaces such as Facebook Messenger, Twitter and Slack. It does not require any additional application. Citizens can interact with the virtual agent by initiating and having a direct conversation in natural language on any of these interfaces.

Along with the chat interface, Citicafe also has a Kibana dashboard [30] that generates visual insights about civic issues that can be used by the civic agencies.

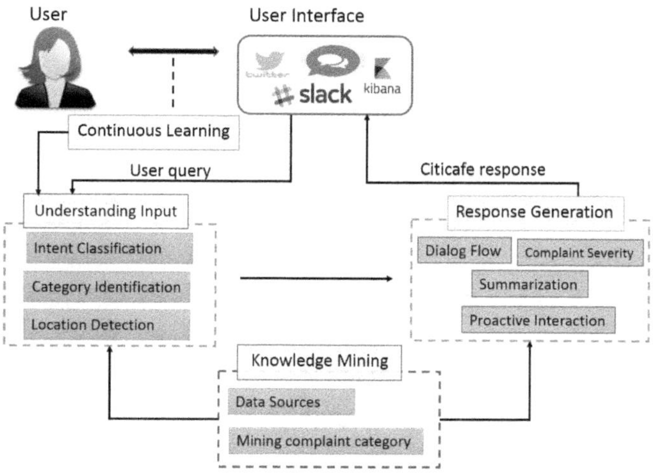

Figure 2: System Components

Understanding Input

Understanding a person's natural language input consists of: i) classifying the intent, ii) identifying the category and iii) detecting the location of the concerned civic issue.

Intent Classification

The main intent of an interaction with the agent is either to *get information* or to *register a complaint*. Apart from this, there may be sub-intents that need to be identified from the user input such as: *affirmative or negative replies, standard greetings, asking for capabilities* etc. In order to identify these intents, we used the intent classifier from Watson Conversation Service [31]. The classifier was bootstrapped using manually curated sample inputs for all the cases.

Category Identification

To understand the underlying category of the concerned civic issue, we used a combination of an entity extractor and an SVM based classifier. The entity extractor, embedded inside the Watson Conversation Service, was trained on a set of keywords that described each category. The classifier was trained on textual description of complaints, which were internally represented as word vectors, using a word2vec model. However, to accurately train the classifier, it was important to identify a good set of initial categories. The process of mining these categories is explained in detail under the section Knowledge Mining. Each mined category was further associated with a civic agency, responsible for that issue. The civic agency (if present) could also be identified from the user input using the entity extractor.

Location Detection

In order to detect the location from the user input, we used a combination of a Conditional Random Field (CRF) model [22] and a Fuzzy Matching Algorithm.

- **Conditional Random Field**: CRF is a very common tool used for sequence labeling of words, wherein the context of the words is important. For example, usually a location word follows words such as *in*, *at*, *near* etc. CRFs are graphical models that can capture dependencies among input observations. A CRF model defines a conditional distribution $p(y|x)$ where y is the corresponding label sequence and x is the observed data sequence. The observation x can be dependent on the current hidden label y, previous n hidden labels and on any of the other observations in an n-order CRF. For our case, the input sequence x corresponds to a series of words from the user query, while the label sequence y corresponds to a set of tags (location or other) assigned to the input sequence. The probabilistic model of a label sequence given some sequence of words is mediated in this model through a set of weighted functions f_i:

$$p(y|x) = \frac{exp(\sum_i \sum_t w_i f_i(y_{t-1}, y_t, x, t))}{Z(x)}$$

where w_i are the weights assigned by the learning algorithm, and $Z(x)$ is a normalization factor over all label sequences.

For the CRF training, we used the complaint descriptions from ichangemycity.com. Apart from having an explicit location tag associated with it, the complaint description could also contain a location. We extracted all sentences from the complaints that contained a location phrase and used the L-O encoding to generate the training data, where each word in the sentence was either labeled as location (L) or other (O). To train our CRF model, we used the Stanford POS Tagger [23] with the following features: unigram features in the [-4,4] offset window from the current word and the POS tag for the current word.

The CRF model extracts a location phrase based on its context. However, the location phrase can contain spelling errors which CRF is unable to correct. This may lead to location not getting identified due to no string matching with a real location. In the next section, we describe the Fuzzy Matching algorithm that can handle any spelling errors.

- **Fuzzy Matching Algorithm**: Fuzzy Matching uses a hybrid similarity metric by combining token-based, character-based and phonetic-based similarity to get the correct location names given the CRF output. The algorithm requires a location lexicon, consisting of various location names in Bangalore as an input, which is represented as a token set S. The output of CRF was also parsed into tokens, representing the set R. We then used a method similar to the one used in [24, 25] as the underlying matching algorithm of token pairs from two token sets R and S. However, Wang et. al's approach doesn't capture the phonetic similarities. In our work, we used phonetic similarity combined with syntactic similarity in the matching algorithm.

We then constructed a weighted bipartite graph between the token sets. Each vertex in the graph represents a token either from R or S. An edge from a token R_i to a token S_j is weighted using the similarity function. We omit pairs of tokens that are too low in similarity, the similarity threshold being 0.75. We, then, used a phonetic algorithm to determine if two tokens were considered close depending on whether they sound alike when pronounced [26].

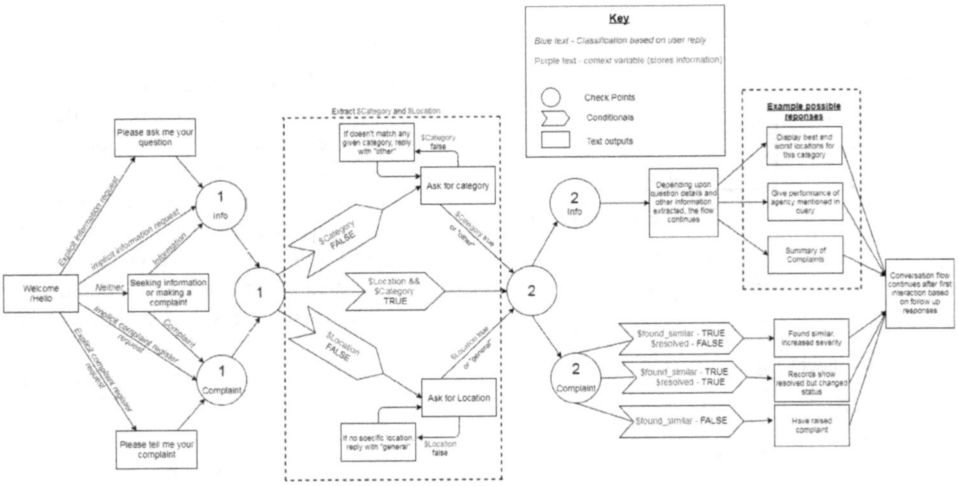

Figure 3: High-level conversation dialog flow

We give below the mathematical formulation for the fuzzy hybrid similarity score:

$$Fuz(R,S) = \sum_{i,j}(W_1 * Phonetic(R_i,S_j) + W_2 * Similarity(R_i,S_j))$$

where W_1 denotes the weight of the string similarity measure, W_2 denotes the weight of the phonetic similarity measure, *Similarity* represents the similarity measure between token i from set R with token j from set S, and *Phonetic* represents the phonetic similarity measure between token i from set R and token j from set S. Given two sets R and S, the final similarity score of a location and the CRF output is defined as

$$Score(R,S) = \frac{Fuz(R,S)}{|R| + |S| - Fuz(R,S)}$$

We got a similarity score between 0 and 1 for each location, which indicated how closely it matched with the user input. The locations were sorted based on their scores in descending order and the top result was used as the final location.

Response Generation

Once the agent appropriately understands the user input, the next step is to generate an appropriate response. Upon receiving the input, the agent first traverses the dialog flow to identify the correct node (explained in the section Dialog Flow). Based on the identified dialog node, the agent further processes the information which is available to generate a response. In case of *registering a complaint flow*, the agent processes the complaint to assign a severity (explained in section Complaint Severity) which forms part of the response. In case of *getting information flow*, the agent respond by summarizing the information relevant to the user request (explained in section Summarization). Apart from responding to user inputs, the agent also initiates an interaction with the user on its own (section Proactive Interaction).

Dialog Flow

We use the Watson Conversation Service to design the dialog flow. The dialog flow consists of around 200 nodes which help the agent to drive the conversation under different scenarios. The scenarios are dictated by the intent of the user input and other information (location, category etc) extracted by the agent from the input.

Figure 3 shows a high-level representation of the dialog flow. In this abstract representation, the first task is to classify the intent of the user input as either *registering a complaint* or *asking for information* (node-1). The next task is to identify the concerned location and the category of the complaint. This is inferred from the user input if provided, otherwise the user is prompted to supply the information. Based on the initial user intent, the agent takes the relevant dialog path and generates appropriate responses (node-2).

Complaint Severity

If the intent of the user input is to register a complaint, the agent assigns a severity to the complaint. We define the severity of a complaint as a function of its sentiment polarity, computed using the Watson Natural Language Understanding tool [32]. For a given input text, the tool outputs a number between -1 to 1, with the magnitude denoting the polarity and the sign denoting the overall sentiment (positive or negative). Before registering the complaint, the agent tries to find a similar complaint in the database, using cosine similarity. In case a similar complaint is found, the severity of the existing complaint is updated by adding the new value to it and no new complaint is registered. In case no similar complaint is found, a new complaint is registered with the computed severity. The severity of the complaint may then be updated based on the fraction of users who validate the complaint. The process of validation via crowd sourcing is explained in Section Proactive Interaction.

Summarization

If the intent of the user input is to get information for a particular location, a category, a civic agency or a combination of these, the agent fetches the relevant information from the data store and then summarizes this information. Summarization includes i) mining aspect-complaints and ii) assigning ratings.

- **Aspect-complaint mining** Aspect-opinion mining, which aims to extract concise opinions on different aspects, is increasing in popularity both in industry and research [33, 34, 35]. We used a similar idea to build an unsupervised method for aspect-complaint mining (Algorithm 1), where we first extract aspects and then extract complaints for each aspect. Given the recent complaints pertaining to a specific category, location or a combination of both, we first identify the part-of-speech tag of each token in the sentence and selected tokens with the POS tags, nouns and noun phrases (*noun clauses*) as candidate aspects. Contiguous aspects are then concatenated together. Aspects that occur in less than α number of sentences are removed. We filter out the overlapping aspects to generate candidate aspects. For example, we filter out "Road" if "Central Road" is an aspect. For each aspect identified, we collect the complaint sentences that have mentions of the aspect. For each sentence, we then identify the adjective and/or verb past particle word(s) (w_i), get the nearest noun phrase (w_j) relative to w_i, and finally get all the words between (and including) w_j and w_i if w_j is positioned before w_i, or between w_i and w_j if w_i is positioned before w_j. These phrases are the complaints for the aspect. Few examples of aspects and their complaints are shown in the Section on Sample Interactions.

- **Rating** A rating assigned to either a location or a civic agency can help in building a profile and draw comparisons. The rating can be with respect to one or more civic issues. For a location, we use the number of complaints to measure the condition of different civic issues. For an agency, we use the number of complaints to measure its load and the number of complaints resolved to measure its performance. The rating is assigned by observing the trend over each day on one of these quantities for the last 30 days. The rating is then converted to an ordinal scale (for example, Bad, Average, Good), taking into account the overall trend.

Proactive Interaction

The agent initiates an interaction with the user by sending a message for the following reasons (i) providing an update on previous complaints registered by the user and (ii) crowd sourcing the validation of new complaints. The latter can help in identifying and removing false complaints and updating severity of pending complaints. For every new complaint or a complaint with a status update, the agent identifies a set of users and sends a direct message to them to validate the complaint. When identifying the set of users, the following factors are considered: (i) user's interests (from past interactions) and (ii) previous messages sent to the user (to avoid spamming).

Knowledge Mining

To enable the bot to effectively understand user queries and generate useful responses, we mined information from varied sources. Further analysis was carried out to enrich this information with tags such as location, category etc. This section details out the data sources and further analysis that was carried out to enrich the data.

```
Input  : Recent Complaints, C
Output : (Aspect, a : Complaints, C(a))
φ(c): Set of all sentences in C
for s ∈ φ(c) : do
    /* R:  Set of all noun clauses in C                              */
    R ← ∅
    foreach noun_clause, N ∈ s do
        R ← R ∪ N
    end
end
/* φ(a):  Final set of noun clauses (aspects)                        */
φ(a) ← ∅
for i = 1 to len(R) do
    /* Get sufficiently common noun clauses                          */
    if freq(R_i, R)/len(φ(c)) > α then
        /* Filter out substring noun clauses                         */
        if R_i not a substring of R_j, where i ≠ j then
            φ(a) ← φ(a) ∪ R_i
    end
end
for a ∈ φ(a) do
    /* C(a):  Set of complaints for aspect a                         */
    C(a) ← ∅
    τ(a): Set of all sentences that contain aspect a
    for s ∈ τ(a) : do
        foreach adj or verb past particle, w ∈ s do
            i ← position of w in s
            j ← position of nearest noun clause in s
            if i < j then
                p ← text between and including i, j
                C(a).append(p)
            end
            else
                p ← text between and including j, i
                C(a).append(p)
            end
        end
    end
end
```

Algorithm 1: Aspect Complaint Mining

Data Sources

We collected information about civic issues in Bangalore from different complaint forums (e.g. ichangemycity.com) and social media (e.g. Twitter). ichangemycity.com is a popular online complaint portal for major cities in India. An important feature of this portal is that each complaint is tagged with the location of the complaint, its category and the agency that is responsible for it. We extracted information from Twitter using its public streaming API. For each category of civic issues, we identified a set of keywords and configured the API to mine all tweets containing those keywords. As of now, our database has more than 50k complaints and around 60 new complaints are coming in every day.

Mining Complaint Categories

In order to identify the initial set of complaint categories, we clustered the complaints mined from ichangemycity.com using

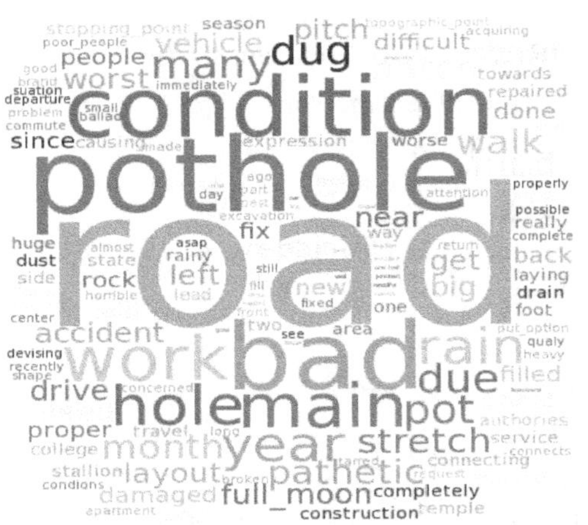

Figure 4: Word Cloud representing the category "Bad Roads"

Latent Dirichlet Allocation (LDA) model [27]. Each cluster of complaints was assigned a topic which was considered as a new category.

An LDA model takes a set of documents as the input and generates a set of k topics (clusters), where any given word in the document set is assigned its own weight with respect to each topic. Let w be a document which can be generated from this set of topics. The probability $p(w)$ of generating this document is given by:

$$p(w) = \int_{\theta} \left(\prod_{n=1}^{N} \sum_{z_n=1}^{k} p(w_n|z_n;\beta)p(z_n|\theta) \right) p(\theta;\alpha)d\theta,$$

where $p(\theta;\alpha)$ is Dirichlet, $p(z_n|\theta)$ is a multinomial parameterized by θ, and $p(w_n|z_n;\beta)$ is a multinomial over the words.

The LDA model used complaint descriptions as the input and generated k clusters of complaints along with the keywords representative of the cluster, each cluster representing a different topic. Figure 4 represents the word cloud of keywords associated with one of the clusters.

Continuous Learning

In order to effectively and efficiently understand the user input, it is important for the agent to continuously learn and update itself based on the historical inputs and the feedback received. To ensure the same, we configured our agent to continuously update and improve its intent classification, category identification and location detection.

The intent classifier can be improved by adding more training data over time. In order to mine the candidate inputs for training data, we extracted all user inputs from the interaction logs where (i) the intent was classified with low confidence, and (ii) a wrong intent was classified with high confidence. If the intent is classified with low confidence, the agent asks for a confirmation from the user, which provides the correct label for the former. The correct label for the latter is identified from the explicit feedback given by the user at the end of each conversation. A combined set of i) and ii) along with their correct labels is then periodically added to the training data.

To further reduce confusion, for every candidate in ii) we also try to identify and remove an existing similar training example that causes the confusion. The complaint classifier was also improved in a similar way by adding more training examples.

The location detection can be improved by adding more location names to the lexicon used by the Fuzzy Matching Algorithm. This can lead to better handling of spelling errors while identifying the correct location. In all cases where the location could not be extracted from the user input, the user was asked to explicitly provide the location. This user input containing the correct location was extracted from the interaction logs and added to the existing lexicon.

SAMPLE INTERACTIONS

In this section, we present examples of interactions with the agent in different scenarios.

1. A citizen is trying to register a complaint with our agent. The agent is able to identify the category and the location of the issue and registers the complaint with the correct agency, along with the severity of the complaint.

   User Input: I'm facing an issue in my locality. A dead dog is lying on the main road of HBR layout. There's a lot of foul smell and the commuters are also facing issues.

   Response: I have registered your complaint under the category ROADS with the location HBR LAYOUT and assigned it to BBMP. The complaint has been marked with HIGH severity.

2. The intent of the user interaction is to compare two neighborhoods in Bangalore city. The agent responds by comparing both the locations in terms of major civic issues and provides a final rating based on that.

   Query: Which neighborhood is better, Indiranagar or Banashankari?
   Response:

   Most civic issues in these localities are related to Garbage, Roads, Electricity and Sewage Drains. In terms of all these issues, Indira Nagar scores better than Banashankari. The overall rating for Banashankari is AVERAGE and the overall rating for Indira Nagar is GOOD.

3. The user wants to know about the conditions of a civic issue in a particular neighborhood. The agent mines all relevant complaints and responds by summarizing the complaints and providing a rating.

Query: How are the roads in Bellandur?
Response:

Aspect	Complaint
Bellandur gate bus stop opposite Dominos	busy stretch
ICICI Bank	entire service road is broken
Service lane	service lane needs to be repaired
Bellandur Central Mall	huge traffic

The condition of Roads in Bellandur is CRITICAL

4. The query is about a particular civic agency operating in Bangalore. In response, the agent provides a summary of the status of complaints assigned to the concerned agency and also assigns a rating to it.

   Query: How is BBMP performing?
   Response:

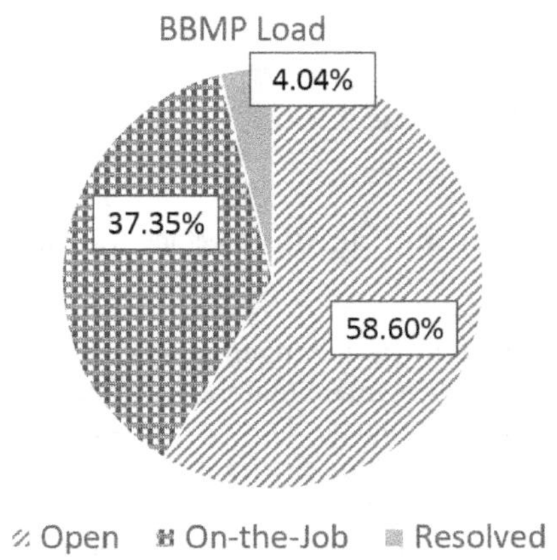

   BBMP is currently functioning under HIGH load with AVERAGE performance

5. The final example presents an interaction initiated by the agent with a user, to validate a complaint registered by another user.

   Message: I hope you're doing good. I just wanted to check if you know about this issue: "A dead dog is lying on the main road of HBR layout. There's a lot of foul smell and the commuters are also facing issues."

EVALUATION

In this section, we present the evaluation of "Citicafe" mainly along two dimensions: a) Accuracy of mining the complaint categories and b) Accuracy of the CRF model.

Mining Complaint Categories

Topic Modeling

While registering a complaint in the online portal ichangemycity.com, a user has the option to choose a category for the complaint. The user can either assign an existing category or define a completely new category. Due to the subjectivity involved in this process, the categories tend to be both inconsistent and ambiguous. We found that the current set of registered complaints correspond to 147 different categories. Out of these, 63 categories have less than ten complaints.

In order to refine the categories, we ran the complaints through a topic modeling process discussed in the section Knowledge Mining. We varied the number of clusters from 5 to 30 and considered the setting that gave the most coherent clusters as the optimum setting. We used UMass topic coherence which is a popular method to measure topic coherence and has been shown to display high correlation with human evaluation [28]. The final setting was with the number of clusters equal to 7. Table 1 shows the major categories and their corresponding keywords generated via the topic model.

Category	LDA Keywords
Bad Roads	road, pothole, bad, condition, main, work, hole, rain, stretch, pot, dug
Garbage	garbage, area, house, shit, collection, people, waste, health, smell, disposal, dump,
Sewage Drains	water, drain, sewage, cross, layout, bwssb, supply, day, issue, pipe, rain
Electricity	light, road, power, bescom, main, dark, layout, pole, night, powercuts, electricity
Stray Dogs	dog, people, child, night, road, stray, walk, difficult, area
Trees,Parks and Playgrounds	lake, park, area, construction, resident, land, tree, building

Table 1: Topic Model Keywords for major categories

On analyzing the clusters and the corresponding set of existing categories, we made the following observations:

- Sometimes a cluster contained issues from multiple categories. For example, one cluster contained complaints from categories like *Bad roads, Footpaths, Potholes*. Another cluster contained complaints from categories *Sewage Drains, Sewage and Storm Water Drains*.
- Few categories were split across multiple clusters. For example, category *Garbage* was split across multiple clusters and provided scope for sub-categorization.
- Few categories like *Air Pollution* and *Noise Pollution* represented separate issues but they could not be split into separate clusters as the number of complaints for these categories was small compared to other major categories.

Based on these observations, we manually curated and finalized 13 categories on the given set of complaints. The set of complaints extracted from ichangemycity.com initially belonged to 25 categories.

Confusion Analysis

Once we had enough data samples (around 11.5k complaints), we trained the classifier by first using the set of 25 categories and then using the final set of 13 categories. We achieved a 5-fold cross validation accuracy of 70.9% with the 25 categories and an accuracy of 90.6% with the 13 categories. Figure 5 compares the category-wise accuracy for three categories before and after the process of topic discovery. We observed that the accuracy for all the three categories had increased after the process of topic discovery. A major reason for this increase in accuracy was due to the merging of categories with high confusion as shown in Figure 6. Initially, category "*Bad Roads*" was confused with the category "*Potholes*" and resulted in 3.8% confusion in the model. On merging these two categories into one category *Bad Roads*, the confusion reduced by more than half. Similarly, combining categories "*Sewage Drains*" and "*Sewage and Storm Water Drains*" increased the accuracy from 52.14% to 79.78% and reduced the confusion from 2.9% to 1.7%.

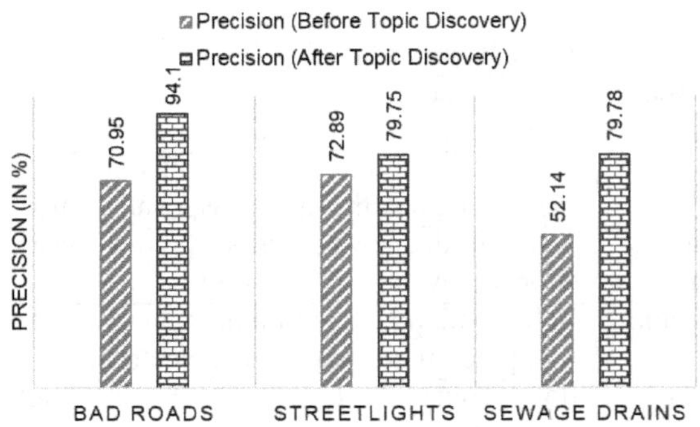

Figure 5: Accuracy (before and after topic discovery)

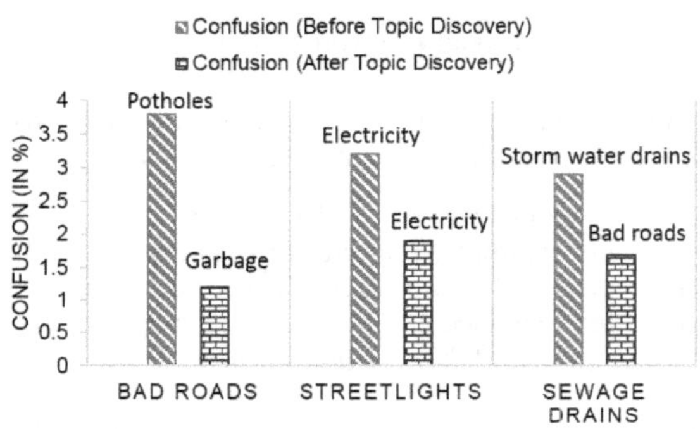

Figure 6: Confusion (before and after topic discovery)

CRF model

We report the 5-fold cross validation accuracy (Precision, Recall and F_1-score) of the CRF model. Table 2 represents a breakdown of accuracy with respect to different feature sets. We observed that adding the context words and the POS Tag of the current word led to an improvement in the accuracy. However, adding the POS Tag of the context words did not improve the accuracy much. We used the current word, the POS tag of the current word, context words in the left window (size = 4) and context words in the right window (size = 4) as the final features.

USER STUDY

Citicafe is designed to perform two main tasks: *registering complaints* and *getting information*. The main aim of this study was to capture user feedback on both these tasks along the following points: (i) usability and ease of use of Citicafe and (ii) comparison of Citicafe with an existing platform.

Features	Precision	Recall	F-score
Current Word	62.01	84.08	71.38
+ POS Tag	75.86	75.36	75.61
+ Context Window [-2,2]	81.02	77.99	79.47
+ Context Window [-4,4]	84.59	80.88	82.69
+ POS Tag of Context	84.43	80.65	82.50

Table 2: Feature-wise performance of CRF model (%) (each row uses features added to the previous rows)

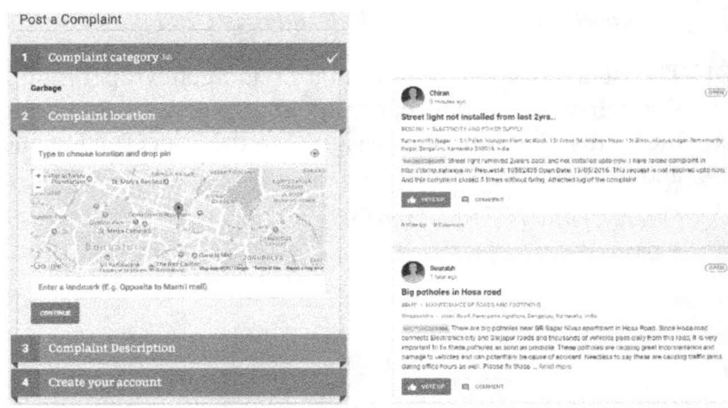

(a) Complaint (b) Information

Figure 7: ICMC interface for user study

For (ii) we choose ichangemycity.com (ICMC), a popular complaint forum in Bangalore, continuously monitored by various civic agencies. This also ensured a fair comparison since ICMC was used as the main data-source for building Citicafe. Figure 7 shows a snapshot of the user interface of ICMC for registering a complaint and getting information. To get information, the users can read complaints about a particular neighborhood, category etc.

Figure 8 shows a snapshot of the user interface of Citicafe. We used the Slack interface for carrying out the study, although Citicafe can support multiple interfaces. Citicafe has the same interface for both the tasks.

Study Design

The study was conducted with 27 participants (18 males and 9 females). The participants resided in different parts of Bangalore city with their age ranging between 21 to 40. All the participants had used some complaint forum in the past and also had prior experience of interacting via social media channels. The study was conducted using a within-subject design. As part of the study, the participants had to perform the two

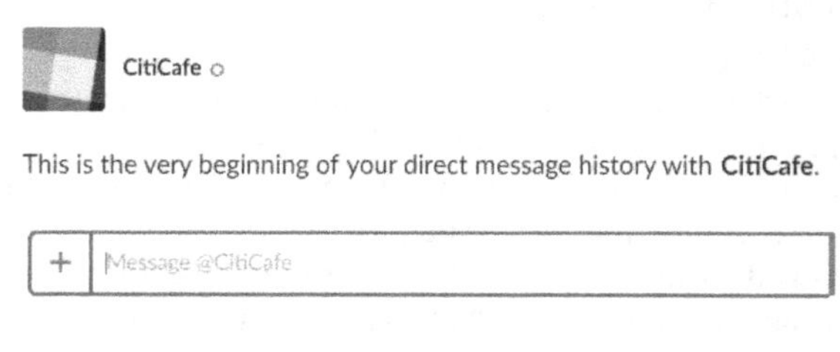

Figure 8: Citicafe interface for user study

Task	Citicafe	ICMC
Information	μ: 78.25 σ: 62.77	μ: 111.16 σ: 84.64
Complaint	μ: 89.77 σ: 60.51	μ: 132.58 σ: 62.99

Table 3: Comparison of time taken (in seconds) on the two platforms

tasks on the two platforms and completed a survey after that. The data generated from the study included survey results, time taken to perform the tasks and correctness of the tasks.

Before starting each task, the participants were asked to know of a civic issue in their neighborhood for registering a complaint (Task 1). They were also asked to think of information on any civic-related amenity that they would like to know about (Task 2).

The order of the two tasks was randomized across participants to remove any bias. Further, half of the participants performed the tasks first on ICMC and then on Citicafe, while the order was reversed for the other half. This was done to take into consideration any bias due to carry-over effects.

Upon completion of the tasks, the participants were asked to answer a questionnaire on the usability of the two platforms, and were also asked to give their written feedback. The usability was measured using the System Usability Scale [29].

The participants were also encouraged to independently explore Citicafe and its functionalities. Citicafe was popularized within our internal community via a social media channel. We next present the results of the analysis carried out on the logs from these out-of-study interactions.

Findings

We now present the results obtained by analyzing the survey results and the logs obtained from the user study.

Time and Correctness

Table 3 shows a comparison of the time taken on different platforms for each task. As shown, the time taken on Citicafe is significantly less than the time taken on ICMC for both the tasks. Further, the results from a *t*-test (assuming unequal variances) show that the difference is statistically significant ($p = 0.0158$). We also measured the correctness of the task in terms of identifying the correct location and the category of the concerned civic issue. On ICMC, the participants had to explicitly provide the location and the category, while Citicafe extracted this information automatically from the user input. We, hence, report the correctness measure for Citicafe only. Based on the feedback from the participants, Citicafe was able to correctly identify the location and the category 70.4% and 77.8% of the times respectively. On analyzing the logs from the study, we found that out of the 12 cases where there were spelling errors in the user input, Citicafe was able to identify the location in 10 cases (83.33% accuracy).

Survey Results

The first part of the survey contained questions on the usability of each platform. Table 4 summarizes the comparison of SUS score for the two platforms. The overall usability score (out of 100) for Citicafe is significantly higher (at $p = 0.0387$) than that of ICMC. (73.6 vs 65.3). For completeness, we also report separate results for the two settings (based on the order of experiment). As shown, Citicafe got a higher usability score in both the settings. There is a difference in the usability score of the same platform under different settings, however, the difference is not statistically significant ($p = 0.136$ & 0.1498). Going forward, we present the combined results for the two settings.

Setting	Citicafe	ICMC
ICMC → Citicafe	μ: 77.11 σ: 11.35	μ: 70.38 σ: 18.84
Citicafe → ICMC	μ: 70.35 σ: 11.08	μ: 60.71 σ: 13.17
Overall	**μ: 73.61 σ: 11.52**	**μ: 65.37 σ: 16.57**

Table 4: SUS Statistics (Score range from 0-100)

We, next, present the questions for comparison of the two platforms along with the summary of participant responses in Table 5. For getting information, 77.8% of the users preferred Citicafe over ICMC. For registering a complaint, 51.9% of the users preferred Citicafe over ICMC. In terms of ease of use and ease of learning, Citicafe was the clear choice, validating the notion that people find it much easier to interact with a virtual agent than getting familiar with a user interface. Majority of the participants felt that ICMC would require more technical help compared to Citicafe, while other participants felt that either of the platforms wouldn't require any technical help.

Subjective Comments

Many participants mentioned that a summarized view for providing information was helpful to get a good overview. This correlated with the above results on user preference for getting information. For registering a complaint, some participants preferred the graphical interface of ICMC, where they could enter all the required information. Some particularly liked the map based interface of ICMC, where they could navigate to point out the location of the issue. One participant found it hard to find the location via the map interface (possibly due to a spelling error). Other participants mentioned that Citicafe's chat interface was much easier as everything was handled by simple exchange of messages. Different participants had different preferences for the choice of platform for registering complaints, which may actually depend upon an individual's choice and familiarity.

Another participant liked Citicafe's feature for getting regular notifications on the status of their complaint, although the feature could not be tested as the study was controlled and the complaints were not actually registered.

To summarize, majority of the participants emphasized on the ease of use and effectiveness of Citicafe. Participants mentioned that getting responses to a query from a virtual agent is quick and reliable. One feature missing was a map-based interface, which along with the existing capability of handling spelling errors, can provide a better user experience.

Question: Which System	Citicafe	ICMC	None
preference for registering complaint?	51.9	44.4	3.7
preference for getting information?	77.8	22.2	0
easiest to use?	85.2	7.4	7.4
quickest to learn?	85.2	7.4	7.4
needs technical help?	14.8	51.9	33.3

Table 5: Objective questionnaire results (in % of participants)

Out of Study Interactions

Overall, we recorded 111 conversations with 35 unique users over a span of 3 weeks. Out of these 111 conversations, 6% of them were aborted in the middle, possibly because the user input couldn't be understood properly. From the conversations that were completed, in 97.3% of the cases, the virtual agent was able to correctly identify the intent of the user query. There were 40 (around 36%) interactions with the intent of registering a complaint. As part of these interactions, 18 new complaints were registered while others had found a similar complaint already registered with the agency. The remaining 71 (64%) interactions were aimed at getting information. We received an explicit feedback on 24 of these, with 19 people indicating they were happy with the interaction (79.16%).

In order to test the learning capabilities at the end of this cycle, we re-trained the different modules based on the new user inputs and the feedback that was captured in the logs. During the re-training process, 19 new training examples were added to the intent classifier, 10 new locations were added to the location lexicon, while no complaints were found that belonged to a new category of civic issue. However, to fully verify the impact of re-training the agent, it would require us to perform multiple rounds of re-training and report the accuracy for each round. Such a detailed study is beyond the scope of this work and may be part of a future study.

Discussion

We conducted a user study that compared the two platforms, Citicafe and ICMC. There was a strong preference for Citicafe to get information on civic-related issues. Ease of use and ease of learning were also some of the features that the users liked. On the other hand, for registering complaints, the preference was not as strong. One of the reasons for that was a map-based interface supported by ICMC, which was useful in identifying locations.

We also list the following observations from the user study:

1. On ICMC, users received a view of all complaints at once without any summarization and found it hard to deduce the specific information that they were looking for. On the other hand, Citicafe summarized the information and engaged in conversation to guide them towards the information they were looking for. This guided question/answer paradigm often helped provide the desired user response across multiple turns. Based on the initial user input, Citicafe requests for more information from the user to better understand the input; provide suggestions regarding additional information available about user's concern; and also handle any follow up queries from the user on the information that was provided. All of this helped in improving the user's attention and engagement with the platform, resulting in an overall improved experience.

2. In some cases, Citicafe also assists users by suggesting possible queries and providing choices. For example, if the user query was about a civic agency, Citicafe also provided the type of information that can be accessed along with a list of civic issues handled by the agency that it can provide information on. The conversation medium guides the user to explore regions where other relevant information can be found. While it can be argued that it may limit the scope of user queries, from our study we observed that this guided exploration allowed users to stay focused on the topic and get relevant, targeted responses.

3. The ability of Citicafe to be integrated with different social media platforms was also appreciated by many.

4. One thing that Citicafe lacked was the ability to support additional graphical interfaces, such as a map-based interface, which made it hard to detect locations in certain cases. While chat based interfaces are good for handling informational queries, designing a hybrid system (chat interface with additional graphical capabilities) can support a wider range of tasks and provide a richer and more dynamic user experience.

CONCLUSION

Effective feedback and communication mechanisms are important for citizens to keep them involved and motivated in improving their neighborhood. In this paper, we develop and build "Citicafe" - a conversation-based platform. The platform considers the interests of both the citizens and public services, and provides a single point of contact to present and answer civic-related queries. The platform learns, curates and assimilates issues discussed in different heterogeneous sources like social media, online blogs, and complaint forums to answer citizen queries. The platform is bundled with various machine learning and natural language processing techniques to effectively understand user input, generate appropriate responses and continue to learn and update itself. The users can engage with our platform through a variety of existing social media avenues making it highly convenient.

In the future, we are planning to extend Citicafe to have it's own graphical interface which can support more functionalities including a map based interface. We also plan to include the capability to automatically identify civic issues from images that are provided by citizens. This can further ease out registering of complaints, effectively making it a single click process.

ACKNOWLEDGMENTS

We would like to thank the participants for their contribution in the user study. We also thank our colleagues for testing our platform and providing valuable suggestions.

REFERENCES

1. D. Agostino. 2013. Using social media to engage citizens: A study of Italian municipalities. Public Relations Review, vol. 39, 232-234.
2. M. M. Skoric, Q. Zhu, D. Goh and N. Pang. 2015. Social media and citizen engagement: A meta-analytic review. New Media and Society, Sage Publishing.
3. M. Karakiza. 2014. The impact of Social Media in the Public Sector. International Conference on Strategic Innovative Marketing, Madrid, Spain, September 1-4.
4. E. Curry, S. Dustdar, Q. Z. Sheng, and A. Sheth. 2016. Smart cities- enabling services and applications. Journal of Internet Services and Applications, vol. 7, no.6.
5. Tibert Verhagen, et al. 2014. Virtual customer service agents: Using social presence and personalization to shape online service encounters. Journal of Computer-Mediated Communication 19.3, 529-545.
6. Pankaj Dhoolia, et al. 2017. A cognitive system for business and technical support: A case study. IBM Journal of Research and Development 61.1, 7-74.
7. ichangemycity. http://www.ichangemycity.com/.
8. ComplaintBoard. https://www.complaintboard.in/.
9. bcity. http://www.bcity.in/.
10. SeeClickFix. http://en.seeclickfix.com/.
11. FixMyStreet Platform. http://www.fixmystreet.com/.
12. Nitish Mittal, Swati Agarwal, and Ashish Sureka. 2016. Got a Complaint?-Keep Calm and Tweet It!. Advanced Data Mining and Applications: 12th International Conference, ADMA 2016, Gold Coast, QLD, Australia, December 12-15.
13. Graeme Mearns, et al. 2014. Tweet my street: a cross-disciplinary collaboration for the analysis of local twitter data. Future Internet 6.2, 378-396.
14. Twitter Seva https://blog.twitter.com/official/en_in/a/2016/the-ministry-of-communication-adopts-twitter-seva-in.html
15. P. Bansal and D. Toshniwal. 2016. Analyzing civic complaints for proactive maintenance in smart city. in IEEE/ACIS 15th International Conference on Computer and Information Science (ICIS). Computer Science and Technologies, vol. 7, no. 1, 403-406.
16. F. Merson and R. Mary. 2017. A text mining approach to identify and analyze prominent issues from public complaints. International Journal of Advanced Research in Computer and Communication Engineering, vol. 6, no. 3.
17. Mahtab Ghazizadeh , Anthony D. McDonald, and John D. Lee. 2014. Text mining to decipher free-response consumer complaints: Insights from the NHTSA vehicle owner's complaint database. Human factors 56.6, 1189-1203.
18. Soon Goo Hong, Hyun Jong Kim, and Hyung Rim Choi. 2016. An Analysis of Civil Traffic Complaints Using Text Mining." International Information Institute (Tokyo). Information 19.11A.
19. Tridib Mukherjee, et al. 2015. Janayuja: A people-centric platform to generate reliable and actionable insights for civic agencies, in Proceedings of the 2015 Annual Symposium on Computing for Development.
20. S. K. Prasad, R. Patil, S. Beldare, and A. Shinde. 2016. Civic complaint application under smart city project, International Journal of Advanced Computing and International Technologies, vol. 3, no. 2.
21. De Melo Borges, Julio, et al. 2016. Estavis: A real-world interactive platform for crowdsourced visual urban analytics, in Proceedings of the Second International Conference on IoT in Urban Space.
22. John Lafferty, Andrew McCallum, and Fernando CN Pereira. 2001. Conditional random fields: Probabilistic models for segmenting and labeling sequence data. in ICML.
23. Kristina Toutanova et al. 2003. Feature-rich part-of-speech tagging with a cyclic dependency network. Proceedings of the 2003 Conference of the North American Chapter of the Association for Computational Linguistics on Human Language Technology-Volume 1. Association for Computational Linguistics.
24. J. Wang, G. Li and J. Fe. 2014. Extending string similarity join to tolerant fuzzy token matching, ACM Transactions Database Systems, vol. 39, no. 1.
25. J. Wang, G. Li and J. Fe. 2011. Fast-join: an efficient method for for fuzzy token matching based sting similarity join, IEEE 27th International Conference on Data Engineering.
26. P. Lawrence. 1990. Hanging on the Metaphone, Computer Language, vol. 7, no. 12.
27. David M. Blei, Andrew Y. Ng, and Michael I. Jordan. 2003. Latent dirichlet allocation." Journal of machine Learning research 3, 993-1022.
28. David Mimno, et al. 2011. Optimizing semantic coherence in topic models. Proceedings of the conference on empirical methods in natural language processing. Association for Computational Linguistics.
29. John Brooke. 1996. SUS-A quick and dirty usability scale. Usability evaluation in industry 189.194, 4-7.
30. ElasticSearch http://www.elastic.co
31. Watson Conversation Service, https://www.ibm.com/watson/developercloud/conversation.html, 2017
32. Natural Language Understanding, https://www.ibm.com/watson/services/natural-language-understanding/, 2017

33. B. Liu, 2012. Sentiment analysis and opinion mining," Synthesis lectures on human language technologies, vol. 5, no. 1, 1-167.

34. R. Wang, W. Huang, W. Chen, T. Wang, and K. Lei. 2015. Asem: Mining aspects and sentiment of events from microblog. in Proceedings of the 24th ACM International on Conference on Information and Knowledge Management, 1923-1926.

35. W. X. Zhao, J. Jiang, H. Yan, and X. Li. 2010. Jointly modeling aspects and opinions with a maxent-lda hybrid. in Proceedings of the 2010 Conference on Empirical Methods in Natural Language Processing. Association for Computational Linguistics, 56-65.

Personal Recommendations for Raising Social Eminence in an Enterprise

Shiri Kremer-Davidson, Inbal Ronen, Lior Leiba, Avi Kaplan, Maya Barnea
IBM Research AI , Haifa, Israel
{shiri, inbal, leiba, avika, mayab}@il.ibm.com

ABSTRACT

Social media sites have become very popular within large enterprises. Still, employees are experiencing difficulties in engaging efficiently. In this paper, we present a study of a personalized action recommendation system in an enterprise social network. Following a previous study on how to raise one's social eminence in the enterprise and a set of interviews, we built an innovative recommendation system which provides employees with concrete personalized recommendations on how and where to engage. Differently from other systems, it presents recommendations in context of limiting social network behavioral patterns. The recommendations' goal is to assist employees in growing out of these patterns. The paper presents the interview findings, the innovative recommendation system and results of a wide survey investigating the effectiveness of such a system.

Author Keywords

action recommendation; social engagement; social eminence; enterprise social media

ACM Classification Keywords

• Human-centered computing~Social recommendation

• Human-centered computing~Reputation systems

INTRODUCTION

Social networking sites and applications play a very significant role in people's interactions on the internet. While many use those mainly for personal social interactions and updates, others also utilize these platforms to build their professional eminence. The Merriam Webster dictionary defines an eminent person as "successful, well-known and respected". Similarly, we define social eminence as being socially successful, well known and respected in the social networking sphere [21]. It can be built, for example, by being active in micro blogs such as Twitter [1], sharing information on LinkedIn[2] or contributing to technical Q&A sites such as Stack Overflow[3] and Quora[4]. But being active alone does not suffice to establish one's social eminence, as eminence is dictated mainly by others' perception of oneself. It can be obtained, for example, through having a considerable number of followers and many interactions from others on one's content. Usually, a person's content needs to be interesting, significant and engaging to motivate others to read and react to it.

Social networking applications have become more and more prevalent also in the intranet of enterprises [25] and serve as a vehicle for employees to express themselves and share their expertise [24]. For many employees, it is important to be socially eminent within the enterprise social network as a path to raising their voice and expanding their influence inside the company. It is thus a beneficial goal for interested employees to strive for [19].

Becoming socially eminent in the enterprise is not an easy task. It requires time investment and socializing in an effective manner to broaden one's crowd. In a recent paper, Kremer-Davidson et al. [20] extracted a comprehensive set of tips and recommendations to help employees become more socially eminent. It turned out that indeed socially eminent employees were exposing certain concrete behaviors in the social sphere to build their eminence. These included among others, engaging with their audience and other employees, contributing meaningful content, and building and maintaining an up to date network. The paper also specified a set of limiting behavioral patterns along with tips on how to overcome them.

Although raising social network eminence might not be a priority to all employees, many of those who understand the value they can gain from it might not know how to do so. To assist employees in conceptualizing their eminence and relative social activity level and efficiency, our company's

IUI'18, March 7–11, 2018, Tokyo, Japan

ACM ISBN 978-1-4503-4945-1/18/03...$15.00
https://doi.org/10.1145/3172944.3172956

[1] https://twitter.com
[2] https://www.linkedin.com/
[3] https://stackoverflow.com/
[4] https://www.quora.com/

social network includes a deployment of a tool called Personal Social Dashboard (PSD) [20]. The PSD provides feedback to employees on how effective they are in the enterprise social network by presenting a set of scores covering various aspects of their social engagement. These scores are computed based on the employee's own activities as well as the reactions they receive and how others perceive them and their content. Employees found the tool and its scores very useful in reflecting their social network status in the organization [20]. Still, just understanding their status is not sufficient. Employees provided feedback that they would like concrete personalized recommendations on where, how, and with whom to engage. Such recommendations could potentially then help them engage more rewarding and effectively and as a side effect also raise their PSD scores. Based on this feedback, we identified the need to extend the tool with personalized social activity recommendations tailored at employees' actual socializing patterns.

In this paper, we explore whether and how a recommender system of concrete personalized actions in the enterprise social network could help employees engage more efficiently and consequently raise their social eminence. Following findings from interviews with very socially eminent employees in [21] we conducted an additional set of interviews with a more diverse set of enterprise social network users to investigate whether they strived to be socially eminent, what limited them and whether and how a recommender system could assist. Based on the paper [21] and these interviews, we built a unique recommender system focused on helping employees to overcome a set of limiting behavioral patterns in the social sphere. The system analyzed employee behavior in the enterprise social network in context of the limiting patterns. It then recommended a set of personalized concrete actions to perform in the network to help employees grow out of those patterns. For example, it recommended where to blog to employees who did not contribute enough content, which people to follow to those whose network was incomplete or not up to date enough and highlighted content which was missing the employee's engagement. We conducted an extensive survey in which we presented action recommendations in context of limiting behavioral patterns to a wide set of participants. Participants were first asked to rate the relevancy of the identified behavioral patterns to them. They were then presented with a set of personalized action recommendations in context of that pattern for which they were asked to rate their relevancy and how likely they would execute those. Our aim was to investigate whether the identified limiting behavioral patterns were indeed relevant from the participant's perspective. Did agreement with a pattern increase a person's likelihood to act upon given personalized action recommendations? Did participants find the recommendations themselves relevant and would they act upon those?

Our results show that participants indeed valued the provided recommendations and that presenting them in context of limiting behavioral patterns raised the probability that they would act upon them.

The paper is organized as follows. The next section provides related work, followed by a description of the research environment and interviews along with their results. We then describe the unique recommender system and the research settings of our survey, followed by survey results, discussion and conclusions.

RELATED WORK

Motivated by today's era of web information overload, recommender systems were developed to process and filter information to predict users' preferences about items of interest. There are many types of recommendation systems as the literature suggests [1,28], which differ from one another by the approach they follow, the types of items they recommend, and the environment in which they are deployed.

There are several common recommendation approaches. Collaborative filtering [8,30,31] recommends items that people with similar preferences liked in the past. With content-based filtering [22,25] items are recommended based on a comparison between the content of the items and a user profile. Knowledge-based recommender systems [32] provide recommendations by gathering knowledge about specific user needs or requirements. Other approaches utilize demographic information [4] and context [2]. An important class of recommender systems are hybrid recommender systems [4], which combine several recommendation approaches and are widely and successfully used.

Social recommender systems [13] target the social domain and provide personalized recommendations related to people (or profiles) and content (or topics). People recommendations are targeted at strengthening one's online social connections by providing users with specific recommendations about who to connect to (or befriend) [5,15] or whom to follow [12,17] on a given social network. Content recommendations aim to expose users to new relevant social content they might not be aware of [16]. One special characteristic of social recommender systems is the underlining structure of the social network which they use to extract recommendations, usually given in the form of a graph, enabling the development of efficient and effective algorithms that exploit graph structure [22, 29].

Not many action recommendation related papers in the enterprise exist. Farzan et al. [9] designed a points system to motivate employees to contribute content in an enterprise social platform. Dugan et al. [7] deployed a topic recommendation system called BlogMuse to make employees blog on topics recommended to them. SuggestBot [6] performed intelligent task routing (matching people with tasks) in Wikipedia. Guy et al. [14] used content recommendation for community owners to share with community members. The motivation in these papers is mostly to increase traffic on the social sites [10] and less the employee's personal benefit as in our paper. Some of the major public social networking sites provide action recommendations. For example, LinkedIn suggests topics for people to endorse their network [3] and recommendation to update one's profile. Facebook recommends people to connect to. Rashid et al [27] conducted an experiment on MovieLens in which users were recommended to rate movies while indicating the benefit they or the community would gain from their ratings. They concluded that explaining value of their contribution to the users increased contributions. In contrast to those systems, our work provides personalized action recommendations in context of behavioral patterns for increasing social eminence in the enterprise.

RESEARCH ENVIRONMENT

Our research was conducted using data extracted from an internal deployment of IBM Connections (Connections) [18] within our company. Connections is an enterprise social networking hub of different collaboration applications which can be used by all company employees. Among other features it includes: Blogs, Micro-blogs, Wikis for Web page co-editing, Files to allow file sharing and Forums for Q&A and discussions. All applications mentioned above support engagement capabilities such as liking and commenting on the entities. Employees have a personal landing page and can explicitly invite others to their network or select who or what to follow. Employees can keep up to date with the activities of the people they follow through Connections' activity stream.

INTERVIEWS

We conducted a set of interviews to get in-depth knowledge on how enterprise social network users feel about becoming more socially eminent and what kind of recommendation system could assist them.

We interviewed 12 employees who volunteered by responding to a post we placed in the enterprise social network. Interviewees originated from six organizations in the company and were located in 3 continents. 7 of them were females. Two of the interviewees worked for 3-5 years in the company, six for 6-10 years, and the rest more than 10 years. 10 interviewees accessed Connections daily and 2 weekly.

The interviews were conducted face to face or over the phone and lasted 15-20 minutes. Each interview consisted of questions related to: interviewee's general usage of Connections, social eminence, their experience with action recommendations in social networks, what should be included in a recommendation system that is to help employees raise their social eminence and what can motivate employees to follow given action recommendations. All questions were open without providing preset answers.

Social Eminence

To conceptualize interviewees' position on social eminence, we first enquired whether they want to be socially eminent. Most (9) responded positively, one negatively, and 2 others were undecided. Regarding what they would gain from being socially eminent, 6 stated increase of their reputation in the company, 3 increase of their visibility, 3 exposure to new people, 2 knowledge gain, and 1 helping others. Although most specified that there was much to gain from being socially eminent, 7 of the interviewees stated they were not socially eminent enough. When asked what they did to increase their social eminence, 6 specified they were not doing anything concrete and 4 stated they were doing some social activity such as adding people to their network, writing thoughtful comments, and sharing information. Interestingly, 2 specified that they were trying to raise their social eminence through interactions outside the social media system. As one said, "I try to reach out on a personal level and build my engagement based on real interactions with people."

When asked what was limiting them to become more socially eminent 4 specified not having enough time to invest, 3 feeling shy or embarrassed to contribute their own content and 1 not knowing what to write. One interviewee said: "when producing content, I need time to explain, create, think." Another stated, "I don't know what to write, what of my knowledge or skills can interest others." Two employees did not feel anything limited them.

We conclude that most employees understand the value they can gain from becoming more socially eminent, however, the journey of becoming eminent includes obstacles such as lack of time, missing knowledge (on how or where to engage), or feeling uncomfortable performing the needed social activities.

Action Recommendations

To conceptualize interviewees experience with action recommendations in social networks we asked them whether they had encountered such recommendations in any social network. Most (10) specified they had, in particular recommendations to connect to others, profile updates, and sharing content suggestions. Interestingly, only half reported they followed these recommendations. Those who followed specified they did so because the recommendations made sense, they were easy to follow and could potentially expose them to new information. Those who did not, stated that recommendations were either not relevant, felt risky (e.g. did not consider company hierarchy), or even felt insincere. One said, "It makes me feel creepy to get a network invitation from someone I do not know.". Another said "I feel such recommendations from external networks are biased – not honest. Some use your data to monetize your content. I don't want to be part of it."

We asked interviewees what should be included in an action recommendation system that aims to help employees raise their social eminence. Almost half mentioned the need for assistance in content contribution based on their specific personal expertise and topics of interest. This was followed by personal guidance of where to contribute content and whom to connect to. Some mentioned the need for getting feedback on their social journey progress. Others stated that recommendations should be provided when and where relevant, with evidence, and in small steps to increase chances of being fulfilled. Some focused on the way the recommendations need to be presented to increase the probability of their adoption. As one stated "use gamification: motivate but in a funny and engaging way" and another stated: "include tips and tricks of little behavior. It has to be in your comfort boundaries."

Apart from the system features, we wanted to understand what could motivate employees to follow action recommendations. 5 of the interviewees wanted a recommendation to include an indication of the value they could gain from following it. As one stated "Getting an answer to: what is in it for me? Why is this important to me?" 4 interviewees mentioned the importance of evidence of why the system decided it was relevant to them. One interviewee emphasized that "the explanation that is given to me needs to be short and truthful." Others added the need to get feedback on how they succeeded in previous similar attempts as well as the need to be easy to follow. Another interesting motivation element raised was to provide evidence on how such a recommendation helped others, as one said: "provide me 'Social Proof' – telling me that others have done this, like 'most people (in your org, in your job) are doing this'." We conclude that personalized action recommendations should be easy to follow, and include evidence of why they were relevant and valuable to the user.

[21] outlined a set of limiting social behavioral patterns and provided tips from socially eminent employees on what to do to grow out of them. We thus wanted to understand if interviewees would gain value from a system that would highlight their potential limiting behavior. Almost all (11) were positive. One interviewee said "I am a real believer in feedback on what I am less good at because this can lead me in the right way to overcome it. I am not familiar with any system that does this." Another stated, "if I knew what behaviors are missing that I am lacking, I would for sure focus on doing them first." Furthermore, an interviewee who felt he was very socially eminent stated: "I may be too of an expert in the area to be honest with myself on behaviors I picked that may be limiting me. Maybe I can improve them with such secret knowledge." The undecided employee explained "It depends on comfort boundaries. Asking me to change behavior that is outside my boundaries will not be successful."

In the last question, we asked participants whether a system that would provide recommendations in context of an explanation of limiting behavioral patterns would motivate them more to follow the recommendations than without such context. As in the previous question, all were positive except for one interviewee who was undecided. When asked why, they stated: "Seeing recommendations in such context will definitely cause me to do more of them. It's like having an angel on your arm forwarding you in the right direction." and "the combination makes the information more valuable. This is a journey. Doing an activity to change a behavior is motivating." Another specified that "if you get insight but nothing with it – it can easily be forgotten."

RECOMMENDATION SYSTEM

Based on limiting behavioral patterns and tips from [21] along with the rich input from the interviews, we built a personalized social action recommendation system.

Social Behavioral Patterns

To meet these qualities one of the main concepts we introduced was a '*Social Behavioral Pattern*'. Logically, each pattern was mapped to a limiting social behavior. A social behavioral pattern thus had the responsibility of quantifying to what extent employee's social behavior matched the limiting behavior denoted as *pattern matching score.* The pattern was an encapsulation of domain expert knowledge into a recommendation generation system. The number of employees a pattern was relevant to could vary significantly between different recommendation patterns.

In the initial implementation of the system we defined three recommendation patterns: *Lead conversations* (Create), *Follow more people* (Follow) and *Sustain your conversations* (Engage). We decided to start with this set as each pattern focuses on a different engagement aspect such as: lack of content creation, insufficient network, and low levels of communication with one's audience. In particular, *Create* focused on employees who were already engaging with other people's content (via liking, commenting and sharing), however rarely actively lead a conversation themselves. *Follow* focused on employees who did not follow enough people. Following the "right" people can potentially expose employees to important insights and open many engagement opportunities which are crucial for getting a voice. *Engage* focused on employees who contributed content but did not engage enough with their commenters. To ensure their knowledge is valued and disseminated, they need to drive conversation around it and thus, dedicate time to respond to those interacting with their content and reward them for their engagement.

Each recommendation pattern was different by nature and required different inputs and time periods of employees' behavior to compute their pattern matching score. For example, among others, *Create* required the number of blog entries an employee created in a defined recent period, *Follow* required the number of people each employee followed, and *Engage* required the recent ratio of unanswered comments on employees' micro-blogs. Thus, employee social behavior was modeled as a set of user characteristics describing basic social features of employees. This information was saved in a 'user profile' database.

Recommendations

Based on the identified social behavioral patterns, our system generated recommendations for guiding and assisting employees in growing out of those identified limiting patterns. The aim was to help them in becoming more socially eminent and increase collaboration and knowledge sharing in the enterprise.

For employees for whom the *Create* pattern was identified as relevant, the system recommended to start driving their own topics and discussions in places where they were already relatively active assuming there was higher potential for them to feel comfortable contributing content there. It identified, for example, communities, blogs, forums, etc. where they reacted (e.g. liked, commented), and recommended them to contribute their own contents there. Despite the existing broad research on recommendations of whom to follow (see related work section), in this initial system for *Follow* we chose to start simple with the incentive stated in [21] that employees should make sure they follow people they regularly interact with, their managers, and their peers. Previous interactions included for example recently writing on one's wall, mentioning a person, commenting on one's content and tagging a person. For employees who were identified relevant to the *Engage* pattern, the system recommended going back to specific entries of their recent content which had engagements from others (e.g. comments), but were missing the employee's responses.

Our system's recommendations had the following qualities: *Actionable*, *Personalized*, *Justifiable* and *Temporal*. *Actionable*, as they encompassed a concrete action (and not just a high-level guideline). For example, a recommendation that guides employees to write a comment on a specific entry in a community (instead of generally recommending to "be more socially active"). They were *Personalized*, as they were based on employees' past actions. For example, which communities they were active on and which people they interacted with. Recommendations were *Justifiable* as each recommendation included a short, natural-language, explanation of why it was suggested to the employee. For example, a recommendation to write a blog entry in a specific community could have an explanation such as: "You commented 8 times and liked 10 times entries in this community." They were also *Temporal*, as they were related to recent user activities. Recommendations may change and become irrelevant over time.

Architecture Overview

All employee interactions with the social network were stored in an enterprise social graph used also by the PSD tool [20] to compute its scores. The graph included for example for a user who created a blog entry: a node for the blog entry, a node for the user, and a connecting edge between them with label *create* and properties such as date. Nodes representing other users who commented or liked the blog entry, would be connected to the node of the blog entry through additional edges. As stated before, the graph did not include the content of the blog entry.

We designed the recommendation system to be extensible to allow easy addition of new social behavioral patterns, as well as reducing the need for each pattern to compute social features that were computed by other patterns. Thus, the system included two separate extensible libraries: the *User Characteristic Computation Library* and the *Social Behavioral Pattern Library*. Figure 1 depicts the architecture of the recommendation system. The User Characteristics Computation Library included computations extracting user specific social characteristics from the enterprise graph such as how many blog entries they created, how many followers they had, the ratio between blog comments they received to blog entries they created, etc. The Social Behavioral Pattern Library included patterns which were implemented as a rule-based algorithm calculating the match between an employee and a limiting pattern. For example, for *Create* it would use computed characteristics such as, the number of blog entries users created during a time period compared to the number of comments and likes they contributed in order to decide whether the user was active but did not produce enough entries. Patterns also included a rule based recommendation generation algorithm which was responsible for generating personal recommendations for users to help them grow out of the

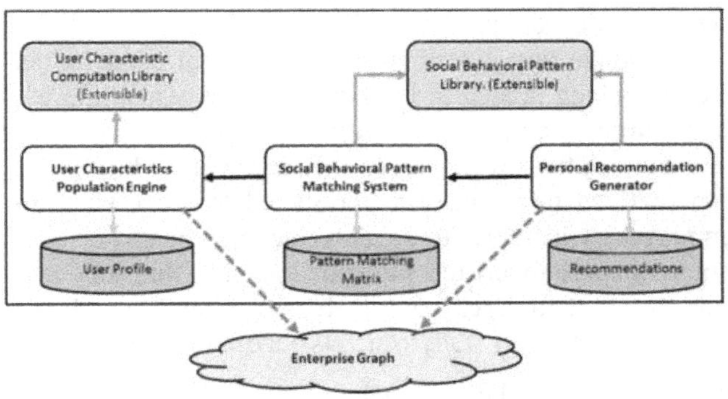

Figure 1 Recommendation System Architecture

identified limiting behavioral pattern. For example, for *Create* it identified which community content users liked or commented on and recommended them to place their own content in that community as well.

To support the recommendations generation process, the system periodically activated the *User Characteristics Population Engine* responsible for calculating the set of user characteristics according to the User Characteristic Computation Library and populating the *User Profile* accordingly. Thus, the User Profile stored all computed user characteristics.

The *Social Behavioral Pattern Matching System* then used the pattern library to calculate a pattern matching score for each employee-pattern pair and stored it in the *Pattern Matching Matrix*. It invoked for each pattern its pattern matching score algorithm according to the Social Behavioral Pattern Library. These algorithms were based on domain expert knowledge and received as input the employee's user profile calculated in the first phase. The output was a score between 0 and 1. To verify that all patterns used a similar logical scale, we defined 5 equally spaced score ranges of relevancy that can be associated with the following levels: *Hardly*, *Borderline*, *Somewhat*, *Relevant* and *Very Relevant*. In general, a score above 0.6 (at least *Relevant*) indicated that the employee possessed the limiting behavioral pattern, and that fixing this habit was relevant for this user.

In the last phase, the *Personal Recommendation Generator* produced recommendations by invoking, for each pattern, a dedicated recommendation generation algorithm which traversed the *Enterprise Graph* to identify what to recommend to each employee according to the criteria mentioned in the subsection above (Recommendations). The output of this algorithm was a set of "personal social action recommendations" that best related to the definition and semantics of the social behavioral pattern that generated them. For example, as stated above, for *Create* it could recommend contributing in a community in which the user was active already through commenting or liking. The 'strength' or quality of the recommendation was defined by a 'Recommendation Score' which considered the match of the recommendation to the user according to the user's activity. For example, if a user was assigned two *Create* recommendations in relation to two different communities, the one which related to the community in which the user was more active, would get a higher score. Only recommendations with a recommendation score higher than a predefined threshold were presented to the user. Thus, employees with only low-quality recommendations would not be exposed to any recommendations. The threshold level was different for each pattern. It was defined based on a pattern specific user study which is out of scope of this work.

Each recommendation included, among others, the following characteristics: descriptive text, action to perform, and evidence. In general, recommendations were produced for all employees regardless of their pattern matching scores.

SYSTEM USAGE SURVEY

We conducted an in-depth investigation of the usability of our Personal Social Recommendation System through a user survey.

Survey Research Settings

The enterprise graph, of our internal deployment of Connections, captured about seven years of historical activities of ~450K company employees including ~40M vertices and ~212M edges. It did not include the content of those activities. The recommendation system provided pattern matching scores for ~326K employees. Out of those it identified recommendations for ~199K employees. For *Create* ~175K, *Engage* ~65K, and for *Follow* ~72K employees. Table 1 summarizes the outputs of each pattern including the number of recommendations and the average number of recommendations it generated for each employee.

Pattern	# of employees with Recommendations	Avg. # per emp. of Recommendations
Create	175,097	3.3
Engage	64,562	1.5
Follow	72,004	2.4

Table 1. Recommendations generated for employees

The user survey consisted of a set of web pages, each focusing on a different social behavioral pattern. Figure 2 shows a sample survey page for the *Engage* pattern. Each participant was exposed to up to 3 patterns, the order of which was randomized. Each pattern page included a short paragraph describing the limiting behavioral pattern it addressed. Participants were asked to rate the relevancy of the pattern to them on a 5-point Likert scale. They could optionally also add a comment. The rating scale was: 1 - Not relevant, 2 - Somewhat Relevant, 3 - Fairly Relevant, 4 - Relevant and 5 - Very Relevant. In the following, relevance is analyzed using this numeric scale.

The pattern page also included the pattern's three top scored recommendations for the participant in randomized order. Participants received only patterns for which they had at least three recommendation candidates. For each recommendation, participants were asked to rate two questions on the scale as above: How relevant this recommendation was to them and to what extent they were likely to follow it. They could also leave an optional comment. Participants could move to the next page only after answering all questions. They could choose to exit the survey on any page. Only fully submitted pages were considered in our analysis. Employees could see evidence of why they received a recommendation by clicking the "i" symbol (marked with a red circle in Figure 2). For example, if the recommendation suggested to contribute a blog entry in a community, it would include insights on the participant's previous engagements in this community such as "you liked a blog entry 3 times" or "you edited a wiki page 2 times."

We defined potential survey participants as employees who were socially active in the past year and had at least 3 recommendations from at least one pattern. We randomly selected 4,160 employees and invited them over email to participate in the survey. Responses were anonymous. 28% (1,165) submitted input to at least one pattern.

Table 2 shows for each pattern the distribution of the number of participants that were exposed to its recommendations in relation to their pattern matching score. Note that we also included participants for whom the pattern was scored as not necessarily relevant (score 0) as such employees were target users of our system as well.

Relevance	Create	Engage	Follow
Not	1033	2	585
Hardly	13	16	125
Borderline	13	3	94
Somewhat	33	10	48
Relevant	14	5	40
Very	51	25	75
Total	**1157**	**61**	**967**

Table 2. Participants pattern matching score distribution

RESULTS

Social Behavioral Patterns

We first examined how participants found the social behavioral patterns they were exposed to in the survey. On average, employees found the patterns relevant where *Create* lead (avg. 3.79, stdev. 1.1, median 4), followed by

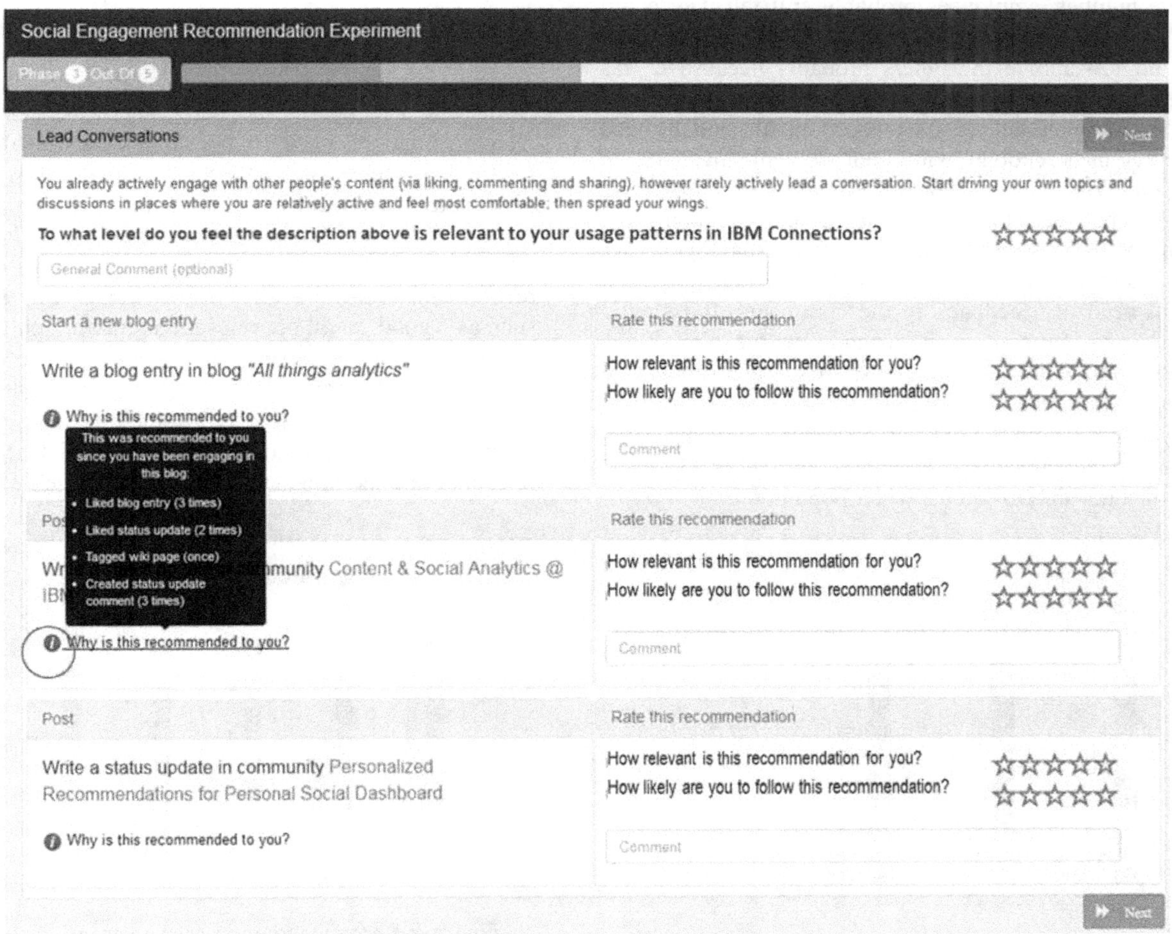

Figure 2: *Engage* Survey Page Example

Follow (avg. 3.44, stdev. 1.23, median 4), and *Engage* (avg. 3.28, stdev. 1.23, median 4). Figure 3 shows the distribution of participants' pattern relevancy ratings. For all patterns, more than 50% of the employees rated them as either *Relevant* or *Very Relevant* (median >= 4). But, as seen in Table 2, the system's pattern matching score algorithms identified the patterns as relevant for only part of the participants who felt it was relevant to them. This discrepancy was strongest for *Create.* We suspect this might be due to the matching score algorithm focusing on actual employee activity, whereas employees based their ratings on their personal perception that they needed to invest much more time in social activity and lead more conversations. Furthermore, as we saw in the interviews, even if they did contribute contents some still found it difficult due to shyness or not knowing what to share. This was also evident in survey comments such as: "I feel that what is interesting to me may not be to others", "I've just started in a new role, once my confidence within the role grows so will my ability to lead." *Follow* got lower average ratings than *Create* (Figure 3), but still there was a discrepancy in relation to the system's relevancy assessment. Even though *Follow* was more quantifiable, as the number of followers constituted a concrete number, employees probably still felt they could invest more in improving their network. *Engage*'s rating was a bit lower than the others probably because it was targeting a narrower community of employees who contributed content but for some reason did not find the need to interact back enough with their content engagers. In contrast to *Create* and *Follow*, for *Engage* we found greater alignment between the system score and the employee perception. In relevant comments, we found mainly excuses for not engaging back such as "most of the contents I created may not need my feedback to the comments. If I should interact with commenters, it depends on the aim of the contents, but not the comments." Our algorithms for computing the matching scores, focused on identifying employees for whom the limiting behavior is evident. From our results we conjecture that we need to further adjust the matching algorithm to catch a wider population.

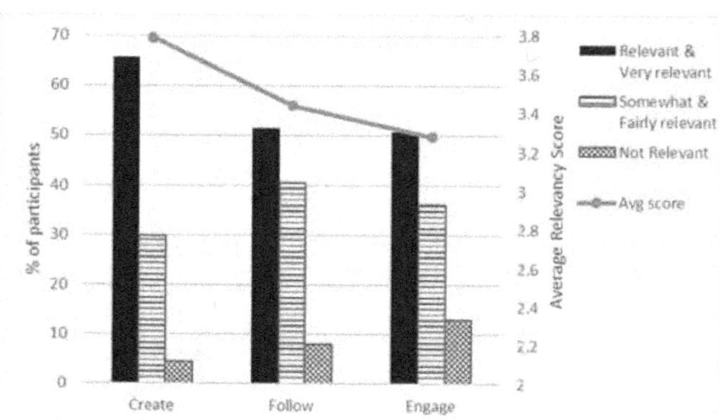

Figure 3: Pattern relevancy distribution and average rating

Recommendations

We first analyzed how participants perceived the recommendations they got using their responses to the two questions: how relevant they found the recommendation and whether they were likely to adopt or follow the recommendation. As each recommendation pattern defines its own recommendation algorithm, we investigated this per recommendation pattern type.

Most employees found their recommendations appropriate and were likely to act on them. On average, *Follow* got highest recommendation relevance average (avg. 3.67, stdev. 1.43, median 4) followed by *Create* (avg. 3.1, stdev. 1.4, median 4) and *Engage* (avg. 3.26, stdev. 1.36, median 3). When focusing on likelihood to adopt the actions, average scores were lower but still the majority found them between somewhat to very relevant. *Follow*'s average was highest (avg. 3.57, stdev. 1.52, median 4), followed by *Create* (avg. 3.1, stdev. 1.47, median 3) and *Engage* (avg. 3.11, stdev. 1.41, median 3). More information can be seen in Figure 4.

Interestingly, when comparing the average distance between relevance and likelihood to adopt we found highest distance for *Create* (0.3) and lowest for *Engage* and *Follow* (0.1). This strengthens our hypothesis that *Create*'s recommendations by nature, although relevant, may be harder to act upon. As our interviewees mentioned, recommendations need to be small and easy to follow. *Follow*'s distance is smallest probably as it is easier to perform and people are more familiar with this type of action recommendations. To further investigate the wider distance in *Create,* we analyzed participants' comments on *Create* recommendations, the gist of which included statements such as: "good catch; not relevant anymore; don't feel I am in the right role to write; I am not expected to contribute there; it's not a common community action; don't think this activity is effective". Indeed, some of these comments exposed additional possible reasons for the distance between relevance and likelihood to adopt, one of which was that the

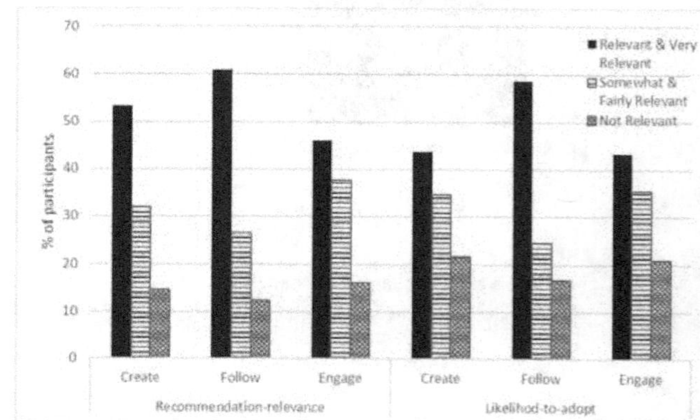

Figure 4: Recommendations relevancy and likelihood to adopt

activity recommended was not a common action in the specific targeted community. For example, participants may have been recommended to write a status update in the community in which it was common to use forums for question and answering. In future versions, we will try to suggest actions according to a community's specific activity patterns and inspect whether results improve. Interestingly, when looking at the number of comments placed on recommendations of each pattern in relation to the employee's relevance rating, we saw that most comments on *Create/Engage* recommendations were from people who found the recommendation not relevant, whereas most comments on *Follow* recommendations were from people who found them very relevant. This may be another indication that people were used and thus more comfortable to perform *Follow* related actions and less so for these new types of recommendations. One type of comment we found for recommendations from all patterns was that the time of opportunity had passed to act on the recommendation. Although only a minority of recommendations got this feedback and the recommendation generation algorithms have a time decay component, we still found this interesting and suspect that different individuals may expect different time decay configurations to their recommendations. In future versions, we should add a learning component that will personalize the time decay configuration based on employee activity rate and interaction with its recommendations.

Across Patterns

We were interested to check whether employees who found recommendations relevant were likely to adopt them. We conducted a Spearman correlation test followed by a Linear Regression test for variables recommendation-relevance and likely-to-adopt. All tests demanded a significance of 0.95 (i.e., = 0.05). We found that the average correlation was very high (0.86) and the linear regression equations suggested a linear dependency where a change in one unit of recommendation-relevance resulted in an average change of more than 0.89 units of likely-to-adopt. Thus, question answers were highly correlated and therefore participants who found the recommendations relevant were very likely to act on them.

To take this one step further, we wanted to check whether participants' perception of their related patterns influenced how they perceived the quality of the recommendations or their likelihood to act on them. This can shed evidence to the actual added value of seeing recommendation in context of the limiting behavioral pattern. Thus, we checked if a relevant pattern lead to relevant recommendations which in turn lead to high likely-to-adopt ratings. We conducted a Spearman correlation test followed by Linear Regression test for the variables mentioned above. All tests demanded a significance of 0.95 (i.e., = 0.05). When checking the influence of the pattern's perception by the user on its average pattern relevancy rating we found a lower average correlation of 0.43 but the linear regression equations revealed a dependency where one-unit change in pattern-rating resulted in 0.42 units change in the recommendation relevance rating. Putting it all together, users tended to adopt recommendations when they were given in the context of a personalized (and hence relevant) pattern.

DISCUSSION AND FUTURE WORK

In this paper, we describe an innovative personal social recommendation system whose aim is to help employees socialize more effectively and as a result raise their social eminence. The system was built following feedback received from users of a social dashboard (PSD) deployed in our organization. Employees expressed that they needed in addition to a set of scores also concrete guidance on how to raise their eminence and become more socially active. The recommendation system was designed following conclusions from [21] and a set of interviews to gain insights on how employees felt about becoming more socially eminent as well as how such a system should be designed to maximize its potential effectiveness for them. Following an initial implementation of the system, we conducted a wide survey analyzing the system's usefulness to employees as well as feedback on how to improve the system in future versions.

Throughout the interviews, employees almost unanimously were intrigued by the idea to gain insights on their limiting behavioral patterns as well as getting action recommendations in context of those. In the survey, many employees found the patterns relevant to them, although there were cases of discrepancy. Furthermore, employees specified their likelihood to adopt recommendations provided in the context of a limiting behavior (that they believed relevant). This strengthens our system's approach that exposing action recommendations in context of limiting behavior, can indeed provide value to employees. We are aware that such systems are potentially more valuable to those who were already beforehand interested in increasing their social eminence and are likely to invest time and effort to do so. But exposing other employees to their limiting behavioral patterns can perhaps motivate them to also strive to change or improve their social engagement. The survey exposed recommendations to all participants regardless of their pattern matching score as there is always room for improvement even when a certain behavioral pattern is not revealed. The matching score, when analyzed over time, can provide employees a reflection of their progress. Furthermore, it could potentially be used to identify employees who are in the process of obtaining a certain limiting behavioral pattern and get them grow out of it before it becomes a habit. In the future, we plan to include in the system's user interface, a score history graph for each pattern conceptualizing users' progress as well as alert them on evolving behaviors that might become a habit.

In the interviews, employees specified many valuable benefits of being socially eminent and expressed their interest to become more so. Still, many did not feel they were socially eminent enough and stated reasons such as not dedicating enough time and not integrating it into their day to day work. According to Kremer-Davidson et al. [21] employees have difficulty in contributing content which is crucial for becoming socially eminent. We were thus not surprised that many employees found the *Create* pattern description relevant to them even when our system algorithms did not. It's generated recommendations also experienced the widest gap between relevancy and likelihood. Though people probably understand the value of contributions, it seems still hard to commit to them. Indeed, taking the stage and contributing content is a hard obstacle for employees who are shy or are not confident enough in what they can say or share. The hope is that following the recommendations employees will start contributing in places they feel more comfortable in, which over time will build employees' confidence, and have them grow out of their impediment behavior.

The initial system included many features raised in the interviews but not all were incorporated into it. Some of missing features focused specifically on means of persuading employees to follow given action recommendations. These included providing indication of the recommendation's potential direct or indirect value, such as how similar actions as those recommended assisted others in raising their social eminence and how they succeeded in following similar recommendations in the past. Some also suggested using gamification to increase probability of adoption.

Our research has some limitations. First, the study did not include a comparison to a ground truth as we were not aware of a similar system to compare to. Second, our enterprise graph did not include the content of the social entities, which did not allow us to consider topical interests or expertise of the users as many suggested in the interviews. In the future, we plan to focus on adding additional limiting behavioral patterns, further adjusting matching score algorithms and improving recommendation generation algorithms of the existing patterns, as well as conducting an additional research to compare how our system recommendations are perceived when they are exposed in context of the limiting behavioral patterns and without.

The system generated recommendations were based on tips provided by experienced socially eminent employees such as motivating employees to lead conversations (take the stage), interact with their contents' audience, and more. Naturally, following such recommendations will raise one's presence in the social arena but still, to increase social eminence, contribution does not suffice. One also needs to get exposed to a wider audience valuing and interacting with those contributions. We believe that the more one contributes valuable content (and in a broad set of locations) and engages with others, the more other employees become exposed to those contents. If those employees in turn find the content valuable, it increases the probability of it impacting them, thus raising one's eminence. As future work, we would like to inspect the impact over time of the recommendations on the scores of employees in the Personal Social Dashboard (PSD) since PSD scores measure the impact on employee social engagement and eminence from various perspectives.

CONCLUSIONS

In this study, we present an innovative personalized social action recommendation system. We report findings from interviews conducted with enterprise social network users on social eminence and whether and how a recommender system could help them raise their social eminence. We then present results of a wide survey investigating the quality and relevancy of our initial system. This study provides several contributions. First, it introduces an innovative recommender system that generates concrete personalized actionable recommendations in context of limiting behavioral patterns that are to help employees grow out of them. Second, it provides evidence to the relevancy and potential adoption level of such a recommender. Third, it introduces a set of features for such systems that can potentially help increase the motivation of employees to adopt such recommendations.

REFERENCES

1. Adomavicius, G., and Tuzhilin, A. 2005. Toward the next generation of recommender systems: A survey of the state-of-the-art and possible extensions. *IEEE transactions on knowledge and data engineering*, *17*(6), 734-749.
2. Adomavicius, G., & Tuzhilin, A. 2015. Context-aware recommender systems. In *Recommender systems handbook* (pp. 191-226). Springer US.
3. Bastian, M., Hayes, M., Vaughan, W., Shah, S., Skomoroch, P., Kim, H., ... & Lloyd, C. 2014. Linkedin skills: large-scale topic extraction and inference. In *RecSys'14.*
4. Burke, R. 2002. Hybrid recommender systems: Survey and experiments. *User modeling and user-adapted interaction*, *12*(4), 331-370.
5. Chen, J., Geyer, W., Dugan, C., Muller, M., & Guy, I. 2009. Make new friends, but keep the old: recommending people on social networking sites. In *Proc. CHI'09*

6. Cosley, D., Frankowski, D., Terveen, L. and Riedl, J., 2007, January. SuggestBot: using intelligent task routing to help people find work in wikipedia. In *Proceedings of the 12th international conference on Intelligent user interfaces (pp. 32-41).*
7. Dugan, C., Geyer, W., & Millen, D. R. 2010. Lessons learned from blog muse: audience-based inspiration for bloggers. In *Proceedings of the SIGCHI Conference on Human Factors in Computing Systems*
8. Ekstrand, M. D., Riedl, J. T., & Konstan, J. A. 2011. Collaborative filtering recommender systems. *Foundations and Trends® in Human–Computer Interaction*, *4*(2), 81-173.
9. Farzan, R., DiMicco, J. M., Millen, D. R., Dugan, C., Geyer, W., & Brownholtz, E. A. 2008. Results from deploying a participation incentive mechanism within the enterprise. In *Proceedings of the SIGCHI conference on Human factors in computing systems* (pp. 563-572). ACM.
10. Freyne, J., Jacovi, M., Guy, I., & Geyer, W. 2009. Increasing engagement through early recommender intervention. In *RecSys'09*
11. Geyer, W., & Dugan, C. 2010. Inspired by the audience: a topic suggestion system for blog writers and readers. In *Proceedings of the 2010 ACM conference on Computer supported cooperative work* (pp. 237-240). ACM.
12. Gupta, P., Goel, A., Lin, J., Sharma, A., Wang, D., & Zadeh, R. 2013. Wtf: The who to follow service at twitter. In *Proceedings of the 22nd international conference on World Wide Web* (pp. 505-514). ACM.
13. Guy, I. 2015. Social recommender systems. In *Recommender Systems Handbook* (pp. 511-543). Springer US.
14. Guy, I., Ronen, I., Kravi, E., & Barnea, M. (2016). Increasing activity in enterprise online communities using content recommendation. *ACM Transactions on Computer-Human Interaction (TOCHI)*, *23*(4), 22.
15. Guy, I., Ronen, I., & Wilcox, E. 2009. Do you know?: recommending people to invite into your social network. In *Proceedings of the 14th international conference on Intelligent user interfaces* (pp. 77-86). ACM.
16. Guy, I., Zwerdling, N., Ronen, I., Carmel, D., & Uziel, E. 2010. Social media recommendation based on people and tags. In *Proc SIGIR'10*
17. Hannon, J., Bennett, M., & Smyth, B. 2010. Recommending twitter users to follow using content and collaborative filtering approaches. In *RecSys'10*
18. IBM Connections: http://www-03.ibm.com/software/products/en/ibmconnsuit
19. Jacovi, M., Guy, I., Kremer-Davidson, S., Porat, S., & Aizenbud-Reshef, N. 2014. The perception of others: inferring reputation from social media in the enterprise. In *Proceedings of the 17th ACM conference on Computer supported cooperative work & social computing*
20. Annonymized.
21. Kremer-Davidson, S., Ronen, I., Leiba, L., Kaplan, A., & Barnea, M. 2016. Raising your Eminence inside the Enterprise Social Network. In *Proceedings of the 19th International Conference on Supporting Group Work*
22. Levin, R., Abassi, H., & Cohen, U. 2016. Guided Walk: A Scalable Recommendation Algorithm for Complex Heterogeneous Social Networks. In *RecSys'16*
23. Lops, P., De Gemmis, M., & Semeraro, G. 2011. Content-based recommender systems: State of the art and trends. In *Recommender systems handbook* (pp. 73-105). Springer US.
24. Mark, G., Guy, I., Kremer-Davidson, S., & Jacovi, M. 2014. Most liked, fewest friends: patterns of enterprise social media use. In *Proceedings of the 17th ACM conference on Computer supported cooperative work & social computing* (pp. 393-404). ACM.
25. http://www.mckinsey.com/business-functions/digital-mckinsey/our-insights/taking-the-measure-of-the-networked-enterprise. Seen March 29, 2017
26. Pazzani, M. J., & Billsus, D. 2007. Content-based recommendation systems. In *The adaptive web* (pp. 325-341). Springer Berlin Heidelberg.
27. Rashid, A. M., Ling, K., Tassone, R. D., Resnick, P., Kraut, R., & Riedl, J. 2006. Motivating participation by displaying the value of contribution. In *Proc CHI'06*
28. Ricci, F., Rokach, L., & Shapira, B. 2011. Introduction to recommender systems handbook (pp. 1-35). springer US.
29. Ronen, I., Shahar, E., Ur, S., Uziel, E., Yogev, S., Zwerdling, N., & Ofek-Koifman, S. 2009. Social networks and discovery in the enterprise (SaND). In *Proceedings of the 32nd international ACM SIGIR conference on Research and development in information retrieval*
30. Sarwar, B., Karypis, G., Konstan, J., & Riedl, J. 2001. Item-based collaborative filtering recommendation algorithms. In *Proceedings of the 10th international conference on World Wide Web* (pp. 285-295). ACM.
31. Schafer, J. H. J. B., Frankowski, D., Herlocker, J., & Sen, S. 2007. Collaborative filtering recommender systems. *The adaptive web*, 291-324.
32. Trewin, S. 2000. Knowledge-based recommender systems. *Encyclopedia of library and information science*, *69* (Supplement 32), 180.

TSCSet: A Crowdsourced Time-Sync Comment Dataset for Exploration of User Experience Improvement

Zhenyu Liao[1]*, Yikun Xian[2]*, Xiao Yang[1], Qinpei Zhao[1], Chenxi Zhang[1], Jiangfeng Li[1] †
[1] Tongji University, Shanghai, China
[2] Rutgers University, New Jersey, USA
102982liaozy@tongji.edu.cn, siriusxyk@gmail.com,
doris.yx@gmail.com, qinpeizhao@tongji.edu.cn, xzhang2000@163.com, lijf@tongji.edu.cn

ABSTRACT
Time-Sync Comment (TSC) is a type of crowdsourced user review embedded in online video websites, which provides better real-time user interaction than traditional user comment type. Various TSC-related problems and approaches have been studied to improve user experience by taking advantage of special characteristics of TSCs such as strong time reliance. However, there are three major drawbacks to these TSC researches. First, they did not explicitly show advantage of TSC features over the traditional features in terms of users' experience. Second, the experiments were conducted on some inconsistent TSC datasets crawled from different source, which makes the effectiveness of their methods less convincing. Third, the methods were manually evaluated by a limited number of so-called "experts" in these experiments, so it is hard for other researchers to obtain the data labels and reproduce the results. In order to overcome these drawbacks, this paper aims to explore the usefulness of TSC data for for the improvement of user experience online by exploiting the TSC pattern inside a new dataset. Specifically, we present a larger-scale TSC dataset with four-level structures and rich self-labeled attributes and formally define a group of TSC-related research problems based on this dataset. The problems are solved by adapted state-of-the-art methods and evaluated through crowdsourced labels in the dataset. The result can be regarded as a baseline for further research.

Author Keywords
Crowdsourced time-sync comment; hierarchical structured dataset; episode representation learning; storyline prediction

INTRODUCTION
As an essential application in Internet, online video websites have been gaining increasing popularity in recent years. In addition to watching videos, users now would like to have more interaction with other audience. Time-sync comment (TSC; also called *Danmu* in Chinese and *Danmaku* in Japanese) is a new textual information on video content that has been applied to many online video websites such as Acfun[1] and Bilibili[2] in China, Niconico[3] in Japan and so forth. TSC is a type of crowdsourced user review organized by video playback time. Audience can bulletin TSCs at any time to share their feelings and opinions about the corresponding video shot. Other audience will see the TSC at the same playback time, so they may react with their own opinions through their TSC. This kind of interaction enriches description of videos and provides a brand new kind of textual data in the analysis of video content and movie reviews. Some substantial researches on TSC have emerged since 2014 including video tagging [35], highlight detection [38] and video key frame recommendation [6]. These studies showed that TSC data embodies great potential in semantic analysis on videos. However, their work on TSC only focused on specific scenarios, lack of a full scale analysis of online clients' experience based on a common dataset. Furthermore, most experiments were conducted on their selected individual datasets. Therefore, these assessments are incomparable on a common ground. As such, a standardized dataset and a complete assessments concerning different aspects are needed.

Based on above motivation and intuition, we present a large scale dataset of TSC in this study, and aim to explore the different levels of assessment methods regarding online users' experience. As shown in Figure 1, TSC data collected from online video websites are reorganized into a four-level structure, season-episode-comment-user, in order to capture hierarchical relation between TSC and other elements. Our full-scale TSC dataset contains nearly 900 seasons of animations, over 17K episodes and over 32 million comments generated by approximately three million users. It not only exceeds any existing TSC datasets, but also contains more abundant attributes, some of which can be regarded as labels as well, such as "tags" and "likes". By taking advantage of this dataset, we are able to study how TSC data can be used to improve user experience through state-of-art techniques in many problems. Our main contributions include:

*These authors contributed equally to this work.
†Corresponding Author

IUI 2018, March 7–11, 2018, Tokyo, Japan.

http://dx.doi.org/10.1145/3172944.3172966

[1] `http://www.acfun.cn` (accessed December 11, 2017)
[2] `https://www.bilibili.com/` (accessed December 11, 2017)
[3] `http://www.nicovideo.jp/` (accessed December 11, 2017)

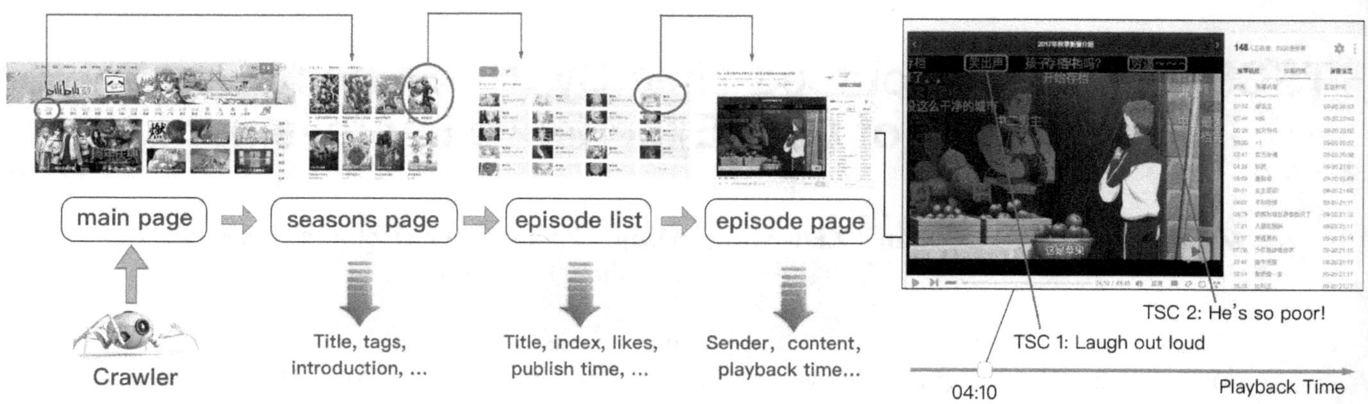

Figure 1: An overview of dataset structure and how our crawler obtained TSC data from Bilibili.com

- Presenting a large-scale TSC dataset with four-level structure and enriched self-labeled attributes collected from the most popular TSC-enabled online video website Bilibili.com through a customized web crawler.
- Formally defining four TSC-related research problems based on our dataset covering topics of high practical value such as representation learning, season tagging, season recommendation and storyline classification.
- Proposing solutions to these problems using state-of-the-art techniques and effective assessment that can be used as baselines for future study.

The rest of this paper is organized as follows. We first summarize existing work on TSC in the past few years, followed by detailed information about the datasets including how the data is obtained and basic statistics. Then, we define a series of TSC-related problems based on this dataset, followed by solutions and evaluations. Finally, the paper is concluded with discussion a summary of our work and some possible future work on this dataset.

RELATED WORK

Crowdsourcing. Large-scale data is everywhere, but usually unlabeled in real world. Crowdsourcing emerging at the right moment provides a suitable way to label data by crowdworkers [2]. For instance, ImageNet [8] and Microsoft coco [21] are two successful crowdsourced datasets in computer vision that lead to numerous research achievements. Crowdsourcing also benefits research areas like natural language processing where human linguistics annotation is expensive and time-consuming [28]. Although noise and bias can hardly be avoided during crowdsourcing process, some advanced techniques are proposed to deal with resulting problems including multiple annotations [34], incorrect annotation [36] and debiasing [7], etc. In this paper, TSC is also a type of crowdsourced data and is similarly generated by "crowdworkers" (users who watch online videos), but one major difference is that these users naturally express their reviews on videos rather than be delibrately asked to label data like real "crowdworkers".

Video Tagging. Traditional video tagging problem aims to automatically generate tags for entire videos and content-based methods have been widely studied and successfully applied [27, 31, 33]. When it comes to TSC, the first substantial research was done by Wu *et al.* [35] who aimed to extract keywords from TSCs as the tags of video shots through a temporal and personalized topic model. Yang *et al.* [40] additionally conducted thorough analysis on TSC features such as semantic relevance, real-time, interdependence and noise data. Xu *et al.* [39] extracted representative comments instead of keywords from TSC because complete sentences convey more meaningful information in terms of video content. However, datasets in these studies didn't provide tags of videos clips and the methods were only evaluated by limited number of "experts".

Popularity Prediction. Video popularity analysis is to study relation between video popularity and video-relevant features and how to leverage them to predict popularity in the future. Some traditional features include intrinsic statistical properties of popularity distributions [5], average viewing rate over some time [25] and "rich get richer" behavior [4], etc. Wu *et al.* [37] firstly investigated the co-relation between volume of TSC and popularity based on number of replays and bookmarks of videos. He *et al.* [12] then introduced concept of Herding Effect on TSC and predicted popularity by considering multiple factors including popular videos, popular TSCs, newly updated videos, uploaders influence and video quality. The work was further extended by He *et al.* [11] to detect leading TSC and predict growth of future TSC. However, characteristics of TSC comments were not fully taken into account, *e.g.* semantic meaning behind comment and user sentiment toward videos reflect upon video popularity trend.

Key Frame Extraction. Video key frame extraction is a process of presenting a summary of an entire video with a small set of representative frames [29]. Traditional methods mainly analyze image information and relation among frames [9, 22, 30]. Another research topic of TSC is to extract key frames in the video. Xian *et al.* [38] first tried extracting highlight shots from video based on temporal topics of TSC. Li *et al.* [20] similarly proposed to detect event in video using

TSC by considering sequence of user behaviors. Lv *et al.* [23] took advantage of special properties of TSC and represented TSC as semantic vectors and then split video to extract and label meaningful video clips by mapping semantic vectors to manually-defined labels. Recently, Chen *et al.* [6] made use of both video images and TSCs for key frame extraction and recommendation. However, the same issue as video tagging is that there is no labeled key frames of video available in these datasets.

These researches did a nice job on enhancement of traditional methods to solve problems like video tagging and key frame extraction using TSC information. However, as abovementioned, most datasets in these studies did not provide any ground truth like tags and key frames. The experiments could only be evaluated by a small group of so-called "experts" and hence the results may be hard to reproduce and not very convincing.

In this paper, we redefine TSC-related research problems in reference to the existing work by taking advantage of our crowdsourced self-labeled dataset. Furthermore, deep learning based methods [19] are adapted and applied to solve these problems in consideration of its tremendous success in many research areas. The breakthrough of deep learning happened in 2012 when AlexNet [17] was proposed to solve image classification on the well-known large-scale ImageNet [8]. New techniques have been invented to make deeper neural network easier to train in order to achieve better performance. For example, residual structure [10] enables neural network to be substantially deeper and works effectively in both visual and non-visual tasks. In the recent work of TSC, Chen *et al.* [6] also used convolutional neural network to analyze video frame together with TSC information. In the area of natural language processing, word embedding techniques such as Word2Vec [24] and Paragraph2Vec [18] outperforms traditional methods like topics models because they can preserve semantic meaning and syntactic relationship. Deep learning was also successfully applied to solving problems including the sentiment analysis of rotten tomato movie reviews [15] and topic categorization of news articles [16] and video caption generation [32], which are similar topics to TSC problems in this paper.

DATASET OVERVIEW AND STATISTICS DESCRIPTION

In this section, we will basically answer following questions. Where and how is TSC data collected and organized into the dataset? What properties do our dataset have as compared with previous work? What are the statistical information hidden in our dataset?

Dataset Overview

A customized web crawler is designed and implemented to collect TSC data in the animation section of Bilibili.com, the most popular TSC-enabled website in China. Firstly, the crawler starts with requesting seasons list in animation section. Information about seasons can be obtained according to the seasons list, which is in JSON format. Then, the crawler enumerates every season in the list and requests their episodes list through another API where each episode uniquely corresponds to one TSC file ID. This enables crawler to download TSC files of XML format according to their file ID. Attributes and content of every single TSC can be retrieved in these XML files and they are stored in a local database, together with season and episode details. Due to the well-functioning APIs provided by Bilibili.com, the data we obtained are almost structured and few data-cleaning works is required during the collection.

Using the crawler mentioned above, we collected two kinds of dataset in this paper for different scenarios: *BL-906* and *BL-D-64*. BL-906 is a larger-scale dataset containing 906 seasons and over 30 million TSCs collected during the period from Aug. 23rd, 2017 to Sept. 3rd, 2017. However, it is not dynamic, *i.e.* changes of TSCs with time are unable to track because the crawler only stores available TSC data when it visits corresponding episode pages. To make up this defect, BL-D-64 is another TSC dataset with dynamic property that is being collected since Sept. 30th, 2017 and will be kept updated in the future. Particularly, a modified crawler is developed to update TSC records in this dataset every two hours in order to keep all the history copies of TSCs in the dataset. The number of seasons in BL-D-64 is relatively smaller than that in BL-906 because we only track hot animations on the air where TSCs were frequently updated during the period.

Therefore, our datasets are different from all existing ones featured by four following characteristics.

1. *Hierarchical Data Structure.* This dataset consists of data organized as a four-level structure (season-episode-comment-user) compared with traditional two-level structure (episode-comment).
2. *Large Data Scale.* This dataset has larger scale than any previous ones in terms of the number of episodes (videos), TSCs, users, etc.
3. *Multi-Dimensional Data Attributes.* This dataset contains more abundant attributes such as season tags, episode coins (likes) and user history that can be regarded as labels for supervised learning problems.
4. *Dynamic Data Update.* This dataset is "dynamic" since it records variation of TSCs for each episode as time elapses while all previous datasets are "static" that only save a single copy at a certain timestamp.

Table 1 illustrates the scale of the dataset and its comparison with previous datasets. In this paper, our work is mainly based on BL-906. The usage of the other dataset will be discussed in the last section. Both datasets are accessible from `https://github.com/Viscount/IUI-Paper`.

Statistics Description

Statistical results of the dataset will be described according to four levels: seasons, episodes, comments and users.

Season-level Statistics

There are 906 seasons in total, all of them are valid, *i.e.* these seasons are associated with a unique set of episodes and TSCs in the dataset. Meanwhile, in a season, there are two useful information: 1) a short passage of animation introduction, and 2) a set of tags of animation styles. There are totally

	BL-906	BL-D-64	Paper[35]	Paper[23]	Paper[12]	Paper[11]	Paper[39]	Paper[6]	Paper[40]
Source	bilibili	bilibili	acfun.tv	bilibili	acfun.tv	acfun.tv	iqiyi	bilibili	acfun.tv
# Seasons	**906**	64	None	None	None	None	2	None	None
# Videos	**17,870**	716	16,414	Unknown	3,623	6,506	6	7166	120
# TSCs	**32,949,297**	7,413,517(i)	1,103,884	133,250	60,956	1,704,930	234,003	11,842,166	227,780
# Users	**3,240,478**	1,482,120	382,752	Unknown	278,520	320,000	Unknown	1,133,750	Unknown
Tags	Yes	Yes	No	No	No	No	No	No	Yes(ii)
Likes	Yes	Yes	No	No	Yes	No	No	No	No
Dynamic	No	**Yes**	No	No	No	No(iii)	No	No	No

(i) The count comes from the copy of BL-D-64 by Dec. 31, 2017.
(ii) It contains videos from only three categories: music, sport and movie.
(iii) It only shows number of TSCs varying with time.

Table 1: Brief summary of this dataset and comparison with previous datasets.

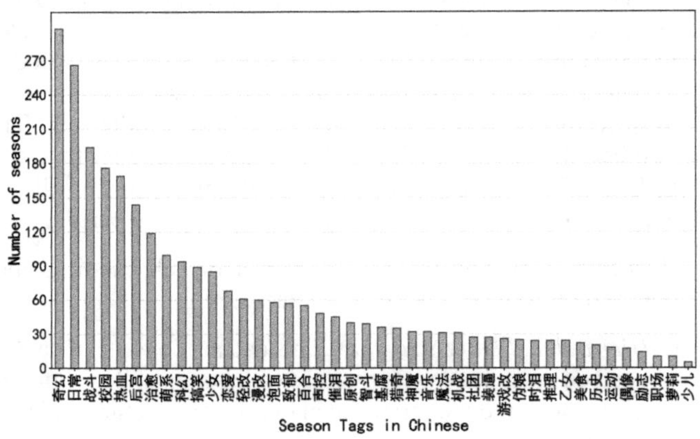

Figure 2: Distribution of number of seasons per tag

43 different tags and each season is assigned around 3 tags on average. The distribution of number of seasons per tag is shown in figure 2.

Episode-level Statistics

There are 17,870 episodes in total and average 19.88 episodes per season. Each season includes one or more episodes and the distribution of number of episodes per season is shown in figure 3a. Aggregated video length of all episodes is 47,835 hours and over 97.63% episodes have video length less than 30 minutes, so only these episodes are considered in this section and its distribution is shown in figure 3b. One useful attribute of episode is "coins" representing how many users like the episode and distribution of ratio of coins within episode is shown in figure 3c.

Comment-level Statistics

There are 32,949,297 TSCs in total, average 36,651 TSCs per season and average 1,857 TSCs per episode. Distribution of number of TSCs per season, number of TSCs along with episode index and number of TSCs along with video playback time are respectively shown in figures 4a, 4b, 4c.

Generally, TSC is featured by following properties:

- *Succinctness.* On average each TSC has 8.71 Chinese characters which is even shorter than Sina Weibo (20 Chinese characters) and Tweet length (30 characters). The distribution of various TSC length is shown in figure 4d. This is because audiences prefer to express their feelings with a few words when watching videos. Otherwise, longer comment may have a negative impact on audience watching experience, for example, to fail to fast read long comments without pausing video.
- *Slanginess.* TSC is usually made of Internet buzzwords among young audiences. Top 40 frequent segmented TSC words are shown in figure 4e. For example, the most frequent word is "233" which is actually not a Chinese word, but a textual expression representing "laugh". Meanwhile, these phrases are not of fixed length because there could be lots of trailing "3"s, and hence it is critical to separately preprocess TSC.
- *Herding Effect.* A user's new comment will be affected by existing comments within a time range. Herding effect on TSC has been deeply studied in [12], so detail will not be covered in this paper.

User-level Statistics

Each TSC is associated with a sender ID that is regarded as visible "audience" or "user" in this paper. We will ignore those who watched the video but didn't leave a comment. We also assume one user is somehow interested in the video if and only if he/she has published at least one TSC for the video. In this dataset, there are totally 3,240,478 such users, the average number of TSCs per user published is 10.17 and average number of seasons watched by a user is 2.66.

TSC-RELATED PROBLEMS

In this section, we formally define four TSC-related research problems to explore user experience improvement by exploiting features and patterns inside time-sync comments. These problems include TSC-based representation learning, season multi-tagging, season recommendation and storyline classification. The significance of selected problems mainly lies in two aspects below:

- Problems like representation learning are the essential researches in machine learning area[3]. Moreover, problems like tagging and recommendation are always hot topics in TSC-related studies.

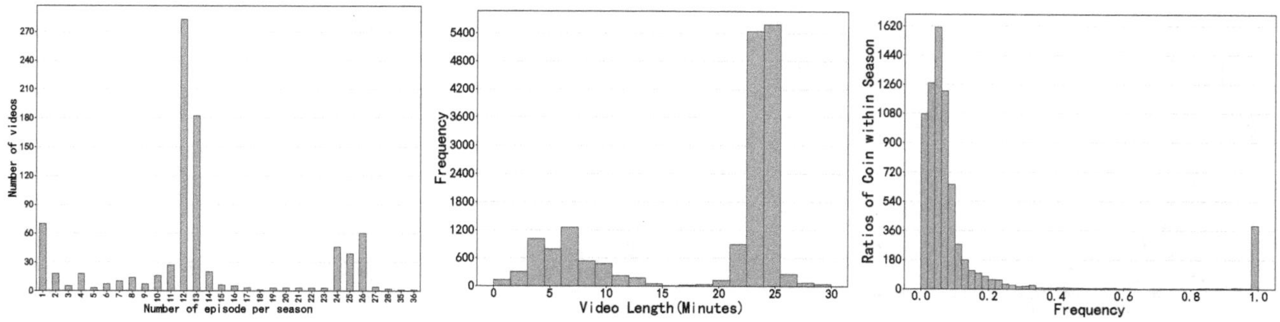

(a) Distribution of number of episodes per season (limited to # episodes ≤40) (b) Distribution of video length per season (limited to length ≤30 minutes) (c) Distribution of ratio of coins within season

Figure 3: Episode-level Statistics

- All the problems are related with a certain business scenario in real world. TSC-enabled online video websites like Bilibili.com will benefit from breakthroughs in the research of these problems.

Formally, the four-level structure of the dataset $\mathbb{D}$ is composed of $\mathbb{S},\mathbb{E},\mathbb{C},\mathbb{U}$, four universal sets respectively representing seasons, episodes (videos), TSCs and users. Basically, each season contains a set of episodes, each episode contains a set of TSCs, and each user can publish a set of TSCs. A TSC $c \in \mathbb{C}$ is defined as a quadruple, i.e. $c \doteq (e,r,t,u)$ where $e \in \mathbb{E}$ is the episode the TSC associated with, r is textual content of user review, t is playback time of TSC in the video, and $u \in \mathbb{U}$ is the one who published the TSC. Let $C_{\cdot|u} \doteq \{c \in \mathbb{C} | c.u = u\}$ be the set of TSCs published by user u, $C_{\cdot|e} \doteq \{c \in \mathbb{C} | c.e = e\}$ be the set of TSCs associated with episode e and $C_{\cdot|s} \doteq \{c \in \mathbb{C} | c.e \in s\}$ be the set of TSCs associated with season s. Let $E_{\cdot|u} \doteq \{e \in \mathbb{E} | \exists c \in \mathbb{C}, c.e = e, c.u = u\}$ to be the set of episodes where user u published any TSCs and $E_{\cdot|s} \doteq \{e \in \mathbb{E} | e \in s\}$ be the set of episodes associated with season s. Let $S_{\cdot|u} \doteq \{s \in \mathbb{S} | \exists c \in \mathbb{C}, c.e \in s, c.u = u\}$ be the set of seasons where user u has published at least one TSC in any episode that belongs to the season.

TSC-based Representation Learning Problem

Scenario Description. One practical problem is how to represent as a vector a set of TSCs associated with an episode or a user? Raw TSC data can hardly be used directly for further analysis in tagging, population detection, key frame extraction, etc, due to special properties of TSC including succinctness and slanginess. Meanwhile, temporal relation between TSCs should be captured in vector representation because the it reflects upon influential factors including previous TSCs and recent video frames. The problem aims to automatically learn feature representation of TSC set and capture abovementioned properties.

Problem Definition. Given any TSC set $C \in \mathbb{C}$, the goal is to represent C as a vector $\mathbf{C}$ such that

1. Given length $d \in \mathbb{N}^+$, $|\mathbf{C}| = d$.
2. Given some similarity measure ρ and error ε, if C is similar to another TSC set C', then their vector representations are also similar, i.e. $\rho(\mathbf{C},\mathbf{C}') < \varepsilon$.
3. $\forall c_i, c_j \in C$, if timestamp t_i of c_i and timestamp t_j of c_j are swapped leading to a new TSC set C', i.e. $c_i = (e_i, r_i, t_j, u_i), c_j = (e_j, r_j, t_i, u_j) \in C'$, then $\mathbf{C} \neq \mathbf{C}'$.

The first constraint ensures that any TSC set C can be mapped to a vector of the same length d. The second constraint states that any vectorized TSC sets will remain similarity under some similarity measure. The third constraint means that temporal relation of every single TSC matters in $\mathbf{C}$. A special case is when $|C| = 1$, the goal is to vectorize a single TSC.

Season Multi-Tagging Problem

Scenario Description. In Bilibili.com, most seasons are assigned with predefined labels based on genre and plot, hence these tags can assist users in searching seasons easily by keywords. For example, the well-known animation *Neon Genesis Evangelion* is tagged with "Sci-Fi", "Action" and "Robot Fight". However, one issue is that all these tags are labeled manually by editors and it takes much time and effort to repeat on thousands of seasons. According to our observation, TSCs vary from each other according to different season tags, so it is possible to infer tags for a new season from its TSC data automatically.

Problem Definition. Given a set of m training examples $\{(x_1,y_1),\ldots,(x_m,y_m)\}$ drawn from an unknown distribution D, the goal is to learn a classifier $f : X \to Y$ with maximum classification score. $x_i \doteq C_{\cdot|s_i}$ is the TSC set associated with season s_i, $y_i \in \{0,1\}^k$ where k is number of tags, X is the space of TSC set $\mathbb{C}$ and Y is the space of binary vector of size k. Classification score here is defined as

$$s_C(f,D) = \sum_{(x_i,y_i)\in X\times Y} D(x_i,y_i) \sum_{j=1}^{k} \mathbb{1}(y_i^j, f_i^j(x)) \quad (1)$$

Season Recommendation Problem

Scenario Description. Recommendation is becoming a fundamental function for any content-sharing website in recent years and it can help users autonomously explore the content in a website with better experience. For example, hundreds

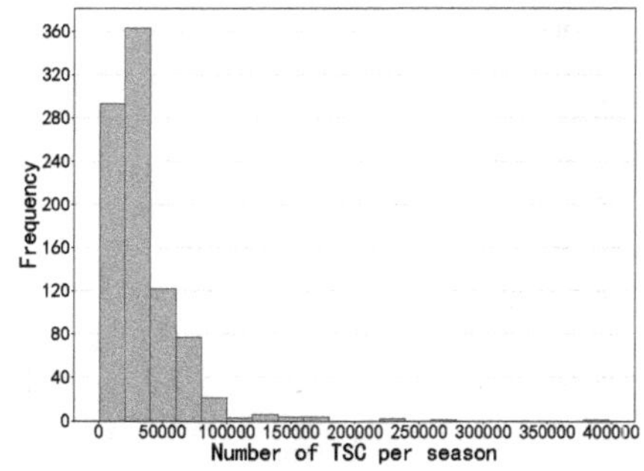

(a) Distribution of number of TSCs per season

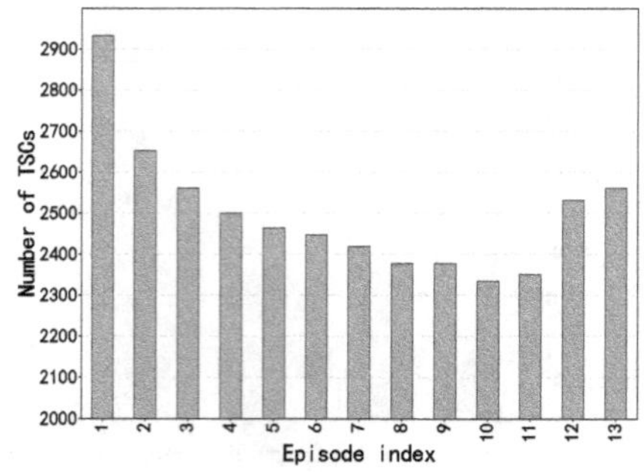

(b) Number of TSCs changing with episodes (limited to the seasons of length 12 or 13)

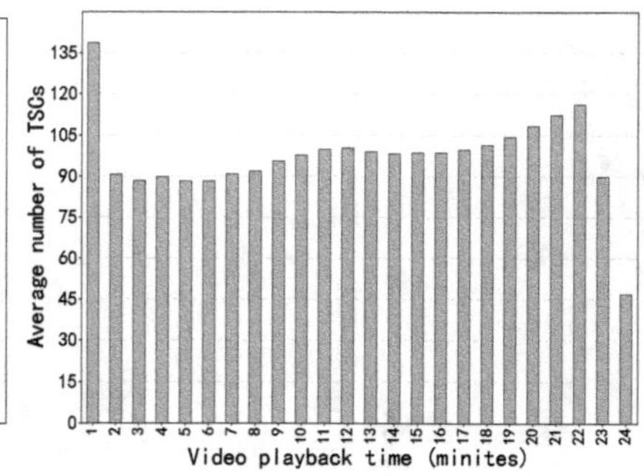

(c) Number of TSCs changing with video playback time (limited to 24-min length)

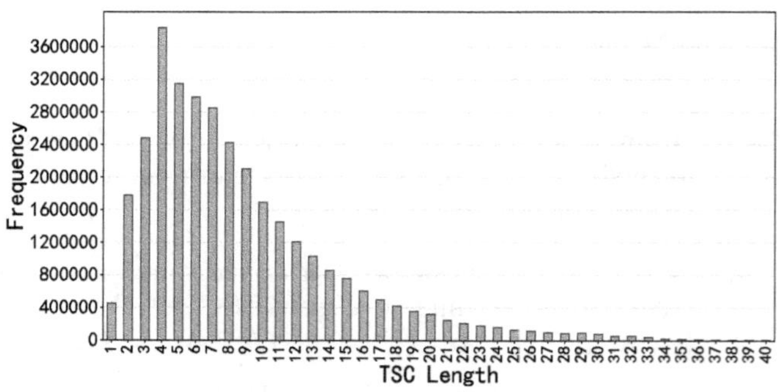

(d) Distribution of TSC length (limited to length ≤ 40)

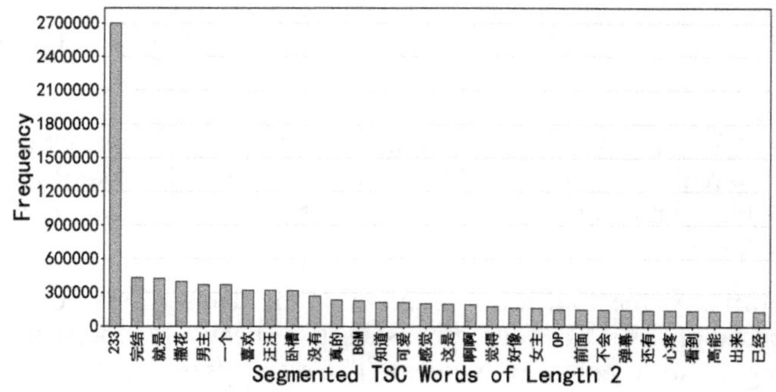

(e) Frequency of segmented TSC words of two Chinese characters (Top 30)

Figure 4: Comment-level Statistics

of animations will be newly released every quarter and users have to watch many reviews before determining which animation to follow. Recommender system can provide a list of new animation seasons that may interest users based on their preference and history. Most existing recommender systems exploit ratings and comments to infer user preferences through collaborative filtering or content-based approach. For TSC-based online video website, larger-scale TSC reviews provide rich detail on video contents, especially overall audience reaction, and hence can be taken into consideration to better improve the quality of recommender system.

Problem Definition. Given a set of n users $U = \{u_1, .., u_n\} \subseteq \mathbb{U}$ and an associated season set $S_{\cdot|u_i}$ for each $u_i \in U$, the goal is to learn a function $f : \mathbb{U} \times \mathbb{S} \to \{0, 1\}$ with maximum recommendation score. In this setting, each u_i is attached with TSC history $C_{\cdot|u_i} \subseteq \mathbb{C}$ that can be taken into consideration by f. Recommendation score is defined as

$$s_R(f, \ell) = \sum_{u \in U} \sum_{s \in \mathbb{S}} \ell(s, f(u, s)|S_{\cdot|u}) \tag{2}$$

where U is the space of user set, S is the space of season set, and $\ell(\cdot)$ is some score function to measure to what level season s interests user u according to history $S_{\cdot|u}$.

Storyline Classification Problem

Scenario Description. According to Freytag's pyramid, the storyline of a drama can be divided into five parts: exposition, rising action, climax, falling action, and denouement [14]. Similarly, every season composes of a complete storyline and each episode of the season belongs to one of these five parts. For example, there are 26 episodes in the well-known animation *Neon Genesis Evangelion*. Episode 24 is considered as a climax because of the depiction of final battle while episode 4 is considered as exposition, for the content in this episode is just Shinji's (lead character) daily life. To simplify the problem, we only consider two aggregated parts: whether one episode is climax or not within a season. From our observation, the content of each episode is highly correlated to user feedback such as TSCs and "likes" that is equivalent to "coins" in our dataset. A very practical problem that can we predict whether an episode is climax or not based on history of associated TSCs?

Problem Definition. Given a set of m seasons $S = \{s_1, .., s_m\}$ where each season s_i is associated with an ordered set of episodes $E_{\cdot|s_i}$ and an ordered set of labels $y_i \in \{0, 1\}^{|E_{\cdot|s_i}|}$ indicating whether an episode $e_{ij} \in E_{\cdot|s_i}$ is climax or not within the season s_i, the goal is to learn a function $f : \mathbb{E} \to \{0, 1\}$ with maximum storyline classification score s_{SC}. In this setting, f can takes as input all episodes e' prior to the current episode e and their associated TSC sets $C_{\cdot|e'}$ and outputs predicts whether e is climax or not. Storyline classification score is defined as

$$s_{SC}(f) = \sum_{s \in \mathbb{S}} \sum_{e_i \in E_{\cdot|s}} \mathbb{1}(f(e_i), y_i) \tag{3}$$

METHODS AND EVALUATIONS

In this section, we will solve four problems by adapting state-of-the-art methods and then evaluate the effectiveness of TSC in improving performance. The pipeline of the complete procedure from data crawling and preprocessing to problem solving can be divided into four steps. First, we crawl TSC data from Bilibili and save the four-level raw data into a relational database. Second, we perform a thorough Chinese textual preprocessing on raw TSC data. This includes removing punctuation, auxiliary word and emojis, replacing slangs with standard words through regular expression, for example substituting "233333" to "233", and splitting every comment into Chinese words. Third, we conduct basic statistics on TSCs to find interesting properties just as shown in the previous section. Finally, we try to solve four selected problems as follows.

Representation Learning Problem

Method. We mainly adapt *paragraph2vec* [18] to the TSC representation learning problem because it can learn continuous vector representation of fixed length as well as take two important factors into account as known as word order in the document and semantic meaning of each word. Analogous to documents and words, we can regard TSC set of an episode as document since temporal dependency of TSC plays as an important role as order of words. Nevertheless, there are two questions worth thinking about.

- What is the granularity in the dataset, *i.e.* taking each TSC as a whole or splitting TSC into words?
- How to choose suitable vector dimension for TSC representation?

For the first question, we prefer to split TSC into words and reconstruct all split words in a TSC set as a "document" in *paragraph2vec*. This is based on following observation with respect to TSC according to our statistical findings in the paper. Although TSC itself is short, taking TSC as a whole may lose semantic information. Some single word in TSC occurs frequently, but they usually mixed with other less-frequent words. For example, let's assume there are two comments r_1 and r_2 and both of them contains some top frequent word w_2, *e.g.* "233". Then, it is most likely that r_1 and r_2 have similar semantic meaning, *e.g.* laughing or interesting video clip. It implies that if we regard r_1 and r_2 as a whole, *paragraph2vec* will treat them as two different "words" and fail to capture similarity between them from context. Therefore, it is better to split each TSC into separate words and treat each of them as a "word" in document. For the second question, in reference to parameter setting in *GloVe* [26], vector size is typically selected from 100 to 300 because dimension less than 100 will lead to very poor performance and dimension greater than 300 makes no significant improvement. We conducted a preliminary experiment on one-vs-42 binary classification in order to evaluate four different choices of vector dimension for TSC representation, *i.e.* , $d = 100, 200, 256, 300$. The result showed that classification performance of $d = 100$ was the worst and other three settings make no big difference in performance. As a rule of thumb, we chose $d = 200$ as the global setting for vector dimension in *paragraph2vec* in consideration of both performance and simplicity.We will discuss evaluation of TSC vector representation in detail through season tag classification problem in the next section.

Season Multi-Tagging Problem

Method. Since each season can be assigned multiple tags, this is actually a multi-label classification problem and we developed two methods to deal with it. The first one is to split the large problem into K binary classification subproblems. For each subproblem, we train a shallow neural network with consistent structure. The input is 200-dimensional encoded vector, followed by three fully-connected layers of size 256, 128 128, and each layer is also connected with one Relu layer and one dropout layer. The advantage of this one-vs-all mode is that each subproblem is very easy to solve even if the labels are imbalanced. However when K is large, it will take lots of time and memory to train and store K binary classifier so it's not suitable for large scale case. The second approach is to create only one deeper neural network to solve this entire problem, and this turns out to be a hard problem. We are inspired by residual network[10] and adapt it to this problem. As shown in figure 5, the input also takes 200-dimensional encoded vector, followed by three residual substructures of size 256, 512, 256. Each residual substructure takes $\mathbf{x}_{in}$ as input and output $\mathbf{x}_{out}$ of the same size:

$$h_1 = p(\sigma(W_1 \mathbf{x}_{in})) \quad (4)$$

$$h_2 = p(\sigma(W_2 h_1)) \quad (5)$$

$$\mathbf{x}_{out} = p(\sigma(W_3 h_2 \oplus h_1)) \quad (6)$$

where $\sigma(\cdot)$ is Relu activation layer, p is dropout layer with keeping probability 0.1, and $\oplus$ is elementwise addition.

The output of the network is a fully connected layer of size K, the same size as number of total tags. Since labels are mostly imbalanced, a modified weighted cross entropy loss is used here. Assume the output of instance $\mathbf{x}_i$ is $\hat{\mathbf{y}}_i$ and the real label vector is $\mathbf{y}_i$, the loss is computed as weighted cross entropy:

$$\ell_i^k = -\mathbf{y}_i^k \log(\sigma(\hat{\mathbf{y}}_i^k)) - (1 - \mathbf{y}_i^k) \log(1 - \sigma(\hat{\mathbf{y}}_i^k)) \quad (7)$$

$$L(\mathbf{y}, \hat{\mathbf{y}}) = \frac{1}{mK} \sum_{i=1}^{m} \sum_{k=1}^{K} w_k \ell_i^k \quad (8)$$

where ℓ_i^k is the cross entropy loss of class k of instance i, m is sample size and w_k is the weight for class k:

$$u_k = \log\left(\frac{1}{m} \sum_{i=1}^{m} \mathbb{1}[\hat{\mathbf{y}}_i^k = 1]\right) \quad (9)$$

$$w_k = 2 - u_k / \min_k\{u_k\} \quad (10)$$

Evaluation. We conduct two sets of experiments to interpret both effectiveness of representation learning using *paragraph2vec* and performance of our method for all-in-one multi-label classification. All models are implemented and tested in Tensorflow [1]. Specifically, minibatch size is 128, learning rate is 10^{-4} and will decay by 5% every 5000 steps, and solver is Adam optimizer.

First, we apply shallow net to three different encoding of textual information of season or episode for one-vs-all binary classifications (42 classes), which is used to reflect upon the usefulness of representation method working for episode encoding. In detail, "Intro2vec" method only utilizes season introduction to encode it into vector through *paragraph2vec*.

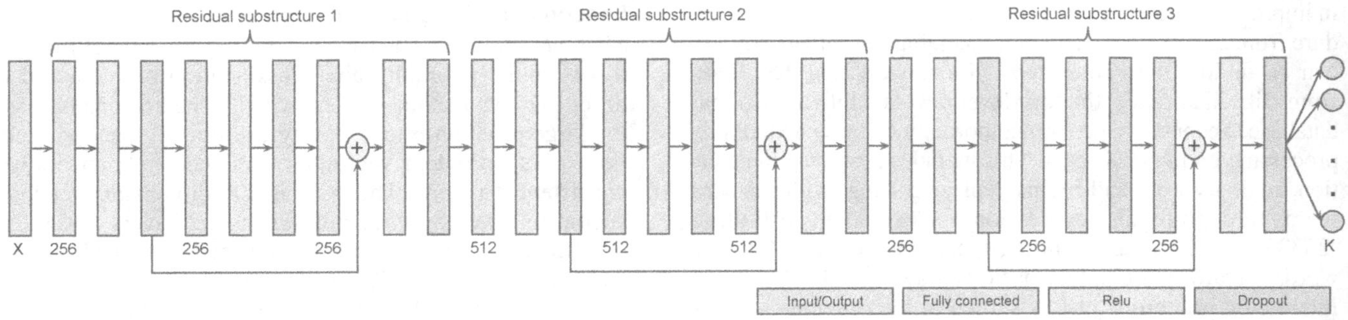

Figure 5: Deep neural network structure for multi-tagging problem

One-vs-42 binary classification (ShallowNet)				
	Accuracy	Precision	Recall	F1 Score
Intro2vec	0.9288	0.1591	0.0511	0.7735
MeanW2v	0.9691	0.8660	0.5807	0.6952
TSC2vec	**0.9820**	**0.9262**	**0.7522**	**0.8302**
42-in-one multi-label classification				
	Accuracy	Precision	Recall	F1 Score
ShallowNet	0.9365	**0.6110**	0.4538	0.5208
DeepNet	**0.9382**	0.6107	**0.5138**	**0.5581**

Table 2: Experiment results of multi-tagging problem

"MeanW2v" method takes TSC set of each episode and encodes it using traditional *word2vec*. "TSC2vec" method that is proposed in this paper also takes TSC set of episode but encodes through *paragraph2vec*. The vector dimension for three cases keeps 200 all the time. Then, we use the shallow network to train 42 binary classifiers mapping these vectors to tags. The entire results of 42 classifiers are shown in figure 6. It is obvious that "TSC2vec" outperforms the other two methods in all metrics evaluation (accuracy, precision, recall, F1). Therefore, we can conclude that TSC data is really useful in representing episode or season.

Second, we compare the proposed deep net to the same shallow net in all-in-one multi-label classification problem. As shown in table 2, the result implies that this is a relatively harder problem than binary classification since the shallow net performs much worse than the previous case. Although our deep net performs pretty same as shallow net in terms of accuracy and precision, it is much better in recall and F1 score. This implies that the model can predict more correct tags among ground truth and it's more useful in practical scenarios.

Season Recommendation Problem

Method. In season recommendation problem, four solutions are proposed, including collaborative filtering, content-based recommendation as well as two methods using TSC data.

- **Collaborative Filtering** Collaborative filtering is a traditional method in recommendation problems. We prefer user-based collaborative filtering in this problem, for it's easier to get users' watching history than to compute the similarity between two seasons. For a target user u, we calculate a score to estimate how a certain season s interests him, defined as

$$score_{u,s} = \sum_{n \in N} \sum_{s \in \mathbb{S}} sim(u,n) * S_{s|n} \quad (11)$$

where N is the space of u's neighbors who have watched at least one same season as u. $sim(u,n)$ is the cosine similarity between u and n, and $S_{s|n}$ is the watching history of neighbor n on season s. Finally, all the scores are normalized into [0,1], a threshold w is set and seasons are recommend to the target user if their score is greater than w.

- **Content-based Method** In content-based method, recommending an item is based upon a description of the item and profiles of users' interests. In this case, we extract semantic features of a season by applying Paragraph2vec model on its introduction text. Seasons are represented by a 200-dimension vector. For each user, a classifier is trained to represent his profile of interest. Finally, we can get the results through his classier that whether a certain season is recommended to this user.

- **Season-level TSC-based Method** In our proposal, we use TSC data instead of season's introduction to train the Paragraph2vec model. To bridge from a single TSC review to a representation of a season, we firstly combine all the TSCs in this season into one document order by episode index and their position in video playback time. A corresponding vector representation for every season can be calculated by Paragraph2vec model, which is also a n-dimension vector (n=200 as mentioned in content-based method). After that, we learn a classifier to represent every user with season representation vector and his watching history, then predict the label of new seasons through this classifier.

- **Episode-level TSC-based Method** The effectiveness of classifier training in season-level method may be affected by the limited number of seasons (only 906 seasons). Thus we expand the season-level method to episode-level (17870 episodes in dataset). That is, we apply Paragraph2vec model with combined TSCs in one episode, and get vector representation for every episode through this model. We feed these episode vector representations for classifier training instead of season vector representations.

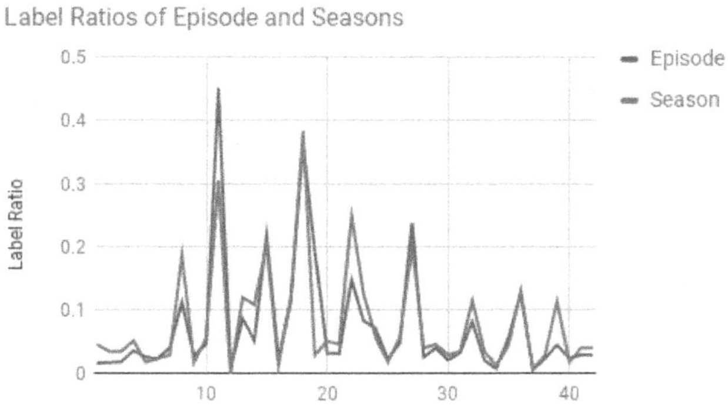

(a) Label ratio

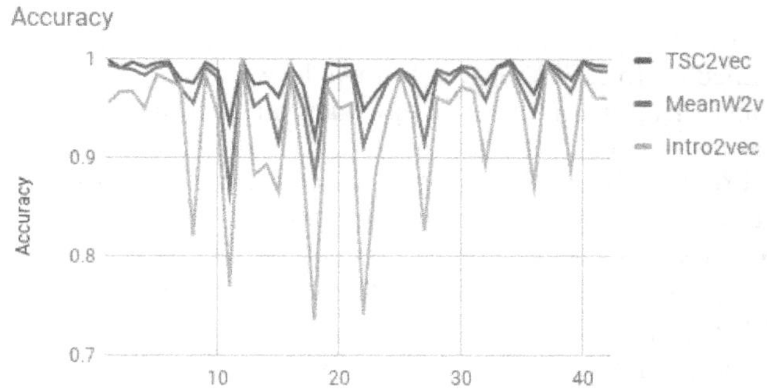

(b) Accuracy

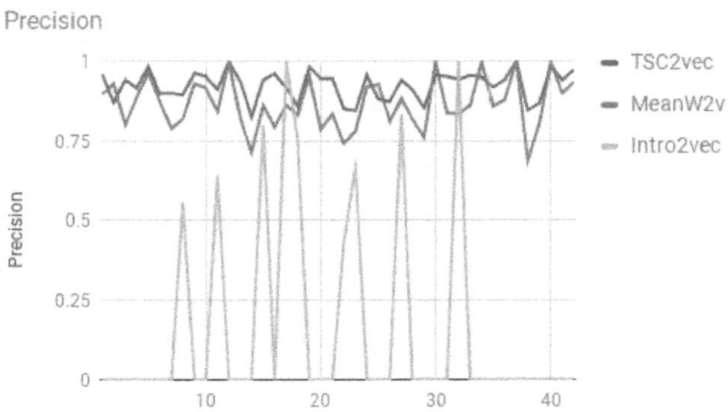

(c) Precision

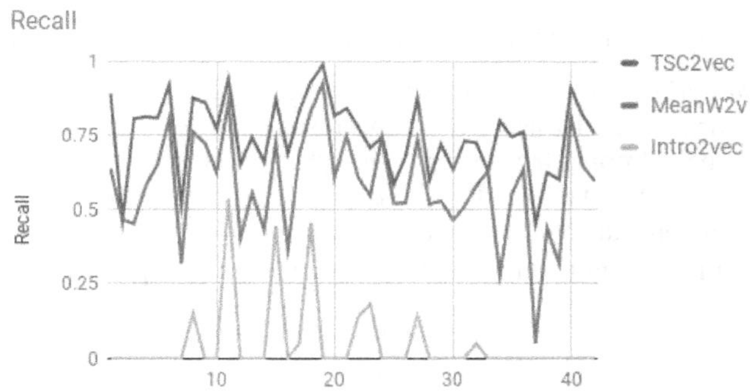

(d) Recall

Figure 6: Experimental results for 42 binary classification subproblems

	Method	Accuracy	Precision	Recall
Naive Bayes	*A*	0.9385	0.5489	0.6197
	B	0.6112	0.1199	0.6459
	C	**0.9593**	**0.7134**	0.3076
	D	0.9210	0.5086	**0.6579**
Neural Network	*A*	0.9385	0.5489	**0.6197**
	B	0.9326	0.3359	0.2577
	C	0.9577	0.6976	0.3030
	D	**0.9655**	**0.7178**	0.4353

Table 3: Experimental results on season recommendation problem. *A*,*B*,*C*,*D* represent Collaborative Filtering, Content-based Method, Season-level TSC-based Method, Episode-level TSC-based Method.

Evaluation. To evaluate forementioned solutions in season recommendation problem, a series of experiments are conducted on current dataset. At first, 2717 users who sent over 500 TSCs in our dataset are selected to avoid cold start problem. For every user, his watching history on 906 seasons is represented as a 906-dimension vector with 0/1 label. 80% of them are selected as a train set, and the other 20% are test set. There are some parameters configuration and model selection issues here. In our experiments, *w* in Collaborative Filtering method is set to 0.5. As for classifier selection, we chose two different models: Naive Bayes and Neural Network. Specifically, for Neural Network, learning rate is 10^{-5}, hidden-layer size is 256, and solver is L-BFGS.

Three typical metrics in classification problems are used to evaluate the effectiveness of methods: accuracy, precision and recall rate. We found that the partition of train set and test set has an important effect on the result. Thus, we choose top 500 users on precision to evaluate the overall effectiveness of methods. The result of experiments are shown in Table 3. Compared with two methods without TSC data, season-level and episode-level TSC-based methods archive higher precision and accuracy, especially when using Neural Network as classifier. We also tried other models, such as SVM and decision tree, but the effectiveness of them are far worse then these two models. However, which is the best classifier model in this problem still needs further study.

Storyline Classification Problem

Method. According to Herding Effect, highlight of current episode depends not only on current TSC set, but also is highly relevant to previous ones. In order to capture such history dependency, we introduce LSTM [13] to solving the problem of predicting whether current episode is highlight or not within some given season. The model takes as input a sequence of TSC sets of episodes, followed by two fully connected layers of sizes 256, 128 respectively and each of them is connected with Relu activation layer and dropout layer with 0.3 keeping probability. An LSTM layer is then added to the network of cell size 128 connected with another dropout layer with 0.3 keeping probability. A final output layer of size two is connected to LSTM layer, followed by cross entropy loss. Considering that number of episodes varies from seasons to seasons, we enable the network to take dynamic size of inputs and outputs by feeding with a prior variable indicating the sequence length. We call this method All-in TSC History Dependent Model (*ATHDM*) because it incorporates cross entropy loss of every single episode within a season. Suppose y_i^j is the climax label for episode i in season j and $\hat{y}_i^j$ is the predicted label, the loss function $L(\mathbf{y},\hat{\mathbf{y}})$ is defined as:

$$L(\mathbf{y},\hat{\mathbf{y}}) = \frac{1}{|S|}\sum_{j=1}^{|S|}\sum_{i=1}\ell(\hat{y}_i^j, y_i^j) \tag{12}$$

where $|S|$ is number of seasons and $\ell(\cdot)$ is cross entropy loss.

Evaluation. We first clarify how climax label can be obtained in our dataset. Basically, climax episode can be measured by number of coins from users. However one issue is that it is infeasible to set a fixed threshold for all episodes because number of coins differs from season to season. Therefore, a variant of ratio of coin is introduced as label y_i^j in this experiment:

$$y_i^j = \mathbb{1}\left[\frac{n_i^j}{\sum_{i=1}^{L_j} n_i^j} > \theta\right] \tag{13}$$

where L_j is number of episodes in season j, n_i^j is number of coins in episode i and θ is the global threshold indicating climax episode in a season. In reference to Figure 3c, θ is set to 0.1, 0.2 and 0.3 in order to verify robustness of our model under different settings of climax labels.

In terms of hyperparameters setting of *ATHDM*, batch size is 64, learning rate is 10^{-5} and decays by 10% every 5000 steps, and total number of steps is 10^5. We compare the method to a basic model named TSC History Independent Model (*THIM*), which treats each episode independently and predicts binary label $\hat{y}_i^j$ of current episode without incorporating history TSC of previous episodes. Since it is similar problem of binary classification, we use the same neural network as tagging problem except hyperparameters setting, *i.e.* batch size=32, learning rate=10^{-5} and number of steps=10^5. The results are shown in table 4, where we can find that *ATHDM* significantly outperforms *THIM* in terms of accuracy, precision, recall and F1 score. Thus we can draw conclusion that highlight of an episode depends both on current TSC content and all previous history.

CONCLUSION AND FUTURE WORK

In this paper, we presented a new crowdsourced TSC dataset with larger scale and richer attributes compared with existing work. In order to improve user experience on online video websites, we explored TSC-related problems by exploiting special characteristics and patterns behind TSCs. Specifically, four research problems were formally defined and deep learning techniques were adapted and applied to these problems. Unlike most previous researches where experiments were manually evaluated by a very small group of "experts", all methods in this paper were evaluated through labels in the dataset. The results showed that TSC-enhanced methods perform better than the methods based on the traditional way, and can be used as a baseline for further studies. One limitation of the dataset is that it only contains textual data but no visual information like video frames due to copyright restriction of video websites.

θ	Method	Accuracy	Precision	Recall	F1
0.1	THIM	0.8692	0.6034	0.5412	0.5706
	ATHDM	**0.9023**	**0.7317**	**0.6186**	**0.6704**
0.2	THIM	0.9512	0.5172	0.2500	0.3371
	ATHDM	**0.9536**	**0.5500**	**0.3667**	**0.4400**
0.3	THIM	0.9743	0.1667	0.0370	0.0606
	ATHDM	**0.9768**	**0.4000**	**0.0741**	**0.1250**

Table 4: Experimental results on storyline classification problem with $\theta = 0.1, 0.2, 0.3$.

In the future, our work can be extended in two directions. The first track is to develop more effective algorithms to solve four proposed problems by incorporating better TSC features and additional visual information like video frames. For example, the sequential character of TSC can be considered in the model for season recommendation problem. The second track is to explore more research problems by using characteristics in this dataset. Some possible problems are listed below.

- *TSC Denoising Problem.* In order to prevent overwhelming TSC displayed on a video screen, the total capacity of TSCs of a video is fixed and dependent on video length. Therefore, TSCs are now being regularly cleaned by human (we have confirmed with Bilibili), which definitely costs lots of time and effort. It would be very useful to solve this denoising problem by learning a filter that can clean TSCs automatically. The filter observes variation of TSCs at different timestamps and learns latent rules similar to what human does.

- *TSC Generation Problem.* A common process for a user to publish a TSC is as follows. When the user watched some attractive shots or read some interesting TSCs by others, he/she is probably willing to write some comments and then publishes as TSC. Since the content is largely influenced by existing TSCs according to Herding Effect, is it possible to provide an intelligent user interface that is able to automatically generate some comments based on current video content for users to choose from?

- *Season Popularity Prediction Problem.* Episode of a season is usually released every week and users will leave feedback like TSCs accordingly. One interesting problem is to predict how popular a season will be by analyzing the trend of popularity among all previous episodes. Unlike some existing work that only studied the amount of likes or comments, our dataset tracks dynamic TSC sets of each episode at different timestamps, so it is possible to analyze season popularity through variation of TSCs of each episode.

ACKNOWLEDGEMENT

This study was funded by the National Natural Science Foundation of China (Grant No.61702372) and the Youth Science and Technology Foundation of Shanghai, China (NO.15YF1412600).

REFERENCES

1. Martín Abadi, Ashish Agarwal, Paul Barham, Eugene Brevdo, Zhifeng Chen, Craig Citro, Greg S Corrado, Andy Davis, Jeffrey Dean, Matthieu Devin, and others. 2016. Tensorflow: Large-scale machine learning on heterogeneous distributed systems. *arXiv preprint arXiv:1603.04467* (2016).
2. Daniel Archambault, Helen Purchase, and Tobias Hoßfeld. 2015. *Evaluation in the Crowd*. Springer.
3. Yoshua Bengio, Aaron Courville, and Pascal Vincent. 2013. *Representation Learning: A Review and New Perspectives*. IEEE Computer Society. 1798–1828 pages.
4. Youmna Borghol, Sebastien Ardon, Niklas Carlsson, Derek Eager, and Anirban Mahanti. 2012. The untold story of the clones: content-agnostic factors that impact YouTube video popularity. In *Proceedings of the 18th ACM SIGKDD international conference on Knowledge discovery and data mining*. ACM, 1186–1194.
5. Meeyoung Cha, Haewoon Kwak, Pablo Rodriguez, Yong-Yeol Ahn, and Sue Moon. 2009. Analyzing the video popularity characteristics of large-scale user generated content systems. *IEEE/ACM Transactions on Networking (TON)* 17, 5 (2009), 1357–1370.
6. Xu Chen, Yongfeng Zhang, Qingyao Ai, Hongteng Xu, Junchi Yan, and Zheng Qin. 2017. Personalized key frame recommendation. In *Proceedings of the 40th International ACM SIGIR Conference on Research and Development in Information Retrieval*. ACM, 315–324.
7. Abhimanyu Das, Sreenivas Gollapudi, Rina Panigrahy, and Mahyar Salek. 2013. Debiasing social wisdom. In *Proceedings of the 19th ACM SIGKDD international conference on Knowledge discovery and data mining*. ACM, 500–508.
8. Jia Deng, Wei Dong, Richard Socher, Li-Jia Li, Kai Li, and Li Fei-Fei. 2009. Imagenet: A large-scale hierarchical image database. In *IEEE Conference on Computer Vision and Pattern Recognition, 2009*. IEEE, 248–255.
9. Yihong Gong and Xin Liu. 2000. Video summarization using singular value decomposition. In *Computer Vision and Pattern Recognition, 2000. Proceedings. IEEE Conference on*, Vol. 2. IEEE, 174–180.
10. Kaiming He, Xiangyu Zhang, Shaoqing Ren, and Jian Sun. 2016b. Deep residual learning for image recognition. In *Proceedings of the IEEE conference on computer vision and pattern recognition*. 770–778.
11. Ming He, Yong Ge, Enhong Chen, Qi Liu, and Xuesong Wang. 2017. Exploring the Emerging Type of Comment for Online Videos: DanMu. *ACM Transactions on the Web (TWEB)* 12, 1 (2017), 1.
12. Ming He, Yong Ge, Le Wu, Enhong Chen, and Chang Tan. 2016a. Predicting the Popularity of DanMu-enabled Videos: A Multi-factor View. In *International Conference on Database Systems for Advanced Applications*. Springer, 351–366.
13. Sepp Hochreiter and Jürgen Schmidhuber. 1997. Long short-term memory. *Neural computation* 9, 8 (1997), 1735–1780.
14. C Hugh Holman and William Harmon. 1992. *A handbook to literature*. Macmillan Publishing Company.
15. Mohit Iyyer, Varun Manjunatha, Jordan Boyd-Graber, and Hal Daumé III. 2015. Deep unordered composition rivals syntactic methods for text classification. In *Proceedings of the 53rd Annual Meeting of the Association for Computational Linguistics and the 7th International Joint Conference on Natural Language Processing (Volume 1: Long Papers)*, Vol. 1. 1681–1691.
16. Rie Johnson and Tong Zhang. 2014. Effective use of word order for text categorization with convolutional neural networks. *arXiv preprint arXiv:1412.1058* (2014).
17. Alex Krizhevsky, Ilya Sutskever, and Geoffrey E Hinton. 2012. Imagenet classification with deep convolutional neural networks. In *Advances in neural information processing systems*. 1097–1105.
18. Quoc Le and Tomas Mikolov. 2014. Distributed representations of sentences and documents. In *Proceedings of the 31st International Conference on Machine Learning (ICML-14)*. 1188–1196.
19. Yann LeCun, Yoshua Bengio, and Geoffrey Hinton. 2015. Deep learning. *Nature* 521, 7553 (2015), 436–444.
20. Jiangfeng Li, Zhenyu Liao, Chenxi Zhang, and Jing Wang. 2016. Event Detection on Online Videos Using Crowdsourced Time-Sync Comment. In *7th International Conference on Cloud Computing and Big Data (CCBD), 2016*. IEEE, 52–57.
21. Tsung-Yi Lin, Michael Maire, Serge Belongie, James Hays, Pietro Perona, Deva Ramanan, Piotr Dollár, and C Lawrence Zitnick. 2014. Microsoft coco: Common objects in context. In *European conference on computer vision*. Springer, 740–755.
22. Tianming Liu, Hong-Jiang Zhang, and Feihu Qi. 2003. A novel video key-frame-extraction algorithm based on perceived motion energy model. *IEEE transactions on circuits and systems for video technology* 13, 10 (2003), 1006–1013.
23. Guangyi Lv, Tong Xu, Enhong Chen, Qi Liu, and Yi Zheng. 2016. Reading the Videos: Temporal Labeling for Crowdsourced Time-Sync Videos Based on Semantic Embedding.. In *AAAI*. 3000–3006.
24. Tomas Mikolov, Kai Chen, Greg Corrado, and Jeffrey Dean. 2013. Efficient estimation of word representations in vector space. *arXiv preprint arXiv:1301.3781* (2013).

25. Siddharth Mitra, Mayank Agrawal, Amit Yadav, Niklas Carlsson, Derek Eager, and Anirban Mahanti. 2011. Characterizing web-based video sharing workloads. *ACM Transactions on the Web (TWEB)* 5, 2 (2011), 8.

26. Jeffrey Pennington, Richard Socher, and Christopher Manning. 2014. Glove: Global vectors for word representation. In *Proceedings of the 2014 conference on empirical methods in natural language processing (EMNLP)*. 1532–1543.

27. Stefan Siersdorfer, Jose San Pedro, and Mark Sanderson. 2009. Automatic video tagging using content redundancy. In *Proceedings of the 32nd international ACM SIGIR conference on Research and development in information retrieval*. ACM, 395–402.

28. Rion Snow, Brendan O'Connor, Daniel Jurafsky, and Andrew Y Ng. 2008. Cheap and fast—but is it good?: evaluating non-expert annotations for natural language tasks. In *Proceedings of the conference on empirical methods in natural language processing*. Association for Computational Linguistics, 254–263.

29. C Sujatha and Uma Mudenagudi. 2011. A study on keyframe extraction methods for video summary. In *International Conference on Computational Intelligence and Communication Networks (CICN), 2011*. IEEE, 73–77.

30. Ba Tu Truong and Svetha Venkatesh. 2007. Video abstraction: A systematic review and classification. *ACM transactions on multimedia computing, communications, and applications (TOMM)* 3, 1 (2007), 3.

31. Adrian Ulges, Christian Schulze, Markus Koch, and Thomas M Breuel. 2010. Learning automatic concept detectors from online video. *Computer vision and Image understanding* 114, 4 (2010), 429–438.

32. Subhashini Venugopalan, Marcus Rohrbach, Jeffrey Donahue, Raymond Mooney, Trevor Darrell, and Kate Saenko. 2015. Sequence to sequence-video to text. In *Proceedings of the IEEE international conference on computer vision*. 4534–4542.

33. Meng Wang, Richang Hong, Guangda Li, Zheng-Jun Zha, Shuicheng Yan, and Tat-Seng Chua. 2012. Event driven web video summarization by tag localization and key-shot identification. *IEEE Transactions on Multimedia* 14, 4 (2012), 975–985.

34. Peter Welinder, Steve Branson, Pietro Perona, and Serge J Belongie. 2010. The multidimensional wisdom of crowds. In *Advances in neural information processing systems*. 2424–2432.

35. Bin Wu, Erheng Zhong, Ben Tan, Andrew Horner, and Qiang Yang. 2014. Crowdsourced time-sync video tagging using temporal and personalized topic modeling. In *Proceedings of the 20th ACM SIGKDD international conference on Knowledge discovery and data mining*. ACM, 721–730.

36. Xian Wu, Wei Fan, and Yong Yu. 2012. Sembler: Ensembling Crowd Sequential Labeling for Improved Quality.. In *AAAI*.

37. Zechen Wu and Eisuke Ito. 2014. Correlation analysis between user's emotional comments and popularity measures. In *IIAI 3rd International Conference on Advanced Applied Informatics (IIAIAAI), 2014*. IEEE, 280–283.

38. Yikun Xian, Jiangfeng Li, Chenxi Zhang, and Zhenyu Liao. 2015. Video highlight shot extraction with time-sync comment. In *Proceedings of the 7th International Workshop on Hot Topics in Planet-scale mObile computing and online Social neTworking*. ACM, 31–36.

39. Linli Xu and Chao Zhang. 2017. Bridging Video Content and Comments: Synchronized Video Description with Temporal Summarization of Crowdsourced Time-Sync Comments.. In *AAAI*. 1611–1617.

40. Wenmian Yang, Na Ruan, Wenyuan Gao, Kun Wang, Wensheng Ran, and Weijia Jia. 2017. Crowdsourced time-sync video tagging using semantic association graph. In *2017 IEEE International Conference on Multimedia and Expo (ICME)*. IEEE, 547–552.

Can We Predict the Scenic Beauty of Locations from Geo-tagged Flickr Images?

Ch. Md. Rakin Haider
Bangladesh University of Engineering and Technology, Dhaka, Bangladesh
rakinhaider@cse.buet.ac.bd

Mohammed Eunus Ali
Bangladesh University of Engineering and Technology, Dhaka, Bangladesh
eunus@cse.buet.ac.bd

ABSTRACT
In this work, we propose a novel technique to determine the aesthetic score of a location from social metadata of Flickr photos. In particular, we built machine learning classifiers to predict the class of a location where each class corresponds to a set of locations having equal aesthetic rating. These models are trained on two empirically build datasets containing locations in two different cities (Rome and Paris) where aesthetic ratings of locations were gathered from *TripAdvisor.com*. In this work we exploit the idea that in a location with higher aesthetic rating, it is more likely for an user to capture a photo and other users are more likely to interact with that photo. Our models achieved as high as 79.48% accuracy (78.60% precision and 79.27% recall) on Rome dataset and 73.78% accuracy(75.62% precision and 78.07% recall) on Paris dataset. The proposed technique can facilitate urban planning, tour planning and recommending aesthetically pleasing paths.

ACM Classification Keywords
Information systems: Data mining; Information systems: Social networks; Computing methodologies: Supervised learning

Author Keywords
Data Mining, Machine Learning, Flickr, Social Metadata.

INTRODUCTION
Aesthetic ratings of locations play a vital role in urban planning and tour planning. Satisfying a certain time and budget constraints, each tourist wishes to visit most attractive places of a city. Such interest have resulted in the increasing popularity of websites like TripAdvisor, Expedia and Travelocity. They help a tourist to choose the best tourist spots in a city. One of the most popular trip recommendation site, TripAdvisor, generates the location ratings based on crowd-sourced reviews and ratings for each location [5]. In this paper, we propose a novel technique to predict TripAdvisor location ratings from the social metadata of photos available in a major social content sharing website, Flickr.

IUI'18, March 7–11, 2018, Tokyo, Japan

DOI: https://doi.org/10.1145/3172944.3173000

The last decade has witnessed an unprecedented rise in the usage of GPS technology and the availability of GPS-enabled camera phones have increased creation of geo-tagged photos. Popular content sharing sites such as Flickr, Instagram and Twitter have already accumulated a large number of user generated photos. In Flickr alone there are about 8 billion existing photos and it is reported that Flickr receives 3.5 million uploads every day. These photos contain metadata such as gps-location, time of the photo taken, number of users viewed and number of favorites. The large amount of geo-tagged photos not only gives us plenty of information about a specific geo-location[6, 12, 4] but also contains patterns of human behavior, photo trails[2, 10], and even transit time [7] between areas of a city. The increased availability of such geographic information in the form of multimedia content such as images have given rise to interesting technologies such as recommendation system, point-of-interest mining, tour planning system etc. Apart from trip planning and route recommendations, research works have also been conducted to find out quantity of ecological phenomena like snow-fall and vegetation density [15], predicting user's home location and gender [8], detecting events that took place [9] etc. each of which used Flickr geo-tagged photos and metadata. In most of these studies geo-tags of photos, temporal metadata, content-based automatically generated tags as well as user generated tags were considered for the task of analysis. However, Flickr contains another set of metadata which are generated from users interaction with the photos and with other users. A few such social metadata are number of views, number of favorites, comments etc. These metadata are mostly overlooked in recent studies.

In this work, we propose a method to predict the aesthetic score of a location from Flickr social metadata. To the best of our knowledge this is the first attempt to predict TripAdvisor location ratings from Flickr social metadata. We exploited the idea that photo capturing patterns in scenic locations should be significantly different than that of lesser ones. We have modeled the problem as a multi-class classification problem were each location is a member of one of the equally rated classes. In TripAdvisor, the ratings are provided on a scale of 0 to 5 with an interval of 0.5. We considered 6 classes with aesthetic rating 2.5, 3, 3.5, 4, 4.5 and 5 respectively and discarded locations with lesser aesthetic ratings. In Paris dataset we have considered an additional class with aesthetic rating 2.0. These classification models can be used to provide suggestions to tourists, artist and urban resource management organizations.

The leading trip recommendation system, TripAdvisor, provides location ratings based on the 500 million reviews and opinions about 7 million attractions, accumulated from 300 million of its users. TripAdvisor considers three factors i.e. quality, recency and quantity of the reviews while computing the ratings. A major drawback of this method of aesthetic rating calculation is the dependancy on crowd-sourced reviews. It is likely that a tourist will prefer to post his photos on social media rather than rating each location he visited in order to help generating aesthetic ratings. The goal of this work is to reduce the dependancy on crowd-sourced ratings. We used aesthetic ratings calculated from TripAdvisor data as ground truth for our work and tried to predict them from the data avaiable in other forms. In this work, we have gathered TripAdvisor ratings of 850 locations in Rome, Italy and 650 locations in Paris, France. For each of the locations we have collected social metadata of photos which are taken within a radius of 100m of that geo-location. We have gathered social metadata of 6 million photos in Rome and 4 million photos in Paris using Flick API. From these metadata we have generated some relevant features for classification. Since significant imbalance was observed in the dataset of both cities, we have applied state-of-art technique, namely SMOTE [3] to balance the classes out. We have trained multiple decision tree variants as our classifier i.e. J48, Random Forrest(RF) and REPTree. Finally, application of ensemble technique further contributed to increasing accuracy. Among the trained models, Random Forrest performed best when combined with bagging ensemble method and achieved 79.48% accuracy on Rome dataset. On the other hand, the best performance(73.78% accuracy) is found when Random Forrest classifier is combined with boosting ensemble technique in Paris dataset.

The major contributions of this work are summarized below.

- We propose a novel approach to predict location ratings from photo capturing, sharing and interaction patterns.
- We build two datasets empirically to facilitate TripAdvisor location rating prediction for the locations of Rome, Italy and Paris, France.
- We train decision tree based classifiers i.e. J48, random forrest, REPTree, whose performance was improved with the help of bagging and boosting ensemble technique. We also handle issues regarding imbalanced dataset by applying SMOTE [3] oversampling technique .
- We test our models on two real world datasets related to two popular tourist destinations, Rome, Italy and Paris, France. Our models demonstrated 79.48% and 73.78% accuracy respectively.

METHODOLOGY

Dataset Generation

There are multiple available datasets related to Flickr that can be considered while choosing the dataset. The first one of them is the *yfcc100m* dataset publised by Yahoo Webscope [13]. This dataset contains a collection of photos and videos, which are compiled from the data available on Yahoo! Flickr. The dataset is divided into three parts. The main part of the dataset contains information about 100 million flickr photos. It contains photo or video identifier, photo/video hash, user information, date in which the photo was taken, upload date, title of the photo, description, user tags (comma-separated), location information, specifications of the device by which the photo or video was captured and URLs of the photo or video. *yfcc100m* also includes machine tags and human readable place information for every photo. An alternative of *yfcc100m* dataset is the Multimedia Commons Repository*(MMC)* [14]. The differences between *yfcc100m* and *MMC* are the supplemental material to *yfcc100m* that the *MMC* offers. *MMC* offers audio, visual and motion features such as LIRE, GIST, SWIFT that are often used by multimedia researchers. There are several other sources such as MIRFLICKR, Flickr API etc., through which one can access large number of flickr photos and their related attributes.

In order to perform the desired task of classification we need a dataset that provides social metadata such as number of views, number of favorites, number of comments etc. of Flickr photos as well as ground truth with respect to the aesthetic scores of geo-locations. From the discussion about *yfcc100m* and *MMC*, we can observe that none of them include social metadata of the photos. Moreover, none of these datasets include any ground truth about a place being aesthetically desirable. To facilitate our classification task we decided to build a new dataset using Flickr social metadata and aesthetic rating of geo-locations from TripAdvisor.

In order to appropriately model photo distribution around a city or country we tried to gather location names and ratings from *TripAdvisor.com.* Since trip advisor does not provide API for research purposes, we used HTML parser to get data from Trip Advisor. From Trip Advisor we have retrieved rating, and number of reviews for around 1200 attractions in Rome, Italy and 1200 attractions in Paris, France. After removing duplicates and attractions such as tours, restaurants and hotels we were left with 850 and 650 locations for consideration respectively. Despite the provided ratings being on a scale of 0-5 with an interval of 0.5, we observed from the data, that most of the ratings associated with top attractions in Rome lies in the range 2.5-5 and within 2-5 in Paris. For each location we retrieved latitude and longitude using *Google Places API.* Then for each geo-location we fetched metadata of all the images that lie within a circle of 100m radius surrounding that particular location from Flick API. Thus we set up two datasets where each location is labeled as one of 7 classes i.e. classes with aesthetic scores $\{2,2.5,3,3.5,4,4.5,5\}$. Let the classes be named as C_i where i is the corresponding aesthetic score. Among the locations in Rome there are points-of-interests(197), museums(130), church and cathedrals(78), historic sites(74), castles(25), gardens(23), parks(10), neighborhoods(13) etc. Similarly, the types of locations considered in Paris are points-of-interests(115), museums(68), neighborhoods(39), church, cathedrals and historic sites (28) and so on.

Feature Extraction

The social metadata related to each photo that are directly available from Flickr are the number of times the photo is viewed, the number of people who have added the photo as favorite, and the number of comments on the photo. We have extracted some aggregate features using these metadata for each location. The major intuitions behind our features are,

- A place with more aesthetic beauty encourages more users to take photos and upload them, resulting in a higher density of photos at that place.
- An aesthetically beautiful place is more likely to draw tourists and the number of distinct users uploading photos at a place should be higher.
- Visitors usually searches for and views photos captured at beautiful locations.
- The more beautiful a place is, it is more likely that people will capture better photos which results in higher number of people adding them to favorites.
- Higher number of views should lead to higher number of favorites and comments.
- The quality of photos, taken at an aesthetic and popular location, usually depends on the surrounding scenario rather than the photographer's skills.

Keeping these points in mind we have generated 11 features for every location. The generated features for each location are photo density, total number of views, total number of favorites, total number of comments, average views per photo, average favorite count, average number of comments per photo, ratio of number of favorites to number of views, ratio of number of comments to number of views, distinct user count per location, and finally maximum number of photo per user. Figure 1 shows the frequency histograms of each feature generated from Rome dataset. The number of instances of a class per histogram bar is represented with appropriate colored portions. Additionally, Figure 1a shows the number of locations for each aesthetic score and their associated color used in the histograms.

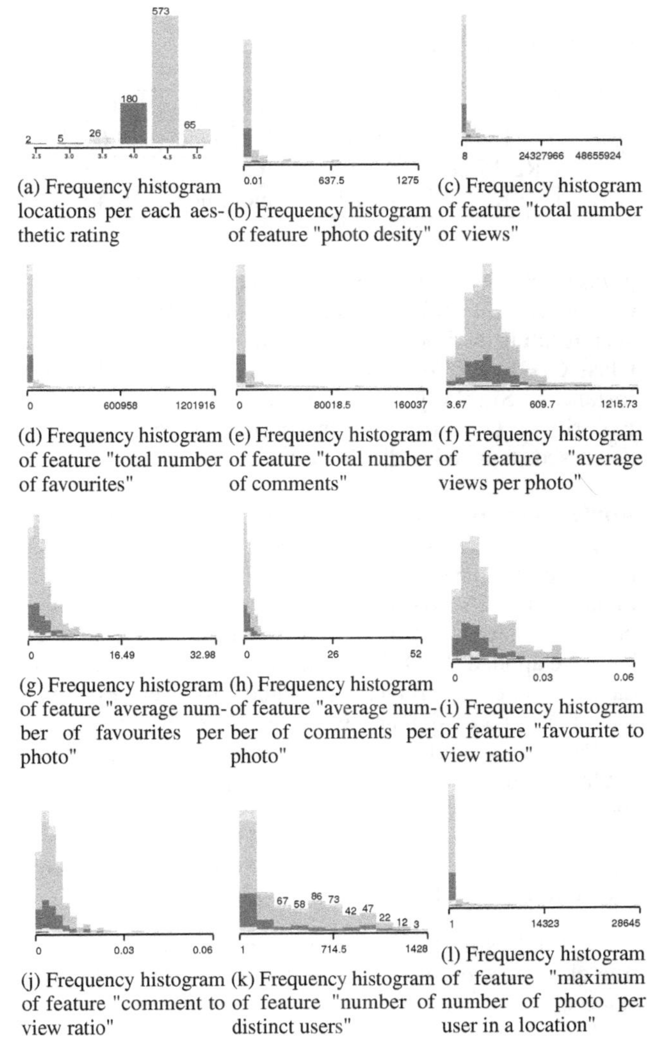

(a) Frequency histogram locations per each aesthetic rating

(b) Frequency histogram of feature "photo desity"

(c) Frequency histogram of feature "total number of views"

(d) Frequency histogram of feature "total number of favourites"

(e) Frequency histogram of feature "total number of comments"

(f) Frequency histogram of feature "average views per photo"

(g) Frequency histogram of feature "average number of favourites per photo"

(h) Frequency histogram of feature "average number of comments per photo"

(i) Frequency histogram of feature "favourite to view ratio"

(j) Frequency histogram of feature "comment to view ratio"

(k) Frequency histogram of feature "number of distinct users"

(l) Frequency histogram of feature "maximum number of photo per user in a location"

Figure 1: Visual Representation of distribution of the features.

Classification

We have trained several classifiers to be able to classify the places as a member of one of the six(or seven in case of Paris dataset) equally rated classes. We evaluated each of their accuracy, precision and recalls to distinguish the best classifier. As our classifiers, we have used J48, REPTree and Random Forrest(RF) decision tree algorithm. To boost the accuracy of classifiers we have also applied Bagging and Boosting technique on the decision tree classifiers.

EXPERIMENTAL RESULTS

Classification

We have considered aesthetic scores as nominal values where a location can have one of 6 aesthetics scores in Rome dataset, starting from 2.5 to 5 with an interval of 0.5. Similarly, a location can have one of 7 possible aesthetic score in Paris dataset, from 2.0 to 5 with 0.5 interval. To solve the classification task we have trained three classifier. The classifiers are different variations of decision tree classifier. They are J48, REPTree and Random Forrest. We have applied 10 fold cross-validation technique to validate the accuracy of classifiers. Table 1 and 2 show the accuracy, precision and recall of each classifier. According to Sokolova et al.[11] the precision and recall of multi-class classifier are the average precision and average recall of all the individual classes.

Table 1: Classifier accuracy, precision and recall of decision tree classifiers on dataset with 851 locations of Rome.

Classifier	Accuracy	Precision	Recall
J48	64.39	Undefined	17.60
REPTree	66.51	Undefined	16.78
RF	60.28	Undefined	19.57

The results in Table 1 and 2 show that the classifiers demonstrate moderate performance with respect to accuracy. However, from the precision and recall measures we can observe that its performance suffers for different classes. The precision values are undefined because there is atleast one class for which the classifier doesn't declare any instance as a member of that class. Additionally the lower average value of recall

Table 2: Classifier accuracy, precision and recall of decision tree classifiers on dataset with 650 locations of Paris.

Classifier	Accuracy	Precision	Recall
J48	36.09	Undefined	18.65
REPTree	41.44	Undefined	16.04
RF	42.81	Undefined	19.46

gives us an idea that the classifier may perform well for one class whereas it performs poorly for others. The reason behind such result is the imbalance between the classes in our dataset. Class $C_{4.5}$ has 573 instances whereas class $C_{2.5}$ has only 2 instances. Similarly in Paris dataset $C_{4.5}$ and $C_{4.0}$ contains majority of the locations. In subsequent sections we have discussed steps to handle this issue.

Applying oversampling technique to handle overfitting

In order to handle the performance issues due to imbalance in dataset, we have applied state-of-the art oversampling technique namely SMOTE [3]. SMOTE uses instances of minority class to generate synthetic instances of corresponding class. We have applied SMOTE for each class to generate a balanced dataset with each class having around 580 instances similar to that of class $C_{4.5}$. Similarly we have balanced out the classes in the Paris dataset. Although any other oversampling techniques could have been chosen and they are reported to have competitive performances [1] on various datasets, to avoid complexity we have chosen to apply SMOTE. The oversampled dataset was used to train classifiers and the result of such classifiers can be found in Table 3 and 4.

Table 3: Classifier accuracy, precision and recall of decision tree classifiers on oversampled Rome dataset with 3417 instances.

Classifier	Accuracy	Precision	Recall
J48	70.00	69.60	69.81
REPTree	67.37	65.97	67.10
RF	77.82	76.94	77.63

Table 4: Classifier accuracy, precision and recall of decision tree classifiers on oversampled Paris dataset with 1598 instances.

Classifier	Accuracy	Precision	Recall
J48	62.20	66.45	67.40
REPTree	58.07	61.86	64.61
RF	69.77	72.35	74.16

Improving classifier accuracy with ensemble method

In order to improve classifier performance, we have applied state-of-art ensemble technique on decision tree classifiers. We have used both Bagging and Boosting technique on the decision tree classifier. Bagging is an ensemble learning method that learns classifier on several different distributions of the training set and uses all the classifiers for classification and applies majority voting to get the desired prediction. On the other hand, in each iteration of boosting technique, it tries to learn classifier on the samples that was wrongly classified using previous classifiers and assign a corresponding weight to each classifier. Both bagging and boosting helps to reduce error rate of an individual classifier. The classifier accuracy after the application of ensemble methods are reported in Table 5 and 6.

Table 5: Classifier accuracy, precision and recall of decision tree classifiers with bagging and boosting technique, on oversampled Rome dataset with 3417 instances.

Classifier	Accuracy	Precision	Recall
Bagging with J48	76.59	75.61	76.35
Bagging with REPTree	74.25	72.78	73.96
Bagging with RF	79.48	78.60	79.27
Boosting with J48	76.76	76.18	76.58
Boosting with REPTree	74.57	73.98	74.37
Boosting with RF	79.10	78.32	78.93

Table 6: Classifier accuracy, precision and recall of decision tree classifiers with bagging and boosting technique, on oversampled Paris dataset with 1598 instances.

Classifier	Accuracy	Precision	Recall
Bagging with J48	68.27	71.25	73.85
Bagging with REPTree	65.02	67.82	71.11
Bagging with RF	72.22	74.28	77.59
Boosting with J48	70.65	73.70	75.17
Boosting with REPTree	64.27	68.79	69.64
Boosting with RF	73.78	75.62	78.07

FUTURE WORKS AND CONCLUSION

In this work, we aimed at using machine learning techniques to score each location with an aesthetic score, which will facilitate urban planning, route recommendation, tour planning etc. We focused on Flickr social metadata to predict TripAdvisor ratings. Having accumulated two real world datasets with 850 locations from Rome and 650 locations from Paris we trained decision tree classifiers to predict the aesthetic score of each location. However, it was observed that the ratings received from TripAdvisor have implicit skewness. The imbalance in dataset resulted in performance issues. Removing the issues of imbalanced dataset using SMOTE technique our proposed models achieved as high as 79% and 73% accuracy on Rome and Paris dataset respectively. Future works may focus on finding aesthetic routes through a city or assigning aesthetic score to each route available through various trajectory datasets. Another direction of study can be attempting to predict aesthetic rating of locations by analyzing Flickr photos rather than assessing their metadata.

REFERENCES

1. Adnan Amin, Sajid Anwar, Awais Adnan, Muhammad Nawaz, Newton Howard, Junaid Qadir, Ahmad Y. A. Hawalah, and Amir Hussain. 2016. Comparing Oversampling Techniques to Handle the Class Imbalance Problem: A Customer Churn Prediction Case Study. *IEEE Access* 4 (2016), 7940–7957. DOI: http://dx.doi.org/10.1109/ACCESS.2016.2619719

2. Yuki Arase, Xing Xie, Takahiro Hara, and Shojiro Nishio. 2010. Mining People's Trips from Large Scale

Geo-tagged Photos. In *Proceedings of the 18th ACM International Conference on Multimedia (MM '10)*. ACM, New York, NY, USA, 133–142. DOI: http://dx.doi.org/10.1145/1873951.1873971

3. Nitesh V. Chawla, Kevin W. Bowyer, Lawrence O. Hall, and W. Philip Kegelmeyer. 2002. SMOTE: Synthetic Minority Over-sampling Technique. *J. Artif. Intell. Res.* 16 (2002), 321–357. DOI: http://dx.doi.org/10.1613/jair.953
4. Livia Hollenstein and Ross Purves. 2010. Exploring place through user-generated content: Using Flickr tags to describe city cores. *J. Spatial Information Science* 1, 1 (2010), 21–48. DOI: http://dx.doi.org/10.5311/JOSIS.2010.1.3
5. TripAdvisor Insight. 2016. Everything You Need to Know About the TripAdvisor Popularity Ranking Algorithm. https://www.tripadvisor.com/TripAdvisorInsights/n2701. (2016). [Accessed October 8th, 2017].
6. Rongrong Ji, Yue Gao, Bineng Zhong, Hongxun Yao, and Qi Tian. 2011. Mining flickr landmarks by modeling reconstruction sparsity. *TOMCCAP* 7, Supplement (2011), 31. DOI: http://dx.doi.org/10.1145/2037676.2037688
7. Adrian Popescu and Gregory Grefenstette. 2009. Deducing trip related information from flickr. In *Proceedings of the 18th International Conference on World Wide Web, WWW 2009, Madrid, Spain, April 20-24, 2009*. 1183–1184. DOI: http://dx.doi.org/10.1145/1526709.1526919
8. Adrian Popescu and Gregory Grefenstette. 2010. Mining User Home Location and Gender from Flickr Tags. In *Proceedings of the Fourth International Conference on Weblogs and Social Media, ICWSM 2010, Washington, DC, USA, May 23-26, 2010.* http://www.aaai.org/ocs/index.php/ICWSM/ICWSM10/paper/view/1477
9. Tye Rattenbury, Nathaniel Good, and Mor Naaman. 2007. Towards automatic extraction of event and place semantics from flickr tags. In *SIGIR 2007: Proceedings of the 30th Annual International ACM SIGIR Conference on Research and Development in Information Retrieval, Amsterdam, The Netherlands, July 23-27, 2007*. 103–110. DOI: http://dx.doi.org/10.1145/1277741.1277762
10. Samia Shafique and Mohammed Eunus Ali. 2016. Recommending most popular travel path within a region of interest from historical trajectory data. In *Proceedings of the 5th ACM SIGSPATIAL International Workshop on Mobile Geographic Information Systems*. 2–11.
11. Marina Sokolova and Guy Lapalme. 2009. A systematic analysis of performance measures for classification tasks. *Inf. Process. Manage.* 45, 4 (2009), 427–437. DOI: http://dx.doi.org/10.1016/j.ipm.2009.03.002
12. Evaggelos Spyrou and Phivos Mylonas. 2016. Analyzing Flickr metadata to extract location-based information and semantically organize its photo content. *Neurocomputing* 172 (2016), 114–133. DOI: http://dx.doi.org/10.1016/j.neucom.2014.12.104
13. Bart Thomee, David A Shamma, Gerald Friedland, Benjamin Elizalde, Karl Ni, Douglas Poland, Damian Borth, and Li-Jia Li. 2016a. Yfcc100m: The new data in multimedia research. *Commun. ACM* 59, 2 (2016), 64–73.
14. Bart Thomee, David A. Shamma, Gerald Friedland, Benjamin Elizalde, Karl Ni, Douglas Poland, Damian Borth, and Li-Jia Li. 2016b. YFCC100M: The New Data in Multimedia Research. *Commun. ACM* 59, 2 (2016), 64–73. http://cacm.acm.org/magazines/2016/2/197425-yfcc100m/fulltext
15. Haipeng Zhang, Mohammed Korayem, David J. Crandall, and Gretchen LeBuhn. 2012. Mining photo-sharing websites to study ecological phenomena. In *Proceedings of the 21st World Wide Web Conference 2012, WWW 2012, Lyon, France, April 16-20, 2012*. 749–758. DOI: http://dx.doi.org/10.1145/2187836.2187938

Explaining Recommendations Using Contexts

Masahiro Sato, Budrul Ahsan, Koki Nagatani, Takashi Sonoda, Qian Zhang, Tomoko Ohkuma
Fuji Xerox
Yokohama, Japan
sato.masahiro/budrul.ahsan/nagatani.koki/sonoda.takashi/qian.zhang/ohkuma.tomoko@fujixerox.co.jp

ABSTRACT

Recommender systems support user decision-making, and explanations of recommendations further facilitate their usefulness. Previous explanation styles are based on similar users, similar items, demographics of users, and contents of items. Contexts, such as "usage scenarios" and "accompanying persons," have not been used for explanations, although they influence user decisions. In this paper, we propose a context style explanation method, presenting contexts suitable for consuming recommended items. The expected impacts of context style explanations are 1) persuasiveness: recognition of suitable context for usage motivates users to consume items, and 2) usefulness: envisioning context helps users to make right choices because the values of items depend on contexts. We evaluate context style persuasiveness and usefulness by a crowdsourcing-based user study in a restaurant recommendation setting. The context style explanation is compared to demographic and content style explanations. We also combine context style and other explanation styles, confirming that hybrid styles improve persuasiveness and usefulness of explanation.

Author Keywords

Recommender System; Explanation; Context-awareness; User Evaluation.

INTRODUCTION

Recommender systems help users to choose items from vast amounts of candidates. Explaining recommendations further supports user decision-making. Several explanation styles have been proposed [21,25,26]. For example, the neighbor style explanation provides ratings from similar users. The influence style explanation shows items related to those recommended from users' purchase histories. The demographic style explanation describes user ages and genders. The content style explanation displays item features, such as keywords for books and user-generated tags for movies. These four styles are based on information related to users or items because these elements influence users' decision processes [11,22]. Contextual factors such as time, location, companion, and purpose are also essential to affect user decision-making [9].

IUI'18, March 7–11, 2018, Tokyo, Japan

ACM ISBN 978-1-4503-4945-1/18/03…$15.00
https://doi.org/10.1145/3172944.3173012

In this study, we propose a new style of explanation using contexts. The context style explanation presents contexts suitable for recommended items. For example, "*This restaurant is recommended to you because the restaurant is suitable for dates with your girlfriend/boyfriend.*" We expect two impacts of contexts in explanations:

- **Persuasiveness**: the exhibited context induces users to picture situations in which they will consume the recommended items in the future, motivating them to make choices.
- **Usefulness**: users select items based on contexts. Therefore, suggested usage contexts should help user decision-making.

In this research, we investigate these aforementioned impacts of context style explanations with the following two aspects: 1) comparison with other explanation styles, and 2) hybridization of context and other styles. To investigate these aspects, we implement a restaurant recommender system with context style explanations, conducting a user study via crowdsourcing.

The remainder of this paper is organized as follows. Related work is presented in next section. Then, the method of context style explanation is described. Afterwards, the experimental details are explained, followed by results and discussion. Conclusion is summarized in the last section.

RELATED WORK

Herlocker et al. [12] compared various explanations with different styles and different visualizations, which included histograms of the user's neighbors' ratings (i.e., neighbor style); similarity to other items in the user's profile (i.e., influence style); and the user's favorite actor or actress (i.e., content style). Demographic information was used for explanations in the tourism domain (i.e., demographic style) [3]. Bilgic et al. [6] demonstrated that explanations using keywords (i.e., content style) or showing items influencing recommendations (i.e., influence style) help users evaluate items effectively. Various kinds of contents and how to visualize them have been explored for content style explanations. User-annotated tags are used for explanations [27] and are displayed in a tagcloud interface [10]. Musto et al. [19] showed that fusing linked open data and choosing specific properties improves explanations. Organizational explanations show pros and cons of items extracted from user reviews, according to users' priorities [18]. Chen et al. [8] further elaborated the organizational explanation by grouping similar trade-off items. Recent research has striven to generate personalized natural language explanations of items [7,17,28], which can be regarded as advanced content style explanations. Chang et al. [7] generated explanations via collaboration of crowdworkers and intelligent systems. State-of-the-art neural network models are also used for that purpose [17,28].

Moreover, hybrids of several explanation styles have been investigated [21,24]. Symeonidis et al. [24] combined content and influence style explanations. Visualization of complex hybrid explanations were also investigated in [16].

Whereas there is vast amount of research on explaining recommendations, most rely on the four types of information shown in Table 1: neighbor, influence, demographic, and content. Besides these four, context significantly influences user decision-making [9]. Contexts have also been used in context-aware recommendations [1,2]. Moreover, Zheng [29] and Papadimitriou [21] alluded to the possibility of using contexts for explanation. However, contexts have not yet been used for explaining recommendations. To the best of our knowledge, this is the first study of context style explanations.

Explanation style	Displayed information
Neighbor	Ratings or the fact of purchases of similar users
Influence	Items related to recommended ones from users' past consumption
Demographic	Gender, age, etc. of users
Content	Keywords, tags, pros and cons of recommended items
Context (ours)	Context when users would consume recommended items

Table 1. Overview of conventional explanation styles and proposed context style explanation.

CONTEXT STYLE EXPLANATION

Generation of context style explanations is composed of two steps: (1) selection of context-item pairs for users, (2) suggestion of the context of a context-item pair as the item's explanation.

Selection of Context-Item Pairs

Our context style explanation suggests contexts that the user might encounter in the future. This means both the context and the item are unknown. In this case, the recommender needs to select appropriate pairs of contexts and items for the users. This requires a) a user-item match, b) an item-context match, and c) a user-context match. For a restaurant recommendation, the recommended restaurant should match the user's preferences, just as with non-contextualized recommender systems. Moreover, the recommended restaurant should match the suggested context. If the context of eating with children is suggested in an explanation, the recommended restaurant should be suitable for that situation. Additionally, the recommended context should be one anticipated by the user. If the user does not have children and lacks many opportunities to eat out with children, a suggestion of eating out with children would likely be inappropriate.

These above three properties can be learned via latent representation of pairwise interactions between features [5,13,23]. Among them, we use field-aware factorization machines (FFMs) [13] for their efficiency and performance. FFM splits features to "fields," and incorporates interaction effects among features of different fields. FFM is formulated as,

$$\sum_{j_1=1}^{n}\sum_{j_2=j_1+1}^{n}(\boldsymbol{w}_{j_1}^{f_2}\cdot\boldsymbol{w}_{j_2}^{f_1})x_{j_1}x_{j_2}, \quad (1)$$

where $\boldsymbol{w}_j^f$ is a latent vector of feature j that interacts with field f; and x_j is the value of feature j. To model interaction among users, items, and contexts, we prepare a user field, an item field, and a context field. If each field takes only one feature, and if the values of features are binary, then Equation (1) is expressed as follows,

$$\boldsymbol{w}_u^{\text{Item}}\cdot\boldsymbol{w}_i^{\text{User}}+\boldsymbol{w}_i^{\text{Context}}\cdot\boldsymbol{w}_c^{\text{Item}}+\boldsymbol{w}_u^{\text{Context}}\cdot\boldsymbol{w}_c^{\text{User}}. \quad (2)$$

Each term in Equation (2) represents a) a user-item match ($\boldsymbol{w}_u^{\text{Item}}\cdot\boldsymbol{w}_i^{\text{User}}$), b) an item-context match ($\boldsymbol{w}_i^{\text{Context}}\cdot\boldsymbol{w}_c^{\text{Item}}$), and c) a user-context match ($\boldsymbol{w}_u^{\text{Context}}\cdot\boldsymbol{w}_c^{\text{User}}$). Context-item pairs are selected by the score of Equation (2).

Suggestion of Context as Explanation

Selected context-item pairs are used to produce recommendations and explanations. If there is a context-item pair with context c and item i, item i is presented to a user as a recommendation and context c is used for an explanation. Explanation is generated using human-crafted templates, for example, "*item i is recommended to you because it is suitable for context c.*"

EXPERIMENT

First, we collected users' restaurant visit logs with context via crowdsourcing. Second, we trained a context-item pair selector using the acquired logs and prepared recommendations and explanations. Finally, we asked the same users to evaluate explanation styles.

Collecting Dataset

Restaurant visit logs were collected using a Japanese crowdsourcing platform. There are three entries per restaurant: name of a visited restaurant, the URL to the restaurant within a restaurant information site, and usage scene of the visit (i.e., contexts). We asked for original contexts of users' visits instead of asking for evaluation under a provided context, because users behave differently under supposed contexts and real contexts [4,20]. Usage scenes were selected from 15 options[1], for example, "with close friends (only eating)," "with colleagues (with drink)," "in solitude," "take-away," and "business entertaining." We asked each crowdworker to input 20 restaurants at maximum. We recruited crowdworkers who lived in certain urban areas in order to confine the areas of visit logs.

We obtained 2,884 visit logs from 155 crowdworkers, after removing logs with improper URLs and crowdworkers who provided improper URLs more than half the time. The genders and approximate ages of the crowdworkers were provided from the crowdsourcing platform. There are 2,730 unique URLs in the remaining visit logs. The average number of visits per restaurant is 1.056 and the sparsity is 99.32%. We crawled the URLs and collected the restaurants' content information, including genres and nearest stations[2]. Note that each restaurant is given many genres (2.3 genres on average). There are 210 unique genres and 473 unique stations.

Training Recommender and Preparing Explanation

We trained the context-item selector using the collected dataset. We use the libffm[3] library for FFM. The features of the user field are user ID, gender, and age. The features of the item field are genre and nearest station. The use of the demographic features of users and the content features of items alleviate the issue of data sparsity. The features of the context field include context ID, which is assigned to 15 usage scenes. Features of the context field include context ID, which is assigned to 15 usage scenes.

Training of the recommender proceeds as follows. First, the dataset is randomly split into 80% training and 20% validation data. Hyper-parameters of FFM are then optimized to maximize the AUC of the validation data. Finally, we train the model using the entire dataset to select context-item pairs.

After training the model, we select seven context-item pairs for each user. Restaurants visited in the past are removed from the list, whereas contexts experienced in the past are not omitted. The same restaurant can be recommended only once per user.

We prepared seven styles of explanations as described in Table 2. Baseline explanation does not include any specific information of demographics, contents, and contexts. This explanation is the same for all users and all recommended items. For the context style explanation, the context of context-item pair is directly assigned. For the demographic style explanation, user age and gender are assigned, because the recommender incorporates gender and age as features, and recommended items should relate to them. For the content style explanation, we select a genre common among the recommended restaurants and those the user visited in the past. Hybrid explanation styles are generated via a combination of the procedures described above.

Style	Sample
Baseline	Recommend based on your visit logs
Demographic	Recommend for "*women in 30s*"
Content	Recommend for who often visit "*Italian restaurant*"
Context	Recommend for use "*with husband/wife*"
Demographic + Context	Recommend for use "*in business entertaining*" of "*men in 50s*"
Content + Context	Recommend for use "*in solitude*" for who often visit "*noodle*"
Demographic + Content + Context	Recommend for use "*with close friends (with drink)*" of "*women in 20s*" who often visit "*cafe*"

Table 2. Samples of seven explanation styles.

Evaluating Explanation Styles

We recruited the 155 crowdworkers who had appropriately submitted restaurant visit logs, and 85 participated in the user study. We presented seven restaurant recommendations with seven different explanation styles to each user. Each recommendation was generated by the same FFM model. We asked the participants not to consult any other information (e.g., restaurant reviews).

The orders of explanation styles are randomly shuffled among users in order to cancel any biases related to the display order. The orders of context-item pairs are also shuffled, assuring recommendation quality does not correlate to the presentation order. We asked the following four evaluation questions using a 7-point Likert scale for each pair of restaurant recommendations and explanations.

- Persuasiveness 1 (P1): The explanation is convincing.
- Persuasiveness 2 (P2): The explanation triggers interest.
- Usefulness 1 (U1): The explanation is useful for choice.
- Usefulness 2 (U2): The explanation is easy to understand.

In addition to these evaluation questions, we asked whether the participants visited the recommended restaurants in the past, and whether they knew of them in advance. There are also free entry fields to express any other comments.

RESULTS AND DISCUSSION

Among restaurants recommended to participants, 21% were visited in the past and 20% were known in advance. This indicates that item recommendation was fairly accurate and that our recommender system works fine.

Responses to the four questions are shown in Figure 1. Responses ranged from strongly disagree (-3) to strongly

[1] We consulted descriptions of usage scenes in several restaurant information sites to prepare the options.

[2] Restaurants are located in urban areas where public transportation is well developed.

[3] https://github.com/guestwalk/libffm

agree (+3). The average response of the context style explanation is higher than that of the demographic style (p = 0.008, 0.10, 0.047, and 0.036 for P1, P2, U1, and U2, respectively, via the Wilcoxon signed rank test). The average response of the context style explanation also tends to be higher than that of content style, though not statistically significant. In terms of the hybrids, the combination of demographic and context styles outperforms demographic-only ($p < 0.01$ for all questions), and the combination of content and context styles outperforms content-only ($p = 0.061$ for P2, and $p < 0.01$ for others).

Sixty-four participants input at least one comment, and 293 comments were obtained in total. User comments indicate two reasons of persuasiveness: 1) relevance of proposed context to users: "*I think I want to go because this situation is probable for me,*" and 2) recognition of appropriate context for usage: "*I think I am going to use this when I organize a drinking party.*" Users also mentioned usefulness of context for decision making. "*I'm afraid of making a wrong choice for girls' night out, so this explanation is useful.*" These findings from qualitative analysis reinforce the importance of context for explanation.

Baseline explanations tend to perform better than the context style, and the hybrid of content and context styles tends to perform better than baseline (both are without statistical significances). Relatively high appraisals of baseline explanation might come from familiarity of the explanation style. Some users commented: "*There is a comfort in this type of explanation,*" and "*This writing style fits into me best.*" The crowdsourcing platform we used provides task recommendation for users with an explanation of this style: "*Recommendation is based on your past task.*" Another reason might be the occasional mismatch of presented context. Evaluation tends to be affected more by negative experiences (i.e., mismatches) than by positive experiences (i.e., good matches). Similar observations are reported in the experiment of personalizing engaging messages [15]. We plan to improve the accuracy of context-item pair selections in future works.

The trio of demographics, contents, and contexts do not produce significant improvement over the duo of contents and contexts. Users may have felt too much complexity. Investigating adequate amounts of information for an explanation would be an interesting challenge.

This work is conducted in a restaurant recommendation domain. We believe that context style explanations can be applied to various domains, though relevant contexts should be unique to those different domains. Those other domains need further study. We compare and hybridize context style explanations with demographic and content styles. Future work will experiment with other conventional explanation styles (e.g., neighbor and influence styles). We evaluated persuasiveness and usefulness to verify our hypothesis of context-style impacts. Evaluation of other factors, such as user trust and decision efficiency, remains for future work.

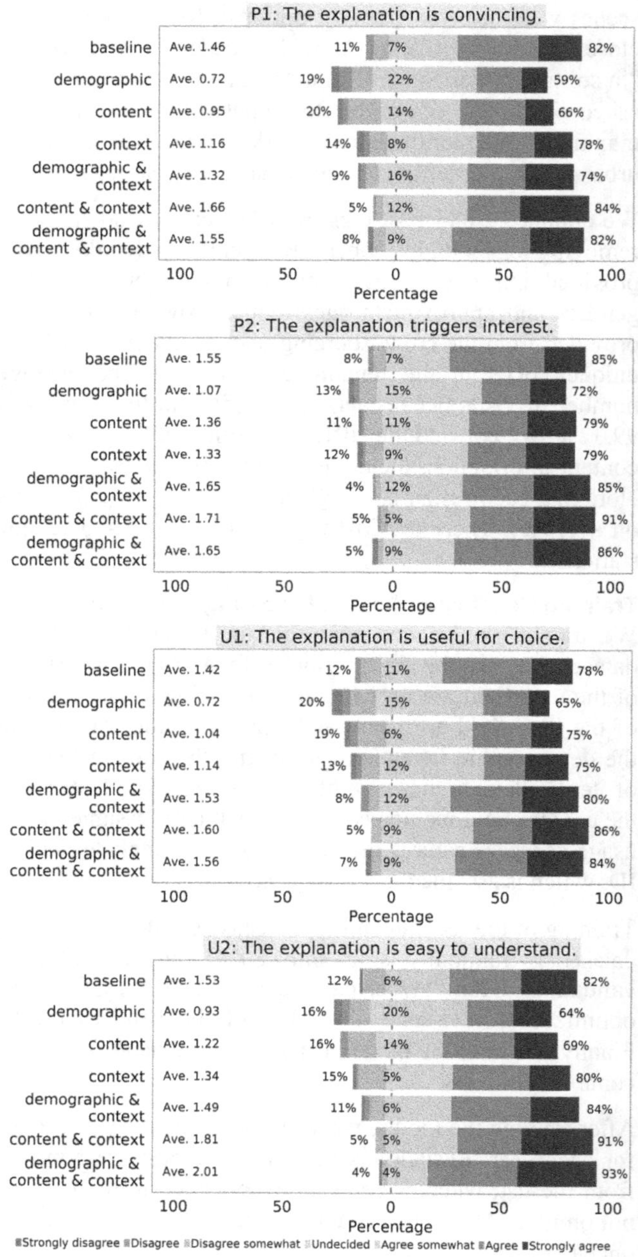

Figure 1. Responses to four questions for each explanation style. Percentages of positive and negative responses are shown in the right and left blanks, respectively. Neutral percentage is shown in the middle. Values of average response are also displayed in the left blanks.

CONCLUSION

In this paper, we proposed the context style explanation for recommenders. We conducted a crowdsourcing-based user study to measure persuasiveness and usefulness. Context style explanations were better than demographic styles. Context styles also tend to perform better than content styles, although not statistically significantly. We further confirmed that hybrids of context style and other explanation styles improve persuasiveness and usefulness. Findings from user comments support these impacts.

REFERENCES

1. Gediminas Adomavicius, Ramesh Sankaranarayanan, Shahana Sen, and Alexander Tuzhilin. 2005. Incorporating contextual information in recommender systems using a multidimensional approach. *ACM Trans. Inf. Syst.* 23, 1: 103-145. http://dx.doi.org/10.1145/1055709.1055714
2. Gediminas Adomavicius and Alexander Tuzhilin. 2015. Context-Aware Recommender Systems. In *Recommender Systems Handbook* (2nd. ed.), Springer, US, 191–226.
3. Liliana Ardissono, Anna Goy, Giovanna Petrone, Marino Segnan, and Pietro Torasso. 2003. Intrigue: personalized recommendation of tourist attractions for desktop and handheld devices. *Applied Artificial Intelligence* 17: 687–714.
4. Hideki Asoh, Yoichi Motomura, and Chihiro Ono. 2010. An analysis of differences between preferences in real and supposed contexts. In *Proceedings of the 2nd Workshop on Context Aware Recommender Systems* (CARS '10).
5. Linas Baltrunas, Bernd Ludwig, and Francesco Ricci. 2011. Matrix factorization techniques for context aware recommendation. In *Proceedings of the fifth ACM conference on Recommender systems* (RecSys '11), 301-304. http://dx.doi.org/10.1145/2043932.2043988
6. Mustafa Bilgic and Raymond J Mooney. 2005. Explaining recommendations: satisfaction vs. promotion. In *Proceedings of the Workshop on the Next Stage of Recommender Systems Research.*
7. Shuo Chang, F. Maxwell Harper, and Loren Gilbert Terveen. 2016. Crowd-based personalized natural language explanations for recommendations. In *Proceedings of the 10th ACM Conference on Recommender Systems* (RecSys '16), 175–182. https://doi.org/10.1145/2959100.2959153
8. Li Chen and Feng Wang. 2017. Explaining recommendations based on feature sentiments in product reviews. In *Proceedings of the 22nd International Conference on Intelligent User Interfaces* (IUI '17), 17–28. https://doi.org/10.1145/3025171.3025173
9. Wei Chen, Christopher Hoyle, and Henk J. Wassenaar. 2013. A Choice Modeling Approach for Usage Context-Based Design. In *Decision-Based Design.* Springer, London, UK, 255-285.
10. Wei Chen, Wynne Hsu, and Mong Li Lee. 2013. Tagcloud-based explanation with feedback for recommender systems. In *Proceedings of the 36th international ACM SIGIR conference on Research and development in information retrieval* (SIGIR '13), 945-948. https://doi.org/10.1145/2484028.2484108
11. Dan Cosley, Shyong K. Lam, Istvan Albert, Joseph A. Konstan, and John Riedl. 2003. Is seeing believing?: how recommender system interfaces affect users' opinions. In *Proceedings of the SIGCHI Conference on Human Factors in Computing Systems* (CHI '03), 585-592. http://dx.doi.org/10.1145/642611.642713
12. Jonathan L. Herlocker, Joseph A. Konstan, and John Riedl. 2000. Explaining collaborative filtering recommendations. In *Proceedings of the 2000 ACM conference on Computer supported cooperative work* (CSCW '00), 241-250. http://dx.doi.org/10.1145/358916.358995
13. Yuchin Juan, Yong Zhuang, Wei-Sheng Chin, and Chih-Jen Lin. 2016. Field-aware factorization machines for CTR prediction. In *Proceedings of the 10th ACM Conference on Recommender Systems* (RecSys '16), 43-50. https://doi.org/10.1145/2959100.2959134
14. Alexandros Karatzoglou, Xavier Amatriain, Linas Baltrunas, and Nuria Oliver. 2010. Multiverse recommendation: n-dimensional tensor factorization for context-aware collaborative filtering. In *Proceedings of the fourth ACM conference on Recommender systems* (RecSys '10), 79-86. https://doi.org/10.1145/1864708.1864727
15. Rafal Kocielnik and Gary Hsieh. 2017. Send me a different message: utilizing cognitive space to create engaging message triggers. In *Proceedings of the 2017 ACM Conference on Computer Supported Cooperative Work and Social Computing* (CSCW '17), 2193-2207. https://doi.org/10.1145/2998181.2998324
16. Pigi Kouki, James Schaffer, Jay Pujara, John O'Donovan, and Lise Getoor. 2017. User preferences for hybrid explanations. In *Proceedings of the Eleventh ACM Conference on Recommender Systems* (RecSys '17), 84–88. https://doi.org/10.1145/3109859.3109915
17. Dong Li, Huang Shaohan, Wei Furu, Lapata Maria, Zhou Ming, and Xu Ke. 2017. Learning to generate product reviews from attributes. In *Proceedings of the 15th Conference of the European Chapter of the Association for Computational Linguistics* (ECACL '17), 623-632.
18. Khalil Ibrahim Muhammad, Aonghus Lawlor, and Barry Smyth. 2016. A live-user study of opinionated explanations for recommender systems. In *Proceedings of the 21st International Conference on Intelligent User Interfaces* (IUI '16), 256–260. https://doi.org/10.1145/2856767.2856813
19. Cataldo Musto, Fedelucio Narducci, Pasquale Lops, Marco De Gemmis, and Giovanni Semeraro. 2016. ExpLOD: a framework for explaining recommendations based on the linked open data cloud. In *Proceedings of the 10th ACM Conference on*

Recommender Systems (RecSys '16), 151–154. https://doi.org/10.1145/2959100.2959173

20. Chihiro Ono, Yasuhiro Takishima, Yoichi Motomura, and Hideki Asoh. 2009. Context-aware preference model based on a study of difference between real and supposed situation data. In *Proceedings of the 17th International Conference on User Modeling, Adaptation, and Personalization* (UMAP '09), 102–113. https://doi.org/10.1007/978-3-642-02247-0_12
21. Alexis Papadimitriou, Panagiotis Symeonidis, and Yannis Manolopoulos. 2012. A generalized taxonomy of explanations styles for traditional and social recommender systems. *Data Mining and Knowledge Discovery* 24, 3: 555–583.
22. Pearl Pu and Li Chen. 2006. Trust building with explanation interfaces. In *Proceedings of the 11th international conference on Intelligent user interfaces* (IUI '06), 93-100. https://doi.org/10.1145/1111449.1111475
23. Steffen Rendle, Zeno Gantner, Christoph Freudenthaler, and Lars Schmidt-Thieme. 2011. Fast context-aware recommendations with factorization machines. In *Proceedings of the 34th international ACM SIGIR conference on Research and development in Information Retrieval* (SIGIR '11), 635-644. http://dx.doi.org/10.1145/2009916.2010002
24. Panagiotis Symeonidis, Alexandros Nanopoulos, and Yannis Manolopoulos. 2009. MoviExplain: a recommender system with explanations. In *Proceedings of the third ACM conference on Recommender systems* (RecSys '09), 317-320. https://doi.org/10.1145/1639714.1639777
25. Nava Tintarev and Judith Masthoff. 2007. A survey of explanations in recommender systems. In *Proceedings of 2007 IEEE 23rd International Conference on Data Engineering Workshop*, 801–810. https://doi.org/10.1109/ICDEW.2007.4401070
26. Tintarev, N. and Masthoff, J. 2015. Explaining Recommendations: Design and Evaluation. In *Recommender Systems Handbook* (2nd. ed.), Springer, US, 353–382.
27. Jesse Vig, Shilad Sen, and John Riedl. 2009. Tagsplanations: explaining recommendations using tags. In *Proceedingsc of the 13th international conference on Intelligent user interfaces* (IUI '09), 47-56. https://doi.org/10.1145/1502650.1502661
28. Lipton, Zachary C., Sharad Vikram, and Julian McAuley. 2015. Generative concatenative nets jointly learn to write and classify reviews. arXiv preprint. arXiv:1511.03683
29. Yong Zheng, Bamshad Mobasher, and Robin Burke. 2016. User-oriented context suggestion. In *Proceedings of the 2016 Conference on User Modeling Adaptation and Personalization* (UMAP '16), 249–258. https://doi.org/10.1145/2930238.2930252

A Technology for Computer-Assisted Stroke Rehabilitation

Min Hun Lee
Carnegie Mellon University
Pittsburgh, PA, 15213 USA
mhlee@cmu.edu

ABSTRACT
Improving functional ability after a stroke requires task-oriented physical rehabilitation with the supervision of a therapist. However, with increasing medical costs and a shortage of rehabilitation specialists, post-stroke survivors sometimes receive a limited amount of individual treatment.

This paper proposes a low-cost computer-assisted rehabilitation system, called Virtual Coach that evaluates and guides a post-stroke survivor to engage in rehabilitation correctly at home with minimal supervision of a therapist. This system includes two major components: 1) motion analysis modules that evaluate exercise performance and guide a desirable joint trajectory and 2) a dialogue interface to provide feedback. The evaluation function of motion analysis modules computed exercise performance scores of 15 post-stroke survivors and achieved a 78% agreement with a practicing clinician. After developing a guidance function, the usability of the system will be evaluated with post-stroke survivors and therapists and iteratively improved.

Author Keywords
Intelligent agent; motion modelling & analysis; uncertainty quantification; stroke rehabilitation.

INTRODUCTION
Stroke is a disease that results in death to cells in part of the brain due to poor blood flow. The damage may lead to an inability to move limbs on one side of the body. Most stroke survivors engage in rehabilitation, which involves a task-oriented exercise to recover functional ability with the guidance of a therapist [4]. A positive functional recovery is highly dependent on receiving motivational and individualized rehabilitation sessions. Unfortunately, post-stroke survivors encounter a difficulty with receiving timely and comprehensive rehabilitation due to the limited time of therapists [5].

In recent years, researchers demonstrate the feasibility of developing low cost computer-based rehabilitation systems [3]. One strategy is to employ a motion based game that motivates a patient's participation [1]. However, this game-based approach does not provide clinical relevance. It is difficult to correlate the results of rehabilitation games with the improvement of a patient's functional ability.

Another approach is to perform action/gesture recognition, which determines the correctness of a motion [2]. Unlike a game-based approach, a gesture recognition-based approach can provide clinical relevance while motivating the patient to increase the number of correct movements. However, the number of correct movements cannot provide the detailed feedback. This binary analysis (i.e. correct or incorrect) may de-motivate the patient, who can only perform part of an exercise. In addition, the same number of incorrect movements does not necessarily represent the same level of functional ability. Even if two patients have the same number of incorrect movements, they may have different degrees of the range of motion. Thus, binary analysis is not sufficient for a therapist to follow the progress of patient's in-home rehabilitation.

To enhance experience of using a computer-based in-home rehabilitation system, this research addresses the following research questions: (1) how can a system automatically provide detailed motion analysis? (2) how closely can the system reproduce therapist's analysis? (3) can this system guide a desirable exercise movement?

PROPOSED RESEARCH
This paper proposes a Virtual Coach system that assists a post-stroke survivor to engage in rehabilitation with minimal supervision of a therapist. Building upon a Kinect sensor, this system utilizes machine learning algorithms to develop two motion analysis modules: evaluation and guidance modules. The evaluation module classifies 'correct' and 'incorrect' movements. It quantifies the probability of performing an correct movements. The guidance module analyzes the desirable joint position of an exercise. When a post-stroke survivor performs an exercise incorrectly, this system can provide corrective instructions. Upon completing an exercise trial, this system provides a performance score to encourage a post-stroke survivor's more active participation in the rehabilitation program. A therapist can easily track the quality of in-home exercise adherence and the progress of a post stroke survivor.

Experimental Design
Based on the discussion with a therapist, this work utilizes three upper limb exercises: E1 - *'Bring a cup to the mouth'*, E2 - *'Switch a light on'*, and E3 - *'Move forward a cane'*. These exercises are examples of task-oriented exercises for stroke rehabilitation. These exercise are selected due to their correspondence with major motion patterns: E1 to elbow flexion, E2 to shoulder flexion, and E3 to elbow extension.

We also specify three performance metrics to evaluate exercise

IUI'18 March 7–11, 2018, Tokyo, Japan

ACM ISBN 978-1-4503-4945-1/18/03.

DOI: https://doi.org/10.1145/3172944.3173146

performance: *'Precision*, *'Smoothness'*, and *'Compensation'*. The *'Precision'* represents how accurately an exercise is performed, the *'Smoothness'* indicates the level of trembling, the *'Compensation'* checks whether a participant involves any compensatory movement (e.g. leaning torso forward)

Data Collection

We utilize a Kinect v2 sensor (Microsoft, Redmond, USA) to record the trajectory of the selected body joints and capture video frames at 30 Hz. We recruit 15 post-stroke survivors with different level of functional abilities and 11 healthy subjects. A post-stroke survivor performed 10 repetitions of each exercise on both affected and unaffected sides. A healthy subject performed 15 repetitions of each exercise on a subject's dominant side. In total, each upper limb exercise contains 465 trials: 315 trials of correct movements and 150 trials of affected movements.

After collecting the dataset, a therapist watched the recorded videos and evaluates an exercise in three performance metrics on 4-point ordinal scale (0-3).

Evaluation and Guidance Modules

To develop motion analysis modules that work across post-stroke patients with different physical conditions, this system computes physical measurements and pre-processes joint coordinates into normalized representations. The evaluation module trains binary classifiers with normalized features to determine the correctness of an exercise movement in terms of the three performance metrics. Based on the results of an experiment that compares classification accuracies between Hidden Markov Model (HMM) and Decision Tree (DT) for each metric, we selected DTs for the *'Precision'* and *'Compensation'* metrics and HMMs for the *'Smoothness'* metric. Using the binary classifiers, this system quantities a probability of being a correct movement and computes a performance score. The guidance module will incorporate motion modeling techniques [6]. As modeling a pixel-level individual motion path is expensive in computation, we will model a motion trajectory in lower-resolution with a bounding box. It can provide an corrective instruction on joint positions when a post-stroke survivor performs an exercise incorrectly.

Dialogue Module

We designed a state machine to provide audio feedback when an user performs an exercise. The dialogue module will communicate with the motion analysis modules. Upon receiving any changes in motion analysis, the state machine will transit to a corresponding state and generate audio outputs. The state machine is composed of four states: *'Initial'*, *'Feedback'*, *'Termination'*, *'Wrap-up'*. In the *'Initial'* status, this system will summarize the main goal of rehabilitation session as specified by a therapist. When a system detects any erroneous movement (e.g. incorrect joint positions or performance metrics), it will switch to the *'Feedback'* state. The system will inform which metric is incorrectly performed or guide how to correctly place a joint. If a post-stroke survivor keeps performing incorrect movements, this system will provide an inspiring message. After finishing each trial of an exercise, the state machine will move to the *'Termination'* state and announce a performance score. Once a participant achieves all pre-specified tasks or gives up in the middle of a session, the state machine will review overall session performance and remind the subject about the next session.

CURRENT PROGRESS AND FUTURE PLAN

For the evaluation module, we have developed binary classifiers to classify incorrect movements in three metrics with the following classification accuracies: above 90% for both precision and compensation metrics and around 82% for the smoothness metric. We have compared the quantified performance scores of the assessment module with the observation scores of a therapist. This system achieves around 78% agreement with a therapist using all three metrics. For the dialogue module, we have designed the state machine and built communication with motion analysis modules.

In the future, we will develop motion trajectory model for the guidance module and the prototype of a Virtual Coach system. We will evaluate the usability of this system with post-stroke survivors and therapists.

CONCLUSION

This research leverages machine learning algorithms to develop a Virtual Coach system that evaluates and guides a stroke rehabilitation program without the presence of a therapist. This technology is not limited to stroke rehabilitation, but applicable to other types of health-care services. The successful completion of this project has a potential to improve the practice of health-care services.

REFERENCES

1. Madeline Balaam, Stefan Rennick Egglestone, Geraldine Fitzpatrick, Tom Rodden, Ann-Marie Hughes, Anna Wilkinson, Thomas Nind, Lesley Axelrod, Eric Harris, Ian Ricketts, and others. 2011. Motivating mobility: designing for lived motivation in stroke rehabilitation. In *Proceedings of the SIGCHI Conference on Human Factors in Computing Systems*. ACM, 3073–3082.
2. Yao-Jen Chang, Wen-Ying Han, and Yu-Chi Tsai. 2013. A Kinect-based upper limb rehabilitation system to assist people with cerebral palsy. *Research in developmental disabilities* 34, 11 (2013), 3654–3659.
3. Michelle J Johnson, Xin Feng, Laura M Johnson, and Jack M Winters. 2007. Potential of a suite of robot/computer-assisted motivating systems for personalized, home-based, stroke rehabilitation. *Journal of NeuroEngineering and Rehabilitation* 4, 1 (2007), 6.
4. Peter Langhorne, Peter Sandercock, and Kameshwar Prasad. 2009. Evidence-based practice for stroke. *The Lancet Neurology* 8, 4 (2009), 308 – 309.
5. Alexandra S Pollock, Lynn Legg, Peter Langhorne, and Cameron Sellars. 2000. Barriers to achieving evidence-based stroke rehabilitation. *Clinical Rehabilitation* 14, 6 (2000), 611–617.
6. Bodo Rosenhahn, Reinhard Klette, and Dimitris Metaxas. 2010. *Human Motion: Understanding, Modelling, Capture, and Animation* (1st ed.). Springer Publishing Company, Incorporated.

Machine Learning Behavioral Recognition to Support Neuropsychological Diagnosis of Cognitive Decline

Raniero A. Lara-Garduno
Texas A&M University
College Station, USA
raniero@tamu.edu

ABSTRACT
With nearly 93,500 deaths were attributed to Alzheimer's Disease in 2014 and numbers projected to climb[1], medical experts have recently placed increasing emphasis in the early detection of Alzheimer's disease and other types of dementia. An open challenge in early detection is developing standardized testing that helps clinicians detect subtle signs of Mild Cognitive Impairment that occur prior to the development of said dementias. In this regard we present our preliminary work on leveraging machine-learning behavioral classification to detect subtle behavioral abnormalities. Our framework consists of detecting behavioral abnormalities through the computerization of an existing paper-based clinical neuropsychological tests as well as the development of novel tests that could only be realized with modern touch tablet technology.

ACM Classification Keywords
I.2.1 Artificial Intelligence: Medicine and Science; H.1.2 Computer Applications: Life and Medical Sciences; H.5.2 Information Systems and Presentation: User Centered Design

Author Keywords
Human-Computer Interaction, Clinical Neuropsychology, Machine Learning Classification, Alzheimer's Disease, Mild Cognitive Impairment

INTRODUCTION
The diagnosis of early signs of Alzheimer's disease and other types of dementia consists of several stages. One such stage is a physical and neuropsychological examination administered by a specialist, who examines a patient's behavior by asking him or her to complete several tasks. These tests are typically administered via paper and pencil and ask the patient to perform various tasks including drawing shapes from memory, identifying target stimuli, connecting dots, and crossing out specific letters among others[7].

An ongoing challenge in this field is enhancing the identification of Mild Cognitive Impairment (MCI). This impairment is inherently comprised of subtle behavioral changes. Proper diagnosis of MCI can help specialists treat patients before the full turnover to dementia, dramatically improving the patient's long-term quality of life. Existing neuropsychological examinations, however, frequently leave the clinician with open interpretations of cognitive decline that can elongate the diagnosis process. We believe that digitizing these examinations and performing machine-learning-assisted behavioral recognition techniques can considerably expedite and standardize the identification of MCI.

RELATED WORK
Machine learning algorithms have previously been employed to identify behavioral abnormalities by training on and classifying medical imaging data. Bron et al.[1] and Greicius et al.[2], and Just et al.[3] are among the many researchers who have trained machine learning algorithms on patient MRI scans to identify subtle behavioral abnormalities, ranging from MCI to suicidal thoughts. Our research intends to employ machine learning algorithms on a quicker, lower-cost and less invasive diagnosis procedure. Machine learning on the neuropsychological exam known as the Clock Drawing test has been explored by Souillard-Mandar et al.[5] [6]. The Clock Drawing Test, however, is but one of many neuropsychological examinations that can test for a subset for a patient's cognitive function. New research questions remain open for other neuropsychological exams, and developing machine learning recognition and classification algorithms for existing and novel exams is not a trivial task.

DESIGN
We have created a computerized version of the classic Trail-Making Test (d-TMT)[4] and have created a novel 3-dimensional version of the Trail-Making Test (3D-TMT) that utilizes touch on a tablet computer to have users manipulate a virtual 2D object and identify labeled boxes in a correct order (submission under review). A digitized version of the Rey-Osterrieth Complex Figure test[7] is under development. These tests collect large volumes of usage data with which to classify behavioral patterns. Our preliminary focus has been classifying for subtle behavioral patterns among healthy populations as stand-ins for what would be behavioral

[1]Centers for Disease Control and Prevention: www.cdc.gov/features/alzheimers-disease-deaths/index.html

IUI 2018, March 7–11, 2018, Tokyo, Japan.
ACM ISBN 978-1-4503-4945-1/18/03.
https://doi.org/10.1145/3172944.3173147

Figure 1. Our digital Trail-Making test (left), our 3D-Trail-Making Test (center), and our digital Rey-Osterrieth Complex Figure test (right)

abnormalities for patients with MCI in the future. Testing so far has been carried out with cognitively healthy populations, classifying for age and country of origin. For the d-TMT, we successfully classified users by age with up to 92% accuracy, and for the 3D-TMT we classified users by country of origin with up to 96% accuracy. These results demonstrate these tests' powerful behavioral recognition capabilities, and are confident we can achieve similar results identifying between healthy patients and those with MCI.

GOALS AND RESEARCH QUESTIONS

Our goals are to expand behavioral recognition technology to a wider range of neuropsychological examinations, and to leverage existing mobile technology to develop new ones. We seek to employ a digital TMT, the 3D-TMT, and a digital Complex Figure test to MCI patients to train classification algorithms. Thus, our research questions, and methods to answer them are as follows:

Which machine learning models can be used on digital input data of neuropsychological exams to identify MCI? We will deploy our developed tests to MCI patients as well as cognitively healthy individuals to serve as training and testing data. Extracting features such as speed, stop-and-go motions, acceleration, smoothness of motions, etc. should help identify subtle behavioral abnormalities.

How do we best communicate our classification model results in a way that a clinician can use the information during diagnosis? We will develop a series of classes of cognitive decline labeled in a spectrum. We will present clinicians with confidence values of our assessment, and conduct qualitative studies with practitioners to elucidate our results in a useful way.

How can modern mobile technology be used to develop novel neuropsychological exams? We will test the efficiency of the 3D-TMT as a successful diagnosis tool for MCI by developing classification algorithms and analyzing how accurately it can predict a patient's cognitive decline. Qualitative studies with practitioners will also yield insights as to how we can further polish and develop this examination to test for functions that traditional paper-based exams cannot (such as depth perception of rotating shapes).

NEXT STEPS

We are currently developing a hierarchical sketch recognition system to automatically grade Complex Figure tests and detect subtle behavioral patterns. We are also communicating with clinical neuropsychologists to begin deploying our systems with patients with MCI. Afterward we will work on data extraction and feature calculation to develop and test behavioral classification algorithms. These steps should provide us with a classification algorithm that we can then integrate to the digital tests for automated behavioral recognition.

REFERENCES

1. Esther E Bron, Marion Smits, Wiesje M Van Der Flier, Hugo Vrenken, Frederik Barkhof, Philip Scheltens, Janne M Papma, Rebecca ME Steketee, Carolina Méndez Orellana, Rozanna Meijboom, and others. 2015. Standardized evaluation of algorithms for computer-aided diagnosis of dementia based on structural MRI: the CADDementia challenge. *NeuroImage* 111 (2015), 562–579.
2. Michael D Greicius and Daniel L Kimmel. 2012. Neuroimaging insights into network-based neurodegeneration. *Current opinion in neurology* 25, 6 (2012), 727–734.
3. Marcel Adam Just, Lisa Pan, Vladimir L. Cherkassky, Christine Cha McMakin, Matthew K. Nock, and David Brent. 2017. Machine learning of neural representations of suicide and emotion concepts identifies suicidal youth. *Nature Human Behaviour* (2017).
4. Raniero Lara-Garduno, Nancy Leslie, and Tracy Hammond. 2016. Smartstrokes: digitizing paper-based neuropsychological tests. In *Revolutionizing Education with Digital Ink*. Springer, 163–175.
5. William Souillard-Mandar, Randall Davis, Cynthia Rudin, Rhoda Au, David J Libon, Rodney Swenson, Catherine C Price, Melissa Lamar, and Dana L Penney. 2015. Learning classification models of cognitive conditions from subtle behaviors in the digital clock drawing test. *Machine learning* 102, 3 (2015), 393–441.
6. William Souillard-Mandar, Randall Davis, Cynthia Rudin, Rhoda Au, and Dana Penney. 2016. Interpretable Machine Learning Models for the Digital Clock Drawing Test. *arXiv preprint arXiv:1606.07163* (2016).
7. Esther Strauss, Elisabeth M. S. Sherman, and Otfried Spreen. 2006. *A Compendium of Neuropsychological Tests: Administration, Norms, and Commentary* (third ed.). Oxford University Press.

Suggestion Models in Geographic Exploratory Search

Noemi Mauro
Computer Science Dept., University of Turin
Torino, Italy
noemi.mauro@unito.it

ABSTRACT
My PhD project focuses on the suggestion of information categories in exploratory search in a geographical domain. Geographical maps may challenge the user in the exploration of possibly complex information spaces, making difficult to find all the relevant data for the completion of her/his search task. I propose different models for concepts suggestion which, given a search query, allow the creation of clusters of categories useful for query expansion as a *"you might be interested in"* function. The training of these models is done by exploiting different types of information: search sessions, users' preferences and social data coming from Twitter.

CCS Concepts
•Information systems → Information retrieval; Query log analysis; Query suggestion; Query reformulation;

Author Keywords
Geographical Information Retrieval; Session-based Concept Suggestion; Query Expansion.

INTRODUCTION
Exploring large datasets can be challenging for users especially when no support for the information navigation is provided by the system. Information search often happens in an "anomalous knowledge status" [3] and the modality of expression and the conceptualization adopted by the system can differ from the user's one. To address these issues, some systems offer different schemes for browsing data categories, such as lists or hierarchies. Sometimes the user deals with the exploration of complex information spaces organized as categories. Thus, users are often exposed to a possibly difficult selection task of the concepts presented. My PhD project focuses on the definition of different suggestion models for exploratory search in a geographical context. Exploratory search is affected by the above issues because the users' information goals are ill-defined; see [7]. I aim to provide users with small clusters of concepts that have the meaning of the suggestion function *"you might be also interested in"*. This may help the exploration of categories belonging to complex information spaces and suggest information related to users' search task.

I aim at answering the following research questions:

H1: *Is it possible to exploit frequently co-occurring concepts in a search session to suggest clusters of concepts relevant to the exploration of complex geographical information spaces?*

H2: *Is it possible to extract from Twitter local common interests of a specific geographical area to suggest clusters of concepts relevant for the user's search task?*

H3: *Is it possible to personalize the suggestion of clusters of concepts taking into account the user's specific information needs extracted from her/his user model?*

In order to answer these questions, I am developing different concepts suggestion models that propose the user a set of possible relevant data categories starting from the queries that he or she has already submitted. The suggested categories are complementary to the concepts that the user has focused on. They are suggested by exploiting different sources of data using different strategies.

RELATED WORK
My PhD project starts from the development of a textual search query interpretation model at a conceptual level. It leverages ontology and linguistic information, following an associative information retrieval model. However, the main focus of my project is the creation of different concepts suggestion models. They are based on the observation of concepts co-occurrence in search sessions, on the examination of population interests in Twitter in a geographical area, and on the creation of user models that represent the specific user's interests within a search session. My work differs from [6] because I aim at finding *concept co-occurrence* in search sessions, while they observe *term co-occurrence* for query expansion. Some works on information filtering and on recommender systems acquire relations among information items observing the users' behavior. For instance, Google Knowledge Graph (https://goo.gl/c56X3D) gather relations among facts, concepts, and items starting from their co-occurrences in queries. Those works are complementary to my PhD project. The main difference is that I employ a knowledge graph to predict further concepts that the user might be interested in, i.e., I aim to suggest topics, instead of recommending individual items.

METHODOLOGY AND SUGGESTION MODELS
I defined the different models starting from the analysis of search sessions from the AOL query log[1]. Since the goal of

[1] https://archive.org/details/AOL_search_data_leak_2006

IUI 2018, March 7–11, 2018, Tokyo, Japan.
ACM ISBN 978-1-4503-4945-1/18/03.
https://doi.org/10.1145/3172944.3173148

my work is the development of an intelligent search support function for Geographical Information Systems, I chose for the experiments an example system, i.e., OnToMap [2, 1]. I pre-processed the AOL search log to work on a smaller dataset composed of search sessions relevant to the geographical information provided by OnToMap. I selected those including at least one query that refers to the concepts of the OnToMap ontology. The ultimate goal of my work is to train different query expansion models suitable for improving information search in OnToMap. The clusters of concepts used as suggestions are created in two steps: (1) First, the creation of a concepts co-occurrence graph in which each node represents a concept and the edges weight reflects the strength of concept co-occurrence in search sessions, or in Twitter (it depends on the model). (2) Secondly, the application of the COPRA [5] community detection algorithm to the co-occurrence graph. COPRA works on weighted graphs and detects overlapping communities. Each community represents a cluster of concepts used as suggestions, while a concept can belong to different clusters at the same time. This supports capturing the fact that different sessions can have different sets of common concepts. Moreover, it is possible to suggest different groups of concepts, starting from the same search queries. In my PhD project, I plan to create different types of concepts suggestion models. They differ from each other by the data source used for the graph creation and from the strategies used to select clusters for query expansion.

Session-based Suggestion of Topics

The concepts co-occurrence graph is created from the analysis of search sessions in the AOL query log and is described in [8]. After the extraction of clusters of concepts from the graph, I analyzed different strategies for the clusters' selection starting from the first query submitted in each search session. Specifically, I investigated three different strategies: (1) Selection of clusters that contain all the concepts referred in the first search query. (2) Selection of clusters that contain at least one concept referred in the first search query. (3) Selection of the best matching cluster with respects to the first query of the search session. The results show that these suggestions strategies have the same accuracy (F1 score) but they differ in precision, or recall, respectively. Thus, depending on the priority of precision with respect to recall, it might be useful to select a specific strategy for suggestions. See [8] for details.

Personalized Suggestion of Topics

Starting from the strategies described in the above section, it could be interesting to analyze if the introduction of ontology-based user models [4] can improve the strategies' accuracy and can better reflect users' information needs. User models try to capture the specific interests of a user and their combination with the general interests of the population might improve the suggestion of more suitable clusters. It is also important to investigate how to tune the temporal span for the generation of the user models.

Suggestion of Topics Exploiting Social Data

Another part of my PhD project concerns the creation of the co-occurrence graph leveraging Twitter data grouped by user in a particular geographical area. In this case, the co-occurrence graph represents the social interests of the population and this information can be used for the construction of a social suggestion model. Starting from the first search query of a search session of AOL query log, the model suggests the clusters built using a social layer of the information.

CONCLUSIONS

I presented different concepts suggestion models helpful to support query expansion during exploratory search in a geographical context. The evaluation of the first model on the AOL log provided satisfactory results about its concept prediction accuracy. I plan an evaluation of the other two models, based on the analysis of search queries (and sessions) of the AOL query log and Twitter data useful for the construction of the clusters described in Section 3.3. In particular, I will evaluate whether the clusters represent the search sessions performed by the users in the AOL log. I also plan some experimentations with real users in order to check whether they explore the suggested concepts. Finally, I plan to combine the different models in order to evaluate whether the accuracy might improve and the models can better support users in the exploration of geographical information space. This work is funded by project MIMOSA (MultIModal Ontology-driven query system for the heterogeneous data of a SmArtcity, "Progetto di Ateneo Torino_call2014_L2_157", 2015-17) and by "Ricerca Autofinanziata"of the University of Turin.

REFERENCES

1. L. Ardissono, M. Lucenteforte, N. Mauro, A. Savoca, A. Voghera, and L. La Riccia. 2017a. Semantic Interpretation of Search Queries for Personalization. In *Proc. of UMAP 2017 Adjunct*. ACM, 101–102.
2. L. Ardissono, M. Lucenteforte, N. Mauro, A. Savoca, A. Voghera, and L. La Riccia. 2017b. OnToMap - Semantic Community Maps for knowledge sharing. In *Proceedings of Hypertext 2017*. ACM, 317–318.
3. N.J. Belkin. 1980. Anomalous states of knowledge as a basis for information retrieval. *Canadian Journal of Information Science* 5 (1980), 133–143.
4. S. Gauch, J. Chaffee, and A. Pretschner. 2003. Ontology-based personalized search and browsing. *Web Intelli. and Agent Sys.* 1, 3-4 (2003), 219–234.
5. S. Gregory. 2010. Finding overlapping communities in networks by label propagation. *New Journal of Physics* 12, 103018 (2010).
6. C.K. Huang, L.F. Chien, and Y.J. Oyang. 2003. Relevant term suggestion in interactive web search based on contextual in formation in query session logs. *Journal of the American Society for Information Science and Technology* 54, 7 (2003), 638–649.
7. G. Marchiorini. 2006. Exploratory search: from finding to understanding. *Commun. ACM* 49, 4 (2006), 41–46.
8. N. Mauro and L. Ardissono. 2018. Session-based Suggestion of Topics for Geographic Exploratory Search. In *Proceedings of the 23rd International Conference on Intelligent User Interfaces (IUI '18)*. ACM.

Leveraging User Input and Feedback for Interactive Sound Event Detection and Annotation

Bongjun Kim
Northwestern University
Evanston, IL, USA
bongjun@u.northwestern.edu

ABSTRACT
Tagging of environment audio events is essential in many areas. However, finding sound events and labeling them within a long audio file is tedious and time-consuming. Building an automatic recognition system using modern machine learning is often not feasible because it requires a large number of human-labeled training examples and it is not reliable enough for all uses. I propose interactive sound event detection to solve the issue by combining machine search with human tagging, specifically focusing on the effectiveness of various types of user-inputs to the interactive sound searching. The types of user inputs that I will explore include binary relevance feedback, segmentation, and vocal imitation. I expect that leveraging one or combination of these user inputs would help users find audio contents of interest quickly and accurately, even in the situation where there are not enough training examples for a typical automated system.

Author Keywords
interactive machine learning; sound event detection; human-in-the-loop system

INTRODUCTION
Searching for sound events within a long audio file can be used in many areas. Sound designers might want to search for sound effects in a long audio recording quickly. Ecologists need tools for labeling bird calls and singing in lengthy recordings (e.g. a 24 hour long recording of a natural scene). Police officers might want to find suspicious sound events in city recording. Speech and language pathologists often wish to label sound and speech events in day-long (24 hours) recordings of patient environments. Collecting audio segments of interest is also an inevitable step when ones want to create an audio dataset from their own recordings, which can be used as sound design library or training dataset for machine learning. The current standard way of searching for audio is text-based search. However, text-based search within a lengthy recording is currently possible only when someone has manually added time-coded text, which is prohibitively labor intensive.

IUI 2018, March 7–11, 2018, Tokyo, Japan.
ACM ISBN 978-1-4503-4945-1/18/03.
https://doi.org/10.1145/3172944.3173149

An obvious solution to the issue is to use an automated audio retrieval system. However, building a fully automated system leveraging machine learning techniques such as deep learning [4] typically requires a large number of training examples (e.g. hundreds of thousands of examples) during system design. On top of that, the set of classes to be identified must be known prior to deployment, meaning end-users cannot define new classes to be identified. Even with lots of training data and model tuning, machine labeling may not be good enough for some applications that require human-level accuracy.

I propose a mixed-initiative audio search system that is useful in a situation where there are no time-coded text labels available in the audio and there are too few training examples to successfully train a statistical machine learner, yet the search task is too time consuming to perform entirely manually. The proposed system allows a user to define a target sound class on-the-fly and helps a user to find the target sound events within a long audio file more quickly than is possible by manual search. The goal of the retrieval system is to speed up the labeling task at hand, rather than to train a generalized machine learning model for later use on different data.

RESEARCH GOALS
I apply a human-in-the-loop approach to content-based audio search. The idea is to engage a user in an interactive process to collaboratively search for sound with machines. The success of interactive retrieval depends on how to incorporate human knowledge into the system. A user can guide and improve the system by providing it with information about a target concept to search for. My research goals are following: 1) Developing new user input and feedback methods to provide machines with more information about a target sound, 2) Implementing a sound event annotation interface that embodies all the interaction methods.

BACKGROUND AND RELATED WORK
Interactive machine learning has been applied to document and image retrieval systems [1, 5], where a user can review retrieved documents or images and provide feedback. This approach is aimed at training the best classifier to retrieve items relevant to a query. My goal is to speed up the labeling task at hand, rather than to train a generalized machine learning model for later use on different data.

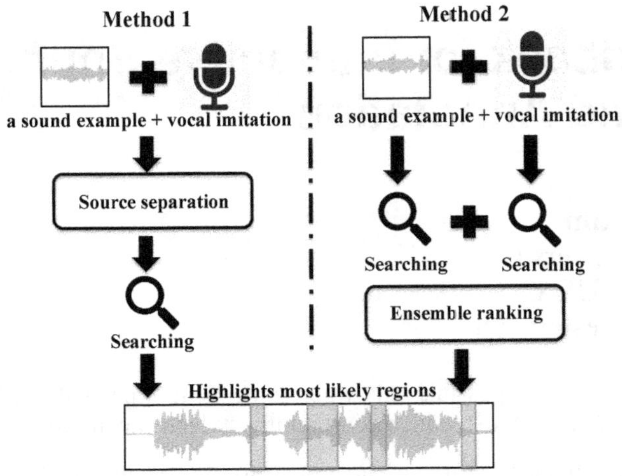

Figure 1. vocal imitation processing methods

How to leverage the user input and feedback in an interactive learning interface could vary depending on the types of data to search (e.g. text, image, or sound). There are only a few works that have applied interactive learning to audio retrieval system [2] and they did not address the difference between audio and other types of data in terms of possible user-inputs for interactive audio retrieval. My focus in this work is how to leverage user input (i.e. human knowledge) in interactive audio retrieval and how much the interaction would help a user to achieve their goal quickly and easily.

CURRENT RESEARCH STATUS

The proposed interface will allow three different types of user inputs: binary relevance feedback (positive or negative), user segmentation (adjusting time-boundaries of retrieved sound segments), and vocal imitation (imitating sound with vocalization). I have implemented my initial proof-of-concept for the proposed system [3] that allows only relevance feedback and user segmentation. How the system works is following. Given a long audio file, a user selects a region that contains a target sound event in the audio track as an initial search key. The system returns the n most similar sound events. Then, the user gives feedback to the system and the importance of audio features is re-weighted so that it can return more relevant examples in the next round. Readers can watch the demo video at `http://www.bongjunkim.com/ised/`. The user study showed that the mixed-intuitive approach speeds up a sound annotation task. I have also learned that, while the interface improves the overall performance of human's audio searching, the human-machine interaction loop causes extra interaction overhead. I will redesign the human-machine interaction to reduce the extra cost during the next iteration of the research.

METHODS AND RESEARCH PLANS

My prior works use two types of user feedback: 1) applying positive or negative labels to each suggested region, 2) adjusting boundaries of the suggested region when its onset and offset are not perfectly aligned with the target sound.

On top of the interaction methods, I plan to develop vocal imitation-based interaction. Vocal imitation is a simple and effective way to describe sound concepts. Unlike texts and images, audio events are often fully overlapped (e.g. a cough is concurrent with television noise). Unless a user tells a system which sound event is the target, the retrieval results would be degraded. In this work, a user will be able to specify the target sound by imitating it. I am exploring two possible approaches to processing the vocal imitation as shown in Figure 1: 1) extracting target source by vocal imitation, 2) combining the two search results from an actual example and its vocal imitation.

I also plan to implement an interface for sound event detection that embodies all the proposed user input and feedback method to speed up the sound labeling task. Based on participants' feedback from the initial experiment [3], I will redesign my initial interface and add a new component for vocal imitation-based interaction where users can quickly monitor or edit their vocal imitation query and feedback.

CONCLUSION AND INTELLECTUAL MERIT

Developing interaction methods that help to speed up sound event search are the main advances of this work. Vocal imitations of sound events would help machines understand perceptually relevant features of audio, and leveraging a combination of various types of user inputs would help users find audio contents of interest quickly and accurately even in the situation where there are not enough training examples for an automated system. I expect that the proposed work will provide insight about how human input and feedback can reduce the gap between human and machine's auditory perception and how they can be applied to an intelligent interactive system.

ACKNOWLEDGMENTS

This work was supported by NSF Grant 1617497.

REFERENCES

1. Saleema Amershi, James Fogarty, Ashish Kapoor, and Desney Tan. 2011. Effective End-user Interaction with Machine Learning. In *Proc. of the AAAI Conference on Artificial Intelligence (AAAI)*. AAAI Press, 1529–1532.
2. Sébastien Gulluni, Slim Essid, Olivier Buisson, and Gaël Richard. 2011. An interactive system for electro-Acoustic music analysis. In *Proc. of the International Society for Music Information Retrieval Conference (ISMIR)*. 145–150.
3. Bongjun Kim and Bryan Pardo. 2017. I-SED: An Interactive Sound Event Detector. In *Proc. of the International Conference on Intelligent User Interfaces (IUI)*. ACM, 553–557.
4. Giambattista Parascandolo, Heikki Huttunen, and Tuomas Virtanen. 2016. Recurrent neural networks for polyphonic sound event detection in real life recordings. In *Proc. of the International Conference on Acoustics, Speech and Signal Processing (ICASSP)*. IEEE, 6440–6444.
5. Burr Settles. 2011. Closing the loop: Fast, interactive semi-supervised annotation with queries on features and instances. In *Proc. of the conference on empirical methods in natural language processing*. Association for Computational Linguistics, 1467–1478.

Analysis of Interaction Design and Evaluation Methods in Full-Body Interaction for Special Needs

Ciera Crowell
University Pompeu Fabra
Barcelona, Spain
ciera.crowell@upf.edu

ABSTRACT
This work is focused on the specific properties and evaluation of full-body interaction design of multi-user mixed reality environments. The main goal is to study how full-body interaction can aid in intervention strategies for children with autism, to improve their understanding and adoption of social behaviors with peers and with society in general. The research is based upon HCI theory, aided by general theories of embodied cognition, embodiment and developmental psychology. The main setting of the research is large scale floor-projected mixed environments, which will allow for testing interaction strategies and evaluation methods of experiences based on collocation of multiple users within a full-body interactive scenario, where they can practice interaction in a natural and uninhibited manner. The research consists of designing playful experiences for the target users in order to promote socialization, collaboration and social inclusion. Topics for analysis include understanding the dynamics of goal-oriented and open-ended gameplay, proxemics, and encouraged group collaboration, on the design of these systems. Assessment methods take into account multimodal analysis, including physiology-based data such as electrodermal activity and heart rate, of the children's behavioral and affective states in the experience.

ACM Classification Keywords
H.5.m. Information Interfaces and Presentation (e.g. HCI): Miscellaneous

Author Keywords
Autism Spectrum Disorder; ASD; full-body interaction; open-ended gameplay; encouraged collaboration

INTRODUCTION
This research investigates how full-body interactive environments can aid in intervention for children with Autism Spectrum Disorder (ASD). These interactive technologies are operated by the natural gestures which we use in daily life to communicate and express ourselves, through the movements of our bodies and understanding humans as active participants in relation to the surrounding space. As children with ASD display marked difficulties in forming and maintaining relationships with peers, we see that full-body interactive systems present an opportunity for children to practice social behaviors face-to-face with others through collaborative activities [2]. As interactive environments are able to adapt and respond to changes in user behavior, we believe this technology could serve as a way to aid psychologists in their work managing the disparity between each child's needs. This work consists of two projects in this research area. The first is a large scale floor projected virtual environment of 6 meters in diameter, called Lands of Fog, which was designed as a play arena to foster exploratory and social behaviors between a child with ASD and a typically developed peer. After testing the environment in both laboratory and classroom settings, the current second generation model is investigating user proxemics, goal oriented behavior, and changes in user affective state via biometrics. This project has inspired a spin-off project called GenPlay, which is undergoing user trials with a Kinect-based prototype. GenPlay is a virtual environment platform which is able to be installed in a standard classroom. By utilizing generative music and visuals, we will aim to increase collaboration between children with ASD and typically developed classmates.

IUI'18 March 7–11, 2018, Tokyo, Japan

ACM ISBN 978-1-4503-4945-1/18/03.

DOI: https://doi.org/10.1145/3172944.3173150

RESEARCH CONTEXT
Full body interactive technologies introduce a novel aspect to the interactive technologies paradigm, placing the body and natural gestures as the focus of interaction [3]. As technological advances have allowed for the proliferation of interactive technologies beyond the traditional keyboard and mouse interface, users are not restricted to external interface elements and can take advantage of more natural and intuitive interactions. In this broadened scope of HCI, we can observe a defined intersection between spatial interaction, motor activity and user interfaces. Full-body technologies in particular hold potential to assist in learning [1], and collocated full-body experiences allow for face-to-face collaboration with other users, which has been seen to foster social behavior [3]. This research shows that full-body interaction systems hold potential for people with social disabilities, such as autism.

The pervasive deficits in social abilities among individuals with ASD frequently result in challenges in developing relationships with others. Individuals with ASD may show difficulties in social-emotional reciprocity, taking part in imaginative play, or initiating social interactions. Thus, children with ASD typically engage in a higher frequency of solitary, nonsocial play and may have a higher incidence of social fragmentation in friendship and classroom circles.

In an attempt to provide engaging and dynamic interventions, many research efforts have utilized Information and Communication Technologies (ICT) to create play and learning experiences for children with ASD. Furthermore, it has been shown that along with an affinity towards science and math skills, children with ASD have a special interest in computerized learning, possibly due to the linear and systematic nature of most computer programs. This clear structure can reduce anxiety for individuals with ASD, as they usually show increased responsiveness to stimuli when events are predictable. Also, with ICT, change can be introduced and mediated in a discrete manner. Projects which use computer graphics displays have been recommended with ASD for the use of visually cued instructions. Examples include hand held devices for aiding communication, tangible user interfaces (TUI) for learning social communication skills, desktop media for language acquisition, and multi-touch tabletops for teaching group collaboration.

RESEARCH GOALS AND METHODOLOGY

With the help of ICT full-body interactive systems, our primary goals include:

1. To study how full-body interactive systems can aid in intervention strategies for children with ASD, improving the understanding and adoption of social behaviors and heightening inclusion with peers and society in general.
2. To better understand the interaction design aspects which create socialization, collaboration, and engagement in interactive games for ASD, such as encouraged collaboration, proxemics and open-ended play.

RESEARCH PLAN AND PROGRESS

Project 1: Lands of Fog

The system Lands of Fog [4] was funded by the Recercaixa 2013 grant, as an interactive play setting to spark social play behaviors in children with ASD. A series of experimental trials was carried out in Barcelona during the summer of 2015. For these trials, a total of 16 children with ASD were recruited from surrounding autism centers to play with 16 typically developed partners. Each child participated in 3 playing sessions of 15 minutes in a controlled laboratory setting. The goal of these trials was to evaluate the efficacy of the system in fostering user engagement, socialization and collaboration within the context of the virtual environment. Multi-modal data analysis revealed an increase in socializations made by users with ASD through the course of the trials. The Lands of Fog system was transported to London in November 2015, where it was installed in an integrated elementary school with a Special Educational Needs program. Over the course of one week, 30 children with ASD played in the system. The goal of these trials was to evaluate the efficacy of the system in an integrated school setting. Multimodal data analysis revealed that the children with ASD felt more comfortable interacting with their partner in the game setting than in a classroom setting, and the typically developed children reported an increased willingness to get to know better their ASD playing partners. In January 2017, work began on a second generation of the Lands of Fog system, with the introduction of biosensing devices to monitor affective states of players through ECG and HRV. Additionally, two gameplay scenarios were developed to test differences in collaboration behaviors in an open ended play vs. goal oriented play format. Finally, a proxemics testing protocol was developed to understand inconsistencies in personal space preferences in typically developed children and children with ASD. Pilot trials were conducted for two months, and the system begun a series of long term trials in June 2017.

Project 2: GenPlay

In 2017, a partnership was formed with the FASIA special education school in Barcelona, where the researcher conducted a 4 session observation and user study. This study revealed the need for in-classroom activities to link typically developed children and children with ASD in integrated school settings. The idea for GenPlay centers around a portable projection system with multiple user tracking, which can be quickly installed and integrated into a classroom. The system is undergoing development of generative audiovisuals which react to patterns in user movements, based on the premise of proxemics and music therapy for autism. Through collaborative gestures, the children can create their own language of interaction with the system. The goal of the system will be to observe a change in social circles in the classroom, towards a more inclusive environment for children with ASD. A finished prototype is due to begin testing in January 2018.

REFERENCES

1. Alissa N. Antle, Greg Corness, and Milena Droumeva. 2009. What the body knows: Exploring the benefits of embodied metaphors in hybrid physical digital environments. *Interacting with Computers* 21, 1-2 (1 2009), 66–75. DOI: http://dx.doi.org/10.1016/j.intcom.2008.10.005
2. Ciera Crowell, Joan Mora-Guiard, and Narcis Pares. 2017. Impact of Interaction Paradigms on Full-Body Interaction Collocated Experiences for Promoting Social Initiation and Collaboration. *HumanâĂŞComputer Interaction* (9 2017), 1–33. DOI: http://dx.doi.org/10.1080/07370024.2017.1374185
3. Joan Mora-Guiard, Ciera Crowell, Narcis Pares, and Pamela Heaton. 2016. Lands of Fog. In *Proceedings of the The 15th International Conference on Interaction Design and Children - IDC '16*. ACM Press, New York, New York, USA, 262–274. DOI: http://dx.doi.org/10.1145/2930674.2930695
4. Joan Mora-Guiard, Ciera Crowell, Narcis Pares, and Pamela Heaton. 2017. Sparking social initiation behaviors in children with Autism through full-body Interaction. *International Journal of Child-Computer Interaction* 11 (1 2017), 62–71. DOI: http://dx.doi.org/10.1016/J.IJCCI.2016.10.006

User Preference Modeling and Exploitation in IoT Scenarios

David Massimo
Free University of Bozen-Bolzano
Bolzano, Italy
damassimo@inf.unibz.it

ABSTRACT
Recommender Systems are commonly used in web applications to support users in finding items of their interest. We here propose to use Recommender Systems in Internet of Things scenarios to support human decision making in the physical world. For instance, users' choices (visit actions) for points of interests (POIs) while they explore a sensor enabled city can be tracked and used to generate recommendations for not yet visited POIs. In this PhD research, we propose a novel learning approach for generating an explainable human behaviour model and relevant recommendations in sensor enabled areas. Moreover, we propose techniques for simulating user behaviour and analyse the collective dynamics of a population of users.

CCS Concepts
•**Information systems** → **Recommender systems;**

Author Keywords
Recommender System; Internet of Things; Inverse Reinforcement Learning; Behaviour Learning.

INTRODUCTION
Recommender Systems (RSs) are software tools that support human decision making by identifying relevant items or actions for a user [9]. Since users' preferences and choices are affected by contextual factors (e.g., being in a group, or the items consumed before) context-aware RSs (CARSs) have also been introduced [1]. Moreover, in order to specifically leverage the knowledge of the specific order in which the user consumes items, pattern-discovery [6, 2, 8] and reinforcement learning [10, 7] approaches have also been proposed. The first approach extracts common patterns from user behaviour logs and learns a predictive model of the next user actions, whereas the latter learns the optimal choice model of the user in order to provide personalised suggestions. However, these approaches are opaque in explaining the predicted user behaviour, i.e., users' preferences and their action-selection policy are black boxes. In addition, these predictive models use the explicit knowledge of the utility a user gets from an action (e.g. in the form of a rating), which, in many practical applications, is unknown. Finally, they often assume that the user selects items according to a simple choice model: he always picks the items with the highest rating.

In our research, we aim at improving the previously mentioned approaches by better modelling and explaining the user's sequential choice process by building an item choice model that can replicate user's observed behaviour and is determined by his preferences. We see this as a prerequisite to tailor the recommendation process to the user. In order to learn the user's choice model in context, we will exploit the observation of the choices of a population that acts in physical areas, which are acquired via Internet of Things (IoT) technologies, i.e., sensors networks that can register users' activities (e.g., movements) and environment conditions (e.g., crowdedness level) [4, 3]. However, IoT sensed data can be noisy and the revealed user actions may not always conform to those of an agent that maximizes his utility, hence specific learning and recommendation techniques must be developed.

Hence, in this PhD research we are firstly focusing on techniques to model/predict user behaviour (his choices) that can explain the observed user's actions in context. Secondly, we propose new techniques to offer compelling (non trivial) recommendations that are adapted to the learned user behaviour but are not trivially offering what the user is predicted to choose. Finally, we propose to reuse the predicted behavioural model to simulate the collective behaviour of a population with alternative environment conditions.

RESEARCH PROGRESS UP TO DATE
In order to address the aforementioned research problems, we propose the usage of Inverse Reinforcement Learning (IRL). IRL has been already successfully used in economics and robotics to simulate agent behaviour, but not yet in RSs. IRL learns user's sequential decision making behaviour by simply observing the user's actions, i.e., without knowing the derived utility for the user (e.g. rating feedback). IRL explicitly represents user's preferences in terms of a reward function, which is usually assumed to be a linear function $r = \vartheta^T \cdot \varphi$ of the features (φ vector) describing the environment state; ϑ is the user preference vector about the environment features. For instance, environmental state variables can describe the location, or the visit context of the visitor in a museum, such as, the crowdedness level of the museum or the time spent in the various museum sections. The user's action-selection policy

IUI'18 March 7–11, 2018, Tokyo, Japan

ACM ISBN 978-1-4503-4945-1/18/03.
DOI: https://doi.org/10.1145/3172944.3173151

is derived from the learned reward function r by exploiting the assumption that observed users act in order to maximise reward while visiting the museum. IRL can also potentially solve the problem of deriving false information on the user utility because of the inherent noise in the user action selection process. This can be done by grouping similar users (e.g., users sharing visit goals) and then by learning user behaviour from grouped observations.

We have implemented this approach in two case studies in the tourism domain: the first one in a closed environment (i.e., a museum) [5] and the second one in an open environment, i.e., a tourist area (under development). In addition, since we conjecture that IRL, in the task of learning users behaviour in a sequential decision making problem, can compete with other novel techniques that are emerging in the field of session-based RSs (e.g., recurrent neural networks), we are comparing our approach to them. Our initial results show that IRL is capable of learning user's preferences and his action-selection policy even from small and noisy datasets. Compared with other techniques for learning/predicting action sequences, such as, recurrent neural networks, the proposed approach has two distinguish aspects. Firstly, it learns to which extent items and context features are "liked" by a user (contribute to the acquired reward), whereas other techniques do not. Secondly, it is able to learn even from small samples.

After the user action selection policy is learnt, recommendations can be generated by comparing the predicted choices of an individual with those of a larger group the user belongs to. For instance, if the policy followed by the individual does not match the predicted group behaviour then he can be recommended to deviate from his own predicted behaviour and consider new opportunities, e.g., to visit a shop that the group seems to like. Alternatively, recommendations can be generated by exploiting external factors that influence the relevance of an item. For instance, if a commuter is understood to like arts and an exhibition is taking place on his way, the system could recommend it to him.

In general, we claim that interesting recommendations should tend to modify the usual user behaviour, rather than, as it was typically done in the state of the art, to simply follow the learnt user behavioural model. However, this is not an easy task since users have a tendency to stick to, even suboptimal behaviours, if not properly instructed. We propose therefore the usage of a proper exploration policy to identify those items/actions that the RS can suggest to a user by knowing his context, preferences and behaviour. For instance, if a tourist is known to daily go to a specific cafeteria in the morning, then the system can recommend him to have breakfast in a bakery nearby. This allows to explore items alternatives and also to nudge a user enabling him to avoid suboptimal choices.

The proposed techniques are going to be implemented in a mobile application that exploits an IoT infrastructure to support tourists' decision making by enabling them to discover new places or shops in an Italian alpine valley. In order to easily bootstrap the application, we are also developing a simulation tool that allows individuals or groups to simulate the experience of visiting a selected POI. Collected data will be used to assess the proposed behaviour learning and recommendation approaches. Evaluations will be performed in both on-line (e.g., A/B testing, questionnaires) and off-line (e.g., algorithms performance) settings.

Finally, we propose to use the learnt behavioural model in order to generate synthetic action sequences of a population under conditions of interest (e.g., the opening of a new road or of a new mall). In this way the system dynamics and the recommender performance can be evaluated by exploiting simulated user actions.

REFERENCES

1. G. Adomavicius and A. Tuzhilin. 2011. *Context-Aware Recommender Systems*. Springer US, Boston, MA, 217–253.
2. D. Jannach, I. Kamehkhosh, and L. Lerche. 2017. Leveraging Multi-dimensional User Models for Personalized Next-track Music Recommendation. In *Proceedings of the Symposium on Applied Computing (SAC '17)*. ACM, New York, NY, USA, 1635–1642.
3. S. Li, Li D. Xu, and S. Zhao. 2015. The internet of things: a survey. *Information Systems Frontiers* 17, 2 (2015), 243–259.
4. Y. Li, M. Hou, H. Liu, and Y. Liu. 2012. Towards a theoretical framework of strategic decision, supporting capability and information sharing under the context of Internet of Things. *Information Technology and Management* 13, 4 (2012), 205–216.
5. D. Massimo, M. Elahi, and F. Ricci. 2017. Learning User Preferences by Observing User-Items Interactions in an IoT Augmented Space. In *2017 Conf. on User Modelling, Adaptation and Personalization*. ACM.
6. B. Mobasher, H. Dao, T. Luo, and M. Nakagawa. 2002. Using Sequential and Non-Sequential Patterns in Predictive Web Usage Mining Tasks. *2002 IEEE International Conference on Data Mining, 2002. Proceedings.* (2002), 669–672.
7. O. Moling, L. Baltrunas, and F. Ricci. 2012. Optimal radio channel recommendations with explicit and implicit feedback. *Proceedings of the 6th ACM conference on Recommender systems - RecSys '12* (2012), 75.
8. E. Palumbo, G. Rizzo, and E. Baralis. 2017. Predicting Your Next Stop-over from Location-based Social Network Data with Recurrent Neural Networks. In *RECSYS 2017, 2nd ACM International Workshop on Recommenders in Tourism (RecTour'17), CEUR Proceedings Vol. 1906, August 27-31, 2017, Como, Italy,*. 1–8.
9. F. Ricci, L. Rokach, and B. Shapira. 2015. *Recommender Systems: Introduction and Challenges*. Springer US, Boston, MA, 1–34.
10. G. Shani, D. Heckerman, and R. I. Brafman. 2005. An mdp-based recommender system. *Journal of Machine Learning Research* (2005), 1265–1295.

Eye Tracking- Single Technology to Handle Multiple Domains

Adil Hamid Malla
Sketch Recognition Lab(SRL),
Texas A&M University
College Station, Texas, USA
adil.hamid@tamu.edu

Tracy Hammond
Sketch Recognition Lab(SRL),
Texas A&M University
College Station, Texas, USA
hammond@tamu.edu

ABSTRACT

Interdisciplinary research always yields an enhanced and different perspective on the problem. Solving a problem using many modalities and technologies gives us the complete picture of the problem and the best solution possible. My thesis is about solving the various problem in different domains using the Eye and Gaze Tracking. My research area currently limits to the application of Eye tracking to three domains i.e. Identification and Authentication, Page Ranking based on the Gaze Interaction, and Data Analytics based on the Gaze Interaction data. In the Authentication and Identification, I have developed different authentication systems [6] which uses Gaze and Eye tracking to authenticate a user with 97% accuracy. For Page ranking of the pages, I have used the eye-tracking interaction to enhance the ranking of the page/link on Google and Bing backed Search Emulator. This project is in progress and will be mostly done in coming two months. The third and the last project is related to using the Eye tracking and Gaze Interaction data for inferences which range from detecting the unique eye moment pattern of the user, the saccades and micro-saccades in both horizontal as well as vertical directions, moreover detecting the eye diseases using the Gaze Interaction data.

Author Keywords

Eye Tracking; Gaze Analysis; Authentication; Identification; Page Ranking; Data Analytics

MOTIVATION & INTRODUCTION

Eye Tracking Based Authentication

Having been around the authentication systems and biometrics authentication for some time, I realized that apart from using the core biometrics which involves the fingerprint, iris or finger vein is quite overkill for some authentication use cases, like unlocking the phone, laptops and other PDA's. Moreover, the high spread spoofing techniques for the fingerprint authentication system motivated me to look for soft biometric authentication techniques which uses something simple and effective. Furthermore, the pin, swipe and password-based authentication systems suffer from the very basic problem- Shoulder Surfing. Shoulder surfing enables an attacker to gain the authentication details of a victim through observations and is becoming a threat to visual privacy. A report on global visual hacking, presented by Ponemon Institute in 2016, found that in business office environments the attacks happen on laptops, tablets, smartphones, etc [3]. They conducted shoulder surfing attacks in eight countries, and a staggering 91% of visual attacks were successful, resulting in 613 units of breached data of various types [5]. Furthermore, 11% (69 units) of the breached data were login credentials. To prevent shoulder surfing, we focus on gaze-based authentication, which has been previously explored by [1] [2] [4]. The existing solutions are limited by low accuracy, the need for precise gaze input, accurate recall of the gestures by users, and susceptibility to video analysis attacks. So we need a system which overcomes these limitations and enhance on top of these systems to make a foolproof system to both hacking as well as shoulder surfing. The results and full information for the system developed can be referenced in our work [6].

IUI'18 March 7–11, 2018, Tokyo, Japan

ACM ISBN 978-1-4503-4945-1/18/03...$15.00

DOI: https://doi.org/10.1145/3172944.3173152

Page Ranking Based on Gaze Interaction

The perception from the eyes is hardly used in the present computing world. Be it watching the movies, the artwork or searching the results. What different users watch can heavily help the developers of these services to target the particular items which majority of the people like to watch. Presently, the Google search results are based on complex ranking algorithms which use the content as well as the behaviour of the users who interact with the pages. When a user searches for a result on Google, the user is presented with results each having following sections, the title of the result, the link for the page and the description of the page in two or three lines. Each user usually looks at these three sections of each result and then decide to click the appropriate result. Since this information of gazing through the results is never used to help rank the results. I am developing a system to address this problem by using the gaze-based input to give a feedback to the ranking system. This project is currently in progress and will be done in two months. I have developed a system where the results are searched using a website powered by Google Search and the feedback is given based on the gaze input to enhance the ranking of the page.

Data Analytics on Gaze Interaction Data

The data obtained by using the authentication system as well as searching systems when analyzed showed many features which can be enhanced and used to derive various information about the users and the conditions. We can see the transition of the movement of the users horizontally and vertically, called saccades. Each user has depicted the unique pattern of how s/he moves the eyes horizontally and vertically. Moreover, the eye movement can help us to detect the condition of the eye muscles. More jittery movements in the gaze points mean the muscles are weak and are not controlled properly. It can mean a possible eye condition. Furthermore, the gaze data can be used to enhance the readability of the text as well as the placement of the ads and other search results to be perceived by the users easily. This project also is under the process and we are trying to get the IRB to conduct the user studies.

DATA ANALYTICS- WHAT RECRUITERS LOOK IN RESUME?

This Project is funded by NSF. We are trying to see how and what the computer science recruiters look at the resume. The Gaze interaction with the resume can help us answer simple questions like what technologies do recruiters like to see on a resume. Also, we would be able to see how they rank the GPA, Side projects, Internships while making a decision on shortlisting a candidate. The project is in the data collection phase. The analytic results will be available soon.

GOAL AND RESEARCH QUESTIONS

The basic questions I am trying to answer through my research are:

1. Can the Eye Tracking help us understand the computational world around us better?
2. Can Eye Tracking and Gaze-based inputs help us solve the problem of continuous interaction with computers and computing technologies?
3. How can we enhance both interactions as well as working with different technologies using Eye Tracking?
4. Can we detect the eye conditions by the way people move their eyes while reading?
5. Can we avoid shoulder surfing and Video Analysis attacks while authentication?

By the end of my research, I would surely want some conclusive results for each of the questions above.

PROGRESS OF RESEARCH AND RESULTS

The authentication and the identification using the Eye tracking is already developed and published [6]. Moreover, I am developing some enhancements which address the limitation of the present system. The overall accuracy of the system achieved was 97.5%. For more information and discussion on the authentication please refer to the paper mentioned in [6]. The progress of the remaining two projects is around 60%. The basic framework for both the projects is ready. I am currently designing the user studies for both the projects. Since the requirement of the IRB is also needed so I am working on that as well. The Gaze Analytics Project will use all of the data collected from various projects which uses the Eye Tracking device and Gaze input. Also, the data will be collected by using some framework of texts and images where the user will have to read through the paragraph and look at different parts of the images. I will be using Stata and other analytical tools to detect the trends and features from the Gaze Data. The Page ranking based on the Gaze data is in progress. I am using the python with flask framework to make a web application to search the Google and use the eye tracking on top of it to enhance the results. The flask framework is already implemented and the backend is powered by using the Google API's. The Gaze interaction is also implemented and stored. Now only the ranking feedback has to be processed in our system so that next time the results hit some link the system enhances the raw Google search results based on previous Gaze interaction with the results. Also, the user studies need to be formulated.

REFERENCES

1. Andreas Bulling, Florian Alt, and Albrecht Schmidt. 2012. Increasing the security of gaze-based cued-recall graphical passwords using saliency masks. In *Proceedings of the SIGCHI Conference on Human Factors in Computing Systems*. ACM, 3011–3020.
2. Dietlind Helene Cymek, Antje Christine Venjakob, Stefan Ruff, Otto Hans-Martin Lutz, Simon Hofmann, and Matthias Roetting. 2014. Entering PIN codes by smooth pursuit eye movements. *Journal of Eye Movement Research* 7, 4 (2014).
3. Ponemon Institute LLC. Global Visual Hacking Experimental Study: Analysis. (????). GlobalVisualHackingExperimentalStudy:Analysis
4. Vijay Rajanna, Seth Polsley, Paul Taele, and Tracy Hammond. 2017. A gaze gesture-based user authentication system to counter shoulder-surfing attacks. In *Proceedings of the 2017 CHI Conference Extended Abstracts on Human Factors in Computing Systems*. ACM, 1978–1986.
5. Mélodie Vidal, Andreas Bulling, and Hans Gellersen. 2013. Pursuits: spontaneous interaction with displays based on smooth pursuit eye movement and moving targets. In *Proceedings of the 2013 ACM international joint conference on Pervasive and ubiquitous computing*. ACM, 439–448.
6. Rajanna Vijay, Adil Hamid Malla, Rahul Ashok Bhagat, and Tracy Hammond. 2018. DyGazePass: A Gaze gesture-Based Dynamic Authentication System to Counter Shoulder Surfing Attacks.. In *IEEE International Conference on Identity, Security and Behavior Analysis (ISBA)*. IEEE.

Automatic Recognition of Hygiene Activities and Personalized Interventions for Chronic Care

Josh Cherian
Texas A&M University
College Station, USA
jcherian14@tamu.edu

ABSTRACT
The number of individuals living with chronic conditions continues to rise. As a result, a significant emphasis has been placed on both improving their quality of life as well as decreasing the cost and burden of caring for them. One particularly promising avenue for achieving this is the use of wearable devices, as they have become both affordable and reliable in recognizing fitness activities. However, while the existing algorithms reliably recognize physically intensive activities (e.g., walking vs. swimming), they fail to recognize personal hygiene actives that have more subtle differences (e.g., brushing teeth vs. washing hands). This research aims to develop novel features and intelligent, multi-stage algorithms that can reliably recognize such personal hygiene activities for chronic care. Additionally, we aim to further supplement this activity recognition with personalized interventions that enable individuals to manage their own personal health.

Author Keywords
Activity Recognition; Machine Learning; Personalized Interventions; Human-Computer Interaction

INTRODUCTION
The development of wearable devices has allowed many people to achieve their own personal fitness goals, as these devices provide users with detailed accounts of their daily physical activity. While wearable devices commonly and accurately measure metrics such as steps walked, calories burned, and sleeping patterns, they have yet to be able to recognize many daily health activities like brushing teeth, washing hands, etc. Keeping track of such activities is especially important for those suffering from chronic conditions as it is estimated that 50% of American households will include someone who suffers from one or more chronic conditions by 2030 [1]. Nearly 20% of the individuals who experience chronic conditions deal with some degree of inability to perform normal everyday activities such as getting in and out of bed, getting dressed, feeding, and basic hygiene activities [1]. The inability to perform normal activities necessitates the aid of one or more caregivers and/or placement into an assisted living or nursing home [2]. This is not only a very expensive paradigm but also one that restricts the independence of those experiencing these conditions.

By developing intelligent algorithms that are capable of recognizing activities that those living with chronic conditions may struggle to do, it becomes possible to reduce their dependence on others. Thus this research will focus on 1) exploring novel features, 2) developing intelligent algorithms that recognize hygiene activities, 3) expanding the range of activities recognized, and 4) developing personalized interventions based on recognition of these activities.

IUI'18 March 7-11, 2018, Tokyo, Japan

ACM ISBN 978-1-4503-4945-1/18/03.
DOI: https://doi.org/10.1145/3172944.3173153

RELATED WORK
Traditionally, the field of activity recognition has mostly focused on recognizing ambulatory activities by placing a variety of sensors on different parts of the body and employing a variety of machine learning algorithms [3]. In recent years this research has begun to incorporate data collected from smartphones and smartwatches, and has expanded the range of studied activities to include activities such as brushing teeth, washing hands, and smoking [3, 4, 5]. While this prior research has shown promising results, most of this work groups these activities together. This makes the recognition impractical for real-world implementation as activities are not being compared against gesturally-similar activities. Our research will place an emphasis on recognizing activities by comparing them to other activities similar in orientation and vigor to ensure that our algorithms are robust enough for real-world applications.

Table 1. Novel features developed for identifying brushing teeth.

Features
Average Amplitude: X, Y, Z
Standard Deviation Amplitude: X, Y, Z
Standard Deviation Height: X
Average Peaks: X, Y, Z
Standard Deviation of Peaks: X, Y, Z
Average Valleys: X, Y, Z
Standard Deviation of Valleys: X, Y, Z
Axis Crossings: XY, XZ, YZ

COMPLETED WORK

The first recognition algorithm we built was to recognize brushing teeth, as those experiencing some form of cognitive decline can struggle with regularly performing this activity [6]. Through a series of three user studies involving 38 participants, we collected approximately 378 hours of accelerometer data from a Pebble smartwatch in an effort to discern between six activities: brushing teeth, washing hands, drinking, taking medication, combing hair, and scratching one's chin and then to identify when participants brushed their teeth. This accelerometer data (sample data can be seen in Figure 1) was analyzed using a novel two-stage recognition system. Stage I took a traditional activity recognition approach to classify 4 second sliding windows of data as either brushing teeth or not. For this stage, 51 features were extracted from each window of data; 21 of these features (shown in Table 1) were derived specifically based on unique patterns in the brushing teeth data. Stage II implemented three thresholds to piece together sequences of 4-second windows of brushing teeth into instances of brushing teeth. Using this methodology we were able to identify brushing teeth in a naturalistic setting with an accuracy of 94% and an F-measure of 0.82 [7].

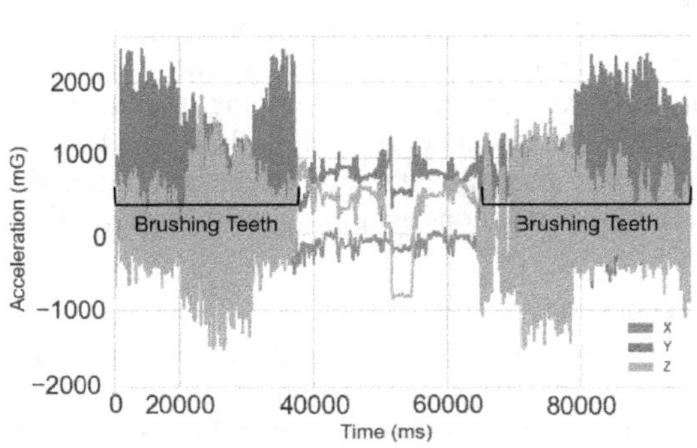

Figure 1. Accelerometer data for brushing teeth with a pause in between

RESEARCH TRAJECTORY

Real-Time Recognition

While we have demonstrated that it is possible to recognize brushing teeth by post-processing the accelerometer data, we have yet to test the recognition in a real-time setting. To do this, we plan to implement our recognition algorithm into a wearable application and test the accuracy and efficacy of basic intervention mechanisms such as reminders and alerts.

Recognizing a Broader Range of Activities

We aim to extend our recognition system to other daily health activities beyond brushing teeth, with washing hands, smoking, and taking medication being the most attractive candidates. Each of these present their own unique challenge. Washing hands is a much shorter activity and is characteristically more chaotic. As such, the accelerometer data does not exhibit clear patterns as brushing teeth does. Smoking is a much longer activity than brushing teeth; however, smokers will often perform other actions such as gesticulating, drinking, and/or using their phone while smoking, complicating the sensor data. Taking medication is the shortest gesture by far, and can be done in several different ways based on the medication container and the individual's personal habits.

Novel Features

In order to accurately recognize brushing teeth we extracted novel features that highlighted the differences between it and other similar activities. Similarly, recognition of these other activities will require the development of features that are specific to that activity's own unique characteristics.

Intelligent, Multi-stage Algorithms

To recognize brushing teeth we developed a two-stage recognition system. We expect that recognizing other activities will require similar multi-stage recognition systems based on the context of these activities and their unique qualities.

Personalized Interventions

Currently, the interventions and notifications generated by wearable devices are broadly applied to all users. While this works well for fitness activities, which are performed fairly similarly by most individuals, it does not work as well for the broader range of health activities which can depend on both the individual and the context. As such, we aim to develop personalized interventions based not only on recognition of the activities that are being performed but also on the context in which the activities are performed. By doing so we can develop systems capable of helping and reassuring the many who live with chronic conditions.

ACKNOWLEDGMENTS

I would like to thank my adviser Dr. Tracy Hammond and the members of the Sketch Recognition Lab for their continued feedback and support.

REFERENCES

1. Gerard F Anderson. *Chronic Care: Making the Case for Ongoing Care*. Robert Wood Johnson Foundation, 2010.
2. Association Alzheimer's. 2015 alzheimer's disease facts and figures. *Alzheimer's & Dementia: the Journal of the Alzheimer's Association*, 11(3):332, 2015.
3. Ling Bao and Stephen Intille. Activity recognition from user-annotated acceleration data. *Pervasive computing*, pages 1–17, 2004.
4. Gary M Weiss, Jessica L Timko, Catherine M Gallagher, Kenichi Yoneda, and Andrew J Schreiber. Smartwatch-based activity recognition: A machine learning approach. In *IEEE-EMBS*, 2016.
5. Stefan Dernbach, Barnan Das, Narayanan C Krishnan, Brian L Thomas, and Diane J Cook. Simple and complex activity recognition through smart phones. In *Intelligent Environments 2012*, pages 214–221. IEEE, 2012.
6. Janet Griffiths and Vicki Jones. *Tracking for health.* Alzheimer's Society, 2015.
7. Josh Cherian, Vijay Rajanna, Daniel Goldberg, and Tracy Hammond. Did you remember to brush? a noninvasive wearable approach to recognizing brushing teeth for elderly care. In *Pervasive Health 2017*, 2017.

An Intelligent Tutoring System for Situated Decision Making in Dental Surgery

Narumol Vannaprathip
Faculty of ICT, Mahidol University, Nakhon Pathom, Thailand
narumol.van@student.mahidol.ac.th

ABSTRACT
We present the design and the partial implementation of a simulation-based intelligent tutoring system for training surgical decision making skill. The simulation combines an immersive virtual environment with a conversational intelligent tutoring system. The pedagogical module has been largely implemented and the result of an initial evaluation of the implemented tutorial interventions is presented.

Author Keywords
surgical decision making; situation awareness; intelligent tutoring system; pedagogical intervention; knowledge representation

ACM Classification Keywords
• Software and its engineering~Virtual worlds training simulations • *Human-centered computing~Virtual reality* • *Computing methodologies~Knowledge representation and reasoning*

MOTIVATION
Surgical skill training has been traditionally based on the Halstedian apprenticeship model whereby a surgical trainee attempts to perform a task with guidance and close supervision from an expert surgeon. But shortened training programs, reduced working hours for residents and limitations on available operating room time have strained this model, resulting in increased interest in use of simulation for training. Surgical simulation has the potential to provide students with increased training time outside the operating room, objective assessment of procedures, and formative feedback. But despite the fact that 75% of the important events in the operating room are related to decision making and only 25% to technical (psychomotor) skills [3], work on surgical simulation has focused mainly on technical skills. The few simulations that exist for teaching decision making [4,6] focus mainly on correct choices of actions rather than teaching the underlying decision making skills.

IUI'18, March 7–11, 2018, Tokyo, Japan

ACM ISBN 978-1-4503-4945-1/18/03.
https://doi.org/10.1145/3172944.3173154

Surgical decision making is a complex and dynamic process in which the state of the patient and consequences of actions must be constantly monitored and evaluated relative to the surgical objective. Thus, situation awareness plays a critical role. Situation awareness (SA) is "the perception of the elements in the environment within a volume of time and space, the comprehension of their meaning, and the projection of their status in the near future" [2]. Lack of sufficient situation awareness has been shown to lead to errors in surgical judgment [1].

To date, there is no intelligent tutoring system that addresses the teaching of situation awareness skill in surgery. The research described here seeks to determine whether situated decision making can be effectively taught through the combination of an immersive virtual environment with a conversational intelligent tutoring system. The research is expected to make the following contributions: a) Identification and classification of key teaching strategies used by expert dental surgeons to teach surgical decision making; b) A novel representation formalism that captures key aspects of surgical procedural knowledge and situation awareness; c) An algorithm to make use of surgical procedural knowledge to generate a large proportion of the identified teaching interventions; d) An immersive interactive simulation that captures key perceptual cues used in surgical decision making.

OBSERVATIONAL STUDY
After approval from the Institutional Ethics Committee, an observational study of 27 teaching sessions at the student clinic in the Faculty of Dentistry, Thammasat University and interviews with dental instructors were conducted to design and identify requirements of the system. Actions and discussions during the teaching sessions were recorded and transcribed. Teaching strategies with their triggering events were identified and the content of interventions was thematically interpreted in terms of situation awareness.

SYSTEM OVERVIEW
We propose an intelligent tutoring system that provides an immersive dental operating room with key relevant cues such that dental students naturally carry out surgical tasks in the simulator. Since the tutoring module needs to be aware of the student's actions being executed, the kinematic motion data from the simulator must be translated into a symbolic representation of actions. For this we plan to use KnowRob [1], a knowledge processing infrastructure for cognition-enabled robots that deduces the symbolic data from

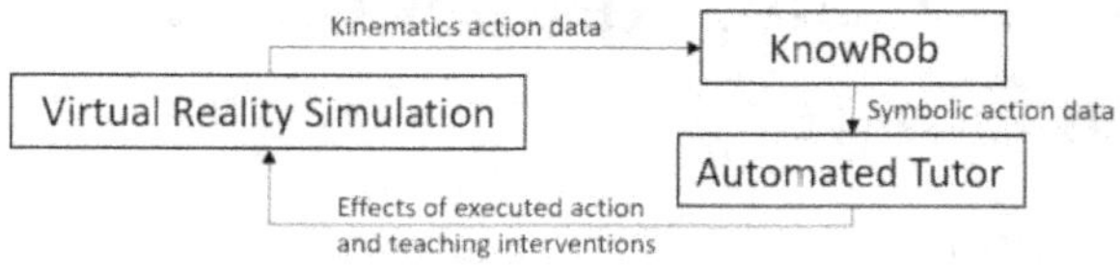

Figure 1. Overall system design

kinematic data. The automated tutor then evaluates the symbolic student action, identifies possible teaching strategies, and generates tutorial interventions. Figure 1 shows the overall system design. In this paper, we present the implemented pedagogical module and an initial evaluation of the implemented tutorial interventions.

AUTOMATED TUTOR

A standard intelligent tutoring system framework is used to develop the automated tutor. The representation of domain knowledge must be expressive enough to represent surgical procedures and situation awareness. We use a subset of the Planning Domain Definition Language (PDDL) to represent domain knowledge because of its mechanisms to represent domain rules and elements of a surgical procedure including action descriptions with conditional effects. The mechanisms support mapping to the key elements of the SA framework: the relations between perception and comprehension are represented by domain rules, and projections are represented in terms of effects [5]. When the student executes an action, the plan projection engine uses this represented domain knowledge to project the effects. These are then evaluated against the desired outcomes. The graph representing domain knowledge and its subset of student's performance is created. The automated tutor utilizes this graph to generate tutorial dialog that focuses on causal relations to give the student a deep understanding of the domain. Figure 2 shows an example of posing a hypothetical situation to explore the breadth of the student's understanding.

```
Suppose that working tooth type is molar, what would be
the correct clamp number?
1) clamp number 9
2) clamp number 14
3) clamp number 2
```

Figure 2. A question about a hypothetical situation

INITIAL EVALUATION

An initial evaluation was conducted to determine the appropriateness of the interventions generated by the automated tutor. Four endodontic clinical instructors who have at least five years of clinical experience were asked to provide tutoring feedback for five different situations from a stage of local anesthesia selection and rubber dam application. Their tutoring feedback and the feedback generated by the automated tutor were blindly scored using a 5-point Likert scale and commented by two endodontic experts who have more than 10 years of clinical experience and are responsible for rating the teaching performance of human instructors. A mean score of each instructor and the automated tutor were computed as well as the average score of the four human instructors. The automated tutor was graded (4.4) above the overall human average (4.2) and only one human tutor achieved better ratings (4.8).

FUTURE WORK

System Development

The virtual dental operating room will be developed to provide perceptual cues. The integration and communication among the virtual dental operating room, KnowRob, and the automated tutor will be established. The scope of the representation will be extended to cover the whole steps of root canal treatment. The representation is not limited to decisions for normal situations but it can also cover the process to recover from errors (e.g., dealing with perforation). We also plan to apply the automated tutor to simple tooth extraction and surgical tooth extraction.

System Evaluation

Two additional evaluations are planned to be conducted. The first evaluation will assess to what extent the simulation helps improving surgical decision making skills. A randomized controlled trial with pre- and posttests will be used to measure the students' knowledge levels related to decision making skill. The second evaluation will extend the scope and rigor of the initial evaluation, by (a) examining more types of situations and (b) increasing the sample size for each.

REFERENCES

1. Dana K Andersen. 2012. How can educators use simulation applications to teach and assess surgical judgment? *Academic Medicine : Journal of the Association of American Medical Colleges* 87,7: 934–41.
2. Mica R. Endsley. 1995. Toward a Theory of Situation Awareness in Dynamic Systems. *Human Factors: The Journal of the Human Factors and Ergonomics Society* 37, 1: 32–64.
3. Frederick Spencer. 1978. Teaching and measuring surgical techniques: the technical evaluation of competence. *Bull Am Coll Surg* 63, 3: 9–12.
4. Linh N Tran, Priyanka Gupta, Lauren H Poniatowski, Shaheen Alanee, Marc a Dall'era, and Robert M Sweet. 2013. Validation study of a computer-based open surgical trainer: SimPraxis(®) simulation platform. *Advances in medical education and practice* 4: 23–30.
5. Narumol Vannaprathip, Peter Haddawy, Holger Schultheis, and Siriwan Suebnukarn. 2017. Generating Tutorial Interventions for Teaching Situation Awareness in Dental Surgery – Preliminary Report. *The 11th Multi-disciplinary International Workshop on Artificial Intelligence*, Springer International Publishing AG.
6. Narumol Vannaprathip, Peter Haddawy, Siriwan Suebnukarn, Patcharapon Sangsartra, Nunnapin Sasikhant, and Sornram Sangutai. 2016. Desitra: A Simulator for Teaching Situated Decision Making in Dental Surgery. *21st International Conference on Intelligent User Interfaces, IUI 2016*, ACM, 397–401.

Facilitating Self-learning in Behavior Change Through Long-term Intelligent Conversational Assistance

Rafal Kocielnik
University of Washington
rkoc@uw.edu

Gary Hsieh
University of Washington
garyhs@uw.edu

ABSTRACT

Despite much recent progress in conversational systems, the vision of a truly "intelligent" agent is still far from being realized. Part of the reason is that current applications focus on offering conversational alternatives to GUI supported tasks. In my research I am focusing on application of dialogue-based interaction in area of self-learning in health behavior change, domain in which conversation can offer unique value. Yet, to be effective in this domain a conversational system needs to be "intelligent". In my research I define aspects of intelligence crucial for supporting long-term self-learning in behavior change through conversation and address the technical as well as design challenges of enabling such intelligent applications.

INTRODUCTION

For decades, the promise of computers that communicate with us through natural language has been depicted in works of science fiction and driven research agendas in artificial intelligence (AI) and human-computer interaction (HCI). Aside from many popular applications, conversational interaction might be especially valuable in the behavior change domain, where such interaction can facilitate users' self-learning and reflection on own behavior data in ways that classical GUI cannot. However, because individual behavior opportunities and barriers are unique, for a conversational agent to be effective in this role, it needs to be "intelligent" and there are a number of technical challenges that make creation of "intelligent" agents difficult.

FACETS OF INTELLIGENT CONVERSTIONAL AGENT

A number of aspects contribute to the intelligence of an agent for the purpose of long-term self-learning.

Facilitation of open exploration of learning-material

To facilitate self-learning and freedom of expression for the user, the conversations should allow for open-ended user responses [8]. While the agent can trigger the user with specific learning-inducting conversation starters, the open expression allows for the learning to take the direction most relevant for user needs. Also in order to facilitate the learning process and challenge the user to consider deeper or new aspects of behavior the agent should be able to provide follow-ups that build up on user responses [6].

IUI'18, March 7–11, 2018, Tokyo, Japan

ACM ISBN 978-1-4503-4945-1/18/03.
https://doi.org/10.1145/3172944.3173156

Conversation around shared knowledge

In order to support meaningful conversations about self-learning, the agent should also have a shared understanding of the relevant learning information (e.g. user physical activity, schedule), to be able to carry out data-driven conversations around relevant topics [7].

Long-term personalization and context awareness

In the context of self-learning in behavior change, the conversational system needs to assist the user for long time. The agent should also assist the user in an ever engaging and novel manner [1]. To do that, it needs to provide novel and diverse conversations each time. It needs to adapt based on the context and knowledge obtained from past conversations, essentially becoming more personalized.

Adaptive behavior change direction

Another aspect of the long-term engagement relates to the need of adapting to user's changing conditions, motivations and challenges to guide the progression of the long-term conversation [11]. In order to evolve with the user the agent needs to adapt the goals and means of carrying out conversations to provide better assistance (e.g. changing from building understanding to providing motivation).

TECHNICAL AND DESIGN CHALLENEGS

Realizing this vision of intelligent conversational assistance requires addressing a number of technical challenges.

Limited training data

There is a limited availability of dialogue data for training conversational systems. This limits the use of data-intensive computational approaches and forces the designers of conversational applications to rely on handcrafting dialogue structures and generating example data themselves [2]. In my research I am interested in exploring ways of dynamically incorporating interaction data to improve agent over time and also look into ways of incorporating dialogue data from different domains, where it is more abundant, using techniques such as transfer learning [10].

Static conversational structure

On top of the limited availability of data, the design of current systems relies on fixed dialogue structure that does not adapt or evolve with time [2]. Such systems do not support dynamic creation of new conversational paths, that may be necessarily if interaction with users takes a directions not designed for in advance. In my work I want to address this limitation by exploring the use of crowd sourcing in combination with machine learning.

Challenges of deep personalization

Current dialogue design tools support personalization through use of templates filled in with user information or through a set of predefined variations on the basic utterances. For long-term adaptive personalization, aspects such as individual behaviors, user specific motivations, values and personality traits are important. These go beyond what can be easily scripted in existing tools. In my research I want to explore how these higher-level information could be incorporated to adapt and personalize conversational interaction on a much deeper level.

RESEARCH GOALS AND CURRENT PROGRESS

My research is thus focused on facilitating the design and development of intelligent agents. I am tackling both the user-centered as a well as technical aspects of the challenge and I have already made significant steps towards realizing the goal of building intelligent agents in behavior change.

I used a crowd-based process for generation and selection of personality-tailored motivational messages for promoting exercise performance [8]. This research has contributed a process of contents diversification in long-term text-message based interaction to improve user engagement.

In subsequent piece of work, I contributed to the creation of a workflow-based scheduling agent with humans in the loop [4], which has since been released as a product. This work used crowd provided feedback to complement automation and generate training data that could be used for improving automated models.

To explore dynamic shaping of the dialogue structure itself, in my recent work I used 2-stage conversational dialogues to support self-learning from self-tracked physical activity data. The dialogues were composed of an initial prompt and a follow-up dynamically tailored based on open-text user response to the initial prompt. We used self-generated artificial examples for training the recognition of user responses. This revealed the difficulty of predicting user responses in design time and the need for dynamic adaptation in the long term. In an earlier piece of work [5] I explored adaptation of the dialogue structure to user culture, which revealed that such adaptation can have significant impact on user experience.

Finally, in another piece of research we explored the use of a mixed-modality coaching agent in a company environment for the purpose of work activity journaling and self-learning. This work highlighted the potential of adaptation to the interaction environment and the importance of domain specific knowledge of conversational agent.

CONCLUSION

My contributions: 1) Systematic exploration and addressing of the challenges involved in building intelligent self-learning adaptive agents; 2) Generation of much needed domain-specific dialogue datasets for long-term conversational exchanges. 3) Creation of tools and techniques for supporting design of intelligent and adaptive conversational systems addressed for designers.

REFERENCES

1. Timothy W. Bickmore and Rosalind W. Picard. 2005. Establishing and maintaining long-term human-computer relationships. *ACM Transactions on Computer-Human Interaction (TOCHI)* 12, 2: 293–327.
2. Antoine Bordes and Jason Weston. 2016. Learning end-to-end goal-oriented dialog. *arXiv preprint arXiv:1605.07683*.
3. Charles S. Carver and Michael F. Scheier. 2000. Autonomy and self-regulation. *Psychological Inquiry* 11, 4: 284–291.
4. Justin Cranshaw, Emad Elwany, Todd Newman, Rafal Kocielnik, Bowen Yu, Sandeep Soni, Jaime Teevan, and Andrés Monroy-Hernández. 2017. Calendar. help: Designing a Workflow-Based Scheduling Agent with Humans in the Loop. In *Proceedings of the 2017 CHI Conference on Human Factors in Computing Systems*, 2382–2393.
5. Beant Dhillon, Rafal Kocielnik, Ioannis Politis, Marc Swerts, and Dalila Szostak. 2011. Culture and facial expressions: A case study with a speech interface. In *IFIP Conference on Human-Computer Interaction*, 392–404.
6. Rowanne Fleck and Geraldine Fitzpatrick. 2010. Reflecting on reflection: framing a design landscape. In *Proceedings of the 22nd Conference of the Computer-Human Interaction Special Interest Group of Australia on Computer-Human Interaction*, 216–223.
7. Yea-Seul Kim and Jessica Hullman. 2015. User-driven Expectation Visualization: Opportunities for Personalized Feedback.
8. Rafal Kocielnik and Gary Hsieh. Send Me a Different Message: Utilizing Cognitive Space to Create Engaging Message Triggers. *Proceedings of the 20th ACM Conference on Computer-Supported Cooperative Work & Social Computing.*: 2017.
9. Min Kyung Lee, Junsung Kim, Jodi Forlizzi, and Sara Kiesler. 2015. Personalization revisited: a reflective approach helps people better personalize health services and motivates them to increase physical activity. In *Proceedings of the 2015 ACM International Joint Conference on Pervasive and Ubiquitous Computing*, 743–754.
10. Sinno Jialin Pan and Qiang Yang. 2010. A survey on transfer learning. *IEEE Transactions on knowledge and data engineering* 22, 10: 1345–1359.
11. James O. Prochaska. 2013. Transtheoretical model of behavior change. In *Encyclopedia of behavioral medicine*. Springer, 1997–2000.

Author Index

www.ingramcontent.com/pod-product-compliance
Lightning Source LLC
LaVergne TN
LVHW082004200926
848481LV00010B/2802